# A CONCORDANCE TO THE COLLECTED POEMS
## OF DYLAN THOMAS

# A Concordance to the
# Collected Poems of
# DYLAN THOMAS

Edited by

ROBERT COLEMAN WILLIAMS, F.R.G.S., F.G.S.

UNIVERSITY OF NEBRASKA PRESS · LINCOLN

Manufactured in the United States of America

# Contents

| | |
|---|---|
| Introduction | vii |
| Alphabetical List of Poems with their numerical designation | xi |
| Entries under A | 3 |
| Entries under B | 26 |
| Entries under C | 70 |
| Entries under D | 107 |
| Entries under E | 139 |
| Entries under F | 150 |
| Entries under G | 181 |
| Entries under H | 204 |
| Entries under I | 245 |
| Entries under J | 254 |
| Entries under K | 257 |
| Entries under L | 262 |
| Entries under M | 294 |
| Entries under N | 325 |
| Entries under O | 342 |
| Entries under P | 353 |
| Entries under Q | 372 |
| Entries under R | 374 |
| Entries under S | 395 |
| Entries under T | 480 |
| Entries under U | 518 |
| Entries under V | 526 |
| Entries under W | 532 |
| Entry under X | 574 |
| Entries under Y | 574 |
| Entries under Z | 579 |

# Introduction

The texts used in the preparation of this concordance were the 1954 reprinting of the *Collected Poems of Dylan Thomas, 1934–1952* (London: J. M. Dent & Sons, Ltd., 1952) and the eighteenth printing of the American edition (New York: New Directions, 1953). The text of the Everyman's Library printing of the *Collected Poems*, published by Dent in 1966, was not available during the preparation of the concordance.

*Index Word*

With the exception of the words listed below, every word in the poems and poem titles of the *Collected Poems* has been included. The words appear in alphabetical order. Hyphenated words which are split on the hyphen to form line endings in the texts are listed as shown in the following example:

COAL-[BLACK]

Whatsoever I did in the coal-

In this case, [BLACK] has been brought forward from the line immediately following the context line to complete the sense of the index word.

The following words were not listed. Because of the high frequency of their occurrence, their inclusion would have added considerably to the size of the volume.

| | | | |
|---|---|---|---|
| A | FOR | OR | THEIR |
| AN | FROM | ON | THIS |
| AND | HIS | OUR | THROUGH |
| AS | I | OUT | TO |
| AT | I'LL | THAT | WAS |
| BUT | IN | THAT'S | WITH |
| BY | MY | THE | YOUR |

*Text Line*

Each indexed word is followed by each line of poetry in which the word occurs. Each of these contextual lines is printed in the sequence in which it appeared in the original texts, and is quoted in full. The contextual presentation of each entry is followed by an index listing the page number and line number for the Dent edition (U.K.) and the New Directions edition (U.S.). The line numbers have been calculated by numbering each line from top to bottom of a page, designating the first full line of poetry as *line one*, the second as *line two*, and so on, in normal numerical sequence. The line numbers refer to full poetic lines, not to "overspill lines" created by the limitations of type-page size. The page numbers are the page numbers which appear in the original editions.

*Poem Title*

Poem titles are indexed by poem number and page number only, and always appear at the end of the entries under the word indexed.

No wd groupg
No hom syp

# INTRODUCTION

*Poem Number*

The column of numbers appearing between the page numbers and page-line numbers for the U.K. and U.S. editions identifies the poems by numerical designations from 1 to 91, derived from the order of their occurrence in the text. Thus "Author's Prologue" is designated as 1; "I see the boys of summer" as 2; and so on. An alphabetical list of the poems with their numerical designation in the concordance appears on pages xi–xiii.

*Variants in the Texts*

The U.S. edition corresponds to the U.K. edition textually in the poems selected and in the order of their presentation from 1 through 90. The poem numbered 91, "Elegy," appears only in the U.S. edition used; however, it appears in later editions of the U.K. text and in the Everyman's Library edition. Although "Elegy" has been reconstructed from manuscript material, it has been fully incorporated into the body of the concordance.

The number of lines and the positioning of stanzas on some of the pages varies in the two editions, with the result that pagination and line-numeration is frequently quite different. The lines of the poems themselves and their order throughout the editions are of course standard, and apart from one difference in stanza layout (noted below), the order of the stanzas does not vary.

Textual differences in the editions are as follows:

1. Poem titles in the U.S. edition are set in small capitals; in the U.K. edition they appear with lower case and capitals mixed.

2. The opening words of poems are set in capitals in the U.K. edition, a practice which has not been followed in the U.S. edition.

3. The lines of "Author's Prologue" are numbered in the U.K. edition, but are unnumbered in the U.S. edition. The numbering runs 1 to 51, then 51 to 1.

4. In "If I were tickled by the rub of love," the words *lovers' rub* appear in the U.S. edition (page 14, line 1), but only the word *lovers* in the U.K. edition.

5. In "Our eunuch dreams," the U.K. edition prints *throwing* (line 18, page 14); the U.S. edition *showing* (line 18, page 16).

6. In "This bread I break" the U.K. edition prints *wind* (pages 39, line 6), the U.S. edition prints *wine* (page 45, line 6).

7. In "I have longed to move away" the U.K. edition prints *For* (page 64, line 8), the U.S. edition prints *From* (page 73, line 8).

8. In sonnet IV of the "Altarwise by Owl-light" sequence, the U.K. edition prints *shroud* (page 73, line 6), the U.S. edition prints *shrowd* (page 82, line 6).

9. In "I make this in a warring absence," two lines grouped at the beginning of the sixth stanza in the U.K. edition (page 79, lines 10–12) occur at the end of the previous stanza in the U.S. edition (page 88, lines 14–15).

10. In "The Conversation of Prayer," the U.K. edition prints *true grave* (page 100, line 18); the U.S. edition prints *made grave* (page 111, line 18).

11. In "Do not go gentle into that good night," the U.K. edition prints *have forked* (page 116, line 5); the U.S. edition prints *had forked* (page 128, line 5).

12. In "Once below a time," the Roman numeral *I* is missing from the U.S. edition (page 147), although it does appear on the next page, as in the U.K. edition.

13. In "Lament," the U.K. edition prints *Slunk* (page 175, line 15); the U.S. edition prints *Slung* (page 195, line 20).

14. In the poem "In the white giant's thigh," the U.K. edition prints *desires* (page 178, line 15), the U.S. edition prints *desirers* (page 199, line 16).

The U.S. edition used includes notes by Vernon Watkins on "Elegy." These notes are of course not in the U.K. edition used, although they appear along with the poem in later printings.

*Acknowledgments*

I would like to thank the Reverend Thomas J. Grace, S.J., former chairman of the Department of the English Language and Literature at the College of the Holy Cross, Worcester, Massachusetts, for his encouragement in this project, and the Reverend William Guindon, S.J., Director of the Holy Cross Data Processing Center, for the energy, patience, and technical skill which made smoother the path toward the completion of this Concordance. I am deeply indebted to the kindness, generosity, and patience of both these priests.

I am also grateful to Father Guindon's secretary, Mrs. Robo, and especially to John Bowen, both members of the staff of the Data Center, who gave considerable assistance to my work. Thanks are also due to Michael Reichel and Terrence Brophy Kearns, ex-students of mine, who volunteered a great deal of time on the early stages of the Concordance. Finally, I commend the patience and editorial tact of my wife, and her spirited tolerance of the whole operation on both sides of the Atlantic.

ROBERT COLEMAN WILLIAMS
*Lecturer in English*
Trinity College
Carmarthen, South Wales

# Alphabetical List of Poems

*with their numerical designation in the concordance*

| *Poem title* | *Number* |
|---|---|
| A grief ago | 33 |
| A process in the weather of the heart | 4 |
| A Refusal to Mourn the Death, by Fire, of a Child in London | 62 |
| A saint about to fall | 58 |
| A Winter's Tale | 72 |
| After the funeral (In memory of Ann Jones) | 52 |
| All all and all the dry world's lever | 19 |
| Altarwise by owl-light | 44 |
| And death shall have no dominion | 42 |
| Author's Prologue | 1 |
| | |
| Ballad of the Long-legged Bait | 83 |
| Because the pleasure-bird whistles | 45 |
| Before I knocked | 5 |
| | |
| Ceremony After a Fire Raid | 77 |
| | |
| Dawn Raid | 80 |
| Deaths and Entrances | 71 |
| Do not go gentle into that good night | 70 |
| Do you not father me | 27 |
| | |
| Ears in the turrets hear | 35 |
| Elegy | 91 |
| Especially when the October wind | 11 |
| | |
| ✓Fern Hill | 85 |
| Find meat on bones | 40 |
| Foster the light | 36 |
| From love's first fever to her plague | 13 |
| | |
| Grief thief of time | 41 |
| | |
| Here in this spring | 26 |
| Hold hard, these ancient minutes in the cuckoo's month | 29 |
| Holy Spring | 84 |
| How shall my animal | 55 |
| How soon the servant sun | 34 |
| | |
| I dreamed my genesis | 17 |
| I fellowed sleep | 16 |

## LIST OF POEMS

I have longed to move away 39
I, in my intricate image 20
I make this in a warring absence 46
I see the boys of summer 2
If I were tickled by the rub of love 9
'If my head hurt a hair's foot' 59
In country sleep 86
In my Craft or Sullen Art 76
In the beginning 14
In the white giant's thigh 90
Incarnate devil 22
Into her Lying Down Head 69
It is the sinners' dust-tongued bell 49

Lament 89
Lie Still, Sleep Becalmed 81
Light breaks where no sun shines 15
Love in the Asylum 66

My hero bares his nerves 7
My world is pyramid 18

Not from this anger 54
Now 31

O make me a mask 50
On a Wedding Anniversary 73
On no work of words 57
On the Marriage of a Virgin 75
Once below a time 78
Once it was the colour of saying 53
Our eunuch dreams 10
Out of the sighs 28
Over Sir John's hill 87

Poem in October 63
Poem on his birthday 88

Shall gods be said to thump the clouds 25
Should lanterns shine 38

The Conversation of Prayer 61
The force that through the green fuse drives the flower 6
The hand that signed the paper 37
The Hunchback in the Park 68
The seed-at-zero 24
The spire cranes 51
The tombstone told when she died 56
Then was my neophyte 43

There was a Saviour                                    74
This bread I break                                     21
This Side of the Truth                                 64
To Others than You                                     65
To-day, this insect                                    23
Twenty-four years                                      60

Unluckily for a Death                                  67

Vision and Prayer                                      82

Was there a time                                       30
We lying by seasand                                    48
When all my five and country senses see               47
When I Woke                                            79
When, like a running grave                             12
When once the twilight locks no longer                  3
Where once the waters of your face                      8
Why east wind chills                                   32

A CONCORDANCE TO THE COLLECTED POEMS
OF DYLAN THOMAS

# ENTRIES UNDER A

|  | U.K. Page | U.K. Line | Poem | U.S. Page | U.S. Line |
|---|---|---|---|---|---|
| **AARON** | | | | | |
| Was who was folded on the rod the aaron | 54 | 13 | 33 | 63 | 13 |
| **ABADDON** | | | | | |
| Abaddon in the hangnail cracked from Adam, | 71 | 3 | 44 | 80 | 3 |
| The horizontal cross-bones of Abaddon, | 71 | 21 | 44 | 80 | 21 |
| **ABED** | | | | | |
| And the lovers lie abed | 128 | 4 | 76 | 142 | 4 |
| **ABOUT** | | | | | |
| Nor damned the sea that sped about my fist, | 4 | 3 | 3 | 4 | 3 |
| There round about your stones the shades | 11 | 16 | 8 | 12 | 16 |
| When no mouth stirred about the hanging famine, | 20 | 5 | 13 | 24 | 5 |
| The secret child, I shift about the sea | 32 | 11 | 18 | 37 | 17 |
| A saint about to fall, | 95 | 1 | 58 | 105 | 1 |
| The conversation of prayers about to be said | 100 | 1 | 61 | 111 | 1 |
| The sound about to be said in the two prayers | 100 | 9 | 61 | 111 | 9 |
| The conversation of prayers about to be said | 100 | 13 | 61 | 111 | 13 |
| Of moving about your death | 105 | 14 | 64 | 116 | 14 |
| About the saint in shades while the endless breviary | 109 | 26 | 67 | 120 | 26 |
| About the lilting house and happy as the grass was green, | 159 | 2 | 85 | 178 | 2 |
| About the happy yard and singing as the farm was home, | 159 | 11 | 85 | 178 | 11 |
| A saint about to fall | 95 | | 58 | 105 | |
| **ABOVE** | | | | | |
| And sleep rolls mute above the beds | 5 | 4 | 3 | 5 | 4 |
| Above the waste allotments the dawn halts. | 25 | 6 | 15 | 30 | 6 |
| Above the farms and the white horses | 102 | 13 | 63 | 113 | 13 |
| Above her folded head, and the soft feathered voice | 122 | 2 | 72 | 135 | 2 |
| The night above the dingle starry, | 159 | 3 | 85 | 178 | 3 |
| Night and the reindeer on the clouds above the haycocks | 164 | 15 | 86 | 184 | 1 |
| Above all he longed for his mother's breast | | | 91 | 200 | 9 |
| **ABRAHAM-MAN** | | | | | |
| Up rose the Abraham-man, mad for my sake, | 46 | 19 | 27 | 54 | 19 |
| **ABROAD** | | | | | |
| And walked abroad in a shower of all my days. | 102 | 16 | 63 | 113 | 16 |

3

# ABSCESSES

| | | U.K. Page | U.K. Line | Poem | U.S. Page | U.S. Line |
|---|---|---|---|---|---|---|
| **ABSCESSES** | | | | | | |
| | Vessel of abscesses and exultation's shell, | 91 | 3 | 55 | 100 | 3 |
| **ABSENCE** | | | | | | |
| | I make this in a warring absence when | 78 | 1 | 46 | 87 | 1 |
| | And a silk pigeon's guilt in her proud absence, | 78 | 17 | 46 | 87 | 17 |
| | I make this in a warring absence | 78 | | 46 | 87 | |
| **ABSTRACTED** | | | | | | |
| | Abstracted all the letters of the void; | 22 | 21 | 14 | 27 | 21 |
| **ACCIDENT** | | | | | | |
| | Hear by death's accident the clocked and dashed-down spire | 83 | 11 | 49 | 92 | 11 |
| **ACHE** | | | | | | |
| | Ache on the lovelorn paper | 10 | 7 | 7 | 11 | 7 |
| | He'll ache too long | 48 | 13 | 28 | 56 | 13 |
| | Bend, if my journey ache, direction like an arc or make | 97 | 14 | 59 | 108 | 14 |
| **ACID** | | | | | | |
| | The milky acid on each hinge, | 4 | 5 | 3 | 4 | 5 |
| | A nitric shape that leaps her, time and acid; | 55 | 7 | 33 | 64 | 10 |
| **ACORN** | | | | | | |
| | The oak is felled in the acorn | 155 | 11 | 83 | 173 | 15 |
| **ACQUAINTED** | | | | | | |
| | Acquainted with the salt adventure | 8 | 9 | 5 | 9 | 9 |
| **ACRE** | | | | | | |
| | Left by the dead who, in their moonless acre, | 21 | 11 | 13 | 25 | 11 |
| | And father all nor fail the fly-lord's acre, | 60 | 13 | 36 | 69 | 13 |
| **ACRES** | | | | | | |
| | What of a bamboo man among your acres? | 73 | 3 | 44 | 82 | 3 |
| **ACRID** | | | | | | |
| | That spill such acrid blood. | 48 | 16 | 28 | 56 | 16 |
| **ACROSS** | | | | | | |
| | Cry, Multitudes of arks! Across | x | 10 | 1 | xviii | 16 |
| | One smile of light across the empty face; | 22 | 2 | 14 | 27 | 2 |
| | One bough of bone across the rooting air, | 22 | 3 | 14 | 27 | 3 |
| | And my heart is cracked across; | 65 | 18 | 40 | 74 | 18 |
| | And bear those tendril hands I touch across | 90 | 6 | 54 | 99 | 6 |
| | Flashed first across his thunderclapping eyes. | 117 | 24 | 71 | 129 | 24 |
| | The sky is torn across | 124 | 1 | 73 | 138 | 1 |
| **ACT** | | | | | | |
| | Is a burning and crested act, | vii | 25 | 1 | xv | 25 |
| | With unforgettably smiling act, | 107 | 11 | 65 | 118 | 11 |
| | Earth, air, water, fire, singing into the white act, | 165 | 16 | 86 | 185 | 6 |
| | And alone in the night's eternal, curving act | 176 | 9 | 90 | 197 | 9 |
| **ACTIONS'** | | | | | | |
| | The actions' end. | 19 | 20 | 12 | 23 | 5 |
| | And, when it quickens, alter the actions' pace | 63 | 12 | 38 | 72 | 12 |
| **ADAM** | | | | | | |
| | Of bud of Adam through his boxy shift, | 19 | 13 | 12 | 22 | 18 |

|  | U.K. | | | U.S. | |
| --- | --- | --- | --- | --- | --- |
|  | *Page* | *Line* | *Poem* | *Page* | *Line* |
| His sea-sucked Adam in the hollow hulk, | 30 | 2 | 18 | 35 | 2 |
| 'Adam I love, my madmen's love is endless, | 41 | 23 | 23 | 48 | 5 |
| Abaddon in the hangnail cracked from Adam, | 71 | 3 | 44 | 80 | 3 |
| Rung bone and blade, the verticals of Adam, | 71 | 23 | 44 | 80 | 23 |
| Rose my Byzantine Adam in the night. | 73 | 16 | 44 | 82 | 16 |
| Cross-stroked salt Adam to the frozen angel | 73 | 21 | 44 | 82 | 21 |
| Adam, time's joker, on a witch of cardboard | 74 | 11 | 44 | 83 | 11 |
| Who sucks the bell-voiced Adam out of magic, | 74 | 23 | 44 | 83 | 23 |
| Adam or Eve, the adorned holy bullock | 130 | 10 | 77 | 144 | 10 |
| O Adam and Eve together | 130 | 18 | 77 | 144 | 18 |
| Of Adam and Eve is never for a second | 130 | 24 | 77 | 145 | 2 |
| And upright Adam | 142 | 5 | 82 | 159 | 5 |
| Shining, it was Adam and maiden, | 160 | 8 | 85 | 179 | 8 |

ADAM'S
| Stale of Adam's brine until, vision | 29 | 3 | 17 | 34 | 7 |
| I, in a wind on fire, from green Adam's cradle, | 38 | 17 | 20 | 44 | 7 |
| That Adam's wether in the flock of horns, | 72 | 7 | 44 | 81 | 7 |

ADDERS
| And loosed the braiding adders from their hairs; | 30 | 22 | 18 | 35 | 22 |

ADMITS
| Who admits the delusive light through the bouncing wall, | 108 | 11 | 66 | 119 | 11 |

ADOLESCENCE
| The thief of adolescence, | 114 | 8 | 69 | 126 | 8 |

ADORATION
| And the lightnings of adoration | 140 | 9 | 82 | 157 | 9 |

ADORE
| Adore my windows for their summer scene? | 46 | 8 | 27 | 54 | 8 |

ADORED
| The adored | 144 | 11 | 82 | 161 | 11 |

ADORNED
| Adam or Eve, the adorned holy bullock | 130 | 10 | 77 | 144 | 10 |

ADORNING
| With dry flesh and earth for adorning and bed. | 133 | 15 | 78 | 148 | 18 |

ADVANCE
| I advance for as long as forever is. | 99 | 9 | 60 | 110 | 9 |

ADVENTURE
| Acquainted with the salt adventure | 8 | 9 | 5 | 9 | 9 |
| Sail on the level, the departing adventure, | 36 | 11 | 20 | 41 | 11 |

ADVICE
| All things are known: the stars' advice | 53 | 16 | 32 | 62 | 16 |

AESOP
| I young Aesop fabling to the near night by the dingle | 168 | 11 | 87 | 188 | 15 |

AFFECTIONATE
| Whispered the affectionate sand | 149 | 9 | 83 | 166 | 9 |

AFLAME
| Juan aflame and savagely young King Lear, | 113 | 11 | 69 | 125 | 11 |

AFLOAT

|  | U.K. | | Poem | U.S. | |
|  | Page | Line |  | Page | Line |
| AFLOAT | | | | | |
| In the throat, burning and turning. All night afloat | 136 | 2 | 81 | 153 | 2 |
| AFRAID | | | | | |
| I have longed to move away but am afraid; | 64 | 11 | 39 | 73 | 11 |
| At the point of love, forsaken and afraid. | 120 | 5 | 72 | 132 | 10 |
| AFTER | | | | | |
| And after came the imprints on the water, | 22 | 9 | 14 | 27 | 9 |
| And that is true after perpetual defeat. | 48 | 9 | 28 | 56 | 9 |
| After such fighting as the weakest know, | 48 | 10 | 28 | 56 | 10 |
| Because the pleasure-bird whistles after the hot wires, | 77 | 1 | 45 | 86 | 1 |
| After the funeral, mule praises, brays, | 87 | 1 | 52 | 96 | 1 |
| After the feast of tear-stuffed time and thistles | 87 | 10 | 52 | 96 | 10 |
| Not from this anger, anticlimax after | 90 | 1 | 54 | 99 | 1 |
| Not from this anger after | 90 | 11 | 54 | 99 | 11 |
| O wake to see, after a noble fall, | 96 | 18 | 58 | 107 | 1 |
| After the first death, there is no other. | 101 | 24 | 62 | 112 | 24 |
| That the phoenix' bid for heaven and the desire after | 110 | 17 | 67 | 121 | 19 |
| After the locks and chains | 112 | 12 | 68 | 124 | 12 |
| After the railings and shrubberies | 112 | 14 | 68 | 124 | 14 |
| Him up and he ran like a wind after the kindling flight | 122 | 9 | 72 | 135 | 9 |
| After a water-face walk, | 134 | 18 | 79 | 150 | 18 |
| Bird after dark and the laughing fish | 154 | 6 | 83 | 172 | 6 |
| To glow after the god stoning night | 158 | 11 | 84 | 177 | 11 |
| So it must have been after the birth of the simple light | 160 | 11 | 85 | 179 | 11 |
| Young as they in the after milking moonlight lay | 176 | 16 | 90 | 197 | 16 |
| Teach me the love that is evergreen after the fall leaved | 178 | 12 | 90 | 199 | 13 |
| Grave, after Beloved on the grass gulfed cross is scrubbed | 178 | 13 | 90 | 199 | 14 |
| After the funeral (In memory of Ann Jones) | 87 | | 52 | 96 | |
| Ceremony After a Fire Raid | 129 | | 77 | 143 | |
| AGAIN | | | | | |
| I dreamed my genesis and died again, shrapnel | 28 | 13 | 17 | 33 | 13 |
| Though they sink through the sea they shall rise again; | 68 | 7 | 42 | 77 | 7 |
| Or like the tide-looped breastknot reefed again | 78 | 11 | 46 | 87 | 11 |
| The old mud hatch again, the horrid | 96 | 19 | 58 | 107 | 2 |
| And I must enter again the round | 101 | 7 | 62 | 112 | 7 |
| Streamed again a wonder of summer | 103 | 18 | 63 | 114 | 18 |
| The sky gathered again | 160 | 9 | 85 | 179 | 9 |
| Daws Sir John's just hill dons, and again the gulled birds hare | 167 | 15 | 87 | 187 | 15 |

| | U.K. | | | U.S. | |
|---|---|---|---|---|---|
| | *Page* | *Line* | *Poem* | *Page* | *Line* |
| We grieve as the blithe birds, never again, leave shingle and elm, | 168 | 9 | 87 | 188 | 13 |
| AGAINST | | | | | |
| 'Rebel against the binding moon | 65 | 9 | 40 | 74 | 9 |
| Rebel against the flesh and bone, | 65 | 14 | 40 | 74 | 14 |
| Rebel against my father's dream | 66 | 3 | 40 | 75 | 3 |
| Under the cloud against love is caught and held and kissed | 109 | 17 | 67 | 120 | 17 |
| Rage, rage against the dying of the light. | 116 | 3 | 70 | 128 | 3 |
| Rage, rage against the dying of the light. | 116 | 9 | 70 | 128 | 9 |
| Rage, rage against the dying of the light. | 116 | 15 | 70 | 128 | 15 |
| Rage, rage against the dying of the light. | 116 | 19 | 70 | 128 | 19 |
| And laid your cheek against a cloud-formed shell: | 125 | 23 | 74 | 139 | 23 |
| AGAPE | | | | | |
| Agape, with woe | ix | 14 | 1 | xvii | 14 |
| AGE | | | | | |
| Drives my green age; that blasts the roots of trees | 9 | 2 | 6 | 10 | 2 |
| In this our age the gunman and his moll, | 14 | 11 | 10 | 16 | 11 |
| Comes, like a scissors stalking, tailor age, | 18 | 6 | 12 | 21 | 6 |
| The time for breast and the green apron age | 20 | 4 | 13 | 24 | 4 |
| Warms youth and seed and burns the seeds of age; | 24 | 8 | 15 | 29 | 8 |
| (My shape of age nagging the wounded whisper). | 72 | 22 | 44 | 81 | 22 |
| The grains beyond age, the dark veins of her mother, | 101 | 21 | 62 | 112 | 21 |
| Old age should burn and rave at close of day; | 116 | 2 | 70 | 128 | 2 |
| Leaves is dancing. Lines of age on the stones weave in a flock. | 121 | 23 | 72 | 134 | 18 |
| Back. Lines of age sleep on the stones till trumpeting dawn. | 123 | 8 | 72 | 136 | 18 |
| The morning is flying on the wings of his age | 135 | 13 | 80 | 152 | 13 |
| His driftwood thirty-fifth wind turned age; | 170 | 8 | 88 | 190 | 8 |
| AGED | | | | | |
| Among those Killed in the Dawn Raid was a Man Aged a Hundred | 135 | | 80 | 152 | |
| AGELESS | | | | | |
| Greek in the Irish sea the ageless voice: | 41 | 22 | 23 | 48 | 4 |
| AGENT | | | | | |
| Hairs of your head, then said the hollow agent, | 72 | 1 | 44 | 81 | 1 |
| AGES | | | | | |
| In the taken body at many ages, | 114 | 17 | 69 | 126 | 17 |
| Round the griefs of the ages, | 128 | 18 | 76 | 142 | 18 |
| AGHAST | | | | | |
| Who razed my wooden folly stands aghast, | 46 | 22 | 27 | 54 | 22 |

| | U.K. | | | U.S. | |
|---|---|---|---|---|---|
| | *Page* | *Line* | *Poem* | *Page* | *Line* |
| **AGO** | | | | | |
| A grief ago, | 54 | 1 | 33 | 63 | 1 |
| In the long ago land that glided the dark door wide | 121 | 12 | 72 | 134 | 7 |
| Of fields. For love, the long ago she bird rises. Look. | 121 | 25 | 72 | 134 | 20 |
| In the far ago land the door of his death glided wide, | 122 | 25 | 72 | 136 | 5 |
| To labour and love though they lay down long ago. | 176 | 5 | 90 | 197 | 5 |
| A grief ago | 54 | | 33 | 63 | |
| **AGONIZED** | | | | | |
| The agonized, two seas. | 90 | 7 | 54 | 99 | 7 |
| **AGONY** | | | | | |
| Before the agony; the spirit grows, | 48 | 3 | 28 | 56 | 3 |
| The stocked heart is forced, and agony has another mouth to feed. | 96 | 17 | 58 | 106 | 17 |
| **AGROUND** | | | | | |
| Dawn ships clouted aground, | 172 | 25 | 88 | 192 | 25 |
| **AHOY** | | | | | |
| Ahoy, old, sea-legged fox, | x | 15 | 1 | xviii | 21 |
| **AIR** | | | | | |
| Or lame the air with leaping from its heats; | 1 | 21 | 2 | 1 | 21 |
| One bough of bone across the rooting air, | 22 | 3 | 14 | 27 | 3 |
| Then all the matter of the living air | 26 | 21 | 16 | 32 | 1 |
| The halves that pierce the pin's point in the air, | 31 | 2 | 18 | 36 | 2 |
| We make me mystic as the arm of air, | 52 | 6 | 31 | 61 | 13 |
| That shapes each bushy item of the air | 60 | 5 | 36 | 69 | 5 |
| For there are ghosts in the air | 64 | 8 | 39 | 73 | 8 |
| And, crackling into the air, leave me half-blind. | 64 | 14 | 39 | 73 | 14 |
| Cudgel great air, wreck east, and topple sun-down, | 79 | 7 | 46 | 88 | 10 |
| And though my love pulls the pale, nippled air, | 80 | 13 | 46 | 89 | 21 |
| Heaven fell with his fall and one crocked bell beat the left air. | 95 | 25 | 58 | 105 | 25 |
| Before I rush in a crouch the ghost with a hammer, air, | 97 | 9 | 59 | 108 | 9 |
| And down the other air and the blue altered sky | 103 | 17 | 63 | 114 | 17 |
| You my friend there with a winning air | 107 | 3 | 65 | 118 | 3 |
| While you displaced a truth in the air, | 107 | 17 | 65 | 118 | 17 |
| Open as to the air to the naked shadow | 115 | 17 | 69 | 127 | 17 |
| Though no sound flowed down the hand folded air | 120 | 15 | 72 | 132 | 20 |
| A voice in the erected air, | 134 | 25 | 79 | 151 | 3 |
| Leads them as children and as air | 155 | 5 | 83 | 173 | 9 |
| Fields high as the house, the tunes from the chimneys, it was air | 159 | 20 | 85 | 178 | 20 |

| | U.K. | | | U.S. | |
|---|---|---|---|---|---|
| | Page | Line | Poem | Page | Line |
| Earth, air, water, fire, singing into the white act, | 165 | 16 | 86 | 185 | 6 |
| And air shaped Heaven where souls grow wild | 172 | 20 | 88 | 192 | 20 |
| AIR-DRAWN | | | | | |
| An air-drawn windmill on a wooden horse, | 41 | 20 | 23 | 48 | 2 |
| AIRY | | | | | |
| And earth and sky were as one airy hill, | 20 | 8 | 13 | 24 | 8 |
| AISLE | | | | | |
| Time marks a black aisle kindle from the brand of ashes, | 83 | 4 | 49 | 92 | 4 |
| AISLES | | | | | |
| Of day, in the thistle aisles, till the white owl crossed | 177 | 12 | 90 | 198 | 11 |
| ALBATROSS | | | | | |
| Hack of the cough, the hanging albatross, | 67 | 10 | 41 | 76 | 10 |
| ALCOVE | | | | | |
| Alcove of words out of cicada shade, | 82 | 4 | 48 | 91 | 4 |
| ALIGHT | | | | | |
| That set alight the weathers from a spark, | 22 | 14 | 14 | 27 | 14 |
| Soon sets alight a long stick from the cradle; | 71 | 20 | 44 | 80 | 20 |
| ALIVE | | | | | |
| The redhaired cancer still alive, | 4 | 20 | 3 | 4 | 20 |
| Over the sea-gut loudening, sets a rock alive; | 49 | 15 | 29 | 58 | 15 |
| Alone alive among his mutton fold, | 72 | 16 | 44 | 81 | 16 |
| To-night shall find no dying but alive and warm | 100 | 15 | 61 | 111 | 15 |
| Sang alive | 104 | 7 | 63 | 115 | 9 |
| A girl alive with his hooks through her lips; | 149 | 22 | 83 | 167 | 2 |
| And terribly lead him home alive | 157 | 6 | 83 | 175 | 18 |
| ALL | | | | | |
| And all the dry seabed unlocked, | 4 | 8 | 3 | 4 | 8 |
| All issue armoured, of the grave, | 4 | 19 | 3 | 4 | 19 |
| All but the briskest riders thrown, | 5 | 17 | 3 | 5 | 17 |
| That utters all love hunger | 10 | 9 | 7 | 11 | 9 |
| Till all our sea-faiths die. | 11 | 24 | 8 | 12 | 24 |
| And all the herrings smelling in the sea, | 13 | 5 | 9 | 14 | 12 |
| Our eunuch dreams, all seedless in the light, | 14 | 1 | 10 | 16 | 1 |
| The shades of girls, all flavoured from their shrouds, | 14 | 7 | 10 | 16 | 7 |
| The signal grass that tells me all I know | 16 | 22 | 11 | 19 | 22 |
| All, men my madmen, the unwholesome wind | 19 | 21 | 12 | 23 | 6 |
| All world was one, one windy nothing, | 20 | 6 | 13 | 24 | 6 |
| Abstracted all the letters of the void; | 22 | 21 | 14 | 27 | 21 |
| Then all the matter of the living air | 26 | 21 | 16 | 32 | 1 |
| Through all the irons in the grass, metal | 28 | 7 | 17 | 33 | 7 |
| All all and all the dry worlds lever, | 33 | 1 | 19 | 38 | 1 |
| All from the oil, the pound of lava. | 33 | 3 | 19 | 38 | 3 |
| All all and all, the corpse's lover, | 33 | 10 | 19 | 38 | 10 |
| All of the flesh, the dry worlds lever. | 33 | 12 | 19 | 38 | 12 |

ALL (continued)

|  | U.K. | | Poem | U.S. | |
|---|---|---|---|---|---|
|  | Page | Line |  | Page | Line |
| All all and all the dry worlds couple, | 34 | 1 | 19 | 39 | 7 |
| All that shapes from the caul and suckle, | 34 | 4 | 19 | 39 | 10 |
| Flower, flower, all all and all. | 34 | 12 | 19 | 39 | 18 |
| All heaven in a midnight of the sun, | 40 | 17 | 22 | 46 | 17 |
| All legends' sweethearts on a tree of stories, | 41 | 25 | 23 | 48 | 7 |
| With tongues that talk all tongues. | 44 | 14 | 25 | 52 | 14 |
| Tell, if at all, the winter's storms | 45 | 10 | 26 | 53 | 10 |
| Am I not all of you by the directed sea | 46 | 13 | 27 | 54 | 13 |
| You are all these, said she who gave me the long suck, | 46 | 17 | 27 | 54 | 17 |
| All these, he said who sacked the children's town, | 46 | 18 | 27 | 54 | 18 |
| Lie all unknowing of the grave sin-eater. | 47 | 8 | 27 | 55 | 8 |
| All could not disappoint; | 48 | 6 | 28 | 56 | 6 |
| The hollow words could bear all suffering | 48 | 22 | 28 | 56 | 22 |
| For all there is to give I offer: | 48 | 28 | 28 | 57 | 5 |
| The child shall question all his days, | 53 | 7 | 32 | 62 | 7 |
| All things are known: the stars' advice | 53 | 16 | 32 | 62 | 16 |
| Shape all her whelps with the long voice of water, | 55 | 2 | 33 | 64 | 5 |
| Unshelve that all my gristles have a gown | 56 | 6 | 34 | 65 | 6 |
| All nerves to serve the sun, | 56 | 15 | 34 | 65 | 15 |
| And all sweet hell, deaf as an hour's ear, | 57 | 5 | 34 | 66 | 12 |
| And father all nor fail the fly-lord's acre, | 60 | 13 | 36 | 69 | 13 |
| From all my mortal lovers with a starboard smile; | 60 | 21 | 36 | 69 | 21 |
| All shall remain and on the graveward gulf | 67 | 27 | 41 | 76 | 27 |
| Split all ends up they shan't crack; | 68 | 17 | 42 | 77 | 17 |
| Knew all His horrible desires | 69 | 10 | 43 | 78 | 10 |
| Death is all metaphors, shape in one history; | 71 | 15 | 44 | 80 | 15 |
| A Bible-leaved of all the written woods | 74 | 16 | 44 | 83 | 16 |
| I by the tree of thieves, all glory's sawbones, | 75 | 15 | 44 | 84 | 15 |
| When all my five and country senses see, | 81 | 1 | 47 | 90 | 1 |
| In all love's countries, that will grope awake; | 81 | 12 | 47 | 90 | 12 |
| And all love's sinners in sweet cloth kneel to a hyleg image, | 84 | 4 | 49 | 93 | 10 |
| But I, Ann's bard on a raised hearth, call all | 87 | 21 | 52 | 96 | 21 |
| That all the charmingly drowned arise to cock-crow and kill. | 89 | 6 | 53 | 98 | 6 |
| To take to give is all, return what is hungrily given | 94 | 4 | 57 | 104 | 4 |
| That will rake at last all currencies of the marked breath | 94 | 8 | 57 | 104 | 8 |
| Cut Christbread spitting vinegar and all | 95 | 16 | 58 | 105 | 16 |
| 'All game phrases fit your ring of a cockfight: | 97 | 6 | 59 | 108 | 6 |
| Nor when all ponderous heaven's host of waters breaks. | 97 | 20 | 59 | 108 | 20 |

10

| | U.K. | | | U.S. | |
|---|---|---|---|---|---|
| | Page | Line | Poem | Page | Line |
| Fathering and all humbling darkness | 101 | 3 | 62 | 112 | 3 |
| And walked abroad in a shower of all my days. | 102 | 16 | 63 | 113 | 16 |
| But all the gardens | 103 | 10 | 63 | 114 | 10 |
| That all is undone, | 105 | 5 | 64 | 116 | 5 |
| And the souls of all men | 105 | 19 | 64 | 116 | 19 |
| And all your deeds and words, | 106 | 10 | 64 | 117 | 10 |
| All love but for the full assemblage in flower | 110 | 12 | 67 | 121 | 14 |
| Made all day until bell time | 112 | 7 | 68 | 124 | 7 |
| All night in the unmade park | 112 | 13 | 68 | 124 | 13 |
| Jealousy cannot forget for all her sakes, | 114 | 11 | 69 | 126 | 11 |
| All blood-signed assailings and vanished marriages in which he had no lovely part | 114 | 20 | 69 | 126 | 20 |
| And all the woken farm at its white trades, | 119 | 25 | 72 | 132 | 5 |
| By losing him all in love, and cast his need | 120 | 27 | 72 | 133 | 12 |
| And all the elements of the slow fall rejoiced | 122 | 4 | 72 | 135 | 4 |
| All night lost and long wading in the wake of the she- | 122 | 18 | 72 | 135 | 18 |
| Unclenched, armless, silk and rough love that breaks all rocks. | 126 | 16 | 74 | 140 | 16 |
| Her heart all ears and eyes, lips catching the avalanche | 127 | 10 | 75 | 141 | 10 |
| With all their griefs in their arms, | 128 | 5 | 76 | 142 | 5 |
| When all the keys shot from the locks, and rang. | 135 | 8 | 80 | 152 | 8 |
| In the throat, burning and turning. All night afloat | 136 | 2 | 81 | 153 | 2 |
| The voices of all the drowned swam on the wind. | 136 | 8 | 81 | 153 | 8 |
| All men | 144 | 10 | 82 | 161 | 10 |
| To know all | 146 | 7 | 82 | 163 | 7 |
| All the fishes were rayed in blood, | 149 | 23 | 83 | 167 | 3 |
| Oh all the wanting flesh his enemy | 152 | 19 | 83 | 170 | 11 |
| And all the lifted waters walk and leap. | 153 | 16 | 83 | 171 | 12 |
| All the horses of his haul of miracles | 156 | 19 | 83 | 175 | 7 |
| Praise that the spring time is all | 158 | 14 | 84 | 177 | 14 |
| All the sun long it was running, it was lovely, the hay | 159 | 19 | 85 | 178 | 19 |
| All the moon long I heard, blessed among stables, the night-jars | 160 | 3 | 85 | 179 | 3 |
| With the dew, come back, the cock on his shoulder: it was all | 160 | 7 | 85 | 179 | 7 |
| In all his tuneful turning so few and such morning songs | 160 | 21 | 85 | 179 | 21 |
| For ever of all not the wolf in his baaing hood | 163 | 13 | 86 | 182 | 13 |
| Leaping! The gospel rooks! All tell, this night, of him | 165 | 9 | 86 | 184 | 17 |
| Ever and ever by all your vows believe and fear | 166 | 8 | 86 | 186 | 8 |
| All praise of the hawk on fire in hawk-eyed dusk be sung, | 168 | 3 | 87 | 188 | 7 |

ALL (continued)

| | U.K. | | | U.S. | |
|---|---|---|---|---|---|
| | *Page* | *Line* | *Poem* | *Page* | *Line* |
| Makes all the music; and I who hear the tune of the slow, | 169 | 9 | 87 | 189 | 18 |
| With all the living, prays, | 172 | 12 | 88 | 192 | 12 |
| All the green leaved little weddings' wives | 174 | 11 | 89 | 194 | 11 |
| I whistled all night in the twisted flues, | 174 | 18 | 89 | 194 | 18 |
| And all the deadly virtues plague my death! | 175 | 31 | 89 | 196 | 12 |
| Hill. Who once in gooseskin winter loved all ice leaved | 176 | 12 | 90 | 197 | 12 |
| All birds and beasts of the linked night uproar and chime | 177 | 15 | 90 | 198 | 14 |
| Or still all the numberless days of his death, though | | | 91 | 200 | 8 |
| Above all he longed for his mother's breast | | | 91 | 200 | 9 |
| All his bones crying, and poor in all but pain, | | | 91 | 200 | 21 |
| O deepest wound of all that he should die | | | 91 | 201 | 16 |
| All all and all the dry worlds lever | 33 | | 19 | 38 | |
| When all my five and country senses see | 81 | | 47 | 90 | |
| ALL-HOLLOWED | | | | | |
| All-hollowed man wept for his white apparel | 38 | 24 | 20 | 44 | 14 |
| ALLOTMENTS | | | | | |
| Above the waste allotments the dawn halts. | 25 | 6 | 15 | 30 | 6 |
| ALLOWS | | | | | |
| And nothing I cared, at my sky blue trades, that time allows | 160 | 20 | 85 | 179 | 20 |
| ALMOST | | | | | |
| On almost the incendiary eve | 117 | 1 | 71 | 129 | 1 |
| On almost the incendiary eve | 117 | 13 | 71 | 129 | 13 |
| On almost the incendiary eve | 117 | 25 | 71 | 130 | 1 |
| ALONE | | | | | |
| We will ride out alone, and then, | x | 8 | 1 | xviii | 14 |
| Alone till the day I die | 58 | 6 | 35 | 67 | 6 |
| Alone alive among his mutton fold, | 72 | 16 | 44 | 81 | 16 |
| An enamoured man alone by the twigs of his eyes, two fires, | 77 | 7 | 45 | 86 | 7 |
| And, pride is last, is like a child alone | 78 | 13 | 46 | 87 | 13 |
| I stand, for this memorial's sake, alone | 87 | 12 | 52 | 96 | 12 |
| Alone between nurses and swans | 112 | 2 | 68 | 124 | 2 |
| Oceanic lover alone | 114 | 10 | 69 | 126 | 10 |
| O she lies alone and still, | 115 | 18 | 69 | 127 | 18 |
| Torn and alone in a farm house in a fold | 119 | 15 | 72 | 131 | 15 |
| And the duck pond glass and the blinding byres alone | 120 | 10 | 72 | 132 | 15 |
| Alone and naked in the engulfing bride, | 120 | 28 | 72 | 133 | 13 |
| That a man knelt alone in the cup of the vales, | 122 | 5 | 72 | 135 | 5 |
| Now see, alone in us, | 126 | 12 | 74 | 140 | 12 |
| Waking alone in a multitude of loves when morning's light | 127 | 1 | 75 | 141 | 1 |

|  | U.K. | | | U.S. | |
| --- | --- | --- | --- | --- | --- |
|  | *Page* | *Line* | *Poem* | *Page* | *Line* |
| Her deepsea pillow where once she married alone, | 127 | 9 | 75 | 141 | 9 |
| But dark alone | 137 | 14 | 82 | 154 | 14 |
| He stands alone at the door of his home, | 157 | 23 | 83 | 176 | 15 |
| That uncalm still it is sure alone to stand and sing | 158 | 21 | 84 | 177 | 21 |
| Alone in the husk of man's home | 158 | 22 | 84 | 177 | 22 |
| He, on the earth of the night, alone | 172 | 11 | 88 | 192 | 11 |
| And my shining men no more alone | 173 | 26 | 88 | 193 | 26 |
| And alone in the night's eternal, curving act | 176 | 9 | 90 | 197 | 9 |
| ALONE'S |  |  |  |  |  |
| Alone's unhurt, so the blind man sees best. | 50 | 9 | 30 | 59 | 9 |
| ALONG |  |  |  |  |  |
| My hero bares his nerves along my wrist | 10 | 1 | 7 | 11 | 1 |
| The knobbly ape that swings along his sex | 13 | 9 | 9 | 14 | 16 |
| So, planing-heeled, I flew along my man | 26 | 4 | 16 | 31 | 4 |
| Here in this spring, stars float along the void; | 45 | 1 | 26 | 53 | 1 |
| That burns along my eyes. | 90 | 14 | 54 | 99 | 14 |
| Along her innocence glided | 113 | 10 | 69 | 125 | 10 |
| ALOUD |  |  |  |  |  |
| Curlews aloud in the congered waves | 170 | 13 | 88 | 190 | 13 |
| Count my blessings aloud: | 172 | 27 | 88 | 192 | 27 |
| ALPHABET |  |  |  |  |  |
| Strip to this tree: a rocking alphabet, | 74 | 17 | 44 | 83 | 17 |
| ALPS |  |  |  |  |  |
| Whales in the wake like capes and Alps | 151 | 1 | 83 | 168 | 9 |
| ALREADY |  |  |  |  |  |
| That the eyes are already murdered, | 96 | 16 | 58 | 106 | 16 |
| ALSO |  |  |  |  |  |
| Glory also this star, bird | viii | 14 | 1 | xvi | 14 |
| ALTAR |  |  |  |  |  |
| You who bow down at cross and altar, | 8 | 19 | 5 | 9 | 19 |
| Grief with dishevelled hands tear out the altar ghost | 83 | 5 | 49 | 92 | 5 |
| On the altar of London, | 130 | 14 | 77 | 144 | 14 |
| ALTARWISE |  |  |  |  |  |
| Altarwise by owl-light in the half-way house | 71 | 1 | 44 | 80 | 1 |
| Altarwise by owl-light | 71 |  | 44 | 80 |  |
| ALTER |  |  |  |  |  |
| And, when it quickens, alter the actions' pace | 63 | 12 | 38 | 72 | 12 |
| ALTERED |  |  |  |  |  |
| And down the other air and the blue altered sky | 103 | 17 | 63 | 114 | 17 |
| ALWAYS |  |  |  |  |  |
| Her holy unholy hours with the always anonymous beast. | 114 | 23 | 69 | 126 | 23 |
| And always known must leave | 117 | 4 | 71 | 129 | 4 |
| In the always desiring centre of the white | 120 | 23 | 72 | 133 | 8 |
| The sky stride of the always slain | 142 | 10 | 82 | 159 | 10 |

ALWAYS (continued)

|  |  | U.K. | | Poem | U.S. | |
|  |  | Page | Line |  | Page | Line |
| Always good-bye to the long-legged bread |  | 152 | 22 | 83 | 170 | 14 |
| Always good-bye to the fires of the face, |  | 153 | 2 | 83 | 170 | 18 |
| Is always lost in her vaulted breath, |  | 153 | 20 | 83 | 171 | 16 |
| Always good-bye, cried the voices through the shell, |  | 154 | 1 | 83 | 172 | 1 |
| Good-bye always for the flesh is cast |  | 154 | 2 | 83 | 172 | 2 |
| Always good luck, praised the finned in the feather |  | 154 | 5 | 83 | 172 | 5 |
| In the moon that is always rising, |  | 160 | 26 | 85 | 180 | 3 |
| Now will be ever is always true, |  | 171 | 24 | 88 | 191 | 24 |

AM

| I am the man your father was. |  | 3 | 4 | 2 | 3 | 10 |
| And I am dumb to tell the hanging man |  | 9 | 14 | 6 | 10 | 14 |
| And I am dumb to tell a weather's wind |  | 9 | 19 | 6 | 10 | 19 |
| And I am dumb to tell the lover's tomb |  | 9 | 21 | 6 | 10 | 21 |
| And I am dumb to tell the crooked rose |  | 9 | 4 | 6 | 10 | 4 |
| And I am dumb to mouth unto my veins |  | 9 | 9 | 6 | 10 | 9 |
| Of love am barer than Cadaver's trap |  | 18 | 8 | 12 | 21 | 8 |
| Do you not mother me, nor, as I am, |  | 46 | 3 | 27 | 54 | 3 |
| Am I not father, too, and the ascending boy, |  | 46 | 9 | 27 | 54 | 9 |
| Am I not sister, too, who is my saviour? |  | 46 | 12 | 27 | 54 | 12 |
| Am I not all of you by the directed sea |  | 46 | 13 | 27 | 54 | 13 |
| Am I not you who front the tidy shore, |  | 46 | 15 | 27 | 54 | 15 |
| I am, the tower told, felled by a timeless stroke, |  | 46 | 21 | 27 | 54 | 21 |
| Let the soil squeal I am the biting man |  | 56 | 20 | 34 | 65 | 20 |
| I have longed to move away but am afraid; |  | 64 | 11 | 39 | 73 | 11 |
| I am the long world's gentleman, he said, |  | 71 | 13 | 44 | 80 | 13 |
| For I was lost who am |  | 140 | 6 | 82 | 157 | 6 |
| Am found. |  | 148 | 10 | 82 | 165 | 10 |
| Now I am lost in the blinding |  | 148 | 16 | 82 | 165 | 16 |
| And I am struck as lonely as a holy maker by the sun. |  | 158 | 12 | 84 | 177 | 12 |
| Now I am a man no more no more |  | 175 | 20 | 89 | 196 | 1 |
| I am not too proud to cry that He and he |  |  |  | 91 | 200 | 19 |

AMBASSADOR

| I sent my own ambassador to light; |  | 5 | 9 | 3 | 5 | 9 |

AMBITION

| Not for ambition or bread |  | 128 | 7 | 76 | 142 | 7 |

AMBULANCE

| The heavenly ambulance drawn by a wound |  | 135 | 10 | 80 | 152 | 10 |

AMBUSH

| Toils towards the ambush of his wounds; |  | 170 | 17 | 88 | 190 | 17 |

AMEN

| And the known dark of the earth amen. |  | 147 | 18 | 82 | 164 | 18 |

AMONG

| Halt among eunuchs, and the nitric stain |  | 18 | 24 | 12 | 22 | 4 |
| Limp in the street of sea, among the rabble |  | 30 | 15 | 18 | 35 | 15 |

14

| | U.K. | | | U.S. | |
|---|---|---|---|---|---|
| | Page | Line | Poem | Page | Line |
| Naked among the bow-and-arrow birds | 60 | 23 | 36 | 69 | 23 |
| And, from his fork, a dog among the fairies, | 71 | 4 | 44 | 80 | 4 |
| Alone alive among his mutton fold, | 72 | 16 | 44 | 81 | 16 |
| What of a bamboo man among your acres? | 73 | 3 | 44 | 82 | 3 |
| Among men later I heard it said | 93 | 16 | 56 | 102 | 16 |
| Lapped among herods wail | 96 | 14 | 58 | 106 | 14 |
| Or a nacreous sleep among soft particles and charms | 97 | 17 | 59 | 108 | 17 |
| Saint carved and sensual among the scudding | 109 | 5 | 67 | 120 | 5 |
| While the boys among willows | 112 | 3 | 68 | 124 | 3 |
| Warning among the folds, and the frozen hold | 119 | 8 | 72 | 131 | 8 |
| When cold as snow he should run the wended vales among | 120 | 20 | 72 | 133 | 5 |
| Among the street burned to tireless death | 129 | 4 | 77 | 143 | 4 |
| She longs among horses and angels, | 150 | 9 | 83 | 167 | 13 |
| Weeps like the risen sun among | 155 | 19 | 83 | 174 | 3 |
| And the bait is drowned among hayricks, | 157 | 16 | 83 | 176 | 8 |
| And honoured among wagons I was prince of the apple towns | 159 | 6 | 85 | 178 | 6 |
| And as I was green and carefree, famous among the barns | 159 | 10 | 85 | 178 | 10 |
| All the moon long I heard, blessed among stables, the night-jars | 160 | 3 | 85 | 179 | 3 |
| And honoured among foxes and pheasants by the gay house | 160 | 15 | 85 | 179 | 15 |
| And staved, and riven among plumes my rider weep. | 162 | 16 | 86 | 181 | 16 |
| Of birds! Among the cocks like fire the red fox | 164 | 20 | 86 | 184 | 6 |
| Of psalms and shadows among the pincered sandcrabs prancing | 167 | 24 | 87 | 188 | 5 |
| In his house on stilts high among beaks | 170 | 4 | 88 | 190 | 4 |
| Young among the long flocks, and never lie lost | | | 91 | 200 | 7 |
| Here among the light of the lording sky | | | 91 | 201 | 8 |
| Among those Killed in the Dawn Raid was a Man Aged a Hundred | 135 | | 80 | 152 | |

ANATOMIST
| Come love's anatomist with sun-gloved hand | 79 | 18 | 46 | 88 | 21 |

ANCESTRALLY
| Or rent ancestrally the roped sea-hymen, | 78 | 12 | 46 | 87 | 12 |

ANCHOR
| The deadrock base and blow the flowered anchor, | 51 | 5 | 31 | 60 | 5 |
| Ships anchor off the bay. | 58 | 20 | 35 | 67 | 20 |
| Ships anchor off the bay, | 59 | 2 | 35 | 68 | 2 |
| Boat with its anchor free and fast | 149 | 6 | 83 | 166 | 6 |
| Where the anchor rode like a gull | 150 | 13 | 83 | 167 | 17 |
| The anchor dives through the floors of a church. | 157 | 20 | 83 | 176 | 12 |

| | U.K. | | | U.S. | |
|---|---|---|---|---|---|
| | *Page* | *Line* | *Poem* | *Page* | *Line* |
| ANCHORED | | | | | |
| Be by the ships' sea broken at the manstring anchored | 38 | 8 | 20 | 43 | 18 |
| Harbours my anchored tongue, slips the quay-stone, | 78 | 3 | 46 | 87 | 3 |
| ANCHORGROUND | | | | | |
| In that bright anchorground where I lay linened, | 79 | 22 | 46 | 89 | 3 |
| ANCIENT | | | | | |
| Hold hard, these ancient minutes in the cuckoo's month, | 49 | 1 | 29 | 58 | 1 |
| The mummy cloths expose an ancient breast. | 63 | 8 | 38 | 72 | 8 |
| Neither by night's ancient fear, | 64 | 15 | 39 | 73 | 15 |
| Each ancient, stone-necked minute of love's season | 78 | 2 | 46 | 87 | 2 |
| Ancient woods of my blood, dash down to the nut of the seas | 94 | 11 | 57 | 104 | 11 |
| The woundward flight of the ancient | 142 | 8 | 82 | 159 | 8 |
| Hold hard, these ancient minutes in the cuckoo's month | 49 | | 29 | 58 | |
| ANDROGYNOUS | | | | | |
| In the androgynous dark, | 110 | 2 | 67 | 121 | 4 |
| ANEMONE | | | | | |
| Sing and howl through sand and anemone | 152 | 17 | 83 | 170 | 9 |
| ANEW | | | | | |
| To shade and knit anew the patch of words | 21 | 10 | 13 | 25 | 10 |
| ANGEL | | | | | |
| The arterial angel. | 30 | 24 | 18 | 35 | 24 |
| Suffer, my topsy-turvies, that a double angel | 37 | 26 | 20 | 43 | 9 |
| Cross-stroked salt Adam to the frozen angel | 73 | 21 | 44 | 82 | 21 |
| A hill touches an angel. Out of a saint's cell | 163 | 4 | 86 | 182 | 4 |
| ANGEL'S | | | | | |
| Binding my angel's hood. | 32 | 6 | 18 | 37 | 12 |
| ANGELIC | | | | | |
| 'But this we tread bears the angelic gangs, | 26 | 13 | 16 | 31 | 13 |
| On the angelic etna of the last whirring feather-lands, | 95 | 11 | 58 | 105 | 11 |
| ANGELS | | | | | |
| As, blowing on the angels, I was lost | 26 | 17 | 16 | 31 | 17 |
| She longs among horses and angels, | 150 | 9 | 83 | 167 | 13 |
| More spanned with angels ride | 173 | 23 | 88 | 193 | 23 |
| In the coal black sky and she bore angels! | 175 | 26 | 89 | 196 | 7 |
| ANGELUS | | | | | |
| Wave's silence, wept white angelus knells. | 171 | 11 | 88 | 191 | 11 |
| ANGER | | | | | |
| Forsake, the fool, the hardiness of anger. | 51 | 7 | 31 | 60 | 7 |
| Brand of the lily's anger on her ring, | 54 | 19 | 33 | 63 | 19 |

|  | U.K. | | | U.S. | |
|---|---|---|---|---|---|
|  | *Page* | *Line* | *Poem* | *Page* | *Line* |
| Not from this anger, anticlimax after | 90 | 1 | 54 | 99 | 1 |
| Not from this anger after | 90 | 11 | 54 | 99 | 11 |
| Not from this anger | 90 | | 54 | 99 | |
| ANGLE | | | | | |
| Star-set at Jacob's angle, | 38 | 3 | 20 | 43 | 13 |
| This was the sky, Jack Christ, each minstrel angle | 75 | 11 | 44 | 84 | 11 |
| Tongue and ear in the thread, angle the temple-bound | 91 | 26 | 55 | 101 | 4 |
| ANGRILY | | | | | |
| Your sport is summer as the spring runs angrily. | 49 | 24 | 29 | 58 | 24 |
| ANGUISH | | | | | |
| To the anguish and carrion, to the infant forever unfree, | 97 | 22 | 59 | 109 | 2 |
| He sings towards anguish; finches fly | 170 | 20 | 88 | 190 | 20 |
| ANIMAL | | | | | |
| At nightbreak born in the fat side, from an animal bed | 84 | 2 | 49 | 93 | 8 |
| How shall my animal | 91 | 1 | 55 | 100 | 1 |
| Curl-locked and animal cavepools of spells and bone, | 91 | 27 | 55 | 101 | 5 |
| Man, animal, or bird | 125 | 13 | 74 | 139 | 13 |
| Sanctum sanctorum the animal eye of the wood | 163 | 7 | 86 | 182 | 7 |
| How shall my animal | 91 | | 55 | 100 | |
| ANIMALS | | | | | |
| But animals thick as thieves | ix | 23 | 1 | xvii | 23 |
| And animals and birds, | 106 | 7 | 64 | 117 | 7 |
| With birds and animals | 155 | 24 | 83 | 174 | 8 |
| ANKLING | | | | | |
| Now on Sir John's hill. The heron, ankling the scaly | 169 | 7 | 87 | 189 | 16 |
| ANN | | | | | |
| In the snivelling hours with dead, humped Ann | 87 | 13 | 52 | 96 | 13 |
| And sculptured Ann is seventy years of stone. | 88 | 7 | 52 | 97 | 7 |
| After the funeral (In memory of Ann Jones) | 87 | | 52 | 96 | |
| ANN'S | | | | | |
| But I, Ann's bard on a raised hearth, call all | 87 | 21 | 52 | 96 | 21 |
| ANNIVERSARY | | | | | |
| This ragged anniversary of two | 124 | 2 | 73 | 138 | 2 |
| On a Wedding Anniversary | 124 | | 73 | 138 | |
| ANNOUNCED | | | | | |
| Close and far she announced the theft of the heart | 114 | 16 | 69 | 126 | 16 |
| ANONYMOUS | | | | | |
| Her holy unholy hours with the always anonymous beast. | 114 | 23 | 69 | 126 | 23 |

|  | U.K. | | Poem | U.S. | |
| --- | --- | --- | --- | --- | --- |
|  | *Page* | *Line* |  | *Page* | *Line* |
| ANOTHER |  |  |  |  |  |
| The stocked heart is forced, and agony has another mouth to feed. | 96 | 17 | 58 | 106 | 17 |
| Your polestar neighbor, sun of another street, | 117 | 17 | 71 | 129 | 17 |
| Time is bearing another son. | 155 | 9 | 83 | 173 | 13 |
| ANSWER |  |  |  |  |  |
| Love's house, they answer, and the tower death | 47 | 7 | 27 | 55 | 7 |
| The yes to death, the yesman and the answer, | 51 | 12 | 31 | 60 | 12 |
| Shall a white answer echo from the rooftops. | 53 | 15 | 32 | 62 | 15 |
| And 'Know no answer,' and I know | 53 | 23 | 32 | 62 | 23 |
| No answer to the children's cry | 53 | 24 | 32 | 62 | 24 |
| Of echo's answer and the man of frost | 53 | 25 | 32 | 62 | 25 |
| ANSWERING |  |  |  |  |  |
| Into the answering skies from the green ground, | 100 | 7 | 61 | 111 | 7 |
| ANSWERS |  |  |  |  |  |
| His lightning answers my | 148 | 14 | 82 | 165 | 14 |
| ANTICLIMAX |  |  |  |  |  |
| Not from this anger, anticlimax after | 90 | 1 | 54 | 99 | 1 |
| ANTIPODES |  |  |  |  |  |
| Said the antipodes, and twice spring chimed. | 72 | 18 | 44 | 81 | 18 |
| An upright man in the antipodes | 77 | 23 | 45 | 86 | 23 |
| ANTISEPTIC |  |  |  |  |  |
| The tray of knives, the antiseptic funeral; | 37 | 3 | 20 | 42 | 9 |
| ANTLERED |  |  |  |  |  |
| And fast through the drifts of the thickets antlered like deer, | 122 | 15 | 72 | 135 | 15 |
| ANTLERS |  |  |  |  |  |
| Combing with antlers, Columbus on fire, | 133 | 9 | 78 | 148 | 12 |
| ANVILS |  |  |  |  |  |
| (A clash of anvils for my | ix | 20 | 1 | xvii | 20 |
| ANY |  |  |  |  |  |
| Would wither up, and any boy of love | 63 | 3 | 38 | 72 | 3 |
| With any further | 101 | 17 | 62 | 112 | 17 |
| Clung to the pitching clouds, or gay with any one | 176 | 15 | 90 | 197 | 15 |
| APART |  |  |  |  |  |
| Not for the proud man apart | 128 | 12 | 76 | 142 | 12 |
| Terror will rage apart | 171 | 16 | 88 | 191 | 16 |
| APE |  |  |  |  |  |
| The knobbly ape that swings along his sex | 13 | 9 | 9 | 14 | 16 |
| APPAREL |  |  |  |  |  |
| All-hollowed man wept for his white apparel | 38 | 24 | 20 | 44 | 14 |
| APPLE |  |  |  |  |  |
| I would not fear the apple nor the flood | 12 | 6 | 9 | 13 | 6 |
| In shapes of sin forked out the bearded apple, | 40 | 4 | 22 | 46 | 4 |
| Now as I was young and easy under the apple boughs | 159 | 1 | 85 | 178 | 1 |

| | U.K. | | | U.S. | |
|---|---|---|---|---|---|
| | *Page* | *Line* | *Poem* | *Page* | *Line* |
| And honoured among wagons I was prince of the apple towns | 159 | 6 | 85 | 178 | 6 |
| Milled dust of the apple tree and the pounded islands | 164 | 10 | 86 | 183 | 17 |
| Apple seed glides, | 164 | 12 | 86 | 183 | 19 |
| APPLES | | | | | |
| And drown the cargoed apples in their tides. | 1 | 6 | 2 | 1 | 6 |
| With apples | 103 | 19 | 63 | 114 | 19 |
| APRIL | | | | | |
| Crack like a spring in a vice, bone breaking April, | 49 | 17 | 29 | 58 | 17 |
| APPROACHING | | | | | |
| Like an approaching wave I sprawl to ruin. | 79 | 12 | 46 | 88 | 15 |
| APRON | | | | | |
| The time for breast and the green apron age | 20 | 4 | 13 | 24 | 4 |
| ARAN | | | | | |
| Sprout from the stony lockers like a tree on Aran. | 37 | 27 | 20 | 43 | 10 |
| ARC | | | | | |
| Under the arc of the sky they are unsafe. | 50 | 5 | 30 | 59 | 5 |
| Bend, if my journey ache, direction like an arc or make | 97 | 14 | 59 | 108 | 14 |
| As the arc of the billhooks that flashed the hedges low | 178 | 7 | 90 | 199 | 8 |
| ARCHED | | | | | |
| Gallop through the arched, green farms, | 156 | 20 | 83 | 175 | 8 |
| ARCHIVES | | | | | |
| From the oracular archives and the parchment, | 75 | 19 | 44 | 84 | 19 |
| ARCLAMPS | | | | | |
| They dance between their arclamps and our skull, | 14 | 17 | 10 | 16 | 17 |
| ARC-LAMPED | | | | | |
| Arc-lamped thrown back upon the cutting flood. | 73 | 10 | 44 | 82 | 10 |
| ARCS | | | | | |
| Shot in the wind, by tilted arcs, | 69 | 26 | 43 | 79 | 2 |
| ARCTIC | | | | | |
| The Arctic scut, and basin of the South, | 31 | 20 | 18 | 37 | 2 |
| ARE | | | | | |
| These boys of light are curdlers in their folly, | 1 | 7 | 2 | 1 | 7 |
| We are the dark deniers, let us summon | 2 | 7 | 2 | 2 | 7 |
| And boys are full and foreign in the pouch. | 3 | 3 | 2 | 3 | 9 |
| We are the sons of flint and pitch. | 3 | 5 | 2 | 3 | 11 |
| O see the poles are kissing as they cross. | 3 | 6 | 2 | 3 | 12 |
| The fences of the light are down, | 5 | 16 | 3 | 5 | 16 |
| The words of death are dryer than his stiff, | 13 | 18 | 9 | 15 | 4 |
| My wordy wounds are printed with your hair | 13 | 19 | 9 | 15 | 5 |

ARE (continued)

|  | U.K. | | | U.S. | |
|---|---|---|---|---|---|
|  | Page | Line | Poem | Page | Line |
| When sunlight goes are sundered from the worm, | 14 | 8 | 10 | 16 | 8 |
| Sweet are their fathered faces in their wings.' | 26 | 14 | 16 | 31 | 14 |
| 'These are but dreaming men. Breathe, and they fade.' | 26 | 15 | 16 | 31 | 15 |
| The broken halves are fellowed in a cripple, | 30 | 13 | 18 | 35 | 13 |
| Rotating halves are horning as they drill | 30 | 23 | 18 | 35 | 23 |
| On casting tides, are tangled in the shells, | 32 | 2 | 18 | 37 | 8 |
| These are your years' recorders. The circular world stands still.) | 37 | 21 | 20 | 143 | 4 |
| When clouds are cursed by thunder, | 44 | 2 | 25 | 52 | 2 |
| When it is rain where are the gods? | 44 | 5 | 25 | 52 | 5 |
| An old god's dugs are pressed and pricked, | 44 | 9 | 25 | 52 | 9 |
| It shall be said that gods are stone. | 44 | 11 | 25 | 52 | 11 |
| Symbols are selected from the years' | 45 | 5 | 26 | 53 | 5 |
| Where bird and shell are babbling in my tower? | 46 | 14 | 27 | 54 | 14 |
| You are all these, said she who gave me the long suck, | 46 | 17 | 27 | 54 | 17 |
| You are your sisters' sire, said seaweedy, | 47 | 2 | 27 | 55 | 2 |
| Under the arc of the sky they are unsafe. | 50 | 5 | 30 | 59 | 5 |
| All things are known: the stars' advice | 53 | 16 | 32 | 62 | 16 |
| The finger joints are cramped with chalk; | 62 | 6 | 37 | 71 | 6 |
| Are formed of flesh, but let the false day come | 63 | 6 | 38 | 72 | 6 |
| For there are ghosts in the air | 64 | 8 | 39 | 73 | 8 |
| Before the ladies' breasts are hags | 65 | 4 | 40 | 74 | 4 |
| And the limbs are torn. | 65 | 5 | 40 | 74 | 5 |
| But when the ladies are cold as stone | 65 | 7 | 40 | 74 | 7 |
| My lips are withered with a kiss, | 65 | 20 | 40 | 74 | 20 |
| My breasts are thin. | 65 | 21 | 40 | 74 | 21 |
| Light and dark are no enemies | 66 | 12 | 40 | 75 | 12 |
| When their bones are picked clean and the clean bones gone, | 68 | 4 | 42 | 77 | 4 |
| Are but the roots of nettles and of feathers | 72 | 2 | 44 | 81 | 2 |
| (Questions are hunchbacks to the poker marrow). | 73 | 2 | 44 | 82 | 2 |
| These are her contraries: the beast who follows | 78 | 24 | 46 | 88 | 1 |
| That her fond wounds are mended bitterly. | 81 | 9 | 47 | 90 | 9 |
| Those craning birds are choice for you, songs that jump back | 86 | 9 | 51 | 95 | 9 |
| That the eyes are already murdered, | 96 | 16 | 58 | 106 | 16 |
| The grave and my calm body are shut to your coming as stone, | 98 | 6 | 59 | 109 | 9 |
| Parish of snow. The carved mouths in the rock are wind swept strings. | 121 | 9 | 72 | 134 | 4 |
| Are you | 137 | 2 | 82 | 154 | 2 |
| Are making under the green, laid veil | 151 | 21 | 83 | 169 | 9 |
| Strike and smoothe, for my decks are drums, | 152 | 5 | 83 | 169 | 17 |
| His decks are drenched with miracles. | 154 | 19 | 83 | 172 | 19 |

|  | U.K. | | | U.S. | |
|---|---|---|---|---|---|
|  | *Page* | *Line* | *Poem* | *Page* | *Line* |
| From the broomed witch's spume you are shielded by fern | 162 | 17 | 86 | 181 | 17 |
| Doing what they are told, | 170 | 12 | 88 | 190 | 12 |
| Though the names on their weed grown stones are rained away, | 176 | 8 | 90 | 197 | 8 |
| ARGUMENT | | | | | |
| Argument of the hewn voice, gesture and psalm, | 88 | 9 | 52 | 97 | 9 |
| ARISE | | | | | |
| That all the charmingly drowned arise to cock-crow and kill. | 89 | 6 | 53 | 98 | 6 |
| Turns in the dark on the sound they know will arise | 100 | 5 | 61 | 111 | 6 |
| Never to awake and arise | 146 | 16 | 82 | 163 | 16 |
| ARISING | | | | | |
| My arising prodigal | 158 | 18 | 84 | 177 | 18 |
| ARK | | | | | |
| I build my bellowing ark | viii | 18 | 1 | xvi | 18 |
| Work ark and the moonshine | x | 1 | 1 | xviii | 7 |
| My ark sings in the sun | x | 17 | 1 | xviii | 23 |
| Shaped my clayfellow, and the heaven's ark | 61 | 2 | 36 | 70 | 2 |
| ARKS | | | | | |
| Cry, Multitudes of arks! Across | x | 10 | 1 | xviii | 16 |
| ARM | | | | | |
| Do you not father me, nor the erected arm | 46 | 1 | 27 | 54 | 1 |
| We make me mystic as the arm of air, | 52 | 6 | 31 | 61 | 13 |
| Bolting the night of the door with her arm her plume. | 108 | 4 | 66 | 119 | 4 |
| Under his downy arm you sighed as he struck, | 125 | 19 | 74 | 139 | 19 |
| For a man sleeps where fire leapt down and she learns through his arm | 127 | 13 | 75 | 141 | 13 |
| On my cleaving arm as I blasted in a wave. | 133 | 20 | 78 | 149 | 3 |
| ARMLESS | | | | | |
| Unclenched, armless, silk and rough love that breaks all rocks. | 126 | 16 | 74 | 140 | 16 |
| ARMOUR | | | | | |
| Felt thud beneath my flesh's armour, | 7 | 9 | 5 | 8 | 9 |
| Who took my flesh and bone for armour | 8 | 21 | 5 | 9 | 21 |
| My Egypt's armour buckling in its sheet, | 31 | 10 | 18 | 36 | 10 |
| My half ghost in armour hold hard in death's corridor, | 35 | 5 | 20 | 40 | 5 |
| Shaped in old armour and oak the countenance of a dunce | 85 | 7 | 50 | 94 | 7 |
| ARMOURED | | | | | |
| All issue armoured, of the grave, | 4 | 19 | 3 | 4 | 19 |
| ARMS | | | | | |
| To Wales in my arms. | ix | 1 | 1 | xvii | 1 |
| Fold in their arms. | 14 | 6 | 10 | 16 | 6 |

ARMS (continued)

|  | U.K. | | | U.S. | |
| --- | --- | --- | --- | --- | --- |
|  | *Page* | *Line* | *Poem* | *Page* | *Line* |
| Under the skysigns they who have no arms | 50 | 7 | 30 | 59 | 7 |
| And taken by light in her arms at long and dear last | 108 | 16 | 66 | 119 | 16 |
| To a haycock couch and the scythes of his arms | 113 | 17 | 69 | 125 | 17 |
| With all their griefs in their arms, | 128 | 5 | 76 | 142 | 5 |
| But for the lovers, their arms | 128 | 17 | 76 | 142 | 17 |
| The mother dug, and its arms full of fires. | 129 | 8 | 77 | 143 | 8 |

ARMY

|  |  |  |  |  |  |
| --- | --- | --- | --- | --- | --- |
| Your monstrous officers and the decaying army, | 37 | 5 | 20 | 42 | 11 |
| Over the barbed and shooting sea assumed an army | 158 | 6 | 84 | 177 | 6 |

AROUND

|  |  |  |  |  |  |
| --- | --- | --- | --- | --- | --- |
| Of skin and vein around the well | 8 | 2 | 5 | 9 | 2 |
| Towns around on a wheel of fire. | 33 | 6 | 19 | 38 | 6 |
| And rivers of the dead around my neck. | 76 | 8 | 44 | 85 | 8 |
| Away but the weather turned around. | 103 | 15 | 63 | 114 | 15 |
| Away but the weather turned around. And the true | 104 | 10 | 63 | 115 | 12 |
| His faith around her flew undone | 114 | 3 | 69 | 126 | 3 |
| Around some coffin carrying | 133 | 2 | 78 | 148 | 5 |
| Of minnows wreathing around their prayer; | 171 | 2 | 88 | 191 | 2 |
| Harpies around me out of her womb! | 175 | 27 | 89 | 196 | 8 |

AROUSE

|  |  |  |  |  |  |
| --- | --- | --- | --- | --- | --- |
| Exiled in us we arouse the soft, | 126 | 15 | 74 | 140 | 15 |

ARRIVAL

|  |  |  |  |  |  |
| --- | --- | --- | --- | --- | --- |
| To the sea-blown arrival. | 36 | 12 | 20 | 41 | 12 |
| Can we fend off rock arrival, | 82 | 22 | 48 | 91 | 22 |

ARROW

|  |  |  |  |  |  |
| --- | --- | --- | --- | --- | --- |
| And heaven crier, arrow now of aspiring | 110 | 10 | 67 | 121 | 12 |

ART

|  |  |  |  |  |  |
| --- | --- | --- | --- | --- | --- |
| In my craft or sullen art | 128 | 1 | 76 | 142 | 1 |
| Nor heed my craft or art. | 128 | 20 | 76 | 142 | 20 |
| In my Craft or Sullen Art | 128 |  | 76 | 142 |  |

ARTERIAL

|  |  |  |  |  |  |
| --- | --- | --- | --- | --- | --- |
| The arterial angel. | 30 | 24 | 18 | 35 | 24 |
| Turn the long sea arterial | 36 | 22 | 20 | 42 | 1 |

ARTERY

|  |  |  |  |  |  |
| --- | --- | --- | --- | --- | --- |
| Weans on an artery the gender's strip; | 71 | 18 | 44 | 80 | 18 |

ASCEND

|  |  |  |  |  |  |
| --- | --- | --- | --- | --- | --- |
| 'See,' drummed the taut masks, 'How the dead ascend: | 79 | 26 | 46 | 89 | 7 |

ASCENDING

|  |  |  |  |  |  |
| --- | --- | --- | --- | --- | --- |
| Am I not father, too, and the ascending boy, | 46 | 9 | 27 | 54 | 9 |

ASCENSION

|  |  |  |  |  |  |
| --- | --- | --- | --- | --- | --- |
| O spiral of ascension | 141 | 11 | 82 | 158 | 11 |

ASH

|  |  |  |  |  |  |
| --- | --- | --- | --- | --- | --- |
| With stones of odyssey for ash and garland | 76 | 7 | 44 | 85 | 7 |

|  | U.K. |  |  | U.S. |  |
|---|---|---|---|---|---|
|  | Page | Line | Poem | Page | Line |
| **ASHEN** |  |  |  |  |  |
| Turns in the earth that turns the ashen | 33 | 5 | 19 | 38 | 5 |
| **ASHES** |  |  |  |  |  |
| Time marks a black aisle kindle from the brand of ashes, | 83 | 4 | 49 | 92 | 4 |
| **ASHPIT** |  |  |  |  |  |
| On the snapping rims of the ashpit, | 132 | 8 | 78 | 147 | 8 |
| **ASIA** |  |  |  |  |  |
| The straws of Asia, lose me as I turn | 31 | 23 | 18 | 37 | 5 |
| The central plains of Asia in his garden, | 40 | 2 | 22 | 46 | 2 |
| A climbing sea from Asia had me down | 73 | 19 | 44 | 82 | 19 |
| **ASIDE** |  |  |  |  |  |
| Dinned aside the coiling crowd, | 134 | 3 | 79 | 150 | 3 |
| **ASK** |  |  |  |  |  |
| When cometh Jack Frost? the children ask. | 53 | 10 | 32 | 62 | 10 |
| Though what the stars ask as they round | 53 | 18 | 32 | 62 | 18 |
| Ask the tall fish swept from the bible east, | 76 | 16 | 44 | 85 | 16 |
| **ASLEEP** |  |  |  |  |  |
| Over the wound asleep | viii | 24 | 1 | xvi | 24 |
| By trick or chance he fell asleep | 5 | 10 | 3 | 5 | 10 |
| His golden yesterday asleep upon the iris | 127 | 3 | 75 | 141 | 3 |
| Who shows to the selves asleep | 153 | 7 | 83 | 171 | 3 |
| In the land of the hearthstone tales, and spelled asleep, | 162 | 2 | 86 | 181 | 2 |
| The haygold haired, my love asleep, and the rift blue | 165 | 17 | 86 | 185 | 7 |
| **ASPIRING** |  |  |  |  |  |
| And heaven crier, arrow now of aspiring | 110 | 10 | 67 | 121 | 12 |
| **ASS** |  |  |  |  |  |
| Winged like a sabbath ass this children's piece | 41 | 16 | 23 | 47 | 16 |
| **ASS'S** |  |  |  |  |  |
| I make a weapon of an ass's skeleton | 79 | 5 | 46 | 88 | 8 |
| **ASSAILINGS** |  |  |  |  |  |
| All blood-signed assailings and vanished marriages in which he had no lovely part | 114 | 20 | 69 | 126 | 20 |
| **ASSASSINS** |  |  |  |  |  |
| With priest's grave foot and hand of five assassins | 78 | 25 | 46 | 88 | 2 |
| **ASSEMBLAGE** |  |  |  |  |  |
| All love but for the full assemblage in flower | 110 | 12 | 67 | 121 | 14 |
| **ASSEMBLED** |  |  |  |  |  |
| Assembled at his tongue | 125 | 5 | 74 | 139 | 5 |
| **ASSEMBLING** |  |  |  |  |  |
| Assembling waits for the spade's ring on the cage. | 135 | 11 | 80 | 152 | 11 |
| **ASSUMED** |  |  |  |  |  |
| Over the barbed and shooting sea assumed an army | 158 | 6 | 84 | 177 | 6 |

|  | U.K. | | | U.S. | |
|---|---|---|---|---|---|
|  | Page | Line | Poem | Page | Line |
| **ASSUMING** |  |  |  |  |  |
| But when the stars, assuming shape, | 4 | 16 | 3 | 4 | 16 |
| **ASTONISH** |  |  |  |  |  |
| I rocketed to astonish | 132 | 25 | 78 | 147 | 25 |
| **ASTOUNDED** |  |  |  |  |  |
| I astounded the sitting tailors, | 132 | 17 | 78 | 147 | 17 |
| **ASTRIDE** |  |  |  |  |  |
| Or flower under the time dying flesh astride. | 120 | 30 | 72 | 133 | 15 |
| The fields of seed and the time dying flesh astride, | 122 | 23 | 72 | 136 | 3 |
| **ASYLUM** |  |  |  |  |  |
| Through the dark asylum, | 96 | 13 | 58 | 106 | 13 |
| Love in the Asylum | 108 |  | 66 | 119 |  |
| **ASYLUMS** |  |  |  |  |  |
| In lairs and asylums of the tremendous shout. | 125 | 16 | 74 | 139 | 16 |
| **ATE** |  |  |  |  |  |
| Death on the mouth that ate the gas. | 28 | 16 | 17 | 33 | 16 |
| **ATLANTIC** |  |  |  |  |  |
| Through the Atlantic corn. | 31 | 24 | 18 | 37 | 6 |
| **ATLAS** |  |  |  |  |  |
| Never shall beast be born to atlas the few seas | 92 | 4 | 55 | 101 | 10 |
| **ATLAS-EATER** |  |  |  |  |  |
| The atlas-eater with a jaw for news, | 71 | 5 | 44 | 80 | 5 |
| **ATLASWISE** |  |  |  |  |  |
| Atlaswise hold half-way off the dummy bay | 76 | 10 | 44 | 85 | 10 |
| **ATONE** |  |  |  |  |  |
| Myselves grieve now, and miracles cannot atone. | 129 | 16 | 77 | 143 | 16 |
| **AUSTRIAN** |  |  |  |  |  |
| Red in an Austrian volley. | 31 | 15 | 18 | 36 | 15 |
| **AUTHOR'S** |  |  |  |  |  |
| Author's Prologue | vii |  | 1 | xv |  |
| **AUTOCRACY** |  |  |  |  |  |
| Autocracy of night and day, | 65 | 12 | 40 | 74 | 12 |
| **AUTUMN** |  |  |  |  |  |
| In autumn teach three seasons' fires | 45 | 7 | 26 | 53 | 7 |
| In rainy autumn | 102 | 15 | 63 | 113 | 15 |
| **AUTUMNAL** |  |  |  |  |  |
| (Some let me make you of autumnal spells, | 17 | 2 | 11 | 20 | 2 |
| **AVALANCHE** |  |  |  |  |  |
| Her heart all ears and eyes, lips catching the avalanche | 127 | 10 | 75 | 141 | 10 |
| **AVIARY** |  |  |  |  |  |
| The spire cranes. Its statue is an aviary. | 86 | 1 | 51 | 95 | 1 |
| **AWAKE** |  |  |  |  |  |
| Awake, my sleeper, to the sun, | 5 | 13 | 3 | 5 | 13 |
| Shall fall awake when cures and their itch | 15 | 2 | 10 | 17 | 2 |
| In shaping-time the circle stung awake, | 40 | 3 | 22 | 46 | 3 |

|  | U.K. | | | U.S. | |
|---|---|---|---|---|---|
|  | *Page* | *Line* | *Poem* | *Page* | *Line* |
| In all love's countries, that will grope awake; | 81 | 12 | 47 | 90 | 12 |
| 'Now to awake husked of gestures and my joy like a cave | 97 | 21 | 59 | 109 | 1 |
| Awake | 145 | 10 | 82 | 162 | 10 |
| Never to awake and arise | 146 | 16 | 82 | 163 | 16 |
| And then to awake, and the farm, like a wanderer white | 160 | 6 | 85 | 179 | 6 |

AWAKING

| He comes to leave her in the lawless sun awaking | 166 | 6 | 86 | 186 | 6 |

AWAY

| Eternal waters away | vii | 18 | 1 | xv | 18 |
| That wipes away not crow's-foot nor the lock | 12 | 23 | 9 | 14 | 2 |
| Wearing the quick away. | 13 | 7 | 9 | 14 | 14 |
| Impose their shots, throwing the nights away; | 14 | 18 | 10 | 16 | 18 |
| Says the world wears away? | 45 | 17 | 26 | 53 | 17 |
| I have longed to move away | 64 | 1 | 39 | 73 | 1 |
| I have longed to move away | 64 | 6 | 39 | 73 | 6 |
| I have longed to move away but am afraid; | 64 | 11 | 39 | 73 | 11 |
| The whispering ears will watch love drummed away | 81 | 6 | 47 | 90 | 6 |
| Watch yellow, wish for wind to blow away | 82 | 19 | 48 | 91 | 19 |
| Away but the weather turned around. | 103 | 15 | 63 | 114 | 15 |
| It turned away from the blithe country | 103 | 16 | 63 | 114 | 16 |
| Away but the weather turned around. And the true | 104 | 10 | 63 | 115 | 12 |
| Blow away like breath, | 105 | 17 | 64 | 116 | 17 |
| O keep his bones away from that common cart, | 135 | 12 | 80 | 152 | 12 |
| Has melted away and is lost | 153 | 19 | 83 | 171 | 15 |
| The hills have footed the waves away, | 156 | 16 | 83 | 175 | 4 |
| As I rode to sleep the owls were bearing the farm away, | 160 | 2 | 85 | 179 | 2 |
| Though the names on their weed grown stones are rained away, | 176 | 8 | 90 | 197 | 8 |
| The darkest way, and did not turn away, |  |  | 91 | 200 | 2 |
| I have longed to move away | 64 |  | 39 | 73 |  |

AWOKE

| Of the town closed as the town awoke. | 102 | 20 | 63 | 113 | 20 |

AXE

| I would not fear the gallows nor the axe | 12 | 13 | 9 | 13 | 13 |

AXLE

| Shall you turn cockwise on a tufted axle. | 60 | 24 | 36 | 69 | 24 |

# ENTRIES UNDER B

| | U.K. | | | U.S. | |
|---|---|---|---|---|---|
| | *Page* | *Line* | *Poem* | *Page* | *Line* |
| BAAING | | | | | |
| For ever of all not the wolf in his baaing hood | 163 | 13 | 86 | 182 | 13 |
| BABBLE | | | | | |
| Let the wax disk babble | 37 | 19 | 20 | 43 | 2 |
| Babble like a bellbuoy over the hymning heads, | 87 | 23 | 52 | 96 | 23 |
| BABBLED | | | | | |
| The fellow seed and shadow as it babbled | 30 | 9 | 18 | 35 | 9 |
| BABBLING | | | | | |
| Where bird and shell are babbling in my tower? | 46 | 14 | 27 | 54 | 14 |
| BABE | | | | | |
| (But nothing bore, no mouthing babe to the veined hives | 178 | 1 | 90 | 199 | 2 |
| BABY | | | | | |
| Even as a baby he had never cried; | | | 91 | 201 | 5 |
| BABY'S | | | | | |
| The itch of man upon the baby's thigh, | 12 | 12 | 9 | 13 | 12 |
| BACK | | | | | |
| Nor blows back moon and midnight as she blows. | 2 | 6 | 2 | 2 | 6 |
| Blowing the old dead back; our shots shall smack | 15 | 18 | 10 | 17 | 18 |
| Blasts back the trumpet voice. | 57 | 6 | 34 | 66 | 13 |
| Nor hammer back a season in the figs, | 60 | 8 | 36 | 69 | 8 |
| Before death takes you, O take back this. | 66 | 17 | 40 | 75 | 17 |
| Call back the castaways | 67 | 7 | 41 | 76 | 7 |
| Cast back the bone of youth | 67 | 11 | 41 | 76 | 11 |
| Arc-lamped thrown back upon the cutting flood. | 73 | 10 | 44 | 82 | 10 |
| Doubled, to fork him back, through the lockjaw bed | 79 | 24 | 46 | 89 | 5 |
| Those craning birds are choice for you, songs that jump back | 86 | 9 | 51 | 95 | 9 |
| Or that rainy tongue beat back | 93 | 13 | 56 | 102 | 13 |
| The lovely gift of the gab bangs back on a blind shaft. | 94 | 6 | 57 | 104 | 6 |
| The breath draw back like a bolt through white oil | 96 | 21 | 58 | 107 | 4 |
| Pack back the downed bone. If the unpricked ball of my breath | 97 | 2 | 59 | 108 | 2 |
| Rage me back to the making house. My hand unravel | 97 | 12 | 59 | 108 | 12 |
| And sear just riders back, | 118 | 6 | 71 | 130 | 10 |

| | U.K. | | | U.S. | |
|---|---|---|---|---|---|
| | Page | Line | Poem | Page | Line |
| Back. Lines of age sleep on the stones till trumpeting dawn. | 123 | 8 | 72 | 136 | 18 |
| Darkness kindled back into beginning | 129 | 12 | 77 | 143 | 12 |
| Beginning crumbled back to darkness | 131 | 6 | 77 | 145 | 12 |
| I set back the clock faced tailors, | 132 | 18 | 78 | 147 | 18 |
| Tell his street on its back he stopped a sun | 135 | 6 | 80 | 152 | 6 |
| Back to black silence melt and mourn | 140 | 10 | 82 | 157 | 10 |
| I would turn back and run | 148 | 4 | 82 | 165 | 4 |
| For my sake sail, and never look back, | 149 | 11 | 83 | 166 | 11 |
| The centuries throw back their hair | 155 | 7 | 83 | 173 | 11 |
| With the dew, come back, the cock on his shoulder: it was all | 160 | 7 | 85 | 179 | 7 |
| **BAD** | | | | | |
| Nor the bad blood of spring. | 12 | 7 | 9 | 13 | 7 |
| And count the taken, forsaken mysteries in a bad dark. | 94 | 9 | 57 | 104 | 9 |
| Good and bad, two ways | 105 | 13 | 64 | 116 | 13 |
| Death, and bad death, and then | 105 | 22 | 64 | 116 | 22 |
| You with a bad coin in your socket, | 107 | 2 | 65 | 118 | 2 |
| Made his bad bed in her good | 114 | 12 | 69 | 126 | 12 |
| God in bed, good and bad, | 134 | 17 | 79 | 150 | 17 |
| **BAGPIPE-BREASTED** | | | | | |
| The bagpipe-breasted ladies in the deadweed | 74 | 13 | 44 | 83 | 13 |
| **BAGS** | | | | | |
| And bags of blood let out their flies; | 4 | 23 | 3 | 4 | 23 |
| **BAIT** | | | | | |
| To the bait that stalked out of the sack, | 149 | 20 | 83 | 166 | 20 |
| But heard his bait buck in the wake | 150 | 5 | 83 | 167 | 9 |
| Deep the great bushed bait with raining lips | 151 | 3 | 83 | 168 | 11 |
| The long-legged beautiful bait their wives. | 151 | 22 | 83 | 169 | 10 |
| And the bait is drowned among hayricks, | 157 | 16 | 83 | 176 | 8 |
| Ballad of the Long-legged Bait | 149 | | 83 | 166 | |
| **BALANCE** | | | | | |
| Time's ship-racked gospel on the globe I balance: | 76 | 11 | 44 | 85 | 11 |
| **BALD** | | | | | |
| From bald pavilions and the house of bread | 75 | 2 | 44 | 84 | 2 |
| **BALL** | | | | | |
| Pick the world's ball of wave and froth | 2 | 16 | 2 | 2 | 16 |
| Ball of the foot depending from the sun, | 19 | 18 | 12 | 23 | 3 |
| So the ball fail, | 51 | 25 | 31 | 61 | 4 |
| The horn and ball of water on the frog | 54 | 15 | 33 | 63 | 15 |
| The ball I threw while playing in the park | 63 | 18 | 38 | 72 | 18 |
| Wound like a ball of lakes | 70 | 5 | 43 | 79 | 9 |
| And the golden ball spins out of the skies; | 90 | 10 | 54 | 99 | 10 |
| Pack back the downed bone. If the unpricked ball of my breath | 97 | 2 | 59 | 108 | 2 |
| Spun on a spout like a long-legged ball | 151 | 8 | 83 | 168 | 16 |

| | U.K. | | | U.S. | |
| --- | --- | --- | --- | --- | --- |
| | Page | Line | Poem | Page | Line |
| **BALLAD** | | | | | |
| Ballad of the Long-legged Bait | 149 | | 83 | 166 | |
| **BAMBOO** | | | | | |
| What of a bamboo man among your acres? | 73 | 3 | 44 | 82 | 3 |
| **BANDAGE** | | | | | |
| Death from a bandage, rants the mask of scholars | 76 | 2 | 44 | 85 | 2 |
| **BANDAGED** | | | | | |
| Broke through her straws, breaking my bandaged string, | 12 | 3 | 9 | 13 | 3 |
| **BANGED** | | | | | |
| Loving on this sea banged guilt | 109 | 15 | 67 | 120 | 15 |
| **BANGS** | | | | | |
| The lovely gift of the gab bangs back on a blind shaft. | 94 | 6 | 57 | 104 | 6 |
| **BAPTISM** | | | | | |
| Bows no baptism | 137 | 13 | 82 | 154 | 13 |
| **BARBED** | | | | | |
| The skull of the earth is barbed with a war of burning brains and hair. | 96 | 9 | 58 | 106 | 9 |
| Over the barbed and shooting sea assumed an army | 158 | 6 | 84 | 177 | 6 |
| Manes, under his quenchless summer barbed gold to the bone, | 177 | 6 | 90 | 198 | 5 |
| **BARD** | | | | | |
| But I, Ann's bard on a raised hearth, call all | 87 | 21 | 52 | 96 | 21 |
| **BARE** | | | | | |
| Gag of a dumbstruck tree to block from bare enemies | 85 | 4 | 50 | 94 | 4 |
| She cried her white-dressed limbs were bare | 93 | 17 | 56 | 102 | 17 |
| And I felt with my bare fall | 93 | 28 | 56 | 103 | 8 |
| Queen Catherine howling bare | 113 | 12 | 69 | 125 | 12 |
| May his hunger go howling on bare white bones | 120 | 8 | 72 | 132 | 13 |
| Bare as the nurseries | 131 | 7 | 77 | 145 | 13 |
| Now shown and mostly bare I would lie down, | 133 | 21 | 78 | 149 | 4 |
| Crouched bare | 141 | 2 | 82 | 158 | 2 |
| There he might wander bare | 172 | 1 | 88 | 192 | 1 |
| Hugged, and barren and bare on Mother Goose's ground | 178 | 2 | 90 | 199 | 3 |
| **BARER** | | | | | |
| Of love am barer than Cadaver's trap | 18 | 8 | 12 | 21 | 8 |
| **BARES** | | | | | |
| My hero bares his nerves along my wrist | 10 | 1 | 7 | 11 | 1 |
| My hero bares my side and sees his heart | 10 | 11 | 7 | 11 | 11 |
| The terrible world my brother bares his skin. | 80 | 7 | 46 | 89 | 15 |
| My hero bares his nerves | 10 | | 7 | 11 | |
| **BARK** | | | | | |
| Soar, with its two bark towers, to that Day | 76 | 20 | 44 | 85 | 20 |

|  | U.K. | | | U.S. | |
|  | *Page* | *Line* | *Poem* | *Page* | *Line* |
| **BARKED** | | | | | |
| Sang to my horn, the foxes on the hills barked clear and cold, | 159 | 16 | 85 | 178 | 16 |
| **BARLEY** | | | | | |
| For the surge is sown with barley, | 156 | 14 | 83 | 175 | 2 |
| Trail with daisies and barley | 159 | 8 | 85 | 178 | 8 |
| And gone that barley dark where their clogs danced in the spring, | 177 | 20 | 90 | 198 | 19 |
| **BARN** | | | | | |
| Crumbs, barn, and halter. | 48 | 29 | 28 | 57 | 6 |
| **BARNROOFS** | | | | | |
| And barnroofs cockcrow war! | ix | 30 | 1 | xviii | 4 |
| **BARNS** | | | | | |
| Past the blind barns and byres of the windless farm. | 122 | 10 | 72 | 135 | 10 |
| And as I was green and carefree, famous among the barns | 159 | 10 | 85 | 178 | 10 |
| **BARREN** | | | | | |
| Lay the gold tithings barren, | 1 | 2 | 2 | 1 | 2 |
| Man in his maggot's barren. | 3 | 2 | 2 | 3 | 8 |
| Where barren as boulders women lie longing still | 176 | 4 | 90 | 197 | 4 |
| Hugged, and barren and bare on Mother Goose's ground | 178 | 2 | 90 | 199 | 3 |
| **BASE** | | | | | |
| The deadrock base and blow the flowered anchor, | 51 | 5 | 31 | 60 | 5 |
| The scudding base of the familiar sky, | 96 | 4 | 58 | 106 | 4 |
| Deep in its black, base bones, | 173 | 7 | 88 | 193 | 7 |
| **BASES** | | | | | |
| That from the solid bases of the light | 22 | 20 | 14 | 27 | 20 |
| And from the cloudy bases of the breath | 22 | 22 | 14 | 27 | 22 |
| **BASIN** | | | | | |
| The Arctic scut, and basin of the South, | 31 | 20 | 18 | 37 | 2 |
| The nurse of giants by the cut sea basin, | 56 | 10 | 34 | 65 | 10 |
| In the fountain basin where I sailed my ship | 111 | 10 | 68 | 123 | 10 |
| **BASKETS** | | | | | |
| And darkness hung the walls with baskets of snakes, | 114 | 4 | 69 | 126 | 4 |
| **BASS** | | | | | |
| Brandy and ripe in my bright, bass prime, | 174 | 28 | 89 | 195 | 4 |
| **BATHE** | | | | | |
| He'll bathe his raining blood in the male sea | 117 | 19 | 71 | 129 | 19 |
| **BATTLE** | | | | | |
| In battle! the happening | 142 | 11 | 82 | 159 | 11 |
| **BAY** | | | | | |
| Drinking Noah of the bay, | x | 2 | 1 | xviii | 8 |
| Marking the flesh and summer in the bay? | 46 | 11 | 27 | 54 | 11 |

BAY (continued)

| | U.K. | | | U.S. | |
|---|---|---|---|---|---|
| | *Page* | *Line* | *Poem* | *Page* | *Line* |
| Ships anchor off the bay. | 58 | 20 | 35 | 67 | 20 |
| Ships anchor off the bay, | 59 | 2 | 35 | 68 | 2 |
| Atlaswise hold half-way off the dummy bay | 76 | 10 | 44 | 85 | 10 |
| Their frail deeds might have danced in a green bay, | 116 | 8 | 70 | 128 | 8 |
| And gallows, up the rays of his eyes the small birds of the bay | 167 | 4 | 87 | 187 | 4 |
| Green chickens of the bay and bushes cluck, 'dilly dilly, | 168 | 7 | 87 | 188 | 11 |
| With the spirits of the horseshoe bay | 172 | 2 | 88 | 192 | 2 |
| Pleading in the waded bay for the seed to flow | 176 | 7 | 90 | 197 | 7 |

BAY'S

| | | | | | |
|---|---|---|---|---|---|
| My dabbed bay's dusk, as I hack | viii | 10 | 1 | xvi | 10 |
| This sandgrain day in the bent bay's grave | 170 | 6 | 88 | 190 | 6 |

BAYING

| | | | | | |
|---|---|---|---|---|---|
| Stream with bells and baying water bounds. The dew rings | 121 | 7 | 72 | 134 | 2 |

BAYONET

| | | | | | |
|---|---|---|---|---|---|
| The bayonet tongue in this undefended prayer-piece, | 85 | 5 | 50 | 94 | 5 |

BE

| | | | | | |
|---|---|---|---|---|---|
| But seasons must be challenged or they totter | 2 | 1 | 2 | 2 | 1 |
| Shall not be latched while magic glides | 11 | 20 | 8 | 12 | 20 |
| There shall be corals in your beds, | 11 | 22 | 8 | 12 | 22 |
| There shall be serpents in your tides, | 11 | 23 | 8 | 12 | 23 |
| Shall it be male or female? say the cells, | 12 | 8 | 9 | 13 | 8 |
| Shall it be male or female? say the fingers | 12 | 15 | 9 | 13 | 15 |
| I would be tickled by the rub that is: | 13 | 20 | 9 | 15 | 6 |
| Man be my metaphor. | 13 | 21 | 9 | 15 | 7 |
| And lets their trash be honoured as the quick. | 15 | 15 | 10 | 17 | 15 |
| For we shall be a shouter like the cock, | 15 | 17 | 10 | 17 | 17 |
| And we shall be fit fellows for a life, | 15 | 20 | 10 | 17 | 20 |
| Dust be your saviour under the conjured soil.) | 37 | 9 | 20 | 42 | 15 |
| Be by your one ghost pierced, his pointed ferrule, | 38 | 1 | 20 | 43 | 11 |
| Be by the ships' sea broken at the manstring anchored | 38 | 8 | 20 | 43 | 18 |
| Shall the star-flanked seed be riddled, | 42 | 16 | 24 | 49 | 16 |
| Shall the star-flanked seed be riddled, | 42 | 23 | 24 | 50 | 2 |
| And a green inch be his bearer; | 43 | 4 | 24 | 50 | 11 |
| And a high sphere be his bearer; | 43 | 11 | 24 | 50 | 18 |
| Shall gods be said to thump the clouds | 44 | | 25 | 52 | |
| Shall gods be said to thump the clouds | 44 | 1 | 25 | 52 | 1 |
| Be said to weep when weather howls? | 44 | 3 | 25 | 52 | 3 |
| Shall Rainbows be their tunics' colour? | 44 | 4 | 25 | 52 | 4 |
| Shall it be said they sprinkle water | 44 | 6 | 25 | 52 | 6 |
| Shall it be said that, venuswise, | 44 | 8 | 25 | 52 | 8 |

| | U.K. | | Poem | U.S. | |
|---|---|---|---|---|---|
| | Page | Line | | Page | Line |
| It shall be said that gods are stone. | 44 | 11 | 25 | 52 | 11 |
| Shall I still be love's house on the widdershin earth, | 47 | 5 | 27 | 55 | 5 |
| There must, be praised, some certainty, | 48 | 7 | 28 | 56 | 7 |
| Man should be cured of distemper. | 48 | 27 | 28 | 57 | 4 |
| Shall not be known till windwell dries | 53 | 2 | 32 | 62 | 2 |
| I hear content, and 'Be content' | 53 | 21 | 32 | 62 | 21 |
| Dead men naked they shall be one | 68 | 2 | 42 | 77 | 2 |
| Though they go mad they shall be sane, | 68 | 6 | 42 | 77 | 6 |
| Though lovers be lost love shall not; | 68 | 8 | 42 | 77 | 8 |
| Though they be mad and dead as nails, | 68 | 24 | 42 | 77 | 24 |
| 'Nor the green nought be hurt; | 70 | 17 | 43 | 79 | 21 |
| Now my saying shall be my undoing, | 89 | 12 | 53 | 98 | 12 |
| Who should be furious, | 91 | 6 | 55 | 100 | 6 |
| Never shall beast be born to atlas the few seas | 92 | 4 | 55 | 101 | 10 |
| The conversation of prayers about to be said | 100 | 1 | 61 | 111 | 1 |
| And the other full of tears that she will be dead, | 100 | 5 | 61 | 111 | 5 |
| The sound about to be said in the two prayers | 100 | 9 | 61 | 111 | 9 |
| Will be the same grief flying. Whom shall they calm? | 100 | 11 | 61 | 111 | 11 |
| Shall the child sleep unharmed or the man be crying? | 100 | 12 | 61 | 111 | 12 |
| The conversation of prayers about to be said | 100 | 13 | 61 | 111 | 13 |
| Still be sung | 104 | 17 | 63 | 115 | 19 |
| The pyre yet to be lighted of my sins and days, | 109 | 3 | 67 | 120 | 3 |
| And the vaulting bird be still. O my true love, hold me. | 110 | 26 | 67 | 122 | 4 |
| Blind eyes could blaze like meteors and be gay, | 116 | 14 | 70 | 128 | 14 |
| There was calm to be done in his safe unrest, | 125 | 11 | 74 | 139 | 11 |
| Bone and be dumb | 144 | 6 | 82 | 161 | 6 |
| And the beating dust be blown | 145 | 15 | 82 | 162 | 15 |
| Be I pray | 147 | 12 | 82 | 164 | 12 |
| But blessed be hail and upheaval | 158 | 20 | 84 | 177 | 20 |
| Time let me play and be | 159 | 13 | 85 | 178 | 13 |
| Safe be and smooth from the bellows of the rushy brood. | 162 | 20 | 86 | 181 | 20 |
| Be shielded by chant and flower and gay may you | 163 | 19 | 86 | 182 | 19 |
| Be you sure the Thief will seek a way sly and sure | 163 | 26 | 86 | 183 | 7 |
| 'Come and be killed,' | 167 | 22 | 87 | 188 | 3 |
| All praise of the hawk on fire in hawk-eyed dusk be sung, | 168 | 3 | 87 | 188 | 7 |
| Now will be ever is always true, | 171 | 24 | 88 | 191 | 24 |
| Be at cloud quaking peace, | 172 | 9 | 88 | 192 | 9 |
| Let him find no rest but be fathered and found, | | | 91 | 200 | 12 |

BEACH

| The beach of flesh, and wind her bloodred plait; | 10 | 13 | 7 | 11 | 13 |
|---|---|---|---|---|---|
| Down breeze and shell to a discordant beach, | 81 | 7 | 47 | 90 | 7 |

| | U.K. | | | U.S. | |
|---|---|---|---|---|---|
| | *Page* | *Line* | *Poem* | *Page* | *Line* |
| **BEAD** | | | | | |
| Zion of the water bead | 101 | 8 | 62 | 112 | 8 |
| **BEADS** | | | | | |
| In the rain telling its beads, and the gravest ghost | 163 | 8 | 86 | 182 | 8 |
| **BEAK** | | | | | |
| Heard her speak through the chipped beak | 93 | 24 | 56 | 103 | 4 |
| Cold Nansen's beak on a boat full of gongs, | 133 | 12 | 78 | 148 | 15 |
| And the beak of slime | 143 | 13 | 82 | 160 | 13 |
| From salt-lipped beak to the kick of the stern | 152 | 9 | 83 | 170 | 1 |
| **BEAKED** | | | | | |
| Yet out of the beaked, web dark and the pouncing boughs | 163 | 25 | 86 | 183 | 6 |
| **BEAKS** | | | | | |
| In your beaks, on the gabbing capes! | ix | 15 | 1 | xvii | 15 |
| In his house on stilts high among beaks | 170 | 4 | 88 | 190 | 4 |
| **BEAR** | | | | | |
| The hollow words could bear all suffering | 48 | 22 | 28 | 56 | 22 |
| By waste seas where the white bear quoted Virgil | 73 | 23 | 44 | 82 | 23 |
| And bear those tendril hands I touch across | 90 | 6 | 54 | 99 | 6 |
| The she mules bear their minotaurs, | 110 | 4 | 67 | 121 | 6 |
| Then, bushily swanked in bear wig and tails, | 132 | 19 | 78 | 147 | 19 |
| **BEARD** | | | | | |
| Whose beard wags in Egyptian wind. | 63 | 15 | 38 | 72 | 15 |
| And his scarving beard from a book, | 134 | 12 | 79 | 150 | 12 |
| **BEARDED** | | | | | |
| In shapes of sin forked out the bearded apple, | 40 | 4 | 22 | 46 | 4 |
| Sussanah's drowned in the bearded stream | 153 | 11 | 83 | 171 | 7 |
| **BEARDING** | | | | | |
| Bearding the unborn devil, | 32 | 3 | 18 | 37 | 9 |
| **BEARER** | | | | | |
| And a green inch be his bearer; | 43 | 4 | 24 | 50 | 11 |
| And a high sphere be his bearer; | 43 | 11 | 24 | 50 | 18 |
| **BEARING** | | | | | |
| And bearing | 143 | 7 | 82 | 160 | 7 |
| Time is bearing another son. | 155 | 9 | 83 | 173 | 13 |
| As I rode to sleep the owls were bearing the farm away, | 160 | 2 | 85 | 179 | 2 |
| **BEARS** | | | | | |
| But this we tread bears the angelic gangs, | 26 | 13 | 16 | 31 | 13 |
| **BEAST** | | | | | |
| Black as the beast and paler than the cross. | 40 | 12 | 22 | 46 | 12 |
| John's beast, Job's patience, and the fibs of vision, | 41 | 21 | 23 | 48 | 3 |
| Convenient bird and beast lie lodged to suffer | 77 | 3 | 45 | 86 | 3 |
| These are her contraries: the beast who follows | 78 | 24 | 46 | 88 | 1 |
| His beast heel cleft in a sandal, | 83 | 3 | 49 | 92 | 3 |

|  | U.K. | | | U.S. | |
| --- | --- | --- | --- | --- | --- |
|  | *Page* | *Line* | *Poem* | *Page* | *Line* |
| Bent like a beast to lap the singular floods | 90 | 3 | 54 | 99 | 3 |
| Never shall beast be born to atlas the few seas | 92 | 4 | 55 | 101 | 10 |
| Lie dry, rest robbed, my beast. | 92 | 14 | 55 | 101 | 20 |
| Bird beast and flower | 101 | 2 | 62 | 112 | 2 |
| Her holy unholy hours with the always anony- mous beast. | 114 | 23 | 69 | 126 | 23 |
| Till every beast blared down in a swerve | 151 | 9 | 83 | 168 | 17 |
| And the black beast of the beetles' pews, | 174 | 14 | 89 | 194 | 14 |
| BEASTHOOD | | | | | |
| (Hail to His beasthood!). | ix | 25 | 1 | xvii | 25 |
| BEASTS | | | | | |
| Beasts who sleep good and thin, | ix | 26 | 1 | xvii | 26 |
| All birds and beasts of the linked night uproar and chime | 177 | 15 | 90 | 198 | 14 |
| BEAT | | | | | |
| Or that rainy tongue beat back | 93 | 13 | 56 | 102 | 13 |
| Heaven fell with his fall and one crocked bell beat the left air. | 95 | 25 | 58 | 105 | 25 |
| Of the wood! Pastoral beat of blood through the laced leaves! | 164 | 22 | 86 | 184 | 8 |
| BEATING | | | | | |
| Greed on man beating near and fire neighbour | 126 | 6 | 74 | 140 | 6 |
| And the beating dust be blown | 145 | 15 | 82 | 162 | 15 |
| BEATS | | | | | |
| Rain beats the sand and slates. | 59 | 3 | 35 | 68 | 3 |
| BEAUTIFUL | | | | | |
| The long-legged beautiful bait their wives. | 151 | 22 | 83 | 169 | 10 |
| BEAUTY | | | | | |
| Nor when he finds a beauty in the breast | 13 | 12 | 9 | 14 | 19 |
| BECALMED | | | | | |
| Lie still, sleep becalmed, sufferer with the wound | 136 | 1 | 81 | 153 | 1 |
| Lie still, sleep becalmed, hide the mouth in the throat, | 136 | 13 | 81 | 153 | 13 |
| Lie Still, Sleep Becalmed | 136 | | 81 | 153 | |
| BECAUSE | | | | | |
| Because the pleasure-bird whistles after the hot wires, | 77 | 1 | 45 | 86 | 1 |
| Because there stands, one story out of the bum city, | 77 | 13 | 45 | 86 | 13 |
| Because their words have forked no lightning they | 116 | 5 | 70 | 128 | 5 |
| Because the pleasure-bird whistles | 77 | | 45 | 86 | |
| BECKON | | | | | |
| The morning beckon | 102 | 5 | 63 | 113 | 5 |
| BED | | | | | |
| I blew the dreaming fellows to their bed | 26 | 19 | 16 | 31 | 19 |
| In the glass bed of grapes with snail and flower, | 36 | 5 | 20 | 41 | 5 |

|  | U.K. | | | U.S. | |
|---|---|---|---|---|---|
|  | Page | Line | Poem | Page | Line |
| Love like a mist or fire through the bed of eels. | 38 | 12 | 20 | 44 | 2 |
| And share my bed with Capricorn and Cancer. | 71 | 14 | 44 | 80 | 14 |
| With priest and pharaoh bed my gentle wound, | 76 | 5 | 44 | 85 | 5 |
| Doubled, to fork him back, through the lockjaw bed | 79 | 24 | 46 | 89 | 5 |
| At nightbreak born in the fat side, from an animal bed | 84 | 2 | 49 | 93 | 8 |
| Before she lay on a stranger's bed | 93 | 11 | 56 | 102 | 11 |
| Flicked from the carbolic city puzzle in a bed of sores | 96 | 3 | 58 | 106 | 3 |
| When you sew the deep door. The bed is a cross place. | 97 | 13 | 59 | 108 | 13 |
| 'No. Not for Christ's dazzling bed | 97 | 16 | 59 | 108 | 16 |
| By the child going to bed and the man on the stairs | 100 | 2 | 61 | 111 | 2 |
| From the man on the stairs and the child by his bed. | 100 | 8 | 61 | 111 | 8 |
| Strait in the mazed bed | 108 | 5 | 66 | 119 | 5 |
| His enemies entered bed, | 113 | 2 | 69 | 125 | 2 |
| Made his bad bed in her good | 114 | 12 | 69 | 126 | 12 |
| Two sand grains together in bed, | 115 | 1 | 69 | 127 | 1 |
| Inhuman cradle and the bride bed forever sought | 120 | 24 | 72 | 133 | 9 |
| Burning in the bride bed of love, in the whirl- | 123 | 17 | 72 | 137 | 7 |
| With dry flesh and earth for adorning and bed. | 133 | 15 | 78 | 148 | 18 |
| God in bed, good and bad, | 134 | 17 | 79 | 150 | 17 |
| Old in her cruel bed. | 152 | 12 | 83 | 170 | 4 |
| Out of a bed of love | 158 | 2 | 84 | 177 | 2 |
| And I lie down but to sleep in bed, | 175 | 6 | 89 | 195 | 11 |
| Or, butter fat goosegirls, bounced in a gambo bed, | 177 | 17 | 90 | 198 | 16 |
| I prayed in the crouching room, by his blind bed, |  |  | 91 | 200 | 13 |
| BEDDED |  |  |  |  |  |
| For the bird lay bedded | 123 | 11 | 72 | 137 | 1 |
| BEDLAM |  |  |  |  |  |
| To the judge blown bedlam | 141 | 6 | 82 | 158 | 6 |
| BEDS |  |  |  |  |  |
| Lovers in the dirt of their leafy beds, | 89 | 9 | 53 | 98 | 9 |
| And the sizzling beds of the town cried, Quick!– | 174 | 20 | 89 | 194 | 20 |
| And sleep rolls mute above the beds | 5 | 4 | 3 | 5 | 4 |
| There shall be corals in your beds, | 11 | 22 | 8 | 12 | 22 |
| The bones of men, the broken in their beds, | 14 | 9 | 10 | 16 | 9 |
| BEDTIME |  |  |  |  |  |
| I died before bedtime came | 93 | 26 | 56 | 103 | 6 |
| BEDWARD |  |  |  |  |  |
| And salt-eyed stumble bedward where she lies | 67 | 12 | 41 | 76 | 12 |
| BEECHES |  |  |  |  |  |
| Some let me make you of the vowelled beeches, | 16 | 13 | 11 | 19 | 13 |

| | U.K. | | | U.S. | |
|---|---|---|---|---|---|
| | Page | Line | Poem | Page | Line |
| **BEEN** | | | | | |
| What had been one was many sounding minded. | 21 | 17 | 13 | 25 | 17 |
| I have been told to reason by the heart, | 63 | 9 | 38 | 72 | 9 |
| I have been told to reason by the pulse, | 63 | 11 | 38 | 72 | 11 |
| So it must have been after the birth of the simple light | 160 | 11 | 85 | 179 | 11 |
| **BEETLES'** | | | | | |
| And the black beast of the beetles' pews, | 174 | 14 | 89 | 194 | 14 |
| **BEFORE** | | | | | |
| Move like two ghosts before the eye. | 6 | 18 | 4 | 6 | 18 |
| Before I knocked and let flesh enter, | 7 | 1 | 5 | 8 | 1 |
| My throat knew thirst before the structure | 8 | 1 | 5 | 9 | 1 |
| Before the pitch was forking to a sun; | 23 | 3 | 14 | 28 | 3 |
| Before the veins were shaking in their sieve, | 23 | 4 | 14 | 28 | 4 |
| A crocodile before the chrysalis, | 41 | 14 | 23 | 47 | 14 |
| Before the fall from love the flying heartbone, | 41 | 15 | 23 | 47 | 15 |
| Before the agony; the spirit grows, | 48 | 3 | 28 | 56 | 3 |
| Rise before dark. | 55 | 5 | 33 | 64 | 8 |
| I tell her this: before the suncock cast | 55 | 8 | 33 | 64 | 11 |
| Look twice before he fell from grace. | 63 | 4 | 38 | 72 | 4 |
| Before the ladies' breasts are hags | 65 | 4 | 40 | 74 | 4 |
| Before death takes you, O take back this. | 66 | 17 | 40 | 75 | 17 |
| Before I heard in my mother's side | 93 | 6 | 56 | 102 | 6 |
| Before she lay on a stranger's bed | 93 | 11 | 56 | 102 | 11 |
| I died before bedtime came | 93 | 26 | 56 | 103 | 6 |
| Before I rush in a crouch the ghost with a hammer, air, | 97 | 9 | 59 | 108 | 9 |
| Before you move to make | 105 | 8 | 64 | 116 | 8 |
| Is cast before you move, | 106 | 9 | 64 | 117 | 9 |
| Before the crowing morning climbed; | 113 | 19 | 69 | 125 | 19 |
| Before the lips blaze and bloom | 144 | 3 | 82 | 161 | 3 |
| Before the children green and golden | 160 | 22 | 85 | 179 | 22 |
| To court the honeyed heart from your side before sunrise | 162 | 13 | 86 | 181 | 13 |
| The owl at its knelling. Fox and holt kneel before blood. | 163 | 9 | 86 | 182 | 9 |
| Before the lunge of the night, the notes on this time-shaken | 169 | 11 | 87 | 189 | 20 |
| Before chains break to a hammer flame | 171 | 17 | 88 | 191 | 17 |
| In the muted house, one minute before | | | 91 | 200 | 14 |
| Before I knocked | 7 | | 5 | 8 | |
| **BEGAN** | | | | | |
| My birthday began with the water- | 102 | 11 | 63 | 113 | 11 |
| **BEGIN** | | | | | |
| Begin | 129 | 9 | 77 | 143 | 9 |
| For my voyage to begin to the end of my wound, | 136 | 11 | 81 | 153 | 11 |

|  | U.K. | | Poem | U.S. | |
|---|---|---|---|---|---|
|  | Page | Line |  | Page | Line |
| **BEGINNING** | | | | | |
| In the beginning was the three-pointed star, | 22 | 1 | 14 | 27 | 1 |
| In the beginning was the pale signature, | 22 | 7 | 14 | 27 | 7 |
| In the beginning was the mounting fire | 22 | 13 | 14 | 27 | 13 |
| In the beginning was the word, the word | 22 | 19 | 14 | 27 | 19 |
| In the beginning was the secret brain. | 23 | 1 | 14 | 28 | 1 |
| Beginning with doom in the bulb, the spring unravels, | 35 | 7 | 20 | 40 | 7 |
| Beginning with doom in the ghost, and the springing marvels, | 35 | 13 | 20 | 40 | 13 |
| This was the god of beginning in the intricate seawhirl, | 38 | 29 | 20 | 44 | 19 |
| And breaks his shell in the last shocked beginning; | 41 | 13 | 23 | 47 | 13 |
| Time, milk, and magic, from the world beginning. | 74 | 24 | 44 | 83 | 24 |
| Green as beginning, let the garden diving | 76 | 19 | 44 | 85 | 19 |
| And the endless beginning of prodigies suffers open.' | 98 | 7 | 59 | 109 | 10 |
| Down the beginning of plants | 106 | 6 | 64 | 117 | 6 |
| Hurling into beginning like Christ the child. | 110 | 24 | 67 | 122 | 2 |
| Darkness kindled back into beginning | 129 | 12 | 77 | 143 | 12 |
| Beginning crumbled back to darkness | 131 | 6 | 77 | 145 | 12 |
| In **the** beginning | 22 | | 14 | 27 | |
| **BEGINS** | | | | | |
| As the flood begins, | viii | 20 | 1 | xvi | 20 |
| **BEGUN** | | | | | |
| Dressed to die, the sensual strut begun, | 99 | 6 | 60 | 110 | 6 |
| **BEHEADED** | | | | | |
| Storm her sped heart, hand with beheaded veins | 79 | 8 | 46 | 88 | 11 |
| **BEHIND** | | | | | |
| Behind a pot of ferns the wagging clock | 16 | 17 | 11 | 19 | 17 |
| Dawn breaks behind the eyes; | 24 | 13 | 15 | 29 | 13 |
| My cross of tales behind the fabulous curtain.' | 41 | 26 | 23 | 48 | 8 |
| Behind my head a square of sky sags over | 90 | 8 | 54 | 99 | 8 |
| Shall her smile breed that mouth, behind the mirror, | 90 | 13 | 54 | 99 | 13 |
| Behind a face of hands, | 95 | 10 | 58 | 105 | 10 |
| Behind the wall thin as a wren's bone? | 137 | 9 | 82 | 154 | 9 |
| Behind the wall's wren | 144 | 5 | 82 | 161 | 5 |
| **BEING** | | | | | |
| Loving and being loth; | 15 | 13 | 10 | 17 | 13 |
| Being innocent, he dreaded that he died | | | 91 | 201 | 1 |
| **BELIEVE** | | | | | |
| Fear or believe that the wolf in a sheepwhite hood | 162 | 3 | 86 | 181 | 3 |

| | U.K. | | | U.S. | |
|---|---|---|---|---|---|
| | *Page* | *Line* | *Poem* | *Page* | *Line* |
| Bell believe or fear that the rustic shade or spell | 162 | 22 | 86 | 181 | 22 |
| Ever and ever by all your vows believe and fear | 166 | 8 | 86 | 186 | 8 |
| **BELIEVED** | | | | | |
| Head, deceived, I believed, my maker, | 133 | 6 | 78 | 148 | 9 |
| **BELIEVER** | | | | | |
| By the believer lost and the hurled outcast of light. | 120 | 25 | 72 | 133 | 10 |
| **BELIEVERS** | | | | | |
| Us your death that myselves the believers | 129 | 19 | 77 | 143 | 19 |
| **BELL** | | | | | |
| Sweetly the diver's bell in the steeple of spindrift | 37 | 11 | 20 | 42 | 17 |
| Under the bell of rocks, | 69 | 3 | 43 | 78 | 3 |
| It is the sinners' dust-tongued bell claps me to churches | 83 | 1 | 49 | 92 | 1 |
| From the emerald; still bell; and from the pacing weather-cock | 83 | 17 | 49 | 92 | 17 |
| Refusal struck like a bell under water | 90 | 12 | 54 | 99 | 12 |
| Heaven fell with his fall and one crocked bell beat the left air. | 95 | 25 | 58 | 105 | 25 |
| Until the Sunday sombre bell at dark | 111 | 6 | 68 | 123 | 6 |
| Made all day until bell time | 112 | 7 | 68 | 124 | 7 |
| Bell believe or fear that the rustic shade or spell | 162 | 22 | 86 | 181 | 22 |
| This night and each vast night until the stern bell talks | 164 | 2 | 86 | 183 | 9 |
| Might cross its planets, the bell weep, night gather her eyes, | 165 | 21 | 86 | 185 | 11 |
| Death clear as a buoy's bell: | 168 | 2 | 87 | 188 | 6 |
| Who tolls his birthday bell, | 170 | 16 | 88 | 190 | 16 |
| To his nimbus bell cool kingdom come | 173 | 4 | 88 | 193 | 4 |
| Who heard the tall bell sail down the Sundays of the dead | 178 | 10 | 90 | 199 | 11 |
| It is the sinners' dust-tongued bell | 83 | | 49 | 92 | |
| **BELLADONNA** | | | | | |
| To veil belladonna and let the dry eyes perceive | 85 | 10 | 50 | 94 | 10 |
| **BELLBUOY** | | | | | |
| Babble like a bellbuoy over the hymning heads, | 87 | 23 | 52 | 96 | 23 |
| **BELLED** | | | | | |
| That belled and bounded with the fossil and the dew reborn. | 123 | 10 | 72 | 136 | 20 |
| **BELL-SPIRE** | | | | | |
| My mast is a bell-spire, | 152 | 4 | 83 | 169 | 16 |
| **BELL-VOICED** | | | | | |
| Who sucks the bell-voiced Adam out of magic, | 74 | 23 | 44 | 83 | 23 |
| **BELLMETAL** | | | | | |
| Strike the sea hour through bellmetal. | 83 | 12 | 49 | 92 | 12 |

| | U.K. | | | U.S. | |
|---|---|---|---|---|---|
| | *Page* | *Line* | *Poem* | *Page* | *Line* |
| **BELLOWED** | | | | | |
| A squall of birds bellowed and fell, | 150 | 15 | 83 | 167 | 19 |
| **BELLOWING** | | | | | |
| I build my bellowing ark | viii | 18 | 1 | xvi | 18 |
| But my womb was bellowing | 93 | 27 | 56 | 103 | 7 |
| **BELLOWS** | | | | | |
| Safe be and smooth from the bellows of the rushy brood. | 162 | 20 | 86 | 181 | 20 |
| **BELLS** | | | | | |
| Only the drowned deep bells | x | 4 | 1 | xviii | 10 |
| There, in his night, the black-tongued bells | 2 | 4 | 2 | 2 | 4 |
| To the built voice, or fly with winter to the bells, | 86 | 10 | 51 | 95 | 10 |
| The vanishing of the musical ship-work and the chucked bells, | 95 | 8 | 58 | 105 | 8 |
| Stream with bells and baying water bounds. The dew rings | 121 | 7 | 72 | 134 | 2 |
| Birds and clocks and cross bells | 134 | 2 | 79 | 150 | 2 |
| No Time, spoke the clocks, no God, rang the bells, | 134 | 28 | 79 | 151 | 6 |
| Thirty-five bells sing struck | 171 | 12 | 88 | 191 | 12 |
| I lie down thin and hear the good bells jaw— | 175 | 24 | 89 | 196 | 5 |
| **BELLY** | | | | | |
| My heart knew love, my belly hunger; | 8 | 5 | 5 | 9 | 5 |
| Belly of the rich year and the big purse of my body | 94 | 2 | 57 | 104 | 2 |
| **BELLYFUL** | | | | | |
| Shall she receive a bellyful of weeds | 90 | 5 | 54 | 99 | 5 |
| **BELONG** | | | | | |
| I pray though I belong | 143 | 14 | 82 | 160 | 14 |
| **BELOVED** | | | | | |
| Grave, after Beloved on the grass gulfed cross is scrubbed | 178 | 13 | 90 | 199 | 14 |
| **BELOW** | | | | | |
| Though the town below lay leaved with October blood. | 104 | 15 | 63 | 115 | 17 |
| Turns of your prayed flesh, nor shall I shoo the bird below me: | 109 | 27 | 67 | 121 | 1 |
| Once below a time, | 132 | 1 | 78 | 147 | 1 |
| And once below a time I lordly had the trees and leaves | 159 | 7 | 85 | 178 | 7 |
| In the river Towy below bows his tilted head-stone. | 167 | 12 | 87 | 187 | 12 |
| Once below a time | 132 | | 78 | 147 | |
| **BEND** | | | | | |
| Bend, if my journey ache, direction like an arc or make | 97 | 14 | 59 | 108 | 14 |
| The rainbow-fish bend in her joys, | 150 | 10 | 83 | 167 | 14 |

| | U.K. | | | U.S. | |
|---|---|---|---|---|---|
| | *Page* | *Line* | *Poem* | *Page* | *Line* |
| **BENDS** | | | | | |
| The rod bends low, divining land, | 155 | 21 | 83 | 174 | 5 |
| **BENEATH** | | | | | |
| Felt thud beneath my flesh's armour, | 7 | 9 | 5 | 8 | 9 |
| I sit and watch the worm beneath my nail | 13 | 6 | 9 | 14 | 13 |
| Beneath my life, that sighs for the seducer's coming | 109 | 13 | 67 | 120 | 13 |
| Mountains and galleries beneath | 152 | 14 | 83 | 170 | 6 |
| **BENT** | | | | | |
| My youth is bent by the same wintry fever. | 9 | 5 | 6 | 10 | 5 |
| Child in white blood bent on its knees | 69 | 2 | 43 | 78 | 2 |
| Bent like three trees and bird-papped through her shift, | 75 | 9 | 44 | 84 | 9 |
| Bless her bent spirit with four, crossing birds. | 87 | 26 | 52 | 96 | 26 |
| Bent like a beast to lap the singular floods | 90 | 3 | 54 | 99 | 3 |
| Towards the studded male in a bent, midnight blaze | 91 | 13 | 55 | 100 | 13 |
| Creep and harp on the tide, sinking their charmed, bent pin | 91 | 24 | 55 | 101 | 2 |
| This sandgrain day in the bent bay's grave | 170 | 6 | 88 | 190 | 6 |
| **BEREFT** | | | | | |
| In the body bereft. | 130 | 6 | 77 | 144 | 6 |
| **BERRY** | | | | | |
| Heigh ho the blood and the berry, | 2 | 20 | 2 | 3 | 2 |
| Grow larked and greener at berry brown | 173 | 20 | 88 | 193 | 20 |
| **BESIDE** | | | | | |
| And put beside her a ram rose. | 65 | 24 | 40 | 74 | 24 |
| **BEST** | | | | | |
| To the best of my love | viii | 19 | 1 | xvi | 19 |
| Alone's unhurt, so the blind man sees best. | 50 | 9 | 30 | 59 | 9 |
| When one at the great least of your best loved | 117 | 3 | 71 | 129 | 3 |
| **BETHELS** | | | | | |
| Cawing from their black bethels soaring, the holy books | 164 | 19 | 86 | 184 | 5 |
| **BETRAY** | | | | | |
| Others betray the lamenting lies of their losses | 85 | 11 | 50 | 94 | 11 |
| **BETRAYAL** | | | | | |
| Libidinous betrayal, | 115 | 8 | 69 | 127 | 8 |
| **BETTER** | | | | | |
| A worm tells summer better than the clock, | 45 | 14 | 26 | 53 | 14 |
| **BETWEEN** | | | | | |
| They dance between their arclamps and our skull, | 14 | 17 | 10 | 16 | 17 |
| Ribbed between desert and water storm, | 82 | 11 | 48 | 91 | 11 |
| Is celebrated there, and communion between suns. | 109 | 24 | 67 | 120 | 24 |
| Propped between trees and water | 111 | 3 | 68 | 123 | 3 |

BETWEEN (continued)

| | U.K. | | | U.S. | |
|---|---|---|---|---|---|
| | *Page* | *Line* | *Poem* | *Page* | *Line* |
| Alone between nurses and swans | 112 | 2 | 68 | 124 | 2 |
| Innocent between two wars, | 115 | 19 | 69 | 127 | 19 |
| And caught between two nights, blindness and death. | | | 91 | 201 | 15 |
| **BEYOND** | | | | | |
| Beyond this island bound | 58 | 10 | 35 | 67 | 10 |
| 'Rest beyond choice in the dust-appointed grain, | 98 | 3 | 59 | 109 | 6 |
| The grains beyond age, the dark veins of her mother, | 101 | 21 | 62 | 112 | 21 |
| Beyond the border and under the lark full cloud. | 103 | 12 | 63 | 114 | 12 |
| Of shades, symbol of desire beyond my hours | 110 | 7 | 67 | 121 | 9 |
| The cloud, the need, the planted stars, the joy beyond | 122 | 22 | 72 | 136 | 2 |
| Child beyond cockcrow, by the fire-dwarfed | 130 | 4 | 77 | 144 | 4 |
| **BIBLE** | | | | | |
| Ask the tall fish swept from the bible east, | 76 | 16 | 44 | 85 | 16 |
| **BIBLE-LEAVED** | | | | | |
| A Bible-leaved of all the written woods | 74 | 16 | 44 | 83 | 16 |
| **BID** | | | | | |
| That the phoenix' bid for heaven and the desire after | 110 | 17 | 67 | 121 | 19 |
| **BIDDEN** | | | | | |
| And the bidden dust upsailing | 141 | 9 | 82 | 158 | 9 |
| **BIDE** | | | | | |
| The country is holy: O bide in that country kind, | 163 | 16 | 86 | 182 | 16 |
| **BIDING** | | | | | |
| The death biding two lie lonely. | 109 | 28 | 67 | 121 | 2 |
| To the sultry, biding herds, I said, | 175 | 4 | 89 | 195 | 9 |
| **BIG** | | | | | |
| Now in the cloud's big breast lie quiet countries, | 80 | 8 | 46 | 89 | 16 |
| Belly of the rich year and the big purse of my body | 94 | 2 | 57 | 104 | 2 |
| I skipped in a blush as the big girls rolled | 174 | 6 | 89 | 194 | 6 |
| **BILLHOOK** | | | | | |
| While a man outside with a billhook, | 134 | 8 | 79 | 150 | 8 |
| **BILLHOOKS** | | | | | |
| As the arc of the billhooks that flashed the hedges low | 178 | 7 | 90 | 199 | 8 |
| **BILLS** | | | | | |
| And the tall grains foamed in their bills; | 153 | 1 | 83 | 170 | 16 |
| **BIND** | | | | | |
| Branded forehead, that could bind | 109 | 9 | 67 | 120 | 9 |
| **BINDING** | | | | | |
| Binding my angel's hood. | 32 | 6 | 18 | 37 | 12 |
| 'Rebel against the binding moon | 65 | 9 | 40 | 74 | 9 |
| **BIRD** | | | | | |
| Glory also this star, bird | viii | 14 | 1 | xvi | 14 |

40

|  | U.K. | | | U.S. | |
|---|---|---|---|---|---|
|  | *Page* | *Line* | *Poem* | *Page* | *Line* |
| This summer buries a spring bird. | 45 | 4 | 26 | 53 | 4 |
| Where bird and shell are babbling in my tower? | 46 | 14 | 27 | 54 | 14 |
| Convenient bird and beast lie lodged to suffer | 77 | 3 | 45 | 86 | 3 |
| Fumed like a tree, and tossed a burning bird; | 80 | 3 | 46 | 89 | 11 |
| The voice of bird on coral prays. | 83 | 18 | 49 | 92 | 18 |
| With carved bird, saint, and sun, the wrack-spiked· maiden mouth | 92 | 9 | 55 | 101 | 15 |
| Of the stone bird guarding her: | 93 | 25 | 56 | 103 | 5 |
| Bird beast and flower | 101 | 2 | 62 | 112 | 2 |
| Turns of your prayed flesh, nor shall I shoo the bird below me: | 109 | 27 | 67 | 121 | 1 |
| And the vaulting bird be still. O my true love, hold me. | 110 | 26 | 67 | 122 | 4 |
| A she bird sleeping brittle by | 115 | 10 | 69 | 127 | 10 |
| A she bird rose and rayed like a burning bride. | 121 | 14 | 72 | 134 | 9 |
| A she bird dawned, and her breast with snow and scarlet downed. | 121 | 15 | 72 | 134 | 10 |
| Of fields. For love, the long ago she bird rises. Look. | 121 | 25 | 72 | 134 | 20 |
| Was flying through the house as though the she bird praised | 122 | 3 | 72 | 135 | 3 |
| Bird through the times and lands and tribes of the slow flakes. | 122 | 19 | 72 | 135 | 19 |
| The sky, the bird, the bride, | 122 | 21 | 72 | 136 | 1 |
| And the bird descended. | 122 | 26 | 72 | 136 | 6 |
| For the bird lay bedded | 123 | 11 | 72 | 137 | 1 |
| Bird, he was brought low, | 123 | 16 | 72 | 137 | 6 |
| Man, animal, or bird | 125 | 13 | 74 | 139 | 13 |
| And the dust shall sing like a bird | 129 | 22 | 77 | 143 | 22 |
| As a bird hooking over the sea, | 149 | 7 | 83 | 166 | 7 |
| Bird after dark and the laughing fish | 154 | 6 | 83 | 172 | 6 |
| Of blood! The bird loud vein! The saga from mermen | 165 | 7 | 86 | 184 | 15 |
| BIRD'S | | | | | |
| Lucifer that bird's dropping | 153 | 17 | 83 | 171 | 13 |
| BIRDMAN | | | | | |
| Birdman or told ghost I hung. | 133 | 3 | 78 | 148 | 6 |
| BIRD-PAPPED | | | | | |
| Bent like three trees and bird-papped through her shift, | 75 | 9 | 44 | 84 | 9 |
| BIRDS | | | | | |
| The fire of birds in | vii | 26 | 1 | xv | 26 |
| Hold up the noisy sea and drop her birds, | 2 | 15 | 2 | 2 | 15 |
| By the sea's side, hearing the noise of birds, | 16 | 5 | 11 | 19 | 5 |
| By the sea's side hear the dark-vowelled birds. | 17 | 8 | 11 | 20 | 8 |
| Man was the scales, the death birds on enamel, | 38 | 19 | 20 | 44 | 9 |
| No birds or flying fish | 58 | 15 | 35 | 67 | 15 |

| | U.K. | | | U.S. | |
|---|---|---|---|---|---|
| | *Page* | *Line* | *Poem* | *Page* | *Line* |
| Lie this fifth month unskated, and the birds have flown; | 49 | 9 | 29 | 58 | 9 |
| Golden Glamorgan straightens, to the falling birds. | 49 | 23 | 29 | 58 | 23 |
| Naked among the bow-and-arrow birds | 60 | 23 | 36 | 69 | 23 |
| Destruction, picked by birds, brays through the jaw-bone, | 79 | 10 | 46 | 88 | 13 |
| Carved birds blunt their striking throats on the salt gravel, | 86 | 3 | 51 | 95 | 3 |
| Those craning birds are choice for you, songs that jump back | 86 | 9 | 51 | 95 | 9 |
| Bless her bent spirit with four, crossing birds. | 87 | 26 | 52 | 96 | 26 |
| Birds and the birds of the winged trees flying my name | 102 | 12 | 63 | 113 | 12 |
| And animals and birds, | 106 | 7 | 64 | 117 | 7 |
| A girl mad as birds | 108 | 3 | 66 | 119 | 3 |
| The duck-billed platypus broody in a milk of birds. | 110 | 5 | 67 | 121 | 7 |
| Like the park birds he came early | 111 | 13 | 68 | 123 | 13 |
| The birds the grass the trees the lake | 112 | 15 | 68 | 124 | 15 |
| The puffed birds hopping and hunting, the milkmaids | 119 | 23 | 72 | 132 | 3 |
| Hunger of birds in the fields of the bread of water, | 120 | 17 | 72 | 133 | 2 |
| Paddocks in the farms of birds. The dead oak walks for love. | 121 | 20 | 72 | 134 | 15 |
| And the sky of birds in the plumed voice charmed | 122 | 8 | 72 | 135 | 8 |
| When black birds died like priests in the cloaked hedge row | 122 | 12 | 72 | 135 | 12 |
| That once cut the figures of birds on the deep bread | 123 | 4 | 72 | 136 | 14 |
| In grottoes I worked with birds, | 132 | 9 | 78 | 147 | 9 |
| Birds and clocks and cross bells | 134 | 2 | 79 | 150 | 2 |
| Where birds ride like leaves and boats like ducks | 134 | 22 | 79 | 150 | 22 |
| Of the birds of burden | 143 | 4 | 82 | 160 | 4 |
| Blackened with birds took a last look | 149 | 2 | 83 | 166 | 2 |
| A squall of birds bellowed and fell, | 150 | 15 | 83 | 167 | 19 |
| Oh the shearwater birds and their boatsized brood | 151 | 19 | 83 | 169 | 7 |
| For the salty birds fluttered and fed | 152 | 24 | 83 | 170 | 17 |
| With birds and animals | 155 | 24 | 83 | 174 | 8 |
| Of birds! Among the cocks like fire the red fox | 164 | 20 | 86 | 184 | 6 |
| Burning! Night and the vein of birds in the winged, sloe wrist | 164 | 21 | 86 | 184 | 7 |
| And gallows, up the rays of his eyes the small birds of the bay | 167 | 4 | 87 | 187 | 4 |

| | U.K. | | | U.S. | |
|---|---|---|---|---|---|
| | *Page* | *Line* | *Poem* | *Page* | *Line* |
| Daws Sir John's just hill dons, and again the gulled birds hare | 167 | 15 | 87 | 187 | 15 |
| We grieve as the blithe birds, never again, leave shingle and elm, | 168 | 9 | 87 | 188 | 13 |
| Of the led-astray birds whom God, for their breast of whistles, | 168 | 19 | 87 | 189 | 4 |
| Stone for the sake of the souls of the slain birds sailing. | 169 | 12 | 87 | 189 | 21 |
| And palavers of birds | 170 | 5 | 88 | 190 | 5 |
| All birds and beasts of the linked night uproar and chime | 177 | 15 | 90 | 198 | 14 |
| BIRDS' | | | | | |
| And four birds' notes. | 45 | 8 | 26 | 53 | 8 |
| And cut the birds' boughs that the minstrel sap ran red. | 178 | 8 | 90 | 199 | 9 |
| BIRTH | | | | | |
| Of birth and death, the two sad knives of thieves, | 10 | 18 | 7 | 11 | 18 |
| First characters of birth and death. | 22 | 24 | 14 | 27 | 24 |
| And power was contagious in my birth, second | 28 | 21 | 17 | 34 | 1 |
| In the birth bloody room unknown | 137 | 10 | 82 | 154 | 10 |
| To the birth bloody room | 144 | 4 | 82 | 161 | 4 |
| So it must have been after the birth of the simple light | 160 | 11 | 85 | 179 | 11 |
| BIRTHDAY | | | | | |
| My birthday began with the water- | 102 | 11 | 63 | 113 | 11 |
| My birthday | 103 | 14 | 63 | 114 | 14 |
| And there could I marvel my birthday | 104 | 9 | 63 | 115 | 11 |
| Who tolls his birthday bell, | 170 | 16 | 88 | 190 | 16 |
| Poem on his birthday | 170 | | 88 | 190 | |
| BISCAY | | | | | |
| Oh the bulls of Biscay and their calves | 151 | 20 | 83 | 169 | 8 |
| BISECTED | | | | | |
| Bisected shadows on the thunder's bone | 30 | 5 | 18 | 35 | 5 |
| BIT | | | | | |
| Bit out the mandrake with to-morrow's scream. | 71 | 6 | 44 | 80 | 6 |
| Till the sweet tooth of my love bit dry, | 107 | 7 | 65 | 118 | 7 |
| Cut-to-measure flesh bit, | 132 | 3 | 78 | 147 | 3 |
| When I was a windy boy and a bit | 174 | 1 | 89 | 194 | 1 |
| Not a boy and a bit in the wick- | 174 | 16 | 89 | 194 | 16 |
| BITCHES | | | | | |
| (Sighed the old ram rod, dying of bitches), | 174 | 15 | 89 | 194 | 15 |
| BITE | | | | | |
| Oh miracle of fishes! The long dead bite! | 154 | 20 | 83 | 172 | 20 |
| BITES | | | | | |
| These stolen bubbles have the bites of snakes | 67 | 23 | 41 | 76 | 23 |
| BITING | | | | | |
| Let the soil squeal I am the biting man | 56 | 20 | 34 | 65 | 20 |

## BITS

|  | U.K. Page | U.K. Line | Poem | U.S. Page | U.S. Line |
|---|---|---|---|---|---|
| **BITS** | | | | | |
| Enticed with twinkling bits of the eye | 107 | 6 | 65 | 118 | 6 |
| **BITTEN** | | | | | |
| That burn the bitten decks, | 69 | 9 | 43 | 78 | 9 |
| Trailing the frost bitten cloth, | 132 | 23 | 78 | 147 | 23 |
| **BITTERLY** | | | | | |
| That her fond wounds are mended bitterly. | 81 | 9 | 47 | 90 | 9 |
| I bitterly take to task my poverty and craft: | 94 | 3 | 57 | 104 | 3 |
| **BLACK** | | | | | |
| Out there, crow black, men | vii | 12 | I | xv | 12 |
| Bring out the black patrol, | 37 | 4 | 20 | 42 | 10 |
| Black as the beast and paler than the cross. | 40 | 12 | 22 | 46 | 12 |
| Both quench his thirst he'll have a black reply. | 53 | 9 | 32 | 62 | 9 |
| Black night still ministers the moon, | 66 | 9 | 40 | 75 | 9 |
| You by the cavern over the black stairs, | 71 | 22 | 44 | 80 | 22 |
| The black ram, shuffling of the year, old winter, | 72 | 15 | 44 | 81 | 15 |
| Pin-legged on pole-hills with a black medusa | 73 | 22 | 44 | 82 | 22 |
| 'A lizard darting with black venom's thread | 79 | 23 | 46 | 89 | 4 |
| Time marks a black aisle kindle from the brand of ashes, | 83 | 4 | 49 | 92 | 4 |
| Grave's foot, blinds down the lids, the teeth in black, | 87 | 4 | 52 | 96 | 4 |
| And the strutting fern lay seeds on the black sill. | 88 | 12 | 52 | 97 | 12 |
| And a black and white patch of girls grew playing; | 89 | 4 | 53 | 98 | 4 |
| The black, burst sea rejoice, | 91 | 19 | 55 | 100 | 19 |
| And her red lips were kissed black, | 93 | 18 | 56 | 102 | 18 |
| With a stub of black buds, | 95 | 21 | 58 | 105 | 21 |
| By the spit and the black pot in the log bright light | 120 | 2 | 72 | 132 | 7 |
| By the spit and the black pot in the log bright light. | 122 | 7 | 72 | 135 | 7 |
| When black birds died like priests in the cloaked hedge row | 122 | 12 | 72 | 135 | 12 |
| Charred on the black breast of the grave | 129 | 7 | 77 | 143 | 7 |
| Seed of sons in the loin of the black husk left. | 130 | 8 | 77 | 144 | 8 |
| Back to black silence melt and mourn | 140 | 10 | 82 | 157 | 10 |
| On the black plume | 143 | 12 | 82 | 160 | 12 |
| Break the black news and paint on a sail | 151 | 23 | 83 | 169 | 11 |
| Cawing from their black bethels soaring, the holy books | 164 | 19 | 86 | 184 | 5 |
| The stream from the priest black wristed spinney and sleeves | 165 | 1 | 86 | 184 | 9 |
| And a black cap of jack- | 167 | 14 | 87 | 187 | 14 |
| Deep in its black, base bones, | 173 | 7 | 88 | 193 | 7 |
| And the black spit of the chapel fold, | 174 | 2 | 89 | 194 | 2 |
| In the coal black bush and let them grieve. | 174 | 12 | 89 | 194 | 12 |

|  | U.K. | | | U.S. | |
|---|---|---|---|---|---|
|  | *Page* | *Line* | *Poem* | *Page* | *Line* |
| And the black beast of the beetles' pews, | 174 | 14 | 89 | 194 | 14 |
| Black night, I left my quivering prints. | 174 | 24 | 89 | 194 | 24 |
| And the black cross of the holy house, | 174 | 26 | 89 | 195 | 2 |
| For my sulking, skulking, coal black soul! | 175 | 7 | 89 | 195 | 12 |
| But a black sheep with a crumpled horn, | 175 | 13 | 89 | 195 | 18 |
| And I shoved it into the coal black sky | 175 | 18 | 89 | 195 | 23 |
| And a black reward for a roaring life, | 175 | 21 | 89 | 196 | 2 |
| In the coal black sky and she bore angels! | 175 | 26 | 89 | 196 | 7 |
| Innocence sweetens my last black breath, | 175 | 29 | 89 | 196 | 10 |
| **BLACK-BACKED** | | | | | |
| Illumination of music! the lulled black-backed | 165 | 11 | 86 | 185 | 1 |
| **BLACKBERRIES** | | | | | |
| Plenty as blackberries in the woods | 171 | 26 | 88 | 191 | 26 |
| **BLACKBIRDS** | | | | | |
| Blackbirds and the sun of October | 102 | 23 | 63 | 113 | 23 |
| **BLACKED** | | | | | |
| Two proud, blacked brothers cry, | 126 | 1 | 74 | 140 | 1 |
| **BLACKENED** | | | | | |
| Blackened with birds took a last look | 149 | 2 | 83 | 166 | 2 |
| **BLACK-TONGUED** | | | | | |
| There, in his night, the black-tongued bells | 2 | 4 | 2 | 2 | 4 |
| Black-tongued and tipsy from salvation's bottle. | 73 | 15 | 44 | 82 | 15 |
| **BLADDERS** | | | | | |
| Of tide-tongued heads and bladders in the deep, | 30 | 16 | 18 | 35 | 16 |
| **BLADE** | | | | | |
| The trigger and scythe, the bridal blade, | 33 | 17 | 19 | 38 | 17 |
| Blunt scythe and water blade. | 70 | 11 | 43 | 79 | 15 |
| Rung bone and blade, the verticals of Adam, | 71 | 23 | 44 | 80 | 23 |
| As their blade marches in | 96 | 15 | 58 | 106 | 15 |
| There the dark blade and wanton sighing her down | 113 | 16 | 69 | 125 | 16 |
| A blade of grass longs with the meadow, | 115 | 15 | 69 | 127 | 15 |
| **BLADES** | | | | | |
| Of hemlock and the blades, rust | 28 | 18 | 17 | 33 | 18 |
| **BLANK** | | | | | |
| From blank and leaking winter sails the child in colour, | 83 | 22 | 49 | 93 | 4 |
| **BLARED** | | | | | |
| Till every beast blared down in a swerve | 151 | 9 | 83 | 168 | 17 |
| **BLASPHEME** | | | | | |
| Nor blaspheme down the stations of the breath | 101 | 16 | 62 | 112 | 16 |
| **BLAST** | | | | | |
| The locks yawned loose and a blast blew them wide, | 135 | 3 | 80 | 152 | 3 |
| **BLASTED** | | | | | |
| The salt person and blasted place | 77 | 20 | 45 | 86 | 20 |
| On my cleaving arm as I blasted in a wave. | 133 | 20 | 78 | 149 | 3 |

|  | U.K. |  | | U.S. | |
| --- | --- | --- | --- | --- | --- |
|  | *Page* | *Line* | *Poem* | *Page* | *Line* |
| BLASTS |  |  |  |  |  |
| Drives my green age; that blasts the roots of trees | 9 | 2 | 6 | 10 | 2 |
| Blasts back the trumpet voice. | 57 | 6 | 34 | 66 | 13 |
| BLAZE |  |  |  |  |  |
| Towards the studded male in a bent, midnight blaze | 91 | 13 | 55 | 100 | 13 |
| Blind eyes could blaze like meteors and be gay, | 116 | 14 | 70 | 128 | 14 |
| Before the lips blaze and bloom | 144 | 3 | 82 | 161 | 3 |
| BLAZING |  |  |  |  |  |
| Blind in the coil scrams round the blazing outline, | 41 | 11 | 23 | 47 | 11 |
| A blazing red harsh head tear up | 93 | 29 | 56 | 103 | 9 |
| Of his blazing | 141 | 4 | 82 | 158 | 4 |
| BLEATING |  |  |  |  |  |
| Loping and bleating roughly and blithely shall leap, | 162 | 4 | 86 | 181 | 4 |
| BLEED |  |  |  |  |  |
| Bleed from my burning fork and smell my heels. | 32 | 4 | 18 | 37 | 10 |
| And the scythed boulders bleed, and the last | 172 | 15 | 88 | 192 | 15 |
| BLESS |  |  |  |  |  |
| Bless her bent spirit with four, crossing birds. | 87 | 26 | 52 | 96 | 26 |
| Curse, bless, me now with your fierce tears, I pray. | 116 | 17 | 70 | 128 | 17 |
| Herons, steeple stemmed, bless. | 170 | 18 | 88 | 190 | 18 |
| BLESSED |  |  |  |  |  |
| Within the hallowed gland, blood blessed the heart, | 20 | 18 | 13 | 24 | 18 |
| When, praise is blessed, her pride in mast and fountain | 78 | 4 | 46 | 87 | 4 |
| With the wild breast and blessed and giant skull | 87 | 28 | 52 | 96 | 28 |
| But blessed by such heroic hosts in your every | 109 | 21 | 67 | 120 | 21 |
| But blessed be hail and upheaval | 158 | 20 | 84 | 177 | 20 |
| All the moon long I heard, blessed among stables, the night-jars | 160 | 3 | 85 | 179 | 3 |
| And star: held and blessed, though you scour the high four | 163 | 22 | 86 | 183 | 3 |
| High riding, held and blessed and true, and so stilly | 165 | 19 | 86 | 185 | 9 |
| With blessed, unborn God and His Ghost, | 172 | 6 | 88 | 192 | 6 |
| BLESSING |  |  |  |  |  |
| Both shall fail if I bow not to your blessing | 110 | 19 | 67 | 121 | 21 |
| Blessing on | 137 | 15 | 82 | 154 | 15 |
| In a blessing of the sudden | 148 | 2 | 82 | 165 | 2 |
| And this last blessing most, | 173 | 9 | 88 | 193 | 9 |
| BLESSINGS |  |  |  |  |  |
| Count my blessings aloud: | 172 | 27 | 88 | 192 | 27 |

| | U.K. | | | U.S. | |
|---|---|---|---|---|---|
| | *Page* | *Line* | *Poem* | *Page* | *Line* |

**BLEST**

| | | | | | |
|---|---|---|---|---|---|
| Roared, sea born, man torn, blood blest. | viii | 15 | 1 | xvi | 15 |
| Wing, and blest shall | 168 | 5 | 87 | 188 | 9 |

**BLEW**

| | | | | | |
|---|---|---|---|---|---|
| He blew like powder to the light | 4 | 14 | 3 | 4 | 14 |
| I blew the dreaming fellows to their bed | 26 | 19 | 16 | 31 | 19 |
| The sea-halved faith that blew time to his knees, | 67 | 4 | 41 | 76 | 4 |
| Where blew a flower may a flower no more | 68 | 22 | 42 | 77 | 22 |
| Which sixth of wind blew out the burning gentry? | 73 | 1 | 44 | 82 | 1 |
| Till tallow I blew from the wax's tower | 74 | 9 | 44 | 83 | 9 |
| Blew out the blood gauze through the wound of manwax. | 74 | 14 | 44 | 83 | 14 |
| The locks yawned loose and a blast blew them wide, | 135 | 3 | 80 | 152 | 3 |
| A cloud blew the rain from its throat; | 150 | 16 | 83 | 167 | 20 |
| He who blew the great fire in | 155 | 13 | 83 | 173 | 17 |

**BLIND**

| | | | | | |
|---|---|---|---|---|---|
| Turning a petrol face blind to the enemy | 36 | 23 | 20 | 42 | 2 |
| Blind in the coil scrams round the blazing out-line, | 41 | 11 | 23 | 47 | 11 |
| Alone's unhurt, so the blind man sees best. | 50 | 9 | 30 | 59 | 9 |
| Shall the blind horse sing sweeter? | 77 | 2 | 45 | 86 | 2 |
| By magnet winds to her blind mother drawn, | 78 | 14 | 46 | 87 | 14 |
| And when blind sleep drops on the spying senses, | 81 | 13 | 47 | 90 | 13 |
| The lovely gift of the gab bangs back on a blind shaft. | 94 | 6 | 57 | 104 | 6 |
| King of your heart in the blind days, | 105 | 16 | 64 | 116 | 16 |
| Made her limbs blind by luminous charms, | 113 | 21 | 69 | 125 | 21 |
| Blind eyes could blaze like meteors and be gay, | 116 | 14 | 70 | 128 | 14 |
| That the snow blind twilight ferries over the lakes | 119 | 2 | 72 | 131 | 2 |
| Of his snow blind love and rush in the white lairs. | 120 | 13 | 72 | 132 | 18 |
| Past the blind barns and byres of the windless farm. | 122 | 10 | 72 | 135 | 10 |
| When the caught tongue nodded blind, | 129 | 13 | 77 | 143 | 13 |
| Blind host to sleep | 145 | 6 | 82 | 162 | 6 |
| He was blind to the eyes of candles | 150 | 3 | 83 | 167 | 7 |
| The blind, clawed stare is cold as sleet. | 153 | 5 | 83 | 171 | 1 |
| And to-morrow weeps in a blind cage | 171 | 15 | 88 | 191 | 15 |
| And I gave my soul a blind, slashed eye, | 175 | 16 | 89 | 195 | 21 |
| Too proud to die; broken and blind he died | | | 91 | 200 | 1 |
| The darkest justice of death, blind and unblessed. | | | 91 | 200 | 11 |
| I prayed in the crouching room, by his blind bed, | | | 91 | 200 | 13 |
| (An old tormented man three-quarters blind, | | | 91 | 200 | 18 |
| An old blind man is with me where I go | | | 91 | 201 | 9 |

47

# BLINDING

|  | U.K. | | | U.S. | |
|---|---|---|---|---|---|
|  | *Page* | *Line* | *Poem* | *Page* | *Line* |
| **BLINDING** | | | | | |
| In the blinding country of youth, | 105 | 4 | 64 | 116 | 4 |
| Grave men, near death, who see with blinding sight | 116 | 13 | 70 | 128 | 13 |
| And the duck pond glass and the blinding byres alone | 120 | 10 | 72 | 132 | 15 |
| Now I am lost in the blinding | 148 | 16 | 82 | 165 | 16 |
| **BLINDLY** | | | | | |
| (Though this for her is a monstrous image blindly | 87 | 16 | 52 | 96 | 16 |
| On to the blindly tossing tops; | 155 | 6 | 83 | 173 | 10 |
| **BLINDNESS** | | | | | |
| The bones of blindness; and the womb | 6 | 8 | 4 | 6 | 8 |
| And caught between two nights, blindness and death. | | | 91 | 201 | 15 |
| **BLINDS** | | | | | |
| Blinds their cloud-tracking eye. | 31 | 6 | 18 | 36 | 6 |
| Grave's foot, blinds down the lids, the teeth in black, | 87 | 4 | 52 | 96 | 4 |
| Blinds my | 140 | 16 | 82 | 157 | 16 |
| **BLISTERED** | | | | | |
| In love torn breeches and blistered jacket | 132 | 7 | 78 | 147 | 7 |
| **BLITHE** | | | | | |
| It turned away from the blithe country | 103 | 16 | 63 | 114 | 16 |
| We grieve as the blithe birds, never again, leave shingle and elm, | 168 | 9 | 87 | 188 | 13 |
| **BLITHELY** | | | | | |
| Loping and bleating roughly and blithely shall leap, | 162 | 4 | 86 | 181 | 4 |
| And blithely they squawk | 167 | 8 | 87 | 187 | 8 |
| **BLOCK** | | | | | |
| Gag of a dumbstruck tree to block from bare enemies | 85 | 4 | 50 | 94 | 4 |
| **BLOOD** | | | | | |
| Roared, sea born, man torn, blood blest. | viii | 15 | 1 | xvi | 15 |
| Heigh ho the blood and the berry, | 2 | 20 | 2 | 3 | 2 |
| And bags of blood let out their flies; | 4 | 23 | 3 | 4 | 23 |
| Turns night to day; blood in their suns | 6 | 5 | 4 | 6 | 5 |
| Unfailing till the blood runs foul; | 8 | 4 | 5 | 9 | 4 |
| Drives my red blood; that dries the mouthing streams | 9 | 7 | 6 | 10 | 7 |
| Love drips and gathers, but the fallen blood | 9 | 17 | 6 | 10 | 17 |
| Nor the bad blood of spring. | 12 | 7 | 9 | 13 | 7 |
| Sheds the syllabic blood and drains her words. | 16 | 8 | 11 | 19 | 8 |
| Of chemic blood, warned of the coming fury. | 17 | 7 | 11 | 20 | 7 |
| When blood, spade-handed, and the logic time | 18 | 13 | 12 | 21 | 13 |
| Despair of blood, faith in the maiden's slime, | 18 | 23 | 12 | 22 | 3 |

| | U.K. | | | U.S. | |
|---|---|---|---|---|---|
| | Page | Line | Poem | Page | Line |
| Within the hallowed gland, blood blessed the heart, | 20 | 18 | 13 | 24 | 18 |
| The blood that touched the crosstree and the grail | 22 | 11 | 14 | 27 | 11 |
| Blood shot and scattered to the winds of light | 23 | 5 | 14 | 28 | 5 |
| From poles of skull and toe the windy blood | 24 | 14 | 15 | 29 | 14 |
| And blood jumps in the sun; | 25 | 5 | 15 | 30 | 5 |
| The inches monkeyed by the blood of man. | 27 | 3 | 16 | 32 | 8 |
| My blood upon the tempered dead, forcing | 28 | 19 | 17 | 33 | 19 |
| And a blood parhelion. | 31 | 12 | 18 | 36 | 12 |
| Fear not the flat, synthetic blood, | 33 | 14 | 19 | 38 | 14 |
| Socket and grave, the brassy blood, | 34 | 11 | 19 | 39 | 17 |
| She threads off the sap and needles, blood and bubble | 35 | 10 | 20 | 40 | 10 |
| Once in this wind the summer blood | 39 | 6 | 21 | 45 | 6 |
| This flesh you break, this blood you let | 39 | 11 | 21 | 45 | 11 |
| That spill such acrid blood. | 48 | 16 | 28 | 56 | 16 |
| Were that enough, bone, blood, and sinew, | 48 | 24 | 28 | 57 | 1 |
| Stalking my children's faces with a tail of blood, | 49 | 20 | 29 | 58 | 20 |
| Why night-time rain and the breast's blood | 53 | 8 | 32 | 62 | 8 |
| The word of the blood, the wily skin, | 65 | 15 | 40 | 74 | 15 |
| Child in white blood bent on its knees | 69 | 2 | 43 | 78 | 2 |
| For loss of blood I fell on Ishmael's plain, | 73 | 17 | 44 | 82 | 17 |
| Blew out the blood gauze through the wound of manwax. | 74 | 14 | 44 | 83 | 14 |
| As tarred with blood as the bright thorns I wept; | 75 | 7 | 44 | 84 | 7 |
| Once where the soft snow's blood was turned to ice. | 80 | 12 | 46 | 89 | 20 |
| Breaks, O my heart's blood, like a heart and hill. | 82 | 24 | 48 | 91 | 24 |
| And clap its great blood down; | 92 | 3 | 55 | 101 | 9 |
| Ancient woods of my blood, dash down to the nut of the seas | 94 | 11 | 57 | 104 | 11 |
| The sweet, fish-gilled boats bringing blood | 95 | 22 | 58 | 105 | 22 |
| Though the town below lay leaved with October blood. | 104 | 15 | 63 | 115 | 17 |
| Fly like the stars' blood, | 105 | 24 | 64 | 116 | 24 |
| He'll bathe his raining blood in the male sea | 117 | 19 | 71 | 129 | 19 |
| That other sun, the jealous coursing of the unrivalled blood. | 127 | 14 | 75 | 141 | 14 |
| Till the blood shall spurt, | 129 | 21 | 77 | 143 | 21 |
| Up to his head in his blood, | 134 | 9 | 79 | 150 | 9 |
| To the sea sound flowing like blood from the loud wound | 136 | 6 | 81 | 153 | 6 |
| And the blood drop's garden | 145 | 4 | 82 | 162 | 4 |
| All the fishes were rayed in blood, | 149 | 23 | 83 | 167 | 3 |
| The whirled boat in the burn of his blood | 151 | 17 | 83 | 169 | 5 |

BLOOD (continued)

|  | U.K. | | | U.S. | |
|---|---|---|---|---|---|
|  | *Page* | *Line* | *Poem* | *Page* | *Line* |
| Shall harrow and snow the blood while you ride wide and near, | 162 | 23 | 86 | 181 | 23 |
| The owl at its knelling. Fox and holt kneel before blood. | 163 | 9 | 86 | 182 | 9 |
| Of the wood! Pastoral beat of blood through the laced leaves! | 164 | 22 | 86 | 184 | 8 |
| Of blood! The bird loud vein! The saga from mermen | 165 | 7 | 86 | 184 | 15 |
| To kill and their own tide daubing blood | 171 | 8 | 88 | 191 | 8 |
| Of, time enough when the blood creeps cold, | 175 | 5 | 89 | 195 | 10 |
| BLOOD'S | | | | | |
| My great blood's iron single | 38 | 15 | 20 | 44 | 5 |
| BLOOD-COUNTING | | | | | |
| The wound-down cough of the blood-counting clock | 95 | 9 | 58 | 105 | 9 |
| BLOOD-RED | | | | | |
| Slapped down the guillotine, the blood-red double | 41 | 6 | 23 | 47 | 6 |
| BLOODRED | | | | | |
| The beach of flesh, and wind her bloodred plait; | 10 | 13 | 7 | 11 | 13 |
| BLOOD-SIGNED | | | | | |
| All blood-signed assailings and vanished marriages in which he had no lovely part | 114 | 20 | 69 | 126 | 20 |
| BLOODY | | | | | |
| Under the mask and the ether, they making bloody | 37 | 2 | 20 | 42 | 8 |
| On no work of words now for three lean months in the bloody | 94 | 1 | 57 | 104 | 1 |
| Strike light, and bloody a loud room. | 97 | 10 | 59 | 108 | 10 |
| In the birth bloody room unknown | 137 | 10 | 82 | 154 | 10 |
| To the birth bloody room | 144 | 4 | 82 | 161 | 4 |
| BLOOM | | | | | |
| The crumpled packs fled past this ghost in bloom, | 80 | 5 | 46 | 89 | 13 |
| Before the lips blaze and bloom | 144 | 3 | 82 | 161 | 3 |
| Who once were a bloom of wayside brides in the hawed house | 177 | 9 | 90 | 198 | 8 |
| BLOOMING | | | | | |
| Of spring and summer were blooming in the tall tales | 103 | 11 | 63 | 114 | 11 |
| BLOOMS | | | | | |
| As the green blooms ride upward, to the drive of time; | 49 | 3 | 29 | 58 | 3 |
| The louder the sun blooms | 173 | 12 | 88 | 193 | 12 |
| BLOW | | | | | |
| I blow the stammel feather in the vein. | 32 | 8 | 18 | 37 | 14 |
| The deadrock base and blow the flowered anchor, | 51 | 5 | 31 | 60 | 5 |

| | U.K. | | | U.S. | |
|---|---|---|---|---|---|
| | *Page* | *Line* | *Poem* | *Page* | *Line* |
| Nor weather winds that blow not down the bone, | 60 | 2 | 36 | 69 | 2 |
| Watch yellow, wish for wind to blow away | 82 | 19 | 48 | 91 | 19 |
| Wind blow cold | 103 | 4 | 63 | 114 | 4 |
| Blow away like breath, | 105 | 17 | 64 | 116 | 17 |
| As the grains blow, as your death grows, through our heart. | 129 | 23 | 77 | 143 | 23 |
| Who knows the rocketing wind will blow | 172 | 13 | 88 | 192 | 13 |
| **BLOWCLOCK** | | | | | |
| And by this blowclock witness of the sun | 75 | 17 | 44 | 84 | 17 |
| **BLOWING** | | | | | |
| Stirs the quicksand; that ropes the blowing wind | 9 | 12 | 6 | 10 | 12 |
| Blowing the old dead back; our shots shall smack | 15 | 18 | 10 | 17 | 18 |
| As, blowing on the angels, I was lost | 26 | 17 | 16 | 31 | 17 |
| **BLOWN** | | | | | |
| And the four winds, that had long blown as one, | 20 | 19 | 13 | 24 | 19 |
| Spot the blown word, and on the seas I image | 76 | 13 | 44 | 85 | 13 |
| And opium head, crow stalk, puffed, cut, and blown, | 78 | 10 | 46 | 87 | 10 |
| The present mouth, and the sweetly blown trumpet of lies, | 85 | 6 | 50 | 94 | 6 |
| To the judge blown bedlam | 141 | 6 | 82 | 158 | 6 |
| And the beating dust be blown | 145 | 15 | 82 | 162 | 15 |
| And sly as snow and meek as dew blown to the thorn, | 164 | 1 | 86 | 183 | 8 |
| Hollows, a grassblade blown in cupped hands, in the looted elms | 169 | 4 | 87 | 189 | 13 |
| **BLOWS** | | | | | |
| Nor blows back moon and midnight as she blows. | 2 | 6 | 2 | 2 | 6 |
| A process blows the moon into the sun, | 6 | 22 | 4 | 7 | 4 |
| Spun to my screws, your dry ghost blows, | 11 | 2 | 8 | 12 | 2 |
| Who blows death's feather? What glory is colour? | 32 | 7 | 18 | 37 | 13 |
| Uncredited blows Jericho on Eden. | 41 | 17 | 23 | 47 | 17 |
| Man morrow blows through food. | 56 | 14 | 34 | 65 | 14 |
| Lift its head to the blows of the rain; | 68 | 23 | 42 | 77 | 23 |
| A calm wind blows that raised the trees like hair | 80 | 11 | 46 | 89 | 19 |
| Sleeps till Silence blows on a cloud | 153 | 15 | 83 | 171 | 11 |
| **BLUE** | | | | | |
| And the dumb swans drub blue | viii | 9 | 1 | xvi | 9 |
| Who moons her blue notes from her nest | ix | 11 | 1 | xvii | 11 |
| Scales the blue wall of spirits; | 83 | 21 | 49 | 93 | 3 |
| And down the other air and the blue altered sky | 103 | 17 | 63 | 114 | 17 |

BLUE (continued)

|  | U.K. | | | U.S. | |
|---|---|---|---|---|---|
|  | Page | Line | Poem | Page | Line |
| King of your blue eyes | 105 | 3 | 64 | 116 | 3 |
| And the groves were blue with sailors | 112 | 6 | 68 | 124 | 6 |
| And nothing I cared, at my sky blue trades, that time allows | 160 | 20 | 85 | 179 | 20 |
| The haygold haired, my love asleep, and the rift blue | 165 | 17 | 86 | 185 | 7 |

BLUNT

| A three-eyed, red-eyed spark, blunt as a flower; | 22 | 15 | 14 | 27 | 15 |
|---|---|---|---|---|---|
| Blunt scythe and water blade. | 70 | 11 | 43 | 79 | 15 |
| To shield the glistening brain and blunt the examiners, | 85 | 8 | 50 | 94 | 8 |
| Carved birds blunt their striking throats on the salt gravel, | 86 | 3 | 51 | 95 | 3 |
| And the mole snout blunt under his pilgrimage of domes, | 177 | 16 | 90 | 198 | 15 |

BLUSH

| I skipped in a blush as the big girls rolled | 174 | 6 | 89 | 194 | 6 |
|---|---|---|---|---|---|

BOARDS

| On the madhouse boards worn thin by my walking tears. | 108 | 15 | 66 | 119 | 15 |
|---|---|---|---|---|---|

BOAT

| Cold Nansen's beak on a boat full of gongs, | 133 | 12 | 78 | 148 | 15 |
|---|---|---|---|---|---|
| Throw wide to the wind the gates of the wandering boat | 136 | 10 | 81 | 153 | 10 |
| Boat with its anchor free and fast | 149 | 6 | 83 | 166 | 6 |
| Miles over the moonstruck boat | 150 | 14 | 83 | 167 | 18 |
| The whirled boat in the burn of his blood | 151 | 17 | 83 | 169 | 5 |
| The boat swims into the six-year weather, | 154 | 9 | 83 | 172 | 9 |
| As the boat skims on with drinking wings! | 154 | 14 | 83 | 172 | 14 |
| In deathbeds of orchards the boat dies down | 157 | 15 | 83 | 176 | 7 |

BOATS

| The sweet, fish-gilled boats bringing blood | 95 | 22 | 58 | 105 | 22 |
|---|---|---|---|---|---|
| And the knock of sailing boats on the net webbed wall | 102 | 7 | 63 | 113 | 7 |
| Then swift from a bursting sea with bottlecork boats | 132 | 13 | 78 | 147 | 13 |
| Where birds ride like leaves and boats like ducks | 134 | 22 | 79 | 150 | 22 |

BOATSIDE

| Toppling up the boatside in a snow of light! | 154 | 18 | 83 | 172 | 18 |
|---|---|---|---|---|---|

BOATSIZED

| Oh the shearwater birds and their boatsized brood | 151 | 19 | 83 | 169 | 7 |
|---|---|---|---|---|---|

BODICE

| Button your bodice on a hump of splinters, | 73 | 5 | 44 | 82 | 5 |
|---|---|---|---|---|---|

BODILESS

| Brass and the bodiless image, on a stick of folly | 38 | 2 | 20 | 43 | 12 |
|---|---|---|---|---|---|

|  | U.K. |  |  | U.S. |  |
|  | Page | Line | Poem | Page | Line |
| **BODY** |  |  |  |  |  |
| The body prospered, teeth in the marrowed gums, | 20 | 16 | 13 | 24 | 16 |
| And need no druid of her broken body). | 87 | 20 | 52 | 96 | 20 |
| Belly of the rich year and the big purse of my body | 94 | 2 | 57 | 104 | 2 |
| The grave and my calm body are shut to your coming as stone, | 98 | 6 | 59 | 109 | 9 |
| My holy lucky body | 109 | 16 | 67 | 120 | 16 |
| In the taken body at many ages, | 114 | 17 | 69 | 126 | 17 |
| In the body bereft. | 130 | 6 | 77 | 144 | 6 |
| The cureless counted body, | 158 | 4 | 84 | 177 | 4 |
| **BOILING** |  |  |  |  |  |
| Sour the boiling honey; | 1 | 8 | 2 | 1 | 8 |
| And in the pincers of the boiling circle, | 38 | 13 | 20 | 44 | 3 |
| **BOLT** |  |  |  |  |  |
| Bolt for the salt unborn. | 30 | 6 | 18 | 35 | 6 |
| The breath draw back like a bolt through white oil | 96 | 21 | 58 | 107 | 4 |
| **BOLTING** |  |  |  |  |  |
| Bolting the night of the door with her arm her plume. | 108 | 4 | 66 | 119 | 4 |
| **BONE** |  |  |  |  |  |
| That globe itself of hair and bone | 4 | 10 | 3 | 4 | 10 |
| A weather in the flesh and bone | 6 | 16 | 4 | 6 | 16 |
| Who took my flesh and bone for armour | 8 | 21 | 5 | 9 | 21 |
| The winging bone that sprouted in the heels, | 12 | 11 | 9 | 13 | 11 |
| An old man's shank one-marrowed with my bone, | 13 | 4 | 9 | 14 | 11 |
| Of the bone inch, | 18 | 10 | 12 | 21 | 10 |
| One bough of bone across the rooting air, | 22 | 3 | 14 | 27 | 3 |
| Day lights the bone; | 24 | 21 | 15 | 29 | 21 |
| Bisected shadows on the thunder's bone | 30 | 5 | 18 | 35 | 5 |
| I scrape through resin to a starry bone | 31 | 11 | 18 | 36 | 11 |
| Know, O my bone, the jointed lever, | 33 | 22 | 19 | 39 | 4 |
| Were that enough, bone, blood, and sinew, | 48 | 24 | 28 | 57 | 1 |
| Crack like a spring in a vice, bone breaking April, | 49 | 17 | 29 | 58 | 17 |
| Her bone to fire, | 55 | 9 | 33 | 64 | 12 |
| (Fog has a bone | 56 | 4 | 34 | 65 | 4 |
| A claw I question from the mouse's bone, | 56 | 17 | 34 | 65 | 17 |
| And a bone coast, | 58 | 12 | 35 | 67 | 12 |
| Nor weather winds that blow not down the bone, | 60 | 2 | 36 | 69 | 2 |
| Rebel against the flesh and bone, | 65 | 14 | 40 | 74 | 14 |
| Cast back the bone of youth | 67 | 11 | 41 | 76 | 11 |
| Rung bone and blade, the verticals of Adam, | 71 | 23 | 44 | 80 | 23 |
| Dipped me breast-deep in the descended bone; | 72 | 14 | 44 | 81 | 14 |

|  | U.K. | | | U.S. | |
| --- | --- | --- | --- | --- | --- |
|  | Page | Line | Poem | Page | Line |
| Out of the font of bone and plants at that stone tocsin | 83 | 20 | 49 | 93 | 2 |
| That breaks one bone to light with a judgment clout, | 87 | 9 | 52 | 96 | 9 |
| Curl-locked and animal cavepools of spells and bone, | 91 | 27 | 55 | 101 | 5 |
| Pack back the downed bone. If the unpricked ball of my breath | 97 | 2 | 59 | 108 | 2 |
| Of the golden ghost who ringed with his streams her mercury bone, | 127 | 11 | 75 | 141 | 11 |
| As quiet as a bone. | 133 | 23 | 78 | 149 | 6 |
| Behind the wall thin as a wren's bone? | 137 | 9 | 82 | 154 | 9 |
| By the wren bone | 138 | 4 | 82 | 155 | 4 |
| Bone writhes down | 139 | 3 | 82 | 156 | 3 |
| The inmost marrow of my heart bone | 143 | 17 | 82 | 160 | 17 |
| Bone and be dumb | 144 | 6 | 82 | 161 | 6 |
| No heart bone | 145 | 11 | 82 | 162 | 11 |
| Till every bone in the rushing grave | 151 | 11 | 83 | 168 | 19 |
| Time and places grip her breast bone, | 156 | 7 | 83 | 174 | 15 |
| Manes, under his quenchless summer barbed gold to the bone, | 177 | 6 | 90 | 198 | 5 |
| BONERAILED |  |  |  |  |  |
| A steeplejack tower, bonerailed and masterless, | 35 | 20 | 20 | 40 | 20 |
| BONES |  |  |  |  |  |
| The bones of blindness; and the womb | 6 | 8 | 4 | 6 | 8 |
| The rack of dreams my lily bones | 7 | 20 | 5 | 8 | 20 |
| The bones of men, the broken in their beds, | 14 | 9 | 10 | 16 | 9 |
| The growing bones, the rumour of manseed | 20 | 17 | 13 | 24 | 17 |
| File through the flesh where no flesh decks the bones. | 24 | 6 | 15 | 29 | 6 |
| A creature in my bones I | 28 | 10 | 17 | 33 | 10 |
| Strewing their bowels from a hill of bones, | 31 | 17 | 18 | 36 | 17 |
| 'Find meat on bones that soon have none, | 65 | 1 | 40 | 74 | 1 |
| When their bones are picked clean and the clean bones gone, | 68 | 4 | 42 | 77 | 4 |
| With bones unbuttoned to the half-way winds, | 71 | 9 | 44 | 80 | 9 |
| Straight and tall from his crooked bones | 112 | 10 | 68 | 124 | 10 |
| May his hunger go howling on bare white bones | 120 | 8 | 72 | 132 | 13 |
| That did not nurse our bones, | 126 | 10 | 74 | 140 | 10 |
| O keep his bones away from that common cart, | 135 | 12 | 80 | 152 | 12 |
| The bones out of the hills, | 172 | 14 | 88 | 192 | 14 |
| Deep in its black, base bones, | 173 | 7 | 88 | 193 | 7 |
| All his bones crying, and poor in all but pain, |  |  | 91 | 200 | 21 |
| Find meat on bones | 65 |  | 40 | 74 |  |
| BONES' |  |  |  |  |  |
| The stoved bones' voyage downward | 38 | 9 | 20 | 43 | 19 |

|  | U.K. Page | U.K. Line | Poem | U.S. Page | U.S. Line |
|---|---|---|---|---|---|
| **BONEYARDS** | | | | | |
| Corset the boneyards for a crooked boy? | 73 | 4 | 44 | 82 | 4 |
| **BONFIRE** | | | | | |
| Who bore him with a bonfire in | 139 | 9 | 82 | 156 | 9 |
| **BOOK** | | | | | |
| He in a book of water tallow-eyed | 74 | 2 | 44 | 83 | 2 |
| And one light's language in the book of trees. | 74 | 19 | 44 | 83 | 19 |
| Grief with drenched book and candle christens the cherub time | 83 | 16 | 49 | 92 | 16 |
| And his scarving beard from a book, | 134 | 12 | 79 | 150 | 12 |
| **BOOKS** | | | | | |
| There was a time they could cry over books, | 50 | 3 | 30 | 59 | 3 |
| Cawing from their black bethels soaring, the holy books | 164 | 19 | 86 | 184 | 5 |
| The sticks of the house were his; his books he owned. | | | 91 | 201 | 4 |
| **BORDER** | | | | | |
| Over the border | 102 | 18 | 63 | 113 | 18 |
| Beyond the border and under the lark full cloud. | 103 | 12 | 63 | 114 | 12 |
| **BORE** | | | | | |
| Who bore him with a bonfire in | 139 | 9 | 82 | 156 | 9 |
| That bore | 144 | 8 | 82 | 161 | 8 |
| In the coal black sky and she bore angels! | 175 | 26 | 89 | 196 | 7 |
| (But nothing bore, no mouthing babe to the veined hives | 178 | 1 | 90 | 199 | 2 |
| **BORED** | | | | | |
| Nor city tar and subway bored to foster | 19 | 9 | 12 | 22 | 14 |
| **BORN** | | | | | |
| Roared, sea born, man torn, blood blest. | viii | 15 | 1 | xvi | 15 |
| I, born of flesh and ghost, was neither | 8 | 13 | 5 | 9 | 13 |
| My Jack of Christ born thorny on the tree? | 13 | 17 | 9 | 15 | 3 |
| Born of the sensual root and sap; | 39 | 14 | 21 | 45 | 14 |
| At nightbreak born in the fat side, from an animal bed | 84 | 2 | 49 | 93 | 8 |
| Never shall beast be born to atlas the few seas | 92 | 4 | 55 | 101 | 10 |
| Who is born | 137 | 3 | 82 | 154 | 3 |
| Until the turbulent new born | 138 | 10 | 82 | 155 | 10 |
| Born sea | 142 | 2 | 82 | 159 | 2 |
| In the sun born over and over, | 160 | 17 | 85 | 179 | 17 |
| This night and each night since the falling star you were born, | 164 | 6 | 86 | 183 | 13 |
| Since you were born; | 166 | 10 | 86 | 186 | 10 |
| **BOTH** | | | | | |
| Both quench his thirst he'll have a black reply. | 53 | 9 | 32 | 62 | 9 |
| And mouth. Both note and plume plunge from the spire's hook. | 86 | 8 | 51 | 95 | 8 |
| Both shall fail if I bow not to your blessing | 110 | 19 | 67 | 121 | 21 |

| | U.K. | | | U.S. | |
|---|---|---|---|---|---|
| | Page | Line | Poem | Page | Line |
| **BOTTLE** | | | | | |
| Black-tongued and tipsy from salvation's bottle. | 73 | 15 | 44 | 82 | 15 |
| **BOTTLECORK** | | | | | |
| Then swift from a bursting sea with bottlecork boats | 132 | 13 | 78 | 147 | 13 |
| **BOTTOM** | | | | | |
| In bottom gear through night-geared man. | 28 | 12 | 17 | 33 | 12 |
| Of the uncaged sea bottom | 141 | 7 | 82 | 158 | 7 |
| **BOUGH** | | | | | |
| One bough of bone across the rooting air, | 22 | 3 | 14 | 27 | 3 |
| It were a wand or subtle bough, | 134 | 14 | 79 | 150 | 14 |
| **BOUGHS** | | | | | |
| Now as I was young and easy under the apple boughs | 159 | 1 | 85 | 178 | 1 |
| Yet out of the beaked, web dark and the pouncing boughs | 163 | 25 | 86 | 183 | 6 |
| And cut the birds' boughs that the minstrel sap ran red. | 178 | 8 | 90 | 199 | 9 |
| **BOULDER** | | | | | |
| They with the simple Jacks were a boulder of wives)— | 178 | 3 | 90 | 199 | 4 |
| **BOULDERS** | | | | | |
| Hurdles and guns and railings, as the boulders heave, | 49 | 16 | 29 | 58 | 16 |
| And the scythed boulders bleed, and the last | 172 | 15 | 88 | 192 | 15 |
| Where barren as boulders women lie longing still | 176 | 4 | 90 | 197 | 4 |
| **BOUNCED** | | | | | |
| O my lost love bounced from a good home; | 97 | 23 | 59 | 109 | 3 |
| Or, butter fat goosegirls, bounced in a gambo bed, | 177 | 17 | 90 | 198 | 16 |
| **BOUNCING** | | | | | |
| Who admits the delusive light through the bouncing wall, | 108 | 11 | 66 | 119 | 11 |
| I hear the bouncing hills | 173 | 19 | 88 | 193 | 19 |
| **BOUND** | | | | | |
| Beyond this island bound | 58 | 10 | 35 | 67 | 10 |
| Bound by a sovereign strip, we lie, | 82 | 18 | 48 | 91 | 18 |
| And his nameless need bound him burning and lost | 120 | 19 | 72 | 133 | 4 |
| **BOUNDED** | | | | | |
| That belled and bounded with the fossil and the dew reborn. | 123 | 10 | 72 | 136 | 20 |
| **BOUNDS** | | | | | |
| Stream with bells and baying water bounds. The dew rings | 121 | 7 | 72 | 134 | 2 |
| **BOW** | | | | | |
| You who bow down at cross and altar, | 8 | 19 | 5 | 9 | 19 |

| | U.K. | | | U.S. | |
|---|---|---|---|---|---|
| | *Page* | *Line* | *Poem* | *Page* | *Line* |
| Bow down the walls of the ferned and foxy woods | 87 | 24 | 52 | 96 | 24 |
| Both shall fail if I bow not to your blessing | 110 | 19 | 67 | 121 | 21 |
| BOW-AND-ARROW | | | | | |
| Naked among the bow-and-arrow birds | 60 | 23 | 36 | 69 | 23 |
| BOWED | | | | | |
| His naked need struck him howling and bowed | 120 | 14 | 72 | 132 | 19 |
| BOWELS | | | | | |
| Strewing their bowels from a hill of bones, | 31 | 17 | 18 | 36 | 17 |
| The bowels turn turtle, | 91 | 20 | 55 | 100 | 20 |
| BOWER | | | | | |
| That out of a bower of red swine | 66 | 4 | 40 | 75 | 4 |
| BOWING | | | | | |
| On the lord's-table of the bowing grass. Fear most | 163 | 12 | 86 | 182 | 12 |
| BOWL | | | | | |
| Or, masted venus, through the paddler's bowl | 54 | 7 | 33 | 63 | 7 |
| Nailed with an open eye, in the bowl of wounds and weed | 92 | 1 | 55 | 101 | 7 |
| BOWS | | | | | |
| Bows no baptism | 137 | 13 | 82 | 154 | 13 |
| The bows glided down, and the coast | 149 | 1 | 83 | 166 | 1 |
| With fuming bows and ram of ice, | 150 | 18 | 83 | 168 | 2 |
| In the river Towy below bows his tilted head-stone. | 167 | 12 | 87 | 187 | 12 |
| BOX | | | | | |
| He holds the wire from this box of nerves | 10 | 16 | 7 | 11 | 16 |
| BOXED | | | | | |
| The country-handed grave boxed into love, | 55 | 4 | 33 | 64 | 7 |
| BOXY | | | | | |
| Of bud of Adam through his boxy shift, | 19 | 13 | 12 | 22 | 18 |
| BOY | | | | | |
| The boy she dropped from darkness at her side | 21 | 2 | 13 | 25 | 2 |
| Am I not father, too, and the ascending boy, | 46 | 9 | 27 | 54 | 9 |
| The boy of woman and the wanton starer | 46 | 10 | 27 | 54 | 10 |
| Would wither up, and any boy of love | 63 | 3 | 38 | 72 | 3 |
| And the masked, headless boy. | 70 | 2 | 43 | 79 | 6 |
| Corset the boneyards for a crooked boy? | 73 | 4 | 44 | 82 | 4 |
| Shakes a desolate boy who slits his throat | 87 | 7 | 52 | 96 | 7 |
| Where a boy | 104 | 2 | 63 | 115 | 4 |
| To the boy of common thread, | 133 | 13 | 78 | 148 | 16 |
| When I was a windy boy and a bit | 174 | 1 | 89 | 194 | 1 |
| Not a boy and a bit in the wick- | 174 | 16 | 89 | 194 | 16 |
| BOYS | | | | | |
| Geese nearly in heaven, boys | vii | 15 | 1 | xv | 15 |
| I see the boys of summer in their ruin | 1 | 1 | 2 | 1 | 1 |
| These boys of light are curdlers in their folly, | 1 | 7 | 2 | 1 | 7 |

| | U.K. | | | U.S. | |
|---|---|---|---|---|---|
| | *Page* | *Line* | *Poem* | *Page* | *Line* |
| I see that from these boys shall men of nothing | 1 | 19 | 2 | 1 | 19 |
| We summer boys in this four-winded spinning, | 2 | 13 | 2 | 2 | 13 |
| O see the poles of promise in the boys. | 2 | 24 | 2 | 3 | 6 |
| I see you boys of summer in your ruin. | 3 | 1 | 2 | 3 | 7 |
| And boys are full and foreign in the pouch. | 3 | 3 | 2 | 3 | 9 |
| Like the mauled pictures of boys? | 77 | 19 | 45 | 86 | 19 |
| When I whistled with mitching boys through a reservoir park | 89 | 7 | 53 | 98 | 7 |
| The truant boys from the town | 111 | 16 | 68 | 123 | 16 |
| While the boys among willows | 112 | 3 | 68 | 124 | 3 |
| And the wild boys innocent as strawberries | 112 | 16 | 68 | 124 | 16 |
| In a spinney of ringed boys and ganders, spike and burn, | 162 | 14 | 86 | 181 | 14 |
| Petticoats galed high, or shy with the rough riding boys, | 176 | 18 | 90 | 197 | 18 |
| I see the boys of summer | 1 | | 2 | 1 | |

BOYS'

| | | | | | |
|---|---|---|---|---|---|
| Whack their boys' limbs; | 14 | 3 | 10 | 16 | 3 |

BRACKEN

| | | | | | |
|---|---|---|---|---|---|
| Where the hay rides now or the bracken kitchens rust | 178 | 6 | 90 | 199 | 7 |

BRAIDING

| | | | | | |
|---|---|---|---|---|---|
| And loosed the braiding adders from their hairs; | 30 | 22 | 18 | 35 | 22 |

BRAIN

| | | | | | |
|---|---|---|---|---|---|
| That, sewn to me by nerve and brain, | 4 | 11 | 3 | 4 | 11 |
| Into the stony idiom of the brain, | 21 | 9 | 13 | 25 | 9 |
| In the beginning was the secret brain. | 23 | 1 | 14 | 28 | 1 |
| The brain was celled and soldered in the thought | 23 | 2 | 14 | 28 | 2 |
| I fellowed sleep who kissed me in the brain, | 26 | 1 | 16 | 31 | 1 |
| The twisted brain, the fair-formed loin, | 48 | 25 | 28 | 57 | 2 |
| Master the night nor serve the snowman's brain | 60 | 4 | 36 | 69 | 4 |
| To shield the glistening brain and blunt the examiners, | 85 | 8 | 50 | 94 | 8 |
| And the doors burn in their brain. | 124 | 12 | 73 | 138 | 12 |

BRAINS

| | | | | | |
|---|---|---|---|---|---|
| And brambles in the wringing brains | 7 | 24 | 5 | 8 | 24 |
| The skull of the earth is barbed with a war of burning brains and hair. | 96 | 9 | 58 | 106 | 9 |

BRAMBLED

| | | | | | |
|---|---|---|---|---|---|
| And, in that brambled void, | 171 | 25 | 88 | 191 | 25 |

BRAMBLES

| | | | | | |
|---|---|---|---|---|---|
| And brambles in the wringing brains | 7 | 24 | 5 | 8 | 24 |
| Rough as cows' tongues and thrashed with brambles their buttermilk | 177 | 5 | 90 | 198 | 4 |

|  | U.K. | | | U.S. | |
|---|---|---|---|---|---|
|  | *Page* | *Line* | *Poem* | *Page* | *Line* |
| BRANCHES |  |  |  |  |  |
| In that proud sailing tree with branches driven | 78 | 6 | 46 | 87 | 6 |
| BRAND |  |  |  |  |  |
| Brand of the lily's anger on her ring, | 54 | 19 | 33 | 63 | 19 |
| Time marks a black aisle kindle from the brand of ashes, | 83 | 4 | 49 | 92 | 4 |
| When his viperish fuse hangs looped with flames under the brand | 168 | 4 | 87 | 188 | 8 |
| BRANDED |  |  |  |  |  |
| Branded forehead, that could bind | 109 | 9 | 67 | 120 | 9 |
| BRANDY |  |  |  |  |  |
| Into the wine burning like brandy, | 131 | 19 | 77 | 146 | 1 |
| Brandy and ripe in my bright, bass prime, | 174 | 28 | 89 | 195 | 4 |
| BRASS |  |  |  |  |  |
| Brass and the bodiless image, on a stick of folly | 38 | 2 | 20 | 43 | 12 |
| BRASSILY |  |  |  |  |  |
| Brassily at my shyest secret, | 107 | 5 | 65 | 118 | 5 |
| BRASSY |  |  |  |  |  |
| Socket and grave, the brassy blood, | 34 | 11 | 19 | 39 | 17 |
| Forged in man's minerals, the brassy orator | 35 | 2 | 20 | 40 | 2 |
| BRAVE |  |  |  |  |  |
| Brave deaths of only ones but never found, | 126 | 11 | 74 | 140 | 11 |
| A cold kind man brave in his narrow pride |  |  | 91 | 200 | 3 |
| An old kind man brave in his burning pride. |  |  | 91 | 201 | 3 |
| BRAWL |  |  |  |  |  |
| Though the brawl of the kiss has not occurred | 109 | 7 | 67 | 120 | 7 |
| BRAWNED |  |  |  |  |  |
| Split up the brawned womb's weathers, | 1 | 14 | 2 | 1 | 14 |
| BRAYS |  |  |  |  |  |
| Destruction, picked by birds, brays through the jaw-bone, | 79 | 10 | 46 | 88 | 13 |
| After the funeral, mule praises, brays, | 87 | 1 | 52 | 96 | 1 |
| BREAD |  |  |  |  |  |
| This bread I break was once the oat, | 39 | 1 | 21 | 45 | 1 |
| Once in this bread | 39 | 8 | 21 | 45 | 8 |
| My wine you drink, my bread you snap. | 39 | 15 | 21 | 45 | 15 |
| From bald pavilions and the house of bread | 75 | 2 | 44 | 84 | 2 |
| Bread and milk mansion in a toothless town. | 78 | 15 | 46 | 87 | 15 |
| With bridebait of gold bread, I with a living skein, | 91 | 25 | 55 | 101 | 3 |
| Eating bread from a newspaper | 111 | 7 | 68 | 123 | 7 |
| On a star of faith pure as the drifting bread, | 119 | 12 | 72 | 131 | 12 |
| And the cup and the cut bread in the dancing shade, | 120 | 3 | 72 | 132 | 8 |
| Hunger of birds in the fields of the bread of water, | 120 | 17 | 72 | 133 | 2 |
| And there outside on the bread of the ground | 121 | 13 | 72 | 134 | 8 |

BREAD (continued)

|  | U.K. | | | U.S. | |
|---|---|---|---|---|---|
|  | Page | Line | Poem | Page | Line |
| On a bread white hill over the cupped farm | 122 | 27 | 72 | 136 | 7 |
| That once cut the figures of birds on the deep bread | 123 | 4 | 72 | 136 | 14 |
| Not for ambition or bread | 128 | 7 | 76 | 142 | 7 |
| Into the bread in a wheatfield of flames, | 131 | 18 | 77 | 145 | 24 |
| Always good-bye to the long-legged bread | 152 | 22 | 83 | 170 | 14 |
| This bread I break | 39 |  | 21 | 45 |  |

BREAD-SIDED

| Stills snapped by night in the bread-sided field, | 73 | 8 | 44 | 82 | 8 |

BREAK

| Here break a kiss in no love's quarry. | 2 | 23 | 2 | 3 | 5 |
| Break on the lovebeds of the weeds; | 11 | 14 | 8 | 12 | 14 |
| This bread I break was once the oat, | 39 | 1 | 21 | 45 | 1 |
| This flesh you break, this blood you let | 39 | 11 | 21 | 45 | 11 |
| Strapped to a wheel, yet they shall not break; | 68 | 14 | 42 | 77 | 14 |
| Or waves break loud on the seashores; | 68 | 21 | 42 | 77 | 21 |
| Break in the sun till the sun breaks down, | 68 | 26 | 42 | 70 | 26 |
| The heart is sensual, though five eyes break. | 81 | 14 | 47 | 90 | 14 |
| Now break a giant tear for the little known fall, | 126 | 8 | 74 | 140 | 8 |
| But let it break | 145 | 12 | 82 | 162 | 12 |
| Break the black news and paint on a sail | 151 | 23 | 83 | 169 | 11 |
| Before chains break to a hammer flame | 171 | 17 | 88 | 191 | 17 |
| This bread I break | 39 |  | 21 | 45 |  |

BREAKERS

| Hear they the salt glass breakers and the tongues of burial. | 37 | 15 | 20 | 42 | 21 |

BREAKING

| Broke through her straws, breaking my bandaged string, | 12 | 3 | 9 | 13 | 3 |
| Hand, the breaking of the hair, | 20 | 11 | 13 | 24 | 11 |
| I dreamed my genesis in sweat of sleep, breaking | 28 | 1 | 17 | 33 | 1 |
| Crack like a spring in a vice, bone breaking April, | 49 | 17 | 29 | 58 | 17 |
| Tells with silence the last light breaking | 101 | 4 | 62 | 112 | 4 |
| Cry my sea town was breaking. | 134 | 27 | 79 | 151 | 5 |
| She is breaking with seasons and clouds; | 156 | 8 | 83 | 174 | 16 |

BREAKNECK

| On a breakneck of rocks | vii | 5 | 1 | xv | 5 |

BREAKS

| Breaks on unangled land. | 6 | 12 | 4 | 6 | 12 |
| Breaks with the wormy winter through the eye. | 16 | 23 | 11 | 19 | 23 |
| Light breaks where no sun shines; | 24 | 1 | 15 | 29 | 1 |
| Dawn breaks behind the eyes; | 24 | 13 | 15 | 29 | 13 |
| Light breaks on secret lots, | 25 | 1 | 15 | 30 | 1 |
| And breaks his shell in the last shocked beginning; | 41 | 13 | 23 | 47 | 13 |
| Break in the sun till the sun breaks down, | 68 | 26 | 42 | 70 | 26 |

|  | U.K. | | | U.S. | |
|  | Page | Line | Poem | Page | Line |
| Love's image till my heartbone breaks | 70 | 7 | 43 | 79 | 11 |
| Nor ever, as the wild tongue breaks its tombs, | 77 | 11 | 45 | 86 | 11 |
| Breaks, O my heart's blood, like a heart and hill. | 82 | 24 | 48 | 91 | 24 |
| That breaks one bone to light with a judgment clout, | 87 | 9 | 52 | 96 | 9 |
| Nor when all ponderous heaven's host of waters breaks. | 97 | 20 | 59 | 108 | 20 |
| The singing breaks in the snow shoed villages of wishes | 123 | 3 | 72 | 136 | 13 |
| Unclenched, armless, silk and rough love that breaks all rocks. | 126 | 16 | 74 | 140 | 16 |
| Light breaks where no sun shines | 24 | | 15 | 29 | |
| BREAST | | | | | |
| And swallowed dry the waters of the breast. | 4 | 6 | 3 | 4 | 6 |
| Nor when he finds a beauty in the breast | 13 | 12 | 9 | 14 | 19 |
| The time for breast and the green apron age | 20 | 4 | 13 | 24 | 4 |
| One breast gave suck the fever's issue; | 21 | 19 | 13 | 26 | 2 |
| The mummy cloths expose an ancient breast. | 63 | 8 | 38 | 72 | 8 |
| Now in the cloud's big breast lie quiet countries, | 80 | 8 | 46 | 89 | 16 |
| With the wild breast and blessed and giant skull | 87 | 28 | 52 | 96 | 28 |
| And dug your grave in my breast. | 92 | 16 | 55 | 101 | 22 |
| At the breast stored with seas. No return | 98 | 4 | 59 | 109 | 7 |
| A she bird dawned, and her breast with snow and scarlet downed. | 121 | 15 | 72 | 134 | 10 |
| Charred on the black breast of the grave | 129 | 7 | 77 | 143 | 7 |
| Under the sad breast of the head stone | 130 | 20 | 77 | 144 | 20 |
| Breast I shall waken | 141 | 5 | 82 | 158 | 5 |
| Time and places grip her breast bone, | 156 | 7 | 83 | 174 | 15 |
| Of the led-astray birds whom God, for their breast of whistles, | 168 | 19 | 87 | 189 | 4 |
| Whenever I doye in a breast high shoal, | 174 | 21 | 89 | 194 | 21 |
| Their breast, the vaulting does roister, the horned bucks climb | 177 | 13 | 90 | 198 | 12 |
| Above all he longed for his mother's breast | | | 91 | 200 | 9 |
| BREAST'S | | | | | |
| Why night-time rain and the breast's blood | 53 | 8 | 32 | 62 | 8 |
| BREASTED | | | | | |
| The woman breasted and the heaven headed | 123 | 15 | 72 | 137 | 5 |
| Her robin breasted tree, three Marys in the rays. | 163 | 6 | 86 | 182 | 6 |
| BREAST-DEEP | | | | | |
| Dipped me breast-deep in the descended bone; | 72 | 14 | 44 | 81 | 14 |
| BREASTKNOT | | | | | |
| Or like the tide-looped breastknot reefed again | 78 | 11 | 46 | 87 | 11 |
| BREASTS | | | | | |
| Before the ladies' breasts are hags | 65 | 4 | 40 | 74 | 4 |
| My breasts are thin. | 65 | 21 | 40 | 74 | 21 |

|  | U.K. | | | U.S. | |
|  | Page | Line | Poem | Page | Line |
| Their breasts full of honey, under their gander king | 177 | 18 | 90 | 198 | 17 |
| **BREATH** |  |  |  |  |  |
| Long breath that carried to my father | 8 | 17 | 5 | 9 | 17 |
| And from the cloudy bases of the breath | 22 | 22 | 14 | 27 | 22 |
| Five sovereign fingers taxed the breath, | 62 | 2 | 37 | 71 | 2 |
| My nostrils see her breath burn like a bush. | 81 | 10 | 47 | 90 | 10 |
| Clips short the gesture of breath. | 92 | 11 | 55 | 101 | 17 |
| That will rake at last all currencies of the marked breath | 94 | 8 | 57 | 104 | 8 |
| The breath draw back like a bolt through white oil | 96 | 21 | 58 | 107 | 4 |
| Pack back the downed bone. If the unpricked ball of my breath | 97 | 2 | 59 | 108 | 2 |
| Nor blaspheme down the stations of the breath | 101 | 16 | 62 | 112 | 16 |
| Blow away like breath, | 105 | 17 | 64 | 116 | 17 |
| Lions and fires of his flying breath, | 117 | 5 | 71 | 129 | 5 |
| The pale breath of cattle at the stealthy sail, | 119 | 5 | 72 | 131 | 5 |
| We hid our fears in that murdering breath, | 125 | 14 | 74 | 139 | 14 |
| Is always lost in her vaulted breath, | 153 | 20 | 83 | 171 | 16 |
| Innocence sweetens my last black breath, | 175 | 29 | 89 | 196 | 10 |
| Last sound, the world going out without a breath: |  |  | 91 | 201 | 13 |
| **BREATH'S** |  |  |  |  |  |
| Is corner-cast, breath's rag, scrawled weed, a vain | 78 | 9 | 46 | 87 | 9 |
| **BREATHE** |  |  |  |  |  |
| 'These are but dreaming men. Breathe, and they fade.' | 26 | 15 | 16 | 31 | 15 |
| To-day, this insect, and the world I breathe, | 41 | 1 | 23 | 47 | 1 |
| **BREATHED** |  |  |  |  |  |
| These once-blind eyes have breathed a wind of visions, | 80 | 1 | 46 | 89 | 9 |
| **BREATHES** |  |  |  |  |  |
| A separate river breathes and runs; | 156 | 12 | 83 | 174 | 20 |
| **BREATH-WHITE** |  |  |  |  |  |
| And the breath-white, curtained mouth of seed.' | 79 | 25 | 46 | 89 | 6 |
| **BRED** |  |  |  |  |  |
| The hand that signed the treaty bred a fever, | 62 | 9 | 37 | 71 | 9 |
| **BREECHES** |  |  |  |  |  |
| In love torn breeches and blistered jacket | 132 | 7 | 78 | 147 | 7 |
| **BREED** |  |  |  |  |  |
| But wishes breed not, neither | 82 | 21 | 48 | 91 | 21 |
| Shall her smile breed that mouth, behind the mirror, | 90 | 13 | 54 | 99 | 13 |
| **BREEZE** |  |  |  |  |  |
| Down breeze and shell to a discordant beach, | 81 | 7 | 47 | 90 | 7 |

| | U.K. | | | U.S. | |
|---|---|---|---|---|---|
| | *Page* | *Line* | *Poem* | *Page* | *Line* |
| BRETHREN | | | | | |
| Brethren for joy has moved within | 143 | 16 | 82 | 160 | 16 |
| BREVIARY | | | | | |
| About the saint in shades while the endless breviary | 109 | 26 | 67 | 120 | 26 |
| BRIARED | | | | | |
| For his briared hands to hoist them | 145 | 2 | 82 | 162 | 2 |
| BRIDAL | | | | | |
| The trigger and scythe, the bridal blade, | 33 | 17 | 19 | 38 | 17 |
| BRIDE | | | | | |
| Grafts on its bride one-sided skins of truth; | 15 | 8 | 10 | 17 | 8 |
| Nutmeg, civet, and sea-parsley serve the plagued groom and bride | 84 | 5 | 49 | 93 | 11 |
| Trespasser and broken bride | 114 | 18 | 69 | 126 | 18 |
| Inhuman cradle and the bride bed forever sought | 120 | 24 | 72 | 133 | 9 |
| Alone and naked in the engulfing bride, | 120 | 28 | 72 | 133 | 13 |
| A she bird rose and rayed like a burning bride. | 121 | 14 | 72 | 134 | 9 |
| The sky, the bird, the bride, | 122 | 21 | 72 | 136 | 1 |
| And through the thighs of the engulfing bride, | 123 | 14 | 72 | 137 | 4 |
| Burning in the bride bed of love, in the whirl- | 123 | 17 | 72 | 137 | 7 |
| O bride and bride groom | 130 | 17 | 77 | 144 | 17 |
| The long, laid minute's bride drifts on | 152 | 11 | 83 | 170 | 3 |
| BRIDEBAIT | | | | | |
| With bridebait of gold bread, I with a living skein, | 91 | 25 | 55 | 101 | 3 |
| BRIDES | | | | | |
| Groom the dark brides, the widows of the night | 14 | 5 | 10 | 16 | 5 |
| Is dumb and gone with his flame of brides. | 153 | 10 | 83 | 171 | 6 |
| Who once were a bloom of wayside brides in the hawed house | 177 | 9 | 90 | 198 | 8 |
| BRIDGED | | | | | |
| That bridged the human halves, | 67 | 26 | 41 | 76 | 26 |
| BRIDLES | | | | | |
| With wild sea fillies and soaking bridles | 156 | 17 | 83 | 175 | 5 |
| BRIGHT | | | | | |
| Bright as a fig; | 24 | 11 | 15 | 29 | 11 |
| Bright as her spinning-wheels, the colic season | 35 | 8 | 20 | 40 | 8 |
| As tarred with blood as the bright thorns I wept; | 75 | 7 | 44 | 84 | 7 |
| In that bright anchorground where I lay linened, | 79 | 22 | 46 | 89 | 3 |
| Carrion, paradise, chirrup my bright yolk. | 115 | 14 | 69 | 127 | 14 |
| Good men, the last wave by, crying how bright | 116 | 7 | 70 | 128 | 7 |
| By the spit and the black pot in the log bright light | 120 | 2 | 72 | 132 | 7 |

|  | U.K. | | | U.S. | |
|---|---|---|---|---|---|
|  | *Page* | *Line* | *Poem* | *Page* | *Line* |
| By the spit and the black pot in the log bright light. | 122 | 7 | 72 | 135 | 7 |
| The bright pretender, the ridiculous sea dandy | 133 | 14 | 78 | 148 | 17 |
| To bright | 138 | 16 | 82 | 155 | 16 |
| Brandy and ripe in my bright, bass prime, | 174 | 28 | 89 | 195 | 4 |
| **BRIGHT-EYED** | | | | | |
| The bright-eyed worm on Davy's lamp, | 2 | 11 | 2 | 2 | 11 |
| **BRIMMING** | | | | | |
| Cloud and the roadside bushes brimming with whistling | 102 | 22 | 63 | 113 | 22 |
| **BRINE** | | | | | |
| Stale of Adam's brine until, vision | 29 | 3 | 17 | 34 | 7 |
| **BRING** | | | | | |
| Bring out the black patrol, | 37 | 4 | 20 | 42 | 10 |
| In winds that bring the fruit and rind | 53 | 4 | 32 | 62 | 4 |
| **BRINGING** | | | | | |
| The sweet, fish-gilled boats bringing blood | ʻ95 | 22 | 58 | 105 | 22 |
| **BRISKEST** | | | | | |
| All but the briskest riders thrown, | 5 | 17 | 3 | 5 | 17 |
| **BRITTLE** | | | | | |
| A she bird sleeping brittle by | 115 | 10 | 69 | 127 | 10 |
| **BROKE** | | | | | |
| Broke through her straws, breaking my bandaged string, | 12 | 3 | 9 | 13 | 3 |
| The sea of scums could drown me as it broke | 12 | 27 | 9 | 14 | 6 |
| Laid the crops low, broke the grape's joy. | 39 | 5 | 21 | 45 | 5 |
| Man broke the sun, pulled the wind down. | 39 | 10 | 21 | 45 | 10 |
| And when the salt sheet broke in a storm of singing | 136 | 7 | 81 | 153 | 7 |
| **BROKEN** | | | | | |
| The bones of men, the broken in their beds, | 14 | 9 | 10 | 16 | 9 |
| And, broken ghosts with glow-worms in their heads, | 24 | 4 | 15 | 29 | 4 |
| The broken halves are fellowed in a cripple, | 30 | 13 | 18 | 35 | 13 |
| Be by the ships' sea broken at the manstring anchored | 38 | 8 | 20 | 43 | 18 |
| That clouts the spittle like bubbles with broken rooms, | 77 | 6 | 45 | 86 | 6 |
| And need no druid of her broken body). | 87 | 20 | 52 | 96 | 20 |
| Her constant, nor the winds of love broken wide | 109 | 10 | 67 | 120 | 10 |
| Trespasser and broken bride | 114 | 18 | 69 | 126 | 18 |
| A star was broken | 129 | 14 | 77 | 143 | 14 |
| Too proud to die; broken and blind he died | | | 91 | 200 | 1 |
| **BRONZE** | | | | | |
| My man of leaves and the bronze root, mortal, unmortal, | 35 | 16 | 20 | 40 | 16 |

| | U.K. | | | U.S. | |
|---|---|---|---|---|---|
| | Page | Line | Poem | Page | Line |
| BROOD | | | | | |
| Oh the shearwater birds and their boatsized brood | 151 | 19 | 83 | 169 | 7 |
| Safe be and smooth from the bellows of the rushy brood. | 162 | 20 | 86 | 181 | 20 |
| BROODY | | | | | |
| The duck-billed platypus broody in a milk of birds. | 110 | 5 | 67 | 121 | 7 |
| BROOMED | | | | | |
| From the broomed witch's spume you are shielded by fern | 162 | 17 | 86 | 181 | 17 |
| BROTHER | | | | | |
| Was brother to Mnetha's daughter | 7 | 5 | 5 | 8 | 5 |
| Do you not brother me, nor, as you climb, | 46 | 7 | 27 | 54 | 7 |
| The terrible world my brother bares his skin. | 80 | 7 | 46 | 89 | 15 |
| With the incestuous secret brother in the seconds to perpetuate the stars, | 115 | 20 | 69 | 127 | 20 |
| BROTHERLESS | | | | | |
| Have brotherless his sister on the handsaw. | 51 | 14 | 31 | 60 | 14 |
| BROTHERS | | | | | |
| Two proud, blacked brothers cry, | 126 | 1 | 74 | 140 | 1 |
| BROUGHT | | | | | |
| Who have brought forth the urchin grief. | 84 | 6 | 49 | 93 | 12 |
| Bird, he was brought low, | 123 | 16 | 72 | 137 | 6 |
| BROW | | | | | |
| The crusted wound nor stroke the brow; | 62 | 14 | 37 | 71 | 14 |
| December's thorn screwed in a brow of holly. | 76 | 14 | 44 | 85 | 14 |
| BROWN | | | | | |
| That her love sing and swing through a brown chapel, | 87 | 25 | 52 | 96 | 25 |
| Brown as owls | 103 | 9 | 63 | 114 | 9 |
| Grow larked and greener at berry brown | 173 | 20 | 88 | 193 | 20 |
| BRUISES | | | | | |
| Drive children up like bruises to the thumb, | 18 | 14 | 12 | 21 | 14 |
| BRUTE | | | | | |
| A brute land in the cool top of the country days | 91 | 15 | 55 | 100 | 15 |
| BRYNS | | | | | |
| Huloo, on plumbed bryns, | ix | 6 | 1 | xvii | 6 |
| BUBBLE | | | | | |
| She threads off the sap and needles, blood and bubble | 35 | 10 | 20 | 40 | 10 |
| But the oil and bubble of the moon, | 150 | 21 | 83 | 168 | 5 |
| BUBBLED | | | | | |
| The fellow half was frozen as it bubbled | 30 | 7 | 18 | 35 | 7 |
| BUBBLES | | | | | |
| With swag of bubbles in a seedy sack | 67 | 17 | 41 | 76 | 17 |
| These stolen bubbles have the bites of snakes | 67 | 23 | 41 | 76 | 23 |

## BUBBLES (continued)

| | U.K. Page | U.K. Line | Poem | U.S. Page | U.S. Line |
|---|---|---|---|---|---|
| That clouts the spittle like bubbles with broken rooms, | 77 | 6 | 45 | 86 | 6 |
| Bump on a spout let the bubbles jump out. | 97 | 3 | 59 | 108 | 3 |
| **BUCK** | | | | | |
| But heard his bait buck in the wake | 150 | 5 | 83 | 167 | 9 |
| **BUCKLE** | | | | | |
| Buckle to lint and cloth their natron footsteps, | 75 | 22 | 44 | 84 | 22 |
| **BUCKLING** | | | | | |
| My Egypt's armour buckling in its sheet, | 31 | 10 | 18 | 36 | 10 |
| **BUCKS** | | | | | |
| Their breast, the vaulting does roister, the horned bucks climb | 177 | 13 | 90 | 198 | 12 |
| **BUD** | | | | | |
| And curling round the bud that forks her eye. | 13 | 3 | 9 | 14 | 10 |
| Of bud of Adam through his boxy shift, | 19 | 13 | 12 | 22 | 18 |
| A million minds gave suck to such a bud | 21 | 22 | 13 | 26 | 5 |
| O light in zenith, the coupled bud, | 34 | 8 | 19 | 39 | 14 |
| Wrenched by my fingerman, the leaden bud | 54 | 11 | 33 | 63 | 11 |
| Of paradise, in the spun bud of the world. | 123 | 19 | 72 | 137 | 9 |
| **BUDS** | | | | | |
| With a stub of black buds, | 95 | 21 | 58 | 105 | 21 |
| **BUGLE** | | | | | |
| Never never oh never to regret the bugle I wore | 133 | 19 | 78 | 149 | 2 |
| **BUILD** | | | | | |
| I build my bellowing ark | viii | 18 | 1 | xvi | 18 |
| **BUILDS** | | | | | |
| When the worm builds with the gold straws of venom | 76 | 21 | 44 | 85 | 21 |
| **BUILT** | | | | | |
| To the built voice, or fly with winter to the bells, | 86 | 10 | 51 | 95 | 10 |
| **BULB** | | | | | |
| Beginning with doom in the bulb, the spring unravels, | 35 | 7 | 20 | 40 | 7 |
| **BULL** | | | | | |
| But a hillocky bull in the swelter | 175 | 2 | 89 | 195 | 7 |
| Or hickory bull in milky grass | 175 | 12 | 89 | 195 | 17 |
| **BULL'S-EYE** | | | | | |
| Bull's-eye the outlaw through a eunuch crack | 67 | 19 | 41 | 76 | 19 |
| **BULLDANCE** | | | | | |
| Whalebed and bulldance, the gold bush of lions, | 78 | 22 | 46 | 87 | 22 |
| **BULLIES** | | | | | |
| Bullies into rough seas you so gentle | 96 | 24 | 58 | 107 | 7 |
| **BULLOCK** | | | | | |
| Adam or Eve, the adorned holy bullock | 130 | 10 | 77 | 144 | 10 |
| **BULLRING** | | | | | |
| A thundering bullring of your silent and girl-circled island. | 96 | 26 | 58 | 107 | 9 |

|  |  | U.K. |  |  | U.S. |  |
| --- | --- | --- | --- | --- | --- | --- |
|  |  | Page | Line | Poem | Page | Line |
| BULLS |  |  |  |  |  |  |
| Oh the bulls of Biscay and their calves |  | 151 | 20 | 83 | 169 | 8 |
| BULLY |  |  |  |  |  |  |
| Than bully ill love in the clouted scene. |  | 97 | 5 | 59 | 108 | 5 |
| BULWARKS |  |  |  |  |  |  |
| And the bulwarks of the dazzled quay. |  | 149 | 10 | 83 | 166 | 10 |
| BUM |  |  |  |  |  |  |
| Because there stands, one story out of the bum city, |  | 77 | 13 | 45 | 86 | 13 |
| BUMP |  |  |  |  |  |  |
| Bump on a spout let the bubbles jump out. |  | 97 | 3 | 59 | 108 | 3 |
| BUNCHED |  |  |  |  |  |  |
| 'If my bunched, monkey coming is cruel |  | 97 | 11 | 59 | 108 | 11 |
| BUOY'S |  |  |  |  |  |  |
| Death clear as a buoy's bell: |  | 168 | 2 | 87 | 188 | 6 |
| BUOYS |  |  |  |  |  |  |
| Chimes of the rocked buoys. |  | 150 | 12 | 83 | 167 | 16 |
| BURDEN |  |  |  |  |  |  |
| Of the birds of burden |  | 143 | 4 | 82 | 160 | 4 |
| BURIAL |  |  |  |  |  |  |
| Hear they the salt glass breakers and the tongues of burial. |  | 37 | 15 | 20 | 42 | 21 |
| Shakes, in crabbed burial shawl, by sorcerer's insect woken, |  | 83 | 23 | 49 | 93 | 5 |
| Endure burial under the spelling wall, |  | 91 | 4 | 55 | 100 | 4 |
| Under the burial song |  | 143 | 3 | 82 | 160 | 3 |
| BURIED |  |  |  |  |  |  |
| The dream that kicks the buried from their sack |  | 15 | 14 | 10 | 17 | 14 |
| Dust in the buried wood, flies on the grains of her wings |  | 121 | 3 | 72 | 133 | 18 |
| BURIES |  |  |  |  |  |  |
| This summer buries a spring bird. |  | 45 | 4 | 26 | 53 | 4 |
| Exultation lies down. Time buries the spring weather |  | 123 | 9 | 72 | 136 | 19 |
| BURN |  |  |  |  |  |  |
| That burn the bitten decks, |  | 69 | 9 | 43 | 78 | 9 |
| My nostrils see her breath burn like a bush. |  | 81 | 10 | 47 | 90 | 10 |
| If I take to burn or return this world which is each man's work. |  | 94 | 12 | 57 | 104 | 12 |
| Old age should burn and rave at close of day; |  | 116 | 2 | 70 | 128 | 2 |
| And the doors burn in their brain. |  | 124 | 12 | 73 | 138 | 12 |
| To the burn and turn of time |  | 137 | 11 | 82 | 154 | 11 |
| I turn the corner of prayer and burn |  | 148 | 1 | 82 | 165 | 1 |
| The whirled boat in the burn of his blood |  | 151 | 17 | 83 | 169 | 5 |
| In a spinney of ringed boys and ganders, spike and burn, |  | 162 | 14 | 86 | 181 | 14 |

|  | U.K. | | | U.S. | |
| --- | --- | --- | --- | --- | --- |
|  | Page | Line | Poem | Page | Line |
| **BURNED** | | | | | |
| And burned sea silence on a wick of words. | 74 | 4 | 44 | 83 | 4 |
| That his tears burned my cheeks and his heart moved in mine. | 103 | 28 | 63 | 115 | 2 |
| The scrolls of fire that burned in his heart and head, | 119 | 14 | 72 | 131 | 14 |
| Among the street burned to tireless death | 129 | 4 | 77 | 143 | 4 |
| And prophets loud on the burned dunes; | 156 | 5 | 83 | 174 | 13 |
| **BURNING** | | | | | |
| Is a burning and crested act, | vii | 25 | 1 | xv | 25 |
| And, burning ciphers on the round of space, | 22 | 5 | 14 | 27 | 5 |
| Bleed from my burning fork and smell my heels. | 32 | 4 | 18 | 37 | 10 |
| Farmer in time of frost the burning leagues, | 60 | 10 | 36 | 69 | 10 |
| Out of the old lie burning on the ground, | 64 | 13 | 39 | 73 | 13 |
| Which sixth of wind blew out the burning gentry? | 73 | 1 | 44 | 82 | 1 |
| Toppling and burning in the muddle of towers and galleries | 77 | 18 | 45 | 86 | 18 |
| Fumed like a tree, and tossed a burning bird; | 80 | 3 | 46 | 89 | 11 |
| The skull of the earth is barbed with a war of burning brains and hair. | 96 | 9 | 58 | 106 | 9 |
| The majesty and burning of the child's death. | 101 | 13 | 62 | 112 | 13 |
| Joy of the long dead child sang burning | 104 | 11 | 63 | 115 | 13 |
| Man was the burning England she was sleep-walking, and the enamouring island | 113 | 20 | 69 | 125 | 20 |
| Of fields. And burning then | 119 | 16 | 72 | 131 | 16 |
| And his nameless need bound him burning and lost | 120 | 19 | 72 | 133 | 4 |
| A she bird rose and rayed like a burning bride. | 121 | 14 | 72 | 134 | 9 |
| The heavens, the heaven, the grave, the burning font. | 122 | 24 | 72 | 136 | 4 |
| Burning in the bride bed of love, in the whirl- | 123 | 17 | 72 | 137 | 7 |
| Into the dead clock burning the hour | 131 | 13 | 77 | 145 | 19 |
| Into the wine burning like brandy, | 131 | 19 | 77 | 146 | 1 |
| In the throat, burning and turning. All night afloat | 136 | 2 | 81 | 153 | 2 |
| Burning! Night and the vein of birds in the winged, sloe wrist | 164 | 21 | 86 | 184 | 7 |
| An old kind man brave in his burning pride. |  |  | 91 | 201 | 3 |
| **BURNS** | | | | | |
| Warms youth and seed and burns the seeds of age; | 24 | 8 | 15 | 29 | 8 |
| That burns along my eyes. | 90 | 14 | 54 | 99 | 14 |
| Burns me his name and his flame | 138 | 11 | 82 | 155 | 11 |
| Cry. My voice burns in his hand. | 148 | 15 | 82 | 165 | 15 |

| | U.K. | | | U.S. | |
|---|---|---|---|---|---|
| | *Page* | *Line* | *Poem* | *Page* | *Line* |
| BURST | | | | | |
| Burst in the roots, pumped from the earth and rock | 22 | 17 | 14 | 27 | 17 |
| The black, burst sea rejoice, | 91 | 19 | 55 | 100 | 19 |
| He dropped where he loved on the burst pavement stone | 135 | 4 | 80 | 152 | 4 |
| BURSTING | | | | | |
| Then swift from a bursting sea with bottlecork boats | 132 | 13 | 78 | 147 | 13 |
| BURSTS | | | | | |
| Of love and light bursts in their throats. | 1 | 23 | 2 | 1 | 23 |
| BURY | | | | | |
| That bury the sweet street slowly, see | 96 | 8 | 58 | 106 | 8 |
| (Bury the dead for fear that they walk to the grave in labour.) | 99 | 2 | 60 | 110 | 2 |
| Forgotten dark, rest' their pulse and bury their dead in her faithless sleep. | 115 | 23 | 69 | 127 | 23 |
| BUSH | | | | | |
| Whalebed and bulldance, the gold bush of lions, | 78 | 22 | 46 | 87 | 22 |
| My nostrils see her breath burn like a bush. | 81 | 10 | 47 | 90 | 10 |
| Lops, as a bush plumed with flames, the rant of the fierce eye, | 92 | 10 | 55 | 101 | 16 |
| In the coal black bush and let them grieve. | 174 | 12 | 89 | 194 | 12 |
| Or with their orchard man in the core of the sun's bush | 177 | 4 | 90 | 198 | 3 |
| BUSHED | | | | | |
| On the departed, snow bushed green, wanton in moon light | 121 | 17 | 72 | 134 | 12 |
| Deep the great bushed bait with raining lips | 151 | 3 | 83 | 168 | 11 |
| BUSHES | | | | | |
| Cloud and the roadside bushes brimming with whistling | 102 | 22 | 63 | 113 | 22 |
| Green chickens of the bay and bushes cluck, 'dilly dilly, | 168 | 7 | 87 | 188 | 11 |
| BUSHILY | | | | | |
| Then, bushily swanked in bear wig and tails, | 132 | 19 | 78 | 147 | 19 |
| BUSHY | | | | | |
| Some dead undid their bushy jaws, | 4 | 22 | 3 | 4 | 22 |
| That shapes each bushy item of the air | 60 | 5 | 36 | 69 | 5 |
| BUSY | | | | | |
| My busy heart who shudders as she talks | 16 | 7 | 11 | 19 | 7 |
| BUTT | | | | | |
| Butt of the tree-tailed worm that mounted Eve, | 72 | 8 | 44 | 81 | 8 |
| BUTTER | | | | | |
| Would leave me cold as butter for the flies, | 12 | 26 | 9 | 14 | 5 |
| Or, butter fat goosegirls, bounced in a gambo bed, | 177 | 17 | 90 | 198 | 16 |

|  | U.K. | | | U.S. | |
| --- | --- | --- | --- | --- | --- |
|  | Page | Line | Poem | Page | Line |
| BUTTERMILK | | | | | |
| Yard of the buttermilk rain on the pail! The sermon | 165 | 6 | 86 | 184 | 14 |
| Rough as cows' tongues and thrashed with brambles their buttermilk | 177 | 5 | 90 | 198 | 4 |
| BUTTON | | | | | |
| Button your bodice on a hump of splinters, | 73 | 5 | 44 | 82 | 5 |
| BYRES | | | | | |
| And the duck pond glass and the blinding byres alone | 120 | 10 | 72 | 132 | 15 |
| Past the blind barns and byres of the windless farm. | 122 | 10 | 72 | 135 | 10 |
| BYZANTINE | | | | | |
| Rose my Byzantine Adam in the night. | 73 | 16 | 44 | 82 | 16 |

# ENTRIES UNDER C

| CADAVER | | | | | |
| --- | --- | --- | --- | --- | --- |
| You hero skull, Cadaver in the hanger | 19 | 4 | 12 | 22 | 9 |
| CADAVER'S | | | | | |
| Of love am barer than Cadaver's trap | 18 | 8 | 12 | 21 | 8 |
| Heart of Cadaver's candle waxes thin, | 18 | 12 | 12 | 21 | 12 |
| Stride through Cadaver's country in my force, | 18 | 21 | 12 | 22 | 1 |
| Joy is the knock of dust, Cadaver's shoot | 19 | 12 | 12 | 22 | 17 |
| Happy Cadaver's hunger as you take | 19 | 24 | 12 | 23 | 9 |
| Man was Cadaver's masker, the harnessing mantle, | 38 | 25 | 20 | 44 | 15 |
| CADAVEROUS | | | | | |
| The cadaverous gravels, falls thick and steadily, | 36 | 20 | 20 | 41 | 20 |
| CAESARED | | | | | |
| Drives out the father from the caesared camp; | 54 | 27 | 33 | 64 | 3 |
| CAGE | | | | | |
| And the cage for the scythe-eyed raven. | 33 | 21 | 19 | 39 | 3 |
| Assembling waits for the spade's ring on the cage. | 135 | 11 | 80 | 152 | 11 |
| And to-morrow weeps in a blind cage | 171 | 15 | 88 | 191 | 15 |
| CAIRO'S | | | | | |
| Draw on the glove of prints, dead Cairo's henna | 75 | 23 | 44 | 84 | 23 |
| CALDRON | | | | | |
| In the caldron | 139 | 15 | 82 | 156 | 15 |
| CALENDAR | | | | | |
| The slug's a living calendar of days; | 45 | 15 | 26 | 53 | 15 |

| | U.K. | | | U.S. | |
|---|---|---|---|---|---|
| | *Page* | *Line* | *Poem* | *Page* | *Line* |

CALF

| | | | | | |
|---|---|---|---|---|---|
| Dipping moon and drunk as a new dropped calf, | 174 | 17 | 89 | 194 | 17 |
| No flailing calf or cat in a flame | 175 | 11 | 89 | 195 | 16 |

CALL

| | | | | | |
|---|---|---|---|---|---|
| Call back the castaways | 67 | 7 | 41 | 76 | 7 |
| But I, Ann's bard on a raised hearth, call all | 87 | 21 | 52 | 96 | 21 |
| With water praying and call of seagull and rook | 102 | 6 | 63 | 113 | 6 |
| Friend by enemy I call you out. | 107 | 1 | 65 | 118 | 1 |
| Call for confessor and wiser mirror but there is none | 158 | 10 | 84 | 177 | 10 |
| When I was a man you could call a man | 174 | 25 | 89 | 195 | 1 |

CALLED

| | | | | | |
|---|---|---|---|---|---|
| Called in my eyes the sound of light. | 20 | 21 | 13 | 24 | 21 |
| And Mister they called Hey mister | 111 | 15 | 68 | 123 | 15 |
| One who called deepest down shall hold his peace | 117 | 9 | 71 | 129 | 9 |

CALLIGRAPHER

| | | | | | |
|---|---|---|---|---|---|
| The lamped calligrapher, the queen in splints, | 75 | 21 | 44 | 84 | 21 |

CALLIGRAPHY

| | | | | | |
|---|---|---|---|---|---|
| Leap, as to trumpets. Calligraphy of the old | 121 | 22 | 72 | 134 | 17 |

CALLING

| | | | | | |
|---|---|---|---|---|---|
| A calling for colour calls with the wind | 82 | 6 | 48 | 91 | 6 |

CALLS

| | | | | | |
|---|---|---|---|---|---|
| Calls some content to travel with the winds, | 53 | 17 | 32 | 62 | 17 |
| And the thunder of calls and notes. | 64 | 10 | 39 | 73 | 10 |
| Calls a green day and night. | 69 | 6 | 43 | 78 | 6 |
| Calls the green rock of light. | 69 | 12 | 43 | 78 | 12 |
| Calls the starved fire herd, is cast in ice, | 79 | 1 | 46 | 88 | 4 |
| A calling for colour calls with the wind | 82 | 6 | 48 | 91 | 6 |
| Shallow and sedge, and 'dilly dilly,' calls the loft hawk, | 167 | 21 | 87 | 188 | 2 |

CALM

| | | | | | |
|---|---|---|---|---|---|
| Shall calm her sores. | 9 | 18 | 6 | 10 | 18 |
| Your calm and cuddled is a scythe of hairs, | 18 | 2 | 12 | 21 | 2 |
| A calm wind blows that raised the trees like hair | 80 | 11 | 46 | 89 | 19 |
| With a one-coloured calm; | 82 | 13 | 48 | 91 | 13 |
| Cathedral calm in the pulled house; | 83 | 15 | 49 | 92 | 15 |
| The grave and my calm body are shut to your coming as stone, | 98 | 6 | 59 | 109 | 9 |
| Will be the same grief flying. Whom shall they calm? | 100 | 11 | 61 | 111 | 11 |
| In the mantle and calm, | 122 | 6 | 72 | 135 | 6 |
| There was calm to be done in his safe unrest, | 125 | 11 | 74 | 139 | 11 |

CALVE

| | | | | | |
|---|---|---|---|---|---|
| If the red tickle as the cattle calve | 12 | 4 | 9 | 13 | 4 |

|  | U.K. | | | U.S. | |
| --- | --- | --- | --- | --- | --- |
|  | *Page* | *Line* | *Poem* | *Page* | *Line* |
| CALVES | | | | | |
| Oh the bulls of Biscay and their calves | 151 | 20 | 83 | 169 | 8 |
| And green and golden I was huntsman and herdsman, the calves | 159 | 15 | 85 | 178 | 15 |
| CAME | | | | | |
| And after came the imprints on the water | 22 | 9 | 14 | 27 | 9 |
| And famine grew, and locusts came; | 62 | 10 | 37 | 71 | 10 |
| And from the windy West came two-gunned Gabriel, | 73 | 11 | 44 | 82 | 11 |
| I died before bedtime came | 93 | 26 | 56 | 103 | 6 |
| Like the park birds he came early | 111 | 13 | 68 | 123 | 13 |
| That came from the wound wrapped in the salt sheet. | 136 | 4 | 81 | 153 | 4 |
| Slunk pouting out when the limp time came; | 175 | 15 | 89 | 195 | 20 |
| On whom a world of ills came down like snow. | | | 91 | 201 | 11 |
| CAMEL'S | | | | | |
| My camel's eyes will needle through the shroud. | 73 | 6 | 44 | 82 | 6 |
| CAMERAS | | | | | |
| When cameras shut they hurry to their hole | 14 | 15 | 10 | 16 | 15 |
| CAMP | | | | | |
| Drives out the father from the caesared camp; | 54 | 27 | 33 | 64 | 3 |
| CAMPED | | | | | |
| Camped in the drug-white shower of nerves and food, | 77 | 8 | 45 | 86 | 8 |
| CAN | | | | | |
| Can never raise the midnight of a chuckle, | 13 | 11 | 9 | 14 | 18 |
| Can time unriddle, and the cupboard stone, | 56 | 3 | 34 | 65 | 3 |
| And the maggot no man can slay.' | 65 | 16 | 40 | 74 | 16 |
| 'The maggot that no man can kill | 66 | 1 | 40 | 75 | 1 |
| And the man no rope can hang | 66 | 2 | 40 | 75 | 2 |
| Nor can I smother the sweet waking.' | 66 | 8 | 40 | 75 | 8 |
| Can we fend off rock arrival, | 82 | 22 | 48 | 91 | 22 |
| That I can hear the womb | 137 | 6 | 82 | 154 | 6 |
| CANALS | | | | | |
| Lapping the still canals, the dry tide-master | 82 | 10 | 48 | 91 | 10 |
| CANCER | | | | | |
| The redhaired cancer still alive, | 4 | 20 | 3 | 4 | 20 |
| The root of tongues ends in a spentout cancer, | 21 | 13 | 13 | 25 | 13 |
| And share my bed with Capricorn and Cancer. | 71 | 14 | 44 | 80 | 14 |
| CANCER'S | | | | | |
| The cancer's fusion, or the summer feather | 19 | 7 | 12 | 22 | 12 |
| CANDLE | | | | | |
| Heart of Cadaver's candle waxes thin, | 18 | 12 | 12 | 21 | 12 |
| A candle in the thighs | 24 | 7 | 15 | 29 | 7 |
| Where no wax is, the candle shows its hairs. | 24 | 12 | 15 | 29 | 12 |
| And a firewind kill the candle. | 83 | 6 | 49 | 92 | 6 |

|  | U.K. | | | U.S. | |
|---|---|---|---|---|---|
|  | Page | Line | Poem | Page | Line |
| Grief with drenched book and candle christens | | | | | |
|     the cherub time | 83 | 16 | 49 | 92 | 16 |
| **CANDLES** | | | | | |
|     He was blind to the eyes of candles | 150 | 3 | 83 | 167 | 7 |
| **CANDLEWOODS** | | | | | |
|     The sun-leaved holy candlewoods | 95 | 19 | 58 | 105 | 19 |
| **CANNONS** | | | | | |
|     Nor the cannons of his kingdom | 43 | 19 | 24 | 51 | 5 |
|     Nor the cannons of his kingdom | 43 | 26 | 24 | 51 | 12 |
| **CANNOT** | | | | | |
|     I cannot murder, like a fool, | 66 | 6 | 40 | 75 | 6 |
|     More the thick stone cannot tell. | 93 | 10 | 56 | 102 | 10 |
|     Jealousy cannot forget for all her sakes, | 114 | 11 | 69 | 126 | 11 |
|     That cannot sink or cease | 117 | 10 | 71 | 129 | 10 |
|     Myselves grieve now, and miracles cannot atone. | 129 | 16 | 77 | 143 | 16 |
| **CANS** | | | | | |
|     From garden cans, or free the floods? | 44 | 7 | 25 | 52 | 7 |
| **CANVAS** | | | | | |
|     Time on the canvas paths. | 69 | 24 | 43 | 78 | 24 |
| **CANYONS** | | | | | |
|     Young from the canyons of oblivion! | 142 | 9 | 82 | 159 | 9 |
| **CAP** | | | | | |
|     The invoked, shrouding veil at the cap of the | | | | | |
|         face, | 91 | 5 | 55 | 100 | 5 |
|     And a black cap of jack- | 167 | 14 | 87 | 187 | 14 |
| **CAPES** | | | | | |
|     In your beaks, on the gabbing capes! | ix | 15 | 1 | xvii | 15 |
|     Whales in the wake like capes and Alps | 151 | 1 | 83 | 168 | 9 |
| **CAPPED** | | | | | |
|     With my cherry capped dangler green as sea- | | | | | |
|         weed | 133 | 17 | 78 | 148 | 20 |
| **CAPRICORN** | | | | | |
|     And share my bed with Capricorn and Cancer. | 71 | 14 | 44 | 80 | 14 |
| **CAPS** | | | | | |
|     Pour like a halo on the caps and serpents. | 75 | 24 | 44 | 84 | 24 |
| **CAPSIZED** | | | | | |
|     With a capsized field where a school sat still | 89 | 3 | 53 | 98 | 3 |
| **CARBOLIC** | | | | | |
|     Flicked from the carbolic city puzzle in a bed of | | | | | |
|         sores | 96 | 3 | 58 | 106 | 3 |
| **CARCASS** | | | | | |
|     And conjured up a carcass shape | 5 | 11 | 3 | 5 | 11 |
| **CARDBOARD** | | | | | |
|     Adam, time's joker, on a witch of cardboard | 74 | 11 | 44 | 83 | 11 |
| **CARE** | | | | | |
|     By these I would not care to die, | 64 | 19 | 39 | 73 | 19 |
|     In the fire of his care his love in the high room. | 100 | 16 | 61 | 111 | 16 |

|  | U.K. | | | U.S. | |
|---|---|---|---|---|---|
|  | Page | Line | Poem | Page | Line |
| **CARED** | | | | | |
| And nothing I cared, at my sky blue trades, that time allows | 160 | 20 | 85 | 179 | 20 |
| Nothing I cared, in the lamb white days, that time would take me | 160 | 24 | 85 | 180 | 1 |
| **CAREFREE** | | | | | |
| And as I was green and carefree, famous among the barns | 159 | 10 | 85 | 178 | 10 |
| **CARGOED** | | | | | |
| And drown the cargoed apples in their tides. | 1 | 6 | 2 | 1 | 6 |
| **CARING** | | | | | |
| The one not caring to whom in his sleep he will move | 100 | 4 | 61 | 111 | 4 |
| And the child not caring to whom he climbs his prayer | 100 | 17 | 61 | 111 | 17 |
| **CARNAL** | | | | | |
| The flight of the carnal skull | 37 | 24 | 20 | 43 | 7 |
| **CARRIED** | | | | | |
| Long breath that carried to my father | 8 | 17 | 5 | 9 | 17 |
| **CARRION** | | | | | |
| To the anguish and carrion, to the infant forever unfree, | 97 | 22 | 59 | 109 | 2 |
| Carrion, paradise, chirrup my bright yolk. | 115 | 14 | 69 | 127 | 14 |
| The swinish plains of carrion | 143 | 2 | 82 | 160 | 2 |
| **CARRY** | | | | | |
| For my tall turrets carry as your sin? | 46 | 6 | 27 | 54 | 6 |
| **CARRYING** | | | | | |
| Carrying cloud, Death strikes their house. | 124 | 8 | 73 | 138 | 8 |
| Around some coffin carrying | 133 | 2 | 78 | 148 | 5 |
| **CART** | | | | | |
| O keep his bones away from that common cart, | 135 | 12 | 80 | 152 | 12 |
| **CARTOON** | | | | | |
| Cartoon of slashes on the tide-traced crater, | 74 | 1 | 44 | 83 | 1 |
| **CARVED** | | | | | |
| Carved birds blunt their striking throats on the salt gravel, | 86 | 3 | 51 | 95 | 3 |
| Is carved from her in a room with a wet window | 88 | 1 | 52 | 97 | 1 |
| With carved bird, saint, and sun, the wrack-spiked maiden mouth | 92 | 9 | 55 | 101 | 15 |
| Saint carved and sensual among the scudding | 109 | 5 | 67 | 120 | 5 |
| I see the wanting nun saint carved in a garb | 110 | 6 | 67 | 121 | 8 |
| Death in the carved nunnery | 110 | 18 | 67 | 121 | 20 |
| Parish of snow. The carved mouths in the rock are wind swept strings. | 121 | 9 | 72 | 134 | 4 |
| The carved limbs in the rock | 121 | 21 | 72 | 134 | 16 |
| **CAST** | | | | | |
| And time cast forth my mortal creature | 8 | 7 | 5 | 9 | 7 |

|  | U.K. | | | U.S. | |
|---|---|---|---|---|---|
|  | *Page* | *Line* | *Poem* | *Page* | *Line* |
| And cast a shadow crab upon the land, | 16 | 4 | 11 | 19 | 4 |
| For my tall tower's sake cast in her stone? | 46 | 2 | 27 | 54 | 2 |
| Rose cast to plague, | 54 | 14 | 33 | 63 | 14 |
| I tell her this: before the suncock cast | 55 | 8 | 33 | 64 | 11 |
| Cast back the bone of youth | 67 | 11 | 41 | 76 | 11 |
| Calls the starved fire herd, is cast in ice, | 79 | 1 | 46 | 88 | 4 |
| I mean by time the cast and curfew rascal of our marriage, | 84 | 1 | 49 | 93 | 7 |
| Cast high, stunned on gilled stone; sly scissors ground in frost | 92 | 7 | 55 | 101 | 13 |
| Is cast before you move, | 106 | 9 | 64 | 117 | 9 |
| By losing him all in love, and cast his need | 120 | 27 | 72 | 133 | 12 |
| Now cast down your rod, for the whole | 150 | 7 | 83 | 167 | 11 |
| Good-bye always for the flesh is cast | 154 | 2 | 83 | 172 | 2 |

CASTAWAYS
| Call back the castaways | 67 | 7 | 41 | 76 | 7 |

CASTING
| On casting tides, are tangled in the shells, | 32 | 2 | 18 | 37 | 8 |
| Casting to-morrow like a thorn | 138 | 8 | 82 | 155 | 8 |

CASTLE
| Hoo, there, in castle keep, | ix | 2 | 1 | xvii | 2 |
| With its horns through mist and the castle | 103 | 8 | 63 | 114 | 8 |

CASTS
| Casts to the pine roots, raising man like a mountain | 35 | 11 | 20 | 40 | 11 |

CAT
| The cattle stirring, the mousing cat stepping shy, | 119 | 22 | 72 | 132 | 2 |
| No flailing calf or cat in a flame | 175 | 11 | 89 | 195 | 16 |

CATARACTED
| The cataracted eyes that filmed their cloth; | 4 | 21 | 3 | 4 | 21 |

CATCH
| Day's night whose towers will catch | vii | 20 | 1 | xv | 20 |
| And the long-tailed lightning lit his catch. | 154 | 8 | 83 | 172 | 8 |
| Strike and sing his catch of fields | 156 | 13 | 83 | 175 | 1 |

CATCHING
| Her heart all ears and eyes, lips catching the avalanche | 127 | 10 | 75 | 141 | 10 |

CATHEDRAL
| Cathedral calm in the pulled house; | 83 | 15 | 49 | 92 | 15 |
| Floated the lost cathedral | 150 | 11 | 83 | 167 | 15 |

CATHEDRALS
| Of the luminous cathedrals, | 131 | 10 | 77 | 145 | 16 |

CATHERINE
| Queen Catherine howling bare | 113 | 12 | 69 | 125 | 12 |

CATTLE
| If the red tickle as the cattle calve | 12 | 4 | 9 | 13 | 4 |
| The pale breath of cattle at the stealthy sail, | 119 | 5 | 72 | 131 | 5 |

CATTLE (continued)

| | U.K. | | | U.S. | |
|---|---|---|---|---|---|
| | Page | Line | Poem | Page | Line |
| The cattle stirring, the mousing cat stepping shy, | 119 | 22 | 72 | 132 | 2 |
| The cattle graze on the covered foam, | 156 | 15 | 83 | 175 | 3 |
| CAUGHT | | | | | |
| Caught by the crabbing sun I walk on fire | 16 | 3 | 11 | 19 | 3 |
| Caught in an octagon of unaccustomed light, | 63 | 2 | 38 | 72 | 2 |
| Under the cloud against love is caught and held and kissed | 109 | 17 | 67 | 120 | 17 |
| Wild men who caught and sang the sun in flight, | 116 | 10 | 70 | 128 | 10 |
| And drown in the drifts of his need, and lie curled caught | 120 | 22 | 72 | 133 | 7 |
| When the caught tongue nodded blind, | 129 | 13 | 77 | 143 | 13 |
| And caught between two nights, blindness and death. | | | 91 | 201 | 15 |
| CAUL | | | | | |
| From the unfolding to the scissored caul, | 20 | 3 | 13 | 24 | 3 |
| This story's monster has a serpent caul, | 41 | 10 | 23 | 47 | 10 |
| All that shapes from the caul and suckle, | 34 | 4 | 19 | 39 | 10 |
| CAULDRON'S | | | | | |
| The cauldron's root through this once-rindless hand | 80 | 2 | 46 | 89 | 10 |
| CAUSES | | | | | |
| And ruin and his causes | 158 | 5 | 84 | 177 | 5 |
| CAVE | | | | | |
| 'Now to awake husked of gestures and my joy like a cave | 97 | 21 | 59 | 109 | 1 |
| CAVEPOOLS | | | | | |
| Curl-locked and animal cavepools of spells and bone, | 91 | 27 | 55 | 101 | 5 |
| CAVERN | | | | | |
| You by the cavern over the black stairs, | 71 | 22 | 44 | 80 | 22 |
| CAVERNOUS | | | | | |
| Whose wizard shape I trace in the cavernous skull, | 91 | 2 | 55 | 100 | 2 |
| In a cavernous, swung | 171 | 10 | 88 | 191 | 10 |
| CAVERNS | | | | | |
| Glint in the staved and siren-printed caverns, | 78 | 20 | 46 | 87 | 20 |
| CAVES | | | | | |
| In the watched dark, quivering through locks and caves, | 118 | 3 | 71 | 130 | 7 |
| CAWING | | | | | |
| Cawing from their black bethels soaring, the holy books | 164 | 19 | 86 | 184 | 5 |
| CEASE | | | | | |
| That cannot sink or cease | 117 | 10 | 71 | 129 | 10 |
| CELEBRATED | | | | | |
| Is celebrated there, and communion between suns. | 109 | 24 | 67 | 120 | 24 |

|  | U.K. | | | U.S. | |
| --- | --- | --- | --- | --- | --- |
|  | *Page* | *Line* | *Poem* | *Page* | *Line* |
| CELEBRATES | | | | | |
| He celebrates and spurns | 170 | 7 | 88 | 190 | 7 |
| CELEBRATING | | | | | |
| Celebrating at her side | 114 | 19 | 69 | 126 | 19 |
| CELL | | | | | |
| A hill touches an angel. Out of a saint's cell | 163 | 4 | 86 | 182 | 4 |
| CELLAR | | | | | |
| Tasselled in cellar and snipping shop | 132 | 11 | 78 | 147 | 11 |
| CELLED | | | | | |
| The brain was celled and soldered in the thought | 23 | 2 | 14 | 28 | 2 |
| CELL-STEPPED | | | | | |
| And the cell-stepped thimble; | 37 | 25 | 20 | 43 | 8 |
| CELLS | | | | | |
| Shall it be male or female? say the cells, | 12 | 8 | 9 | 13 | 8 |
| CELLULOID | | | | | |
| Flavoured of celluloid give love the lie. | 14 | 20 | 10 | 16 | 20 |
| CEMENTED | | | | | |
| (Give, summer, over), the cemented skin, | 19 | 19 | 12 | 23 | 4 |
| CEMENTING | | | | | |
| A stem cementing, wrestled up the tower, | 54 | 5 | 33 | 63 | 5 |
| CENTAUR | | | | | |
| Horses, centaur dead, turn and tread the drenched white | 121 | 19 | 72 | 134 | 14 |
| Of nightingale and centaur dead horse. The springs wither | 123 | 7 | 72 | 136 | 17 |
| CENTRAL | | | | | |
| The central plains of Asia in his garden, | 40 | 2 | 22 | 46 | 2 |
| CENTRE | | | | | |
| Should he, for centre sake, hop in the dust, | 51 | 6 | 31 | 60 | 6 |
| Erect a walking centre in the shroud, | 56 | 27 | 34 | 66 | 6 |
| In the always desiring centre of the white | 120 | 23 | 72 | 133 | 8 |
| Pool at the wanting centre, in the folds | 123 | 18 | 72 | 137 | 8 |
| From the chill, silent centre | 132 | 22 | 78 | 147 | 22 |
| In the centre of dark I pray him | 144 | 17 | 82 | 161 | 17 |
| CENTRED | | | | | |
| Your corkscrew grave centred in navel and nipple, | 36 | 27 | 20 | 42 | 6 |
| CENTURIES | | | | | |
| Into the centuries of the child | 129 | 15 | 77 | 143 | 15 |
| The centuries throw back their hair | 155 | 7 | 83 | 173 | 11 |
| CENTURY | | | | | |
| In your young years the vegetable century. | 60 | 12 | 36 | 69 | 12 |
| CEREMONY | | | | | |
| Is certain god, and the ceremony of souls | 109 | 23 | 67 | 120 | 23 |
| Ceremony After a Fire Raid | 129 | | 77 | 143 | |
| CERTAIN | | | | | |
| The insect certain is the plague of fables. | 41 | 9 | 23 | 47 | 9 |

CERTAIN (continued)

|  | U.K. | | | U.S. | |
|---|---|---|---|---|---|
|  | Page | Line | Poem | Page | Line |
| The insect fable is the certain promise. | 41 | 18 | 23 | 47 | 18 |
| No tell-tale lover has an end more certain, | 41 | 24 | 23 | 48 | 6 |
| Is certain god, and the ceremony of souls | 109 | 23 | 67 | 120 | 23 |
| CERTAINTY |  |  |  |  |  |
| There must, be praised, some certainty, | 48 | 7 | 28 | 56 | 7 |
| CHAIN |  |  |  |  |  |
| He pulls the chain, the cistern moves. | 10 | 20 | 7 | 11 | 20 |
| And Love and his patients roar on a chain; | 124 | 6 | 73 | 138 | 6 |
| CHAINED |  |  |  |  |  |
| Drinking water from the chained cup | 111 | 8 | 68 | 123 | 8 |
| But nobody chained him up. | 111 | 12 | 68 | 123 | 12 |
| CHAINS |  |  |  |  |  |
| After the locks and chains | 112 | 12 | 68 | 124 | 12 |
| One voice in chains declaims | 115 | 6 | 69 | 127 | 6 |
| Dig no more for the chains of his grey-haired heart. | 135 | 9 | 80 | 152 | 9 |
| Though I sang in my chains like the sea. | 161 | 6 | 85 | 180 | 9 |
| Before chains break to a hammer flame | 171 | 17 | 88 | 191 | 17 |
| CHALK |  |  |  |  |  |
| That chalk the walls with green girls and their men. | 12 | 16 | 9 | 13 | 16 |
| The finger joints are cramped with chalk; | 62 | 6 | 37 | 71 | 6 |
| Under the conceiving moon, on the high chalk hill, | 176 | 2 | 90 | 197 | 2 |
| CHALLENGED |  |  |  |  |  |
| But seasons must be challenged or they totter | 2 | 1 | 2 | 2 | 1 |
| CHANCE |  |  |  |  |  |
| By trick or chance he fell asleep | 5 | 10 | 3 | 5 | 10 |
| CHANGE |  |  |  |  |  |
| And many years should see some change. | 63 | 17 | 38 | 72 | 17 |
| My dear would I change my tears on your iron head. | 97 | 18 | 59 | 108 | 18 |
| CHANGES |  |  |  |  |  |
| We rung our weathering changes on the ladder, | 72 | 17 | 44 | 81 | 17 |
| CHANNEL |  |  |  |  |  |
| Turning the riderless dead by the channel wall. | 36 | 24 | 20 | 42 | 3 |
| What rhubarb man peeled in her foam-blue channel | 76 | 17 | 44 | 85 | 17 |
| CHANNELS |  |  |  |  |  |
| To cut the channels at their source | 11 | 11 | 8 | 12 | 11 |
| CHANT |  |  |  |  |  |
| Over the choir minute I hear the hour chant: | 83 | 7 | 49 | 92 | 7 |
| Never shall my self chant | 109 | 25 | 67 | 120 | 25 |
| Street we chant the flying sea | 130 | 5 | 77 | 144 | 5 |
| Be shielded by chant and flower and gay may you | 163 | 19 | 86 | 182 | 19 |
| CHANTER |  |  |  |  |  |
| Gulled and chanter in young Heaven's fold | 172 | 8 | 88 | 192 | 8 |

| | U.K. Page | Line | Poem | U.S. Page | Line |
|---|---|---|---|---|---|
| **CHAPEL** | | | | | |
| That her love sing and swing through a brown chapel, | 87 | 25 | 52 | 96 | 25 |
| And the black spit of the chapel fold, | 174 | 2 | 89 | 194 | 2 |
| **CHAPELS** | | | | | |
| And the legends of the green chapels | 103 | 25 | 63 | 114 | 25 |
| **CHAPTER** | | | | | |
| Like exodus a chapter from the garden, | 54 | 18 | 33 | 63 | 18 |
| **CHARACTERS** | | | | | |
| First characters of birth and death. | 22 | 24 | 14 | 27 | 24 |
| Heads of the characters hammer through daisies; | 68 | 25 | 42 | 70 | 25 |
| **CHARGE** | | | | | |
| My fuses timed to charge his heart, | 4 | 13 | 3 | 4 | 13 |
| **CHARMED** | | | | | |
| Creep and harp on the tide, sinking their charmed, bent pin' | 91 | 24 | 55 | 101 | 2 |
| And the sky of birds in the plumed voice charmed | 122 | 8 | 72 | 135 | 8 |
| **CHARMINGLY** | | | | | |
| That all the charmingly drowned arise to cockcrow and kill. | 89 | 6 | 53 | 98 | 6 |
| **CHARMS** | | | | | |
| Or a nacreous sleep among soft particles and charms | 97 | 17 | 59 | 108 | 17 |
| Made her limbs blind by luminous charms, | 113 | 21 | 69 | 125 | 21 |
| Or the strut and trade of charms | 128 | 8 | 76 | 142 | 8 |
| **CHARRED** | | | | | |
| Charred on the black breast of the grave | 129 | 7 | 77 | 143 | 7 |
| **CHARTING** | | | | | |
| Of the charting sleepers prays | 146 | 15 | 82 | 163 | 15 |
| **CHASE** | | | | | |
| No silver whistles chase him down the weeks' | 67 | 21 | 41 | 76 | 21 |
| **CHASER** | | | | | |
| Chaste and the chaser, man with the cockshut eye, | 18 | 17 | 12 | 21 | 17 |
| **CHASTE** | | | | | |
| Chaste and the chaser, man with the cockshut eye, | 18 | 17 | 12 | 21 | 17 |
| **CHASTITY** | | | | | |
| Chastity prays for me, piety sings, | 175 | 28 | 89 | 196 | 9 |
| **CHEAT** | | | | | |
| An inch in froth. Chimes cheat the prison spire, pelter | 86 | 5 | 51 | 95 | 5 |
| **CHECK** | | | | | |
| Too proud to cry, to frail to check the tears, | | | 91 | 201 | 14 |
| **CHEEK** | | | | | |
| And laid your cheek against a cloud-formed shell: | 125 | 23 | 74 | 139 | 23 |

| | | | U.K. | | | U.S. | |
|---|---|---|---|---|---|---|---|
| | | | Page | Line | Poem | Page | Line |
| **CHEEKS** | | | | | | | |
| | That his tears burned my cheeks and his heart moved in mine. | | 103 | 28 | 63 | 115 | 2 |
| **CHEMIC** | | | | | | | |
| | Of chemic blood, warned of the coming fury. | | 17 | 7 | 11 | 20 | 7 |
| **CHERRY** | | | | | | | |
| | With my cherry capped dangler green as sea-weed | | 133 | 17 | 78 | 148 | 20 |
| **CHERUB** | | | | | | | |
| | The twelve triangles of the cherub wind | | 54 | 23 | 33 | 63 | 23 |
| | Grief with drenched book and candle christens the cherub time | | 83 | 16 | 49 | 92 | 16 |
| **CHICKENS** | | | | | | | |
| | Green chickens of the bay and bushes cluck, 'dilly dilly, | | 168 | 7 | 87 | 188 | 11 |
| **CHILD** | | | | | | | |
| | Turns ghost to ghost; each mothered child | | 6 | 20 | 4 | 7 | 2 |
| | The secret child, I shift about the sea | | 32 | 11 | 18 | 37 | 17 |
| | The child shall question all his days, | | 53 | 7 | 32 | 62 | 7 |
| | Child in white blood bent on its knees | | 69 | 2 | 43 | 78 | 2 |
| | That the green child see like a grail | | 69 | 22 | 43 | 78 | 22 |
| | The child that sucketh long is shooting up, | | 71 | 16 | 44 | 80 | 16 |
| | Child of the short spark in a shapeless country | | 71 | 19 | 44 | 80 | 19 |
| | And, pride is last, is like a child alone | | 78 | 13 | 46 | 87 | 13 |
| | Forever it is a white child in the dark-skinned summer | | 83 | 19 | 49 | 93 | 1 |
| | From blank and leaking winter sails the child in colour, | | 83 | 22 | 49 | 93 | 4 |
| | To the room of a secret child, | | 93 | 15 | 56 | 102 | 15 |
| | By the child going to bed and the man on the stairs | | 100 | 2 | 61 | 111 | 2 |
| | From the man on the stairs and the child by his bed. | | 100 | 8 | 61 | 111 | 8 |
| | Shall the child sleep unharmed or the man be crying? | | 100 | 12 | 61 | 111 | 12 |
| | And the child not caring to whom he climbs his prayer | | 100 | 17 | 61 | 111 | 17 |
| | A Refusal to Mourn the Death, by Fire, of a child in London | | 101 | | 62 | 112 | |
| | Joy of the long dead child sang burning | | 104 | 11 | 63 | 115 | 13 |
| | Hurling into beginning like Christ the child. | | 110 | 24 | 67 | 122 | 2 |
| | A child of a few hours | | 129 | 5 | 77 | 143 | 5 |
| | Into the centuries of the child | | 129 | 15 | 77 | 143 | 15 |
| | Child beyond cockcrow, by the fire-dwarfed | | 130 | 4 | 77 | 144 | 4 |
| | Child who was priest and servants, | | 130 | 28 | 77 | 145 | 6 |
| | Child. | | 137 | 17 | 82 | 154 | 17 |

| | U.K. | | | U.S. | |
|---|---|---|---|---|---|
| | *Page* | *Line* | *Poem* | *Page* | *Line* |
| CHILD'S | | | | | |
| The majesty and burning of the child's death. | 101 | 13 | 62 | 112 | 13 |
| And I saw in the turning so clearly a child's | 103 | 21 | 63 | 114 | 21 |
| Summoning a child's voice from a webfoot stone, | 133 | 18 | 78 | 149 | 1 |
| And the shrill child's play | 167 | 5 | 87 | 187 | 5 |
| CHILDISH | | | | | |
| The darted hail, the childish snow, | 7 | 14 | 5 | 8 | 14 |
| CHILDLESS | | | | | |
| And wake to the farm forever fled from the childless land. | 161 | 3 | 85 | 180 | 6 |
| CHILDREN | | | | | |
| I see the summer children in their mothers | 1 | 13 | 2 | 1 | 13 |
| Of children go who, from their voids, | 11 | 17 | 8 | 12 | 17 |
| Of the star-gestured children in the park. | 16 | 12 | 11 | 19 | 12 |
| Drive children up like bruises to the thumb, | 18 | 14 | 12 | 21 | 14 |
| Drives forth my mén, my children, from the hanging south. | 49 | 6 | 29 | 58 | 6 |
| Hold hard, my country children in the world of tales, | 49 | 10 | 29 | 58 | 10 |
| Should he who split his children with a cure | 51 | 13 | 31 | 60 | 13 |
| When cometh Jack Frost? the children ask. | 53 | 10 | 32 | 62 | 10 |
| Children from homes and children's parks | 69 | 28 | 43 | 79 | 4 |
| Suffer the heaven's children through my heart-beat. | 75 | 18 | 44 | 84 | 18 |
| That the children filled with gravel | 111 | 9 | 68 | 123 | 9 |
| Children kept from the sun | 125 | 4 | 74 | 139 | 4 |
| The voice of children says | 125 | 9 | 74 | 139 | 9 |
| O the wings of the children! | 142 | 7 | 82 | 159 | 7 |
| Leads them as children and as air | 155 | 5 | 83 | 173 | 9 |
| Before the children green and golden | 160 | 22 | 85 | 179 | 22 |
| CHILDREN'S | | | | | |
| Winged like a sabbath ass this children's piece | 41 | 16 | 23 | 47 | 16 |
| All these, he said who sacked the children's town, | 46 | 18 | 27 | 54 | 18 |
| Stalking my children's faces with a tail of blood, | 49 | 20 | 29 | 58 | 20 |
| In children's circuses could stay their troubles? | 50 | 2 | 30 | 59 | 2 |
| Sprinkles in children's eyes a long-last sleep | 53 | 13 | 32 | 62 | 13 |
| And dusk is crowded with the children's ghosts, | 53 | 14 | 32 | 62 | 14 |
| No answer to the children's cry | 53 | 24 | 32 | 62 | 24 |
| Children from homes and children's parks | 69 | 28 | 43 | 79 | 4 |
| CHILL | | | | | |
| Roosts sleeping chill till the flame of the cock crow | 119 | 19 | 72 | 131 | 19 |
| From the chill, silent centre | 132 | 22 | 78 | 147 | 22 |
| CHILLS | | | | | |
| Why east wind chills and south wind cools | 53 | 1 | 32 | 62 | 1 |
| Why east wind chills | 53 | | 32 | 62 | |

|  | U.K. Page | Line | Poem | U.S. Page | Line |
|---|---|---|---|---|---|
| **CHIME** |  |  |  |  |  |
| As they drown, the chime travels, | 37 | 10 | 20 | 42 | 16 |
| Flung gravel chime? Let the stones speak | 44 | 13 | 25 | 52 | 13 |
| All birds and beasts of the linked night uproar and chime | 177 | 15 | 90 | 198 | 14 |
| **CHIMED** |  |  |  |  |  |
| Said the antipodes, and twice spring chimed. | 72 | 18 | 44 | 81 | 18 |
| **CHIMES** |  |  |  |  |  |
| An inch in froth. Chimes cheat the prison spire, pelter | 86 | 5 | 51 | 95 | 5 |
| Chimes of the rocked buoys. | 150 | 12 | 83 | 167 | 16 |
| **CHIMING** |  |  |  |  |  |
| Into a chiming quarter | 2 | 2 | 2 | 2 | 2 |
| **CHIMNEYS** |  |  |  |  |  |
| Good-bye to chimneys and funnels, | 150 | 1 | 83 | 167 | 5 |
| Fields high as the house, the tunes from the chimneys, it was air | 159 | 20 | 85 | 178 | 20 |
| **CHIPPED** |  |  |  |  |  |
| Heard her speak through the chipped beak | 93 | 24 | 56 | 103 | 4 |
| **CHIRRUP** |  |  |  |  |  |
| Tangled with chirrup and fruit, | vii | 6 | 1 | xv | 6 |
| Carrion, paradise, chirrup my bright yolk. | 115 | 14 | 69 | 127 | 14 |
| **CHOICE** |  |  |  |  |  |
| Those craning birds are choice for you, songs that jump back | 86 | 9 | 51 | 95 | 9 |
| 'Rest beyond choice in the dust-appointed grain, | 98 | 3 | 59 | 109 | 6 |
| **CHOIR** |  |  |  |  |  |
| Of mortal voices to the ninnies' choir, | 60 | 16 | 36 | 69 | 16 |
| Over the choir minute I hear the hour chant: | 83 | 7 | 49 | 92 | 7 |
| To the wind the choir and cloister | 109 | 11 | 67 | 120 | 11 |
| In a choir of wings, as though she slept or died, | 123 | 12 | 72 | 137 | 2 |
| **CHOIRS** |  |  |  |  |  |
| The liquid choirs of his tribes. | 155 | 20 | 83 | 174 | 4 |
| **CHOKE** |  |  |  |  |  |
| To choke the deserts with her tides, | 2 | 17 | 2 | 2 | 17 |
| **CHOSEN** |  |  |  |  |  |
| Or the chosen virgin | 130 | 12 | 77 | 144 | 12 |
| **CHRIST** |  |  |  |  |  |
| The message of his dying christ. | 8 | 18 | 5 | 9 | 18 |
| My Jack of Christ born thorny on the tree? | 13 | 17 | 9 | 15 | 3 |
| This was the sky, Jack Christ, each minstrel angle | 75 | 11 | 44 | 84 | 11 |
| With immortality at my side like Christ the sky. | 110 | 21 | 67 | 121 | 23 |
| Hurling into beginning like Christ the child. | 110 | 24 | 67 | 122 | 2 |
| **CHRIST'S** |  |  |  |  |  |
| 'No. Not for Christ's dazzling bed | 97 | 16 | 59 | 108 | 16 |

|  | U.K. |  | Poem | U.S. |  |
|---|---|---|---|---|---|
|  | Page | Line |  | Page | Line |
| **CHRISTBREAD** |  |  |  |  |  |
| Cut Christbread spitting vinegar and all | 95 | 16 | 58 | 105 | 16 |
| **CHRIST-CROSS-ROW** |  |  |  |  |  |
| He had by heart the Christ-cross-row of death. | 4 | 24 | 3 | 4 | 24 |
| **CHRISTENED** |  |  |  |  |  |
| My world was christened in a stream of milk. | 20 | 7 | 13 | 24 | 7 |
| **CHRISTENS** |  |  |  |  |  |
| Grief with drenched book and candle christens the cherub time | 83 | 16 | 49 | 92 | 16 |
| Christens down | 148 | 7 | 82 | 165 | 7 |
| **CHRISTIAN** |  |  |  |  |  |
| Let the tale's sailor from a Christian voyage | 76 | 9 | 44 | 85 | 9 |
| **CHRISTWARD** |  |  |  |  |  |
| That night of time under the Christward shelter: | 71 | 12 | 44 | 80 | 12 |
| **CHRYSALIS** |  |  |  |  |  |
| A crocodile before the chrysalis, | 41 | 14 | 23 | 47 | 14 |
| A chrysalis unwrinkling on the iron, | 54 | 10 | 33 | 63 | 10 |
| **CHUCKED** |  |  |  |  |  |
| The vanishing of the musical ship-work and the chucked bells, | 95 | 8 | 58 | 105 | 8 |
| **CHUCKLE** |  |  |  |  |  |
| Can never raise the midnight of a chuckle, | 13 | 11 | 9 | 14 | 18 |
| **CHURCH** |  |  |  |  |  |
| And over the sea wet church the size of a snail | 103 | 7 | 63 | 114 | 7 |
| The anchor dives through the floors of a church. | 157 | 20 | 83 | 176 | 12 |
| **CHURCHES** |  |  |  |  |  |
| Of sheep and churches noise | x | 5 | I | xviii | 11 |
| It is the sinners' dust-tongued bell claps me to churches | 83 | 1 | 49 | 92 | 1 |
| In the churches of his tears, | 125 | 18 | 74 | 139 | 18 |
| **CICADA** |  |  |  |  |  |
| Alcove of words out of cicada shade, | 82 | 4 | 48 | 91 | 4 |
| **CINDER** |  |  |  |  |  |
| Shapes in a cinder death; love for his trick, | 19 | 23 | 12 | 23 | 8 |
| In the cinder of the little skull, | 130 | 16 | 77 | 144 | 16 |
| In the cinder of the little skull, | 131 | 2 | 77 | 145 | 8 |
| **CINDER-NESTING** |  |  |  |  |  |
| Her molten flight up cinder-nesting columns, | 78 | 26 | 46 | 88 | 3 |
| **CIPHER** |  |  |  |  |  |
| Did twist into a living cipher, | 7 | 21 | 5 | 8 | 21 |
| **CIPHERS** |  |  |  |  |  |
| And, burning ciphers on the round of space, | 22 | 5 | 14 | 27 | 5 |
| **CIRCLE** |  |  |  |  |  |
| Square in these worlds the mortal circle. | 34 | 6 | 19 | 39 | 12 |
| And in the pincers of the boiling circle, | 38 | 13 | 20 | 44 | 3 |
| In shaping-time the circle stung awake, | 40 | 3 | 22 | 46 | 3 |

CIRCLE (continued)

|  | U.K. | | Poem | U.S. | |
| --- | --- | --- | --- | --- | --- |
|  | Page | Line |  | Page | Line |
| But strip the twelve-winded marrow from his circle; | 60 | 3 | 36 | 69 | 3 |
| A merry manshape of your walking circle. | 61 | 6 | 36 | 70 | 6 |
| The natural circle of the discovered skies | 91 | 10 | 55 | 100 | 10 |
| CIRCLES |  |  |  |  |  |
| The planet-ducted pelican of circles | 71 | 17 | 44 | 80 | 17 |
| Rippling in twelve-winded circles, | 131 | 12 | 77 | 145 | 18 |
| CIRCULAR |  |  |  |  |  |
| These are your years' recorders. The circular world stands still.) | 37 | 21 | 20 | 143 | 4 |
| The circular smile tossed from lover to lover | 90 | 9 | 54 | 99 | 9 |
| CIRCUSES |  |  |  |  |  |
| In children's circuses could stay their troubles? | 50 | 2 | 30 | 59 | 2 |
| CISTERN |  |  |  |  |  |
| He pulls the chain, the cistern moves. | 10 | 20 | 7 | 11 | 20 |
| CITIES |  |  |  |  |  |
| From the cities of nine | vii, | 19 | 1 | xv | 19 |
| CITIES' |  |  |  |  |  |
| Escapes to the flat cities' sails | 69 | 16 | 43 | 78 | 16 |
| CITY |  |  |  |  |  |
| Nor city tar and subway bored to foster | 19 | 9 | 12 | 22 | 14 |
| City of spring, the governed flower, | 33 | 4 | 19 | 38 | 4 |
| Time at the city spectacles, and half | 41 | 3 | 23 | 47 | 3 |
| The hand that signed the paper felled a city; | 62 | 1 | 37 | 71 | 1 |
| Because there stands, one story out of the bum city, | 77 | 13 | 45 | 86 | 13 |
| Flicked from the carbolic city puzzle in a bed of sores | 96 | 3 | 58 | 106 | 3 |
| CIVET |  |  |  |  |  |
| Nutmeg, civet, and sea-parsley serve the plagued groom and bride | 84 | 5 | 49 | 93 | 11 |
| CLACK |  |  |  |  |  |
| Clack through the thicket of strength, love hewn in pillars drops | 92 | 8 | 55 | 101 | 14 |
| CLAN |  |  |  |  |  |
| Ho, hullabaloing clan | ix | 13 | 1 | xvii | 13 |
| CLANGOUR |  |  |  |  |  |
| Clangour as I hew and smite | ix | 19 | 1 | xvii | 19 |
| CLAP |  |  |  |  |  |
| And clap its great blood down; | 92 | 3 | 55 | 101 | 9 |
| CLAPPED |  |  |  |  |  |
| And, clapped in water till the triton dangles, | 37 | 13 | 20 | 42 | 19 |
| CLAPS |  |  |  |  |  |
| It is the sinners' dust-tongued bell claps me to churches | 83 | 1 | 49 | 92 | 1 |
| CLASH |  |  |  |  |  |
| (A clash of anvils for my | ix | 20 | 1 | xvii | 20 |
| Clash out the mounting dolphin's day, | 152 | 3 | 83 | 169 | 15 |

| | U.K. | | | U.S. | |
|---|---|---|---|---|---|
| | *Page* | *Line* | *Poem* | *Page* | *Line* |

CLASP
| Shall they clasp a comet in their fists? | 53 | 11 | 32 | 62 | 11 |
| To clasp my fury on ground | 92 | 2 | 55 | 101 | 8 |
| Now clasp me to their grains in the gigantic glade, | 176 | 19 | 90 | 197 | 19 |

CLAW
| A claw I question from the mouse's bone, | 56 | 17 | 34 | 65 | 17 |
| Claw of the crabbed veins squeeze from each red particle | 91 | 21 | 55 | 100 | 21 |
| Claw fold and hole for the rotten | 133 | 5 | 78 | 148 | 8 |
| In the claw tracks of hawks | 170 | 21 | 88 | 190 | 21 |

CLAWED
| No man more magical, clawed out the crocodile. | 38 | 18 | 20 | 44 | 8 |
| The blind, clawed stare is cold as sleet. | 153 | 5 | 83 | 171 | 1 |

CLAWS
| Of the sharp, enamelled eyes and the spectacled claws | 85 | 2 | 50 | 94 | 2 |
| In a hoisted cloud, at drop of dusk, he pulls to his claws | 167 | 3 | 87 | 187 | 3 |

CLAY
| How of my clay is made the hangman's lime. | 9 | 15 | 6 | 10 | 15 |
| My clay unsuckled and my salt unborn, | 32 | 10 | 18 | 37 | 16 |
| Sigh long, clay cold, lie shorn, | 92 | 6 | 55 | 101 | 12 |
| On the clay cold mouth, on the fire | 109 | 8 | 67 | 120 | 8 |
| In common clay clothes disguised as scales, | 132 | 15 | 78 | 147 | 15 |
| And the colour of clay | 147 | 15 | 82 | 164 | 15 |

CLAYFELLOW
| Shaped my clayfellow, and the heaven's ark | 61 | 2 | 36 | 70 | 2 |

CLEAN
| When their bones are picked clean and the clean bones gone, | 68 | 4 | 42 | 77 | 4 |

CLEANEST
| Have cleanest hands, and, as the heartless ghost | 50 | 8 | 30 | 59 | 8 |

CLEAR
| Sang to my horn, the foxes on the hills barked clear and cold, | 159 | 16 | 85 | 178 | 16 |
| Or skulks in the dell moon but moonshine echoing clear | 163 | 2 | 86 | 182 | 2 |
| Death clear as a buoy's bell: | 168 | 2 | 87 | 188 | 6 |

CLEARLY
| And I saw in the turning so clearly a child's | 103 | 21 | 63 | 114 | 21 |
| Running when he had heard them clearly | 111 | 17 | 68 | 123 | 17 |

CLEAVING
| On my cleaving arm as I blasted in a wave. | 133 | 20 | 78 | 149 | 3 |

CLEFT
| His beast heel cleft in a sandal, | 83 | 3 | 49 | 92 | 3 |

| | U.K. | | | U.S. | |
|---|---|---|---|---|---|
| | Page | Line | Poem | Page | Line |
| **CLENCHED** | | | | | |
| Her fist of a face died clenched on a round pain; | 88 | 6 | 52 | 97 | 6 |
| **CLIMATES** | | | | | |
| Here were fond climates and sweet singers suddenly | 103 | 1 | 63 | 114 | 1 |
| **CLIMB** | | | | | |
| They climb the country pinnacle, | 36 | 13 | 20 | 41 | 13 |
| Do you not brother me, nor, as you climb, | 46 | 7 | 27 | 54 | 7 |
| The cloud climb of the exhaling tomb | 141 | 8 | 82 | 158 | 8 |
| I climb to greet the war in which I have no heart but only | 158 | 8 | 84 | 177 | 8 |
| Time let me hail and climb | 159 | 4 | 85 | 178 | 4 |
| Their breast, the vaulting does roister, the horned bucks climb | 177 | 13 | 90 | 198 | 12 |
| **CLIMBED** | | | | | |
| I fled the earth and, naked, climbed the weather, | 26 | 6 | 16 | 31 | 6 |
| Before the crowing morning climbed; | 113 | 19 | 69 | 125 | 19 |
| **CLIMBER** | | | | | |
| The climber of the water sex | 69 | 11 | 43 | 78 | 11 |
| **CLIMBING** | | | | | |
| Raised up a voice, and, climbing on the words, | 26 | 22 | 16 | 32 | 2 |
| An old, mad man still climbing in his ghost, | 27 | 4 | 16 | 32 | 9 |
| My fathers' ghost is climbing in the rain. | 27 | 5 | 16 | 32 | 10 |
| And three dead seasons on a climbing grave | 72 | 6 | 44 | 81 | 6 |
| A climbing sea from Asia had me down | 73 | 19 | 44 | 82 | 19 |
| **CLIMBS** | | | | | |
| Who climbs to his dying love in her high room, | 100 | 3 | 61 | 111 | 3 |
| And the child not caring to whom he climbs his prayer | 100 | 17 | 61 | 111 | 17 |
| Clings to her drifting hair, and climbs; | 155 | 17 | 83 | 174 | 1 |
| **CLING** | | | | | |
| Of waters cluck and cling, | ix | 29 | 1 | xviii | 3 |
| His fathers cling to the hand of the girl | 155 | 3 | 83 | 173 | 7 |
| **CLINGS** | | | | | |
| See what clings to hair and skull | 154 | 13 | 83 | 172 | 13 |
| Clings to her drifting hair, and climbs; | 155 | 17 | 83 | 174 | 1 |
| **CLIPS** | | | | | |
| Clips short the gesture of breath. | 92 | 11 | 55 | 101 | 17 |
| **CLOAKED** | | | | | |
| When black birds died like priests in the cloaked hedge row | 122 | 12 | 72 | 135 | 12 |
| **CLOCK** | | | | | |
| Behind a pot of ferns the wagging clock | 16 | 17 | 11 | 19 | 17 |
| A worm tells summer better than the clock, | 45 | 14 | 26 | 53 | 14 |
| The wound-down cough of the blood-counting clock | 95 | 9 | 58 | 105 | 9 |

|  | U.K. | | | U.S. | |
| --- | --- | --- | --- | --- | --- |
|  | Page | Line | Poem | Page | Line |
| Into the dead clock burning the hour | 131 | 13 | 77 | 145 | 19 |
| I set back the clock faced tailors, | 132 | 18 | 78 | 147 | 18 |
| CLOCKED | | | | | |
| Hear by death's accident the clocked and dashed-down spire | 83 | 11 | 49 | 92 | 11 |
| CLOCKING | | | | | |
| Invisible, your clocking tides | 11 | 13 | 8 | 12 | 13 |
| CLOCKS | | | | | |
| Birds and clocks and cross bells | 134 | 2 | 79 | 150 | 2 |
| No Time, spoke the clocks, no God, rang the bells, | 134 | 28 | 79 | 151 | 6 |
| The dust of their kettles and clocks swings to and fro | 178 | 5 | 90 | 199 | 6 |
| CLOCKWISE | | | | | |
| Voyaging clockwise off the symboled harbour, | 36 | 8 | 20 | 41 | 8 |
| The winder of the clockwise scene | 70 | 4 | 43 | 79 | 8 |
| CLOGS | | | | | |
| Gentle in their clogs over the fallen sky, | 119 | 24 | 72 | 132 | 4 |
| And gone that barley dark where their clogs danced in the spring, | 177 | 20 | 90 | 198 | 19 |
| CLOISTER | | | | | |
| To the wind the choir and cloister | 109 | 11 | 67 | 120 | 11 |
| CLOSE | | | | | |
| And close her fist. | 55 | 13 | 33 | 64 | 16 |
| Close and far she announced the theft of the heart | 114 | 16 | 69 | 126 | 16 |
| Old age should burn and rave at close of day; | 116 | 2 | 70 | 128 | 2 |
| CLOSED | | | | | |
| The frank, closed pearl, the sea-girls' lineaments | 78 | 19 | 46 | 87 | 19 |
| Of the town closed as the town awoke. | 102 | 20 | 63 | 113 | 20 |
| CLOSE-UP | | | | | |
| Once close-up smiling in the wall of pictures, | 73 | 9 | 44 | 82 | 9 |
| CLOSER | | | | | |
| That the closer I move | 173 | 10 | 88 | 193 | 10 |
| CLOTH | | | | | |
| The cataracted eyes that filmed their cloth; | 4 | 21 | 3 | 4 | 21 |
| Buckle to lint and cloth their natron footsteps, | 75 | 22 | 44 | 84 | 22 |
| And all love's sinners in sweet cloth kneel to a hyleg image, | 84 | 4 | 49 | 93 | 10 |
| And over the cloth of counties the far hills rode near, | 122 | 13 | 72 | 135 | 13 |
| Trailing the frost bitten cloth, | 132 | 23 | 78 | 147 | 23 |
| CLOTHES | | | | | |
| In common clay clothes disguised as scales, | 132 | 15 | 78 | 147 | 15 |
| He put on his clothes and stepped out and he died, | 135 | 2 | 80 | 152 | 2 |
| CLOTHS | | | | | |
| The mummy cloths expose an ancient breast. | 63 | 8 | 38 | 72 | 8 |

|  |  | U.K. |  |  | U.S. |  |
|  |  | Page | Line | Poem | Page | Line |
| CLOTTED |  |  |  |  |  |  |
| In the stitched wound and clotted wind, muzzled | | 28 | 15 | 17 | 33 | 15 |
| CLOUD |  |  |  |  |  |  |
| Touched the first cloud and left a sign. | | 22 | 12 | 14 | 27 | 12 |
| On that cloud coast to each grave-gabbing shade; | | 26 | 18 | 16 | 31 | 18 |
| A handmade moon half holy in a cloud, | | 40 | 8 | 22 | 46 | 8 |
| The two-a-vein, the foreskin, and the cloud. | | 52 | 7 | 31 | 61 | 14 |
| Or spirit up a cloud, | | 56 | 26 | 34 | 66 | 5 |
| High lord esquire, speak up the singing cloud, | | 60 | 17 | 36 | 69 | 17 |
| Time tracks the sound of shape on man and cloud, | | 75 | 3 | 44 | 84 | 3 |
| And, mild as pardon from a cloud of pride, | | 80 | 6 | 46 | 89 | 14 |
| Cloud and the roadside bushes brimming with whistling | | 102 | 22 | 63 | 113 | 22 |
| Beyond the border and under the lark full cloud. | | 103 | 12 | 63 | 114 | 12 |
| With their heads in a cunning cloud. | | 107 | 21 | 65 | 118 | 21 |
| Under the cloud against love is caught and held and kissed | | 109 | 17 | 67 | 120 | 17 |
| CLOUD |  |  |  |  |  |  |
| And fires where he should prowl down the cloud | | 120 | 12 | 72 | 132 | 17 |
| The cloud, the need, the planted stars, the joy beyond | | 122 | 22 | 72 | 136 | 2 |
| Carrying cloud, Death strikes their house. | | 124 | 8 | 73 | 138 | 8 |
| Or decked on a cloud swallower, | | 132 | 12 | 78 | 147 | 12 |
| The cloud perched tailors' master with nerves for cotton. | | 133 | 7 | 78 | 148 | 10 |
| The cloud climb of the exhaling tomb | | 141 | 8 | 82 | 158 | 8 |
| A cloud blew the rain from its throat; | | 150 | 16 | 83 | 167 | 20 |
| Sleeps till Silence blows on a cloud | | 153 | 15 | 83 | 171 | 11 |
| And steeples pierce the cloud on her shoulder | | 157 | 1 | 83 | 175 | 13 |
| In a hoisted cloud, at drop of dusk, he pulls to his claws | | 167 | 3 | 87 | 187 | 3 |
| Under a serpent cloud, | | 171 | 5 | 88 | 191 | 5 |
| Be at cloud quaking peace, | | 172 | 9 | 88 | 192 | 9 |
| CLOUD'S |  |  |  |  |  |  |
| Now in the cloud's big breast lie quiet countries, | | 80 | 8 | 46 | 89 | 16 |
| CLOUD-FORMED |  |  |  |  |  |  |
| And laid your cheek against a cloud-formed shell: | | 125 | 23 | 74 | 139 | 23 |
| CLOUD-SOPPED |  |  |  |  |  |  |
| These cloud-sopped, marble hands, this monumental | | 88 | 8 | 52 | 97 | 8 |
| CLOUD-TRACKING |  |  |  |  |  |  |
| Blinds their cloud-tracking eye. | | 31 | 6 | 18 | 36 | 6 |

| | U.K. | | | U.S. | |
|---|---|---|---|---|---|
| | Page | Line | Poem | Page | Line |

CLOUDS

| | | | | | |
|---|---|---|---|---|---|
| Tackled with clouds, who kneel | vii | 13 | I | xv | 13 |
| How deep the waking in the worlded clouds. | 26 | 25 | 16 | 32 | 5 |
| Shall gods be said to thump the clouds | 44 | 1 | 25 | 52 | 1 |
| When clouds are cursed by thunder, | 44 | 2 | 25 | 52 | 2 |
| The lofty roots of the clouds. | 96 | 5 | 58 | 106 | 5 |
| She deludes the heaven-proof house with entering clouds | 108 | 6 | 66 | 119 | 6 |
| She is breaking with seasons and clouds; | 156 | 8 | 83 | 174 | 16 |
| Under the new made clouds and happy as the heart was long, | 160 | 16 | 85 | 179 | 16 |
| Night and the reindeer on the clouds above the haycocks | 164 | 15 | 86 | 184 | 1 |
| And surely he sails like the ship shape clouds. Oh he | 165 | 28 | 86 | 185 | 18 |
| Clung to the pitching clouds, or gay with any one | 176 | 15 | 90 | 197 | 15 |
| Shall gods be said to thump the clouds | 44 | | 25 | 52 | |

CLOUDY

| | | | | | |
|---|---|---|---|---|---|
| And from the cloudy bases of the breath | 22 | 22 | 14 | 27 | 22 |

CLOUT

| | | | | | |
|---|---|---|---|---|---|
| That breaks one bone to light with a judgment clout, | 87 | 9 | 52 | 96 | 9 |

CLOUTED

| | | | | | |
|---|---|---|---|---|---|
| Than bully ill love in the clouted scene. | 97 | 5 | 59 | 108 | 5 |
| Dawn ships clouted aground, | 172 | 25 | 88 | 192 | 25 |

CLOUTS

| | | | | | |
|---|---|---|---|---|---|
| That clouts the spittle like bubbles with broken rooms, | 77 | 6 | 45 | 86 | 6 |

CLOVEN

| | | | | | |
|---|---|---|---|---|---|
| The patchwork halves were cloven as they scudded | 30 | 19 | 18 | 35 | 19 |
| The fellow halves that, cloven as they swivel | 32 | 1 | 18 | 37 | 7 |
| Hell in a horn of sulphur and the cloven myth, | 40 | 16 | 22 | 46 | 16 |

CLOVER

| | | | | | |
|---|---|---|---|---|---|
| Wherever I ramped in the clover quilts, | 174 | 22 | 89 | 194 | 22 |

CLUCK

| | | | | | |
|---|---|---|---|---|---|
| Of waters cluck and cling, | ix | 29 | I | xviii | 3 |
| Green chickens of the bay and bushes cluck, 'dilly dilly, | 168 | 7 | 87 | 188 | 11 |

CLUNG

| | | | | | |
|---|---|---|---|---|---|
| Clung to the pitching clouds, or gay with any one | 176 | 15 | 90 | 197 | 15 |

COAL

| | | | | | |
|---|---|---|---|---|---|
| In the coal black bush and let them grieve. | 174 | 12 | 89 | 194 | 12 |
| For my sulking, skulking, coal black soul! | 175 | 7 | 89 | 195 | 12 |
| And I shoved it into the coal black sky | 175 | 18 | 89 | 195 | 23 |
| In the coal black sky and she bore angels! | 175 | 26 | 89 | 196 | 7 |

COAL-[BLACK]

|  | U.K. | | | U.S. | |
|---|---|---|---|---|---|
|  | *Page* | *Line* | *Poem* | *Page* | *Line* |
| COAL-[BLACK]* | | | | | |
| Whatsoever I did in the coal- | 174 | 23 | 89 | 194 | 23 |
| COAST | | | | | |
| On that cloud coast to each grave-gabbing shade; | 26 | 18 | 16 | 31 | 18 |
| And a bone coast, | 58 | 12 | 35 | 67 | 12 |
| The bows glided down, and the coast | 149 | 1 | 83 | 166 | 1 |
| COASTS | | | | | |
| Slow rounding of four seasons' coasts, | 45 | 6 | 26 | 53 | 6 |
| COAT | | | | | |
| I, that time's jacket or the coat of ice | 18 | 18 | 12 | 21 | 18 |
| COBBLED | | | | | |
| The country tide is cobbled with towns, | 156 | 24 | 83 | 175 | 12 |
| COBBLES | | | | | |
| The trodden town rang its cobbles for luck. | 149 | 4 | 83 | 166 | 4 |
| Where the sea cobbles sail, | 168 | 14 | 87 | 188 | 18 |
| COBWEB | | | | | |
| With loud, torn tooth and tail and cobweb drum | 80 | 4 | 46 | 89 | 12 |
| COCK | | | | | |
| For we shall be a shouter like the cock, | 15 | 17 | 10 | 17 | 17 |
| And tells the windy weather in the cock. | 16 | 20 | 11 | 19 | 20 |
| Old cock from nowheres and the heaven's egg, | 71 | 8 | 44 | 80 | 8 |
| Pluck, cock, my sea eye, said Medusa's scripture, | 74 | 5 | 44 | 83 | 5 |
| Old cock from nowheres lopped the minstrel tongue | 74 | 8 | 44 | 83 | 8 |
| Roosts sleeping chill till the flame of the cock crow | 119 | 19 | 72 | 131 | 19 |
| With the dew, come back, the cock on his shoulder: it was all | 160 | 7 | 85 | 179 | 7 |
| COCKCROW | | | | | |
| And barnroofs cockcrow war! | ix | 30 | 1 | xviii | 4 |
| That all the charmingly drowned arise to cock-crow and kill. | 89 | 6 | 53 | 98 | 6 |
| Child beyond cockcrow, by the fire-dwarfed | 130 | 4 | 77 | 144 | 4 |
| COCKEREL'S | | | | | |
| The cockerel's tide upcasting from the fire. | 51 | 21 | 31 | 60 | 21 |
| Murmur of spring nor crush the cockerel's eggs, | 60 | 7 | 36 | 69 | 7 |
| COCKFIGHT | | | | | |
| 'All game phrases fit your ring of a cockfight: | 97 | 6 | 59 | 108 | 6 |
| COCK-ON-A-DUNGHILL | | | | | |
| A cock-on-a-dunghill | 37 | 7 | 20 | 42 | 13 |

*[BLACK] in COAL-[BLACK], listed above, occurs in the line following the contextual line given in the original texts. It is bracketed and appended to the index word-entry in order to clarify the full meaning of the hyphenated words, otherwise disjointed by the split at the end of the quoted line. Other occurrences of bracketed follow-on words are: HARE-[HEELED], JACK-[DAWS], KNEE-[DEEP], SHE-[BIRD], WATER-[BIRDS], WHIRL-[POOL], WICK-[DIPPING], and WIND-[MILLED].

| | U.K. | | | U.S. | |
|---|---|---|---|---|---|
| | *Page* | *Line* | *Poem* | *Page* | *Line* |
| COCKLES | | | | | |
| Gulls, pipers, cockles, and sails, | vii | 11 | 1 | xv | 11 |
| COCKS | | | | | |
| Of birds! Among the cocks like fire the red fox | 164 | 20 | 86 | 184 | 6 |
| And no green cocks or hens | 169 | 5 | 87 | 189 | 14 |
| COCKSHUT | | | | | |
| Chaste and the chaser, man with the cockshut eye, | 18 | 17 | 12 | 21 | 17 |
| COCKWISE | | | | | |
| Shall you turn cockwise on a tufted axle. | 60 | 24 | 36 | 69 | 24 |
| CODE | | | | | |
| The code of night tapped on my tongue; | 21 | 16 | 13 | 25 | 16 |
| COFFIN | | | | | |
| In the dark of the coffin and sheds dry leaves, | 87 | 8 | 52 | 96 | 8 |
| Around some coffin carrying | 133 | 2 | 78 | 148 | 5 |
| COIL | | | | | |
| Blind in the coil scrams round the blazing outline, | 41 | 11 | 23 | 47 | 11 |
| Trap I with coil and sheet, | 56 | 19 | 34 | 65 | 19 |
| Through veil and fin and fire and coil | 69 | 23 | 43 | 78 | 23 |
| In the groin's endless coil a man is tangled.' | 79 | 27 | 46 | 89 | 8 |
| Coil from the thoroughfares of her hair | 157 | 5 | 83 | 175 | 17 |
| COILING | | | | | |
| Dinned aside the coiling crowd, | 134 | 3 | 79 | 150 | 3 |
| COILS | | | | | |
| And the hewn coils of his trade perceives | 170 | 26 | 88 | 190 | 26 |
| COIN | | | | | |
| You with a bad coin in your socket, | 107 | 2 | 65 | 118 | 2 |
| COINS | | | | | |
| And the coins on my eyelids sang like shells. | 134 | 30 | 79 | 151 | 8 |
| COLD | | | | | |
| Would leave me cold as butter for the flies, | 12 | 26 | 9 | 14 | 5 |
| Where no cold is, the skinning gales unpin | 24 | 22 | 15 | 29 | 22 |
| But when the ladies are cold as stone | 65 | 7 | 40 | 74 | 7 |
| Who scales a hailing hill in her cold flintsteps | 79 | 3 | 46 | 88 | 6 |
| Where at night we stoned the cold and cuckoo | 89 | 8 | 53 | 98 | 8 |
| Sigh long, clay cold, lie shorn, | 92 | 6 | 55 | 101 | 12 |
| The rain through her cold heart speak | 93 | 8 | 56 | 102 | 8 |
| Wind blow cold | 103 | 4 | 63 | 114 | 4 |
| On the clay cold mouth, on the fire | 109 | 8 | 67 | 120 | 8 |
| And the stars falling cold, | 119 | 6 | 72 | 131 | 6 |
| He knelt on the cold stones, | 120 | 6 | 72 | 132 | 11 |
| When cold as snow he should run the wended vales among | 120 | 20 | 72 | 133 | 5 |
| Cold Nansen's beak on a boat full of gongs, | 133 | 12 | 78 | 148 | 15 |
| The blind, clawed stare is cold as sleet. | 153 | 5 | 83 | 171 | 1 |
| Sang to my horn, the foxes on the hills barked clear and cold, | 159 | 16 | 85 | 178 | 16 |

## COLD (continued)

|  | U.K. | | Poem | U.S. | |
|---|---|---|---|---|---|
|  | Page | Line |  | Page | Line |
| Flounders, gulls, on their cold, dying trails, | 170 | 11 | 88 | 190 | 11 |
| Of, time enough when the blood creeps cold, | 175 | 5 | 89 | 195 | 10 |
| A cold kind man brave in his narrow pride |  |  | 91 | 200 | 3 |

### COLIC
| | | | | | |
|---|---|---|---|---|---|
| Bright as her spinning-wheels, the colic season | 35 | 8 | 20 | 40 | 8 |

### COLLAR
| | | | | | |
|---|---|---|---|---|---|
| Spiked with a mastiff collar, | 132 | 10 | 78 | 147 | 10 |

### COLOSSAL
| | | | | | |
|---|---|---|---|---|---|
| The colossal intimacies of silent | 113 | 14 | 69 | 125 | 14 |

### COLOUR
| | | | | | |
|---|---|---|---|---|---|
| What colour is glory? death's feather? tremble | 31 | 1 | 18 | 36 | 1 |
| Who blows death's feather? What glory is colour? | 32 | 7 | 18 | 37 | 13 |
| Shall rainbows be their tunics' colour? | 44 | 4 | 25 | 52 | 4 |
| Who gave these seas their colour in a shape, | 61 | 1 | 36 | 70 | 1 |
| A calling for colour calls with the wind | 82 | 6 | 48 | 91 | 6 |
| From blank and leaking winter sails the child in colour, | 83 | 22 | 49 | 93 | 4 |
| Once it was the colour of saying | 89 | 1 | 53 | 98 | 1 |
| And the colour of clay | 147 | 15 | 82 | 164 | 15 |
| Once it was the colour of saying | 89 | | 53 | 98 | |

### COLOURED
| | | | | | |
|---|---|---|---|---|---|
| Dry as a tomb, your coloured lids | 11 | 19 | 8 | 12 | 19 |
| In time at flood filled with his coloured doubles; | 61 | 3 | 36 | 70 | 3 |

### COLTS
| | | | | | |
|---|---|---|---|---|---|
| With salty colts and gales in their limbs | 156 | 18 | 83 | 175 | 6 |

### COLUMBUS
| | | | | | |
|---|---|---|---|---|---|
| Combing with antlers, Columbus on fire, | 133 | 9 | 78 | 148 | 12 |

### COLUMN-MEMBERED
| | | | | | |
|---|---|---|---|---|---|
| A furnace-nostrilled column-membered | 114 | 5 | 69 | 126 | 5 |

### COLUMNS
| | | | | | |
|---|---|---|---|---|---|
| Her molten flight up cinder-nesting columns, | 78 | 26 | 46 | 88 | 3 |

### COMB
| | | | | | |
|---|---|---|---|---|---|
| And comb the county gardens for a wreath. | 2 | 18 | 2 | 2 | 18 |
| I'll comb the snared woods with a glove on a lamp, | 97 | 7 | 59 | 108 | 7 |

### COMBED
| | | | | | |
|---|---|---|---|---|---|
| And the streets that the fisherman combed | 157 | 2 | 83 | 175 | 14 |

### COMBING
| | | | | | |
|---|---|---|---|---|---|
| Combing with antlers, Columbus on fire, | 133 | 9 | 78 | 148 | 12 |

### COMBS
| | | | | | |
|---|---|---|---|---|---|
| Combs through the mantled yards and the morning men | 119 | 20 | 72 | 131 | 20 |

### COME
| | | | | | |
|---|---|---|---|---|---|
| Come unto sea-stuck towers, at the fibre scaling, | 37 | 23 | 20 | 43 | 6 |
| Over the water come | 69 | 27 | 43 | 79 | 3 |
| Are formed of flesh, but let the false day come | 63 | 6 | 38 | 72 | 6 |

| | U.K. | | | U.S. | |
|---|---|---|---|---|---|
| | *Page* | *Line* | *Poem* | *Page* | *Line* |
| Is come of the sea tumbling in harness | 101 | 6 | 62 | 112 | 6 |
| Come in the morning where I wandered and listened | 103 | 2 | 63 | 114 | 2 |
| A stranger has come | 108 | 1 | 66 | 119 | 1 |
| She has come possessed | 108 | 10 | 66 | 119 | 10 |
| Vales where he prayed to come to the last harm | 122 | 29 | 72 | 136 | 9 |
| They come together whom their love parted: | 124 | 10 | 73 | 138 | 10 |
| Swarms on the kingdom come | 139 | 6 | 82 | 156 | 6 |
| For I was lost who have come | 140 | 11 | 82 | 157 | 11 |
| And we have come | 146 | 6 | 82 | 163 | 6 |
| With the dew, come back, the cock on his shoulder: it was all | 160 | 7 | 85 | 179 | 7 |
| Naked and forsaken to grieve he will not come. | 166 | 7 | 86 | 186 | 7 |
| 'Come and be killed,' | 167 | 22 | 87 | 188 | 3 |
| Come let us die.' | 168 | 8 | 87 | 188 | 12 |
| To his nimbus bell cool kingdom come | 173 | 4 | 88 | 193 | 4 |
| Of summer come in his great good time | 175 | 3 | 89 | 195 | 8 |
| COME-A-CROPPER | | | | | |
| The come-a-cropper rider of the flower. | 51 | 28 | 31 | 61 | 7 |
| COMERS | | | | | |
| And the second comers, the severers, the enemies from the deep | 115 | 22 | 69 | 127 | 22 |
| COMES | | | | | |
| Comes, like a scissors stalking, tailor age, | 18 | 6 | 12 | 21 | 6 |
| Out of the sighs a little comes, | 48 | 1 | 28 | 56 | 1 |
| A little comes, is tasted and found good; | 48 | 5 | 28 | 56 | 5 |
| Comes love's anatomist with sun-gloved hand | 79 | 18 | 46 | 88 | 21 |
| Who comes as red as the fox and sly as the heeled wind. | 165 | 10 | 86 | 184 | 18 |
| Round the sun, he comes to my love like the designed snow, | 165 | 25 | 86 | 185 | 15 |
| Comes designed to my love to steal not her tide raking | 166 | 1 | 86 | 186 | 1 |
| He comes to take | 166 | 4 | 86 | 186 | 4 |
| He comes to leave her in the lawless sun awaking | 166 | 6 | 86 | 186 | 6 |
| My dear this night he comes and night without end my dear | 166 | 9 | 86 | 186 | 9 |
| COMET | | | | | |
| Shall they clasp a comet in their fists? | 53 | 11 | 32 | 62 | 11 |
| COMETH | | | | | |
| When cometh Jack Frost? the children ask. | 53 | 10 | 32 | 62 | 10 |
| COMETS | | | | | |
| And ghostly comets over the raised fists. | 53 | 26 | 32 | 62 | 26 |
| COMING | | | | | |
| Of chemic blood, warned of the coming fury. | 17 | 7 | 11 | 20 | 7 |
| 'If my bunched, monkey coming is cruel | 97 | 11 | 59 | 108 | 11 |

|  | U.K. | | | U.S. | |
|---|---|---|---|---|---|
|  | *Page* | *Line* | *Poem* | *Page* | *Line* |
| The grave and my calm body are shut to your coming as stone, | 98 | 6 | 59 | 109 | 9 |
| Beneath my life, that sighs for the seducer's coming | 109 | 13 | 67 | 120 | 13 |
| And heard the lewd, wooed field flow to the coming frost, | 177 | 10 | 90 | 198 | 9 |
| COMMIT | | | | | |
| In seizure of silence commit the dead nuisance: | 35 | 23 | 20 | 40 | 23 |
| COMMON | | | | | |
| But for the common wages | 128 | 10 | 76 | 142 | 10 |
| In common clay clothes disguised as scales, | 132 | 15 | 78 | 147 | 15 |
| To the boy of common thread, | 133 | 13 | 78 | 148 | 16 |
| O keep his bones away from that common cart, | 135 | 12 | 80 | 152 | 12 |
| Now common lazarus | 146 | 14 | 82 | 163 | 14 |
| Ninepin down on the donkeys' common, | 174 | 7 | 89 | 194 | 7 |
| COMMONER | | | | | |
| Commoner than water, crueller than truth; | 125 | 3 | 74 | 139 | 3 |
| COMMUNION | | | | | |
| Is celebrated there, and communion between suns. | 109 | 24 | 67 | 120 | 24 |
| COMPANION | | | | | |
| But one companion. | 66 | 13 | 40 | 75 | 13 |
| CONCEIVING | | | | | |
| Under the conceiving moon, on the high chalk hill, | 176 | 2 | 90 | 197 | 2 |
| CONDENSE | | | | | |
| Youth did condense; the tears of spring | 21 | 24 | 13 | 26 | 7 |
| CONFESSOR | | | | | |
| Call for confessor and wiser mirror but there is none | 158 | 10 | 84 | 177 | 10 |
| CONGERED | | | | | |
| Curlews aloud in the congered waves | 170 | 13 | 88 | 190 | 13 |
| CONJURE | | | | | |
| Whom now I conjure to stand as thief | 107 | 9 | 65 | 118 | 9 |
| CONJURED | | | | | |
| And conjured up a carcass shape | 5 | 11 | 3 | 5 | 11 |
| Dust be your saviour under the conjured soil.) | 37 | 9 | 20 | 42 | 15 |
| CONSTANT | | | | | |
| Her constant, nor the winds of love broken wide | 109 | 10 | 67 | 120 | 10 |
| CONSUMPTIVES' | | | | | |
| On the consumptives' terrace taking their two farewells, | 36 | 10 | 20 | 41 | 10 |
| CONTAGES | | | | | |
| With whistler's cough contages, time on track | 19 | 22 | 12 | 23 | 7 |
| CONTAGION | | | | | |
| And, for that murder's sake, dark with contagion | 79 | 11 | 46 | 88 | 14 |

|  | U.K. Page | U.K. Line | Poem | U.S. Page | U.S. Line |
|---|---|---|---|---|---|
| **CONTAGIOUS** | | | | | |
| And power was contagious in my birth, second | 28 | 21 | 17 | 34 | 1 |
| Ghost with her ghost, contagious man | 34 | 2 | 19 | 39 | 8 |
| **CONTENT** | | | | | |
| Calls some content to travel with the winds, | 53 | 17 | 32 | 62 | 17 |
| I hear content, and 'Be content' | 53 | 21 | 32 | 62 | 21 |
| **CONTINENCE** | | | | | |
| Continence. I see the unfired phoenix, herald | 110 | 9 | 67 | 121 | 11 |
| **CONTINENT** | | | | | |
| And a continent deny? | 43 | 2 | 24 | 50 | 9 |
| And a continent deny? | 43 | 9 | 24 | 50 | 16 |
| In the continent of a fossil | 154 | 24 | 83 | 173 | 4 |
| **CONTINUAL** | | | | | |
| And the old terrors' continual cry | 64 | 3 | 39 | 73 | 3 |
| **CONTRARIES** | | | | | |
| These are her contraries: the beast who follows | 78 | 24 | 46 | 88 | 1 |
| **CONVENIENT** | | | | | |
| Convenient bird and beast lie lodged to suffer | 77 | 3 | 45 | 86 | 3 |
| **CONVENTION** | | | | | |
| Half convention and half lie. | 64 | 20 | 39 | 73 | 20 |
| **CONVERSATION** | | | | | |
| The conversation of prayers about to be said | 100 | 1 | 61 | 111 | 1 |
| The conversation of prayers about to be said | 100 | 13 | 61 | 111 | 13 |
| The Conversation of Prayer | 100 | | 61 | 111 | |
| **COO** | | | | | |
| Coo rooing the woods' praise, | ix | 10 | 1 | xvii | 10 |
| **COOED** | | | | | |
| Tidy and cursed in my dove cooed room | 175 | 23 | 89 | 196 | 4 |
| **COOL** | | | | | |
| A brute land in the cool top of the country days | 91 | 15 | 55 | 100 | 15 |
| Nor walk in the cool of your mortal garden | 110 | 20 | 67 | 121 | 22 |
| Trees cool and dry in the whirlpool of ships | 156 | 2 | 83 | 174 | 10 |
| And the multitude's sultry tear turns cool on the weeping wall, | 158 | 17 | 84 | 177 | 17 |
| Cool in your vows. | 163 | 24 | 86 | 183 | 5 |
| To his nimbus bell cool kingdom come | 173 | 4 | 88 | 193 | 4 |
| **COOLS** | | | | | |
| Why east wind chills and south wind cools | 53 | 1 | 32 | 62 | 1 |
| **CORAL** | | | | | |
| And the five-fathomed Hamlet on his father's coral, | 38 | 5 | 20 | 43 | 15 |
| Time's coral saint and the salt grief drown a foul sepulchre | 83 | 8 | 49 | 92 | 8 |
| The voice of bird on coral prays. | 83 | 18 | 49 | 92 | 18 |
| **CORALS** | | | | | |
| There shall be corals in your beds, | 11 | 22 | 8 | 12 | 22 |

95

| | U.K. | | | U.S. | |
| --- | --- | --- | --- | --- | --- |
| | *Page* | *Line* | *Poem* | *Page* | *Line* |
| CORD | | | | | |
| Into the tided cord, there goes | 11 | 8 | 8 | 12 | 8 |
| CORE | | | | | |
| Or with their orchard man in the core of the sun's bush | 177 | 4 | 90 | 198 | 3 |
| CORKSCREW | | | | | |
| Your corkscrew grave centred in navel and nipple, | 36 | 27 | 20 | 42 | 6 |
| CORMORANTS | | | | | |
| Where the cormorants scud, | 170 | 3 | 88 | 190 | 3 |
| CORN | | | | | |
| Through the Atlantic corn. | 31 | 24 | 18 | 37 | 6 |
| And the synagogue of the ear of corn | 101 | 9 | 62 | 112 | 9 |
| In high corn and the harvest melting on their tongues. | 120 | 18 | 72 | 133 | 3 |
| CORNER | | | | | |
| Corner the mounted meadows in the hill corral; | 36 | 15 | 20 | 41 | 15 |
| I turn the corner of prayer and burn | 148 | 1 | 82 | 165 | 1 |
| CORNER-CAST | | | | | |
| Is corner-cast, breath's rag, scrawled weed, a vain | 78 | 9 | 46 | 87 | 9 |
| CORPSE'S | | | | | |
| All all and all, the corpse's lover, | 33 | 10 | 19 | 38 | 10 |
| CORRAL | | | | | |
| Corner the mounted meadows in the hill corral; | 36 | 15 | 20 | 41 | 15 |
| CORRIDOR | | | | | |
| My half ghost in armour hold hard in death's corridor, | 35 | 5 | 20 | 40 | 5 |
| CORRIDORS | | | | | |
| Ring like a handbell through the corridors, | 53 | 22 | 32 | 62 | 22 |
| CORROSIVE | | | | | |
| Corrosive spring out of the iceberg's crop, | 30 | 8 | 18 | 35 | 8 |
| CORSET | | | | | |
| Corset the boneyards for a crooked boy? | 73 | 4 | 44 | 82 | 4 |
| COSTLY | | | | | |
| Heir to the scalding veins that hold love's drop, costly | 28 | 9 | 17 | 33 | 9 |
| COTTON | | | | | |
| The cloud perched tailors' master with nerves for cotton. | 133 | 7 | 78 | 148 | 10 |
| COUCH | | | | | |
| Has a voice and a house, and there and here you must couch and cry. | 98 | 2 | 59 | 109 | 5 |
| To a haycock couch and the scythes of his arms | 113 | 17 | 69 | 125 | 17 |
| COUGH | | | | | |
| Hearing the raven cough in winter sticks, | 16 | 6 | 11 | 19 | 6 |
| With whistler's cough contages, time on track | 19 | 22 | 12 | 23 | 7 |

|  | U.K. | | | U.S. | |
|---|---|---|---|---|---|
|  | Page | Line | Poem | Page | Line |
| Hack of the cough, the hanging albatross, | 67 | 10 | 41 | 76 | 10 |
| The wound-down cough of the blood-counting clock | 95 | 9 | 58 | 105 | 9 |

COULD

| | | | | | |
|---|---|---|---|---|---|
| The sea of scums could drown me as it broke | 12 | 27 | 9 | 14 | 6 |
| In sacred waters that no frost could harden, | 40 | 14 | 22 | 46 | 14 |
| All could not disappoint; | 48 | 6 | 28 | 56 | 6 |
| The hollow words could bear all suffering | 48 | 22 | 28 | 56 | 22 |
| In children's circuses could stay their troubles? | 50 | 2 | 30 | 59 | 2 |
| There was a time they could cry over books, | 50 | 3 | 30 | 59 | 3 |
| 'Who could snap off the shapeless print | 70 | 12 | 43 | 79 | 16 |
| Who could hack out your unsucked heart, | 70 | 18 | 43 | 79 | 22 |
| There could I marvel | 103 | 13 | 63 | 114 | 13 |
| And there could I marvel my birthday | 104 | 9 | 63 | 115 | 11 |
| Branded forehead, that could bind | 109 | 9 | 67 | 120 | 9 |
| Nor could share, for his pride, to the least | 114 | 21 | 69 | 126 | 21 |
| Blind eyes could blaze like meteors and be gay, | 116 | 14 | 70 | 128 | 14 |
| O you who could not cry | 125 | 20 | 74 | 139 | 20 |
| O we who could not stir | 126 | 4 | 74 | 140 | 4 |
| The whole of the moon I could love and leave | 174 | 10 | 89 | 194 | 10 |
| When I was a man you could call a man | 174 | 25 | 89 | 195 | 1 |
| On that darkest day. Oh, he could hide | | | 91 | 201 | 17 |

COUNT

| | | | | | |
|---|---|---|---|---|---|
| ˅The five kings count the dead but do not soften | 62 | 13 | 37 | 71 | 13 |
| ⌐ And count the taken, forsaken mysteries in a bad dark. | 94 | 9 | 57 | 104 | 9 |
| ˅ Count my blessings aloud: | 172 | 27 | 88 | 192 | 27 |

COUNTED

| | | | | | |
|---|---|---|---|---|---|
| Who'd raise the organs of the counted dust | 117 | 7 | 71 | 129 | 7 |
| The cureless counted body, | 158 | 4 | 84 | 177 | 4 |

COUNTENANCE

| | | | | | |
|---|---|---|---|---|---|
| Shaped in old armour and oak the countenance of a dunce | 85 | 7 | 50 | 94 | 7 |

COUNTIES

| | | | | | |
|---|---|---|---|---|---|
| And over the cloth of counties the far hills rode near, | 122 | 13 | 72 | 135 | 13 |

COUNTING

| | | | | | |
|---|---|---|---|---|---|
| Counting the denials of the grains | 155 | 16 | 83 | 173 | 20 |

COUNTRIES

| | | | | | |
|---|---|---|---|---|---|
| Now in the cloud's big breast lie quiet countries, | 80 | 8 | 46 | 89 | 16 |
| In all love's countries, that will grope awake: | 81 | 12 | 47 | 90 | 12 |
| Who once, green countries since, were a hedge-row of joys. | 176 | 20 | 90 | 197 | 20 |

COUNTRY

| | | | | | |
|---|---|---|---|---|---|
| Stride through Cadaver's country in my force, | 18 | 21 | 12 | 22 | 1 |
| They climb the country pinnacle, | 36 | 13 | 20 | 41 | 13 |

|  | U.K. | | | U.S. | |
| --- | --- | --- | --- | --- | --- |
|  | Page | Line | Poem | Page | Line |
| Country, your sport is summer, and December's pools | 49 | 7 | 29 | 58 | 7 |
| Hold hard, my country children in the world of tales, | 49 | 10 | 29 | 58 | 10 |
| But graft these four-fruited ridings on your country; | 60 | 9 | 36 | 69 | 9 |
| Doubled the globe of dead and halved a country; | 62 | 3 | 37 | 71 | 3 |
| Child of the short spark in a shapeless country | 71 | 19 | 44 | 80 | 19 |
| When all my five and country senses see, | 81 | 1 | 47 | 90 | 1 |
| A brute land in the cool top of the country days | 91 | 15 | 55 | 100 | 15 |
| It turned away from the blithe country | 103 | 16 | 63 | 114 | 16 |
| In the blinding country of youth, | 105 | 4 | 64 | 116 | 4 |
| Star and country to the legion | 146 | 2 | 82 | 163 | 2 |
| For the country of death is the heart's size | 146 | 17 | 82 | 163 | 17 |
| The country tide is cobbled with towns, | 156 | 24 | 83 | 175 | 12 |
| And flower of country sleep and the greenwood keep. | 162 | 18 | 86 | 181 | 18 |
| The country is holy: O bide in that country kind, | 163 | 16 | 86 | 182 | 16 |
| And you shall wake, from country sleep, this dawn and each first dawn, | 166 | 11 | 86 | 186 | 11 |
| When all my five and country senses see | 81 |  | 47 | 90 |  |
| In country sleep | 162 |  | 86 | 181 |  |

COUNTRY-HANDED
| The country-handed grave boxed into love, | 55 | 4 | 33 | 64 | 7 |

COUNTY
| And comb the county gardens for a wreath. | 2 | 18 | 2 | 2 | 18 |
| Time, in a folly's rider, like a county man | 49 | 4 | 29 | 58 | 4 |
| Hold hard, my county darlings, for a hawk descends, | 49 | 22 | 29 | 58 | 22 |

COUPLE
| All all and all the dry worlds couple, | 34 | 1 | 19 | 39 | 7 |

COUPLED
| O light in zenith, the coupled bud, | 34 | 8 | 19 | 39 | 14 |

COURSE
| Plunging and piercing in his course | 150 | 22 | 83 | 168 | 6 |

COURSING
| That other sun, the jealous coursing of the unrivalled blood. | 127 | 14 | 75 | 141 | 14 |

COURT
| To court the honeyed heart from your side before sunrise | 162 | 13 | 86 | 181 | 13 |

COURTERS'
| In the courters' lanes, or twined in the ox roasting sun | 176 | 13 | 90 | 197 | 13 |
| Love for ever meridian through the courters' trees | 178 | 18 | 90 | 199 | 19 |

|  | U.K. | | | U.S. | |
|---|---|---|---|---|---|
|  | *Page* | *Line* | *Poem* | *Page* | *Line* |
| COVERED | | | | | |
| The cattle graze on the covered foam, | 156 | 15 | 83 | 175 | 3 |
| COVERING | | | | | |
| The covering sea their nightfall with no names; | 115 | 4 | 69 | 127 | 4 |
| COWL | | | | | |
| Flocked with the sheep white smoke of the farm house cowl | 119 | 9 | 72 | 131 | 9 |
| COWS' | | | | | |
| Rough as cows' tongues and thrashed with brambles their buttermilk | 177 | 5 | 90 | 198 | 4 |
| CRAB | | | | | |
| And cast a shadow crab upon the land, | 16 | 4 | 11 | 19 | 4 |
| CRAB-BACKED | | | | | |
| For the crab-backed dead on the sea-bed rose | 153 | 3 | 83 | 170 | 19 |
| CRABBED | | | | | |
| Shakes, in crabbed burial shawl, by sorcerer's insect woken, | 83 | 23 | 49 | 93 | 5 |
| Claw of the crabbed veins squeeze from each red particle | 91 | 21 | 55 | 100 | 21 |
| CRABBING | | | | | |
| Caught by the crabbing sun I walk on fire | 16 | 3 | 11 | 19 | 3 |
| CRABS | | | | | |
| Time and the crabs and the sweethearting crib | 12 | 25 | 9 | 14 | 4 |
| CRACK | | | | | |
| Crack like a spring in a vice, bone breaking April, | 49 | 17 | 29 | 58 | 17 |
| Bull's-eye the outlaw through a eunuch crack | 67 | 19 | 41 | 76 | 19 |
| Split all ends up they shan't crack; | 68 | 17 | 42 | 77 | 17 |
| Flash, and the plumes crack, | 167 | 13 | 87 | 187 | 13 |
| CRACKED | | | | | |
| And my heart is cracked across; | 65 | 18 | 40 | 74 | 18 |
| Abaddon in the hangnail cracked from Adam, | 71 | 3 | 44 | 80 | 3 |
| Glory cracked like a flea. | 95 | 18 | 58 | 105 | 18 |
| CRACKLING | | | | | |
| And, crackling into the air, leave me half-blind. | 64 | 14 | 39 | 73 | 14 |
| CRADLE | | | | | |
| I, in a wind on fire, from green Adam's cradle, | 38 | 17 | 20 | 44 | 7 |
| Scraped at my cradle in a walking word | 71 | 11 | 44 | 80 | 11 |
| Soon sets alight a long stick from the cradle; | 71 | 20 | 44 | 80 | 20 |
| And, Rip Van Winkle from a timeless cradle, | 72 | 13 | 44 | 81 | 13 |
| Inhuman cradle and the bride bed forever sought | 120 | 24 | 72 | 133 | 9 |
| CRAFT | | | | | |
| In my craft or sullen art | 128 | 1 | 76 | 142 | 1 |
| I bitterly take to task my poverty and craft: | 94 | 3 | 57 | 104 | 3 |
| Nor heed my craft or art. | 128 | 20 | 76 | 142 | 20 |
| In my Craft or Sullen Art | 128 | | 76 | 142 | |

| | | U.K. | | | U.S. | |
|---|---|---|---|---|---|---|
| | | Page | Line | Poem | Page | Line |
| CRAGS | | | | | | |
| | And drink in the two milked crags, | 65 | 2 | 40 | 74 | 2 |
| CRAMP | | | | | | |
| | A muscling life from lovers in their cramp, | 2 | 9 | 2 | 2 | 9 |
| | Lie with religion in their cramp, her threadbare | 88 | 4 | 52 | 97 | 4 |
| CRAMPED | | | | | | |
| | The finger joints are cramped with chalk; | 62 | 6 | 37 | 71 | 6 |
| CRANE | | | | | | |
| | By crane and water-tower by the seedy trees | 49 | 8 | 29 | 58 | 8 |
| CRANES | | | | | | |
| | The spire cranes. Its statue is an aviary. | 86 | 1 | 51 | 95 | 1 |
| | And wharves of water where the walls dance and the white cranes stilt. | 168 | 15 | 87 | 188 | 19 |
| | The spire cranes | 86 | | 51 | 95 | |
| CRANING | | | | | | |
| | Those craning birds are choice for you, songs that jump back | 86 | 9 | 51 | 95 | 9 |
| CRASHES | | | | | | |
| | Crashes, and slowly the fishing holy stalking heron | 167 | 11 | 87 | 187 | 11 |
| CRATER | | | | | | |
| | Cartoon of slashes on the tide-traced crater, | 74 | 1 | 44 | 83 | 1 |
| | From every true or crater | 124 | 7 | 73 | 138 | 7 |
| CRATERS | | | | | | |
| | And the craters of his eyes grew springshoots and fire | 135 | 7 | 80 | 152 | 7 |
| CRAWLING | | | | | | |
| | Roaring, crawling, quarrel | 91 | 8 | 55 | 100 | 8 |
| CRAWLS | | | | | | |
| | Grief thief of time crawls off, | 67 | 1 | 41 | 76 | 1 |
| | And through the sundered water crawls | 155 | 22 | 83 | 174 | 6 |
| CREASING | | | | | | |
| | Off from the creasing flesh, filed | 28 | 6 | 17 | 33 | 6 |
| CREATE | | | | | | |
| | Create this twin miracle. | 35 | 18 | 20 | 40 | 18 |
| CREATURE | | | | | | |
| | I sent my creature scouting on the globe, | 4 | 9 | 3 | 4 | 9 |
| | And time cast forth my mortal creature | 8 | 7 | 5 | 9 | 7 |
| | A creature in my bones I | 28 | 10 | 17 | 33 | 10 |
| | Were once such a creature, so gay and frank | 107 | 14 | 65 | 118 | 14 |
| CREEP | | | | | | |
| | Creep and harp on the tide, sinking their charmed, bent pin | 91 | 24 | 55 | 101 | 2 |
| CREEPS | | | | | | |
| | Of, time enough when the blood creeps cold, | 175 | 5 | 89 | 195 | 10 |
| CREST | | | | | | |
| | He wept from the crest of grief, he prayed to the veiled sky | 120 | 7 | 72 | 132 | 12 |

|  | U.K. | | | U.S. | |
|---|---|---|---|---|---|
|  | Page | Line | Poem | Page | Line |
| Mountains and galleries to the crest! | 154 | 12 | 83 | 172 | 12 |
| CRESTED |  |  |  |  |  |
| Is a burning and crested act, | vii | 25 | 1 | xv | 25 |
| CRIB |  |  |  |  |  |
| Time and the crabs and the sweethearting crib | 12 | 25 | 9 | 14 | 4 |
| CRIED |  |  |  |  |  |
| Cried the topless, inchtaped lips from hank and hood | 79 | 21 | 46 | 89 | 2 |
| She cried her white-dressed limbs were bare | 93 | 17 | 56 | 102 | 17 |
| Deliver him, he cried, | 120 | 26 | 72 | 133 | 11 |
| Always good-bye, cried the voices through the shell, | 154 | 1 | 83 | 172 | 1 |
| The rude owl cried like a telltale tit, | 174 | 5 | 89 | 194 | 5 |
| And the sizzling beds of the town cried, Quick!— | 174 | 20 | 89 | 194 | 20 |
| Even as a baby he had never cried; |  |  | 91 | 201 | 5 |
| He cried as he died, fearing at last the spheres' |  |  | 91 | 201 | 12 |
| CRIER |  |  |  |  |  |
| And heaven crier, arrow now of aspiring | 110 | 10 | 67 | 121 | 12 |
| CRIERS |  |  |  |  |  |
| The criers of Shabby and Shorten, | 132 | 27 | 78 | 148 | 2 |
| CRIES |  |  |  |  |  |
| Forgets, and cries; | 48 | 4 | 28 | 56 | 4 |
| The womb-eyed, cries, | 57 | 4 | 34 | 66 | 11 |
| The old forget the cries, | 67 | 5 | 41 | 76 | 5 |
| CRIME |  |  |  |  |  |
| Do you not sister me, nor the erected crime | 46 | 5 | 27 | 54 | 5 |
| CRIMSON |  |  |  |  |  |
| May the crimson | 147 | 13 | 82 | 164 | 13 |
| CRIPPLE |  |  |  |  |  |
| The broken halves are fellowed in a cripple, | 30 | 13 | 18 | 35 | 13 |
| CROCKED |  |  |  |  |  |
| Heaven fell with his fall and one crocked bell beat the left air. | 95 | 25 | 58 | 105 | 25 |
| CROCODILE |  |  |  |  |  |
| No man more magical, clawed out the crocodile. | 38 | 18 | 20 | 44 | 8 |
| A crocodile before the chrysalis, | 41 | 14 | 23 | 47 | 14 |
| CROOK |  |  |  |  |  |
| Now Jack my fathers let the time-faced crook, | 67 | 15 | 41 | 76 | 15 |
| CROOKED |  |  |  |  |  |
| And I am dumb to tell the crooked rose | 9 | 4 | 6 | 10 | 4 |
| How at my sheet goes the same crooked worm. | 9 | 22 | 6 | 10 | 22 |
| Corset the boneyards for a crooked boy? | 73 | 4 | 44 | 82 | 4 |
| In a fiercely mourning house in a crooked year. | 88 | 2 | 52 | 97 | 2 |
| Straight and tall from his crooked bones | 112 | 10 | 68 | 124 | 10 |
| CROP |  |  |  |  |  |
| Corrosive spring out of the iceberg's crop, | 30 | 8 | 18 | 35 | 8 |

|  | U.K. | | | U.S. | |
|  | Page | Line | Poem | Page | Line |
|---|---|---|---|---|---|
| **CROPS** | | | | | |
| Laid the crops low, broke the grape's joy. | 39 | 5 | 21 | 45 | 5 |
| **CROSS** | | | | | |
| With their fishwife cross | vii | 10 | I | xv | 10 |
| In spring we cross our foreheads with the holly, | 2 | 19 | 2 | 3 | 1 |
| O see the poles are kissing as they cross. | 3 | 6 | 2 | 3 | 12 |
| And flesh was snipped to cross the lines | 7 | 22 | 5 | 8 | 22 |
| You who bow down at cross and altar, | 8 | 19 | 5 | 9 | 19 |
| Lit on the cuddled tree, the cross of fever, | 19 | 8 | 12 | 22 | 13 |
| Black as the beast and paler than the cross. | 40 | 12 | 22 | 46 | 12 |
| My cross of tales behind the fabulous curtain.' | 41 | 26 | 23 | 48 | 8 |
| So cross her hand with their grave gipsy eyes, | 55 | 12 | 33 | 64 | 15 |
| When you sew the deep door. The bed is a cross place. | 97 | 13 | 59 | 108 | 13 |
| Birds and clocks and cross bells | 134 | 2 | 79 | 150 | 2 |
| Might cross its planets, the bell weep, night gather her eyes, | 165 | 21 | 86 | 185 | 11 |
| And the black cross of the holy house, | 174 | 26 | 89 | 195 | 2 |
| Grave, after Beloved on the grass gulfed cross is scrubbed | 178 | 13 | 90 | 199 | 14 |
| **CROSSED** | | | | | |
| Nor the crossed sticks of war. | 12 | 14 | 9 | 13 | 14 |
| Of day, in the thistle aisles, till the white owl crossed | 177 | 12 | 90 | 198 | 11 |
| He lie lightly, at last, on the last, crossed | | | 91 | 200 | 5 |
| **CROSSES** | | | | | |
| Of gallow crosses on the liver | 7 | 23 | 5 | 8 | 23 |
| **CROSSING** | | | | | |
| My grave is watered by the crossing Jordan. | 31 | 19 | 18 | 37 | 1 |
| Bless her bent spirit with four, crossing birds. | 87 | 26 | 52 | 96 | 26 |
| **CROSS-BONED** | | | | | |
| Nor when my love lies in the cross-boned drift | 60 | 22 | 36 | 69 | 22 |
| **CROSS-BONES** | | | | | |
| The horizontal cross-bones of Abaddon, | 71 | 21 | 44 | 80 | 21 |
| **CROSS-STROKED** | | | | | |
| Cross-stroked salt Adam to the frozen angel | 73 | 21 | 44 | 82 | 21 |
| **CROSSLY** | | | | | |
| Crossly out of the town noises | 134 | 24 | 79 | 151 | 2 |
| **CROSSTREE** | | | | | |
| The blood that touched the crosstree and the grail | 22 | 11 | 14 | 27 | 11 |
| **CROTCH** | | | | | |
| Of the crotch of the squawking shores, | 96 | 2 | 58 | 106 | 2 |
| And guilts, great crotch and giant | 110 | 8 | 67 | 121 | 10 |
| **CROUCH** | | | | | |
| Before I rush in a crouch the ghost with a hammer, air, | 97 | 9 | 59 | 108 | 9 |

| | U.K. | | | U.S. | |
|---|---|---|---|---|---|
| | Page | Line | Poem | Page | Line |
| **CROUCHED** | | | | | |
| In the groin of the natural doorway I crouched like a tailor | 99 | 3 | 60 | 110 | 3 |
| Crouched bare | 141 | 2 | 82 | 158 | 2 |
| Who slaves to his crouched, eternal end | 171 | 4 | 88 | 191 | 4 |
| **CROUCHING** | | | | | |
| I prayed in the crouching room, by his blind bed, | | | 91 | 200 | 13 |
| **CROW** | | | | | |
| Out there, crow black, men | vii | 12 | I | xv | 12 |
| And this, nor this, is shade, the landed crow, | 51 | 19 | 31 | 60 | 19 |
| And opium head, crow stalk, puffed, cut, and blown, | 78 | 10 | 46 | 87 | 10 |
| Roosts sleeping chill till the flame of the cock crow | 119 | 19 | 72 | 131 | 19 |
| **CROW'S-FOOT** | | | | | |
| That wipes away not crow's-foot nor the lock | 12 | 23 | 9 | 14 | 2 |
| **CROWD** | | | | | |
| Dinned aside the coiling crowd, | 134 | 3 | 79 | 150 | 3 |
| **CROWDED** | | | | | |
| And dusk is crowded with the children's ghosts, | 53 | 14 | 32 | 62 | 14 |
| **CROWED** | | | | | |
| Rose and crowed and fell! | 151 | 12 | 83 | 168 | 20 |
| **CROWING** | | | | | |
| Crowing to Lazarus the morning is vanity, | 37 | 8 | 20 | 42 | 14 |
| Before the crowing morning climbed; | 113 | 19 | 69 | 125 | 19 |
| **CROWN** | | | | | |
| By his torrid crown | 138 | 13 | 82 | 155 | 13 |
| On the mountain crown | 145 | 13 | 82 | 162 | 13 |
| **CRUCIFIXION** | | | | | |
| This was the crucifixion on the mountain, | 75 | 5 | 44 | 84 | 5 |
| **CRUEL** | | | | | |
| In quick, sweet, cruel light till the locked ground sprout out, | 91 | 18 | 55 | 100 | 18 |
| 'If my bunched, monkey coming is cruel | 97 | 11 | 59 | 108 | 11 |
| Old in her cruel bed. | 152 | 12 | 83 | 170 | 4 |
| **CRUELLER** | | | | | |
| Commoner than water, crueller than truth; | 125 | 3 | 74 | 139 | 3 |
| **CRUMBLE** | | | | | |
| Crumble and undie | viii | 6 | I | xvi | 6 |
| **CRUMBLED** | | | | | |
| Beginning crumbled back to darkness | 131 | 6 | 77 | 145 | 12 |
| Streets or hungering in the crumbled wood: to these | 178 | 16 | 90 | 199 | 17 |
| **CRUMBS** | | | | | |
| Crumbs, barn, and halter. | 48 | 29 | 28 | 57 | 6 |

|  | U.K. | | | U.S. | |
|  | Page | Line | Poem | Page | Line |
| **CRUMPLED** |  |  |  |  |  |
| The crumpled packs fled past this ghost in bloom, | 80 | 5 | 46 | 89 | 13 |
| But a black sheep with a crumpled horn, | 175 | 13 | 89 | 195 | 18 |
| **CRUSH** |  |  |  |  |  |
| Murmur of spring nor crush the cockerel's eggs, | 60 | 7 | 36 | 69 | 7 |
| **CRUSHED** |  |  |  |  |  |
| Till every turtle crushed from his shell | 151 | 10 | 83 | 168 | 18 |
| **CRUST** |  |  |  |  |  |
| Up through the lubber crust of Wales | 132 | 24 | 78 | 147 | 24 |
| **CRUSTED** |  |  |  |  |  |
| The crusted wound nor stroke the brow; | 62 | 14 | 37 | 71 | 14 |
| **CRUTCH** |  |  |  |  |  |
| The crutch that marrow taps upon their sleep, | 30 | 14 | 18 | 35 | 14 |
| **CRY** |  |  |  |  |  |
| Cry, Multitudes of arks! Across | x | 10 | 1 | xviii | 16 |
| Cry to the dolphined sea. | 11 | 18 | 8 | 12 | 18 |
| Cry Eloi to the guns. | 31 | 18 | 18 | 36 | 18 |
| There was a time they could cry over books, | 50 | 3 | 30 | 59 | 3 |
| No answer to the children's cry | 53 | 24 | 32 | 62 | 24 |
| And the old terrors' continual cry | 64 | 3 | 39 | 73 | 3 |
| No more may gulls cry at their ears | 68 | 20 | 42 | 77 | 20 |
| And, lashed to syllables, the lynx tongue cry | 81 | 8 | 47 | 90 | 8 |
| The stuffed lung of the fox twitch and cry Love | 88 | 11 | 52 | 97 | 11 |
| Cry joy that this witchlike midwife second | 96 | 23 | 58 | 107 | 6 |
| Has a voice and a house, and there and here you must couch and cry. | 98 | 2 | 59 | 109 | 5 |
| With every cry since light | 117 | 23 | 71 | 129 | 23 |
| O you who could not cry | 125 | 20 | 74 | 139 | 20 |
| Two proud, blacked brothers cry, | 126 | 1 | 74 | 140 | 1 |
| Cry, | 130 | 3 | 77 | 144 | 3 |
| Cry my sea town was breaking. | 134 | 27 | 79 | 151 | 5 |
| Cry. | 140 | 17 | 82 | 157 | 17 |
| Cry. My voice burns in his hand. | 148 | 15 | 82 | 165 | 15 |
| Yet, though I cry with tumbledown tongue, | 172 | 26 | 88 | 192 | 26 |
| Through throats where many rivers meet, the curlews cry, | 176 | 1 | 90 | 197 | 1 |
| Now curlew cry me down to kiss the mouths of their dust. | 178 | 4 | 90 | 199 | 5 |
| I am not too proud to cry that He and he |  |  | 91 | 200 | 19 |
| Too proud to cry, too frail to check the tears, |  |  | 91 | 201 | 14 |
| The tears out of his eyes, too proud to cry. |  |  | 91 | 201 | 18 |
| **CRYING** |  |  |  |  |  |
| Was muscled, matted, wise to the crying thigh | 21 | 4 | 13 | 25 | 4 |
| Shall the child sleep unharmed or the man be crying? | 100 | 12 | 61 | 111 | 12 |
| Go crying through you and me | 105 | 18 | 64 | 116 | 18 |

| | U.K. | | | U.S. | |
|---|---|---|---|---|---|
| | Page | Line | Poem | Page | Line |
| Crying, white gowned, from the middle moonlit stages | 114 | 14 | 69 | 126 | 14 |
| Good men, the last wave by, crying how bright | 116 | 7 | 70 | 128 | 7 |
| Crying | 130 | 1 | 77 | 144 | 1 |
| Crying in vain | 139 | 14 | 82 | 156 | 14 |
| Crying at the man drenched throne | 140 | 7 | 82 | 157 | 7 |
| Is crying from nets to knives, | 151 | 18 | 83 | 169 | 6 |
| All his bones crying, and poor in all but pain, | | | 91 | 200 | 21 |
| CRYSTAL | | | | | |
| Crystal harbour vale | 168 | 13 | 87 | 188 | 17 |
| CUBBED | | | | | |
| Save by their long desirers in the fox cubbed | 178 | 15 | 90 | 199 | 16 |
| CUCKOO | | | | | |
| Where at night we stoned the cold and cuckoo | 89 | 8 | 53 | 98 | 8 |
| CUCKOO'S | | | | | |
| Hold hard, these ancient minutes in the cuckoo's month, | 49 | 1 | 29 | 58 | 1 |
| Hold hard, these ancient minutes in the cuckoo's month | 49 | | 29 | 58 | |
| CUCKOOING | | | | | |
| I should learn spring by the cuckooing, | 45 | 12 | 26 | 53 | 12 |
| CUDDLED | | | | | |
| Your calm and cuddled is a scythe of hairs, | 18 | 2 | 12 | 21 | 2 |
| Lit on the cuddled tree, the cross of fever, | 19 | 8 | 12 | 22 | 13 |
| CUDGEL | | | | | |
| Cudgel great air, wreck east, and topple sundown, | 79 | 7 | 46 | 88 | 10 |
| CUDGELLING | | | | | |
| And immemorial sons of the cudgelling, hacked | 176 | 11 | 90 | 197 | 11 |
| CUNNING | | | | | |
| With their heads in a cunning cloud. | 107 | 21 | 65 | 118 | 21 |
| CUP | | | | | |
| Drinking water from the chained cup | 111 | 8 | 68 | 123 | 8 |
| And floating fields from the farm in the cup of the vales, | 119 | 3 | 72 | 131 | 3 |
| And the cup and the cut bread in the dancing shade, | 120 | 3 | 72 | 132 | 8 |
| That a man knelt alone in the cup of the vales, | 122 | 5 | 72 | 135 | 5 |
| CUPBOARD | | | | | |
| Can time unriddle, and the cupboard stone, | 56 | 3 | 34 | 65 | 3 |
| CUPPED | | | | | |
| On a bread white hill over the cupped farm | 122 | 27 | 72 | 136 | 7 |
| Hollows, a grassblade blown in cupped hands, in the looted elms | 169 | 4 | 87 | 189 | 13 |
| CURDLERS | | | | | |
| These boys of light are curdlers in their folly, | 1 | 7 | 2 | 1 | 7 |

|  | U.K. | | | U.S. | |
|---|---|---|---|---|---|
|  | Page | Line | Poem | Page | Line |
| **CURE** |  |  |  |  |  |
| And cure me of ills. | 48 | 23 | 28 | 56 | 23 |
| Should he who split his children with a cure | 51 | 13 | 31 | 60 | 13 |
| Should cure our ills of the water | 82 | 12 | 48 | 91 | 12 |
| **CURED** |  |  |  |  |  |
| Man should be cured of distemper. | 48 | 27 | 28 | 57 | 4 |
| **CURELESS** |  |  |  |  |  |
| The cureless counted body, | 158 | 4 | 84 | 177 | 4 |
| **CURES** |  |  |  |  |  |
| Shall fall awake when cures and their itch | 15 | 2 | 10 | 17 | 2 |
| **CURFEW** |  |  |  |  |  |
| I mean by time the cast and curfew rascal of our marriage, | 84 | 1 | 49 | 93 | 7 |
| **CURLED** |  |  |  |  |  |
| And drown in the drifts of his need, and lie curled caught | 120 | 22 | 72 | 133 | 7 |
| **CURLEW** |  |  |  |  |  |
| Down to the curlew herd! | ix | 12 | 1 | xvii | 12 |
| Now curlew cry me down to kiss the mouths of their dust. | 178 | 4 | 90 | 199 | 5 |
| **CURLEWS** |  |  |  |  |  |
| Curlews aloud in the congered waves | 170 | 13 | 88 | 190 | 13 |
| Through throats where many rivers meet, the curlews cry, | 176 | 1 | 90 | 197 | 1 |
| They yearn with tongues of curlews for the unconceived | 176 | 10 | 90 | 197 | 10 |
| **CURLING** |  |  |  |  |  |
| And curling round the bud that forks her eye. | 13 | 3 | 9 | 14 | 10 |
| **CURL-LOCKED** |  |  |  |  |  |
| Curl-locked and animal cavepools of spells and bone, | 91 | 27 | 55 | 101 | 5 |
| **CURRANTS** |  |  |  |  |  |
| Pears and red currants | 103 | 20 | 63 | 114 | 20 |
| **CURRENCIES** |  |  |  |  |  |
| That will rake at last all currencies of the marked breath | 94 | 8 | 57 | 104 | 8 |
| **CURSE** |  |  |  |  |  |
| Curse, bless, me now with your fierce tears, I pray. | 116 | 17 | 70 | 128 | 17 |
| **CURSED** |  |  |  |  |  |
| When clouds are cursed by thunder, | 44 | 2 | 25 | 52 | 2 |
| Tidy and cursed in my dove cooed room | 175 | 23 | 89 | 196 | 4 |
| **CURTAIN** |  |  |  |  |  |
| My cross of tales behind the fabulous curtain.' | 41 | 26 | 23 | 48 | 8 |
| **CURTAINED** |  |  |  |  |  |
| And the breath-white, curtained mouth of seed.' | 79 | 25 | 46 | 89 | 6 |

|  |  | U.K. |  |  | U.S. |  |
|---|---|---|---|---|---|---|
|  |  | *Page* | *Line* | *Poem* | *Page* | *Line* |
| CURTAINS | Pulls down the shabby curtains of the skin; | 6 | 23 | 4 | 7 | 5 |
| CURVE | By the curve of the nude mouth or the laugh up the sleeve. | 85 | 12 | 50 | 94 | 12 |
| CURVING | And alone in the night's eternal, curving act | 176 | 9 | 90 | 197 | 9 |
| CUT | To cut the channels at their source | 11 | 11 | 8 | 12 | 11 |
|  | The nurse of giants by the cut sea basin, | 56 | 10 | 34 | 65 | 10 |
|  | And opium head, crow stalk, puffed, cut, and blown, | 78 | 10 | 46 | 87 | 10 |
|  | Die in red feathers when the flying heaven's cut, | 92 | 12 | 55 | 101 | 18 |
|  | Cut Christbread spitting vinegar and all | 95 | 16 | 58 | 105 | 16 |
|  | Cut to the still star in the order of the quick | 109 | 20 | 67 | 120 | 20 |
|  | And the cup and the cut bread in the dancing shade, | 120 | 3 | 72 | 132 | 8 |
|  | That once cut the figures of birds on the deep bread | 123 | 4 | 72 | 136 | 14 |
|  | And cut the birds' boughs that the minstrel sap ran red. | 178 | 8 | 90 | 199 | 9 |
| CUT-TO-MEASURE | Cut-to-measure flesh bit, | 132 | 3 | 78 | 147 | 3 |
| CUTTING | Arc-lamped thrown back upon the cutting flood. | 73 | 10 | 44 | 82 | 10 |
|  | Cutting the morning off, | 134 | 10 | 79 | 150 | 10 |
| CYANIDE | Sucking the dark, kissed on the cyanide, | 30 | 21 | 18 | 35 | 21 |
| CYCLONE | Cyclone of his wing | 140 | 5 | 82 | 157 | 5 |
|  | As the world falls, silent as the cyclone of silence. | 164 | 14 | 86 | 183 | 21 |
| CYPRESS | My world is cypress, and an English valley. | 31 | 13 | 18 | 36 | 13 |
| CYPRESSES | Hill of cypresses! The din and tale in the skimmed | 165 | 5 | 86 | 184 | 13 |

# ENTRIES UNDER D

|  |  | viii | 10 | 1 | xvi | 10 |
|---|---|---|---|---|---|---|
| DABBED | My dabbed bay's dusk, as I hack | viii | 10 | 1 | xvi | 10 |
| DABBLES | Half of the fellow mother as she dabbles | 30 | 3 | 18 | 35 | 3 |

DAB-FILLED

|  |  | U.K. |  |  | U.S. |  |
|  |  | Page | Line | Poem | Page | Line |
|---|---|---|---|---|---|---|
| DAB-FILLED |  |  |  |  |  |  |
| In the pebbly dab-filled | | 167 | 20 | 87 | 188 | I |
| DAFT |  |  |  |  |  |  |
| Daft with the drug that's smoking in a girl | | 13 | 2 | 9 | 14 | 9 |
| The dear, daft time I take to nudge the sentence, | | 41 | 4 | 23 | 47 | 4 |
| DAI |  |  |  |  |  |  |
| Tom tit and Dai mouse! | | x | 16 | I | xviii | 22 |
| DAISIES |  |  |  |  |  |  |
| Heads of the characters hammer through daisies; | | 68 | 25 | 42 | 70 | 25 |
| Trail with daisies and barley | | 159 | 8 | 85 | 178 | 8 |
| DAM |  |  |  |  |  |  |
| The salt sucked dam and darlings of the land | | 47 | 3 | 27 | 55 | 3 |
| DAMNED |  |  |  |  |  |  |
| Nor damned the sea that sped about my fist, | | 4 | 3 | 3 | 4 | 3 |
| Sun. In the name of the damned | | 148 | 3 | 82 | 165 | 3 |
| DAMP |  |  |  |  |  |  |
| Here love's damp muscle dries and dies, | | 2 | 22 | 2 | 3 | 4 |
| Turns damp to dry; the golden shot | | 6 | 2 | 4 | 6 | 2 |
| Is damp and dry; the quick and dead | | 6 | 17 | 4 | 6 | 17 |
| From damp love-darkness and the nurse's twist | | 13 | 10 | 9 | 14 | 17 |
| I damp the waxlights in your tower dome. | | 19 | 11 | 12 | 22 | 16 |
| Shames and the damp dishonours, the relic scraping. | | 37 | 20 | 20 | 43 | 3 |
| Whisper in a damp word, her wits drilled hollow, | | 88 | 5 | 52 | 97 | 5 |
| DAMS |  |  |  |  |  |  |
| Of sun and moon they paint their dams | | I | 17 | 2 | I | 17 |
| DANCE |  |  |  |  |  |  |
| They dance between their arclamps and our skull, | | 14 | 17 | 10 | 16 | 17 |
| Peck, sprint, dance on fountains and duck time | | 97 | 8 | 59 | 108 | 8 |
| And wharves of water where the walls dance and the white cranes stilt. | | 168 | 15 | 87 | 188 | 19 |
| DANCED |  |  |  |  |  |  |
| Their frail deeds might have danced in a green bay, | | 116 | 8 | 70 | 128 | 8 |
| And gone that barley dark where their clogs danced in the spring, | | 177 | 20 | 90 | 198 | 19 |
| DANCERS |  |  |  |  |  |  |
| Was there a time when dancers with their fiddles | | 50 | I | 30 | 59 | I |
| Look. And the dancers move | | 121 | 16 | 72 | 134 | 11 |
| DANCING |  |  |  |  |  |  |
| At a wood's dancing hoof, | | vii | 8 | I | xv | 8 |
| And the cup and the cut bread in the dancing shade, | | 120 | 3 | 72 | 132 | 8 |
| Leaves is dancing. Lines of age on the stones weave in a flock. | | 121 | 23 | 72 | 134 | 18 |

|  | U.K. |  |  | U.S. |  |
|---|---|---|---|---|---|
|  | Page | Line | Poem | Page | Line |
| The dancing perishes | 123 | 1 | 72 | 136 | 11 |
| DANDY |  |  |  |  |  |
| The bright pretender, the ridiculous sea dandy | 133 | 14 | 78 | 148 | 17 |
| DANGLER |  |  |  |  |  |
| With my cherry capped dangler green as seaweed | 133 | 17 | 78 | 148 | 20 |
| DANGLES |  |  |  |  |  |
| And, clapped in water till the triton dangles, | 37 | 13 | 20 | 42 | 19 |
| DARK |  |  |  |  |  |
| In the hooting, nearly dark | ix | 8 | 1 | xvii | 8 |
| And dark shoals every holy field. | x | 7 | 1 | xviii | 13 |
| Of doubt and dark they feed their nerves; | 1 | 11 | 2 | 1 | 11 |
| We are the dark deniers, let us summon | 2 | 7 | 2 | 2 | 7 |
| Groom the dark brides, the widows of the night | 14 | 5 | 10 | 16 | 5 |
| Sucking the dark, kissed on the cyanide, | 30 | 21 | 18 | 35 | 21 |
| Rise before dark. | 55 | 5 | 33 | 64 | 8 |
| The features in their private dark | 63 | 5 | 38 | 72 | 5 |
| Light and dark are no enemies | 66 | 12 | 40 | 75 | 12 |
| And, for that murder's sake, dark with contagion | 79 | 11 | 46 | 88 | 14 |
| There is loud and dark directly under the dumb flame, | 83 | 13 | 49 | 92 | 13 |
| In the dark of the coffin and sheds dry leaves, | 87 | 8 | 52 | 96 | 8 |
| And a lamp of lightning for the poor in the dark; | 89 | 11 | 53 | 98 | 11 |
| You have kicked from a dark den, leaped up the whinnying light, | 92 | 15 | 55 | 101 | 21 |
| And count the taken, forsaken mysteries in a bad dark. | 94 | 9 | 57 | 104 | 9 |
| Through the dark asylum, | 96 | 13 | 58 | 106 | 13 |
| Turns in the dark on the sound they know will arise | 100 | 6 | 61 | 111 | 6 |
| And mark the dark eyed wave, through the eyes of sleep, | 100 | 19 | 61 | 111 | 19 |
| The grains beyond age, the dark veins of her mother, | 101 | 21 | 62 | 112 | 21 |
| Into the winding dark | 105 | 11 | 64 | 116 | 11 |
| Dark, and the guilty dark, and good | 105 | 21 | 64 | 116 | 21 |
| Of the descending day, the dark our folly, | 109 | 19 | 67 | 120 | 19 |
| In the androgynous dark, | 110 | 2 | 67 | 121 | 4 |
| Until the Sunday sombre bell at dark | 111 | 6 | 68 | 123 | 6 |
| To his kennel in the dark. | 112 | 18 | 68 | 124 | 18 |
| There the dark blade and wanton sighing her down | 113 | 16 | 69 | 125 | 16 |
| Forgotten dark, rest their pulse and bury their dead in her faithless sleep. | 115 | 23 | 69 | 127 | 23 |
| Though wise men at their end know dark is right, | 116 | 4 | 70 | 128 | 4 |

DARK (continued)

|  | U.K. | | Poem | U.S. | |
|---|---|---|---|---|---|
|  | *Page* | *Line* |  | *Page* | *Line* |
| In the watched dark, quivering through locks and caves, | 118 | 3 | 71 | 130 | 7 |
| In the long ago land that glided the dark door wide | 121 | 12 | 72 | 134 | 7 |
| Now in the dark there is only yourself and myself. | 125 | 24 | 74 | 139 | 24 |
| Opening and the dark run | 137 | 7 | 82 | 154 | 7 |
| But dark alone | 137 | 14 | 82 | 154 | 14 |
| And the dark thrown | 138 | 14 | 82 | 155 | 14 |
| In the centre of dark I pray him | 144 | 17 | 82 | 161 | 17 |
| In the dark | 145 | 7 | 82 | 162 | 7 |
| And the known dark of the earth amen. | 147 | 18 | 82 | 164 | 18 |
| He sped into the drinking dark; | 149 | 14 | 83 | 166 | 14 |
| White springs in the dark. | 153 | 24 | 83 | 171 | 20 |
| Bird after dark and the laughing fish | 154 | 6 | 83 | 172 | 6 |
| That one dark I owe my light, | 158 | 9 | 84 | 177 | 9 |
| Flashing into the dark. | 160 | 5 | 85 | 179 | 5 |
| Yet out of the beaked, web dark and the pouncing boughs | 163 | 25 | 86 | 183 | 6 |
| And love unbolts the dark | 171 | 18 | 88 | 191 | 18 |
| Dark is a way and light is a place, | 171 | 22 | 88 | 191 | 22 |
| But dark is a long way. | 172 | 10 | 88 | 192 | 10 |
| And gone that barley dark where their clogs danced in the spring, | 177 | 20 | 90 | 198 | 19 |

DARKENED
| To shut the sun, plunge, mount your darkened keys | 118 | 5 | 71 | 130 | 9 |

DARKEST
| The darkest way, and did not turn away, |  |  | 91 | 200 | 2 |
| On that darkest day. Oh, forever may |  |  | 91 | 200 | 4 |
| The darkest justice of death, blind and unblessed. |  |  | 91 | 200 | 11 |
| On that darkest day. Oh, he could hide |  |  | 91 | 201 | 17 |

DARKNESS
| A darkness in the weather of the eye | 6 | 10 | 4 | 6 | 10 |
| The boy she dropped from darkness at her side | 21 | 2 | 13 | 25 | 2 |
| Mister and master, darkness for his eyes, | 57 | 3 | 34 | 66 | 10 |
| Fathering and all humbling darkness | 101 | 3 | 62 | 112 | 3 |
| And darkness hung the walls with baskets of snakes, | 114 | 4 | 69 | 126 | 4 |
| Darkness kindled back into beginning | 129 | 12 | 77 | 143 | 12 |
| Beginning crumbled back to darkness | 131 | 6 | 77 | 145 | 12 |
| And the daughters of darkness flame like Fawkes fires still. | 178 | 19 | 90 | 199 | 20 |

DARK-SKINNED
| Forever it is a white child in the dark-skinned summer | 83 | 19 | 49 | 93 | 1 |

|  | U.K. |  |  | U.S. |  |
|---|---|---|---|---|---|
|  | *Page* | *Line* | *Poem* | *Page* | *Line* |
| DARK-VOWELLED |  |  |  |  |  |
| By the sea's side hear the dark-vowelled birds. | 17 | 8 | 11 | 20 | 8 |
| DARLINGS |  |  |  |  |  |
| The salt sucked dam and darlings of the land | 47 | 3 | 27 | 55 | 3 |
| Hold hard, my county darlings, for a hawk descends, | 49 | 22 | 29 | 58 | 22 |
| DARTED |  |  |  |  |  |
| The darted hail, the childish snow, | 7 | 14 | 5 | 8 | 14 |
| DARTING |  |  |  |  |  |
| 'A lizard darting with black venom's thread | 79 | 23 | 46 | 89 | 4 |
| DASH |  |  |  |  |  |
| Ancient woods of my blood, dash down to the nut of the seas | 94 | 11 | 57 | 104 | 11 |
| DASHED-DOWN |  |  |  |  |  |
| Hear by death's accident the clocked and dashed-down spire | 83 | 11 | 49 | 92 | 11 |
| DAUBING |  |  |  |  |  |
| To kill and their own tide daubing blood | 171 | 8 | 88 | 191 | 8 |
| DAUGHTER |  |  |  |  |  |
| Was brother to Mnetha's daughter | 7 | 5 | 5 | 8 | 5 |
| Thrust, my daughter or son, to escape, there is none, none, none, | 97 | 19 | 59 | 108 | 19 |
| Deep with the first dead lies London's daughter, | 101 | 19 | 62 | 112 | 19 |
| DAUGHTERS |  |  |  |  |  |
| And the grave its daughters. | 110 | 14 | 67 | 121 | 16 |
| Off by the sun and Daughters no longer grieved | 178 | 14 | 90 | 199 | 15 |
| And the daughters of darkness flame like Fawkes fires still. | 178 | 19 | 90 | 199 | 20 |
| DAVY'S |  |  |  |  |  |
| The bright-eyed worm on Davy's lamp, | 2 | 11 | 2 | 2 | 11 |
| DAWN |  |  |  |  |  |
| Dawn breaks behind the eyes; | 24 | 13 | 15 | 29 | 13 |
| Above the waste allotments the dawn halts. | 25. | 6 | 15 | 30 | 6 |
| Back. Lines of age sleep on the stones till trumpeting dawn. | 123 | 8 | 72 | 136 | 18 |
| And the first dawn | 139 | 4 | 82 | 156 | 4 |
| And you shall wake, from country sleep, this dawn and each first dawn, | 166 | 11 | 86 | 186 | 11 |
| Dawn ships clouted aground, | 172 | 25 | 88 | 192 | 25 |
| Among those Killed in the Dawn Raid was a Man Aged a Hundred | 135 |  | 80 | 152 |  |
| DAWNED |  |  |  |  |  |
| A she bird dawned, and her breast with snow and scarlet downed. | 121 | 15 | 72 | 134 | 10 |
| DAWS |  |  |  |  |  |
| Daws Sir John's just hill dons, and again the gulled birds hare | 167 | 15 | 87 | 187 | 15 |

# DAY

|  | U.K. Page | U.K. Line | Poem | U.S. Page | U.S. Line |
|---|---|---|---|---|---|
| **DAY** | | | | | |
| This day winding down now | vii | 1 | 1 | xv | 1 |
| Divide the night and day with fairy thumbs; | 1 | 15 | 2 | 1 | 15 |
| Turns night to day; blood in their suns | 6 | 5 | 4 | 6 | 5 |
| Ungotten I knew night and day. | 7 | 18 | 5 | 8 | 18 |
| Down in the yard of day. | 14 | 16 | 10 | 16 | 16 |
| Day lights the bone; | 24 | 21 | 15 | 29 | 21 |
| Man in the day or wind at night | 39 | 4 | 21 | 45 | 4 |
| Alone till the day I die | 58 | 6 | 35 | 67 | 6 |
| Or stay till the day I die | 58 | 23 | 35 | 67 | 23 |
| Or stay till the day I die? | 59 | 6 | 35 | 68 | 6 |
| Calls a green day and night. | 69 | 6 | 43 | 78 | 6 |
| Are formed of flesh, but let the false day come | 63 | 6 | 38 | 72 | 6 |
| Growing more terrible as the day | 64 | 4 | 39 | 73 | 4 |
| Autocracy of night and day, | 65 | 12 | 40 | 74 | 12 |
| Dayed peaks to day to death, | 67 | 22 | 41 | 76 | 22 |
| Soar, with its two bark towers, to that Day | 76 | 20 | 44 | 85 | 20 |
| Or poise the day on a horn. | 92 | 5 | 55 | 101 | 11 |
| That I struck one day by luck, | 93 | 5 | 56 | 102 | 5 |
| Of the descending day, the dark our folly, | 109 | 19 | 67 | 120 | 19 |
| Made all day until bell time | 112 | 7 | 68 | 124 | 7 |
| Old age should burn and rave at close of day; | 116 | 2 | 70 | 128 | 2 |
| Clash out the mounting dolphin's day, | 152 | 3 | 83 | 169 | 15 |
| And the sun grew round that very day. | 160 | 10 | 85 | 179 | 10 |
| This sandgrain day in the bent bay's grave | 170 | 6 | 88 | 190 | 6 |
| Of day, in the thistle aisles, till the white owl crossed | 177 | 12 | 90 | 198 | 11 |
| On that darkest day. Oh, forever may | | | 91 | 200 | 4 |
| On that darkest day. Oh, he could hide | | | 91 | 201 | 17 |
| **DAY'S** | | | | | |
| Day's night whose towers will catch | vii | 20 | 1 | xv | 20 |
| And this day's sun leapt up the sky out of her thighs | 127 | 4 | 75 | 141 | 4 |
| **DAYBREAK** | | | | | |
| Over the whirling ditch of daybreak | 131 | 15 | 77 | 145 | 21 |
| **DAYED** | | | | | |
| Dayed peaks to day to death, | 67 | 22 | 41 | 76 | 22 |
| **DAYLIGHT** | | | | | |
| Pack off the shapes of daylight and their starch, | 15 | 4 | 10 | 17 | 4 |
| **DAYS** | | | | | |
| By sipping at the vine of days. | 8 | 12 | 5 | 9 | 12 |
| The slug's a living calendar of days; | 45 | 15 | 26 | 53 | 15 |
| The child shall question all his days, | 53 | 7 | 32 | 62 | 7 |
| Tugged through the days | 54 | 20 | 33 | 63 | 20 |
| A brute land in the cool top of the country days | 91 | 15 | 55 | 100 | 15 |
| And walked abroad in a shower of all my days. | 102 | 16 | 63 | 113 | 16 |
| King of your heart in the blind days, | 105 | 16 | 64 | 116 | 16 |

| | U.K. | | | U.S. | |
|---|---|---|---|---|---|
| | Page | Line | Poem | Page | Line |
| The pyre yet to be lighted of my sins and days, | 109 | 3 | 67 | 120 | 3 |
| Nothing I cared, in the lamb white days, that time would take me | 160 | 24 | 85 | 180 | 1 |
| Or still all the numberless days of his death, though | | | 91 | 200 | 8 |
| DAZZLE | | | | | |
| Dazzle this face of voices on the moon-turned table, | 37 | 18 | 20 | 43 | 1 |
| DAZZLED | | | | | |
| And the bulwarks of the dazzled quay. | 149 | 10 | 83 | 166 | 10 |
| DAZZLER | | | | | |
| Of the dazzler of heaven | 139 | 7 | 82 | 156 | 7 |
| DAZZLING | | | | | |
| Sailed and set dazzling by the handshaped ocean, | 78 | 5 | 46 | 87 | 5 |
| 'No. Not for Christ's dazzling bed | 97 | 16 | 59 | 108 | 16 |
| The dazzling prison | 144 | 13 | 82 | 161 | 13 |
| DEAD | | | | | |
| The dingle furred deer dead! | ix | 5 | 1 | xvii | 5 |
| From the fair dead who flush the sea | 2 | 10 | 2 | 2 | 10 |
| Some dead undid their bushy jaws, | 4 | 22 | 3 | 4 | 22 |
| Gives up its dead to such a working sea; | 5 | 3 | 3 | 5 | 3 |
| Is damp and dry; the quick and dead | 6 | 17 | 4 | 6 | 17 |
| And the heart gives up its dead. | 6 | 24 | 4 | 7 | 6 |
| The dead turns up its eye; | 11 | 3 | 8 | 12 | 3 |
| Dead on the sweethearts' toes. | 12 | 28 | 9 | 14 | 7 |
| Blowing the old dead back; our shots shall smack | 15 | 18 | 10 | 17 | 18 |
| Left by the dead who, in their moonless acre, | 21 | 11 | 13 | 25 | 11 |
| My blood upon the tempered dead, forcing | 28 | 19 | 17 | 33 | 19 |
| I hear, through dead men's drums, the riddled lads, | 31 | 16 | 18 | 36 | 16 |
| Drip on my dead house garden. | 31 | 21 | 18 | 37 | 3 |
| In seizure of silence commit the dead nuisance: | 35 | 23 | 20 | 40 | 23 |
| Turning the riderless dead by the channel wall. | 36 | 24 | 20 | 42 | 3 |
| Rings out the Dead Sea scale; | 37 | 12 | 20 | 42 | 18 |
| Yea the dead stir, | 51 | 18 | 31 | 60 | 18 |
| Let her inhale her dead, through seed and solid | 55 | 10 | 33 | 64 | 13 |
| And the velvet dead inch out. | 56 | 21 | 34 | 65 | 21 |
| Doubled the globe of dead and halved a country; | 62 | 3 | 37 | 71 | 3 |
| The five kings count the dead but do not soften | 62 | 13 | 37 | 71 | 13 |
| Dead men naked they shall be one | 68 | 2 | 42 | 77 | 2 |
| Though they be mad and dead as nails, | 68 | 24 | 42 | 77 | 24 |
| And three dead seasons on a climbing grave | 72 | 6 | 44 | 81 | 6 |
| Draw on the glove of prints, dead Cairo's henna | 75 | 23 | 44 | 84 | 23 |
| And rivers of the dead around my neck. | 76 | 8 | 44 | 85 | 8 |
| If the dead starve, their stomachs turn to tumble | 77 | 22 | 45 | 86 | 22 |

|  | U.K. | | | U.S. | |
|---|---|---|---|---|---|
|  | Page | Line | Poem | Page | Line |
| And walk the warring sands by the dead town, | 79 | 6 | 46 | 88 | 9 |
| 'See,' drummed the taut masks, 'how the dead ascend: | 79 | 26 | 46 | 89 | 7 |
| In the snivelling hours with dead, humped Ann | 87 | 13 | 52 | 96 | 13 |
| (Bury the dead for fear that they walk to the grave in labour.) | 99 | 2 | 60 | 110 | 2 |
| And the other full of tears that she will be dead, | 100 | 5 | 61 | 111 | 5 |
| Turns on the quick and the dead, and the man on the stairs | 100 | 14 | 61 | 111 | 14 |
| Dragging him up the stairs to one who lies dead. | 100 | 20 | 61 | 111 | 20 |
| Deep with the first dead lies London's daughter, | 101 | 19 | 62 | 112 | 19 |
| Summertime of the dead whispered the truth of his joy | 104 | 4 | 63 | 115 | 6 |
| Joy of the long dead child sang burning | 104 | 11 | 63 | 115 | 13 |
| Like the dust of the dead. | 105 | 12 | 64 | 116 | 12 |
| At large as the dead, | 108 | 8 | 66 | 119 | 8 |
| Dead and gone, dedicate forever to my self | 109 | 6 | 67 | 120 | 6 |
| Forgotten dark, rest their pulse and bury their dead in her faithless sleep. | 115 | 23 | 69 | 127 | 23 |
| Who strode for your own dead | 117 | 20 | 71 | 129 | 20 |
| And spells on the winds of the dead his winter's tale. | 121 | 4 | 72 | 133 | 19 |
| Time sings through the intricately dead snow drop. Listen. | 121 | 10 | 72 | 134 | 5 |
| Horses, centaur dead, turn and tread the drenched white | 121 | 19 | 72 | 134 | 14 |
| Paddocks in the farms of birds. The dead oak walks for love. | 121 | 20 | 72 | 134 | 15 |
| Of nightingale and centaur dead horse. The springs minstrel dead, | 123 | 2 | 72 | 136 | 12 |
| On the white, no longer growing green, and, wither | 123 | 7 | 72 | 136 | 17 |
| Nor for the towering dead | 128 | 15 | 76 | 142 | 15 |
| Over the dead infants | 130 | 26 | 77 | 145 | 4 |
| Into the dead clock burning the hour | 131 | 13 | 77 | 145 | 19 |
| That he let the dead lie though they moan | 145 | 1 | 82 | 162 | 1 |
| Sing how the seal has kissed her dead! | 152 | 10 | 83 | 170 | 2 |
| For the crab-backed dead on the sea-bed rose | 153 | 3 | 83 | 170 | 19 |
| Oh miracle of fishes! The long dead bite! | 154 | 20 | 83 | 172 | 20 |
| And the dead hand leads the past. | 155 | 4 | 83 | 173 | 8 |
| The Thief fall on the dead like the willy nilly dew, | 165 | 22 | 86 | 185 | 12 |
| The dead grow for His joy. | 171 | 27 | 88 | 191 | 27 |
| Or the stars' seashore dead, | 172 | 3 | 88 | 192 | 3 |
| Trounced by his wings in the hissing shippen, long dead | 177 | 19 | 90 | 198 | 18 |
| Who heard the tall bell sail down the Sundays of the dead | 178 | 10 | 90 | 199 | 11 |

|  | U.K. | | | U.S. | |
|  | Page | Line | Poem | Page | Line |
| Hale dead and deathless do the women of the hill | 178 | 17 | 90 | 199 | 18 |
| Noon, and night, and light. The rivers of the dead |  |  | 91 | 200 | 15 |
| **DEADLY** |  |  |  |  |  |
| Savours the lick of the times through a deadly wood of hair | 77 | 9 | 45 | 86 | 9 |
| The female, deadly, and male | 115 | 7 | 69 | 127 | 7 |
| And all the deadly virtues plague my death! | 175 | 31 | 89 | 196 | 12 |
| **DEADROCK** |  |  |  |  |  |
| The deadrock base and blow the flowered anchor, | 51 | 5 | 31 | 60 | 5 |
| **DEADWEED** |  |  |  |  |  |
| The bagpipe-breasted ladies in the deadweed | 74 | 13 | 44 | 83 | 13 |
| **DEAF** |  |  |  |  |  |
| I who was deaf to spring and summer, | 7 | 7 | 5 | 8 | 7 |
| And all sweet hell, deaf as an hour's ear, | 57 | 5 | 34 | 66 | 12 |
| **DEAR** |  |  |  |  |  |
| The dear, daft time I take to nudge the sentence, | 41 | 4 | 23 | 47 | 4 |
| And the dear floods of his hair. | 93 | 30 | 56 | 103 | 10 |
| My dear would I change my tears on your iron head. | 97 | 18 | 59 | 108 | 18 |
| And taken by light in her arms at long and dear last | 108 | 16 | 66 | 119 | 16 |
| My dear, my dear, | 162 | 5 | 86 | 181 | 5 |
| My dear this night he comes and night without end my dear | 166 | 9 | 86 | 186 | 9 |
| And fabulous, dear God. | 171 | 21 | 88 | 191 | 21 |
| **DEATH** |  |  |  |  |  |
| Where, punctual as death, we ring the stars; | 2 | 3 | 2 | 2 | 3 |
| Death from a summer woman, | 2 | 8 | 2 | 2 | 8 |
| He had by heart the Christ-cross-row of death. | 4 | 24 | 3 | 4 | 24 |
| Drives in a death as life leaks out. | 6 | 9 | 4 | 6 | 9 |
| Of birth and death, the two sad knives of thieves, | 10 | 18 | 7 | 11 | 18 |
| The words of death are dryer than his stiff, | 13 | 18 | 9 | 15 | 4 |
| Shapes in a cinder death; love for his trick, | 19 | 23 | 12 | 23 | 8 |
| First characters of birth and death. | 22 | 24 | 14 | 27 | 24 |
| Death on the mouth that ate the gas. | 28 | 16 | 17 | 33 | 16 |
| Sharp in my second death I marked the hills, harvest | 28 | 17 | 17 | 33 | 17 |
| I dreamed my genesis in sweat of death, fallen | 29 | 1 | 17 | 34 | 5 |
| No death more natural; | 35 | 21 | 20 | 40 | 21 |
| (Death instrumental, | 36 | 25 | 20 | 42 | 4 |
| Man was the scales, the death birds on enamel, | 38 | 19 | 20 | 44 | 9 |
| Death: death of Hamlet and the nightmare madmen, | 41 | 19 | 23 | 48 | 1 |
| Love's house, they answer, and the tower death | 47 | 7 | 27 | 55 | 7 |

|  | U.K. | | | U.S. | |
|  | Page | Line | Poem | Page | Line |
| Death to the yes, | 51 | 11 | 31 | 60 | 11 |
| The yes to death, the yesman and the answer, | 51 | 12 | 31 | 60 | 12 |
| Death hairy-heeled, and the tapped ghost in wood, | 52 | 5 | 31 | 61 | 12 |
| These five kings did a king to death. | 62 | 4 | 37 | 71 | 4 |
| Before death takes you, O take back this. | 66 | 17 | 40 | 75 | 17 |
| Death flashing from his sleeve, | 67 | 16 | 41 | 76 | 16 |
| Dayed peaks to day to death, | 67 | 22 | 41 | 76 | 22 |
| And death shall have no dominion. | 68 | 1 | 42 | 77 | 1 |
| And death shall have no dominion. | 68 | 9 | 42 | 77 | 9 |
| And death shall have no dominion. | 68 | 10 | 42 | 77 | 10 |
| And death shall have no dominion. | 68 | 18 | 42 | 77 | 18 |
| And death shall have no dominion. | 68 | 19 | 42 | 77 | 19 |
| And death shall have no dominion. | 68 | 27 | 42 | 77 | 27 |
| Death is all metaphors, shape in one history; | 71 | 15 | 44 | 80 | 15 |
| Death from a bandage, rants the mask of scholars | 76 | 2 | 44 | 85 | 2 |
| Magnified out of praise; her death was a still drop; | 87 | 17 | 52 | 96 | 17 |
| Death and this mad heroine | 93 | 22 | 56 | 103 | 2 |
| To lift to leave from the treasures of man is pleasing death | 94 | 7 | 57 | 104 | 7 |
| The majesty and burning of the child's death. | 101 | 13 | 62 | 112 | 13 |
| After the first death, there is no other. | 101 | 24 | 62 | 112 | 24 |
| Of moving about your death | 105 | 14 | 64 | 116 | 14 |
| Death, and bad death, and then | 105 | 22 | 64 | 116 | 22 |
| Unluckily for a death | 109 | 1 | 67 | 120 | 1 |
| The death biding two lie lonely. | 109 | 28 | 67 | 121 | 2 |
| Death in the carved nunnery | 110 | 18 | 67 | 121 | 20 |
| Grave men, near death, who see with blinding sight | 116 | 13 | 70 | 128 | 13 |
| In the far ago land the door of his death glided wide, | 122 | 25 | 72 | 136 | 5 |
| Carrying cloud, Death strikes their house. | 124 | 8 | 73 | 138 | 8 |
| Among the street burned to tireless death | 129 | 4 | 77 | 143 | 4 |
| Us your death that myselves the believers | 129 | 19 | 77 | 143 | 19 |
| As the grains blow, as your death grows, through our heart. | 129 | 23 | 77 | 143 | 23 |
| For the country of death is the heart's size | 146 | 17 | 82 | 163 | 17 |
| Rejoicing for that drifting death | 152 | 16 | 83 | 170 | 8 |
| Death clear as a buoy's bell: | 168 | 2 | 87 | 188 | 6 |
| Work at their ways to death, | 170 | 14 | 88 | 190 | 14 |
| To death, one man through his sundered hulks, | 173 | 11 | 88 | 193 | 11 |
| And all the deadly virtues plague my death! | 175 | 31 | 89 | 196 | 12 |
| Or still all the numberless days of his death, though |  |  | 91 | 200 | 8 |

| | U.K. | | | U.S. | |
|---|---|---|---|---|---|
| | Page | Line | Poem | Page | Line |
| The darkest justice of death, blind and un-blessed. | | | 91 | 200 | 11 |
| And caught between two nights, blindness and death. | | | 91 | 201 | 15 |
| And death shall have no dominion | 68 | | 42 | 77 | |
| A Refusal to Mourn the Death, by Fire, of a child in London | 101 | | 62 | 112 | |
| Unluckily for a Death | 109 | | 67 | 120 | |
| DEATH'S | | | | | |
| And I was struck down by death's feather. | 8 | 15 | 5 | 9 | 15 |
| And what's the rub? Death's feather on the nerve? | 13 | 15 | 9 | 15 | 1 |
| What colour is glory? Death's feather? Tremble | 31 | 1 | 18 | 36 | 1 |
| Who blows death's feather? What glory is colour? | 32 | 7 | 18 | 37 | 13 |
| My half ghost in armour hold hard in death's corridor, | 35 | 5 | 20 | 40 | 5 |
| Shall I fall to death's feather. | 64 | 18 | 39 | 73 | 18 |
| Hear by death's accident the clocked and dashed-down spire | 83 | 11 | 49 | 92 | 11 |
| DEATHBEDS | | | | | |
| In deathbeds of orchards the boat dies down | 157 | 15 | 83 | 176 | 7 |
| DEATHLESS | | | | | |
| Your faith as deathless as the outcry of the ruled sun. | 166 | 12 | 86 | 186 | 12 |
| Hale dead and deathless do the women of the hill | 178 | 17 | 90 | 199 | 18 |
| DEATHS | | | | | |
| Through the devilish years and innocent deaths | 93 | 14 | 56 | 102 | 14 |
| Of several near deaths, | 117 | 2 | 71 | 129 | 2 |
| Of deaths and entrances, | 117 | 26 | 71 | 130 | 2 |
| Brave deaths of only ones but never found, | 126 | 11 | 74 | 140 | 11 |
| Deaths and Entrances | 117 | | 71 | 129 | |
| DEATH-STAGGED | | | | | |
| The death-stagged scatter-breath | 134 | 19 | 79 | 150 | 19 |
| DECAYING | | | | | |
| Your monstrous officers and the decaying army, | 37 | 5 | 20 | 42 | 11 |
| DECEIVED | | | | | |
| Head, deceived, I believed, my maker, | 133 | 6 | 78 | 148 | 9 |
| DECEMBER'S | | | | | |
| Country, your sport is summer, and December's pools | 49 | 7 | 29 | 58 | 7 |
| December's thorn screwed in a brow of holly. | 76 | 14 | 44 | 85 | 14 |
| DECK | | | | | |
| Good-bye to the man on the sea-legged deck | 149 | 18 | 83 | 166 | 18 |
| DECKED | | | | | |
| Knocked in the flesh that decked the vine, | 39 | 7 | 21 | 45 | 7 |
| Or decked on a cloud swallower, | 132 | 12 | 78 | 147 | 12 |

|  | U.K. | | | U.S. | |
| --- | --- | --- | --- | --- | --- |
|  | Page | Line | Poem | Page | Line |
| DECKS | | | | | |
| File through the flesh where no flesh decks the bones. | 24 | 6 | 15 | 29 | 6 |
| That burn the bitten decks, | 69 | 9 | 43 | 78 | 9 |
| Strike and smoothe, for my decks are drums, | 152 | 5 | 83 | 169 | 17 |
| His decks are drenched with miracles. | 154 | 19 | 83 | 172 | 19 |
| DECLAIMS | | | | | |
| Flies on the shafted disk, declaims the morning | 16 | 19 | 11 | 19 | 19 |
| One voice in chains declaims | 115 | 6 | 69 | 127 | 6 |
| DECLENSION | | | | | |
| And from the first declension of the flesh | 21 | 7 | 13 | 25 | 7 |
| DEDICATE | | | | | |
| Dead and gone, dedicate forever to my self | 109 | 6 | 67 | 120 | 6 |
| DEEDS | | | | | |
| And all your deeds and words, | 106 | 10 | 64 | 117 | 10 |
| Their frail deeds might have danced in a green bay, | 116 | 8 | 70 | 128 | 8 |
| DEEP | | | | | |
| Only the drowned deep bells | x | 4 | 1 | xviii | 10 |
| There in the deep with quartered shades | 1 | 16 | 2 | 1 | 16 |
| How deep the waking in the worlded clouds. | 26 | 25 | 16 | 32 | 5 |
| Of tide-tongued heads and bladders in the deep, | 30 | 16 | 18 | 35 | 16 |
| Goes over the hill into the deep sea; | 64 | 5 | 39 | 73 | 5 |
| Flood of her heart's fame; she would lie dumb and deep | 87 | 19 | 52 | 96 | 19 |
| When you sew the deep door. The bed is a cross place. | 97 | 13 | 59 | 108 | 13 |
| Shall drown in a grief as deep as his true grave, | 100 | 18 | 61 | 111 | 18 |
| Deep with the first dead lies London's daughter, | 101 | 19 | 62 | 112 | 19 |
| And the second comers, the severers, the enemies from the deep | 115 | 22 | 69 | 127 | 22 |
| Deep hillocks and loud on the numbed lakes, | 122 | 17 | 72 | 135 | 17 |
| That once cut the figures of birds on the deep bread | 123 | 4 | 72 | 136 | 14 |
| And deep | 145 | 8 | 82 | 162 | 8 |
| Quaked the sick sea and snouted deep, | 151 | 2 | 83 | 168 | 10 |
| Deep the great bushed bait with raining lips | 151 | 3 | 83 | 168 | 11 |
| Sleep, good, for ever, slow and deep, spelled rare and wise, | 162 | 8 | 86 | 181 | 8 |
| Deep in its black, base bones, | 173 | 7 | 88 | 193 | 7 |
| DEEPEST | | | | | |
| One who called deepest down shall hold his peace | 117 | 9 | 71 | 129 | 9 |
| O deepest wound of all that he should die | | | 91 | 201 | 16 |
| DEEPSEA | | | | | |
| Her deepsea pillow where once she married alone, | 127 | 9 | 75 | 141 | 9 |

| | U.K. Page | U.K. Line | Poem | U.S. Page | U.S. Line |
|---|---|---|---|---|---|
| **DEER** | | | | | |
| The dingle furred deer dead! | ix | 5 | 1 | xvii | 5 |
| The greenwood dying as the deer fall in their tracks, | 49 | 11 | 29 | 58 | 11 |
| And fast through the drifts of the thickets antlered like deer, | 122 | 15 | 72 | 135 | 15 |
| **DEFEAT** | | | | | |
| And that is true after perpetual defeat. | 48 | 9 | 28 | 56 | 9 |
| **DEFYING** | | | | | |
| So fast I move defying time, the quiet gentleman | 63 | 14 | 38 | 72 | 14 |
| **DELIVER** | | | | | |
| Deliver me who, timid in my tribe, | 18 | 7 | 12 | 21 | 7 |
| Deliver me, my masters, head and heart, | 18 | 11 | 12 | 21 | 11 |
| Deliver him, he cried, | 120 | 26 | 72 | 133 | 11 |
| **DELIVERED** | | | | | |
| Delivered seas my love from her proud place | 80 | 9 | 46 | 89 | 17 |
| **DELL** | | | | | |
| Or skulks in the dell moon but moonshine echoing clear | 163 | 2 | 86 | 182 | 2 |
| **DELUDES** | | | | | |
| She deludes the heaven-proof house with entering clouds | 108 | 6 | 66 | 119 | 6 |
| Yet she deludes with walking the nightmarish room, | 108 | 7 | 66 | 119 | 7 |
| **DELUGING** | | | | | |
| To mourn his deluging | 146 | 4 | 82 | 163 | 4 |
| **DELUSIVE** | | | | | |
| Who admits the delusive light through the bouncing wall, | 108 | 11 | 66 | 119 | 11 |
| **DEN** | | | | | |
| You have kicked from a dark den, leaped up the whinnying light, | 92 | 15 | 55 | 101 | 21 |
| **DENIALS** | | | | | |
| Counting the denials of the grains | 155 | 16 | 83 | 173 | 20 |
| **DENIERS** | | | | | |
| We are the dark deniers, let us summon | 2 | 7 | 2 | 2 | 7 |
| Doom on deniers at the wind-turned statement. | 74 | 20 | 44 | 83 | 20 |
| **DENS** | | | | | |
| The dens of shape | 55 | 1 | 33 | 64 | 4 |
| **DENY** | | | | | |
| And a continent deny? | 43 | 2 | 24 | 50 | 9 |
| And a continent deny? | 43 | 9 | 24 | 50 | 16 |
| **DEPARTED** | | | | | |
| In the departed villages. The nightingale, | 121 | 2 | 72 | 133 | 17 |
| On the departed, snow bushed green, wanton in moon light | 121 | 17 | 72 | 134 | 12 |

| | U.K. | | | U.S. | |
|---|---|---|---|---|---|
| | Page | Line | Poem | Page | Line |
| **DEPARTING** | | | | | |
| Sail on the level, the departing adventure, | 36 | 11 | 20 | 41 | 11 |
| **DEPENDING** | | | | | |
| Ball of the foot depending from the sun, | 19 | 18 | 12 | 23 | 3 |
| **DERIDE** | | | | | |
| And the grave sea, mock who deride | 82 | 2 | 48 | 91 | 2 |
| **DESCENDED** | | | | | |
| Dipped me breast-deep in the descended bone; | 72 | 14 | 44 | 81 | 14 |
| And the bird descended. | 122 | 26 | 72 | 136 | 6 |
| **DESCENDING** | | | | | |
| No, no, you lover skull, descending hammer | 19 | 2 | 12 | 22 | 7 |
| Of the descending day, the dark our folly, | 109 | 19 | 67 | 120 | 19 |
| **DESCENDS** | | | | | |
| Descends, my masters, on the entered honour. | 19 | 3 | 12 | 22 | 8 |
| Hold hard, my county darlings, for a hawk descends, | 49 | 22 | 29 | 58 | 22 |
| **DESERT** | | | | | |
| Weeps on the desert ochre and the salt | 31 | 8 | 18 | 36 | 8 |
| This was the resurrection in the desert, | 76 | 1 | 44 | 85 | 1 |
| Ribbed between desert and water storm, | 82 | 11 | 48 | 91 | 11 |
| **DESERTS** | | | | | |
| To choke the deserts with her tides, | 2 | 17 | 2 | 2 | 17 |
| **DESIGNED** | | | | | |
| Round the sun, he comes to my love like the designed snow, | 165 | 25 | 86 | 185 | 15 |
| Comes designed to my love to steal not her tide raking | 166 | 1 | 86 | 186 | 1 |
| **DESIRE** | | | | | |
| Of shades, symbol of desire beyond my hours | 110 | 7 | 67 | 121 | 9 |
| That the phoenix' bid for heaven and the desire after | 110 | 17 | 67 | 121 | 19 |
| No longer will the vibrations of the sun desire on | 127 | 8 | 75 | 141 | 8 |
| With no more desire than a ghost. | 154 | 4 | 83 | 172 | 4 |
| **DESIRELESS** | | | | | |
| A desireless familiar | 107 | 15 | 65 | 118 | 15 |
| **DESIRERS** | | | | | |
| Save by their long desirers in the fox cubbed | 178 | 15 | 90 | 199 | 16 |
| **DESIRES** | | | | | |
| Knew all His horrible desires | 69 | 10 | 43 | 78 | 10 |
| **DESIRING** | | | | | |
| In the always desiring centre of the white | 120 | 23 | 72 | 133 | 8 |
| **DESOLATE** | | | | | |
| Shakes a desolate boy who slits his throat | 87 | 7 | 52 | 96 | 7 |
| **DESOLATION** | | | | | |
| Make desolation in the vein, | 39 | 12 | 21 | 45 | 12 |
| **DESPAIR** | | | | | |
| Despair of blood, faith in the maiden's slime, | 18 | 23 | 12 | 22 | 3 |

|  | U.K. | | | U.S. | |
| --- | --- | --- | --- | --- | --- |
|  | *Page* | *Line* | *Poem* | *Page* | *Line* |
| DESTINY | | | | | |
| War on the destiny of man! | 66 | 15 | 40 | 75 | 15 |
| DESTROYER | | | | | |
| Is my destroyer. | 9 | 3 | 6 | 10 | 3 |
| DESTROYING | | | | | |
| Do you not father me on the destroying sand? | 47 | 1 | 27 | 55 | 1 |
| DESTRUCTION | | | | | |
| And the slug should teach me destruction. | 45 | 13 | 26 | 53 | 13 |
| Destruction, picked by birds, brays through the jaw-bone, | 79 | 10 | 46 | 88 | 13 |
| DEVIL | | | | | |
| I would not fear the devil in the loin | 12 | 20 | 9 | 13 | 20 |
| Bearding the unborn devil, | 32 | 3 | 18 | 37 | 9 |
| Thus the shadowless man or ox, and the pictured devil, | 35 | 22 | 20 | 40 | 22 |
| Incarnate devil in a talking snake, | 40 | 1 | 22 | 46 | 1 |
| Incarnate devil | 40 | | 22 | 46 | |
| DEVIL'S | | | | | |
| This world is half the devil's and my own, | 13 | 1 | 9 | 14 | 8 |
| DEVILISH | | | | | |
| Through the devilish years and innocent deaths | 93 | 14 | 56 | 102 | 14 |
| DEW | | | | | |
| Wind in me leaped, the hellborn dew; | 7 | 16 | 5 | 8 | 16 |
| Puffing the pounds of manna up through the dew to heaven, | 94 | 5 | 57 | 104 | 5 |
| Stream with bells and baying water bounds. The dew rings | 121 | 7 | 72 | 134 | 2 |
| That belled and bounded with the fossil and the dew reborn. | 123 | 10 | 72 | 136 | 20 |
| With the dew, come back, the cock on his shoulder: it was all | 160 | 7 | 85 | 179 | 7 |
| Out of a lair in the flocked leaves in the dew dipped year | 162 | 6 | 86 | 181 | 6 |
| And mire of love, but the Thief as meek as the dew. | 163 | 15 | 86 | 182 | 15 |
| And sly as snow and meek as dew blown to the thorn, | 164 | 1 | 86 | 183 | 8 |
| Through the haygold stalls, as the dew falls on the wind- | 164 | 9 | 86 | 183 | 16 |
| The Thief fall on the dead like the willy nilly dew, | 165 | 22 | 86 | 185 | 12 |
| Fall and the dew larks sing | 173 | 21 | 88 | 193 | 21 |
| DEW'S | | | | | |
| Flows to the strand of flowers like the dew's ruly sea, | 165 | 27 | 86 | 185 | 17 |
| DIAMOND | | | | | |
| Who picks the live heart on a diamond. | 79 | 19 | 46 | 88 | 22 |

|  | U.K. Page | U.K. Line | Poem | U.S. Page | U.S. Line |
|---|---|---|---|---|---|
| **DICTATORSHIP** | | | | | |
| Dictatorship of sun. | 65 | 13 | 40 | 74 | 13 |
| **DICTIONARY** | | | | | |
| What is the metre of the dictionary? | 72 | 19 | 44 | 81 | 19 |
| **DID** | | | | | |
| As yet ungotten, I did suffer; | 7 | 19 | 5 | 8 | 19 |
| Did twist into a living cipher, | 7 | 21 | 5 | 8 | 21 |
| Youth did condense; the tears of spring | 21 | 24 | 13 | 26 | 7 |
| These five kings did a king to death. | 62 | 4 | 37 | 71 | 4 |
| That did not nurse our bones, | 126 | 10 | 74 | 140 | 10 |
| Whatsoever I did in the coal- | 174 | 23 | 89 | 194 | 23 |
| The darkest way, and did not turn away, | | | 91 | 200 | 2 |
| Nor did he now, save to his secret wound. | | | 91 | 201 | 6 |
| **DIE** | | | | | |
| Till all our sea-faiths die. | 11 | 24 | 8 | 12 | 24 |
| When logics die, | 25 | 3 | 15 | 30 | 3 |
| Alone till the day I die | 58 | 6 | 35 | 67 | 6 |
| Or stay till the day I die | 58 | 23 | 35 | 67 | 23 |
| Or stay till the day I die? | 59 | 6 | 35 | 68 | 6 |
| By these I would not care to die, | 64 | 19 | 39 | 73 | 19 |
| They lying long shall not die windily; | 68 | 12 | 42 | 77 | 12 |
| Die in red feathers when the flying heaven's cut, | 92 | 12 | 55 | 101 | 18 |
| Dressed to die, the sensual strut begun, | 99 | 6 | 60 | 110 | 6 |
| Die in unjudging love. | 106 | 12 | 64 | 117 | 12 |
| Was the first to die | 130 | 15 | 77 | 144 | 15 |
| Die. | 142 | 17 | 82 | 159 | 17 |
| Come let us die.' | 168 | 8 | 87 | 188 | 12 |
| As I sail out to die. | 173 | 27 | 88 | 193 | 27 |
| Too proud to die; broken and blind he died | | | 91 | 200 | 1 |
| O deepest wound of all that he should die | | | 91 | 201 | 16 |
| Until I die he will not leave my side.) | | | 91 | 201 | 19 |
| **DIED** | | | | | |
| I dreamed my genesis and died again, shrapnel | 28 | 13 | 17 | 33 | 13 |
| Her fist of a face died clenched on a round pain; | 88 | 6 | 52 | 97 | 6 |
| The tombstone told when she died. | 93 | 1 | 56 | 102 | 1 |
| I died before bedtime came | 93 | 26 | 56 | 103 | 6 |
| When black birds died like priests in the cloaked hedge row | 122 | 12 | 72 | 135 | 12 |
| In a choir of wings, as though she slept or died, | 123 | 12 | 72 | 137 | 2 |
| On to the ground when a man died | 125 | 21 | 74 | 139 | 21 |
| He put on his clothes and stepped out and he died, | 135 | 2 | 80 | 152 | 2 |
| And died on a hiss of flames | 155 | 14 | 83 | 173 | 18 |
| Too proud to die; broken and blind he died | | | 91 | 200 | 1 |
| Being innocent, he dreaded that he died | | | 91 | 201 | 1 |
| He cried as he died, fearing at last the spheres' | | | 91 | 201 | 12 |
| The tombstone told when she died | 93 | | 56 | 102 | |

|  | U.K. Page | U.K. Line | Poem | U.S. Page | U.S. Line |
|---|---|---|---|---|---|
| **DIES** |  |  |  |  |  |
| Here love's damp muscle dries and dies, | 2 | 22 | 2 | 3 | 4 |
| For the sleep in a safe land and the love who dies | 100 | 10 | 61 | 111 | 10 |
| In deathbeds of orchards the boat dies down | 157 | 15 | 83 | 176 | 7 |
| **DIG** |  |  |  |  |  |
| Dig no more for the chains of his grey-haired heart. | 135 | 9 | 80 | 152 | 9 |
| **DILLY** |  |  |  |  |  |
| Shallow and sedge, and 'dilly dilly,' calls the loft hawk, | 167 | 21 | 87 | 188 | 2 |
| Green chickens of the bay and bushes cluck, 'dilly dilly, | 168 | 7 | 87 | 188 | 11 |
| **DIN** |  |  |  |  |  |
| Of the nightingale's din and tale! The upgiven ghost | 165 | 3 | 86 | 184 | 11 |
| Hill of cypresses! The din and tale in the skimmed | 165 | 5 | 86 | 184 | 13 |
| **DING** |  |  |  |  |  |
| Ding dong from the mute turrets. | 83 | 24 | 49 | 93 | 6 |
| **DINGLE** |  |  |  |  |  |
| The dingle furred deer dead! | ix | 5 | 1 | xvii | 5 |
| The night above the dingle starry, | 159 | 3 | 85 | 178 | 3 |
| Nor the innocent lie in the rooting dingle wooed | 162 | 15 | 86 | 181 | 15 |
| Of the dingle torn to singing and the surpliced | 165 | 4 | 86 | 184 | 12 |
| I young Aesop fabling to the near night by the dingle | 168 | 11 | 87 | 188 | 15 |
| **DINNED** |  |  |  |  |  |
| Dinned aside the coiling crowd, | 134 | 3 | 79 | 150 | 3 |
| **DIP** |  |  |  |  |  |
| And fled their love in a weaving dip. | 151 | 5 | 83 | 168 | 13 |
| **DIPPED** |  |  |  |  |  |
| Dipped me breast-deep in the descended bone; | 72 | 14 | 44 | 81 | 14 |
| Out of a lair in the flocked leaves in the dew dipped year | 162 | 6 | 86 | 181 | 6 |
| **DIPPING** |  |  |  |  |  |
| Dipping moon and drunk as a new dropped calf, | 174 | 17 | 89 | 194 | 17 |
| **DIRECTED** |  |  |  |  |  |
| Am I not all of you by the directed sea | 46 | 13 | 27 | 54 | 13 |
| **DIRECTION** |  |  |  |  |  |
| Bend, if my journey ache, direction like an arc or make | 97 | 14 | 59 | 108 | 14 |
| In the final direction of the elementary town | 99 | 8 | 60 | 110 | 8 |
| **DIRECTLY** |  |  |  |  |  |
| There is loud and dark directly under the dumb flame, | 83 | 13 | 49 | 92 | 13 |
| **DIRT** |  |  |  |  |  |
| Lovers in the dirt of their leafy beds, | 89 | 9 | 53 | 98 | 9 |

| | U.K. | | | U.S. | |
|---|---|---|---|---|---|
| | Page | Line | Poem | Page | Line |
| DISAPPOINT | | | | | |
| All could not disappoint; | 48 | 6 | 28 | 56 | 6 |
| DISCIPLE | | | | | |
| Ducked in the twelve, disciple seas | 69 | 4 | 43 | 78 | 4 |
| DISCORDANT | | | | | |
| Down breeze and shell to a discordant beach, | 81 | 7 | 47 | 90 | 7 |
| DISCOVERED | | | | | |
| The natural circle of the discovered skies | 91 | 10 | 55 | 100 | 10 |
| DISGUISED | | | | | |
| In common clay clothes disguised as scales, | 132 | 15 | 78 | 147 | 15 |
| DISHEVELLED | | | | | |
| Grief with dishevelled hands tear out the altar ghost | 83 | 5 | 49 | 92 | 5 |
| DISHONOURS | | | | | |
| Shames and the damp dishonours, the relic scraping. | 37 | 20 | 20 | 43 | 3 |
| DISHRAG | | | | | |
| Woe drip from the dishrag hands and the pressed sponge of the forehead, | 96 | 20 | 58 | 107 | 3 |
| DISK | | | | | |
| Flies on the shafted disk, declaims the morning | 16 | 19 | 11 | 19 | 19 |
| Let the wax disk babble | 37 | 19 | 20 | 43 | 2 |
| DISPELLED | | | | | |
| The next-door sea dispelled | 134 | 6 | 79 | 150 | 6 |
| DISPLACED | | | | | |
| While you displaced a truth in the air, | 107 | 17 | 65 | 118 | 17 |
| DISSOLVED | | | | | |
| Dissolved in summer and the hundred seasons; | 21 | 25 | 13 | 26 | 8 |
| DISSOLVING | | | | | |
| Golden dissolving under the water veil. | 115 | 9 | 69 | 127 | 9 |
| DISTANT | | | | | |
| Of eels, saint heron hymning in the shell-hung distant | 168 | 12 | 87 | 188 | 16 |
| DISTEMPER | | | | | |
| Man should be cured of distemper. | 48 | 27 | 28 | 57 | 4 |
| DISTURB | | | | | |
| Disturb no winding-sheets, my son, | 65 | 6 | 40 | 74 | 6 |
| DISTURBS | | | | | |
| Disturbs this island's rest. | 58 | 16 | 35 | 67 | 16 |
| DITCH | | | | | |
| Over the whirling ditch of daybreak | 131 | 15 | 77 | 145 | 21 |
| DITCHES | | | | | |
| Midwives grew in the midnight ditches, | 174 | 19 | 89 | 194 | 19 |
| DIVE | | | | | |
| The flickering runs and dive | ix | 4 | 1 | xvii | 4 |
| As they dive, the dust settles, | 36 | 19 | 20 | 41 | 19 |
| Will dive up to his tears. | 117 | 18 | 71 | 129 | 18 |

124

| | U.K. | | | U.S. | |
|---|---|---|---|---|---|
| | Page | Line | Poem | Page | Line |
| Dolphins dive in their turnturtle dust, | 171 | 6 | 88 | 191 | 6 |
| DIVED | | | | | |
| High tide and the heron dived when I took the road | 102 | 17 | 63 | 113 | 17 |
| She nipped and dived in the nick of love, | 151 | 7 | 83 | 168 | 15 |
| DIVER | | | | | |
| To-morrow's diver in her horny milk, | 30 | 4 | 18 | 35 | 4 |
| DIVER'S | | | | | |
| Sweetly the diver's bell in the steeple of spindrift | 37 | 11 | 20 | 42 | 17 |
| DIVES | | | | | |
| The anchor dives through the floors of a church. | 157 | 20 | 83 | 176 | 12 |
| DIVIDE | | | | | |
| Divide the night and day with fairy thumbs; | 1 | 15 | 2 | 1 | 15 |
| DIVIDED | | | | | |
| In trust and tale have I divided sense, | 41 | 5 | 23 | 47 | 5 |
| DIVINELY | | | | | |
| Dumbly and divinely stumbling | 42 | 6 | 24 | 49 | 6 |
| Dumbly and divinely leaping | 42 | 13 | 24 | 49 | 13 |
| DIVING | | | | | |
| Green as beginning, let the garden diving | 76 | 19 | 44 | 85 | 19 |
| Pierce the spilt sky with diving wing in weed and heel | 86 | 4 | 51 | 95 | 4 |
| DIVINING | | | | | |
| Divining in a smile the oil of tears. | 24 | 18 | 15 | 29 | 18 |
| The rod bends low, divining land, | 155 | 21 | 83 | 174 | 5 |
| DIVORCING | | | | | |
| From the divorcing sky I learnt the double, | 21 | 20 | 13 | 26 | 3 |
| DO | | | | | |
| Do you not father me, nor the erected arm | 46 | 1 | 27 | 54 | 1 |
| Do you not mother me, nor, as I am, | 46 | 3 | 27 | 54 | 3 |
| Do you not sister me, nor the erected crime | 46 | 5 | 27 | 54 | 5 |
| Do you not brother me, nor, as you climb, | 46 | 7 | 27 | 54 | 7 |
| Do you not father me on the destroying sand? | 47 | 1 | 27 | 55 | 1 |
| The five kings count the dead but do not soften | 62 | 13 | 37 | 71 | 13 |
| But do not travel down dumb wind like prodigals. | 86 | 11 | 51 | 95 | 11 |
| Do not go gentle into that good night, | 116 | 1 | 70 | 128 | 1 |
| Do not go gentle into that good night. | 116 | 6 | 70 | 128 | 6 |
| Do not go gentle into that good night. | 116 | 12 | 70 | 128 | 12 |
| Do not go gentle into that good night. | 116 | 18 | 70 | 128 | 18 |
| Silence, silence to do, when earth grew loud, | 125 | 15 | 74 | 139 | 15 |
| Hale dead and deathless do the women of the hill | 178 | 17 | 90 | 199 | 18 |
| Do you not father me | 46 | | 27 | 54 | |
| Do not go gentle into that good night | 116 | | 70 | 128 | |
| DODGING | | | | | |
| Dodging the park keeper | 111 | 23 | 68 | 123 | 23 |

| | U.K. | | | U.S. | |
|---|---|---|---|---|---|
| | *Page* | *Line* | *Poem* | *Page* | *Line* |
| DOES | | | | | |
| From the stone nest it does not let the feathery | 86 | 2 | 51 | 95 | 2 |
| Their breast, the vaulting docs roister, the horned bucks climb | 177 | 13 | 90 | 198 | 12 |
| DOG | | | | | |
| And, from his fork, a dog among the fairies, | 71 | 4 | 44 | 80 | 4 |
| Slept at night in a dog kennel | 111 | 11 | 68 | 123 | 11 |
| And the old dog sleeper | 112 | 1 | 68 | 124 | 1 |
| DOG'S | | | | | |
| Groping for matter under the dog's plate, | 48 | 26 | 28 | 57 | 3 |
| DOGDAYED | | | | | |
| Into the dogdayed night. | viii | 7 | 1 | xvi | 7 |
| There from their hearts the dogdayed pulse | 1 | 22 | 2 | 1 | 22 |
| DOING | | | | | |
| Doing what they are told, | 170 | 12 | 88 | 190 | 12 |
| DOLPHIN'S | | | | | |
| Clash out the mounting dolphin's day, | 152 | 3 | 83 | 169 | 15 |
| DOLPHINED | | | | | |
| Cry to the dolphined sea. | 11 | 18 | 8 | 12 | 18 |
| DOLPHINS | | | | | |
| Dolphins dive in their turnturtle dust, | 171 | 6 | 88 | 191 | 6 |
| DOME | | | | | |
| Swung by my father from his dome. | 7 | 12 | 5 | 8 | 12 |
| Hauled to the dome, | 18 | 5 | 12 | 21 | 5 |
| I damp the waxlights in your tower dome. | 19 | 11 | 12 | 22 | 16 |
| DOMED | | | | | |
| And out of every domed and soil-based shell | 115 | 5 | 69 | 127 | 5 |
| DOMES | | | | | |
| The nightbird lauds through nunneries and domes of leaves | 163 | 5 | 86 | 182 | 5 |
| And the lost, moonshine domes, | 173 | 5 | 88 | 193 | 5 |
| And the mole snout blunt under his pilgrimage of domes, | 177 | 16 | 90 | 198 | 15 |
| DOMINION | | | | | |
| Great is the hand that holds dominion over | 62 | 11 | 37 | 71 | 11 |
| And death shall have no dominion. | 68 | 1 | 42 | 77 | 1 |
| And death shall have no dominion. | 68 | 9 | 42 | 77 | 9 |
| And death shall have no dominion. | 68 | 10 | 42 | 77 | 10 |
| And death shall have no dominion. | 68 | 18 | 42 | 77 | 18 |
| And death shall have no dominion. | 68 | 19 | 42 | 77 | 19 |
| And death shall have no dominion. | 68 | 27 | 42 | 77 | 27 |
| And death shall have no dominion | 68 | | 42 | 77 | |
| DONE | | | | | |
| There was calm to be done in his safe unrest, | 125 | 11 | 74 | 139 | 11 |
| DONG | | | | | |
| Ding dong from the mute turrets. | 83 | 24 | 49 | 93 | 6 |

| | U.K. | | | U.S. | |
|---|---|---|---|---|---|
| | *Page* | *Line* | *Poem* | *Page* | *Line* |
| DONKEYS' | | | | | |
| Ninepin down on the donkeys' common, | 174 | 7 | 89 | 194 | 7 |
| DONS | | | | | |
| Daws Sir John's just hill dons, and again the gulled birds hare | 167 | 15 | 87 | 187 | 15 |
| DOOM | | | | | |
| Sir, is your doom. | 19 | 15 | 12 | 22 | 20 |
| Beginning with doom in the bulb, the spring unravels, | 35 | 7 | 20 | 40 | 7 |
| Beginning with doom in the ghost, and the springing marvels, | 35 | 13 | 20 | 40 | 13 |
| Doom on the sun!' | 66 | 16 | 40 | 75 | 16 |
| Doom on deniers at the wind-turned statement. | 74 | 20 | 44 | 83 | 20 |
| DOOR | | | | | |
| Hands grumble on the door, | 58 | 2 | 35 | 67 | 2 |
| Hands grumble on the door, | 59 | 1 | 35 | 68 | 1 |
| When you sew the deep door. The bed is a cross place. | 97 | 13 | 59 | 108 | 13 |
| Bolting the night of the door with her arm her plume. | 108 | 4 | 66 | 119 | 4 |
| In the long ago land that glided the dark door wide | 121 | 12 | 72 | 134 | 7 |
| In the far ago land the door of his death glided wide, | 122 | 25 | 72 | 136 | 5 |
| He stands alone at the door of his home, | 157 | 23 | 83 | 176 | 15 |
| DOORS | | | | | |
| And the doors burn in their brain. | 124 | 12 | 73 | 138 | 12 |
| Ride through the doors of our unentered house. | 126 | 14 | 74 | 140 | 14 |
| DOORWAY | | | | | |
| In the groin of the natural doorway I crouched like a tailor | 99 | 3 | 60 | 110 | 3 |
| DOUBLE | | | | | |
| Sits in their double shade. | 6 | 21 | 4 | 7 | 3 |
| From the divorcing sky I learnt the double, | 21 | 20 | 13 | 26 | 3 |
| The scales of this twin world tread on the double, | 35 | 4 | 20 | 40 | 4 |
| Suffer, my topsy-turvies, that a double angel | 37 | 26 | 20 | 43 | 9 |
| Slapped down the guillotine, the blood-red double | 41 | 6 | 23 | 47 | 6 |
| The warm-veined double of Time | 134 | 11 | 79 | 150 | 11 |
| DOUBLED | | | | | |
| Doubled the globe of dead and halved a country; | 62 | 3 | 37 | 71 | 3 |
| Doubled, to fork him back, through the lockjaw bed | 79 | 24 | 46 | 89 | 5 |
| DOUBLECROSSED | | | | | |
| And doublecrossed my mother's womb. | 8 | 22 | 5 | 9 | 22 |

DOUBLES

|  |  |  | U.K. | | Poem | U.S. | |
|  |  |  | Page | Line |  | Page | Line |
| **DOUBLES** | | | | | | | |
| Half of the fellow father as he doubles | | | 30 | 1 | 18 | 35 | 1 |
| In time at flood filled with his coloured doubles; | | | 61 | 3 | 36 | 70 | 3 |
| **DOUBT** | | | | | | | |
| Of doubt and dark they feed their nerves; | | | 1 | 11 | 2 | 1 | 11 |
| **DOUSING** | | | | | | | |
| Winds, from the dousing shade and the roarer at the latch, | | | 163 | 23 | 86 | 183 | 4 |
| **DOVE** | | | | | | | |
| O my ruffled ring dove | | | ix | 7 | 1 | xvii | 7 |
| Huloo, my prowed dove with a flute! | | | x | 14 | 1 | xviii | 20 |
| And Noah's rekindled now unkind dove | | | 113 | 5 | 69 | 125 | 5 |
| Whenever I dove in a breast high shoal, | | | 174 | 21 | 89 | 194 | 21 |
| Tidy and cursed in my dove cooed room | | | 175 | 23 | 89 | 196 | 4 |
| **DOVES** | | | | | | | |
| And the shipyards of Galilee's footprints hide a navy of doves. | | | 127 | 7 | 75 | 141 | 7 |
| **DOWN** | | | | | | | |
| This day winding down now | | | vii | 1 | 1 | xv | 1 |
| Down to the curlew herd! | | | ix | 12 | 1 | xvii | 12 |
| The fences of the light are down, | | | 5 | 16 | 3 | 5 | 16 |
| Forks half its fruit; and half droops down, | | | 6 | 14 | 4 | 6 | 14 |
| Pulls down the shabby curtains of the skin; | | | 6 | 23 | 4 | 7 | 5 |
| And I was struck down by death's feather. | | | 8 | 15 | 5 | 9 | 15 |
| You who bow down at cross and altar, | | | 8 | 19 | 5 | 9 | 19 |
| Down in the yard of day. | | | 14 | 16 | 10 | 16 | 16 |
| When, like a running grave, time tracks you down, | | | 18 | 1 | 12 | 21 | 1 |
| Man broke the sun, pulled the wind down. | | | 39 | 10 | 21 | 45 | 10 |
| And played down pardon from the heavens' hill. | | | 40 | 6 | 22 | 46 | 6 |
| Slapped down the guillotine, the blood-red double | | | 41 | 6 | 23 | 47 | 6 |
| No god-in-hero tumble down | | | 42 | 4 | 24 | 49 | 4 |
| No god-in-hero tumble down | | | 42 | 11 | 24 | 49 | 11 |
| Down pelts the naked weather; | | | 45 | 3 | 26 | 53 | 3 |
| But not of grief, for I have knocked down that | | | 48 | 2 | 28 | 56 | 2 |
| Down fall four padding weathers on the scarlet lands, | | | 49 | 19 | 29 | 58 | 19 |
| Nor weather winds that blow not down the bone, | | | 60 | 2 | 36 | 69 | 2 |
| I laid her down and told her sin, | | | 65 | 23 | 40 | 74 | 23 |
| And the sky lays down her laws, | | | 66 | 10 | 40 | 75 | 10 |
| Sneak down the stallion grave, | | | 67 | 18 | 41 | 76 | 18 |
| No silver whistles chase him down the weeks' | | | 67 | 21 | 41 | 76 | 21 |
| Break in the sun till the sun breaks down, | | | 68 | 26 | 42 | 70 | 26 |
| Horned down with skullfoot and the skull of toes | | | 72 | 9 | 44 | 81 | 9 |
| A climbing sea from Asia had me down | | | 73 | 19 | 44 | 82 | 19 |

| | U.K. | | | U.S. | |
|---|---|---|---|---|---|
| | Page | Line | Poem | Page | Line |
| Down the stacked sea and water-pillared shade, | 79 | 14 | 46 | 88 | 17 |
| Down breeze and shell to a discordant beach, | 81 | 7 | 47 | 90 | 7 |
| But do not travel down dumb wind like prodigals. | 86 | 11 | 51 | 95 | 11 |
| Grave's foot, blinds down the lids, the teeth in black, | 87 | 4 | 52 | 96 | 4 |
| Bow down the walls of the ferned and foxy woods | 87 | 24 | 52 | 96 | 24 |
| Draw down to its weird eyes? | 91 | 11 | 55 | 100 | 11 |
| And clap its great blood down; | 92 | 3 | 55 | 101 | 9 |
| Ancient woods of my blood, dash down to the nut of the seas | 94 | 11 | 57 | 104 | 11 |
| Drivelled down to one singeing tree | 95 | 20 | 58 | 105 | 20 |
| Nor blaspheme down the stations of the breath | 101 | 16 | 62 | 112 | 16 |
| And down the other air and the blue altered sky | 103 | 17 | 63 | 114 | 17 |
| Down the beginning of plants | 106 | 6 | 64 | 117 | 6 |
| Like the water he sat down | 111 | 14 | 68 | 123 | 14 |
| Into her lying down head | 113 | 1 | 69 | 125 | 1 |
| There the dark blade and wanton sighing her down | 113 | 16 | 69 | 125 | 16 |
| One who called deepest down shall hold his peace | 117 | 9 | 71 | 129 | 9 |
| And fires where he should prowl down the cloud | 120 | 12 | 72 | 132 | 17 |
| Though no sound flowed down the hand folded air | 120 | 15 | 72 | 132 | 20 |
| Rags and prayers down the knee- | 122 | 16 | 72 | 135 | 16 |
| Exultation lies down. Time buries the spring weather | 123 | 9 | 72 | 136 | 19 |
| Down the long walks of their vows. | 124 | 4 | 73 | 138 | 4 |
| For a man sleeps where fire leapt down and she learns through his arm | 127 | 13 | 75 | 141 | 13 |
| Now shown and mostly bare I would lie down, | 133 | 21 | 78 | 149 | 4 |
| Lie down, lie down and live | 133 | 22 | 78 | 149 | 5 |
| Slashed down the last snake as though | 134 | 13 | 79 | 150 | 13 |
| Bone writhes down | 139 | 3 | 82 | 156 | 3 |
| Down to the river rooting plain | 145 | 16 | 82 | 162 | 16 |
| Christens down | 148 | 7 | 82 | 165 | 7 |
| The bows glided down, and the coast | 149 | 1 | 83 | 166 | 1 |
| Now cast down your rod, for the whole | 150 | 7 | 83 | 167 | 11 |
| Till every beast blared down in a swerve | 151 | 9 | 83 | 168 | 17 |
| Up and down the greater waves | 156 | 11 | 83 | 174 | 19 |
| Down, down, down, under the ground, | 157 | 9 | 83 | 176 | 1 |
| In deathbeds of orchards the boat dies down | 157 | 15 | 83 | 176 | 7 |
| Down the rivers of the windfall light. | 159 | 9 | 85 | 178 | 9 |
| The rippled seals streak down | 171 | 7 | 88 | 191 | 7 |
| Ninepin down on the donkeys' common, | 174 | 7 | 89 | 194 | 7 |
| And I lie down but to sleep in bed, | 175 | 6 | 89 | 195 | 11 |

129

DOWN (continued)

|  | U.K. | | | U.S. | |
|---|---|---|---|---|---|
|  | *Page* | *Line* | *Poem* | *Page* | *Line* |
| I lie down thin and hear the good bells jaw— | 175 | 24 | 89 | 196 | 5 |
| To labour and love though they lay down long ago. | 176 | 5 | 90 | 197 | 5 |
| Now curlew cry me down to kiss the mouths of their dust. | 178 | 4 | 90 | 199 | 5 |
| Who heard the tall bell sail down the Sundays of the dead | 178 | 10 | 90 | 199 | 11 |
| On whom a world of ills came down like snow. |  |  | 91 | 201 | 11 |
| Into her Lying Down Head | 113 |  | 69 | 125 |  |
| DOWNED |  |  |  |  |  |
| Pack back the downed bone. If the unpricked ball of my breath | 97 | 2 | 59 | 108 | 2 |
| A she bird dawned, and her breast with snow and scarlet downed. | 121 | 15 | 72 | 134 | 10 |
| DOWNFALL |  |  |  |  |  |
| (Sighed the old ram rod, dying of downfall), | 175, | 10 | 89 | 195 | 15 |
| DOWNWARD |  |  |  |  |  |
| The stoved bones' voyage downward | 38 | 9 | 20 | 43 | 19 |
| DOWNY |  |  |  |  |  |
| Under his downy arm you sighed as he struck, | 125 | 19 | 74 | 139 | 19 |
| DOWSE |  |  |  |  |  |
| The scurrying, furred small friars squeal, in the dowse | 177 | 11 | 90 | 198 | 10 |
| DRAGGING |  |  |  |  |  |
| Dragging him up the stairs to one who lies dead. | 100 | 20 | 61 | 111 | 20 |
| DRAGS |  |  |  |  |  |
| See what the gold gut drags from under | 154 | 11 | 83 | 172 | 11 |
| DRAINED |  |  |  |  |  |
| The heart is drained that, spelling in the scurry | 17 | 6 | 11 | 20 | 6 |
| DRAINS |  |  |  |  |  |
| Sheds the syllabic blood and drains her words. | 16 | 8 | 11 | 19 | 8 |
| DRAKED |  |  |  |  |  |
| And ducked and draked white lake that harps to a hail stone. | 177 | 8 | 90 | 198 | 7 |
| DRAMATIC |  |  |  |  |  |
| By a dramatic sea. | 70 | 8 | 43 | 79 | 12 |
| DRANK |  |  |  |  |  |
| Sails drank the wind, and white as milk | 149 | 13 | 83 | 166 | 13 |
| As the sails drank up the hail of thunder | 154 | 7 | 83 | 172 | 7 |
| DRAW |  |  |  |  |  |
| Draw in their seas, | 55 | 11 | 33 | 64 | 14 |
| Draw on the glove of prints, dead Cairo's henna | 75 | 23 | 44 | 84 | 23 |
| Draw down to its weird eyes? | 91 | 11 | 55 | 100 | 11 |
| The breath draw back like a bolt through white oil | 96 | 21 | 58 | 107 | 4 |
| DRAWN |  |  |  |  |  |
| By magnet winds to her blind mother drawn, | 78 | 14 | 46 | 87 | 14 |

| | U.K. | | | U.S. | |
|---|---|---|---|---|---|
| | *Page* | *Line* | *Poem* | *Page* | *Line* |
| The heavenly ambulance drawn by a wound | 135 | 10 | 80 | 152 | 10 |
| DREADED | | | | | |
| Being innocent, he dreaded that he died | | | 91 | 201 | 1 |
| DREAM | | | | | |
| He drowned his father's magics in a dream. | 4 | 18 | 3 | 4 | 18 |
| The dream has sucked the sleeper of his faith | 15 | 9 | 10 | 17 | 9 |
| The dream that kicks the buried from their sack | 15 | 14 | 10 | 17 | 14 |
| Rebel against my father's dream | 66 | 3 | 40 | 75 | 3 |
| DREAMED | | | | | |
| I dreamed my genesis in sweat of sleep, breaking | 28 | 1 | 17 | 33 | 1 |
| I dreamed my genesis and died again, shrapnel | 28 | 13 | 17 | 33 | 13 |
| I dreamed my genesis in sweat of death, fallen | 29 | 1 | 17 | 34 | 5 |
| I dreamed my genesis | 28 | | 17 | 33 | |
| DREAMING | | | | | |
| 'These are but dreaming men. Breathe, and they fade.' | 26 | 15 | 16 | 31 | 15 |
| I blew the dreaming fellows to their bed | 26 | 19 | 16 | 31 | 19 |
| And dropped on dreaming and the upward sky. | 26 | 5 | 16 | 31 | 5 |
| DREAMS | | | | | |
| The rack of dreams my lily bones | 7 | 20 | 5 | 8 | 20 |
| Our eunuch dreams, all seedless in the light, | 14 | 1 | 10 | 16 | 1 |
| Our eunuch dreams | 14 | | 10 | 16 | |
| DREGS | | | | | |
| The merriest marrow and the dregs | 65 | 3 | 40 | 74 | 3 |
| DRENCHED | | | | | |
| Grief with drenched book and candle christens the cherub time | 83 | 16 | 49 | 92 | 16 |
| Horses, centaur dead, turn and tread the drenched white | 121 | 19 | 72 | 134 | 14 |
| Crying at the man drenched throne | 140 | 7 | 82 | 157 | 7 |
| His decks are drenched with miracles. | 154 | 19 | 83 | 172 | 19 |
| DRESSED | | | | | |
| Dressed to die, the sensual strut begun, | 99 | 6 | 60 | 110 | 6 |
| DREW | | | | | |
| Drew in his eyes the straws of sleep, | 4 | 17 | 3 | 4 | 17 |
| I drew the white sheet over the islands | 134 | 29 | 79 | 151 | 7 |
| DRIES | | | | | |
| Here love's damp muscle dries and dies, | 2 | 22 | 2 | 3 | 4 |
| Drives my red blood; that dries the mouthing streams | 9 | 7 | 6 | 10 | 7 |
| Shall not be known till windwell dries | 53 | 2 | 32 | 62 | 2 |
| DRIFT | | | | | |
| To drift or drown upon the seas | 8 | 8 | 5 | 9 | 8 |
| Nor when my love lies in the cross-boned drift | 60 | 22 | 36 | 69 | 22 |
| That frozen wife whose juices drift like a fixed sea | 77 | 14 | 45 | 86 | 14 |
| DRIFTING | | | | | |
| On a star of faith pure as the drifting bread, | 119 | 12 | 72 | 131 | 12 |

| | U.K. | | | U.S. | |
|---|---|---|---|---|---|
| | *Page* | *Line* | *Poem* | *Page* | *Line* |
| Rejoicing for that drifting death | 152 | 16 | 83 | 170 | 8 |
| Clings to her drifting hair, and climbs; | 155 | 17 | 83 | 174 | 1 |
| DRIFTS | | | | | |
| And drown in the drifts of his need, and lie curled caught | 120 | 22 | 72 | 133 | 7 |
| And fast through the drifts of the thickets antlered like deer, | 122 | 15 | 72 | 135 | 15 |
| The long, laid minute's bride drifts on | 152 | 11 | 83 | 170 | 3 |
| DRIFTWOOD | | | | | |
| His driftwood thirty-fifth wind turned age; | 170 | 8 | 88 | 190 | 8 |
| DRILL | | | | | |
| As motor muscle on the drill, driving | 28 | 3 | 17 | 33 | 3 |
| Rotating halves are horning as they drill | 30 | 23 | 18 | 35 | 23 |
| DRILLED | | | | | |
| Whisper in a damp word, her wits drilled hollow, | 88 | 5 | 52 | 97 | 5 |
| DRINK | | | | | |
| My wine you drink, my bread you snap. | 39 | 15 | 21 | 45 | 15 |
| And drink in the two milked crags, | 65 | 2 | 40 | 74 | 2 |
| DRINKING | | | | | |
| Drinking Noah of the bay, | x | 2 | 1 | xviii | 8 |
| Drinking water from the chained cup | 111 | 8 | 68 | 123 | 8 |
| He sped into the drinking dark; | 149 | 14 | 83 | 166 | 14 |
| As the boat skims on with drinking wings! | 154 | 14 | 83 | 172 | 14 |
| DRIP | | | | | |
| Drip on my dead house garden. | 31 | 21 | 18 | 37 | 3 |
| Woe drip from the dishrag hands and the pressed sponge of the forehead, | 96 | 20 | 58 | 107 | 3 |
| DRIPS | | | | | |
| Love drips and gathers, but the fallen blood | 9 | 17 | 6 | 10 | 17 |
| DRIVE | | | | | |
| Or drive the night-geared forth. | 15 | 6 | 10 | 17 | 6 |
| Drive children up like bruises to the thumb, | 18 | 14 | 12 | 21 | 14 |
| The secret oils that drive the grass. | 22 | 18 | 14 | 27 | 18 |
| Out of the sea, the drive of oil, | 34 | 10 | 19 | 39 | 16 |
| As the green blooms ride upward, to the drive of time; | 49 | 3 | 29 | 58 | 3 |
| DRIVELLED | | | | | |
| Drivelled down to one singeing tree | 95 | 20 | 58 | 105 | 20 |
| DRIVEN | | | | | |
| And the face to the driven lover. | 33 | 24 | 19 | 39 | 6 |
| In that proud sailing tree with branches driven | 78 | 6 | 46 | 87 | 6 |
| DRIVES | | | | | |
| Drives in a death as life leaks out. | 6 | 9 | 4 | 6 | 9 |
| The force that through the green fuse drives the flower | 9 | 1 | 6 | 10 | 1 |
| Drives my green age; that blasts the roots of trees | 9 | 2 | 6 | 10 | 2 |

| | U.K. | | Poem | U.S. | |
|---|---|---|---|---|---|
| | Page | Line | | Page | Line |
| The force that drives the water through the rocks | 9 | 6 | 6 | 10 | 6 |
| Drives my red blood; that dries the mouthing streams | 9 | 7 | 6 | 10 | 7 |
| Drives forth my men, my children, from the hanging south. | 49 | 6 | 29 | 58 | 6 |
| She holding me? The people's sea drives on her, | 54 | 26 | 33 | 64 | 2 |
| Drives out the father from the caesared camp; | 54 | 27 | 33 | 64 | 3 |
| And a whirlpool drives the prayerwheel; | 83 | 9 | 49 | 92 | 9 |
| The force that through the green fuse drives the flower | 9 | | 6 | 10 | |
| DRIVING | | | | | |
| As motor muscle on the drill, driving | 28 | 3 | 17 | 33 | 3 |
| DROOPED | | | | | |
| And a tear-stained widower grief drooped from the lashes | 85 | 9 | 50 | 94 | 9 |
| DROOPING | | | | | |
| For the drooping of homes | 126 | 9 | 74 | 140 | 9 |
| DROOPS | | | | | |
| Forks half its fruit; and half droops down, | 6 | 14 | 4 | 6 | 14 |
| DROP | | | | | |
| Hold up the noisy sea and drop her birds, | 2 | 15 | 2 | 2 | 15 |
| And drop the plum like fire from the flesh. | 12 | 9 | 9 | 13 | 9 |
| Heir to the scalding veins that hold love's drop, costly | 28 | 9 | 17 | 33 | 9 |
| Magnified out of praise; her death was a still drop; | 87 | 17 | 52 | 96 | 17 |
| Sooner drop with the worm of the ropes round my throat | 97 | 4 | 59 | 108 | 4 |
| Time sings through the intricately dead snow drop. Listen. | 121 | 10 | 72 | 134 | 5 |
| In a hoisted cloud, at drop of dusk, he pulls to his claws | 167 | 3 | 87 | 187 | 3 |
| DROP'S | | | | | |
| And the blood drop's garden | 145 | 4 | 82 | 162 | 4 |
| DROPPED | | | | | |
| The boy she dropped from darkness at her side | 21 | 2 | 13 | 25 | 2 |
| And dropped on dreaming and the upward sky. | 26 | 5 | 16 | 31 | 5 |
| Shall a dropped stone drum on the ground, | 44 | 12 | 25 | 52 | 12 |
| Ruin, the room of errors, one rood dropped | 79 | 13 | 46 | 88 | 16 |
| He dropped where he loved on the burst pavement stone | 135 | 4 | 80 | 152 | 4 |
| Over the ghost and the dropped son | 137 | 8 | 82 | 154 | 8 |
| Dipping moon and drunk as a new dropped calf, | 174 | 17 | 89 | 194 | 17 |
| DROPPERS | | | | | |
| The famous stitch droppers. | 132 | 28 | 78 | 148 | 3 |

|  | U.K. | | | U.S. | |
|---|---|---|---|---|---|
|  | *Page* | *Line* | *Poem* | *Page* | *Line* |
| **DROPPING** | | | | | |
| Lucifer that bird's dropping | 153 | 17 | 83 | 171 | 13 |
| **DROPS** | | | | | |
| And when blind sleep drops on the spying senses, | 81 | 13 | 47 | 90 | 13 |
| Clack through the thicket of strength, love hewn in pillars drops | 92 | 8 | 55 | 101 | 14 |
| **DROVE** | | | | | |
| Drove in the heaven-driven of the nails | 75 | 12 | 44 | 84 | 12 |
| **DROWN** | | | | | |
| And drown the cargoed apples in their tides. | 1 | 6 | 2 | 1 | 6 |
| To drift or drown upon the seas | 8 | 8 | 5 | 9 | 8 |
| The sea of scums could drown me as it broke | 12 | 27 | 9 | 14 | 6 |
| As they drown, the chime travels, | 37 | 10 | 20 | 42 | 16 |
| The strata of the shore and drown red rock; | 82 | 20 | 48 | 91 | 20 |
| Time's coral saint and the salt grief drown a foul sepulchre | 83 | 8 | 49 | 92 | 8 |
| Shall drown in a grief as deep as his true grave, | 100 | 18 | 61 | 111 | 18 |
| And drown in the drifts of his need, and lie curled caught | 120 | 22 | 72 | 133 | 7 |
| It was sweet to drown in the readymade handy water | 133 | 16 | 78 | 148 | 19 |
| Scald me and drown | 148 | 12 | 82 | 165 | 12 |
| **DROWNED** | | | | | |
| Only the drowned deep bells | x | 4 | 1 | xviii | 10 |
| He drowned his father's magics in a dream. | 4 | 18 | 3 | 4 | 18 |
| And west's no longer drowned | 53 | 3 | 32 | 62 | 3 |
| Round the parched worlds of Wales and drown- ed each sun | 87 | 15 | 52 | 96 | 15 |
| That all the charmingly drowned arise to cock- crow and kill. | 89 | 6 | 53 | 98 | 6 |
| And Samson drowned in his hair. | 113 | 13 | 69 | 125 | 13 |
| The voices of all the drowned swam on the wind. | 136 | 8 | 81 | 153 | 8 |
| Or we shall obey, and ride with you through the drowned. | 136 | 14 | 81 | 153 | 14 |
| Heavy with the drowned | 143 | 5 | 82 | 160 | 5 |
| Sussanah's drowned in the bearded stream | 153 | 11 | 83 | 171 | 7 |
| And the bait is drowned among hayricks, | 157 | 16 | 83 | 176 | 8 |
| Through wynds and shells of drowned | 170 | 23 | 88 | 190 | 23 |
| **DRUB** | | | | | |
| And the dumb swans drub blue | viii | 9 | 1 | xvi | 9 |
| **DRUG** | | | | | |
| Daft with the drug that's smoking in a girl | 13 | 2 | 9 | 14 | 9 |
| **DRUG-WHITE** | | | | | |
| Camped in the drug-white shower of nerves and food, | 77 | 8 | 45 | 86 | 8 |
| **DRUID** | | | | | |
| And need no druid of her broken body). | 87 | 20 | 52 | 96 | 20 |

|  | U.K. | | | U.S. | |
|---|---|---|---|---|---|
|  | *Page* | *Line* | *Poem* | *Page* | *Line* |
| And druid herons' vows | 172 | 23 | 88 | 192 | 23 |

DRUM

| | | | | | |
|---|---|---|---|---|---|
| Shall a dropped stone drum on the ground, | 44 | 12 | 25 | 52 | 12 |
| With loud, torn tooth and tail and cobweb drum | 80 | 4 | 46 | 89 | 12 |
| Through the rippled drum of the hair-buried ear; | 113 | 4 | 69 | 125 | 4 |

DRUMMED

| | | | | | |
|---|---|---|---|---|---|
| 'See,' drummed the taut masks, 'how the dead ascend: | 79 | 26 | 46 | 89 | 7 |
| The whispering ears will watch love drummed away | 81 | 6 | 47 | 90 | 6 |

DRUMS

| | | | | | |
|---|---|---|---|---|---|
| I hear, through dead men's drums, the riddled lads, | 31 | 16 | 18 | 36 | 16 |
| Strike and smoothe, for my decks are drums, | 152 | 5 | 83 | 169 | 17 |

DRUNK

| | | | | | |
|---|---|---|---|---|---|
| Drunk as a vineyard snail, flailed like an octopus, | 91 | 7 | 55 | 100 | 7 |
| Dipping moon and drunk as a new dropped calf, | 174 | 17 | 89 | 194 | 17 |

DRUNKEN

| | | | | | |
|---|---|---|---|---|---|
| Seaports by a drunken shore | 43 | 6 | 24 | 50 | 13 |
| Have their drunken sailors hide him. | 43 | 14 | 24 | 50 | 21 |

DRY

| | | | | | |
|---|---|---|---|---|---|
| Like stalks of tall, dry straw, | vii | 22 | 1 | xv | 22 |
| And swallowed dry the waters of the breast. | 4 | 6 | 3 | 4 | 6 |
| And all the dry seabed unlocked, | 4 | 8 | 3 | 4 | 8 |
| The dry Sargasso of the tomb | 5 | 2 | 3 | 5 | 2 |
| Turns damp to dry; the golden shot | 6 | 2 | 4 | 6 | 2 |
| Is damp and dry; the quick and dead | 6 | 17 | 4 | 6 | 17 |
| Spun to my screws, your dry ghost blows, | 11 | 2 | 8 | 12 | 2 |
| Pushed up their hair, the dry wind steers | 11 | 5 | 8 | 12 | 5 |
| The weed of love's left dry; | 11 | 15 | 8 | 12 | 15 |
| Dry as a tomb, your coloured lids | 11 | 19 | 8 | 12 | 19 |
| Dry in the half-tracked thigh. | 32 | 12 | 18 | 37 | 18 |
| All all and all the dry worlds lever, | 33 | 1 | 19 | 38 | 1 |
| All of the flesh, the dry worlds lever. | 33 | 12 | 19 | 38 | 12 |
| All all and all the dry worlds couple, | 34 | 1 | 19 | 39 | 7 |
| Man dry man, | 51 | 3 | 31 | 60 | 3 |
| Dry lover mine | 51 | 4 | 31 | 60 | 4 |
| Lapping the still canals, the dry tide-master | 82 | 10 | 48 | 91 | 10 |
| To veil belladonna and let the dry eyes perceive | 85 | 10 | 50 | 94 | 10 |
| In the dark of the coffin and sheds dry leaves, | 87 | 8 | 52 | 96 | 8 |
| Lie dry, rest robbed, my beast. | 92 | 14 | 55 | 101 | 20 |
| Till the sweet tooth of my love bit dry, | 107 | 7 | 65 | 118 | 7 |
| With dry flesh and earth for adorning and bed. | 133 | 15 | 78 | 148 | 18 |
| High and dry by the top of the mast, | 149 | 8 | 83 | 166 | 8 |
| Dry as echoes and insect-faced, | 155 | 2 | 83 | 173 | 6 |
| Trees cool and dry in the whirlpool of ships | 156 | 2 | 83 | 174 | 10 |
| All all and all the dry worlds lever | 33 | | 19 | 38 | |

| | U.K. | | | U.S. | |
|---|---|---|---|---|---|
| | *Page* | *Line* | *Poem* | *Page* | *Line* |
| **DRY-AS-PASTE** | | | | | |
| For man-begetters in the dry-as-paste, | 46 | 23 | 27 | 54 | 23 |
| **DRYER** | | | | | |
| The words of death are dryer than his stiff, | 13 | 18 | 9 | 15 | 4 |
| **DUCK** | | | | | |
| Peck, sprint, dance on fountains and duck time | 97 | 8 | 59 | 108 | 8 |
| And the duck pond glass and the blinding byres alone | 120 | 10 | 72 | 132 | 15 |
| **DUCK-BILLED** | | | | | |
| The duck-billed platypus broody in a milk of birds. | 110 | 5 | 67 | 121 | 7 |
| **DUCKED** | | | | | |
| Ducked in the twelve, disciple seas | 69 | 4 | 43 | 78 | 4 |
| And ducked and draked white lake that harps to a hail stone. | 177 | 8 | 90 | 198 | 7 |
| **DUCKS** | | | | | |
| Where birds ride like leaves and boats like ducks | 134 | 22 | 79 | 150 | 22 |
| **DUG** | | | | | |
| Dug of the sea, the glanded morrow, | 33 | 8 | 19 | 38 | 8 |
| And dug your grave in my breast. | 92 | 16 | 55 | 101 | 22 |
| The mother dug, and its arms full of fires. | 129 | 8 | 77 | 143 | 8 |
| **DUGS** | | | | | |
| An old god's dugs are pressed and pricked, | 44 | 9 | 25 | 52 | 9 |
| **DULLED** | | | | | |
| Resembling to her dulled sense | 114 | 7 | 69 | 126 | 7 |
| **DUMB** | | | | | |
| And the dumb swans drub blue | viii | 9 | 1 | xvi | 9 |
| And I am dumb to tell the hanging man | 9 | 14 | 6 | 10 | 14 |
| And I am dumb to tell a weather's wind | 9 | 19 | 6 | 10 | 19 |
| And I am dumb to tell the lover's tomb | 9 | 21 | 6 | 10 | 21 |
| And I am dumb to tell the crooked rose | 9 | 4 | 6 | 10 | 4 |
| And I am dumb to mouth unto my veins | 9 | 9 | 6 | 10 | 9 |
| And to the first dumb wonder at the flesh, | 20 | 13 | 13 | 24 | 13 |
| The ghost is dumb that stammered in the straw, | 31 | 4 | 18 | 36 | 4 |
| There is loud and dark directly under the dumb flame, | 83 | 13 | 49 | 92 | 13 |
| But do not travel down dumb wind like prodigals. | 86 | 11 | 51 | 95 | 11 |
| Flood of her heart's fame; she would lie dumb and deep | 87 | 19 | 52 | 96 | 19 |
| Bone and be dumb | 144 | 6 | 82 | 161 | 6 |
| Is dumb and gone with his flame of brides. | 153 | 10 | 83 | 171 | 6 |
| **DUMBFOUNDING** | | | | | |
| To dumbfounding haven | 140 | 12 | 82 | 157 | 12 |
| **DUMBLY** | | | | | |
| Dumbly and divinely stumbling | 42 | 6 | 24 | 49 | 6 |
| Dumbly and divinely leaping | 42 | 13 | 24 | 49 | 13 |

|  | U.K. Page | Line | Poem | U.S. Page | Line |
|---|---|---|---|---|---|
| DUMBSTRUCK | | | | | |
| Gag of a dumbstruck tree to block from bare enemies | 85 | 4 | 50 | 94 | 4 |
| DUMMY | | | | | |
| Atlaswise hold half-way off the dummy bay | 76 | 10 | 44 | 85 | 10 |
| DUNCE | | | | | |
| Shaped in old armour and oak the countenance of a dunce | 85 | 7 | 50 | 94 | 7 |
| DUNES | | | | | |
| And prophets loud on the burned dunes; | 156 | 5 | 83 | 174 | 13 |
| DUNG | | | | | |
| And the dung hills white as wool and the hen | 119 | 18 | 72 | 131 | 18 |
| DUNGHILL | | | | | |
| Light of his thighs, spreadeagle to the dunghill sky, | 177 | 3 | 90 | 198 | 2 |
| DUSK | | | | | |
| My dabbed bay's dusk, as I hack | viii | 10 | 1 | xvi | 10 |
| And dusk is crowded with the children's ghosts, | 53 | 14 | 32 | 62 | 14 |
| In a hoisted cloud, at drop of dusk, he pulls to his claws | 167 | 3 | 87 | 187 | 3 |
| Of the sparrows and such who swansing, dusk, in wrangling hedges. | 167 | 7 | 87 | 187 | 7 |
| All praise of the hawk on fire in hawk-eyed dusk be sung, | 168 | 3 | 87 | 188 | 7 |
| Of dusk and water I see the tilting whispering | 168 | 24 | 87 | 189 | 9 |
| DUST | | | | | |
| Feet in the rubbing dust. | 13 | 14 | 9 | 14 | 21 |
| Joy is the knock of dust, Cadaver's shoot | 19 | 12 | 12 | 22 | 17 |
| As they dive, the dust settles, | 36 | 19 | 20 | 41 | 19 |
| Dust be your saviour under the conjured soil.) | 37 | 9 | 20 | 42 | 15 |
| Not till, from high and low, their dust | 53 | 12 | 32 | 62 | 12 |
| Should he, for centre sake, hop in the dust, | 51 | 6 | 31 | 60 | 6 |
| Like the dust of the dead. | 105 | 12 | 64 | 116 | 12 |
| She sleeps in the narrow trough yet she walks the dust | 108 | 13 | 66 | 119 | 13 |
| Who'd raise the organs of the counted dust | 117 | 7 | 71 | 129 | 7 |
| Dust in the buried wood, flies on the grains of her wings | 121 | 3 | 72 | 133 | 18 |
| The voice of the dust of water from the withered spring | 121 | 5 | 72 | 133 | 20 |
| As a dust of pigeons. Exulting, the grave hooved | 121 | 18 | 72 | 134 | 13 |
| And the harp shaped voice of the water's dust plucks in a fold | 121 | 24 | 72 | 134 | 19 |
| Our own true strangers' dust | 126 | 13 | 74 | 140 | 13 |
| And the dust shall sing like a bird | 129 | 22 | 77 | 143 | 22 |
| And the bidden dust upsailing | 141 | 9 | 82 | 158 | 9 |
| And the green dust | 143 | 6 | 82 | 160 | 6 |

DUST (continued)

|  | U.K. | | Poem | U.S. | |
|---|---|---|---|---|---|
|  | *Page* | *Line* | | *Page* | *Line* |
| And the beating dust be blown | 145 | 15 | 82 | 162 | 15 |
| One by one in dust and shawl, | 155 | 1 | 83 | 173 | 5 |
| Milled dust of the apple tree and the pounded islands | 164 | 10 | 86 | 183 | 17 |
| Dolphins dive in their turnturtle dust, | 171 | 6 | 88 | 191 | 6 |
| Time by, their dust was flesh the swineherd rooted sly, | 177 | 1 | 90 | 197 | 21 |
| Now curlew cry me down to kiss the mouths of their dust. | 178 | 4 | 90 | 199 | 5 |
| The dust of their kettles and clocks swings to and fro | 178 | 5 | 90 | 199 | 6 |
| Which was rest and dust, and in the kind ground |  |  | 91 | 200 | 10 |

DUSTERS

| For, sunday faced, with dusters in my glove, | 18 | 16 | 12 | 21 | 16 |

DUST-APPOINTED

| 'Rest beyond choice in the dust-appointed grain, | 98 | 3 | 59 | 109 | 6 |

DUST-TONGUED

| It is the sinners' dust-tongued bell claps me to churches | 83 | 1 | 49 | 92 | 1 |
| It is the sinners' dust-tongued bell | 83 | | 49 | 92 | |

DUSTS

| Weds my long gentleman to dusts and furies; | 76 | 4 | 44 | 85 | 4 |

DWINDLING

| Pale rain over the dwindling harbour | 103 | 6 | 63 | 114 | 6 |

DWINDLING

| Said the dwindling ships. | 149 | 24 | 83 | 167 | 4 |

DYING

| The message of his dying christ. | 8 | 18 | 5 | 9 | 18 |
| There's more than dying; | 48 | 11 | 28 | 56 | 11 |
| The greenwood dying as the deer fall in their tracks, | 49 | 11 | 29 | 58 | 11 |
| Who climbs to his dying love in her high room, | 100 | 3 | 61 | 111 | 3 |
| To-night shall find no dying but alive and warm | 100 | 15 | 61 | 111 | 15 |
| Rage, rage against the dying of the light. | 116 | 3 | 70 | 128 | 3 |
| Rage, rage against the dying of the light. | 116 | 9 | 80 | 128 | 9 |
| Rage, rage against the dying of the light. | 116 | 15 | 70 | 128 | 15 |
| Rage, rage against the dying of the light. | 116 | 19 | 70 | 128 | 19 |
| Or flower under the time dying flesh astride. | 120 | 30 | 72 | 133 | 15 |
| The fields of seed and the time dying flesh astride, | 122 | 23 | 72 | 136 | 3 |
| Your dying | 130 | 2 | 77 | 144 | 2 |
| Time held me green and dying | 161 | 5 | 85 | 180 | 8 |
| Flounders, gulls, on their cold, dying trails, | 170 | 11 | 88 | 190 | 11 |
| (Sighed the old ram rod, dying of women), | 174 | 3 | 89 | 194 | 3 |
| (Sighed the old ram rod, dying of bitches), | 174 | 15 | 89 | 194 | 15 |
| (Sighed the old ram rod, dying of welcome), | 174 | 27 | 89 | 195 | 3 |
| (Sighed the old ram rod, dying of downfall), | 175 | 10 | 89 | 195 | 15 |
| (Sighed the old ram rod, dying of strangers), | 175 | 22 | 89 | 196 | 3 |

# ENTRIES UNDER E

|  | U.K. | | | U.S. | |
|---|---|---|---|---|---|
|  | *Page* | *Line* | *Poem* | *Page* | *Line* |
| EACH | | | | | |
| The milky acid on each hinge, | 4 | 5 | 3 | 4 | 5 |
| Turns ghost to ghost; each mothered child | 6 | 20 | 4 | 7 | 2 |
| Each golden grain spat life into its fellow, | 20 | 23 | 13 | 24 | 23 |
| On that cloud coast to each grave-gabbing shade; | 26 | 18 | 16 | 31 | 18 |
| Each rung a love or losing to the last, | 27 | 2 | 16 | 32 | 7 |
| That shapes each bushy item of the air | 60 | 5 | 36 | 69 | 5 |
| This was the sky, Jack Christ, each minstrel angle | 75 | 11 | 44 | 84 | 11 |
| Each ancient, stone-necked minute of love's season | 78 | 2 | 46 | 87 | 2 |
| Round the parched worlds of Wales and drowned each sun | 87 | 15 | 52 | 96 | 15 |
| Claw of the crabbed veins squeeze from each red particle | 91 | 21 | 55 | 100 | 21 |
| If I take to burn or return this world which is each man's work. | 94 | 12 | 57 | 104 | 12 |
| Each truth, each lie, | 106 | 11 | 64 | 117 | 11 |
| On the first of each hardship, | 132 | 5 | 78 | 147 | 5 |
| This night and each vast night until the stern bell talks | 164 | 2 | 86 | 183 | 9 |
| This night and each night since the falling star you were born, | 164 | 6 | 86 | 183 | 13 |
| But her faith that each vast night and the saga of prayer | 166 | 3 | 86 | 186 | 3 |
| And you shall wake, from country sleep, this dawn and each first dawn, | 166 | 11 | 86 | 186 | 11 |
| EAGLE | | | | | |
| The polar eagle with his tread of snow. | 152 | 8 | 83 | 169 | 20 |
| EAGLES | | | | | |
| Marrow of eagles, the roots of whales | 172 | 4 | 88 | 192 | 4 |
| EAR | | | | | |
| He lying low with ruin in his ear, | 51 | 20 | 31 | 60 | 20 |
| And all sweet hell, deaf as an hour's ear, | 57 | 5 | 34 | 66 | 12 |
| Tongue and ear in the thread, angle the temple-bound | 91 | 26 | 55 | 101 | 4 |
| And the synagogue of the ear of corn | 101 | 9 | 62 | 112 | 9 |
| Through the rippled drum of the hair-buried ear; | 113 | 4 | 69 | 125 | 4 |

139

EARDRUM

|  | U.K. | | Poem | U.S. | |
|  | Page | Line | | Page | Line |
|---|---|---|---|---|---|

EARDRUM

| Raise the live rafters of the eardrum, | 96 | 11 | 58 | 106 | 11 |

EARLY

| Like the park birds he came early | 111 | 13 | 68 | 123 | 13 |
| Early imaginary half remembered | 114 | 9 | 69 | 126 | 9 |

EARS

| Shone in my ears the light of sound, | 20 | 20 | 13 | 24 | 20 |
| Ears in the turrets hear | 58 | 1 | 35 | 67 | 1 |
| Ears in this island hear | 58 | 17 | 35 | 67 | 17 |
| No more may gulls cry at their ears | 68 | 20 | 42 | 77 | 20 |
| The whispering ears will watch love drummed away | 81 | 6 | 47 | 90 | 6 |
| Windshake of sailshaped ears, muffle-toed tap | 87 | 2 | 52 | 96 | 2 |
| Her heart all ears and eyes, lips catching the avalanche | 127 | 10 | 75 | 141 | 10 |
| Ears in the turrets hear | 58 | | 35 | 67 | |

EARTH

| Sage on the earth and sky; | 11 | 21 | 8 | 12 | 21 |
| Raise up this red-eyed earth? | 15 | 3 | 10 | 17 | 3 |
| And earth and sky were as one airy hill, | 20 | 8 | 13 | 24 | 8 |
| The earth and sky were as two mountains meeting. | 20 | 15 | 13 | 24 | 15 |
| Burst in the roots, pumped from the earth and rock | 22 | 17 | 14 | 27 | 17 |
| I fled the earth and, naked, climbed the weather, | 26 | 6 | 16 | 31 | 6 |
| Turns in the earth that turns the ashen | 33 | 5 | 19 | 38 | 5 |
| And in the mighty mornings of the earth; | 40 | 15 | 22 | 46 | 15 |
| Shall I still be love's house on the widdershin earth, | 47 | 5 | 27 | 55 | 5 |
| And roll with the knocked earth: | 92 | 13 | 55 | 101 | 19 |
| The skull of the earth is barbed with a war of burning brains and hair. | 96 | 9 | 58 | 106 | 9 |
| Water and light, the earth and sky, | 106 | 8 | 64 | 117 | 8 |
| And the living earth your sons. | 110 | 28 | 67 | 122 | 6 |
| Silence, silence to do, when earth grew loud, | 125 | 15 | 74 | 139 | 15 |
| From the kangaroo foot of the earth, | 132 | 21 | 78 | 147 | 21 |
| With dry flesh and earth for adorning and bed. | 133 | 15 | 78 | 148 | 18 |
| Everybody's earth. | 134 | 21 | 79 | 150 | 21 |
| And the known dark of the earth amen. | 147 | 18 | 82 | 164 | 18 |
| Or walked on the earth in the evening | 155 | 15 | 83 | 173 | 19 |
| Under the earth the loud sea walks, | 157 | 14 | 83 | 176 | 6 |
| Earth, air, water, fire, singing into the white act, | 165 | 16 | 86 | 185 | 6 |
| Only for the turning of the earth in her holy | 165 | 23 | 86 | 185 | 13 |
| He, on the earth of the night, alone | 172 | 11 | 88 | 192 | 11 |

EASE

| Were that enough, enough to ease the pain, | 48 | 17 | 28 | 56 | 17 |

|  | U.K. | | | U.S. | |
| --- | --- | --- | --- | --- | --- |
|  | *Page* | *Line* | *Poem* | *Page* | *Line* |
| EAST |  |  |  |  |  |
| Why east wind chills and south wind cools | 53 | 1 | 32 | 62 | 1 |
| Ask the tall fish swept from the bible east, | 76 | 16 | 44 | 85 | 16 |
| Cudgel great air, wreck east, and topple sundown, | 79 | 7 | 46 | 88 | 10 |
| Why east wind chills | 53 |  | 32 | 62 |  |
| EASTERN |  |  |  |  |  |
| My veins flowed with the Eastern weather; | 7 | 17 | 5 | 8 | 17 |
| Twined good and evil on an eastern tree; | 40 | 10 | 22 | 46 | 10 |
| EASY |  |  |  |  |  |
| Now as I was young and easy under the apple boughs | 159 | 1 | 85 | 178 | 1 |
| Oh as I was young and easy in the mercy of his means, | 161 | 4 | 85 | 180 | 7 |
| EAT |  |  |  |  |  |
| To eat your heart in the house in the rosy wood. | 162 | 7 | 86 | 181 | 7 |
| EATING |  |  |  |  |  |
| Eating bread from a newspaper | 111 | 7 | 68 | 123 | 7 |
| EAVES |  |  |  |  |  |
| For who unmanningly haunts the mountain ravened eaves | 163 | 1 | 86 | 182 | 1 |
| ECHO |  |  |  |  |  |
| Shall a white answer echo from the rooftops. | 53 | 15 | 32 | 62 | 15 |
| Shade without shape? the shape of Pharaoh's echo? | 72 | 21 | 44 | 81 | 21 |
| ECHO'S |  |  |  |  |  |
| Of echo's answer and the man of frost | 53 | 25 | 32 | 62 | 25 |
| ECHOES |  |  |  |  |  |
| And ghostly echoes on paper, | 64 | 9 | 39 | 73 | 9 |
| Dry as echoes and insect-faced, | 155 | 2 | 83 | 173 | 6 |
| ECHOING |  |  |  |  |  |
| Or skulks in the dell moon but moonshine echoing clear | 163 | 2 | 86 | 182 | 2 |
| EDEN |  |  |  |  |  |
| We in our Eden knew the secret guardian | 40 | 13 | 22 | 46 | 13 |
| Murder of Eden and green genesis. | 41 | 8 | 23 | 47 | 8 |
| Uncredited blows Jericho on Eden. | 41 | 17 | 23 | 47 | 17 |
| Of the garden of Eden. | 130 | 22 | 77 | 144 | 22 |
| EEL |  |  |  |  |  |
| Is old as water and plain as an eel; | 152 | 21 | 83 | 170 | 13 |
| EELS |  |  |  |  |  |
| Love like a mist or fire through the bed of eels. | 38 | 12 | 20 | 44 | 2 |
| Of eels, saint heron hymning in the shell-hung distant | 168 | 12 | 87 | 188 | 16 |
| EGG |  |  |  |  |  |
| And the naked egg stand straight, | 56 | 7 | 34 | 65 | 7 |
| Old cock from nowheres and the heaven's egg, | 71 | 8 | 44 | 80 | 8 |

EGG (continued)

|  | U.K. | | | U.S. | |
|---|---|---|---|---|---|
|  | Page | Line | Poem | Page | Line |
| And the hawk in the egg kills the wren. | 155 | 12 | 83 | 173 | 16 |
| EGGS | | | | | |
| Murmur of spring nor crush the cockerel's eggs, | 60 | 7 | 36 | 69 | 7 |
| EGYPT'S | | | | | |
| My Egypt's armour buckling in its sheet, | 31 | 10 | 18 | 36 | 10 |
| EGYPTIAN | | | | | |
| Whose beard wags in Egyptian wind. | 63 | 15 | 38 | 72 | 15 |
| EITHER | | | | | |
| Sleeping on either hand. | 82 | 8 | 48 | 91 | 8 |
| ELBOW | | | | | |
| Faded my elbow ghost, the mothers-eyed, | 26 | 16 | 16 | 31 | 16 |
| They shall have stars at elbow and foot; | 68 | 5 | 42 | 77 | 5 |
| ELEGIAC | | | | | |
| Where the elegiac fisherbird stabs and paddles | 167 | 19 | 87 | 187 | 19 |
| ELEGY | | | | | |
| Elegy of innocence and youth. | 101 | 18 | 62 | 112 | 18 |
| Elegy | | | 91 | 200 | |
| ELEMENT | | | | | |
| In the last element | 105 | 23 | 64 | 116 | 23 |
| ELEMENTARY | | | | | |
| In the final direction of the elementary town | 99 | 8 | 60 | 110 | 8 |
| ELEMENTS | | | | | |
| And all the elements of the slow fall rejoiced | 122 | 4 | 72 | 135 | 4 |
| Music of elements, that a miracle makes! | 165 | 15 | 86 | 185 | 5 |
| Four elements and five | 173 | 1 | 88 | 193 | 1 |
| ELM | | | | | |
| Straight as a young elm | 112 | 9 | 68 | 124 | 9 |
| We grieve as the blithe birds, never again, leave shingle and elm, | 168 | 9 | 87 | 188 | 13 |
| ELMED | | | | | |
| It is the heron and I, under judging Sir John's elmed | 168 | 16 | 87 | 189 | 1 |
| ELMS | | | | | |
| To fiery tyburn over the wrestle of elms until | 167 | 9 | 87 | 187 | 9 |
| Hollows, a grassblade blown in cupped hands, in the looted elms | 169 | 4 | 87 | 189 | 13 |
| ELOI | | | | | |
| Cry Eloi to the guns. | 31 | 18 | 18 | 36 | 18 |
| EMERALD | | | | | |
| Where, wound in emerald linen and sharp wind, | 79 | 16 | 46 | 88 | 19 |
| From the emerald, still bell; and from the pacing weather-cock | 83 | 17 | 49 | 92 | 17 |
| EMPEROR | | | | | |
| And the hunger's emperor; | 10 | 19 | 7 | 11 | 19 |
| Moonfall and sailing emperor, pale as their tide-print, | 83 | 10 | 49 | 92 | 10 |

|  | U.K. | | | U.S. | |
| --- | --- | --- | --- | --- | --- |
|  | *Page* | *Line* | *Poem* | *Page* | *Line* |
| EMPTY | | | | | |
| And tells the page the empty ill. | 10 | 10 | 7 | 11 | 10 |
| One smile of light across the empty face; | 22 | 2 | 14 | 27 | 2 |
| ENAMEL | | | | | |
| Man was the scales, the death birds on enamel, | 38 | 19 | 20 | 44 | 9 |
| ENAMELLED | | | | | |
| Of the sharp, enamelled eyes and the spectacled claws | 85 | 2 | 50 | 94 | 2 |
| ENAMOURED | | | | | |
| An enamoured man alone by the twigs of his eyes, two fires, | 77 | 7 | 45 | 86 | 7 |
| ENAMOURING | | | | | |
| Man was the burning England she was sleep-walking, and the enamouring island | 113 | 20 | 69 | 125 | 20 |
| ENCOUNTER | | | | | |
| Twelve winds encounter by the white host at pasture, | 36 | 14 | 20 | 41 | 14 |
| ENCUMBERED | | | | | |
| Under the encumbered eyelid, | 113 | 3 | 69 | 125 | 3 |
| END | | | | | |
| At God speeded summer's end | vii | 2 | 1 | xv | 2 |
| At God speeded summer's end | x | 18 | 1 | xviii | 24 |
| The actions' end. | 19 | 20 | 12 | 23 | 5 |
| No tell-tale lover has an end more certain, | 41 | 24 | 23 | 48 | 6 |
| A goose's quill has put an end to murder | 62 | 7 | 37 | 71 | 7 |
| That put an end to talk. | 62 | 8 | 37 | 71 | 8 |
| Though wise men at their end know dark is right, | 116 | 4 | 70 | 128 | 4 |
| For my voyage to begin to the end of my wound, | 136 | 11 | 81 | 153 | 11 |
| One. The sun roars at the prayer's end | 148 | 17 | 82 | 165 | 17 |
| My dear this night he comes and night without end my dear | 166 | 9 | 86 | 186 | 9 |
| Who slaves to his crouched, eternal end | 171 | 4 | 88 | 191 | 4 |
| ENDED | | | | | |
| And the home of prayers and fires, the tale ended. | 122 | 30 | 72 | 136 | 10 |
| ENDING | | | | | |
| Everything ends, the tower ending and, | 19 | 16 | 12 | 23 | 1 |
| Intricate manhood of ending, the invalid rivals, | 36 | 7 | 20 | 41 | 7 |
| ENDLESS | | | | | |
| 'Adam I love, my madmen's love is endless, | 41 | 23 | 23 | 48 | 5 |
| In the groin's endless coil a man is tangled.' | 79 | 27 | 46 | 89 | 8 |
| And the endless beginning of prodigies suffers open.' | 98 | 7 | 59 | 109 | 10 |
| About the saint in shades while the endless breviary | 109 | 26 | 67 | 120 | 26 |

ENDLESS (continued)

|  | U.K. | | | U.S. | |
|---|---|---|---|---|---|
|  | *Page* | *Line* | *Poem* | *Page* | *Line* |
| Of the endless fall. | 146 | 13 | 82 | 163 | 13 |
| ENDLESSLY | | | | | |
| Endlessly to his wound | 117 | 11 | 71 | 129 | 11 |
| ENDS | | | | | |
| Everything ends, the tower ending and, | 19 | 16 | 12 | 23 | 1 |
| The root of tongues ends in a spentout cancer, | 21 | 13 | 13 | 25 | 13 |
| Split all ends up they shan't crack; | 68 | 17 | 42 | 77 | 17 |
| ENDURE | | | | | |
| Endure burial under the spelling wall, | 91 | 4 | 55 | 100 | 4 |
| Endure the stone | 145 | 5 | 82 | 162 | 5 |
| ENEMIES | | | | | |
| Light and dark are no enemies | 66 | 12 | 40 | 75 | 12 |
| Gag of a dumbstruck tree to block from bare enemies | 85 | 4 | 50 | 94 | 4 |
| My friends were enemies on stilts | 107 | 20 | 65 | 118 | 20 |
| His enemies entered bed, | 113 | 2 | 69 | 125 | 2 |
| And the second comers, the severers, the enemies from the deep | 115 | 22 | 69 | 127 | 22 |
| ENEMY | | | | | |
| Turning a petrol face blind to the enemy | 36 | 23 | 20 | 42 | 2 |
| Friend by enemy I call you out. | 107 | 1 | 65 | 118 | 1 |
| One enemy, of many, who knows well | 118 | 1 | 71 | 130 | 5 |
| Oh all the wanting flesh his enemy | 152 | 19 | 83 | 170 | 11 |
| ENGLAND | | | | | |
| And now the horns of England, in the sound of shape, | 49 | 13 | 29 | 58 | 13 |
| Man was the burning England she was sleep-walking, and the enamouring island | 113 | 20 | 69 | 125 | 20 |
| ENGLISH | | | | | |
| My world is cypress, and an English valley. | 31 | 13 | 18 | 36 | 13 |
| ENGRAVING | | | | | |
| Engraving going. | 54 | 24 | 33 | 63 | 24 |
| ENGULFING | | | | | |
| Alone and naked in the engulfing bride, | 120 | 28 | 72 | 133 | 13 |
| And through the thighs of the engulfing bride, | 123 | 14 | 72 | 137 | 4 |
| ENJOYED | | | | | |
| Night, and enjoyed as he would. | 114 | 13 | 69 | 126 | 13 |
| ENOUGH | | | | | |
| Were that enough, enough to ease the pain, | 48 | 17 | 28 | 56 | 17 |
| Were vaguenesses enough and the sweet lies plenty, | 48 | 21 | 28 | 56 | 21 |
| Were that enough, bone, blood, and sinew, | 48 | 24 | 28 | 57 | 1 |
| Of, time enough when the blood creeps cold, | 175 | 5 | 89 | 195 | 10 |
| ENTER | | | | | |
| Before I knocked and let flesh enter, | 7 | 1 | 5 | 8 | 1 |
| And a stranger enter like iron. | 96 | 22 | 58 | 107 | 5 |
| And I must enter again the round | 101 | 7 | 62 | 112 | 7 |

| | U.K. | | | U.S. | |
|---|---|---|---|---|---|
| | *Page* | *Line* | *Poem* | *Page* | *Line* |
| That lets the trees and water enter | 111 | 5 | 68 | 123 | 5 |
| Erupt, fountain, and enter to utter for ever | 131 | 23 | 77 | 146 | 5 |
| **ENTERED** | | | | | |
| Descends, my masters, on the entered honour. | 19 | 3 | 12 | 22 | 8 |
| His enemies entered bed, | 113 | 2 | 69 | 125 | 2 |
| **ENTERING** | | | | | |
| She deludes the heaven-proof house with entering clouds | 108 | 6 | 66 | 119 | 6 |
| **ENTICED** | | | | | |
| Enticed with twinkling bits of the eye | 107 | 6 | 65 | 118 | 6 |
| **ENTRAIL** | | | | | |
| Out of the naked entrail. | 35 | 12 | 20 | 40 | 12 |
| **ENTRANCES** | | | | | |
| Of deaths and entrances, | 117 | 26 | 71 | 130 | 2 |
| Deaths and Entrances | 117 | | 71 | 129 | |
| **ENVIOUS** | | | | | |
| The mazes of his praise and envious tongue were worked in flames and shells. | 95 | 17 | 58 | 105 | 17 |
| **ERECT** | | | | | |
| Erect a walking centre in the shroud, | 56 | 27 | 34 | 66 | 6 |
| **ERECTED** | | | | | |
| Do you not father me, nor the erected arm | 46 | 1 | 27 | 54 | 1 |
| Do you not sister me, nor the erected crime | 46 | 5 | 27 | 54 | 5 |
| A voice in the erected air, | 134 | 25 | 79 | 151 | 3 |
| **ERROR** | | | | | |
| Praising the mortal error | 10 | 17 | 7 | 11 | 17 |
| **ERRORS** | | | | | |
| Ruin, the room of errors, one rood dropped | 79 | 13 | 46 | 88 | 16 |
| **ERUPT** | | | | | |
| Erupt, fountain, and enter to utter for ever | 131 | 23 | 77 | 146 | 5 |
| **ESCAPE** | | | | | |
| Thrust, my daughter or son, to escape, there is none, none, none, | 97 | 19 | 59 | 108 | 19 |
| **ESCAPES** | | | | | |
| Escapes to the flat cities' sails | 69 | 16 | 43 | 78 | 16 |
| **ESPECIALLY** | | | | | |
| Especially when the October wind | 16 | 1 | 11 | 19 | 1 |
| Especially when the October wind | 17 | 1 | 11 | 20 | 1 |
| Especially when the October wind | 16 | | 11 | 19 | |
| **ESQUIRE** | | | | | |
| High lord esquire, speak up the singing cloud, | 60 | 17 | 36 | 69 | 17 |
| **ESTRANGING** | | | | | |
| In many married London's estranging grief. | 117 | 12 | 71 | 129 | 12 |
| **ETERNAL** | | | | | |
| Eternal waters away | vii | 18 | 1 | xv | 18 |
| Who slaves to his crouched, eternal end | 171 | 4 | 88 | 191 | 4 |
| And alone in the night's eternal, curving act | 176 | 9 | 90 | 197 | 9 |

145

|  | U.K. | | | U.S. | |
| --- | --- | --- | --- | --- | --- |
|  | *Page* | *Line* | *Poem* | *Page* | *Line* |
| **ETHER** |  |  |  |  |  |
| Under the mask and the ether, they making bloody | 37 | 2 | 20 | 42 | 8 |
| **ETNA** |  |  |  |  |  |
| On the angelic etna of the last whirring featherlands, | 95 | 11 | 58 | 105 | 11 |
| **EUNUCH** |  |  |  |  |  |
| Our eunuch dreams, all seedless in the light, | 14 | 1 | 10 | 16 | 1 |
| Bull's-eye the outlaw through a eunuch crack | 67 | 19 | 41 | 76 | 19 |
| Our eunuch dreams | 14 |  | 10 | 16 |  |
| **EUNUCHS** |  |  |  |  |  |
| Halt among eunuchs, and the nitric stain | 18 | 24 | 12 | 22 | 4 |
| **EVE** |  |  |  |  |  |
| Butt of the tree-tailed worm that mounted Eve, | 72 | 8 | 44 | 81 | 8 |
| On almost the incendiary eve | 117 | 1 | 71 | 129 | 1 |
| On almost the incendiary eve | 117 | 13 | 71 | 129 | 13 |
| On almost the incendiary eve | 117 | 25 | 71 | 130 | 1 |
| Adam or Eve, the adorned holy bullock | 130 | 10 | 77 | 144 | 10 |
| O Adam and Eve together | 130 | 18 | 77 | 144 | 18 |
| Of Adam and Eve is never for a second | 130 | 24 | 77 | 145 | 2 |
| **EVEN** |  |  |  |  |  |
| Even as a baby he had never cried; |  |  | 91 | 201 | 5 |
| **EVENING** |  |  |  |  |  |
| In the interpreted evening | 147 | 17 | 82 | 164 | 17 |
| Or walked on the earth in the evening | 155 | 15 | 83 | 173 | 19 |
| **EVER** |  |  |  |  |  |
| Nor ever, as the wild tongue breaks its tombs, | 77 | 11 | 45 | 86 | 11 |
| Erupt, fountain, and enter to utter for ever | 131 | 23 | 77 | 146 | 5 |
| Sleep, good, for ever, slow and deep, spelled rare and wise, | 162 | 8 | 86 | 181 | 8 |
| For ever of all not the wolf in his baaing hood | 163 | 13 | 86 | 182 | 13 |
| Ever and ever he finds a way, as the snow falls, | 164 | 7 | 86 | 183 | 14 |
| Ever and ever by all your vows believe and fear | 166 | 8 | 86 | 186 | 8 |
| Now will be ever is always true, | 171 | 24 | 88 | 191 | 24 |
| Than ever was since the world was said, | 173 | 17 | 88 | 193 | 17 |
| Love for ever meridian through the courters' trees | 178 | 18 | 90 | 199 | 19 |
| **EVERGREEN** |  |  |  |  |  |
| Teach me the love that is evergreen after the fall leaved | 178 | 12 | 90 | 199 | 13 |
| **EVERY** |  |  |  |  |  |
| And dark shoals every holy field. | x | 7 | 1 | xviii | 13 |
| The hero's head lies scraped of every legend, | 79 | 17 | 46 | 88 | 20 |
| And every stone I wind off like a reel. | 89 | 13 | 53 | 98 | 13 |
| But blessed by such heroic hosts in your every | 109 | 21 | 67 | 120 | 21 |
| In your every inch and glance is the globe of genesis spun, | 110 | 27 | 67 | 122 | 5 |

|  | U.K. | | | U.S. | |
|---|---|---|---|---|---|
|  | *Page* | *Line* | *Poem* | *Page* | *Line* |
| And out of every domed and soil-based shell | 115 | 5 | 69 | 127 | 5 |
| With every cry since light | 117 | 23 | 71 | 129 | 23 |
| From every true or crater | 124 | 7 | 73 | 138 | 7 |
| Every morning I make, | 134 | 16 | 79 | 150 | 16 |
| With his flame in every grain. | 141 | 10 | 82 | 158 | 10 |
| Till every beast blared down in a swerve | 151 | 9 | 83 | 168 | 17 |
| Till every turtle crushed from his shell | 151 | 10 | 83 | 168 | 18 |
| Till every bone in the rushing grave | 151 | 11 | 83 | 168 | 19 |
| And every soul His priest, | 172 | 7 | 88 | 192 | 7 |
| And every wave of the way | 173 | 14 | 88 | 193 | 14 |
| With every simmering woman his mouse | 175 | 1 | 89 | 195 | 6 |
| EVERYBODY'S | | | | | |
| Everybody's earth. | 134 | 21 | 79 | 150 | 21 |
| EVERYTHING | | | | | |
| Everything ends, the tower ending and, | 19 | 16 | 12 | 23 | 1 |
| EVIL | | | | | |
| Twined good and evil on an eastern tree; | 40 | 10 | 22 | 46 | 10 |
| Spelt out the seven seas, an evil index, | 74 | 12 | 44 | 83 | 12 |
| EVILS | | | | | |
| And the unicorn evils run them through; | 68 | 16 | 42 | 77 | 16 |
| EWE | | | | | |
| Or the white ewe lamb | 130 | 11 | 77 | 144 | 11 |
| EXAMINERS | | | | | |
| To shield the glistening brain and blunt the examiners, | 85 | 8 | 50 | 94 | 8 |
| EXERCISED | | | | | |
| Exercised in the still night | 128 | 2 | 76 | 142 | 2 |
| EXHALING | | | | | |
| The cloud climb of the exhaling tomb | 141 | 8 | 82 | 158 | 8 |
| EXILED | | | | | |
| Exiled in us we arouse the soft, | 126 | 15 | 74 | 140 | 15 |
| EXODUS | | | | | |
| Like exodus a chapter from the garden, | 54 | 18 | 33 | 63 | 18 |
| EXPENSIVE | | | | | |
| To surrender now is to pay the expensive ogre twice. | 94 | 10 | 57 | 104 | 10 |
| EXPLODE | | | | | |
| Some life, yet unspent, might explode | 64 | 12 | 39 | 73 | 12 |
| EXPOSE | | | | | |
| The mummy cloths expose an ancient breast. | 63 | 8 | 38 | 72 | 8 |
| EXULTATION | | | | | |
| Exultation lies down. Time buries the spring weather | 123 | 9 | 72 | 136 | 19 |
| EXULTATION'S | | | | | |
| Vessel of abscesses and exultation's shell, | 91 | 3 | 55 | 100 | 3 |
| EXULTING | | | | | |
| As a dust of pigeons. Exulting, the grave hooved | 121 | 18 | 72 | 134 | 13 |

|  |  | U.K. |  |  | U.S. |  |
|  |  | Page | Line | Poem | Page | Line |
| EXULTS |  |  |  |  |  |  |
| And the tusked, ramshackling sea exults; | 173 | 13 | 88 | 193 | 13 |
| EYE |  |  |  |  |  |  |
| A process in the eye forwarns | 6 | 7 | 4 | 6 | 7 |
| A darkness in the weather of the eye | 6 | 10 | 4 | 6 | 10 |
| Move like two ghosts before the eye. | 6 | 18 | 4 | 6 | 18 |
| The dead turns up its eye; | 11 | 3 | 8 | 12 | 3 |
| And curling round the bud that forks her eye. | 13 | 3 | 9 | 14 | 10 |
| Strange to our solid eye, | 14 | 13 | 10 | 16 | 13 |
| The photograph is married to the eye, | 15 | 7 | 10 | 17 | 7 |
| Breaks with the wormy winter through the eye. | 16 | 23 | 11 | 19 | 23 |
| Chaste and the chaser, man with the cockshut eye, | 18 | 17 | 12 | 21 | 17 |
| As forks my eye; | 21 | 23 | 13 | 26 | 6 |
| The secret of the soil grows through the eye, | 25 | 4 | 15 | 30 | 4 |
| Let fall the tear of time; the sleeper's eye, | 26 | 2 | 16 | 31 | 2 |
| Blinds their cloud-tracking eye. | 31 | 6 | 18 | 36 | 6 |
| Splitting the long eye open, and the spiral turnkey, | 36 | 26 | 20 | 42 | 5 |
| No third eye probe into a rainbow's sex | 67 | 25 | 41 | 76 | 25 |
| With oracle for eye?' | 70 | 14 | 43 | 79 | 18 |
| Pluck, cock, my sea eye, said medusa's scripture, | 74 | 5 | 44 | 83 | 5 |
| And love plucked out the stinging siren's eye, | 74 | 7 | 44 | 83 | 7 |
| How, through the halfmoon's vegetable eye, | 81 | 3 | 47 | 90 | 3 |
| Nailed with an open eye, in the bowl of wounds and weed | 92 | 1 | 55 | 101 | 7 |
| Lops, as a bush plumed with flames, the rant of the fierce eye, | 92 | 10 | 55 | 101 | 16 |
| Enticed with twinkling bits of the eye | 107 | 6 | 65 | 118 | 6 |
| At his thrashing hair and whale-blue eye; | 149 | 3 | 83 | 166 | 3 |
| Sanctum sanctorum the animal eye of the wood | 163 | 7 | 86 | 182 | 7 |
| And I gave my soul a blind, slashed eye, | 175 | 16 | 89 | 195 | 21 |
| Walking in the meadows of his son's eye |  |  | 91 | 201 | 10 |
| EYED |  |  |  |  |  |  |
| And mark the dark eyed wave, through the eyes of sleep, | 100 | 19 | 61 | 111 | 19 |
| Eyed, in the haloed house, in her rareness and hilly | 165 | 18 | 86 | 185 | 8 |
| EYE-TEETH |  |  |  |  |  |  |
| And the undead eye-teeth, | 67 | 24 | 41 | 76 | 24 |
| EYELID |  |  |  |  |  |  |
| Under the encumbered eyelid, | 113 | 3 | 69 | 125 | 3 |
| The tempter under the eyelid | 153 | 6 | 83 | 171 | 2 |
| EYELIDS |  |  |  |  |  |  |
| Its wringing shell, and let her eyelids fasten. | 79 | 9 | 46 | 88 | 12 |
| And the coins on my eyelids sang like shells. | 134 | 30 | 79 | 151 | 8 |

| | U.K. | | | U.S. | |
| --- | --- | --- | --- | --- | --- |
| | Page | Line | Poem | Page | Line |

EYES

| | U.K. Page | Line | Poem | U.S. Page | Line |
| --- | --- | --- | --- | --- | --- |
| Drew in his eyes the straws of sleep, | 4 | 17 | 3 | 4 | 17 |
| The cataracted eyes that filmed their cloth; | 4 | 21 | 3 | 4 | 21 |
| Called in my eyes the sound of light. | 20 | 21 | 13 | 24 | 21 |
| Dawn breaks behind the eyes; | 24 | 13 | 15 | 29 | 13 |
| Sprinkles in children's eyes a long-last sleep | 53 | 13 | 32 | 62 | 13 |
| So cross her hand with their grave gipsy eyes, | 55 | 12 | 33 | 64 | 15 |
| Mister and master, darkness for his eyes, | 57 | 3 | 34 | 66 | 10 |
| Eyes in the gables see | 58 | 3 | 35 | 67 | 3 |
| Eyes in this island see | 58 | 19 | 35 | 67 | 19 |
| My camel's eyes will needle through the shroud. | 73 | 6 | 44 | 82 | 6 |
| So shall winged harbours through the rockbirds' eyes | 76 | 12 | 44 | 85 | 12 |
| An enamoured man alone by the twigs of his eyes, two fires, | 77 | 7 | 45 | 86 | 7 |
| These once-blind eyes have breathed a wind of visions, | 80 | 1 | 46 | 89 | 9 |
| Prides of to-morrow suckling in her eyes, | 80 | 14 | 46 | 89 | 22 |
| The heart is sensual, though five eyes break. | 81 | 14 | 47 | 90 | 14 |
| Of the sharp, enamelled eyes and the spectacled claws | 85 | 2 | 50 | 94 | 2 |
| To veil belladonna and let the dry eyes perceive | 85 | 10 | 50 | 94 | 10 |
| The spittled eyes, the salt ponds in the sleeves, | 87 | 5 | 52 | 96 | 5 |
| That burns along my eyes. | 90 | 14 | 54 | 99 | 14 |
| Draw down o its weird eyes? | 91 | 11 | 55 | 100 | 11 |
| Talked and tore though her eyes smiled. | 93 | 20 | 56 | 102 | 20 |
| That the eyes are already murdered, | 96 | 16 | 58 | 106 | 16 |
| Twenty-four years remind the tears of my eyes. | 99 | 1 | 60 | 110 | 1 |
| And mark the dark eyed wave, through the eyes of sleep, | 100 | 19 | 61 | 111 | 19 |
| King of your blue eyes | 105 | 3 | 64 | 116 | 3 |
| Tongue of your translating eyes. The young stars told me, | 110 | 23 | 67 | 122 | 1 |
| Made the tigers jump out of their eyes | 112 | 4 | 68 | 124 | 4 |
| Blind eyes could blaze like meteors and be gay, | 116 | 14 | 70 | 128 | 14 |
| Flashed first across his thunderclapping eyes. | 117 | 24 | 71 | 129 | 24 |
| Prisoners of wishes locked their eyes | 125 | 7 | 74 | 139 | 7 |
| Surprised in the opening of her nightlong eyes | 127 | 2 | 75 | 141 | 2 |
| Her heart all ears and eyes, lips catching the avalanche | 127 | 10 | 75 | 141 | 10 |
| I was pierced by the idol tailor's eyes, | 133 | 10 | 78 | 148 | 13 |
| And the craters of his eyes grew springshoots and fire | 135 | 7 | 80 | 152 | 7 |
| And the star of the lost the shape of the eyes. | 147 | 1 | 82 | 164 | 1 |
| He was blind to the eyes of candles | 150 | 3 | 83 | 167 | 7 |
| And scuttled over her eyes, | 153 | 4 | 83 | 170 | 20 |
| Golden in the heydays of his eyes, | 159 | 5 | 85 | 178 | 5 |

149

| | U.K. | | | U.S. | |
| --- | --- | --- | --- | --- | --- |
| | *Page* | *Line* | *Poem* | *Page* | *Line* |
| Gull, on the wave with sand in its eyes! And the foal moves | 165 | 12 | 86 | 185 | 2 |
| Might cross its planets, the bell weep, night gather her eyes, | 165 | 21 | 86 | 185 | 11 |
| Wound, nor her riding high, nor her eyes, nor kindled hair, | 166 | 2 | 86 | 186 | 2 |
| And gallows, up the rays of his eyes the small birds of the bay | 167 | 4 | 87 | 187 | 4 |
| Holier then their eyes, | 173 | 25 | 88 | 193 | 25 |
| Whoever I would with my wicked eyes, | 174 | 9 | 89 | 194 | 9 |
| Through his unseeing eyes to the roots of the sea. | | | 91 | 200 | 17 |
| Out of his eyes I saw the last light glide. | | | 91 | 201 | 7 |
| The tears out of his eyes, too proud to cry. | | | 91 | 201 | 18 |

# ENTRIES UNDER F

FABLE

| | U.K. | | | U.S. | |
| --- | --- | --- | --- | --- | --- |
| The insect fable is the certain promise. | 41 | 18 | 23 | 47 | 18 |
| I furnish with the meat of a fable; | 77 | 21 | 45 | 86 | 21 |

FABLES

| | | | | | |
| --- | --- | --- | --- | --- | --- |
| The insect certain is the plague of fables. | 41 | 9 | 23 | 47 | 9 |
| The star rise at pasture and nightlong the fables graze | 163 | 11 | 86 | 182 | 11 |

FABLING

| | | | | | |
| --- | --- | --- | --- | --- | --- |
| I young Aesop fabling to the near night by the dingle | 168 | 11 | 87 | 188 | 15 |

FABULOUS

| | | | | | |
| --- | --- | --- | --- | --- | --- |
| My cross of tales behind the fabulous curtain.' | 41 | 26 | 23 | 48 | 8 |
| And fabulous, dear God. | 171 | 21 | 88 | 191 | 21 |

FACE

| | | | | | |
| --- | --- | --- | --- | --- | --- |
| Where once the waters of your face | 11 | 1 | 8 | 12 | 1 |
| On fork and face. | 18 | 25 | 12 | 22 | 5 |
| One smile of light across the empty face; | 22 | 2 | 14 | 27 | 2 |
| Stamp of the minted face upon the moon; | 22 | 10 | 14 | 27 | 10 |
| And the face to the driven lover. | 33 | 24 | 19 | 39 | 6 |
| Turning a petrol face blind to the enemy | 36 | 23 | 20 | 42 | 2 |
| Dazzle this face of voices on the moon-turned table, | 37 | 18 | 20 | 43 | 1 |
| Should lanterns shine, the holy face, | 63 | 1 | 38 | 72 | 1 |
| My face is haggard in the glass, | 65 | 19 | 40 | 74 | 19 |
| Walks with no wound, nor lightning in her face, | 80 | 10 | 46 | 89 | 18 |

|  | U.K. |  |  | U.S. |  |
|---|---|---|---|---|---|
|  | Page | Line | Poem | Page | Line |
| Rape and rebellion in the nurseries of my face, | 85 | 3 | 50 | 94 | 3 |
| Her fist of a face died clenched on a round pain; | 88 | 6 | 52 | 97 | 6 |
| The invoked, shrouding veil at the cap of the face, | 91 | 5 | 55 | 100 | 5 |
| And the sun killed in her face. | 93 | 9 | 56 | 102 | 9 |
| Behind a face of hands, | 95 | 10 | 58 | 105 | 10 |
| And nothing shone on the water's face | 150 | 20 | 83 | 168 | 4 |
| Always good-bye to the fires of the face, | 153 | 2 | 83 | 170 | 18 |
| Where once the waters of your face | 11 |  | 8 | 12 |  |
| FACED |  |  |  |  |  |
| For, sunday faced, with dusters in my glove, | 18 | 16 | 12 | 21 | 16 |
| I set back the clock faced tailors, | 132 | 18 | 78 | 147 | 18 |
| FACES |  |  |  |  |  |
| Sweet are their fathered faces in their wings.' | 26 | 14 | 16 | 31 | 14 |
| Stalking my children's faces with a tail of blood, | 49 | 20 | 29 | 58 | 20 |
| FADE |  |  |  |  |  |
| 'These are but dreaming men. Breathe, and they fade.' | 26 | 15 | 16 | 31 | 15 |
| FADED |  |  |  |  |  |
| Faded my elbow ghost, the mothers-eyed, | 26 | 16 | 16 | 31 | 16 |
| And from her lips the faded pigments fall, | 63 | 7 | 38 | 72 | 7 |
| And the rain wring out its tongues on the faded yard, | 178 | 11 | 90 | 199 | 12 |
| FAIL |  |  |  |  |  |
| May fail to fasten with a virgin o | 18 | 19 | 12 | 21 | 19 |
| Tells the stick, 'fail'. | 19 | 5 | 12 | 22 | 10 |
| So the ball fail, | 51 | 25 | 31 | 61 | 4 |
| And father all nor fail the fly-lord's acre, | 60 | 13 | 36 | 69 | 13 |
| I may without fail | 108 | 17 | 66 | 119 | 17 |
| Both shall fail if I bow not to your blessing | 110 | 19 | 67 | 121 | 21 |
| FAIR |  |  |  |  |  |
| From the fair dead who flush the sea | 2 | 10 | 2 | 2 | 10 |
| And the wings of the great roc ribboned for the fair! | 164 | 16 | 86 | 184 | 2 |
| FAIR-FORMED |  |  |  |  |  |
| The twisted brain, the fair-formed loin, | 48 | 25 | 28 | 57 | 2 |
| FAIRIES |  |  |  |  |  |
| And, from his fork, a dog among the fairies, | 71 | 4 | 44 | 80 | 4 |
| FAIRY |  |  |  |  |  |
| Divide the night and day with fairy thumbs; | 1 | 15 | 2 | 1 | 15 |
| FAITH |  |  |  |  |  |
| The dream has sucked the sleeper of his faith | 15 | 9 | 10 | 17 | 9 |
| This is the world. Have faith. | 15 | 16 | 10 | 17 | 16 |
| Despair of blood, faith in the maiden's slime, | 18 | 23 | 12 | 22 | 3 |
| The sea-halved faith that blew time to his knees, | 67 | 4 | 41 | 76 | 4 |
| Faith in their hands shall snap in two, | 68 | 15 | 42 | 77 | 15 |
| His faith around her flew undone | 114 | 3 | 69 | 126 | 3 |

|  | U.K. | | | U.S. | |
| --- | --- | --- | --- | --- | --- |
|  | Page | Line | Poem | Page | Line |
| On a star of faith pure as the drifting bread, | 119 | 12 | 72 | 131 | 12 |
| But her faith that each vast night and the saga of prayer | 166 | 3 | 86 | 186 | 3 |
| Her faith that this last night for his unsacred sake | 166 | 5 | 86 | 186 | 5 |
| Your faith as deathless as the outcry of the ruled sun. | 166 | 12 | 86 | 186 | 12 |
| With more triumphant faith | 173 | 16 | 88 | 193 | 16 |
| Under the lighted shapes of faith and their moonshade | 176 | 17 | 90 | 197 | 17 |
| **FAITHLESS** | | | | | |
| Forgotten dark, rest their pulse and bury their dead in her faithless sleep. | 115 | 23 | 69 | 127 | 23 |
| **FAITHLESSLY** | | | | | |
| Faithlessly unto Him | 172 | 18 | 88 | 192 | 18 |
| **FAKE** | | | | | |
| Said the fake gentleman in suit of spades, | 73 | 14 | 44 | 82 | 14 |
| **FALL** | | | | | |
| That will fly and fall | viii | 4 | 1 | xvi | 4 |
| Shall fall awake when cures and their itch | 15 | 2 | 10 | 17 | 2 |
| Let fall the tear of time; the sleeper's eye, | 26 | 2 | 16 | 31 | 2 |
| Hearing the weather fall. | 36 | 6 | 20 | 41 | 6 |
| Before the fall from love the flying heartbone, | 41 | 15 | 23 | 47 | 15 |
| The greenwood dying as the deer fall in their tracks, | 49 | 11 | 29 | 58 | 11 |
| Down fall four padding weathers on the scarlet lands, | 49 | 19 | 29 | 58 | 19 |
| So star fall, | 51 | 24 | 31 | 61 | 3 |
| And from her lips the faded pigments fall, | 63 | 7 | 38 | 72 | 7 |
| Shall I fall to death's feather. | 64 | 18 | 39 | 73 | 18 |
| And I felt with my bare fall | 93 | 28 | 56 | 103 | 8 |
| A saint about to fall, | 95 | 1 | 58 | 105 | 1 |
| Heaven fell with his fall and one crocked bell beat the left air. | 95 | 25 | 58 | 105 | 25 |
| O wake to see, after a noble fall, | 96 | 18 | 58 | 107 | 1 |
| And all the elements of the slow fall rejoiced | 122 | 4 | 72 | 135 | 4 |
| Now break a giant tear for the little known fall, | 126 | 8 | 74 | 140 | 8 |
| Night fall and the fruit like a sun, | 131 | 4 | 77 | 145 | 10 |
| Of the endless fall. | 146 | 13 | 82 | 163 | 13 |
| And the flakes fall like hills. | 154 | 16 | 83 | 172 | 16 |
| The Thief fall on the dead like the willy nilly dew, | 165 | 22 | 86 | 185 | 12 |
| In the thistledown fall, | 170 | 19 | 88 | 190 | 19 |
| Fall and the dew larks sing | 173 | 21 | 88 | 193 | 21 |
| Teach me the love that is evergreen after the fall leaved | 178 | 12 | 90 | 199 | 13 |
| A saint about to fall | 95 | | 58 | 105 | |

| | U.K. | | | U.S. | |
|---|---|---|---|---|---|
| | *Page* | *Line* | *Poem* | *Page* | *Line* |
| **FALLEN** | | | | | |
| Love drips and gathers, but the fallen blood | 9 | 17 | 6 | 10 | 17 |
| Of sick old manhood on the fallen jaws, | 12 | 24 | 9 | 14 | 3 |
| I dreamed my genesis in sweat of death, fallen | 29 | 1 | 17 | 34 | 5 |
| Gentle in their clogs over the fallen sky, | 119 | 24 | 72 | 132 | 4 |
| **FALLING** | | | | | |
| Golden Glamorgan straightens, to the falling birds. | 49 | 23 | 29 | 58 | 23 |
| And the stars falling cold, | 119 | 6 | 72 | 131 | 6 |
| Under the night forever falling. | 145 | 17 | 82 | 162 | 17 |
| Forever falling night is a known | 146 | 1 | 82 | 163 | 1 |
| Oh, Jericho was falling in their lungs! | 151 | 6 | 83 | 168 | 14 |
| This night and each night since the falling star you were born, | 164 | 6 | 86 | 183 | 13 |
| Steered by the falling stars. | 171 | 14 | 88 | 191 | 14 |
| **FALLOW** | | | | | |
| Worm in the scalp, the staked and fallow. | 33 | 9 | 19 | 38 | 9 |
| **FALLS** | | | | | |
| The cadaverous gravels, falls thick and steadily, | 36 | 20 | 20 | 41 | 20 |
| Of many a hundred falls; | 53 | 5 | 32 | 62 | 5 |
| Nor falls to His green myths? | 69 | 18 | 43 | 78 | 18 |
| Falls on a ring of summers and locked noons. | 79 | 4 | 46 | 88 | 7 |
| And falls, and flowers in the yawning wound at our sides, | 163 | 13 | 86 | 183 | 20 |
| Ever and ever he finds a way, as the snow falls, | 164 | 7 | 86 | 183 | 14 |
| As the rain falls, hail on the fleece, as the vale mist rides | 164 | 8 | 86 | 183 | 15 |
| Through the haygold stalls, as the dew falls on the wind- | 164 | 9 | 86 | 183 | 16 |
| Of the morning leaves, as the star falls, as the winged | 164 | 11 | 86 | 183 | 18 |
| As the world falls, silent as the cyclone of silence. | 164 | 14 | 86 | 183 | 21 |
| **FALSE** | | | | | |
| Are formed of flesh, but let the false day come | 63 | 6 | 38 | 72 | 6 |
| **FAME** | | | | | |
| Flood of her heart's fame; she would lie dumb and deep | 87 | 19 | 52 | 96 | 19 |
| **FAMILIAR** | | | | | |
| The scudding base of the familiar sky, | 96 | 4 | 58 | 106 | 4 |
| A desireless familiar | 107 | 15 | 65 | 118 | 15 |
| **FAMINE** | | | | | |
| When no mouth stirred about the hanging famine, | 20 | 5 | 13 | 24 | 5 |
| And famine grew, and locusts came; | 62 | 10 | 37 | 71 | 10 |
| **FAMOUS** | | | | | |
| The famous stitch droppers. | 132 | 28 | 78 | 148 | 3 |

| | U.K. | | | U.S. | |
|---|---|---|---|---|---|
| | *Page* | *Line* | *Poem* | *Page* | *Line* |
| Of the pacing, famous sea but its speech, | 157 | 18 | 83 | 176 | 10 |
| And as I was green and carefree, famous among the barns | 159 | 10 | 85 | 178 | 10 |
| In the unknown, famous light of great | 171 | 20 | 88 | 191 | 20 |
| FANCY | | | | | |
| Time is a foolish fancy, time and fool. | 19 | 1 | 12 | 22 | 6 |
| FAR | | | | | |
| Reaching a second ground far from the stars; | 26 | 7 | 16 | 31 | 7 |
| Close and far she announced the theft of the heart | 114 | 16 | 69 | 126 | 16 |
| And the smell of hay in the snow, and the far owl | 119 | 7 | 72 | 131 | 7 |
| And over the cloth of counties the far hills rode near, | 122 | 13 | 72 | 135 | 13 |
| In the far ago land the door of his death glided wide, | 122 | 25 | 72 | 136 | 5 |
| Never and never, my girl riding far and near | 162 | 1 | 86 | 181 | 1 |
| And far at sea he knows, | 171 | 3 | 88 | 191 | 3 |
| FARAWAY | | | | | |
| In the wood faraway under me. | 103 | 5 | 63 | 114 | 5 |
| FAREWELLS | | | | | |
| On the consumptives' terrace taking their two farewells, | 36 | 10 | 20 | 41 | 10 |
| FARING | | | | | |
| Praise to our faring hearts. | 15 | 22 | 10 | 18 | 2 |
| FARM | | | | | |
| And floating fields from the farm in the cup of the vales, | 119 | 3 | 72 | 131 | 3 |
| Flocked with the sheep white smoke of the farm house cowl | 119 | 9 | 72 | 131 | 9 |
| Torn and alone in a farm house in a fold | 119 | 15 | 72 | 131 | 15 |
| And all the woken farm at its white trades, | 119 | 25 | 72 | 132 | 5 |
| Past the blind barns and byres of the windless farm. | 122 | 10 | 72 | 135 | 10 |
| On a bread white hill over the cupped farm | 122 | 27 | 72 | 136 | 7 |
| About the happy yard and singing as the farm was home, | 159 | 11 | 85 | 178 | 11 |
| As I rode to sleep the owls were bearing the farm away, | 160 | 2 | 85 | 179 | 2 |
| And then to awake, and the farm, like a wanderer white | 160 | 6 | 85 | 179 | 6 |
| Nor the tusked prince, in the ruttish farm, at the rind | 163 | 14 | 86 | 182 | 14 |
| And wake to the farm forever fled from the childless land. | 161 | 3 | 85 | 180 | 6 |
| FARMER | | | | | |
| Farmer in time of frost the burning leagues, | 60 | 10 | 36 | 69 | 10 |

|  | U.K. | | | U.S. | |
| --- | --- | --- | --- | --- | --- |
|  | *Page* | *Line* | *Poem* | *Page* | *Line* |
| **FARMS** | | | | | |
| Sheep white hollow farms | viii | 25 | 1 | xvi | 25 |
| Hollow farms in a throng | ix | 28 | 1 | xviii | 2 |
| Above the farms and the white horses | 102 | 13 | 63 | 113 | 13 |
| Paddocks in the farms of birds. The dead oak walks for love. | 121 | 20 | 72 | 134 | 15 |
| Gallop through the arched, green farms, | 156 | 20 | 82 | 175 | 8 |
| **FAST** | | | | | |
| So fast I move defying time, the quiet gentleman | 63 | 14 | 38 | 72 | 14 |
| And fast through the drifts of the thickets antlered like deer, | 122 | 15 | 72 | 135 | 15 |
| Boat with its anchor free and fast | 149 | 6 | 83 | 166 | 6 |
| A wind throws a shadow and it freezes fast. | 154 | 10 | 83 | 172 | 10 |
| Lie fast and soothed, | 162 | 19 | 86 | 181 | 19 |
| **FASTEN** | | | | | |
| May fail to fasten with a virgin o | 18 | 19 | 12 | 21 | 19 |
| Its wringing shell, and let her eyelids fasten. | 79 | 9 | 46 | 88 | 12 |
| **FAT** | | | | | |
| At nightbreak born in the fat side, from an animal bed | 84 | 2 | 49 | 93 | 8 |
| Through the waves of the fat streets nor the skeleton's thin ways. | 98 | 5 | 59 | 109 | 8 |
| Or, butter fat goosegirls, bounced in a gambo bed, | 177 | 17 | 90 | 198 | 16 |
| **FATE** | | | | | |
| Love, my fate got luckily, | 110 | 15 | 67 | 121 | 17 |
| **FATHER** | | | | | |
| I am the man your father was. | 3 | 4 | 2 | 3 | 10 |
| Swung by my father from his dome. | 7 | 12 | 5 | 8 | 12 |
| Long breath that carried to my father | 8 | 17 | 5 | 9 | 17 |
| Half of the fellow father as he doubles | 30 | 1 | 18 | 35 | 1 |
| Do you not father me, nor the erected arm | 46 | 1 | 27 | 54 | 1 |
| Am I not father, too, and the ascending boy, | 46 | 9 | 27 | 54 | 9 |
| Do you not father me on the destroying sand? | 47 | 1 | 27 | 55 | 1 |
| Drives out the father from the caesared camp; | 54 | 27 | 33 | 64 | 3 |
| And father all nor fail the fly-lord's acre, | 60 | 13 | 36 | 69 | 13 |
| And you, my father, there on the sad height, | 116 | 16 | 70 | 128 | 16 |
| Sun the father his quiver full of the infants of pure fire, | 158 | 19 | 84 | 177 | 19 |
| Do you not father me | 46 | | 27 | 54 | |
| **FATHER'S** | | | | | |
| He drowned his father's magics in a dream. | 4 | 18 | 3 | 4 | 18 |
| And the five-fathomed Hamlet on his father's coral, | 38 | 5 | 20 | 43 | 15 |
| Rebel against my father's dream | 66 | 3 | 40 | 75 | 3 |
| Of his father's house in the sands, | 95 | 7 | 58 | 105 | 7 |
| **FATHERED** | | | | | |
| Sweet are their fathered faces in their wings.' | 26 | 14 | 16 | 31 | 14 |

FATHERED (continued)

| | U.K. | | | U.S. | |
|---|---|---|---|---|---|
| | Page | Line | Poem | Page | Line |
| Let him find no rest but be fathered and found, | | | 91 | 200 | 12 |

FATHERING

| | | | | | |
|---|---|---|---|---|---|
| And sister to the fathering worm. | 7 | 6 | 5 | 8 | 6 |
| Fathering and all humbling darkness | 101 | 3 | 62 | 112 | 3 |

FATHERLESS

| | | | | | |
|---|---|---|---|---|---|
| In the name of the fatherless | 147 | 2 | 82 | 164 | 2 |

FATHERS

| | | | | | |
|---|---|---|---|---|---|
| Now Jack my fathers let the time-faced crook, | 67 | 15 | 41 | 76 | 15 |
| His fathers cling to the hand of the girl | 155 | 3 | 83 | 173 | 7 |

FATHERS'

| | | | | | |
|---|---|---|---|---|---|
| 'My fathers' globe knocks on its nave and sings.' | 26 | 11 | 16 | 31 | 11 |
| 'This that we tread was, too, your fathers' land.' | 26 | 12 | 16 | 31 | 12 |
| My fathers' ghost is climbing in the rain. | 27 | 5 | 16 | 32 | 10 |
| Shape with my fathers' thieves. | 67 | 28 | 41 | 76 | 28 |

FATHOM

| | | | | | |
|---|---|---|---|---|---|
| Windily master of man was the rotten fathom, | 38 | 26 | 20 | 44 | 16 |

FATHOMED

| | | | | | |
|---|---|---|---|---|---|
| Is half its light; the fathomed sea | 6 | 11 | 4 | 6 | 11 |

FATS

| | | | | | |
|---|---|---|---|---|---|
| She who was who I hold, the fats and flower, | 54 | 2 | 33 | 63 | 2 |
| The fats of midnight when the salt was singing; | 74 | 10 | 44 | 83 | 10 |

FAULT

| | | | | | |
|---|---|---|---|---|---|
| A woman figure without fault | 112 | 8 | 68 | 124 | 8 |

FAULTS

| | | | | | |
|---|---|---|---|---|---|
| That though I loved them for their faults | 107 | 18 | 65 | 118 | 18 |

FAWKES

| | | | | | |
|---|---|---|---|---|---|
| And the daughters of darkness flame like Fawkes fires still. | 178 | 19 | 90 | 199 | 20 |

FEAR

| | | | | | |
|---|---|---|---|---|---|
| Of fear, rage red, manalive, | viii | 22 | 1 | xvi | 22 |
| I would not fear the apple nor the flood | 12 | 6 | 9 | 13 | 6 |
| I would not fear the gallows nor the axe | 12 | 13 | 9 | 13 | 13 |
| I would not fear the muscling-in of love | 12 | 17 | 9 | 13 | 17 |
| I would not fear the devil in the loin | 12 | 20 | 9 | 13 | 20 |
| Fear not the working world, my mortal, | 33 | 13 | 19 | 38 | 13 |
| Fear not the flat, synthetic blood, | 33 | 14 | 19 | 38 | 14 |
| Fear not the tread, the seeded milling, | 33 | 16 | 19 | 38 | 16 |
| Fear not the screws that turn the voice, | 33 | 23 | 19 | 39 | 5 |
| Neither by night's ancient fear, | 64 | 15 | 39 | 73 | 15 |
| Throw your fear a parcel of stone | 96 | 12 | 58 | 106 | 12 |
| (Bury the dead for fear that they walk to the grave in labour.) | 99 | 2 | 60 | 110 | 2 |
| Fear or believe that the wolf in a sheepwhite hood | 162 | 3 | 86 | 181 | 3 |
| Bell believe or fear that the rustic shade or spell | 162 | 22 | 86 | 181 | 22 |
| On the lord's-table of the bowing grass. Fear most | 163 | 12 | 86 | 182 | 12 |

| | U.K. Page | U.K. Line | Poem | U.S. Page | U.S. Line |
|---|---|---|---|---|---|
| Ever and ever by all your vows believe and fear | 166 | 8 | 86 | 186 | 8 |
| FEARING | | | | | |
| He cried as he died, fearing at last the spheres' | | | 91 | 201 | 12 |
| FEARS | | | | | |
| We hid our fears in that murdering breath, | 125 | 14 | 74 | 139 | 14 |
| FEAST | | | | | |
| After the feast of tear-stuffed time and thistles | 87 | 10 | 52 | 96 | 10 |
| FEATHER | | | | | |
| And I was struck down by death's feather. | 8 | 15 | 5 | 9 | 15 |
| And what's the rub? Death's feather on the nerve? | 13 | 15 | 9 | 15 | 1 |
| The cancer's fusion, or the summer feather | 19 | 7 | 12 | 22 | 12 |
| I fled that ground as lightly as a feather. | 26 | 10 | 16 | 31 | 10 |
| What colour is glory? Death's feather? tremble | 31 | 1 | 18 | 36 | 1 |
| Who blows death's feather? What glory is colour? | 32 | 7 | 18 | 37 | 13 |
| I blow the stammel feather in the vein. | 32 | 8 | 18 | 37 | 14 |
| Shall I fall to death's feather. | 64 | 18 | 39 | 73 | 18 |
| Always good luck, praised the finned in the feather | 154 | 5 | 83 | 172 | 5 |
| FEATHERED | | | | | |
| Above her folded head, and the soft feathered voice | 122 | 2 | 72 | 135 | 2 |
| Hopping hot leaved and feathered | 132 | 20 | 78 | 147 | 20 |
| FEATHERLANDS | | | | | |
| On the angelic etna of the last whirring feather-lands, | 95 | 11 | 58 | 105 | 11 |
| FEATHERS | | | | | |
| Are but the roots of nettles and of feathers | 72 | 2 | 44 | 81 | 2 |
| Die in red feathers when the flying heaven's cut, | 92 | 12 | 55 | 101 | 18 |
| As the snapt feathers snow, | 169 | 2 | 87 | 189 | 11 |
| FEATHERY | | | | | |
| From the stone nest it does not let the feathery | 86 | 2 | 51 | 95 | 2 |
| FEATURES | | | | | |
| The features in their private dark | 63 | 5 | 38 | 72 | 5 |
| Love's reflection of the mushroom features, | 73 | 7 | 44 | 82 | 7 |
| Gold on such features, and the linen spirit | 76 | 3 | 44 | 85 | 3 |
| FED | | | | | |
| Where fishes' food is fed the shades | 5 | 5 | 3 | 5 | 5 |
| One sun, one manna, warmed and fed. | 21 | 26 | 13 | 26 | 9 |
| For the salty birds fluttered and fed | 152 | 24 | 83 | 170 | 17 |
| FEED | | | | | |
| Of doubt and dark they feed their nerves; | 1 | 11 | 2 | 1 | 11 |
| The stocked heart is forced, and agony has another mouth to feed. | 96 | 17 | 58 | 106 | 17 |
| FEEDING | | | | | |
| Twice in the feeding sea, grown | 29 | 2 | 17 | 34 | 6 |

FEELING

| | U.K. | | | U.S. | |
|---|---|---|---|---|---|
| | Page | Line | Poem | Page | Line |

FEELING
Feeling regret when this is wasted

| | 48 | 18 | 28 | 56 | 18 |

FEET
Feet in the rubbing dust.

| | 13 | 14 | 9 | 14 | 21 |

FELL
By trick or chance he fell asleep

| | 5 | 10 | 3 | 5 | 10 |

Look twice before he fell from grace.

| | 63 | 4 | 38 | 72 | 4 |

For loss of blood I fell on Ishmael's plain,

| | 73 | 17 | 44 | 82 | 17 |

Whose hooded, fountain heart once fell in puddles

| | 87 | 14 | 52 | 96 | 14 |

Heaven fell with his fall and one crocked bell beat the left air.

| | 95 | 25 | 58 | 105 | 25 |

A squall of birds bellowed and fell,

| | 150 | 15 | 83 | 167 | 19 |

Rose and crowed and fell!

| | 151 | 12 | 83 | 168 | 20 |

FELLED
Felled and quilled, flash to my patch

| | ix | 32 | 1 | xviii | 6 |

I am, the tower told, felled by a timeless stroke,

| | 46 | 21 | 27 | 54 | 21 |

The hand that signed the paper felled a city;

| | 62 | 1 | 37 | 71 | 1 |

The oak is felled in the acorn

| | 155 | 11 | 83 | 173 | 15 |

FELLOW
Each golden grain spat life into its fellow,

| | 20 | 23 | 13 | 24 | 23 |

Half of the fellow father as he doubles

| | 30 | 1 | 18 | 35 | 1 |

Half of the fellow mother as she dabbles

| | 30 | 3 | 18 | 35 | 3 |

The fellow half was frozen as it bubbled

| | 30 | 7 | 18 | 35 | 7 |

The fellow seed and shadow as it babbled

| | 30 | 9 | 18 | 35 | 9 |

The fellow halves that, cloven as they swivel

| | 32 | 1 | 18 | 37 | 7 |

How now my flesh, my naked fellow,

| | 33 | 7 | 19 | 38 | 7 |

FELLOWED
I fellowed sleep who kissed me in the brain,

| | 26 | 1 | 16 | 31 | 1 |

The broken halves are fellowed in a cripple,

| | 30 | 13 | 18 | 35 | 13 |

I fellowed sleep

| | 26 | | 16 | 31 | |

FELLOWS
And we shall be fit fellows for a life,

| | 15 | 20 | 10 | 17 | 20 |

I blew the dreaming fellows to their bed

| | 26 | 19 | 16 | 31 | 19 |

FELT
Felt thud beneath my flesh's armour,

| | 7 | 9 | 5 | 8 | 9 |

And I felt with my bare fall

| | 93 | 28 | 56 | 103 | 8 |

FEMALE
Shall it be male or female? say the cells,

| | 12 | 8 | 9 | 13 | 8 |

Shall it be male or female? say the fingers

| | 12 | 15 | 9 | 13 | 15 |

The female, deadly, and male

| | 115 | 7 | 69 | 127 | 7 |

FENCED
Nor fenced, nor staked, the gushers of the sky

| | 24 | 16 | 15 | 29 | 16 |

FENCES
The fences of the light are down,

| | 5 | 16 | 3 | 5 | 16 |

FEND
Can we fend off rock arrival,

| | 82 | 22 | 48 | 91 | 22 |

| | U.K. Page | Line | Poem | U.S. Page | Line |
|---|---|---|---|---|---|
| **FERN** | | | | | |
| In a room with a stuffed fox and a stale fern, | 87 | 11 | 52 | 96 | 11 |
| And the strutting fern lay seeds on the black sill. | 88 | 12 | 52 | 97 | 12 |
| From the broomed witch's spume you are shielded by fern | 162 | 17 | 86 | 181 | 17 |
| Fern Hill | 159 | | 85 | 178 | |
| **FERNED** | | | | | |
| Bow down the walls of the ferned and foxy woods | 87 | 24 | 52 | 96 | 24 |
| **FERNS** | | | | | |
| Behind a pot of ferns the wagging clock | 16 | 17 | 11 | 19 | 17 |
| **FERRIES** | | | | | |
| That the snow blind twilight ferries over the lakes | 119 | 2 | 72 | 131 | 2 |
| **FERRULE** | | | | | |
| Be by your one ghost pierced, his pointed ferrule, | 38 | 1 | 20 | 43 | 11 |
| **FETCH** | | | | | |
| Of frozen loves they fetch their girls, | 1 | 5 | 2 | 1 | 5 |
| **FEVER** | | | | | |
| My youth is bent by the same wintry fever. | 9 | 5 | 6 | 10 | 5 |
| Lit on the cuddled tree, the cross of fever, | 19 | 8 | 12 | 22 | 13 |
| From love's first fever to her plague, from the soft second | 20 | 1 | 13 | 24 | 1 |
| The hand that signed the treaty bred a fever, | 62 | 9 | 37 | 71 | 9 |
| From love's first fever to her plague | 20 | | 13 | 24 | |
| **FEVER'S** | | | | | |
| One breast gave suck the fever's issue; | 21 | 19 | 13 | 26 | 2 |
| **FEW** | | | | | |
| Never shall beast be born to atlas the few seas | 92 | 4 | 55 | 101 | 10 |
| A child of a few hours | 129 | 5 | 77 | 143 | 5 |
| In all his tuneful turning so few and such morning songs | 160 | 21 | 85 | 179 | 21 |
| **FIBRE** | | | | | |
| Come unto sea-stuck towers, at the fibre scaling, | 37 | 23 | 20 | 43 | 6 |
| Prophets and fibre kings in oil and letter, | 75 | 20 | 44 | 84 | 20 |
| **FIBS** | | | | | |
| John's beast, Job's patience, and the fibs of vision, | 41 | 21 | 23 | 48 | 3 |
| **FIDDLE** | | | | | |
| Hubbub and fiddle, this tune | ix | 21 | 1 | xvii | 21 |
| **FIDDLED** | | | | | |
| A serpent fiddled in the shaping-time. | 40 | 18 | 22 | 46 | 18 |
| **FIDDLES** | | | | | |
| Was there a time when dancers with their fiddles | 50 | 1 | 30 | 59 | 1 |
| **FIDDLING** | | | | | |
| And God walked there who was a fiddling warden | 40 | 5 | 22 | 46 | 5 |
| **FIELD** | | | | | |
| And dark shoals every holy field. | x | 7 | 1 | xviii | 13 |

FIELD (continued)

|  | U.K. | | | U.S. | |
|---|---|---|---|---|---|
|  | *Page* | *Line* | *Poem* | *Page* | *Line* |
| On field and sand | 54 | 22 | 33 | 63 | 22 |
| Till field and roof lie level and the same | 63 | 13 | 38 | 72 | 13 |
| Stills snapped by night in the bread-sided field, | 73 | 8 | 44 | 82 | 8 |
| With a capsized field where a school sat still | 89 | 3 | 53 | 98 | 3 |
| And heard the lewd, wooed field flow to the coming frost, | 177 | 10 | 90 | 198 | 9 |

FIELDS

| From the foreign fields of space, | 43 | 16 | 24 | 51 | 2 |
|---|---|---|---|---|---|
| From the star-flanked fields of space, | 43 | 23 | 24 | 51 | 9 |
| And the twice told fields of infancy | 103 | 26 | 63 | 115 | 1 |
| And floating fields from the farm in the cup of the vales, | 119 | 3 | 72 | 131 | 3 |
| Of fields. And burning then | 119 | 16 | 72 | 131 | 16 |
| Hunger of birds in the fields of the bread of water, | 120 | 17 | 72 | 133 | 2 |
| Never to flourish in the fields of the white seed | 120 | 29 | 72 | 133 | 14 |
| Of fields. For love, the long ago she bird rises. Look. | 121 | 25 | 72 | 134 | 20 |
| The fields of seed and the time dying flesh astride, | 122 | 23 | 72 | 136 | 3 |
| And the lakes and floating fields and the river wended | 122 | 28 | 72 | 136 | 8 |
| Strike and sing his catch of fields | 156 | 13 | 83 | 175 | 1 |
| Fields high as the house, the tunes from the chimneys, it was air | 159 | 20 | 85 | 178 | 20 |
| On to the fields of praise | 160 | 14 | 85 | 179 | 14 |
| I should hear him fly with the high fields | 161 | 2 | 85 | 180 | 5 |

FIEND

| Howls the foul fiend to heel. | 66 | 5 | 40 | 75 | 5 |
|---|---|---|---|---|---|

FIERCE

| Lops, as a bush plumed with flames, the rant of the fierce eye, | 92 | 10 | 55 | 101 | 16 |
|---|---|---|---|---|---|
| Curse, bless, me now with your fierce tears, I pray. | 116 | 17 | 70 | 128 | 17 |

FIERCELY

| In a fiercely mourning house in a crooked year. | 88 | 2 | 52 | 97 | 2 |
|---|---|---|---|---|---|

FIERY

| His fiery reel sings off its flames, | 151 | 16 | 83 | 169 | 4 |
|---|---|---|---|---|---|
| To fiery tyburn over the wrestle of elms until | 167 | 9 | 87 | 187 | 9 |
| The mansouled fiery islands! Oh, | 173 | 24 | 88 | 193 | 24 |

FIFTH

| Lie this fifth month unskated, and the birds have flown; | 49 | 9 | 29 | 58 | 9 |
|---|---|---|---|---|---|

FIG

| Bright as a fig; | 24 | 11 | 15 | 29 | 11 |
|---|---|---|---|---|---|
| A fig for | 52 | 3 | 31 | 61 | 10 |

FIGHTING

| After such fighting as the weakest know, | 48 | 10 | 28 | 56 | 10 |
|---|---|---|---|---|---|

|  | U.K. | | | U.S. | |
|  | Page | Line | Poem | Page | Line |
|---|---|---|---|---|---|
| **FIGS** | | | | | |
| Nor hammer back a season in the figs, | 60 | 8 | 36 | 69 | 8 |
| **FIGURE** | | | | | |
| A woman figure without fault | 112 | 8 | 68 | 124 | 8 |
| **FIGURES** | | | | | |
| That once cut the figures of birds on the deep bread | 123 | 4 | 72 | 136 | 14 |
| **FILE** | | | | | |
| File through the flesh where no flesh decks the bones. | 24 | 6 | 15 | 29 | 6 |
| **FILED** | | | | | |
| Off from the creasing flesh, filed | 28 | 6 | 17 | 33 | 6 |
| **FILLED** | | | | | |
| In time at flood filled with his coloured doubles; | 61 | 3 | 36 | 70 | 3 |
| That the children filled with gravel | 111 | 9 | 68 | 123 | 9 |
| **FILLIES** | | | | | |
| With wild sea fillies and soaking bridles | 156 | 17 | 83 | 175 | 5 |
| **FILM** | | | | | |
| The film of spring is hanging from the lids. | 24 | 24 | 15 | 29 | 24 |
| I who saw in a hurried film | 93 | 21 | 56 | 103 | 1 |
| **FILMED** | | | | | |
| The cataracted eyes that filmed their cloth; | 4 | 21 | 3 | 4 | 21 |
| **FILMS** | | | | | |
| He films my vanity. | 69 | 25 | 43 | 79 | 1 |
| **FIN** | | | | | |
| Froth, flute, fin and quill | vii | 7 | 1 | xv | 7 |
| Through veil and fin and fire and coil | 69 | 23 | 43 | 78 | 23 |
| **FINAL** | | | | | |
| Finding the water final, | 36 | 9 | 20 | 41 | 9 |
| In the final direction of the elementary town | 99 | 8 | 60 | 110 | 8 |
| **FINCHES** | | | | | |
| He sings towards anguish; finches fly | 170 | 20 | 88 | 190 | 20 |
| **FIND** | | | | | |
| Let the hero seed find harbour, | 43 | 5 | 24 | 50 | 12 |
| Let the hero seed find harbour, | 43 | 12 | 24 | 50 | 19 |
| 'Find meat on bones that soon have none, | 65 | 1 | 40 | 74 | 1 |
| To-night shall find no dying but alive and warm | 100 | 15 | 61 | 111 | 15 |
| To find a woman's soul for a wife. | 175 | 19 | 89 | 195 | 24 |
| Let him find no rest but be fathered and found, | | | 91 | 200 | 12 |
| Find meat on bones | 65 | | 40 | 74 | |
| **FINDING** | | | | | |
| Finding the water final, | 36 | 9 | 20 | 41 | 9 |
| And the finding one | 140 | 13 | 82 | 157 | 13 |
| The finding one | 142 | 4 | 82 | 159 | 4 |
| **FINDS** | | | | | |
| Nor when he finds a beauty in the breast | 13 | 12 | 9 | 14 | 19 |
| Ever and ever he finds a way, as the snow falls, | 164 | 7 | 86 | 183 | 14 |

|  |  | U.K. |  |  | U.S. |  |
|  |  | Page | Line | Poem | Page | Line |
| **FINGER** |  |  |  |  |  |  |
| The jacks of frost they finger in the hives; | | 1 | 9 | 2 | 1 | 9 |
| Locked in the long worm of my finger | | 4 | 2 | 3 | 4 | 2 |
| The finger joints are cramped with chalk; | | 62 | 6 | 37 | 71 | 6 |
| Who speak on a finger and thumb, | | 70 | 1 | 43 | 79 | 5 |
| **FINGERMAN** |  |  |  |  |  |  |
| Wrenched by my fingerman, the leaden bud | | 54 | 11 | 33 | 63 | 11 |
| **FINGERS** |  |  |  |  |  |  |
| Shall it be male or female? say the fingers | | 12 | 15 | 9 | 13 | 15 |
| With frosty fingers punishes my hair, | | 16 | 2 | 11 | 19 | 2 |
| The fingers at the locks. | | 58 | 4 | 35 | 67 | 4 |
| Five sovereign fingers taxed the breath, | | 62 | 2 | 37 | 71 | 2 |
| The fingers will forget green thumbs and mark | | 81 | 2 | 47 | 90 | 2 |
| **FIN-GREEN** |  |  |  |  |  |  |
| Suffer the slash of vision by the fin-green stubble, | | 38 | 7 | 20 | 43 | 17 |
| **FINNED** |  |  |  |  |  |  |
| O kingdom of neighbours, finned | | ix | 31 | 1 | xviii | 5 |
| Always good luck, praised the finned in the feather | | 154 | 5 | 83 | 172 | 5 |
| **FINS** |  |  |  |  |  |  |
| Slipped the fins of those humpbacked tons | | 151 | 4 | 83 | 168 | 12 |
| To the hawk on fire, the halter height, over Towy's fins, | | 167 | 16 | 87 | 187 | 16 |
| **FIRE** |  |  |  |  |  |  |
| The fire of birds in | | vii | 26 | 1 | xv | 26 |
| And drop the plum like fire from the flesh. | | 12 | 9 | 9 | 13 | 9 |
| Caught by the crabbing sun I walk on fire | | 16 | 3 | 11 | 19 | 3 |
| In the beginning was the mounting fire | | 22 | 13 | 14 | 27 | 13 |
| Towns around on a wheel of fire. | | 33 | 6 | 19 | 38 | 6 |
| Love like a mist or fire through the bed of eels. | | 38 | 12 | 20 | 44 | 2 |
| I, in a wind on fire, from green Adam's cradle, | | 38 | 17 | 20 | 44 | 7 |
| The cockerel's tide upcasting from the fire. | | 51 | 21 | 31 | 60 | 21 |
| The seal of fire, | | 52 | 4 | 31 | 61 | 11 |
| Her bone to fire, | | 55 | 9 | 33 | 64 | 12 |
| The wind pass like a fire, | | 58 | 18 | 35 | 67 | 18 |
| Through veil and fin and fire and coil | | 69 | 23 | 43 | 78 | 23 |
| Calls the starved fire herd, is cast in ice, | | 79 | 1 | 46 | 88 | 4 |
| In the fire of his care his love in the high room. | | 100 | 16 | 61 | 111 | 16 |
| And fire, the flying rant | | 106 | 3 | 64 | 117 | 3 |
| Suffer the first vision that set fire to the stars. | | 108 | 18 | 66 | 119 | 18 |
| On the clay cold mouth, on the fire | | 109 | 8 | 67 | 120 | 8 |
| The scrolls of fire that burned in his heart and head, | | 119 | 14 | 72 | 131 | 14 |
| Greed on man beating near and fire neighbour | | 126 | 6 | 74 | 140 | 6 |
| For a man sleeps where fire leapt down and she learns through his arm | | 127 | 13 | 75 | 141 | 13 |
| Over the sun's hovel and the slum of fire | | 131 | 16 | 77 | 145 | 22 |

|  | U.K. | | | U.S. | |
|---|---|---|---|---|---|
|  | *Page* | *Line* | *Poem* | *Page* | *Line* |
| Combing with antlers, Columbus on fire, | 133 | 9 | 78 | 148 | 12 |
| And the craters of his eyes grew springshoots and fire | 135 | 7 | 80 | 152 | 7 |
| Fire on starlight, rake Jesu's stream; | 150 | 19 | 83 | 168 | 3 |
| He who blew the great fire in | 155 | 13 | 83 | 173 | 17 |
| When his long-legged flesh was a wind on fire | 157 | 3 | 83 | 175 | 15 |
| Sun the father his quiver full of the infants of pure fire, | 158 | 19 | 84 | 177 | 19 |
| And fire green as grass. | 159 | 22 | 85 | 178 | 22 |
| Into a homestall king or hamlet of fire | 162 | 11 | 86 | 181 | 11 |
| Of birds! Among the cocks like fire the red fox | 164 | 20 | 86 | 184 | 6 |
| Earth, air, water, fire, singing into the white act, | 165 | 16 | 86 | 185 | 6 |
| The hawk on fire hangs still; | 167 | 2 | 87 | 187 | 2 |
| To the hawk on fire, the halter height, over Towy's fins, | 167 | 16 | 87 | 187 | 16 |
| All praise of the hawk on fire in hawk-eyed dusk be sung, | 168 | 3 | 87 | 188 | 7 |
| A Refusal to Mourn the Death, by Fire, of a Child in London | 101 | | 62 | 112 | |
| Ceremony After a Fire Raid | 129 | | 77 | 143 | |
| FIREBALL | | | | | |
| Wind-heeled foot in the hole of a fireball, | 95 | 12 | 58 | 105 | 12 |
| FIRE-DWARFED | | | | | |
| Child beyond cockcrow, by the fire-dwarfed | 130 | 4 | 77 | 144 | 4 |
| FIREFLY | | | | | |
| And their firefly hairpins flew, and the ricks ran round— | 177 | 21 | 90 | 199 | 1 |
| FIRELIT | | | | | |
| In his firelit island ringed by the winged snow | 119 | 17 | 72 | 131 | 17 |
| FIRES | | | | | |
| In autumn teach three seasons' fires | 45 | 7 | 26 | 53 | 7 |
| Snail of man in His ship of fires | 69 | 8 | 43 | 78 | 8 |
| An enamoured man alone by the twigs of his eyes, two fires, | 77 | 7 | 45 | 86 | 7 |
| Lions and fires of his flying breath, | 117 | 5 | 71 | 129 | 5 |
| And fires where he should prowl down the cloud | 120 | 12 | 72 | 132 | 17 |
| And the home of prayers and fires, the tale ended. | 122 | 30 | 72 | 136 | 10 |
| The mother dug, and its arms full of fires. | 129 | 8 | 77 | 143 | 8 |
| Always good-bye to the fires of the face, | 153 | 2 | 83 | 170 | 18 |
| And the daughters of darkness flame like Fawkes fires still. | 178 | 19 | 90 | 199 | 20 |
| FIREWIND | | | | | |
| And a firewind kill the candle. | 83 | 6 | 49 | 92 | 6 |
| FIREWORKS | | | | | |
| Storm, snow, and fountain in the weather of fireworks, | 83 | 14 | 49 | 92 | 14 |

| | U.K. | | | U.S. | |
|---|---|---|---|---|---|
| | *Page* | *Line* | *Poem* | *Page* | *Line* |
| **FIRST** | | | | | |
| From love's first fever to her plague, from the soft second | 20 | 1 | 13 | 24 | 1 |
| From the first print of the unshodden foot, the lifting | 20 | 10 | 13 | 24 | 10 |
| From the first secret of the heart, the warning ghost, | 20 | 12 | 13 | 24 | 12 |
| And to the first dumb wonder at the flesh, | 20 | 13 | 13 | 24 | 13 |
| And from the first declension of the flesh | 21 | 7 | 13 | 25 | 7 |
| The substance forked that marrowed the first sun; | 22 | 4 | 14 | 27 | 4 |
| Touched the first cloud and left a sign. | 22 | 12 | 14 | 27 | 12 |
| First characters of birth and death. | 22 | 24 | 14 | 27 | 24 |
| This first and steepled season, to the summer's game. | 49 | 12 | 29 | 58 | 12 |
| First there was the lamb on knocking knees | 72 | 5 | 44 | 81 | 5 |
| Let the first Peter from a rainbow's quayrail | 76 | 15 | 44 | 85 | 15 |
| Deep with the first dead lies London's daughter, | 101 | 19 | 62 | 112 | 19 |
| After the first death, there is no other. | 101 | 24 | 62 | 112 | 24 |
| Suffer the first vision that set fire to the stars. | 108 | 18 | 66 | 119 | 18 |
| Flashed first across his thunderclapping eyes. | 117 | 24 | 71 | 129 | 24 |
| Was the first to die | 130 | 15 | 77 | 144 | 15 |
| On the first of each hardship, | 132 | 5 | 78 | 147 | 5 |
| And the first dawn | 139 | 4 | 82 | 156 | 4 |
| In the first fury of his stream | 140 | 8 | 82 | 157 | 8 |
| In the first, spinning place, the spellbound horses walking warm | 160 | 12 | 85 | 179 | 12 |
| And you shall wake, from country sleep, this dawn and each first dawn, | 166 | 11 | 86 | 186 | 11 |
| From love's first fever to her plague | 20 | | 13 | 24 | |
| **FISH** | | | | | |
| From fish to jumping hill! Look: | viii | 17 | 1 | xvi | 17 |
| No birds or flying fish | 58 | 15 | 35 | 67 | 15 |
| Ask the tall fish swept from the bible east, | 76 | 16 | 44 | 85 | 16 |
| To the trees and the stones and the fish in the tide. | 104 | 5 | 63 | 115 | 7 |
| The lured fish under the foam | 150 | 23 | 83 | 168 | 7 |
| Bird after dark and the laughing fish | 154 | 6 | 83 | 172 | 6 |
| With moving fish and rounded stones | 156 | 10 | 83 | 174 | 18 |
| **FISHERBIRD** | | | | | |
| Where the elegiac fisherbird stabs and paddles | 167 | 19 | 87 | 187 | 19 |
| **FISHERMAN** | | | | | |
| And the fisherman winds his reel | 154 | 3 | 83 | 172 | 3 |
| And the streets that the fisherman combed | 157 | 2 | 83 | 175 | 14 |
| To the fisherman lost on the land. | 157 | 22 | 83 | 176 | 14 |
| **FISHERMANNED** | | | | | |
| Then good-bye to the fishermanned | 149 | 5 | 83 | 166 | 5 |

|  | U.K. | | | U.S. | |
|  | Page | Line | Poem | Page | Line |
| **FISHERMEN** | | | | | |
| Fishermen of mermen | 91 | 23 | 55 | 101 | 1 |
| **FISHES** | | | | | |
| And over the glazed lakes skated the shapes of fishes | 123 | 5 | 72 | 136 | 15 |
| Was miraculous virginity old as loaves and fishes, | 127 | 5 | 75 | 141 | 5 |
| All the fishes were rayed in blood, | 149 | 23 | 83 | 167 | 3 |
| Oh miracle of fishes! The long dead bite! | 154 | 20 | 83 | 172 | 20 |
| Metropolis of fishes, | 157 | 12 | 83 | 176 | 4 |
| On a seizing sky; small fishes glide | 170 | 22 | 88 | 190 | 22 |
| Masts and fishes to the still quick stars, | 172 | 17 | 88 | 192 | 17 |
| **FISHES'** | | | | | |
| Where fishes' food is fed the shades | 5 | 5 | 3 | 5 | 5 |
| Furled on the fishes' house and hell, | 69 | 17 | 43 | 78 | 17 |
| **FISH-GILLED** | | | | | |
| The sweet, fish-gilled boats bringing blood | 95 | 22 | 58 | 105 | 22 |
| **FISHING** | | | | | |
| Crashes, and slowly the fishing holy stalking heron | 167 | 11 | 87 | 187 | 11 |
| Fishing in the tear of the Towy. Only a hoot owl | 169 | 3 | 87 | 189 | 12 |
| **FISHWIFE** | | | | | |
| With their fishwife cross | vii | 10 | 1 | xv | 10 |
| **FIST** | | | | | |
| Nor damned the sea that sped about my fist, | 4 | 3 | 3 | 4 | 3 |
| And close her fist. | 55 | 13 | 33 | 64 | 16 |
| Her fist of a face died clenched on a round pain; | 88 | 6 | 52 | 97 | 6 |
| **FISTS** | | | | | |
| With fists of turnips punishes the land, | 17 | 4 | 11 | 20 | 4 |
| Shall they clasp a comet in their fists? | 53 | 11 | 32 | 62 | 11 |
| And ghostly comets over the raised fists. | 53 | 26 | 32 | 62 | 26 |
| **FIT** | | | | | |
| And we shall be fit fellows for a life, | 15 | 20 | 10 | 17 | 20 |
| 'All game phrases fit your ring of a cockfight: | 97 | 6 | 59 | 108 | 6 |
| **FIVE** | | | | | |
| Five sovereign fingers taxed the breadth, | 62 | 2 | 37 | 71 | 2 |
| These five kings did a king to death. | 62 | 4 | 37 | 71 | 4 |
| The five kings count the dead but do not soften | 62 | 13 | 37 | 71 | 13 |
| With priest's grave foot and hand of five assassins | 78 | 25 | 46 | 88 | 2 |
| When all my five and country senses see, | 81 | 1 | 47 | 90 | 1 |
| The heart is sensual, though five eyes break. | 81 | 14 | 47 | 90 | 14 |
| Four elements and five | 173 | 1 | 88 | 193 | 1 |
| When all my five and country senses see | 81 | | 47 | 90 | |
| **FIVE-FATHOMED** | | | | | |
| And the five-fathomed Hamlet on his father's coral, | 38 | 5 | 20 | 43 | 15 |

| | U.K. | | | U.S. | |
|---|---|---|---|---|---|
| | Page | Line | Poem | Page | Line |

FIX

The scaled sea-sawers, fix in a naked sponge ... 74 / 22 / 44 / 83 / 22

FIXED

That frozen wife whose juices drift like a fixed
sea ... 77 / 14 / 45 / 86 / 14

FLAILED

Drunk as a vineyard snail, flailed like an octo-
pus, ... 91 / 7 / 55 / 100 / 7

FLAILING

No flailing calf or cat in a flame ... 175 / 11 / 89 / 195 / 16

FLAKES

Gliding windless through the hand folded flakes, ... 119 / 4 / 72 / 131 / 4

Bird through the times and lands and tribes of
the slow flakes. ... 122 / 19 / 72 / 135 / 19

And the flakes fall like hills. ... 154 / 16 / 83 / 172 / 16

FLAME

And the flame in the flesh's vision. ... 34 / 9 / 19 / 39 / 15

There is loud and dark directly under the dumb
flame, ... 83 / 13 / 49 / 92 / 13

Roosts sleeping chill till the flame of the cock
crow ... 119 / 19 / 72 / 131 / 19

The reptile profligates in a flame, ... 134 / 4 / 79 / 150 / 4

Burns me his name and his flame ... 138 / 11 / 82 / 155 / 11

With his flame in every grain. ... 141 / 10 / 82 / 158 / 10

Is dumb and gone with his flame of brides. ... 153 / 10 / 83 / 171 / 6

And his loin was a hunting flame ... 157 / 4 / 83 / 175 / 16

Before chains break to a hammer flame ... 171 / 17 / 88 / 191 / 17

No flailing calf or cat in a flame ... 175 / 11 / 89 / 195 / 16

And the daughters of darkness flame like Fawkes
fires still. ... 178 / 19 / 90 / 199 / 20

FLAMES

Lops, as a bush plumed with flames, the rant of
the fierce eye, ... 92 / 10 / 55 / 101 / 16

The mazes of his praise and envious tongue were
worked in flames and shells. ... 95 / 17 / 58 / 105 / 17

As the food and flames of the snow, a man unrolled ... 119 / 13 / 72 / 131 / 13

Into the bread in a wheatfield of flames, ... 131 / 18 / 77 / 145 / 24

His fiery reel sings off its flames, ... 151 / 16 / 83 / 169 / 4

And died on a hiss of flames ... 155 / 14 / 83 / 173 / 18

When his viperish fuse hangs looped with flames
under the brand ... 168 / 4 / 87 / 188 / 8

FLARED

Flared in the reek of the wiving sty with the rush ... 177 / 2 / 90 / 198 / 1

FLASH

Felled and quilled, flash to my patch ... ix / 32 / 1 / xviii / 6

The flash the noosed hawk ... 167 / 10 / 87 / 187 / 10

|  | U.K. | | | U.S. | |
|---|---|---|---|---|---|
|  | *Page* | *Line* | *Poem* | *Page* | *Line* |
| Flash, and the plumes crack, | 167 | 13 | 87 | 187 | 13 |
| FLASHED | | | | | |
| Flashed first across his thunderclapping eyes. | 117 | 24 | 71 | 129 | 24 |
| As the arc of the billhooks that flashed the hedges low | 178 | 7 | 90 | 199 | 8 |
| FLASHING | | | | | |
| Death flashing from his sleeve, | 67 | 16 | 41 | 76 | 16 |
| The flashing needle rock of squatters, | 132 | 26 | 78 | 148 | 1 |
| Flashing into the dark. | 160 | 5 | 85 | 179 | 5 |
| FLASK | | | | | |
| Had stringed my flask of matter to his rib. | 4 | 12 | 3 | 4 | 12 |
| FLAT | | | | | |
| Fear not the flat, synthetic blood, | 33 | 14 | 19 | 38 | 14 |
| Escapes to the flat cities' sails | 69 | 16 | 43 | 78 | 16 |
| FLATS | | | | | |
| The stained flats of heaven hit and razed | 95 | 2 | 58 | 105 | 2 |
| FLAVOURED | | | | | |
| The shades of girls, all flavoured from their shrouds, | 14 | 7 | 10 | 16 | 7 |
| Flavoured of celluloid give love the lie. | 14 | 20 | 10 | 16 | 20 |
| FLAXEN | | | | | |
| Strung by the flaxen whale-weed, from the hangman's raft, | 37 | 14 | 20 | 42 | 20 |
| FLEA | | | | | |
| Glory cracked like a flea. | 95 | 18 | 58 | 105 | 18 |
| FLED | | | | | |
| I fled the earth and, naked, climbed the weather, | 26 | 6 | 16 | 31 | 6 |
| I fled that ground as lightly as a feather. | 26 | 10 | 16 | 31 | 10 |
| The crumpled packs fled past this ghost in bloom, | 80 | 5 | 46 | 89 | 13 |
| And fled their love in a weaving dip. | 151 | 5 | 83 | 168 | 13 |
| And wake to the farm forever fled from the childless land. | 161 | 3 | 85 | 180 | 6 |
| FLEECE | | | | | |
| With pelt, and scale, and fleece: | x | 3 | 1 | xviii | 9 |
| As the rain falls, hail on the fleece, as the vale mist rides | 164 | 8 | 86 | 183 | 15 |
| FLESH | | | | | |
| A weather in the flesh and bone | 6 | 16 | 4 | 6 | 16 |
| Before I knocked and let flesh enter, | 7 | 1 | 5 | 8 | 1 |
| And flesh was snipped to cross the lines | 7 | 22 | 5 | 8 | 22 |
| I, born of flesh and ghost, was neither | 8 | 13 | 5 | 9 | 13 |
| Who took my flesh and bone for armour | 8 | 21 | 5 | 9 | 21 |
| The beach of flesh, and wind her bloodred plait; | 10 | 13 | 7 | 11 | 13 |
| And drop the plum like fire from the flesh. | 12 | 9 | 9 | 13 | 9 |

FLESH (continued)

|  | U.K. | | | U.S. | |
|---|---|---|---|---|---|
|  | Page | Line | Poem | Page | Line |
| And to the first dumb wonder at the flesh, | 20 | 13 | 13 | 24 | 13 |
| And from the first declension of the flesh | 21 | 7 | 13 | 25 | 7 |
| File through the flesh where no flesh decks the bones. | 24 | 6 | 15 | 29 | 6 |
| Off from the creasing flesh, filed | 28 | 6 | 17 | 33 | 6 |
| I piece my flesh that rattled on the yards | 31 | 14 | 18 | 36 | 14 |
| How now my flesh, my naked fellow, | 33 | 7 | 19 | 38 | 7 |
| All of the flesh, the dry worlds lever. | 33 | 12 | 19 | 38 | 12 |
| Man of my flesh, the jawbone riven, | 33 | 19 | 19 | 39 | 1 |
| Stroke of mechanical flesh on mine, | 34 | 5 | 19 | 39 | 11 |
| Knocked in the flesh that decked the vine, | 39 | 7 | 21 | 45 | 7 |
| This flesh you break, this blood you let | 39 | 11 | 21 | 45 | 11 |
| Marking the flesh and summer in the bay? | 46 | 11 | 27 | 54 | 11 |
| By a thin sea of flesh | 58 | 11 | 35 | 67 | 11 |
| Are formed of flesh, but let the false day come | 63 | 6 | 38 | 72 | 6 |
| Rebel against the flesh and bone, | 65 | 14 | 40 | 74 | 14 |
| Her flesh was meek as milk, but this skyward statue | 87 | 27 | 52 | 96 | 27 |
| Turns of your prayed flesh, nor shall I shoo the bird below me: | 109 | 27 | 67 | 121 | 1 |
| Of the living flesh is monstrous or immortal, | 110 | 13 | 67 | 121 | 15 |
| Or flower under the time dying flesh astride. | 120 | 30 | 72 | 133 | 15 |
| The fields of seed and the time dying flesh astride, | 122 | 23 | 72 | 136 | 3 |
| Cut-to-measure flesh bit, | 132 | 3 | 78 | 147 | 3 |
| With dry flesh and earth for adorning and bed. | 133 | 15 | 78 | 148 | 18 |
| Oh all the wanting flesh his enemy | 152 | 19 | 83 | 170 | 11 |
| Good-bye always for the flesh is cast | 154 | 2 | 83 | 172 | 2 |
| When his long-legged flesh was a wind on fire | 157 | 3 | 83 | 175 | 15 |
| Lulling of spheres in the seashell flesh, | 173 | 8 | 88 | 193 | 8 |
| Time by, their dust was flesh the swineherd rooted sly, | 177 | 1 | 90 | 197 | 21 |
| FLESH'S | | | | | |
| Felt thud beneath my flesh's armour, | 7 | 9 | 5 | 8 | 9 |
| Know now the flesh's lock and vice, | 33 | 20 | 19 | 39 | 2 |
| And the flame in the flesh's vision. | 34 | 9 | 19 | 39 | 15 |
| FLEW | | | | | |
| So, planing-heeled, I flew along my man | 26 | 4 | 16 | 31 | 4 |
| The ghost that hatched his havoc as he flew | 31 | 5 | 18 | 36 | 5 |
| Flew man-bearing there. | 113 | 6 | 69 | 125 | 6 |
| His faith around her flew undone | 114 | 3 | 69 | 126 | 3 |
| And their firefly hairpins flew, and the ricks ran round— | 177 | 21 | 90 | 199 | 1 |
| FLICK | | | | | |
| And makes with a flick of the thumb and sun | 96 | 25 | 58 | 107 | 8 |
| FLICKED | | | | | |
| Flicked from the carbolic city puzzle in a bed of sores | 96 | 3 | 58 | 106 | 3 |

|  | U.K. |  | Poem | U.S. |  |
|  | Page | Line |  | Page | Line |
| FLICKERING |  |  |  |  |  |
| The flickering runs and dive | ix | 4 | 1 | xviii | 4 |
| FLIES |  |  |  |  |  |
| And bags of blood let out their flies; | 4 | 23 | 3 | 4 | 23 |
| Would leave me cold as butter for the flies, | 12 | 26 | 9 | 14 | 5 |
| Flies on the shafted disk, declaims the morning | 16 | 19 | 11 | 19 | 19 |
| Dust in the buried wood, flies on the grains of her wings | 121 | 3 | 72 | 133 | 18 |
| FLIGHT |  |  |  |  |  |
| The flight of the carnal skull | 37 | 24 | 20 | 43 | 7 |
| Her molten flight up cinder-nesting columns, | 78 | 26 | 46 | 88 | 3 |
| Her lover's wings that fold to-morrow's flight, | 115 | 11 | 69 | 127 | 11 |
| Wild men who caught and sang the sun in flight, | 116 | 10 | 70 | 128 | 10 |
| Him up and he ran like a wind after the kindling flight | 122 | 9 | 72 | 135 | 9 |
| The woundward flight of the ancient | 142 | 8 | 82 | 159 | 8 |
| FLINT |  |  |  |  |  |
| We are the sons of flint and pitch. | 3 | 5 | 2 | 3 | 11 |
| Nor the flint in the lover's mauling. | 33 | 18 | 19 | 38 | 18 |
| The year-hedged row is lame with flint, | 70 | 10 | 43 | 79 | 14 |
| FLINTSTEPS |  |  |  |  |  |
| Who scales a hailing hill in her cold flintsteps | 79 | 3 | 46 | 88 | 6 |
| FLOAT |  |  |  |  |  |
| Here in this spring, stars float along the void; | 45 | 1 | 26 | 53 | 1 |
| FLOATED |  |  |  |  |  |
| Floated the lost cathedral | 150 | 11 | 83 | 167 | 15 |
| FLOATING |  |  |  |  |  |
| And floating fields from the farm in the cup of the vales, | 119 | 3 | 72 | 131 | 3 |
| And the lakes and floating fields and the river wended | 122 | 28 | 72 | 136 | 8 |
| Under the floating villages, | 157 | 10 | 83 | 176 | 2 |
| FLOCK |  |  |  |  |  |
| That Adam's wether in the flock of horns, | 72 | 7 | 44 | 81 | 7 |
| Hymned his shrivelling flock, | 95 | 13 | 58 | 105 | 13 |
| Leaves is dancing. Lines of age on the stones weave in a flock. | 121 | 23 | 72 | 134 | 18 |
| FLOCKED |  |  |  |  |  |
| Flocked with the sheep white smoke of the farm house cowl | 119 | 9 | 72 | 131 | 9 |
| Out of a lair in the flocked leaves in the dew dipped year | 162 | 6 | 86 | 181 | 6 |
| FLOCKS |  |  |  |  |  |
| Young among the long flocks, and never lie lost |  |  | 91 | 200 | 7 |
| FLOOD |  |  |  |  |  |
| As the flood begins, | viii | 20 | 1 | xvi | 20 |

FLOOD (continued)

|  | U.K. Page | U.K. Line | Poem | U.S. Page | U.S. Line |
|---|---|---|---|---|---|
| Hears, there, this fox light, my flood ship's | ix | 18 | 1 | xvii | 18 |
| And the flood flowers now | x | 19 | 1 | xviii | 25 |
| I would not fear the apple nor the flood | 12 | 6 | 9 | 13 | 6 |
| In time at flood filled with his coloured doubles; | 61 | 3 | 36 | 70 | 3 |
| Arc-lamped thrown back upon the cutting flood. | 73 | 10 | 44 | 82 | 10 |
| Flood of her heart's fame; she would lie dumb and deep | 87 | 19 | 52 | 96 | 19 |
| Put a tear for joy in the unearthly flood | 125 | 22 | 74 | 139 | 22 |
| May hold it in a great flood | 129 | 20 | 77 | 143 | 20 |
| For we saw him throw to the swift flood | 149 | 21 | 83 | 167 | 1 |

FLOODS

|  | U.K. Page | U.K. Line | Poem | U.S. Page | U.S. Line |
|---|---|---|---|---|---|
| There in their heat the winter floods | 1 | 4 | 2 | 1 | 4 |
| From garden cans, or free the floods? | 44 | 7 | 25 | 52 | 7 |
| Bent like a beast to lap the singular floods | 90 | 3 | 54 | 99 | 3 |
| And the dear floods of his hair. | 93 | 30 | 56 | 103 | 10 |
| Milk in your mouth, at the sour floods | 96 | 7 | 58 | 106 | 7 |

FLOOR

|  | U.K. Page | U.K. Line | Poem | U.S. Page | U.S. Line |
|---|---|---|---|---|---|
| Two heels of water on the floor of seed), | 56 | 24 | 34 | 66 | 3 |
| And the funeral grains of the slaughtered floor. | 135 | 5 | 80 | 152 | 5 |
| Over the gardens of the floor | 152 | 2 | 83 | 169 | 14 |

FLOORS

|  | U.K. Page | U.K. Line | Poem | U.S. Page | U.S. Line |
|---|---|---|---|---|---|
| The anchor dives through the floors of a church. | 157 | 20 | 83 | 176 | 12 |

FLOUNDERS

|  | U.K. Page | U.K. Line | Poem | U.S. Page | U.S. Line |
|---|---|---|---|---|---|
| Flounders, gulls, on their cold, dying trails, | 170 | 11 | 88 | 190 | 11 |

FLOURISH

|  | U.K. Page | U.K. Line | Poem | U.S. Page | U.S. Line |
|---|---|---|---|---|---|
| Never to flourish in the fields of the white seed | 120 | 29 | 72 | 133 | 14 |

FLOW

|  | U.K. Page | U.K. Line | Poem | U.S. Page | U.S. Line |
|---|---|---|---|---|---|
| Hands have no tears to flow. | 62 | 16 | 37 | 71 | 16 |
| Pleading in the waded bay for the seed to flow | 176 | 7 | 90 | 197 | 7 |
| And heard the lewd, wooed field flow to the coming frost, | 177 | 10 | 90 | 198 | 9 |

FLOWED

|  | U.K. Page | U.K. Line | Poem | U.S. Page | U.S. Line |
|---|---|---|---|---|---|
| My veins flowed with the Eastern weather; | 7 | 17 | 5 | 8 | 17 |
| The word flowed up, translating to the heart | 22 | 23 | 14 | 27 | 23 |
| Though no sound flowed down the hand folded air | 120 | 15 | 72 | 132 | 20 |

FLOWER

|  | U.K. Page | U.K. Line | Poem | U.S. Page | U.S. Line |
|---|---|---|---|---|---|
| The force that through the green fuse drives the flower | 9 | 1 | 6 | 10 | 1 |
| And who remain shall flower as they love, | 15 | 21 | 10 | 18 | 1 |
| A three-eyed, red-eyed spark, blunt as a flower; | 22 | 15 | 14 | 27 | 15 |
| City of spring, the governed flower, | 33 | 4 | 19 | 38 | 4 |
| Flower, flower the people's fusion, | 34 | 7 | 19 | 39 | 13 |
| Flower, flower, all all and all. | 34 | 12 | 19 | 39 | 18 |
| In the glass bed of grapes with snail and flower, | 36 | 5 | 20 | 41 | 5 |
| The haring snail go giddily round the flower, | 36 | 17 | 20 | 41 | 17 |
| The come-a-cropper rider of the flower. | 51 | 28 | 31 | 61 | 7 |

| | U.K. | | | U.S. | |
|---|---|---|---|---|---|
| | *Page* | *Line* | *Poem* | *Page* | *Line* |
| She who was who I hold, the fats and flower, | 54 | 2 | 33 | 63 | 2 |
| Where blew a flower may a flower no more | 68 | 22 | 42 | 77 | 22 |
| Refusal struck her loin and the lame flower | 90 | 2 | 54 | 99 | 2 |
| Bird beast and flower | 101 | 2 | 62 | 112 | 2 |
| All love but for the full assemblage in flower | 110 | 12 | 67 | 121 | 14 |
| Or flower under the time dying flesh astride. | 120 | 30 | 72 | 133 | 15 |
| And flower of country sleep and the greenwood keep. | 162 | 18 | 86 | 181 | 18 |
| Be shielded by chant and flower and gay may you | 163 | 19 | 86 | 182 | 19 |
| The force that through the green fuse drives the flower | 9 | | 6 | 10 | |

FLOWERED

| | | | | | |
|---|---|---|---|---|---|
| The deadrock base and blow the flowered anchor, | 51 | 5 | 31 | 60 | 5 |

FLOWERING

| | | | | | |
|---|---|---|---|---|---|
| And she rose with him flowering in her melting snow. | 123 | 20 | 72 | 137 | 10 |

FLOWERS

| | | | | | |
|---|---|---|---|---|---|
| And the flood flowers now | x | 19 | 1 | xviii | 25 |
| Who periscope through flowers to the sky. | 5 | 6 | 3 | 5 | 6 |
| And falls, and flowers in the yawning wound at our sides, | 163 | 13 | 86 | 183 | 20 |
| Flows to the strand of flowers like the dew's ruly sea, | 165 | 27 | 86 | 185 | 17 |

FLOWING

| | | | | | |
|---|---|---|---|---|---|
| To the sea sound flowing like blood from the loud wound | 136 | 6 | 81 | 153 | 6 |

FLOWN

| | | | | | |
|---|---|---|---|---|---|
| Lie this fifth month unskated, and the birds have flown; | 49 | 9 | 29 | 58 | 9 |

FLOWS

| | | | | | |
|---|---|---|---|---|---|
| Flows open | 142 | 15 | 82 | 159 | 15 |
| Flows to the strand of flowers like the dew's ruly sea, | 165 | 27 | 86 | 185 | 17 |

FLUES

| | | | | | |
|---|---|---|---|---|---|
| I whistled all night in the twisted flues, | 174 | 18 | 89 | 194 | 18 |

FLUIDS

| | | | | | |
|---|---|---|---|---|---|
| To rob me of my fluids in his heart. | 5 | 12 | 3 | 5 | 12 |

FLUNG

| | | | | | |
|---|---|---|---|---|---|
| Flung gravel chime? Let the stones speak | 44 | 13 | 25 | 52 | 13 |

FLUSH

| | | | | | |
|---|---|---|---|---|---|
| From the fair dead who flush the sea | 2 | 10 | 2 | 2 | 10 |

FLUTE

| | | | | | |
|---|---|---|---|---|---|
| Froth, flute, fin and quill | vii | 7 | 1 | xv | 7 |
| Huloo, my prowed dove with a flute! | x | 14 | 1 | xviii | 20 |

FLUTTERED

| | | | | | |
|---|---|---|---|---|---|
| For the salty birds fluttered and fed | 152 | 24 | 83 | 170 | 17 |

| | | U.K. | | | U.S. | |
|---|---|---|---|---|---|---|
| | | Page | Line | Poem | Page | Line |
| **FLY** | | | | | | |
| | That will fly and fall | viii | 4 | 1 | xvi | 4 |
| | That shrouded men might marrow as they fly. | 15 | 10 | 10 | 17 | 10 |
| | To the built voice, or fly with winter to the bells, | 86 | 10 | 51 | 95 | 10 |
| | Fly like the stars' blood, | 105 | 24 | 64 | 116 | 24 |
| | I should hear him fly with the high fields | 161 | 2 | 85 | 180 | 5 |
| | He sings towards anguish; finches fly | 170 | 20 | 88 | 190 | 20 |
| **FLYING** | | | | | | |
| | And, as for oils and ointments on the flying grail, | 38 | 23 | 20 | 44 | 13 |
| | Before the fall from love the flying heartbone, | 41 | 15 | 23 | 47 | 15 |
| | No birds or flying fish | 58 | 15 | 35 | 67 | 15 |
| | Has sown a flying garden round that sea-ghost? | 76 | 18 | 44 | 85 | 18 |
| | Die in red feathers when the flying heaven's cut, | 92 | 12 | 55 | 101 | 18 |
| | Will be the same grief flying. Whom shall they calm? | 100 | 11 | 61 | 111 | 11 |
| | Birds and the birds of the winged trees flying my name | 102 | 12 | 63 | 113 | 12 |
| | And fire, the flying rant | 106 | 3 | 64 | 117 | 3 |
| | Lions and fires of his flying breath, | 117 | 5 | 71 | 129 | 5 |
| | Was flying through the house as though the she bird praised | 122 | 3 | 72 | 135 | 3 |
| | Flying. The rite is shorn | 123 | 6 | 72 | 136 | 16 |
| | Street we chant the flying sea | 130 | 5 | 77 | 144 | 5 |
| | The morning is flying on the wings of his age | 135 | 13 | 80 | 152 | 13 |
| | Flying with the ricks, and the horses | 160 | 4 | 85 | 179 | 4 |
| **FLY-LORD'S** | | | | | | |
| | And father all nor fail the fly-lord's acre, | 60 | 13 | 36 | 69 | 13 |
| **FOAL** | | | | | | |
| | Gull, on the wave with sand in its eyes! And the foal moves | 165 | 12 | 86 | 185 | 2 |
| **FOAM** | | | | | | |
| | The lured fish under the foam | 150 | 23 | 83 | 168 | 7 |
| | The cattle graze on the covered foam, | 156 | 15 | 83 | 175 | 3 |
| | As horses in the foam: | 172 | 21 | 88 | 192 | 21 |
| **FOAM-BLUE** | | | | | | |
| | What rhubarb man peeled in her foam-blue channel | 76 | 17 | 44 | 85 | 17 |
| **FOAMED** | | | | | | |
| | And the tall grains foamed in their bills; | 153 | 1 | 83 | 170 | 16 |
| **FOAMING** | | | | | | |
| | Skinny as sin, the foaming marrow, | 33 | 11 | 19 | 38 | 11 |
| **FOAMS** | | | | | | |
| | Quick in the wood at love, where a torch of foxes foams, | 177 | 14 | 90 | 198 | 13 |
| **FOG** | | | | | | |
| | (Fog has a bone | 56 | 4 | 34 | 65 | 4 |
| | (Fog by his spring | 56 | 11 | 34 | 65 | 11 |

|  | U.K. |  |  | U.S. |  |
|  | Page | Line | Poem | Page | Line |

**FOLD**

Fold in their arms. — 14 · 6 · 10 · 16 · 6
Alone alive among his mutton fold, — 72 · 16 · 44 · 81 · 16
Her lover's wings that fold to-morrow's flight, — 115 · 11 · 69 · 127 · 11
Torn and alone in a farm house in a fold — 119 · 15 · 72 · 131 · 15
And the harp shaped voice of the water's dust plucks in a fold — 121 · 24 · 72 · 134 · 19
Claw fold and hole for the rotten — 133 · 5 · 78 · 148 · 8
Gulled and chanter in young Heaven's fold — 172 · 8 · 88 · 192 · 8
And the black spit of the chapel fold, — 174 · 2 · 89 · 194 · 2

**FOLDED**

Was who was folded on the rod the aaron — 54 · 13 · 33 · 63 · 13
Gliding windless through the hand folded flakes, — 119 · 4 · 72 · 131 · 4
Though no sound flowed down the hand folded air — 120 · 15 · 72 · 132 · 20
Above her folded head, and the soft feathered voice — 122 · 2 · 72 · 135 · 2

**FOLDS**

Warning among the folds, and the frozen hold — 119 · 8 · 72 · 131 · 8
Pool at the wanting centre, in the folds — 123 · 18 · 72 · 137 · 8

**FOLLOW**

Who follow the red rivers, hollow — 82 · 3 · 48 · 91 · 3
Follow him out of grace, — 160 · 23 · 85 · 179 · 23

**FOLLOWED**

Had followed the hunchback — 112 · 17 · 68 · 124 · 17

**FOLLOWS**

These are her contraries: the beast who follows — 78 · 24 · 46 · 88 · 1

**FOLLY**

These boys of light are curdlers in their folly, — 1 · 7 · 2 · 1 · 7
Brass and the bodiless image, on a stick of folly — 38 · 2 · 20 · 43 · 12
Who razed my wooden folly stands aghast, — 46 · 22 · 27 · 54 · 22
Under the lank, fourth folly on Glamorgan's hill, — 49 · 2 · 29 · 58 · 2
Of the descending day, the dark our folly, — 109 · 19 · 67 · 120 · 19

**FOLLY'S**

Time, in a folly's rider, like a county man — 49 · 4 · 29 · 58 · 4
Spill the lank folly's hunter and the hard-held hope. — 49 · 18 · 29 · 58 · 18

**FOND**

That her fond wounds are mended bitterly. — 81 · 9 · 47 · 90 · 9
Here were fond climates and sweet singers suddenly — 103 · 1 · 63 · 114 · 1

**FONT**

Out of the font of bone and plants at that stone tocsin — 83 · 20 · 49 · 93 · 2
The heavens, the heaven, the grave, the burning font. — 122 · 24 · 72 · 136 · 4

| | U.K. | | | U.S. | |
|---|---|---|---|---|---|
| | Page | Line | Poem | Page | Line |
| **FOOD** | | | | | |
| Where fishes' food is fed the shades | 5 | 5 | 3 | 5 | 5 |
| Man morrow blows through food. | 56 | 14 | 34 | 65 | 14 |
| Camped in the drug-white shower of nerves and food, | 77 | 8 | 45 | 86 | 8 |
| As the food and flames of the snow, a man un-rolled | 119 | 13 | 72 | 131 | 13 |
| **FOOL** | | | | | |
| Time is a foolish fancy, time and fool. | 19 | 1 | 12 | 22 | 6 |
| Forsake, the fool, the hardiness of anger. | 51 | 7 | 31 | 60 | 7 |
| I cannot murder, like a fool, | 66 | 6 | 40 | 75 | 6 |
| **FOOLISH** | | | | | |
| Time is a foolish fancy, time and fool. | 19 | 1 | 12 | 22 | 6 |
| **FOOT** | | | | | |
| Ball of the foot depending from the sun, | 19 | 18 | 12 | 23 | 3 |
| From the first print of the unshodden foot, the lifting | 20 | 10 | 13 | 24 | 10 |
| They shall have stars at elbow and foot; | 68 | 5 | 42 | 77 | 5 |
| With priest's grave foot and hand of five assassins | 78 | 25 | 46 | 88 | 2 |
| Grave's foot, blinds down the lids, the teeth in black, | 87 | 4 | 52 | 96 | 4 |
| Wind-heeled foot in the hole of a fireball, | 95 | 12 | 58 | 105 | 12 |
| 'If my head hurt a hair's foot | 97 | 1 | 59 | 108 | 1 |
| Myself to set foot | 102 | 8 | 63 | 113 | 8 |
| From the kangaroo foot of the earth, | 132 | 21 | 78 | 147 | 21 |
| 'If my head hurt a hair's foot' | 97 | | 59 | 108 | |
| **FOOTED** | | | | | |
| Robbed of the foxy tongue, his footed tape | 18 | 9 | 12 | 21 | 9 |
| The hills have footed the waves away, | 156 | 16 | 83 | 175 | 4 |
| **FOOTFALL** | | | | | |
| Mount on man's footfall, | 36 | 3 | 20 | 41 | 3 |
| **FOOTPRINTS** | | | | | |
| And the shipyards of Galilee's footprints hide a navy of doves. | 127 | 7 | 75 | 141 | 7 |
| **FOOTSTEPS** | | | | | |
| Buckle to lint and cloth their natron footsteps, | 75 | 22 | 44 | 84 | 22 |
| **FORCE** | | | | | |
| The force that through the green fuse drives the flower | 9 | 1 | 6 | 10 | 1 |
| The force that drives the water through the rocks | 9 | 6 | 6 | 10 | 6 |
| Stride through Cadaver's country in my force, | 18 | 21 | 12 | 22 | 1 |
| The force that through the green fuse drives the flower | 9 | | 6 | 10 | |
| **FORCED** | | | | | |
| The stocked heart is forced, and agony has another mouth to feed. | 96 | 17 | 58 | 106 | 17 |

| | U.K. | | | U.S. | |
|---|---|---|---|---|---|
| | *Page* | *Line* | *Poem* | *Page* | *Line* |
| FORCING | | | | | |
| My blood upon the tempered dead, forcing | 28 | 19 | 17 | 33 | 19 |
| Forcing forth through the harebell, | 35 | 15 | 20 | 40 | 15 |
| FOREHEAD | | | | | |
| Woe drip from the dishrag hands and the pressed sponge of the forehead, | 96 | 20 | 58 | 107 | 3 |
| Branded forehead, that could bind | 109 | 9 | 67 | 120 | 9 |
| FOREHEADS | | | | | |
| In spring we cross our foreheads with the holly, | 2 | 19 | 2 | 3 | 1 |
| FOREIGN | | | | | |
| And boys are full and foreign in the pouch. | 3 | 3 | 2 | 3 | 9 |
| This wine upon a foreign tree | 39 | 2 | 21 | 45 | 2 |
| From the foreign fields of space, | 43 | 16 | 24 | 51 | 2 |
| Thunders on the foreign town | 43 | 24 | 24 | 51 | 10 |
| FORESKIN | | | | | |
| The two-a-vein, the foreskin, and the cloud. | 52 | 7 | 31 | 61 | 14 |
| FOREST | | | | | |
| The seed that makes a forest of the loin | 6 | 13 | 4 | 6 | 13 |
| FOREVER | | | | | |
| Forever it is a white child in the dark-skinned summer | 83 | 19 | 49 | 93 | 1 |
| Storm me forever over her grave until | 88 | 10 | 52 | 97 | 10 |
| To the anguish and carrion, to the infant forever unfree, | 97 | 22 | 59 | 109 | 2 |
| I advance for as long as forever is. | 99 | 9 | 60 | 110 | 9 |
| Dead and gone, dedicate forever to my self | 109 | 6 | 67 | 120 | 6 |
| Inhuman cradle and the bride bed forever sought | 120 | 24 | 72 | 133 | 9 |
| Under the night forever falling. | 145 | 17 | 82 | 162 | 17 |
| Forever falling night is a known | 146 | 1 | 82 | 163 | 1 |
| And wake to the farm forever fled from the childless land. | 161 | 3 | 85 | 180 | 6 |
| On that darkest day. Oh, forever may | | | 91 | 200 | 4 |
| FORGED | | | | | |
| Forged in man's minerals, the brassy orator | 35 | 2 | 20 | 40 | 2 |
| Forged in man's mineral. | 38 | 28 | 20 | 44 | 18 |
| FORGET | | | | | |
| The old forget the cries, | 67 | 5 | 41 | 76 | 5 |
| The old forget the grief, | 67 | 9 | 41 | 76 | 9 |
| The fingers will forget green thumbs and mark | 81 | 2 | 47 | 90 | 2 |
| Jealousy cannot forget for all her sakes, | 114 | 11 | 69 | 126 | 11 |
| FORGETS | | | | | |
| Forgets, and cries; | 48 | 4 | 28 | 56 | 4 |
| FORGIVE | | | | | |
| Forgive | 129 | 17 | 77 | 143 | 17 |
| Us forgive | 129 | 18 | 77 | 143 | 18 |
| FORGIVING | | | | | |
| Yet this I make in a forgiving presence. | 80 | 15 | 46 | 89 | 23 |

FORGOTTEN

| | U.K. Page | Line | Poem | U.S. Page | Line |
|---|---|---|---|---|---|
| **FORGOTTEN** | | | | | |
| Forgotten mornings when he walked with his mother | 103 | 22 | 63 | 114 | 22 |
| Forgotten dark, rest their pulse and bury their dead in her faithless sleep. | 115 | 23 | 69 | 127 | 23 |
| **FORK** | | | | | |
| On fork and face. | 18 | 25 | 12 | 22 | 5 |
| Bleed from my burning fork and smell my heels. | 32 | 4 | 18 | 37 | 10 |
| And, from his fork, a dog among the fairies, | 71 | 4 | 44 | 80 | 4 |
| Lop, love, my fork tongue, said the pin-hilled nettle; | 74 | 6 | 44 | 83 | 6 |
| Doubled, to fork him back, through the lockjaw bed | 79 | 24 | 46 | 89 | 5 |
| **FORKED** | | | | | |
| The substance forked that marrowed the first sun; | 22 | 4 | 14 | 27 | 4 |
| In shapes of sin forked out the bearded apple, | 40 | 4 | 22 | 46 | 4 |
| Because their words have forked no lightning they | 116 | 5 | 70 | 128 | 5 |
| **FORKING** | | | | | |
| Before the pitch was forking to a sun; | 23 | 3 | 14 | 28 | 3 |
| **FORKS** | | | | | |
| Forks half its fruit; and half droops down, | 6 | 14 | 4 | 6 | 14 |
| And curling round the bud that forks her eye. | 13 | 3 | 9 | 14 | 10 |
| As forks my eye; | 21 | 23 | 13 | 26 | 6 |
| **FORM** | | | | | |
| As yet was in a molten form, | 7 | 10 | 5 | 8 | 10 |
| **FORMED** | | | | | |
| Are formed of flesh, but let the false day come | 63 | 6 | 38 | 72 | 6 |
| **FORSAKE** | | | | | |
| Forsake, the fool, the hardiness of anger. | 51 | 7 | 31 | 60 | 7 |
| **FORSAKEN** | | | | | |
| And count the taken, forsaken mysteries in a bad dark. | 94 | 9 | 57 | 104 | 9 |
| At the point of love, forsaken and afraid. | 120 | 5 | 72 | 132 | 10 |
| Naked and forsaken to grieve he will not come. | 166 | 7 | 86 | 186 | 7 |
| **FORTH** | | | | | |
| And time cast forth my mortal creature | 8 | 7 | 5 | 9 | 7 |
| Or drive the night-geared forth. | 15 | 6 | 10 | 17 | 6 |
| Forcing forth through the harebell, | 35 | 15 | 20 | 40 | 15 |
| Drives forth my men, my children, from the hanging south. | 49 | 6 | 29 | 58 | 6 |
| Who have brought forth the urchin grief. | 84 | 6 | 49 | 93 | 12 |
| In the still sleeping town and set forth. | 102 | 10 | 63 | 113 | 10 |
| **FORTUNE** | | | | | |
| This is the fortune of manhood: the natural peril, | 35 | 19 | 20 | 40 | 19 |

|  | U.K. | | Poem | U.S. | |
| --- | --- | --- | --- | --- | --- |
|  | Page | Line | | Page | Line |
| **FORWARNS** | | | | | |
| A process in the eye forwarns | 6 | 7 | 4 | 6 | 7 |
| **FOSSIL** | | | | | |
| That belled and bounded with the fossil and the dew reborn. | 123 | 10 | 72 | 136 | 20 |
| In the continent of a fossil | 154 | 24 | 83 | 173 | 4 |
| **FOSTER** | | | | | |
| Nor city tar and subway bored to foster | 19 | 9 | 12 | 22 | 14 |
| Foster the light nor veil the manshaped moon, | 60 | 1 | 36 | 69 | 1 |
| Foster the light | 60 | | 36 | 69 | |
| **FOUL** | | | | | |
| Unfailing till the blood runs foul; | 8 | 4 | 5 | 9 | 4 |
| Howls the foul fiend to heel. | 66 | 5 | 40 | 75 | 5 |
| Time's coral saint and the salt grief drown a foul sepulchre | 83 | 8 | 49 | 92 | 8 |
| Mutter and foul wingbeat of the solemnizing nightpriest | 114 | 22 | 69 | 126 | 22 |
| At last the soul from its foul mousehole | 175 | 14 | 89 | 195 | 19 |
| **FOUND** | | | | | |
| A little comes, is tasted and found good; | 48 | 5 | 28 | 56 | 5 |
| Brave deaths of only ones but never found, | 126 | 11 | 74 | 140 | 11 |
| Am found. | 148 | 10 | 82 | 165 | 10 |
| For, oh, my soul found a sunday wife | 175 | 25 | 89 | 196 | 6 |
| Let him find no rest but be fathered and found, | | | 91 | 200 | 12 |
| **FOUNTAIN** | | | | | |
| The lips of time leech to the fountain head; | 9 | 16 | 6 | 10 | 16 |
| When, praise is blessed, her pride in mast and fountain | 78 | 4 | 46 | 87 | 4 |
| Storm, snow, and fountain in the weather of fireworks, | 83 | 14 | 49 | 92 | 14 |
| Whose hooded, fountain heart once fell in puddles | 87 | 14 | 52 | 96 | 14 |
| In the fountain basin where I sailed my ship | 111 | 10 | 68 | 123 | 10 |
| Erupt, fountain, and enter to utter for ever | 131 | 23 | 77 | 146 | 5 |
| **FOUNTAINHEAD** | | | | | |
| Out of the fountainhead | viii | 21 | 1 | xvi | 21 |
| **FOUNTAINS** | | | | | |
| Peck, sprint, dance on fountains and duck time | 97 | 8 | 59 | 108 | 8 |
| In fountains of origin gave up their love, | 113 | 9 | 69 | 125 | 9 |
| **FOUR** | | | | | |
| And the four winds, that had long blown as one, | 20 | 19 | 13 | 24 | 19 |
| Slow rounding of four seasons' coasts, | 45 | 6 | 26 | 53 | 6 |
| And four birds' notes. | 45 | 8 | 26 | 53 | 8 |
| Down fall four padding weathers on the scarlet lands, | 49 | 19 | 29 | 58 | 19 |
| Bless her bent spirit with four, crossing birds. | 87 | 26 | 52 | 96 | 26 |

| | U.K. | | | U.S. | |
|---|---|---|---|---|---|
| | Page | Line | Poem | Page | Line |
| And star: held and blessed, though you scour the high four | 163 | 22 | 86 | 183 | 3 |
| Four elements and five | 173 | 1 | 88 | 193 | 1 |
| FOUR-FRUITED | | | | | |
| But graft these four-fruited ridings on your country; | 60 | 9 | 36 | 69 | 9 |
| FOUR-STRINGED | | | | | |
| Summon your snowy horsemen, and the four-stringed hill, | 49 | 14 | 29 | 58 | 14 |
| FOUR-WINDED | | | | | |
| We summer boys in this four-winded spinning, | 2 | 13 | 2 | 2 | 13 |
| FOURTH | | | | | |
| Under the lank, fourth folly on Glamorgan's hill, | 49 | 2 | 29 | 58 | 2 |
| FOX | | | | | |
| Hears, there, this fox light, my flood ship's | ix | 18 | 1 | xvii | 18 |
| Ahoy, old, sea-legged fox, | x | 15 | 1 | xviii | 21 |
| In a room with a stuffed fox and a stale fern, | 87 | 11 | 52 | 96 | 11 |
| The stuffed lung of the fox twitch and cry Love | 88 | 11 | 52 | 97 | 11 |
| The owl at its knelling. Fox and holt kneel before blood. | 163 | 9 | 86 | 182 | 9 |
| Of birds! Among the cocks like fire the red fox | 164 | 20 | 86 | 184 | 6 |
| Who comes as red as the fox and sly as the heeled wind. | 165 | 10 | 86 | 184 | 18 |
| Save by their long desirers in the fox cubbed | 178 | 15 | 90 | 199 | 16 |
| FOXES | | | | | |
| Sang to my horn, the foxes on the hills barked clear and cold, | 159 | 16 | 85 | 178 | 16 |
| And honoured among foxes and pheasants by the gay house | 160 | 15 | 85 | 179 | 15 |
| Quick in the wood at love, where a torch of foxes foams, | 177 | 14 | 90 | 198 | 13 |
| FOXY | | | | | |
| Robbed of the foxy tongue, his footed tape | 18 | 9 | 12 | 21 | 9 |
| Bow down the walls of the ferned and foxy woods | 87 | 24 | 52 | 96 | 24 |
| FRAIL | | | | | |
| Their frail deeds might have danced in a green bay, | 116 | 8 | 70 | 128 | 8 |
| Too proud to cry, too frail to check the tears, | | | 91 | 201 | 14 |
| FRANK | | | | | |
| The frank, closed pearl, the sea-girls' lineaments | 78 | 19 | 46 | 87 | 19 |
| Were once such a creature, so gay and frank | 107 | 14 | 65 | 118 | 14 |
| FREE | | | | | |
| From garden cans, or free the floods? | 44 | 7 | 25 | 52 | 7 |
| And free the twin-boxed grief, | 67 | 20 | 41 | 76 | 20 |

|  | U.K. | | | U.S. | |
|  | Page | Line | Poem | Page | Line |
| Boat with its anchor free and fast | 149 | 6 | 83 | 166 | 6 |
| FREELY |  |  |  |  |  |
| And freely he goes lost | 171 | 19 | 88 | 191 | 19 |
| FREEZE |  |  |  |  |  |
| Setting no store by harvest, freeze the soils; | 1 | 3 | 2 | 1 | 3 |
| FREEZES |  |  |  |  |  |
| A wind throws a shadow and it freezes fast. | 154 | 10 | 83 | 172 | 10 |
| FREEZING |  |  |  |  |  |
| Storms in the freezing tomb. | 6 | 3 | 4 | 6 | 3 |
| FRESH |  |  |  |  |  |
| Round her trailed wrist fresh water weaves, | 156 | 9 | 83 | 174 | 17 |
| FRIARS |  |  |  |  |  |
| The scurrying, furred small friars squeal, in the dowse | 177 | 11 | 90 | 198 | 10 |
| FRIEND |  |  |  |  |  |
| Friend by enemy I call you out. | 107 | 1 | 65 | 118 | 1 |
| You my friend there with a winning air | 107 | 3 | 65 | 118 | 3 |
| FRIENDS |  |  |  |  |  |
| Robed in the long friends, | 101 | 20 | 62 | 112 | 20 |
| My friends were enemies on stilts | 107 | 20 | 65 | 118 | 20 |
| Of your immortal friends | 117 | 6 | 71 | 129 | 6 |
| FRIGID |  |  |  |  |  |
| There in the sun the frigid threads | 1 | 10 | 2 | 1 | 10 |
| FRO |  |  |  |  |  |
| The dust of their kettles and clocks swings to and fro | 178 | 5 | 90 | 199 | 6 |
| FROG |  |  |  |  |  |
| The horn and ball of water on the frog | 54 | 15 | 33 | 63 | 15 |
| FROGS |  |  |  |  |  |
| Frogs and satans and woman-luck, | 134 | 7 | 79 | 150 | 7 |
| FRONT |  |  |  |  |  |
| Am I not you who front the tidy shore, | 46 | 15 | 27 | 54 | 15 |
| FROST |  |  |  |  |  |
| The jacks of frost they finger in the hives; | 1 | 9 | 2 | 1 | 9 |
| In sacred waters that no frost could harden, | 40 | 14 | 22 | 46 | 14 |
| When cometh Jack Frost? the children ask. | 53 | 10 | 32 | 62 | 10 |
| Of echo's answer and the man of frost | 53 | 25 | 32 | 62 | 25 |
| Farmer in time of frost the burning leagues, | 60 | 10 | 36 | 69 | 10 |
| Love in the frost is pared and wintered by, | 81 | 5 | 47 | 90 | 5 |
| Cast high, stunned on gilled stone; sly scissors ground in frost | 92 | 7 | 55 | 101 | 13 |
| Trailing the frost bitten cloth, | 132 | 23 | 78 | 147 | 23 |
| Of thistling frost | 165 | 2 | 86 | 184 | 10 |
| And heard the lewd, wooed field flow to the coming frost, | 177 | 10 | 90 | 198 | 9 |
| FROSTY |  |  |  |  |  |
| With frosty fingers punishes my hair, | 16 | 2 | 11 | 19 | 2 |

|  | U.K. | | | U.S. | |
|---|---|---|---|---|---|
|  | *Page* | *Line* | *Poem* | *Page* | *Line* |
| **FROTH** |  |  |  |  |  |
| Froth, flute, fin and quill | vii | 7 | 1 | xv | 7 |
| Pick the world's ball of wave and froth | 2 | 16 | 2 | 2 | 16 |
| An inch in froth. Chimes cheat the prison spire, pelter | 86 | 5 | 51 | 95 | 5 |
| **FROZEN** |  |  |  |  |  |
| Of frozen loves they fetch their girls, | 1 | 5 | 2 | 1 | 5 |
| The fellow half was frozen as it bubbled | 30 | 7 | 18 | 35 | 7 |
| Cross-stroked salt Adam to the frozen angel | 73 | 21 | 44 | 82 | 21 |
| That frozen wife whose juices drift like a fixed sea | 77 | 14 | 45 | 86 | 14 |
| Warning among the folds, and the frozen hold | 119 | 8 | 72 | 131 | 8 |
| **FRUIT** |  |  |  |  |  |
| Tangled with chirrup and fruit, | vii | 6 | 1 | xv | 6 |
| Forks half its fruit; and half droops down, | 6 | 14 | 4 | 6 | 14 |
| The fruit of man unwrinkles in the stars, | 24 | 10 | 15 | 29 | 10 |
| Plunged in its fruit; | 39 | 3 | 21 | 45 | 3 |
| In winds that bring the fruit and rind | 53 | 4 | 32 | 62 | 4 |
| Night fall and the fruit like a sun, | 131 | 4 | 77 | 145 | 10 |
| **FRUITS** |  |  |  |  |  |
| And lay the wet fruits low. | 11 | 12 | 8 | 12 | 12 |
| **FULL** |  |  |  |  |  |
| And boys are full and foreign in the pouch. | 3 | 3 | 2 | 3 | 9 |
| With my red veins full of money, | 99 | 7 | 60 | 110 | 7 |
| And the other full of tears that she will be dead, | 100 | 5 | 61 | 111 | 5 |
| Beyond the border and under the lark full cloud. | 103 | 12 | 63 | 114 | 12 |
| All love but for the full assemblage in flower | 110 | 12 | 67 | 121 | 14 |
| The mother dug, and its arms full of fires. | 129 | 8 | 77 | 143 | 8 |
| Cold Nansen's beak on a boat full of gongs, | 133 | 12 | 78 | 148 | 15 |
| Sun the father his quiver full of the infants of pure fire, | 158 | 19 | 84 | 177 | 19 |
| By full tilt river and switchback sea | 170 | 2 | 88 | 190 | 2 |
| Their breasts full of honey, under their gander king | 177 | 18 | 90 | 198 | 17 |
| **FUMED** |  |  |  |  |  |
| Fumed like a tree, and tossed a burning bird; | 80 | 3 | 46 | 89 | 11 |
| **FUMING** |  |  |  |  |  |
| With fuming bows and ram of ice, | 150 | 18 | 83 | 168 | 2 |
| **FUNERAL** |  |  |  |  |  |
| The tray of knives, the antiseptic funeral; | 37 | 3 | 20 | 42 | 9 |
| Or the funeral of the sun; | 45 | 11 | 26 | 53 | 11 |
| After the funeral, mule praises, brays, | 87 | 1 | 52 | 96 | 1 |
| And the funeral grains of the slaughtered floor. | 135 | 5 | 80 | 152 | 5 |
| After the funeral (In memory of Ann Jones) | 87 |  | 52 | 96 |  |
| **FUNNELS** |  |  |  |  |  |
| Funnels and masts went by in a whirl. | 149 | 17 | 83 | 166 | 17 |
| Good-bye to chimneys and funnels, | 150 | 1 | 83 | 167 | 5 |

| | U.K. | | | U.S. | |
|---|---|---|---|---|---|
| | *Page* | *Line* | *Poem* | *Page* | *Line* |
| FURIED | | | | | |
| Furied by his stream | 139 | 5 | 82 | 156 | 5 |
| FURIES | | | | | |
| The gentleman lay graveward with his furies; | 71 | 2 | 44 | 80 | 2 |
| Weds my long gentleman to dusts and furies; | 76 | 4 | 44 | 85 | 4 |
| FURIOUS | | | | | |
| Who should be furious, | 91 | 6 | 55 | 100 | 6 |
| The furious ox-killing house of love. | 157 | 8 | 83 | 175 | 20 |
| FURLED | | | | | |
| Furled on the fishes' house and hell, | 69 | 17 | 43 | 78 | 17 |
| FURNACE-NOSTRILLED | | | | | |
| A furnace-nostrilled column-membered | 114 | 5 | 69 | 126 | 5 |
| FURNISH | | | | | |
| I furnish with the meat of a fable; | 77 | 21 | 45 | 86 | 21 |
| FURRED | | | | | |
| The dingle furred deer dead! | ix | 5 | 1 | xvii | 5 |
| The scurrying, furred small friars squeal, in the dowse | 177 | 11 | 90 | 198 | 10 |
| FURTHER | | | | | |
| With any further | 101 | 17 | 62 | 112 | 17 |
| FURY | | | | | |
| Of chemic blood, warned of the coming fury. | 17 | 7 | 11 | 20 | 7 |
| To clasp my fury on ground | 92 | 2 | 55 | 101 | 8 |
| In the first fury of his stream | 140 | 8 | 82 | 157 | 8 |
| FUSE | | | | | |
| The force that through the green fuse drives the flower | 9 | 1 | 6 | 10 | 1 |
| When his viperish fuse hangs looped with flames under the brand | 168 | 4 | 87 | 188 | 8 |
| The force that through the green fuse drives the flower | 9 | | 6 | 10 | |
| FUSES | | | | | |
| My fuses timed to charge his heart, | 4 | 13 | 3 | 4 | 13 |
| FUSION | | | | | |
| The cancer's fusion, or the summer feather | 19 | 7 | 12 | 22 | 12 |
| Flower, flower the people's fusion, | 34 | 7 | 19 | 39 | 13 |
| I, in my fusion of rose and male motion, | 35 | 17 | 20 | 40 | 17 |

# ENTRIES UNDER G

| GAB | | | | | |
|---|---|---|---|---|---|
| The lovely gift of the gab bangs back on a blind shaft. | 94 | 6 | 57 | 104 | 6 |

| | U.K. Page | U.K. Line | Poem | U.S. Page | U.S. Line |
|---|---|---|---|---|---|
| **GABBING** | | | | | |
| In your beaks, on the gabbing capes! | ix | 15 | 1 | xvii | 15 |
| **GABLES** | | | | | |
| Eyes in the gables see | 58 | 3 | 35 | 67 | 3 |
| **GABRIEL** | | | | | |
| And from the windy West came two-gunned Gabriel, | 73 | 11 | 44 | 82 | 11 |
| Gabriel and radiant shrubbery as the morning grows joyful | 158 | 15 | 84 | 177 | 15 |
| **GAG** | | | | | |
| Gag of a dumbstruck tree to block from bare enemies | 85 | 4 | 50 | 94 | 4 |
| **GALACTIC** | | | | | |
| When the galactic sea was sucked | 4 | 7 | 3 | 4 | 7 |
| **GALE** | | | | | |
| And gale I tackle, the whole world of then, | 173 | 15 | 88 | 193 | 15 |
| **GALED** | | | | | |
| Petticoats galed high, or shy with the rough riding boys, | 176 | 18 | 90 | 197 | 18 |
| Where no cold is, the skinning gales unpin | 24 | 22 | 15 | 29 | 22 |
| With salty colts and gales in their limbs | 156 | 18 | 83 | 175 | 6 |
| **GALILEE'S** | | | | | |
| And the shipyards of Galilee's footprints hide a navy of doves. | 127 | 7 | 75 | 141 | 7 |
| **GALLERIES** | | | | | |
| Toppling and burning in the muddle of towers and galleries | 77 | 18 | 45 | 86 | 18 |
| Mountains and galleries beneath | 152 | 14 | 83 | 170 | 6 |
| Mountains and galleries to the crest! | 154 | 12 | 83 | 172 | 12 |
| **GALLOP** | | | | | |
| Gallop through the arched, green farms, | 156 | 20 | 83 | 175 | 8 |
| Trot and gallop with gulls upon them | 156 | 21 | 83 | 175 | 9 |
| **GALLOW** | | | | | |
| Of gallow crosses on the liver· | 7 | 23 | 5 | 8 | 23 |
| Time's nerve in vinegar, the gallow grave | 75 | 6 | 44 | 84 | 6 |
| **GALLOWS** | | | | | |
| I would not fear the gallows nor the axe | 12 | 13 | 9 | 13 | 13 |
| And gallows, up the rays of his eyes the small birds of the bay | 167 | 4 | 87 | 187 | 4 |
| **GAMBO** | | | | | |
| Or, butter fat goosegirls, bounced in a gambo bed, | 177 | 17 | 90 | 198 | 16 |
| **GAME** | | | | | |
| This first and steepled season, to the summer's game. | 49 | 12 | 29 | 58 | 12 |
| 'All game phrases fit your ring of a cockfight: | 97 | 6 | 59 | 108 | 6 |
| **GANDER** | | | | | |
| Their breasts full of honey, under their gander king | 177 | 18 | 90 | 198 | 17 |

|  |  | U.K. |  |  | U.S. |  |
|  |  | Page | Line | Poem | Page | Line |
| GANDERS |  |  |  |  |  |  |
| In a spinney of ringed boys and ganders, spike and burn, |  | 162 | 14 | 86 | 181 | 14 |
| GANGS |  |  |  |  |  |  |
| 'But this we tread bears the angelic gangs, |  | 26 | 13 | 16 | 31 | 13 |
| GARB |  |  |  |  |  |  |
| I see the wanting nun saint carved in a garb |  | 110 | 6 | 67 | 121 | 8 |
| GARDEN |  |  |  |  |  |  |
| Drip on my dead house garden. |  | 31 | 21 | 18 | 37 | 3 |
| The central plains of Asia in his garden, |  | 40 | 2 | 22 | 46 | 2 |
| The wisemen tell me that the garden gods |  | 40 | 9 | 22 | 46 | 9 |
| Measures his own length on the garden wall |  | 41 | 12 | 23 | 47 | 12 |
| From garden cans, or free the floods? |  | 44 | 7 | 25 | 52 | 7 |
| Like exodus a chapter from the garden, |  | 54 | 18 | 33 | 63 | 18 |
| On thunderous pavements in the garden time; |  | 72 | 10 | 44 | 81 | 10 |
| Has sown a flying garden round that sea-ghost? |  | 76 | 18 | 44 | 85 | 18 |
| Green as beginning, let the garden diving |  | 76 | 19 | 44 | 85 | 19 |
| Nor walk in the cool of your mortal garden |  | 110 | 20 | 67 | 121 | 22 |
| From the opening of the garden lock |  | 111 | 4 | 68 | 123 | 4 |
| Of the garden of Eden. |  | 130 | 22 | 77 | 144 | 22 |
| Of the garden of wilderness. |  | 131 | 8 | 77 | 145 | 14 |
| And the blood drop's garden |  | 145 | 4 | 82 | 162 | 4 |
| A garden holding to her hand |  | 155 | 23 | 83 | 174 | 7 |
| GARDENS |  |  |  |  |  |  |
| And comb the county gardens for a wreath. |  | 2 | 18 | 2 | 2 | 18 |
| But all the gardens |  | 103 | 10 | 63 | 114 | 10 |
| Over the gardens of the floor |  | 152 | 2 | 83 | 169 | 14 |
| GARLAND |  |  |  |  |  |  |
| With stones of odyssey for ash and garland |  | 76 | 7 | 44 | 85 | 7 |
| GARRISON |  |  |  |  |  |  |
| With a star-flanked garrison, |  | 43 | 18 | 24 | 51 | 4 |
| With a sand-bagged garrison, |  | 43 | 25 | 24 | 51 | 11 |
| GARRISONED |  |  |  |  |  |  |
| The sexton sentinel, garrisoned under thistles, |  | 37 | 6 | 20 | 42 | 12 |
| GAS |  |  |  |  |  |  |
| Death on the mouth that ate the gas. |  | 28 | 16 | 17 | 33 | 16 |
| GATHER |  |  |  |  |  |  |
| Might cross its planets, the bell weep, night gather her eyes, |  | 165 | 21 | 86 | 185 | 11 |
| GATHERED |  |  |  |  |  |  |
| Is gathered and spilt |  | 105 | 10 | 64 | 116 | 10 |
| The sky gathered again |  | 160 | 9 | 85 | 179 | 9 |
| GATHERS |  |  |  |  |  |  |
| Love drips and gathers, but the fallen blood |  | 9 | 17 | 6 | 10 | 17 |
| GATES |  |  |  |  |  |  |
| And the gates |  | 102 | 19 | 63 | 113 | 19 |

|  | U.K. | | | U.S. | |
|---|---|---|---|---|---|
|  | *Page* | *Line* | *Poem* | *Page* | *Line* |
| Throw wide to the wind the gates of the wandering boat | 136 | 10 | 81 | 153 | 10 |
| GAUZE | | | | | |
| Blew out the blood gauze through the wound of manwax. | 74 | 14 | 44 | 83 | 14 |
| GAVE | | | | | |
| One breast gave suck the fever's issue; | 21 | 19 | 13 | 26 | 2 |
| A million minds gave suck to such a bud | 21 | 22 | 13 | 26 | 5 |
| You are all these, said she who gave me the long suck, | 46 | 17 | 27 | 54 | 17 |
| Who gave these seas their colour in a shape, | 61 | 1 | 36 | 70 | 1 |
| In fountains of origin gave up their love, | 113 | 9 | 69 | 125 | 9 |
| And I gave my soul a blind, slashed eye, | 175 | 16 | 89 | 195 | 21 |
| GAY | | | | | |
| That's grave and gay as grave and sea | 82 | 7 | 48 | 91 | 7 |
| Of the grave, gay, seaside land. | 82 | 17 | 48 | 91 | 17 |
| Were once such a creature, so gay and frank | 107 | 14 | 65 | 118 | 14 |
| Blind eyes could blaze like meteors and be gay, | 116 | 14 | 70 | 128 | 14 |
| And honoured among foxes and pheasants by the gay house | 160 | 15 | 85 | 179 | 15 |
| Be shielded by chant and flower and gay may you | 163 | 19 | 86 | 182 | 19 |
| Clung to the pitching clouds, or gay with any one | 176 | 15 | 90 | 197 | 15 |
| GEAR | | | | | |
| Love in her gear is slowly through the house, | 18 | 3 | 12 | 21 | 3 |
| In bottom gear through night-geared man. | 28 | 12 | 17 | 33 | 12 |
| GEESE | | | | | |
| Geese nearly in heaven, boys | vii | 15 | 1 | xv | 15 |
| And wishbones of wild geese, | 172 | 5 | 88 | 192 | 5 |
| GENDER | | | | | |
| The size of genesis? the short spark's gender? | 72 | 20 | 44 | 81 | 20 |
| GENDER'S | | | | | |
| Weans on an artery the gender's strip; | 71 | 18 | 44 | 80 | 18 |
| GENESIS | | | | | |
| I dreamed my genesis in sweat of sleep, breaking | 28 | 1 | 17 | 33 | 1 |
| I dreamed my genesis and died again, shrapnel | 28 | 13 | 17 | 33 | 13 |
| I dreamed my genesis in sweat of death, fallen | 29 | 1 | 17 | 34 | 5 |
| Murder of Eden and green genesis. | 41 | 8 | 23 | 47 | 8 |
| The size of genesis? the short spark's gender? | 72 | 20 | 44 | 81 | 20 |
| Genesis in the root, the scarecrow word, | 74 | 18 | 44 | 83 | 18 |
| In your every inch and glance is the globe of genesis spun, | 110 | 27 | 67 | 122 | 5 |
| I dreamed my genesis | 28 | | 17 | 33 | |
| GENESIS' | | | | | |
| The sundering ultimate kingdom of genesis' thunder. | 131 | 25 | 77 | 146 | 7 |

| | U.K. | | | U.S. | |
|---|---|---|---|---|---|
| | *Page* | *Line* | *Poem* | *Page* | *Line* |
| **GENTLE** | | | | | |
| With priest and pharaoh bed my gentle wound, | 76 | 5 | 44 | 85 | 5 |
| The gentle seaslides of saying I must undo | 89 | 5 | 53 | 98 | 5 |
| Bullies into rough seas you so gentle | 96 | 24 | 58 | 107 | 7 |
| Do not go gentle into that good night, | 116 | 1 | 70 | 128 | 1 |
| Do not go gentle into that good night. | 116 | 6 | 70 | 128 | 6 |
| Do not go gentle into that good night. | 116 | 12 | 70 | 128 | 12 |
| Do not go gentle into that good night. | 116 | 18 | 70 | 128 | 18 |
| Gentle in their clogs over the fallen sky, | 119 | 24 | 72 | 132 | 4 |
| Do not go gentle into that good night | 116 | | 70 | 128 | |
| **GENTLEMAN** | | | | | |
| Who play the proper gentleman and lady. | 47 | 4 | 27 | 55 | 4 |
| So fast I move defying time, the quiet gentleman | 63 | 14 | 38 | 72 | 14 |
| The gentleman lay graveward with his furies; | 71 | 2 | 44 | 80 | 2 |
| Then, penny-eyed, that gentleman of wounds, | 71 | 7 | 44 | 80 | 7 |
| I am the long world's gentleman, he said, | 71 | 13 | 44 | 80 | 13 |
| Said the fake gentleman in suit of spades, | 73 | 14 | 44 | 82 | 14 |
| Weds my long gentleman to dusts and furies; | 76 | 4 | 44 | 85 | 4 |
| **GENTLEMEN** | | | | | |
| The sunny gentlemen, the Welshing rich, | 15 | 5 | 10 | 17 | 5 |
| **GENTRY** | | | | | |
| Which sixth of wind blew out the burning gentry? | 73 | 1 | 44 | 82 | 1 |
| **GESTURE** | | | | | |
| Argument of the hewn voice, gesture and psalm, | 88 | 9 | 52 | 97 | 9 |
| Clips short the gesture of breath. | 92 | 11 | 55 | 101 | 17 |
| One gesture of the heart or head, | 105 | 9 | 64 | 116 | 9 |
| **GESTURES** | | | | | |
| 'Now to awake husked of gestures and my joy like a cave | 97 | 21 | 59 | 109 | 1 |
| **GHOST** | | | | | |
| Turns ghost to ghost; each mothered child | 6 | 20 | 4 | 7 | 2 |
| I, born of flesh and ghost, was neither | 8 | 13 | 5 | 9 | 13 |
| A ghost nor man, but mortal ghost. | 8 | 14 | 5 | 9 | 14 |
| Unpacks the head that, like a sleepy ghost, | 10 | 3 | 7 | 11 | 3 |
| Spun to my screws, your dry ghost blows, | 11 | 2 | 8 | 12 | 2 |
| From the first secret of the heart, the warning ghost, | 20 | 12 | 13 | 24 | 12 |
| Faded my elbow ghost, the mothers-eyed, | 26 | 16 | 16 | 31 | 16 |
| Where still they sleep unknowing of their ghost. | 26 | 20 | 16 | 31 | 20 |
| An old, mad man still climbing in his ghost, | 27 | 4 | 16 | 32 | 9 |
| My fathers' ghost is climbing in the rain. | 27 | 5 | 16 | 32 | 10 |
| Rerobing of the naked ghost. Manhood | 28 | 23 | 17 | 34 | 3 |
| And the unplanted ghost. | 30 | 12 | 18 | 35 | 12 |
| The ghost is dumb that stammered in the straw, | 31 | 4 | 18 | 36 | 4 |
| The ghost that hatched his havoc as he flew | 31 | 5 | 18 | 36 | 5 |

GHOST (continued)

|  | U.K. | | | U.S. | |
|---|---|---|---|---|---|
|  | Page | Line | Poem | Page | Line |
| Ghost with her ghost, contagious man | 34 | 2 | 19 | 39 | 8 |
| Laying my ghost in metal, | 35 | 3 | 20 | 40 | 3 |
| My half ghost in armour hold hard in death's corridor, | 35 | 5 | 20 | 40 | 5 |
| Beginning with doom in the ghost, and the springing marvels, | 35 | 13 | 20 | 40 | 13 |
| Be by your one ghost pierced, his pointed ferrule, | 38 | 1 | 20 | 43 | 11 |
| My ghost in his metal neptune | 38 | 27 | 20 | 44 | 17 |
| The ringed-sea ghost, rise grimly from the wrack. | 46 | 24 | 27 | 54 | 24 |
| Have cleanest hands, and, as the heartless ghost | 50 | 8 | 30 | 59 | 8 |
| Death hairy-heeled, and the tapped ghost in wood, | 52 | 5 | 31 | 61 | 12 |
| The crumpled packs fled past this ghost in bloom, | 80 | 5 | 46 | 89 | 13 |
| Grief with dishevelled hands tear out the altar ghost | 83 | 5 | 49 | 92 | 5 |
| Before I rush in a crouch the ghost with a hammer, air, | 97 | 9 | 59 | 108 | 9 |
| Of the golden ghost who ringed with his streams her mercury bone, | 127 | 11 | 75 | 141 | 11 |
| Birdman or told ghost I hung. | 133 | 3 | 78 | 148 | 6 |
| Over the ghost and the dropped son | 137 | 8 | 82 | 154 | 8 |
| The ghost | 143 | 8 | 82 | 160 | 8 |
| With no more desire than a ghost. | 154 | 4 | 83 | 172 | 4 |
| In the rain telling its beads, and the gravest ghost | 163 | 8 | 86 | 182 | 8 |
| Of the nightingale's din and tale! The upgiven ghost | 165 | 3 | 86 | 184 | 11 |
| With blessed, unborn God and His Ghost, | 172 | 6 | 88 | 192 | 6 |
| GHOSTLY | | | | | |
| And there we wept, I and a ghostly other, | 26 | 8 | 16 | 31 | 8 |
| And ghostly comets over the raised fists. | 53 | 26 | 32 | 62 | 26 |
| And ghostly echoes on paper, | 64 | 9 | 39 | 73 | 9 |
| GHOSTS | | | | | |
| Move like two ghosts before the eye. | 6 | 18 | 4 | 6 | 18 |
| Two one-dimensioned ghosts, love on a reel, | 14 | 12 | 10 | 16 | 12 |
| And, broken ghosts with glow-worms in their heads, | 24 | 4 | 15 | 29 | 4 |
| That town of ghosts, the trodden womb | 42 | 2 | 24 | 49 | 2 |
| That town of ghosts, the manwaged womb | 42 | 9 | 24 | 49 | 9 |
| And dusk is crowded with the children's ghosts, | 53 | 14 | 32 | 62 | 14 |
| For there are ghosts in the air | 64 | 8 | 39 | 73 | 8 |
| GIANT | | | | | |
| With the wild breast and blessed and giant skull | 87 | 28 | 52 | 96 | 28 |
| And guilts, great crotch and giant | 110 | 8 | 67 | 121 | 10 |

|  | U.K. | | | U.S. | |
|---|---|---|---|---|---|
|  | *Page* | *Line* | *Poem* | *Page* | *Line* |
| Now break a giant tear for the little known fall, | 126 | 8 | 74 | 140 | 8 |
| GIANT'S |  |  |  |  |  |
| And there this night I walk in the white giant's thigh | 176 | 3 | 90 | 197 | 3 |
| In the white giant's thigh | 176 |  | 90 | 197 |  |
| GIANTS |  |  |  |  |  |
| The nurse of giants by the cut sea basin, | 56 | 10 | 34 | 65 | 10 |
| GIDDILY |  |  |  |  |  |
| The haring snail go giddily round the flower, | 36 | 17 | 20 | 41 | 17 |
| GIFT |  |  |  |  |  |
| The lovely gift of the gab bangs back on a blind shaft. | 94 | 6 | 57 | 104 | 6 |
| GIGANTIC |  |  |  |  |  |
| Now clasp me to their grains in the gigantic glade, | 176 | 19 | 90 | 197 | 19 |
| GILLED |  |  |  |  |  |
| Cast high, stunned on gilled stone; sly scissors ground in frost | 92 | 7 | 55 | 101 | 13 |
| GIPSY |  |  |  |  |  |
| So cross her hand with their grave gipsy eyes, | 55 | 12 | 33 | 64 | 15 |
| GIRDERED |  |  |  |  |  |
| Through vision and the girdered nerve. | 28 | 4 | 17 | 33 | 4 |
| GIRL |  |  |  |  |  |
| A rooking girl who stole me for her side, | 12 | 2 | 9 | 13 | 2 |
| Daft with the drug that's smoking in a girl | 13 | 2 | 9 | 14 | 9 |
| A merry girl took me for man, | 65 | 22 | 40 | 74 | 22 |
| Season and sunshine, grace and girl, | 66 | 7 | 40 | 75 | 7 |
| A girl mad as birds | 108 | 3 | 66 | 119 | 3 |
| A girl alive with his hooks through her lips; | 149 | 22 | 83 | 167 | 2 |
| Thrown to the sea in the shell of a girl | 152 | 20 | 83 | 170 | 12 |
| His fathers cling to the hand of the girl | 155 | 3 | 83 | 173 | 7 |
| Never and never, my girl riding far and near | 162 | 1 | 86 | 181 | 1 |
| My girl ranging the night in the rose and shire | 162 | 9 | 86 | 181 | 9 |
| Never, my girl, until tolled to sleep by the stern | 162 | 21 | 86 | 181 | 21 |
| GIRL-CIRCLED |  |  |  |  |  |
| A thundering bullring of your silent and girl-circled island. | 96 | 26 | 58 | 107 | 9 |
| GIRLS |  |  |  |  |  |
| Of frozen loves they fetch their girls, | 1 | 5 | 2 | 1 | 5 |
| That chalk the walls with green girls and their men. | 12 | 16 | 9 | 13 | 16 |
| The shades of girls, all flavoured from their shrouds, | 14 | 7 | 10 | 16 | 7 |
| And a black and white patch of girls grew playing; | 89 | 4 | 53 | 98 | 4 |
| I skipped in a blush as the big girls rolled | 174 | 6 | 89 | 194 | 6 |

| | U.K. | | | U.S. | |
|---|---|---|---|---|---|
| | *Page* | *Line* | *Poem* | *Page* | *Line* |
| **GIVE** | | | | | |
| Flavoured of celluloid give love the lie. | 14 | 20 | 10 | 16 | 20 |
| (Give, summer, over), the cemented skin, | 19 | 19 | 12 | 23 | 4 |
| Give over, lovers, locking, and the seawax struggle, | 38 | 11 | 20 | 44 | 1 |
| For all there is to give I offer: | 48 | 28 | 28 | 57 | 5 |
| Twisting on racks when sinews give way, | 68 | 13 | 42 | 77 | 13 |
| To take to give is all, return what is hungrily given | 94 | 4 | 57 | 104 | 4 |
| **GIVEN** | | | | | |
| To take to give is all, return what is hungrily given | 94 | 4 | 57 | 104 | 4 |
| **GIVES** | | | | | |
| Gives up its dead to such a working sea; | 5 | 3 | 3 | 5 | 3 |
| And the heart gives up its dead. | 6 | 24 | 4 | 7 | 6 |
| **GLADE** | | | | | |
| Now clasp me to their grains in the gigantic glade, | 176 | 19 | 90 | 197 | 19 |
| **GLAMORGAN** | | | | | |
| Golden Glamorgan straightens, to the falling birds. | 49 | 23 | 29 | 58 | 23 |
| **GLAMORGAN'S** | | | | | |
| Under the lank, fourth folly on Glamorgan's hill, | 49 | 2 | 29 | 58 | 2 |
| **GLANCE** | | | | | |
| Inch and glance that the wound | 109 | 22 | 67 | 120 | 22 |
| In your every inch and glance is the globe of genesis spun, | 110 | 27 | 67 | 122 | 5 |
| **GLAND** | | | | | |
| Within the hallowed gland, blood blessed the heart, | 20 | 18 | 13 | 24 | 18 |
| **GLANDED** | | | | | |
| Dug of the sea, the glanded morrow, | 33 | 8 | 19 | 38 | 8 |
| **GLARED** | | | | | |
| Glared through shark mask and navigating head, | 133 | 11 | 78 | 148 | 14 |
| **GLASS** | | | | | |
| In the glass bed of grapes with snail and flower, | 36 | 5 | 20 | 41 | 5 |
| Hear they the salt glass breakers and the tongues of burial. | 37 | 15 | 20 | 42 | 21 |
| My face is haggard in the glass, | 65 | 19 | 40 | 74 | 19 |
| And the duck pond glass and the blinding byres alone | 120 | 10 | 72 | 132 | 15 |
| **GLAZED** | | | | | |
| And over the glazed lakes skated the shapes of fishes | 123 | 5 | 72 | 136 | 15 |
| **GLIDE** | | | | | |
| The tongues of heaven gossip as I glide | 32 | 5 | 18 | 37 | 11 |

| | U.K. | | | U.S. | |
|---|---|---|---|---|---|
| | Page | Line | Poem | Page | Line |
| On a seizing sky; small fishes glide | 170 | 22 | 88 | 190 | 22 |
| Out of his eyes I saw the last light glide. | | | 91 | 201 | 7 |
| GLIDED | | | | | |
| Along her innocence glided | 113 | 10 | 69 | 125 | 10 |
| In the long ago land that glided the dark door wide | 121 | 12 | 72 | 134 | 7 |
| In the far ago land the door of his death glided wide, | 122 | 25 | 72 | 136 | 5 |
| And the wings glided wide and he was hymned and wedded, | 123 | 13 | 72 | 137 | 3 |
| The bows glided down, and the coast | 149 | 1 | 83 | 166 | 1 |
| GLIDES | | | | | |
| Shall not be latched while magic glides | 11 | 20 | 8 | 12 | 20 |
| Apple seed glides, | 164 | 12 | 86 | 183 | 19 |
| GLIDING | | | | | |
| Gliding windless through the hand folded flakes, | 119 | 4 | 72 | 131 | 4 |
| GLINT | | | | | |
| Glint in the staved and siren-printed caverns, | 78 | 20 | 46 | 87 | 20 |
| GLISTENING | | | | | |
| To shield the glistening brain and blunt the examiners, | 85 | 8 | 50 | 94 | 8 |
| On the gristed leaves and the long gone glistening | 121 | 8 | 72 | 134 | 3 |
| GLOBE | | | | | |
| I sent my creature scouting on the globe, | 4 | 9 | 3 | 4 | 9 |
| That globe itself of hair and bone | 4 | 10 | 3 | 4 | 10 |
| The two-framed globe that spun into a score; | 21 | 21 | 13 | 26 | 4 |
| 'My fathers' globe knocks on its nave and sings.' | 26 | 11 | 16 | 31 | 11 |
| Rounded my globe of heritage, journey | 28 | 11 | 17 | 33 | 11 |
| Doubled the globe of dead and halved a country; | 62 | 3 | 37 | 71 | 3 |
| Time's ship-racked gospel on the globe I balance: | 76 | 11 | 44 | 85 | 11 |
| In your every inch and glance is the globe of genesis spun, | 110 | 27 | 67 | 122 | 5 |
| And wind his globe out of your water thread | 117 | 21 | 71 | 129 | 21 |
| GLOBES | | | | | |
| Like some pitch moon, the limit of the globes; | 24 | 20 | 15 | 29 | 20 |
| GLORY | | | | | |
| Glory also this star, bird | viii | 14 | 1 | xvi | 14 |
| What colour is glory? death's feather? tremble | 31 | 1 | 18 | 36 | 1 |
| Who blows death's feather? What glory is colour? | 32 | 7 | 18 | 37 | 13 |
| The loin is glory in a working pallor. | 32 | 9 | 18 | 37 | 15 |
| O who is glory in the shapeless maps, | 61 | 4 | 36 | 70 | 4 |
| Glory cracked like a flea. | 95 | 18 | 58 | 105 | 18 |
| There was glory to hear | 125 | 17 | 74 | 139 | 17 |

GLORY (continued)

| | U.K. | | | U.S. | |
|---|---|---|---|---|---|
| | Page | Line | Poem | Page | Line |
| Glory glory glory | 131 | 24 | 77 | 146 | 6 |
| In the name of the lost who glory in | 143 | 1 | 82 | 160 | 1 |
| GLORY'S | | | | | |
| I by the tree of thieves, all glory's sawbones, | 75 | 15 | 44 | 84 | 15 |
| GLOVE | | | | | |
| For, sunday faced, with dusters in my glove, | 18 | 16 | 12 | 21 | 16 |
| Draw on the glove of prints, dead Cairo's henna | 75 | 23 | 44 | 84 | 23 |
| I'll comb the snared woods with a glove on a lamp, | 97 | 7 | 59 | 108 | 7 |
| Quickness of hand in the velvet glove | 107 | 12 | 65 | 118 | 12 |
| GLOW | | | | | |
| To glow after the god stoning night | 158 | 11 | 84 | 177 | 11 |
| GLOW-WORMS | | | | | |
| And, broken ghosts with glow-worms in their heads, | 24 | 4 | 15 | 29 | 4 |
| GO | | | | | |
| Of children go who, from their voids, | 11 | 17 | 8 | 12 | 17 |
| The haring snail go giddily round the flower, | 36 | 17 | 20 | 41 | 17 |
| Is heard but little till the stars go out. | 53 | 20 | 32 | 62 | 20 |
| Though they go mad they shall be sane, | 68 | 6 | 42 | 77 | 6 |
| Go crying through you and me | 105 | 18 | 64 | 116 | 18 |
| Do not go gentle into that good night, | 116 | 1 | 70 | 128 | 1 |
| Do not go gentle into that good night. | 116 | 6 | 70 | 128 | 6 |
| Do not go gentle into that good night. | 116 | 12 | 70 | 128 | 12 |
| Do not go gentle into that good night. | 116 | 18 | 70 | 128 | 18 |
| May his hunger go howling on bare white bones | 120 | 8 | 72 | 132 | 13 |
| Heart! Slyly, slowly, hearing the wound in her side go | 165 | 24 | 86 | 185 | 14 |
| Heron, mirrored, go, | 169 | 1 | 87 | 189 | 10 |
| Under and round him go | 170 | 10 | 88 | 190 | 10 |
| Will never go out of my mind: | | | 91 | 200 | 20 |
| An old blind man is with me where I go | | | 91 | 201 | 9 |
| Do not go gentle into that good night | 116 | | 70 | 128 | |
| GOBLIN-SUCKER | | | | | |
| Nor sprout on owl-seed like a goblin-sucker, | 60 | 14 | 36 | 69 | 14 |
| GOD | | | | | |
| At God speeded summer's end | vii | 2 | 1 | xv | 2 |
| At God speeded summer's end | x | 18 | 1 | xviii | 24 |
| This was the god of beginning in the intricate seawhirl, | 38 | 29 | 20 | 44 | 19 |
| And God walked there who was a fiddling warden | 40 | 5 | 22 | 46 | 5 |
| Is certain god, and the ceremony of souls | 109 | 23 | 67 | 120 | 23 |
| God in bed, good and bad, | 134 | 17 | 79 | 150 | 17 |
| No Time, spoke the clocks, no God, rang the bells, | 134 | 28 | 79 | 151 | 6 |
| To glow after the god stoning night | 158 | 11 | 84 | 177 | 11 |
| Of the led-astray birds whom God, for their breast of whistles, | 168 | 19 | 87 | 189 | 4 |

| | U.K. | | | U.S. | |
|---|---|---|---|---|---|
| | Page | Line | Poem | Page | Line |
| God in his whirlwind silence save, who marks the sparrows hail, | 168 | 21 | 87 | 189 | 6 |
| And fabulous, dear God. | 171 | 21 | 88 | 191 | 21 |
| With blessed, unborn God and His Ghost, | 172 | 6 | 88 | 192 | 6 |
| Hating his God, but what he was was plain: | | | 91 | 201 | 2 |
| GOD'S | | | | | |
| On God's rough tumbling grounds | ix | 24 | 1 | xvii | 24 |
| An old god's dugs are pressed and pricked, | 44 | 9 | 25 | 52 | 9 |
| The world's my wound, God's Mary in her grief, | 75 | 8 | 44 | 84 | 8 |
| GOD-IN-HERO | | | | | |
| No god-in-hero tumble down | 42 | 4 | 24 | 49 | 4 |
| No god-in-hero tumble down | 42 | 11 | 24 | 49 | 11 |
| GODS | | | | | |
| The wisemen tell me that the garden gods | 40 | 9 | 22 | 46 | 9 |
| Shall gods be said to thump the clouds | 44 | 1 | 25 | 52 | 1 |
| When it is rain where are the gods? | 44 | 5 | 25 | 52 | 5 |
| It shall be said that gods are stone. | 44 | 11 | 25 | 52 | 11 |
| Shall gods be said to thump the clouds | 44 | | 25 | 52 | |
| GOES | | | | | |
| How at my sheet goes the same crooked worm. | 9 | 22 | 6 | 10 | 22 |
| Into the tided cord, there goes | 11 | 8 | 8 | 12 | 8 |
| When sunlight goes are sundered from the worm, | 14 | 8 | 10 | 16 | 8 |
| Goes over the hill into the deep sea; | 64 | 5 | 39 | 73 | 5 |
| And freely he goes lost | 171 | 19 | 88 | 191 | 19 |
| GOING | | | | | |
| Engraving going. | 54 | 24 | 33 | 63 | 24 |
| By the child going to bed and the man on the stairs | 100 | 2 | 61 | 111 | 2 |
| The mankind of her going with a grave truth | 101 | 15 | 62 | 112 | 15 |
| Last sound, the world going out without a breath: | | | 91 | 201 | 13 |
| GOLD | | | | | |
| Lay the gold tithings barren, | 1 | 2 | 2 | 1 | 2 |
| Gold on such features, and the linen spirit | 76 | 3 | 44 | 85 | 3 |
| When the worm builds with the gold straws of venom | 76 | 21 | 44 | 85 | 21 |
| Whalebed and bulldance, the gold bush of lions, | 78 | 22 | 46 | 87 | 22 |
| With bridebait of gold bread, I with a living skein, | 91 | 25 | 55 | 101 | 3 |
| To the gold gut that sings on his reel | 149 | 19 | 83 | 166 | 19 |
| Gold gut is a lightning thread | 151 | 15 | 83 | 169 | 3 |
| See what the gold gut drags from under | 154 | 11 | 83 | 172 | 11 |
| Manes, under his quenchless summer barbed gold to the bone, | 177 | 6 | 90 | 198 | 5 |
| GOLDEN | | | | | |
| Turns damp to dry; the golden shot | 6 | 2 | 4 | 6 | 2 |

GOLDEN (continued)

|  | U.K. | | | U.S. | |
|---|---|---|---|---|---|
|  | *Page* | *Line* | *Poem* | *Page* | *Line* |
| Each golden grain spat life into its fellow, | 20 | 23 | 13 | 24 | 23 |
| Golden Glamorgan straightens, to the falling birds. | 49 | 23 | 29 | 58 | 23 |
| Hiding the golden mountains and mansions | 82 | 16 | 48 | 91 | 16 |
| Lie watching yellow until the golden weather | 82 | 23 | 48 | 91 | 23 |
| And the golden ball spins out of the skies; | 90 | 10 | 54 | 99 | 10 |
| Golden dissolving under the water veil. | 115 | 9 | 69 | 127 | 9 |
| To hear the golden note turn in a groove, | 125 | 6 | 74 | 139 | 6 |
| His golden yesterday asleep upon the iris | 127 | 3 | 75 | 141 | 3 |
| Of the golden ghost who ringed with his streams her mercury bone, | 127 | 11 | 75 | 141 | 11 |
| Who under the lids of her windows hoisted his golden luggage, | 127 | 12 | 75 | 141 | 12 |
| And the golden pavements laid in requiems, | 131 | 17 | 77 | 145 | 23 |
| Golden in the heydays of his eyes, | 159 | 5 | 85 | 178 | 5 |
| Golden in the mercy of his means, | 159 | 14 | 85 | 178 | 14 |
| And green and golden I was huntsman and herdsman, the calves | 159 | 15 | 85 | 178 | 15 |
| Before the children green and golden | 160 | 22 | 85 | 179 | 22 |
| GONE | | | | | |
| 'The thirst is quenched, the hunger gone, | 65 | 17 | 40 | 74 | 17 |
| When their bones are picked clean and the clean bones gone, | 68 | 4 | 42 | 77 | 4 |
| Dead and gone, dedicate forever to my self | 109 | 6 | 67 | 120 | 6 |
| On the gristed leaves and the long gone glistening | 121 | 8 | 72 | 134 | 3 |
| Is dumb and gone with his flame of brides. | 153 | 10 | 83 | 171 | 6 |
| And gone that barley dark where their clogs danced in the spring, | 177 | 20 | 90 | 198 | 19 |
| GONGS | | | | | |
| Cold Nansen's beak on a boat full of gongs, | 133 | 12 | 78 | 148 | 15 |
| GOOD | | | | | |
| Beasts who sleep good and thin, | ix | 26 | 1 | xvii | 26 |
| Twined good and evil on an eastern tree; | 40 | 10 | 22 | 46 | 10 |
| A little comes, is tasted and found good; | 48 | 5 | 28 | 56 | 5 |
| O my lost love bounced from a good home; | 97 | 23 | 59 | 109 | 3 |
| Good and bad, two ways | 105 | 13 | 64 | 116 | 13 |
| Dark, and the guilty dark, and good | 105 | 21 | 64 | 116 | 21 |
| As much as for their good, | 107 | 19 | 65 | 118 | 19 |
| Made his bad bed in her good | 114 | 12 | 69 | 126 | 12 |
| Do not go gentle into that good night, | 116 | 1 | 70 | 128 | 1 |
| Do not go gentle into that good night. | 116 | 6 | 70 | 128 | 6 |
| Good men, the last wave by, crying how bright | 116 | 7 | 70 | 128 | 7 |
| Do not go gentle into that good night. | 116 | 12 | 70 | 128 | 12 |
| Do not go gentle into that good night. | 116 | 18 | 70 | 128 | 18 |
| God in bed, good and bad, | 134 | 17 | 79 | 150 | 17 |
| Good luck to the hand on the rod, | 151 | 13 | 83 | 169 | 1 |

|  | U.K. | | | U.S. | |
|---|---|---|---|---|---|
|  | Page | Line | Poem | Page | Line |
| Always good luck, praised the finned in the feather | 154 | 5 | 83 | 172 | 5 |
| Good-bye, good luck, struck the sun and the moon, | 157 | 21 | 83 | 176 | 13 |
| Sleep, good, for ever, slow and deep, spelled rare and wise, | 162 | 8 | 86 | 181 | 8 |
| Know the green good, | 163 | 17 | 86 | 182 | 17 |
| Slides good in the sleek mouth | 171 | 9 | 88 | 191 | 9 |
| Of summer come in his great good time | 175 | 3 | 89 | 195 | 8 |
| I lie down thin and hear the good bells jaw— | 175 | 24 | 89 | 196 | 5 |
| Do not go gentle into that good night | 116 | | 70 | 128 | |

GOOD-BYE

| Then good-bye to the fishermanned | 149 | 5 | 83 | 166 | 5 |
|---|---|---|---|---|---|
| Good-bye to the man on the sea-legged deck | 149 | 18 | 83 | 166 | 18 |
| Good-bye to chimneys and funnels, | 150 | 1 | 83 | 167 | 5 |
| Always good-bye to the long-legged bread | 152 | 22 | 83 | 170 | 14 |
| Always good-bye to the fires of the face, | 153 | 2 | 83 | 170 | 18 |
| Always good-bye, cried the voices through the shell, | 154 | 1 | 83 | 172 | 1 |
| Good-bye always for the flesh is cast | 154 | 2 | 83 | 172 | 2 |
| Good-bye, good luck, struck the sun and the moon, | 157 | 21 | 83 | 176 | 13 |

GOOSE

| In a wind that plucked a goose, | 77 | 10 | 45 | 86 | 10 |
|---|---|---|---|---|---|
| Listen and look where she sails the goose plucked sea, | 122 | 20 | 72 | 135 | 20 |

GOOSE'S

| A goose's quill has put an end to murder | 62 | 7 | 37 | 71 | 7 |
|---|---|---|---|---|---|
| Hugged, and barren and bare on Mother Goose's ground | 178 | 2 | 90 | 199 | 3 |

GOOSEBERRY

| I tiptoed shy in the gooseberry wood, | 174 | 4 | 89 | 194 | 4 |
|---|---|---|---|---|---|

GOOSEGIRLS

| Or, butter fat goosegirls, bounced in a gambo bed, | 177 | 17 | 90 | 198 | 16 |
|---|---|---|---|---|---|

GOOSEHERD

| Of the hobnail tales: No gooseherd or swine will turn | 162 | 10 | 86 | 181 | 10 |
|---|---|---|---|---|---|

GOOSESKIN

| Hill. Who once in gooseskin winter loved all ice leaved | 176 | 12 | 90 | 197 | 12 |
|---|---|---|---|---|---|

GOSPEL

| Time's ship-racked gospel on the globe I balance: | 76 | 11 | 44 | 85 | 11 |
|---|---|---|---|---|---|
| Leaping! The gospel rooks! All tell, this night, of him | 165 | 9 | 86 | 184 | 17 |

GOSSIP

| The tongues of heaven gossip as I glide | 32 | 5 | 18 | 37 | 11 |
|---|---|---|---|---|---|

|  | U.K. | | | U.S. | |
|---|---|---|---|---|---|
|  | *Page* | *Line* | *Poem* | *Page* | *Line* |
| **GOT** | | | | | |
| Love, my fate got luckily, | 110 | 15 | 67 | 121 | 17 |
| **GOVERNED** | | | | | |
| City of spring, the governed flower, | 33 | 4 | 19 | 38 | 4 |
| **GOWN** | | | | | |
| Unshelve that all my gristles have a gown | 56 | 6 | 34 | 65 | 6 |
| **GOWNED** | | | | | |
| Crying, white gowned, from the middle moonlit stages | 114 | 14 | 69 | 126 | 14 |
| **GRACE** | | | | | |
| Look twice before he fell from grace. | 63 | 4 | 38 | 72 | 4 |
| Season and sunshine, grace and girl, | 66 | 7 | 40 | 75 | 7 |
| Over the past table I repeat this present grace. | 77 | 25 | 45 | 86 | 25 |
| Follow him out of grace, | 160 | 23 | 85 | 179 | 23 |
| Lie in grace. Sleep spelled at rest in the lowly house | 163 | 20 | 86 | 183 | 1 |
| **GRAFT** | | | | | |
| But graft these four-fruited ridings on your country; | 60 | 9 | 36 | 69 | 9 |
| **GRAFTS** | | | | | |
| Grafts on its bride one-sided skins of truth; | 15 | 8 | 10 | 17 | 8 |
| **GRAIL** | | | | | |
| The blood that touched the crosstree and the grail | 22 | 11 | 14 | 27 | 11 |
| And, as for oils and ointments on the flying grail, | 38 | 23 | 20 | 44 | 13 |
| That the green child see like a grail | 69 | 22 | 43 | 78 | 22 |
| **GRAIN** | | | | | |
| Each golden grain spat life into its fellow, | 20 | 23 | 13 | 24 | 23 |
| Now stamp the Lord's Prayer on a grain of rice, | 74 | 15 | 44 | 83 | 15 |
| The grain that hurries this way from the rim of the grave | 98 | 1 | 59 | 109 | 4 |
| 'Rest beyond choice in the dust-appointed grain, | 98 | 3 | 59 | 109 | 6 |
| With his flame in every grain. | 141 | 10 | 82 | 158 | 10 |
| **GRAINS** | | | | | |
| Sounds with the grains as they hurry | 82 | 15 | 48 | 91 | 15 |
| The grains beyond age, the dark veins of her mother, | 101 | 21 | 62 | 112 | 21 |
| Two sand grains together in bed, | 115 | 1 | 69 | 127 | 1 |
| Dust in the buried wood, flies on the grains of her wings | 121 | 3 | 72 | 133 | 18 |
| As the grains blow, as your death grows, through our heart. | 129 | 23 | 77 | 143 | 23 |
| And the funeral grains of the slaughtered floor. | 135 | 5 | 80 | 152 | 5 |
| And the tall grains foamed in their bills; | 153 | 1 | 83 | 170 | 16 |
| Counting the denials of the grains | 155 | 16 | 83 | 173 | 20 |
| Now clasp me to their grains in the gigantic glade, | 176 | 19 | 90 | 197 | 19 |

|  |  | U.K. |  | | U.S. | |
|---|---|---|---|---|---|---|
|  |  | Page | Line | Poem | Page | Line |
| GRAPE |  |  |  |  |  |  |
| Were oat and grape | | 39 | 13 | 21 | 45 | 13 |
| GRAPE'S |  |  |  |  |  |  |
| Laid the crops low, broke the grape's joy. | | 39 | 5 | 21 | 45 | 5 |
| GRAPES |  |  |  |  |  |  |
| In the glass bed of grapes with snail and flower, | | 36 | 5 | 20 | 41 | 5 |
| Hands, hold you poison or grapes? | | 58 | 9 | 35 | 67 | 9 |
| Ships, hold you poison or grapes? | | 58 | 25 | 35 | 67 | 25 |
| Hold you poison or grapes? | | 59 | 8 | 35 | 68 | 8 |
| GRAPPLE |  |  |  |  |  |  |
| He shall grapple with the guard | | 42 | 20 | 24 | 49 | 20 |
| He shall grapple with the guard | | 42 | 27 | 24 | 50 | 6 |
| GRASS |  |  |  |  |  |  |
| The signal grass that tells me all I know | | 16 | 22 | 11 | 19 | 22 |
| The secret oils that drive the grass. | | 22 | 18 | 14 | 27 | 18 |
| Through all the irons in the grass, metal | | 28 | 7 | 17 | 33 | 7 |
| My second struggling from the grass. | | 28 | 20 | 17 | 33 | 20 |
| The birds the grass the trees the lake | | 112 | 15 | 68 | 124 | 15 |
| A blade of grass longs with the meadow, | | 115 | 15 | 69 | 127 | 15 |
| About the lilting house and happy as the grass was green, | | 159 | 2 | 85 | 178 | 2 |
| And fire green as grass. | | 159 | 22 | 85 | 178 | 22 |
| On the lord's-table of the bowing grass. Fear most | | 163 | 12 | 86 | 182 | 12 |
| Or hickory bull in milky grass | | 175 | 12 | 89 | 195 | 17 |
| Grave, after Beloved on the grass gulfed cross is scrubbed | | 178 | 13 | 90 | 199 | 14 |
| Hill, under the grass, in love, and there grow | | | | 91 | 200 | 6 |
| GRASSBLADE |  |  |  |  |  |  |
| Hollows, a grassblade blown in cupped hands, in the looted elms | | 169 | 4 | 87 | 189 | 13 |
| GRAVE |  |  |  |  |  |  |
| All issue armoured, of the grave, | | 4 | 19 | 3 | 4 | 19 |
| Nor the outspoken grave. | | 12 | 21 | 9 | 13 | 21 |
| When, like a running grave, time tracks you down, | | 18 | 1 | 12 | 21 | 1 |
| In the straight grave, | | 18 | 20 | 12 | 21 | 20 |
| And stake the sleepers in the savage grave | | 30 | 17 | 18 | 35 | 17 |
| My grave is watered by the crossing Jordan. | | 31 | 19 | 18 | 37 | 1 |
| Socket and grave, the brassy blood, | | 34 | 11 | 19 | 39 | 17 |
| Your corkscrew grave centred in navel and nipple, | | 36 | 27 | 20 | 42 | 6 |
| Lie all unknowing of the grave sin-eater. | | 47 | 8 | 27 | 55 | 8 |
| The country-handed grave boxed into love, | | 55 | 4 | 33 | 64 | 7 |
| So cross her hand with their grave gipsy eyes, | | 55 | 12 | 33 | 64 | 15 |
| The moon-drawn grave, with the seafaring years, | | 67 | 2 | 41 | 76 | 2 |
| Sneak down the stallion grave, | | 67 | 18 | 41 | 76 | 18 |

|  | U.K. | | | U.S. | |
| --- | --- | --- | --- | --- | --- |
|  | Page | Line | Poem | Page | Line |
| And three dead seasons on a climbing grave | 72 | 6 | 44 | 81 | 6 |
| Time's nerve in vinegar, the gallow grave | 75 | 6 | 44 | 84 | 6 |
| With priest's grave foot and hand of five assassins | 78 | 25 | 46 | 88 | 2 |
| And the grave sea, mock who deride | 82 | 2 | 48 | 91 | 2 |
| For in this yellow grave of sand and sea | 82 | 5 | 48 | 91 | 5 |
| That's grave and gay as grave and sea | 82 | 7 | 48 | 91 | 7 |
| Of the grave, gay, seaside land. | 82 | 17 | 48 | 91 | 17 |
| Storm me forever over her grave until | 88 | 10 | 52 | 97 | 10 |
| And dug your grave in my breast. | 92 | 16 | 55 | 101 | 22 |
| The grain that hurries this way from the rim of the grave | 98 | 1 | 59 | 109 | 4 |
| The grave and my calm body are shut to your coming as stone, | 98 | 6 | 59 | 109 | 9 |
| (Bury the dead for fear that they walk to the grave in labour.) | 99 | 2 | 60 | 110 | 2 |
| Shall drown in a grief as deep as his true grave, | 100 | 18 | 61 | 111 | 18 |
| The mankind of her going with a grave truth | 101 | 15 | 62 | 112 | 15 |
| And the grave its daughters. | 110 | 14 | 67 | 121 | 16 |
| Whales unreined from the green grave | 113 | 8 | 69 | 125 | 8 |
| Grave men, near death, who see with blinding sight | 116 | 13 | 70 | 128 | 13 |
| Have sought your single grave, | 117 | 28 | 71 | 130 | 4 |
| As a dust of pigeons. Exulting, the grave hooved | 121 | 18 | 72 | 134 | 13 |
| The heavens, the heaven, the grave, the burning font. | 122 | 24 | 72 | 136 | 4 |
| Charred on the black breast of the grave | 129 | 7 | 77 | 143 | 7 |
| Sun spin a grave grey | 147 | 14 | 82 | 164 | 14 |
| Till every bone in the rushing grave | 151 | 11 | 83 | 168 | 19 |
| Wear-willow river, grave, | 169 | 10 | 87 | 189 | 19 |
| This sandgrain day in the bent bay's grave | 170 | 6 | 88 | 190 | 6 |
| Grave, after Beloved on the grass gulfed cross is scrubbed | 178 | 13 | 90 | 199 | 14 |
| When, like a running grave | 18 |  | 12 | 21 |  |

GRAVE'S

| | | | | | |
| --- | --- | --- | --- | --- | --- |
| Grave's foot, blinds down the lids, the teeth in black, | 87 | 4 | 52 | 96 | 4 |

GRAVE-GABBING

| | | | | | |
| --- | --- | --- | --- | --- | --- |
| On that cloud coast to each grave-gabbing shade; | 26 | 18 | 16 | 31 | 18 |

GRAVE-GROPING

| | | | | | |
| --- | --- | --- | --- | --- | --- |
| Range from the grave-groping place. | 43 | 28 | 24 | 51 | 14 |

GRAVEL

| | | | | | |
| --- | --- | --- | --- | --- | --- |
| Flung gravel chime? Let the stones speak | 44 | 13 | 25 | 52 | 13 |
| Carved birds blunt their striking throats on the salt gravel; | 86 | 3 | 51 | 95 | 3 |
| That the children filled with gravel | 111 | 9 | 68 | 123 | 9 |

| | U.K. | | | U.S. | |
|---|---|---|---|---|---|
| | *Page* | *Line* | *Poem* | *Page* | *Line* |
| GRAVELS | | | | | |
| The cadaverous gravels, falls thick and steadily, | 36 | 20 | 20 | 41 | 20 |
| GRAVES | | | | | |
| Quarters and graves | 146 | 12 | 82 | 163 | 12 |
| GRAVEST | | | | | |
| In the rain telling its beads, and the gravest ghost | 163 | 8 | 86 | 182 | 8 |
| GRAVEWARD | | | | | |
| All shall remain and on the graveward gulf | 67 | 27 | 41 | 76 | 27 |
| The gentleman lay graveward with his furies; | 71 | 2 | 44 | 80 | 2 |
| GRAVEYARD | | | | | |
| Over the graveyard in the water | 152 | 13 | 83 | 170 | 5 |
| GRAZE | | | | | |
| The cattle graze on the covered foam, | 156 | 15 | 83 | 175 | 3 |
| The star rise at pasture and nightlong the fables graze | 163 | 11 | 86 | 182 | 11 |
| GREAT | | | | | |
| My great blood's iron single | 38 | 15 | 20 | 44 | 5 |
| Lose the great pains or stuff the wound, | 48 | 12 | 28 | 56 | 12 |
| Great is the hand that holds dominion over | 62 | 11 | 37 | 71 | 11 |
| Cudgel great air, wreck east, and topple sun-down, | 79 | 7 | 46 | 88 | 10 |
| And clap its great blood down; | 92 | 3 | 55 | 101 | 9 |
| And guilts, great crotch and giant | 110 | 8 | 67 | 121 | 10 |
| When one at the great least of your best loved | 117 | 3 | 71 | 129 | 3 |
| May hold it in a great flood | 129 | 20 | 77 | 143 | 20 |
| Deep the great bushed bait with raining lips | 151 | 3 | 83 | 168 | 11 |
| The statues of great rain stand still, | 154 | 15 | 83 | 172 | 15 |
| He who blew the great fire in | 155 | 13 | 83 | 173 | 17 |
| And the wings of the great roc ribboned for the fair! | 164 | 16 | 86 | 184 | 2 |
| In the unknown, famous light of great | 171 | 20 | 88 | 191 | 20 |
| Of summer come in his great good time | 175 | 3 | 89 | 195 | 8 |
| GREATER | | | | | |
| Up and down the greater waves | 156 | 11 | 83 | 174 | 19 |
| GREED | | | | | |
| Greed on man beating near and fire neighbour | 126 | 6 | 74 | 140 | 6 |
| GREEK | | | | | |
| Greek in the Irish sea the ageless voice: | 41 | 22 | 23 | 48 | 4 |
| GREEN | | | | | |
| Green of the seaweed's iron, | 2 | 14 | 2 | 2 | 14 |
| The force that through the green fuse drives the flower | 9 | 1 | 6 | 10 | 1 |
| Drives my green age; that blasts the roots of trees | 9 | 2 | 6 | 10 | 2 |
| Where once your green knots sank their splice | 11 | 7 | 8 | 12 | 7 |
| The green unraveller | 11 | 9 | 8 | 12 | 9 |
| That chalk the walls with green girls and their men. | 12 | 16 | 9 | 13 | 16 |

197

|  | U.K. | | | U.S. | |
|  | Page | Line | Poem | Page | Line |
| The time for breast and the green apron age | 20 | 4 | 13 | 24 | 4 |
| Green was the singing house. | 20 | 24 | 13 | 24 | 24 |
| No tread more perilous, the green steps and spire | 36 | 2 | 20 | 41 | 2 |
| I, in a wind on fire, from green Adam's cradle, | 38 | 17 | 20 | 44 | 7 |
| Murder of Eden and green genesis. | 41 | 8 | 23 | 47 | 8 |
| A hemisphere green may scold him | 43 | 3 | 24 | 50 | 10 |
| And a green inch be his bearer; | 43 | 4 | 24 | 50 | 11 |
| A village green may scold him | 43 | 10 | 24 | 50 | 17 |
| As the green blooms ride upward, to the drive of time; | 49 | 3 | 29 | 58 | 3 |
| Calls a green day and night. | 69 | 6 | 43 | 78 | 6 |
| Calls the green rock of light. | 69 | 12 | 43 | 78 | 12 |
| Nor falls to His green myths? | 69 | 18 | 43 | 78 | 18 |
| That the green child see like a grail | 69 | 22 | 43 | 78 | 22 |
| 'Nor the green nought be hurt; | 70 | 17 | 43 | 79 | 21 |
| O green and unborn and undead?' | 70 | 19 | 43 | 79 | 23 |
| Green as beginning, let the garden diving | 76 | 19 | 44 | 85 | 19 |
| The fingers will forget green thumbs and mark | 81 | 2 | 47 | 90 | 2 |
| Into the answering skies from the green ground, | 100 | 7 | 61 | 111 | 7 |
| And the legends of the green chapels | 103 | 25 | 63 | 114 | 25 |
| Whales unreined from the green grave | 113 | 8 | 69 | 125 | 8 |
| Their frail deeds might have danced in a green bay, | 116 | 8 | 70 | 128 | 8 |
| On the departed, snow bushed green, wanton in moon light | 121 | 17 | 72 | 134 | 12 |
| On the white, no longer growing green, and, minstrel dead, | 123 | 2 | 72 | 136 | 12 |
| With my cherry capped dangler green as seaweed | 133 | 17 | 78 | 148 | 20 |
| And the green dust | 143 | 6 | 82 | 160 | 6 |
| Are making under the green, laid veil | 151 | 21 | 83 | 169 | 9 |
| And stunned and still on the green, laid veil | 156 | 3 | 83 | 174 | 11 |
| Gallop through the arched, green farms, | 156 | 20 | 83 | 175 | 8 |
| About the lilting house and happy as the grass was green, | 159 | 2 | 85 | 178 | 2 |
| And as I was green and carefree, famous among the barns | 159 | 10 | 85 | 178 | 10 |
| And green and golden I was huntsman and herdsman, the calves | 159 | 15 | 85 | 178 | 15 |
| And fire green as grass. | 159 | 22 | 85 | 178 | 22 |
| Out of the whinnying green stable | 160 | 13 | 85 | 179 | 13 |
| Before the children green and golden | 160 | 22 | 85 | 179 | 22 |
| Time held me green and dying | 161 | 5 | 85 | 180 | 8 |
| Know the green good, | 163 | 17 | 86 | 182 | 17 |
| Green chickens of the bay and bushes cluck, 'dilly dilly, | 168 | 7 | 87 | 188 | 11 |
| And no green cocks or hens | 169 | 5 | 87 | 189 | 14 |

|  | U.K. |  |  | U.S. |  |
|---|---|---|---|---|---|
|  | Page | Line | Poem | Page | Line |
| All the green leaved little weddings' wives | 174 | 11 | 89 | 194 | 11 |
| Who once, green countries since, were a hedge-row of joys. | 176 | 20 | 90 | 197 | 20 |
| The force that through the green fuse drives the flower | 9 |  | 6 | 10 |  |
| GREENER |  |  |  |  |  |
| Grow larked and greener at berry brown | 173 | 20 | 88 | 193 | 20 |
| GREENSWARD |  |  |  |  |  |
| Through the shaken greensward lake, silent, on moonshod hooves, | 165 | 13 | 86 | 185 | 3 |
| GREENWOOD |  |  |  |  |  |
| The greenwood dying as the deer fall in their tracks, | 49 | 11 | 29 | 58 | 11 |
| And flower of country sleep and the greenwood keep. | 162 | 18 | 86 | 181 | 18 |
| GREET |  |  |  |  |  |
| I climb to greet the war in which I have no heart but only | 158 | 8 | 84 | 177 | 8 |
| GREW |  |  |  |  |  |
| Into the sided lap of light grew strong, | 21 | 3 | 13 | 25 | 3 |
| And famine grew, and locusts came; | 62 | 10 | 37 | 71 | 10 |
| And a black and white patch of girls grew playing; | 89 | 4 | 53 | 98 | 4 |
| Silence, silence to do, when earth grew loud, | 125 | 15 | 74 | 139 | 15 |
| And the craters of his eyes grew springshoots and fire | 135 | 7 | 80 | 152 | 7 |
| And the sun grew round that very day. | 160 | 10 | 85 | 179 | 10 |
| Midwives grew in the midnight ditches, | 174 | 19 | 89 | 194 | 19 |
| GREY |  |  |  |  |  |
| The sun was red, the moon was grey, | 20 | 14 | 13 | 24 | 14 |
| Sun spin a grave grey | 147 | 14 | 82 | 164 | 14 |
| GREY-HAIRED |  |  |  |  |  |
| Dig no more for the chains of his grey-haired heart. | 135 | 9 | 80 | 152 | 9 |
| GRIEF |  |  |  |  |  |
| But not of grief, for I have knocked down that | 48 | 2 | 28 | 56 | 2 |
| A grief ago, | 54 | 1 | 33 | 63 | 1 |
| Who is my grief, | 54 | 9 | 33 | 63 | 9 |
| Grief thief of time crawls off, | 67 | 1 | 41 | 76 | 1 |
| The old forget the grief, | 67 | 9 | 41 | 76 | 9 |
| And free the twin-boxed grief, | 67 | 20 | 41 | 76 | 20 |
| The landscape grief, love in His oils | 69 | 20 | 43 | 78 | 20 |
| The world's my wound, God's Mary in her grief, | 75 | 8 | 44 | 84 | 8 |
| Grief with dishevelled hands tear out the altar ghost | 83 | 5 | 49 | 92 | 5 |
| Time's coral saint and the salt grief drown a foul sepulchre | 83 | 8 | 49 | 92 | 8 |

GRIEF (continued)

| | U.K. | | | U.S. | |
| --- | --- | --- | --- | --- | --- |
| | Page | Line | Poem | Page | Line |
| Grief with drenched book and candle christens the cherub time | 83 | 16 | 49 | 92 | 16 |
| Who have brought forth the urchin grief. | 84 | 6 | 49 | 93 | 12 |
| And a tear-stained widower grief drooped from the lashes | 85 | 9 | 50 | 94 | 9 |
| Will be the same grief flying. Whom shall they calm? | 100 | 11 | 61 | 111 | 11 |
| Shall drown in a grief as deep as his true grave, | 100 | 18 | 61 | 111 | 18 |
| In many married London's estranging grief. | 117 | 12 | 71 | 129 | 12 |
| He wept from the crest of grief, he prayed to the veiled sky | 120 | 7 | 72 | 132 | 12 |
| A grief ago | 54 | | 33 | 63 | |
| Grief thief of time | 67 | | 41 | 76 | |
| GRIEFS | | | | | |
| With all their griefs in their arms, | 128 | 5 | 76 | 142 | 5 |
| Round the griefs of the ages, | 128 | 18 | 76 | 142 | 18 |
| GRIEVE | | | | | |
| Grieve | 129 | 3 | 77 | 143 | 3 |
| Myselves grieve now, and miracles cannot atone. | 129 | 16 | 77 | 143 | 16 |
| Naked and forsaken to grieve he will not come. | 166 | 7 | 86 | 186 | 7 |
| We grieve as the blithe birds, never again, leave shingle and elm, | 168 | 9 | 87 | 188 | 13 |
| In the coal black bush and let them grieve. | 174 | 12 | 89 | 194 | 12 |
| GRIEVED | | | | | |
| And learn, too late, they grieved it on its way, | 116 | 11 | 70 | 128 | 11 |
| Off by the sun and Daughters no longer grieved | 178 | 14 | 90 | 199 | 15 |
| GRIEVERS | | | | | |
| The grievers | 129 | 2 | 77 | 143 | 2 |
| GRIEVES | | | | | |
| Now the heron grieves in the weeded verge. Through windows | 168 | 23 | 87 | 189 | 8 |
| GRIMLY | | | | | |
| The ringed-sea ghost, rise grimly from the wrack. | 46 | 24 | 27 | 54 | 24 |
| GRINDING | | | | | |
| By the grinding sea, | 105 | 15 | 64 | 116 | 15 |
| GRIP | | | | | |
| Time and places grip her breast bone, | 156 | 7 | 83 | 174 | 15 |
| GRISTED | | | | | |
| On the gristed leaves and the long gone glistening | 121 | 8 | 72 | 134 | 3 |
| GRISTLE | | | | | |
| Gristle and rind, and a roarers' life, | 175 | 17 | 89 | 195 | 22 |
| GRISTLES | | | | | |
| Unshelve that all my gristles have a gown | 56 | 6 | 34 | 65 | 6 |

|  | U.K. | | Poem | U.S. | |
| --- | --- | --- | --- | --- | --- |
|  | *Page* | *Line* |  | *Page* | *Line* |
| GROIN |  |  |  |  |  |
| In the groin of the natural doorway I crouched like a tailor | 99 | 3 | 60 | 110 | 3 |
| GROIN'S |  |  |  |  |  |
| In the groin's endless coil a man is tangled.' | 79 | 27 | 46 | 89 | 8 |
| GROOM |  |  |  |  |  |
| Groom the dark brides, the widows of the night | 14 | 5 | 10 | 16 | 5 |
| Nutmeg, civet, and sea-parsley serve the plagued groom and bride | 84 | 5 | 49 | 93 | 11 |
| O bride and bride groom | 130 | 17 | 77 | 144 | 17 |
| GROOVE |  |  |  |  |  |
| To hear the golden note turn in a groove, | 125 | 6 | 74 | 139 | 6 |
| GROOVED |  |  |  |  |  |
| The grooved land rotating, that the stylus of lightning | 37 | 17 | 20 | 42 | 23 |
| GROPE |  |  |  |  |  |
| In all love's countries, that will grope awake; | 81 | 12 | 47 | 90 | 12 |
| GROPING |  |  |  |  |  |
| Groping for matter under the dog's plate, | 48 | 26 | 28 | 57 | 3 |
| GROTTOES |  |  |  |  |  |
| In grottoes I worked with birds, | 132 | 9 | 78 | 147 | 9 |
| GROUND |  |  |  |  |  |
| Reaching a second ground far from the stars; | 26 | 7 | 16 | 31 | 7 |
| I fled that ground as lightly as a feather. | 26 | 10 | 16 | 31 | 10 |
| Manna for the rumbling ground, | 42 | 17 | 24 | 49 | 17 |
| Manna for the guarded ground, | 42 | 24 | 24 | 50 | 3 |
| Shall a dropped stone drum on the ground, | 44 | 12 | 25 | 52 | 12 |
| Has not yet reached the ground. | 63 | 19 | 38 | 72 | 19 |
| Out of the old lie burning on the ground, | 64 | 13 | 39 | 73 | 13 |
| In quick, sweet, cruel light till the locked ground sprout out, | 91 | 18 | 55 | 100 | 18 |
| To clasp my fury on ground | 92 | 2 | 55 | 101 | 8 |
| Cast high, stunned on gilled stone; sly scissors ground in frost | 92 | 7 | 55 | 101 | 13 |
| Into the answering skies from the green ground, | 100 | 7 | 61 | 111 | 7 |
| And there outside on the bread of the ground | 121 | 13 | 72 | 134 | 8 |
| On to the ground when a man died | 125 | 21 | 74 | 139 | 21 |
| The ground | 143 | 10 | 82 | 160 | 10 |
| Down, down, down, under the ground, | 157 | 9 | 83 | 176 | 1 |
| Hugged, and barren and bare on Mother Goose's ground | 178 | 2 | 90 | 199 | 3 |
| Which was rest and dust, and in the kind ground |  |  | 91 | 200 | 10 |
| GROUNDS |  |  |  |  |  |
| On God's rough tumbling grounds | ix | 24 | 1 | xvii | 24 |
| GROUNDWORKS |  |  |  |  |  |
| Over these groundworks thrusting through a pavement | 72 | 3 | 44 | 81 | 3 |

201

|  | | U.K. | | | U.S. | |
| --- | --- | --- | --- | --- | --- | --- |
|  |  | Page | Line | Poem | Page | Line |
| GROVE | | | | | | |
| In the squirrel nimble grove, under linen and thatch | | 163 | 21 | 86 | 183 | 2 |
| GROVES | | | | | | |
| Through the loud zoo of the willow groves | | 111 | 22 | 68 | 123 | 22 |
| And the groves were blue with sailors | | 112 | 6 | 68 | 124 | 6 |
| GROW | | | | | | |
| The dead grow for His joy. | | 171 | 27 | 88 | 191 | 27 |
| And air shaped Heaven where souls grow wild | | 172 | 20 | 88 | 192 | 20 |
| Grow larked and greener at berry brown | | 173 | 20 | 88 | 193 | 20 |
| Hill, under the grass, in love, and there grow | | | | 91 | 200 | 6 |
| GROWING | | | | | | |
| The growing bones, the rumour of manseed | | 20 | 17 | 13 | 24 | 17 |
| Growing more terrible as the day | | 64 | 4 | 39 | 73 | 4 |
| On the white, no longer growing green, and, minstrel dead, | | 123 | 2 | 72 | 136 | 12 |
| GROWN | | | | | | |
| Twice in the feeding sea, grown | | 29 | 2 | 17 | 34 | 6 |
| Though the names on their weed grown stones are rained away, | | 176 | 8 | 90 | 197 | 8 |
| GROWS | | | | | | |
| The secret of the soil grows through the eye, | | 25 | 4 | 15 | 30 | 4 |
| There grows the hours' ladder to the sun, | | 27 | 1 | 16 | 32 | 6 |
| Before the agony; the spirit grows, | | 48 | 3 | 28 | 56 | 3 |
| As the grains blow, as your death grows, through our heart. | | 129 | 23 | 77 | 143 | 23 |
| Gabriel and radiant shrubbery as the morning grows joyful | | 158 | 15 | 84 | 177 | 15 |
| GROYNE | | | | | | |
| Through the last vault and vegetable groyne, | | 78 | 7 | 46 | 87 | 7 |
| GRUMBLE | | | | | | |
| Hands grumble on the door, | | 58 | 2 | 35 | 67 | 2 |
| Hands grumble on the door, | | 59 | 1 | 35 | 68 | 1 |
| GUARD | | | | | | |
| He shall grapple with the guard | | 42 | 20 | 24 | 49 | 20 |
| He shall grapple with the guard | | 42 | 27 | 24 | 50 | 6 |
| GUARDED | | | | | | |
| Manna for the guarded ground, | | 42 | 24 | 24 | 50 | 3 |
| GUARDIAN | | | | | | |
| We in our Eden knew the secret guardian | | 40 | 13 | 22 | 46 | 13 |
| GUARDING | | | | | | |
| Of the stone bird guarding her: | | 93 | 25 | 56 | 103 | 5 |
| GUIDED | | | | | | |
| When we were strangers to the guided seas, | | 40 | 7 | 22 | 46 | 7 |
| GUILLOTINE | | | | | | |
| Slapped down the guillotine, the blood-red double | | 41 | 6 | 23 | 47 | 6 |

|  |  | U.K. |  |  | U.S. |  |
|  | Page | Line | Poem | Page | Line |
| GUILT |  |  |  |  |  |  |
| And a silk pigeon's guilt in her proud absence, | 78 | 17 | 46 | 87 | 17 |
| Of innocence and guilt | 105 | 7 | 64 | 116 | 7 |
| Loving on this sea banged guilt | 109 | 15 | 67 | 120 | 15 |
| Guilt | 168 | 18 | 87 | 189 | 3 |
| GUILTS |  |  |  |  |  |  |
| And guilts, great crotch and giant | 110 | 8 | 67 | 121 | 10 |
| GUILTY |  |  |  |  |  |  |
| Dark, and the guilty dark, and good | 105 | 21 | 64 | 116 | 21 |
| GULF |  |  |  |  |  |  |
| All shall remain and on the graveward gulf | 67 | 27 | 41 | 76 | 27 |
| GULFED |  |  |  |  |  |  |
| Grave, after Beloved on the grass gulfed cross is scrubbed | 178 | 13 | 90 | 199 | 14 |
| GULL |  |  |  |  |  |  |
| Where the anchor rode like a gull | 150 | 13 | 83 | 167 | 17 |
| Gull, on the wave with sand in its eyes! And the foal moves | 165 | 12 | 86 | 185 | 2 |
| GULLED |  |  |  |  |  |  |
| Daws Sir John's just hill dons, and again the gulled birds hare | 167 | 15 | 87 | 187 | 15 |
| Gulled and chanter in young Heaven's fold | 172 | 8 | 88 | 192 | 8 |
| GULLS |  |  |  |  |  |  |
| Gulls, pipers, cockles, and sails, | vii | 11 | 1 | xv | 11 |
| No more may gulls cry at their ears | 68 | 20 | 42 | 77 | 20 |
| Trot and gallop with gulls upon them | 156 | 21 | 83 | 175 | 9 |
| Flounders, gulls, on their cold, dying trails, | 170 | 11 | 88 | 190 | 11 |
| GUMS |  |  |  |  |  |  |
| The body prospered, teeth in the marrowed gums, | 20 | 16 | 13 | 24 | 16 |
| GUNMAN |  |  |  |  |  |  |
| In this our age the gunman and his moll, | 14 | 11 | 10 | 16 | 11 |
| GUNS |  |  |  |  |  |  |
| Cry Eloi to the guns. | 31 | 18 | 18 | 36 | 18 |
| Hurdles and guns and railings, as the boulders heave, | 49 | 16 | 29 | 58 | 16 |
| GUSHERS |  |  |  |  |  |  |
| Nor fenced, nor staked, the gushers of the sky | 24 | 16 | 15 | 29 | 16 |
| GUSTY |  |  |  |  |  |  |
| When I was a gusty man and a half | 174 | 13 | 89 | 194 | 13 |
| GUT |  |  |  |  |  |  |
| To the gold gut that sings on his reel | 149 | 19 | 83 | 166 | 19 |
| Gold gut is a lightning thread, | 151 | 15 | 83 | 169 | 3 |
| See what the gold gut drags from under | 154 | 11 | 83 | 172 | 11 |

# ENTRIES UNDER H

|  |  | U.K. | | Poem | U.S. | |
|---|---|---|---|---|---|---|
|  |  | Page | Line |  | Page | Line |
| HACK | | | | | | |
| | My dabbed bay's dusk, as I hack | viii | 10 | 1 | xvi | 10 |
| | Hack of the cough, the hanging albatross, | 67 | 10 | 41 | 76 | 10 |
| | Who could hack out your unsucked heart, | 70 | 18 | 43 | 79 | 22 |
| HACKED | | | | | | |
| | They said, who hacked and humoured, they were mine. | 46 | 20 | 27 | 54 | 20 |
| | And immemorial sons of the cudgelling, hacked | 176 | 11 | 90 | 197 | 11 |
| HAD | | | | | | |
| | Had stringed my flask of matter to his rib. | 4 | 12 | 3 | 4 | 12 |
| | He had by heart the Christ-cross-row of death. | 4 | 24 | 3 | 4 | 24 |
| | And the four winds, that had long blown as one, | 20 | 19 | 13 | 24 | 19 |
| | I learnt the verbs of will, and had my secret; | 21 | 15 | 13 | 25 | 15 |
| | What had been one was many sounding minded. | 21 | 17 | 13 | 25 | 17 |
| | From limbs that had the measure of the worm, shuffled | 28 | 5 | 17 | 33 | 5 |
| | A climbing sea from Asia had me down | 73 | 19 | 44 | 82 | 19 |
| | 'His mother's womb had a tongue that lapped up mud,' | 79 | 20 | 46 | 89 | 1 |
| | Running when he had heard them clearly | 111 | 17 | 68 | 123 | 17 |
| | Had followed the hunchback | 112 | 17 | 68 | 124 | 17 |
| | All blood-signed assailings and vanished marriages in which he had no lovely part | 114 | 20 | 69 | 126 | 20 |
| | Sin who had a woman's shape | 153 | 14 | 83 | 171 | 10 |
| | And once below a time I lordly had the trees and leaves | 159 | 7 | 85 | 178 | 7 |
| | Even as a baby he had never cried; | | | 91 | 201 | 5 |
| HAGGARD | | | | | | |
| | My face is haggard in the glass, | 65 | 19 | 40 | 74 | 19 |
| HAGS | | | | | | |
| | Before the ladies' breasts are hags | 65 | 4 | 40 | 74 | 4 |
| HAIL | | | | | | |
| | (Hail to His beasthood!). | ix | 25 | 1 | xvii | 25 |
| | The darted hail, the childish snow, | 7 | 14 | 5 | 8 | 14 |
| | As the sails drank up the hail of thunder | 154 | 7 | 83 | 172 | 7 |
| | But blessed be hail and upheaval | 158 | 20 | 84 | 177 | 20 |
| | Time let me hail and climb | 159 | 4 | 85 | 178 | 4 |

| | U.K. | | | U.S. | |
|---|---|---|---|---|---|
| | *Page* | *Line* | *Poem* | *Page* | *Line* |
| As the rain falls, hail on the fleece, as the vale mist rides | 164 | 8 | 86 | 183 | 15 |
| God in his whirlwind silence save, who marks the sparrows hail, | 168 | 21 | 87 | 189 | 6 |
| And ducked and draked white lake that harps to a hail stone. | 177 | 8 | 90 | 198 | 7 |
| HAILING | | | | | |
| Who scales a hailing hill in her cold flintsteps | 79 | 3 | 46 | 88 | 6 |
| HAIR | | | | | |
| That globe itself of hair and bone | 4 | 10 | 3 | 4 | 10 |
| Pushed up their hair, the dry wind steers | 11 | 5 | 8 | 12 | 5 |
| If I were tickled by the hatching hair, | 12 | 10 | 9 | 13 | 10 |
| My wordy wounds are printed with your hair | 13 | 19 | 9 | 15 | 5 |
| With frosty fingers punishes my hair, | 16 | 2 | 11 | 19 | 2 |
| Hand, the breaking of the hair, | 20 | 11 | 13 | 24 | 11 |
| I spelt my vision with a hand and hair, | 26 | 23 | 16 | 32 | 3 |
| With the wind in my hair, | 58 | 22 | 35 | 67 | 22 |
| The parting of hat from hair, | 64 | 16 | 39 | 73 | 16 |
| And Jonah's Moby snatched me by the hair, | 73 | 20 | 44 | 82 | 20 |
| Savours the lick of the times through a deadly wood of hair | 77 | 9 | 45 | 86 | 9 |
| A calm wind blows that raised the trees like hair | 80 | 11 | 46 | 89 | 19 |
| With a hand plunged through her hair, | 93 | 12 | 56 | 102 | 12 |
| And the dear floods of his hair. | 93 | 30 | 56 | 103 | 10 |
| The skull of the earth is barbed with a war of burning brains and hair. | 96 | 9 | 58 | 106 | 9 |
| And Samson drowned in his hair. | 113 | 13 | 69 | 125 | 13 |
| At his thrashing hair and whale-blue eye; | 149 | 3 | 83 | 166 | 3 |
| See what clings to hair and skull | 154 | 13 | 83 | 172 | 13 |
| The centuries throw back their hair | 155 | 7 | 83 | 173 | 11 |
| Clings to her drifting hair, and climbs; | 155 | 17 | 83 | 174 | 1 |
| Coil from the thoroughfares of her hair | 157 | 5 | 83 | 175 | 17 |
| Wound, nor her riding high, nor her eyes, nor kindled hair, | 166 | 2 | 86 | 186 | 2 |
| HAIR'S | | | | | |
| 'If my head hurt a hair's foot | 97 | 1 | 59 | 108 | 1 |
| 'If my head hurt a hair's foot' | 97 | | 59 | 108 | |
| HAIRED | | | | | |
| The haygold haired, my love asleep, and the rift blue | 165 | 17 | 86 | 185 | 7 |
| HAIR-BURIED | | | | | |
| Through the rippled drum of the hair-buried ear; | 113 | 4 | 69 | 125 | 4 |
| HAIRPINS | | | | | |
| And their firefly hairpins flew, and the ricks ran round— | 177 | 21 | 90 | 199 | 1 |
| HAIRS | | | | | |
| Your calm and cuddled is a scythe of hairs, | 18 | 2 | 12 | 21 | 2 |

HAIRS (continued)

|  | U.K. | | | U.S. | |
|---|---|---|---|---|---|
|  | *Page* | *Line* | *Poem* | *Page* | *Line* |
| Where no wax is, the candle shows its hairs. | 24 | 12 | 15 | 29 | 12 |
| And loosed the braiding adders from their hairs; | 30 | 22 | 18 | 35 | 22 |
| Hairs of your head, then said the hollow agent, | 72 | 1 | 44 | 81 | 1 |
| HAIRY-HEELED | | | | | |
| Death hairy-heeled, and the tapped ghost in wood, | 52 | 5 | 31 | 61 | 12 |
| HALE | | | | | |
| Hale dead and deathless do the women of the hill | 178 | 17 | 90 | 199 | 18 |
| HALF | | | | | |
| Is half its light; the fathomed sea | 6 | 11 | 4 | 6 | 11 |
| Forks half its fruit; and half droops down, | 6 | 14 | 4 | 6 | 14 |
| This world is half the devil's and my own, | 13 | 1 | 9 | 14 | 8 |
| Half of the fellow father as he doubles | 30 | 1 | 18 | 35 | 1 |
| Half of the fellow mother as she dabbles | 30 | 3 | 18 | 35 | 3 |
| The fellow half was frozen as it bubbled | 30 | 7 | 18 | 35 | 7 |
| For half of love was planted in the lost, | 30 | 11 | 18 | 35 | 11 |
| My half ghost in armour hold hard in death's corridor, | 35 | 5 | 20 | 40 | 5 |
| A handmade moon half holy in a cloud, | 40 | 8 | 22 | 46 | 8 |
| Time at the city spectacles, and half | 41 | 3 | 23 | 47 | 3 |
| Half convention and half lie. | 64 | 20 | 39 | 73 | 20 |
| Early imaginary half remembered | 114 | 9 | 69 | 126 | 9 |
| When I was a gusty man and a half | 174 | 13 | 89 | 194 | 13 |
| When I was a half the man I was | 175 | 8 | 89 | 195 | 13 |
| HALF-BLIND | | | | | |
| And, crackling into the air, leave me half-blind. | 64 | 14 | 39 | 73 | 14 |
| HALFMOON'S | | | | | |
| How, through the halfmoon's vegetable eye, | 81 | 3 | 47 | 90 | 3 |
| HALF-TRACKED | | | | | |
| Dry in the half-tracked thigh. | 32 | 12 | 18 | 37 | 18 |
| HALF-WAY | | | | | |
| Atlaswise by owl-light in the half-way house | 71 | 1 | 44 | 80 | 1 |
| With bones unbuttoned to the half-way winds, | 71 | 9 | 44 | 80 | 9 |
| Atlaswise hold half-way off the dummy bay | 76 | 10 | 44 | 85 | 10 |
| HALLOWED | | | | | |
| Within the hallowed gland, blood blessed the heart, | 20 | 18 | 13 | 24 | 18 |
| HALO | | | | | |
| Pour like a halo on the caps and serpents. | 75 | 24 | 44 | 84 | 24 |
| HALOED | | | | | |
| Eyed, in the haloed house, in her rareness and hilly | 165 | 18 | 86 | 185 | 8 |
| HALT | | | | | |
| Halt among eunuchs, and the nitric stain | 18 | 24 | 12 | 22 | 4 |
| HALTER | | | | | |
| Crumbs, barn, and halter. | 48 | 29 | 28 | 57 | 6 |

|  | U.K. | | | U.S. | |
| --- | Page | Line | Poem | Page | Line |
| To the hawk on fire, the halter height, over Towy's fins, | 167 | 16 | 87 | 187 | 16 |
| HALTS |  |  |  |  |  |
| Above the waste allotments the dawn halts. | 25 | 6 | 15 | 30 | 6 |
| HALVED |  |  |  |  |  |
| Doubled the globe of dead and halved a country; | 62 | 3 | 37 | 71 | 3 |
| HALVES |  |  |  |  |  |
| The broken halves are fellowed in a cripple, | 30 | 13 | 18 | 35 | 13 |
| The patchwork halves were cloven as they scudded | 30 | 19 | 18 | 35 | 19 |
| Rotating halves are horning as they drill | 30 | 23 | 18 | 35 | 23 |
| The halves that pierce the pin's point in the air, | 31 | 2 | 18 | 36 | 2 |
| The fellow halves that, cloven as they swivel | 32 | 1 | 18 | 37 | 7 |
| That bridged the human halves, | 67 | 26 | 41 | 76 | 26 |
| HAMLET |  |  |  |  |  |
| And the five-fathomed Hamlet on his father's coral, | 38 | 5 | 20 | 43 | 15 |
| Death: death of Hamlet and the nightmare madmen, | 41 | 19 | 23 | 48 | 1 |
| Into a homestall king or hamlet of fire | 162 | 11 | 86 | 181 | 11 |
| HAMMER |  |  |  |  |  |
| The leaden stars, the rainy hammer | 7 | 11 | 5 | 8 | 11 |
| No, no, you lover skull, descending hammer | 19 | 2 | 12 | 22 | 7 |
| Nor hammer back a season in the figs, | 60 | 8 | 36 | 69 | 8 |
| Heads of the characters hammer through daisies; | 68 | 25 | 42 | 70 | 25 |
| Before I rush in a crouch the ghost with a hammer, air | 97 | 9 | 59 | 108 | 9 |
| And my whole heart under your hammer, | 107 | 13 | 65 | 118 | 13 |
| Before chains break to a hammer flame | 171 | 17 | 88 | 191 | 17 |
| HAND |  |  |  |  |  |
| The hand that whirls the water in the pool | 9 | 11 | 6 | 10 | 11 |
| Hand, the breaking of the hair, | 20 | 11 | 13 | 24 | 11 |
| I spelt my vision with a hand and hair, | 26 | 23 | 16 | 32 | 3 |
| So cross her hand with their grave gipsy eyes, | 55 | 12 | 33 | 64 | 15 |
| The hand that signed the paper felled a city; | 62 | 1 | 37 | 71 | 1 |
| The mighty hand leads to a sloping shoulder, | 62 | 5 | 37 | 71 | 5 |
| The hand that signed the treaty bred a fever, | 62 | 9 | 37 | 71 | 9 |
| Great is the hand that holds dominion over | 62 | 11 | 37 | 71 | 11 |
| A hand rules pity as a hand rules heaven; | 62 | 15 | 37 | 71 | 15 |
| With priest's grave foot and hand of five assassins | 78 | 25 | 46 | 88 | 2 |
| Storm her sped heart, hand with beheaded veins | 79 | 8 | 46 | 88 | 11 |
| Comes love's anatomist with sun-gloved hand | 79 | 18 | 46 | 88 | 21 |
| The cauldron's root through this once-rindless hand | 80 | 2 | 46 | 89 | 10 |
| Sleeping on either hand. | 82 | 8 | 48 | 91 | 8 |

HAND (continued)

| | U.K. | | | U.S. | |
|---|---|---|---|---|---|
| | *Page* | *Line* | *Poem* | *Page* | *Line* |
| With a hand plunged through her hair, | 93 | 12 | 56 | 102 | 12 |
| Rage me back to the making house. My hand unravel | 97 | 12 | 59 | 108 | 12 |
| Quickness of hand in the velvet glove | 107 | 12 | 65 | 118 | 12 |
| Gliding windless through the hand folded flakes, | 119 | 4 | 72 | 131 | 4 |
| Though no sound flowed down the hand folded air | 120 | 15 | 72 | 132 | 20 |
| It was a hand or sound | 121 | 11 | 72 | 134 | 6 |
| And a hundred storks perch on the sun's right hand. | 135 | 14 | 80 | 152 | 14 |
| Cry. My voice burns in his hand. | 148 | 15 | 82 | 165 | 15 |
| Good luck to the hand on the rod, | 151 | 13 | 83 | 169 | 1 |
| His fathers cling to the hand of the girl | 155 | 3 | 83 | 173 | 7 |
| And the dead hand leads the past. | 155 | 4 | 83 | 173 | 8 |
| A garden holding to her hand | 155 | 23 | 83 | 174 | 7 |
| With his long-legged heart in his hand. | 157 | 24 | 83 | 176 | 16 |
| Up to the swallow thronged loft by the shadow of my hand, | 160 | 25 | 85 | 180 | 2 |
| Veined his poor hand I held, and I saw | | | 91 | 200 | 16 |
| The hand that signed the paper | 62 | | 37 | 71 | |

HANDBELL
| Ring like a handbell through the corridors, | 53 | 22 | 32 | 62 | 22 |
|---|---|---|---|---|---|

HANDFULL
| Husk of young stars and handfull zodiac, | 81 | 4 | 47 | 90 | 4 |
|---|---|---|---|---|---|

HANDMADE
| A handmade moon half holy in a cloud, | 40 | 8 | 22 | 46 | 8 |
|---|---|---|---|---|---|

HANDPRINT
| On rose and icicle the ringing handprint. | 75 | 4 | 44 | 84 | 4 |
|---|---|---|---|---|---|

HANDS
| With liquid hands tapped on the womb, | 7 | 2 | 5 | 8 | 2 |
|---|---|---|---|---|---|
| Have cleanest hands, and, as the heartless ghost | 50 | 8 | 30 | 59 | 8 |
| Hands grumble on the door, | 58 | 2 | 35 | 67 | 2 |
| Hands, hold you poison or grapes? | 58 | 9 | 35 | 67 | 9 |
| Hands grumble on the door, | 59 | 1 | 35 | 68 | 1 |
| Hands of the stranger and holds of the ships, | 59 | 7 | 35 | 68 | 7 |
| Hands have no tears to flow. | 62 | 16 | 37 | 71 | 16 |
| Faith in their hands shall snap in two, | 68 | 15 | 42 | 77 | 15 |
| Grief with dishevelled hands tear out the altar ghost | 83 | 5 | 49 | 92 | 5 |
| Time for the swimmers' hands, music for silver lock | 86 | 7 | 51 | 95 | 7 |
| I know her scrubbed and sour humble hands | 88 | 3 | 52 | 97 | 3 |
| These cloud-sopped, marble hands, this monumental | 88 | 8 | 52 | 97 | 8 |
| And bear those tendril hands I touch across | 90 | 6 | 54 | 99 | 6 |
| Behind a face of hands, | 95 | 10 | 58 | 105 | 10 |

|  | U.K. | | | U.S. | |
| --- | --- | --- | --- | --- | --- |
|  | *Page* | *Line* | *Poem* | *Page* | *Line* |
| Woe drip from the dishrag hands and the pressed sponge of the forehead, | 96 | 20 | 58 | 107 | 3 |
| For his briared hands to hoist them | 145 | 2 | 82 | 162 | 2 |
| Hands or instruments | 147 | 6 | 82 | 164 | 6 |
| Hollows, a grassblade blown in cupped hands, in the looted elms | 169 | 4 | 87 | 189 | 13 |
| HANDSAW | | | | | |
| Have brotherless his sister on the handsaw. | 51 | 14 | 31 | 60 | 14 |
| HANDSHAPED | | | | | |
| Sailed and set dazzling by the handshaped ocean, | 78 | 5 | 46 | 87 | 5 |
| HANDY | | | | | |
| It was sweet to drown in the readymade handy water | 133 | 16 | 78 | 148 | 19 |
| HANG | | | | | |
| And worlds hang on the trees. | 5 | 18 | 3 | 5 | 18 |
| Then hang a ram rose over the rags. | 65 | 8 | 40 | 74 | 8 |
| And the man no rope can hang | 66 | 2 | 40 | 75 | 2 |
| HANGER | | | | | |
| You hero skull, Cadaver in the hanger | 19 | 4 | 12 | 22 | 9 |
| HANGING | | | | | |
| And I am dumb to tell the hanging man | 9 | 14 | 6 | 10 | 14 |
| When no mouth stirred about the hanging famine, | 20 | 5 | 13 | 24 | 5 |
| The film of spring is hanging from the lids. | 24 | 24 | 15 | 29 | 24 |
| Drives forth my men, my children, from the hanging south. | 49 | 6 | 29 | 58 | 6 |
| Hack of the cough, the hanging albatross, | 67 | 10 | 41 | 76 | 10 |
| HANGMAN'S | | | | | |
| How of my clay is made the hangman's lime. | 9 | 15 | 6 | 10 | 15 |
| Strung by the flaxen whale-weed, from the hangman's raft, | 37 | 14 | 20 | 42 | 20 |
| HANGNAIL | | | | | |
| Abaddon in the hangnail cracked from Adam, | 71 | 3 | 44 | 80 | 3 |
| HANGS | | | | | |
| The hawk on fire hangs still; | 167 | 2 | 87 | 187 | 2 |
| When his viperish fuse hangs looped with flames under the brand | 168 | 4 | 87 | 188 | 8 |
| HANK | | | | | |
| Cried the topless, inchtaped lips from hank and hood | 79 | 21 | 46 | 89 | 2 |
| HAPPENING | | | | | |
| In battle! the happening | 142 | 11 | 82 | 159 | 11 |
| HAPPILY | | | | | |
| Tap happily of one peg in the thick | 87 | 3 | 52 | 96 | 3 |
| HAPPY | | | | | |
| Happy Cadaver's hunger as you take | 19 | 24 | 12 | 23 | 9 |
| That made me happy in the sun, | 48 | 19 | 28 | 56 | 19 |

|  | U.K. | | | U.S. | |
|---|---|---|---|---|---|
|  | Page | Line | Poem | Page | Line |
| How much was happy while it lasted, | 48 | 20 | 28 | 56 | 20 |
| About the lilting house and happy as the grass was green, | 159 | 2 | 85 | 178 | 2 |
| About the happy yard and singing as the farm was home, | 159 | 11 | 85 | 178 | 11 |
| Under the new made clouds and happy as the heart was long, | 160 | 16 | 85 | 179 | 16 |
| HARBOUR | | | | | |
| Voyaging clockwise off the symboled harbour, | 36 | 8 | 20 | 41 | 8 |
| Let the hero seed find harbour, | 43 | 5 | 24 | 50 | 12 |
| Let the hero seed find harbour, | 43 | 12 | 24 | 50 | 19 |
| Woke to my hearing from harbour and neighbour wood | 102 | 2 | 63 | 113 | 2 |
| Pale rain over the dwindling harbour | 103 | 6 | 63 | 114 | 6 |
| Crystal harbour vale | 168 | 13 | 87 | 188 | 17 |
| HARBOURS | | | | | |
| So shall winged harbours through the rockbirds' eyes | 76 | 12 | 44 | 85 | 12 |
| Harbours my anchored tongue, slips the quay-stone, | 78 | 3 | 46 | 87 | 3 |
| HARD . | | | | | |
| My half ghost in armour hold hard in death's corridor, | 35 | 5 | 20 | 40 | 5 |
| Hold hard, these ancient minutes in the cuckoo's month, | 49 | 1 | 29 | 58 | 1 |
| Hold hard, my county children in the world of tales, | 49 | 10 | 29 | 58 | 10 |
| Hold hard, my county darlings, for a hawk descends, | 49 | 22 | 29 | 58 | 22 |
| Insects and valleys hold her thighs hard, | 156 | 6 | 83 | 174 | 14 |
| They from houses where the harvest kneels, hold me hard, | 178 | 9 | 90 | 199 | 10 |
| Hold hard, these ancient minutes in the cuckoo's month | 49 | | 29 | 58 | |
| HARDEN | | | | | |
| In sacred waters that no frost could harden, | 40 | 14 | 22 | 46 | 14 |
| HARDINESS | | | | | |
| Forsake, the fool, the hardiness of anger. | 51 | 7 | 31 | 60 | 7 |
| HARD-HELD | | | | | |
| Spill the lank folly's hunter and the hard-held hope. | 49 | 18 | 29 | 58 | 18 |
| HARDLY | | | | | |
| My silly suit, hardly yet suffered for, | 133 | 1 | 78 | 148 | 4 |
| HARDSHIP | | | | | |
| On the first of each hardship, | 132 | 5 | 78 | 147 | 5 |
| HARE | | | | | |
| Whisking hare! who | ix | 17 | 1 | xvii | 17 |

| | U.K. | | | U.S. | |
|---|---|---|---|---|---|
| | *Page* | *Line* | *Poem* | *Page* | *Line* |
| HARE-[HEELED] | | | | | |
| The leaping saga of prayer! And high, there, on the hare- | 164 | 17 | 86 | 184 | 3 |
| HARE | | | | | |
| Daws Sir John's just hill dons, and again the gulled birds hare | 167 | 15 | 87 | 187 | 15 |
| HAREBELL | | | | | |
| Forcing forth through the harebell, | 35 | 15 | 20 | 40 | 15 |
| HARING | | | | | |
| The haring snail go giddily round the flower, | 36 | 17 | 20 | 41 | 17 |
| HARK | | | | | |
| Hark: I trumpet the place, | viii | 16 | 1 | xvi | 16 |
| HARM | | | | | |
| Vales where he prayed to come to the last harm | 122 | 29 | 72 | 136 | 9 |
| HARNESS | | | | | |
| Is come of the sea tumbling in harness | 101 | 6 | 62 | 112 | 6 |
| HARNESSED | | | | | |
| Time, in a rider rising, from the harnessed valley; | 49 | 21 | 29 | 58 | 21 |
| HARNESSING | | | | | |
| Man was Cadaver's masker, the harnessing mantle, | 38 | 25 | 20 | 44 | 15 |
| HARP | | | | | |
| Creep and harp on the tide, sinking their charmed, bent pin | 91 | 24 | 55 | 101 | 2 |
| And the harp shaped voice of the water's dust plucks in a fold | 121 | 24 | 72 | 134 | 19 |
| HARPIES | | | | | |
| Harpies around me out of her womb! | 175 | 27 | 89 | 196 | 8 |
| HARPS | | | | | |
| And ducked and draked white lake that harps to a hail stone. | 177 | 8 | 90 | 198 | 7 |
| HARROW | | | | | |
| Shall harrow and snow the blood while you ride wide and near, | 162 | 23 | 86 | 181 | 23 |
| HARSH | | | | | |
| A blazing red harsh head tear up | 93 | 29 | 56 | 103 | 9 |
| HARVEST | | | | | |
| Setting no store by harvest, freeze the soils; | 1 | 3 | 2 | 1 | 3 |
| Sharp in my second death I marked the hills, harvest | 28 | 17 | 17 | 33 | 17 |
| In high corn and the harvest melting on their tongues. | 120 | 18 | 72 | 133 | 3 |
| They from houses where the harvest kneels, hold me hard, | 178 | 9 | 90 | 199 | 10 |
| HAS | | | | | |
| How time has tickled a heaven round the stars. | 9 | 20 | 6 | 10 | 20 |

211

|  | U.K. | | | U.S. | |
|---|---|---|---|---|---|
|  | Page | Line | Poem | Page | Line |
| The dream has sucked the sleeper of his faith | 15 | 9 | 10 | 17 | 9 |
| This story's monster has a serpent caul, | 41 | 10 | 23 | 47 | 10 |
| No tell-tale lover has an end more certain, | 41 | 24 | 23 | 48 | 6 |
| But time has set its maggot on their track. | 50 | 4 | 30 | 59 | 4 |
| (Fog has a bone | 56 | 4 | 34 | 65 | 4 |
| A goose's quill has put an end to murder | 62 | 7 | 37 | 71 | 7 |
| Has not yet reached the ground. | 63 | 19 | 38 | 72 | 19 |
| Has sown a flying garden round that sea-ghost? | 76 | 18 | 44 | 85 | 18 |
| My one and noble heart has witnesses | 81 | 11 | 47 | 90 | 11 |
| The stocked heart is forced, and agony has another mouth to feed. | 96 | 17 | 58 | 106 | 17 |
| Has a voice and a house, and there and here you must couch and cry. | 98 | 2 | 59 | 109 | 5 |
| A stranger has come | 108 | 1 | 66 | 119 | 1 |
| She has come possessed | 108 | 10 | 66 | 119 | 10 |
| Though the brawl of the kiss has not occurred | 109 | 7 | 67 | 120 | 7 |
| Brethren for joy has moved within | 148 | 16 | 82 | 160 | 16 |
| Sing how the seal has kissed her dead! | 152 | 10 | 83 | 170 | 2 |
| Has melted away and is lost | 153 | 19 | 83 | 171 | 15 |
| **HAT** | | | | | |
| The parting of hat from hair, | 64 | 16 | 39 | 73 | 16 |
| **HATCH** | | | | | |
| The old mud hatch again, the horrid | 96 | 19 | 58 | 107 | 2 |
| **HATCHED** | | | | | |
| The ghost that hatched his havoc as he flew | 31 | 5 | 18 | 36 | 5 |
| Hatched from the windy salvage on one leg, | 71 | 10 | 44 | 80 | 10 |
| **HATCHING** | | | | | |
| If I were tickled by the hatching hair, | 12 | 10 | 9 | 13 | 10 |
| **HATING** | | | | | |
| Hating his God, but what he was was plain: | | | 91 | 201 | 2 |
| **HAUL** | | | | | |
| Sing and strike his heavy haul | 154 | 17 | 83 | 172 | 17 |
| All the horses of his haul of miracles | 156 | 19 | 83 | 175 | 7 |
| **HAULED** | | | | | |
| Hauled to the dome, | 18 | 5 | 12 | 21 | 5 |
| **HAULS** | | | | | |
| Hauls my shroud sail. | 9 | 13 | 6 | 10 | 13 |
| **HAUNTS** | | | | | |
| For who unmanningly haunts the mountain ravened eaves | 163 | 1 | 86 | 182 | 1 |
| **HAVE** | | | | | |
| This is the world. Have faith. | 15 | 16 | 10 | 17 | 16 |
| (Have with the house of wind), the leaning scene, | 19 | 17 | 12 | 23 | 2 |
| That but a name, where maggots have their X. | 21 | 14 | 13 | 25 | 14 |
| Now that my symbols have outelbowed space, | 41 | 2 | 23 | 47 | 2 |
| In trust and tale have I divided sense, | 41 | 5 | 23 | 47 | 5 |

|  | U.K. | | | U.S. | |
| --- | --- | --- | --- | --- | --- |
|  | Page | Line | Poem | Page | Line |
| Have their thirsty sailors hide him. | 43 | 7 | 24 | 50 | 14 |
| Have their drunken sailors hide him. | 43 | 14 | 24 | 50 | 21 |
| But not of grief, for I have knocked down that | 48 | 2 | 28 | 56 | 2 |
| Lie this fifth month unskated, and the birds have flown; | 49 | 9 | 29 | 58 | 9 |
| Under the skysigns they who have no arms | 50 | 7 | 30 | 59 | 7 |
| Have cleanest hands, and, as the heartless ghost | 50 | 8 | 30 | 59 | 8 |
| Have brotherless his sister on the handsaw. | 51 | 14 | 31 | 60 | 14 |
| Both quench his thirst he'll have a black reply. | 53 | 9 | 32 | 62 | 9 |
| That she I have, | 55 | 3 | 33 | 64 | 6 |
| Unshelve that all my gristles have a gown | 56 | 6 | 34 | 65 | 6 |
| Now make the world of me as I have made | 61 | 5 | 36 | 70 | 5 |
| Hands have no tears to flow. | 62 | 16 | 37 | 71 | 16 |
| I have been told to reason by the heart, | 63 | 9 | 38 | 72 | 9 |
| I have been told to reason by the pulse, | 63 | 11 | 38 | 72 | 11 |
| I have heard many years of telling, | 63 | 16 | 38 | 72 | 16 |
| I have longed to move away | 64 | 1 | 39 | 73 | 1 |
| I have longed to move away | 64 | 6 | 39 | 73 | 6 |
| I have longed to move away but am afraid; | 64 | 11 | 39 | 73 | 11 |
| 'Find meat on bones that soon have none, | 65 | 1 | 40 | 74 | 1 |
| These stolen bubbles have the bites of snakes | 67 | 23 | 41 | 76 | 23 |
| And death shall have no dominion. | 68 | 1 | 42 | 77 | 1 |
| They shall have stars at elbow and foot; | 68 | 5 | 42 | 77 | 5 |
| And death shall have no dominion. | 68 | 9 | 42 | 77 | 9 |
| And death shall have no dominion. | 68 | 10 | 42 | 77 | 10 |
| And death shall have no dominion. | 68 | 18 | 42 | 77 | 18 |
| And death shall have no dominion. | 68 | 19 | 42 | 77 | 19 |
| And death shall have no dominion. | 68 | 27 | 42 | 77 | 27 |
| These once-blind eyes have breathed a wind of visions, | 80 | 1 | 46 | 89 | 9 |
| Who have brought forth the urchin grief. | 84 | 6 | 49 | 93 | 12 |
| She would not have me sinking in the holy | 87 | 18 | 52 | 96 | 18 |
| You have kicked from a dark den, leaped up the whinnying light, | 92 | 15 | 55 | 101 | 21 |
| Because their words have forked no lightning they | 116 | 5 | 70 | 128 | 5 |
| Their frail deeds might have danced in a green bay, | 116 | 8 | 70 | 128 | 8 |
| Have sought your single grave, | 117 | 28 | 71 | 130 | 4 |
| On the silent sea we have heard the sound | 136 | 3 | 81 | 153 | 3 |
| For I was lost who have come | 140 | 11 | 82 | 157 | 11 |
| And we have come | 146 | 6 | 82 | 163 | 6 |
| The hills have footed the waves away, | 156 | 16 | 83 | 175 | 4 |
| I climb to greet the war in which I have no heart but only | 158 | 8 | 84 | 177 | 8 |
| So it must have been after the birth of the simple light | 160 | 11 | 85 | 179 | 11 |

HAVE (continued)

|  | U.K. | | | U.S. | |
|---|---|---|---|---|---|
|  | Page | Line | Poem | Page | Line |
| Have mercy on, | 168 | 20 | 87 | 189 | 5 |
| I have longed to move away | 64 | | 39 | 73 | |
| And death shall have no dominion | 68 | | 42 | 77 | |
| HAVEN | | | | | |
| To dumbfounding haven | 140 | 12 | 82 | 157 | 12 |
| HAVOC | | | | | |
| The ghost that hatched his havoc as he flew | 31 | 5 | 18 | 36 | 5 |
| HAWED | | | | | |
| Who once were a bloom of wayside brides in the hawed house | 177 | 9 | 90 | 198 | 8 |
| HAWK | | | | | |
| Hold hard, my county darlings, for a hawk descends, | 49 | 22 | 29 | 58 | 22 |
| Sings to the treading hawk | 115 | 13 | 69 | 127 | 13 |
| And the hawk in the egg kills the wren. | 155 | 12 | 83 | 173 | 16 |
| The hawk on fire hangs still; | 167 | 2 | 87 | 187 | 2 |
| The flash the noosed hawk | 167 | 10 | 87 | 187 | 10 |
| To the hawk on fire, the halter height, over Towy's fins, | 167 | 16 | 87 | 187 | 16 |
| Shallow and sedge, and 'dilly dilly,' calls the loft hawk, | 167 | 21 | 87 | 188 | 2 |
| All praise of the hawk on fire in hawk-eyed dusk be sung, | 168 | 3 | 87 | 188 | 7 |
| HAWK-EYED | | | | | |
| All praise of the hawk on fire in hawk-eyed dusk be sung, | 168 | 3 | 87 | 188 | 7 |
| HAWKS | | | | | |
| In the claw tracks of hawks | 170 | 21 | 88 | 190 | 21 |
| HAY | | | | | |
| And the smell of hay in the snow, and the far owl | 119 | 7 | 72 | 131 | 7 |
| All the sun long it was running, it was lovely, the hay | 159 | 19 | 85 | 178 | 19 |
| My wishes raced through the house high hay | 160 | 19 | 85 | 179 | 19 |
| In the wains tonned so high that the wisps of the hay | 176 | 14 | 90 | 197 | 14 |
| Where the hay rides now or the bracken kitchens rust | 178 | 6 | 90 | 199 | 7 |
| HAYBEDS | | | | | |
| To trot with a loud mate the haybeds of a mile, | 91 | 16 | 55 | 100 | 16 |
| HAYCOCK | | | | | |
| To a haycock couch and the scythes of his arms | 113 | 17 | 69 | 125 | 17 |
| HAYCOCKS | | | | | |
| Night and the reindeer on the clouds above the haycocks | 164 | 15 | 86 | 184 | 1 |
| HAYGOLD | | | | | |
| Through the haygold stalls, as the dew falls on the wind- | 164 | 9 | 86 | 183 | 16 |

|  | U.K. | | | U.S. | |
|---|---|---|---|---|---|
|  | Page | Line | Poem | Page | Line |
| The haygold haired, my love asleep, and the rift blue | 165 | 17 | 86 | 185 | 7 |
| HAYRICKS | | | | | |
| And the bait is drowned among hayricks, | 157 | 16 | 83 | 176 | 8 |
| HAYSTACKED | | | | | |
| Hist, in hogsback woods! The haystacked | ix | 27 | 1 | xviii | 1 |
| HE | | | | | |
| He blew like powder to the light | 4 | 14 | 3 | 4 | 14 |
| He drowned his father's magics in a dream. | 4 | 18 | 3 | 4 | 18 |
| He had by heart the Christ-cross-row of death. | 4 | 24 | 3 | 4 | 24 |
| By trick or chance he fell asleep | 5 | 10 | 3 | 5 | 10 |
| And leave the poppied pickthank where he lies; | 5 | 15 | 3 | 5 | 15 |
| He promises a secret heat. | 10 | 15 | 7 | 11 | 15 |
| He holds the wire from this box of nerves | 10 | 16 | 7 | 11 | 16 |
| He pulls the chain, the cistern moves. | 10 | 20 | 7 | 11 | 20 |
| Nor when he finds a beauty in the breast | 13 | 12 | 9 | 14 | 19 |
| Half of the fellow father as he doubles | 30 | 1 | 18 | 35 | 1 |
| The ghost that hatched his havoc as he flew | 31 | 5 | 18 | 36 | 5 |
| He shall grapple with the guard | 42 | 20 | 24 | 49 | 20 |
| He shall grapple with the guard | 42 | 27 | 24 | 50 | 6 |
| All these, he said who sacked the children's town, | 46 | 18 | 27 | 54 | 18 |
| Should he, for centre sake, hop in the dust, | 51 | 6 | 31 | 60 | 6 |
| Should he who split his children with a cure | 51 | 13 | 31 | 60 | 13 |
| He lying low with ruin in his ear, | 51 | 20 | 31 | 60 | 20 |
| Look twice before he fell from grace. | 63 | 4 | 38 | 72 | 4 |
| He films my vanity. | 69 | 25 | 43 | 79 | 1 |
| 'Time shall not murder you,' He said, | 70 | 16 | 43 | 79 | 20 |
| I am the long world's gentleman, he said, | 71 | 13 | 44 | 80 | 13 |
| He in a book of water tallow-eyed | 74 | 2 | 44 | 83 | 2 |
| The one not caring to whom in his sleep he will move | 100 | 4 | 61 | 111 | 4 |
| And the child not caring to whom he climbs his prayer | 100 | 17 | 61 | 111 | 17 |
| Forgotten mornings when he walked with his mother | 103 | 22 | 63 | 114 | 22 |
| Like the park birds he came early | 111 | 13 | 68 | 123 | 13 |
| Like the water he sat down | 111 | 14 | 68 | 123 | 14 |
| Running when he had heard them clearly | 111 | 17 | 68 | 123 | 17 |
| Laughing when he shook his paper | 111 | 20 | 68 | 123 | 20 |
| Night, and enjoyed as he would. | 114 | 13 | 69 | 126 | 13 |
| All blood-signed assailings and vanished marriages in which he had no lovely part | 114 | 20 | 69 | 126 | 20 |
| He knelt, he wept, he prayed, | 120 | 1 | 72 | 132 | 6 |
| He knelt on the cold stones, | 120 | 6 | 72 | 132 | 11 |
| He wept from the crest of grief, he prayed to the veiled sky | 120 | 7 | 72 | 132 | 12 |

215

| | U.K. | | | U.S. | |
|---|---|---|---|---|---|
| | Page | Line | Poem | Page | Line |
| And fires where he should prowl down the cloud | 120 | 12 | 72 | 132 | 17 |
| When cold as snow he should run the wended vales among | 120 | 20 | 72 | 133 | 5 |
| Deliver him, he cried, | 120 | 26 | 72 | 133 | 11 |
| Him up and he ran like a wind after the kindling flight | 122 | 9 | 72 | 135 | 9 |
| Vales where he prayed to come to the last harm | 122 | 29 | 72 | 136 | 9 |
| And the wings glided wide and he was hymned and wedded, | 123 | 13 | 72 | 137 | 3 |
| Bird, he was brought low, | 123 | 16 | 72 | 137 | 6 |
| Under his downy arm you sighed as he struck, | 125 | 19 | 74 | 139 | 19 |
| He put on his clothes and stepped out and he died, | 135 | 2 | 80 | 152 | 2 |
| He dropped where he loved on the burst pavement stone | 135 | 4 | 80 | 152 | 4 |
| Tell his street on its back he stopped a sun | 135 | 6 | 80 | 152 | 6 |
| That he who learns now the sun and moon | 144 | 1 | 82 | 161 | 1 |
| That he let the dead lie though they moan | 145 | 1 | 82 | 162 | 1 |
| He sped into the drinking dark; | 149 | 14 | 83 | 166 | 14 |
| He was blind to the eyes of candles | 150 | 3 | 83 | 167 | 7 |
| He saw the storm smoke out to kill | 150 | 17 | 83 | 168 | 1 |
| He who blew the great fire in | 155 | 13 | 83 | 173 | 17 |
| And he who taught their lips to sing | 155 | 18 | 83 | 174 | 2 |
| He stands alone at the door of his home, | 157 | 23 | 83 | 176 | 15 |
| Ever and ever he finds a way, as the snow falls, | 164 | 7 | 86 | 183 | 14 |
| Round the sun, he comes to my love like the designed snow, | 165 | 25 | 86 | 185 | 15 |
| And truly he | 165 | 26 | 86 | 185 | 16 |
| And surely he sails like the ship shape clouds. Oh he | 165 | 28 | 86 | 185 | 18 |
| And surely he sails like the ship shape clouds. Oh he | 165 | 28 | 86 | 185 | 18 |
| He comes to take | 166 | 4 | 86 | 186 | 4 |
| He comes to leave her in the lawless sun awaking | 166 | 6 | 86 | 186 | 6 |
| Naked and forsaken to grieve he will not come. | 166 | 7 | 86 | 186 | 7 |
| My dear this night he comes and night without end my dear | 166 | 9 | 86 | 186 | 9 |
| In a hoisted cloud, at drop of dusk, he pulls to his claws | 167 | 3 | 87 | 187 | 3 |
| He celebrates and spurns | 170 | 7 | 88 | 190 | 7 |
| He sings towards anguish; finches fly | 170 | 20 | 88 | 190 | 20 |
| Ship towns to pastures of otters. He | 170 | 24 | 88 | 190 | 24 |
| And far at sea he knows, | 171 | 3 | 88 | 191 | 3 |
| And freely he goes lost | 171 | 19 | 88 | 191 | 19 |
| There he might wander bare | 172 | 1 | 88 | 192 | 1 |

|  | U.K. | | | U.S. | |
|  | Page | Line | Poem | Page | Line |
| He, on the earth of the night, alone | 172 | 11 | 88 | 192 | 11 |
| Too proud to die; broken and blind he died |  |  | 91 | 200 | 1 |
| He lie lightly, at last, on the last, crossed |  |  | 91 | 200 | 5 |
| Above all he longed for his mother's breast |  |  | 91 | 200 | 9 |
| I am not too proud to cry that He and he |  |  | 91 | 200 | 19 |
| Being innocent, he dreaded that he died |  |  | 91 | 201 | 1 |
| Hating his God, but what he was was plain: |  |  | 91 | 201 | 2 |
| The sticks of the house were his; his books he owned. |  |  | 91 | 201 | 4 |
| Even as a baby he had never cried; |  |  | 91 | 201 | 5 |
| Nor did he now, save to his secret wound. |  |  | 91 | 201 | 6 |
| He cried as he died, fearing at last the spheres' |  |  | 91 | 201 | 12 |
| O deepest wound of all that he should die |  |  | 91 | 201 | 16 |
| On that darkest day. Oh, he could hide |  |  | 91 | 201 | 17 |
| Until I die he will not leave my side.) |  |  | 91 | 201 | 19 |

HE-GOD'S

| As a he-god's paddling water skirts, | 132 | 16 | 78 | 147 | 16 |

HE'LL

| He'll ache too long | 48 | 13 | 28 | 56 | 13 |
| Both quench his thirst he'll have a black reply. | 53 | 9 | 32 | 62 | 9 |
| He'll trumpet into meat), | 56 | 5 | 34 | 65 | 5 |
| He'll bathe his raining blood in the male sea | 117 | 19 | 71 | 129 | 19 |

HEAD

| The lips of time leech to the fountain head; | 9 | 16 | 6 | 10 | 16 |
| Unpacks the head that, like a sleepy ghost, | 10 | 3 | 7 | 11 | 3 |
| Deliver me, my masters, head and heart, | 18 | 11 | 12 | 21 | 11 |
| From maid and head, | 18 | 15 | 12 | 21 | 15 |
| Of head and tail made witnesses to this | 41 | 7 | 23 | 47 | 7 |
| But heart, like head, leads helpessly; | 63 | 10 | 38 | 72 | 10 |
| Lift its head to the blows of the rain; | 68 | 23 | 42 | 77 | 23 |
| Hairs of your head, then said the hollow agent, | 72 | 1 | 44 | 81 | 1 |
| And opium head, crow stalk, puffed, cut, and blown, | 78 | 10 | 46 | 87 | 10 |
| The hero's head lies scraped of every legend, | 79 | 17 | 46 | 88 | 20 |
| Behind my head a square of sky sags over | 90 | 8 | 54 | 99 | 8 |
| A blazing red harsh head tear up | 93 | 29 | 56 | 103 | 9 |
| 'If my head hurt a hair's foot | 97 | 1 | 59 | 108 | 1 |
| My dear would I change my tears on your iron head. | 97 | 18 | 59 | 108 | 18 |
| One gesture of the heart or head, | 105 | 9 | 64 | 116 | 9 |
| To share my room in the house not right in the head, | 108 | 2 | 66 | 119 | 2 |
| Into her lying down head | 113 | 1 | 69 | 125 | 1 |
| Head to heaven-circling head, | 115 | 2 | 69 | 127 | 2 |
| The scrolls of fire that burned in his heart and head, | 119 | 14 | 72 | 131 | 14 |

|  | U.K. | | | U.S. | |
|  | Page | Line | Poem | Page | Line |
| Above her folded head, and the soft feathered voice | 122 | 2 | 72 | 135 | 2 |
| Under the sad breast of the head stone | 130 | 20 | 77 | 144 | 20 |
| Head, deceived, I believed, my maker, | 133 | 6 | 78 | 148 | 9 |
| Glared through shark mask and navigating head, | 133 | 11 | 78 | 148 | 14 |
| Up to his head in his blood, | 134 | 9 | 79 | 150 | 9 |
| And the shadowed head of pain | 138 | 7 | 82 | 155 | 7 |
| 'If my head hurt a hair's foot' | 97 |  | 59 | 108 |  |
| Into her Lying Down Head | 113 |  | 69 | 125 |  |

HEADED
| The woman breasted and the heaven headed | 123 | 15 | 72 | 137 | 5 |

HEADLESS
| And the masked, headless boy. | 70 | 2 | 43 | 79 | 6 |

HEADS
| As sunlight paints the shelling of their heads. | 1 | 18 | 2 | 1 | 18 |
| And, broken ghosts with glow-worms in their heads, | 24 | 4 | 15 | 29 | 4 |
| Of tide-tongued heads and bladders in the deep, | 30 | 16 | 18 | 35 | 16 |
| Heads of the characters hammer through daisies; | 68 | 25 | 42 | 70 | 25 |
| Babble like a bellbuoy over the hymning heads, | 87 | 23 | 52 | 96 | 23 |
| With their heads in a cunning cloud. | 107 | 21 | 65 | 118 | 21 |

HEADSTONE
| In the river Towy below bows his tilted head-stone. | 167 | 12 | 87 | 187 | 12 |

HEAR
| By the sea's side hear the dark-vowelled birds. | 17 | 8 | 11 | 20 | 8 |
| I hear, through dead men's drums, the riddled lads, | 31 | 16 | 18 | 36 | 16 |
| Hear they the salt glass breakers and the tongues of burial. | 37 | 15 | 20 | 42 | 21 |
| I hear content, and 'Be content' | 53 | 21 | 32 | 62 | 21 |
| Ears in the turrets hear | 58 | 1 | 35 | 67 | 1 |
| Ears in this island hear | 58 | 17 | 35 | 67 | 17 |
| Over the choir minute I hear the hour chant: | 83 | 7 | 49 | 92 | 7 |
| Hear by death's accident the clocked and dashed-down spire | 83 | 11 | 49 | 92 | 11 |
| To hear the golden note turn in a groove, | 125 | 6 | 74 | 139 | 6 |
| There was glory to hear | 125 | 17 | 74 | 139 | 17 |
| That I can hear the womb | 137 | 6 | 82 | 154 | 6 |
| I should hear him fly with the high fields | 161 | 2 | 85 | 180 | 5 |
| Makes all the music; and I who hear the tune of the slow, | 169 | 9 | 87 | 189 | 18 |
| I hear the bouncing hills | 173 | 19 | 88 | 193 | 19 |
| I lie down thin and hear the good bells jaw- | 175 | 24 | 89 | 196 | 5 |
| Ears in the turrets hear | 58 |  | 35 | 67 |  |

|  | U.K. | | | U.S. | |
|---|---|---|---|---|---|
|  | *Page* | *Line* | *Poem* | *Page* | *Line* |
| **HEARD** | | | | | |
| Is heard but little till the stars go out. | 53 | 20 | 32 | 62 | 20 |
| I have heard many years of telling, | 63 | 16 | 38 | 72 | 16 |
| Before I heard in my mother's side | 93 | 6 | 56 | 102 | 6 |
| Among men later I heard it said | 93 | 16 | 56 | 102 | 16 |
| Heard her speak through the chipped beak | 93 | 24 | 56 | 103 | 4 |
| Running when he had heard them clearly | 111 | 17 | 68 | 123 | 17 |
| One lean sigh when we heard | 126 | 5 | 74 | 140 | 5 |
| I heard, this morning, waking, | 134 | 23 | 79 | 151 | 1 |
| On the silent sea we have heard the sound | 136 | 3 | 81 | 153 | 3 |
| We heard the sea sound sing, we saw the salt sheet tell. | 136 | 12 | 81 | 153 | 12 |
| But heard his bait buck in the wake | 150 | 5 | 83 | 167 | 9 |
| All the moon long I heard, blessed among stables, the night-jars | 160 | 3 | 85 | 179 | 3 |
| And heard the lewd, wooed field flow to the coming frost, | 177 | 10 | 90 | 198 | 9 |
| Who heard the tall bell sail down the Sundays of the dead | 178 | 10 | 90 | 199 | 11 |
| **HEARING** | | | | | |
| By the sea's side, hearing the noise of birds, | 16 | 5 | 11 | 19 | 5 |
| Hearing the raven cough in winter sticks, | 16 | 6 | 11 | 19 | 6 |
| Hearing the weather fall. | 36 | 6 | 20 | 41 | 6 |
| Woke to my hearing from harbour and neighbour wood | 102 | 2 | 63 | 113 | 2 |
| Out to the tiered and hearing tide, | 114 | 15 | 69 | 126 | 15 |
| Wall hearing the moan | 138 | 5 | 82 | 155 | 5 |
| Heart! Slyly, slowly, hearing the wound in her side go | 165 | 24 | 86 | 185 | 14 |
| **HEARS** | | | | | |
| Hears, there, this fox light, my flood ship's | ix | 18 | 1 | xvii | 18 |
| **HEARSE** | | | | | |
| Up naked stairs, a turtle in a hearse, | 18 | 4 | 12 | 21 | 4 |
| **HEART** | | | | | |
| My fuses timed to charge his heart, | 4 | 13 | 3 | 4 | 13 |
| He had by heart the Christ-cross-row of death. | 4 | 24 | 3 | 4 | 24 |
| To rob me of my fluids in his heart. | 5 | 12 | 3 | 5 | 12 |
| A process in the weather of the heart | 6 | 1 | 4 | 6 | 1 |
| And the heart gives up its dead. | 6 | 24 | 4 | 7 | 6 |
| My heart knew love, my belly hunger; | 8 | 5 | 5 | 9 | 5 |
| My hero bares my side and sees his heart | 10 | 11 | 7 | 11 | 11 |
| Of light and love, the tempers of the heart, | 14 | 2 | 10 | 16 | 2 |
| My busy heart who shudders as she talks | 16 | 7 | 11 | 19 | 7 |
| The heart is drained that, spelling in the scurry | 17 | 6 | 11 | 20 | 6 |
| Deliver me, my masters, head and heart, | 18 | 11 | 12 | 21 | 11 |
| Heart of Cadaver's candle waxes thin, | 18 | 12 | 12 | 21 | 12 |

| | U.K. | | | U.S. | |
|---|---|---|---|---|---|
| | *Page* | *Line* | *Poem* | *Page* | *Line* |
| From the first secret of the heart, the warning ghost, | 20 | 12 | 13 | 24 | 12 |
| Within the hallowed gland, blood blessed the heart, | 20 | 18 | 13 | 24 | 18 |
| The word flowed up, translating to the heart | 22 | 23 | 14 | 27 | 23 |
| Where no sea runs, the waters of the heart | 24 | 2 | 15 | 29 | 2 |
| Rammed in the marching heart, hole | 28 | 14 | 17 | 33 | 14 |
| Nor the heart in the ribbing metal. | 33 | 15 | 19 | 38 | 15 |
| I have been told to reason by the heart, | 63 | 9 | 38 | 72 | 9 |
| But heart, like head, leads helplessly; | 63 | 10 | 38 | 72 | 10 |
| And my heart is cracked across; | 65 | 18 | 40 | 74 | 18 |
| Who could hack out your unsucked heart, | 70 | 18 | 43 | 79 | 22 |
| The sheath-decked jacks, queen with a shuffled heart; | 73 | 13 | 44 | 82 | 13 |
| Storm her sped heart, hand with beheaded veins | 79 | 8 | 46 | 88 | 11 |
| Who picks the live heart on a diamond. | 79 | 19 | 46 | 88 | 22 |
| My one and noble heart has witnesses | 81 | 11 | 47 | 90 | 11 |
| The heart is sensual, though five eyes break. | 81 | 14 | 47 | 90 | 14 |
| Breaks, O my heart's blood, like a heart and hill. | 82 | 24 | 48 | 91 | 24 |
| Whose hooded, fountain heart once fell in puddles | 87 | 14 | 52 | 96 | 14 |
| That melts the lionhead's heel and horseshoe of the heart, | 91 | 14 | 55 | 100 | 14 |
| The rain through her cold heart speak | 93 | 8 | 56 | 102 | 8 |
| The stocked heart is forced, and agony has another mouth to feed. | 96 | 17 | 58 | 106 | 17 |
| That his tears burned my cheeks and his heart moved in mine. | 103 | 28 | 63 | 115 | 2 |
| One gesture of the heart or head, | 105 | 9 | 64 | 116 | 9 |
| King of your heart in the blind days, | 105 | 16 | 64 | 116 | 16 |
| And my whole heart under your hammer, | 107 | 13 | 65 | 118 | 13 |
| Close and far she announced the theft of the heart | 114 | 16 | 69 | 126 | 16 |
| Your heart is luminous | 118 | 2 | 71 | 130 | 6 |
| The scrolls of fire that burned in his heart and head, | 119 | 14 | 72 | 131 | 14 |
| The windows pour into their heart | 124 | 11 | 73 | 138 | 11 |
| Her heart all ears and eyes, lips catching the avalanche | 127 | 10 | 75 | 141 | 10 |
| Of their most secret heart. | 128 | 11 | 76 | 142 | 11 |
| As the grains blow, as your death grows, through our heart. | 129 | 23 | 77 | 143 | 23 |
| Dig no more for the chains of his grey-haired heart. | 135 | 9 | 80 | 152 | 9 |
| And the heart print of man | 137 | 12 | 82 | 154 | 12 |
| The inmost marrow of my heart bone | 143 | 17 | 82 | 160 | 17 |

| | U.K. | | | U.S. | |
|---|---|---|---|---|---|
| | *Page* | *Line* | *Poem* | *Page* | *Line* |
| No heart bone | 145 | 11 | 82 | 162 | 11 |
| With his long-legged heart in his hand. | 157 | 24 | 83 | 176 | 16 |
| I climb to greet the war in which I have no heart but only | 158 | 8 | 84 | 177 | 8 |
| Under the new made clouds and happy as the heart was long, | 160 | 16 | 85 | 179 | 16 |
| To eat your heart in the house in the rosy wood. | 162 | 7 | 86 | 181 | 7 |
| To court the honeyed heart from your side before sunrise | 162 | 13 | 86 | 181 | 13 |
| Heart! Slyly, slowly, hearing the wound in her side go | 165 | 24 | 86 | 185 | 14 |
| A process in the weather of the heart | 6 | | 4 | 6 | |
| HEART'S | | | | | |
| Breaks, O my heart's blood, like a heart and hill. | 82 | 24 | 48 | 91 | 24 |
| Flood of her heart's fame; she would lie dumb and deep | 87 | 19 | 52 | 96 | 19 |
| O may my heart's truth | 104 | 16 | 63 | 115 | 18 |
| For the country of death is the heart's size | 146 | 17 | 82 | 163 | 17 |
| HEARTBEAT | | | | | |
| Suffer the heaven's children through my heartbeat. | 75 | 18 | 44 | 84 | 18 |
| HEARTBONE | | | | | |
| Before the fall from love the flying heartbone, | 41 | 15 | 23 | 47 | 15 |
| Love's image till my heartbone breaks | 70 | 7 | 43 | 79 | 11 |
| HEARTBREAK | | | | | |
| Time is the tune my ladies lend their heartbreak, | 75 | 1 | 44 | 84 | 1 |
| HEARTH | | | | | |
| But I, Ann's bard on a raised hearth, call all | 87 | 21 | 52 | 96 | 21 |
| HEARTHSTONE | | | | | |
| In the land of the hearthstone tales, and spelled asleep, | 162 | 2 | 86 | 181 | 2 |
| Of the hearthstone tales my own, lost love; and the soul walks | 164 | 4 | 86 | 183 | 11 |
| HEARTLESS | | | | | |
| Some let me make you of the heartless words. | 17 | 5 | 11 | 20 | 5 |
| Have cleanest hands, and, as the heartless ghost | 50 | 8 | 30 | 59 | 8 |
| HEARTS | | | | | |
| There from their hearts the dogdayed pulse | 1 | 22 | 2 | 1 | 22 |
| Praise to our faring hearts. | 15 | 22 | 10 | 18 | 2 |
| HEART-SHAPED | | | | | |
| But rail with your wizard's ribs the heart-shaped planet; | 60 | 15 | 36 | 69 | 15 |
| HEAT | | | | | |
| There in their heat the winter floods | 1 | 4 | 2 | 1 | 4 |

|  | U.K. |  |  | U.S. |  |
|---|---|---|---|---|---|
|  | *Page* | *Line* | *Poem* | *Page* | *Line* |
| He promises a secret heat. | 10 | 15 | 7 | 11 | 15 |
| Rehearsing heat upon a raw-edged nerve. | 12 | 19 | 9 | 13 | 19 |
| HEATS |  |  |  |  |  |
| Or lame the air with leaping from its heats; | 1 | 21 | 2 | 1 | 21 |
| HEAVE |  |  |  |  |  |
| Hurdles and guns and railings, as the boulders heave, | 49 | 16 | 29 | 58 | 16 |
| HEAVEN |  |  |  |  |  |
| Geese nearly in heaven, boys | vii | 15 | 1 | xv | 15 |
| How time has tickled a heaven round the stars. | 9 | 20 | 6 | 10 | 20 |
| Heaven and hell mixed as they spun. | 22 | 6 | 14 | 27 | 6 |
| And prick the thumb-stained heaven through the thimble. | 31 | 3 | 18 | 36 | 3 |
| The tongues of heaven gossip as I glide | 32 | 5 | 18 | 37 | 11 |
| All heaven in a midnight of the sun, | 40 | 17 | 22 | 46 | 17 |
| A hand rules pity as a hand rules heaven; | 62 | 15 | 37 | 71 | 15 |
| And this weak house to marrow-columned heaven, | 78 | 8 | 46 | 87 | 8 |
| Puffing the pounds of manna up through the dew to heaven, | 94 | 5 | 57 | 104 | 5 |
| The stained flats of heaven hit and razed | 95 | 2 | 58 | 105 | 2 |
| Sang heaven hungry and the quick | 95 | 15 | 58 | 105 | 15 |
| Heaven fell with his fall and one crocked bell beat the left air. | 95 | 25 | 58 | 105 | 25 |
| It was my thirtieth year to heaven | 102 | 1 | 63 | 113 | 1 |
| Year to heaven stood there then in the summer noon | 104 | 14 | 63 | 115 | 16 |
| And heaven crier, arrow now of aspiring | 110 | 10 | 67 | 121 | 12 |
| That the phoenix' bid for heaven and the desire after | 110 | 17 | 67 | 121 | 19 |
| The heavens, the heaven, the grave, the burning font. | 122 | 24 | 72 | 136 | 4 |
| The woman breasted and the heaven headed | 123 | 15 | 72 | 137 | 5 |
| Of the dazzler of heaven | 139 | 7 | 82 | 156 | 7 |
| Heaven that never was | 171 | 23 | 88 | 191 | 23 |
| And air shaped Heaven where souls grow wild | 172 | 20 | 88 | 192 | 20 |
| HEAVEN'S |  |  |  |  |  |
| And my images roared and rose on heaven's hill. | 38 | 30 | 20 | 44 | 20 |
| Shaped my clayfellow, and the heaven's ark | 61 | 2 | 36 | 70 | 2 |
| Old cock from nowheres and the heaven's egg, | 71 | 8 | 44 | 80 | 8 |
| Suffer the heaven's children through my heart-beat. | 75 | 18 | 44 | 84 | 18 |
| Die in red feathers when the flying heaven's cut, | 92 | 12 | 55 | 101 | 18 |
| Nor when all ponderous heaven's host of waters breaks. | 97 | 20 | 59 | 108 | 20 |

| | U.K. | | | U.S. | |
|---|---|---|---|---|---|
| | *Page* | *Line* | *Poem* | *Page* | *Line* |
| Gulled and chanter in young Heaven's fold | 172 | 8 | 88 | 192 | 8 |
| HEAVEN-CIRCLING | | | | | |
| Head to heaven-circling head, | 115 | 2 | 69 | 127 | 2 |
| HEAVEN-DRIVEN | | | | | |
| Drove in the heaven-driven of the nails | 75 | 12 | 44 | 84 | 12 |
| HEAVEN-PROOF | | | | | |
| She deludes the heaven-proof house with entering clouds | 108 | 6 | 66 | 119 | 6 |
| HEAVENLY | | | | | |
| The heavenly music over the sand | 82 | 14 | 48 | 91 | 14 |
| The heavenly ambulance drawn by a wound | 135 | 10 | 80 | 152 | 10 |
| HEAVENS | | | | | |
| The heavens, the heaven, the grave, the burning font. | 122 | 24 | 72 | 136 | 4 |
| HEAVENS' | | | | | |
| And played down pardon from the heavens' hill. | 40 | 6 | 22 | 46 | 6 |
| HEAVY | | | | | |
| Heavy with the drowned | 143 | 5 | 82 | 160 | 5 |
| Sing and strike his heavy haul | 154 | 17 | 83 | 172 | 17 |
| HEDGE | | | | | |
| When black birds died like priests in the cloaked hedge row | 122 | 12 | 72 | 135 | 12 |
| HEDGEROW | | | | | |
| Who once, green countries since, were a hedge-row of joys. | 176 | 20 | 90 | 197 | 20 |
| HEDGES | | | | | |
| Of the sparrows and such who swansing, dusk, in wrangling hedges. | 167 | 7 | 87 | 187 | 7 |
| As the arc of the billhooks that flashed the hedges low | 178 | 7 | 90 | 199 | 8 |
| HEED | | | | | |
| Nor heed my craft or art. | 128 | 20 | 76 | 142 | 20 |
| HEEDLESS | | | | | |
| I ran my heedless ways, | 160 | 18 | 85 | 179 | 18 |
| HEEL | | | | | |
| Over the vault of ridings with his hound at heel, | 49 | 5 | 29 | 58 | 5 |
| Howls the foul fiend to heel. | 66 | 5 | 40 | 75 | 5 |
| His beast heel cleft in a sandal, | 83 | 3 | 49 | 92 | 3 |
| Pierce the spilt sky with diving wing in weed and heel | 86 | 4 | 51 | 95 | 4 |
| That melts the lionhead's heel and horseshoe of the heart, | 91 | 14 | 55 | 100 | 14 |
| And the owl hood, the heel hider, | 133 | 4 | 78 | 148 | 7 |
| HEELED | | | | | |
| Heeled winds the rooks | 164 | 18 | 86 | 184 | 4 |
| Who comes as red as the fox and sly as the heeled wind. | 165 | 10 | 86 | 184 | 18 |

|  | U.K. | | Poem | U.S. | |
|---|---|---|---|---|---|
|  | Page | Line |  | Page | Line |
| **HEELS** |  |  |  |  |  |
| The winging bone that sprouted in the heels, | 12 | 11 | 9 | 13 | 11 |
| Bleed from my burning fork and smell my heels. | 32 | 4 | 18 | 37 | 10 |
| Two heels of water on the floor of seed), | 56 | 24 | 34 | 66 | 3 |
| Scattered in the paths of his heels | 152 | 23 | 83 | 170 | 15 |
| **HEIGH** |  |  |  |  |  |
| Heigh, on horseback hill, jack | ix | 16 | 1 | xvii | 16 |
| Heigh ho the blood and the berry, | 2 | 20 | 2 | 3 | 2 |
| **HEIGHT** |  |  |  |  |  |
| And you, my father, there on the sad height, | 116 | 16 | 70 | 128 | 16 |
| To the hawk on fire, the halter height, over Towy's fins, | 167 | 16 | 87 | 187 | 16 |
| **HEIR** |  |  |  |  |  |
| Heir to the scalding veins that hold love's drop, costly | 28 | 9 | 17 | 33 | 9 |
| **HELD** |  |  |  |  |  |
| And held a little sabbath with the sun, | 4 | 15 | 3 | 4 | 15 |
| Under the cloud against love is caught and held and kissed | 109 | 17 | 67 | 120 | 17 |
| Time held me green and dying | 161 | 5 | 85 | 180 | 8 |
| And star: held and blessed, though you scour the high four | 163 | 22 | 86 | 183 | 3 |
| High riding, held and blessed and true, and so stilly | 165 | 19 | 86 | 185 | 9 |
| Veined his poor hand I held, and I saw |  |  | 91 | 200 | 16 |
| **HELL** |  |  |  |  |  |
| Heaven and hell mixed as they spun. | 22 | 6 | 14 | 27 | 6 |
| Hell in a horn of sulphur and the cloven myth, | 40 | 16 | 22 | 46 | 16 |
| Hell wind and sea, | 54 | 4 | 33 | 63 | 4 |
| And all sweet hell, deaf as an hour's ear, | 57 | 5 | 34 | 66 | 12 |
| Furled on the fishes' house and hell, | 69 | 17 | 43 | 78 | 17 |
| **HELLBORN** |  |  |  |  |  |
| Wind in me leaped, the hellborn dew; | 7 | 16 | 5 | 8 | 16 |
| **HELPLESSLY** |  |  |  |  |  |
| But heart, like head, leads helplessly; | 63 | 10 | 38 | 72 | 10 |
| **HEMISPHERE** |  |  |  |  |  |
| A hemisphere green may scold him | 43 | 3 | 24 | 50 | 10 |
| **HEMLOCK** |  |  |  |  |  |
| Of hemlock and the blades, rust | 28 | 18 | 17 | 33 | 18 |
| **HEMLOCK-HEADED** |  |  |  |  |  |
| And hemlock-headed in the wood of weathers | 72 | 4 | 44 | 81 | 4 |
| **HEMS** |  |  |  |  |  |
| To the kissed kite hems of his shawl, | 95 | 3 | 58 | 105 | 3 |
| **HEN** |  |  |  |  |  |
| And the dung hills white as wool and the hen | 119 | 18 | 72 | 131 | 18 |
| **HENNA** |  |  |  |  |  |
| Draw on the glove of prints, dead Cairo's henna | 75 | 23 | 44 | 84 | 23 |

| | U.K. | | Poem | U.S. | |
|---|---|---|---|---|---|
| | *Page* | *Line* | *Poem* | *Page* | *Line* |
| **HENS** | | | | | |
| And no green cocks or hens | 169 | 5 | 87 | 189 | 14 |
| **HER** | | | | | |
| Who moons her blue notes from her nest | ix | 11 | 1 | xvii | 11 |
| Hold up the noisy sea and drop her birds, | 2 | 15 | 2 | 2 | 15 |
| To choke the deserts with her tides, | 2 | 17 | 2 | 2 | 17 |
| Shall calm her sores. | 9 | 18 | 6 | 10 | 18 |
| The beach of flesh, and wind her bloodred plait; | 10 | 13 | 7 | 11 | 13 |
| A rooking girl who stole me for her side, | 12 | 2 | 9 | 13 | 2 |
| Broke through her straws, breaking my bandage string, | 12 | 3 | 9 | 13 | 3 |
| And curling round the bud that forks her eye. | 13 | 3 | 9 | 14 | 10 |
| Sheds the syllabic blood and drains her words. | 16 | 8 | 11 | 19 | 8 |
| Love in her gear is slowly through the house, | 18 | 3 | 12 | 21 | 3 |
| From love's first fever to her plague, from the soft second | 20 | 1 | 13 | 24 | 1 |
| The boy she dropped from darkness at her side | 21 | 2 | 13 | 25 | 2 |
| To-morrow's diver in her horny milk, | 30 | 4 | 18 | 35 | 4 |
| Ghost with her ghost, contagious man | 34 | 2 | 19 | 39 | 8 |
| Bright as her spinning-wheels, the colic season | 35 | 8 | 20 | 40 | 8 |
| With her rampart to his tapping, | 42 | 3 | 24 | 49 | 3 |
| With her rampart to his tapping, | 42 | 10 | 24 | 49 | 10 |
| For my tall tower's sake cast in her stone? | 46 | 2 | 27 | 54 | 2 |
| For her soldier stained with spilt words | 48 | 15 | 28 | 56 | 15 |
| Brand of the lily's anger on her ring; | 54 | 19 | 33 | 63 | 19 |
| Her ropes of heritage, the wars of pardon, | 54 | 21 | 33 | 63 | 21 |
| She holding me? The people's sea drives on her, | 54 | 26 | 33 | 64 | 2 |
| Shape all her whelps with the long voice of water, | 55 | 2 | 33 | 64 | 5 |
| A nitric shape that leaps her, time and acid; | 55 | 7 | 33 | 64 | 10 |
| I tell her this: before the suncock cast | 55 | 8 | 33 | 64 | 11 |
| Her bone to fire, | 55 | 9 | 33 | 64 | 12 |
| Let her inhale her dead, through seed and solid | 55 | 10 | 33 | 64 | 13 |
| So cross her hand with their grave gipsy eyes, | 55 | 12 | 33 | 64 | 15 |
| And close her fist. | 55 | 13 | 33 | 64 | 16 |
| And from her lips the faded pigments fall, | 63 | 7 | 38 | 72 | 7 |
| I laid her down and told her sin, | 65 | 23 | 40 | 74 | 23 |
| And put beside her a ram rose. | 65 | 24 | 40 | 74 | 24 |
| And the sky lays down her laws, | 66 | 10 | 40 | 75 | 10 |
| The world's my wound, God's Mary in her grief, | 75 | 8 | 44 | 84 | 8 |
| Bent like three trees and bird-papped through her shift, | 75 | 9 | 44 | 84 | 9 |
| What rhubarb man peeled in her foam-blue channel | 76 | 17 | 44 | 85 | 17 |
| When, praise is blessed, her pride in mast and fountain | 78 | 4 | 46 | 87 | 4 |

| | U.K. | | | U.S. | |
|---|---|---|---|---|---|
| | Page | Line | Poem | Page | Line |
| By magnet winds to her blind mother drawn, | 78 | 14 | 46 | 87 | 14 |
| And a silk pigeon's guilt in her proud absence, | 78 | 17 | 46 | 87 | 17 |
| These are her contraries: the beast who follows | 78 | 24 | 46 | 88 | 1 |
| Her molten flight up cinder-nesting columns, | 78 | 26 | 46 | 88 | 3 |
| Who scales a hailing hill in her cold flintsteps | 79 | 3 | 46 | 88 | 6 |
| Storm her sped heart, hand with beheaded veins | 79 | 8 | 46 | 88 | 11 |
| Its wringing shell, and let her eyelids fasten. | 79 | 9 | 46 | 88 | 12 |
| Delivered seas my love from her proud place | 80 | 9 | 46 | 89 | 17 |
| Walks with no wound, nor lightning in her face, | 80 | 10 | 46 | 89 | 18 |
| Prides of to-morrow suckling in her eyes, | 80 | 14 | 46 | 89 | 22 |
| That her fond wounds are mended bitterly. | 81 | 9 | 47 | 90 | 9 |
| My nostrils see her breath burn like a bush. | 81 | 10 | 47 | 90 | 10 |
| (Though this for her is a monstrous image blindly | 87 | 16 | 52 | 96 | 16 |
| Magnified out of praise; her death was a still drop; | 87 | 17 | 52 | 96 | 17 |
| Flood of her heart's fame; she would lie dumb and deep | 87 | 19 | 52 | 96 | 19 |
| And need no druid of her broken body). | 87 | 20 | 52 | 96 | 20 |
| The seas to service that her wood-tongued virtue | 87 | 22 | 52 | 96 | 22 |
| That her love sing and swing through a brown chapel, | 87 | 25 | 52 | 96 | 25 |
| Bless her bent spirit with four, crossing birds. | 87 | 26 | 52 | 96 | 26 |
| Her flesh was meek as milk, but this skyward statue | 87 | 27 | 52 | 96 | 27 |
| Is carved from her in a room with a wet window | 88 | 1 | 52 | 97 | 1 |
| I know her scrubbed and sour humble hands | 88 | 3 | 52 | 97 | 3 |
| Lie with religion in their cramp, her threadbare | 88 | 4 | 52 | 97 | 4 |
| Whisper in a damp word, her wits drilled hollow, | 88 | 5 | 52 | 97 | 5 |
| Her fist of a face died clenched on a round pain; | 88 | 6 | 52 | 97 | 6 |
| Storm me forever over her grave until | 88 | 10 | 52 | 97 | 10 |
| Refusal struck her loin and the lame flower | 90 | 2 | 54 | 99 | 2 |
| Shall her smile breed that mouth, behind the mirror, | 90 | 13 | 54 | 99 | 13 |
| Her two surnames stopped me still. | 93 | 2 | 56 | 102 | 2 |
| The rain through her cold heart speak | 93 | 8 | 56 | 102 | 8 |
| And the sun killed in her face. | 93 | 9 | 56 | 102 | 9 |
| With a hand plunged through her hair, | 93 | 12 | 56 | 102 | 12 |
| She cried her white-dressed limbs were bare | 93 | 17 | 56 | 102 | 17 |
| And her red lips were kissed black, | 93 | 18 | 56 | 102 | 18 |
| She wept in her pain and made mouths, | 93 | 19 | 56 | 102 | 19 |
| Talked and tore though her eyes smiled. | 93 | 20 | 56 | 102 | 20 |
| Heard her speak through the chipped beak | 93 | 24 | 56 | 103 | 4 |
| Of the stone bird guarding her: | 93 | 25 | 56 | 103 | 5 |
| Who climbs to his dying love in her high room, | 100 | 3 | 61 | 111 | 3 |
| The mankind of her going with a grave truth | 101 | 15 | 62 | 112 | 15 |

| | U.K. | | | U.S. | |
|---|---|---|---|---|---|
| | Page | Line | Poem | Page | Line |
| The grains beyond age, the dark veins of her mother, | 101 | 21 | 62 | 112 | 21 |
| Bolting the night of the door with her arm her plume. | 108 | 4 | 66 | 119 | 4 |
| Yet raves at her will | 108 | 14 | 66 | 119 | 14 |
| And taken by light in her arms at long and dear last | 108 | 16 | 66 | 119 | 16 |
| Her constant, nor the winds of love broken wide | 109 | 10 | 67 | 120 | 10 |
| Into her lying down head | 113 | 1 | 69 | 125 | 1 |
| Along her innocence glided | 113 | 10 | 69 | 125 | 10 |
| There the dark blade and wanton sighing her down | 113 | 16 | 69 | 125 | 16 |
| Made her limbs blind by luminous charms, | 113 | 21 | 69 | 125 | 21 |
| His faith around her flew undone | 114 | 3 | 69 | 126 | 3 |
| Resembling to her dúlled sense | 114 | 7 | 69 | 126 | 7 |
| Jealousy cannot forget for all her sakes, | 114 | 11 | 69 | 126 | 11 |
| Made his bad bed in her good | 114 | 12 | 69 | 126 | 12 |
| Celebrating at her side | 114 | 19 | 69 | 126 | 19 |
| Her holy unholy hours with the always anonymous beast. | 114 | 23 | 69 | 126 | 23 |
| Her lover's wings that fold to-morrow's flight, | 115 | 11 | 69 | 127 | 11 |
| Forgotten dark, rest their pulse and bury their dead in her faithless sleep. | 115 | 23 | 69 | 127 | 23 |
| Dust in the buried wood, flies on the grains of her wings | 121 | 3 | 72 | 133 | 18 |
| A she bird dawned, and her breast with snow and scarlet downed. | 121 | 15 | 72 | 134 | 10 |
| Above her folded head, and the soft feathered voice | 122 | 2 | 72 | 135 | 2 |
| And she rose with him flowering in her melting snow. | 123 | 20 | 72 | 137 | 10 |
| Surprised in the opening of her nightlong eyes | 127 | 2 | 75 | 141 | 2 |
| And this day's sun leapt up the sky out of her thighs | 127 | 4 | 75 | 141 | 4 |
| Her deepsea pillow where once she married alone, | 127 | 9 | 75 | 141 | 9 |
| Her heart all ears and eyes, lips catching the avalanche | 127 | 10 | 75 | 141 | 10 |
| Of the golden ghost who ringed with his streams her mercury bone, | 127 | 11 | 75 | 141 | 11 |
| Who under the lids of her windows hoisted his golden luggage, | 127 | 12 | 75 | 141 | 12 |
| Laid in her snow | 130 | 13 | 77 | 144 | 13 |
| A girl alive with his hooks through her lips; | 149 | 22 | 83 | 167 | 2 |
| The rainbow-fish bend in her joys, | 150 | 10 | 83 | 167 | 14 |
| The octopus walking into her limbs | 152 | 7 | 83 | 169 | 19 |

|  | U.K. | | | U.S. | |
| --- | --- | --- | --- | --- | --- |
|  | *Page* | *Line* | *Poem* | *Page* | *Line* |
| Sing how the seal has kissed her dead! | 152 | 10 | 83 | 170 | 2 |
| Old in her cruel bed. | 152 | 12 | 83 | 170 | 4 |
| And scuttled over her eyes, | 153 | 4 | 83 | 170 | 20 |
| Is always lost in her vaulted breath, | 153 | 20 | 83 | 171 | 16 |
| Venus lies star-struck in her wound | 153 | 21 | 83 | 171 | 17 |
| Kill Time! She turns in her pain! | 155 | 10 | 83 | 173 | 14 |
| Clings to her drifting hair, and climbs; | 155 | 17 | 83 | 174 | 1 |
| A garden holding to her hand | 155 | 23 | 83 | 174 | 7 |
| Insects and valleys hold her thighs hard, | 156 | 6 | 83 | 174 | 14 |
| Time and places grip her breast bone, | 156 | 7 | 83 | 174 | 15 |
| Round her trailed wrist fresh water weaves, | 156 | 9 | 83 | 174 | 17 |
| And steeples pierce the cloud on her shoulder | 157 | 1 | 83 | 175 | 13 |
| Coil from the thoroughfares of her hair | 157 | 5 | 83 | 175 | 17 |
| Lead her prodigal home to his terror, | 157 | 7 | 83 | 175 | 19 |
| Her robin breasted tree, three Marys in the rays. | 163 | 6 | 86 | 182 | 6 |
| Eyed, in the haloed house, in her rareness and hilly | 165 | 18 | 86 | 185 | 8 |
| Might cross its planets, the bell weep, night gather her eyes, | 165 | 21 | 86 | 185 | 11 |
| Only for the turning of the earth in her holy | 165 | 23 | 86 | 185 | 13 |
| Heart! Slyly, slowly, hearing the wound in her side go | 165 | 24 | 86 | 185 | 14 |
| Comes designed to my love to steal not her tide raking | 166 | 1 | 86 | 186 | 1 |
| Wound, nor her riding high, nor her eyes, nor kindled hair, | 166 | 2 | 86 | 186 | 2 |
| But her faith that each vast night and the saga of prayer | 166 | 3 | 86 | 186 | 3 |
| Her faith that this last night for his unsacred sake | 166 | 5 | 86 | 186 | 5 |
| He comes to leave her in the lawless sun awaking | 166 | 6 | 86 | 186 | 6 |
| Harpies around me out of her womb! | 175 | 27 | 89 | 196 | 8 |
| Modesty hides my thighs in her wings, | 175 | 30 | 89 | 196 | 11 |
| From love's first fever to her plague | 20 |  | 13 | 24 |  |
| Into her Lying Down Head | 113 |  | 69 | 125 |  |

**HERALD**

| Continence. I see the unfired phoenix, herald | 110 | 9 | 67 | 121 | 11 |

**HERD**

| Down to the curlew herd! | ix | 12 | 1 | xvii | 12 |
| Calls the starved fire herd, is cast in ice, | 79 | 1 | 46 | 88 | 4 |

**HERDS**

| To the sultry, biding herds, I said, | 175 | 4 | 89 | 195 | 9 |

**HERDSMAN**

| And green and golden I was huntsman and herdsman, the calves | 159 | 15 | 85 | 178 | 15 |

| | U.K. | | | U.S. | |
|---|---|---|---|---|---|
| | Page | Line | Poem | Page | Line |
| **HERE** | | | | | |
| Here love's damp muscle dries and dies, | 2 | 22 | 2 | 3 | 4 |
| Here break a kiss in no love's quarry. | 2 | 23 | 2 | 3 | 5 |
| Here is this spring, stars float along the void; | 45 | 1 | 26 | 53 | 1 |
| Here in this ornamental winter | 45 | 2 | 26 | 53 | 2 |
| Has a voice and a house, and there and here you must couch and cry. | 98 | 2 | 59 | 109 | 5 |
| Here were fond climates and sweet singers suddenly | 103 | 1 | 63 | 114 | 1 |
| Here among the light of the lording sky | | | 91 | 201 | 8 |
| Here in this spring | 45 | | 26 | 53 | |
| **HERITAGE** | | | | | |
| Rounded my globe of heritage, journey | 28 | 11 | 17 | 33 | 11 |
| Her ropes of heritage, the wars of pardon, | 54 | 21 | 33 | 63 | 21 |
| **HERMAPHRODITE** | | | | | |
| My sea hermaphrodite, | 69 | 7 | 43 | 78 | 7 |
| **HERO** | | | | | |
| My hero bares his nerves along my wrist | 10 | 1 | 7 | 11 | 1 |
| My hero bares my side and sees his heart | 10 | 11 | 7 | 11 | 11 |
| You hero skull, Cadaver in the hanger | 19 | 4 | 12 | 22 | 9 |
| Let the hero seed find harbour, | 43 | 5 | 24 | 50 | 12 |
| Let the hero seed find harbour, | 43 | 12 | 24 | 50 | 19 |
| My hero bares his nerves | 10 | | 7 | 11 | |
| **HERO'S** | | | | | |
| The hero's head lies scraped of every legend, | 79 | 17 | 46 | 88 | 20 |
| **HERO-IN-TOMORROW** | | | | | |
| Shall the hero-in-tomorrow | 43 | 20 | 24 | 51 | 6 |
| **HERO-IN-TO-MORROW** | | | | | |
| Shall the hero-in-to-morrow | 43 | 27 | 24 | 51 | 13 |
| **HERODS** | | | | | |
| Lapped among herods wail | 96 | 14 | 58 | 106 | 14 |
| **HEROIC** | | | | | |
| But blessed by such heroic hosts in your every | 109 | 21 | 67 | 120 | 21 |
| **HEROINE** | | | | | |
| Death and this mad heroine | 93 | 22 | 56 | 103 | 2 |
| **HERON** | | | | | |
| And the mussel pooled and the heron | 102 | 3 | 63 | 113 | 3 |
| High tide and the heron dived when I took the road | 102 | 17 | 63 | 113 | 17 |
| Crashes, and slowly the fishing holy stalking heron | 167 | 11 | 87 | 187 | 11 |
| The heron and I, | 168 | 10 | 87 | 188 | 14 |
| Of eels, saint heron hymning in the shell-hung distant | 168 | 12 | 87 | 188 | 16 |
| It is the heron and I, under judging Sir John's elmed | 168 | 16 | 87 | 189 | 1 |

|  | U.K. | | | U.S. | |
| --- | --- | --- | --- | --- | --- |
|  | *Page* | *Line* | *Poem* | *Page* | *Line* |
| Now the heron grieves in the weeded verge. Through windows | 168 | 23 | 87 | 189 | 8 |
| Heron, mirrored, go, | 169 | 1 | 87 | 189 | 10 |
| Now on Sir John's hill. The heron, ankling the scaly | 169 | 7 | 87 | 189 | 16 |
| HERONS |  |  |  |  |  |
| Stabbing, and herons, and shells | vii | 16 | 1 | xv | 16 |
| Herons spire and spear. | 170 | 9 | 88 | 190 | 9 |
| Herons, steeple stemmed, bless. | 170 | 18 | 88 | 190 | 18 |
| Herons walk in their shroud, | 170 | 27 | 88 | 190 | 27 |
| HERONS' |  |  |  |  |  |
| And druid herons' vows | 172 | 23 | 88 | 192 | 23 |
| HERRINGS |  |  |  |  |  |
| And all the herrings smelling in the sea, | 13 | 5 | 9 | 14 | 12 |
| HEWN |  |  |  |  |  |
| Argument of the hewn voice, gesture and psalm, | 88 | 9 | 52 | 97 | 9 |
| Clack through the thicket of strength, love hewn in pillars drops | 92 | 8 | 55 | 101 | 14 |
| And the hewn coils of his trade perceives | 170 | 26 | 88 | 190 | 26 |
| HEW |  |  |  |  |  |
| Clangour as I hew and smite | ix | 19 | 1 | xvii | 19 |
| HEY |  |  |  |  |  |
| And Mister they called Hey mister | 111 | 15 | 68 | 123 | 15 |
| HEYDAYS |  |  |  |  |  |
| Golden in the heydays of his eyes, | 159 | 5 | 85 | 178 | 5 |
| HICKORY |  |  |  |  |  |
| Or hickory bull in milky grass | 175 | 12 | 89 | 195 | 17 |
| HID |  |  |  |  |  |
| We hid our fears in that murdering breath, | 125 | 14 | 74 | 139 | 14 |
| HIDDEN |  |  |  |  |  |
| Of the mother hidden | 138 | 6 | 82 | 155 | 6 |
| To the hidden land | 148 | 5 | 82 | 165 | 5 |
| HIDE |  |  |  |  |  |
| Have their thirsty sailors hide him. | 43 | 7 | 24 | 50 | 14 |
| Have their drunken sailors hide him. | 43 | 14 | 24 | 50 | 21 |
| And the shipyards of Galilee's footprints hide a navy of doves. | 127 | 7 | 75 | 141 | 7 |
| Lie still, sleep becalmed, hide the mouth in the throat, | 136 | 13 | 81 | 153 | 13 |
| On that darkest day. Oh, he could hide |  |  | 91 | 201 | 17 |
| HIDER |  |  |  |  |  |
| And the owl hood, the heel hider, | 133 | 4 | 78 | 148 | 7 |
| HIDES |  |  |  |  |  |
| And the sea that hides his secret selves | 173 | 6 | 88 | 193 | 6 |
| Modesty hides my thighs in her wings, | 175 | 30 | 89 | 196 | 11 |
| HIDING |  |  |  |  |  |
| Hiding the golden mountains and mansions | 82 | 16 | 48 | 91 | 16 |

| | U.K. | | | U.S. | |
|---|---|---|---|---|---|
| | Page | Line | Poem | Page | Line |

HIGH

| | | | | | |
|---|---|---|---|---|---|
| And a high sphere be his bearer; | 43 | 11 | 24 | 50 | 18 |
| Not till, from high and low, their dust | 53 | 12 | 32 | 62 | 12 |
| High lord esquire, speak up the singing cloud, | 60 | 17 | 36 | 69 | 17 |
| Who tossed the high tide in a time of stories | 67 | 13 | 41 | 76 | 13 |
| Cast high, stunned on gilled stones; sly scissors ground in frost | 92 | 7 | 55 | 101 | 13 |
| Who climbs to his dying love in her high room, | 100 | 3 | 61 | 111 | 3 |
| In the fire of his care his love in the high room. | 100 | 16 | 61 | 111 | 16 |
| High tide and the heron dived when I took the road | 102 | 17 | 63 | 113 | 17 |
| On this high hill in a year's turning. | 104 | 18 | 63 | 115 | 20 |
| In high corn and the harvest melting on their tongues. | 120 | 18 | 72 | 133 | 3 |
| And the high noon | 140 | 14 | 82 | 157 | 14 |
| High and dry by the top of the mast, | 149 | 8 | 83 | 166 | 8 |
| Fields high as the house, the tunes from the chimneys, it was air | 159 | 20 | 85 | 178 | 20 |
| My wishes raced through the house high hay | 160 | 19 | 85 | 179 | 19 |
| I should hear him fly with the high fields | 161 | 2 | 85 | 180 | 5 |
| And star: held and blessed, though you scour the high four | 163 | 22 | 86 | 183 | 3 |
| The leaping saga of prayer! And high, there, on the hare- | 164 | 17 | 86 | 184 | 3 |
| High riding, held and blessed and true, and so stilly | 165 | 19 | 86 | 185 | 9 |
| Wound, nor her riding high, nor her eyes, nor kindled hair, | 166 | 2 | 86 | 186 | 2 |
| In his house on stilts high among beaks | 170 | 4 | 88 | 190 | 4 |
| Whenever I dove in a breast high shoal, | 174 | 21 | 89 | 194 | 21 |
| Under the conceiving moon, on the high chalk hill, | 176 | 2 | 90 | 197 | 2 |
| In the wains tonned so high that the wisps of the hay | 176 | 14 | 90 | 197 | 14 |
| Petticoats galed high, or shy with the rough riding boys, | 176 | 18 | 90 | 197 | 18 |

HIGHROAD

| | | | | | |
|---|---|---|---|---|---|
| The highroad of water where the seabear and mackerel | 36 | 21 | 20 | 41 | 21 |

HILL

| | | | | | |
|---|---|---|---|---|---|
| From fish to jumping hill! Look: | viii | 17 | 1 | xvi | 17 |
| Heigh, on horseback hill, jack | ix | 16 | 1 | xvii | 16 |
| Like wooden islands, hill to hill. | x | 13 | 1 | xviii | 19 |
| The spider-tongued, and the loud hill of Wales) | 17 | 3 | 11 | 20 | 3 |
| And earth and sky were as one airy hill, | 20 | 8 | 13 | 24 | 8 |
| Strewing their bowels from a hill of bones, | 31 | 17 | 18 | 36 | 17 |

|  | U.K. | | | U.S. | |
|---|---|---|---|---|---|
|  | Page | Line | Poem | Page | Line |
| Corner the mounted meadows in the hill corral; | 36 | 15 | 20 | 41 | 15 |
| Smoke hill and hophead's valley, | 38 | 4 | 20 | 43 | 14 |
| And my images roared and rose on heaven's hill. | 38 | 30 | 20 | 44 | 20 |
| And played down pardon from the heavens' hill. | 40 | 6 | 22 | 46 | 6 |
| Under the lank, fourth folly on Glamorgan's hill, | 49 | 2 | 29 | 58 | 2 |
| Summon your snowy horsemen, and the four-stringed hill, | 49 | 14 | 29 | 58 | 14 |
| Goes over the hill into the deep sea; | 64 | 5 | 39 | 73 | 5 |
| Who scales a hailing hill in her cold flintsteps | 79 | 3 | 46 | 88 | 6 |
| Breaks, O my heart's blood, like a heart and hill. | 82 | 24 | 48 | 91 | 24 |
| Soaked my table the uglier side of a hill | 89 | 2 | 53 | 98 | 2 |
| On this high hill in a year's turning. | 104 | 18 | 63 | 115 | 20 |
| A stone lies lost and locked in the lark-high hill. | 115 | 16 | 69 | 127 | 16 |
| On a bread white hill over the cupped farm | 122 | 27 | 72 | 136 | 7 |
| A hill touches an angel. Out of a saint's cell | 163 | 4 | 86 | 182 | 4 |
| Hill of cypresses! The din and tale in the skimmed | 165 | 5 | 86 | 184 | 13 |
| Over Sir John's hill, | 167 | 1 | 87 | 187 | 1 |
| Daws Sir John's just hill dons, and again the gulled birds hare | 167 | 15 | 87 | 187 | 15 |
| Hill, tell-tale the knelled | 168 | 17 | 87 | 189 | 2 |
| Now on Sir John's hill. The heron, ankling the scaly | 169 | 7 | 87 | 189 | 16 |
| Under the conceiving moon, on the high chalk hill, | 176 | 2 | 90 | 197 | 2 |
| Hill. Who once in gooseskin winter loved all ice leaved | 176 | 12 | 90 | 197 | 12 |
| Hale dead and deathless do the women of the hill | 178 | 17 | 90 | 199 | 18 |
| Hill, under the grass, in love, and there grow |  |  | 91 | 200 | 6 |
| Fern Hill | 159 |  | 85 | 178 |  |
| Over Sir John's hill | 167 |  | 87 | 187 |  |
| HILL'S |  |  |  |  |  |
| On the hill's shoulder, | 102 | 25 | 63 | 113 | 25 |
| HILLOCKS |  |  |  |  |  |
| Deep hillocks and loud on the numbed lakes, | 122 | 17 | 72 | 135 | 17 |
| HILLOCKY |  |  |  |  |  |
| But a hillocky bull in the swelter | 175 | 2 | 89 | 195 | 7 |
| HILLS |  |  |  |  |  |
| Sharp in my second death I marked the hills, harvest | 28 | 17 | 17 | 33 | 17 |
| And the hills out of mind. | 58 | 14 | 35 | 67 | 14 |

| | U.K. | | | U.S. | |
|---|---|---|---|---|---|
| | Page | Line | Poem | Page | Line |
| And the dung hills white as wool and the hen | 119 | 18 | 72 | 131 | 18 |
| And over the cloth of counties the far hills rode near, | 122 | 13 | 72 | 135 | 13 |
| And the flakes fall like hills. | 154 | 16 | 83 | 172 | 16 |
| The hills have footed the waves away, | 156 | 16 | 83 | 175 | 4 |
| Sang to my horn, the foxes on the hills barked clear and cold, | 159 | 16 | 85 | 178 | 16 |
| The bones out of the hills, | 172 | 14 | 88 | 192 | 14 |
| I hear the bouncing hills | 173 | 19 | 88 | 193 | 19 |

HILLY

| | U.K. | | | U.S. | |
|---|---|---|---|---|---|
| Of the sea is hilly with whales, | 150 | 8 | 83 | 167 | 12 |
| Eyed, in the haloed house, in her rareness and hilly | 165 | 18 | 86 | 185 | 8 |

HIM

| | U.K. | | | U.S. | |
|---|---|---|---|---|---|
| Remember me and pity Him | 8 | 20 | 5 | 9 | 20 |
| A hemisphere green may scold him | 43 | 3 | 24 | 50 | 10 |
| Have their thirsty sailors hide him. | 43 | 7 | 24 | 50 | 14 |
| A village green may scold him | 43 | 10 | 24 | 50 | 17 |
| Have their drunken sailors hide him. | 43 | 14 | 24 | 50 | 21 |
| No silver whistles chase him down the weeks' | 67 | 21 | 41 | 76 | 21 |
| Doubled, to fork him back, through the lockjaw bed | 79 | 24 | 46 | 89 | 5 |
| Dragging him up the stairs to one who lies dead. | 100 | 20 | 61 | 111 | 20 |
| But nobody chained him up. | 111 | 12 | 68 | 123 | 12 |
| His naked need struck him howling and bowed | 120 | 14 | 72 | 132 | 19 |
| And his nameless need bound him burning and lost | 120 | 19 | 72 | 133 | 4 |
| Deliver him, he cried, | 120 | 26 | 72 | 133 | 11 |
| By losing him all in love, and cast his need | 120 | 27 | 72 | 133 | 12 |
| Him up and he ran like a wind after the kindling flight | 122 | 9 | 72 | 135 | 9 |
| And she rose with him flowering in her melting snow. | 123 | 20 | 72 | 137 | 10 |
| Who bore him with a bonfire in | 139 | 9 | 82 | 156 | 9 |
| His mouth and rocked him like a storm | 139 | 10 | 82 | 156 | 10 |
| In the centre of dark I pray him | 144 | 17 | 82 | 161 | 17 |
| O let him | 148 | 11 | 82 | 165 | 11 |
| For we saw him throw to the swift flood | 149 | 21 | 83 | 167 | 1 |
| And terribly lead him home alive | 157 | 6 | 83 | 175 | 18 |
| Follow him out of grace, | 160 | 23 | 85 | 179 | 23 |
| I should hear him fly with the high fields | 161 | 2 | 85 | 180 | 5 |
| Leaping! The gospel rooks! All tell, this night, of him | 165 | 9 | 86 | 184 | 17 |
| Under and round him go | 170 | 10 | 88 | 190 | 10 |
| Faithlessly unto Him | 172 | 18 | 88 | 192 | 18 |
| Let him find no rest but be fathered and found, | | | 91 | 200 | 12 |

HINDERING

| | U.K. | | | U.S. | |
|---|---|---|---|---|---|
| When hindering man hurt | 125 | 12 | 74 | 139 | 12 |

| | | U.K. | | | U.S. | |
|---|---|---|---|---|---|---|
| | | Page | Line | Poem | Page | Line |
| **HINGE** | | | | | | |
| The milky acid on each hinge, | | 4 | 5 | 3 | 4 | 5 |
| **HISS** | | | | | | |
| And died on a hiss of flames | | 155 | 14 | 83 | 173 | 18 |
| **HISSING** | | | | | | |
| From the hissing of the spent lie | | 64 | 2 | 39 | 73 | 2 |
| Trounced by his wings in the hissing shippen, long dead | | 177 | 19 | 90 | 198 | 18 |
| **HIST** | | | | | | |
| Hist, in hogsback woods! The haystacked | | ix | 27 | 1 | xviii | 1 |
| **HISTORY** | | | | | | |
| Who kills my history? | | 70 | 9 | 43 | 79 | 13 |
| Death is all metaphors, shape in one history; | | 71 | 15 | 44 | 80 | 15 |
| **HIT** | | | | | | |
| The stained flats of heaven hit and razed | | 95 | 2 | 58 | 105 | 2 |
| **HIVES** | | | | | | |
| The jacks of frost they finger in the hives; | | 1 | 9 | 2 | 1 | 9 |
| (But nothing bore, no mouthing babe to the veined hives | | 178 | 1 | 90 | 199 | 2 |
| **HO** | | | | | | |
| Ho, hullaballoing clan | | ix | 13 | 1 | xvii | 13 |
| Heigh ho the blood and the berry, | | 2 | 20 | 2 | 3 | 2 |
| **HOBNAIL** | | | | | | |
| Of the hobnail tales: no gooseherd or swine will turn | | 162 | 10 | 86 | 181 | 10 |
| **HOGSBACK** | | | | | | |
| Hist, in hogsback woods! The haystacked | | ix | 27 | 1 | xviii | 1 |
| **HOIST** | | | | | | |
| For his briared hands to hoist them | | 145 | 2 | 82 | 162 | 2 |
| **HOISTED** | | | | | | |
| Who under the lids of her windows hoisted his golden luggage, | | 127 | 12 | 75 | 141 | 12 |
| In a hoisted cloud, at drop of dusk, he pulls to his claws | | 167 | 3 | 87 | 187 | 3 |
| **HOLD** | | | | | | |
| Hold up the noisy sea and drop her birds, | | 2 | 15 | 2 | 2 | 15 |
| Heir to the scalding veins that hold love's drop, costly | | 28 | 9 | 17 | 33 | 9 |
| My half ghost in armour hold hard in death's corridor, | | 35 | 5 | 20 | 40 | 5 |
| Hold hard, these ancient minutes in the cuckoo's month, | | 49 | 1 | 29 | 58 | 1 |
| Hold hard, my country children in the world of tales, | | 49 | 10 | 29 | 58 | 10 |
| Hold hard, my county darlings, for a hawk descends, | | 49 | 22 | 29 | 58 | 22 |
| She who was who I hold, the fats and flower, | | 54 | 2 | 33 | 63 | 2 |

| | U.K. | | | U.S. | |
|---|---|---|---|---|---|
| | *Page* | *Line* | *Poem* | *Page* | *Line* |
| Hands, hold you poison or grapes? | 58 | 9 | 35 | 67 | 6 |
| Ships, hold you poison or grapes? | 58 | 25 | 35 | 67 | 25 |
| Hold you poison or grapes? | 59 | 8 | 35 | 68 | 8 |
| Atlaswise hold half-way off the dummy bay | 76 | 10 | 44 | 85 | 10 |
| With a hold of leeches and straws, | 95 | 24 | 58 | 105 | 24 |
| And the vaulting bird be still. O my true love, hold me. | 110 | 26 | 67 | 122 | 4 |
| One who called deepest down shall hold his peace | 117 | 9 | 71 | 129 | 9 |
| Warning among the folds, and the frozen hold | 119 | 8 | 72 | 131 | 8 |
| May hold it in a great flood | 129 | 20 | 77 | 143 | 20 |
| Insects and valleys hold her thighs hard, | 156 | 6 | 83 | 174 | 14 |
| They from houses where the harvest kneels, hold me hard, | 178 | 9 | 90 | 199 | 10 |
| Hold hard, these ancient minutes in the cuckoo's month | 49 | | 29 | 58 | |
| **HOLDING** | | | | | |
| She holding me? The people's sea drives on her, | 54 | 26 | 33 | 64 | 2 |
| A garden holding to her hand | 155 | 23 | 83 | 174 | 7 |
| **HOLDS** | | | | | |
| He holds the wire from this box of nerves | 10 | 16 | 7 | 11 | 16 |
| Hands of the stranger and holds of the ships, | 59 | 7 | 35 | 68 | 7 |
| Great is the hand that holds dominion over | 62 | 11 | 37 | 71 | 11 |
| Out of the house that holds a town | 154 | 23 | 83 | 173 | 3 |
| **HOLE** | | | | | |
| When cameras shut they hurry to their hole | 14 | 15 | 10 | 16 | 15 |
| Rammed in the marching heart, hole | 28 | 14 | 17 | 33 | 14 |
| Wind-heeled foot in the hole of a fireball, | 95 | 12 | 58 | 105 | 12 |
| Claw fold and hole for the rotten | 133 | 5 | 78 | 148 | 8 |
| **HOLIER** | | | | | |
| Holier then their eyes, | 173 | 25 | 88 | 193 | 25 |
| **HOLLOW** | | | | | |
| Sheep white hollow farms | viii | 25 | I | xvi | 25 |
| Hollow farms in a throng | ix | 28 | L | xviii | 2 |
| And to the hollow minute of the womb, | 20 | 2 | 13 | 24 | 2 |
| His sea-sucked Adam in the hollow hulk, | 30 | 2 | 18 | 35 | 2 |
| The hollow words could bear all suffering | 48 | 22 | 28 | 56 | 22 |
| Hairs of your head, then said the hollow agent, | 72 | 1 | 44 | 81 | 1 |
| Who follow the red rivers, hollow | 82 | 3 | 48 | 91 | 3 |
| Whisper in a damp word, her wits drilled hollow, | 88 | 5 | 52 | 97 | 5 |
| To this inhospitable hollow year, | 126 | 3 | 74 | 140 | 3 |
| **HOLLOWS** | | | | | |
| Hollows, a grassblade blown in cupped hands, in the looted elms | 169 | 4 | 87 | 189 | 13 |
| **HOLLY** | | | | | |
| In spring we cross our foreheads with the holly, | 2 | 19 | 2 | 3 | I |
| December's thorn screwed in a brow of holly. | 76 | 14 | 44 | 85 | 14 |

# HOLOCAUST

|  | U.K. Page | U.K. Line | Poem | U.S. Page | U.S. Line |
|---|---|---|---|---|---|
| **HOLOCAUST** | | | | | |
| His striped and noon maned tribe striding to holocaust, | 110 | 3 | 67 | 121 | 5 |
| **HOLT** | | | | | |
| The owl at its knelling. Fox and holt kneel before blood. | 163 | 9 | 86 | 182 | 9 |
| **HOLY** | | | | | |
| And dark shoals every holy field. | x | 7 | 1 | xviii | 13 |
| A handmade moon half holy in a cloud, | 40 | 8 | 22 | 46 | 8 |
| Should lanterns shine, the holy face, | 63 | 1 | 38 | 72 | 1 |
| In a holy room in a wave; | 84 | 3 | 49 | 93 | 9 |
| She would not have me sinking in the holy | 87 | 18 | 52 | 96 | 18 |
| The sun-leaved holy candlewoods | 95 | 19 | 58 | 105 | 19 |
| My holy lucky body | 109 | 16 | 67 | 120 | 16 |
| Her holy unholy hours with the always anonymous beast. | 114 | 23 | 69 | 126 | 23 |
| Adam or Eve, the adorned holy bullock | 130 | 10 | 77 | 144 | 10 |
| And I am struck as lonely as a holy maker by the sun. | 158 | 12 | 84 | 177 | 12 |
| And the mother and toppling house of the holy spring, | 158 | 23 | 84 | 177 | 23 |
| In the pebbles of the holy streams. | 159 | 18 | 85 | 178 | 18 |
| The country is holy: O bide in that country kind, | 163 | 16 | 86 | 182 | 16 |
| Cawing from their black bethels soaring, the holy books | 164 | 19 | 86 | 184 | 5 |
| Only for the turning of the earth in her holy | 165 | 23 | 86 | 185 | 13 |
| Crashes, and slowly the fishing holy stalking heron | 167 | 11 | 87 | 187 | 11 |
| And the black cross of the holy house, | 174 | 26 | 89 | 195 | 2 |
| Holy spring | 158 | | 84 | 177 | |
| **HOME** | | | | | |
| That shaped the Jordan near my home | 7 | 4 | 5 | 8 | 4 |
| O my lost love bounced from a good home; | 97 | 23 | 59 | 109 | 3 |
| Into the home of prayers | 120 | 11 | 72 | 132 | 16 |
| And the home of prayers and fires, the tale ended. | 122 | 30 | 72 | 136 | 10 |
| The world winding home! | 142 | 13 | 82 | 159 | 13 |
| And terribly lead him home alive | 157 | 6 | 83 | 175 | 18 |
| Lead her prodigal home to his terror, | 157 | 7 | 83 | 175 | 19 |
| He stands alone at the door of his home, | 157 | 23 | 83 | 176 | 15 |
| Alone in the husk of man's home | 158 | 22 | 84 | 177 | 22 |
| About the happy yard and singing as the farm was home, | 159 | 11 | 85 | 178 | 11 |
| **HOMES** | | | | | |
| Children from homes and children's parks | 69 | 28 | 43 | 79 | 4 |
| For the drooping of homes | 126 | 9 | 74 | 140 | 9 |

|  | U.K. | | | U.S. | |
| --- | --- | --- | --- | --- | --- |
|  | *Page* | *Line* | *Poem* | *Page* | *Line* |
| **HOMESTALL** | | | | | |
| Into a homestall king or hamlet of fire | 162 | 11 | 86 | 181 | 11 |
| **HONEY** | | | | | |
| Sour the boiling honey; | 1 | 8 | 2 | 1 | 8 |
| Their breasts full of honey, under their gander king | 177 | 18 | 90 | 198 | 17 |
| **HONEYED** | | | | | |
| To court the honeyed heart from your side before sunrise | 162 | 13 | 86 | 181 | 13 |
| **HONOUR** | | | | | |
| Descends, my masters, on the entered honour. | 19 | 3 | 12 | 22 | 8 |
| **HONOURED** | | | | | |
| And lets their trash be honoured as the quick. | 15 | 15 | 10 | 17 | 15 |
| And honoured among wagons I was prince of the apple towns | 159 | 6 | 85 | 178 | 6 |
| And honoured among foxes and pheasants by the gay house | 160 | 15 | 85 | 179 | 15 |
| **HOO** | | | | | |
| Hoo, there, in castle keep, | ix | 2 | 1 | xvii | 2 |
| **HOOD** | | | | | |
| Binding my angel's hood. | 32 | 6 | 18 | 37 | 12 |
| Cried the topless, inchtaped lips from hank and hood | 79 | 21 | 46 | 89 | 2 |
| And the owl hood, the heel hider, | 133 | 4 | 78 | 148 | 7 |
| Fear or believe that the wolf in 'a sheepwhite hood | 162 | 3 | 86 | 181 | 3 |
| For ever of all not the wolf in his baaing hood | 163 | 13 | 86 | 182 | 13 |
| **HOODED** | | | | | |
| Whose hooded, fountain heart once fell in puddles | 87 | 14 | 52 | 96 | 14 |
| The once hooded room | 139 | 13 | 82 | 156 | 13 |
| **HOOF** | | | | | |
| At a wood's dancing hoof, | vii | 8 | 1 | xv | 8 |
| **HOOK** | | | | | |
| And mouth. Both note and plume plunge from the spire's hook. | 86 | 8 | 51 | 95 | 8 |
| **HOOKING** | | | | | |
| As a bird hooking over the sea, | 149 | 7 | 83 | 166 | 7 |
| **HOOKS** | | | | | |
| A girl alive with his hooks through her lips; | 149 | 22 | 83 | 167 | 2 |
| **HOOT** | | | | | |
| Fishing in the tear of the Towy. Only a hoot owl | 169 | 3 | 87 | 189 | 12 |
| **HOOTING** | | | | | |
| In the hooting, nearly dark | ix | 8 | 1 | xvii | 8 |
| **HOOVED** | | | | | |
| As a dust of pigeons. Exulting, the grave hooved | 121 | 18 | 72 | 134 | 13 |

|  | U.K. | | | U.S. | |
|---|---|---|---|---|---|
|  | Page | Line | Poem | Page | Line |
| **HOOVES** | | | | | |
| Through the shaken greensward lake, silent, on moonshod hooves, | 165 | 13 | 86 | 185 | 3 |
| **HOP** | | | | | |
| Should he, for centre sake, hop in the dust, | 51 | 6 | 31 | 60 | 6 |
| **HOPE** | | | | | |
| Spill the lank folly's hunter and the hard-held hope. | 49 | 18 | 29 | 58 | 18 |
| **HOPHEAD'S** | | | | | |
| Smoke hill and hophead's valley, | 38 | 4 | 20 | 43 | 14 |
| **HOPPING** | | | | | |
| The puffed birds hopping and hunting, the milk-maids | 119 | 23 | 72 | 132 | 3 |
| Hopping hot leaved and feathered | 132 | 20 | 78 | 147 | 20 |
| **HORIZON** | | | | | |
| On the horizon walking like the trees | 16 | 10 | 11 | 19 | 10 |
| **HORIZONTAL** | | | | | |
| The horizontal cross-bones of Abaddon, | 71 | 21 | 44 | 80 | 21 |
| **HORN** | | | | | |
| Hell in a horn of sulphur and the cloven myth, | 40 | 16 | 22 | 46 | 16 |
| The horn and ball of water on the frog | 54 | 15 | 33 | 63 | 15 |
| Or poise the day on a horn. | 92 | 5 | 55 | 101 | 11 |
| Sang to my horn, the foxes on the hills barked clear and cold, | 159 | 16 | 85 | 178 | 16 |
| But a black sheep with a crumpled horn, | 175 | 13 | 89 | 195 | 18 |
| **HORNED** | | | | | |
| Horned down with skullfoot and the skull of toes | 72 | 9 | 44 | 81 | 9 |
| Their breast, the vaulting does roister, the horned bucks climb | 177 | 13 | 90 | 198 | 12 |
| **HORNING** | | | | | |
| Rotating halves are horning as they drill | 30 | 23 | 18 | 35 | 23 |
| **HORNS** | | | | | |
| And now the horns of England, in the sound of shape, | 49 | 13 | 29 | 58 | 13 |
| That Adam's wether in the flock of horns, | 72 | 7 | 44 | 81 | 7 |
| With its horns through mist and the castle | 103 | 8 | 63 | 114 | 8 |
| **HORNY** | | | | | |
| To-morrow's diver in her horny milk, | 30 | 4 | 18 | 35 | 4 |
| **HORRIBLE** | | | | | |
| Knew all His horrible desires | 69 | 10 | 43 | 78 | 10 |
| **HORRID** | | | | | |
| The old mud hatch again, the horrid | 96 | 19 | 58 | 107 | 2 |
| **HORSE** | | | | | |
| An air-drawn windmill on a wooden horse, | 41 | 20 | 23 | 48 | 2 |
| Shall the blind horse sing sweeter? | 77 | 2 | 45 | 86 | 2 |

|  | U.K. | | | U.S. | |
| --- | --- | --- | --- | --- | --- |
|  | *Page* | *Line* | *Poem* | *Page* | *Line* |
| Of nightingale and centaur dead horse. The springs wither | 123 | 7 | 72 | 136 | 17 |
| **HORSEBACK** | | | | | |
| Heigh, on horseback hill, jack | ix | 16 | 1 | xvii | 16 |
| **HORSEMEN** | | | | | |
| Summon your snowy horsemen, and the four-stringed hill, | 49 | 14 | 29 | 58 | 14 |
| **HORSES** | | | | | |
| Above the farms and the white horses | 102 | 13 | 63 | 113 | 13 |
| Horses, centaur dead, turn and tread the drenched white | 121 | 19 | 72 | 134 | 14 |
| She longs among horses and angels, | 150 | 9 | 83 | 167 | 13 |
| All the horses of his haul of miracles | 156 | 19 | 83 | 175 | 7 |
| Flying with the ricks, and the horses | 160 | 4 | 85 | 179 | 4 |
| In the first, spinning place, the spellbound horses walking warm | 160 | 12 | 85 | 179 | 12 |
| As horses in the foam: | 172 | 21 | 88 | 192 | 21 |
| **HORSESHOE** | | | | | |
| That melts the lionhead's heel and horseshoe of the heart, | 91 | 14 | 55 | 100 | 14 |
| With the spirits of the horseshoe bay | 172 | 2 | 88 | 192 | 2 |
| **HOSPITAL** | | | | | |
| When that immortal hospital made one more move to soothe | 158 | 3 | 84 | 177 | 3 |
| **HOST** | | | | | |
| Twelve winds encounter by the white host at pasture, | 36 | 14 | 20 | 41 | 14 |
| Nor when all ponderous heaven's host of waters breaks. | 97 | 20 | 59 | 108 | 20 |
| Blind host to sleep | 145 | 6 | 82 | 162 | 6 |
| **HOSTS** | | | | | |
| But blessed by such heroic hosts in your every | 109 | 21 | 67 | 120 | 21 |
| **HOT** | | | | | |
| Because the pleasure-bird whistles after the hot wires, | 77 | 1 | 45 | 86 | 1 |
| Shall I, struck on the hot and rocking street, | 77 | 16 | 45 | 86 | 16 |
| Hopping hot leaved and feathered | 132 | 20 | 78 | 147 | 20 |
| No springtailed tom in the red hot town | 174 | 29 | 89 | 195 | 5 |
| **HOUND** | | | | | |
| Over the vault of ridings with his hound at heel, | 49 | 5 | 29 | 58 | 5 |
| **HOUR** | | | | | |
| Over the choir minute I hear the hour chant: | 83 | 7 | 49 | 92 | 7 |
| Strike the sea hour through bellmetal. | 83 | 12 | 49 | 92 | 12 |
| And the still hour | 101 | 5 | 62 | 112 | 5 |
| Into the dead clock burning the hour | 131 | 13 | 77 | 145 | 19 |
| **HOUR'S** | | | | | |
| Tells me the hour's word, the neural meaning | 16 | 18 | 11 | 19 | 18 |

|  | U.K. | | | U.S. | |
|---|---|---|---|---|---|
|  | *Page* | *Line* | *Poem* | *Page* | *Line* |
| And all sweet hell, deaf as an hour's ear, | 57 | 5 | 34 | 66 | 12 |
| HOURGLASS | | | | | |
| When, with his torch and hourglass, like a sulphur priest, | 83 | 2 | 49 | 92 | 2 |
| HOURLESS | | | | | |
| Time in the hourless houses | 38 | 21 | 20 | 44 | 11 |
| HOURS' | | | | | |
| There grows the hours' ladder to the sun, | 27 | 1 | 16 | 32 | 6 |
| HOURS | | | | | |
| In the snivelling hours with dead, humped Ann | 87 | 13 | 52 | 96 | 13 |
| Of shades, symbol of desire beyond my hours | 110 | 7 | 67 | 121 | 9 |
| Her holy unholy hours with the always anonymous beast. | 114 | 23 | 69 | 126 | 23 |
| A child of a few hours | 129 | 5 | 77 | 143 | 5 |
| HOUSE | | | | | |
| In my seashaken house | vii | 4 | 1 | xv | 4 |
| Love in her gear is slowly through the house, | 18 | 3 | 12 | 21 | 3 |
| (Have with the house of wind), the leaning scene, | 19 | 17 | 12 | 23 | 2 |
| Green was the singing house. | 20 | 24 | 13 | 24 | 24 |
| Drip on my dead house garden. | 31 | 21 | 18 | 37 | 3 |
| The lovers' house, lie suffering my stain? | 46 | 4 | 27 | 54 | 4 |
| Shall I still be love's house on the widdershin earth, | 47 | 5 | 27 | 55 | 5 |
| Love's house, they answer, and the tower death | 47 | 7 | 27 | 55 | 7 |
| In this white house? | 58 | 8 | 35 | 67 | 8 |
| Furled on the fishes' house and hell, | 69 | 17 | 43 | 78 | 17 |
| Altarwise by owl-light in the half-way house | 71 | 1 | 44 | 80 | 1 |
| From bald pavilions and the house of bread | 75 | 2 | 44 | 84 | 2 |
| And this weak house to marrow-columned heaven, | 78 | 8 | 46 | 87 | 8 |
| Cathedral calm in the pulled house; | 83 | 15 | 49 | 92 | 15 |
| In a fiercely mourning house in a crooked year. | 88 | 2 | 52 | 97 | 2 |
| Of his father's house in the sands, | 95 | 7 | 58 | 105 | 7 |
| O wake in me in my house in the mud | 96 | 1 | 58 | 106 | 1 |
| From an odd room in a split house stare, | 96 | 6 | 58 | 106 | 6 |
| Rage me back to the making house. My hand unravel | 97 | 12 | 59 | 108 | 12 |
| Has a voice and a house, and there and here you must couch and cry. | 98 | 2 | 59 | 109 | 5 |
| To share my room in the house not right in the head, | 108 | 2 | 66 | 119 | 2 |
| She deludes the heaven-proof house with entering clouds | 108 | 6 | 66 | 119 | 6 |
| Flocked with the sheep white smoke of the farm house cowl | 119 | 9 | 72 | 131 | 9 |

|  | U.K. | | | U.S. | |
| --- | --- | --- | --- | --- | --- |
|  | *Page* | *Line* | *Poem* | *Page* | *Line* |
| Torn and alone in a farm house in a fold | 119 | 15 | 72 | 131 | 15 |
| In the muffled house, in the quick of night, | 120 | 4 | 72 | 132 | 9 |
| Was flying through the house as though the she bird praised | 122 | 3 | 72 | 135 | 3 |
| Carrying cloud, death strikes their house. | 124 | 8 | 73 | 138 | 8 |
| Ride through the doors of our unentered house. | 126 | 14 | 74 | 140 | 14 |
| Out of the house that holds a town | 154 | 23 | 83 | 173 | 3 |
| The furious ox-killing house of love. | 157 | 8 | 83 | 175 | 20 |
| And the mother and toppling house of the holy spring, | 158 | 23 | 84 | 177 | 23 |
| About the lilting house and happy as the grass was green, | 159 | 2 | 85 | 178 | 2 |
| Fields high as the house, the tunes from the chimneys, it was air | 159 | 20 | 85 | 178 | 20 |
| And honoured among foxes and pheasants by the gay house | 160 | 15 | 85 | 179 | 15 |
| My wishes raced through the house high hay | 160 | 19 | 85 | 179 | 19 |
| To eat your heart in the house in the rosy wood. | 162 | 7 | 86 | 181 | 7 |
| Lie in grace. Sleep spelled at rest in the lowly house | 163 | 20 | 86 | 183 | 1 |
| Eyed, in the haloed house, in her rareness and hilly | 165 | 18 | 86 | 185 | 8 |
| In his house on stilts high among beaks | 170 | 4 | 88 | 190 | 4 |
| In his slant, racking house | 170 | 25 | 88 | 190 | 25 |
| And the black cross of the holy house, | 174 | 26 | 89 | 195 | 2 |
| Who once were a bloom of wayside brides in the hawed house | 177 | 9 | 90 | 198 | 8 |
| In the muted house, one minute before |  |  | 91 | 200 | 14 |
| The sticks of the house were his; his books he owned. |  |  | 91 | 201 | 4 |
| HOUSED |  |  |  |  |  |
| Housed in the side. | 54 | 16 | 33 | 63 | 16 |
| HOUSES |  |  |  |  |  |
| Time in the hourless houses | 38 | 21 | 20 | 44 | 11 |
| And swept into our wounds and houses, | 158 | 7 | 84 | 177 | 7 |
| They from houses where the harvest kneels, hold me hard, | 178 | 9 | 90 | 199 | 10 |
| HOVEL |  |  |  |  |  |
| Over the sun's hovel and the slum of fire | 131 | 16 | 77 | 145 | 22 |
| HOW |  |  |  |  |  |
| How I, a spinning man, | viii | 13 | 1 | xvi | 13 |
| How of my clay is made the hangman's lime. | 9 | 15 | 6 | 10 | 15 |
| How time has tickled a heaven round the stars. | 9 | 20 | 6 | 10 | 20 |
| How at my sheet goes the same crooked worm. | 9 | 22 | 6 | 10 | 22 |
| How at the mountain spring the same mouth sucks. | 9 | 10 | 6 | 10 | 10 |
| How light the sleeping on this soily star, | 26 | 24 | 16 | 32 | 4 |

|  | U.K. | | | U.S. | |
| --- | --- | --- | --- | --- | --- |
|  | Page | Line | Poem | Page | Line |
| How deep the waking in the worlded clouds. | 26 | 25 | 16 | 32 | 5 |
| How now my flesh, my naked fellow, | 33 | 7 | 19 | 38 | 7 |
| How much was happy while it lasted, | 48 | 20 | 28 | 56 | 20 |
| How soon the servant sun, | 56 | 1 | 34 | 65 | 1 |
| How soon my level, lord, | 56 | 22 | 34 | 66 | 1 |
| 'See,' drummed the taut masks, 'how the dead ascend: | 79 | 26 | 46 | 89 | 7 |
| How, through the halfmoon's vegetable eye, | 81 | 3 | 47 | 90 | 3 |
| How shall my animal | 91 | 1 | 55 | 100 | 1 |
| How shall it magnetize, | 91 | 12 | 55 | 100 | 12 |
| Good men, the last wave by, crying how bright | 116 | 7 | 70 | 128 | 7 |
| Sing how the seal has kissed her dead! | 152 | 10 | 83 | 170 | 2 |
| Taller this thunderclap spring, and how | 173 | 22 | 88 | 193 | 22 |
| How soon the servant sun | 56 | | 34 | 65 | |
| How shall my animal | 91 | | 55 | 100 | |

HOWL

| Sing and howl through sand and anemone | 152 | 17 | 83 | 170 | 9 |

HOWLING

| Queen Catherine howling bare | 113 | 12 | 69 | 125 | 12 |
| May his hunger go howling on bare white bones | 120 | 8 | 72 | 132 | 13 |
| His naked need struck him howling and bowed | 120 | 14 | 72 | 132 | 19 |

HOWLS

| Be said to weep when weather howls? | 44 | 3 | 25 | 52 | 3 |
| Howls the foul fiend to heel. | 66 | 5 | 40 | 75 | 5 |

HUBBUB

| Hubbub and fiddle, this tune | ix | 21 | 1 | xvii | 21 |

HUG

| I hug to love with my unruly scrawl | 10 | 8 | 7 | 11 | 8 |

HUGE

| Proud as a sucked stone and huge as sandgrains. | 78 | 23 | 46 | 87 | 23 |
| Huge weddings in the waves, | 151 | 24 | 83 | 169 | 12 |

HUGGED

| Hugged, and barren and bare on Mother Goose's ground | 178 | 2 | 90 | 199 | 3 |

HULK

| His sea-sucked Adam in the hollow hulk, | 30 | 2 | 18 | 35 | 2 |
| And the moon swam out of its hulk. | 149 | 16 | 83 | 166 | 16 |

HULKS

| To death, one man through his sundered hulks, | 173 | 11 | 88 | 193 | 11 |

HULLABALLOING

| Ho, hullaballoing clan | ix | 13 | 1 | xvii | 13 |

HULOO

| Huloo, on plumbed bryns, | ix | 6 | 1 | xvii | 6 |
| Huloo, my prowed dove with a flute! | x | 14 | 1 | xviii | 20 |

HUMAN

| That bridged the human halves, | 67 | 26 | 41 | 76 | 26 |

|  | U.K. | | | U.S. | |
| --- | --- | --- | --- | --- | --- |
|  | *Page* | *Line* | *Poem* | *Page* | *Line* |
| HUMBLE |  |  |  |  |  |
| May a humble village labour | 43 | 1 | 24 | 50 | 8 |
| May a humble planet labour | 43 | 8 | 24 | 50 | 15 |
| I know her scrubbed and sour humble hands | 88 | 3 | 52 | 97 | 3 |
| HUMBLING |  |  |  |  |  |
| Fathering and all humbling darkness | 101 | 3 | 62 | 112 | 3 |
| HUMOURED |  |  |  |  |  |
| They said, who hacked and humoured, they were mine. | 46 | 20 | 27 | 54 | 20 |
| HUMP |  |  |  |  |  |
| Button your bodice on a hump of splinters, | 73 | 5 | 44 | 82 | 5 |
| HUMPBACKED |  |  |  |  |  |
| Slipped the fins of those humpbacked tons | 151 | 4 | 83 | 168 | 12 |
| HUMPED |  |  |  |  |  |
| In the snivelling hours with dead, humped Ann | 87 | 13 | 52 | 96 | 13 |
| HUNCHBACK |  |  |  |  |  |
| The hunchback in the park | 111 | 1 | 68 | 123 | 1 |
| Had followed the hunchback | 112 | 17 | 68 | 124 | 17 |
| The Hunchback in the Park | 111 |  | 68 | 123 |  |
| HUNCHBACKED |  |  |  |  |  |
| Hunchbacked in mockery | 111 | 21 | 68 | 123 | 21 |
| HUNCHBACKS |  |  |  |  |  |
| (Questions are hunchbacks to the poker marrow). | 73 | 2 | 44 | 82 | 2 |
| HUNDRED |  |  |  |  |  |
| Dissolved in summer and the hundred seasons; | 21 | 25 | 13 | 26 | 8 |
| Of many a hundred falls; | 53 | 5 | 32 | 62 | 5 |
| Rode and whistled a hundred times | 113 | 18 | 69 | 125 | 18 |
| And a hundred storks perch on the sun's right hand. | 135 | 14 | 80 | 152 | 14 |
| Among those Killed in the Dawn Raid was a Man Aged a Hundred | 135 |  | 80 | 152 |  |
| HUNG |  |  |  |  |  |
| His scissors oiled, his knife hung loose | 11 | 10 | 8 | 12 | 10 |
| And darkness hung the walls with baskets of snakes, | 114 | 4 | 69 | 126 | 4 |
| Birdman or told ghost I hung. | 133 | 3 | 78 | 148 | 6 |
| HUNGER |  |  |  |  |  |
| My heart knew love, my belly hunger; | 8 | 5 | 5 | 9 | 5 |
| That utters all love hunger | 10 | 9 | 7 | 11 | 9 |
| Happy Cadaver's hunger as you take | 19 | 24 | 12 | 23 | 9 |
| And to the voice that, like a voice of hunger, | 21 | 5 | 13 | 25 | 5 |
| 'The thirst is quenched, the hunger gone, | 65 | 17 | 40 | 74 | 17 |
| Under the milky mushrooms slew my hunger, | 73 | 18 | 44 | 82 | 18 |
| In a land strapped by hunger | 90 | 4 | 54 | 99 | 4 |
| May his hunger go howling on bare white bones | 120 | 8 | 72 | 132 | 13 |

# HUNGER (continued)

|  | U.K. Page | U.K. Line | Poem | U.S. Page | U.S. Line |
|---|---|---|---|---|---|
| Hunger of birds in the fields of the bread of water, | 120 | 17 | 72 | 133 | 2 |
| HUNGER'S |  |  |  |  |  |
| And the hunger's emperor; | 10 | 19 | 7 | 11 | 19 |
| HUNGERING |  |  |  |  |  |
| Streets or hungering in the crumbled wood: to these | 178 | 16 | 90 | 199 | 17 |
| HUNGERS |  |  |  |  |  |
| If I were tickled by the urchin hungers | 12 | 18 | 9 | 13 | 18 |
| HUNGRILY |  |  |  |  |  |
| To take to give is all, return what is hungrily given | 94 | 4 | 57 | 104 | 4 |
| HUNGRY |  |  |  |  |  |
| Sang heaven hungry and the quick | 95 | 15 | 58 | 105 | 15 |
| But the hungry kings of the tides; | 153 | 13 | 83 | 171 | 9 |
| HUNTER |  |  |  |  |  |
| Spill the lank folly's hunter and the hard-held hope. | 49 | 18 | 29 | 58 | 18 |
| HUNTING |  |  |  |  |  |
| The puffed birds hopping and hunting, the milkmaids | 119 | 23 | 72 | 132 | 3 |
| And his loin was a hunting flame | 157 | 4 | 83 | 175 | 16 |
| HUNTSMAN |  |  |  |  |  |
| And green and golden I was huntsman and herdsman, the calves | 159 | 15 | 85 | 178 | 15 |
| HURDLES |  |  |  |  |  |
| Hurdles and guns and railings, as the boulders heave, | 49 | 16 | 29 | 58 | 16 |
| HURLED |  |  |  |  |  |
| By the believer lost and the hurled outcast of light. | 120 | 25 | 72 | 133 | 10 |
| HURLING |  |  |  |  |  |
| Hurling into beginning like Christ the child. | 110 | 24 | 67 | 122 | 2 |
| HURRIED |  |  |  |  |  |
| I who saw in a hurried film | 93 | 21 | 56 | 103 | 1 |
| HURRIES |  |  |  |  |  |
| The grain that hurries this way from the rim of the grave | 98 | 1 | 59 | 109 | 4 |
| HURRY |  |  |  |  |  |
| When cameras shut they hurry to their hole | 14 | 15 | 10 | 16 | 15 |
| Sounds with the grains as they hurry | 82 | 15 | 48 | 91 | 15 |
| HURT |  |  |  |  |  |
| 'Nor the green nought be hurt; | 70 | 17 | 43 | 79 | 21 |
| 'If my head hurt a hair's foot | 97 | 1 | 59 | 108 | 1 |
| When hindering man hurt | 125 | 12 | 74 | 139 | 12 |
| 'If my head hurt a hair's foot' | 97 |  | 59 | 108 |  |

|  | U.K. | | | U.S. | |
| --- | --- | --- | --- | --- | --- |
|  | *Page* | *Line* | *Poem* | *Page* | *Line* |
| **HUSK** | | | | | |
| Husk of young stars and handfull zodiac, | 81 | 4 | 47 | 90 | 4 |
| Seed of sons in the loin of the black husk left. | 130 | 8 | 77 | 144 | 8 |
| Alone in the husk of man's home | 158 | 22 | 84 | 177 | 22 |
| **HUSKED** | | | | | |
| 'Now to awake husked of gestures and my joy like a cave | 97 | 21 | 59 | 109 | 1 |
| **HYENA** | | | | | |
| Nightingale and hyena | 152 | 15 | 83 | 170 | 7 |
| **HYLEG** | | | | | |
| And all love's sinners in sweet cloth kneel to a hyleg image, | 84 | 4 | 49 | 93 | 10 |
| **HYMNED** | | | | | |
| Hymned his shrivelling flock, | 95 | 13 | 58 | 105 | 13 |
| And the wings glided wide and he was hymned and wedded, | 123 | 13 | 72 | 137 | 3 |
| **HYMNING** | | | | | |
| Babble like a bellbuoy over the hymning heads, | 87 | 23 | 52 | 96 | 23 |
| Of eels, saint heron hymning in the shell-hung distant | 168 | 12 | 87 | 188 | 16 |

# ENTRIES UNDER I

| **ICE** | | | | | |
| --- | --- | --- | --- | --- | --- |
| O see the pulse of summer in the ice. | 1 | 24 | 2 | 1 | 24 |
| Where once the mermen through your ice | 11 | 4 | 8 | 12 | 4 |
| I, that time's jacket or the coat of ice | 18 | 18 | 12 | 21 | 18 |
| Stage of the ice, the solid ocean, | 33 | 2 | 19 | 38 | 2 |
| Calls the starved fire herd, is cast in ice, | 79 | 1 | 46 | 88 | 4 |
| Once where the soft snow's blood was turned to ice. | 80 | 12 | 46 | 89 | 20 |
| With fuming bows and ram of ice, | 150 | 18 | 83 | 168 | 2 |
| And prince of ice | 162 | 12 | 86 | 181 | 12 |
| Hill. Who once in gooseskin winter loved all ice leaved | 176 | 12 | 90 | 197 | 12 |
| **ICEBERG'S** | | | | | |
| Corrosive spring out of the iceberg's crop, | 30 | 8 | 18 | 35 | 8 |
| **ICICLE** | | | | | |
| Into a polestar pointed on an icicle. | 60 | 6 | 36 | 69 | 6 |
| On rose and icicle the ringing handprint. | 75 | 4 | 44 | 84 | 4 |
| **IDIOM** | | | | | |
| Into the stony idiom of the brain, | 21 | 9 | 13 | 25 | 9 |
| **IDOL** | | | | | |
| I was pierced by the idol tailor's eyes, | 133 | 10 | 78 | 148 | 13 |

|  | U.K. Page | Line | Poem | U.S. Page | Line |
|---|---|---|---|---|---|
| **IF** | | | | | |
| If I were tickled by the rub of love, | 12 | 1 | 9 | 13 | 1 |
| If the red tickle as the cattle calve | 12 | 4 | 9 | 13 | 4 |
| If I were tickled by the hatching hair, | 12 | 10 | 9 | 13 | 10 |
| If I were tickled by the urchin hungers | 12 | 18 | 9 | 13 | 18 |
| If I were tickled by the lovers' rub | 12 | 22 | 9 | 14 | 1 |
| Tell, if at all, the winter's storms | 45 | 10 | 26 | 53 | 10 |
| What shall it tell me if a timeless insect | 45 | 16 | 26 | 53 | 16 |
| If not of loving well, then not, | 48 | 8 | 28 | 56 | 8 |
| If the dead starve, their stomachs turn to tumble | 77 | 22 | 45 | 86 | 22 |
| If I take to burn or return this world which is each man's work. | 94 | 12 | 57 | 104 | 12 |
| 'If my head hurt a hair's foot | 97 | 1 | 59 | 108 | 1 |
| Pack back the downed bone. If the unpricked ball of my breath | 97 | 2 | 59 | 108 | 2 |
| 'If my bunched, monkey coming is cruel | 97 | 11 | 59 | 108 | 11 |
| Bend, if my journey ache, direction like an arc or make | 97 | 14 | 59 | 108 | 14 |
| Both shall fail if I bow not to your blessing | 110 | 19 | 67 | 121 | 21 |
| If only for a last time. | 158 | 24 | 84 | 177 | 24 |
| If I were tickled by the rub of love | 12 | | 9 | 13 | |
| 'If my head hurt a hair's foot' | 97 | | 59 | 108 | |
| **ILL** | | | | | |
| And tells the page the empty ill. | 10 | 10 | 7 | 11 | 10 |
| Than bully ill love in the clouted scene. | 97 | 5 | 59 | 108 | 5 |
| **ILLS** | | | | | |
| And cure me of ills. | 48 | 23 | 28 | 56 | 23 |
| Should cure our ills of the water | 82 | 12 | 48 | 91 | 12 |
| On whom a world of ills came down like snow. | | | 91 | 201 | 11 |
| **ILLUMINATION** | | | | | |
| Illumination of music! the lulled black-backed | 165 | 11 | 86 | 185 | 1 |
| **IMAGE** | | | | | |
| The image from the plates; | 15 | 19 | 10 | 17 | 19 |
| I, in my intricate image, stride on two levels, | 35 | 1 | 20 | 40 | 1 |
| Image of images, my metal phantom | 35 | 14 | 20 | 40 | 14 |
| Brass and the bodiless image, on a stick of folly | 38 | 2 | 20 | 43 | 12 |
| Love's image till my heartbone breaks | 70 | 7 | 43 | 79 | 11 |
| Spot the blown word, and on the seas I image | 76 | 13 | 44 | 85 | 13 |
| And all love's sinners in sweet cloth kneel to a hyleg image, | 84 | 4 | 49 | 93 | 10 |
| (Though this for her is a monstrous image blindly | 87 | 16 | 52 | 96 | 16 |
| I, in my intricate image | 35 | | 20 | 40 | |
| **IMAGES** | | | | | |
| Image of images, my metal phantom | 35 | 14 | 20 | 40 | 14 |

|  | U.K. | | | U.S. | |
|---|---|---|---|---|---|
|  | Page | Line | Poem | Page | Line |
| My images stalk the trees and the slant sap's tunnel, | 36 | 1 | 20 | 41 | 1 |
| And my images roared and rose on heaven's hill. | 38 | 30 | 20 | 44 | 20 |
| IMAGINARY |  |  |  |  |  |
| Early imaginary half remembered | 114 | 9 | 69 | 126 | 9 |
| IMAGINED |  |  |  |  |  |
| Or rides the imagined oceans of the male wards. | 108 | 9 | 66 | 119 | 9 |
| IMMEMORIAL |  |  |  |  |  |
| And immemorial sons of the cudgelling, hacked | 176 | 11 | 90 | 197 | 11 |
| IMMORTAL |  |  |  |  |  |
| Of the living flesh is monstrous or immortal, | 110 | 13 | 67 | 121 | 15 |
| Of your immortal friends | 117 | 6 | 71 | 129 | 6 |
| When that immortal hospital made one more move to soothe | 158 | 3 | 84 | 177 | 3 |
| IMMORTALITY |  |  |  |  |  |
| With immortality at my side like Christ the sky. | 110 | 21 | 67 | 121 | 23 |
| IMPOSE |  |  |  |  |  |
| Impose their shots, throwing the nights away; | 14 | 18 | 10 | 16 | 18 |
| IMPRINTS |  |  |  |  |  |
| And after came the imprints on the water, | 22 | 9 | 14 | 27 | 9 |
| INCARNATE |  |  |  |  |  |
| Incarnate devil in a talking snake, | 40 | 1 | 22 | 46 | 1 |
| Incarnate devil | 40 |  | 22 | 46 |  |
| INCENDIARY |  |  |  |  |  |
| On almost the incendiary eve | 117 | 1 | 71 | 129 | 1 |
| On almost the incendiary eve | 117 | 13 | 71 | 129 | 13 |
| On almost the incendiary eve | 117 | 25 | 71 | 130 | 1 |
| INCESTUOUS |  |  |  |  |  |
| With the incestuous secret brother in the seconds to perpetuate the stars, | 115 | 20 | 69 | 127 | 20 |
| INCH |  |  |  |  |  |
| Of the bone inch, | 18 | 10 | 12 | 21 | 10 |
| And a green inch be his bearer; | 43 | 4 | 24 | 50 | 11 |
| And the velvet dead inch out. | 56 | 21 | 34 | 65 | 21 |
| An inch in froth. Chimes cheat the prison spire, pelter | 86 | 5 | 51 | 95 | 5 |
| Inch and glance that the wound | 109 | 22 | 67 | 120 | 22 |
| In your every inch and glance is the globe of genesis spun, | 110 | 27 | 67 | 122 | 5 |
| INCHES |  |  |  |  |  |
| The inches monkeyed by the blood of man. | 27 | 3 | 16 | 32 | 8 |
| INCHTAPED |  |  |  |  |  |
| Cried the topless, inchtaped lips from hank and hood | 79 | 21 | 46 | 89 | 2 |
| INCISING |  |  |  |  |  |
| Incising summer. | 31 | 9 | 18 | 36 | 9 |

247

# INDEX

|  | U.K. | | | U.S. | |
|  | Page | Line | Poem | Page | Line |
|---|---|---|---|---|---|
| **INDEX** | | | | | |
| Spelt out the seven seas, an evil index, | 74 | 12 | 44 | 83 | 12 |
| **INFANCY** | | | | | |
| And the twice told fields of infancy | 103 | 26 | 63 | 115 | 1 |
| **INFANT** | | | | | |
| To the anguish and carrion, to the infant forever unfree, | 97 | 22 | 59 | 109 | 2 |
| Infant light or | 144 | 12 | 82 | 161 | 12 |
| **INFANT-BEARING** | | | | | |
| The masses of the infant-bearing sea | 131 | 22 | 77 | 146 | 4 |
| **INFANTS** | | | | | |
| Over the dead infants | 130 | 26 | 77 | 145 | 4 |
| Sun the father his quiver full of the infants of pure fire, | 158 | 19 | 84 | 177 | 19 |
| **INHALE** | | | | | |
| Let her inhale her dead, through seed and solid | 55 | 10 | 33 | 64 | 13 |
| **INHOSPITABLE** | | | | | |
| To this inhospitable hollow year, | 126 | 3 | 74 | 140 | 3 |
| **INHUMAN** | | | | | |
| Inhuman cradle and the bride bed forever sought | 120 | 24 | 72 | 133 | 9 |
| **INMOST** | | | | | |
| The inmost marrow of my heart bone | 143 | 17 | 82 | 160 | 17 |
| **INNOCENCE** | | | | | |
| She makes for me a nettle's innocence | 78 | 16 | 46 | 87 | 16 |
| Elegy of innocence and youth. | 101 | 18 | 62 | 112 | 18 |
| Of innocence and guilt | 105 | 7 | 64 | 116 | 7 |
| Along her innocence glided | 113 | 10 | 69 | 125 | 10 |
| Innocence sweetens my last black breath, | 175 | 29 | 89 | 196 | 10 |
| **INNOCENT** | | | | | |
| Through the devilish years and innocent deaths | 93 | 14 | 56 | 102 | 14 |
| Into the innocent | 105 | 20 | 64 | 116 | 20 |
| And the wild boys innocent as strawberries | 112 | 16 | 68 | 124 | 16 |
| Innocent between two wars, | 115 | 19 | 69 | 127 | 19 |
| Nor the innocent lie in the rooting dingle wooed | 162 | 15 | 86 | 181 | 15 |
| Being innocent, he dreaded that he died | | | 91 | 201 | 1 |
| **INSECT** | | | | | |
| I with the wooden insect in the tree of nettles, | 36 | 4 | 20 | 41 | 4 |
| To-day, this insect, and the world I breathe, | 41 | 1 | 23 | 47 | 1 |
| The insect certain is the plague of fables. | 41 | 9 | 23 | 47 | 9 |
| The insect fable is the certain promise. | 41 | 18 | 23 | 47 | 18 |
| What shall it tell me if a timeless insect | 45 | 16 | 26 | 53 | 16 |
| Shakes, in crabbed burial shawl, by sorcerer's insect woken, | 83 | 23 | 49 | 93 | 5 |
| To-day, this insect | 41 | | 23 | 47 | |

|  | U.K. | | | U.S. | |
|  | Page | Line | Poem | Page | Line |
|---|---|---|---|---|---|
| INSECT-FACED | | | | | |
| Dry as echoes and insect-faced, | 155 | 2 | 83 | 173 | 6 |
| INSECTS | | | | | |
| Insects and valleys hold her thighs hard, | 156 | 6 | 83 | 174 | 14 |
| INSTRUMENT | | | | | |
| The sea and instrument, nicked in the locks of time, | 38 | 14 | 20 | 44 | 4 |
| INSTRUMENTAL | | | | | |
| (Death instrumental, | 36 | 25 | 20 | 42 | 4 |
| INSTRUMENTS | | | | | |
| Hands or instruments | 147 | 6 | 82 | 164 | 6 |
| INTERPRETED | | | | | |
| In the interpreted evening | 147 | 17 | 82 | 164 | 17 |
| INTIMACIES | | | | | |
| The colossal intimacies of silent | 113 | 14 | 69 | 125 | 14 |
| INTO | | | | | |
| Into the dogdayed night. | viii | 7 | I | xvi | 7 |
| Into a chiming quarter | 2 | 2 | 2 | 2 | 2 |
| A process blows the moon into the sun, | 6 | 22 | 4 | 7 | 4 |
| Did twist into a living cipher, | 7 | 21 | 5 | 8 | 21 |
| Into the tided cord, there goes | 11 | 8 | 8 | 12 | 8 |
| Each golden grain spat life into its fellow, | 20 | 23 | 13 | 24 | 23 |
| Into the sided lap of light grew strong, | 21 | 3 | 13 | 25 | 3 |
| Into the stony idiom of the brain, | 21 | 9 | 13 | 25 | 9 |
| The two-framed globe that spun into a score; | 21 | 21 | 13 | 26 | 4 |
| The country-handed grave boxed into love, | 55 | 4 | 33 | 64 | 7 |
| He'll trumpet into meat), | 56 | 5 | 34 | 65 | 5 |
| Into a polestar pointed on an icicle. | 60 | 6 | 36 | 69 | 6 |
| Goes over the hill into the deep sea; | 64 | 5 | 39 | 73 | 5 |
| And, crackling into the air, leave me half-blind. | 64 | 14 | 39 | 73 | 14 |
| No third eye probe into a rainbow's sex | 67 | 25 | 41 | 76 | 25 |
| Bullies into rough seas you so gentle | 96 | 24 | 58 | 107 | 7 |
| Into the answering skies from the green ground, | 100 | 7 | 61 | 111 | 7 |
| Into the winding dark | 105 | 11 | 64 | 116 | 11 |
| Into the innocent | 105 | 20 | 64 | 116 | 20 |
| Hurling into beginning like Christ the child. | 110 | 24 | 67 | 122 | 2 |
| Into her lying down head | 113 | 1 | 69 | 125 | 1 |
| Do not go gentle into that good night, | 116 | 1 | 70 | 128 | 1 |
| Do not go gentle into that good night. | 116 | 6 | 70 | 128 | 6 |
| Do not go gentle into that good night. | 116 | 12 | 70 | 128 | 12 |
| Do not go gentle into that good night. | 116 | 18 | 70 | 128 | 18 |
| Into the home of prayers | 120 | 11 | 72 | 132 | 16 |
| The windows pour into their heart | 124 | 11 | 73 | 138 | 11 |
| Darkness kindled back into beginning | 129 | 12 | 77 | 143 | 12 |
| Into the centuries of the child | 129 | 15 | 77 | 143 | 15 |
| Into the organpipes and steeples | 131 | 9 | 77 | 145 | 15 |
| Into the weathercocks' molten mouths | 131 | 11 | 77 | 145 | 17 |

|  | U.K. | | | U.S. | |
| --- | --- | --- | --- | --- | --- |
|  | Page | Line | Poem | Page | Line |
| Into the dead clock burning the hour | 131 | 13 | 77 | 145 | 19 |
| Into the bread in a wheatfield of flames, | 131 | 18 | 77 | 145 | 24 |
| Into the wine burning like brandy, | 131 | 19 | 77 | 146 | 1 |
| He sped into the drinking dark; | 149 | 14 | 83 | 166 | 14 |
| The octopus walking into her limbs | 152 | 7 | 83 | 169 | 19 |
| The boat swims into the six-year weather, | 154 | 9 | 83 | 172 | 9 |
| And into its talkative seven tombs | 157 | 19 | 83 | 176 | 11 |
| And swept into our wounds and houses, | 158 | 7 | 84 | 177 | 7 |
| Flashing into the dark. | 160 | 5 | 85 | 179 | 5 |
| Into a homestall king or hamlet of fire | 162 | 11 | 86 | 181 | 11 |
| Earth, air, water, fire, singing into the white act, | 165 | 16 | 86 | 185 | 6 |
| And I shoved it into the coal black sky | 175 | 18 | 89 | 195 | 23 |
| Into her Lying Down Head | 113 | | 69 | 125 | |
| Do not go gentle into that good night | 116 | | 70 | 128 | |
| **INTRICATE** | | | | | |
| I, in my intricate image, stride on two levels, | 35 | 1 | 20 | 40 | 1 |
| Intricate manhood of ending, the invalid rivals, | 36 | 7 | 20 | 41 | 7 |
| This was the god of beginning in the intricate seawhirl, | 38 | 29 | 20 | 44 | 19 |
| I, in my intricate image | 35 | | 20 | 40 | |
| **INTRICATELY** | | | | | |
| Time sings through the intricately dead snow drop. Listen. | 121 | 10 | 72 | 134 | 5 |
| **INVALID** | | | | | |
| Intricate manhood of ending, the invalid rivals, | 36 | 7 | 20 | 41 | 7 |
| **INVISIBLE** | | | | | |
| Invisible, your clocking tides | 11 | 13 | 8 | 12 | 13 |
| Invisible on the stump | 56 | 28 | 34 | 66 | 7 |
| **INVOKED** | | | | | |
| The invoked, shrouding veil at the cap of the face, | 91 | 5 | 55 | 100 | 5 |
| **INWARD** | | | | | |
| This inward sir, | 57 | 2 | 34 | 66 | 9 |
| **IRIS** | | | | | |
| His golden yesterday asleep upon the iris | 127 | 3 | 75 | 141 | 3 |
| **IRISH** | | | | | |
| Greek in the Irish sea the ageless voice: | 41 | 22 | 23 | 48 | 4 |
| **IRON** | | | | | |
| Green of the seaweed's iron, | 2 | 14 | 2 | 2 | 14 |
| Thrusting the tom-thumb vision up the iron mile. | 38 | 6 | 20 | 43 | 16 |
| My great blood's iron single | 38 | 15 | 20 | 44 | 5 |
| A chrysalis unwrinkling on the iron, | 54 | 10 | 33 | 63 | 10 |
| And a stranger enter like iron. | 96 | 22 | 58 | 107 | 5 |
| My dear would I change my tears on your iron head. | 97 | 18 | 59 | 108 | 18 |

|  | U.K. | | | U.S. | |
|---|---|---|---|---|---|
|  | *Page* | *Line* | *Poem* | *Page* | *Line* |
| IRONS | | | | | |
| Through all the irons in the grass, metal | 28 | 7 | 17 | 33 | 7 |
| ISHMAEL'S | | | | | |
| For loss of blood I fell on Ishmael's plain, | 73 | 17 | 44 | 82 | 17 |
| ISLAND | | | | | |
| Beyond this island bound | 58 | 10 | 35 | 67 | 10 |
| Ears in this island hear | 58 | 17 | 35 | 67 | 17 |
| Eyes in this island see | 58 | 19 | 35 | 67 | 19 |
| A thundering bullring of your silent and girl-circled island. | 96 | 26 | 58 | 107 | 9 |
| Man was the burning England she was sleep-walking, and the enamouring island | 113 | 20 | 69 | 125 | 20 |
| In his firelit island ringed by the winged snow | 119 | 17 | 72 | 131 | 17 |
| ISLAND'S | | | | | |
| Disturbs this island's rest. | 58 | 16 | 35 | 67 | 16 |
| ISLANDS | | | | | |
| Like wooden islands, hill to hill. | x | 13 | 1 | xviii | 19 |
| And the renouncing of islands. | 110 | 11 | 67 | 121 | 13 |
| I drew the white sheet over the islands | 134 | 29 | 79 | 151 | 7 |
| Milled dust of the apple tree and the pounded islands | 164 | 10 | 86 | 183 | 17 |
| The mansouled fiery islands! Oh, | 173 | 24 | 88 | 193 | 24 |
| ISSUE | | | | | |
| All issue armoured, of the grave, | 4 | 19 | 3 | 4 | 19 |
| One breast gave suck the fever's issue; | 21 | 19 | 13 | 26 | 2 |
| IT | | | | | |
| Shall it be male or female? say the cells, | 12 | 8 | 9 | 13 | 8 |
| Shall it be male or female? say the fingers | 12 | 15 | 9 | 13 | 15 |
| The sea of scums could drown me as it broke | 12 | 27 | 9 | 14 | 6 |
| The fellow half was frozen as it bubbled | 30 | 7 | 18 | 35 | 7 |
| The fellow seed and shadow as it babbled | 30 | 9 | 18 | 35 | 9 |
| And when the moon rose windily it was | 40 | 11 | 22 | 46 | 11 |
| When it is rain where are the gods? | 44 | 5 | 25 | 52 | 5 |
| Shall it be said they sprinkle water | 44 | 6 | 25 | 52 | 6 |
| Shall it be said that, venuswise, | 44 | 8 | 25 | 52 | 8 |
| It shall be said that gods are stone. | 44 | 11 | 25 | 52 | 11 |
| What shall it tell me if a timeless insect | 45 | 16 | 26 | 53 | 16 |
| How much was happy while it lasted, | 48 | 20 | 28 | 56 | 20 |
| And, when it quickens, alter the actions' pace | 63 | 12 | 38 | 72 | 12 |
| It is the sinners' dust-tongued bell claps me to churches | 83 | 1 | 49 | 92 | 1 |
| Forever it is a white child in the dark-skinned summer | 83 | 19 | 49 | 93 | 1 |
| From the stone nest it does not let the feathery | 86 | 2 | 51 | 95 | 2 |
| Once it was the colour of saying | 89 | 1 | 53 | 98 | 1 |
| How shall it magnetize, | 91 | 12 | 55 | 100 | 12 |
| Among men later I heard it said | 93 | 16 | 56 | 102 | 16 |

| | U.K. | | | U.S. | |
|---|---|---|---|---|---|
| | Page | Line | Poem | Page | Line |
| It was my thirtieth year to heaven | 102 | 1 | 63 | 113 | 1 |
| It turned away from the blithe country | 103 | 16 | 63 | 114 | 16 |
| It was my thirtieth | 104 | 13 | 63 | 115 | 15 |
| And learn, too late, they grieved it on its way, | 116 | 11 | 70 | 128 | 11 |
| It is a winter's tale | 119 | 1 | 72 | 131 | 1 |
| It was a hand or sound | 121 | 11 | 72 | 134 | 6 |
| May hold it in a great flood | 129 | 20 | 77 | 143 | 20 |
| It was sweet to drown in the readymade handy water | 133 | 16 | 78 | 148 | 19 |
| It were a wand or subtle bough, | 134 | 14 | 79 | 150 | 14 |
| But let it break | 145 | 12 | 82 | 162 | 12 |
| A wind throws a shadow and it freezes fast. | 154 | 10 | 83 | 172 | 10 |
| That uncalm still it is sure alone to stand and sing | 158 | 21 | 84 | 177 | 21 |
| All the sun long it was running, it was lovely, the hay | 159 | 19 | 85 | 178 | 19 |
| Fields high as the house, the tunes from the chimneys, it was air | 159 | 20 | 85 | 178 | 20 |
| With the dew, come back, the cock on his shoulder: it was all | 160 | 7 | 85 | 179 | 7 |
| Shining, it was Adam and maiden, | 160 | 8 | 85 | 179 | 8 |
| So it must have been after the birth of the simple light | 160 | 11 | 85 | 179 | 11 |
| It is the heron and I, under judging Sir John's elmed | 168 | 16 | 87 | 189 | 1 |
| And I shoved it into the coal black sky | 175 | 18 | 89 | 195 | 23 |
| It is the sinners' dust-tongued bell | 83 | | 49 | 92 | |
| Once it was the colour of saying | 89 | | 53 | 98 | |
| ITCH | | | | | |
| The itch of man upon the baby's thigh, | 12 | 12 | 9 | 13 | 12 |
| Shall fall awake when cures and their itch | 15 | 2 | 10 | 17 | 2 |
| ITCHED | | | | | |
| Itched in the noise of wind and sun. | 21 | 6 | 13 | 25 | 6 |
| ITEM | | | | | |
| That shapes each bushy item of the air | 60 | 5 | 36 | 69 | 5 |
| ITS | | | | | |
| Or lame the air with leaping from its heats; | 1 | 21 | 2 | 1 | 21 |
| Gives up its dead to such a working sea; | 5 | 3 | 3 | 5 | 3 |
| Is half its light; the fathomed sea | 6 | 11 | 4 | 6 | 11 |
| Forks half its fruit; and half droops down, | 6 | 14 | 4 | 6 | 14 |
| And the heart gives up its dead. | 6 | 24 | 4 | 7 | 6 |
| The dead turns up its eye; | 11 | 3 | 8 | 12 | 3 |
| Grafts on its bride one-sided skins of truth; | 15 | 8 | 10 | 17 | 8 |
| Each golden grain spat life into its fellow, | 20 | 23 | 13 | 24 | 23 |
| Where no wax is, the candle shows its hairs. | 24 | 12 | 15 | 29 | 12 |
| 'My fathers' globe knocks on its nave and sings.' | 26 | 11 | 16 | 31 | 11 |
| My Egypt's armour buckling in its sheet, | 31 | 10 | 18 | 36 | 10 |

| | U.K. | | | U.S. | |
|---|---|---|---|---|---|
| | *Page* | *Line* | *Poem* | *Page* | *Line* |
| Plunged in its fruit; | 39 | 3 | 21 | 45 | 3 |
| But time has set its maggot on their track. | 50 | 4 | 30 | 59 | 4 |
| Lift its head to the blows of the rain; | 68 | 23 | 42 | 77 | 23 |
| Child in white blood bent on its knees | 69 | 2 | 43 | 78 | 2 |
| Soar, with its two bark towers, to that Day | 76 | 20 | 44 | 85 | 20 |
| Nor ever, as the wild tongue breaks its tombs, | 77 | 11 | 45 | 86 | 11 |
| Its wringing shell, and let her eyelids fasten. | 79 | 9 | 46 | 88 | 12 |
| The spire cranes. Its statue is an aviary. | 86 | 1 | 51 | 95 | 1 |
| Draw down to its weird eyes? | 91 | 11 | 55 | 100 | 11 |
| And clap its great blood down; | 92 | 3 | 55 | 101 | 9 |
| With its horns through mist and the castle | 103 | 8 | 63 | 114 | 8 |
| And the grave its daughters. | 110 | 14 | 67 | 121 | 16 |
| And learn, too late, they grieved it on its way, | 116 | 11 | 70 | 128 | 11 |
| And all the woken farm at its white trades, | 119 | 25 | 72 | 132 | 5 |
| With its kneading mouth | 129 | 6 | 77 | 143 | 6 |
| The mother dug, and its arms full of fires. | 129 | 8 | 77 | 143 | 8 |
| Its tongue peeled in the wrap of a leaf. | 134 | 15 | 79 | 150 | 15 |
| Tell his street on its back he stopped a sun | 135 | 6 | 80 | 152 | 6 |
| The trodden town rang its cobbles for luck. | 149 | 4 | 83 | 166 | 4 |
| Boat with its anchor free and fast | 149 | 6 | 83 | 166 | 6 |
| And the moon swam out of its hulk. | 149 | 16 | 83 | 166 | 16 |
| A cloud blew the rain from its throat; | 150 | 16 | 83 | 167 | 20 |
| There is thunder under its thumbs; | 151 | 14 | 83 | 169 | 2 |
| His fiery reel sings off its flames, | 151 | 16 | 83 | 169 | 4 |
| Sand with legends in its virgin laps | 156 | 4 | 83 | 174 | 12 |
| There is nothing left of the sea but its sound, | 157 | 13 | 83 | 176 | 5 |
| Of the pacing, famous sea but its speech, | 157 | 18 | 83 | 176 | 10 |
| And into its talkative seven tombs | 157 | 19 | 83 | 176 | 11 |
| In the rain telling its beads, and the gravest ghost | 163 | 8 | 86 | 182 | 8 |
| The owl at its knelling. Fox and holt kneel before blood. | 163 | 9 | 86 | 182 | 9 |
| Gull, on the wave with sand in its eyes! And the foal moves | 165 | 12 | 86 | 185 | 2 |
| Might cross its planets, the bell weep, night gather her eyes, | 165 | 21 | 86 | 185 | 11 |
| Deep in its black, base bones, | 173 | 7 | 88 | 193 | 7 |
| Spins its morning of praise, | 173 | 18 | 88 | 193 | 18 |
| At last the soul from its foul mousehole | 175 | 14 | 89 | 195 | 19 |
| And the rain wring out its tongues on the faded yard, | 178 | 11 | 90 | 199 | 12 |
| ITSELF | | | | | |
| That globe itself of hair and bone | 4 | 10 | 3 | 4 | 10 |
| IVORY | | | | | |
| On the ivory stages | 128 | 9 | 76 | 142 | 9 |

# ENTRIES UNDER J

| | | U.K. | | | U.S. | |
|---|---|---|---|---|---|---|
| | | Page | Line | Poem | Page | Line |
| JACK | | | | | | |
| | Heigh, on horseback hill, jack | ix | 16 | 1 | xvii | 16 |
| | My Jack of Christ born thorny on the tree? | 13 | 17 | 9 | 15 | 3 |
| | When cometh Jack Frost? the children ask. | 53 | 10 | 32 | 62 | 10 |
| | Now Jack my fathers let the time-faced crook, | 67 | 15 | 41 | 76 | 15 |
| | This was the sky, Jack Christ, each minstrel angle | 75 | 11 | 44 | 84 | 11 |
| JACK-[DAWS] | | | | | | |
| | And a black cap of jack- | 167 | 14 | 87 | 187 | 14 |
| JACKET | | | | | | |
| | I, that time's jacket or the coat of ice | 18 | 18 | 12 | 21 | 18 |
| | In love torn breeches and blistered jacket | 132 | 7 | 78 | 147 | 7 |
| JACKS | | | | | | |
| | The jacks of frost they finger in the hives; | 1 | 9 | 2 | 1 | 9 |
| | The sheath-decked jacks, queen with a shuffled heart; | 73 | 13 | 44 | 82 | 13 |
| | They with the simple Jacks were a boulder of wives)— | 178 | 3 | 90 | 199 | 4 |
| JACOB | | | | | | |
| | And, manned by midnight, Jacob to the stars. | 71 | 24 | 44 | 80 | 24 |
| JACOB'S | | | | | | |
| | Star-set at Jacob's angle, | 38 | 3 | 20 | 43 | 13 |
| JAILS | | | | | | |
| | In the jails and studies of his keyless smiles. | 125 | 8 | 74 | 139 | 8 |
| JAW | | | | | | |
| | The atlas-eater with a jaw for news, | 71 | 5 | 44 | 80 | 5 |
| | I lie down thin and hear the good bells jaw— | 175 | 24 | 89 | 196 | 5 |
| JAWBONE | | | | | | |
| | Man of my flesh, the jawbone riven, | 33 | 19 | 19 | 39 | 1 |
| JAW-BONE | | | | | | |
| | Destruction, picked by birds, brays through the jaw-bone, | 79 | 10 | 46 | 88 | 13 |
| JAWS | | | | | | |
| | Some dead undid their bushy jaws, | 4 | 22 | 3 | 4 | 22 |
| | Of sick old manhood on the fallen jaws, | 12 | 24 | 9 | 14 | 3 |
| JEALOUS | | | | | | |
| | That other sun, the jealous coursing of the unrivalled blood. | 127 | 14 | 75 | 141 | 14 |

| | | U.K. | | | U.S. | |
|---|---|---|---|---|---|---|
| | | Page | Line | Poem | Page | Line |
| JEALOUSY | | | | | | |
| | Jealousy cannot forget for all her sakes, | 114 | 11 | 69 | 126 | 11 |
| JERICHO | | | | | | |
| | Uncredited blows Jericho on Eden. | 41 | 17 | 23 | 47 | 17 |
| | Oh, Jericho was falling in their lungs! | 151 | 6 | 83 | 168 | 14 |
| JESU'S | | | | | | |
| | From Jesu's sleeve trumped up the king of spots, | 73 | 12 | 44 | 82 | 12 |
| | Fire on starlight, rake Jesu's stream; | 150 | 19 | 83 | 168 | 3 |
| JOB'S | | | | | | |
| | John's beast, Job's patience, and the fibs of vision, | 41 | 21 | 23 | 48 | 3 |
| JOHN'S | | | | | | |
| | John's beast, Job's patience, and the fibs of vision, | 41 | 21 | 23 | 48 | 3 |
| | Over Sir John's Hill, | 167 | 1 | 87 | 187 | 1 |
| | Daws Sir John's just hill dons, and again the gulled birds hare | 167 | 15 | 87 | 187 | 15 |
| | It is the heron and I, under judging Sir John's elmed | 168 | 16 | 87 | 189 | 1 |
| | Now on Sir John's hill. The heron, ankling the scaly | 169 | 7 | 87 | 189 | 16 |
| | Over Sir John's hill | 167 | | 87 | 187 | |
| JOINTED | | | | | | |
| | Know, O my bone, the jointed lever, | 33 | 22 | 19 | 39 | 4 |
| JOINTS | | | | | | |
| | The finger joints are cramped with chalk; | 62 | 6 | 37 | 71 | 6 |
| JOKER | | | | | | |
| | Adam, time's joker, on a witch of cardboard | 74 | 11 | 44 | 83 | 11 |
| JONAH'S | | | | | | |
| | And Jonah's Moby snatched me by the hair, | 73 | 20 | 44 | 82 | 20 |
| JONES | | | | | | |
| | After the funeral (in memory of Ann Jones) | 87 | | 52 | 96 | |
| JORDAN | | | | | | |
| | That shaped the Jordan near my home | 7 | 4 | 5 | 8 | 4 |
| | My grave is watered by the crossing Jordan. | 31 | 19 | 18 | 37 | 1 |
| JOURNEY | | | | | | |
| | Rounded my globe of heritage, journey | 28 | 11 | 17 | 33 | 11 |
| | Bend, if my journey ache, direction like an arc or make | 97 | 14 | 59 | 108 | 14 |
| | Sewing a shroud for a journey | 99 | 4 | 60 | 110 | 4 |
| JOY | | | | | | |
| | Joy is no knocking nation, sir and madam, | 19 | 6 | 12 | 22 | 11 |
| | Joy is the knock of dust, Cadaver's shoot | 19 | 12 | 12 | 22 | 17 |
| | Laid the crops low, broke the grape's joy. | 39 | 5 | 21 | 45 | 5 |
| | Cry joy that this witchlike midwife second | 96 | 23 | 58 | 107 | 6 |
| | 'Now to awake husked of gestures and my joy like a cave | 97 | 21 | 59 | 109 | 1 |

JOY (continued)

|  | U.K. | | | U.S. | |
|---|---|---|---|---|---|
|  | Page | Line | Poem | Page | Line |
| Summertime of the dead whispered the truth of his joy | 104 | 4 | 63 | 115 | 6 |
| Joy of the long dead child sang burning | 104 | 11 | 63 | 115 | 13 |
| The cloud, the need, the planted stars, the joy beyond | 122 | 22 | 72 | 136 | 2 |
| Put a tear for joy in the unearthly flood | 125 | 22 | 74 | 139 | 22 |
| Brethren for joy has moved within | 143 | 16 | 82 | 160 | 16 |
| The dead grow for His joy. | 171 | 27 | 88 | 191 | 27 |

JOYFUL

| Gabriel and radiant shrubbery as the morning grows joyful | 158 | 15 | 84 | 177 | 15 |

JOYS

| The rainbow-fish bend in her joys, | 150 | 10 | 83 | 167 | 14 |
| Who once, green countries since, were a hedge-row of joys. | 176 | 20 | 90 | 197 | 20 |

JUAN

| Juan aflame and savagely young King Lear, | 113 | 11 | 69 | 125 | 11 |

JUDGE

| To the judge blown bedlam | 141 | 6 | 82 | 158 | 6 |

JUDGING

| It is the heron and I, under judging Sir John's elmed | 168 | 16 | 87 | 189 | 1 |

JUDGMENT

| That breaks one bone to light with a judgment clout, | 87 | 9 | 52 | 96 | 9 |

JUICES

| That frozen wife whose juices drift like a fixed sea | 77 | 14 | 45 | 86 | 14 |

JUMP

| Those craning birds are choice for you, songs that jump back | 86 | 9 | 51 | 95 | 9 |
| Bump on a spout let the bubbles jump out. | 97 | 3 | 59 | 108 | 3 |
| Made the tigers jump out of their eyes | 112 | 4 | 68 | 124 | 4 |

JUMPING

| From fish to jumping hill! Look: | viii | 17 | 1 | xvi | 17 |

JUMPS

| And blood jumps in the sun; | 25 | 5 | 15 | 30 | 5 |

JUST

| And sear just riders back, | 118 | 6 | 71 | 130 | 10 |
| Daws Sir John's just hill dons, and again the gulled birds hare | 167 | 15 | 87 | 187 | 15 |

JUSTICE

| The darkest justice of death, blind and un-blessed. |  |  | 91 | 200 | 11 |

# ENTRIES UNDER K

|  | U.K. Page | Line | Poem | U.S. Page | Line |
|---|---|---|---|---|---|
| KANGAROO | | | | | |
| From the kangaroo foot of the earth, | 132 | 21 | 78 | 147 | 21 |
| KEEP | | | | | |
| Hoo, there, in castle keep, | ix | 2 | I | xvii | 2 |
| O keep his bones away from that common cart, | 135 | 12 | 80 | 152 | 12 |
| And flower of country sleep and the greenwood keep. | 162 | 18 | 86 | 181 | 18 |
| KEEPER | | | | | |
| And the keeper of the key. | 42 | 21 | 24 | 49 | 21 |
| Dodging the park keeper | 111 | 23 | 68 | 123 | 23 |
| KENNEL | | | | | |
| Slept at night in a dog kennel | 111 | 11 | 68 | 123 | 11 |
| To his kennel in the dark. | 112 | 18 | 68 | 124 | 18 |
| KEPT | | | | | |
| Children kept from the sun | 125 | 4 | 74 | 139 | 4 |
| KETTLES | | | | | |
| The dust of their kettles and clocks swings to and fro | 178 | 5 | 90 | 199 | 6 |
| KEY | | | | | |
| And the keeper of the key. | 42 | 21 | 24 | 49 | 21 |
| And the loser of the key. | 42 | 28 | 24 | 50 | 7 |
| KEYLESS | | | | | |
| In the jails and studies of his keyless smiles. | 125 | 8 | 74 | 139 | 8 |
| KEYS | | | | | |
| When at your lips and keys, | 117 | 14 | 71 | 129 | 14 |
| To shut the sun, plunge, mount your darkened keys | 118 | 5 | 71 | 130 | 9 |
| When all the keys shot from the locks, and rang. | 135 | 8 | 80 | 152 | 8 |
| KICK | | | | | |
| From salt-lipped beak to the kick of the stern | 152 | 9 | 83 | 170 | 1 |
| Rage shattered waters kick | 172 | 16 | 88 | 192 | 16 |
| KICKED | | | | | |
| You have kicked from a dark den, leaped up the whinnying light, | 92 | 15 | 55 | 101 | 21 |
| KICKS | | | | | |
| The dream that kicks the buried from their sack | 15 | 14 | 10 | 17 | 14 |
| KILL | | | | | |
| We watch the show of shadows kiss or kill, | 14 | 19 | 10 | 16 | 19 |

KILL (continued)

|  | U.K. | | | U.S. | |
|---|---|---|---|---|---|
|  | *Page* | *Line* | *Poem* | *Page* | *Line* |
| 'The maggot that no man can kill | 66 | 1 | 40 | 75 | 1 |
| And a firewind kill the candle. | 83 | 6 | 49 | 92 | 6 |
| That all the charmingly drowned arise to cock-crow and kill. | 89 | 6 | 53 | 98 | 6 |
| Love and labour and kill | 91 | 17 | 55 | 100 | 17 |
| He saw the storm smoke out to kill | 150 | 17 | 83 | 168 | 1 |
| Kill Time! She turns in her pain! | 155 | 10 | 83 | 173 | 14 |
| To kill and their own tide daubing blood | 171 | 8 | 88 | 191 | 8 |
| KILLED | | | | | |
| And the sun killed in her face. | 93 | 9 | 56 | 102 | 9 |
| 'Come and be killed,' | 167 | 22 | 87 | 188 | 3 |
| Among those Killed in the Dawn Raid was a Man Aged a Hundred | 135 | | 80 | 152 | |
| KILLS | | | | | |
| Who kills my history? | 70 | 9 | 43 | 79 | 13 |
| Time kills me terribly. | 70 | 15 | 43 | 79 | 19 |
| And the hawk in the egg kills the wren. | 153 | 12 | 83 | 173 | 16 |
| KIND | | | | | |
| The country is holy: O bide in that country kind, | 163 | 16 | 86 | 182 | 16 |
| A cold kind man brave in his narrow pride | | | 91 | 200 | 3 |
| Which was rest and dust, and in the kind ground | | | 91 | 200 | 10 |
| An old kind man brave in his burning pride. | | | 91 | 201 | 3 |
| KINDLE | | | | | |
| Time marks a black aisle kindle from the brand of ashes, | 83 | 4 | 49 | 92 | 4 |
| KINDLED | | | | | |
| Darkness kindled back into beginning | 129 | 12 | 77 | 143 | 12 |
| Wound, nor her riding high, nor her eyes, nor kindled hair, | 166 | 2 | 86 | 186 | 2 |
| KINDLING | | | | | |
| Him up and he ran like a wind after the kindling flight | 122 | 9 | 72 | 135 | 9 |
| KING | | | | | |
| You king singsong owls, who moonbeam. | ix | 3 | 1 | xvii | 3 |
| These five kings did a king to death. | 62 | 4 | 37 | 71 | 4 |
| From Jesu's sleeve trumped up the king of spots, | 73 | 12 | 44 | 82 | 12 |
| King of your blue eyes | 105 | 3 | 64 | 116 | 3 |
| King of your heart in the blind days, | 105 | 16 | 64 | 116 | 16 |
| Of the sky, king of your six years. | 106 | 4 | 64 | 117 | 4 |
| Juan aflame and savagely young King Lear, | 113 | 11 | 69 | 125 | 11 |
| Into a homestall king or hamlet of fire | 162 | 11 | 86 | 181 | 11 |
| Their breasts full of honey, under their gander king | 177 | 18 | 90 | 198 | 17 |
| KINGCRAFTS | | | | | |
| The kingcrafts of the wicked sea, | 65 | 11 | 40 | 74 | 11 |

|  | U.K. | | | U.S. | |
|---|---|---|---|---|---|
|  | *Page* | *Line* | *Poem* | *Page* | *Line* |
| KINGDOM |  |  |  |  |  |
| O kingdom of neighbours, finned | ix | 31 | 1 | xviii | 5 |
| Nor the cannons of his kingdom | 43 | 19 | 24 | 51 | 5 |
| Nor the cannons of his kingdom | 43 | 26 | 24 | 51 | 12 |
| The sundering ultimate kingdom of genesis' thunder. | 131 | 25 | 77 | 146 | 7 |
| Swarms on the kingdom come | 139 | 6 | 82 | 156 | 6 |
| To his nimbus bell cool kingdom come | 173 | 4 | 88 | 193 | 4 |
| KINGLY |  |  |  |  |  |
| The sea speaks in a kingly voice, | 66 | 11 | 40 | 75 | 11 |
| KINGS |  |  |  |  |  |
| These five kings did a king to death. | 62 | 4 | 37 | 71 | 4 |
| The five kings count the dead but do not soften | 62 | 13 | 37 | 71 | 13 |
| Prophets and fibre kings in oil and letter, | 75 | 20 | 44 | 84 | 20 |
| But the hungry kings of the tides; | 153 | 13 | 83 | 171 | 9 |
| KISS |  |  |  |  |  |
| Here break a kiss in no love's quarry. | 2 | 23 | 2 | 3 | 5 |
| Your mouth, my love, the thistle in the kiss? | 13 | 16 | 9 | 15 | 2 |
| We watch the show of shadows kiss or kill, | 14 | 19 | 10 | 16 | 19 |
| My lips are withered with a kiss, | 65 | 20 | 40 | 74 | 20 |
| Though the brawl of the kiss has not occurred | 109 | 7 | 67 | 120 | 7 |
| Kiss | 139 | 17 | 82 | 156 | 17 |
| Witnessed with a kiss. | 150 | 24 | 83 | 168 | 8 |
| Now curlew cry me down to kiss the mouths of their dust. | 178 | 4 | 90 | 199 | 5 |
| KISSED |  |  |  |  |  |
| I fellowed sleep who kissed me in the brain, | 26 | 1 | 16 | 31 | 1 |
| Sucking the dark, kissed on the cyanide, | 30 | 21 | 18 | 35 | 21 |
| And her red lips were kissed black, | 93 | 18 | 56 | 102 | 18 |
| To the kissed kite hems of his shawl, | 95 | 3 | 58 | 105 | 3 |
| Under the cloud against love is caught and held and kissed | 109 | 17 | 67 | 120 | 17 |
| Sing how the seal has kissed her dead! | 152 | 10 | 83 | 170 | 2 |
| KISSING |  |  |  |  |  |
| O see the poles are kissing as they cross. | 3 | 6 | 2 | 3 | 12 |
| KISSPROOF |  |  |  |  |  |
| The kissproof world. | 19 | 25 | 12 | 23 | 10 |
| KITCHENS |  |  |  |  |  |
| Where the hay rides now or the bracken kitchens rust | 178 | 6 | 90 | 199 | 7 |
| KITE |  |  |  |  |  |
| To the kissed kite hems of his shawl, | 95 | 3 | 58 | 105 | 3 |
| KNAVE |  |  |  |  |  |
| The knave of pain steals off | 67 | 3 | 41 | 76 | 3 |
| KNEADING |  |  |  |  |  |
| With its kneading mouth | 129 | 6 | 77 | 143 | 6 |

|  | U.K. Page | U.K. Line | Poem | U.S. Page | U.S. Line |
|---|---|---|---|---|---|
| KNEE-[DEEP] |  |  |  |  |  |
| Rags and prayers down the knee- | 122 | 16 | 72 | 135 | 16 |
| KNEEL |  |  |  |  |  |
| Tackled with clouds, who kneel | vii | 13 | 1 | xv | 13 |
| And all love's sinners in sweet cloth kneel to a hyleg image, | 84 | 4 | 49 | 93 | 10 |
| The owl at its knelling. Fox and holt kneel before blood. | 163 | 9 | 86 | 182 | 9 |
| KNEELS |  |  |  |  |  |
| They from houses where the harvest kneels, hold me hard, | 178 | 9 | 90 | 199 | 10 |
| KNEES |  |  |  |  |  |
| The sea-halved faith that blew time to his knees, | 67 | 4 | 41 | 76 | 4 |
| Child in white blood bent on its knees | 69 | 2 | 43 | 78 | 2 |
| First there was the lamb on knocking knees | 72 | 5 | 44 | 81 | 5 |
| KNELLED |  |  |  |  |  |
| Hill, tell-tale the knelled | 168 | 17 | 87 | 189 | 2 |
| KNELLING |  |  |  |  |  |
| The owl at its knelling. Fox and holt kneel before blood. | 163 | 9 | 86 | 182 | 9 |
| KNELLS |  |  |  |  |  |
| Wave's silence, wept white angelus knells. | 171 | 11 | 88 | 191 | 11 |
| KNELT |  |  |  |  |  |
| He knelt, he wept, he prayed, | 120 | 1 | 72 | 132 | 6 |
| He knelt on the cold stones, | 120 | 6 | 72 | 132 | 11 |
| That a man knelt alone in the cup of the vales, | 122 | 5 | 72 | 135 | 5 |
| KNEW |  |  |  |  |  |
| Who knew not sun and moon by name, | 7 | 8 | 5 | 8 | 8 |
| I knew the message of the winter, | 7 | 13 | 5 | 8 | 13 |
| Ungotten I knew night and day. | 7 | 18 | 5 | 8 | 18 |
| My throat knew thirst before the structure | 8 | 1 | 5 | 9 | 1 |
| My heart knew love, my belly hunger; | 8 | 5 | 5 | 9 | 5 |
| We in our Eden knew the secret guardian | 40 | 13 | 22 | 46 | 13 |
| Knew all His horrible desires | 69 | 10 | 43 | 78 | 10 |
| KNIFE |  |  |  |  |  |
| His scissors oiled, his knife hung loose | 11 | 10 | 8 | 12 | 10 |
| KNIT |  |  |  |  |  |
| To shade and knit anew the patch of words | 21 | 10 | 13 | 25 | 10 |
| KNIVES |  |  |  |  |  |
| Of birth and death, the two sad knives of thieves, | 10 | 18 | 7 | 11 | 18 |
| The tray of knives, the antiseptic funeral; | 37 | 3 | 20 | 42 | 9 |
| The supper and knives of a mood. | 77 | 4 | 45 | 86 | 4 |
| Is crying from nets to knives, | 151 | 18 | 83 | 169 | 6 |
| KNOBBLY |  |  |  |  |  |
| The knobbly ape that swings along his sex | 13 | 9 | 9 | 14 | 16 |
| KNOCK |  |  |  |  |  |
| Joy is the knock of dust, Cadaver's shoot | 19 | 12 | 12 | 22 | 17 |

| | U.K. | | | U.S. | |
|---|---|---|---|---|---|
| | *Page* | *Line* | *Poem* | *Page* | *Line* |
| And the knock of sailing boats on the net webbed wall | 102 | 7 | 63 | 113 | 7 |
| KNOCKED | | | | | |
| Before I knocked and let flesh enter, | 7 | 1 | 5 | 8 | 1 |
| Knocked in the flesh that decked the vine, | 39 | 7 | 21 | 45 | 7 |
| But not of grief, for I have knocked down that | 48 | 2 | 28 | 56 | 2 |
| And roll with the knocked earth: | 92 | 13 | 55 | 101 | 19 |
| Before I knocked | 7 | | 5 | 8 | |
| KNOCKING | | | | | |
| Joy is no knocking nation, sir and madam, | 19 | 6 | 12 | 22 | 11 |
| First there was the lamb on knocking knees | 72 | 5 | 44 | 81 | 5 |
| KNOCKS | | | | | |
| 'My fathers' globe knocks on its nave and sings.' | 26 | 11 | 16 | 31 | 11 |
| KNOW | | | | | |
| For you to know | viii | 12 | 1 | xvi | 12 |
| The signal grass that tells me all I know | 16 | 22 | 11 | 19 | 22 |
| Know now the flesh's lock and vice, | 33 | 20 | 19 | 39 | 2 |
| Know, O my bone, the jointed lever, | 33 | 22 | 19 | 39 | 4 |
| After such fighting as the weakest know, | 48 | 10 | 28 | 56 | 10 |
| And 'Know no answer,' and I know | 53 | 23 | 32 | 62 | 23 |
| I know her scrubbed and sour humble hands | 88 | 3 | 52 | 97 | 3 |
| Turns in the dark on the sound they know will arise | 100 | 6 | 61 | 111 | 6 |
| This I know from the native | 110 | 22 | 67 | 121 | 24 |
| Though wise men at their end know dark is right, | 116 | 4 | 70 | 128 | 4 |
| I know not whether | 130 | 9 | 77 | 144 | 9 |
| I know the legend | 130 | 23 | 77 | 145 | 1 |
| To know all | 146 | 7 | 82 | 163 | 7 |
| Know the green good, | 163 | 17 | 86 | 182 | 17 |
| KNOWN | | | | | |
| What's never known is safest in this life. | 50 | 6 | 30 | 59 | 6 |
| Shall not be known till windwell dries | 53 | 2 | 32 | 62 | 2 |
| All things are known: the stars' advice | 53 | 16 | 32 | 62 | 16 |
| And always known must leave | 117 | 4 | 71 | 129 | 4 |
| Now break a giant tear for the little known fall, | 126 | 8 | 74 | 140 | 8 |
| Forever falling night is a known | 146 | 1 | 82 | 163 | 1 |
| And the known dark of the earth amen. | 147 | 18 | 82 | 164 | 18 |
| KNOWS | | | | | |
| One enemy, of many, who knows well | 118 | 1 | 71 | 130 | 5 |
| And far at sea he knows, | 171 | 3 | 88 | 191 | 3 |
| Who knows the rocketing wind will blow | 172 | 13 | 88 | 192 | 13 |
| KNOTS | | | | | |
| Where once your green knots sank their splice | 11 | 7 | 8 | 12 | 7 |

# ENTRIES UNDER L

|  | U.K. | | | U.S. | |
| --- | --- | --- | --- | --- | --- |
|  | Page | Line | Poem | Page | Line |
| LABOUR | | | | | |
| May a humble village labour | 43 | 1 | 24 | 50 | 8 |
| May a humble planet labour | 43 | 8 | 24 | 50 | 15 |
| Love and labour and kill | 91 | 17 | 55 | 100 | 17 |
| (Bury the dead for fear that they walk to the grave in labour.) | 99 | 2 | 60 | 110 | 2 |
| I labour by singing light | 128 | 6 | 76 | 142 | 6 |
| To labour and love though they lay down long ago. | 176 | 5 | 90 | 197 | 5 |
| LABYRINTHS | | | | | |
| Who in these labyrinths, | 69 | 13 | 43 | 78 | 13 |
| LACED | | | | | |
| Of the wood! Pastoral beat of blood through the laced leaves! | 164 | 22 | 86 | 184 | 8 |
| LADDER | | | | | |
| There grows the hours' ladder to the sun, | 27 | 1 | 16 | 32 | 6 |
| We rung our weathering changes on the ladder, | 72 | 17 | 44 | 81 | 17 |
| LADIES | | | | | |
| But when the ladies are cold as stone | 65 | 7 | 40 | 74 | 7 |
| The bagpipe-breasted ladies in the deadweed | 74 | 13 | 44 | 83 | 13 |
| Time's tune my ladies with the teats of music, | 74 | 21 | 44 | 83 | 21 |
| Time is the tune my ladies lend their heart-break, | 75 | 1 | 44 | 84 | 1 |
| LADIES' | | | | | |
| Before the ladies' breasts are hags | 65 | 4 | 40 | 74 | 4 |
| LADS | | | | | |
| I hear, through dead men's drums, the riddled lads, | 31 | 16 | 18 | 36 | 16 |
| LADY | | | | | |
| Who play the proper gentleman and lady. | 47 | 4 | 27 | 55 | 4 |
| LADY'S | | | | | |
| And sirens singing from our lady's sea-straw. | 73 | 24 | 44 | 82 | 24 |
| LAID | | | | | |
| Laid the crops low, broke the grape's joy. | 39 | 5 | 21 | 45 | 5 |
| I laid her down and told her sin, | 65 | 23 | 40 | 74 | 23 |
| And laid your cheek against a cloud-formed shell: | 125 | 23 | 74 | 139 | 23 |
| Laid in her snow | 130 | 13 | 77 | 144 | 13 |

| | U.K. | | | U.S. | |
|---|---|---|---|---|---|
| | *Page* | *Line* | *Poem* | *Page* | *Line* |
| And the golden pavements laid in requiems, | 131 | 17 | 77 | 145 | 23 |
| Are making under the green, laid veil | 151 | 21 | 83 | 169 | 9 |
| The long, laid minute's bride drifts on | 152 | 11 | 83 | 170 | 3 |
| And stunned and still on the green, laid veil | 156 | 3 | 83 | 174 | 11 |

LAIR

| | | | | | |
|---|---|---|---|---|---|
| Out of a lair in the flocked leaves in the dew dipped year | 162 | 6 | 86 | 181 | 6 |

LAIRS

| | | | | | |
|---|---|---|---|---|---|
| Of his snow blind love and rush in the white lairs. | 120 | 13 | 72 | 132 | 18 |
| In lairs and asylums of the tremendous shout. | 125 | 16 | 74 | 139 | 16 |

LAKE

| | | | | | |
|---|---|---|---|---|---|
| Past lake and rockery | 111 | 19 | 68 | 123 | 19 |
| The birds the grass the trees the lake | 112 | 15 | 68 | 124 | 15 |
| Through the shaken greensward lake, silent, on moonshod hooves, | 165 | 13 | 86 | 185 | 3 |
| And ducked and draked white lake that harps to a hail stone. | 177 | 8 | 90 | 198 | 7 |

LAKES

| | | | | | |
|---|---|---|---|---|---|
| Wound like a ball of lakes | 70 | 5 | 43 | 79 | 9 |
| That the snow blind twilight ferries over the lakes | 119 | 2 | 72 | 131 | 2 |
| Deep hillocks and loud on the numbed lakes, | 122 | 17 | 72 | 135 | 17 |
| And the lakes and floating fields and the river wended | 122 | 28 | 72 | 136 | 8 |
| And over the glazed lakes skated the shapes of fishes | 123 | 5 | 72 | 136 | 15 |

LAMB

| | | | | | |
|---|---|---|---|---|---|
| First there was the lamb on knocking knees | 72 | 5 | 44 | 81 | 5 |
| Or the white ewe lamb | 130 | 11 | 77 | 144 | 11 |
| Nothing I cared, in the lamb white days, that time would take me | 160 | 24 | 85 | 180 | 1 |

LAME

| | | | | | |
|---|---|---|---|---|---|
| Or lame the air with leaping from its heats; | 1 | 21 | 2 | 1 | 21 |
| The year-hedged row is lame with flint, | 70 | 10 | 43 | 79 | 14 |
| Refusal struck her loin and the lame flower | 90 | 2 | 54 | 99 | 2 |

LAMENT

| | | | | | |
|---|---|---|---|---|---|
| Lament | 174 | | 89 | 194 | |

LAMENTING

| | | | | | |
|---|---|---|---|---|---|
| Others betray the lamenting lies of their losses | 85 | 11 | 50 | 94 | 11 |
| Not wholly to that lamenting | 143 | 15 | 82 | 160 | 15 |

LAMP

| | | | | | |
|---|---|---|---|---|---|
| The bright-eyed worm on Davy's lamp, | 2 | 11 | 2 | 2 | 11 |
| Shall raise a lamp | 56 | 25 | 34 | 66 | 4 |
| And a lamp of lightning for the poor in the dark; | 89 | 11 | 53 | 98 | 11 |
| I'll comb the snared woods with a glove on a lamp, | 97 | 7 | 59 | 108 | 7 |

|  | U.K. | | | U.S. | |
|  | Page | Line | Poem | Page | Line |
|---|---|---|---|---|---|
| **LAMPED** | | | | | |
| The lamped calligrapher, the queen in splints, | 75 | 21 | 44 | 84 | 21 |
| **LAND** | | | | | |
| Breaks on unangled land. | 6 | 12 | 4 | 6 | 12 |
| And cast a shadow crab upon the land, | 16 | 4 | 11 | 19 | 4 |
| With fists of turnips punishes the land, | 17 | 4 | 11 | 20 | 4 |
| 'This that we tread was, too, your fathers' land.' | 26 | 12 | 16 | 31 | 12 |
| The grooved land rotating, that the stylus of lightning | 37 | 17 | 20 | 42 | 23 |
| The salt sucked dam and darlings of the land | 47 | 3 | 27 | 55 | 3 |
| The land lies out of sound | 58 | 13 | 35 | 67 | 13 |
| Of the grave, gay, seaside land. | 82 | 17 | 48 | 91 | 17 |
| In a land strapped by hunger | 90 | 4 | 54 | 99 | 4 |
| A brute land in the cool top of the country days | 91 | 15 | 55 | 100 | 15 |
| For the sleep in a safe land and the love who dies | 100 | 10 | 61 | 111 | 10 |
| In the long ago land that glided the dark door wide | 121 | 12 | 72 | 134 | 7 |
| In the far ago land the door of his death glided wide, | 122 | 25 | 72 | 136 | 5 |
| The land | 141 | 15 | 82 | 158 | 15 |
| To the hidden land | 148 | 5 | 82 | 165 | 5 |
| Said the looking land. | 149 | 12 | 83 | 166 | 12 |
| The rod bends low, divining land, | 155 | 21 | 83 | 174 | 5 |
| Land, land, land, nothing remains | 157 | 17 | 83 | 176 | 9 |
| To the fisherman lost on the land. | 157 | 22 | 83 | 176 | 14 |
| And wake to the farm forever fled from the childless land. | 161 | 3 | 85 | 180 | 6 |
| In the land of the hearthstone tales, and spelled asleep, | 162 | 2 | 86 | 181 | 2 |
| **LANDED** | | | | | |
| And this, nor this, is shade, the landed crow, | 51 | 19 | 31 | 60 | 19 |
| **LANDS** | | | | | |
| The water lidded lands, | x | 11 | 1 | xviii | 17 |
| Down fall four padding weathers on the scarlet lands, | 49 | 19 | 29 | 58 | 19 |
| Bird through the times and lands and tribes of the slow flakes. | 122 | 19 | 72 | 135 | 19 |
| **LANDSCAPE** | | | | | |
| The landscape grief, love in His oils | 69 | 20 | 43 | 78 | 20 |
| World in the sand, on the triangle landscape, | 76 | 6 | 44 | 85 | 6 |
| **LANDWARD** | | | | | |
| Who seek me landward, marking in my mouth | 31 | 22 | 18 | 37 | 4 |
| **LANE** | | | | | |
| This tidethread and the lane of scales, | 69 | 14 | 43 | 78 | 14 |
| **LANES** | | | | | |
| In the courters' lanes, or twined in the ox roasting sun | 176 | 13 | 90 | 197 | 13 |

| | U.K. | | | U.S. | |
|---|---|---|---|---|---|
| | *Page* | *Line* | *Poem* | *Page* | *Line* |
| LANGUAGE | | | | | |
| And one light's language in the book of trees. | 74 | 19 | 44 | 83 | 19 |
| LANK | | | | | |
| Under the lank, fourth folly on Glamorgan's hill, | 49 | 2 | 29 | 58 | 2 |
| Spill the lank folly's hunter and the hard-held hope. | 49 | 18 | 29 | 58 | 18 |
| LANTERNS | | | | | |
| Should lanterns shine, the holy face, | 63 | 1 | 38 | 72 | 1 |
| Should lanterns shine | 63 | | 38 | 72 | |
| LAP | | | | | |
| Into the sided lap of light grew strong, | 21 | 3 | 13 | 25 | 3 |
| Bent like a beast to lap the singular floods | 90 | 3 | 54 | 99 | 3 |
| LAPPED | | | | | |
| 'His mother's womb had a tongue that lapped up mud,' | 79 | 20 | 46 | 89 | 1 |
| Lapped among herods wail | 96 | 14 | 58 | 106 | 14 |
| LAPPING | | | | | |
| Lapping the still canals, the dry tide-master | 82 | 10 | 48 | 91 | 10 |
| LAPS | | | | | |
| Sand with legends in its virgin laps | 156 | 4 | 83 | 174 | 12 |
| LARGE | | | | | |
| At large as the dead, | 108 | 8 | 66 | 119 | 8 |
| LARK | | | | | |
| Beyond the border and under the lark full cloud. | 103 | 12 | 63 | 114 | 12 |
| LARKED | | | | | |
| Grow larked and greener at berry brown | 173 | 20 | 88 | 193 | 20 |
| LARK-HIGH | | | | | |
| A stone lies lost and locked in the lark-high hill. | 115 | 16 | 69 | 127 | 16 |
| LARKS | | | | | |
| A springful of larks in a rolling | 102 | 21 | 63 | 113 | 21 |
| Fall and the dew larks sing | 173 | 21 | 88 | 193 | 21 |
| LASHED | | | | | |
| And, lashed to syllables, the lynx tongue cry | 81 | 8 | 47 | 90 | 8 |
| LASHES | | | | | |
| And a tear-stained widower grief drooped from the lashes | 85 | 9 | 50 | 94 | 9 |
| LAST | | | | | |
| I was a mortal to the last | 8 | 16 | 5 | 9 | 16 |
| Each rung a love or losing to the last, | 27 | 2 | 16 | 32 | 7 |
| And breaks his shell in the last shocked beginning; | 41 | 13 | 23 | 47 | 13 |
| Through the last vault and vegetable groyne, | 78 | 7 | 46 | 87 | 7 |
| And, pride is last, is like a child alone | 78 | 13 | 46 | 87 | 13 |
| That will rake at last all currencies of the marked breath | 94 | 8 | 57 | 104 | 8 |
| On the last street wave praised | 95 | 4 | 58 | 105 | 4 |

|  | U.K. | | | U.S. | |
|---|---|---|---|---|---|
|  | *Page* | *Line* | *Poem* | *Page* | *Line* |
| On the angelic etna of the last whirring feather-lands, | 95 | 11 | 58 | 105 | 11 |
| On the last rick's tip by spilled wine-wells | 95 | 14 | 58 | 105 | 14 |
| Tells with silence the last light breaking | 101 | 4 | 63 | 112 | 4 |
| In the last element | 105 | 23 | 64 | 116 | 23 |
| Rasped at last, and I stumbled and sucked, | 107 | 8 | 65 | 118 | 8 |
| And taken by light in her arms at long and dear last | 108 | 16 | 66 | 119 | 16 |
| Last night in a raping wave | 113 | 7 | 69 | 125 | 7 |
| Good men, the last wave by, crying how bright | 116 | 7 | 70 | 128 | 7 |
| Looms the last Samson of your zodiac. | 118 | 8 | 71 | 130 | 12 |
| Vales where he prayed to come to the last harm | 122 | 29 | 72 | 136 | 9 |
| Love is the last light spoken. Oh | 130 | 7 | 77 | 144 | 7 |
| Slashed down the last snake as though | 134 | 13 | 79 | 150 | 13 |
| Blackened with birds took a last look | 149 | 2 | 83 | 166 | 2 |
| If only for a last time. | 158 | 24 | 84 | 177 | 24 |
| Her faith that this last night for his unsacred sake | 166 | 5 | 86 | 186 | 5 |
| And the scythed boulders bleed, and the last | 172 | 15 | 88 | 192 | 15 |
| And this last blessing most, | 173 | 9 | 88 | 193 | 9 |
| At last the soul from its foul mousehole | 175 | 14 | 89 | 195 | 19 |
| Innocence sweetens my last black breath, | 175 | 29 | 89 | 196 | 10 |
| He lie lightly, at last, on the last, crossed |  |  | 91 | 200 | 5 |
| Out of his eyes I saw the last light glide. |  |  | 91 | 201 | 7 |
| He cried as he died, fearing at last the spheres' |  |  | 91 | 201 | 12 |
| Last sound, the world going out without a breath: |  |  | 91 | 201 | 13 |
| **LASTED** |  |  |  |  |  |
| How much was happy while it lasted, | 48 | 20 | 28 | 56 | 20 |
| **LATCH** |  |  |  |  |  |
| Winds, from the dousing shade and the roarer at the latch, | 163 | 23 | 86 | 183 | 4 |
| **LATCHED** |  |  |  |  |  |
| Shall not be latched while magic glides | 11 | 20 | 8 | 12 | 20 |
| **LATE** |  |  |  |  |  |
| And learn, too late, they grieved it on its way, | 116 | 11 | 70 | 128 | 11 |
| Too late in the wrong rain | 124 | 9 | 73 | 138 | 9 |
| My paid-for slaved-for own too late | 132 | 6 | 78 | 147 | 6 |
| **LATER** |  |  |  |  |  |
| Among men later I heard it said | 93 | 16 | 56 | 102 | 16 |
| **LATERAL** |  |  |  |  |  |
| (Turn the sea-spindle lateral, | 37 | 16 | 20 | 42 | 22 |
| **LAUDS** |  |  |  |  |  |
| The nightbird lauds through nunneries and domes of leaves | 163 | 5 | 86 | 182 | 5 |
| **LAUGH** |  |  |  |  |  |
| That the vampire laugh. | 30 | 18 | 18 | 35 | 18 |

|  | U.K. | | | U.S. | |
|---|---|---|---|---|---|
|  | *Page* | *Line* | *Poem* | *Page* | *Line* |
| By the curve of the nude mouth or the laugh up the sleeve. | 85 | 12 | 50 | 94 | 12 |
| LAUGHING |  |  |  |  |  |
| Laughing when he shook his paper | 111 | 20 | 68 | 123 | 20 |
| Bird after dark and the laughing fish | 154 | 6 | 83 | 172 | 6 |
| LAUGHTER |  |  |  |  |  |
| Still set to scratch a laughter from my lung, | 12 | 5 | 9 | 13 | 5 |
| LAVA |  |  |  |  |  |
| All from the oil, the pound of lava. | 33 | 3 | 19 | 38 | 3 |
| LAVA'S |  |  |  |  |  |
| By lava's light split through the oyster vowels | 74 | 3 | 44 | 83 | 3 |
| LAWLESS |  |  |  |  |  |
| He comes to leave her in the lawless sun awaking | 166 | 6 | 86 | 186 | 6 |
| LAWS |  |  |  |  |  |
| And the sky lays down her laws, | 66 | 10 | 40 | 75 | 10 |
| LAY |  |  |  |  |  |
| Lay the gold tithings barren, | 1 | 2 | 2 | 1 | 2 |
| And lay the wet fruits low. | 11 | 12 | 8 | 12 | 12 |
| The gentleman lay graveward with his furies; | 71 | 2 | 44 | 80 | 2 |
| In that bright anchorground where I lay linened, | 79 | 22 | 46 | 89 | 3 |
| And the strutting fern lay seeds on the black sill. | 88 | 12 | 52 | 97 | 12 |
| Before she lay on a stranger's bed | 93 | 11 | 56 | 102 | 11 |
| Though the town below lay leaved with October blood. | 104 | 15 | 63 | 115 | 17 |
| For the bird lay bedded | 123 | 11 | 72 | 137 | 1 |
| To labour and love though they lay down long ago. | 176 | 5 | 90 | 197 | 5 |
| Young as they in the after milking moonlight lay | 176 | 16 | 90 | 197 | 16 |
| LAYING |  |  |  |  |  |
| Laying my ghost in metal, | 35 | 3 | 20 | 40 | 3 |
| LAYS |  |  |  |  |  |
| And the sky lays down her laws, | 66 | 10 | 40 | 75 | 10 |
| LAZARUS |  |  |  |  |  |
| Crowing to lazarus the morning is vanity, | 37 | 8 | 20 | 42 | 14 |
| Now common lazarus | 146 | 14 | 82 | 163 | 14 |
| LEAD |  |  |  |  |  |
| And terribly lead him home alive | 157 | 6 | 83 | 175 | 18 |
| Lead her prodigal home to his terror, | 157 | 7 | 83 | 175 | 19 |
| LEADEN |  |  |  |  |  |
| The leaden stars, the rainy hammer | 7 | 11 | 5 | 8 | 11 |
| Wrenched by my fingerman, the leaden bud | 54 | 11 | 33 | 63 | 11 |
| LEADS |  |  |  |  |  |
| The mighty hand leads to a sloping shoulder, | 62 | 5 | 37 | 71 | 5 |

LEADS (continued)

|  | U.K. | | | U.S. | |
|---|---|---|---|---|---|
|  | Page | Line | Poem | Page | Line |
| But heart, like head, leads helplessly; | 63 | 10 | 38 | 72 | 10 |
| And the dead hand leads the past. | 155 | 4 | 83 | 173 | 8 |
| Leads them as children and as air | 155 | 5 | 83 | 173 | 9 |

LEAF

| | | | | | |
|---|---|---|---|---|---|
| Shot through the leaf, | 54 | 12 | 33 | 63 | 12 |
| Its tongue peeled in the wrap of a leaf. | 134 | 15 | 79 | 150 | 15 |

LEAFY

| | | | | | |
|---|---|---|---|---|---|
| Lovers in the dirt of their leafy beds, | 89 | 9 | 53 | 98 | 9 |

LEAGUES

| | | | | | |
|---|---|---|---|---|---|
| Farmer in time of frost the burning leagues, | 60 | 10 | 36 | 69 | 10 |

LEAKING

| | | | | | |
|---|---|---|---|---|---|
| From blank and leaking winter sails the child in colour, | 83 | 22 | 49 | 93 | 4 |

LEAKS

| | | | | | |
|---|---|---|---|---|---|
| Drives in a death as life leaks out. | 6 | 9 | 4 | 6 | 9 |

LEAN

| | | | | | |
|---|---|---|---|---|---|
| Lean time on tide and times the wind stood rough, | 67 | 6 | 41 | 76 | 6 |
| On no work of words now for three lean months in the bloody | 94 | 1 | 57 | 104 | 1 |
| One lean sigh when we heard | 126 | 5 | 74 | 140 | 5 |

LEANING

| | | | | | |
|---|---|---|---|---|---|
| (Have with the house of wind), the leaning scene, | 19 | 17 | 12 | 23 | 2 |

LEANS

| | | | | | |
|---|---|---|---|---|---|
| Leans on my mortal ruler, | 10 | 4 | 7 | 11 | 4 |

LEAP

| | | | | | |
|---|---|---|---|---|---|
| A limp and riderless shape to leap nine thinning months.' | 97 | 15 | 59 | 108 | 15 |
| Leap, as to trumpets. Calligraphy of the old | 121 | 22 | 72 | 134 | 17 |
| And all the lifted waters walk and leap. | 153 | 16 | 83 | 171 | 12 |
| Loping and bleating roughly and blithely shall leap, | 162 | 4 | 86 | 181 | 4 |

LEAPED

| | | | | | |
|---|---|---|---|---|---|
| Wind in me leaped, the hellborn dew; | 7 | 16 | 5 | 8 | 16 |
| You have kicked from a dark den, leaped up the whinnying light, | 92 | 15 | 55 | 101 | 21 |

LEAPING

| | | | | | |
|---|---|---|---|---|---|
| Or lame the air with leaping from its heats; | 1 | 21 | 2 | 1 | 21 |
| Dumbly and divinely leaping | 42 | 13 | 24 | 49 | 13 |
| The leaping saga of prayer! And high, there, on the hare- | 164 | 17 | 86 | 184 | 3 |
| Leaping! The gospel rooks! All tell, this night, of him | 165 | 9 | 86 | 184 | 17 |

LEAPS

| | | | | | |
|---|---|---|---|---|---|
| The sun that leaps on petals through a nought, | 51 | 27 | 31 | 61 | 6 |
| A nitric shape that leaps her, time and acid; | 55 | 7 | 33 | 64 | 10 |

| | U.K. Page | Line | Poem | U.S. Page | Line |
|---|---|---|---|---|---|
| **LEAPT** | | | | | |
| From pole to pole leapt round the snail-waked world. | 75 | 14 | 44 | 84 | 14 |
| And this day's sun leapt up the sky out of her thighs | 127 | 4 | 75 | 141 | 4 |
| For a man sleeps where fire leapt down and she learns through his arm | 127 | 13 | 75 | 141 | 13 |
| **LEAR** | | | | | |
| Juan aflame and savagely young King Lear, | 113 | 11 | 69 | 125 | 11 |
| **LEARN** | | | | | |
| I should learn spring by the cuckooing, | 45 | 12 | 26 | 53 | 12 |
| And learn, too late, they grieved it on its way, | 116 | 11 | 70 | 128 | 11 |
| **LEARNS** | | | | | |
| For a man sleeps where fire leapt down and she learns through his arm | 127 | 13 | 75 | 141 | 13 |
| That he who learns now the sun and moon | 144 | 1 | 82 | 161 | 1 |
| **LEARNT** | | | | | |
| I learnt man's tongue, to twist the shapes of thoughts | 21 | 8 | 13 | 25 | 8 |
| I learnt the verbs of will, and had my secret; | 21 | 15 | 13 | 25 | 15 |
| From the divorcing sky I learnt the double, | 21 | 20 | 13 | 26 | 3 |
| **LEAST** | | | | | |
| In the least valley of sackcloth to mourn | 101 | 12 | 62 | 112 | 12 |
| Nor could share, for his pride, to the least | 114 | 21 | 69 | 126 | 21 |
| When one at the great least of your best loved | 117 | 3 | 71 | 129 | 3 |
| Until that one loved least | 118 | 7 | 71 | 130 | 11 |
| **LEAVE** | | | | | |
| And leave the poppied pickthank where he lies; | 5 | 15 | 3 | 5 | 15 |
| Would leave me cold as butter for the flies, | 12 | 26 | 9 | 14 | 5 |
| And, crackling into the air, leave me half-blind. | 64 | 14 | 39 | 73 | 14 |
| To lift to leave from the treasures of man is pleasing death | 94 | 7 | 57 | 104 | 7 |
| And always known must leave | 117 | 4 | 71 | 129 | 4 |
| He comes to leave her in the lawless sun awaking | 166 | 6 | 86 | 186 | 6 |
| We grieve as the blithe birds, never again, leave shingle and elm, | 168 | 9 | 87 | 188 | 13 |
| The whole of the moon I could love and leave | 174 | 10 | 89 | 194 | 10 |
| Until I die he will not leave my side.) | | | 91 | 201 | 19 |
| **LEAVED** | | | | | |
| Though the town below lay leaved with October blood. | 104 | 15 | 63 | 115 | 17 |
| Under the one leaved trees ran a scarecrow of snow | 122 | 14 | 72 | 135 | 14 |
| Hopping hot leaved and feathered | 132 | 20 | 78 | 147 | 20 |
| All the green leaved little weddings' wives | 174 | 11 | 89 | 194 | 11 |

|  | U.K. | | | U.S. | |
|---|---|---|---|---|---|
|  | *Page* | *Line* | *Poem* | *Page* | *Line* |
| Hill. Who once in gooseskin winter loved all ice leaved | 176 | 12 | 90 | 197 | 12 |
| Teach me the love that is evergreen after the fall leaved | 178 | 12 | 90 | 199 | 13 |
| **LEAVES** | | | | | |
| Out of these seathumbed leaves | viii | 3 | 1 | xvi | 3 |
| Like leaves of trees and as soon | viii | 5 | 1 | xvi | 5 |
| My man of leaves and the bronze root, mortal, unmortal, | 35 | 16 | 20 | 40 | 16 |
| In the dark of the coffin and sheds dry leaves, | 87 | 8 | 52 | 96 | 8 |
| With his stick that picked up leaves. | 111 | 24 | 68 | 123 | 24 |
| On the gristed leaves and the long gone glistening | 121 | 8 | 72 | 134 | 3 |
| Leaves is dancing. Lines of age on the stones weave in a flock. | 121 | 23 | 72 | 134 | 18 |
| Where birds ride like leaves and boats like ducks | 134 | 22 | 79 | 150 | 22 |
| And once below a time I lordly had the trees and leaves | 159 | 7 | 85 | 178 | 7 |
| Out of a lair in the flocked leaves in the dew dipped year | 162 | 6 | 86 | 181 | 6 |
| The nightbird lauds through nunneries and domes of leaves | 163 | 5 | 86 | 182 | 5 |
| Of the morning leaves, as the star falls, as the winged | 164 | 11 | 86 | 183 | 18 |
| Of the wood! Pastoral beat of blood through the laced leaves! | 164 | 22 | 86 | 184 | 8 |
| I open the leaves of the water at a passage | 167 | 23 | 87 | 188 | 4 |
| **LEAVING** | | | | | |
| Through no regret of leaving woman waiting | 48 | 14 | 28 | 56 | 14 |
| **LED-ASTRAY** | | | | | |
| Of the led-astray birds whom God, for their breast of whistles, | 168 | 19 | 87 | 189 | 4 |
| **LEECH** | | | | | |
| The lips of time leech to the fountain head; | 9 | 16 | 6 | 10 | 16 |
| **LEECHES** | | | | | |
| With a hold of leeches and straws, | 95 | 24 | 58 | 105 | 24 |
| **LEFT** | | | | | |
| The weed of love's left dry; | 11 | 15 | 8 | 12 | 15 |
| Left by the dead who, in their moonless acre, | 21 | 11 | 13 | 25 | 11 |
| Touched the first cloud and left a sign. | 22 | 12 | 14 | 27 | 12 |
| Heaven fell with his fall and one crocked bell beat the left air. | 95 | 25 | 58 | 105 | 5 |
| Seed of sons in the loin of the black husk left. | 130 | 8 | 77 | 144 | 8 |
| There is nothing left of the sea but its sound, | 157 | 13 | 83 | 176 | 5 |
| Black night, I left my quivering prints. | 174 | 24 | 89 | 194 | 24 |
| **LEG** | | | | | |
| A leg as long as trees, | 57 | 1 | 34 | 66 | 8 |

| | U.K. | | | U.S. | |
|---|---|---|---|---|---|
| | *Page* | *Line* | *Poem* | *Page* | *Line* |
| Hatched from the windy salvage on one leg, | 71 | 10 | 44 | 80 | 10 |

LEGEND

| | | | | | |
|---|---|---|---|---|---|
| The hero's head lies scraped of every legend, | 79 | 17 | 46 | 88 | 20 |
| I know the legend | 130 | 23 | 77 | 145 | 1 |

LEGENDS

| | | | | | |
|---|---|---|---|---|---|
| And the legends of the green chapels | 103 | 25 | 63 | 114 | 25 |
| Sand with legends in its virgin laps | 156 | 4 | 83 | 174 | 12 |

LEGENDS'

| | | | | | |
|---|---|---|---|---|---|
| All legends' sweethearts on a tree of stories, | 41 | 25 | 23 | 48 | 7 |

LEGION

| | | | | | |
|---|---|---|---|---|---|
| Star and country to the legion | 146 | 2 | 82 | 163 | 2 |

LEND

| | | | | | |
|---|---|---|---|---|---|
| Time is the tune my ladies lend their heartbreak, | 75 | 1 | 44 | 84 | 1 |

LENGTH

| | | | | | |
|---|---|---|---|---|---|
| Measures his own length on the garden wall | 41 | 12 | 23 | 47 | 12 |

LET

| | | | | | |
|---|---|---|---|---|---|
| We are the dark deniers, let us summon | 2 | 7 | 2 | 2 | 7 |
| And bags of blood let out their flies; | 4 | 23 | 3 | 4 | 23 |
| Before I knocked and let flesh enter, | 7 | 1 | 5 | 8 | 1 |
| Some let me make you of the vowelled beeches, | 16 | 13 | 11 | 19 | 13 |
| Some let me make you of the water's speeches. | 16 | 16 | 11 | 19 | 16 |
| Some let me make you of the meadow's signs; | 16 | 21 | 11 | 19 | 21 |
| Some let me tell you of the raven's sins. | 16 | 24 | 11 | 19 | 24 |
| (Some let me make you of autumnal spells, | 17 | 2 | 11 | 20 | 2 |
| Some let me make you of the heartless words. | 17 | 5 | 11 | 20 | 5 |
| Let fall the tear of time; the sleeper's eye, | 26 | 2 | 16 | 31 | 2 |
| Let the wax disk babble | 37 | 19 | 20 | 43 | 2 |
| This flesh you break, this blood you let | 39 | 11 | 21 | 45 | 11 |
| Let the hero seed find harbour, | 43 | 5 | 24 | 50 | 12 |
| Let the hero seed find harbour, | 43 | 12 | 24 | 50 | 19 |
| Flung gravel chime? Let the stones speak | 44 | 13 | 25 | 52 | 13 |
| Let her inhale her dead, through seed and solid | 55 | 10 | 33 | 64 | 13 |
| Let the soil squeal I am the biting man | 56 | 20 | 34 | 65 | 20 |
| Shall I let in the stranger, | 59 | 4 | 35 | 68 | 4 |
| Are formed of flesh, but let the false day come | 63 | 6 | 38 | 72 | 6 |
| Now Jack my fathers let the time-faced crook, | 67 | 15 | 41 | 76 | 15 |
| Let the tale's sailor from a Christian voyage | 76 | 9 | 44 | 85 | 9 |
| Let the first Peter from a rainbow's quayrail | 76 | 15 | 44 | 85 | 15 |
| Green as beginning, let the garden diving | 76 | 19 | 44 | 85 | 19 |
| Its wringing shell, and let her eyelids fasten. | 79 | 9 | 46 | 88 | 12 |
| To veil belladonna and let the dry eyes perceive | 85 | 10 | 50 | 94 | 10 |
| From the stone nest it does not let the feathery | 86 | 2 | 51 | 95 | 2 |
| Bump on a spout let the bubbles jump out. | 97 | 3 | 59 | 108 | 3 |
| Shall I let pray the shadow of a sound | 101 | 10 | 62 | 121 | 10 |
| That he let the dead lie though they moan | 145 | 1 | 82 | 162 | 1 |
| But let it break | 145 | 12 | 82 | 162 | 12 |
| O let him | 148 | 11 | 82 | 165 | 11 |

LET (continued)

| | U.K. | | | U.S. | |
|---|---|---|---|---|---|
| | *Page* | *Line* | *Poem* | *Page* | *Line* |
| Time let me hail and climb | 159 | 4 | 85 | 178 | 4 |
| Time let me play and be | 159 | 13 | 85 | 178 | 13 |
| Come let us die.' | 168 | 8 | 87 | 188 | 12 |
| Oh, let me midlife mourn by the shrined | 172 | 22 | 88 | 192 | 22 |
| In the coal black bush and let them grieve. | 174 | 12 | 89 | 194 | 12 |
| Let him find no rest but be fathered and found, | | | 91 | 200 | 12 |

LETS

| | | | | | |
|---|---|---|---|---|---|
| And lets their trash be honoured as the quick. | 15 | 15 | 10 | 17 | 15 |
| That lets the trees and water enter | 111 | 5 | 68 | 123 | 5 |

LETTER

| | | | | | |
|---|---|---|---|---|---|
| Prophets and fibre kings in oil and letter, | 75 | 20 | 44 | 84 | 20 |

LETTERS

| | | | | | |
|---|---|---|---|---|---|
| Abstracted all the letters of the void; | 22 | 21 | 14 | 27 | 21 |

LEVEL

| | | | | | |
|---|---|---|---|---|---|
| Sail on the level, the departing adventure, | 36 | 11 | 20 | 41 | 11 |
| How soon my level, lord, | 56 | 22 | 34 | 66 | 1 |
| Till field and roof lie level and the same | 63 | 13 | 38 | 72 | 13 |

LEVELS

| | | | | | |
|---|---|---|---|---|---|
| I, in my intricate image, stride on two levels, | 35 | 1 | 20 | 40 | 1 |

LEVER

| | | | | | |
|---|---|---|---|---|---|
| All all and all the dry worlds lever, | 33 | 1 | 19 | 38 | 1 |
| All of the flesh, the dry worlds lever. | 33 | 12 | 19 | 38 | 12 |
| Know, O my bone, the jointed lever, | 33 | 22 | 19 | 39 | 4 |
| All all and all the dry worlds lever | 33 | | 19 | 38 | |

LEWD

| | | | | | |
|---|---|---|---|---|---|
| And heard the lewd, wooed field flow to the coming frost, | 177 | 10 | 90 | 198 | 9 |

LIBIDINOUS

| | | | | | |
|---|---|---|---|---|---|
| Libidinous betrayal, | 115 | 8 | 69 | 127 | 8 |

LICK

| | | | | | |
|---|---|---|---|---|---|
| Savours the lick of the times through a deadly wood of hair | 77 | 9 | 45 | 86 | 9 |

LIDDED

| | | | | | |
|---|---|---|---|---|---|
| The water lidded lands, | x | 11 | 1 | xviii | 17 |

LIDS

| | | | | | |
|---|---|---|---|---|---|
| Dry as a tomb, your coloured lids | 11 | 19 | 8 | 12 | 19 |
| The film of spring is hanging from the lids. | 24 | 24 | 15 | 29 | 24 |
| Grave's foot, blinds down the lids, the teeth in black, | 87 | 4 | 52 | 96 | 4 |
| Who under the lids of her windows hoisted his golden luggage, | 127 | 12 | 75 | 141 | 12 |

LIE

| | | | | | |
|---|---|---|---|---|---|
| Flavoured of celluloid give love the lie. | 14 | 20 | 10 | 16 | 20 |
| The lovers' house, lie suffering my stain? | 46 | 4 | 27 | 54 | 4 |
| Lie all unknowing of the grave sin-eater. | 47 | 8 | 27 | 55 | 8 |
| Lie this fifth month unskated, and the birds have flown; | 49 | 9 | 29 | 58 | 9 |

| | U.K. | | | U.S. | |
|---|---|---|---|---|---|
| | Page | Line | Poem | Page | Line |
| Till field and roof lie level and the same | 63 | 13 | 38 | 72 | 13 |
| From the hissing of the spent lie | 64 | 2 | 39 | 73 | 2 |
| Out of the old lie burning on the ground, | 64 | 13 | 39 | 73 | 13 |
| Half convention and half lie. | 64 | 20 | 39 | 73 | 20 |
| Convenient bird and beast lie lodged to suffer | 77 | 3 | 45 | 86 | 3 |
| Now in the cloud's big breast lie quiet countries, | 80 | 8 | 46 | 89 | 16 |
| Bound by a sovereign strip, we lie, | 82 | 18 | 48 | 91 | 18 |
| Lie watching yellow until the golden weather | 82 | 23 | 48 | 91 | 23 |
| Flood of her heart's fame; she would lie dumb and deep | 87 | 19 | 52 | 96 | 19 |
| Lie with religion in their cramp, her threadbare | 88 | 4 | 52 | 97 | 4 |
| Sigh long, clay cold, lie shorn, | 92 | 6 | 55 | 101 | 12 |
| Lie dry, rest robbed, my beast. | 92 | 14 | 55 | 101 | 20 |
| Each truth, each lie, | 106 | 11 | 64 | 117 | 11 |
| Who palmed the lie on me when you looked | 107 | 4 | 65 | 118 | 4 |
| The death biding two lie-lonely. | 109 | 28 | 67 | 121 | 2 |
| Lucklessly she must lie patient | 110 | 25 | 67 | 122 | 3 |
| Singly lie with the whole wide shore, | 115 | 3 | 69 | 127 | 3 |
| And drown in the drifts of his need, and lie curled caught | 120 | 22 | 72 | 133 | 7 |
| And the lovers lie abed | 128 | 4 | 76 | 142 | 4 |
| Now shown and mostly bare I would lie down, | 133 | 21 | 78 | 149 | 4 |
| Lie down, lie down and live | 133 | 22 | 78 | 149 | 5 |
| Lie still, sleep becalmed, sufferer with the wound | 136 | 1 | 81 | 153 | 1 |
| Lie still, sleep becalmed, hide the mouth in the throat, | 136 | 13 | 81 | 153 | 13 |
| Must lie | 138 | 2 | 82 | 155 | 2 |
| That he let the dead lie though they moan | 145 | 1 | 82 | 162 | 1 |
| Nor the innocent lie in the rooting dingle wooed | 162 | 15 | 86 | 181 | 15 |
| Lie fast and soothed, | 162 | 19 | 86 | 181 | 19 |
| Lie in grace. Sleep spelled at rest in the lowly house | 163 | 20 | 86 | 183 | 1 |
| On skull and scar where his loves lie wrecked, | 171 | 13 | 88 | 191 | 13 |
| And I lie down but to sleep in bed, | 175 | 6 | 89 | 195 | 11 |
| I lie down thin and hear the good bells jaw— | 175 | 24 | 89 | 196 | 5 |
| Where barren as boulders women lie longing still | 176 | 4 | 90 | 197 | 4 |
| He lie lightly, at last, on the last, crossed | | | 91 | 200 | 5 |
| Young among the long flocks, and never lie lost | | | 91 | 200 | 7 |
| Lie Still, Sleep Becalmed | 136 | | 81 | 153 | |

LIES

| And leave the poppied pickthank where he lies; | 5 | 15 | 3 | 5 | 15 |
|---|---|---|---|---|---|
| Were vaguenesses enough and the sweet lies plenty, | 48 | 21 | 28 | 56 | 21 |

LIES (continued)

|  | U.K. | | | U.S. | |
|---|---|---|---|---|---|
|  | Page | Line | Poem | Page | Line |
| And she who lies, | 54 | 17 | 33 | 63 | 17 |
| The land lies out of sound | 58 | 13 | 35 | 67 | 13 |
| Nor when my love lies in the cross-boned drift | 60 | 22 | 36 | 69 | 22 |
| And salt-eyed stumble bedward where she lies | 67 | 12 | 41 | 76 | 12 |
| And timelessly lies loving with the thief. | 67 | 14 | 41 | 76 | 14 |
| The hero's head lies scraped of every legend, | 79 | 17 | 46 | 88 | 20 |
| The present mouth, and the sweetly blown trumpet of lies, | 85 | 6 | 50 | 94 | 6 |
| Others betray the lamenting lies of their losses | 85 | 11 | 50 | 94 | 11 |
| Dragging him up the stairs to one who lies dead. | 100 | 20 | 61 | 111 | 20 |
| Deep with the first dead lies London's daughter, | 101 | 19 | 62 | 112 | 19 |
| A stone lies lost and locked in the lark-high hill. | 115 | 16 | 69 | 127 | 16 |
| O she lies alone and still, | 115 | 18 | 69 | 127 | 18 |
| Exultation lies down. Time buries the spring weather | 123 | 9 | 72 | 136 | 19 |
| Now their love lies a loss | 124 | 5 | 73 | 138 | 5 |
| Venus lies star-struck in her wound | 153 | 21 | 83 | 171 | 17 |

LIFE

| A muscling life from lovers in their cramp, | 2 | 9 | 2 | 2 | 9 |
|---|---|---|---|---|---|
| Drives in a death as life leaks out. | 6 | 9 | 4 | 6 | 9 |
| And we shall be fit fellows for a life, | 15 | 20 | 10 | 17 | 20 |
| Each golden grain spat life into its fellow, | 20 | 23 | 13 | 24 | 23 |
| Life rose and spouted from the rolling seas, | 22 | 16 | 14 | 27 | 16 |
| What's never known is safest in this life. | 50 | 6 | 30 | 59 | 6 |
| Some life, yet unspent, might explode | 64 | 12 | 39 | 73 | 12 |
| Beneath my life, that sighs for the seducer's coming | 109 | 13 | 67 | 120 | 13 |
| Gristle and rind, and a roarers' life, | 175 | 17 | 89 | 195 | 22 |
| And a black reward for a roaring life, | 175 | 21 | 89 | 196 | 2 |

LIFT

| Lift its head to the blows of the rain; | 68 | 23 | 42 | 77 | 23 |
|---|---|---|---|---|---|
| To lift to leave from the treasures of man is pleasing death | 94 | 7 | 57 | 104 | 7 |

LIFTED

| And all the lifted waters walk and leap. | 153 | 16 | 83 | 171 | 12 |
|---|---|---|---|---|---|

LIFTING

| From the first print of the unshodden foot, the lifting | 20 | 10 | 13 | 24 | 10 |
|---|---|---|---|---|---|

LIGHT

| Hears, there, this fox light, my flood ship's | ix | 18 | 1 | xvii | 18 |
|---|---|---|---|---|---|
| These boys of light are curdlers in their folly, | 1 | 7 | 2 | 1 | 7 |
| Of love and light bursts in their throats. | 1 | 23 | 2 | 1 | 23 |
| He blew like powder to the light | 4 | 14 | 3 | 4 | 14 |
| I sent my own ambassador to light; | 5 | 9 | 3 | 5 | 9 |
| The fences of the light are down, | 5 | 16 | 3 | 5 | 16 |
| Is half its light; the fathomed sea | 6 | 11 | 4 | 6 | 11 |
| Our eunuch dreams, all seedless in the light, | 14 | 1 | 10 | 16 | 1 |

|  | U.K. | | | U.S. | |
| --- | --- | --- | --- | --- | --- |
|  | Page | Line | Poem | Page | Line |
| Of light and love, the tempers of the heart, | 14 | 2 | 10 | 16 | 2 |
| The sun and moon shed one white light. | 20 | 9 | 13 | 24 | 9 |
| Shone in my ears the light of sound, | 20 | 20 | 13 | 24 | 20 |
| Called in my eyes the sound of light. | 20 | 21 | 13 | 24 | 21 |
| Into the sided lap of light grew strong, | 21 | 3 | 13 | 25 | 3 |
| One smile of light across the empty face; | 22 | 2 | 14 | 27 | 2 |
| That from the solid bases of the light | 22 | 20 | 14 | 27 | 20 |
| Blood shot and scattered to the winds of light | 23 | 5 | 14 | 28 | 5 |
| Light breaks where no sun shines; | 24 | 1 | 15 | 29 | 1 |
| The things of light | 24 | 5 | 15 | 29 | 5 |
| Light breaks on secret lots, | 25 | 1 | 15 | 30 | 1 |
| Shifting to light, turned on me like a moon. | 26 | 3 | 16 | 31 | 3 |
| How light the sleeping on this soily star, | 26 | 24 | 16 | 32 | 4 |
| O light in zenith, the coupled bud, | 34 | 8 | 19 | 39 | 14 |
| So solve the mystic sun, the wife of light, | 51 | 26 | 31 | 61 | 5 |
| The rite of light, | 56 | 16 | 34 | 65 | 16 |
| Foster the light nor veil the manshaped moon, | 60 | 1 | 36 | 69 | 1 |
| Caught in an octagon of unaccustomed light, | 63 | 2 | 38 | 72 | 2 |
| Light and dark are no enemies | 66 | 12 | 40 | 75 | 12 |
| Riding the sea light on a sunken path, | 67 | 8 | 41 | 76 | 8 |
| Calls the green rock of light. | 69 | 12 | 43 | 78 | 12 |
| By lava's light split through the oyster vowels | 74 | 3 | 44 | 83 | 3 |
| That breaks one bone to light with a judgment clout, | 87 | 9 | 52 | 96 | 9 |
| In quick, sweet, cruel light till the locked ground sprout out, | 91 | 18 | 55 | 100 | 18 |
| You have kicked from a dark den, leaped up the whinnying light, | 92 | 15 | 55 | 101 | 21 |
| Strike light, and bloody a loud room. | 97 | 10 | 59 | 108 | 10 |
| By the light of the meat-eating sun. | 99 | 5 | 60 | 110 | 5 |
| Tells with silence the last light breaking | 101 | 4 | 62 | 112 | 4 |
| Of sun light | 103 | 24 | 63 | 114 | 24 |
| Water and light, the earth and sky, | 106 | 8 | 64 | 117 | 8 |
| Who admits the delusive light through the bouncing wall, | 108 | 11 | 66 | 119 | 11 |
| And taken by light in her arms at long and dear last | 108 | 16 | 66 | 119 | 16 |
| Rage, rage against the dying of the light. | 116 | 3 | 70 | 128 | 3 |
| Rage, rage against the dying of the light. | 116 | 9 | 70 | 128 | 9 |
| Rage, rage against the dying of the light. | 116 | 15 | 70 | 128 | 15 |
| Rage, rage against the dying of the light. | 116 | 19 | 70 | 128 | 19 |
| With every cry since light | 117 | 23 | 71 | 129 | 23 |
| By the spit and the black pot in the log bright light | 120 | 2 | 72 | 132 | 7 |
| By the believer lost and the hurled outcast of light. | 120 | 25 | 72 | 133 | 10 |

|  | U.K. | | | U.S. | |
|  | Page | Line | Poem | Page | Line |
| On the departed, snow bushed green, wanton in moon light | 121 | 17 | 72 | 134 | 12 |
| By the spit and the black pot in the log bright light. | 122 | 7 | 72 | 135 | 7 |
| Waking alone in a multitude of loves when morning's light | 127 | 1 | 75 | 141 | 1 |
| I labour by singing light | 128 | 6 | 76 | 142 | 6 |
| Love is the last light spoken. Oh | 130 | 7 | 77 | 144 | 7 |
| Light. | 138 | 17 | 82 | 155 | 17 |
| Infant light or | 144 | 12 | 82 | 161 | 12 |
| Light through sea and soil | 146 | 5 | 82 | 163 | 5 |
| Toppling up the boatside in a snow of light! | 154 | 18 | 83 | 172 | 18 |
| That one dark I owe my light, | 158 | 9 | 84 | 177 | 9 |
| Down the rivers of the windfall light. | 159 | 9 | 85 | 178 | 9 |
| So it must have been after the birth of the simple light | 160 | 11 | 85 | 179 | 11 |
| In the unknown, famous light of great | 171 | 20 | 88 | 191 | 20 |
| Dark is a way and light is a place, | 171 | 22 | 88 | 191 | 22 |
| Who is the light of old | 172 | 19 | 88 | 192 | 19 |
| Light of his thighs, spreadeagle to the dunghill sky, | 177 | 3 | 90 | 198 | 2 |
| Noon, and night, and light. The rivers of the dead |  |  | 91 | 200 | 15 |
| Out of his eyes I saw the last light glide. |  |  | 91 | 201 | 7 |
| Here among the light of the lording sky |  |  | 91 | 201 | 8 |
| Light breaks where no sun shines | 24 |  | 15 | 29 |  |
| Foster the light | 60 |  | 36 | 69 |  |
| LIGHT'S |  |  |  |  |  |
| And one light's language in the book of trees. | 74 | 19 | 44 | 83 | 19 |
| LIGHTED |  |  |  |  |  |
| The pyre yet to be lighted of my sins and days, | 109 | 3 | 67 | 120 | 3 |
| Under the lighted shapes of faith and their moonshade | 176 | 17 | 90 | 197 | 17 |
| LIGHTLY |  |  |  |  |  |
| I fled that ground as lightly as a feather. | 26 | 10 | 16 | 31 | 10 |
| He lie lightly, at last, on the last, crossed |  |  | 91 | 200 | 5 |
| LIGHTNING |  |  |  |  |  |
| The grooved land rotating, that the stylus of lightning | 37 | 17 | 20 | 42 | 23 |
| Walks with no wound, nor lightning in her face, | 80 | 10 | 46 | 89 | 18 |
| And a lamp of lightning for the poor in the dark; | 89 | 11 | 53 | 98 | 11 |
| Because their words have forked no lightning they | 116 | 5 | 70 | 128 | 5 |
| Though the moment of a miracle is unending lightning | 127 | 6 | 75 | 141 | 6 |

| | U.K. | | | U.S. | |
|---|---|---|---|---|---|
| | *Page* | *Line* | *Poem* | *Page* | *Line* |
| His lightning answers my | 148 | 14 | 82 | 165 | 14 |
| Gold gut is a lightning thread, | 151 | 15 | 83 | 169 | 3 |
| And the long-tailed lightning lit his catch. | 154 | 8 | 83 | 172 | 8 |
| LIGHTNINGS | | | | | |
| And the lightnings of adoration | 140 | 9 | 82 | 157 | 9 |
| LIGHTS | | | | | |
| Lights up the living worm. | 6 | 6 | 4 | 6 | 6 |
| Day lights the bone; | 24 | 21 | 15 | 29 | 21 |
| LIKE | | | | | |
| Like stalks of tall, dry straw, | vii | 22 | 1 | xv | 22 |
| Like leaves of trees and as soon | viii | 5 | 1 | xvi | 5 |
| Like wooden islands, hill to hill. | x | 13 | 1 | xviii | 19 |
| The mouth of time sucked, like a sponge, | 4 | 4 | 3 | 4 | 4 |
| He blew like powder to the light | 4 | 14 | 3 | 4 | 14 |
| Move like two ghosts before the eye. | 6 | 18 | 4 | 6 | 18 |
| Unpacks the head that, like a sleepy ghost, | 10 | 3 | 7 | 11 | 3 |
| Tread, like a naked Venus, | 10 | 12 | 7 | 11 | 12 |
| And drop the plum like fire from the flesh. | 12 | 9 | 9 | 13 | 9 |
| For we shall be a shouter like the cock, | 15 | 17 | 10 | 17 | 17 |
| On the horizon walking like the trees | 16 | 10 | 11 | 19 | 10 |
| When, like a running grave, time tracks you down, | 18 | 1 | 12 | 21 | 1 |
| Comes, like a scissors stalking, tailor age, | 18 | 6 | 12 | 21 | 6 |
| Drive children up like bruises to the thumb, | 18 | 14 | 12 | 21 | 14 |
| And to the voice that, like a voice of hunger, | 21 | 5 | 13 | 25 | 5 |
| Slides like a sea; | 24 | 15 | 15 | 29 | 15 |
| Like some pitch moon, the limit of the globes; | 24 | 20 | 15 | 29 | 20 |
| Shifting to light, turned on me like a moon. | 26 | 3 | 16 | 31 | 3 |
| Casts to the pine roots, raising man like a mountain | 35 | 11 | 20 | 40 | 11 |
| Sprout from the stony lockers like a tree on Aran. | 37 | 27 | 20 | 43 | 10 |
| Love like a mist or fire through the bed of eels. | 38 | 12 | 20 | 44 | 2 |
| Winged like a sabbath ass this children's piece | 41 | 16 | 23 | 47 | 16 |
| Like a tower on the town | 42 | 5 | 24 | 49 | 5 |
| Like a tower on the town | 42 | 12 | 24 | 49 | 12 |
| The wet night scolds me like a nurse? | 44 | 10 | 25 | 52 | 10 |
| Time, in a folly's rider, like a county man | 49 | 4 | 29 | 58 | 4 |
| Crack like a spring in a vice, bone breaking April, | 49 | 17 | 29 | 58 | 17 |
| Ring like a handbell through the corridors, | 53 | 22 | 32 | 62 | 22 |
| Like exodus a chapter from the garden, | 54 | 18 | 33 | 63 | 18 |
| The wind pass like a fire, | 58 | 18 | 35 | 67 | 18 |
| Nor sprout on owl-seed like a goblin-sucker, | 60 | 14 | 36 | 69 | 14 |
| But heart, like head, leads helplessly; | 63 | 10 | 38 | 72 | 10 |
| I cannot murder, like a fool, | 66 | 6 | 40 | 75 | 6 |
| That the green child see like a grail | 69 | 22 | 43 | 78 | 22 |

|  | U.K. | | | U.S. | |
|---|---|---|---|---|---|
|  | *Page* | *Line* | *Poem* | *Page* | *Line* |
| Wound like a ball of lakes | 70 | 5 | 43 | 79 | 9 |
| Bent like three trees and bird-papped through her shift, | 75 | 9 | 44 | 84 | 9 |
| Pour like a halo on the caps and serpents. | 75 | 24 | 44 | 84 | 24 |
| That clouts the spittle like bubbles with broken rooms, | 77 | 6 | 45 | 86 | 6 |
| That frozen wife whose juices drift like a fixed sea | 77 | 14 | 45 | 86 | 14 |
| Like the mauled pictures of boys? | 77 | 19 | 45 | 86 | 19 |
| Or like the tide-looped breastknot reefed again | 78 | 11 | 46 | 87 | 11 |
| And, pride is last, is like a child alone | 78 | 13 | 46 | 87 | 13 |
| Like an approaching wave I sprawl to ruin. | 79 | 12 | 46 | 88 | 15 |
| Fumed like a tree, and tossed a burning bird; | 80 | 3 | 46 | 89 | 11 |
| A calm wind blows that raised the trees like hair | 80 | 11 | 46 | 89 | 19 |
| My nostrils see her breath burn like a bush. | 81 | 10 | 47 | 90 | 10 |
| Breaks, O my heart's blood, like a heart and hill. | 82 | 24 | 48 | 91 | 24 |
| When, with his torch and hourglass, like a sulphur priest, | 83 | 2 | 49 | 92 | 2 |
| In time like outlaw rains on that priest, water, | 86 | 6 | 51 | 95 | 6 |
| But do not travel down dumb wind like prodigals. | 86 | 11 | 51 | 95 | 11 |
| Babble like a bellbuoy over the hymning heads, | 87 | 23 | 52 | 96 | 23 |
| And every stone I wind off like a reel. | 89 | 13 | 53 | 98 | 13 |
| Bent like a beast to lap the singular floods | 90 | 3 | 54 | 99 | 3 |
| Refusal struck like a bell under water | 90 | 12 | 54 | 99 | 12 |
| Drunk as a vineyard snail, flailed like an octopus, | 91 | 7 | 55 | 100 | 7 |
| Glory cracked like a flea. | 95 | 18 | 58 | 105 | 18 |
| The breath draw back like a bolt through white oil | 96 | 21 | 58 | 107 | 4 |
| And a stranger enter like iron. | 96 | 22 | 58 | 107 | 5 |
| Bend, if my journey ache, direction like an arc or make | 97 | 14 | 59 | 108 | 14 |
| 'Now to awake husked of gestures and my joy like a cave | 97 | 21 | 59 | 109 | 1 |
| In the groin of the natural doorway I crouched like a tailor | 99 | 3 | 60 | 110 | 3 |
| Like the dust of the dead. | 105 | 12 | 64 | 116 | 12 |
| Blow away like breath, | 105 | 17 | 64 | 116 | 17 |
| Fly like the stars' blood, | 105 | 24 | 64 | 116 | 24 |
| Like the sun's tears, | 106 | 1 | 64 | 117 | 1 |
| Like the moon's seed, rubbish | 106 | 2 | 64 | 117 | 2 |
| With immortality at my side like Christ the sky. | 110 | 21 | 67 | 121 | 23 |
| Hurling into beginning like Christ the child. | 110 | 24 | 67 | 122 | 2 |
| Like the park birds he came early | 111 | 13 | 68 | 123 | 13 |
| Like the water he sat down | 111 | 14 | 68 | 123 | 14 |

|  | U.K. | | | U.S. | |
|---|---|---|---|---|---|
|  | *Page* | *Line* | *Poem* | *Page* | *Line* |
| Blind eyes could blaze like meteors and be gay, | 116 | 14 | 70 | 128 | 14 |
| A she bird rose and rayed like a burning bride. | 121 | 14 | 72 | 134 | 9 |
| Him up and he ran like a wind after the kindling flight | 122 | 9 | 72 | 135 | 9 |
| When black birds died like priests in the cloaked hedge row | 122 | 12 | 72 | 135 | 12 |
| And fast through the drifts of the thickets antlered like deer, | 122 | 15 | 72 | 135 | 15 |
| And the dust shall sing like a bird | 129 | 22 | 77 | 143 | 22 |
| Night fall and the fruit like a sun, | 131 | 4 | 77 | 145 | 10 |
| Into the wine burning like brandy, | 131 | 19 | 77 | 146 | 1 |
| Where birds ride like leaves and boats like ducks | 134 | 22 | 79 | 150 | 22 |
| And the coins on my eyelids sang like shells. | 134 | 30 | 79 | 151 | 8 |
| To the sea sound flowing like blood from the loud wound | 136 | 6 | 81 | 153 | 6 |
| Casting to-morrow like a thorn | 138 | 8 | 82 | 155 | 8 |
| His mouth and rocked him like a storm | 139 | 10 | 82 | 156 | 10 |
| Like pollen | 143 | 11 | 82 | 160 | 11 |
| Where the anchor rode like a gull | 150 | 13 | 83 | 167 | 17 |
| Whales in the wake like capes and Alps | 151 | 1 | 83 | 168 | 9 |
| Spun on a spout like a long-legged ball | 151 | 8 | 83 | 168 | 16 |
| And the flakes fall like hills. | 154 | 16 | 83 | 172 | 16 |
| Weeps like the risen sun among | 155 | 19 | 83 | 174 | 3 |
| And then to awake, and the farm, like a wanderer white | 160 | 6 | 85 | 179 | 6 |
| Though I sang in my chains like the sea. | 161 | 6 | 85 | 180 | 9 |
| Of birds! Among the cocks like fire the red fox | 164 | 20 | 86 | 184 | 6 |
| The thief fall on the dead like the willy nilly dew, | 165 | 22 | 86 | 185 | 12 |
| Round the sun, he comes to my love like the designed snow, | 165 | 25 | 86 | 185 | 15 |
| Flows to the strand of flowers like the dew's ruly sea, | 165 | 27 | 86 | 185 | 17 |
| And surely he sails like the ship shape clouds. Oh he | 165 | 28 | 86 | 185 | 18 |
| The rude owl cried like a telltale tit, | 174 | 5 | 89 | 194 | 5 |
| And the daughters of darkness flame like Fawkes fires still. | 178 | 19 | 90 | 199 | 20 |
| On whom a world of ills came down like snow. |  |  | 91 | 201 | 11 |
| When, like a running grave | 18 |  | 12 | 21 |  |
| LIKENESS |  |  |  |  |  |
| This is the world: the lying likeness of | 15 | 11 | 10 | 17 | 11 |
| LILTING |  |  |  |  |  |
| About the lilting house and happy as the grass was green, | 159 | 2 | 85 | 178 | 2 |

|  | U.K. Page | Line | Poem | U.S. Page | Line |
|---|---|---|---|---|---|
| LILY |  |  |  |  |  |
| The rack of dreams my lily bones | 7 | 20 | 5 | 8 | 20 |
| LILY'S |  |  |  |  |  |
| Brand of the lily's anger on her ring, | 54 | 19 | 33 | 63 | 19 |
| LIMBS |  |  |  |  |  |
| Whack their boys' limbs, | 14 | 3 | 10 | 16 | 3 |
| From limbs that had the measure of the worm, shuffled | 28 | 5 | 17 | 33 | 5 |
| And the limbs are torn. | 65 | 5 | 40 | 74 | 5 |
| She cried her white-dressed limbs were bare | 93 | 17 | 56 | 102 | 17 |
| Made her limbs blind by luminous charms, | 113 | 21 | 69 | 125 | 21 |
| The carved limbs in the rock | 121 | 21 | 72 | 134 | 16 |
| The octopus walking into her limbs | 152 | 7 | 83 | 169 | 19 |
| With salty colts and gales in their limbs | 156 | 18 | 83 | 175 | 6 |
| LIME |  |  |  |  |  |
| How of my clay is made the hangman's lime. | 9 | 15 | 6 | 10 | 15 |
| LIMIT |  |  |  |  |  |
| Like some pitch moon, the limit of the globes; | 24 | 20 | 15 | 29 | 20 |
| LIMP |  |  |  |  |  |
| Limp in the street of sea, among the rabble | 30 | 15 | 18 | 35 | 15 |
| A limp and riderless shape to leap nine thinning months.' | 97 | 15 | 59 | 108 | 15 |
| Slunk pouting out when the limp time came; | 175 | 15 | 89 | 195 | 20 |
| LIMP-TREED |  |  |  |  |  |
| Lost in a limp-treed and uneating silence, | 79 | 2 | 46 | 88 | 5 |
| LINE |  |  |  |  |  |
| Over the manwaging line. | 42 | 7 | 24 | 49 | 7 |
| Over the warbearing line | 42 | 14 | 24 | 49 | 14 |
| LINEAMENTS |  |  |  |  |  |
| The frank, closed pearl, the sea-girls' lineaments | 78 | 19 | 46 | 87 | 19 |
| LINEN |  |  |  |  |  |
| Gold on such features, and the linen spirit | 76 | 3 | 44 | 85 | 3 |
| Where, wound in emerald linen and sharp wind, | 79 | 16 | 46 | 88 | 19 |
| In the squirrel nimble grove, under linen and thatch | 163 | 21 | 86 | 183 | 2 |
| LINENED |  |  |  |  |  |
| In that bright anchorground where I lay linened, | 79 | 22 | 46 | 89 | 3 |
| LINES |  |  |  |  |  |
| And flesh was snipped to cross the lines | 7 | 22 | 5 | 8 | 22 |
| Leaves is dancing. Lines of age on the stones weave in a flock. | 121 | 23 | 72 | 134 | 18 |
| Back. Lines of age sleep on the stones till trumpeting dawn. | 123 | 8 | 72 | 136 | 18 |
| LINKED |  |  |  |  |  |
| All birds and beasts of the linked night uproar and chime | 177 | 15 | 90 | 198 | 14 |

|  | U.K. | | | U.S. | |
|---|---|---|---|---|---|
|  | Page | Line | Poem | Page | Line |
| **LINT** |  |  |  |  |  |
| Buckle to lint and cloth their natron footsteps, | 75 | 22 | 44 | 84 | 22 |
| **LIONHEAD'S** |  |  |  |  |  |
| That melts the lionhead's heel and horseshoe of the heart, | 91 | 14 | 55 | 100 | 14 |
| **LIONS** |  |  |  |  |  |
| Whalebed and bulldance, the gold bush of lions, | 78 | 22 | 46 | 87 | 22 |
| Lions and fires of his flying breath, | 117 | 5 | 71 | 129 | 5 |
| **LIPS** |  |  |  |  |  |
| The lips of time leech to the fountain head; | 9 | 16 | 6 | 10 | 16 |
| And from her lips the faded pigments fall, | 63 | 7 | 38 | 72 | 7 |
| Pursed lips at the receiver, | 64 | 17 | 39 | 73 | 17 |
| My lips are withered with a kiss, | 65 | 20 | 40 | 74 | 20 |
| Cried the topless, inchtaped lips from hank and hood | 79 | 21 | 46 | 89 | 2 |
| And her red lips were kissed black, | 93 | 18 | 56 | 102 | 18 |
| When at your lips and keys, | 117 | 14 | 71 | 129 | 14 |
| Her heart all ears and eyes, lips catching the avalanche | 127 | 10 | 75 | 141 | 10 |
| Before the lips blaze and bloom | 144 | 3 | 82 | 161 | 3 |
| A girl alive with his hooks through her lips; | 149 | 22 | 83 | 167 | 2 |
| Deep the great bushed bait with raining lips | 151 | 3 | 83 | 168 | 11 |
| And the old men sing from newborn lips: | 155 | 8 | 83 | 173 | 12 |
| And he who taught their lips to sing | 155 | 18 | 83 | 174 | 2 |
| **LIQUID** |  |  |  |  |  |
| With liquid hands tapped on the womb, | 7 | 2 | 5 | 8 | 2 |
| Seasons over the liquid world, | 153 | 23 | 83 | 171 | 19 |
| The liquid choirs of his tribes. | 155 | 20 | 83 | 174 | 4 |
| **LISTEN** |  |  |  |  |  |
| Listen. The minstrels sing | 121 | 1 | 72 | 133 | 16 |
| Time sings through the intricately dead snow drop. Listen. | 121 | 10 | 72 | 134 | 5 |
| Listen and look where she sails the goose plucked sea, | 122 | 20 | 72 | 135 | 20 |
| **LISTENED** |  |  |  |  |  |
| Come in the morning where I wandered and listened | 103 | 2 | 63 | 114 | 2 |
| **LISTENING** |  |  |  |  |  |
| In the listening | 104 | 3 | 63 | 115 | 5 |
| Under the mile off moon we trembled listening | 136 | 5 | 81 | 153 | 5 |
| **LIT** |  |  |  |  |  |
| Lit on the cuddled tree, the cross of fever, | 19 | 8 | 12 | 22 | 13 |
| And the long-tailed lightning lit his catch. | 154 | 8 | 83 | 172 | 8 |
| **LITTLE** |  |  |  |  |  |
| And held a little sabbath with the sun, | 4 | 15 | 3 | 4 | 15 |
| Out of the sighs a little comes, | 48 | 1 | 28 | 56 | 1 |
| A little comes, is tasted and found good; | 48 | 5 | 28 | 56 | 5 |

# LITTLE (continued)

|  | U.K. | | | U.S. | |
|---|---|---|---|---|---|
|  | *Page* | *Line* | *Poem* | *Page* | *Line* |
| Is heard but little till the stars go out. | 53 | 20 | 32 | 62 | 20 |
| Now break a giant tear for the little known fall, | 126 | 8 | 74 | 140 | 8 |
| In the cinder of the little skull, | 130 | 16 | 77 | 144 | 16 |
| In the cinder of the little skull, | 131 | 2 | 77 | 145 | 8 |
| All the green leaved little weddings' wives | 174 | 11 | 89 | 194 | 11 |

## LIVE

| | | | | | |
|---|---|---|---|---|---|
| Who picks the live heart on a diamond. | 79 | 19 | 46 | 88 | 22 |
| Raise the live rafters of the eardrum, | 96 | 11 | 58 | 106 | 11 |
| Lie down, lie down and live | 133 | 22 | 78 | 149 | 5 |

## LIVELONG

| | | | | | |
|---|---|---|---|---|---|
| The livelong river's robe | 171 | 1 | 88 | 191 | 1 |

## LIVER

| | | | | | |
|---|---|---|---|---|---|
| Of gallow crosses on the liver | 7 | 23 | 5 | 8 | 23 |

## LIVING

| | | | | | |
|---|---|---|---|---|---|
| Lights up the living worm. | 6 | 6 | 4 | 6 | 6 |
| Did twist into a living cipher, | 7 | 21 | 5 | 8 | 21 |
| Then all the matter of the living air | 26 | 21 | 16 | 32 | 1 |
| The slug's a living calendar of days; | 45 | 15 | 26 | 53 | 15 |
| With bridebait of gold bread, I with a living skein, | 91 | 25 | 55 | 101 | 3 |
| Of the living flesh is monstrous or immortal, | 110 | 13 | 67 | 121 | 15 |
| And the living earth your sons. | 110 | 28 | 67 | 122 | 6 |
| With all the living, prays, | 172 | 12 | 88 | 192 | 12 |

## LIZARD

| | | | | | |
|---|---|---|---|---|---|
| 'A lizard darting with black venom's thread | 79 | 23 | 46 | 89 | 4 |

## LLEWELYN

| | | | | | |
|---|---|---|---|---|---|
| This Side of the Truth (for Llewelyn) | 105 | | 64 | 116 | |

## LOAD

| | | | | | |
|---|---|---|---|---|---|
| And load the throats of shells | 117 | 22 | 71 | 129 | 22 |

## LOAVES

| | | | | | |
|---|---|---|---|---|---|
| Was miraculous virginity old as loaves and fishes, | 127 | 5 | 75 | 141 | 5 |

## LOCK

| | | | | | |
|---|---|---|---|---|---|
| That wipes away not crow's-foot nor the lock | 12 | 23 | 9 | 14 | 2 |
| Know now the flesh's lock and vice, | 33 | 20 | 19 | 39 | 2 |
| Time for the swimmers' hands, music for silver lock | 86 | 7 | 51 | 95 | 7 |
| From the opening of the garden lock | 111 | 4 | 68 | 123 | 4 |

## LOCKED

| | | | | | |
|---|---|---|---|---|---|
| Locked in the long worm of my finger | 4 | 2 | 3 | 4 | 2 |
| Falls on a ring of summers and locked noons. | 79 | 4 | 46 | 88 | 7 |
| In quick, sweet, cruel light till the locked ground sprout out, | 91 | 18 | 55 | 100 | 18 |
| A stone lies lost and locked in the lark-high hill. | 115 | 16 | 69 | 127 | 16 |
| Prisoners of wishes locked their eyes | 125 | 7 | 74 | 139 | 7 |

## LOCKERS

| | | | | | |
|---|---|---|---|---|---|
| Sprout from the stony lockers like a tree on Aran. | 37 | 27 | 20 | 43 | 10 |

|  | U.K. | | | U.S. | |
|  | Page | Line | Poem | Page | Line |
| **LOCKING** | | | | | |
| Give over, lovers, locking, and the seawax struggle, | 38 | 11 | 20 | 44 | 1 |
| Locking, unlocking, the murdered strangers weave, | 117 | 15 | 71 | 129 | 15 |
| **LOCKJAW** | | | | | |
| Doubled, to fork him back, through the lockjaw bed | 79 | 24 | 46 | 89 | 5 |
| **LOCKS** | | | | | |
| When once the twilight locks no longer | 4 | 1 | 3 | 4 | 1 |
| The sea and instrument, nicked in the locks of time, | 38 | 14 | 20 | 44 | 4 |
| The fingers at the locks. | 58 | 4 | 35 | 67 | 4 |
| After the locks and chains | 112 | 12 | 68 | 124 | 12 |
| In the watched dark, quivering through locks and caves, | 118 | 3 | 71 | 130 | 7 |
| The locks yawned loose and a blast blew them wide, | 135 | 3 | 80 | 152 | 3 |
| When all the keys shot from the locks, and rang. | 135 | 8 | 80 | 152 | 8 |
| When once the twilight locks no longer | 4 | | 3 | 4 | |
| **LOCUSTS** | | | | | |
| And famine grew, and locusts came; | 62 | 10 | 37 | 71 | 10 |
| **LODGED** | | | | | |
| Convenient bird and beast lie lodged to suffer | 77 | 3 | 45 | 86 | 3 |
| **LOFT** | | | | | |
| Up to the swallow thronged loft by the shadow of my hand, | 160 | 25 | 85 | 180 | 2 |
| Shallow and sedge, and 'dilly dilly,' calls the loft hawk, | 167 | 21 | 87 | 188 | 2 |
| **LOFTY** | | | | | |
| The lofty roots of the clouds. | 96 | 5 | 58 | 106 | 5 |
| **LOG** | | | | | |
| By the spit and the black pot in the log bright light | 120 | 2 | 72 | 132 | 7 |
| By the spit and the black pot in the log bright light. | 122 | 7 | 72 | 135 | 7 |
| **LOGIC** | | | | | |
| When blood, spade-handed, and the logic time | 18 | 13 | 12 | 21 | 13 |
| **LOGICS** | | | | | |
| When logics die, | 25 | 3 | 15 | 30 | 3 |
| **LOIN** | | | | | |
| The seed that makes a forest of the loin | 6 | 13 | 4 | 6 | 13 |
| Stripping my loin of promise, | 10 | 14 | 7 | 11 | 14 |
| I would not fear the devil in the loin | 12 | 20 | 9 | 13 | 20 |
| The loin is glory in a working pallor. | 32 | 9 | 18 | 37 | 15 |
| The twisted brain, the fair-formed loin, | 48 | 25 | 28 | 57 | 2 |
| Refusal struck her loin and the lame flower | 90 | 2 | 54 | 99 | 2 |

|  | U.K. | | | U.S. | |
|  | Page | Line | Poem | Page | Line |
| Seed of sons in the loin of the black husk left. | 130 | 8 | 77 | 144 | 8 |
| From his loin | 138 | 15 | 82 | 155 | 15 |
| And his loin was a hunting flame | 157 | 4 | 83 | 175 | 16 |
| **LOIN-LEAF** | | | | | |
| Sleep to a newborn sleep in a swaddling loin-leaf stroked and sang | 113 | 22 | 69 | 125 | 22 |
| **LONDON** | | | | | |
| On the altar of London, | 130 | 14 | 77 | 144 | 14 |
| O Rome and Sodom To-morrow and London | 156 | 23 | 83 | 175 | 11 |
| A Refusal to Mourn the Death, by Fire, of a child in London | 101 | | 62 | 112 | |
| **LONDON's** | | | | | |
| Deep with the first dead lies London's daughter, | 101 | 19 | 62 | 112 | 19 |
| In many married London's estranging grief. | 117 | 12 | 71 | 129 | 12 |
| When near and strange wounded on London's waves | 117 | 27 | 71 | 130 | 3 |
| **LONELY** | | | | | |
| The death biding two lie lonely. | 109 | 28 | 67 | 121 | 2 |
| And I am struck as lonely as a holy maker by the sun. | 158 | 12 | 84 | 177 | 12 |
| **LONG** | | | | | |
| Locked in the long worm of my finger | 4 | 2 | 3 | 4 | 2 |
| Long breath that carried to my father | 8 | 17 | 5 | 9 | 17 |
| And the four winds, that had long blown as one, | 20 | 19 | 13 | 24 | 19 |
| Turn the long sea arterial | 36 | 22 | 20 | 42 | 1 |
| Splitting the long eye open, and the spiral turnkey, | 36 | 26 | 20 | 42 | 5 |
| You are all these, said she who gave me the long suck, | 46 | 17 | 27 | 54 | 17 |
| He'll ache too long | 48 | 13 | 28 | 56 | 13 |
| Shape all her whelps with the long voice of water, | 55 | 2 | 33 | 64 | 5 |
| A leg as long as trees, | 57 | 1 | 34 | 66 | 8 |
| They lying long shall not die windily; | 68 | 12 | 42 | 77 | 12 |
| I am the long world's gentleman, he said, | 71 | 13 | 44 | 80 | 13 |
| The child that sucketh long is shooting up, | 71 | 16 | 44 | 80 | 16 |
| Soon sets alight a long stick from the cradle; | 71 | 20 | 44 | 80 | 20 |
| With pins for teardrops is the long wound's woman. | 75 | 10 | 44 | 84 | 10 |
| Weds my long gentleman to dusts and furies; | 76 | 4 | 44 | 85 | 4 |
| Sigh long, clay cold, lie shorn, | 92 | 6 | 55 | 101 | 12 |
| I advance for as long as forever is. | 99 | 9 | 60 | 110 | 9 |
| Robed in the long friends, | 101 | 20 | 62 | 112 | 20 |
| Joy of the long dead child sang burning | 104 | 11 | 63 | 115 | 13 |
| And taken by light in her arms at long and dear last | 108 | 16 | 66 | 119 | 16 |

|  | U.K. | | | U.S. | |
|---|---|---|---|---|---|
|  | *Page* | *Line* | *Poem* | *Page* | *Line* |
| On the gristed leaves and the long gone glistening | 121 | 8 | 72 | 134 | 3 |
| In the long ago land that glided the dark door wide | 121 | 12 | 72 | 134 | 7 |
| Of fields. For love, the long ago she bird rises. Look. | 121 | 25 | 72 | 134 | 20 |
| All night lost and long wading in the wake of the she- | 122 | 18 | 72 | 135 | 18 |
| Down the long walks of their vows. | 124 | 4 | 73 | 138 | 4 |
| The long, laid minute's bride drifts on | 152 | 11 | 83 | 170 | 3 |
| Oh miracle of fishes! The long dead bite! | 154 | 20 | 83 | 172 | 20 |
| All the sun long it was running, it was lovely, the hay | 159 | 19 | 85 | 178 | 19 |
| All the moon long I heard, blessed among stables, the night-jars | 160 | 3 | 85 | 179 | 3 |
| Under the new made clouds and happy as the heart was long, | 160 | 16 | 85 | 179 | 16 |
| And the rhymer in the long tongued room, | 170 | 15 | 88 | 190 | 15 |
| But dark is a long way. | 172 | 10 | 88 | 192 | 10 |
| To labour and love though they lay down long ago. | 176 | 5 | 90 | 197 | 5 |
| Trounced by his wings in the hissing shippen, long dead | 177 | 19 | 90 | 198 | 18 |
| Save by their long desirers in the fox cubbed | 178 | 15 | 90 | 199 | 16 |
| Young among the long flocks, and never lie lost |  |  | 91 | 200 | 7 |
| LONGED |  |  |  |  |  |
| I have longed to move away | 64 | 1 | 39 | 73 | 1 |
| I have longed to move away | 64 | 6 | 39 | 73 | 6 |
| I have longed to move away but am afraid; | 64 | 11 | 39 | 73 | 11 |
| Above all he longed for his mother's breast |  |  | 91 | 200 | 9 |
| I have longed to move away | 64 |  | 39 | 73 |  |
| LONGER |  |  |  |  |  |
| When once the twilight locks no longer | 4 | 1 | 3 | 4 | 1 |
| And west's no longer drowned | 53 | 3 | 32 | 62 | 3 |
| On the white, no longer growing green, and, minstrel dead, | 123 | 2 | 72 | 136 | 12 |
| No longer will the vibrations of the sun desire on | 127 | 8 | 75 | 141 | 8 |
| Off by the sun and Daughters no longer grieved | 178 | 14 | 90 | 199 | 15 |
| When once the twilight locks no longer | 4 |  | 3 | 4 |  |
| LONGING |  |  |  |  |  |
| Where barren as boulders women lie longing still | 176 | 4 | 90 | 197 | 4 |
| LONG-LAST |  |  |  |  |  |
| Sprinkles in children's eyes a long-last sleep | 53 | 13 | 32 | 62 | 13 |
| LONG-LEGGED |  |  |  |  |  |
| Spun on a spout like a long-legged ball | 151 | 8 | 83 | 168 | 16 |
| The long-legged beautiful bait their wives. | 151 | 22 | 83 | 169 | 10 |

## LONG-LEGGED (continued)

| | U.K. | | | U.S. | |
|---|---|---|---|---|---|
| | *Page* | *Line* | *Poem* | *Page* | *Line* |
| Always good-bye to the long-legged bread | 152 | 22 | 83 | 170 | 14 |
| When his long-legged flesh was a wind on fire | 157 | 3 | 83 | 175 | 15 |
| With his long-legged heart in his hand. | 157 | 24 | 83 | 176 | 16 |
| Ballad of the Long-legged Bait | 149 | | 83 | 166 | |
| **LONG-TAILED** | | | | | |
| The long-tailed stone | 56 | 18 | 34 | 65 | 18 |
| And the long-tailed lightning lit his catch. | 154 | 8 | 83 | 172 | 8 |
| **LONGS** | | | | | |
| A blade of grass longs with the meadow, | 115 | 15 | 69 | 127 | 15 |
| She longs among horses and angels, | 150 | 9 | 83 | 167 | 13 |
| **LOOK** | | | | | |
| From fish to jumping hill! Look: | viii | 17 | 1 | xvi | 17 |
| Look twice before he fell from grace. | 63 | 4 | 38 | 72 | 4 |
| Rounds to look at the red, wagged root. | 77 | 12 | 45 | 86 | 12 |
| Look. And the dancers move | 121 | 16 | 72 | 134 | 11 |
| Of fields. For love, the long ago she bird rises. Look. | 121 | 25 | 72 | 134 | 20 |
| Listen and look where she sails the goose plucked sea, | 122 | 20 | 72 | 135 | 20 |
| Blackened with birds took a last look | 149 | 2 | 83 | 166 | 2 |
| For my sake sail, and never look back, | 149 | 11 | 83 | 166 | 11 |
| **LOOKED** | | | | | |
| Who palmed the lie on me when you looked | 107 | 4 | 65 | 118 | 4 |
| **LOOKING** | | | | | |
| Said the looking land. | 149 | 12 | 83 | 166 | 12 |
| **LOOKING-GLASS** | | | | | |
| Or saw in the looking-glass shell | 93 | 7 | 56 | 102 | 7 |
| **LOOMS** | | | | | |
| Looms the last Samson of your zodiac. | 118 | 8 | 71 | 130 | 12 |
| **LOOPED** | | | | | |
| When his viperish fuse hangs looped with flames under the brand | 168 | 4 | 87 | 188 | 8 |
| **LOOSE** | | | | | |
| His scissors oiled, his knife hung loose | 11 | 10 | 8 | 12 | 10 |
| The locks yawned loose and a blast blew them wide, | 135 | 3 | 80 | 152 | 3 |
| **LOOSED** | | | | | |
| And loosed the braiding adders from their hairs; | 30 | 22 | 18 | 35 | 22 |
| **LOOTED** | | | | | |
| Hollows, a grassblade blown in cupped hands, in the looted elms | 169 | 4 | 87 | 189 | 13 |
| **LOP** | | | | | |
| Lop, love, my fork tongue, said the pin-hilled nettle; | 74 | 6 | 44 | 83 | 6 |
| **LOPING** | | | | | |
| Loping and bleating roughly and blithely shall leap, | 162 | 4 | 86 | 181 | 4 |

|  | U.K. | | | U.S. | |
|  | Page | Line | Poem | Page | Line |
|---|---|---|---|---|---|
| **LOPPED** | | | | | |
| Old cock from nowheres lopped the minstrel tongue | 74 | 8 | 44 | 83 | 8 |
| **LOPS** | | | | | |
| Lops, as a bush plumed with flames, the rant of the fierce eye, | 92 | 10 | 55 | 101 | 16 |
| **LORD** | | | | | |
| How soon my level, lord, | 56 | 22 | 34 | 66 | 1 |
| High lord esquire, speak up the singing cloud, | 60 | 17 | 36 | 69 | 17 |
| **LORD'S** | | | | | |
| Now stamp the Lord's Prayer on a grain of rice, | 74 | 15 | 44 | 83 | 15 |
| **LORD'S-TABLE** | | | | | |
| On the lord's-table of the bowing grass. Fear most | 163 | 12 | 86 | 182 | 12 |
| **LORDING** | | | | | |
| Here among the light of the lording sky | | | 91 | 201 | 8 |
| **LORDLY** | | | | | |
| And once below a time I lordly had the trees and leaves | 159 | 7 | 85 | 178 | 7 |
| **LOSE** | | | | | |
| The straws of Asia, lose me as I turn | 31 | 23 | 18 | 37 | 5 |
| Lose the great pains or stuff the wound, | 48 | 12 | 28 | 56 | 12 |
| **LOSER** | | | | | |
| And the loser of the key. | 42 | 28 | 24 | 50 | 7 |
| **LOSING** | | | | | |
| Each rung a love or losing to the last, | 27 | 2 | 16 | 32 | 7 |
| By losing him all in love, and cast his need | 120 | 27 | 72 | 133 | 12 |
| **LOSS** | | | | | |
| For loss of blood I fell on Ishmael's plain, | 73 | 17 | 44 | 82 | 17 |
| Now their love lies a loss | 124 | 5 | 73 | 138 | 5 |
| **LOSSES** | | | | | |
| Others betray the lamenting lies of their losses | 85 | 11 | 50 | 94 | 11 |
| **LOST** | | | | | |
| As, blowing on the angels, I was lost | 26 | 17 | 16 | 31 | 17 |
| For half of love was planted in the lost, | 30 | 11 | 18 | 35 | 11 |
| Though lovers be lost love shall not; | 68 | 8 | 42 | 77 | 8 |
| Lost in a limp-treed and uneating silence, | 79 | 2 | 46 | 88 | 5 |
| O my lost love bounced from a good home; | 97 | 23 | 59 | 109 | 3 |
| A stone lies lost and locked in the lark-high hill. | 115 | 16 | 69 | 127 | 16 |
| And his nameless need bound him burning and lost | 120 | 19 | 72 | 133 | 4 |
| By the believer lost and the hurled outcast of light. | 120 | 25 | 72 | 133 | 10 |
| All night lost and long wading in the wake of the she- | 122 | 18 | 72 | 135 | 18 |
| From a lost wilderness | 125 | 10 | 74 | 139 | 10 |
| I shall run lost in sudden | 139 | 11 | 82 | 156 | 11 |

LOST (continued)

|  | U.K. | | | U.S. | |
|---|---|---|---|---|---|
|  | *Page* | *Line* | *Poem* | *Page* | *Line* |
| For I was lost who am | 140 | 6 | 82 | 157 | 6 |
| For I was lost who have come | 140 | 11 | 82 | 157 | 11 |
| In the name of the lost who glory in | 143 | 1 | 82 | 160 | 1 |
| Lost on the unchristened mountain | 144 | 16 | 82 | 161 | 16 |
| And the star of the lost the shape of the eyes. | 147 | 1 | 82 | 164 | 1 |
| Now I am lost in the blinding | 148 | 16 | 82 | 165 | 16 |
| Floated the lost cathedral | 150 | 11 | 83 | 167 | 15 |
| Has melted away and is lost | 153 | 19 | 83 | 171 | 15 |
| Is always lost in her vaulted breath, | 153 | 20 | 83 | 171 | 16 |
| To the fisherman lost on the land. | 157 | 22 | 83 | 176 | 14 |
| Of the hearthstone tales my own, lost love; and the soul walks | 164 | 4 | 86 | 183 | 11 |
| And freely he goes lost | 171 | 19 | 88 | 191 | 19 |
| And the lost, moonshine domes, | 173 | 5 | 88 | 193 | 5 |
| Young among the long flocks, and never lie lost |  |  | 91 | 200 | 7 |
| LOTS |  |  |  |  |  |
| Light breaks on secret lots, | 25 | 1 | 15 | 30 | 1 |
| LOTH |  |  |  |  |  |
| Loving and being loth; | 15 | 13 | 10 | 17 | 13 |
| LOUD |  |  |  |  |  |
| The spider-tongued, and the loud hill of Wales) | 17 | 3 | 11 | 20 | 3 |
| Or waves break loud on the seashores; | 68 | 21 | 42 | 77 | 21 |
| With loud, torn tooth and tail and cobweb drum | 80 | 4 | 46 | 89 | 12 |
| There is loud and dark directly under the dumb flame, | 83 | 13 | 49 | 92 | 13 |
| To trot with a loud mate the haybeds of a mile, | 91 | 16 | 55 | 100 | 16 |
| Strike light, and bloody a loud room. | 97 | 10 | 59 | 108 | 10 |
| Through the loud zoo of the willow groves | 111 | 22 | 68 | 123 | 22 |
| Deep hillocks and loud on the numbed lakes, | 122 | 17 | 72 | 135 | 17 |
| Silence, silence to do, when earth grew loud, | 125 | 15 | 74 | 139 | 15 |
| To the sea sound flowing like blood from the loud wound | 136 | 6 | 81 | 153 | 6 |
| So loud to my own | 137 | 5 | 82 | 154 | 5 |
| But the loud sun | 148 | 6 | 82 | 165 | 6 |
| And prophets loud on the burned dunes; | 156 | 5 | 83 | 174 | 13 |
| Under the earth the loud sea walks, | 157 | 14 | 83 | 176 | 6 |
| Of blood! The bird loud vein! The saga from mermen | 165 | 7 | 86 | 184 | 15 |
| LOUDENING |  |  |  |  |  |
| Over the sea-gut loudening, sets a rock alive; | 49 | 15 | 29 | 58 | 15 |
| LOUDER |  |  |  |  |  |
| The louder the sun blooms | 173 | 12 | 88 | 193 | 12 |
| LOVE |  |  |  |  |  |
| To the best of my love | viii | 19 | 1 | xvi | 19 |
| Of love and light bursts in their throats. | 1 | 23 | 2 | 1 | 23 |
| My heart knew love, my belly hunger; | 8 | 5 | 5 | 9 | 5 |
| Love drips and gathers, but the fallen blood | 9 | 17 | 6 | 10 | 17 |

| | U.K. | | | U.S. | |
|---|---|---|---|---|---|
| | Page | Line | Poem | Page | Line |
| I hug to love with my unruly scrawl | 10 | 8 | 7 | 11 | 8 |
| That utters all love hunger | 10 | 9 | 7 | 11 | 9 |
| If I were tickled by the rub of love, | 12 | 1 | 9 | 13 | 1 |
| I would not fear the muscling-in of love | 12 | 17 | 9 | 13 | 17 |
| Your mouth, my love, the thistle in the kiss? | 13 | 16 | 9 | 15 | 2 |
| Of light and love, the tempers of the heart, | 14 | 2 | 10 | 16 | 2 |
| Two one-dimensioned ghosts, love on a reel, | 14 | 12 | 10 | 16 | 12 |
| Flavoured of celluloid give love the lie. | 14 | 20 | 10 | 16 | 20 |
| And who remain shall flower as they love, | 15 | 21 | 10 | 18 | 1 |
| Love in her gear is slowly through the house, | 18 | 3 | 12 | 21 | 3 |
| Of love am barer than Cadaver's trap | 18 | 8 | 12 | 21 | 8 |
| Shapes in a cinder death; love for his trick, | 19 | 23 | 12 | 23 | 8 |
| The ribbed original of love. | 23 | 6 | 14 | 28 | 6 |
| Each rung a love or losing to the last, | 27 | 2 | 16 | 32 | 7 |
| For half of love was planted in the lost, | 30 | 11 | 18 | 35 | 11 |
| Love like a mist or fire through the bed of eels. | 38 | 12 | 20 | 44 | 2 |
| Before the fall from love the flying heartbone, | 41 | 15 | 23 | 47 | 15 |
| 'Adam I love, my madmen's love is endless, | 41 | 23 | 23 | 48 | 5 |
| The country-handed grave boxed into love, | 55 | 4 | 33 | 64 | 7 |
| Nor when my love lies in the cross-boned drift | 60 | 22 | 36 | 69 | 22 |
| Would wither up, and any boy of love | 63 | 3 | 38 | 72 | 3 |
| Though lovers be lost love shall not; | 68 | 8 | 42 | 77 | 8 |
| The landscape grief, love in His oils | 69 | 20 | 43 | 78 | 20 |
| Lop, love, my fork tongue, said the pin-hilled nettle; | 74 | 6 | 44 | 83 | 6 |
| And love plucked out the stinging siren's eye, | 74 | 7 | 44 | 83 | 7 |
| Delivered seas my love from her proud place | 80 | 9 | 46 | 89 | 17 |
| And though my love pulls the pale, nippled air, | 80 | 13 | 46 | 89 | 21 |
| Love in the frost is pared and wintered by, | 81 | 5 | 47 | 90 | 5 |
| The whispering ears will watch love drummed away | 81 | 6 | 47 | 90 | 6 |
| That her love sing and swing through a brown chapel, | 87 | 25 | 52 | 96 | 25 |
| The stuffed lung of the fox twitch and cry Love | 88 | 11 | 52 | 97 | 11 |
| Love and labour and kill | 91 | 17 | 55 | 100 | 17 |
| Clack through the thicket of strength, love hewn in pillars drops | 92 | 8 | 55 | 101 | 14 |
| Than bully ill love in the clouted scene. | 97 | 5 | 59 | 108 | 5 |
| O my lost love bounced from a good home; | 97 | 23 | 59 | 109 | 3 |
| Who climbs to his dying love in her high room, | 100 | 3 | 61 | 111 | 3 |
| For the sleep in a safe land and the love who dies | 100 | 10 | 61 | 111 | 10 |
| In the fire of his care his love in the high room. | 100 | 16 | 61 | 111 | 16 |
| Die in unjudging love. | 106 | 12 | 64 | 117 | 12 |
| Till the sweet tooth of my love bit dry, | 107 | 7 | 65 | 118 | 7 |
| Her constant, nor the winds of love broken wide | 109 | 10 | 67 | 120 | 10 |
| Under the cloud against love is caught and held and kissed | 109 | 17 | 67 | 120 | 17 |

|  | U.K. | | | U.S. | |
| --- | --- | --- | --- | --- | --- |
|  | Page | Line | Poem | Page | Line |
| All love but for the full assemblage in flower | 110 | 12 | 67 | 121 | 14 |
| Love, my fate got luckily, | 110 | 15 | 67 | 121 | 17 |
| And the vaulting bird be still. O my true love, hold me. | 110 | 26 | 67 | 122 | 4 |
| In fountains of origin gave up their love, | 113 | 9 | 69 | 125 | 9 |
| At the point of love, forsaken and afraid. | 120 | 5 | 72 | 132 | 10 |
| Of his snow blind love and rush in the white lairs. | 120 | 13 | 72 | 132 | 18 |
| By losing him all in love, and cast his need | 120 | 27 | 72 | 133 | 12 |
| Paddocks in the farms of birds. The dead oak walks for love. | 121 | 20 | 72 | 134 | 15 |
| Of fields. For love, the long ago she bird rises. Look. | 121 | 25 | 72 | 134 | 20 |
| Burning in the bride bed of love, in the whirl- | 123 | 17 | 72 | 137 | 7 |
| Now their love lies a loss | 124 | 5 | 73 | 138 | 5 |
| And love and his patients roar on a chain; | 124 | 6 | 73 | 138 | 6 |
| They come together whom their love parted: | 124 | 10 | 73 | 138 | 10 |
| Unclenched, armless, silk and rough love that breaks all rocks. | 126 | 16 | 74 | 140 | 16 |
| Love is the last light spoken. Oh | 130 | 7 | 77 | 144 | 7 |
| In love torn breeches and blistered jacket | 132 | 7 | 78 | 147 | 7 |
| And fled their love in a weaving dip. | 151 | 5 | 83 | 168 | 13 |
| She nipped and dived in the nick of love, | 151 | 7 | 83 | 168 | 15 |
| The furious ox-killing house of love. | 157 | 8 | 83 | 175 | 20 |
| Out of a bed of love | 158 | 2 | 84 | 177 | 2 |
| And mire of love, but the Thief as meek as the dew. | 163 | 15 | 86 | 182 | 15 |
| Of the hearthstone tales my own, lost love; and the soul walks | 164 | 4 | 86 | 183 | 11 |
| The haygold haired, my love asleep, and the rift blue | 165 | 17 | 86 | 185 | 7 |
| Round the sun, he comes to my love like the designed snow, | 165 | 25 | 86 | 185 | 15 |
| Comes designed to my love to steal not her tide raking | 166 | 1 | 86 | 186 | 1 |
| And love unbolts the dark | 171 | 18 | 88 | 191 | 18 |
| Senses, and man a spirit in love | 173 | 2 | 88 | 193 | 2 |
| The whole of the moon I could love and leave | 174 | 10 | 89 | 194 | 10 |
| To labour and love though they lay down long ago. | 176 | 5 | 90 | 197 | 5 |
| Quick in the wood at love, where a torch of foxes foams, | 177 | 14 | 90 | 198 | 13 |
| Teach me the love that is evergreen after the fall leaved | 178 | 12 | 90 | 199 | 13 |
| Love for ever meridian through the courters' trees | 178 | 18 | 90 | 199 | 19 |
| Hill, under the grass, in love, and there grow |  |  | 91 | 200 | 6 |

| | U.K. | | | U.S. | |
|---|---|---|---|---|---|
| | Page | Line | Poem | Page | Line |
| If I were tickled by the rub of love | 12 | | 9 | 13 | |
| Love in the Asylum | 108 | | 66 | 119 | |
| LOVE'S | | | | | |
| Here love's damp muscle dries and dies, | 2 | 22 | 2 | 3 | 4 |
| Here break a kiss in no love's quarry. | 2 | 23 | 2 | 3 | 5 |
| The weed of love's left dry; | 11 | 15 | 8 | 12 | 15 |
| Love's twilit nation and the skull of state, | 19 | 14 | 12 | 22 | 19 |
| From love's first fever to her plague, from the soft second | 20 | 1 | 13 | 24 | 1 |
| Heir to the scalding veins that hold love's drop, costly | 28 | 9 | 17 | 33 | 9 |
| Shall I still be love's house on the widdershin earth, | 47 | 5 | 27 | 55 | 5 |
| Love's house, they answer, and the tower death | 47 | 7 | 27 | 55 | 7 |
| Love's image till my heartbone breaks | 70 | 7 | 43 | 79 | 11 |
| Love's reflection of the mushroom features, | 73 | 7 | 44 | 82 | 7 |
| Each ancient, stone-necked minute of love's season | 78 | 2 | 46 | 87 | 2 |
| Comes love's anatomist with sun-gloved hand | 79 | 18 | 46 | 88 | 21 |
| In all love's countries, that will grope awake; | 81 | 12 | 47 | 90 | 12 |
| And all love's sinners in sweet cloth kneel to a hyleg image, | 84 | 4 | 49 | 93 | 10 |
| From love's first fever to her plague | 20 | | 13 | 24 | |
| LOVEBEDS | | | | | |
| Break on the lovebeds of the weeds; | 11 | 14 | 8 | 12 | 14 |
| LOVED | | | | | |
| That though I loved them for their faults | 107 | 18 | 65 | 118 | 18 |
| When one at the great least of your best loved | 117 | 3 | 71 | 129 | 3 |
| Until that one loved least | 118 | 7 | 71 | 130 | 11 |
| He dropped where he loved on the burst pavement stone | 135 | 4 | 80 | 152 | 4 |
| Hill. Who once in gooseskin winter loved all ice leaved | 176 | 12 | 90 | 197 | 12 |
| LOVE-DARKNESS | | | | | |
| From damp love-darkness and the nurse's twist | 13 | 10 | 9 | 14 | 17 |
| LOVELORN | | | | | |
| Ache on the lovelorn paper | 10 | 7 | 7 | 11 | 7 |
| LOVELY | | | | | |
| The lovely gift of the gab bangs back on a blind shaft. | 94 | 6 | 57 | 104 | 6 |
| All blood-signed assailings and vanished marriages in which he had no lovely part | 114 | 20 | 69 | 126 | 20 |
| Walking in wishes and lovely for shame | 153 | 9 | 83 | 171 | 5 |
| All the sun long it was running, it was lovely, the hay | 159 | 19 | 85 | 178 | 19 |
| And playing, lovely and watery | 159 | 21 | 85 | 178 | 21 |

# LOVER

|  | U.K. Page | U.K. Line | Poem | U.S. Page | U.S. Line |
|---|---|---|---|---|---|
| **LOVER** | | | | | |
| Of lover, mother, lovers, or his six | 13 | 13 | 9 | 14 | 20 |
| No, no, you lover skull, descending hammer | 19 | 2 | 12 | 22 | 7 |
| All all and all, the corpse's lover, | 33 | 10 | 19 | 38 | 10 |
| And the face to the driven lover. | 33 | 24 | 19 | 39 | 6 |
| No tell-tale lover has an end more certain, | 41 | 24 | 23 | 48 | 6 |
| Dry lover mine | 51 | 4 | 31 | 60 | 4 |
| The circular smile tossed from lover to lover | 90 | 9 | 54 | 99 | 9 |
| Oceanic lover alone | 114 | 10 | 69 | 126 | 10 |
| **LOVER'S** | | | | | |
| And I am dumb to tell the lover's tomb | 9 | 21 | 6 | 10 | 21 |
| Nor the flint in the lover's mauling. | 33 | 18 | 19 | 38 | 18 |
| Her lover's wings that fold to-morrow's flight, | 115 | 11 | 69 | 127 | 11 |
| **LOVERS** | | | | | |
| A muscling life from lovers in their cramp, | 2 | 9 | 2 | 2 | 9 |
| Of lover, mother, lovers, or his six | 13 | 13 | 9 | 14 | 20 |
| Give over, lovers, locking, and the seawax struggle, | 38 | 11 | 20 | 44 | 1 |
| From all my mortal lovers with a starboard smile; | 60 | 21 | 36 | 69 | 21 |
| Though lovers be lost love shall not; | 68 | 8 | 42 | 77 | 8 |
| Lovers in the dirt of their leafy beds, | 89 | 9 | 53 | 98 | 9 |
| And the lovers lie abed | 128 | 4 | 76 | 142 | 4 |
| But for the lovers, their arms | 128 | 17 | 76 | 142 | 17 |
| **LOVERS'** | | | | | |
| If I were tickled by the lovers' rub | 12 | 22 | 9 | 14 | 1 |
| The lovers' house, lie suffering my stain? | 46 | 4 | 27 | 54 | 4 |
| **LOVES** | | | | | |
| Manned with their loves they'll move, | x | 12 | 1 | xviii | 18 |
| Of frozen loves they fetch their girls, | 1 | 5 | 2 | 1 | 5 |
| Waking alone in a multitude of loves when morning's light | 127 | 1 | 75 | 141 | 1 |
| And tussle in a shoal of loves. | 150 | 6 | 83 | 167 | 10 |
| On skull and scar where his loves lie wrecked, | 171 | 13 | 88 | 191 | 13 |
| **LOVING** | | | | | |
| Loving and being loth; | 15 | 13 | 10 | 17 | 13 |
| If not of loving well, then not, | 48 | 8 | 28 | 56 | 8 |
| And timelessly lies loving with the thief. | 67 | 14 | 41 | 76 | 14 |
| Loving on this sea banged guilt | 109 | 15 | 67 | 120 | 15 |
| **LOW** | | | | | |
| And lay the wet fruits low. | 11 | 12 | 8 | 12 | 12 |
| Laid the crops low, broke the grape's joy. | 39 | 5 | 21 | 45 | 5 |
| He lying low with ruin in his ear, | 51 | 20 | 31 | 60 | 20 |
| Not till, from high and low, their dust | 53 | 12 | 32 | 62 | 12 |
| Bird, he was brought low, | 123 | 16 | 72 | 137 | 6 |
| The rod bends low, divining land, | 155 | 21 | 83 | 174 | 5 |
| As the arc of the billhooks that flashed the hedges low | 178 | 7 | 90 | 199 | 8 |

|  | U.K. |  |  | U.S. |  |
|---|---|---|---|---|---|
|  | Page | Line | Poem | Page | Line |
| **LOWLANDS** |  |  |  |  |  |
| Lowlands of the waves, | 169 | 8 | 87 | 189 | 17 |
| **LOWLY** |  |  |  |  |  |
| Lie in grace. Sleep spelled at rest in the lowly house | 163 | 20 | 86 | 183 | 1 |
| **LUBBER** |  |  |  |  |  |
| Up through the lubber crust of Wales | 132 | 24 | 78 | 147 | 24 |
| **LUCIFER** |  |  |  |  |  |
| Lucifer that bird's dropping | 153 | 17 | 83 | 171 | 13 |
| **LUCK** |  |  |  |  |  |
| That I struck one day by luck, | 93 | 5 | 56 | 102 | 5 |
| The trodden town rang its cobbles for luck. | 149 | 4 | 83 | 166 | 4 |
| Good luck to the hand on the rod, | 151 | 13 | 83 | 169 | 1 |
| Always good luck, praised the finned in the feather | 154 | 5 | 83 | 172 | 5 |
| Good-bye, good luck, struck the sun and the moon, | 157 | 21 | 83 | 176 | 13 |
| **LUCKILY** |  |  |  |  |  |
| Love, my fate got luckily, | 110 | 15 | 67 | 121 | 17 |
| **LUCKLESSLY** |  |  |  |  |  |
| Lucklessly she must lie patient | 110 | 25 | 67 | 122 | 3 |
| **LUCKY** |  |  |  |  |  |
| My holy lucky body | 109 | 16 | 67 | 120 | 16 |
| **LUGGAGE** |  |  |  |  |  |
| Who under the lids of her windows hoisted his golden luggage, | 127 | 12 | 75 | 141 | 12 |
| **LULL** |  |  |  |  |  |
| Lying in the lull | 130 | 19 | 77 | 144 | 19 |
| **LULLED** |  |  |  |  |  |
| Illumination of music! the lulled black-backed | 165 | 11 | 86 | 185 | 1 |
| **LULLING** |  |  |  |  |  |
| Lulling of spheres in the seashell flesh, | 173 | 8 | 88 | 193 | 8 |
| **LUMINOUS** |  |  |  |  |  |
| Made her limbs blind by luminous charms, | 113 | 21 | 69 | 125 | 21 |
| Your heart is luminous | 118 | 2 | 71 | 130 | 6 |
| Of the luminous cathedrals, | 131 | 10 | 77 | 145 | 16 |
| **LUNAR** |  |  |  |  |  |
| The lunar silences, the silent tide | 82 | 9 | 48 | 91 | 9 |
| **LUNG** |  |  |  |  |  |
| Still set to scratch a laughter from my lung, | 12 | 5 | 9 | 13 | 5 |
| The stuffed lung of the fox twitch and cry Love | 88 | 11 | 52 | 97 | 11 |
| **LUNGE** |  |  |  |  |  |
| Before the lunge of the night, the notes on this time-shaken | 169 | 11 | 87 | 189 | 20 |
| **LUNGS** |  |  |  |  |  |
| Oh, Jericho was falling in their lungs! | 151 | 6 | 83 | 168 | 14 |

| | U.K. | | | U.S. | |
|---|---|---|---|---|---|
| | Page | Line | Poem | Page | Line |
| **LURCHED** | | | | | |
| Lurched through a scuttled sea | 95 | 23 | 58 | 105 | 23 |
| **LURED** | | | | | |
| The lured fish under the foam | 150 | 23 | 83 | 168 | 7 |
| **LUST** | | | | | |
| Of the wintry nunnery of the order of lust | 109 | 12 | 67 | 120 | 12 |
| **LYING** | | | | | |
| This is the world: the lying likeness of | 15 | 11 | 10 | 17 | 11 |
| He lying low with ruin in his ear, | 51 | 20 | 31 | 60 | 20 |
| They lying long shall not die windily; | 68 | 12 | 42 | 77 | 12 |
| We lying by seasand, watching yellow | 82 | 1 | 48 | 91 | 1 |
| Into her lying down head | 113 | 1 | 69 | 125 | 1 |
| Lying in the lull | 130 | 19 | 77 | 144 | 19 |
| Lying the sky | 165 | 20 | 86 | 185 | 10 |
| We lying by seasand | 82 | | 48 | 91 | |
| Into her Lying Down Head | 113 | | 69 | 125 | |
| **LYNX** | | | | | |
| And, lashed to syllables, the lynx tongue cry | 81 | 8 | 47 | 90 | 8 |

# ENTRIES UNDER M

| | U.K. | | | U.S. | |
|---|---|---|---|---|---|
| **MACADAM** | | | | | |
| Man through macadam. | 19 | 10 | 12 | 22 | 15 |
| **MACKEREL** | | | | | |
| The highroad of water where the seabear and mackerel | 36 | 21 | 20 | 41 | 21 |
| **MAD** | | | | | |
| An old, mad man still climbing in his ghost, | 27 | 4 | 16 | 32 | 9 |
| Up rose the Abraham-man, mad for my sake, | 46 | 19 | 27 | 54 | 19 |
| Though they go mad they shall be sane, | 68 | 6 | 42 | 77 | 6 |
| Though they be mad and dead as nails, | 68 | 24 | 42 | 77 | 24 |
| Death and this mad heroine | 93 | 22 | 56 | 103 | 2 |
| A girl mad as birds | 108 | 3 | 66 | 119 | 3 |
| **MADAM** | | | | | |
| Joy is no knocking nation, sir and madam, | 19 | 6 | 12 | 22 | 11 |
| **MADE** | | | | | |
| How of my clay is made the hangman's lime. | 9 | 15 | 6 | 10 | 15 |
| I who was rich was made the richer | 8 | 11 | 5 | 9 | 11 |
| Of head and tail made witnesses to this | 41 | 7 | 23 | 47 | 7 |
| Now make the world of me as I have made | 61 | 5 | 36 | 70 | 5 |
| That made me happy in the sun, | 48 | 19 | 28 | 56 | 19 |
| She wept in her pain and made mouths, | 93 | 19 | 56 | 102 | 19 |

|  | U.K. | | | U.S. | |
|---|---|---|---|---|---|
|  | *Page* | *Line* | *Poem* | *Page* | *Line* |
| Made the tigers jump out of their eyes | 112 | 4 | 68 | 124 | 4 |
| Made all day until bell time | 112 | 7 | 68 | 124 | 7 |
| Made her limbs blind by luminous charms, | 113 | 21 | 69 | 125 | 21 |
| Made his bad bed in her good | 114 | 12 | 69 | 126 | 12 |
| When that immortal hospital made one more move to soothe | 158 | 3 | 84 | 177 | 3 |
| Under the new made clouds and happy as the heart was long, | 160 | 16 | 85 | 179 | 16 |
| MADHOUSE | | | | | |
| On the madhouse boards worn thin by my walking tears. | 108 | 15 | 66 | 119 | 15 |
| MADMEN | | | | | |
| All, men my madmen, the unwholesome wind | 19 | 21 | 12 | 23 | 6 |
| Death: death of Hamlet and the nightmare madmen, | 41 | 19 | 23 | 48 | 1 |
| MADMEN'S | | | | | |
| 'Adam I love, my madmen's love is endless, | 41 | 23 | 23 | 48 | 5 |
| MAGGOT | | | | | |
| I smelt the maggot in my stool. | 8 | 6 | 5 | 9 | 6 |
| But time has set its maggot on their track. | 50 | 4 | 30 | 59 | 4 |
| And the maggot no man can slay.' | 65 | 16 | 40 | 74 | 16 |
| 'The maggot that no man can kill | 66 | 1 | 40 | 75 | 1 |
| MAGGOT'S | | | | | |
| Man in his maggot's barren. | 3 | 2 | 2 | 3 | 8 |
| MAGGOTS | | | | | |
| That but a name, where maggots have their X. | 21 | 14 | 13 | 25 | 14 |
| MAGIC | | | | | |
| Shall not be latched while magic glides | 11 | 20 | 8 | 12 | 20 |
| Who sucks the bell-voiced Adam out of magic, | 74 | 23 | 44 | 83 | 23 |
| Time, milk, and magic, from the world beginning. | 74 | 24 | 44 | 83 | 24 |
| MAGICAL | | | | | |
| No man more magical, clawed out the crocodile. | 38 | 18 | 20 | 44 | 8 |
| MAGICS | | | | | |
| He drowned his father's magics in a dream. | 4 | 18 | 3 | 4 | 18 |
| MAGNET | | | | | |
| By magnet winds to her blind mother drawn, | 78 | 14 | 46 | 87 | 14 |
| MAGNETIZE | | | | | |
| How shall it magnetize, | 91 | 12 | 55 | 100 | 12 |
| MAGNIFIED | | | | | |
| Magnified out of praise; her death was a still drop, | 87 | 17 | 52 | 96 | 17 |
| MAID | | | | | |
| From maid and head, | 18 | 15 | 12 | 21 | 15 |
| Rose maid and male, | 54 | 6 | 33 | 63 | 6 |
| MAIDEN | | | | | |
| Is maiden in the shameful oak, omens | 78 | 21 | 46 | 87 | 21 |

|  | U.K. | | | U.S. | |
|---|---|---|---|---|---|
|  | *Page* | *Line* | *Poem* | *Page* | *Line* |
| With carved bird, saint, and sun, the wrack-spiked maiden mouth | 92 | 9 | 55 | 101 | 15 |
| And the splashed mothering maiden | 139 | 8 | 82 | 156 | 8 |
| Shining, it was Adam and maiden, | 160 | 8 | 85 | 179 | 8 |
| MAIDEN'S | | | | | |
| Despair of blood, faith in the maiden's slime, | 18 | 23 | 12 | 22 | 3 |
| MAJESTY | | | | | |
| The majesty and burning of the child's death. | 101 | 13 | 62 | 112 | 13 |
| MAKE | | | | | |
| Where words and water make a mixture | 8 | 3 | 5 | 9 | 3 |
| Some let me make you of the vowelled beeches, | 16 | 13 | 11 | 19 | 13 |
| Some let me make you of the water's speeches. | 16 | 16 | 11 | 19 | 16 |
| Some let me make you of the meadow's signs; | 16 | 21 | 11 | 19 | 21 |
| (Some let me make you of autumnal spells, | 17 | 2 | 11 | 20 | 2 |
| Some let me make you of the heartless words. | 17 | 5 | 11 | 20 | 5 |
| Make desolation in the vein, | 39 | 12 | 21 | 45 | 12 |
| We make me mystic as the arm of air, | 52 | 6 | 31 | 61 | 13 |
| Now make the world of me as I have made | 61 | 5 | 36 | 70 | 5 |
| I make this in a warring absence when | 78 | 1 | 46 | 87 | 1 |
| I make a weapon of an ass's skeleton | 79 | 5 | 46 | 88 | 8 |
| Yet this I make in a forgiving presence. | 80 | 15 | 46 | 89 | 23 |
| O make me a mask and a wall to shut from your spies | 85 | 1 | 50 | 94 | 1 |
| Bend, if my journey ache, direction like an arc or make | 97 | 14 | 59 | 108 | 14 |
| Before you move to make | 105 | 8 | 64 | 116 | 8 |
| Every morning I make, | 134 | 16 | 79 | 150 | 16 |
| And the sensual ruins make | 153 | 22 | 83 | 171 | 18 |
| I make this in a warring absence | 78 | | 46 | 87 | |
| O make me a mask | 85 | | 50 | 94 | |
| MAKER | | | | | |
| Head, deceived, I believed, my maker, | 133 | 6 | 78 | 148 | 9 |
| And I am struck as lonely as a holy maker by the sun. | 158 | 12 | 84 | 177 | 12 |
| MAKES | | | | | |
| The seed that makes a forest of the loin | 6 | 13 | 4 | 6 | 13 |
| She makes for me a nettle's innocence | 78 | 16 | 46 | 87 | 16 |
| And makes with a flick of the thumb and sun | 96 | 25 | 58 | 107 | 8 |
| Music of elements, that a miracle makes! | 165 | 15 | 86 | 185 | 5 |
| Makes all the music; and I who hear the tune of the slow, | 169 | 9 | 87 | 189 | 18 |
| MAKING | | | | | |
| Under the mask and the ether, they making bloody | 37 | 2 | 20 | 42 | 8 |
| Rage me back to the making house. My hand unravel | 97 | 12 | 59 | 108 | 12 |
| Never until the mankind making | 101 | 1 | 62 | 112 | 1 |

|  | U.K. | | | U.S. | |
|---|---|---|---|---|---|
|  | *Page* | *Line* | *Poem* | *Page* | *Line* |
| Are making under the green, laid veil | 151 | 21 | 83 | 169 | 9 |
| MALE | | | | | |
| Shall it be male or female? say the cells, | 12 | 8 | 9 | 13 | 8 |
| Shall it be male or female? say the fingers | 12 | 15 | 9 | 13 | 15 |
| I, in my fusion of rose and male motion, | 35 | 17 | 20 | 40 | 17 |
| Rose maid and male, | 54 | 6 | 33 | 63 | 6 |
| Towards the studded male in a bent, midnight blaze | 91 | 13 | 55 | 100 | 13 |
| Or rides the imagined oceans of the male wards. | 108 | 9 | 66 | 119 | 9 |
| Wound their room with a male moan, | 114 | 2 | 69 | 126 | 2 |
| The female, deadly, and male | 115 | 7 | 69 | 127 | 7 |
| He'll bathe his raining blood in the male sea | 117 | 19 | 71 | 129 | 19 |
| MAMMOTH | | | | | |
| Mammoth and sparrowfall | 134 | 20 | 79 | 150 | 20 |
| MAN | | | | | |
| How I, a spinning man, | viii | 13 | 1 | xvi | 13 |
| Roared, sea born, man torn, blood blest. | viii | 15 | 1 | xvi | 15 |
| The sleepy man of winter pulls, | 2 | 5 | 2 | 2 | 5 |
| And from the planted womb the man of straw. | 2 | 12 | 2 | 2 | 12 |
| Man in his maggot's barren. | 3 | 2 | 2 | 3 | 8 |
| I am the man your father was. | 3 | 4 | 2 | 3 | 10 |
| And I am dumb to tell the hanging man | 9 | 14 | 6 | 10 | 14 |
| A ghost nor man, but mortal ghost. | 8 | 14 | 5 | 9 | 14 |
| The itch of man upon the baby's thigh, | 12 | 12 | 9 | 13 | 12 |
| Man be my metaphor. | 13 | 21 | 9 | 15 | 7 |
| Chaste and the chaser, man with the cockshut eye, | 18 | 17 | 12 | 21 | 17 |
| Man through macadam. | 19 | 10 | 12 | 22 | 15 |
| The fruit of man unwrinkles in the stars, | 24 | 10 | 15 | 29 | 10 |
| So, planing-heeled, I flew along my man | 26 | 4 | 16 | 31 | 4 |
| The inches monkeyed by the blood of man. | 27 | 3 | 16 | 32 | 8 |
| An old, mad man still climbing in his ghost, | 27 | 4 | 16 | 32 | 9 |
| In bottom gear through night-geared man. | 28 | 12 | 17 | 33 | 12 |
| Of new man strength, I seek the sun. | 29 | 4 | 17 | 34 | 8 |
| Man of my flesh, the jawbone riven, | 33 | 19 | 19 | 39 | 1 |
| Ghost with her ghost, contagious man | 34 | 2 | 19 | 39 | 8 |
| Casts to the pine roots, raising man like a mountain | 35 | 11 | 20 | 40 | 11 |
| My man of leaves and the bronze root, mortal, unmortal, | 35 | 16 | 20 | 40 | 16 |
| Thus the shadowless man or ox, and the pictured devil, | 35 | 22 | 20 | 40 | 22 |
| No man more magical, clawed out the crocodile. | 38 | 18 | 20 | 44 | 8 |
| Man was the scales, the death birds on enamel, | 38 | 19 | 20 | 44 | 9 |
| All-hollowed man wept for his white apparel | 38 | 24 | 20 | 44 | 14 |
| Man was Cadaver's masker, the harnessing mantle, | 38 | 25 | 20 | 44 | 15 |

|  | U.K. | | | U.S. | |
| --- | --- | --- | --- | --- | --- |
|  | *Page* | *Line* | *Poem* | *Page* | *Line* |
| Windily master of man was the rotten fathom, | 38 | 26 | 20 | 44 | 16 |
| Man in the day or wind at night | 39 | 4 | 21 | 45 | 4 |
| Man broke the sun, pulled the wind down. | 39 | 10 | 21 | 45 | 10 |
| Man should be cured of distemper. | 48 | 27 | 28 | 57 | 4 |
| Time, in a folly's rider, like a county man | 49 | 4 | 29 | 58 | 4 |
| Alone's unhurt, so the blind man sees best. | 50 | 9 | 30 | 59 | 9 |
| Man dry man, | 51 | 3 | 31 | 60 | 3 |
| Of echo's answer and the man of frost | 53 | 25 | 32 | 62 | 25 |
| Man morrow blows through food. | 56 | 14 | 34 | 65 | 14 |
| Let the soil squeal I am the biting man | 56 | 20 | 34 | 65 | 20 |
| Man by a scribbled name. | 62 | 12 | 37 | 71 | 12 |
| And the maggot no man can slay.' | 65 | 16 | 40 | 74 | 16 |
| A merry girl took me for man, | 65 | 22 | 40 | 74 | 22 |
| 'The maggot that no man can kill | 66 | 1 | 40 | 75 | 1 |
| And the man no rope can hang | 66 | 2 | 40 | 75 | 2 |
| War on the destiny of man! | 66 | 15 | 40 | 75 | 15 |
| With the man in the wind and the west moon; | 68 | 3 | 42 | 77 | 3 |
| Snail of man in His ship of fires | 69 | 8 | 43 | 78 | 8 |
| Mirror from man to whale | 69 | 21 | 43 | 78 | 21 |
| What of a bamboo man among your acres? | 73 | 3 | 44 | 82 | 3 |
| Time tracks the sound of shape on man and cloud, | 75 | 3 | 44 | 84 | 3 |
| What rhubarb man peeled in her foam-blue channel | 76 | 17 | 44 | 85 | 17 |
| An enamoured man alone by the twigs of his eyes, two fires, | 77 | 7 | 45 | 86 | 7 |
| An upright man in the antipodes | 77 | 23 | 45 | 86 | 23 |
| In the groin's endless coil a man is tangled.' | 79 | 27 | 46 | 89 | 8 |
| To lift to leave from the treasures of man is pleasing death | 94 | 7 | 57 | 104 | 7 |
| By the child going to bed and the man on the stairs | 100 | 2 | 61 | 111 | 2 |
| From the man on the stairs and the child by his bed. | 100 | 8 | 61 | 111 | 8 |
| Shall the child sleep unharmed or the man be crying? | 100 | 12 | 61 | 111 | 12 |
| Turns on the quick and the dead, and the man on the stairs | 100 | 14 | 61 | 111 | 14 |
| Man was the burning England she was sleep-walking, and the enamouring island | 113 | 20 | 69 | 125 | 20 |
| Super-or-near man | 114 | 6 | 69 | 126 | 6 |
| A man torn up mourns in the sole night. | 115 | 21 | 69 | 127 | 21 |
| As the food and flames of the snow, a man un-rolled | 119 | 13 | 72 | 131 | 13 |
| That a man knelt alone in the cup of the vales, | 122 | 5 | 72 | 135 | 5 |
| When hindering man hurt | 125 | 12 | 74 | 139 | 12 |
| Man, animal, or bird | 125 | 13 | 74 | 139 | 13 |

| | U.K. | | | U.S. | |
|---|---|---|---|---|---|
| | Page | Line | Poem | Page | Line |
| On to the ground when a man died | 125 | 21 | 74 | 139 | 21 |
| Greed on man beating near and fire neighbour | 126 | 6 | 74 | 140 | 6 |
| For a man sleeps where fire leapt down and she learns through his arm | 127 | 13 | 75 | 141 | 13 |
| Not for the proud man apart | 128 | 12 | 76 | 142 | 12 |
| Man and woman undone, | 131 | 5 | 77 | 145 | 11 |
| While a man outside with a billhook, | 134 | 8 | 79 | 150 | 8 |
| And the heart print of man | 137 | 12 | 82 | 154 | 12 |
| Crying at the man drenched throne | 140 | 7 | 82 | 157 | 7 |
| Of man when | 141 | 14 | 82 | 158 | 14 |
| Good-bye to the man on the sea-legged deck | 149 | 18 | 83 | 166 | 18 |
| Out of the urn the size of a man | 154 | 21 | 83 | 173 | 1 |
| Senses, and man a spirit in love | 173 | 2 | 88 | 193 | 2 |
| To death, one man through his sundered hulks, | 173 | 11 | 88 | 193 | 11 |
| When I was a gusty man and a half | 174 | 13 | 89 | 194 | 13 |
| When I was a man you could call a man | 174 | 25 | 89 | 195 | 1 |
| When I was a half the man I was | 175 | 8 | 89 | 195 | 13 |
| Now I am a man no more no more | 175 | 20 | 89 | 196 | 1 |
| Or with their orchard man in the core of the sun's bush | 177 | 4 | 90 | 198 | 3 |
| A cold kind man brave in his narrow pride | | | 91 | 200 | 3 |
| (An old tormented man three-quarters blind, | | | 91 | 200 | 18 |
| An old kind man brave in his burning pride. | | | 91 | 201 | 3 |
| An old blind man is with me where I go | | | 91 | 201 | 9 |
| Among those Killed in the Dawn Raid was a Man Aged a Hundred | 135 | | 80 | 152 | |

MAN'S

| | | | | | |
|---|---|---|---|---|---|
| An old man's shank one-marrowed with my bone, | 13 | 4 | 9 | 14 | 11 |
| I learnt man's tongue, to twist the shapes of thoughts | 21 | 8 | 13 | 25 | 8 |
| Forged in man's minerals, the brassy orator | 35 | 2 | 20 | 40 | 2 |
| Mount on man's footfall, | 36 | 3 | 20 | 41 | 3 |
| Forged in man's mineral. | 38 | 28 | 20 | 44 | 18 |
| If I take to burn or return this world which is each man's work. | 94 | 12 | 57 | 104 | 12 |
| Alone in the husk of man's home | 158 | 22 | 84 | 177 | 22 |

MANALIVE

| | | | | | |
|---|---|---|---|---|---|
| Of fear, rage red, manalive, | viii | 22 | 1 | xvi | 22 |

MAN-BEARING

| | | | | | |
|---|---|---|---|---|---|
| Flew man-bearing there. | 113 | 6 | 69 | 125 | 6 |

MAN-BEGETTERS

| | | | | | |
|---|---|---|---|---|---|
| For man-begetters in the dry-as-paste, | 46 | 23 | 27 | 54 | 23 |

MANDRAKE

| | | | | | |
|---|---|---|---|---|---|
| And pluck a mandrake music from the marrow-root. | 60 | 18 | 36 | 69 | 18 |
| Bit out the mandrake with to-morrow's scream. | 71 | 6 | 44 | 80 | 6 |

| | U.K. | | | U.S. | |
|---|---|---|---|---|---|
| | Page | Line | Poem | Page | Line |

MANED
His striped and noon maned tribe striding to holocaust, — 110, 3, 67, 121, 5

MANES
And thunderbolts in their manes. — 156, 22, 83, 175, 10
Manes, under his quenchless summer barbed gold to the bone, — 177, 6, 90, 198, 5

MANHOOD
Of sick old manhood on the fallen jaws, — 12, 24, 9, 14, 3
Rerobing of the naked ghost. Manhood — 28, 23, 17, 34, 3
This is the fortune of manhood: the natural peril, — 35, 19, 20, 40, 19
Intricate manhood of ending, the invalid rivals, — 36, 7, 20, 41, 7

MAN-IN-SEED
Man-in-seed, in seed-at-zero, — 43, 15, 24, 51, 1
Man-in-seed, in seed-at-zero, — 43, 22, 24, 51, 8

MAN-IRON
To my man-iron sidle. — 35, 6, 20, 40, 6

MANKIND
Never until the mankind making — 101, 1, 62, 112, 1
The mankind of her going with a grave truth — 101, 15, 62, 112, 15

MAN-MELTING
Of suns in the man-melting night. — 28, 8, 17, 33, 8

MANNA
One sun, one manna, warmed and fed. — 21, 26, 13, 26, 9
Manna for the rumbling ground, — 42, 17, 24, 49, 17
Manna for the guarded ground, — 42, 24, 24, 50, 3
Puffing the pounds of manna up through the dew to heaven, — 94, 5, 57, 104, 5

MANNED
Manned with their loves they'll move, — x, 12, 1, xviii, 18
And, manned by midnight, Jacob to the stars. — 71, 24, 44, 80, 24

MANSEED
The growing bones, the rumour of manseed — 20, 17, 13, 24, 17

MANSHAPE
A merry manshape of your walking circle. — 61, 6, 36, 70, 6

MANSHAPED
Foster the light nor veil the manshaped moon, — 60, 1, 36, 69, 1

MANSION
Bread and milk mansion in a toothless town. — 78, 15, 46, 87, 15

MANSIONS
Hiding the golden mountains and mansions — 82, 16, 48, 91, 16

MANSOULED
The mansouled fiery islands! Oh, — 173, 24, 88, 193, 24

MANSTRING
Be by the ships' sea broken at the manstring anchored — 38, 8, 20, 43, 18

| | U.K. | | | U.S. | |
|---|---|---|---|---|---|
| | *Page* | *Line* | *Poem* | *Page* | *Line* |

MANTLE

Man was Cadaver's masker, the harnessing
mantle, — 38 — 25 — 20 — 44 — 15

In the mantle and calm, — 122 — 6 — 72 — 135 — 6

MANTLED

Combs through the mantled yards and the
morning men — 119 — 20 — 72 — 131 — 20

MANWAGED

That town of ghosts, the manwaged womb — 42 — 9 — 24 — 49 — 9

MANWAGING

Over the manwaging line. — 42 — 7 — 24 — 49 — 7

MANWAX

Blew out the blood gauze through the wound of
manwax. — 74 — 14 — 44 — 83 — 14

MANY

Of many a thorny shire tell you notes, — 16 — 15 — 11 — 19 — 15

What had been one was many sounding minded. — 21 — 17 — 13 — 25 — 17

Of many a hundred falls; — 53 — 5 — 32 — 62 — 5

I have heard many years of telling, — 63 — 16 — 38 — 72 — 16

And many years should see some change. — 63 — 17 — 38 — 72 — 17

The shade of their trees was a word of many
shades — 89 — 10 — 53 — 98 — 10

In the taken body at many ages, — 114 — 17 — 69 — 126 — 17

In many married London's estranging grief. — 117 — 12 — 71 — 129 — 12

One enemy, of many, who knows well — 118 — 1 — 71 — 130 — 5

Through throats where many rivers meet, the
curlews cry, — 176 — 1 — 90 — 197 — 1

Through throats where many rivers meet, the
women pray, — 176 — 6 — 90 — 197 — 6

MAPS

O who is glory in the shapeless maps, — 61 — 4 — 36 — 70 — 4

MARBLE

These cloud-sopped, marble hands, this monu-
mental — 88 — 8 — 52 — 97 — 8

MARCHES

As their blade marches in — 96 — 15 — 58 — 106 — 15

MARCHING

Rammed in the marching heart, hole — 28 — 14 — 17 — 33 — 14

MARK

Shut, too, in a tower of words, I mark — 16 — 9 — 11 — 19 — 9

(Sir morrow mark), — 56 — 2 — 34 — 65 — 2

The fingers will forget green thumbs and mark — 81 — 2 — 47 — 90 — 2

And mark the dark eyed wave, through the eyes
of sleep, — 100 — 19 — 61 — 111 — 19

MARKED

Sharp in my second death I marked the hills,
harvest — 28 — 17 — 17 — 33 — 17

301

MARKED (continued)

|  | U.K. | | | U.S. | |
|---|---|---|---|---|---|
|  | *Page* | *Line* | *Poem* | *Page* | *Line* |
| That will rake at last all currencies of the marked breath | 94 | 8 | 57 | 104 | 8 |
| MARKING | | | | | |
| Who seek me landward, marking in my mouth | 31 | 22 | 18 | 37 | 4 |
| Marking the flesh and summer in the bay? | 46 | 11 | 27 | 54 | 11 |
| MARKS | | | | | |
| Time marks a black aisle kindle from the brand of ashes, | 83 | 4 | 49 | 92 | 4 |
| God in his whirlwind silence save, who marks the sparrows hail, | 168 | 21 | 87 | 189 | 6 |
| MARRIAGE | | | | | |
| I mean by time the cast and curfew rascal of our marriage, | 84 | 1 | 49 | 93 | 7 |
| On the Marriage of a Virgin | 127 | | 75 | 141 | |
| MARRIAGES | | | | | |
| All blood-signed assailings and vanished marriages in which he had no lovely part | 114 | 20 | 69 | 126 | 20 |
| MARRIED | | | | | |
| The photograph is married to the eye, | 15 | 7 | 10 | 17 | 7 |
| A virgin married at rest. | 93 | 3 | 56 | 102 | 3 |
| She married in this pouring place, | 93 | 4 | 56 | 102 | 4 |
| In many married London's estranging grief. | 117 | 12 | 71 | 129 | 12 |
| Her deepsea pillow where once she married alone, | 127 | 9 | 75 | 141 | 9 |
| MARROW | | | | | |
| That shrouded men might marrow as they fly. | 15 | 10 | 10 | 17 | 10 |
| The crutch that marrow taps upon their sleep, | 30 | 14 | 18 | 35 | 14 |
| Skinny as sin, the foaming marrow, | 33 | 11 | 19 | 38 | 11 |
| But strip the twelve-winded marrow from his circle; | 60 | 3 | 36 | 69 | 3 |
| The merriest marrow and the dregs | 65 | 3 | 40 | 74 | 3 |
| (Questions are hunchbacks to the poker marrow). | 73 | 2 | 44 | 82 | 2 |
| The inmost marrow of my heart bone | 143 | 17 | 82 | 160 | 17 |
| Marrow of eagles, the roots of whales | 172 | 4 | 88 | 192 | 4 |
| MARROW-COLUMNED | | | | | |
| And his weak house to marrow-columned heaven, | 78 | 8 | 46 | 87 | 8 |
| MARROWED | | | | | |
| The body prospered, teeth in the marrowed gums, | 20 | 16 | 13 | 24 | 16 |
| The substance forked that marrowed the first sun; | 22 | 4 | 14 | 27 | 4 |
| MARROW-LADLE | | | | | |
| Rip of the vaults, I took my marrow-ladle | 72 | 11 | 44 | 81 | 11 |
| MARROWROOT | | | | | |
| And pluck a mandrake music from the marrowroot. | 60 | 18 | 36 | 69 | 18 |

|  | U.K. | | | U.S. | |
| --- | --- | --- | --- | --- | --- |
|  | *Page* | *Line* | *Poem* | *Page* | *Line* |
| MARTYRDOM | | | | | |
| Stream upon his martyrdom | 147 | 16 | 82 | 164 | 16 |
| MARVEL | | | | | |
| There could I marvel | 103 | 13 | 63 | 114 | 13 |
| And there could I marvel my birthday | 104 | 9 | 63 | 115 | 11 |
| MARVELS | | | | | |
| Beginning with doom in the ghost, and the springing marvels, | 35 | 13 | 20 | 40 | 13 |
| MARY | | | | | |
| The world's my wound, God's Mary in her grief, | 75 | 8 | 44 | 84 | 8 |
| MARYS | | | | | |
| Her robin breasted tree, three Marys in the rays. | 163 | 6 | 86 | 182 | 6 |
| MASK | | | | | |
| Under the mask and the ether, they making bloody | 37 | 2 | 20 | 42 | 8 |
| Death from a bandage, rants the mask of scholars | 76 | 2 | 44 | 85 | 2 |
| O make me a mask and a wall to shut from your spies | 85 | 1 | 50 | 94 | 1 |
| Glared through shark mask and navigating head, | 133 | 11 | 78 | 148 | 14 |
| O make me a mask | 85 | | 50 | 94 | |
| MASKED | | | | | |
| And the masked, headless boy. | 70 | 2 | 43 | 79 | 6 |
| MASKER | | | | | |
| Man was Cadaver's masker, the harnessing mantle, | 38 | 25 | 20 | 44 | 15 |
| MASKS | | | | | |
| 'See,' drummed the taut masks, 'how the dead ascend: | 79 | 26 | 46 | 89 | 7 |
| MASONS | | | | | |
| Woe to the windy masons at my shelter? | 47 | 6 | 27 | 55 | 6 |
| MASSES | | | | | |
| The masses of the sea | 131 | 20 | 77 | 146 | 2 |
| The masses of the sea under | 131 | 21 | 77 | 146 | 3 |
| The masses of the infant-bearing sea | 131 | 22 | 77 | 146 | 4 |
| MAST | | | | | |
| When, praise is blessed, her pride in mast and fountain | 78 | 4 | 46 | 87 | 4 |
| High and dry by the top of the mast, | 149 | 8 | 83 | 166 | 8 |
| My mast is a bell-spire, | 152 | 4 | 83 | 169 | 16 |
| MASTED | | | | | |
| Or, masted venus, through the paddler's bowl | 54 | 7 | 33 | 63 | 7 |
| MASTER | | | | | |
| Windily master of man was the rotten fathom, | 38 | 26 | 20 | 44 | 16 |
| Mister and master, darkness for his eyes, | 57 | 3 | 34 | 66 | 10 |
| Master the night nor serve the snowman's brain | 60 | 4 | 36 | 69 | 4 |

303

|  | U.K. | | Poem | U.S. | |
|---|---|---|---|---|---|
|  | Page | Line |  | Page | Line |
| The cloud perched tailors' master with nerves for cotton. | 133 | 7 | 78 | 148 | 10 |
| MASTERLESS | | | | | |
| A steeplejack tower, bonerailed and masterless, | 35 | 20 | 20 | 40 | 20 |
| MASTERS | | | | | |
| Deliver me, my masters, head and heart, | 18 | 11 | 12 | 21 | 11 |
| My pickbrain masters morsing on the stone | 18 | 22 | 12 | 22 | 2 |
| Descends, my masters, on the entered honour. | 19 | 3 | 12 | 22 | 8 |
| Tells you and you, my masters, as his strange | 56 | 13 | 34 | 65 | 13 |
| MAST-HIGH | | | | | |
| Mast-high moon-white women naked | 153 | 8 | 83 | 171 | 4 |
| MASTIFF | | | | | |
| Spiked with a mastiff collar, | 132 | 10 | 78 | 147 | 10 |
| MASTS | | | | | |
| Funnels and masts went by in a whirl. | 149 | 17 | 83 | 166 | 17 |
| Masts and fishes to the still quick stars, | 172 | 17 | 88 | 192 | 17 |
| MATE | | | | | |
| To trot with a loud mate the haybeds of a mile, | 91 | 16 | 55 | 100 | 16 |
| MATTED | | | | | |
| Was muscled, matted, wise to the crying thigh | 21 | 4 | 13 | 25 | 4 |
| MATTER | | | | | |
| Had stringed my flask of matter to his rib. | 4 | 12 | 3 | 4 | 12 |
| One womb, one mind, spewed out the matter, | 21 | 18 | 13 | 26 | 1 |
| Then all the matter of the living air | 26 | 21 | 16 | 32 | 1 |
| Groping for matter under the dog's plate, | 48 | 26 | 28 | 57 | 3 |
| MATURED | | | | | |
| The plum my mother picked matured slowly, | 21 | 1 | 13 | 25 | 1 |
| MAULED | | | | | |
| Like the mauled pictures of boys? | 77 | 19 | 45 | 86 | 91 |
| MAULING | | | | | |
| Nor the flint in the lover's mauling. | 33 | 18 | 19 | 38 | 18 |
| MAY | | | | | |
| May fail to fasten with a virgin o | 18 | 19 | 12 | 21 | 19 |
| May a humble village labour | 43 | 1 | 24 | 50 | 8 |
| A hemisphere green may scold him | 43 | 3 | 24 | 50 | 10 |
| May a humble planet labour | 43 | 8 | 24 | 50 | 15 |
| A village green may scold him | 43 | 10 | 24 | 50 | 17 |
| No more may gulls cry at their ears | 68 | 20 | 42 | 77 | 20 |
| Where blew a flower may a flower no more | 68 | 22 | 42 | 77 | 22 |
| O may my heart's truth | 104 | 16 | 63 | 115 | 18 |
| You may not see, my son, | 105 | 2 | 64 | 116 | 2 |
| I may without fail | 108 | 17 | 66 | 119 | 17 |
| May his hunger go howling on bare white bones | 120 | 8 | 72 | 132 | 13 |
| May hold it in a great flood | 129 | 20 | 77 | 143 | 20 |
| Of his mother's milk may return | 144 | 2 | 82 | 161 | 2 |
| May the crimson | 147 | 13 | 82 | 164 | 13 |
| Be shielded by chant and flower and gay may you | 163 | 19 | 86 | 182 | 19 |

|  | U.K. | | Poem | U.S. | |
|---|---|---|---|---|---|
|  | *Page* | *Line* |  | *Page* | *Line* |
| On that darkest day. Oh, forever may |  |  | 91 | 200 | 4 |
| **MAZED** |  |  |  |  |  |
| Strait in the mazed bed | 108 | 5 | 66 | 119 | 5 |
| **MAZES** |  |  |  |  |  |
| The mazes of his praise and envious tongue were worked in flames and shells. | 95 | 17 | 58 | 105 | 17 |
| Mazes | 146 | 10 | 82 | 163 | 10 |
| **ME** |  |  |  |  |  |
| That, sewn to me by nerve and brain, | 4 | 11 | 3 | 4 | 11 |
| To rob me of my fluids in his heart. | 5 | 12 | 3 | 5 | 12 |
| Remember me and pity Him | 8 | 20 | 5 | 9 | 20 |
| Wind in me leaped, the hellborn dew; | 7 | 16 | 5 | 8 | 16 |
| A rooking girl who stole me for her side, | 12 | 2 | 9 | 13 | 2 |
| Would leave me cold as butter for the flies, | 12 | 26 | 9 | 14 | 5 |
| The sea of scums could drown me as it broke | 12 | 27 | 9 | 14 | 6 |
| Some let me make you of the vowelled beeches, | 16 | 13 | 11 | 19 | 13 |
| Some let me make you of the water's speeches. | 16 | 16 | 11 | 19 | 16 |
| Tells me the hour's word, the neural meaning | 16 | 18 | 11 | 19 | 18 |
| Some let me make you of the meadow's signs; | 16 | 21 | 11 | 19 | 21 |
| The signal grass that tells me all I know | 16 | 22 | 11 | 19 | 22 |
| Some let me tell you of the raven's sins. | 16 | 24 | 11 | 19 | 24 |
| (Some let me make you of autumnal spells, | 17 | 2 | 11 | 20 | 2 |
| Some let me make you of the heartless words. | 17 | 5 | 11 | 20 | 5 |
| Deliver me who, timid in my tribe, | 18 | 7 | 12 | 21 | 7 |
| Deliver me, my masters, head and heart, | 18 | 11 | 12 | 21 | 11 |
| I fellowed sleep who kissed me in the brain, | 26 | 1 | 16 | 31 | 1 |
| Shifting to light, turned on me like a moon. | 26 | 3 | 16 | 31 | 3 |
| Who seek me landward, marking in my mouth | 31 | 22 | 18 | 37 | 4 |
| The straws of Asia, lose me as I turn | 31 | 23 | 18 | 37 | 5 |
| The wisemen tell me that the garden gods | 40 | 9 | 22 | 46 | 9 |
| The wet night scolds me like a nurse? | 44 | 10 | 25 | 52 | 10 |
| And the slug should teach me destruction. | 45 | 13 | 26 | 53 | 13 |
| What shall it tell me if a timeless insect | 45 | 16 | 26 | 53 | 16 |
| Do you not father me, nor the erected arm | 46 | 1 | 27 | 54 | 1 |
| Do you not mother me, nor, as I am, | 46 | 3 | 27 | 54 | 3 |
| Do you not sister me, nor the erected crime | 46 | 5 | 27 | 54 | 5 |
| Do you not brother me, nor, as you climb, | 46 | 7 | 27 | 54 | 7 |
| You are all these, said she who gave me the long suck, | 46 | 17 | 27 | 54 | 17 |
| Do you not father me on the destroying sand? | 47 | 1 | 27 | 55 | 1 |
| That made me happy in the sun, | 48 | 19 | 28 | 56 | 19 |
| And cure me of ills. | 48 | 23 | 28 | 56 | 23 |
| We make me mystic as the arm of air, | 52 | 6 | 31 | 61 | 13 |
| She holding me? The people's sea drives on her, | 54 | 26 | 33 | 64 | 2 |
| Now make the world of me as I have made | 61 | 5 | 36 | 70 | 5 |
| And, crackling into the air, leave me half-blind. | 64 | 14 | 39 | 73 | 14 |

|  | U.K. | | | U.S. | |
|---|---|---|---|---|---|
|  | Page | Line | Poem | Page | Line |
| A merry girl took me for man, | 65 | 22 | 40 | 74 | 22 |
| Time kills me terribly. | 70 | 15 | 43 | 79 | 19 |
| I saw time murder me. | 70 | 20 | 43 | 79 | 24 |
| Dipped me breast-deep in the descended bone; | 72 | 14 | 44 | 81 | 14 |
| A climbing sea from Asia had me down | 73 | 19 | 44 | 82 | 19 |
| And Jonah's Moby snatched me by the hair, | 73 | 20 | 44 | 82 | 20 |
| She makes for me a nettle's innocence | 78 | 16 | 46 | 87 | 16 |
| It is the sinners' dust-tongued bell claps me to churches | 83 | 1 | 49 | 92 | 1 |
| O make me a mask and a wall to shut from your spies | 85 | 1 | 50 | 94 | 1 |
| She would not have me sinking in the holy | 87 | 18 | 52 | 96 | 18 |
| Storm me forever over her grave until | 88 | 10 | 52 | 97 | 10 |
| Her two surnames stopped me still. | 93 | 2 | 56 | 102 | 2 |
| O wake in me in my house in the mud | 96 | 1 | 58 | 106 | 1 |
| Rage me back to the making house. My hand unravel | 97 | 12 | 59 | 108 | 12 |
| In the wood faraway under me. | 103 | 5 | 63 | 114 | 5 |
| Go crying through you and me | 105 | 18 | 64 | 116 | 18 |
| Who palmed the lie on me when you looked | 107 | 4 | 65 | 118 | 4 |
| Turns of your prayed flesh, nor shall I shoo the bird below me: | 109 | 27 | 67 | 121 | 1 |
| Tongue of your translating eyes. The young stars told me, | 110 | 23 | 67 | 122 | 1 |
| And the vaulting bird be still. O my true love, hold me. | 110 | 26 | 67 | 122 | 4 |
| Curse, bless, me now with your fierce tears, I pray. | 116 | 17 | 70 | 128 | 17 |
| Burns me his name and his flame | 138 | 11 | 82 | 155 | 11 |
| Scald me and drown | 148 | 12 | 82 | 165 | 12 |
| Me in his world's wound. | 148 | 13 | 82 | 165 | 13 |
| Time let me hail and climb | 159 | 4 | 85 | 178 | 4 |
| Time let me play and be | 159 | 13 | 85 | 178 | 13 |
| Nothing I cared, in the lamb white days, that time would take me | 160 | 24 | 85 | 180 | 1 |
| Time held me green and dying | 161 | 5 | 85 | 180 | 8 |
| Oh, let me midlife mourn by the shrined | 172 | 22 | 88 | 192 | 22 |
| And serve me right as the preachers warn, | 175 | 9 | 89 | 195 | 14 |
| Harpies around me out of her womb! | 175 | 27 | 89 | 196 | 8 |
| Chastity prays for me, piety sings, | 175 | 28 | 89 | 196 | 9 |
| Now clasp me to their grains in the gigantic glade, | 176 | 19 | 90 | 197 | 19 |
| Now curlew cry me down to kiss the mouths of their dust. | 178 | 4 | 90 | 199 | 5 |
| They from houses where the harvest kneels, hold me hard, | 178 | 9 | 90 | 199 | 10 |

|  | U.K. | | | U.S. | |
| --- | --- | --- | --- | --- | --- |
|  | Page | Line | Poem | Page | Line |
| Teach me the love that is evergreen after the fall leaved | 178 | 12 | 90 | 199 | 13 |
| An old blind man is with me where I go |  |  | 91 | 201 | 9 |
| Do you not father me | 46 |  | 27 | 54 |  |
| O make me a mask | 85 |  | 50 | 94 |  |
| **MEADOW** |  |  |  |  |  |
| A blade of grass longs with the meadow, | 115 | 15 | 69 | 127 | 15 |
| **MEADOW'S** |  |  |  |  |  |
| Some let me make you of the meadow's signs; | 16 | 21 | 11 | 19 | 21 |
| **MEADOWS** |  |  |  |  |  |
| Corner the mounted meadows in the hill corral; | 36 | 15 | 20 | 41 | 15 |
| Walking in the meadows of his son's eye |  |  | 91 | 201 | 10 |
| **MEAN** |  |  |  |  |  |
| I mean by time the cast and curfew rascal of our marriage, | 84 | 1 | 49 | 93 | 7 |
| **MEANING** |  |  |  |  |  |
| Tells me the hour's word, the neural meaning | 16 | 18 | 11 | 19 | 18 |
| **MEANS** |  |  |  |  |  |
| Golden in the mercy of his means, | 159 | 14 | 85 | 178 | 14 |
| Oh as I was young and easy in the mercy of his means, | 161 | 4 | 85 | 180 | 7 |
| **MEASURE** |  |  |  |  |  |
| From limbs that had the measure of the worm, shuffled | 28 | 5 | 17 | 33 | 5 |
| **MEASURES** |  |  |  |  |  |
| Measures his own length on the garden wall | 41 | 12 | 23 | 47 | 12 |
| **MEAT** |  |  |  |  |  |
| He'll trumpet into meat), | 56 | 5 | 34 | 65 | 5 |
| 'Find meat on bones that soon have none, | 65 | 1 | 40 | 74 | 1 |
| I furnish with the meat of a fable; | 77 | 21 | 45 | 86 | 21 |
| Find meat on bones | 65 |  | 40 | 74 |  |
| **MEAT-EATING** |  |  |  |  |  |
| By the light of the meat-eating sun. | 99 | 5 | 60 | 110 | 5 |
| **MECHANICAL** |  |  |  |  |  |
| Stroke of mechanical flesh on mine, | 34 | 5 | 19 | 39 | 11 |
| **MEDUSA** |  |  |  |  |  |
| Pin-legged on pole-hills with a black medusa | 73 | 22 | 44 | 82 | 22 |
| **MEDUSA'S** |  |  |  |  |  |
| Pluck, cock, my sea eye, said medusa's scripture, | 74 | 5 | 44 | 83 | 5 |
| **MEEK** |  |  |  |  |  |
| Her flesh was meek as milk, but this skyward statue | 87 | 27 | 52 | 96 | 27 |
| And mire of love, but the Thief as meek as the dew. | 163 | 15 | 86 | 182 | 15 |
| And sly as snow and meek as dew blown to the thorn, | 164 | 1 | 86 | 183 | 8 |

|  | U.K. | | | U.S. | |
|---|---|---|---|---|---|
|  | *Page* | *Line* | *Poem* | *Page* | *Line* |
| **MEET** |  |  |  |  |  |
| Meet once on a mortal wall | 93 | 23 | 56 | 103 | 3 |
| Through throats where many rivers meet, the curlews cry, | 176 | 1 | 90 | 197 | 1 |
| Through throats where many rivers meet, the women pray, | 176 | 6 | 90 | 197 | 6 |
| **MEETING** |  |  |  |  |  |
| The earth and sky were as two mountains meeting. | 20 | 15 | 13 | 24 | 15 |
| **MELT** |  |  |  |  |  |
| Back to black silence melt and mourn | 140 | 10 | 82 | 157 | 10 |
| **MELTED** |  |  |  |  |  |
| Has melted away and is lost | 153 | 19 | 83 | 171 | 15 |
| **MELTING** |  |  |  |  |  |
| In high corn and the harvest melting on their tongues. | 120 | 18 | 72 | 133 | 3 |
| And she rose with him flowering in her melting snow. | 123 | 20 | 72 | 137 | 10 |
| **MELTS** |  |  |  |  |  |
| That melts the lionhead's heel and horseshoe of the heart, | 91 | 14 | 55 | 100 | 14 |
| **MEMORIAL'S** |  |  |  |  |  |
| I stand, for this memorial's sake, alone | 87 | 12 | 52 | 96 | 12 |
| **MEMORY** |  |  |  |  |  |
| In the memory worked by mirrors, | 107 | 10 | 65 | 118 | 10 |
| After the funeral (In memory of Ann Jones) | 87 |  | 52 | 96 |  |
| **MEN** |  |  |  |  |  |
| Out there, crow black, men | vii | 12 | 1 | xv | 12 |
| I see that from these boys shall men of nothing | 1 | 19 | 2 | 1 | 19 |
| That chalk the walls with green girls and their men. | 12 | 16 | 9 | 13 | 16 |
| The bones of men, the broken in their beds, | 14 | 9 | 10 | 16 | 9 |
| That shrouded men might marrow as they fly. | 15 | 10 | 10 | 17 | 10 |
| All, men my madmen, the unwholesome wind | 19 | 21 | 12 | 23 | 6 |
| 'These are but dreaming men. Breathe, and they fade.' | 26 | 15 | 16 | 31 | 15 |
| Drives forth my men, my children, from the hanging south. | 49 | 6 | 29 | 58 | 6 |
| Dead men naked they shall be one | 68 | 2 | 42 | 77 | 2 |
| Among men later I heard it said | 93 | 16 | 56 | 102 | 16 |
| And the souls of all men | 105 | 19 | 64 | 116 | 19 |
| Though wise men at their end know dark is right, | 116 | 4 | 70 | 128 | 4 |
| Good men, the last wave by, crying how bright | 116 | 7 | 70 | 128 | 7 |
| Wild men who caught and sang the sun in flight, | 116 | 10 | 70 | 128 | 10 |
| Grave men, near death, who see with blinding sight | 116 | 13 | 70 | 128 | 13 |

|  | U.K. |  |  | U.S. |  |
| --- | --- | --- | --- | --- | --- |
|  | *Page* | *Line* | *Poem* | *Page* | *Line* |
| Combs through the mantled yards and the morning men | 119 | 20 | 72 | 131 | 20 |
| All men | 144 | 10 | 82 | 161 | 10 |
| And the old men sing from newborn lips: | 155 | 8 | 83 | 173 | 12 |
| With men and women and waterfalls | 156 | 1 | 83 | 174 | 9 |
| And my shining men no more alone | 173 | 26 | 88 | 193 | 26 |
| MEN'S |  |  |  |  |  |
| I hear, through dead men's drums, the riddled lads, | 31 | 16 | 18 | 36 | 16 |
| MENDED |  |  |  |  |  |
| That her fond wounds are mended bitterly. | 81 | 9 | 47 | 90 | 9 |
| MERCIES |  |  |  |  |  |
| My nest of mercies in the rude, red tree. | 76 | 22 | 44 | 85 | 22 |
| MERCURY |  |  |  |  |  |
| Of the golden ghost who ringed with his streams her mercury bone, | 127 | 11 | 75 | 141 | 11 |
| MERCY |  |  |  |  |  |
| Golden in the mercy of his means, | 159 | 14 | 85 | 178 | 14 |
| Oh as I was young and easy in the mercy of his means, | 161 | 4 | 85 | 180 | 7 |
| Have mercy on, | 168 | 20 | 87 | 189 | 5 |
| MERIDIAN |  |  |  |  |  |
| Love for ever meridian through the courters' trees | 178 | 18 | 90 | 199 | 19 |
| MERMEN |  |  |  |  |  |
| Where once the mermen through your ice | 11 | 4 | 8 | 12 | 4 |
| Fishermen of mermen | 91 | 23 | 55 | 101 | 1 |
| Of blood! The bird loud vein! The saga from mermen | 165 | 7 | 86 | 184 | 15 |
| MERRIEST |  |  |  |  |  |
| The merriest marrow and the dregs | 65 | 3 | 40 | 74 | 3 |
| MERRY |  |  |  |  |  |
| And nail the merry squires to the trees; | 2 | 21 | 2 | 3 | 3 |
| The oat was merry in the wind; | 39 | 9 | 21 | 45 | 9 |
| A merry manshape of your walking circle. | 61 | 6 | 36 | 70 | 6 |
| A merry girl took me for man, | 65 | 22 | 40 | 74 | 22 |
| MESSAGE |  |  |  |  |  |
| I knew the message of the winter, | 7 | 13 | 5 | 8 | 13 |
| The message of his dying christ. | 8 | 18 | 5 | 9 | 18 |
| METAL |  |  |  |  |  |
| Through all the irons in the grass, metal | 28 | 7 | 17 | 33 | 7 |
| Nor the heart in the ribbing metal. | 33 | 15 | 19 | 38 | 15 |
| Laying my ghost in metal, | 35 | 3 | 20 | 40 | 3 |
| Image of images, my metal phantom | 35 | 14 | 20 | 40 | 14 |
| My ghost in his metal neptune | 38 | 27 | 20 | 44 | 17 |
| METAPHOR |  |  |  |  |  |
| Man be my metaphor. | 13 | 21 | 9 | 15 | 7 |

| | U.K. | | | U.S. | |
|---|---|---|---|---|---|
| | Page | Line | Poem | Page | Line |
| **METAPHORS** | | | | | |
| Death is all metaphors, shape in one history; | 71 | 15 | 44 | 80 | 15 |
| **METEORS** | | | | | |
| Blind eyes could blaze like meteors and be gay, | 116 | 14 | 70 | 128 | 14 |
| **METRE** | | | | | |
| What is the metre of the dictionary? | 72 | 19 | 44 | 81 | 19 |
| **METROPOLIS** | | | | | |
| Metropolis of fishes, | 157 | 12 | 83 | 176 | 4 |
| **MIDDLE** | | | | | |
| Crying, white gowned, from the middle moonlit stages | 114 | 14 | 69 | 126 | 14 |
| **MIDLIFE** | | | | | |
| Oh, let me midlife mourn by the shrined | 172 | 22 | 88 | 192 | 22 |
| **MIDNIGHT** | | | | | |
| Nor blows back moon and midnight as she blows. | 2 | 6 | 2 | 2 | 6 |
| Can never raise the midnight of a chuckle, | 13 | 11 | 9 | 14 | 18 |
| By midnight pulleys that unhouse the tomb. | 14 | 10 | 10 | 16 | 10 |
| And speak their midnight nothings as they swell; | 14 | 14 | 10 | 16 | 14 |
| All heaven in a midnight of the sun, | 40 | 17 | 22 | 46 | 17 |
| And, manned by midnight, Jacob to the stars. | 71 | 24 | 44 | 80 | 24 |
| The fats of midnight when the salt was singing; | 74 | 10 | 44 | 83 | 10 |
| Towards the studded male in a bent, midnight blaze | 91 | 13 | 55 | 100 | 13 |
| Midwives grew in the midnight ditches, | 174 | 19 | 89 | 194 | 19 |
| **MIDST** | | | | | |
| In the mill of the midst | 109 | 18 | 67 | 120 | 18 |
| **MIDWIFE** | | | | | |
| Cry joy that this witchlike midwife second | 96 | 23 | 58 | 107 | 6 |
| **MIDWIVES** | | | | | |
| And the midwives of miracle sing | 138 | 9 | 82 | 155 | 9 |
| Midwives grew in the midnight ditches, | 174 | 19 | 89 | 194 | 19 |
| **MIDWIVING** | | | | | |
| Of midwiving morning's | 147 | 5 | 82 | 164 | 5 |
| **MIGHT** | | | | | |
| That shrouded men might marrow as they fly. | 15 | 10 | 10 | 17 | 10 |
| Some life, yet unspent, might explode | 64 | 12 | 39 | 73 | 12 |
| That she might stand in the night | 112 | 11 | 68 | 124 | 11 |
| Their frail deeds might have danced in a green bay, | 116 | 8 | 70 | 128 | 8 |
| Might cross its planets, the bell weep, night gather her eyes, | 165 | 21 | 86 | 185 | 11 |
| There he might wander bare | 172 | 1 | 88 | 192 | 1 |
| **MIGHTY** | | | | | |
| And in the mighty mornings of the earth; | 40 | 15 | 22 | 46 | 15 |
| The mighty hand leads to a sloping shoulder, | 62 | 5 | 37 | 71 | 5 |

|  |  | U.K. | | | U.S. | |
|---|---|---|---|---|---|---|
|  |  | Page | Line | Poem | Page | Line |
| **MILD** | | | | | | |
| | And, mild as pardon from a cloud of pride, | 80 | 6 | 46 | 89 | 14 |
| **MILE** | | | | | | |
| | Thrusting the tom-thumb vision up the iron mile. | 38 | 6 | 20 | 43 | 16 |
| | To trot with a loud mate the haybeds of a mile, | 91 | 16 | 55 | 100 | 16 |
| | Under the mile off moon we trembled listening | 136 | 5 | 81 | 153 | 5 |
| **MILES** | | | | | | |
| | Miles over the moonstruck boat | 150 | 14 | 83 | 167 | 18 |
| **MILK** | | | | | | |
| | And mother milk was stiff as sand, | 5 | 8 | 3 | 5 | 8 |
| | My world was christened in a stream of milk. | 20 | 7 | 13 | 24 | 7 |
| | To-morrow's diver in her horny milk, | 30 | 4 | 18 | 35 | 4 |
| | The swing of milk was tufted in the pap, | 30 | 10 | 18 | 35 | 10 |
| | Time, milk, and magic, from the world beginning. | 74 | 24 | 44 | 83 | 24 |
| | Bread and milk mansion in a toothless town. | 78 | 15 | 46 | 87 | 15 |
| | Her flesh was meek as milk, but this skyward statue | 87 | 27 | 52 | 96 | 27 |
| | Milk in your mouth, at the sour floods | 96 | 7 | 58 | 106 | 7 |
| | The duck-billed platypus broody in a milk of birds. | 110 | 5 | 67 | 121 | 7 |
| | Of his mother's milk may return | 144 | 2 | 82 | 161 | 2 |
| | Sails drank the wind, and white as milk | 149 | 13 | 83 | 166 | 13 |
| **MILKED** | | | | | | |
| | And drink in the two milked crags, | 65 | 2 | 40 | 74 | 2 |
| **MILKING** | | | | | | |
| | Young as they in the after milking moonlight lay | 176 | 16 | 90 | 197 | 16 |
| **MILKMAIDS** | | | | | | |
| | The puffed birds hopping and hunting, the milkmaids | 119 | 23 | 72 | 132 | 3 |
| **MILKY** | | | | | | |
| | The milky acid on each hinge, | 4 | 5 | 3 | 4 | 5 |
| | Under the milky mushrooms slew my hunger, | 73 | 18 | 44 | 82 | 18 |
| | Or hickory bull in milky grass | 175 | 12 | 89 | 195 | 17 |
| **MILL** | | | | | | |
| | In the mill of the midst | 109 | 18 | 67 | 120 | 18 |
| **MILLED** | | | | | | |
| | Milled dust of the apple tree and the pounded islands | 164 | 10 | 86 | 183 | 17 |
| **MILLING** | | | | | | |
| | Fear not the tread, the seeded milling, | 33 | 16 | 19 | 38 | 16 |
| **MILLION** | | | | | | |
| | A million minds gave suck to such a bud | 21 | 22 | 13 | 26 | 5 |
| **MIND** | | | | | | |
| | One womb, one mind, spewed out the matter, | 21 | 18 | 13 | 26 | 1 |
| | And the hills out of mind. | 58 | 14 | 35 | 67 | 14 |

MIND (continued)

|  | U.K. | | | U.S. | |
|---|---|---|---|---|---|
|  | *Page* | *Line* | *Poem* | *Page* | *Line* |
| Will never go out of my mind. |  |  | 91 | 200 | 20 |
| MINDED |  |  |  |  |  |
| What had been one was many sounding minded. | 21 | 17 | 13 | 25 | 17 |
| MINDS |  |  |  |  |  |
| A million minds gave suck to such a bud | 21 | 22 | 13 | 26 | 5 |
| MINE |  |  |  |  |  |
| Turns mine to wax. | 9 | 8 | 6 | 10 | 8 |
| Stroke of mechanical flesh on mine, | 34 | 5 | 19 | 39 | 11 |
| They said, who hacked and humoured, they were mine. | 46 | 20 | 27 | 54 | 20 |
| Dry lover mine | 51 | 4 | 31 | 60 | 4 |
| That his tears burned my cheeks and his heart moved in mine. | 103 | 28 | 63 | 115 | 2 |
| No prophet-progeny of mine, | 134 | 26 | 79 | 151 | 4 |
| MINERAL |  |  |  |  |  |
| Forged in man's mineral. | 38 | 28 | 20 | 44 | 18 |
| MINERALS |  |  |  |  |  |
| Forged in man's minerals, the brassy orator | 35 | 2 | 20 | 40 | 2 |
| MINISTERS |  |  |  |  |  |
| Black night still ministers the moon, | 66 | 9 | 40 | 75 | 9 |
| MINNOWS |  |  |  |  |  |
| Of minnows wreathing around their prayer; | 171 | 2 | 88 | 191 | 2 |
| MINOTAURS |  |  |  |  |  |
| The she mules bear their minotaurs, | 110 | 4 | 67 | 121 | 6 |
| MINSTREL |  |  |  |  |  |
| Old cock from nowheres lopped the minstrel tongue | 74 | 8 | 44 | 83 | 8 |
| This was the sky, Jack Christ, each minstrel angle | 75 | 11 | 44 | 84 | 11 |
| On the white, no longer growing green, and, minstrel dead, | 123 | 2 | 72 | 136 | 12 |
| And cut the birds' boughs that the minstrel sap ran red. | 178 | 8 | 90 | 199 | 9 |
| MINSTRELS |  |  |  |  |  |
| Listen. The minstrels sing | 121 | 1 | 72 | 133 | 16 |
| MINTED |  |  |  |  |  |
| Stamp of the minted face upon the moon; | 22 | 10 | 14 | 27 | 10 |
| MINUTE |  |  |  |  |  |
| And to the hollow minute of the womb, | 20 | 2 | 13 | 24 | 2 |
| In the muted house, one minute before |  |  | 91 | 200 | 14 |
| Unsex the skeleton this mountain minute, | 75 | 16 | 44 | 84 | 16 |
| Each ancient, stone-necked minute of love's season | 78 | 2 | 46 | 87 | 2 |
| Over the choir minute I hear the hour chant: | 83 | 7 | 49 | 92 | 7 |
| MINUTE'S |  |  |  |  |  |
| The long, laid minute's bride drifts on | 152 | 11 | 83 | 170 | 3 |

| | U.K. | | | U.S. | |
|---|---|---|---|---|---|
| | *Page* | *Line* | *Poem* | *Page* | *Line* |
| MINUTES | | | | | |
| Hold hard, these ancient minutes in the cuckoo's month, | 49 | 1 | 29 | 58 | 1 |
| Hold hard, these ancient minutes in the cuckoo's month | 49 | | 29 | 58 | |
| MIRACLE | | | | | |
| Create this twin miracle. | 35 | 18 | 20 | 40 | 18 |
| Though the moment of a miracle is unending lightning | 127 | 6 | 75 | 141 | 6 |
| And the midwives of miracle sing | 138 | 9 | 82 | 155 | 9 |
| Oh miracle of fishes! The long dead bite! | 154 | 20 | 83 | 172 | 20 |
| Music of elements, that a miracle makes! | 165 | 15 | 86 | 185 | 5 |
| MIRACLES | | | | | |
| Myselves grieve now, and miracles cannot atone. | 129 | 16 | 77 | 143 | 16 |
| His decks are drenched with miracles. | 154 | 19 | 83 | 172 | 19 |
| All the horses of his haul of miracles | 156 | 19 | 83 | 175 | 7 |
| MIRACULOUS | | | | | |
| Was miraculous virginity old as loaves and fishes, | 127 | 5 | 75 | 141 | 5 |
| MIRE | | | | | |
| And mire of love, but the Thief as meek as the dew. | 163 | 15 | 86 | 182 | 15 |
| MIRROR | | | | | |
| Mirror from man to whale | 69 | 21 | 43 | 78 | 21 |
| Shall her smile breed that mouth, behind the mirror, | 90 | 13 | 54 | 99 | 13 |
| Call for confessor and wiser mirror but there is none | 158 | 10 | 84 | 177 | 10 |
| MIRRORED | | | | | |
| Heron, mirrored, go, | 169 | 1 | 87 | 189 | 10 |
| MIRRORS | | | | | |
| In the memory worked by mirrors, | 107 | 10 | 65 | 118 | 10 |
| MIST | | | | | |
| Love like a mist or fire through the bed of eels. | 38 | 12 | 20 | 44 | 2 |
| With its horns through mist and the castle | 103 | 8 | 63 | 114 | 8 |
| As the rain falls, hail on the fleece, as the vale mist rides | 164 | 8 | 86 | 183 | 15 |
| MISTER | | | | | |
| Mister and master, darkness for his eyes, | 57 | 3 | 34 | 66 | 10 |
| A solitary mister | 111 | 2 | 68 | 123 | 2 |
| And Mister they called Hey mister | 111 | 15 | 68 | 123 | 15 |
| MITCHING | | | | | |
| When I whistled with mitching boys through a reservoir park | 89 | 7 | 53 | 98 | 7 |
| MIXTURE | | | | | |
| Where words and water make a mixture | 8 | 3 | 5 | 9 | 3 |

| | U.K. | | | U.S. | |
|---|---|---|---|---|---|
| | *Page* | *Line* | *Poem* | *Page* | *Line* |
| MIXED | | | | | |
| Heaven and hell mixed as they spun. | 22 | 6 | 14 | 27 | 6 |
| MNETHA'S | | | | | |
| Was brother to Mnetha's daughter | 7 | 5 | 5 | 8 | 5 |
| MOAN | | | | | |
| Wound their room with a male moan, | 114 | 2 | 69 | 126 | 2 |
| Wall hearing the moan | 138 | 5 | 82 | 155 | 5 |
| That he let the dead lie though they moan | 145 | 1 | 82 | 162 | 1 |
| MOBY | | | | | |
| And Jonah's Moby snatched me by the hair, | 73 | 20 | 44 | 82 | 20 |
| MOCK | | | | | |
| And the grave sea, mock who deride | 82 | 2 | 48 | 91 | 2 |
| MOCKERY | | | | | |
| Hunchbacked in mockery | 111 | 21 | 68 | 123 | 21 |
| MODESTY | | | | | |
| Modesty hides my thighs in her wings, | 175 | 30 | 89 | 196 | 11 |
| MOLE | | | | | |
| And the mole snout blunt under his pilgrimage of domes, | 177 | 16 | 90 | 198 | 15 |
| MOLESTED | | | | | |
| In the molested rocks the shell of virgins, | 78 | 18 | 46 | 87 | 18 |
| MOLL | | | | | |
| In this our age the gunman and his moll, | 14 | 11 | 10 | 16 | 11 |
| MOLTEN | | | | | |
| Molten and mountainous to stream | viii | 23 | 1 | xvi | 23 |
| As yet was in a molten form, | 7 | 10 | 5 | 8 | 10 |
| Her molten flight up cinder-nesting columns, | 78 | 26 | 46 | 88 | 3 |
| Into the weathercocks' molten mouths | 131 | 11 | 77 | 145 | 17 |
| MOMENT | | | | | |
| Though the moment of a miracle is unending lightning | 127 | 6 | 75 | 141 | 6 |
| MONEY | | | | | |
| With my red veins full of money, | 99 | 7 | 60 | 110 | 7 |
| MONKEY | | | | | |
| 'If my bunched, monkey coming is cruel | 97 | 11 | 59 | 108 | 11 |
| MONKEYED | | | | | |
| The inches monkeyed by the blood of man. | 27 | 3 | 16 | 32 | 8 |
| MONSTER | | | | | |
| This story's monster has a serpent caul, | 41 | 10 | 23 | 47 | 10 |
| MONSTROUS | | | | | |
| Your monstrous officers and the decaying army, | 37 | 5 | 20 | 42 | 11 |
| (Though this for her is a monstrous image blindly | 87 | 16 | 52 | 96 | 16 |
| Of the living flesh is monstrous or immortal, | 110 | 13 | 67 | 121 | 15 |
| MONTH | | | | | |
| Hold hard, these ancient minutes in the cuckoo's month, | 49 | 1 | 29 | 58 | 1 |

|  | U.K. | | | U.S. | |
| --- | --- | --- | --- | --- | --- |
|  | Page | Line | Poem | Page | Line |
| Lie this fifth month unskated, and the birds have flown; | 49 | 9 | 29 | 58 | 9 |
| Hold hard, these ancient minutes in the cuckoo's month | 49 |  | 29 | 58 |  |
| **MONTHS** | | | | | |
| On no work of words now for three lean months in the bloody | 94 | 1 | 57 | 104 | 1 |
| A limp and riderless shape to leap nine thinning months.' | 97 | 15 | 59 | 108 | 15 |
| **MONUMENTAL** | | | | | |
| These cloud-sopped, marble hands, this monumental | 88 | 8 | 52 | 97 | 8 |
| **MOOD** | | | | | |
| The supper and knives of a mood. | 77 | 4 | 45 | 86 | 4 |
| **MOON** | | | | | |
| The signal moon is zero in their voids. | 1 | 12 | 2 | 1 | 12 |
| Of sun and moon they paint their dams | 1 | 17 | 2 | 1 | 17 |
| Nor blows back moon and midnight as she blows. | 2 | 6 | 2 | 2 | 6 |
| A process blows the moon into the sun, | 6 | 22 | 4 | 7 | 4 |
| Who knew not sun and moon by name, | 7 | 8 | 5 | 8 | 8 |
| The sun and moon shed one white light. | 20 | 9 | 13 | 24 | 9 |
| The sun was red, the moon was grey, | 20 | 14 | 13 | 24 | 14 |
| Stamp of the minted face upon the moon; | 22 | 10 | 14 | 27 | 10 |
| Like some pitch moon, the limit of the globes; | 24 | 20 | 15 | 29 | 20 |
| Shifting to light, turned on me like a moon. | 26 | 3 | 16 | 31 | 3 |
| A handmade moon half holy in a cloud, | 40 | 8 | 22 | 46 | 8 |
| And when the moon rose windily it was | 40 | 11 | 22 | 46 | 11 |
| Foster the light nor veil the manshaped moon, | 60 | 1 | 36 | 69 | 1 |
| 'Rebel against the binding moon | 65 | 9 | 40 | 74 | 9 |
| Black night still ministers the moon, | 66 | 9 | 40 | 75 | 9 |
| With the man in the wind and the west moon; | 68 | 3 | 42 | 77 | 3 |
| On the departed, snow bushed green, wanton in moon light | 121 | 17 | 72 | 134 | 12 |
| When only the moon rages | 128 | 3 | 76 | 142 | 3 |
| From the raging moon I write | 128 | 13 | 76 | 142 | 13 |
| Under the mile off moon we trembled listening | 136 | 5 | 81 | 153 | 5 |
| That he who learns now the sun and moon | 144 | 1 | 82 | 161 | 1 |
| And the moon swam out of its hulk. | 149 | 16 | 83 | 166 | 16 |
| But the oil and bubble of the moon, | 150 | 21 | 83 | 168 | 5 |
| Good-bye, good luck, struck the sun and the moon, | 157 | 21 | 83 | 176 | 13 |
| In the moon that is always rising, | 160 | 26 | 85 | 180 | 3 |
| All the moon long I heard, blessed among stables, the night-jars | 160 | 3 | 85 | 179 | 3 |
| Or skulks in the dell moon but moonshine echoing clear | 163 | 2 | 86 | 182 | 2 |

MOON (continued)

|  | U.K. | | | U.S. | |
|---|---|---|---|---|---|
|  | *Page* | *Line* | *Poem* | *Page* | *Line* |
| Under the prayer wheeling moon in the rosy wood | 163 | 18 | 86 | 182 | 18 |
| The whole of the moon I could love and leave | 174 | 10 | 89 | 194 | 10 |
| Dipping moon and drunk as a new dropped calf, | 174 | 17 | 89 | 194 | 17 |
| Under the conceiving moon, on the high chalk hill, | 176 | 2 | 90 | 197 | 2 |
| Or rippling soft in the spinney moon as the silk | 177 | 7 | 90 | 198 | 6 |
| MOON'S | | | | | |
| Like the moon's seed, rubbish | 106 | 2 | 64 | 117 | 2 |
| MOONBEAM | | | | | |
| You king singsong owls, who moonbeam. | ix | 3 | 1 | xvii | 3 |
| MOON-BLOWN | | | | | |
| Twine in a moon-blown shell, | 69 | 15 | 43 | 78 | 15 |
| MOON-CHAINED | | | | | |
| Turns the moon-chained and water-wound | 157 | 11 | 83 | 176 | 3 |
| MOON-DRAWN | | | | | |
| The moon-drawn grave, with the seafaring years, | 67 | 2 | 41 | 76 | 2 |
| MOONFALL | | | | | |
| Moonfall and sailing emperor, pale as their tide-print, | 83 | 10 | 49 | 92 | 10 |
| MOONLESS | | | | | |
| Left by the dead who, in their moonless acre, | 21 | 11 | 13 | 25 | 11 |
| MOONLIGHT | | | | | |
| Young as they in the after milking moonlight lay | 176 | 16 | 90 | 197 | 16 |
| MOONLIT | | | | | |
| Crying, white gowned, from the middle moonlit stages | 114 | 14 | 69 | 126 | 14 |
| MOONS | | | | | |
| Who moons her blue notes from her nest | ix | 11 | 1 | xvii | 11 |
| MOONSHADE | | | | | |
| Under the lighted shapes of faith and their moonshade | 176 | 17 | 90 | 197 | 17 |
| MOONSHINE | | | | | |
| Work ark and the moonshine | x | 1 | 1 | xviii | 7 |
| Or skulks in the dell moon but moonshine echoing clear | 163 | 2 | 86 | 182 | 2 |
| And the lost, moonshine domes, | 173 | 5 | 88 | 193 | 5 |
| MOONSHOD | | | | | |
| Through the shaken greensward lake, silent, on moonshod hooves, | 165 | 13 | 86 | 185 | 3 |
| MOONSTRUCK | | | | | |
| Miles over the moonstruck boat | 150 | 14 | 83 | 167 | 18 |
| MOON-TURNED | | | | | |
| Dazzle this face of voices on the moon-turned table, | 37 | 18 | 20 | 43 | 1 |

|  | U.K. | | Poem | U.S. | |
|---|---|---|---|---|---|
|  | Page | Line |  | Page | Line |

MOON-WHITE

| Mast-high moon-white women naked | 153 | 8 | 83 | 171 | 4 |

MORE

| No death more natural; | 35 | 21 | 20 | 40 | 21 |
| No tread more perilous, the green steps and spire | 36 | 2 | 20 | 41 | 2 |
| No man more magical, clawed out the crocodile. | 38 | 18 | 20 | 44 | 8 |
| No tell-tale lover has an end more certain, | 41 | 24 | 23 | 48 | 6 |
| There's more than dying; | 48 | 11 | 28 | 56 | 11 |
| Growing more terrible as the day | 64 | 4 | 39 | 73 | 4 |
| No more may gulls cry at their ears | 68 | 20 | 42 | 77 | 20 |
| Where blew a flower may a flower no more | 68 | 22 | 42 | 77 | 22 |
| More the thick stone cannot tell. | 93 | 10 | 56 | 102 | 10 |
| Dig no more for the chains of his grey-haired heart. | 135 | 9 | 80 | 152 | 9 |
| With no more desire than a ghost. | 154 | 4 | 83 | 172 | 4 |
| When that immortal hospital made one more move to soothe | 158 | 3 | 84 | 177 | 3 |
| With more triumphant faith | 173 | 16 | 88 | 193 | 16 |
| More spanned with angels ride | 173 | 23 | 88 | 193 | 23 |
| And my shining men no more alone | 173 | 26 | 88 | 193 | 26 |
| Now I am a man no more no more | 175 | 20 | 89 | 196 | 1 |

MORNING

| A worker in the morning town, | 5 | 14 | 3 | 5 | 14 |
| Flies on the shafted disk, declaims the morning | 16 | 19 | 11 | 19 | 19 |
| Crowing to Lazarus the morning is vanity, | 37 | 8 | 20 | 42 | 14 |
| Morning smack of the spade that wakes up sleep, | 87 | 6 | 52 | 96 | 6 |
| The morning beckon | 102 | 5 | 63 | 113 | 5 |
| Come in the morning where I wandered and listened | 103 | 2 | 63 | 114 | 2 |
| Before the crowing morning climbed; | 113 | 19 | 69 | 125 | 19 |
| Combs through the mantled yards and the morning men | 119 | 20 | 72 | 131 | 20 |
| Cutting the morning off, | 134 | 10 | 79 | 150 | 10 |
| Every morning I make, | 134 | 16 | 79 | 150 | 16 |
| I heard, this morning, waking, | 134 | 23 | 79 | 151 | 1 |
| When the morning was waking over the war | 135 | 1 | 80 | 152 | 1 |
| The morning is flying on the wings of his age | 135 | 13 | 80 | 152 | 13 |
| Of the morning | 141 | 13 | 82 | 158 | 13 |
| Gabriel and radiant shrubbery as the morning grows joyful | 158 | 15 | 84 | 177 | 15 |
| In all his tuneful turning so few and such morning songs | 160 | 21 | 85 | 179 | 21 |
| Of the morning leaves, as the star falls, as the winged | 164 | 11 | 86 | 183 | 18 |
| Spins its morning of praise, | 173 | 18 | 88 | 193 | 18 |

MORNING'S

| Waking alone in a multitude of loves when morning's light | 127 | 1 | 75 | 141 | 1 |

|  | U.K. |  |  | U.S. |  |
|---|---|---|---|---|---|
|  | *Page* | *Line* | *Poem* | *Page* | *Line* |
| Of midwiving morning's | 147 | 5 | 82 | 164 | 5 |

MORNINGS

| And in the mighty mornings of the earth; | 40 | 15 | 22 | 46 | 15 |
| Forgotten mornings when he walked with his mother | 103 | 22 | 63 | 114 | 22 |

MORROW

| Dug of the sea, the glanded morrow, | 33 | 8 | 19 | 38 | 8 |
| Man morrow blows through food. | 56 | 14 | 34 | 65 | 14 |
| (Sir morrow stamps | 56 | 23 | 34 | 66 | 2 |
| (Sir morrow mark), | 56 | 2 | 34 | 65 | 2 |
| Sir morrow at his sponge, | 56 | 8 | 34 | 65 | 8 |

MORSING

| My pickbrain masters morsing on the stone | 18 | 22 | 12 | 22 | 2 |

MORTAL

| A ghost nor man, but mortal ghost. | 8 | 14 | 5 | 9 | 14 |
| I was a mortal to the last | 8 | 16 | 5 | 9 | 16 |
| And time cast forth my mortal creature | 8 | 7 | 5 | 9 | 7 |
| Leans on my mortal ruler, | 10 | 4 | 7 | 11 | 4 |
| Praising the mortal error | 10 | 17 | 7 | 11 | 17 |
| Fear not the working world, my mortal, | 33 | 13 | 19 | 38 | 13 |
| Square in these worlds the mortal circle. | 34 | 6 | 19 | 39 | 12 |
| My man of leaves and the bronze root, mortal, unmortal, | 35 | 16 | 20 | 40 | 16 |
| Of mortal voices to the ninnies' choir, | 60 | 16 | 36 | 69 | 16 |
| From all my mortal lovers with a starboard smile; | 60 | 21 | 36 | 69 | 21 |
| Meet once on a mortal wall | 93 | 23 | 56 | 103 | 3 |
| Nor walk in the cool of your mortal garden | 110 | 20 | 67 | 121 | 22 |

MOST

| One who is most unknown, | 117 | 16 | 71 | 129 | 16 |
| Of their most secret heart. | 128 | 11 | 76 | 142 | 11 |
| On the lord's-table of the bowing grass. Fear most | 163 | 12 | 86 | 182 | 12 |
| And this last blessing most, | 173 | 9 | 88 | 193 | 9 |

MOSTLY

| Now shown and mostly bare I would lie down, | 133 | 21 | 78 | 149 | 4 |

MOTHER

| And mother milk was stiff as sand, | 5 | 8 | 3 | 5 | 8 |
| Of lover, mother, lovers, or his six | 13 | 13 | 9 | 14 | 20 |
| The plum my mother picked matured slowly, | 21 | 1 | 13 | 25 | 1 |
| Half of the fellow mother as she dabbles | 30 | 3 | 18 | 35 | 3 |
| Do you not mother me, nor, as I am, | 46 | 3 | 27 | 54 | 3 |
| By magnet winds to her blind mother drawn, | 78 | 14 | 46 | 87 | 14 |
| The grains beyond age, the dark veins of her mother, | 101 | 21 | 62 | 112 | 21 |
| Forgotten mornings when he walked with his mother | 103 | 22 | 63 | 114 | 22 |

|  | U.K. |  |  | U.S. |  |
| --- | --- | --- | --- | --- | --- |
|  | Page | Line | Poem | Page | Line |
| The mother dug, and its arms full of fires. | 129 | 8 | 77 | 143 | 8 |
| Of the mother hidden | 138 | 6 | 82 | 155 | 6 |
| And the mother and toppling house of the holy spring, | 158 | 23 | 84 | 177 | 23 |
| Hugged, and barren and bare on Mother Goose's ground | 178 | 2 | 90 | 199 | 3 |
| MOTHER'S |  |  |  |  |  |
| And double-crossed my mother's womb. | 8 | 22 | 5 | 9 | 22 |
| 'His mother's womb had a tongue that lapped up mud,' | 79 | 20 | 46 | 89 | 1 |
| Before I heard in my mother's side | 93 | 6 | 56 | 102 | 6 |
| Of his mother's milk may return | 144 | 2 | 82 | 161 | 2 |
| Above all he longed for his mother's breast |  |  | 91 | 200 | 9 |
| MOTHERED |  |  |  |  |  |
| Turns ghost to ghost; each mothered child | 6 | 20 | 4 | 7 | 2 |
| MOTHERING |  |  |  |  |  |
| And the splashed mothering maiden | 139 | 8 | 82 | 156 | 8 |
| MOTHERS |  |  |  |  |  |
| I see the summer children in their mothers | 1 | 13 | 2 | 1 | 13 |
| MOTHERS-EYED |  |  |  |  |  |
| My mothers-eyed, upon the tops of trees; | 26 | 9 | 16 | 31 | 9 |
| Faded my elbow ghost, the mothers-eyed, | 26 | 16 | 16 | 31 | 16 |
| MOTION |  |  |  |  |  |
| I, in my fusion of rose and male motion, | 35 | 17 | 20 | 40 | 17 |
| MOTOR |  |  |  |  |  |
| As motor muscle on the drill, driving | 28 | 3 | 17 | 33 | 3 |
| MOUNT |  |  |  |  |  |
| Mount on man's footfall, | 36 | 3 | 20 | 41 | 3 |
| To shut the sun, plunge, mount your darkened keys | 118 | 5 | 71 | 130 | 9 |
| MOUNTAIN |  |  |  |  |  |
| How at the mountain spring the same mouth sucks. | 9 | 10 | 6 | 10 | 10 |
| Casts to the pine roots, raising man like a mountain | 35 | 11 | 20 | 40 | 11 |
| This was the crucifixion on the mountain, | 75 | 5 | 44 | 84 | 5 |
| Unsex the skeleton this mountain minute, | 75 | 16 | 44 | 84 | 16 |
| Lost on the unchristened mountain | 144 | 16 | 82 | 161 | 16 |
| On the mountain crown | 145 | 13 | 82 | 162 | 13 |
| For who unmanningly haunts the mountain ravened eaves | 163 | 1 | 86 | 182 | 1 |
| MOUNTAINOUS |  |  |  |  |  |
| Molten and mountainous to stream | viii | 23 | 1 | xvi | 23 |
| MOUNTAINS |  |  |  |  |  |
| The earth and sky were as two mountains meeting. | 20 | 15 | 13 | 24 | 15 |
| Hiding the golden mountains and mansions | 82 | 16 | 48 | 91 | 16 |

# MOUNTAINS (continued)

| | U.K. | | | U.S. | |
|---|---|---|---|---|---|
| | *Page* | *Line* | *Poem* | *Page* | *Line* |
| Mountains and galleries beneath | 152 | 14 | 83 | 170 | 6 |
| Mountains and galleries to the crest! | 154 | 12 | 83 | 172 | 12 |
| **MOUNTED** | | | | | |
| Corner the mounted meadows in the hill corral; | 36 | 15 | 20 | 41 | 15 |
| Butt of the tree-tailed worm that mounted Eve, | 72 | 8 | 44 | 81 | 8 |
| **MOUNTING** | | | | | |
| In the beginning was the mounting fire | 22 | 13 | 14 | 27 | 13 |
| Clash out the mounting dolphin's day, | 152 | 3 | 83 | 169 | 15 |
| **MOURN** | | | | | |
| In the least valley of sackcloth to mourn | 101 | 12 | 62 | 112 | 12 |
| Back to black silence melt and mourn | 140 | 10 | 82 | 157 | 10 |
| To mourn his deluging | 146 | 4 | 82 | 163 | 4 |
| Oh, let me midlife mourn by the shrined | 172 | 22 | 88 | 192 | 22 |
| A Refusal to Mourn the Death, by Fire, of a child in London | 101 | | 62 | 112 | |
| **MOURNING** | | | | | |
| In a fiercely mourning house in a crooked year. | 88 | 2 | 52 | 97 | 2 |
| **MOURNS** | | | | | |
| A man torn up mourns in the sole night. | 115 | 21 | 69 | 127 | 21 |
| **MOUSE** | | | | | |
| Tom tit and Dai mouse! | x | 16 | 1 | xviii | 22 |
| With every simmering woman his mouse | 175 | 1 | 89 | 195 | 6 |
| **MOUSE'S** | | | | | |
| A claw I question from the mouse's bone, | 56 | 17 | 34 | 65 | 17 |
| **MOUSEHOLE** | | | | | |
| At last the soul from its foul mousehole | 175 | 14 | 89 | 195 | 19 |
| **MOUSING** | | | | | |
| The cattle stirring, the mousing cat stepping shy, | 119 | 22 | 72 | 132 | 2 |
| **MOUTH** | | | | | |
| The mouth of time sucked, like a sponge, | 4 | 4 | 3 | 4 | 4 |
| And I am dumb to mouth unto my veins | 9 | 9 | 6 | 10 | 9 |
| How at the mountain spring the same mouth sucks. | 9 | 10 | 6 | 10 | 10 |
| Your mouth, my love, the thistle in the kiss? | 13 | 16 | 9 | 15 | 2 |
| When no mouth stirred about the hanging famine, | 20 | 5 | 13 | 24 | 5 |
| Death on the mouth that ate the gas. | 28 | 16 | 17 | 33 | 16 |
| Who seek me landward, marking in my mouth | 31 | 22 | 18 | 37 | 4 |
| And the breath-white, curtained mouth of seed.' | 79 | 25 | 46 | 89 | 6 |
| The present mouth, and the sweetly blown trumpet of lies, | 85 | 6 | 50 | 94 | 6 |
| By the curve of the nude mouth or the laugh up the sleeve. | 85 | 12 | 50 | 94 | 12 |
| And mouth. Both note and plume plunge from the spire's hook. | 86 | 8 | 51 | 95 | 8 |
| Shall her smile breed that mouth, behind the mirror, | 90 | 13 | 54 | 99 | 13 |

|  | U.K. Page | U.K. Line | Poem | U.S. Page | U.S. Line |
|---|---|---|---|---|---|
| With carved bird, saint, and sun, the wrack-spiked maiden mouth | 92 | 9 | 55 | 101 | 15 |
| Milk in your mouth, at the sour floods | 96 | 7 | 58 | 106 | 7 |
| The stocked heart is forced, and agony has another mouth to feed. | 96 | 17 | 58 | 106 | 17 |
| On the clay cold mouth, on the fire | 109 | 8 | 67 | 120 | 8 |
| With its kneading mouth | 129 | 6 | 77 | 143 | 6 |
| Lie still, sleep becalmed, hide the mouth in the throat, | 136 | 13 | 81 | 153 | 13 |
| His mouth and rocked him like a storm | 139 | 10 | 82 | 156 | 10 |
| Slides good in the sleek mouth | 171 | 9 | 88 | 191 | 9 |

MOUTHED

| The rivers mouthed in night, | 120 | 21 | 72 | 133 | 6 |

MOUTHING

| Drives my red blood; that dries the mouthing streams | 9 | 7 | 6 | 10 | 7 |
| (But nothing bore, no mouthing babe to the veined hives | 178 | 1 | 90 | 199 | 2 |

MOUTHS

| She wept in her pain and made mouths, | 93 | 19 | 56 | 102 | 19 |
| Parish of snow. The carved mouths in the rock are wind swept strings. | 121 | 9 | 72 | 134 | 4 |
| Into the weathercocks' molten mouths | 131 | 11 | 77 | 145 | 17 |
| Now curlew cry me down to kiss the mouths of their dust. | 178 | 4 | 90 | 199 | 5 |

MOVE

| Manned with their loves they'll move, | x | 12 | 1 | xviii | 18 |
| Move like two ghosts before the eye. | 6 | 18 | 4 | 6 | 18 |
| Our strips of stuff that tatter as we move | 15 | 12 | 10 | 17 | 12 |
| So fast I move defying time, the quiet gentleman | 63 | 14 | 38 | 72 | 14 |
| I have longed to move away | 64 | 1 | 39 | 73 | 1 |
| I have longed to move away | 64 | 6 | 39 | 73 | 6 |
| I have longed to move away but am afraid; | 64 | 11 | 39 | 73 | 11 |
| The one not caring to whom in his sleep he will move | 100 | 4 | 61 | 111 | 4 |
| Before you move to make | 105 | 8 | 64 | 116 | 8 |
| Is cast before you move, | 106 | 9 | 64 | 117 | 9 |
| Look. And the dancers move | 121 | 16 | 72 | 134 | 11 |
| When that immortal hospital made one more move to soothe | 158 | 3 | 84 | 177 | 3 |
| That the closer I move | 173 | 10 | 88 | 193 | 10 |
| I have longed to move away | 64 |  | 39 | 73 |  |

MOVED

| That his tears burned my cheeks and his heart moved in mine. | 103 | 28 | 63 | 115 | 2 |
| Who moved for three years in tune | 124 | 3 | 73 | 138 | 3 |
| Brethren for joy has moved within | 143 | 16 | 82 | 160 | 16 |

|  |  | U.K. |  |  | U.S. |  |
| --- | --- | --- | --- | --- | --- | --- |
|  |  | Page | Line | Poem | Page | Line |
| **MOVES** |  |  |  |  |  |  |
|  | He pulls the chain, the cistern moves. | 10 | 20 | 7 | 11 | 20 |
|  | Gull, on the wave with sand in its eyes! And the foal moves | 165 | 12 | 86 | 185 | 2 |
| **MOVING** |  |  |  |  |  |  |
|  | Of moving about your death | 105 | 14 | 64 | 116 | 14 |
|  | With moving fish and rounded stones | 156 | 10 | 83 | 174 | 18 |
| **MUCH** |  |  |  |  |  |  |
|  | How much was happy while it lasted, | 48 | 20 | 28 | 56 | 20 |
|  | As much as for their good, | 107 | 19 | 65 | 118 | 19 |
| **MUD** |  |  |  |  |  |  |
|  | 'His mother's womb had a tongue that lapped up mud,' | 79 | 20 | 46 | 89 | 1 |
|  | O wake in me in my house in the mud | 96 | 1 | 58 | 106 | 1 |
|  | The old mud hatch again, the horrid | 96 | 19 | 58 | 107 | 2 |
| **MUDDLE** |  |  |  |  |  |  |
|  | Toppling and burning in the muddle of towers and galleries | 77 | 18 | 45 | 86 | 18 |
| **MUFFLED** |  |  |  |  |  |  |
|  | In the muffled house, in the quick of night, | 120 | 4 | 72 | 132 | 9 |
| **MUFFLE-TOED** |  |  |  |  |  |  |
|  | Windshake of sailshaped ears, muffle-toed tap | 87 | 2 | 52 | 96 | 2 |
| **MULE** |  |  |  |  |  |  |
|  | After the funeral, mule praises, brays, | 87 | 1 | 52 | 96 | 1 |
| **MULES** |  |  |  |  |  |  |
|  | The she mules bear their minotaurs, | 110 | 4 | 67 | 121 | 6 |
| **MULTIPLYING** |  |  |  |  |  |  |
|  | And yellow was the multiplying sand, | 20 | 22 | 13 | 24 | 22 |
| **MULTITUDE** |  |  |  |  |  |  |
|  | Waking alone in a multitude of loves when morning's light | 127 | 1 | 75 | 141 | 1 |
| **MULTITUDE'S** |  |  |  |  |  |  |
|  | And the multitude's sultry tear turns cool on the weeping wall, | 158 | 17 | 84 | 177 | 17 |
| **MULTITUDES** |  |  |  |  |  |  |
|  | Cry, Multitudes of arks! Across | x | 10 | 1 | xviii | 16 |
| **MUMMER** |  |  |  |  |  |  |
|  | My world is pyramid. The padded mummer | 31 | 7 | 18 | 36 | 7 |
| **MUMMY** |  |  |  |  |  |  |
|  | The mummy cloths expose an ancient breast. | 63 | 8 | 38 | 72 | 8 |
| **MURDER** |  |  |  |  |  |  |
|  | Murder of Eden and green genesis. | 41 | 8 | 23 | 47 | 8 |
|  | A goose's quill has put an end to murder | 62 | 7 | 37 | 71 | 7 |
|  | I cannot murder, like a fool, | 66 | 6 | 40 | 75 | 6 |
|  | 'Time shall not murder you.' He said, | 70 | 16 | 43 | 79 | 20 |
|  | I saw time murder me. | 70 | 20 | 43 | 79 | 24 |
|  | I shall not murder | 101 | 14 | 62 | 112 | 14 |

| | U.K. | | | U.S. | |
|---|---|---|---|---|---|
| | *Page* | *Line* | *Poem* | *Page* | *Line* |
| MURDER'S | | | | | |
| And, for that murder's sake, dark with contagion | 79 | 11 | 46 | 88 | 14 |
| MURDERED | | | | | |
| That the eyes are already murdered, | 96 | 16 | 58 | 106 | 16 |
| Locking, unlocking, the murdered strangers weave, | 117 | 15 | 71 | 129 | 15 |
| MURDERING | | | | | |
| We hid our fears in that murdering breath, | 125 | 14 | 74 | 139 | 14 |
| MURMUR | | | | | |
| Murmur of spring nor crush the cockerel's eggs, | 60 | 7 | 36 | 69 | 7 |
| MUSCLE | | | | | |
| Here love's damp muscle dries and dies, | 2 | 22 | 2 | 3 | 4 |
| As motor muscle on the drill, driving | 28 | 3 | 17 | 33 | 3 |
| In the shipwreck of muscle; | 38 | 10 | 20 | 43 | 20 |
| MUSCLED | | | | | |
| Was muscled, matted, wise to the crying thigh | 21 | 4 | 13 | 25 | 4 |
| MUSCLING | | | | | |
| A muscling life from lovers in their cramp, | 2 | 9 | 2 | 2 | 9 |
| MUSCLING-IN | | | | | |
| I would not fear the muscling-in of love | 12 | 17 | 9 | 13 | 17 |
| MUSHROOM | | | | | |
| Love's reflection of the mushroom features, | 73 | 7 | 44 | 82 | 7 |
| MUSHROOMS | | | | | |
| Under the milky mushrooms slew my hunger, | 73 | 18 | 44 | 82 | 18 |
| MUSIC | | | | | |
| And pluck a mandrake music from the marrow-root. | 60 | 18 | 36 | 69 | 18 |
| Time's tune my ladies with the teats of music, | 74 | 21 | 44 | 83 | 21 |
| The heavenly music over the sand | 82 | 14 | 48 | 91 | 14 |
| Time for the swimmers' hands, music for silver lock | 86 | 7 | 51 | 95 | 7 |
| Illumination of music! the lulled black-backed | 165 | 11 | 86 | 185 | 1 |
| Music of elements, that a miracle makes! | 165 | 15 | 86 | 185 | 5 |
| Makes all the music; and I who hear the tune of the slow, | 169 | 9 | 87 | 189 | 18 |
| MUSICAL | | | | | |
| The vanishing of the musical ship-work and the chucked bells, | 95 | 8 | 58 | 105 | 8 |
| MUSSEL | | | | | |
| And the mussel pooled and the heron | 102 | 3 | 63 | 113 | 3 |
| MUST | | | | | |
| But seasons must be challenged or they totter | 2 | 1 | 2 | 2 | 1 |
| There must, be praised, some certainty, | 48 | 7 | 28 | 56 | 7 |
| The gentle seaslides of saying I must undo | 89 | 5 | 53 | 98 | 5 |
| Has a voice and a house, and there and here you must couch and cry. | 98 | 2 | 59 | 109 | 5 |

MUST (continued)

|  | U.K. | | | U.S. | |
|---|---|---|---|---|---|
|  | Page | Line | Poem | Page | Line |
| And I must enter again the round | 101 | 7 | 62 | 112 | 7 |
| Lucklessly she must lie patient | 110 | 25 | 67 | 122 | 3 |
| And always known must leave | 117 | 4 | 71 | 129 | 4 |
| Must lie | 138 | 2 | 82 | 155 | 2 |
| So it must have been after the birth of the simple light | 160 | 11 | 85 | 179 | 11 |
| The voyage to ruin I must run, | 172 | 24 | 88 | 192 | 24 |
| MUSTARDSEED | | | | | |
| In the mustardseed sun, | 170 | 1 | 88 | 190 | 1 |
| MUTE | | | | | |
| And sleep rolls mute above the beds | 5 | 4 | 3 | 5 | 4 |
| Ding dong from the mute turrets. | 83 | 24 | 49 | 93 | 6 |
| MUTED | | | | | |
| In the muted house, one minute before | | | 91 | 200 | 14 |
| MUTTER | | | | | |
| Mutter and foul wingbeat of the solemnizing nightpriest | 114 | 22 | 69 | 126 | 22 |
| MUTTON | | | | | |
| Alone alive among his mutton fold, | 72 | 16 | 44 | 81 | 16 |
| MUZZLED | | | | | |
| In the stitched wound and clotted wind, muzzled | 28 | 15 | 17 | 33 | 15 |
| MYSELF | | | | | |
| Myself to set foot | 102 | 8 | 63 | 113 | 8 |
| Now in the dark there is only yourself and myself. | 125 | 24 | 74 | 139 | 24 |
| MYSELVES | | | | | |
| Myselves | 129 | 1 | 77 | 143 | 1 |
| Myselves grieve now, and miracles cannot atone. | 129 | 16 | 77 | 143 | 16 |
| Us your death that myselves the believers | 129 | 19 | 77 | 143 | 19 |
| MYSTERIES | | | | | |
| And count the taken, forsaken mysteries in a bad dark. | 94 | 9 | 57 | 104 | 9 |
| MYSTERY | | | | | |
| His reels and mystery | 70 | 3 | 43 | 79 | 7 |
| And the mystery | 104 | 6 | 63 | 115 | 8 |
| MYSTIC | | | | | |
| So solve the mystic sun, the wife of light, | 51 | 26 | 31 | 61 | 5 |
| We make me mystic as the arm of air, | 52 | 6 | 31 | 61 | 13 |
| MYTHS | | | | | |
| Nor falls to His green myths? | 69 | 18 | 43 | 78 | 18 |
| MYTH | | | | | |
| Hell in a horn of sulphur and the cloven myth, | 40 | 16 | 22 | 46 | 16 |

# ENTRIES UNDER N

| | U.K. | | | U.S. | |
|---|---|---|---|---|---|
| | Page | Line | Poem | Page | Line |
| **NACREOUS** | | | | | |
| Or a nacreous sleep among soft particles and charms | 97 | 17 | 59 | 108 | 17 |
| **NAGGING** | | | | | |
| (My shape of age nagging the wounded whisper). | 72 | 22 | 44 | 81 | 22 |
| **NAIL** | | | | | |
| And nail the merry squires to the trees; | 2 | 21 | 2 | 3 | 3 |
| I sit and watch the worm beneath my nail | 13 | 6 | 9 | 14 | 13 |
| **NAILED** | | | | | |
| Nailed with an open eye, in the bowl of wounds and weed | 92 | 1 | 55 | 101 | 7 |
| **NAILS** | | | | | |
| Though they be mad and dead as nails, | 68 | 24 | 42 | 77 | 24 |
| Drove in the heaven-driven of the nails | 75 | 12 | 44 | 84 | 12 |
| **NAKED** | | | | | |
| Tread, like a naked Venus, | 10 | 12 | 7 | 11 | 12 |
| Up naked stairs, a turtle in a hearse, | 18 | 4 | 12 | 21 | 4 |
| I fled the earth and, naked, climbed the weather, | 26 | 6 | 16 | 31 | 6 |
| Rerobing of the naked ghost. Manhood | 28 | 23 | 17 | 34 | 3 |
| How now my flesh, my naked fellow, | 33 | 7 | 19 | 38 | 7 |
| Out of the naked entrail. | 35 | 12 | 20 | 40 | 12 |
| Down pelts the naked weather; | 45 | 3 | 26 | 53 | 3 |
| And the naked egg stand straight, | 56 | 7 | 34 | 65 | 7 |
| Naked among the bow-and-arrow birds | 60 | 23 | 36 | 69 | 23 |
| Dead men naked they shall be one | 68 | 2 | 42 | 77 | 2 |
| The scaled sea-sawers, fix in a naked sponge | 74 | 22 | 44 | 83 | 22 |
| Open as to the air to the naked shadow | 115 | 17 | 69 | 127 | 17 |
| His naked need struck him howling and bowed | 120 | 14 | 72 | 132 | 19 |
| Alone and naked in the engulfing bride, | 120 | 28 | 72 | 133 | 13 |
| Mast-high moon-white women naked | 153 | 8 | 83 | 171 | 4 |
| Naked and forsaken to grieve he will not come. | 166 | 7 | 86 | 186 | 7 |
| **NAME** | | | | | |
| Who knew not sun and moon by name, | 7 | 8 | 5 | 8 | 8 |
| That but a name, where maggots have their X. | 21 | 14 | 13 | 25 | 14 |

|  | U.K. | | | U.S. | |
|---|---|---|---|---|---|
|  | *Page* | *Line* | *Poem* | *Page* | *Line* |
| Man by a scribbled name. | 62 | 12 | 37 | 71 | 12 |
| Birds and the birds of the winged trees flying my name | 102 | 12 | 63 | 113 | 12 |
| Burns me his name and his flame | 138 | 11 | 82 | 155 | 11 |
| In the name of the lost who glory in | 143 | 1 | 82 | 160 | 1 |
| In the name of the wanton | 144 | 15 | 82 | 161 | 15 |
| In the name of the fatherless | 147 | 2 | 82 | 164 | 2 |
| In the name of the unborn | 147 | 3 | 82 | 164 | 3 |
| O in the name | 147 | 7 | 82 | 164 | 7 |
| Sun. In the name of the damned | 148 | 3 | 82 | 165 | 3 |
| NAMELESS | | | | | |
| And his nameless need bound him burning and lost | 120 | 19 | 72 | 133 | 4 |
| NAMES | | | | | |
| The covering sea their nightfall with no names; | 115 | 4 | 69 | 127 | 4 |
| Though the names on their weed grown stones are rained away, | 176 | 8 | 90 | 197 | 8 |
| NANSEN'S | | | | | |
| Cold Nansen's beak on a boat full of gongs, | 133 | 12 | 78 | 148 | 15 |
| NARROW | | | | | |
| She sleeps in the narrow trough yet she walks the dust | 108 | 13 | 66 | 119 | 13 |
| A cold kind man brave in his narrow pride | | | 91 | 200 | 3 |
| NATION | | | | | |
| Joy is no knocking nation, sir and madam, | 19 | 6 | 12 | 22 | 11 |
| Love's twilit nation and the skull of state, | 19 | 14 | 12 | 22 | 19 |
| NATIVE | | | | | |
| This I know from the native | 110 | 22 | 67 | 121 | 24 |
| NATRON | | | | | |
| Buckle to lint and cloth their natron footsteps, | 75 | 22 | 44 | 84 | 22 |
| NATURAL | | | | | |
| This is the fortune of manhood: the natural peril, | 35 | 19 | 20 | 40 | 19 |
| No death more natural; | 35 | 21 | 20 | 40 | 21 |
| The natural parallel. | 35 | 24 | 20 | 40 | 24 |
| The natural circle of the discovered skies | 91 | 10 | 55 | 100 | 10 |
| In the groin of the natural doorway I crouched like a tailor | 99 | 3 | 60 | 110 | 3 |
| NAVE | | | | | |
| 'My fathers' globe knocks on its nave and sings.' | 26 | 11 | 16 | 31 | 11 |
| NAVEL | | | | | |
| Your corkscrew grave centred in navel and nipple, | 36 | 27 | 20 | 42 | 6 |
| NAVIGATES | | | | | |
| Sleep navigates the tides of time; | 5 | 1 | 3 | 5 | 1 |
| NAVIGATING | | | | | |
| Glared through shark mask and navigating head, | 133 | 11 | 78 | 148 | 14 |

|  | U.K. | | | U.S. | |
|  | Page | Line | Poem | Page | Line |
|---|---|---|---|---|---|
| **NAVY** | | | | | |
| And the shipyards of Galilee's footprints hide a navy of doves. | 127 | 7 | 75 | 141 | 7 |
| **NAY** | | | | | |
| Say nay, | 51 | 2 | 31 | 60 | 2 |
| Say nay, | 51 | 9 | 31 | 60 | 9 |
| Say nay, | 51 | 16 | 31 | 60 | 16 |
| Say nay, | 51 | 23 | 31 | 61 | 2 |
| Say nay | 52 | 2 | 31 | 61 | 9 |
| **NEAR** | | | | | |
| That shaped the Jordan near my home | 7 | 4 | 5 | 8 | 4 |
| The night is near, | 55 | 6 | 33 | 64 | 9 |
| Grave men, near death, who see with blinding sight | 116 | 13 | 70 | 128 | 13 |
| Of several near deaths, | 117 | 2 | 71 | 129 | 2 |
| When near and strange wounded on London's waves | 117 | 27 | 71 | 130 | 3 |
| And over the cloth of counties the far hills rode near, | 122 | 13 | 72 | 135 | 13 |
| Greed on man beating near and fire neighbour | 126 | 6 | 74 | 140 | 6 |
| Never and never, my girl riding far and near | 162 | 1 | 86 | 181 | 1 |
| Shall harrow and snow the blood while you ride wide and near, | 162 | 23 | 86 | 181 | 23 |
| I young Aesop fabling to the near night by the dingle | 168 | 11 | 87 | 188 | 15 |
| **NEARLY** | | | | | |
| Geese nearly in heaven, boys | vii | 15 | I | xv | 15 |
| In the hooting, nearly dark | ix | 8 | I | xvii | 8 |
| **NECK** | | | | | |
| The neck of the nostril, | 37 | 1 | 20 | 42 | 7 |
| And rivers of the dead around my neck. | 76 | 8 | 44 | 85 | 8 |
| **NEED** | | | | | |
| Need no word's warmth. | 21 | 12 | 13 | 25 | 12 |
| And need no druid of her broken body). | 87 | 20 | 52 | 96 | 20 |
| His naked need struck him howling and bowed | 120 | 14 | 72 | 132 | 19 |
| And his nameless need bound him burning and lost | 120 | 19 | 72 | 133 | 4 |
| And drown in the drifts of his need, and lie curled caught | 120 | 22 | 72 | 133 | 7 |
| By losing him all in love, and cast his need | 120 | 27 | 72 | 133 | 12 |
| The cloud, the need, the planted stars, the joy beyond | 122 | 22 | 72 | 136 | 2 |
| **NEEDLE** | | | | | |
| My camel's eyes will needle through the shroud. | 73 | 6 | 44 | 82 | 6 |
| The flashing needle rock of squatters, | 132 | 26 | 78 | 148 | 1 |

| | U.K. Page | Line | Poem | U.S. Page | Line |
|---|---|---|---|---|---|
| **NEEDLES** | | | | | |
| She threads off the sap and needles, blood and bubble | 35 | 10 | 20 | 40 | 10 |
| **NEIGHBOR** | | | | | |
| Your polestar neighbor, sun of another street, | 117 | 17 | 71 | 129 | 17 |
| **NEIGHBOUR** | | | | | |
| Woke to my hearing from harbour and neighbour wood | 102 | 2 | 63 | 113 | 2 |
| Greed on man beating near and fire neighbour | 126 | 6 | 74 | 140 | 6 |
| **NEIGHBOURS** | | | | | |
| O kingdom of neighbours, finned | ix | 31 | 1 | xviii | 5 |
| **NEITHER** | | | | | |
| I, born of flesh and ghost, was neither | 8 | 13 | 5 | 9 | 13 |
| Neither by night's ancient fear, | 64 | 15 | 39 | 73 | 15 |
| But wishes breed not, neither | 82 | 21 | 48 | 91 | 21 |
| **NEOPHYTE** | | | | | |
| Then was my neophyte, | 69 | 1 | 43 | 78 | 1 |
| Then was my neophyte | 69 | | 43 | 78 | |
| **NEPTUNE** | | | | | |
| My ghost in his metal neptune | 38 | 27 | 20 | 44 | 17 |
| **NERVE** | | | | | |
| That, sewn to me by nerve and brain, | 4 | 11 | 3 | 4 | 11 |
| Rehearsing heat upon a raw-edged nerve. | 12 | 19 | 9 | 13 | 19 |
| And what's the rub? Death's feather on the nerve? | 13 | 15 | 9 | 15 | 1 |
| Through vision and the girdered nerve. | 28 | 4 | 17 | 33 | 4 |
| Time's nerve in vinegar, the gallow grave | 75 | 6 | 44 | 84 | 6 |
| **NERVES** | | | | | |
| Of doubt and dark they feed their nerves; | 1 | 11 | 2 | 1 | 11 |
| My hero bares his nerves along my wrist | 10 | 1 | 7 | 11 | 1 |
| And these poor nerves so wired to the skull | 10 | 6 | 7 | 11 | 6 |
| He holds the wire from this box of nerves | 10 | 16 | 7 | 11 | 16 |
| All nerves to serve the sun, | 56 | 15 | 34 | 65 | 15 |
| Camped in the drug-white shower of nerves and food, | 77 | 8 | 45 | 86 | 8 |
| The cloud perched tailors' master with nerves for cotton. | 133 | 7 | 78 | 148 | 10 |
| My hero bares his nerves | 10 | | 7 | 11 | |
| **NEST** | | | | | |
| Who moons her blue notes from her nest | ix | 11 | 1 | xvii | 11 |
| My nest of mercies in the rude, red tree. | 76 | 22 | 44 | 85 | 22 |
| From the stone nest it does not let the feathery | 86 | 2 | 51 | 95 | 2 |
| **NESTED** | | | | | |
| Within the nested treefork | 115 | 12 | 69 | 127 | 12 |
| But wailed and nested in the sky-blue wall | 126 | 7 | 74 | 140 | 7 |
| **NETS** | | | | | |
| To the sunset nets, | vii | 14 | 1 | xv | 14 |

| | U.K. | | | U.S. | |
|---|---|---|---|---|---|
| | Page | Line | Poem | Page | Line |
| Is crying from nets to knives, | 151 | 18 | 83 | 169 | 6 |
| **NETTLE** | | | | | |
| Lop, love, my fork tongue, said the pin-hilled nettle; | 74 | 6 | 44 | 83 | 6 |
| **NETTLE'S** | | | | | |
| She makes for me a nettle's innocence | 78 | 16 | 46 | 87 | 16 |
| **NETTLES** | | | | | |
| I with the wooden insect in the tree of nettles, | 36 | 4 | 20 | 41 | 4 |
| Are but the roots of nettles and of feathers | 72 | 2 | 44 | 81 | 2 |
| **NET** | | | | | |
| And the knock of sailing boats on the net webbed wall | 102 | 7 | 63 | 113 | 7 |
| **NEURAL** | | | | | |
| Tells me the hour's word, the neural meaning | 16 | 18 | 11 | 19 | 18 |
| **NEVER** | | | | | |
| Of tides that never touch the shores. | 8 | 10 | 5 | 9 | 10 |
| Can never raise the midnight of a chuckle, | 13 | 11 | 9 | 14 | 18 |
| What's never known is safest in this life. | 50 | 6 | 30 | 59 | 6 |
| Never shall beast be born to atlas the few seas | 92 | 4 | 55 | 101 | 10 |
| Never until the mankind making | 101 | 1 | 62 | 112 | 1 |
| I never thought to utter or think | 107 | 16 | 65 | 118 | 16 |
| Never shall my self chant | 109 | 25 | 67 | 120 | 25 |
| Never to flourish in the fields of the white seed | 120 | 29 | 72 | 133 | 14 |
| Brave deaths of only ones but never found, | 126 | 11 | 74 | 140 | 11 |
| Of Adam and Eve is never for a second | 130 | 24 | 77 | 145 | 2 |
| Never never oh never to regret the bugle I wore | 133 | 19 | 78 | 149 | 2 |
| Never to awake and arise | 146 | 16 | 82 | 163 | 16 |
| For my sake sail, and never look back, | 149 | 11 | 83 | 166 | 11 |
| Never and never, my girl riding far and near | 162 | 1 | 86 | 181 | 1 |
| Never, my girl, until tolled to sleep by the stern | 162 | 21 | 86 | 181 | 21 |
| We grieve as the blithe birds, never again, leave shingle and elm, | 168 | 9 | 87 | 188 | 13 |
| Heaven that never was | 171 | 23 | 88 | 191 | 23 |
| Young among the long flocks, and never lie lost | | | 91 | 200 | 7 |
| Will never go out of my mind: | | | 91 | 200 | 20 |
| Even as a baby he had never cried; | | | 91 | 201 | 5 |
| **NEWS** | | | | | |
| The atlas-eater with a jaw for news, | 71 | 5 | 44 | 80 | 5 |
| Break the black news and paint on a sail | 151 | 23 | 83 | 169 | 11 |
| **NEWSPAPER** | | | | | |
| Eating bread from a newspaper | 111 | 7 | 68 | 123 | 7 |
| **NEW** | | | | | |
| Of new man strength, I seek the sun. | 29 | 4 | 17 | 34 | 8 |
| Until the turbulent new born | 138 | 10 | 82 | 155 | 10 |
| Under the new made clouds and happy as the heart was long, | 160 | 16 | 85 | 179 | 16 |
| Dipping moon and drunk as a new dropped calf, | 174 | 17 | 89 | 194 | 17 |

# NEWBORN

|  | U.K. | | | U.S. | |
|---|---|---|---|---|---|
|  | *Page* | *Line* | *Poem* | *Page* | *Line* |
| **NEWBORN** | | | | | |
| Sleep to a newborn sleep in a swaddling loin-leaf stroked and sang | 113 | 22 | 69 | 125 | 22 |
| And the old men sing from newborn lips: | 155 | 8 | 83 | 173 | 12 |
| **NEXT** | | | | | |
| In the next room | 137 | 4 | 82 | 154 | 4 |
| **NEXT-DOOR** | | | | | |
| The next-door sea dispelled | 134 | 6 | 79 | 150 | 6 |
| **NIBBLES** | | | | | |
| They suffer the undead water where the turtle nibbles, | 37 | 22 | 20 | 43 | 5 |
| **NICK** | | | | | |
| She nipped and dived in the nick of love, | 151 | 7 | 83 | 168 | 15 |
| **NICKED** | | | | | |
| The sea and instrument, nicked in the locks of time, | 38 | 14 | 20 | 44 | 4 |
| **NIGHT** | | | | | |
| Day's night whose towers will catch | vii | 20 | I | xv | 20 |
| Into the dogdayed night. | viii | 7 | I | xvi | 7 |
| Divide the night and day with fairy thumbs; | I | 15 | 2 | I | 15 |
| There, in his night, the black-tongued bells | 2 | 4 | 2 | 2 | 4 |
| Turns night to day; blood in their suns | 6 | 5 | 4 | 6 | 5 |
| Ungotten I knew night and day. | 7 | 18 | 5 | 8 | 18 |
| Groom the dark brides, the widows of the night | 14 | 5 | 10 | 16 | 5 |
| The code of night tapped on my tongue; | 21 | 16 | 13 | 25 | 16 |
| Night in the sockets rounds, | 24 | 19 | 15 | 29 | 19 |
| Of suns in the man-melting night. | 28 | 8 | 17 | 33 | 8 |
| Man in the day or wind at night | 39 | 4 | 21 | 45 | 4 |
| The wet night scolds me like a nurse? | 44 | 10 | 25 | 52 | 10 |
| The night is near, | 55 | 6 | 33 | 64 | 9 |
| Master the night nor serve the snowman's brain | 60 | 4 | 36 | 69 | 4 |
| Autocracy of night and day, | 65 | 12 | 40 | 74 | 12 |
| Black night still ministers the moon, | 66 | 9 | 40 | 75 | 9 |
| Calls a green day and night. | 69 | 6 | 43 | 78 | 6 |
| That night of time under the Christward shelter: | 71 | 12 | 44 | 80 | 12 |
| Stills snapped by night in the bread-sided field, | 73 | 8 | 44 | 82 | 8 |
| Rose my Byzantine Adam in the night. | 73 | 16 | 44 | 82 | 16 |
| Where at night we stoned the cold and cuckoo | 89 | 8 | 53 | 98 | 8 |
| Bolting the night of the door with her arm her plume. | 108 | 4 | 66 | 119 | 4 |
| Slept at night in a dog kennel | 111 | 11 | 68 | 123 | 11 |
| That she might stand in the night | 112 | 11 | 68 | 124 | 11 |
| All night in the unmade park | 112 | 13 | 68 | 124 | 13 |
| Last night in a raping wave | 113 | 7 | 69 | 125 | 7 |
| Night, and enjoyed as he would. | 114 | 13 | 69 | 126 | 13 |
| A man torn up mourns in the sole night. | 115 | 21 | 69 | 127 | 21 |

| | U.K. | | | U.S. | |
|---|---|---|---|---|---|
| | Page | Line | Poem | Page | Line |
| Do not go gentle into that good night, | 116 | 1 | 70 | 128 | 1 |
| Do not go gentle into that good night. | 116 | 6 | 70 | 128 | 6 |
| Do not go gentle into that good night. | 116 | 12 | 70 | 128 | 12 |
| Do not go gentle into that good night. | 116 | 18 | 70 | 128 | 18 |
| In the muffled house, in the quick of night, | 120 | 4 | 72 | 132 | 9 |
| The rivers mouthed in night, | 120 | 21 | 72 | 133 | 6 |
| All night lost and long wading in the wake of the she- | 122 | 18 | 72 | 135 | 18 |
| Exercised in the still night | 128 | 2 | 76 | 142 | 2 |
| Night fall and the fruit like a sun, | 131 | 4 | 77 | 145 | 10 |
| In the throat, burning and turning. All night afloat | 136 | 2 | 81 | 153 | 2 |
| Under the night forever falling. | 145 | 17 | 82 | 162 | 17 |
| Forever falling night is a known | 146 | 1 | 82 | 163 | 1 |
| To glow after the god stoning night | 158 | 11 | 84 | 177 | 11 |
| The night above the dingle starry, | 159 | 3 | 85 | 178 | 3 |
| My girl ranging the night in the rose and shire | 162 | 9 | 86 | 181 | 9 |
| This night and each vast night until the stern bell talks | 164 | 2 | 86 | 183 | 9 |
| This night and each night since the falling star you were born, | 164 | 6 | 86 | 183 | 13 |
| Night and the reindeer on the clouds above the haycocks | 164 | 15 | 86 | 184 | 1 |
| Burning! Night and the vein of birds in the winged, sloe wrist | 164 | 21 | 86 | 184 | 7 |
| Leaping! The gospel rooks! All tell, this night, of him | 165 | 9 | 86 | 184 | 17 |
| Might cross its planets, the bell weep, night gather her eyes, | 165 | 21 | 86 | 185 | 11 |
| But her faith that each vast night and the saga of prayer | 166 | 3 | 86 | 186 | 3 |
| Her faith that this last night for his unsacred sake | 166 | 5 | 86 | 186 | 5 |
| My dear this night he comes and night without end my dear | 166 | 9 | 86 | 186 | 9 |
| I young Aesop fabling to the near night by the dingle | 168 | 11 | 87 | 188 | 15 |
| Before the lunge of the night, the notes on this time-shaken | 169 | 11 | 87 | 189 | 20 |
| He, on the earth of the night, alone | 172 | 11 | 88 | 192 | 11 |
| I whistled all night in the twisted flues, | 174 | 18 | 89 | 194 | 18 |
| Black night, I left my quivering prints. | 174 | 24 | 89 | 194 | 24 |
| And there this night I walk in the white giant's thigh | 176 | 3 | 90 | 197 | 3 |
| All birds and beasts of the linked night uproar and chime | 177 | 15 | 90 | 198 | 14 |
| Noon, and night, and light. The rivers of the dead | | | 91 | 200 | 15 |

331

|  | U.K. | | | U.S. | |
|  | Page | Line | Poem | Page | Line |
| Do not go gentle into that good night | 116 |  | 70 | 128 |  |
| NIGHT'S |  |  |  |  |  |
| Neither by night's ancient fear, | 64 | 15 | 39 | 73 | 15 |
| And alone in the night's eternal, curving act | 176 | 9 | 90 | 197 | 9 |
| NIGHTBIRD |  |  |  |  |  |
| The nightbird lauds through nunneries and domes of leaves | 163 | 5 | 86 | 182 | 5 |
| NIGHTBREAK |  |  |  |  |  |
| At nightbreak born in the fat side, from an animal bed | 84 | 2 | 49 | 93 | 8 |
| NIGHTFALL |  |  |  |  |  |
| The covering sea their nightfall with no names; | 115 | 4 | 69 | 127 | 4 |
| NIGHTINGALE |  |  |  |  |  |
| In the departed villages. The nightingale, | 121 | 2 | 72 | 133 | 17 |
| Of nightingale and centaur dead horse. The springs wither | 123 | 7 | 72 | 136 | 17 |
| Nightingale and hyena | 152 | 15 | 83 | 170 | 7 |
| NIGHTINGALE'S |  |  |  |  |  |
| Of the nightingale's din and tale! The upgiven ghost | 165 | 3 | 86 | 184 | 11 |
| NIGHTINGALES |  |  |  |  |  |
| With their nightingales and psalms | 128 | 16 | 76 | 142 | 16 |
| NIGHT-GEARED |  |  |  |  |  |
| Or drive the night-geared forth. | 15 | 6 | 10 | 17 | 6 |
| In bottom gear through night-geared man. | 28 | 12 | 17 | 33 | 12 |
| NIGHT-JARS |  |  |  |  |  |
| All the moon long I heard, blessed among stables, the night-jars | 160 | 3 | 85 | 179 | 3 |
| NIGHT-TIME |  |  |  |  |  |
| Why night-time rain and the breast's blood | 53 | 8 | 32 | 62 | 8 |
| NIGHTLONG |  |  |  |  |  |
| Surprised in the opening of her nightlong eyes | 127 | 2 | 75 | 141 | 2 |
| The star rise at pasture and nightlong the fables graze | 163 | 11 | 86 | 182 | 11 |
| NIGHTLY |  |  |  |  |  |
| And nightly under the simple stars | 160 | 1 | 85 | 179 | 1 |
| NIGHTMARE |  |  |  |  |  |
| Death: death of Hamlet and the nightmare madmen, | 41 | 19 | 23 | 48 | 1 |
| NIGHTMARISH |  |  |  |  |  |
| Yet she deludes with walking the nightmarish room, | 108 | 7 | 66 | 119 | 7 |
| NIGHTPRIEST |  |  |  |  |  |
| Mutter and foul wingbeat of the solemnizing nightpriest | 114 | 22 | 69 | 126 | 22 |
| NIGHTS |  |  |  |  |  |
| Impose their shots, throwing the nights away; | 14 | 18 | 10 | 16 | 18 |

|  | U.K. | | | U.S. | |
|  | Page | Line | Poem | Page | Line |
| And on seesaw sunday nights I wooed | 174 | 8 | 89 | 194 | 8 |
| And caught between two nights, blindness and death | | | 91 | 201 | 15 |
| **NILE** | | | | | |
| Tail, Nile, and snout, a saddler of the rushes, | 38 | 20 | 20 | 44 | 10 |
| **NILLY** | | | | | |
| The Thief fall on the dead like the willy nilly dew, | 165 | 22 | 86 | 185 | 12 |
| **NIMBLE** | | | | | |
| In the squirrel nimble grove, under linen and thatch | 163 | 21 | 86 | 183 | 2 |
| **NIMBUS** | | | | | |
| To his nimbus bell cool kingdom come | 173 | 4 | 88 | 193 | 4 |
| **NINE** | | | | | |
| From the cities of nine | vii | 19 | 1 | xv | 19 |
| A limp and riderless shape to leap nine thinning months.' | 97 | 15 | 59 | 108 | 15 |
| **NINEPIN** | | | | | |
| Ninepin down on the donkeys' common, | 174 | 7 | 89 | 194 | 7 |
| **NINNIES'** | | | | | |
| Of mortal voices to the ninnies' choir, | 60 | 16 | 36 | 69 | 16 |
| **NIPPED** | | | | | |
| She nipped and dived in the nick of love, | 151 | 7 | 83 | 168 | 15 |
| **NIPPLE** | | | | | |
| Your corkscrew grave centred in navel and nipple, | 36 | 27 | 20 | 42 | 6 |
| **NIPPLED** | | | | | |
| And though my love pulls the pale, nippled air, | 80 | 13 | 46 | 89 | 21 |
| **NIPPLES** | | | | | |
| Till the three-coloured rainbow from my nipples | 75 | 13 | 44 | 84 | 13 |
| **NITRIC** | | | | | |
| Halt among eunuchs, and the nitric stain | 18 | 24 | 12 | 22 | 4 |
| A nitric shape that leaps her, time and acid; | 55 | 7 | 33 | 64 | 10 |
| **NO** | | | | | |
| Setting no store by harvest, freeze the soils; | 1 | 3 | 2 | 1 | 3 |
| Here break a kiss in no love's quarry. | 2 | 23 | 2 | 3 | 5 |
| When once the twilight locks no longer | 4 | 1 | 3 | 4 | 1 |
| No, no, you lover skull, descending hammer | 19 | 2 | 12 | 22 | 7 |
| Joy is no knocking nation, sir and madam, | 19 | 6 | 12 | 22 | 11 |
| When no mouth stirred about the hanging famine, | 20 | 5 | 13 | 24 | 5 |
| Need no word's warmth. | 21 | 12 | 13 | 25 | 12 |
| Light breaks where no sun shines; | 24 | 1 | 15 | 29 | 1 |
| Where no sea runs, the waters of the heart | 24 | 2 | 15 | 29 | 2 |
| File through the flesh where no flesh decks the bones. | 24 | 6 | 15 | 29 | 6 |
| Where no seed stirs. | 24 | 9 | 15 | 29 | 9 |

333

|  | U.K. |  |  | U.S. |  |
|---|---|---|---|---|---|
|  | Page | Line | Poem | Page | Line |
| Where no wax is, the candle shows its hairs. | 24 | 12 | 15 | 29 | 12 |
| Where no cold is, the skinning gales unpin | 24 | 22 | 15 | 29 | 22 |
| No death more natural; | 35 | 21 | 20 | 40 | 21 |
| No tread more perilous, the green steps and spire | 36 | 2 | 20 | 41 | 2 |
| No man more magical, clawed out the crocodile. | 38 | 18 | 20 | 44 | 8 |
| In sacred waters that no frost could harden, | 40 | 14 | 22 | 46 | 14 |
| No tell-tale lover has an end more certain, | 41 | 24 | 23 | 48 | 6 |
| No god-in-hero tumble down | 42 | 4 | 24 | 49 | 4 |
| No god-in-hero tumble down | 42 | 11 | 24 | 49 | 11 |
| Through no regret of leaving woman waiting | 48 | 14 | 28 | 56 | 14 |
| Under the skysigns they who have no arms | 50 | 7 | 30 | 59 | 7 |
| Sir no say, | 51 | 10 | 31 | 60 | 10 |
| No say sir | 51 | 17 | 31 | 60 | 17 |
| And west's no longer drowned | 53 | 3 | 32 | 62 | 3 |
| And 'Know no answer,' and I know | 53 | 23 | 32 | 62 | 23 |
| No answer to the children's cry | 53 | 24 | 32 | 62 | 24 |
| No birds or flying fish | 58 | 15 | 35 | 67 | 15 |
| And welcome no sailor? | 58 | 24 | 35 | 67 | 24 |
| Hands have no tears to flow. | 62 | 16 | 37 | 71 | 16 |
| Disturb no winding-sheets, my son, | 65 | 6 | 40 | 74 | 6 |
| And the maggot no man can slay.' | 65 | 16 | 40 | 74 | 16 |
| 'The maggot that no man can kill | 66 | 1 | 40 | 75 | 1 |
| And the man no rope can hang | 66 | 2 | 40 | 75 | 2 |
| Light and dark are no enemies | 66 | 12 | 40 | 75 | 12 |
| No silver whistles chase him down the weeks' | 67 | 21 | 41 | 76 | 21 |
| No third eye probe into a rainbow's sex | 67 | 25 | 41 | 76 | 25 |
| And death shall have no dominion. | 68 | 1 | 42 | 77 | 1 |
| And death shall have no dominion. | 68 | 9 | 42 | 77 | 9 |
| And death shall have no dominion. | 68 | 10 | 42 | 77 | 10 |
| And death shall have no dominion. | 68 | 18 | 42 | 77 | 18 |
| And death shall have no dominion. | 68 | 19 | 42 | 77 | 19 |
| No more may gulls cry at their ears | 68 | 20 | 42 | 77 | 20 |
| Where blew a flower may a flower no more | 68 | 22 | 42 | 77 | 22 |
| And death shall have no dominion. | 68 | 27 | 42 | 77 | 27 |
| Walks with no wound, nor lightning in her face, | 80 | 10 | 46 | 89 | 18 |
| And need no druid of her broken body). | 87 | 20 | 52 | 96 | 20 |
| On no work of words now for three lean months in the bloody | 94 | 1 | 57 | 104 | 1 |
| 'No. Not for Christ's dazzling bed | 97 | 16 | 59 | 108 | 16 |
| At the breast stored with seas. No return | 98 | 4 | 59 | 109 | 7 |
| To-night shall find no dying but alive and warm | 100 | 15 | 61 | 111 | 15 |
| After the first death, there is no other. | 101 | 24 | 62 | 112 | 24 |
| Teaches with no telling | 110 | 16 | 67 | 121 | 18 |
| All blood-signed assailings and vanished marriages in which he had no lovely part | 114 | 20 | 69 | 126 | 20 |
| The covering sea their nightfall with no names; | 115 | 4 | 69 | 127 | 4 |

|  | U.K. | | Poem | U.S. | |
|---|---|---|---|---|---|
|  | Page | Line |  | Page | Line |
| Because their words have forked no lightning they | 116 | 5 | 70 | 128 | 5 |
| Though no sound flowed down the hand folded air | 120 | 15 | 72 | 132 | 20 |
| On the white, no longer growing green, and, minstrel dead, | 123 | 2 | 72 | 136 | 12 |
| No longer will the vibrations of the sun desire on | 127 | 8 | 75 | 141 | 8 |
| Who pay no praise or wages | 128 | 19 | 76 | 142 | 19 |
| No prophet-progeny of mine, | 134 | 26 | 79 | 151 | 4 |
| No Time, spoke the clocks, no God, rang the bells, | 134 | 28 | 79 | 151 | 6 |
| Dig no more for the chains of his grey-haired heart. | 135 | 9 | 80 | 152 | 9 |
| Bows no baptism | 137 | 13 | 82 | 154 | 13 |
| No heart bone | 145 | 11 | 82 | 162 | 11 |
| Of no one | 147 | 8 | 82 | 164 | 8 |
| No | 147 | 10 | 82 | 164 | 10 |
| With no more desire than a ghost. | 154 | 4 | 83 | 172 | 4 |
| No | 158 | 13 | 84 | 177 | 13 |
| I climb to greet the war in which I have no heart but only | 158 | 8 | 84 | 177 | 8 |
| Of the hobnail tales: no gooseherd or swine will turn | 162 | 10 | 86 | 181 | 10 |
| And no green cocks or hens | 169 | 5 | 87 | 189 | 14 |
| And my shining men no more alone | 173 | 26 | 88 | 193 | 26 |
| No springtailed tom in the red hot town | 174 | 29 | 89 | 195 | 5 |
| No flailing calf or cat in a flame | 175 | 11 | 89 | 195 | 16 |
| Now I am a man no more no more | 175 | 20 | 89 | 196 | 1 |
| (But nothing bore, no mouthing babe to the veined hives | 178 | 1 | 90 | 199 | 2 |
| Off by the sun and Daughters no longer grieved | 178 | 14 | 90 | 199 | 15 |
| Let him find no rest but be fathered and found, |  |  | 91 | 200 | 12 |
| When once the twilight locks no longer | 4 |  | 3 | 4 |  |
| Light breaks where no sun shines | 24 |  | 15 | 29 |  |
| And death shall have no dominion | 68 |  | 42 | 77 |  |
| On no work of words | 94 |  | 57 | 104 |  |
| NOAH |  |  |  |  |  |
| Drinking Noah of the bay, | x | 2 | 1 | xviii | 8 |
| NOAH'S |  |  |  |  |  |
| And Noah's rekindled now unkind dove | 113 | 5 | 69 | 125 | 5 |
| NOBLE |  |  |  |  |  |
| My one and noble heart has witnesses | 81 | 11 | 47 | 90 | 11 |
| O wake to see, after a noble fall, | 96 | 18 | 58 | 107 | 1 |
| NOBODY |  |  |  |  |  |
| But nobody chained him up. | 111 | 12 | 68 | 123 | 12 |
| NODDED |  |  |  |  |  |
| When the caught tongue nodded blind, | 129 | 13 | 77 | 143 | 13 |

|  | U.K. | | | U.S. | |
|---|---|---|---|---|---|
|  | *Page* | *Line* | *Poem* | *Page* | *Line* |
| **NOISE** | | | | | |
| Of sheep and churches noise | x | 5 | 1 | xviii | 11 |
| By the sea's side, hearing the noise of birds, | 16 | 5 | 11 | 19 | 5 |
| Itched in the noise of wind and sun. | 21 | 6 | 13 | 25 | 6 |
| **NOISES** | | | | | |
| Crossly out of the town noises | 134 | 24 | 79 | 151 | 2 |
| **NOISY** | | | | | |
| Hold up the noisy sea and drop her birds, | 2 | 15 | 2 | 2 | 15 |
| **NONE** | | | | | |
| 'Find meat on bones that soon have none, | 65 | 1 | 40 | 74 | 1 |
| Thrust, my daughter or son, to escape, there is none, none, none, | 97 | 19 | 59 | 108 | 19 |
| Call for confessor and wiser mirror but there is none | 158 | 10 | 84 | 177 | 10 |
| **NO-ONE** | | | | | |
| And no-one stirs at Sheba's side | 153 | 12 | 83 | 171 | 8 |
| **NOON** | | | | | |
| Year to heaven stood there then in the summer noon | 104 | 14 | 63 | 115 | 16 |
| His striped and noon maned tribe striding to holocaust, | 110 | 3 | 67 | 121 | 5 |
| And the high noon | 140 | 14 | 82 | 157 | 14 |
| Noon, and night, and light. The rivers of the dead | | | 91 | 200 | 15 |
| **NOONS** | | | | | |
| Falls on a ring of summers and locked noons. | 79 | 4 | 46 | 88 | 7 |
| **NOOSED** | | | | | |
| The flash the noosed hawk | 167 | 10 | 87 | 187 | 10 |
| **NOR** | | | | | |
| Nor blows back moon and midnight as she blows. | 2 | 6 | 2 | 2 | 6 |
| Nor damned the sea that sped about my fist, | 4 | 3 | 3 | 4 | 3 |
| A ghost nor man, but mortal ghost. | 8 | 14 | 5 | 9 | 14 |
| I would not fear the apple nor the flood | 12 | 6 | 9 | 13 | 6 |
| Nor the bad blood of spring. | 12 | 7 | 9 | 13 | 7 |
| I would not fear the gallows nor the axe | 12 | 13 | 9 | 13 | 13 |
| Nor the crossed sticks of war. | 12 | 14 | 9 | 13 | 14 |
| Nor the outspoken grave. | 12 | 21 | 9 | 13 | 21 |
| That wipes away not crow's-foot nor the lock | 12 | 23 | 9 | 14 | 2 |
| Nor when he finds a beauty in the breast | 13 | 12 | 9 | 14 | 19 |
| Nor city tar and subway bored to foster | 19 | 9 | 12 | 22 | 14 |
| Nor fenced, nor staked, the gushers of the sky | 24 | 16 | 15 | 29 | 16 |
| Nor the heart in the ribbing metal. | 33 | 15 | 19 | 38 | 15 |
| Nor the flint in the lover's mauling. | 33 | 18 | 19 | 38 | 18 |
| Nor the cannons of his kingdom | 43 | 19 | 24 | 51 | 5 |
| Nor the cannons of his kingdom | 43 | 26 | 24 | 51 | 12 |
| Do you not father me, nor the erected arm | 46 | 1 | 27 | 54 | 1 |

| | U.K. | | | U.S. | |
|---|---|---|---|---|---|
| | Page | Line | Poem | Page | Line |
| Do you not mother me, nor, as I am, | 46 | 3 | 27 | 54 | 3 |
| Do you not sister me, nor the erected crime | 46 | 5 | 27 | 54 | 5 |
| Do you not brother me, nor, as you climb, | 46 | 7 | 27 | 54 | 7 |
| Nor roof of sand, nor yet the towering tiler? | 46 | 16 | 27 | 54 | 16 |
| And this, nor this, is shade, the landed crow, | 51 | 19 | 31 | 60 | 19 |
| Foster the light nor veil the manshaped moon, | 60 | 1 | 36 | 69 | 1 |
| Nor weather winds that blow not down the bone, | 60 | 2 | 36 | 69 | 2 |
| Master the night nor serve the snowman's brain | 60 | 4 | 36 | 69 | 4 |
| Murmur of spring nor crush the cockerel's eggs, | 60 | 7 | 36 | 69 | 7 |
| Nor hammer back a season in the figs, | 60 | 8 | 36 | 69 | 8 |
| And father all nor fail the fly-lord's acre, | 60 | 13 | 36 | 69 | 13 |
| Nor sprout on owl-seed like a goblin-sucker, | 60 | 14 | 36 | 69 | 14 |
| O ring of seas, nor sorrow as I shift | 60 | 20 | 36 | 69 | 20 |
| Nor when my love lies in the cross-boned drift | 60 | 22 | 36 | 69 | 22 |
| The crusted wound nor stroke the brow; | 62 | 14 | 37 | 71 | 14 |
| Nor can I smother the sweet waking.' | 66 | 8 | 40 | 75 | 8 |
| Nor falls to His green myths? | 69 | 18 | 43 | 78 | 18 |
| 'Nor the green nought be hurt; | 70 | 17 | 43 | 79 | 21 |
| Nor ever, as the wild tongue breaks its tombs, | 77 | 11 | 45 | 86 | 11 |
| Walks with no wound, nor lightning in her face, | 80 | 10 | 46 | 89 | 18 |
| Nor when all ponderous heaven's host of waters breaks. | 97 | 20 | 59 | 108 | 20 |
| Through the waves of the fat streets nor the skeleton's thin ways. | 98 | 5 | 59 | 109 | 8 |
| Nor blaspheme down the stations of the breath | 101 | 16 | 62 | 112 | 16 |
| Her constant, nor the winds of love broken wide | 109 | 10 | 67 | 120 | 10 |
| Turns of your prayed flesh, nor shall I shoo the bird below me: | 109 | 27 | 67 | 121 | 1 |
| Nor walk in the cool of your mortal garden | 110 | 20 | 67 | 121 | 22 |
| Nor could share, for his pride, to the least | 114 | 21 | 69 | 126 | 21 |
| Nor for the towering dead | 128 | 15 | 76 | 142 | 15 |
| Nor heed my craft or art. | 128 | 20 | 76 | 142 | 20 |
| Nor that riding to sleep | 161 | 1 | 85 | 180 | 4 |
| Nor the innocent lie in the rooting dingle wooed | 162 | 15 | 86 | 181 | 15 |
| Nor the tusked prince, in the ruttish farm, at the rind | 163 | 14 | 86 | 182 | 14 |
| Wound, nor her riding high, nor her eyes, nor kindled hair, | 166 | 2 | 86 | 186 | 2 |
| Nor did he now, save to his secret wound. | | | 91 | 201 | 6 |
| NORTH | | | | | |
| Out of the sides of the north | 153 | 18 | 83 | 171 | 14 |
| NOSTRIL | | | | | |
| The neck of the nostril, | 37 | 1 | 20 | 42 | 7 |
| NOSTRILS | | | | | |
| My nostrils see her breath burn like a bush. | 81 | 10 | 47 | 90 | 10 |
| NOT | | | | | |
| Who knew not sun and moon by name, | 7 | 8 | 5 | 8 | 8 |

| | U.K. | | | U.S. | |
|---|---|---|---|---|---|
| | *Page* | *Line* | *Poem* | *Page* | *Line* |
| Shall not be latched while magic glides | 11 | 20 | 8 | 12 | 20 |
| I would not fear the apple nor the flood | 12 | 6 | 9 | 13 | 6 |
| I would not fear the gallows nor the axe | 12 | 13 | 9 | 13 | 13 |
| I would not fear the muscling-in of love | 12 | 17 | 9 | 13 | 17 |
| I would not fear the devil in the loin | 12 | 20 | 9 | 13 | 20 |
| That wipes away not crow's-foot nor the lock | 12 | 23 | 9 | 14 | 2 |
| Fear not the working world, my mortal, | 33 | 13 | 19 | 38 | 13 |
| Fear not the flat, synthetic blood, | 33 | 14 | 19 | 38 | 14 |
| Fear not the tread, the seeded milling, | 33 | 16 | 19 | 38 | 16 |
| Fear not the screws that turn the voice, | 33 | 23 | 19 | 39 | 5 |
| The seed-at-zero shall not storm | 42 | 1 | 24 | 49 | 1 |
| The seed-at-zero shall not storm | 42 | 8 | 24 | 49 | 8 |
| Shall not thunder on the town | 43 | 17 | 24 | 51 | 3 |
| Do you not father me, nor the erected arm | 46 | 1 | 27 | 54 | 1 |
| Do you not mother me, nor, as I am, | 46 | 3 | 27 | 54 | 3 |
| Do you not sister me, nor the erected crime | 46 | 5 | 27 | 54 | 5 |
| Do you not brother me, nor, as you climb, | 46 | 7 | 27 | 54 | 7 |
| Am I not father, too, and the ascending boy, | 46 | 9 | 27 | 54 | 9 |
| Am I not sister, too, who is my saviour? | 46 | 12 | 27 | 54 | 12 |
| Am I not all of you by the directed sea | 46 | 13 | 27 | 54 | 13 |
| Am I not you who front the tidy shore, | 46 | 15 | 27 | 54 | 15 |
| Do you not father me on the destroying sand? | 47 | 1 | 27 | 55 | 1 |
| But not of grief, for I have knocked down that | 48 | 2 | 28 | 56 | 2 |
| All could not disappoint; | 48 | 6 | 28 | 56 | 6 |
| If not of loving well, then not, | 48 | 8 | 28 | 56 | 8 |
| Shall not be known till windwell dries | 53 | 2 | 32 | 62 | 2 |
| Not till, from high and low, their dust | 53 | 12 | 32 | 62 | 12 |
| Nor weather winds that blow not down the bone, | 60 | 2 | 36 | 69 | 2 |
| The five kings count the dead but do not soften | 62 | 13 | 37 | 71 | 13 |
| Has not yet reached the ground. | 63 | 19 | 38 | 72 | 19 |
| By these I would not care to die, | 64 | 19 | 39 | 73 | 19 |
| Though lovers be lost love shall not; | 68 | 8 | 42 | 77 | 8 |
| They lying long shall not die windily; | 68 | 12 | 42 | 77 | 12 |
| Strapped to a wheel, yet they shall not break; | 68 | 14 | 42 | 77 | 14 |
| 'Time shall not murder you,' He said, | 70 | 16 | 43 | 79 | 20 |
| Not spin to stare at an old year | 77 | 17 | 45 | 86 | 17 |
| But wishes breed not, neither | 82 | 21 | 48 | 91 | 21 |
| From the stone nest it does not let the feathery | 86 | 2 | 51 | 95 | 2 |
| But do not travel down dumb wind like prodigals. | 86 | 11 | 51 | 95 | 11 |
| She would not have me sinking in the holy | 87 | 18 | 52 | 96 | 18 |
| Not from this anger, anticlimax after | 90 | 1 | 54 | 99 | 1 |
| Not from this anger after | 90 | 11 | 54 | 99 | 11 |
| 'No. Not for Christ's dazzling bed | 97 | 16 | 59 | 108 | 16 |
| The one not caring to whom in his sleep he will move | 100 | 4 | 61 | 111 | 4 |
| And the child not caring to whom he climbs his prayer | 100 | 17 | 61 | 111 | 17 |

|  | U.K. | | | U.S. | |
| --- | --- | --- | --- | --- | --- |
|  | *Page* | *Line* | *Poem* | *Page* | *Line* |
| I shall not murder | 101 | 14 | 62 | 112 | 14 |
| You may not see, my son, | 105 | 2 | 64 | 116 | 2 |
| To share my room in the house not right in the head, | 108 | 2 | 66 | 119 | 2 |
| Though the brawl of the kiss has not occurred | 109 | 7 | 67 | 120 | 7 |
| Both shall fail if I bow not to your blessing | 110 | 19 | 67 | 121 | 21 |
| Do not go gentle into that good night, | 116 | 1 | 70 | 128 | 1 |
| Do not go gentle into that good night. | 116 | 6 | 70 | 128 | 6 |
| Do not go gentle into that good night. | 116 | 12 | 70 | 128 | 12 |
| Do not go gentle into that good night. | 116 | 18 | 70 | 128 | 18 |
| O you who could not cry | 125 | 20 | 74 | 139 | 20 |
| O we who could not stir | 126 | 4 | 74 | 140 | 4 |
| That did not nurse our bones, | 126 | 10 | 74 | 140 | 10 |
| Not for ambition or bread | 128 | 7 | 76 | 142 | 7 |
| Not for the proud man apart | 128 | 12 | 76 | 142 | 12 |
| I know not whether | 130 | 9 | 77 | 144 | 9 |
| Not wholly to that lamenting | 143 | 15 | 82 | 160 | 15 |
| For ever of all not the wolf in his baaing hood | 163 | 13 | 86 | 182 | 13 |
| Comes designed to my love to steal not her tide raking | 166 | 1 | 86 | 186 | 1 |
| Naked and forsaken to grieve he will not come. | 166 | 7 | 86 | 186 | 7 |
| Not a boy and a bit in the wick- | 174 | 16 | 89 | 194 | 16 |
| The darkest way, and did not turn away, |  |  | 91 | 200 | 2 |
| I am not too proud to cry that He and he |  |  | 91 | 200 | 19 |
| Until I die he will not leave my side.) |  |  | 91 | 201 | 19 |
| Do you not father me | 46 |  | 27 | 54 |  |
| Not from this anger | 90 |  | 54 | 99 |  |
| Do not go gentle into that good night | 116 |  | 70 | 128 |  |

NOTE
| And mouth. Both note and plume plunge from the spire's hook. | 86 | 8 | 51 | 95 | 8 |
| To hear the golden note turn in a groove, | 125 | 6 | 74 | 139 | 6 |

NOTES
| Who moons her blue notes from her nest | ix | 11 | 1 | xvii | 11 |
| Of many a thorny shire tell you notes, | 16 | 15 | 11 | 19 | 15 |
| And four birds' notes. | 45 | 8 | 26 | 53 | 8 |
| And the thunder of calls and notes. | 64 | 10 | 39 | 73 | 10 |
| Before the lunge of the night, the notes on this time-shaken | 169 | 11 | 87 | 189 | 20 |

NOTHING
| I see that from these boys shall men of nothing | 1 | 19 | 2 | 1 | 19 |
| All world was one, one windy nothing, | 20 | 6 | 13 | 24 | 6 |
| And nothing shone on the water's face | 150 | 20 | 83 | 168 | 4 |
| There is nothing left of the sea but its sound, | 157 | 13 | 83 | 176 | 5 |
| Land, land, land, nothing remains | 157 | 17 | 83 | 176 | 9 |
| And nothing I cared, at my sky blue trades, that time allows | 160 | 20 | 85 | 179 | 20 |

|  | U.K. | | Poem | U.S. | |
|  | Page | Line | Poem | Page | Line |
| Nothing I cared, in the lamb white days, that time would take me | 160 | 24 | 85 | 180 | I |
| (But nothing bore, no mouthing babe to the veined hives | 178 | I | 90 | 199 | 2 |
| NOTHINGS |  |  |  |  |  |
| And speak their midnight nothings as they swell; | 14 | 14 | 10 | 16 | 14 |
| NOUGHT |  |  |  |  |  |
| The sun that leaps on petals through a nought, | 51 | 27 | 31 | 61 | 6 |
| 'Nor the green nought be hurt; | 70 | 17 | 43 | 79 | 21 |
| NOW |  |  |  |  |  |
| This day winding down now | vii | I | I | xv | I |
| And the flood flowers now | x | 19 | I | xviii | 25 |
| How now my flesh, my naked fellow, | 33 | 7 | 19 | 38 | 7 |
| Know now the flesh's lock and vice, | 33 | 20 | 19 | 39 | 2 |
| Now that my symbols have outelbowed space, | 41 | 2 | 23 | 47 | 2 |
| And now the horns of England, in the sound of shape, | 49 | 13 | 29 | 58 | 13 |
| Now | 51 | I | 31 | 60 | I |
| Now | 51 | 8 | 31 | 60 | 8 |
| Now | 51 | 15 | 31 | 60 | 15 |
| Now | 51 | 22 | 31 | 61 | I |
| Now | 52 | I | 31 | 61 | 8 |
| Now make the world of me as I have made | 61 | 5 | 36 | 70 | 5 |
| Now Jack my fathers let the time-faced crook, | 67 | 15 | 41 | 76 | 15 |
| Now stamp the Lord's Prayer on a grain of rice, | 74 | 15 | 44 | 83 | 15 |
| Now in the cloud's big breast lie quiet countries, | 80 | 8 | 46 | 89 | 16 |
| Now my saying shall be my undoing, | 89 | 12 | 53 | 98 | 12 |
| On no work of words now for three lean months in the bloody | 94 | I | 57 | 104 | I |
| To surrender now is to pay the expensive ogre twice. | 94 | 10 | 57 | 104 | 10 |
| 'Now to awake husked of gestures and my joy like a cave | 97 | 21 | 59 | 109 | I |
| Whom now I conjure to stand as thief | 107 | 9 | 65 | 118 | 9 |
| And heaven crier, arrow now of aspiring | 110 | 10 | 67 | 121 | 12 |
| And Noah's rekindled now unkind dove | 113 | 5 | 69 | 125 | 5 |
| Curse, bless, me now with your fierce tears, I pray. | 116 | 17 | 70 | 128 | 17 |
| Now their love lies a loss | 124 | 5 | 73 | 138 | 5 |
| Now in the dark there is only yourself and my-self. | 125 | 24 | 74 | 139 | 24 |
| Now break a giant tear for the little known fall, | 126 | 8 | 74 | 140 | 8 |
| Now see, alone in us, | 126 | 12 | 74 | 140 | 12 |
| Myselves grieve now, and miracles cannot atone. | 129 | 16 | 77 | 143 | 16 |
| Now shown and mostly bare I would lie down, | 133 | 21 | 78 | 149 | 4 |
| That he who learns now the sun and moon | 144 | I | 82 | 161 | I |

|  | U.K. | | | U.S. | |
|  | Page | Line | Poem | Page | Line |
| Now common lazarus | 146 | 14 | 82 | 163 | 14 |
| Now or | 147 | 9 | 82 | 164 | 9 |
| Now I am lost in the blinding | 148 | 16 | 82 | 165 | 16 |
| Now cast down your rod, for the whole | 150 | 7 | 83 | 167 | 11 |
| Now as I was young and easy under the apple boughs | 159 | 1 | 85 | 178 | 1 |
| Now the tales praise | 163 | 10 | 86 | 182 | 10 |
| Now the heron grieves in the weeded verge. Through windows | 168 | 23 | 87 | 189 | 8 |
| Now on Sir John's hill. The heron, ankling the scaly | 169 | 7 | 87 | 189 | 16 |
| Now will be ever is always true, | 171 | 24 | 88 | 191 | 24 |
| Now I am a man no more no more | 175 | 20 | 89 | 196 | 1 |
| Now clasp me to their grains in the gigantic glade, | 176 | 19 | 90 | 197 | 19 |
| Now curlew cry me down to kiss the mouths of their dust. | 178 | 4 | 90 | 199 | 5 |
| Where the hay rides now or the bracken kitchens rust | 178 | 6 | 90 | 199 | 7 |
| Nor did he now, save to his secret wound. |  |  | 91 | 201 | 6 |
| Now | 51 |  | 31 | 60 |  |

NOWHERES

| Old cock from nowheres and the heaven's egg, | 71 | 8 | 44 | 80 | 8 |
| Old cock from nowheres lopped the minstrel tongue | 74 | 8 | 44 | 83 | 8 |

NUDE

| By the curve of the nude mouth or the laugh up the sleeve. | 85 | 12 | 50 | 94 | 12 |

NUDGE

| The dear, daft time I take to nudge the sentence, | 41 | 4 | 23 | 47 | 4 |

NUISANCE

| In seizure of silence commit the dead nuisance: | 35 | 23 | 20 | 40 | 23 |

NUMBED

| Deep hillocks and loud on the numbed lakes, | 122 | 17 | 72 | 135 | 17 |

NUMBERLESS

| There where a numberless tongue | 114 | 1 | 69 | 126 | 1 |
| Or still all the numberless days of his death, though |  |  | 91 | 200 | 8 |

NUN

| I see the wanting nun saint carved in a garb | 110 | 6 | 67 | 121 | 8 |

NUNNERIES

| The nightbird lauds through nunneries and domes of leaves | 163 | 5 | 86 | 182 | 5 |

NUNNERY

| Of the wintry nunnery of the order of lust | 109 | 12 | 67 | 120 | 12 |
| Death in the carved nunnery | 110 | 18 | 67 | 121 | 20 |

|  | U.K. | | | U.S. | |
|---|---|---|---|---|---|
|  | *Page* | *Line* | *Poem* | *Page* | *Line* |
| NURSE | | | | | |
| The wet night scolds me like a nurse? | 44 | 10 | 25 | 52 | 10 |
| The nurse of giants by the cut sea basin, | 56 | 10 | 34 | 65 | 10 |
| That did not nurse our bones, | 126 | 10 | 74 | 140 | 10 |
| NURSE'S | | | | | |
| From damp love-darkness and the nurse's twist | 13 | 10 | 9 | 14 | 17 |
| NURSERIES | | | | | |
| Rape and rebellion in the nurseries of my face, | 85 | 3 | 50 | 94 | 3 |
| Bare as the nurseries | 131 | 7 | 77 | 145 | 13 |
| NURSES | | | | | |
| Alone between nurses and swans | 112 | 2 | 68 | 124 | 2 |
| NUT | | | | | |
| Ancient woods of my blood, dash down to the nut of the seas | 94 | 11 | 57 | 104 | 11 |
| NUTMEG | | | | | |
| Nutmeg, civet, and sea-parsley serve the plagued groom and bride | 84 | 5 | 49 | 93 | 11 |

# ENTRIES UNDER O

| O | U.K. | | | U.S. | |
|---|---|---|---|---|---|
| O my ruffled ring dove | ix | 7 | 1 | xvii | 7 |
| O kingdom of neighbours, finned | ix | 31 | 1 | xviii | 5 |
| O see the pulse of summer in the ice. | 1 | 24 | 2 | 1 | 24 |
| O see the poles of promise in the boys. | 2 | 24 | 2 | 3 | 6 |
| O see the poles are kissing as they cross. | 3 | 6 | 2 | 3 | 12 |
| May fail to fasten with a virgin o | 18 | 19 | 12 | 21 | 19 |
| Know, O my bone, the jointed lever, | 33 | 22 | 19 | 39 | 4 |
| O light in zenith, the coupled bud, | 34 | 8 | 19 | 39 | 14 |
| O ring of seas, nor sorrow as I shift | 60 | 20 | 36 | 69 | 20 |
| O who is glory in the shapeless maps, | 61 | 4 | 36 | 70 | 4 |
| Before death takes you, O take back this. | 66 | 17 | 40 | 75 | 17 |
| O green and unborn and undead?' | 70 | 19 | 43 | 79 | 23 |
| Breaks, O my heart's blood, like a heart and hill. | 82 | 24 | 48 | 91 | 24 |
| O make me a mask and a wall to shut from your spies | 85 | 1 | 50 | 94 | 1 |
| O wake in me in my house in the mud | 96 | 1 | 58 | 106 | 1 |
| O wake to see, after a noble fall, | 96 | 18 | 58 | 107 | 1 |
| O my lost love bounced from a good home; | 97 | 23 | 59 | 109 | 3 |
| O may my heart's truth | 104 | 16 | 63 | 115 | 18 |
| And the vaulting bird be still. O my true love, hold me. | 110 | 26 | 67 | 122 | 4 |
| O she lies alone and still, | 115 | 18 | 69 | 127 | 18 |

| | U.K. | | | U.S. | |
|---|---|---|---|---|---|
| | Page | Line | Poem | Page | Line |
| O you who could not cry | 125 | 20 | 74 | 139 | 20 |
| O we who could not stir | 126 | 4 | 74 | 140 | 4 |
| O bride and bride groom | 130 | 17 | 77 | 144 | 17 |
| O Adam and Eve together | 130 | 18 | 77 | 144 | 18 |
| O keep his bones away from that common cart, | 135 | 12 | 80 | 152 | 12 |
| O spiral of ascension | 141 | 11 | 82 | 158 | 11 |
| O the wings of the children! | 142 | 7 | 82 | 159 | 7 |
| O in the name | 147 | 7 | 82 | 164 | 7 |
| O let him | 148 | 11 | 82 | 165 | 11 |
| O Rome and Sodom To-morrow and London | 156 | 23 | 83 | 175 | 11 |
| O | 158 | 1 | 84 | 177 | 1 |
| The country is holy: O bide in that country kind, | 163 | 16 | 86 | 182 | 16 |
| O make me a mask | 85 | | 50 | 94 | |
| O deepest wound of all that he should die | | | 91 | 201 | 16 |
| OAK | | | | | |
| Is maiden in the shameful oak, omens | 78 | 21 | 46 | 87 | 21 |
| Shaped in old armour and oak the countenance of a dunce | 85 | 7 | 50 | 94 | 7 |
| Paddocks in the farms of birds. The dead oak walks for love. | 121 | 20 | 72 | 134 | 15 |
| The oak is felled in the acorn | 155 | 11 | 83 | 173 | 15 |
| OAKEN | | | | | |
| Some of the oaken voices, from the roots | 16 | 14 | 11 | 19 | 14 |
| OAT | | | | | |
| This bread I break was once the oat, | 39 | 1 | 21 | 45 | 1 |
| The oat was merry in the wind; | 39 | 9 | 21 | 45 | 9 |
| Were oat and grape | 39 | 13 | 21 | 45 | 13 |
| OBEY | | | | | |
| Or we shall obey, and ride with you through the drowned. | 136 | 14 | 81 | 153 | 14 |
| OBLIVION | | | | | |
| Young from the canyons of oblivion! | 142 | 9 | 82 | 159 | 9 |
| OCCURRED | | | | | |
| Though the brawl of the kiss has not occurred | 109 | 7 | 67 | 120 | 7 |
| OCEAN | | | | | |
| Stage of the ice, the solid ocean, | 33 | 2 | 19 | 38 | 2 |
| Sailed and set dazzling by the handshaped ocean, | 78 | 5 | 46 | 87 | 5 |
| OCEANIC | | | | | |
| Oceanic lover alone | 114 | 10 | 69 | 126 | 10 |
| OCEANS | | | | | |
| Or rides the imagined oceans of the male wards. | 108 | 9 | 66 | 119 | 9 |
| OCHRE | | | | | |
| Weeps on the desert ochre and the salt | 31 | 8 | 18 | 36 | 8 |
| OCTAGON | | | | | |
| Caught in an octagon of unaccustomed light, | 63 | 2 | 38 | 72 | 2 |

|  |  | U.K. |  | Poem | U.S. |  |
|  |  | Page | Line |  | Page | Line |
| OCTOBER |  |  |  |  |  |  |
| Especially when the October wind | 16 | 1 | 11 | 19 | 1 |
| Especially when the October wind | 17 | 1 | 11 | 20 | 1 |
| Blackbirds and the sun of October | 102 | 23 | 63 | 113 | 23 |
| Though the town below lay leaved with October blood. | 104 | 15 | 63 | 115 | 17 |
| Especially when the October wind | 16 |  | 11 | 19 |  |
| Poem in October | 102 |  | 63 | 113 |  |
| OCTOPUS |  |  |  |  |  |  |
| Drunk as a vineyard snail, flailed like an octopus, | 91 | 7 | 55 | 100 | 7 |
| The octopus walking into her limbs | 152 | 7 | 83 | 169 | 19 |
| ODD |  |  |  |  |  |  |
| From an odd room in a split house stare, | 96 | 6 | 58 | 106 | 6 |
| ODYSSEY |  |  |  |  |  |  |
| With stones of odyssey for ash and garland | 76 | 7 | 44 | 85 | 7 |
| OFF |  |  |  |  |  |  |
| Pack off the shapes of daylight and their starch, | 15 | 4 | 10 | 17 | 4 |
| Off from the creasing flesh, filed | 28 | 6 | 17 | 33 | 6 |
| She threads off the sap and needles, blood and bubble | 35 | 10 | 20 | 40 | 10 |
| Voyaging clockwise off the symboled harbour, | 36 | 8 | 20 | 41 | 8 |
| Ships anchor off the bay. | 58 | 20 | 35 | 67 | 20 |
| Ships anchor off the bay, | 59 | 2 | 35 | 68 | 2 |
| Grief thief of time crawls off, | 67 | 1 | 41 | 76 | 1 |
| The knave of pain steals off | 67 | 3 | 41 | 76 | 3 |
| 'Who could snap off the shapeless print | 70 | 12 | 43 | 79 | 16 |
| Atlaswise hold half-way off the dummy bay | 76 | 10 | 44 | 85 | 10 |
| Can we fend off rock arrival, | 82 | 22 | 48 | 91 | 22 |
| And every stone I wind off like a reel. | 89 | 13 | 53 | 98 | 13 |
| Cutting the morning off, | 134 | 10 | 79 | 150 | 10 |
| Under the mile off moon we trembled listening | 136 | 5 | 81 | 153 | 5 |
| His fiery reel sings off its flames, | 151 | 16 | 83 | 169 | 4 |
| Off by the sun and Daughters no longer grieved | 178 | 14 | 90 | 199 | 15 |
| OFFER |  |  |  |  |  |  |
| For all there is to give I offer: | 48 | 28 | 28 | 57 | 5 |
| OFFICERS |  |  |  |  |  |  |
| Your monstrous officers and the decaying army, | 37 | 5 | 20 | 42 | 11 |
| OGRE |  |  |  |  |  |  |
| To surrender now is to pay the expensive ogre twice. | 94 | 10 | 57 | 104 | 10 |
| OH |  |  |  |  |  |  |
| Love is the last light spoken. Oh | 130 | 7 | 77 | 144 | 7 |
| Never never oh never to regret the bugle I wore | 133 | 19 | 78 | 149 | 2 |
| Oh, Jericho was falling in their lungs! | 151 | 6 | 83 | 168 | 14 |
| Oh the shearwater birds and their boatsized brood | 151 | 19 | 83 | 169 | 7 |
| Oh the bulls of Biscay and their calves | 151 | 20 | 83 | 169 | 8 |

| | U.K. | | | U.S. | |
| --- | --- | --- | --- | --- | --- |
| | Page | Line | Poem | Page | Line |
| Oh all the wanting flesh his enemy | 152 | 19 | 83 | 170 | 11 |
| Oh miracle of fishes! The long dead bite! | 154 | 20 | 83 | 172 | 20 |
| Oh as I was young and easy in the mercy of his means, | 161 | 4 | 85 | 180 | 7 |
| And surely he sails like the ship shape clouds. Oh he | 165 | 28 | 86 | 185 | 18 |
| Oh, let me midlife mourn by the shrined | 172 | 22 | 88 | 192 | 22 |
| The mansouled fiery islands! Oh, | 173 | 24 | 88 | 193 | 24 |
| For, oh, my soul found a sunday wife | 175 | 25 | 89 | 196 | 6 |
| On that darkest day. Oh, forever may | | | 91 | 200 | 4 |
| On that darkest day. Oh, he could hide | | | 91 | 201 | 17 |

OIL

| | | | | | |
| --- | --- | --- | --- | --- | --- |
| Divining in a smile the oil of tears. | 24 | 18 | 15 | 29 | 18 |
| All from the oil, the pound of lava. | 33 | 3 | 19 | 38 | 3 |
| Out of the sea, the drive of oil, | 34 | 10 | 19 | 39 | 16 |
| Prophets and fibre kings in oil and letter, | 75 | 20 | 44 | 84 | 20 |
| The breath draw back like a bolt through white oil | 96 | 21 | 58 | 107 | 4 |
| But the oil and bubble of the moon, | 150 | 21 | 83 | 168 | 5 |

OILED

| | | | | | |
| --- | --- | --- | --- | --- | --- |
| His scissors oiled, his knife hung loose | 11 | 10 | 8 | 12 | 10 |

OILS

| | | | | | |
| --- | --- | --- | --- | --- | --- |
| The secret oils that drive the grass. | 22 | 18 | 14 | 27 | 18 |
| And, as for oils and ointments on the flying grail, | 38 | 23 | 20 | 44 | 13 |
| The landscape grief, love in His oils | 69 | 20 | 43 | 78 | 20 |

OINTMENTS

| | | | | | |
| --- | --- | --- | --- | --- | --- |
| And, as for oils and ointments on the flying grail, | 38 | 23 | 20 | 44 | 13 |

OLD

| | | | | | |
| --- | --- | --- | --- | --- | --- |
| Ahoy, old, sea-legged fox, | x | 15 | 1 | xviii | 21 |
| Of sick old manhood on the fallen jaws, | 12 | 24 | 9 | 14 | 3 |
| An old man's shank one-marrowed with my bone, | 13 | 4 | 9 | 14 | 11 |
| Blowing the old dead back; our shots shall smack | 15 | 18 | 10 | 17 | 18 |
| An old, mad man still climbing in his ghost, | 27 | 4 | 16 | 32 | 9 |
| An old god's dugs are pressed and pricked, | 44 | 9 | 25 | 52 | 9 |
| And the old terrors' continual cry | 64 | 3 | 39 | 73 | 3 |
| Out of the old lie burning on the ground, | 64 | 13 | 39 | 73 | 13 |
| The old forget the cries, | 67 | 5 | 41 | 76 | 5 |
| The old forget the grief, | 67 | 9 | 41 | 76 | 9 |
| Old cock from nowheres and the heaven's egg, | 71 | 8 | 44 | 80 | 8 |
| The black ram, shuffling of the year, old winter, | 72 | 15 | 44 | 81 | 15 |
| Old cock from nowheres lopped the minstrel tongue | 74 | 8 | 44 | 83 | 8 |
| Not spin to stare at an old year | 77 | 17 | 45 | 86 | 17 |

|  | U.K. | | | U.S. | |
|---|---|---|---|---|---|
|  | Page | Line | Poem | Page | Line |
| Shaped in old armour and oak the countenance of a dunce | 85 | 7 | 50 | 94 | 7 |
| The old mud hatch again, the horrid | 96 | 19 | 58 | 107 | 2 |
| And the old dog sleeper | 112 | 1 | 68 | 124 | 1 |
| Old age should burn and rave at close of day; | 116 | 2 | 70 | 128 | 2 |
| Once when the world turned old | 119 | 11 | 72 | 131 | 11 |
| Leap, as to trumpets. Calligraphy of the old | 121 | 22 | 72 | 134 | 17 |
| Was miraculous virginity old as loaves and fishes, | 127 | 5 | 75 | 141 | 5 |
| On the old seas from stories, thrashing my wings, | 133 | 8 | 78 | 148 | 11 |
| Old wives that spin in the smoke, | 150 | 2 | 83 | 167 | 6 |
| Old in her cruel bed. | 152 | 12 | 83 | 170 | 4 |
| Is old as water and plain as an eel; | 152 | 21 | 83 | 170 | 13 |
| And the old men sing from newborn lips: | 155 | 8 | 83 | 173 | 12 |
| Who is the light of old | 172 | 19 | 88 | 192 | 19 |
| (Sighed the old ram rod, dying of women), | 174 | 3 | 89 | 194 | 3 |
| (Sighed the old ram rod, dying of bitches), | 174 | 15 | 89 | 194 | 15 |
| (Sighed the old ram rod, dying of welcome), | 174 | 27 | 89 | 195 | 3 |
| (Sighed the old ram rod, dying of downfall), | 175 | 10 | 89 | 195 | 15 |
| (Sighed the old ram rod, dying of strangers), | 175 | 22 | 89 | 196 | 3 |
| (An old tormented man three-quarters blind, |  |  | 91 | 200 | 18 |
| An old kind man brave in his burning pride. |  |  | 91 | 201 | 3 |
| An old blind man is with me where I go |  |  | 91 | 201 | 9 |
| OMENS |  |  |  |  |  |
| Is maiden in the shameful oak, omens | 78 | 21 | 46 | 87 | 21 |
| ONCE |  |  |  |  |  |
| When once the twilight locks no longer | 4 | 1 | 3 | 4 | 1 |
| When once the twilight screws were turned, | 5 | 7 | 3 | 5 | 7 |
| Where once the waters of your face | 11 | 1 | 8 | 12 | 1 |
| Where once the mermen through your ice | 11 | 4 | 8 | 12 | 4 |
| Where once your green knots sank their splice | 11 | 7 | 8 | 12 | 7 |
| This bread I break was once the oat, | 39 | 1 | 21 | 45 | 1 |
| Once in this wind the summer blood | 39 | 6 | 21 | 45 | 6 |
| Once in this bread | 39 | 8 | 21 | 45 | 8 |
| Once close-up smiling in the wall of pictures, | 73 | 9 | 44 | 82 | 9 |
| Once where the soft snow's blood was turned to ice. | 80 | 12 | 46 | 89 | 20 |
| Whose hooded, fountain heart once fell in puddles | 87 | 14 | 52 | 96 | 14 |
| Once it was the colour of saying | 89 | 1 | 53 | 98 | 1 |
| Meet once on a mortal wall | 93 | 23 | 56 | 103 | 3 |
| Were once such a creature, so gay and frank | 107 | 14 | 65 | 118 | 14 |
| Once seen strangers or shades on a stair; | 113 | 15 | 69 | 125 | 15 |
| Once when the world turned old | 119 | 11 | 72 | 131 | 11 |
| That once cut the figures of birds on the deep bread | 123 | 4 | 72 | 136 | 14 |

| | U.K. | | Poem | U.S. | |
|---|---|---|---|---|---|
| | *Page* | *Line* | | *Page* | *Line* |
| Her deepsea pillow where once she married alone, | 127 | 9 | 75 | 141 | 9 |
| Once below a time, | 132 | 1 | 78 | 147 | 1 |
| The once hooded room | 139 | 13 | 82 | 156 | 13 |
| And once below a time I lordly had the trees and leaves | 159 | 7 | 85 | 178 | 7 |
| In the sun that is young once only, | 159 | 12 | 85 | 178 | 12 |
| Hill. Who once in gooseskin winter loved all ice leaved | 176 | 12 | 90 | 197 | 12 |
| Who once, green countries since, were a hedge-row of joys. | 176 | 20 | 90 | 197 | 20 |
| Who once were a bloom of wayside brides in the hawed house | 177 | 9 | 90 | 198 | 8 |
| When once the twilight locks no longer | 4 | | 3 | 4 | |
| Where once the waters of your face | 11 | | 8 | 12 | |
| Once it was the colour of saying | 89 | | 53 | 98 | |
| Once below a time | 132 | | 78 | 147 | |

ONCE-BLIND

| | | | | | |
|---|---|---|---|---|---|
| These once-blind eyes have breathed a wind of visions, | 80 | 1 | 46 | 89 | 9 |

ONCE-RINDLESS

| | | | | | |
|---|---|---|---|---|---|
| The cauldron's root through this once-rindless hand | 80 | 2 | 46 | 89 | 10 |

ONE

| | | | | | |
|---|---|---|---|---|---|
| All world was one, one windy nothing, | 20 | 6 | 13 | 24 | 6 |
| And earth and sky were as one airy hill, | 20 | 8 | 13 | 24 | 8 |
| The sun and moon shed one white light. | 20 | 9 | 13 | 24 | 9 |
| And the four winds, that had long blown as one, | 20 | 19 | 13 | 24 | 19 |
| What had been one was many sounding minded. | 21 | 17 | 13 | 25 | 17 |
| One womb, one mind, spewed out the matter, | 21 | 18 | 13 | 26 | 1 |
| One breast gave suck the fever's issue; | 21 | 19 | 13 | 26 | 2 |
| One sun, one manna, warmed and fed. | 21 | 26 | 13 | 26 | 9 |
| One smile of light across the empty face; | 22 | 2 | 14 | 27 | 2 |
| One bough of bone across the rooting air, | 22 | 3 | 14 | 27 | 3 |
| Be by your one ghost pierced, his pointed ferrule, | 38 | 1 | 20 | 43 | 11 |
| But one companion. | 66 | 13 | 40 | 75 | 13 |
| Dead men naked they shall be one | 68 | 2 | 42 | 77 | 2 |
| Hatched from the windy salvage on one leg, | 71 | 10 | 44 | 80 | 10 |
| Death is all metaphors, shape in one history; | 71 | 15 | 44 | 80 | 15 |
| And one light's language in the book of trees. | 74 | 19 | 44 | 83 | 19 |
| Because there stands, one story out of the bum city, | 77 | 13 | 45 | 86 | 13 |
| Ruin, the room of errors, one rood dropped | 79 | 13 | 46 | 88 | 16 |
| My one and noble heart has witnesses | 81 | 11 | 47 | 90 | 11 |
| Tap happily of one peg in the thick | 87 | 3 | 52 | 96 | 3 |
| That breaks one bone to light with a judgment clout, | 87 | 9 | 52 | 96 | 9 |

|  | U.K. | | | U.S. | |
| --- | --- | --- | --- | --- | --- |
|  | Page | Line | Poem | Page | Line |
| That I struck one day by luck, | 93 | 5 | 56 | 102 | 5 |
| Drivelled down to one singeing tree | 95 | 20 | 58 | 105 | 20 |
| Heaven fell with his fall and one crocked bell beat the left air. | 95 | 25 | 58 | 105 | 25 |
| The one not caring to whom in his sleep he will move | 100 | 4 | 61 | 111 | 4 |
| Dragging him up the stairs to one who lies dead. | 100 | 20 | 61 | 111 | 20 |
| One gesture of the heart or head, | 105 | 9 | 64 | 116 | 9 |
| One voice in chains declaims | 115 | 6 | 69 | 127 | 6 |
| When one at the great least of your best loved | 117 | 3 | 71 | 129 | 3 |
| One who called deepest down shall hold his peace | 117 | 9 | 71 | 129 | 9 |
| One who is most unknown, | 117 | 16 | 71 | 129 | 16 |
| One enemy, of many, who knows well | 118 | 1 | 71 | 130 | 5 |
| Until that one loved least | 118 | 7 | 71 | 130 | 11 |
| Under the one leaved trees ran a scarecrow of snow | 122 | 14 | 72 | 135 | 14 |
| One lean sigh when we heard | 126 | 5 | 74 | 140 | 5 |
| Over the one | 130 | 27 | 77 | 145 | 5 |
| And the finding one | 140 | 13 | 82 | 157 | 13 |
| The finding one | 142 | 4 | 82 | 159 | 4 |
| Of no one | 147 | 8 | 82 | 164 | 8 |
| One to | 147 | 11 | 82 | 164 | 11 |
| One. The sun roars at the prayer's end | 148 | 17 | 82 | 165 | 17 |
| One by one in dust and shawl, | 155 | 1 | 83 | 173 | 5 |
| When that immortal hospital made one more move to soothe | 158 | 3 | 84 | 177 | 3 |
| That one dark I owe my light, | 158 | 9 | 84 | 177 | 9 |
| To death, one man through his sundered hulks, | 173 | 11 | 88 | 193 | 11 |
| Clung to the pitching clouds, or gay with any one | 176 | 15 | 90 | 197 | 15 |
| In the muted house, one minute before |  |  | 91 | 200 | 14 |
| ONE-COLOURED |  |  |  |  |  |
| With a one-coloured calm; | 82 | 13 | 48 | 91 | 13 |
| ONE-DIMENSIONED |  |  |  |  |  |
| Two one-dimensioned ghosts, love on a reel, | 14 | 12 | 10 | 16 | 12 |
| ONE-MARROWED |  |  |  |  |  |
| An old man's shank one-marrowed with my bone, | 13 | 4 | 9 | 14 | 11 |
| ONE-SIDED |  |  |  |  |  |
| Grafts on its bride one-sided skins of truth; | 15 | 8 | 10 | 17 | 8 |
| ONES |  |  |  |  |  |
| Brave deaths of only ones but never found, | 126 | 11 | 74 | 140 | 11 |
| ONLY |  |  |  |  |  |
| Only the drowned deep bells | x | 4 | 1 | xviii | 10 |
| And that's the rub, the only rub that tickles. | 13 | 8 | 9 | 14 | 15 |
| But only the wind strung | 120 | 16 | 72 | 133 | 1 |

| | U.K. | | | U.S. | |
|---|---|---|---|---|---|
| | Page | Line | Poem | Page | Line |
| Now in the dark there is only yourself and my-self. | 125 | 24 | 74 | 139 | 24 |
| Brave deaths of only ones but never found, | 126 | 11 | 74 | 140 | 11 |
| When only the moon rages | 128 | 3 | 76 | 142 | 3 |
| I climb to greet the war in which I have no heart but only | 158 | 8 | 84 | 177 | 8 |
| If only for a last time. | 158 | 24 | 84 | 177 | 24 |
| In the sun that is young once only, | 159 | 12 | 85 | 178 | 12 |
| Only for the turning of the earth in her holy | 165 | 23 | 86 | 185 | 13 |
| Fishing in the tear of the Towy. Only a hoot owl | 169 | 3 | 87 | 189 | 12 |

**OPEN**

| | | | | | |
|---|---|---|---|---|---|
| Splitting the long eye open, and the spiral turnkey, | 36 | 26 | 20 | 42 | 5 |
| Nailed with an open eye, in the bowl of wounds and weed | 92 | 1 | 55 | 101 | 7 |
| And the endless beginning of prodigies suffers open.' | 98 | 7 | 59 | 109 | 10 |
| Open as to the air to the naked shadow | 115 | 17 | 69 | 127 | 17 |
| Open a pathway through the slow sad sail, | 136 | 9 | 81 | 153 | 9 |
| Flows open | 142 | 15 | 82 | 159 | 15 |
| I open the leaves of the water at a passage | 167 | 23 | 87 | 188 | 4 |

**OPENING**

| | | | | | |
|---|---|---|---|---|---|
| From the opening of the garden lock | 111 | 4 | 68 | 123 | 4 |
| Surprised in the opening of her nightlong eyes | 127 | 2 | 75 | 141 | 2 |
| Opening and the dark run | 137 | 7 | 82 | 154 | 7 |

**OPIUM**

| | | | | | |
|---|---|---|---|---|---|
| And opium head, crow stalk, puffed, cut, and blown, | 78 | 10 | 46 | 87 | 10 |

**ORACLE**

| | | | | | |
|---|---|---|---|---|---|
| With oracle for eye?' | 70 | 14 | 43 | 79 | 18 |

**ORACULAR**

| | | | | | |
|---|---|---|---|---|---|
| From the oracular archives and the parchment, | 75 | 19 | 44 | 84 | 19 |

**ORATOR**

| | | | | | |
|---|---|---|---|---|---|
| Forged in man's minerals, the brassy orator | 35 | 2 | 20 | 40 | 2 |

**ORCHARD**

| | | | | | |
|---|---|---|---|---|---|
| Or with their orchard man in the core of the sun's bush | 177 | 4 | 90 | 198 | 3 |

**ORCHARDS**

| | | | | | |
|---|---|---|---|---|---|
| By red-eyed orchards sow the seeds of snow, | 60 | 11 | 36 | 69 | 11 |
| In deathbeds of orchards the boat dies down | 157 | 15 | 83 | 176 | 7 |

**ORDER**

| | | | | | |
|---|---|---|---|---|---|
| Of the wintry nunnery of the order of lust | 109 | 12 | 67 | 120 | 12 |
| Cut to the still star in the order of the quick | 109 | 20 | 67 | 120 | 20 |

**ORGANPIPES**

| | | | | | |
|---|---|---|---|---|---|
| Into the organpipes and steeples | 131 | 9 | 77 | 145 | 15 |

**ORGANS**

| | | | | | |
|---|---|---|---|---|---|
| Who'd raise the organs of the counted dust | 117 | 7 | 71 | 129 | 7 |

|  | U.K. | | | U.S. | |
|  | Page | Line | Poem | Page | Line |
|---|---|---|---|---|---|
| **ORIGIN** |  |  |  |  |  |
| In fountains of origin gave up their love, | 113 | 9 | 69 | 125 | 9 |
| Sang upon origin! | 142 | 6 | 82 | 159 | 6 |
| **ORIGINAL** |  |  |  |  |  |
| The ribbed original of love. | 23 | 6 | 14 | 28 | 6 |
| **ORNAMENTAL** |  |  |  |  |  |
| Here in this ornamental winter | 45 | 2 | 26 | 53 | 2 |
| **OTHER** |  |  |  |  |  |
| And there we wept, I and a ghostly other, | 26 | 8 | 16 | 31 | 8 |
| And the other full of tears that she will be dead, | 100 | 5 | 61 | 111 | 5 |
| After the first death, there is no other. | 101 | 24 | 62 | 112 | 24 |
| And down the other air and the blue altered sky | 103 | 17 | 63 | 114 | 17 |
| That other sun, the jealous coursing of the un-rivalled blood. | 127 | 14 | 75 | 141 | 14 |
| **OTHERS** |  |  |  |  |  |
| Others betray the lamenting lies of their losses | 85 | 11 | 50 | 94 | 11 |
| To others than You | 107 |  | 65 | 118 |  |
| **OTTERS** |  |  |  |  |  |
| Ship towns to pastures of otters. He | 170 | 24 | 88 | 190 | 24 |
| **OUTCAST** |  |  |  |  |  |
| By the believer lost and the hurled outcast of light. | 120 | 25 | 72 | 133 | 10 |
| **OUTCRY** |  |  |  |  |  |
| Your faith as deathless as the outcry of the ruled sun. | 166 | 12 | 86 | 186 | 12 |
| **OUTELBOWED** |  |  |  |  |  |
| Now that my symbols have outelbowed space, | 41 | 2 | 23 | 47 | 2 |
| **OUTLAW** |  |  |  |  |  |
| Bull's-eye the outlaw through a eunuch crack | 67 | 19 | 41 | 76 | 19 |
| In time like outlaw rains on that priest, water, | 86 | 6 | 51 | 95 | 6 |
| **OUTLINE** |  |  |  |  |  |
| Blind in the coil scrams round the blazing out-line, | 41 | 11 | 23 | 47 | 11 |
| **OUT-OF-PERSPECTIVE** |  |  |  |  |  |
| And out-of-perspective sailors, | 132 | 14 | 78 | 147 | 14 |
| **OUTSIDE** |  |  |  |  |  |
| With the outside weathers, | 91 | 9 | 55 | 100 | 9 |
| And there outside on the bread of the ground | 121 | 13 | 72 | 134 | 8 |
| While a man outside with a billhook, | 134 | 8 | 79 | 150 | 8 |
| **OUTSPOKEN** |  |  |  |  |  |
| Nor the outspoken grave. | 12 | 21 | 9 | 13 | 21 |
| **OVER** |  |  |  |  |  |
| Over the wound asleep | viii | 24 | 1 | xvi | 24 |
| (Give, summer, over), the cemented skin, | 19 | 19 | 12 | 23 | 4 |
| Give over, lovers, locking, and the seawax struggle, | 38 | 11 | 20 | 44 | 1 |
| Over the manwaging line. | 42 | 7 | 24 | 49 | 7 |

| | U.K. | | | U.S. | |
|---|---|---|---|---|---|
| | *Page* | *Line* | *Poem* | *Page* | *Line* |
| Over the warbearing line | 42 | 14 | 24 | 49 | 14 |
| Over the vault of ridings with his hound at heel, | 49 | 5 | 29 | 58 | 5 |
| Over the sea-gut loudening, sets a rock alive; | 49 | 15 | 29 | 58 | 15 |
| There was a time they could cry over books, | 50 | 3 | 30 | 59 | 3 |
| And ghostly comets over the raised fists. | 53 | 26 | 32 | 62 | 26 |
| Roll unmanly over this turning tuft, | 60 | 19 | 36 | 69 | 19 |
| Great is the hand that holds dominion over | 62 | 11 | 37 | 71 | 11 |
| Goes over the hill into the deep sea; | 64 | 5 | 39 | 73 | 5 |
| Then hang a ram rose over the rags. | 65 | 8 | 40 | 74 | 8 |
| Over the water come | 69 | 27 | 43 | 79 | 3 |
| You by the cavern over the black stairs, | 71 | 22 | 44 | 80 | 22 |
| Over these groundworks thrusting through a pavement | 72 | 3 | 44 | 81 | 3 |
| Over the past table I repeat this present grace. | 77 | 25 | 45 | 86 | 25 |
| The heavenly music over the sand | 82 | 14 | 48 | 91 | 14 |
| Over the choir minute I hear the hour chant: | 83 | 7 | 49 | 92 | 7 |
| Babble like a bellbuoy over the hymning heads, | 87 | 23 | 52 | 96 | 23 |
| Storm me forever over her grave until | 88 | 10 | 52 | 97 | 10 |
| Behind my head a square of sky sags over | 90 | 8 | 54 | 99 | 8 |
| Over the border | 102 | 18 | 63 | 113 | 18 |
| Pale rain over the dwindling harbour | 103 | 6 | 63 | 114 | 6 |
| And over the sea wet church the size of a snail | 103 | 7 | 63 | 114 | 7 |
| That the snow blind twilight ferries over the lakes | 119 | 2 | 72 | 131 | 2 |
| Gentle in their clogs over the fallen sky, | 119 | 24 | 72 | 132 | 4 |
| And over the cloth of counties the far hills rode near, | 122 | 13 | 72 | 135 | 13 |
| On a bread white hill over the cupped farm | 122 | 27 | 72 | 136 | 7 |
| And over the glazed lakes skated the shapes of fishes | 123 | 5 | 72 | 136 | 15 |
| Over the dead infants | 130 | 26 | 77 | 145 | 4 |
| Over the one | 130 | 27 | 77 | 145 | 5 |
| Over the urn of sabbaths | 131 | 14 | 77 | 145 | 20 |
| Over the whirling ditch of daybreak | 131 | 15 | 77 | 145 | 21 |
| Over the sun's hovel and the slum of fire | 131 | 16 | 77 | 145 | 22 |
| I drew the white sheet over the islands | 134 | 29 | 79 | 151 | 7 |
| When the morning was waking over the war | 135 | 1 | 80 | 152 | 1 |
| Over the ghost and the dropped son | 137 | 8 | 82 | 154 | 8 |
| As a bird hooking over the sea, | 149 | 7 | 83 | 166 | 7 |
| Miles over the moonstruck boat | 150 | 14 | 83 | 167 | 18 |
| Over the wakeward-flashing spray | 152 | 1 | 83 | 169 | 13 |
| Over the gardens of the floor | 152 | 2 | 83 | 169 | 14 |
| Over the graveyard in the water | 152 | 13 | 83 | 170 | 5 |
| And scuttled over her eyes, | 153 | 4 | 83 | 170 | 20 |
| Seasons over the liquid world, | 153 | 23 | 83 | 171 | 19 |
| Over the barbed and shooting sea assumed an army | 158 | 6 | 84 | 177 | 6 |

OVER (continued)

|  | U.K. | | | U.S. | |
|  | Page | Line | Poem | Page | Line |
| In the sun born over and over, | 160 | 17 | 85 | 179 | 17 |
| In the tower and tolls to sleep over the stalls | 164 | 3 | 86 | 183 | 10 |
| Over Sir John's hill, | 167 | 1 | 87 | 187 | 1 |
| To fiery tyburn over the wrestle of elms until | 167 | 9 | 87 | 187 | 9 |
| To the hawk on fire, the halter height, over Towy's fins, | 167 | 16 | 87 | 187 | 16 |
| Over Sir John's hill | 167 |  | 87 | 187 |  |
| **OWE** | | | | | |
| That one dark I owe my light, | 158 | 9 | 84 | 177 | 9 |
| **OWL** | | | | | |
| And the smell of hay in the snow, and the far owl | 119 | 7 | 72 | 131 | 7 |
| And the owl hood, the heel hider, | 133 | 4 | 78 | 148 | 7 |
| The owl at its knelling. Fox and holt kneel before blood. | 163 | 9 | 86 | 182 | 9 |
| Fishing in the tear of the Towy. Only a hoot owl | 169 | 3 | 87 | 189 | 12 |
| The rude owl cried like a telltale tit, | 174 | 5 | 89 | 194 | 5 |
| Of day, in the thistle aisles, till the white owl crossed | 177 | 12 | 90 | 198 | 11 |
| **OWL-LIGHT** | | | | | |
| Altarwise by owl-light in the half-way house | 71 | 1 | 44 | 80 | 1 |
| Altarwise by owl-light | 71 |  | 44 | 80 |  |
| **OWL-SEED** | | | | | |
| Nor sprout on owl-seed like a goblin-sucker, | 60 | 14 | 36 | 69 | 14 |
| **OWLS** | | | | | |
| You king singsong owls, who moonbeam. | ix | 3 | 1 | xvii | 3 |
| Brown as owls | 103 | 9 | 63 | 114 | 9 |
| As I rode to sleep the owls were bearing the farm away, | 160 | 2 | 85 | 179 | 2 |
| **OWN** | | | | | |
| I sent my own ambassador to light; | 5 | 9 | 3 | 5 | 9 |
| This world is half the devil's and my own, | 13 | 1 | 9 | 14 | 8 |
| Measures his own length on the garden wall | 41 | 12 | 23 | 47 | 12 |
| Who strode for your own dead | 117 | 20 | 71 | 129 | 20 |
| Our own true strangers' dust | 126 | 13 | 74 | 140 | 13 |
| My paid-for slaved-for own too late | 132 | 6 | 78 | 147 | 6 |
| So loud to my own | 137 | 5 | 82 | 154 | 5 |
| Of the hearthstone tales my own, lost love; and the soul walks | 164 | 4 | 86 | 183 | 11 |
| To kill and their own tide daubing blood | 171 | 8 | 88 | 191 | 8 |
| **OWNED** | | | | | |
| The sticks of the house were his; his books he owned. |  |  | 91 | 201 | 4 |
| **OX** | | | | | |
| Thus the shadowless man or ox, and the pictured devil, | 35 | 22 | 20 | 40 | 22 |
| In the courters' lanes, or twined in the ox roasting sun | 176 | 13 | 90 | 197 | 13 |

| | | PAID-FOR | | |
| | U.K. | | U.S. | |
| | Page | Line | Poem | Page | Line |
|---|---|---|---|---|---|

OX-KILLING
The furious ox-killing house of love. — 157 / 8 / 83 / 175 / 20

OYSTER
By lava's light split through the oyster vowels — 74 / 3 / 44 / 83 / 3

# ENTRIES UNDER P

| | U.K. Page | Line | Poem | U.S. Page | Line |
|---|---|---|---|---|---|
| PACE | | | | | |
| And, when it quickens, alter the actions' pace | 63 | 12 | 38 | 72 | 12 |
| PACING | | | | | |
| From the emerald, still bell; and from the pacing weather-cock | 83 | 17 | 49 | 92 | 17 |
| Of the pacing, famous sea but its speech, | 157 | 18 | 83 | 176 | 10 |
| PACK | | | | | |
| Pack off the shapes of daylight and their starch, | 15 | 4 | 10 | 17 | 4 |
| Pack back the downed bone. If the unpricked ball of my breath | 97 | 2 | 59 | 108 | 2 |
| PACKS | | | | | |
| The crumpled packs fled past this ghost in bloom, | 80 | 5 | 46 | 89 | 13 |
| PADDED | | | | | |
| My world is pyramid. The padded mummer | 31 | 7 | 18 | 36 | 7 |
| PADDING | | | | | |
| Down fall four padding weathers on the scarlet lands, | 49 | 19 | 29 | 58 | 19 |
| PADDLER'S | | | | | |
| Or, masted venus, through the paddler's bowl | 54 | 7 | 33 | 63 | 7 |
| PADDLES | | | | | |
| Where the elegiac fisherbird stabs and paddles | 167 | 19 | 87 | 187 | 19 |
| PADDLING | | | | | |
| As a he-god's paddling water skirts, | 132 | 16 | 78 | 147 | 16 |
| PADDOCKS | | | | | |
| Paddocks in the farms of birds. The dead oak walks for love. | 121 | 20 | 72 | 134 | 15 |
| PAGE | | | | | |
| And tells the page the empty ill. | 10 | 10 | 7 | 11 | 10 |
| PAGES | | | | | |
| On these spindrift pages | 128 | 14 | 76 | 142 | 14 |
| PAID-FOR | | | | | |
| My paid-for slaved-for own too late | 132 | 6 | 78 | 147 | 6 |

353

| | | U.K. | | | U.S. | |
|---|---|---|---|---|---|---|
| | | Page | Line | Poem | Page | Line |
| PAIL | | | | | | |
| | Yard of the buttermilk rain on the pail! The sermon | 165 | 6 | 86 | 184 | 14 |
| PAIN | | | | | | |
| | Spat up from the resuffered pain. | 28 | 24 | 17 | 34 | 4 |
| | Were that enough, enough to ease the pain, | 48 | 17 | 28 | 56 | 17 |
| | The knave of pain steals off | 67 | 3 | 41 | 76 | 3 |
| | Her fist of a face died clenched on a round pain; | 88 | 6 | 52 | 97 | 6 |
| | She wept in her pain and made mouths, | 93 | 19 | 56 | 102 | 19 |
| | And the shadowed head of pain | 138 | 7 | 82 | 155 | 7 |
| | And the whole pain | 142 | 14 | 82 | 159 | 14 |
| | Kill Time! She turns in her pain! | 155 | 10 | 83 | 173 | 14 |
| | All his bones crying, and poor in all but pain, | | | 91 | 200 | 21 |
| PAINS | | | | | | |
| | Lose the great pains or stuff the wound, | 48 | 12 | 28 | 56 | 12 |
| PAINT | | | | | | |
| | Of sun and moon they paint their dams | 1 | 17 | 2 | 1 | 17 |
| | Break the black news and paint on a sail | 151 | 23 | 83 | 169 | 11 |
| PAINTS | | | | | | |
| | As sunlight paints the shelling of their heads. | 1 | 18 | 2 | 1 | 18 |
| PALAVERS | | | | | | |
| | And palavers of birds | 170 | 5 | 88 | 190 | 5 |
| PALE | | | | | | |
| | In the beginning was the pale signature, | 22 | 7 | 14 | 27 | 7 |
| | And though my love pulls the pale, nippled air, | 80 | 13 | 46 | 89 | 21 |
| | Moonfall and sailing emperor, pale as their tide-print, | 83 | 10 | 49 | 92 | 10 |
| | Pale rain over the dwindling harbour | 103 | 6 | 63 | 114 | 6 |
| | The pale breath of cattle at the stealthy sail, | 119 | 5 | 72 | 131 | 5 |
| PALER | | | | | | |
| | Black as the beast and paler than the cross. | 40 | 12 | 22 | 46 | 12 |
| PALLOR | | | | | | |
| | The loin is glory in a working pallor. | 32 | 9 | 18 | 37 | 15 |
| PALMED | | | | | | |
| | Who palmed the lie on me when you looked | 107 | 4 | 65 | 118 | 4 |
| PAP | | | | | | |
| | The swing of milk was tufted in the pap, | 30 | 10 | 18 | 35 | 10 |
| PAPER | | | | | | |
| | Ache on the lovelorn paper | 10 | 7 | 7 | 11 | 7 |
| | The hand that signed the paper felled a city; | 62 | 1 | 37 | 71 | 1 |
| | And ghostly echoes on paper, | 64 | 9 | 39 | 73 | 9 |
| | Laughing when he shook his paper | 111 | 20 | 68 | 123 | 20 |
| | The hand that signed the paper | 62 | | 37 | 71 | |
| PARABLES | | | | | | |
| | Through the parables | 103 | 23 | 63 | 114 | 23 |
| PARADISE | | | | | | |
| | Carrion, paradise, chirrup my bright yolk. | 115 | 14 | 69 | 127 | 14 |

| | U.K. | | | U.S. | |
|---|---|---|---|---|---|
| | Page | Line | Poem | Page | Line |
| Of paradise, in the spun bud of the world. | 123 | 19 | 72 | 137 | 9 |
| PARALLEL | | | | | |
| The natural parallel. | 35 | 24 | 20 | 40 | 24 |
| PARCEL | | | | | |
| Throw your fear a parcel of stone | 96 | 12 | 58 | 106 | 12 |
| PARCHED | | | | | |
| Round the parched worlds of Wales and drowned each sun | 87 | 15 | 52 | 96 | 15 |
| The parched and raging voice? | 91 | 22 | 55 | 100 | 22 |
| PARCHMENT | | | | | |
| From the oracular archives and the parchment, | 75 | 19 | 44 | 84 | 19 |
| PARDON | | | | | |
| And played down pardon from the heavens' hill. | 40 | 6 | 22 | 46 | 6 |
| Her ropes of heritage, the wars of pardon, | 54 | 21 | 33 | 63 | 21 |
| And, mild as pardon from a cloud of pride, | 80 | 6 | 46 | 89 | 14 |
| PARED | | | | | |
| Love in the frost is pared and wintered by, | 81 | 5 | 47 | 90 | 5 |
| PARHELION | | | | | |
| And a blood parhelion. | 31 | 12 | 18 | 36 | 12 |
| PARISH | | | | | |
| Parish of snow. The carved mouths in the rock are wind swept strings. | 121 | 9 | 72 | 134 | 4 |
| PARK | | | | | |
| Of the star-gestured children in the park. | 16 | 12 | 11 | 19 | 12 |
| The ball I threw while playing in the park | 63 | 18 | 38 | 72 | 18 |
| When I whistled with mitching boys through a reservoir park | 89 | 7 | 53 | 98 | 7 |
| The hunchback in the park | 111 | 1 | 68 | 123 | 1 |
| Like the park birds he came early | 111 | 13 | 68 | 123 | 13 |
| Dodging the park keeper | 111 | 23 | 68 | 123 | 23 |
| All night in the unmade park | 112 | 13 | 68 | 124 | 13 |
| The hunchback in the Park | 111 | | 68 | 123 | |
| PARKS | | | | | |
| Children from homes and children's parks | 69 | 28 | 43 | 79 | 4 |
| PARLIAMENT | | | | | |
| And the parliament of sky, | 65 | 10 | 40 | 74 | 10 |
| PART | | | | | |
| All blood-signed assailings and vanished marriages in which he had no lovely part | 114 | 20 | 69 | 126 | 20 |
| PARTED | | | | | |
| They come together whom their love parted: | 124 | 10 | 73 | 138 | 10 |
| PARTICLE | | | | | |
| Claw of the crabbed veins squeeze from each red particle | 91 | 21 | 55 | 100 | 21 |
| PARTICLES | | | | | |
| Or a nacreous sleep among soft particles and charms | 97 | 17 | 59 | 108 | 17 |

|  | U.K. | | | U.S. | |
| --- | --- | --- | --- | --- | --- |
|  | Page | Line | Poem | Page | Line |
| PARTING |  |  |  |  |  |
| The parting of hat from hair, | 64 | 16 | 39 | 73 | 16 |
| PASS |  |  |  |  |  |
| The wind pass like a fire, | 58 | 18 | 35 | 67 | 18 |
| PASSAGE |  |  |  |  |  |
| I open the leaves of the water at a passage | 167 | 23 | 87 | 188 | 4 |
| PASSAGES |  |  |  |  |  |
| Passages | 146 | 11 | 82 | 163 | 11 |
| PAST |  |  |  |  |  |
| Over the past table I repeat this present grace. | 77 | 25 | 45 | 86 | 25 |
| The crumpled packs fled past this ghost in bloom, | 80 | 5 | 46 | 89 | 13 |
| Past lake and rockery | 111 | 19 | 68 | 123 | 19 |
| Past the statues of the stables and the sky roofed sties | 120 | 9 | 72 | 132 | 14 |
| Past the blind barns and byres of the windless farm. | 122 | 10 | 72 | 135 | 10 |
| And the dead hand leads the past. | 155 | 4 | 83 | 173 | 8 |
| PASTORAL |  |  |  |  |  |
| Of the wood! Pastoral beat of blood through the laced leaves! | 164 | 22 | 86 | 184 | 8 |
| PASTURE |  |  |  |  |  |
| Twelve winds encounter by the white host at pasture, | 36 | 14 | 20 | 41 | 14 |
| The star rise at pasture and nightlong the fables graze | 163 | 11 | 86 | 182 | 11 |
| PASTURES |  |  |  |  |  |
| Ship towns to pastures of otters. He | 170 | 24 | 88 | 190 | 24 |
| PATHS |  |  |  |  |  |
| Time on the canvas paths. | 69 | 24 | 43 | 78 | 24 |
| Scattered in the paths of his heels | 152 | 23 | 83 | 170 | 15 |
| PATHWAY |  |  |  |  |  |
| Open a pathway through the slow sad sail, | 136 | 9 | 81 | 153 | 9 |
| PATIENCE |  |  |  |  |  |
| John's beast, Job's patience, and the fibs of vision, | 41 | 21 | 23 | 48 | 3 |
| PATIENT |  |  |  |  |  |
| Lucklessly she must lie patient | 110 | 25 | 67 | 122 | 3 |
| PATIENTS |  |  |  |  |  |
| And Love and his patients roar on a chain; | 124 | 6 | 73 | 138 | 6 |
| PATROL |  |  |  |  |  |
| Bring out the black patrol, | 37 | 4 | 20 | 42 | 10 |
| PATCH |  |  |  |  |  |
| Felled and quilled, flash to my patch | ix | 32 | 1 | xviii | 6 |
| To shade and knit anew the patch of words | 21 | 10 | 13 | 25 | 10 |
| And a black and white patch of girls grew playing; | 89 | 4 | 53 | 98 | 4 |

| | U.K. | | | U.S. | |
|---|---|---|---|---|---|
| | Page | Line | Poem | Page | Line |
| **PATCHWORK** | | | | | |
| The patchwork halves were cloven as they scudded | 30 | 19 | 18 | 35 | 19 |
| **PATH** | | | | | |
| Riding the sea light on a sunken path, | 67 | 8 | 41 | 76 | 8 |
| **PAVILIONS** | | | | | |
| From bald pavilions and the house of bread | 75 | 2 | 44 | 84 | 2 |
| **PAVEMENT** | | | | | |
| Over these groundworks thrusting through a pavement | 72 | 3 | 44 | 81 | 3 |
| He dropped where he loved on the burst pavement stone | 135 | 4 | 80 | 152 | 4 |
| **PAVEMENTS** | | | | | |
| On thunderous pavements in the garden time; | 72 | 10 | 44 | 81 | 10 |
| And the golden pavements laid in requiems, | 131 | 17 | 77 | 145 | 23 |
| **PAY** | | | | | |
| To surrender now is to pay the expensive ogre twice. | 94 | 10 | 57 | 104 | 10 |
| Who pay no praise or wages | 128 | 19 | 76 | 142 | 19 |
| **PEACE** | | | | | |
| At poor peace I sing | vii | 23 | I | xv | 23 |
| Poor peace as the sun sets | x | 6 | I | xviii | 12 |
| One who called deepest down shall hold his peace | 117 | 9 | 71 | 129 | 9 |
| Be at cloud quaking peace, | 172 | 9 | 88 | 192 | 9 |
| **PEAKS** | | | | | |
| Dayed peaks to day to death, | 67 | 22 | 41 | 76 | 22 |
| **PEARL** | | | | | |
| The frank, closed pearl, the sea-girls' lineaments | 78 | 19 | 46 | 87 | 19 |
| The sun shipwrecked west on a pearl | 149 | 15 | 83 | 166 | 15 |
| **PEARS** | | | | | |
| Pears and red currants | 103 | 20 | 63 | 114 | 20 |
| **PEBBLES** | | | | | |
| In the pebbles of the holy streams. | 159 | 18 | 85 | 178 | 18 |
| **PEBBLY** | | | | | |
| In the pebbly dab-filled | 167 | 20 | 87 | 188 | I |
| **PECK** | | | | | |
| Peck, sprint, dance on fountains and duck time | 97 | 8 | 59 | 108 | 8 |
| **PEELED** | | | | | |
| What rhubarb man peeled in her foam-blue channel | 76 | 17 | 44 | 85 | 17 |
| Its tongue peeled in the wrap of a leaf. | 134 | 15 | 79 | 150 | 15 |
| **PEG** | | | | | |
| Tap happily of one peg in the thick | 87 | 3 | 52 | 96 | 3 |
| **PELICAN** | | | | | |
| The planet-ducted pelican of circles | 71 | 17 | 44 | 80 | 17 |

| | U.K. | | Poem | U.S. | |
|---|---|---|---|---|---|
| | *Page* | *Line* | | *Page* | *Line* |
| PELT | | | | | |
| With pelt, and scale, and fleece: | x | 3 | 1 | xviii | 9 |
| PELTER | | | | | |
| An inch in froth. Chimes cheat the prison spire, pelter | 86 | 5 | 51 | 95 | 5 |
| PELTS | | | | | |
| Down pelts the naked weather; | 45 | 3 | 26 | 53 | 3 |
| PENNY-EYED | | | | | |
| Then, penny-eyed, that gentleman of wounds, | 71 | 7 | 44 | 80 | 7 |
| PEOPLE | | | | | |
| With the womb of his shapeless people. | 34 | 3 | 19 | 39 | 9 |
| PEOPLE'S | | | | | |
| Flower, flower the people's fusion, | 34 | 7 | 19 | 39 | 13 |
| She holding me? The people's sea drives on her, | 54 | 26 | 33 | 64 | 2 |
| PERCEIVE | | | | | |
| To veil belladonna and let the dry eyes perceive | 85 | 10 | 50 | 94 | 10 |
| PERCEIVES | | | | | |
| And the hewn coils of his trade perceives | 170 | 26 | 88 | 190 | 26 |
| PERCH | | | | | |
| And a hundred storks perch on the sun's right hand. | 135 | 14 | 80 | 152 | 14 |
| PERCHED | | | | | |
| The cloud perched tailors' master with nerves for cotton. | 133 | 7 | 78 | 148 | 10 |
| PERIL | | | | | |
| This is the fortune of manhood: the natural peril, | 35 | 19 | 20 | 40 | 19 |
| PERILOUS | | | | | |
| No tread more perilous, the green steps and spire | 36 | 2 | 20 | 41 | 2 |
| PERISCOPE | | | | | |
| Who periscope through flowers to the sky. | 5 | 6 | 3 | 5 | 6 |
| PERISHES | | | | | |
| The dancing perishes | 123 | 1 | 72 | 136 | 11 |
| PERPETUAL | | | | | |
| And that is true after perpetual defeat. | 48 | 9 | 28 | 56 | 9 |
| PERPETUATE | | | | | |
| With the incestuous secret brother in the seconds to perpetuate the stars, | 115 | 20 | 69 | 127 | 20 |
| PERSON | | | | | |
| The salt person and blasted place | 77 | 20 | 45 | 86 | 20 |
| PETALS | | | | | |
| Worked on a world of petals; | 35 | 9 | 20 | 40 | 9 |
| The sun that leaps on petals through a nought, | 51 | 27 | 31 | 61 | 6 |
| PETER | | | | | |
| Let the first Peter from a rainbow's quayrail | 76 | 15 | 44 | 85 | 15 |
| PETROL | | | | | |
| Turning a petrol face blind to the enemy | 36 | 23 | 20 | 42 | 2 |

| | U.K. | | | U.S. | |
|---|---|---|---|---|---|
| | Page | Line | Poem | Page | Line |
| PETTICOATS | | | | | |
| Petticoats galed high, or shy with the rough riding boys, | 176 | 18 | 90 | 197 | 18 |
| PEWS | | | | | |
| And the black beast of the beetles' pews, | 174 | 14 | 89 | 194 | 14 |
| PHANTOM | | | | | |
| Image of images, my metal phantom | 35 | 14 | 20 | 40 | 14 |
| PHARAOH | | | | | |
| With priest and pharaoh bed my gentle wound, | 76 | 5 | 44 | 85 | 5 |
| PHARAOH'S | | | | | |
| Shade without shape? the shape of Pharaoh's echo? | 72 | 21 | 44 | 81 | 21 |
| PHEASANTS | | | | | |
| And honoured among foxes and pheasants by the gay house | 160 | 15 | 85 | 179 | 15 |
| PHOENIX | | | | | |
| Waiting with phoenix under | 109 | 2 | 67 | 120 | 2 |
| Continence. I see the unfired phoenix, herald | 110 | 9 | 67 | 121 | 11 |
| PHOENIX' | | | | | |
| That the phoenix' bid for heaven and the desire after | 110 | 17 | 67 | 121 | 19 |
| PHOTOGRAPH | | | | | |
| The photograph is married to the eye, | 15 | 7 | 10 | 17 | 7 |
| PHOTOGRAPHS | | | | | |
| Stretch the salt photographs, | 69 | 19 | 43 | 78 | 19 |
| PHRASES | | | | | |
| 'All game phrases fit your ring of a cockfight: | 97 | 6 | 59 | 108 | 6 |
| PICK | | | | | |
| Pick the world's ball of wave and froth | 2 | 16 | 2 | 2 | 16 |
| PICKBRAIN | | | | | |
| My pickbrain masters morsing on the stone | 18 | 22 | 12 | 22 | 2 |
| PICKED | | | | | |
| The plum my mother picked matured slowly, | 21 | 1 | 13 | 25 | 1 |
| When their bones are picked clean and the clean bones gone, | 68 | 4 | 42 | 77 | 4 |
| Destruction, picked by birds, brays through the jaw-bone, | 79 | 10 | 46 | 88 | 13 |
| With his stick that picked up leaves. | 111 | 24 | 68 | 123 | 24 |
| PICKS | | | | | |
| Who picks the live heart on a diamond. | 79 | 19 | 46 | 88 | 22 |
| PICKTHANK | | | | | |
| And leave the poppied pickthank where he lies; | 5 | 15 | 3 | 5 | 15 |
| PICTURED | | | | | |
| Thus the shadowless man or ox, and the pictured devil, | 35 | 22 | 20 | 40 | 22 |
| PICTURES | | | | | |
| Once close-up smiling in the wall of pictures, | 73 | 9 | 44 | 82 | 9 |

# PICTURES (continued)

|  | U.K. | | | U.S. | |
|---|---|---|---|---|---|
|  | Page | Line | Poem | Page | Line |
| Like the mauled pictures of boys? | 77 | 19 | 45 | 86 | 19 |
| PIECE |  |  |  |  |  |
| I piece my flesh that rattled on the yards | 31 | 14 | 18 | 36 | 14 |
| Winged like a sabbath ass this children's piece | 41 | 16 | 23 | 47 | 16 |
| PIERCE |  |  |  |  |  |
| The halves that pierce the pin's point in the air, | 31 | 2 | 18 | 36 | 2 |
| Pierce the spilt sky with diving wing in weed and heel | 86 | 4 | 51 | 95 | 4 |
| And steeples pierce the cloud on her shoulder | 157 | 1 | 83 | 175 | 13 |
| PIERCED |  |  |  |  |  |
| Be by your one ghost pierced, his pointed ferrule, | 38 | 1 | 20 | 43 | 11 |
| I was pierced by the idol tailor's eyes, | 133 | 10 | 78 | 148 | 13 |
| PIERCING |  |  |  |  |  |
| Plunging and piercing in his course | 150 | 22 | 83 | 168 | 6 |
| PIETY |  |  |  |  |  |
| Chastity prays for me, piety sings, | 175 | 28 | 89 | 196 | 9 |
| PIGEON'S |  |  |  |  |  |
| And a silk pigeon's guilt in her proud absence, | 78 | 17 | 46 | 87 | 17 |
| PIGEONS |  |  |  |  |  |
| As a dust of pigeons. Exulting, the grave hooved | 121 | 18 | 72 | 134 | 13 |
| PIGMENTS |  |  |  |  |  |
| And from her lips the faded pigments fall, | 63 | 7 | 38 | 72 | 7 |
| PIGS' |  |  |  |  |  |
| The wild pigs' wood, and slime upon the trees, | 30 | 20 | 18 | 35 | 20 |
| PILGRIMAGE |  |  |  |  |  |
| And the mole snout blunt under his pilgrimage of domes, | 177 | 16 | 90 | 198 | 15 |
| PILLARS |  |  |  |  |  |
| Clack through the thicket of strength, love hewn in pillars drops | 92 | 8 | 55 | 101 | 14 |
| PILLOW |  |  |  |  |  |
| Her deepsea pillow where once she married alone, | 127 | 9 | 75 | 141 | 9 |
| PIN |  |  |  |  |  |
| Creep and harp on the tide, sinking their charmed, bent pin | 91 | 24 | 55 | 101 | 2 |
| PIN'S |  |  |  |  |  |
| The halves that pierce the pin's point in the air, | 31 | 2 | 18 | 36 | 2 |
| PINCERED |  |  |  |  |  |
| Of psalms and shadows among the pincered sandcrabs prancing | 167 | 24 | 87 | 188 | 5 |
| PINCERS |  |  |  |  |  |
| And in the pincers of the boiling circle, | 38 | 13 | 20 | 44 | 3 |
| PINE |  |  |  |  |  |
| Casts to the pine roots, raising man like a mountain | 35 | 11 | 20 | 40 | 11 |

| | U.K. | | | U.S. | |
|---|---|---|---|---|---|
| | Page | Line | Poem | Page | Line |

**PIN-HILLED**

Lop, love, my fork tongue, said the pin-hilled
    nettle; — 74, 6, 44, 83, 6

**PIN-LEGGED**

Pin-legged on pole-hills with a black medusa — 73, 22, 44, 82, 22

**PINNACLE**

They climb the country pinnacle, — 36, 13, 20, 41, 13

**PINNED-AROUND-THE-SPIRIT**

When my pinned-around-the-spirit — 132, 2, 78, 147, 2

**PINS**

With pins for teardrops is the long wound's
    woman. — 75, 10, 44, 84, 10

**PIPERS**

Gulls, pipers, cockles, and sails, — vii, 11, I, xv, 11

**PITY**

Remember me and and pity Him — 8, 20, 5, 9, 20
A hand rules pity as a hand rules heaven; — 62, 15, 37, 71, 15

**PITCH**

We are the sons of flint and pitch. — 3, 5, 2, 3, 11
Before the pitch was forking to a sun; — 23, 3, 14, 28, 3
Like some pitch moon, the limit of the
    globes; — 24, 20, 15, 29, 20

**PITCHING**

Clung to the pitching clouds, or gay with any
    one — 176, 15, 90, 197, 15

**PLACE**

Hark: I trumpet the place, — viii, 16, I, xvi, 16
Range on the sky-scraping place. — 43, 21, 24, 51, 7
Range from the grave-groping place. — 43, 28, 24, 51, 14
The salt person and blasted place — 77, 20, 45, 86, 20
Delivered seas my love from her proud place — 80, 9, 46, 89, 17
She married in this pouring place, — 93, 4, 56, 102, 4
When you sew the deep door. The bed is a cross
    place. — 97, 13, 59, 108, 13
In the first, spinning place, the spellbound horses
    walking warm — 160, 12, 85, 179, 12
Dark is a way and light is a place, — 171, 22, 88, 191, 22

**PLACES**

Places — 146, 8, 82, 163, 8
Time and places grip her breast bone, — 156, 7, 83, 174, 15

**PLAGUE**

From love's first fever to her plague, from the
    soft second — 20, 1, 13, 24, 1
The insect certain is the plague of fables. — 41, 9, 23, 47, 9
Rose cast to plague, — 54, 14, 33, 63, 14
And all the deadly virtues plague my death! — 175, 31, 89, 196, 12
From love's first fever to her plague — 20, , 13, 24,

| | U.K. Page | Line | Poem | U.S. Page | Line |
|---|---|---|---|---|---|
| **PLAGUED** | | | | | |
| Nutmeg, civet, and sea-parsley serve the plagued groom and bride | 84 | 5 | 49 | 93 | 11 |
| **PLAIN** | | | | | |
| For loss of blood I fell on Ishmael's plain, | 73 | 17 | 44 | 82 | 17 |
| Down to the river rooting plain | 145 | 16 | 82 | 162 | 16 |
| Is old as water and plain as an eel; | 152 | 21 | 83 | 170 | 13 |
| Hating his God, but what he was was plain: | | | 91 | 201 | 2 |
| **PLAINS** | | | | | |
| The central plains of Asia in his garden, | 40 | 2 | 22 | 46 | 2 |
| The swinish plains of carrion | 143 | 2 | 82 | 160 | 2 |
| **PLAIT** | | | | | |
| The beach of flesh, and wind her bloodred plait; | 10 | 13 | 7 | 11 | 13 |
| **PLANET** | | | | | |
| May a humble planet labour | 43 | 8 | 24 | 50 | 15 |
| But rail with your wizard's ribs the heart-shaped planet; | 60 | 15 | 36 | 69 | 15 |
| **PLANET-DUCTED** | | | | | |
| The planet-ducted pelican of circles | 71 | 17 | 44 | 80 | 17 |
| **PLANETS** | | | | | |
| Might cross its planets, the bell weep, night gather her eyes, | 165 | 21 | 86 | 185 | 11 |
| **PLANING-HEELED** | | | | | |
| So, planing-heeled, I flew along my man | 26 | 4 | 16 | 31 | 4 |
| **PLANTED** | | | | | |
| And from the planted womb the man of straw. | 2 | 12 | 2 | 2 | 12 |
| For half of love was planted in the lost, | 30 | 11 | 18 | 35 | 11 |
| The cloud, the need, the planted stars, the joy beyond | 122 | 22 | 72 | 136 | 2 |
| **PLANTS** | | | | | |
| Out of the font of bone and plants at that stone tocsin | 83 | 20 | 49 | 93 | 2 |
| Down the beginning of plants | 106 | 6 | 64 | 117 | 6 |
| **PLATE** | | | | | |
| Groping for matter under the dog's plate, | 48 | 26 | 28 | 57 | 3 |
| **PLATES** | | | | | |
| The image from the plates; | 15 | 19 | 10 | 17 | 19 |
| **PLATYPUS** | | | | | |
| The duck-billed platypus broody in a milk of birds. | 110 | 5 | 67 | 121 | 7 |
| **PLAY** | | | | | |
| Who play the proper gentleman and lady. | 47 | 4 | 27 | 55 | 4 |
| Time let me play and be | 159 | 13 | 85 | 178 | 13 |
| And the shrill child's play | 167 | 5 | 87 | 187 | 5 |
| **PLAYED** | | | | | |
| And played down pardon from the heavens' hill. | 40 | 6 | 22 | 46 | 6 |

| | U.K. | | | U.S. | |
|---|---|---|---|---|---|
| | *Page* | *Line* | *Poem* | *Page* | *Line* |
| **PLAYING** | | | | | |
| The ball I threw while playing in the park | 63 | 18 | 38 | 72 | 18 |
| And a black and white patch of girls grew playing; | 89 | 4 | 53 | 98 | 4 |
| And playing, lovely and watery | 159 | 21 | 85 | 178 | 21 |
| **PLEADING** | | | | | |
| Pleading in the waded bay for the seed to flow | 176 | 7 | 90 | 197 | 7 |
| **PLEASING** | | | | | |
| To lift to leave from the treasures of man is pleasing death . | 94 | 7 | 57 | 104 | 7 |
| **PLEASURE-BIRD** | | | | | |
| Because the pleasure-bird whistles after the hot wires, | 77 | 1 | 45 | 86 | 1 |
| Because the pleasure-bird whistles | 77 | | 45 | 86 | |
| **PLENTY** | | | | | |
| Were vaguenesses enough and the sweet lies plenty, | 48 | 21 | 28 | 56 | 21 |
| Plenty as blackberries in the woods | 171 | 26 | 88 | 191 | 26 |
| **PLUM** | | | | | |
| And drop the plum like fire from the flesh. | 12 | 9 | 9 | 13 | 9 |
| The plum my mother picked matured slowly, | 21 | 1 | 13 | 25 | 1 |
| **PLUMBED** | | | | | |
| Huloo, on plumbed bryns, | ix | 6 | 1 | xvii | 6 |
| **PLUME** | | | | | |
| And mouth. Both note and plume plunge from the spire's hook. | 86 | 8 | 51 | 95 | 8 |
| Bolting the night of the door with her arm her plume. | 108 | 4 | 66 | 119 | 4 |
| On the black plume | 143 | 12 | 82 | 160 | 12 |
| **PLUMED** | | | | | |
| Lops, as a bush plumed with flames, the rant of the fierce eye, | 92 | 10 | 55 | 101 | 16 |
| And the sky of birds in the plumed voice charmed | 122 | 8 | 72 | 135 | 8 |
| **PLUMES** | | | | | |
| And staved, and riven among plumes my rider weep. | 162 | 16 | 86 | 181 | 16 |
| Flash, and the plumes crack, | 167 | 13 | 87 | 187 | 13 |
| **PLUNGE** | | | | | |
| And mouth. Both note and plume plunge from the spire's hook. | 86 | 8 | 51 | 95 | 8 |
| To shut the sun, plunge, mount your darkened keys | 118 | 5 | 71 | 130 | 9 |
| **PLUNGED** | | | | | |
| Plunged in its fruit; | 39 | 3 | 21 | 45 | 3 |
| With a hand plunged through her hair, | 93 | 12 | 56 | 102 | 12 |
| **PLUNGING** | | | | | |
| Plunging and piercing in his course | 150 | 22 | 83 | 168 | 6 |

|  | U.K. | | | U.S. | |
| --- | --- | --- | --- | --- | --- |
|  | *Page* | *Line* | *Poem* | *Page* | *Line* |

**PLUCK**

And pluck a mandrake music from the marrow-root. — 60 / 18 / 36 / 69 / 18

Pluck, cock, my sea eye, said medusa's scripture, — 74 / 5 / 44 / 83 / 5

**PLUCKED**

And love plucked out the stinging siren's eye, — 74 / 7 / 44 / 83 / 7

In a wind that plucked a goose, — 77 / 10 / 45 / 86 / 10

Listen and look where she sails the goose plucked sea, — 122 / 20 / 72 / 135 / 20

**PLUCKS**

And the harp shaped voice of the water's dust plucks in a fold — 121 / 24 / 72 / 134 / 19

**POEM**

Poem in October — 102 / / 63 / 113 /

Poem on his birthday — 170 / / 88 / 190 /

**POINT**

The halves that pierce the pin's point in the air, — 31 / 2 / 18 / 36 / 2

At the point of love, forsaken and afraid. — 120 / 5 / 72 / 132 / 10

**POINTED**

Be by your one ghost pierced, his pointed ferrule, — 38 / 1 / 20 / 43 / 11

Into a polestar pointed on an icicle. — 60 / 6 / 36 / 69 / 6

**POISE**

Or poise the day on a horn. — 92 / 5 / 55 / 101 / 11

**POISON**

Hands, hold you poison or grapes? — 58 / 9 / 35 / 67 / 9

Ships, hold you poison or grapes? — 58 / 25 / 35 / 67 / 25

Hold you poison or grapes? — 59 / 8 / 35 / 68 / 8

**POKER**

(Questions are hunchbacks to the poker marrow). — 73 / 2 / 44 / 82 / 2

**POKERS**

Spoilers and pokers of sleep, — 134 / 5 / 79 / 150 / 5

**POLAR**

The polar eagle with his tread of snow. — 152 / 8 / 83 / 169 / 20

**POLE**

From pole to pole leapt round the snail-waked world. — 75 / 14 / 44 / 84 / 14

**POLE-HILLS**

Pin-legged on pole-hills with a black medusa — 73 / 22 / 44 / 82 / 22

**POLES**

O see the poles of promise in the boys. — 2 / 24 / 2 / 3 / 6

O see the poles are kissing as they cross. — 3 / 6 / 2 / 3 / 12

From poles of skull and toe the windy blood — 24 / 14 / 15 / 29 / 14

In the poles of the year — 122 / 11 / 72 / 135 / 11

**POLESTAR**

Into a polestar pointed on an icicle. — 60 / 6 / 36 / 69 / 6

Your polestar neighbor, sun of another street, — 117 / 17 / 71 / 129 / 17

|  | U.K. |  |  | U.S. |  |
|---|---|---|---|---|---|
|  | Page | Line | Poem | Page | Line |
| **POLLEN** |  |  |  |  |  |
| Like pollen | 143 | 11 | 82 | 160 | 11 |
| **POND** |  |  |  |  |  |
| And the duck pond glass and the blinding byres alone | 120 | 10 | 72 | 132 | 15 |
| **PONDEROUS** |  |  |  |  |  |
| Nor when all ponderous heaven's host of waters breaks. | 97 | 20 | 59 | 108 | 20 |
| **PONDS** |  |  |  |  |  |
| The spittled eyes, the salt ponds in the sleeves, | 87 | 5 | 52 | 96 | 5 |
| **POOL** |  |  |  |  |  |
| The hand that whirls the water in the pool | 9 | 11 | 6 | 10 | 11 |
| Pool at the wanting centre, in the folds | 123 | 18 | 72 | 137 | 8 |
| **POOLED** |  |  |  |  |  |
| And the mussel pooled and the heron | 102 | 3 | 63 | 113 | 3 |
| **POOLS** |  |  |  |  |  |
| Country, your sport is summer, and December's pools | 49 | 7 | 29 | 58 | 7 |
| **POOR** |  |  |  |  |  |
| At poor peace I sing | vii | 23 | 1 | xv | 23 |
| Poor peace as the sun sets | x | 6 | 1 | xviii | 12 |
| And these poor nerves so wired to the skull | 10 | 6 | 7 | 11 | 6 |
| And a lamp of lightning for the poor in the dark; | 89 | 11 | 53 | 98 | 11 |
| Veined his poor hand I held, and I saw |  |  | 91 | 200 | 16 |
| All his bones crying, and poor in all but pain, |  |  | 91 | 200 | 21 |
| **POPPIED** |  |  |  |  |  |
| And leave the poppied pickthank where he lies; | 5 | 15 | 3 | 5 | 15 |
| **POSSESSED** |  |  |  |  |  |
| She has come possessed | 108 | 10 | 66 | 119 | 10 |
| Possessed by the skies | 108 | 12 | 66 | 119 | 12 |
| **POT** |  |  |  |  |  |
| Behind a pot of ferns the wagging clock | 16 | 17 | 11 | 19 | 17 |
| By the spit and the black pot in the log bright light | 120 | 2 | 72 | 132 | 7 |
| By the spit and the black pot in the log bright light. | 122 | 7 | 72 | 135 | 7 |
| **POUNCING** |  |  |  |  |  |
| Yet out of the beaked, web dark and the pouncing boughs | 163 | 25 | 86 | 183 | 6 |
| **POUND** |  |  |  |  |  |
| All from the oil, the pound of lava. | 33 | 3 | 19 | 38 | 3 |
| **POUNDED** |  |  |  |  |  |
| Milled dust of the apple tree and the pounded islands | 164 | 10 | 86 | 183 | 17 |
| **POUNDS** |  |  |  |  |  |
| Puffing the pounds of manna up through the dew to heaven, | 94 | 5 | 57 | 104 | 5 |

POUR

| | U.K. Page | U.K. Line | Poem | U.S. Page | U.S. Line |
|---|---|---|---|---|---|
| **POUR** | | | | | |
| Pour like a halo on the caps and serpents. | 75 | 24 | 44 | 84 | 24 |
| The windows pour into their heart | 124 | 11 | 73 | 138 | 11 |
| **POURED** | | | | | |
| In the sniffed and poured snow on the tip of the tongue of the year | 77 | 5 | 45 | 86 | 5 |
| **POURING** | | | | | |
| In the pouring town, | 38 | 16 | 20 | 44 | 6 |
| She married in this pouring place, | 93 | 4 | 56 | 102 | 4 |
| **POUTING** | | | | | |
| Slunk pouting out when the limp time came; | 175 | 15 | 89 | 195 | 20 |
| **POUCH** | | | | | |
| And boys are full and foreign in the pouch. | 3 | 3 | 2 | 3 | 9 |
| **POVERTY** | | | | | |
| I bitterly take to task my poverty and craft: | 94 | 3 | 57 | 104 | 3 |
| **POWDER** | | | | | |
| He blew like powder to the light | 4 | 14 | 3 | 4 | 14 |
| **POWER** | | | | | |
| And power was contagious in my birth, second | 28 | 21 | 17 | 34 | 1 |
| **PRAISE** | | | | | |
| Coo rooing the woods' praise, | ix | 10 | 1 | xvii | 10 |
| Praise to our faring hearts. | 15 | 22 | 10 | 18 | 2 |
| When, praise is blessed, her pride in mast and fountain | 78 | 4 | 46 | 87 | 4 |
| Magnified out of praise; her death was a still drop; | 87 | 17 | 52 | 96 | 17 |
| The mazes of his praise and envious tongue were worked in flames and shells. | 95 | 17 | 58 | 105 | 17 |
| To shoot and sing your praise, | 117 | 8 | 71 | 129 | 8 |
| Who pay no praise or wages | 128 | 19 | 76 | 142 | 19 |
| Praise that the spring time is all | 158 | 14 | 84 | 177 | 14 |
| On to the fields of praise | 160 | 14 | 85 | 179 | 14 |
| Now the tales praise | 163 | 10 | 86 | 182 | 10 |
| All praise of the hawk on fire in hawk-eyed dusk be sung, | 168 | 3 | 87 | 188 | 7 |
| Spins its morning of praise, | 173 | 18 | 88 | 193 | 18 |
| **PRAISED** | | | | | |
| There must, be praised, some certainty, | 48 | 7 | 28 | 56 | 7 |
| On the last street wave praised | 95 | 4 | 58 | 105 | 4 |
| Was flying through the house as though the she bird praised | 122 | 3 | 72 | 135 | 3 |
| Praised the sun | 142 | 3 | 82 | 159 | 3 |
| Always good luck, praised the finned in the feather | 154 | 5 | 83 | 172 | 5 |
| **PRAISES** | | | | | |
| After the funeral, mule praises, brays, | 87 | 1 | 52 | 96 | 1 |
| **PRAISING** | | | | | |
| Praising the mortal error | 10 | 17 | 7 | 11 | 17 |

| | U.K. | | | U.S. | |
|---|---|---|---|---|---|
| | Page | Line | Poem | Page | Line |
| **PRANCING** | | | | | |
| Of psalms and shadows among the pincered sandcrabs prancing | 167 | 24 | 87 | 188 | 5 |
| **PRAY** | | | | | |
| Shall I let pray the shadow of a sound | 101 | 10 | 62 | 112 | 10 |
| Curse, bless, me now with your fierce tears, I pray. | 116 | 17 | 70 | 128 | 17 |
| I pray though I belong | 143 | 14 | 82 | 160 | 14 |
| In the centre of dark I pray him | 144 | 17 | 82 | 161 | 17 |
| Be I pray | 147 | 12 | 82 | 164 | 12 |
| Through throats where many rivers meet, the women pray, | 176 | 6 | 90 | 197 | 6 |
| **PRAYED** | | | | | |
| Turns of your prayed flesh, nor shall I shoo the bird below me: | 109 | 27 | 67 | 121 | 1 |
| He knelt, he wept, he prayed, | 120 | 1 | 72 | 132 | 6 |
| He wept from the crest of grief, he prayed to the veiled sky | 120 | 7 | 72 | 132 | 12 |
| Vales where he prayed to come to the last harm | 122 | 29 | 72 | 136 | 9 |
| I prayed in the crouching room, by his blind bed, | | | 91 | 200 | 13 |
| **PRAYER** | | | | | |
| Now stamp the Lord's Prayer on a grain of rice, | 74 | 15 | 44 | 83 | 15 |
| And the child not caring to whom he climbs his prayer | 100 | 17 | 61 | 111 | 17 |
| I turn the corner of prayer and burn | 148 | 1 | 82 | 165 | 1 |
| Under the prayer wheeling moon in the rosy wood | 163 | 18 | 86 | 182 | 18 |
| The leaping saga of prayer! And high, there, on the hare- | 164 | 17 | 86 | 184 | 3 |
| But her faith that each vast night and the saga of prayer | 166 | 3 | 86 | 186 | 3 |
| Of minnows wreathing around their prayer; | 171 | 2 | 88 | 191 | 2 |
| The Conversation of Prayer | 100 | | 61 | 111 | |
| Vision and Prayer | 137 | | 82 | 154 | |
| **PRAYER'S** | | | | | |
| One. The sun roars at the prayer's end | 148 | 17 | 82 | 165 | 17 |
| **PRAYERPIECE** | | | | | |
| The bayonet tongue in this undefended prayer-piece, | 85 | 5 | 50 | 94 | 5 |
| **PRAYERS** | | | | | |
| The conversation of prayers about to be said | 100 | 1 | 61 | 111 | 1 |
| The sound about to be said in the two prayers | 100 | 9 | 61 | 111 | 9 |
| The conversation of prayers about to be said | 100 | 13 | 61 | 111 | 13 |
| Into the home of prayers | 120 | 11 | 72 | 132 | 16 |
| Rags and prayers down the knee- | 122 | 16 | 72 | 135 | 16 |
| And the home of prayers and fires, the tale ended. | 122 | 30 | 72 | 136 | 10 |

| | U.K. | | | U.S. | |
|---|---|---|---|---|---|
| | Page | Line | Poem | Page | Line |
| **PRAYERWHEEL** | | | | | |
| And a whirlpool drives the prayerwheel; | 83 | 9 | 49 | 92 | 9 |
| **PRAYING** | | | | | |
| With water praying and call of seagull and rook | 102 | 6 | 63 | 113 | 6 |
| In the praying windows of waves | 150 | 4 | 83 | 167 | 8 |
| **PRAYS** | | | | | |
| The voice of bird on coral prays. | 83 | 18 | 49 | 92 | 18 |
| Of the charting sleepers prays | 146 | 15 | 82 | 163 | 15 |
| With all the living, prays, | 172 | 12 | 88 | 192 | 12 |
| Chastity prays for me, piety sings, | 175 | 28 | 89 | 196 | 9 |
| **PREACHERS** | | | | | |
| And serve me right as the preachers warn, | 175 | 9 | 89 | 195 | 14 |
| **PRESENCE** | | | | | |
| Yet this I make in a forgiving presence. | 80 | 15 | 46 | 89 | 23 |
| **PRESENT** | | | | | |
| Over the past table I repeat this present grace. | 77 | 25 | 45 | 86 | 25 |
| The present mouth, and the sweetly blown trumpet of lies, | 85 | 6 | 50 | 94 | 6 |
| **PRESSED** | | | | | |
| An old god's dugs are pressed and pricked, | 44 | 9 | 25 | 52 | 9 |
| Woe drip from the dishrag hands and the pressed sponge of the forehead, | 96 | 20 | 58 | 107 | 3 |
| **PRETENDER** | | | | | |
| The bright pretender, the ridiculous sea dandy | 133 | 14 | 78 | 148 | 17 |
| **PRICK** | | | | | |
| And prick the thumb-stained heaven through the thimble. | 31 | 3 | 18 | 36 | 3 |
| **PRICKED** | | | | | |
| An old god's dugs are pressed and pricked, | 44 | 9 | 25 | 52 | 9 |
| **PRIDE** | | | | | |
| When, praise is blessed, her pride in mast and fountain | 78 | 4 | 46 | 87 | 4 |
| And, pride is last, is like a child alone | 78 | 13 | 46 | 87 | 13 |
| And, mild as pardon from a cloud of pride, | 80 | 6 | 46 | 89 | 14 |
| Nor could share, for his pride, to the least | 114 | 21 | 69 | 126 | 21 |
| A cold kind man brave in his narrow pride | | | 91 | 200 | 3 |
| An old kind man brave in his burning pride. | | | 91 | 201 | 3 |
| **PRIDES** | | | | | |
| Prides of to-morrow suckling in her eyes, | 80 | 14 | 46 | 89 | 22 |
| **PRIEST** | | | | | |
| With priest and pharaoh bed my gentle wound, | 76 | 5 | 44 | 85 | 5 |
| When, with his torch and hourglass, like a sulphur priest, | 83 | 2 | 49 | 92 | 2 |
| In time like outlaw rains on that priest, water, | 86 | 6 | 51 | 95 | 6 |
| Child who was priest and servants, | 130 | 28 | 77 | 145 | 6 |
| The stream from the priest black wristed spinney and sleeves | 165 | 1 | 86 | 184 | 9 |

|  | U.K. | | | U.S. | |
|  | Page | Line | Poem | Page | Line |
| And every soul His priest, | 172 | 7 | 88 | 192 | 7 |
| PRIEST'S |  |  |  |  |  |
| With priest's grave foot and hand of five assassins | 78 | 25 | 46 | 88 | 2 |
| PRIESTED |  |  |  |  |  |
| Priested shore | 102 | 4 | 63 | 113 | 4 |
| PRIESTS |  |  |  |  |  |
| When black birds died like priests in the cloaked hedge row | 122 | 12 | 72 | 135 | 12 |
| PRIME |  |  |  |  |  |
| Brandy and ripe in my bright, bass prime, | 174 | 28 | 89 | 195 | 4 |
| PRINCE |  |  |  |  |  |
| And honoured among wagons I was prince of the apple towns | 159 | 6 | 85 | 178 | 6 |
| And prince of ice | 162 | 12 | 86 | 181 | 12 |
| Nor the tusked prince, in the ruttish farm, at the rind | 163 | 14 | 86 | 182 | 14 |
| PRINT |  |  |  |  |  |
| From the first print of the unshodden foot, the lifting | 20 | 10 | 13 | 24 | 10 |
| 'Who could snap off the shapeless print | 70 | 12 | 43 | 79 | 16 |
| And the heart print of man | 137 | 12 | 82 | 154 | 12 |
| PRINTED |  |  |  |  |  |
| My wordy wounds are printed with your hair | 13 | 19 | 9 | 15 | 5 |
| PRINTS |  |  |  |  |  |
| Draw on the glove of prints, dead Cairo's henna | 75 | 23 | 44 | 84 | 23 |
| Black night, I left my quivering prints. | 174 | 24 | 89 | 194 | 24 |
| PRISON |  |  |  |  |  |
| An inch in froth. Chimes cheat the prison spire, pelter | 86 | 5 | 51 | 95 | 5 |
| The dazzling prison | 144 | 13 | 82 | 161 | 13 |
| PRISONERS |  |  |  |  |  |
| Prisoners of wishes locked their eyes | 125 | 7 | 74 | 139 | 7 |
| PRIVATE |  |  |  |  |  |
| The features in their private dark | 63 | 5 | 38 | 72 | 5 |
| PROBE |  |  |  |  |  |
| No third eye probe into a rainbow's sex | 67 | 25 | 41 | 76 | 25 |
| PROCESS |  |  |  |  |  |
| A process in the weather of the heart | 6 | 1 | 4 | 6 | 1 |
| A process in the eye forwarns | 6 | 7 | 4 | 6 | 7 |
| A process in the weather of the world | 6 | 19 | 4 | 7 | 1 |
| A process blows the moon into the sun, | 6 | 22 | 4 | 7 | 4 |
| A process in the weather of the heart | 6 |  | 4 | 6 |  |
| PRODIGAL |  |  |  |  |  |
| Lead her prodigal home to his terror, | 157 | 7 | 83 | 175 | 19 |
| My arising prodigal | 158 | 18 | 84 | 177 | 18 |
| PRODIGALS |  |  |  |  |  |
| But do not travel down dumb wind like prodigals. | 86 | 11 | 51 | 95 | 11 |

369

|  |  | U.K. |  |  | U.S. |  |
|---|---|---|---|---|---|---|
|  |  | *Page* | *Line* | *Poem* | *Page* | *Line* |
| **PRODIGIES** |  |  |  |  |  |  |
| And the endless beginning of prodigies suffers open.' |  | 98 | 7 | 59 | 109 | 10 |
| **PROFLIGATES** |  |  |  |  |  |  |
| The reptile profligates in a flame, |  | 134 | 4 | 79 | 150 | 4 |
| **PROLOGUE** |  |  |  |  |  |  |
| Author's Prologue |  | vii |  | 1 | xv |  |
| **PROMISE** |  |  |  |  |  |  |
| O see the poles of promise in the boys. |  | 2 | 24 | 2 | 3 | 6 |
| Stripping my loin of promise, |  | 10 | 14 | 7 | 11 | 14 |
| The insect fable is the certain promise. |  | 41 | 18 | 23 | 47 | 18 |
| **PROMISES** |  |  |  |  |  |  |
| He promises a secret heat. |  | 10 | 15 | 7 | 11 | 15 |
| **PROPER** |  |  |  |  |  |  |
| Who play the proper gentleman and lady. |  | 47 | 4 | 27 | 55 | 4 |
| **PROPHET-PROGENY** |  |  |  |  |  |  |
| No prophet-progeny of mine, |  | 134 | 26 | 79 | 151 | 4 |
| **PROPHETS** |  |  |  |  |  |  |
| Prophets and fibre kings in oil and letter, |  | 75 | 20 | 44 | 84 | 20 |
| And prophets loud on the burned dunes; |  | 156 | 5 | 83 | 174 | 13 |
| **PROPPED** |  |  |  |  |  |  |
| Propped between trees and water |  | 111 | 3 | 68 | 123 | 3 |
| **PROSPERED** |  |  |  |  |  |  |
| The body prospered, teeth in the marrowed gums, |  | 20 | 16 | 13 | 24 | 16 |
| **PROUD** |  |  |  |  |  |  |
| The proud spine spurning turn and twist. |  | 10 | 5 | 7 | 11 | 5 |
| In that proud sailing tree with branches driven |  | 78 | 6 | 46 | 87 | 6 |
| And a silk pigeon's guilt in her proud absence, |  | 78 | 17 | 46 | 87 | 17 |
| Proud as a sucked stone and huge as sand-grains. |  | 78 | 23 | 46 | 87 | 23 |
| Weighed in rock shroud, is my proud pyramid; |  | 79 | 15 | 46 | 88 | 18 |
| Delivered seas my love from her proud place |  | 80 | 9 | 46 | 89 | 17 |
| Two proud, blacked brothers cry, |  | 126 | 1 | 74 | 140 | 1 |
| Not for the proud man apart |  | 128 | 12 | 76 | 142 | 12 |
| Too proud to die; broken and blind he died |  |  |  | 91 | 200 | 1 |
| I am not too proud to cry that He and he |  |  |  | 91 | 200 | 19 |
| Too proud to cry, too frail to check the tears, |  |  |  | 91 | 201 | 14 |
| The tears out of his eyes, too proud to cry. |  |  |  | 91 | 201 | 18 |
| **PROW** |  |  |  |  |  |  |
| Sing through the water-spoken prow |  | 152 | 6 | 83 | 169 | 18 |
| **PROWED** |  |  |  |  |  |  |
| Huloo, my prowed dove with a flute! |  | x | 14 | 1 | xviii | 20 |
| **PROWL** |  |  |  |  |  |  |
| And fires where he should prowl down the cloud |  | 120 | 12 | 72 | 132 | 17 |
| **PSALM** |  |  |  |  |  |  |
| Argument of the hewn voice, gesture and psalm, |  | 88 | 9 | 52 | 97 | 9 |

|  | U.K. |  | Poem | U.S. |  |
|---|---|---|---|---|---|
|  | Page | Line |  | Page | Line |
| **PSALMS** | | | | | |
| With their nightingales and psalms | 128 | 16 | 76 | 142 | 16 |
| Of psalms and shadows among the pincered sandcrabs prancing | 167 | 24 | 87 | 188 | 5 |
| **PUDDLES** | | | | | |
| Whose hooded, fountain heart once fell in puddles | 87 | 14 | 52 | 96 | 14 |
| **PUFFBALL** | | | | | |
| On a tongued puffball) | ix | 22 | 1 | xvii | 22 |
| **PUFFED** | | | | | |
| And opium head, crow stalk, puffed, cut, and blown, | 78 | 10 | 46 | 87 | 10 |
| The puffed birds hopping and hunting, the milkmaids | 119 | 23 | 72 | 132 | 3 |
| **PUFFING** | | | | | |
| Puffing the pounds of manna up through the dew to heaven, | 94 | 5 | 57 | 104 | 5 |
| **PULL** | | | | | |
| Will pull the thunderbolts | 118 | 4 | 71 | 130 | 8 |
| **PULLED** | | | | | |
| Man broke the sun, pulled the wind down. | 39 | 10 | 21 | 45 | 10 |
| Cathedral calm in the pulled house; | 83 | 15 | 49 | 92 | 15 |
| **PULLEYS** | | | | | |
| By midnight pulleys that unhouse the tomb. | 14 | 10 | 10 | 16 | 10 |
| **PULLS** | | | | | |
| The sleepy man of winter pulls, | 2 | 5 | 2 | 2 | 5 |
| Pulls down the shabby curtains of the skin; | 6 | 23 | 4 | 7 | 5 |
| He pulls the chain, the cistern moves. | 10 | 20 | 7 | 11 | 20 |
| And though my love pulls the pale, nippled air, | 80 | 13 | 46 | 89 | 21 |
| In a hoisted cloud, at drop of dusk, he pulls to his claws | 167 | 3 | 87 | 187 | 3 |
| **PULSE** | | | | | |
| There from their hearts the dogdayed pulse | 1 | 22 | 2 | 1 | 22 |
| O see the pulse of summer in the ice. | 1 | 24 | 2 | 1 | 24 |
| I have been told to reason by the pulse, | 63 | 11 | 38 | 72 | 11 |
| Forgotten dark, rest their pulse and bury their dead in her faithless sleep. | 115 | 23 | 69 | 127 | 23 |
| **PUMPED** | | | | | |
| Burst in the roots, pumped from the earth and rock | 22 | 17 | 14 | 27 | 17 |
| **PUNCTUAL** | | | | | |
| Where, punctual as death, we ring the stars; | 2 | 3 | 2 | 2 | 3 |
| **PUNISHES** | | | | | |
| With frosty fingers punishes my hair, | 16 | 2 | 11 | 19 | 2 |
| With fists of turnips punishes the land, | 17 | 4 | 11 | 20 | 4 |
| **PURE** | | | | | |
| On a star of faith pure as the drifting bread, | 119 | 12 | 72 | 131 | 12 |

PURE (continued)

| | U.K. | | | U.S. | |
|---|---|---|---|---|---|
| | *Page* | *Line* | *Poem* | *Page* | *Line* |
| Sun the father his quiver full of the infants of pure fire, | 158 | 19 | 84 | 177 | 19 |
| PURSE | | | | | |
| Belly of the rich year and the big purse of my body | 94 | 2 | 57 | 104 | 2 |
| PURSED | | | | | |
| Pursed lips at the receiver, | 64 | 17 | 39 | 73 | 17 |
| PUSH | | | | | |
| Push in their tides; | 24 | 3 | 15 | 29 | 3 |
| PUSHED | | | | | |
| Pushed up their hair, the dry wind steers | 11 | 5 | 8 | 12 | 5 |
| PUT | | | | | |
| A goose's quill has put an end to murder | 62 | 7 | 37 | 71 | 7 |
| That put an end to talk. | 62 | 8 | 37 | 71 | 8 |
| And put beside her a ram rose. | 65 | 24 | 40 | 74 | 24 |
| Put a tear for joy in the unearthly flood | 125 | 22 | 74 | 139 | 22 |
| He put on his clothes and stepped out and he died, | 135 | 2 | 80 | 152 | 2 |
| PUZZLE | | | | | |
| Flicked from the carbolic city puzzle in a bed of sores | 96 | 3 | 58 | 106 | 3 |
| PYRAMID | | | | | |
| My world is pyramid. The padded mummer | 31 | 7 | 18 | 36 | 7 |
| Weighed in rock shroud, is my proud pyramid; | 79 | 15 | 46 | 88 | 18 |
| My world is pyramid | 30 | | 18 | 35 | |
| PYRE | | | | | |
| The pyre yet to be lighted of my sins and days, | 109 | 3 | 67 | 120 | 3 |
| Out of the woebegone pyre | 158 | 16 | 84 | 177 | 16 |

# ENTRIES UNDER Q

| | | | | | |
|---|---|---|---|---|---|
| QUAKED | | | | | |
| Quaked the sick sea and snouted deep, | 151 | 2 | 83 | 168 | 10 |
| QUAKING | | | | | |
| Be at cloud quaking peace, | 172 | 9 | 88 | 192 | 9 |
| QUARREL | | | | | |
| A quarrel of weathers and trees in the windy spiral. | 36 | 18 | 20 | 41 | 18 |
| Roaring, crawling, quarrel | 91 | 8 | 55 | 100 | 8 |
| QUARRY | | | | | |
| Here break a kiss in no love's quarry. | 2 | 23 | 2 | 3 | 5 |

| | U.K. | | | U.S. | |
|---|---|---|---|---|---|
| | *Page* | *Line* | *Poem* | *Page* | *Line* |
| QUARTER | | | | | |
| Into a chiming quarter | 2 | 2 | 2 | 2 | 2 |
| A weather in the quarter of the veins | 6 | 4 | 4 | 6 | 4 |
| QUARTERED | | | | | |
| There in the deep with quartered shades | 1 | 16 | 2 | 1 | 16 |
| QUARTERS | | | | | |
| Quarters and graves | 146 | 12 | 82 | 163 | 12 |
| QUAY | | | | | |
| And the bulwarks of the dazzled quay. | 149 | 10 | 83 | 166 | 10 |
| QUAYRAIL | | | | | |
| Let the first Peter from a rainbow's quayrail | 76 | 15 | 44 | 85 | 15 |
| QUAYSTONE | | | | | |
| Harbours my anchored tongue, slips the quay-stone, | 78 | 3 | 46 | 87 | 3 |
| QUEEN | | | | | |
| The sheath-decked jacks, queen with a shuffled heart; | 73 | 13 | 44 | 82 | 13 |
| The lamped calligrapher, the queen in splints, | 75 | 21 | 44 | 84 | 21 |
| Queen Catherine howling bare | 113 | 12 | 69 | 125 | 12 |
| QUENCH | | | | | |
| Both quench his thirst he'll have a black reply. | 53 | 9 | 32 | 62 | 9 |
| QUENCHED | | | | | |
| 'The thirst is quenched, the hunger gone, | 65 | 17 | 40 | 74 | 17 |
| QUENCHLESS | | | | | |
| Manes, under his quenchless summer barbed gold to the bone, | 177 | 6 | 90 | 198 | 5 |
| QUESTION | | | | | |
| The child shall question all his days, | 53 | 7 | 32 | 62 | 7 |
| A claw I question from the mouse's bone, | 56 | 17 | 34 | 65 | 17 |
| QUESTIONS | | | | | |
| (Questions are hunchbacks to the poker marrow). | 73 | 2 | 44 | 82 | 2 |
| QUICK | | | | | |
| Is damp and dry; the quick and dead | 6 | 17 | 4 | 6 | 17 |
| Wearing the quick away. | 13 | 7 | 9 | 14 | 14 |
| And lets their trash be honoured as the quick. | 15 | 15 | 10 | 17 | 15 |
| In quick, sweet, cruel light till the locked ground sprout out, | 91 | 18 | 55 | 100 | 18 |
| Sang heaven hungry and the quick | 95 | 15 | 58 | 105 | 15 |
| Turns on the quick and the dead, and the man on the stairs | 100 | 14 | 61 | 111 | 14 |
| Cut to the still star in the order of the quick | 109 | 20 | 67 | 120 | 20 |
| In the muffled house, in the quick of night, | 120 | 4 | 72 | 132 | 9 |
| Masts and fishes to the still quick stars, | 172 | 17 | 88 | 192 | 17 |
| And the sizzling beds of the town cried, Quick!— | 174 | 20 | 89 | 194 | 20 |
| Quick in the wood at love, where a torch of foxes foams, | 177 | 14 | 90 | 198 | 13 |

| | U.K. | | | U.S. | |
| --- | --- | --- | --- | --- | --- |
| | Page | Line | Poem | Page | Line |
| QUICKENING | | | | | |
| Quickening for the riddled sea; | 42 | 18 | 24 | 49 | 18 |
| Quickening for the virgin sea; | 42 | 25 | 24 | 50 | 4 |
| QUICKENS | | | | | |
| And, when it quickens, alter the actions' pace | 63 | 12 | 38 | 72 | 12 |
| QUICKNESS | | | | | |
| Quickness of hand in the velvet glove | 107 | 12 | 65 | 118 | 12 |
| QUICKSAND | | | | | |
| Stirs the quicksand; that ropes the blowing wind | 9 | 12 | 6 | 10 | 12 |
| QUIET | | | | | |
| So fast I move defying time, the quiet gentleman | 63 | 14 | 38 | 72 | 14 |
| Now in the cloud's big breast lie quiet countries, | 80 | 8 | 46 | 89 | 16 |
| As quiet as a bone. | 133 | 23 | 78 | 149 | 6 |
| QUILL | | | | | |
| Froth, flute, fin and quill | vii | 7 | 1 | xv | 7 |
| A goose's quill has put an end to murder | 62 | 7 | 37 | 71 | 7 |
| QUILLED | | | | | |
| Felled and quilled, flash to my patch | ix | 32 | 1 | xviii | 6 |
| QUILTS | | | | | |
| Wherever I ramped in the clover quilts, | 174 | 22 | 89 | 194 | 22 |
| QUIVER | | | | | |
| Sun the father his quiver full of the infants of pure fire, | 158 | 19 | 84 | 177 | 19 |
| QUIVERING | | | | | |
| In the watched dark, quivering through locks and caves, | 118 | 3 | 71 | 130 | 7 |
| Black night, I left my quivering prints. | 174 | 24 | 89 | 194 | 24 |
| QUOTED | | | | | |
| By waste seas where the white bear quoted Virgil | 73 | 23 | 44 | 82 | 23 |

# ENTRIES UNDER R

| RABBLE | | | | | |
| --- | --- | --- | --- | --- | --- |
| Limp in the street of sea, among the rabble | 30 | 15 | 18 | 35 | 15 |
| RACED | | | | | |
| My wishes raced through the house high hay | 160 | 19 | 85 | 179 | 19 |
| RACK | | | | | |
| The rack of dreams my lily bones | 7 | 20 | 5 | 8 | 20 |
| RACKING | | | | | |
| In his slant, racking house | 170 | 25 | 88 | 190 | 25 |
| RACKS | | | | | |
| Twisting on racks when sinews give way, | 68 | 13 | 42 | 77 | 13 |

|  |  | U.K. |  |  | U.S. |  |
|---|---|---|---|---|---|---|
|  |  | *Page* | *Line* | *Poem* | *Page* | *Line* |
| RADIANT |  |  |  |  |  |  |
|  | Gabriel and radiant shrubbery as the morning grows joyful | 158 | 15 | 84 | 177 | 15 |
| RADIUM |  |  |  |  |  |  |
|  | Rarer than radium, | 125 | 2 | 74 | 139 | 2 |
| RAFT |  |  |  |  |  |  |
|  | Strung by the flaxen whale-weed, from the hangman's raft, | 37 | 14 | 20 | 42 | 20 |
| RAFTERS |  |  |  |  |  |  |
|  | Raise the live rafters of the eardrum, | 96 | 11 | 58 | 106 | 11 |
| RAG |  |  |  |  |  |  |
|  | Is corner-cast, breath's rag, scrawled weed, a vain | 78 | 9 | 46 | 87 | 9 |
| RAGE |  |  |  |  |  |  |
|  | Of fear, rage red, manalive, | viii | 22 | 1 | xvi | 22 |
|  | Rage me back to the making house. My hand unravel | 97 | 12 | 59 | 108 | 12 |
|  | Rage, rage against the dying of the light. | 116 | 3 | 70 | 128 | 3 |
|  | Rage, rage against the dying of the light. | 116 | 9 | 70 | 128 | 9 |
|  | Rage, rage against the dying of the light. | 116 | 15 | 70 | 128 | 15 |
|  | Rage, rage against the dying of the light. | 116 | 19 | 70 | 128 | 19 |
|  | Terror will rage apart | 171 | 16 | 88 | 191 | 16 |
|  | Rage shattered waters kick | 172 | 16 | 88 | 192 | 16 |
| RAGES |  |  |  |  |  |  |
|  | When only the moon rages | 128 | 3 | 76 | 142 | 3 |
| RAGGED |  |  |  |  |  |  |
|  | This ragged anniversary of two | 124 | 2 | 73 | 138 | 2 |
| RAGING |  |  |  |  |  |  |
|  | The parched and raging voice? | 91 | 22 | 55 | 100 | 22 |
|  | From the raging moon I write | 128 | 13 | 76 | 142 | 13 |
| RAGS |  |  |  |  |  |  |
|  | Then hang a ram rose over the rags. | 65 | 8 | 40 | 74 | 8 |
|  | Rags and prayers down the knee- | 122 | 16 | 72 | 135 | 16 |
| RAID |  |  |  |  |  |  |
|  | Ceremony After a Fire Raid | 129 |  | 77 | 143 |  |
|  | Among those Killed in the Dawn Raid was a Man Aged a Hundred | 135 |  | 80 | 152 |  |
| RAIL |  |  |  |  |  |  |
|  | But rail with your wizard's ribs the heart-shaped planet; | 60 | 15 | 36 | 69 | 15 |
| RAILINGS |  |  |  |  |  |  |
|  | Hurdles and guns and railings, as the boulders heave, | 49 | 16 | 29 | 58 | 16 |
|  | After the railings and shrubberies | 112 | 14 | 68 | 124 | 14 |
| RAIN |  |  |  |  |  |  |
|  | On tips of thought where thoughts smell in the rain; | 25 | 2 | 15 | 30 | 2 |

|  | U.K. | | | U.S. | |
|  | Page | Line | Poem | Page | Line |
| My fathers' ghost is climbing in the rain. | 27 | 5 | 16 | 32 | 10 |
| When it is rain where are the gods? | 44 | 5 | 25 | 52 | 5 |
| Why night-time rain and the breast's blood | 53 | 8 | 32 | 62 | 8 |
| Rain beats the sand and slates. | 59 | 3 | 35 | 68 | 3 |
| Lift its head to the blows of the rain; | 68 | 23 | 42 | 77 | 23 |
| The rain through her cold heart speak | 93 | 8 | 56 | 102 | 8 |
| To the rain wringing | 103 | 3 | 63 | 114 | 3 |
| Pale rain over the dwindling harbour | 103 | 6 | 63 | 114 | 6 |
| Too late in the wrong rain | 124 | 9 | 73 | 138 | 9 |
| A cloud blew the rain from its throat; | 150 | 16 | 83 | 167 | 20 |
| The statues of great rain stand still, | 154 | 15 | 83 | 172 | 15 |
| In the rain telling its beads, and the gravest ghost | 163 | 8 | 86 | 182 | 8 |
| As the rain falls, hail on the fleece, as the vale mist rides | 164 | 8 | 86 | 183 | 15 |
| Yard of the buttermilk rain on the pail! The sermon | 165 | 6 | 86 | 184 | 14 |
| And the rain wring out its tongues on the faded yard, | 178 | 11 | 90 | 199 | 12 |
| RAINBOW | | | | | |
| Till the three-coloured rainbow from my nipples | 75 | 13 | 44 | 84 | 13 |
| RAINBOW'S | | | | | |
| No third eye probe into a rainbow's sex | 67 | 25 | 41 | 76 | 25 |
| Let the first Peter from a rainbow's quayrail | 76 | 15 | 44 | 85 | 15 |
| RAINBOW-FISH | | | | | |
| The rainbow-fish bend in her joys, | 150 | 10 | 83 | 167 | 14 |
| RAINBOWS | | | | | |
| Shall rainbows be their tunics' colour? | 44 | 4 | 25 | 52 | 4 |
| RAINED | | | | | |
| Though the names on their weed grown stones are rained away, | 176 | 8 | 90 | 197 | 8 |
| RAINING | | | | | |
| He'll bathe his raining blood in the male sea | 117 | 19 | 71 | 129 | 19 |
| Deep the great bushed bait with raining lips | 151 | 3 | 83 | 168 | 11 |
| RAINS | | | | | |
| In time like outlaw rains on that priest, water, | 86 | 6 | 51 | 95 | 6 |
| RAINY | | | | | |
| The leaden stars, the rainy hammer | 7 | 11 | 5 | 8 | 11 |
| Or that rainy tongue beat back | 93 | 13 | 56 | 102 | 13 |
| In rainy autumn | 102 | 15 | 63 | 113 | 15 |
| RAISE | | | | | |
| Can never raise the midnight of a chuckle, | 13 | 11 | 9 | 14 | 18 |
| Raise up this red-eyed earth? | 15 | 3 | 10 | 17 | 3 |
| Shall raise a lamp | 56 | 25 | 34 | 66 | 4 |
| Raise the live rafters of the eardrum, | 96 | 11 | 58 | 106 | 11 |
| Who'd raise the organs of the counted dust | 117 | 7 | 71 | 129 | 7 |

|  | U.K. | | | U.S. | |
|---|---|---|---|---|---|
|  | *Page* | *Line* | *Poem* | *Page* | *Line* |
| RAISED | | | | | |
| Raised up a voice, and, climbing on the words, | 26 | 22 | 16 | 32 | 2 |
| And ghostly comets over the raised fists. | 53 | 26 | 32 | 62 | 26 |
| A calm wind blows that raised the trees like hair | 80 | 11 | 46 | 89 | 19 |
| But I, Ann's bard on a raised hearth, call all | 87 | 21 | 52 | 96 | 21 |
| And the wild wings were raised | 122 | 1 | 72 | 135 | 1 |
| RAISING | | | | | |
| Casts to the pine roots, raising man like a mountain | 35 | 11 | 20 | 40 | 11 |
| RAKE | | | | | |
| That will rake at last all currencies of the marked breath | 94 | 8 | 57 | 104 | 8 |
| Fire on starlight, rake Jesu's stream; | 150 | 19 | 83 | 168 | 3 |
| RAKING | | | | | |
| Comes designed to my love to steal not her tide raking | 166 | 1 | 86 | 186 | 1 |
| RAM | | | | | |
| Then hang a ram rose over the rags. | 65 | 8 | 40 | 74 | 8 |
| And put beside her a ram rose. | 65 | 24 | 40 | 74 | 24 |
| The black ram, shuffling of the year, old winter, | 72 | 15 | 44 | 81 | 15 |
| With fuming bows and ram of ice, | 150 | 18 | 83 | 168 | 2 |
| (Sighed the old ram rod, dying of women), | 174 | 3 | 89 | 194 | 3 |
| (Sighed the old ram rod, dying of bitches), | 174 | 15 | 89 | 194 | 15 |
| (Sighed the old ram rod, dying of welcome), | 174 | 27 | 89 | 195 | 3 |
| (Sighed the old ram rod, dying of downfall), | 175 | 10 | 89 | 195 | 15 |
| (Sighed the old ram rod, dying of strangers), | 175 | 22 | 89 | 196 | 3 |
| RAMMED | | | | | |
| Rammed in the marching heart, hole | 28 | 14 | 17 | 33 | 14 |
| RAMPART | | | | | |
| With her rampart to his tapping, | 42 | 3 | 24 | 49 | 3 |
| With her rampart to his tapping, | 42 | 10 | 24 | 49 | 10 |
| Through the rampart of the sky | 42 | 15 | 24 | 49 | 15 |
| Through the rampart of the sky | 42 | 22 | 24 | 50 | 1 |
| RAMPED | | | | | |
| Wherever I ramped in the clover quilts, | 174 | 22 | 89 | 194 | 22 |
| RAMSHACKLING | | | | | |
| And the tusked, ramshackling sea exults; | 173 | 13 | 88 | 193 | 13 |
| RAN | | | | | |
| Him up and he ran like a wind after the kindling flight | 122 | 9 | 72 | 135 | 9 |
| Under the one leaved trees ran a scarecrow of snow | 122 | 14 | 72 | 135 | 14 |
| I ran my heedless ways, | 160 | 18 | 85 | 179 | 18 |
| And their firefly hairpins flew, and the ricks ran round— | 177 | 21 | 90 | 199 | 1 |
| And cut the birds' boughs that the minstrel sap ran red. | 178 | 8 | 90 | 199 | 9 |

|  |  | U.K. |  |  | U.S. |  |
|  |  | Page | Line | Poem | Page | Line |
| **RANG** |  |  |  |  |  |  |
| No Time, spoke the clocks, no God, rang the bells, |  | 134 | 28 | 79 | 151 | 6 |
| When all the keys shot from the locks, and rang. |  | 135 | 8 | 80 | 152 | 8 |
| The trodden town rang its cobbles for luck. |  | 149 | 4 | 83 | 166 | 4 |
| And the sabbath rang slowly |  | 159 | 17 | 85 | 178 | 17 |
| **RANGE** |  |  |  |  |  |  |
| Range on the sky-scraping place. |  | 43 | 21 | 24 | 51 | 7 |
| Range from the grave-groping place. |  | 43 | 28 | 24 | 51 | 14 |
| **RANGING** |  |  |  |  |  |  |
| My girl ranging the night in the rose and shire |  | 162 | 9 | 86 | 181 | 9 |
| **RANT** |  |  |  |  |  |  |
| Lops, as a bush plumed with flames, the rant of the fierce eye, |  | 92 | 10 | 55 | 101 | 16 |
| And fire, the flying rant |  | 106 | 3 | 64 | 117 | 3 |
| **RANTS** |  |  |  |  |  |  |
| Death from a bandage, rants the mask of scholars |  | 76 | 2 | 44 | 85 | 2 |
| **RAPE** |  |  |  |  |  |  |
| Rape and rebellion in the nurseries of my face, |  | 85 | 3 | 50 | 94 | 3 |
| **RAPING** |  |  |  |  |  |  |
| Last night in a raping wave |  | 113 | 7 | 69 | 125 | 7 |
| **RARE** |  |  |  |  |  |  |
| Sleep, good, for ever, slow and deep, spelled rare and wise, |  | 162 | 8 | 86 | 181 | 8 |
| **RARENESS** |  |  |  |  |  |  |
| Eyed, in the haloed house, in her rareness and hilly |  | 165 | 18 | 86 | 185 | 8 |
| **RARER** |  |  |  |  |  |  |
| Rarer than radium, |  | 125 | 2 | 74 | 139 | 2 |
| **RASCAL** |  |  |  |  |  |  |
| I mean by time the cast and curfew rascal of our marriage, |  | 84 | 1 | 49 | 93 | 7 |
| **RASPED** |  |  |  |  |  |  |
| Rasped at last, and I stumbled and sucked, |  | 107 | 8 | 65 | 118 | 8 |
| **RATTLED** |  |  |  |  |  |  |
| I piece my flesh that rattled on the yards |  | 31 | 14 | 18 | 36 | 14 |
| **RAVE** |  |  |  |  |  |  |
| Old age should burn and rave at close of day; |  | 116 | 2 | 70 | 128 | 2 |
| **RAVEN** |  |  |  |  |  |  |
| Hearing the raven cough in winter sticks, |  | 16 | 6 | 11 | 19 | 6 |
| And the cage for the scythe-eyed raven. |  | 33 | 21 | 19 | 39 | 3 |
| **RAVEN'S** |  |  |  |  |  |  |
| Some let me tell you of the raven's sins. |  | 16 | 24 | 11 | 19 | 24 |
| **RAVENED** |  |  |  |  |  |  |
| For who unmanningly haunts the mountain ravened eaves |  | 163 | 1 | 86 | 182 | 1 |

|  | U.K. |  |  | U.S. |  |
|  | Page | Line | Poem | Page | Line |
|---|---|---|---|---|---|
| **RAVES** |  |  |  |  |  |
| Yet raves at her will | 108 | 14 | 66 | 119 | 14 |
| **RAW-EDGED** |  |  |  |  |  |
| Rehearsing heat upon a raw-edged nerve. | 12 | 19 | 9 | 13 | 19 |
| **RAYS** |  |  |  |  |  |
| Her robin breasted tree, three Marys in the rays. | 163 | 6 | 86 | 182 | 6 |
| And gallows, up the rays of his eyes the small birds of the bay | 167 | 4 | 87 | 187 | 4 |
| **RAYED** |  |  |  |  |  |
| A she bird rose and rayed like a burning bride. | 121 | 14 | 72 | 134 | 9 |
| All the fishes were rayed in blood, | 149 | 23 | 83 | 167 | 3 |
| **RAZED** |  |  |  |  |  |
| Who razed my wooden folly stands aghast, | 46 | 22 | 27 | 54 | 22 |
| The stained flats of heaven hit and razed | 95 | 2 | 58 | 105 | 2 |
| **REACHED** |  |  |  |  |  |
| Has not yet reached the ground. | 63 | 19 | 38 | 72 | 19 |
| **REACHING** |  |  |  |  |  |
| Reaching a second ground far from the stars; | 26 | 7 | 16 | 31 | 7 |
| **READ** |  |  |  |  |  |
| And read, in a shell, | 168 | 1 | 87 | 188 | 5 |
| **READYMADE** |  |  |  |  |  |
| It was sweet to drown in the readymade handy water | 133 | 16 | 78 | 148 | 19 |
| **REASON** |  |  |  |  |  |
| I have been told to reason by the heart, | 63 | 9 | 38 | 72 | 9 |
| I have been told to reason by the pulse, | 63 | 11 | 38 | 72 | 11 |
| **REBEL** |  |  |  |  |  |
| 'Rebel against the binding moon | 65 | 9 | 40 | 74 | 9 |
| Rebel against the flesh and bone, | 65 | 14 | 40 | 74 | 14 |
| Rebel against my father's dream | 66 | 3 | 40 | 75 | 3 |
| **REBELLION** |  |  |  |  |  |
| Rape and rebellion in the nurseries of my face, | 85 | 3 | 50 | 94 | 3 |
| **REBORN** |  |  |  |  |  |
| That belled and bounded with the fossil and the dew reborn. | 123 | 10 | 72 | 136 | 20 |
| **RECEIVE** |  |  |  |  |  |
| Shall she receive a bellyful of weeds | 90 | 5 | 54 | 99 | 5 |
| **RECEIVER** |  |  |  |  |  |
| Pursed lips at the receiver, | 64 | 17 | 39 | 73 | 17 |
| **RECORDERS** |  |  |  |  |  |
| These are your years' recorders. The circular world stands still.) | 37 | 21 | 20 | 143 | 4 |
| **RECORDS** |  |  |  |  |  |
| (The wound records), | 56 | 9 | 34 | 65 | 9 |
| **RED** |  |  |  |  |  |
| Of fear, rage red, manalive, | viii | 22 | 1 | xvi | 22 |

379

RED (continued)

|  | U.K. | | | U.S. | |
|---|---|---|---|---|---|
|  | Page | Line | Poem | Page | Line |
| Drives my red blood; that dries the mouthing streams | 9 | 7 | 6 | 10 | 7 |
| If the red tickle as the cattle calve | 12 | 4 | 9 | 13 | 4 |
| The sun was red, the moon was grey, | 20 | 14 | 13 | 24 | 14 |
| Red in an Austrian volley. | 31 | 15 | 18 | 36 | 15 |
| That out of a bower of red swine | 66 | 4 | 40 | 75 | 4 |
| My nest of mercies in the rude, red tree. | 76 | 22 | 44 | 85 | 22 |
| Rounds to look at the red, wagged root. | 77 | 12 | 45 | 86 | 12 |
| Who follow the red rivers, hollow | 82 | 3 | 48 | 91 | 3 |
| The strata of the shore and drown red rock; | 82 | 20 | 48 | 91 | 20 |
| Claw of the crabbed veins squeeze from each red particle | 91 | 21 | 55 | 100 | 21 |
| Die in red feathers when the flying heaven's cut, | 92 | 12 | 55 | 101 | 18 |
| And her red lips were kissed black, | 93 | 18 | 56 | 102 | 18 |
| A blazing red harsh head tear up | 93 | 29 | 56 | 103 | 9 |
| With my red veins full of money, | 99 | 7 | 60 | 110 | 7 |
| Pears and red currants | 103 | 20 | 63 | 114 | 20 |
| Of birds! Among the cocks like fire the red fox | 164 | 20 | 86 | 184 | 6 |
| Who comes as red as the fox and sly as the heeled wind. | 165 | 10 | 86 | 184 | 18 |
| No springtailed tom in the red hot town | 174 | 29 | 89 | 195 | 5 |
| And cut the birds' boughs that the minstrel sap ran red. | 178 | 8 | 90 | 199 | 9 |
| RED-EYED | | | | | |
| Raise up this red-eyed earth? | 15 | 3 | 10 | 17 | 3 |
| A three-eyed, red-eyed spark, blunt as a flower; | 22 | 15 | 14 | 27 | 15 |
| By red-eyed orchards sow the seeds of snow, | 60 | 11 | 36 | 69 | 11 |
| REDHAIRED | | | | | |
| The redhaired cancer still alive, | 4 | 20 | 3 | 4 | 20 |
| REEFED | | | | | |
| Or like the tide-looped breastknot reefed again | 78 | 11 | 46 | 87 | 11 |
| REEK | | | | | |
| Flared in the reek of the wiving sty with the rush | 177 | 2 | 90 | 198 | 1 |
| REEL | | | | | |
| Two one-dimensioned ghosts, love on a reel, | 14 | 12 | 10 | 16 | 12 |
| And every stone I wind off like a reel. | 89 | 13 | 53 | 98 | 13 |
| To the gold gut that sings on his reel | 149 | 19 | 83 | 166 | 19 |
| His fiery reel sings off its flames, | 151 | 16 | 83 | 169 | 4 |
| And the fisherman winds his reel | 154 | 3 | 83 | 172 | 3 |
| REELS | | | | | |
| His reels and mystery | 70 | 3 | 43 | 79 | 7 |
| REFLECTION | | | | | |
| Love's reflection of the mushroom features, | 73 | 7 | 44 | 82 | 7 |
| REFUSAL | | | | | |
| Refusal struck her loin and the lame flower | 90 | 2 | 54 | 99 | 2 |
| Refusal struck like a bell under water | 90 | 12 | 54 | 99 | 12 |

| | U.K. | | | U.S. | |
|---|---|---|---|---|---|
| | Page | Line | Poem | Page | Line |
| A Refusal to Mourn the Death, by Fire, of a child in London | 101 | | 62 | 112 | |
| REGRET | | | | | |
| Through no regret of leaving woman waiting | 48 | 14 | 28 | 56 | 14 |
| Feeling regret when this is wasted | 48 | 18 | 28 | 56 | 18 |
| Never never oh never to regret the bugle I wore | 133 | 19 | 78 | 149 | 2 |
| REHEARSING | | | | | |
| Rehearsing heat upon a raw-edged nerve. | 12 | 19 | 9 | 13 | 19 |
| REINDEER | | | | | |
| Night and the reindeer on the clouds above the haycocks | 164 | 15 | 86 | 184 | 1 |
| REJOICE | | | | | |
| The black, burst sea rejoice, | 91 | 19 | 55 | 100 | 19 |
| REJOICED | | | | | |
| And all the elements of the slow fall rejoiced | 122 | 4 | 72 | 135 | 4 |
| REJOICING | | | | | |
| Rejoicing for that drifting death | 152 | 16 | 83 | 170 | 8 |
| REKINDLED | | | | | |
| And Noah's rekindled now unkind dove | 113 | 5 | 69 | 125 | 5 |
| RELIC | | | | | |
| Shames and the damp dishonours, the relic scraping. | 37 | 20 | 20 | 43 | 3 |
| RELIGION | | | | | |
| Lie with religion in their cramp, her threadbare | 88 | 4 | 52 | 97 | 4 |
| RELIGIOUS | | | | | |
| In the religious wind | vii | 21 | 1 | xvi | 21 |
| REMAIN | | | | | |
| And who remain shall flower as they love, | 15 | 21 | 10 | 18 | 1 |
| All shall remain and on the graveward gulf | 67 | 27 | 41 | 76 | 27 |
| REMAINS | | | | | |
| Land, land, land, nothing remains | 157 | 17 | 83 | 176 | 9 |
| REMEMBER | | | | | |
| Remember me and pity Him | 8 | 20 | 5 | 9 | 20 |
| REMEMBERED | | | | | |
| Early imaginary half remembered | 114 | 9 | 69 | 126 | 9 |
| REMIND | | | | | |
| Twenty-four years remind the tears of my eyes. | 99 | 1 | 60 | 110 | 1 |
| RENOUNCING | | | | | |
| And the renouncing of islands. | 110 | 11 | 67 | 121 | 13 |
| RENT | | | | | |
| Or rent ancestrally the roped sea-hymen, | 78 | 12 | 46 | 87 | 12 |
| REPEAT | | | | | |
| Over the past table I repeat this present grace. | 77 | 25 | 45 | 86 | 25 |
| REPETITION | | | | | |
| From the repetition of salutes, | 64 | 7 | 39 | 73 | 7 |
| REPLY | | | | | |
| Both quench his thirst he'll have a black reply. | 53 | 9 | 32 | 62 | 9 |

|  | U.K. | | | U.S. | |
|---|---|---|---|---|---|
|  | Page | Line | Poem | Page | Line |
| **REPTILE** | | | | | |
| The reptile profligates in a flame, | 134 | 4 | 79 | 150 | 4 |
| **REQUIEMS** | | | | | |
| And the golden pavements laid in requiems, | 131 | 17 | 77 | 145 | 23 |
| **REROBING** | | | | | |
| Rerobing of the naked ghost. Manhood | 28 | 23 | 17 | 34 | 3 |
| **RESEMBLING** | | | | | |
| Resembling to her dulled sense | 114 | 7 | 69 | 126 | 7 |
| **RESERVOIR** | | | | | |
| When I whistled with mitching boys through a reservoir park | 89 | 7 | 53 | 98 | 7 |
| **RESIN** | | | | | |
| I scape through resin to a starry bone | 31 | 11 | 18 | 36 | 11 |
| **REST** | | | | | |
| Disturbs this island's rest. | 58 | 16 | 35 | 67 | 16 |
| Lie dry, rest robbed, my beast. | 92 | 14 | 55 | 101 | 20 |
| A virgin married at rest. | 93 | 3 | 56 | 102 | 3 |
| 'Rest beyond choice in the dust-appointed grain, | 98 | 3 | 59 | 109 | 6 |
| Forgotten dark, rest their pulse and bury their dead in her faithless sleep. | 115 | 23 | 69 | 127 | 23 |
| Lie in grace. Sleep spelled at rest in the lowly house | 163 | 20 | 86 | 183 | 1 |
| Which was rest and dust, and in the kind ground |  |  | 91 | 200 | 10 |
| Let him find no rest but be fathered and found, |  |  | 91 | 200 | 12 |
| **RESUFFERED** | | | | | |
| Spat up from the resuffered pain. | 28 | 24 | 17 | 34 | 4 |
| **RESURRECTION** | | | | | |
| This was the resurrection in the desert, | 76 | 1 | 44 | 85 | 1 |
| **RETURN** | | | | | |
| To take to give is all, return what is hungrily given | 94 | 4 | 57 | 104 | 4 |
| If I take to burn or return this world which is each man's work. | 94 | 12 | 57 | 104 | 12 |
| At the breast stored with seas. No return | 98 | 4 | 59 | 109 | 7 |
| Of his mother's milk may return | 144 | 2 | 82 | 161 | 2 |
| **REVERENT** | | | | | |
| With Welsh and reverent rook, | ix | 9 | 1 | xvii | 9 |
| **REWARD** | | | | | |
| And a black reward for a roaring life, | 175 | 21 | 89 | 196 | 2 |
| **RHUBARB** | | | | | |
| What rhubarb man peeled in her foam-blue channel | 76 | 17 | 44 | 85 | 17 |
| **RHYMER** | | | | | |
| And the rhymer in the long tongued room, | 170 | 15 | 88 | 190 | 15 |
| **RIB** | | | | | |
| Has stringed my flask of matter to his rib. | 4 | 12 | 3 | 4 | 12 |

| | U.K. | | | U.S. | |
|---|---|---|---|---|---|
| | *Page* | *Line* | *Poem* | *Page* | *Line* |
| RIBBED | | | | | |
| The ribbed original of love. | 23 | 6 | 14 | 28 | 6 |
| Ribbed between desert and water storm, | 82 | 11 | 48 | 91 | 11 |
| RIBBING | | | | | |
| Nor the heart in the ribbing metal. | 33 | 15 | 19 | 38 | 15 |
| RIBBONED | | | | | |
| And the wings of the great roc ribboned for the fair! | 164 | 16 | 86 | 184 | 2 |
| RIBS | | | | | |
| But rail with your wizard's ribs the heart-shaped planet; | 60 | 15 | 36 | 69 | 15 |
| RICE | | | | | |
| Now stamp the Lord's Prayer on a grain of rice, | 74 | 15 | 44 | 83 | 15 |
| RICH | | | | | |
| I who was rich was made the richer | 8 | 11 | 5 | 9 | 11 |
| The sunny gentlemen, the Welshing rich, | 15 | 5 | 10 | 17 | 5 |
| Belly of the rich year and the big purse of my body | 94 | 2 | 57 | 104 | 2 |
| RICHER | | | | | |
| I who was rich was made the richer | 8 | 11 | 5 | 9 | 11 |
| RICK'S | | | | | |
| On the last rick's tip by spilled wine-wells | 95 | 14 | 58 | 105 | 14 |
| RICKS | | | | | |
| Flying with the ricks, and the horses | 160 | 4 | 85 | 179 | 4 |
| And their firefly hairpins flew, and the ricks ran round— | 171 | 21 | 90 | 199 | 1 |
| RIDDLED | | | | | |
| I hear, through dead men's drums, the riddled lads, | 31 | 16 | 18 | 36 | 16 |
| Shall the star-flanked seed be riddled, | 42 | 16 | 24 | 49 | 16 |
| Quickening for the riddled sea; | 42 | 18 | 24 | 49 | 18 |
| Shall the star-flanked seed be riddled, | 42 | 23 | 24 | 50 | 2 |
| Settling on a riddled stronghold | 42 | 26 | 24 | 50 | 5 |
| RIDE | | | | | |
| We will ride out alone, and then, | x | 8 | 1 | xviii | 14 |
| As the green blooms ride upward, to the drive of time; | 49 | 3 | 29 | 58 | 3 |
| Ride through the doors of our unentered house. | 126 | 14 | 74 | 140 | 14 |
| Where birds ride like leaves and boats like ducks | 134 | 22 | 79 | 150 | 22 |
| Or we shall obey, and ride with you through the drowned. | 136 | 14 | 81 | 153 | 14 |
| Shall harrow and snow the blood while you ride wide and near, | 162 | 23 | 86 | 181 | 23 |
| More spanned with angels ride | 173 | 23 | 88 | 193 | 23 |
| RIDER | | | | | |
| Time, in a folly's rider, like a county man | 49 | 4 | 29 | 58 | 4 |

383

|  | U.K. | | | U.S. | |
|  | Page | Line | Poem | Page | Line |
| Time, in a rider rising, from the harnessed valley; | 49 | 21 | 29 | 58 | 21 |
| The come-a-cropper rider of the flower. | 51 | 28 | 31 | 61 | 7 |
| And staved, and riven among plumes my rider weep. | 162 | 16 | 86 | 181 | 16 |
| **RIDERLESS** | | | | | |
| Turning the riderless dead by the channel wall. | 36 | 24 | 20 | 42 | 3 |
| A limp and riderless shape to leap nine thinning months.' | 97 | 15 | 59 | 108 | 15 |
| **RIDERS** | | | | | |
| All but the briskest riders thrown, | 5 | 17 | 3 | 5 | 17 |
| And sear just riders back, | 118 | 6 | 71 | 130 | 10 |
| **RIDES** | | | | | |
| Or rides the imagined oceans of the male wards. | 108 | 9 | 66 | 119 | 9 |
| As the rain falls, hail on the fleece, as the vale mist rides | 164 | 8 | 86 | 183 | 15 |
| Where the hay rides now or the bracken kitchens rust | 178 | 6 | 90 | 199 | 7 |
| **RIDICULOUS** | | | | | |
| The bright pretender, the ridiculous sea dandy | 133 | 14 | 78 | 148 | 17 |
| **RIDING** | | | | | |
| Riding the sea light on a sunken path, | 67 | 8 | 41 | 76 | 8 |
| Of the riding Thames. | 101 | 23 | 62 | 112 | 23 |
| Nor that riding to sleep | 161 | 1 | 85 | 180 | 4 |
| Never and never, my girl riding far and near | 162 | 1 | 86 | 181 | 1 |
| High riding, held and blessed and true, and so stilly | 165 | 19 | 86 | 185 | 9 |
| Wound, nor her riding high, nor her eyes, nor kindled hair, | 166 | 2 | 86 | 186 | 2 |
| Petticoats galed high, or shy with the rough riding boys, | 176 | 18 | 90 | 197 | 18 |
| **RIDINGS** | | | | | |
| Over the vault of ridings with his hound at heel, | 49 | 5 | 29 | 58 | 5 |
| But graft these four-fruited ridings on your country; | 60 | 9 | 36 | 69 | 9 |
| **RIFT** | | | | | |
| The haygold haired, my love asleep, and the rift blue | 165 | 17 | 86 | 185 | 7 |
| **RIGHT** | | | | | |
| To share my room in the house not right in the head, | 108 | 2 | 66 | 119 | 2 |
| Though wise men at their end know dark is right, | 116 | 4 | 70 | 128 | 4 |
| And a hundred storks perch on the sun's right hand. | 135 | 14 | 80 | 152 | 14 |
| And serve me right as the preachers warn, | 175 | 9 | 89 | 195 | 14 |

|  | U.K. | | | U.S. | |
|---|---|---|---|---|---|
|  | *Page* | *Line* | *Poem* | *Page* | *Line* |
| RIM | | | | | |
| The grain that hurries this way from the rim of the grave | 98 | 1 | 59 | 109 | 4 |
| RIMS | | | | | |
| On the snapping rims of the ashpit, | 132 | 8 | 78 | 147 | 8 |
| RIND | | | | | |
| In winds that bring the fruit and rind | 53 | 4 | 32 | 62 | 4 |
| Nor the tusked prince, in the ruttish farm, at the rind | 163 | 14 | 86 | 182 | 14 |
| Gristle and rind, and a roarers' life, | 175 | 17 | 89 | 195 | 22 |
| RING | | | | | |
| O my ruffled ring dove | ix | 7 | 1 | xvii | 7 |
| Where, punctual as death, we ring the stars; | 2 | 3 | 2 | 2 | 3 |
| Ring like a handbell through the corridors, | 53 | 22 | 32 | 62 | 22 |
| Brand of the lily's anger on her ring, | 54 | 19 | 33 | 63 | 19 |
| O ring of seas, nor sorrow as I shift | 60 | 20 | 36 | 69 | 20 |
| Falls on a ring of summers and locked noons. | 79 | 4 | 46 | 88 | 7 |
| 'All game phrases fit your ring of a cockfight: | 97 | 6 | 59 | 108 | 6 |
| Assembling waits for the spade's ring on the cage. | 135 | 11 | 80 | 152 | 11 |
| RINGED | | | | | |
| In his firelit island ringed by the winged snow | 119 | 17 | 72 | 131 | 17 |
| Of the golden ghost who ringed with his streams her mercury bone, | 127 | 11 | 75 | 141 | 11 |
| In a spinney of ringed boys and ganders, spike and burn, | 162 | 14 | 86 | 181 | 14 |
| RINGED-SEA | | | | | |
| The ringed-sea ghost, rise grimly from the wrack. | 46 | 24 | 27 | 54 | 24 |
| RINGING | | | | | |
| On rose and icicle the ringing handprint. | 75 | 4 | 44 | 84 | 4 |
| RINGS | | | | | |
| Rings out the Dead Sea scale; | 37 | 12 | 20 | 42 | 18 |
| Stream with bells and baying water bounds. The dew rings | 121 | 7 | 72 | 134 | 2 |
| RIP | | | | | |
| Rip of the vaults, I took my marrow-ladle | 72 | 11 | 44 | 81 | 11 |
| And, Rip Van Winkle from a timeless cradle, | 72 | 13 | 44 | 81 | 13 |
| RIPE | | | | | |
| Brandy and ripe in my bright, bass prime, | 174 | 28 | 89 | 195 | 4 |
| RIPPLED | | | | | |
| Through the rippled drum of the hair-buried ear; | 113 | 4 | 69 | 125 | 4 |
| The rippled seals streak down | 171 | 7 | 88 | 191 | 7 |
| RIPPLING | | | | | |
| Rippling in twelve-winded circles, | 131 | 12 | 77 | 145 | 18 |
| Or rippling soft in the spinney moon as the silk | 177 | 7 | 90 | 198 | 6 |

|  |  | U.K. |  |  | U.S. |  |
|---|---|---|---|---|---|---|
|  |  | Page | Line | Poem | Page | Line |
| **RISE** |  |  |  |  |  |  |
| | Rise of the skeleton and | 28 | 22 | 17 | 34 | 2 |
| | The ringed-sea ghost, rise grimly from the wrack. | 46 | 24 | 27 | 54 | 24 |
| | Rise before dark. | 55 | 5 | 33 | 64 | 8 |
| | Though they sink through the sea they shall rise again; | 68 | 7 | 42 | 77 | 7 |
| | The star rise at pasture and nightlong the fables graze | 163 | 11 | 86 | 182 | 11 |
| **RISEN** |  |  |  |  |  |  |
| | Weeps like the risen sun among | 155 | 19 | 83 | 174 | 3 |
| **RISES** |  |  |  |  |  |  |
| | Of fields. For love, the long ago she bird rises. Look. | 121 | 25 | 72 | 134 | 20 |
| **RISING** |  |  |  |  |  |  |
| | Time, in a rider rising, from the harnessed valley; | 49 | 21 | 29 | 58 | 21 |
| | In the moon that is always rising, | 160 | 26 | 85 | 180 | 3 |
| **RITE** |  |  |  |  |  |  |
| | The rite of light, | 56 | 16 | 34 | 65 | 16 |
| | Flying. The rite is shorn | 123 | 6 | 72 | 136 | 16 |
| **RIVALS** |  |  |  |  |  |  |
| | Intricate manhood of ending, the invalid rivals, | 36 | 7 | 20 | 41 | 7 |
| **RIVEN** |  |  |  |  |  |  |
| | Man of my flesh, the jawbone riven, | 33 | 19 | 19 | 39 | 1 |
| | And staved, and riven among plumes my rider weep. | 162 | 16 | 86 | 181 | 16 |
| **RIVER** |  |  |  |  |  |  |
| | These were the woods the river and sea | 104 | 1 | 63 | 115 | 3 |
| | In the river wended vales where the tale was told. | 119 | 10 | 72 | 131 | 10 |
| | And the lakes and floating fields and the river wended | 122 | 28 | 72 | 136 | 8 |
| | Down to the river rooting plain | 145 | 16 | 82 | 162 | 16 |
| | A separate river breathes and runs; | 156 | 12 | 83 | 174 | 20 |
| | In the river Towy below bows his tilted head-stone. | 167 | 12 | 87 | 187 | 12 |
| | Wear-willow river, grave, | 169 | 10 | 87 | 189 | 19 |
| | By full tilt river and switchback sea | 170 | 2 | 88 | 190 | 2 |
| **RIVER'S** |  |  |  |  |  |  |
| | The livelong river's robe | 171 | 1 | 88 | 191 | 1 |
| **RIVERS** |  |  |  |  |  |  |
| | And rivers of the dead around my neck. | 76 | 8 | 44 | 85 | 8 |
| | Who follow the red rivers, hollow | 82 | 3 | 48 | 91 | 3 |
| | The rivers mouthed in night, | 120 | 21 | 72 | 133 | 6 |
| | Down the rivers of the windfall light. | 159 | 9 | 85 | 178 | 9 |
| | Through throats where many rivers meet, the curlews cry, | 176 | 1 | 90 | 197 | 1 |

|  | U.K. | | | U.S. | |
|---|---|---|---|---|---|
|  | *Page* | *Line* | *Poem* | *Page* | *Line* |
| Through throats where many rivers meet, the women pray, | 176 | 6 | 90 | 197 | 6 |
| Noon, and night, and light. The rivers of the dead | | | 91 | 200 | 15 |
| ROAD | | | | | |
| High tide and the heron dived when I took the road | 102 | 17 | 63 | 113 | 17 |
| ROADSIDE | | | | | |
| Cloud and the roadside bushes brimming with whistling | 102 | 22 | 63 | 113 | 22 |
| ROAR | | | | | |
| To roar on the rockery stones | 112 | 5 | 68 | 124 | 5 |
| And Love and his patients roar on a chain; | 124 | 6 | 73 | 138 | 6 |
| ROARED | | | | | |
| Roared, sea born, man torn, blood blest. | viii | 15 | 1 | xvi | 15 |
| And my images roared and rose on heaven's hill. | 38 | 30 | 20 | 44 | 20 |
| ROARER | | | | | |
| Winds, from the dousing shade and the roarer at the latch, | 163 | 23 | 86 | 183 | 4 |
| ROARERS' | | | | | |
| Gristle and rind, and a roarers' life, | 175 | 17 | 89 | 195 | 22 |
| ROARING | | | | | |
| Roaring, crawling, quarrel | 91 | 8 | 55 | 100 | 8 |
| And a black reward for a roaring life, | 175 | 21 | 89 | 196 | 2 |
| ROARS | | | | | |
| One. The sun roars at the prayer's end | 148 | 17 | 82 | 165 | 17 |
| ROASTING | | | | | |
| In the courters' lanes, or twined in the ox roasting sun | 176 | 13 | 90 | 197 | 13 |
| ROB | | | | | |
| To rob me of my fluids in his heart. | 5 | 12 | 3 | 5 | 12 |
| ROBBED | | | | | |
| Robbed of the foxy tongue, his footed tape | 18 | 9 | 12 | 21 | 9 |
| Lie dry, rest robbed, my beast. | 92 | 14 | 55 | 101 | 20 |
| ROBE | | | | | |
| The livelong river's robe | 171 | 1 | 88 | 191 | 1 |
| ROBED | | | | | |
| Robed in the long friends, | 101 | 20 | 62 | 112 | 20 |
| ROBES | | | | | |
| The winter's robes; | 24 | 23 | 15 | 29 | 23 |
| ROBIN | | | | | |
| Her robin breasted tree, three Marys in the rays. | 163 | 6 | 86 | 182 | 6 |
| ROC | | | | | |
| And the wings of the great Roc ribboned for the fair! | 164 | 16 | 86 | 184 | 2 |
| ROCK | | | | | |
| Burst in the roots, pumped from the earth and rock | 22 | 17 | 14 | 27 | 17 |

|  | U.K. | | | U.S. | |
|  | Page | Line | Poem | Page | Line |
| Over the sea-gut loudening, sets a rock alive; | 49 | 15 | 29 | 58 | 15 |
| Calls the green rock of light. | 69 | 12 | 43 | 78 | 12 |
| Weighed in rock shroud, is my proud pyramid; | 79 | 15 | 46 | 88 | 18 |
| The strata of the shore and drown red rock; | 82 | 20 | 48 | 91 | 20 |
| Can we fend off rock arrival, | 82 | 22 | 48 | 91 | 22 |
| The unwinding, song by rock, | 95 | 5 | 58 | 105 | 5 |
| Parish of snow. The carved mouths in the rock are wind swept strings. | 121 | 9 | 72 | 134 | 4 |
| The carved limbs in the rock | 121 | 21 | 72 | 134 | 16 |
| The flashing needle rock of squatters, | 132 | 26 | 78 | 148 | 1 |
| Rock | 145 | 9 | 82 | 162 | 9 |

**ROCKBIRDS'**

| So shall winged harbours through the rockbirds' eyes | 76 | 12 | 44 | 85 | 12 |

**ROCK-CHESTED**

| Or spray-based and rock-chested sea: | 77 | 24 | 45 | 86 | 24 |

**ROCKED**

| His mouth and rocked him like a storm | 139 | 10 | 82 | 156 | 10 |
| Chimes of the rocked buoys. | 150 | 12 | 83 | 167 | 16 |

**ROCKERY**

| Past lake and rockery | 111 | 19 | 68 | 123 | 19 |
| To roar on the rockery stones | 112 | 5 | 68 | 124 | 5 |

**ROCKETED**

| I rocketed to astonish | 132 | 25 | 78 | 147 | 25 |

**ROCKETING**

| Who knows the rocketing wind will blow | 172 | 13 | 88 | 192 | 13 |

**ROCKING**

| Strip to this tree: a rocking alphabet, | 74 | 17 | 44 | 83 | 17 |
| Shall I, struck on the hot and rocking street, | 77 | 16 | 45 | 86 | 16 |

**ROCKS**

| On a breakneck of rocks | vii | 5 | 1 | xvi | 5 |
| The force that drives the water through the rocks | 9 | 6 | 6 | 10 | 6 |
| Under the bell of rocks, | 69 | 3 | 43 | 78 | 3 |
| In the molested rocks the shell of virgins, | 78 | 18 | 46 | 87 | 18 |
| Unclenched, armless, silk and rough love that breaks all rocks. | 126 | 16 | 74 | 140 | 16 |

**ROD**

| Spout to the rod | 24 | 17 | 15 | 29 | 17 |
| Was who was folded on the rod the aaron | 54 | 13 | 33 | 63 | 13 |
| Now cast down your rod, for the whole | 150 | 7 | 83 | 167 | 11 |
| Good luck to the hand on the rod, | 151 | 13 | 83 | 169 | 1 |
| The rod bends low, divining land, | 155 | 21 | 83 | 174 | 5 |
| (Sighed the old ram rod, dying of women), | 174 | 3 | 89 | 194 | 3 |
| (Sighed the old ram rod, dying of bitches), | 174 | 15 | 89 | 194 | 15 |
| (Sighed the old ram rod, dying of welcome), | 174 | 27 | 89 | 195 | 3 |
| (Sighed the old ram rod, dying of downfall), | 175 | 10 | 89 | 195 | 15 |

| | U.K. | | | U.S. | |
|---|---|---|---|---|---|
| | *Page* | *Line* | *Poem* | *Page* | *Line* |
| (Sighed the old ram rod, dying of strangers), | 175 | 22 | 89 | 196 | 3 |
| RODE | | | | | |
| Rode and whistled a hundred times | 113 | 18 | 69 | 125 | 18 |
| And over the cloth of counties the far hills rode near, | 122 | 13 | 72 | 135 | 13 |
| Where the anchor rode like a gull | 150 | 13 | 83 | 167 | 17 |
| As I rode to sleep the owls were bearing the farm away, | 160 | 2 | 85 | 179 | 2 |
| ROE | | | | | |
| Through salt and root and roe. | 11 | 6 | 8 | 12 | 6 |
| ROISTER | | | | | |
| Their breast, the vaulting does roister, the horned bucks climb | 177 | 13 | 90 | 198 | 12 |
| ROLL | | | | | |
| Roll unmanly over this turning tuft, | 60 | 19 | 36 | 69 | 19 |
| And roll with the knocked earth: | 92 | 13 | 55 | 101 | 19 |
| ROLLED | | | | | |
| I skipped in a blush as the big girls rolled | 174 | 6 | 89 | 194 | 6 |
| ROLLING | | | | | |
| Life rose and spouted from the rolling seas, | 22 | 16 | 14 | 27 | 16 |
| A springful of larks in a rolling | 102 | 21 | 63 | 113 | 21 |
| ROLLS | | | | | |
| And sleep rolls mute above the beds | 5 | 4 | 3 | 5 | 4 |
| ROME | | | | | |
| O Rome and Sodom To-morrow and London | 156 | 23 | 83 | 175 | 11 |
| ROOD | | | | | |
| Ruin, the room of errors, one rood dropped | 79 | 13 | 46 | 88 | 16 |
| ROOF | | | | | |
| Nor roof of sand, nor yet the towering tiler? | 46 | 16 | 27 | 54 | 16 |
| Till field and roof lie level and the same | 63 | 13 | 38 | 72 | 13 |
| ROOFED | | | | | |
| Past the statues of the stables and the sky roofed sties | 120 | 9 | 72 | 132 | 14 |
| ROOFTOPS | | | | | |
| Shall a white answer echo from the rooftops. | 53 | 15 | 32 | 62 | 15 |
| ROOING | | | | | |
| Coo rooing the woods' praise, | ix | 10 | 1 | xvii | 10 |
| ROOK | | | | | |
| With Welsh and reverent rook, | ix | 9 | 1 | xvii | 9 |
| With water praying and call of seagull and rook | 102 | 6 | 63 | 113 | 6 |
| ROOKING | | | | | |
| A rooking girl who stole me for her side, | 12 | 2 | 9 | 13 | 2 |
| ROOKS | | | | | |
| Heeled winds the rooks | 164 | 18 | 86 | 184 | 4 |
| Leaping! The gospel rooks! All tell, this night, of him | 165 | 9 | 86 | 184 | 17 |

| | U.K. Page | Line | Poem | U.S. Page | Line |
|---|---|---|---|---|---|
| **ROOM** | | | | | |
| Ruin, the room of errors, one rood dropped | 79 | 13 | 46 | 88 | 16 |
| In a holy room in a wave; | 84 | 3 | 49 | 93 | 9 |
| In a room with a stuffed fox and a stale fern, | 87 | 11 | 52 | 96 | 11 |
| Is carved from her in a room with a wet window | 88 | 1 | 52 | 97 | 1 |
| To the room of a secret child, | 93 | 15 | 56 | 102 | 15 |
| From an odd room in a split house stare, | 96 | 6 | 58 | 106 | 6 |
| Strike light, and bloody a loud room. | 97 | 10 | 59 | 108 | 10 |
| Who climbs to his dying love in her high room, | 100 | 3 | 61 | 111 | 3 |
| In the fire of his care his love in the high room. | 100 | 16 | 61 | 111 | 16 |
| To share my room in the house not right in the head, | 108 | 2 | 66 | 119 | 2 |
| Yet she deludes with walking the nightmarish room, | 108 | 7 | 66 | 119 | 7 |
| Wound their room with a male moan, | 114 | 2 | 69 | 126 | 2 |
| In the next room | 137 | 4 | 82 | 154 | 4 |
| In the birth bloody room unknown | 137 | 10 | 82 | 154 | 10 |
| The once hooded room | 139 | 13 | 82 | 156 | 13 |
| To the birth bloody room | 144 | 4 | 82 | 161 | 4 |
| Out of the room the weight of his trouble | 154 | 22 | 83 | 173 | 2 |
| And the rhymer in the long tongued room, | 170 | 15 | 88 | 190 | 15 |
| Tidy and cursed in my dove cooed room | 175 | 23 | 89 | 196 | 4 |
| I prayed in the crouching room, by his blind bed, | | | 91 | 200 | 13 |
| **ROOMS** | | | | | |
| That clouts the spittle like bubbles with broken rooms, | 77 | 6 | 45 | 86 | 6 |
| **ROOSTS** | | | | | |
| Roosts sleeping chill till the flame of the cock crow | 119 | 19 | 72 | 131 | 19 |
| **ROOT** | | | | | |
| Through salt and root and roe. | 11 | 6 | 8 | 12 | 6 |
| The root of tongues ends in a spentout cancer, | 21 | 13 | 13 | 25 | 13 |
| My man of leaves and the bronze root, mortal, unmortal, | 35 | 16 | 20 | 40 | 16 |
| Born of the sensual root and sap; | 39 | 14 | 21 | 45 | 14 |
| Genesis in the root, the scarecrow word, | 74 | 18 | 44 | 83 | 18 |
| Rounds to look at the red, wagged root. | 77 | 12 | 45 | 86 | 12 |
| The cauldron's root through this once-rindless hand | 80 | 2 | 46 | 89 | 10 |
| **ROOTED** | | | | | |
| Time by, their dust was flesh the swineherd rooted sly, | 177 | 1 | 90 | 197 | 21 |
| **ROOTING** | | | | | |
| One bough of bone across the rooting air, | 22 | 3 | 14 | 27 | 3 |
| Down to the river rooting plain | 145 | 16 | 82 | 162 | 16 |
| Nor the innocent lie in the rooting dingle wooed | 162 | 15 | 86 | 181 | 15 |

| | U.K. | | | U.S. | |
|---|---|---|---|---|---|
| | *Page* | *Line* | *Poem* | *Page* | *Line* |
| ROOTS | | | | | |
| Drives my green age; that blasts the roots of trees | 9 | 2 | 6 | 10 | 2 |
| Some of the oaken voices, from the roots | 16 | 14 | 11 | 19 | 14 |
| Burst in the roots, pumped from the earth and rock | 22 | 17 | 14 | 27 | 17 |
| Casts to the pine roots, raising man like a mountain | 35 | 11 | 20 | 40 | 11 |
| Are but the roots of nettles and of feathers | 72 | 2 | 44 | 81 | 2 |
| The lofty roots of the clouds. | 96 | 5 | 58 | 106 | 5 |
| Marrow of eagles, the roots of whales | 172 | 4 | 88 | 192 | 4 |
| Through his unseeing eyes to the roots of the sea. | | | 91 | 200 | 17 |
| ROPE | | | | | |
| And the man no rope can hang | 66 | 2 | 40 | 75 | 2 |
| ROPED | | | | | |
| Or rent ancestrally the roped sea-hymen, | 78 | 12 | 46 | 87 | 12 |
| ROPES | | | | | |
| Stirs the quicksand; that ropes the blowing wind | 9 | 12 | 6 | 10 | 12 |
| Her ropes of heritage, the wars of pardon, | 54 | 21 | 33 | 63 | 21 |
| Sooner drop with the worm of the ropes round my throat | 97 | 4 | 59 | 108 | 4 |
| ROSE | | | | | |
| And I am dumb to tell the crooked rose | 9 | 4 | 6 | 10 | 4 |
| Life rose and spouted from the rolling seas, | 22 | 16 | 14 | 27 | 16 |
| I, in my fusion of rose and male motion, | 35 | 17 | 20 | 40 | 17 |
| And my images roared and rose on heaven's hill. | 38 | 30 | 20 | 44 | 20 |
| And when the moon rose windily it was | 40 | 11 | 22 | 46 | 11 |
| Up rose the Abraham-man, mad for my sake, | 46 | 19 | 27 | 54 | 19 |
| Rose maid and male, | 54 | 6 | 33 | 63 | 6 |
| Rose cast to plague, | 54 | 14 | 33 | 63 | 14 |
| Then hang a ram rose over the rags. | 65 | 8 | 40 | 74 | 8 |
| And put beside her a ram rose. | 65 | 24 | 40 | 74 | 24 |
| Rose my Byzantine Adam in the night. | 73 | 16 | 44 | 82 | 16 |
| On rose and icicle the ringing handprint. | 75 | 4 | 44 | 84 | 4 |
| And I rose | 102 | 14 | 63 | 113 | 14 |
| A she bird rose and rayed like a burning bride. | 121 | 14 | 72 | 134 | 9 |
| And she rose with him flowering in her melting snow. | 123 | 20 | 72 | 137 | 10 |
| Rose and crowed and fell! | 151 | 12 | 83 | 168 | 20 |
| For the crab-backed dead on the sea-bed rose | 153 | 3 | 83 | 170 | 19 |
| My girl ranging the night in the rose and shire | 162 | 9 | 86 | 181 | 9 |
| ROSY | | | | | |
| To eat your heart in the house in the rosy wood. | 162 | 7 | 86 | 181 | 7 |
| Under the prayer wheeling moon in the rosy wood | 163 | 18 | 86 | 182 | 18 |

391

|  | U.K. | | | U.S. | |
| --- | --- | --- | --- | --- | --- |
|  | *Page* | *Line* | *Poem* | *Page* | *Line* |
| ROTATING | | | | | |
| Through the rotating shell, strong | 28 | 2 | 17 | 33 | 2 |
| Rotating halves are horning as they drill | 30 | 23 | 18 | 35 | 23 |
| The grooved land rotating, that the stylus of lightning | 37 | 17 | 20 | 43 | 23 |
| ROTTEN | | | | | |
| Windily master of man was the rotten fathom, | 38 | 26 | 20 | 44 | 16 |
| Claw fold and hole for the rotten | 133 | 5 | 78 | 148 | 8 |
| ROUGH | | | | | |
| On God's rough tumbling grounds | ix | 24 | 1 | xvii | 24 |
| Lean time on tide and times the wind stood rough, | 67 | 6 | 41 | 76 | 6 |
| Bullies into rough seas you so gentle | 96 | 24 | 58 | 107 | 7 |
| Unclenched, armless, silk and rough love that breaks all rocks. | 126 | 16 | 74 | 140 | 16 |
| Petticoats galed high, or shy with the rough riding boys, | 176 | 18 | 90 | 197 | 18 |
| Rough as cows' tongues and thrashed with brambles their buttermilk | 177 | 5 | 90 | 198 | 4 |
| ROUGHLY | | | | | |
| Loping and bleating roughly and blithely shall leap, | 162 | 4 | 86 | 181 | 4 |
| ROUND | | | | | |
| How time has ticked a heaven round the stars. | 9 | 20 | 6 | 10 | 20 |
| There round about your stones the shades | 11 | 16 | 8 | 12 | 16 |
| And curling round the bud that forks her eye. | 13 | 3 | 9 | 14 | 10 |
| And, burning ciphers on the round of space, | 22 | 5 | 14 | 27 | 5 |
| The haring snail go giddily round the flower, | 36 | 17 | 20 | 41 | 17 |
| Blind in the coil scrams round the blazing outline, | 41 | 11 | 23 | 47 | 11 |
| Though what the stars ask as they round | 53 | 18 | 32 | 62 | 18 |
| From pole to pole leapt round the snail-waked world. | 75 | 14 | 44 | 84 | 14 |
| Has sown a flying garden round that sea-ghost? | 76 | 18 | 44 | 85 | 18 |
| Round the parched worlds of Wales and drowned each sun | 87 | 15 | 52 | 96 | 15 |
| Her fist of a face died clenched on a round pain; | 88 | 6 | 52 | 97 | 6 |
| Sooner drop with the worm of the ropes round my throat | 97 | 4 | 59 | 108 | 4 |
| And I must enter again the round | 101 | 7 | 62 | 112 | 7 |
| Round the griefs of the ages, | 128 | 18 | 76 | 142 | 18 |
| Round her trailed wrist fresh water weaves, | 156 | 9 | 83 | 174 | 17 |
| And the sun grew round that very day. | 160 | 10 | 85 | 179 | 10 |
| Round the sun, he comes to my love like the designed snow, | 165 | 25 | 86 | 185 | 15 |
| Under and round him go | 170 | 10 | 88 | 190 | 10 |

| | U.K. | | | U.S. | |
|---|---|---|---|---|---|
| | *Page* | *Line* | *Poem* | *Page* | *Line* |
| And their firefly hairpins flew, and the ricks ran round— | 177 | 21 | 90 | 199 | 1 |
| **ROUNDED** | | | | | |
| Rounded my globe of heritage, journey | 28 | 11 | 17 | 33 | 11 |
| With moving fish and rounded stones | 156 | 10 | 83 | 174 | 18 |
| **ROUNDING** | | | | | |
| Slow rounding of four season's coasts, | 45 | 6 | 26 | 53 | 6 |
| **ROUNDS** | | | | | |
| Night in the sockets rounds, | 24 | 19 | 15 | 29 | 19 |
| Rounds to look at the red, wagged root. | 77 | 12 | 45 | 86 | 12 |
| **ROWS** | | | | | |
| The wordy shapes of women, and the rows | 16 | 11 | 11 | 19 | 11 |
| **ROW** | | | | | |
| The year-hedged row is lame with flint, | 70 | 10 | 43 | 79 | 14 |
| When black birds died like priests in the cloaked hedge row | 122 | 12 | 72 | 135 | 12 |
| **RUB** | | | | | |
| If I were tickled by the rub of love, | 12 | 1 | 9 | 13 | 1 |
| If I were tickled by the lovers' rub | 12 | 22 | 9 | 14 | 1 |
| And that's the rub, the only rub that tickles. | 13 | 8 | 9 | 14 | 15 |
| And what's the rub? Death's feather on the nerve? | 13 | 15 | 9 | 15 | 1 |
| I would be tickled by the rub that is: | 13 | 20 | 9 | 15 | 6 |
| If I were tickled by the rub of love | 12 | | 9 | 13 | |
| **RUBBING** | | | | | |
| Feet in the rubbing dust. | 13 | 14 | 9 | 14 | 21 |
| **RUBBISH** | | | | | |
| Like the moon's seed, rubbish | 106 | 2 | 64 | 117 | 2 |
| **RUDE** | | | | | |
| My nest of mercies in the rude, red tree. | 76 | 22 | 44 | 85 | 22 |
| The rude owl cried like a telltale tit, | 174 | 5 | 89 | 194 | 5 |
| **RUFFLED** | | | | | |
| O my ruffled ring dove | ix | 7 | 1 | xvii | 7 |
| **RUIN** | | | | | |
| I see the boys of summer in their ruin | 1 | 1 | 2 | 1 | 1 |
| I see you boys of summer in your ruin. | 3 | 1 | 2 | 3 | 7 |
| He lying low with ruin in his ear, | 51 | 20 | 31 | 60 | 20 |
| Like an approaching wave I sprawl to ruin. | 79 | 12 | 46 | 88 | 15 |
| Ruin, the room of errors, one rood dropped | 79 | 13 | 46 | 88 | 16 |
| And ruin and his causes | 158 | 5 | 84 | 177 | 5 |
| The voyage to ruin I must run, | 172 | 24 | 88 | 192 | 24 |
| **RUINS** | | | | | |
| And the sensual ruins make | 153 | 22 | 83 | 171 | 18 |
| **RULED** | | | | | |
| Your faith as deathless as the outcry of the ruled sun. | 166 | 12 | 86 | 186 | 12 |

|  | U.K. | | Poem | U.S. | |
|---|---|---|---|---|---|
|  | Page | Line |  | Page | Line |
| **RULER** |  |  |  |  |  |
| Leans on my mortal ruler, | 10 | 4 | 7 | 11 | 4 |
| **RULES** |  |  |  |  |  |
| That rules from wrist to shoulder, | 10 | 2 | 7 | 11 | 2 |
| A hand rules pity as a hand rules heaven; | 62 | 15 | 37 | 71 | 15 |
| **RULY** |  |  |  |  |  |
| Flows to the strand of flowers like the dew's ruly sea, | 165 | 27 | 86 | 185 | 17 |
| **RUMBLING** |  |  |  |  |  |
| Manna for the rumbling ground, | 42 | 17 | 24 | 49 | 17 |
| **RUMOUR** |  |  |  |  |  |
| The growing bones, the rumour of manseed | 20 | 17 | 13 | 24 | 17 |
| **RUMPUS** |  |  |  |  |  |
| This rumpus of shapes | viii | 11 | 1 | xvi | 11 |
| **RUN** |  |  |  |  |  |
| Shall I run to the ships | 58 | 21 | 35 | 67 | 21 |
| And the unicorn evils run them through; | 68 | 16 | 42 | 77 | 16 |
| When cold as snow he should run the wended vales among | 120 | 20 | 72 | 133 | 5 |
| Opening and the dark run | 137 | 7 | 82 | 154 | 7 |
| I shall run lost in sudden | 139 | 11 | 82 | 156 | 11 |
| I would turn back and run | 148 | 4 | 82 | 165 | 4 |
| The voyage to ruin I must run, | 172 | 24 | 88 | 192 | 24 |
| **RUNG** |  |  |  |  |  |
| Each rung a love or losing to the last, | 27 | 2 | 16 | 32 | 7 |
| Rung bone and blade, the verticals of Adam, | 71 | 23 | 44 | 80 | 23 |
| We rung our weathering changes on the ladder, | 72 | 17 | 44 | 81 | 17 |
| **RUNNING** |  |  |  |  |  |
| When, like a running grave, time tracks you down, | 18 | 1 | 12 | 21 | 1 |
| Running when he had heard them clearly | 111 | 17 | 68 | 123 | 17 |
| All the sun long it was running, it was lovely, the hay | 159 | 19 | 85 | 178 | 19 |
| When, like a running grave | 18 |  | 12 | 21 |  |
| **RUNS** |  |  |  |  |  |
| The flickering runs and dive | ix | 4 | 1 | xvii | 4 |
| Unfailing till the blood runs foul; | 8 | 4 | 5 | 9 | 4 |
| Where no sea runs, the waters of the heart | 24 | 2 | 15 | 29 | 2 |
| Your sport is summer as the spring runs angrily. | 49 | 24 | 29 | 58 | 24 |
| A separate river breathes and runs; | 156 | 12 | 83 | 174 | 20 |
| **RUSH** |  |  |  |  |  |
| Before I rush in a crouch the ghost with a hammer, air, | 97 | 9 | 59 | 108 | 9 |
| Of his snow blind love and rush in the white lairs. | 120 | 13 | 72 | 132 | 18 |
| Flared in the reek of the wiving sty with the rush | 177 | 2 | 90 | 198 | 1 |

| | U.K. | | | U.S. | |
|---|---|---|---|---|---|
| | *Page* | *Line* | *Poem* | *Page* | *Line* |

RUSHES
Tail, Nile, and snout, a saddler of the rushes, — 38 — 20 — 20 — 44 — 10

RUSHING
Till every bone in the rushing grave — 151 — 11 — 83 — 168 — 19

RUSHY
Safe be and smooth from the bellows of the rushy brood. — 162 — 20 — 86 — 181 — 20

RUST
Of hemlock and the blades, rust — 28 — 18 — 17 — 33 — 18
Where the hay rides now or the bracken kitchens rust — 178 — 6 — 90 — 199 — 7

RUSTIC
Bell believe or fear that the rustic shade or spell — 162 — 22 — 86 — 181 — 22

RUTTISH
Nor the tusked prince, in the ruttish farm, at the rind — 163 — 14 — 86 — 182 — 14

# ENTRIES UNDER S

SABBATH
And held a little sabbath with the sun, — 4 — 15 — 3 — 4 — 15
Winged like a sabbath ass this children's piece — 41 — 16 — 23 — 47 — 16
And the sabbath rang slowly — 159 — 17 — 85 — 178 — 17

SABBATHS
Over the urn of sabbaths — 131 — 14 — 77 — 145 — 20

SACK
The dream that kicks the buried from their sack — 15 — 14 — 10 — 17 — 14
With swag of bubbles in a seedy sack — 67 — 17 — 41 — 76 — 17
To the bait that stalked out of the sack, — 149 — 20 — 83 — 166 — 20

SACKCLOTH
In the least valley of sackcloth to mourn — 101 — 12 — 62 — 112 — 12

SACKED
All these, he said who sacked the children's town, — 46 — 18 — 27 — 54 — 18

SACRED
In sacred waters that no frost could harden, — 40 — 14 — 22 — 46 — 14

SAD
Of birth and death, the two sad knives of thieves, — 10 — 18 — 7 — 11 — 18
And you, my father, there on the sad height, — 116 — 16 — 70 — 128 — 16
Under the sad breast of the head stone — 130 — 20 — 77 — 144 — 20
Open a pathway through the slow sad sail, — 136 — 9 — 81 — 153 — 9

| | U.K. | | | U.S. | |
|---|---|---|---|---|---|
| | *Page* | *Line* | *Poem* | *Page* | *Line* |
| SADDLER | | | | | |
| Tail, Nile, and snout, a saddler of the rushes, | 38 | 20 | 20 | 44 | 10 |
| SAFE | | | | | |
| For the sleep in a safe land and the love who dies | 100 | 10 | 61 | 111 | 10 |
| There was calm to be done in his safe unrest, | 125 | 11 | 74 | 139 | 11 |
| Safe be and smooth from the bellows of the rushy brood. | 162 | 20 | 86 | 181 | 20 |
| SAFEST | | | | | |
| What's never known is safest in this life. | 50 | 6 | 30 | 59 | 6 |
| SAGA | | | | | |
| The leaping saga of prayer! And high, there, on the hare- | 164 | 17 | 86 | 184 | 3 |
| Of blood! The bird loud vein! The saga from mermen | 165 | 7 | 86 | 184 | 15 |
| But her faith that each vast night and the saga of prayer | 166 | 3 | 86 | 186 | 3 |
| SAGE | | | | | |
| Sage on the earth and sky; | 11 | 21 | 8 | 12 | 21 |
| SAGS | | | | | |
| Behind my head a square of sky sags over | 90 | 8 | 54 | 99 | 8 |
| SAHARA | | | | | |
| Valley and sahara in a shell, | 152 | 18 | 83 | 170 | 10 |
| SAID | | | | | |
| Shall gods be said to thump the clouds | 44 | 1 | 25 | 52 | 1 |
| Be said to weep when weather howls? | 44 | 3 | 25 | 52 | 3 |
| Shall it be said they sprinkle water | 44 | 6 | 25 | 52 | 6 |
| Shall it be said that, venuswise, | 44 | 8 | 25 | 52 | 8 |
| It shall be said that gods are stone. | 44 | 11 | 25 | 52 | 11 |
| You are all these, said she who gave me the long suck, | 46 | 17 | 27 | 54 | 17 |
| All these, he said who sacked the children's town, | 46 | 18 | 27 | 54 | 18 |
| They **said,** who hacked and humoured, they were **mine.** | 46 | 20 | 27 | 54 | 20 |
| You are your sisters' sire, said seaweedy, | 47 | 2 | 27 | 55 | 2 |
| 'Time shall not murder you,' He said, | 70 | 16 | 43 | 79 | 20 |
| I am the long world's gentleman, he said, | 71 | 13 | 44 | 80 | 13 |
| Hairs of your head, then said the hollow agent, | 72 | 1 | 44 | 81 | 1 |
| Said the antipodes, and twice spring chimed. | 72 | 18 | 44 | 81 | 18 |
| Said the fake gentleman in suit of spades, | 73 | 14 | 44 | 82 | 14 |
| Pluck, cock, my sea eye, said medusa's scripture, | 74 | 5 | 44 | 83 | 5 |
| Lop, love, my fork tongue, said the pin-hilled nettle; | 74 | 6 | 44 | 83 | 6 |
| Among men later I heard it said | 93 | 16 | 56 | 102 | 16 |
| The conversation of prayers about to be said | 100 | 1 | 61 | 111 | 1 |
| The sound about to be said in the two prayers | 100 | 9 | 61 | 111 | 9 |

|  | U.K. | | | U.S. | |
| --- | --- | --- | --- | --- | --- |
|  | *Page* | *Line* | *Poem* | *Page* | *Line* |
| The conversation of prayers about to be said | 100 | 13 | 61 | 111 | 13 |
| Said the looking land. | 149 | 12 | 83 | 166 | 12 |
| Said the dwindling ships. | 149 | 24 | 83 | 167 | 4 |
| Than ever was since the world was said, | 173 | 17 | 88 | 193 | 17 |
| To the sultry, biding herds, I said, | 175 | 4 | 89 | 195 | 9 |
| Shall gods be said to thump the clouds | 44 |  | 25 | 52 |  |
| SAIL |  |  |  |  |  |
| Hauls my shroud sail. | 9 | 13 | 6 | 10 | 13 |
| Sail on the level, the departing adventure, | 36 | 11 | 20 | 41 | 11 |
| The pale breath of cattle at the stealthy sail, | 119 | 5 | 72 | 131 | 5 |
| Open a pathway through the slow sad sail, | 136 | 9 | 81 | 153 | 9 |
| For my sake sail, and never look back, | 149 | 11 | 83 | 166 | 11 |
| Break the black news and paint on a sail | 151 | 23 | 83 | 169 | 11 |
| Where the sea cobbles sail, | 168 | 14 | 87 | 188 | 18 |
| As I sail out to die. | 173 | 27 | 88 | 193 | 27 |
| Who heard the tall bell sail down the Sundays of the dead | 178 | 10 | 90 | 199 | 11 |
| SAILED |  |  |  |  |  |
| Sailed up the sun; | 54 | 8 | 33 | 63 | 8 |
| Sailed and set dazzling by the handshaped ocean, | 78 | 5 | 46 | 87 | 5 |
| In the fountain basin where I sailed my ship | 111 | 10 | 68 | 123 | 10 |
| SAILING |  |  |  |  |  |
| In that proud sailing tree with branches driven | 78 | 6 | 46 | 87 | 6 |
| Moonfall and sailing emperor, pale as their tide-print, | 83 | 10 | 49 | 92 | 10 |
| And the knock of sailing boats on the net webbed wall | 102 | 7 | 63 | 113 | 7 |
| Stone for the sake of the souls of the slain birds sailing. | 169 | 12 | 87 | 189 | 21 |
| SAILOR |  |  |  |  |  |
| And welcome no sailor? | 58 | 24 | 35 | 67 | 24 |
| Shall I welcome the sailor, | 59 | 5 | 35 | 68 | 5 |
| Let the tale's sailor from a Christian voyage | 76 | 9 | 44 | 85 | 9 |
| SAILORS |  |  |  |  |  |
| Have their thirsty sailors hide him. | 43 | 7 | 24 | 50 | 14 |
| Have their drunken sailors hide him. | 43 | 14 | 24 | 50 | 21 |
| And the groves were blue with sailors | 112 | 6 | 68 | 124 | 6 |
| And out-of-perspective sailors, | 132 | 14 | 78 | 147 | 14 |
| SAILS |  |  |  |  |  |
| Gulls, pipers, cockles, and sails, | vii | 11 | 1 | xv | 11 |
| Escapes to the flat cities' sails | 69 | 16 | 43 | 78 | 16 |
| From blank and leaking winter sails the child in colour, | 83 | 22 | 49 | 93 | 4 |
| Listen and look where she sails the goose plucked sea, | 122 | 20 | 72 | 135 | 20 |
| Sails drank the wind, and white as milk | 149 | 13 | 83 | 166 | 13 |
| As the sails drank up the hail of thunder | 154 | 7 | 83 | 172 | 7 |

SAILS (continued)

|  | U.K. | | | U.S. | |
|---|---|---|---|---|---|
|  | *Page* | *Line* | *Poem* | *Page* | *Line* |
| And surely he sails like the ship shape clouds. Oh he | 165 | 28 | 86 | 185 | 18 |
| SAILSHAPED | | | | | |
| Windshake of sailshaped ears, muffle-toed tap | 87 | 2 | 52 | 96 | 2 |
| SAINT | | | | | |
| Time's coral saint and the salt grief drown a foul sepulchre | 83 | 8 | 49 | 92 | 8 |
| With carved bird, saint, and sun, the wrack-spiked maiden mouth | 92 | 9 | 55 | 101 | 15 |
| A saint about to fall, | 95 | 1 | 58 | 105 | 1 |
| Saint carved and sensual among the scudding | 109 | 5 | 67 | 120 | 5 |
| About the saint in shades while the endless breviary | 109 | 26 | 67 | 120 | 26 |
| I see the wanting nun saint carved in a garb | 110 | 6 | 67 | 121 | 8 |
| Of eels, saint heron hymning in the shell-hung distant | 168 | 12 | 87 | 188 | 16 |
| A saint about to fall | 95 | | 58 | 105 | |
| SAINT'S | | | | | |
| A hill touches an angel. Out of a saint's cell | 163 | 4 | 86 | 182 | 4 |
| SAINTS | | | | | |
| Of saints to their vision! | 142 | 12 | 82 | 159 | 12 |
| SAKE | | | | | |
| For my tall tower's sake cast in her stone? | 46 | 2 | 27 | 54 | 2 |
| Up rose the Abraham-man, mad for my sake, | 46 | 19 | 27 | 54 | 19 |
| Should he, for centre sake, hop in the dust, | 51 | 6 | 31 | 60 | 6 |
| And, for that murder's sake, dark with contagion | 79 | 11 | 46 | 88 | 14 |
| I stand, for this memorial's sake, alone | 87 | 12 | 52 | 96 | 12 |
| For my sake sail, and never look back, | 149 | 11 | 83 | 166 | 11 |
| Her faith that this last night for his unsacred sake | 166 | 5 | 86 | 186 | 5 |
| Stone for the sake of the souls of the slain birds sailing. | 169 | 12 | 87 | 189 | 21 |
| SAKES | | | | | |
| Jealousy cannot forget for all her sakes, | 114 | 11 | 69 | 126 | 11 |
| SALMON | | | | | |
| In the torrent salmon sun, | vii | 3 | 1 | xv | 3 |
| Seaward the salmon, sucked sun slips, | viii | 8 | 1 | xvi | 8 |
| SALT | | | | | |
| Acquainted with the salt adventure | 8 | 9 | 5 | 9 | 9 |
| Through salt and root and roe. | 11 | 6 | 8 | 12 | 6 |
| Bolt for the salt unborn. | 30 | 6 | 18 | 35 | 6 |
| Weeps on the desert ochre and the salt | 31 | 8 | 18 | 36 | 8 |
| My clay unsuckled and my salt unborn, | 32 | 10 | 18 | 37 | 16 |
| Hear they the salt glass breakers and the tongues of burial. | 37 | 15 | 20 | 42 | 21 |
| The salt sucked dam and darlings of the land | 47 | 3 | 27 | 55 | 3 |
| Stretch the salt photographs, | 69 | 19 | 43 | 78 | 19 |

| | U.K. | | | U.S. | |
|---|---|---|---|---|---|
| | Page | Line | Poem | Page | Line |
| Cross-stroked salt Adam to the frozen angel | 73 | 21 | 44 | 82 | 21 |
| The fats of midnight when the salt was singing; | 74 | 10 | 44 | 83 | 10 |
| The salt person and blasted place | 77 | 20 | 45 | 86 | 20 |
| Time's coral saint and the salt grief drown a foul sepulchre | 83 | 8 | 48 | 92 | 8 |
| Carved birds blunt their striking throats on the salt gravel, | 86 | 3 | 51 | 95 | 3 |
| The spittled eyes, the salt ponds in the sleeves, | 87 | 5 | 52 | 96 | 5 |
| Or sow my salt seed | 101 | 11 | 62 | 112 | 11 |
| That came from the wound wrapped in the salt sheet. | 136 | 4 | 81 | 153 | 4 |
| And when the salt sheet broke in a storm of singing | 136 | 7 | 81 | 153 | 7 |
| We heard the sea sound sing, we saw the salt sheet tell. | 136 | 12 | 81 | 153 | 12 |
| SALT-EYED | | | | | |
| And salt-eyed stumble bedward where she lies | 67 | 12 | 41 | 76 | 12 |
| SALT-LIPPED | | | | | |
| From salt-lipped beak to the kick of the stern | 152 | 9 | 83 | 170 | 1 |
| SALTY | | | | | |
| For the salty birds fluttered and fed | 152 | 24 | 83 | 170 | 17 |
| With salty colts and gales in their limbs | 156 | 18 | 83 | 175 | 6 |
| SALUTES | | | | | |
| From the repetition of salutes, | 64 | 7 | 39 | 73 | 7 |
| SALVAGE | | | | | |
| Hatched from the windy salvage on one leg, | 71 | 10 | 44 | 80 | 10 |
| SALVATION'S | | | | | |
| Black-tongued and tipsy from salvation's bottle. | 73 | 15 | 44 | 82 | 15 |
| SAME | | | | | |
| My youth is bent by the same wintry fever. | 9 | 5 | 6 | 10 | 5 |
| How at the mountain spring the same mouth sucks. | 9 | 10 | 6 | 10 | 10 |
| How at my sheet goes the same crooked worm. | 9 | 22 | 6 | 10 | 22 |
| Till field and roof lie level and the same | 63 | 13 | 38 | 72 | 13 |
| Will be the same grief flying. Whom shall they calm? | 100 | 11 | 61 | 111 | 11 |
| SAMSON | | | | | |
| And Samson drowned in his hair. | 113 | 13 | 69 | 125 | 13 |
| Looms the last Samson of your zodiac. | 118 | 8 | 71 | 130 | 12 |
| SANCTORUM | | | | | |
| Sanctum sanctorum the animal eye of the wood | 163 | 7 | 86 | 182 | 7 |
| SANCTUM | | | | | |
| Sanctum sanctorum the animal eye of the wood | 163 | 7 | 86 | 182 | 7 |
| SAND | | | | | |
| And mother milk was stiff as sand, | 5 | 8 | 3 | 5 | 8 |
| And yellow was the multiplying sand, | 20 | 22 | 13 | 24 | 22 |
| Nor roof of sand, nor yet the towering tiler? | 46 | 16 | 27 | 54 | 16 |

## SAND (continued)

|  | U.K. Page | U.K. Line | Poem | U.S. Page | U.S. Line |
|---|---|---|---|---|---|
| Do you not father me on the destroying sand? | 47 | 1 | 27 | 55 | 1 |
| On field and sand | 54 | 22 | 33 | 63 | 22 |
| Rain beats the sand and slates. | 59 | 3 | 35 | 68 | 3 |
| World in the sand, on the triangle landscape, | 76 | 6 | 44 | 85 | 6 |
| For in this yellow grave of sand and sea | 82 | 5 | 48 | 91 | 5 |
| The heavenly music over the sand | 82 | 14 | 48 | 91 | 14 |
| Two sand grains together in bed, | 115 | 1 | 69 | 127 | 1 |
| Whispered the affectionate sand | 149 | 9 | 83 | 166 | 9 |
| Sing and howl through sand and anemone | 152 | 17 | 83 | 170 | 9 |
| Sand with legends in its virgin laps | 156 | 4 | 83 | 174 | 12 |
| Gull, on the wave with sand in its eyes! And the foal moves | 165 | 12 | 86 | 185 | 2 |

### SANDAL
| His beast heel cleft in a sandal, | 83 | 3 | 49 | 92 | 3 |
|---|---|---|---|---|---|

### SAND-BAGGED
| With a sand-bagged garrison, | 43 | 25 | 24 | 51 | 11 |
|---|---|---|---|---|---|

### SANDCRABS
| Of psalms and shadows among the pincered sandcrabs prancing | 167 | 24 | 87 | 188 | 5 |
|---|---|---|---|---|---|

### SANDGRAIN
| This sandgrain day in the bent bay's grave | 170 | 6 | 88 | 190 | 6 |
|---|---|---|---|---|---|

### SANDGRAINS
| Proud as a sucked stone and huge as sandgrains. | 78 | 23 | 46 | 87 | 23 |
|---|---|---|---|---|---|

### SANDS
| By scummed, starfish sands | vii | 9 | 1 | xv | 9 |
|---|---|---|---|---|---|
| And walk the warring sands by the dead town, | 79 | 6 | 46 | 88 | 9 |
| Of his father's house in the sands, | 95 | 7 | 58 | 105 | 7 |

### SANE
| Though they go mad they shall be sane, | 68 | 6 | 42 | 77 | 6 |
|---|---|---|---|---|---|

### SANG
| Sang heaven hungry and the quick | 95 | 15 | 58 | 105 | 15 |
|---|---|---|---|---|---|
| Sang alive | 104 | 7 | 63 | 115 | 9 |
| Joy of the long dead child sang burning | 104 | 11 | 63 | 115 | 13 |
| Sleep to a newborn sleep in a swaddling loin-leaf stroked and sang | 113 | 22 | 69 | 125 | 22 |
| Wild men who caught and sang the sun in flight, | 116 | 10 | 70 | 128 | 10 |
| And the coins on my eyelids sang like shells. | 134 | 30 | 79 | 151 | 8 |
| Sang upon origin! | 142 | 6 | 82 | 159 | 6 |
| Sang to my horn, the foxes on the hills barked clear and cold, | 159 | 16 | 85 | 178 | 16 |
| Though I sang in my chains like the sea. | 161 | 6 | 85 | 180 | 9 |

### SANK
| Where once your green knots sank their splice | 11 | 7 | 8 | 12 | 7 |
|---|---|---|---|---|---|

### SAP
| She threads off the sap and needles, blood and bubble | 35 | 10 | 20 | 40 | 10 |
|---|---|---|---|---|---|
| Born of the sensual root and sap; | 39 | 14 | 21 | 45 | 14 |

| | U.K. | | | U.S. | |
|---|---|---|---|---|---|
| | *Page* | *Line* | *Poem* | *Page* | *Line* |
| And cut the birds' boughs that the minstrel sap ran red. | 178 | 8 | 90 | 199 | 9 |
| SAP'S | | | | | |
| My images stalk the trees and the slant sap's tunnel, | 36 | 1 | 20 | 41 | 1 |
| SARGASSO | | | | | |
| The dry Sargasso of the tomb | 5 | 2 | 3 | 5 | 2 |
| SAT | | | | | |
| With a capsized field where a school sat still | 89 | 3 | 53 | 98 | 3 |
| Like the water he sat down | 111 | 14 | 68 | 123 | 14 |
| SATANS | | | | | |
| Frogs and satans and woman-luck, | 134 | 7 | 79 | 150 | 7 |
| SAVAGE | | | | | |
| And stake the sleepers in the savage grave | 30 | 17 | 18 | 35 | 17 |
| SAVAGELY | | | | | |
| Juan aflame and savagely young King Lear, | 113 | 11 | 69 | 125 | 11 |
| SAVE | | | | | |
| God in his whirlwind silence save, who marks the sparrows hail, | 168 | 21 | 87 | 189 | 6 |
| Save by their long desirers in the fox cubbed | 178 | 15 | 90 | 199 | 16 |
| Nor did he now, save to his secret wound. | | | 91 | 201 | 6 |
| SAVIOUR | | | | | |
| Dust be your saviour under the conjured soil.) | 37 | 9 | 20 | 42 | 15 |
| Am I not sister, too, who is my saviour? | 46 | 12 | 27 | 54 | 12 |
| There was a saviour | 125 | 1 | 74 | 139 | 1 |
| There was a Saviour | 125 | | 74 | 139 | |
| SAVOURS | | | | | |
| Savours the lick of the times through a deadly wood of hair | 77 | 9 | 45 | 86 | 9 |
| SAW | | | | | |
| I saw time murder me. | 70 | 20 | 43 | 79 | 24 |
| Or saw in the looking-glass shell | 93 | 7 | 56 | 102 | 7 |
| I who saw in a hurried film | 93 | 21 | 56 | 103 | 1 |
| And I saw in the turning so clearly a child's | 103 | 21 | 63 | 114 | 21 |
| We heard the sea sound sing, we saw the salt sheet tell. | 136 | 12 | 81 | 153 | 12 |
| For we saw him throw to the swift flood | 149 | 21 | 83 | 167 | 1 |
| He saw the storm smoke out to kill | 150 | 17 | 83 | 168 | 1 |
| Veined his poor hand I held, and I saw | | | 91 | 200 | 16 |
| Out of his eyes I saw the last light glide. | | | 91 | 201 | 7 |
| SAWBONES | | | | | |
| I by the tree of thieves, all glory's sawbones, | 75 | 15 | 44 | 84 | 15 |
| SAWN | | | | | |
| For my sawn, splay sounds), | viii | 2 | 1 | xvi | 2 |
| SAY | | | | | |
| Shall it be male or female? say the cells, | 12 | 8 | 9 | 13 | 8 |
| Shall it be male or female? say the fingers | 12 | 15 | 9 | 13 | 15 |

SAY (continued)

| | U.K. | | | U.S. | |
|---|---|---|---|---|---|
| | *Page* | *Line* | *Poem* | *Page* | *Line* |
| Say nay, | 51 | 2 | 31 | 60 | 2 |
| Say nay, | 51 | 9 | 31 | 60 | 9 |
| Sir no say, | 51 | 10 | 31 | 60 | 10 |
| Say nay, | 51 | 16 | 31 | 60 | 16 |
| No say sir | 51 | 17 | 31 | 60 | 17 |
| Say nay, | 51 | 23 | 31 | 61 | 2 |
| Say nay | 52 | 2 | 31 | 61 | 9 |

SAYING

| | | | | | |
|---|---|---|---|---|---|
| Once it was the colour of saying | 89 | 1 | 53 | 98 | 1 |
| The gentle seaslides of saying I must undo | 89 | 5 | 53 | 98 | 5 |
| Now my saying shall be my undoing, | 89 | 12 | 53 | 98 | 12 |
| Once it was the colour of saying | 89 | | 53 | 98 | |

SAYS

| | | | | | |
|---|---|---|---|---|---|
| Says the world wears away? | 45 | 17 | 26 | 53 | 17 |
| The voice of children says | 125 | 9 | 74 | 139 | 9 |

SCALD

| | | | | | |
|---|---|---|---|---|---|
| Scald me and drown | 148 | 12 | 82 | 165 | 12 |

SCALDING

| | | | | | |
|---|---|---|---|---|---|
| Heir to the scalding veins that hold love's drop, costly | 28 | 9 | 17 | 33 | 9 |

SCALE

| | | | | | |
|---|---|---|---|---|---|
| With pelt, and scale, and fleece: | x | 3 | 1 | xviii | 9 |
| Rings out the Dead Sea scale; | 37 | 12 | 20 | 42 | 18 |

SCALED

| | | | | | |
|---|---|---|---|---|---|
| The scaled sea-sawers, fix in a naked sponge | 74 | 22 | 44 | 83 | 22 |

SCALES

| | | | | | |
|---|---|---|---|---|---|
| The scales of this twin world tread on the double, | 35 | 4 | 20 | 40 | 4 |
| Man was the scales, the death birds on enamel, | 38 | 19 | 20 | 44 | 9 |
| This tidethread and the lane of scales, | 69 | 14 | 43 | 78 | 14 |
| Who scales a hailing hill in her cold flintsteps | 79 | 3 | 46 | 88 | 6 |
| Scales the blue wall of spirits; | 83 | 21 | 49 | 93 | 3 |
| In common clay clothes disguised as scales, | 132 | 15 | 78 | 147 | 15 |

SCALING

| | | | | | |
|---|---|---|---|---|---|
| Come unto sea-stuck towers, at the fibre scaling, | 37 | 23 | 20 | 43 | 6 |

SCALP

| | | | | | |
|---|---|---|---|---|---|
| Worm in the scalp, the staked and fallow. | 33 | 9 | 19 | 38 | 9 |

SCALY

| | | | | | |
|---|---|---|---|---|---|
| Now on Sir John's hill. The heron, ankling the scaly | 169 | 7 | 87 | 189 | 16 |

SCAR

| | | | | | |
|---|---|---|---|---|---|
| On skull and scar where his loves lie wrecked, | 171 | 13 | 88 | 191 | 13 |

SCARECROW

| | | | | | |
|---|---|---|---|---|---|
| Genesis in the root, the scarecrow word, | 74 | 18 | 44 | 83 | 18 |
| Under the one leaved trees ran a scarecrow of snow | 122 | 14 | 72 | 135 | 14 |

SCARLET

| | | | | | |
|---|---|---|---|---|---|
| Down fall four padding weathers on the scarlet lands, | 49 | 19 | 29 | 58 | 19 |

|  | U.K. | | | U.S. | |
|  | Page | Line | Poem | Page | Line |
| A she bird dawned, and her breast with snow and scarlet downed. | 121 | 15 | 72 | 134 | 10 |
| SCARVING |  |  |  |  |  |
| And his scarving beard from a book, | 134 | 12 | 79 | 150 | 12 |
| SCATTER-BREATH |  |  |  |  |  |
| The death-stagged scatter-breath | 134 | 19 | 79 | 150 | 19 |
| SCATTERED |  |  |  |  |  |
| Blood shot and scattered to the winds of light | 23 | 5 | 14 | 28 | 5 |
| Scattered in the paths of his heels | 152 | 23 | 83 | 170 | 15 |
| SCENE |  |  |  |  |  |
| (Have with the house of wind), the leaning scene, | 19 | 17 | 12 | 23 | 2 |
| Adore my windows for their summer scene? | 46 | 8 | 27 | 54 | 8 |
| The winder of the clockwise scene | 70 | 4 | 43 | 79 | 8 |
| Than bully ill love in the clouted scene. | 97 | 5 | 59 | 108 | 5 |
| SCHOLARS |  |  |  |  |  |
| Death from a bandage, rants the mask of scholars | 76 | 2 | 44 | 85 | 2 |
| SCHOOL |  |  |  |  |  |
| With a capsized field where a school sat still | 89 | 3 | 53 | 98 | 3 |
| SCISSORED |  |  |  |  |  |
| From the unfolding to the scissored caul, | 20 | 3 | 13 | 24 | 3 |
| SCISSORS |  |  |  |  |  |
| His scissors oiled, his knife hung loose | 11 | 10 | 8 | 12 | 10 |
| Comes, like a scissors stalking, tailor age, | 18 | 6 | 12 | 21 | 6 |
| Cast high, stunned on gilled stone; sly scissors ground in frost | 92 | 7 | 55 | 101 | 13 |
| SCOLD |  |  |  |  |  |
| A hemisphere green may scold him | 43 | 3 | 24 | 50 | 10 |
| A village green may scold him | 43 | 10 | 24 | 50 | 17 |
| SCOLDS |  |  |  |  |  |
| The wet night scolds me like a nurse? | 44 | 10 | 25 | 52 | 10 |
| SCORE |  |  |  |  |  |
| The two-framed globe that spun into a score; | 21 | 21 | 13 | 26 | 4 |
| SCOUR |  |  |  |  |  |
| And star: held and blessed, though you scour the high four | 163 | 22 | 86 | 183 | 3 |
| SCOUTING |  |  |  |  |  |
| I sent my creature scouting on the globe, | 4 | 9 | 3 | 4 | 9 |
| SCRAMS |  |  |  |  |  |
| Blind in the coil scrams round the blazing outline, | 41 | 11 | 23 | 47 | 11 |
| SCRAPE |  |  |  |  |  |
| I scrape through resin to a starry bone | 31 | 11 | 18 | 36 | 11 |
| SCRAPED |  |  |  |  |  |
| Scraped at my cradle in a walking word | 71 | 11 | 44 | 80 | 11 |

403

SCRAPED (continued)

| | U.K. | | | U.S. | |
|---|---|---|---|---|---|
| | *Page* | *Line* | *Poem* | *Page* | *Line* |
| The hero's head lies scraped of every legend, | 79 | 17 | 46 | 88 | 20 |
| SCRAPING | | | | | |
| Shames and the damp dishonours, the relic scraping. | 37 | 20 | 20 | 43 | 3 |
| SCRATCH | | | | | |
| Still set to scratch a laughter from my lung, | 12 | 5 | 9 | 13 | 5 |
| SCRAWL | | | | | |
| I hug to love with my unruly scrawl | 10 | 8 | 7 | 11 | 8 |
| SCRAWLED | | | | | |
| Is corner-cast, breath's rag, scrawled weed, a vain | 78 | 9 | 46 | 87 | 9 |
| SCREAM | | | | | |
| Bit out the mandrake with to-morrow's scream. | 71 | 6 | 44 | 80 | 6 |
| SCREEN | | | | | |
| Then threw on that tide-hoisted screen | 70 | 6 | 43 | 79 | 10 |
| SCREWED | | | | | |
| December's thorn screwed in a brow of holly. | 76 | 14 | 44 | 85 | 14 |
| SCREWS | | | | | |
| When once the twilight screws were turned, | 5 | 7 | 3 | 5 | 7 |
| Spun to my screws, your dry ghost blows, | 11 | 2 | 8 | 12 | 2 |
| Fear not the screws that turn the voice, | 33 | 23 | 19 | 39 | 5 |
| SCRIBBLED | | | | | |
| Man by a scribbled name. | 62 | 12 | 37 | 71 | 12 |
| SCRIPTURE | | | | | |
| Pluck, cock, my sea eye, said medusa's scripture, | 74 | 5 | 44 | 83 | 5 |
| SCROLLS | | | | | |
| The scrolls of fire that burned in his heart and head, | 119 | 14 | 72 | 131 | 14 |
| SCRUBBED | | | | | |
| I know her scrubbed and sour humble hands | 88 | 3 | 52 | 97 | 3 |
| Grave, after Beloved on the grass gulfed cross is scrubbed | 178 | 13 | 90 | 199 | 14 |
| SCUD | | | | | |
| Where the cormorants scud, | 170 | 3 | 88 | 190 | 3 |
| SCUDDED | | | | | |
| The patchwork halves were cloven as they scudded | 30 | 19 | 18 | 35 | 19 |
| SCUDDING | | | | | |
| The scudding base of the familiar sky, | 96 | 4 | 58 | 106 | 4 |
| Saint carved and sensual among the scudding | 109 | 5 | 67 | 120 | 5 |
| SCULPTURED | | | | | |
| And sculptured Ann is seventy years of stone. | 88 | 7 | 52 | 97 | 7 |
| SCUMMED | | | | | |
| By scummed, starfish sands | vii | 9 | 1 | xv | 9 |
| SCUMS | | | | | |
| The sea of scums could drown me as it broke | 12 | 27 | 9 | 14 | 6 |

|  | U.K. | | | U.S. | |
|---|---|---|---|---|---|
|  | Page | Line | Poem | Page | Line |
| **SCURRY** | | | | | |
| The heart is drained that, spelling in the scurry | 17 | 6 | 11 | 20 | 6 |
| **SCURRYING** | | | | | |
| The scurrying, furred small friars squeal, in the dowse | 177 | 11 | 90 | 198 | 10 |
| **SCUT** | | | | | |
| The Arctic scut, and basin of the South, | 31 | 20 | 18 | 37 | 2 |
| **SCUTTLED** | | | | | |
| Lurched through a scuttled sea | 95 | 23 | 58 | 105 | 23 |
| And scuttled over her eyes, | 153 | 4 | 83 | 170 | 20 |
| **SCYTHE** | | | | | |
| Your calm and cuddled is a scythe of hairs, | 18 | 2 | 12 | 21 | 2 |
| The trigger and scythe, the bridal blade, | 33 | 17 | 19 | 38 | 17 |
| Blunt scythe and water blade. | 70 | 11 | 43 | 79 | 15 |
| **SCYTHED** | | | | | |
| And the scythed boulders bleed, and the last | 172 | 15 | 88 | 192 | 15 |
| **SCYTHE-EYED** | | | | | |
| And the cage for the scythe-eyed raven. | 33 | 21 | 19 | 39 | 3 |
| **SCYTHE-SIDED** | | | | | |
| Or, water-lammed, from the scythe-sided thorn, | 54 | 3 | 33 | 63 | 3 |
| **SCYTHES** | | | | | |
| To a haycock couch and the scythes of his arms | 113 | 17 | 69 | 125 | 17 |
| **SEA** | | | | | |
| Roared, sea born, man torn, blood blest. | viii | 15 | 1 | xvi | 15 |
| From the fair dead who flush the sea | 2 | 10 | 2 | 2 | 10 |
| Hold up the noisy sea and drop her birds, | 2 | 15 | 2 | 2 | 15 |
| Nor damned the sea that sped about my fist, | 4 | 3 | 3 | 4 | 3 |
| When the galactic sea was sucked | 4 | 7 | 3 | 4 | 7 |
| Gives up its dead to such a working sea; | 5 | 3 | 3 | 5 | 3 |
| Is half its light; the fathomed sea | 6 | 11 | 4 | 6 | 11 |
| Cry to the dolphined sea. | 11 | 18 | 8 | 12 | 18 |
| The sea of scums could drown me as it broke | 12 | 27 | 9 | 14 | 6 |
| And all the herrings smelling in the sea, | 13 | 5 | 9 | 14 | 12 |
| Where no sea runs, the waters of the heart | 24 | 2 | 15 | 29 | 2 |
| Slides like a sea; | 24 | 15 | 15 | 29 | 15 |
| Twice in the feeding sea, grown | 29 | 2 | 17 | 34 | 6 |
| Limp in the street of sea, among the rabble | 30 | 15 | 18 | 35 | 15 |
| The secret child, I shift about the sea | 32 | 11 | 18 | 37 | 17 |
| Dug of the sea, the glanded morrow, | 33 | 8 | 19 | 38 | 8 |
| Out of the sea, the drive of oil, | 34 | 10 | 19 | 39 | 16 |
| Turn the long sea arterial | 36 | 22 | 20 | 42 | 1 |
| Rings out the Dead Sea scale; | 37 | 12 | 20 | 42 | 18 |
| Be by the ships' sea broken at the manstring anchored | 38 | 8 | 20 | 43 | 18 |
| The sea and instrument, nicked in the locks of time, | 38 | 14 | 20 | 44 | 4 |
| Greek in the Irish sea the ageless voice: | 41 | 22 | 23 | 48 | 4 |

|  | U.K. | | | U.S. | |
| --- | --- | --- | --- | --- | --- |
|  | *Page* | *Line* | *Poem* | *Page* | *Line* |
| Quickening for the riddled sea; | 42 | 18 | 24 | 49 | 18 |
| Quickening for the virgin sea; | 42 | 25 | 24 | 50 | 4 |
| Am I not all of you by the directed sea | 46 | 13 | 27 | 54 | 13 |
| Hell wind and sea, | 54 | 4 | 33 | 63 | 4 |
| She holding me? The people's sea drives on her, | 54 | 26 | 33 | 64 | 2 |
| The nurse of giants by the cut sea basin, | 56 | 10 | 34 | 65 | 10 |
| By a thin sea of flesh | 58 | 11 | 35 | 67 | 11 |
| Goes over the hill into the deep sea; | 64 | 5 | 39 | 73 | 5 |
| The kingcrafts of the wicked sea, | 65 | 11 | 40 | 74 | 11 |
| The sea speaks in a kingly voice, | 66 | 11 | 40 | 75 | 11 |
| Riding the sea light on a sunken path, | 67 | 8 | 41 | 76 | 8 |
| Though they sink through the sea they shall rise again; | 68 | 7 | 42 | 77 | 7 |
| Under the windings of the sea | 68 | 11 | 42 | 77 | 11 |
| My sea hermaphrodite, | 69 | 7 | 43 | 78 | 7 |
| By a dramatic sea. | 70 | 8 | 43 | 79 | 12 |
| A climbing sea from Asia had me down | 73 | 19 | 44 | 82 | 19 |
| And burned sea silence on a wick of words. | 74 | 4 | 44 | 83 | 4 |
| Pluck, cock, my sea eye, said medusa's scripture, | 74 | 5 | 44 | 83 | 5 |
| That frozen wife whose juices drift like a fixed sea | 77 | 14 | 45 | 86 | 14 |
| Or spray-based and rock-chested sea: | 77 | 24 | 45 | 86 | 24 |
| Down the stacked sea and water-pillared shade, | 79 | 14 | 46 | 88 | 17 |
| And the grave sea, mock who deride | 82 | 2 | 48 | 91 | 2 |
| For in this yellow grave of sand and sea | 82 | 5 | 48 | 91 | 5 |
| That's grave and gay as grave and sea | 82 | 7 | 48 | 91 | 7 |
| Strike the sea hour through bellmetal. | 83 | 12 | 49 | 92 | 12 |
| The black, burst sea rejoice, | 91 | 19 | 55 | 100 | 19 |
| Lurched through a scuttled sea | 95 | 23 | 58 | 105 | 23 |
| Is come of the sea tumbling in harness | 101 | 6 | 62 | 112 | 6 |
| And over the sea wet church the size of a snail | 103 | 7 | 63 | 114 | 7 |
| These were the woods the river and sea | 104 | 1 | 63 | 115 | 3 |
| By the grinding sea, | 105 | 15 | 64 | 116 | 15 |
| Loving on this sea banged guilt | 109 | 15 | 67 | 120 | 15 |
| The covering sea their nightfall with no names; | 115 | 4 | 69 | 127 | 4 |
| He'll bathe his raining blood in the male sea | 117 | 19 | 71 | 129 | 19 |
| Listen and look where she sails the goose plucked sea, | 122 | 20 | 72 | 135 | 20 |
| Street we chant the flying sea | 130 | 5 | 77 | 144 | 5 |
| The masses of the sea | 131 | 20 | 77 | 146 | 2 |
| The masses of the sea under | 131 | 21 | 77 | 146 | 3 |
| The masses of the infant-bearing sea | 131 | 22 | 77 | 146 | 4 |
| Then swift from a bursting sea with bottlecork boats | 132 | 13 | 78 | 147 | 13 |
| The bright pretender, the ridiculous sea dandy | 133 | 14 | 78 | 148 | 17 |
| The next-door sea dispelled | 134 | 6 | 79 | 150 | 6 |
| Cry my sea town was breaking. | 134 | 27 | 79 | 151 | 5 |

|  | U.K. | | | U.S. | |
|---|---|---|---|---|---|
|  | *Page* | *Line* | *Poem* | *Page* | *Line* |
| On the silent sea we have heard the sound | 136 | 3 | 81 | 153 | 3 |
| To the sea sound flowing like blood from the loud wound | 136 | 6 | 81 | 153 | 6 |
| We heard the sea sound sing, we saw the salt sheet tell. | 136 | 12 | 81 | 153 | 12 |
| Of the uncaged sea bottom | 141 | 7 | 82 | 158 | 7 |
| Born sea | 142 | 2 | 82 | 159 | 2 |
| Light through sea and soil | 146 | 5 | 82 | 163 | 5 |
| As a bird hooking over the sea, | 149 | 7 | 83 | 166 | 7 |
| Of the sea is hilly with whales, | 150 | 8 | 83 | 167 | 12 |
| Quaked the sick sea and snouted deep, | 151 | 2 | 83 | 168 | 10 |
| Thrown to the sea in the shell of a girl | 152 | 20 | 83 | 170 | 12 |
| With wild sea fillies and soaking bridles | 156 | 17 | 83 | 175 | 5 |
| There is nothing left of the sea but its sound, | 157 | 13 | 83 | 176 | 5 |
| Under the earth the loud sea walks, | 157 | 14 | 83 | 176 | 6 |
| Of the pacing, famous sea but its speech, | 157 | 18 | 83 | 176 | 10 |
| Over the barbed and shooting sea assumed an army | 158 | 6 | 84 | 177 | 6 |
| Though I sang in my chains like the sea. | 161 | 6 | 85 | 180 | 9 |
| Flows to the strand of flowers like the dew's ruly sea, | 165 | 27 | 86 | 185 | 17 |
| Where the sea cobbles sail, | 168 | 14 | 87 | 188 | 18 |
| By full tilt river and switchback sea | 170 | 2 | 88 | 190 | 2 |
| And far at sea he knows, | 171 | 3 | 88 | 191 | 3 |
| And the sea that hides his secret selves | 173 | 6 | 88 | 193 | 6 |
| And the tusked, ramshackling sea exults; | 173 | 13 | 88 | 193 | 13 |
| Through his unseeing eyes to the roots of the sea. | | | 91 | 200 | 17 |
| SEA'S | | | | | |
| By the sea's side, hearing the noise of birds, | 16 | 5 | 11 | 19 | 5 |
| By the sea's side hear the dark-vowelled birds. | 17 | 8 | 11 | 20 | 8 |
| SEABEAR | | | | | |
| The highroad of water where the seabear and mackerel | 36 | 21 | 20 | 41 | 21 |
| SEABED | | | | | |
| And all the dry seabed unlocked, | 4 | 8 | 3 | 4 | 8 |
| SEA-BED | | | | | |
| For the crab-backed dead on the sea-bed rose | 153 | 3 | 83 | 170 | 19 |
| SEA-BLOWN | | | | | |
| To the sea-blown arrival. | 36 | 12 | 20 | 41 | 12 |
| SEA-FAITHS | | | | | |
| Till all our sea-faiths die. | 11 | 24 | 8 | 12 | 24 |
| SEAFARING | | | | | |
| The moon-drawn grave, with the seafaring years, | 67 | 2 | 41 | 76 | 2 |
| SEA-GHOST | | | | | |
| Has sown a flying garden round that sea-ghost? | 76 | 18 | 44 | 85 | 18 |

|  | U.K. | | | U.S. | |
|---|---|---|---|---|---|
|  | Page | Line | Poem | Page | Line |
| SEA-GIRLS' | | | | | |
| The frank, closed pearl, the sea-girls' lineaments | 78 | 19 | 46 | 87 | 19 |
| SEAGULL | | | | | |
| With water praying and call of seagull and rook | 102 | 6 | 63 | 113 | 6 |
| SEA-GUT | | | | | |
| Over the sea-gut loudening, sets a rock alive; | 49 | 15 | 29 | 58 | 15 |
| SEA-HALVED | | | | | |
| The sea-halved faith that blew time to his knees, | 67 | 4 | 41 | 76 | 4 |
| SEA-HATCHED | | | | | |
| Shaking the sea-hatched skull, | 38 | 22 | 20 | 44 | 12 |
| SEA-HYMEN | | | | | |
| Or rent ancestrally the roped sea-hymen, | 78 | 12 | 46 | 87 | 12 |
| SEA-LEGGED | | | | | |
| Ahoy, old, sea-legged fox, | x | 15 | 1 | xviii | 21 |
| Good-bye to the man on the sea-legged deck | 149 | 18 | 83 | 166 | 18 |
| SEA-PARSLEY | | | | | |
| Nutmeg, civet, and sea-parsley serve the plagued groom and bride | 84 | 5 | 49 | 93 | 11 |
| SEA-SAWERS | | | | | |
| The scaled sea-sawers, fix in a naked sponge | 74 | 22 | 44 | 83 | 22 |
| SEA-SPINDLE | | | | | |
| (Turn the sea-spindle lateral, | 37 | 16 | 20 | 42 | 22 |
| SEA-STRAW | | | | | |
| And sirens singing from our lady's sea-straw. | 73 | 24 | 44 | 82 | 24 |
| SEA-STUCK | | | | | |
| Come unto sea-stuck towers, at the fibre scaling, | 37 | 23 | 20 | 43 | 6 |
| SEA-SUCKED | | | | | |
| His sea-sucked Adam in the hollow hulk, | 30 | 2 | 18 | 35 | 2 |
| SEAL | | | | | |
| The seal of fire, | 52 | 4 | 31 | 61 | 11 |
| Sing how the seal has kissed her dead! | 152 | 10 | 83 | 170 | 2 |
| SEALS | | | | | |
| The rippled seals streak down | 171 | 7 | 88 | 191 | 7 |
| SEAPORTS | | | | | |
| Seaports by a drunken shore | 43 | 6 | 24 | 50 | 13 |
| Seaports by a thirsty shore | 43 | 13 | 24 | 50 | 20 |
| SEAR | | | | | |
| And sear just riders back, | 118 | 6 | 71 | 130 | 10 |
| SEAS | | | | | |
| That speak seven seas, | vii | 17 | 1 | xv | 17 |
| To drift or drown upon the seas | 8 | 8 | 5 | 9 | 8 |
| Life rose and spouted from the rolling seas, | 22 | 16 | 14 | 27 | 16 |
| When we were strangers to the guided seas, | 40 | 7 | 22 | 46 | 7 |
| Draw in their seas, | 55 | 11 | 33 | 64 | 14 |
| O ring of seas, nor sorrow as I shift | 60 | 20 | 36 | 69 | 20 |

|  | U.K. | | | U.S. | |
|---|---|---|---|---|---|
|  | Page | Line | Poem | Page | Line |
| Who gave these seas their colour in a shape, | 61 | 1 | 36 | 70 | 1 |
| Ducked in the twelve, disciple seas | 69 | 4 | 43 | 78 | 4 |
| By waste seas where the white bear quoted Virgil | 73 | 23 | 44 | 82 | 23 |
| Spelt out the seven seas, an evil index, | 74 | 12 | 44 | 83 | 12 |
| Spot the blown word, and on the seas I image | 76 | 13 | 44 | 85 | 13 |
| Delivered seas my love from her proud place | 80 | 9 | 46 | 89 | 17 |
| The seas to service that her wood-tongued virtue | 87 | 22 | 52 | 96 | 22 |
| The agonized, two seas. | 90 | 7 | 54 | 99 | 7 |
| Never shall beast be born to atlas the few seas | 92 | 4 | 55 | 101 | 10 |
| Ancient woods of my blood, dash down to the nut of the seas | 94 | 11 | 57 | 104 | 11 |
| Bullies into rough seas you so gentle | 96 | 24 | 58 | 107 | 7 |
| At the breast stored with seas. No return | 98 | 4 | 59 | 109 | 7 |
| On the old seas from stories, thrashing my wings, | 133 | 8 | 78 | 148 | 11 |
| SEASAND |  |  |  |  |  |
| We lying by seasand, watching yellow | 82 | 1 | 48 | 91 | 1 |
| We lying by seasand | 82 |  | 48 | 91 |  |
| SEASHAKEN |  |  |  |  |  |
| In my seashaken house | vii | 4 | 1 | xv | 4 |
| SEASHELL |  |  |  |  |  |
| Lulling of spheres in the seashell flesh, | 173 | 8 | 88 | 193 | 8 |
| SEASHORE |  |  |  |  |  |
| Or the stars' seashore dead, | 172 | 3 | 88 | 192 | 3 |
| SEASHORES |  |  |  |  |  |
| Or waves break loud on the seashores; | 68 | 21 | 42 | 77 | 21 |
| SEASIDE |  |  |  |  |  |
| Of the grave, gay, seaside land. | 82 | 17 | 48 | 91 | 17 |
| SEASLIDES |  |  |  |  |  |
| The gentle seaslides of saying I must undo | 89 | 5 | 53 | 98 | 5 |
| SEASON |  |  |  |  |  |
| Bright as her spinning-wheels, the colic season | 35 | 8 | 20 | 40 | 8 |
| This first and steepled season, to the summer's game. | 49 | 12 | 29 | 58 | 12 |
| Nor hammer back a season in the figs, | 60 | 8 | 36 | 69 | 8 |
| Season and sunshine, grace and girl, | 66 | 7 | 40 | 75 | 7 |
| Each ancient, stone-necked minute of love's season | 78 | 2 | 46 | 87 | 2 |
| SEASONS |  |  |  |  |  |
| But seasons must be challenged or they totter | 2 | 1 | 2 | 2 | 1 |
| Dissolved in summer and the hundred seasons; | 21 | 25 | 13 | 26 | 8 |
| And three dead seasons on a climbing grave | 72 | 6 | 44 | 81 | 6 |
| Seasons over the liquid world, | 153 | 23 | 83 | 171 | 19 |
| She is breaking with seasons and clouds; | 156 | 8 | 83 | 174 | 16 |
| SEASONS' |  |  |  |  |  |
| Slow rounding of four seasons' coasts, | 45 | 6 | 26 | 53 | 6 |
| In autumn teach three seasons' fires | 45 | 7 | 26 | 53 | 7 |

SEATHUMBED

| | | U.K. | | | U.S. | |
|---|---|---|---|---|---|---|
| | | *Page* | *Line* | *Poem* | *Page* | *Line* |
| **SEATHUMBED** | | | | | | |
| Out of these seathumbed leaves | | viii | 3 | 1 | xvi | 3 |
| **SEAWARD** | | | | | | |
| Seaward the salmon, sucked sun slips, | | viii | 8 | 1 | xvi | 8 |
| **SEAWAX** | | | | | | |
| Give over, lovers, locking, and the seawax struggle, | | 38 | 11 | 20 | 44 | 1 |
| **SEAWEED** | | | | | | |
| With my cherry capped dangler green as seaweed | | 133 | 17 | 78 | 148 | 20 |
| **SEAWEED'S** | | | | | | |
| Green of the seaweed's iron, | | 2 | 14 | 2 | 2 | 14 |
| **SEAWEEDY** | | | | | | |
| You are your sisters' sire, said seaweedy, | | 47 | 2 | 27 | 55 | 2 |
| **SEAWHIRL** | | | | | | |
| This was the god of beginning in the intricate seawhirl, | | 38 | 29 | 20 | 44 | 19 |
| **SECOND** | | | | | | |
| From love's first fever to her plague, from the soft second | | 20 | 1 | 13 | 24 | 1 |
| Reaching a second ground far from the stars; | | 26 | 7 | 16 | 31 | 7 |
| Sharp in my second death I marked the hills, harvest | | 28 | 17 | 17 | 33 | 17 |
| My second struggling from the grass. | | 28 | 20 | 17 | 33 | 20 |
| And power was contagious in my birth, second | | 28 | 21 | 17 | 34 | 1 |
| Cry joy that this witchlike midwife second | | 96 | 23 | 58 | 107 | 6 |
| That second | | 102 | 9 | 63 | 113 | 9 |
| And the second comers, the severers, the enemies from the deep | | 115 | 22 | 69 | 127 | 22 |
| Of Adam and Eve is never for a second | | 130 | 24 | 77 | 145 | 2 |
| **SECONDS** | | | | | | |
| With the incestuous secret brother in the seconds to perpetuate the stars, | | 115 | 20 | 69 | 127 | 20 |
| **SECRET** | | | | | | |
| He promises a secret heat. | | 10 | 15 | 7 | 11 | 15 |
| From the first secret of the heart, the warning ghost, | | 20 | 12 | 13 | 24 | 12 |
| I learnt the verbs of will, and had my secret; | | 21 | 15 | 13 | 25 | 15 |
| The secret oils that drive the grass. | | 22 | 18 | 14 | 27 | 18 |
| In the beginning was the secret brain. | | 23 | 1 | 14 | 28 | 1 |
| Light breaks on secret lots, | | 25 | 1 | 15 | 30 | 1 |
| The secret of the soil grows through the eye, | | 25 | 4 | 15 | 30 | 4 |
| The secret child, I shift about the sea | | 32 | 11 | 18 | 37 | 17 |
| We in our Eden knew the secret guardian | | 40 | 13 | 22 | 46 | 13 |
| To the room of a secret child, | | 93 | 15 | 56 | 102 | 15 |
| Secret by the unmourning water | | 101 | 22 | 62 | 112 | 22 |
| Brassily at my shyest secret, | | 107 | 5 | 65 | 118 | 5 |

| | U.K. Page | Line | Poem | U.S. Page | Line |
|---|---|---|---|---|---|
| With the incestuous secret brother in the seconds to perpetuate the stars, | 115 | 20 | 69 | 127 | 20 |
| Of their most secret heart. | 128 | 11 | 76 | 142 | 11 |
| And the sea that hides his secret selves | 173 | 6 | 88 | 193 | 6 |
| Nor did he now, save to his secret wound. | | | 91 | 201 | 6 |
| SECRETLY | | | | | |
| Secretly in statuary, | 77 | 15 | 45 | 86 | 15 |
| SEDGE | | | | | |
| Shallow and sedge, and 'dilly dilly,' calls the loft hawk, | 167 | 21 | 87 | 188 | 2 |
| SEDUCER'S | | | | | |
| Beneath my life, that sighs for the seducer's coming | 109 | 13 | 67 | 120 | 13 |
| SEE | | | | | |
| I see the boys of summer in their ruin | 1 | 1 | 2 | 1 | 1 |
| I see the summer children in their mothers | 1 | 13 | 2 | 1 | 13 |
| I see that from these boys shall men of nothing | 1 | 19 | 2 | 1 | 19 |
| O see the pulse of summer in the ice. | 1 | 24 | 2 | 1 | 24 |
| O see the poles of promise in the boys. | 2 | 24 | 2 | 3 | 6 |
| I see you boys of summer in your ruin. | 3 | 1 | 2 | 3 | 7 |
| O see the poles are kissing as they cross. | 3 | 6 | 2 | 3 | 12 |
| They see the squirrel stumble, | 36 | 16 | 20 | 41 | 16 |
| Eyes in the gables see | 58 | 3 | 35 | 67 | 3 |
| Eyes in this island see | 58 | 19 | 35 | 67 | 19 |
| And many years should see some change. | 63 | 17 | 38 | 72 | 17 |
| That the green child see like a grail | 69 | 22 | 43 | 78 | 22 |
| 'See,' drummed the taut masks, 'how the dead ascend: | 79 | 26 | 46 | 89 | 7 |
| When all my five and country senses see, | 81 | 1 | 47 | 90 | 1 |
| My nostrils see her breath burn like a bush. | 81 | 10 | 47 | 90 | 10 |
| That bury the sweet street slowly, see | 96 | 8 | 58 | 106 | 8 |
| O wake to see, after a noble fall, | 96 | 18 | 58 | 107 | 1 |
| You may not see, my son, | 105 | 2 | 64 | 116 | 2 |
| I see the tigron in tears | 110 | 1 | 67 | 121 | 3 |
| I see the wanting nun saint carved in a garb | 110 | 6 | 67 | 121 | 8 |
| Continence. I see the unfired phoenix, herald | 110 | 9 | 67 | 121 | 11 |
| Grave men, near death, who see with blinding sight | 116 | 13 | 70 | 128 | 13 |
| Now see, alone in us, | 126 | 12 | 74 | 140 | 12 |
| See what the gold gut drags from under | 154 | 11 | 83 | 172 | 11 |
| See what clings to hair and skull | 154 | 13 | 83 | 172 | 13 |
| Of dusk and water I see the tilting whispering | 168 | 24 | 87 | 189 | 9 |
| I see the boys of summer | 1 | | 2 | 1 | |
| When all my five and country senses see | 81 | | 47 | 90 | |
| SEED | | | | | |
| The seed that makes a forest of the loin | 6 | 13 | 4 | 6 | 13 |
| Warms youth and seed and burns the seeds of age; | 24 | 8 | 15 | 29 | 8 |

# SEED (continued)

|  | U.K. |  |  | U.S. |  |
|---|---|---|---|---|---|
|  | Page | Line | Poem | Page | Line |
| Where no seed stirs, | 24 | 9 | 15 | 29 | 9 |
| The fellow seed and shadow as it babbled | 30 | 9 | 18 | 35 | 9 |
| Shall the star-flanked seed be riddled, | 42 | 16 | 24 | 49 | 16 |
| Shall the star-flanked seed be riddled, | 42 | 23 | 24 | 50 | 2 |
| Let the hero seed find harbour, | 43 | 5 | 24 | 50 | 12 |
| Let the hero seed find harbour, | 43 | 12 | 24 | 50 | 19 |
| Let her inhale her dead, through seed and solid | 55 | 10 | 33 | 64 | 13 |
| Two heels of water on the floor of seed), | 56 | 24 | 34 | 66 | 3 |
| And the breath-white, curtained mouth of seed.' | 79 | 25 | 46 | 89 | 6 |
| Or sow my salt seed | 101 | 11 | 62 | 112 | 11 |
| Like the moon's seed, rubbish | 106 | 2 | 64 | 117 | 2 |
| Never to flourish in the fields of the white seed | 120 | 29 | 72 | 133 | 14 |
| The fields of seed and the time dying flesh astride, | 122 | 23 | 72 | 136 | 3 |
| Seed of sons in the loin of the black husk left. | 130 | 8 | 77 | 144 | 8 |
| Apple seed glides, | 164 | 12 | 86 | 183 | 19 |
| Pleading in the waded bay for the seed to flow | 176 | 7 | 90 | 197 | 7 |
| SEED-AT-ZERO |  |  |  |  |  |
| The seed-at-zero shall not storm | 42 | 1 | 24 | 49 | 1 |
| The seed-at-zero shall not storm | 42 | 8 | 24 | 49 | 8 |
| Man-in-seed, in seed-at-zero, | 43 | 15 | 24 | 51 | 1 |
| Man-in-seed, in seed-at-zero, | 43 | 22 | 24 | 51 | 8 |
| The seed-at-zero | 42 |  | 24 | 49 |  |
| SEEDED |  |  |  |  |  |
| Fear not the tread, the seeded milling, | 33 | 16 | 19 | 38 | 16 |
| SEEDLESS |  |  |  |  |  |
| Our eunuch dreams, all seedless in the light, | 14 | 1 | 10 | 16 | 1 |
| SEEDS |  |  |  |  |  |
| Warms youth and seed and burns the seeds of age; | 24 | 8 | 15 | 29 | 8 |
| By red-eyed orchards sow the seeds of snow, | 60 | 11 | 36 | 69 | 11 |
| And the strutting fern lay seeds on the black sill. | 88 | 12 | 52 | 97 | 12 |
| SEEDY |  |  |  |  |  |
| Stature by seedy shifting, | 1 | 20 | 2 | 1 | 20 |
| By crane and water-tower by the seedy trees | 49 | 8 | 29 | 58 | 8 |
| With swag of bubbles in a seedy sack | 67 | 17 | 41 | 76 | 17 |
| SEEK |  |  |  |  |  |
| Of new man strength, I seek the sun. | 29 | 4 | 17 | 34 | 8 |
| Who seek me landward, marking in my mouth | 31 | 22 | 18 | 37 | 4 |
| Be you sure the Thief will seek a way sly and sure | 163 | 26 | 86 | 183 | 7 |
| SEEN |  |  |  |  |  |
| Once seen strangers or shades on a stair; | 113 | 15 | 69 | 125 | 15 |
| SEES |  |  |  |  |  |
| My hero bares my side and sees his heart | 10 | 11 | 7 | 11 | 11 |
| Alone's unhurt, so the blind man sees best. | 50 | 9 | 30 | 59 | 9 |

| | U.K. | | | U.S. | |
|---|---|---|---|---|---|
| | Page | Line | Poem | Page | Line |
| SEESAW | | | | | |
| And on seesaw sunday nights I wooed | 174 | 8 | 89 | 194 | 8 |
| SEIZING | | | | | |
| On a seizing sky; small fishes glide | 170 | 22 | 88 | 190 | 22 |
| SEIZURE | | | | | |
| In seizure of silence commit the dead nuisance: | 35 | 23 | 20 | 40 | 23 |
| SELECTED | | | | | |
| Symbols are selected from the years' | 45 | 5 | 26 | 53 | 5 |
| SELF | | | | | |
| Dead and gone, dedicate forever to my self | 109 | 6 | 67 | 120 | 6 |
| Never shall my self chant | 109 | 25 | 67 | 120 | 25 |
| SELVES | | | | | |
| Who shows to the selves asleep | 153 | 7 | 83 | 171 | 3 |
| And the sea that hides his secret selves | 173 | 6 | 88 | 193 | 6 |
| SENSE | | | | | |
| In trust and tale have I divided sense, | 41 | 5 | 23 | 47 | 5 |
| Resembling to her dulled sense | 114 | 7 | 69 | 126 | 7 |
| SENSES | | | | | |
| When all my five and country senses see, | 81 | 1 | 47 | 90 | 1 |
| And when blind sleep drops on the spying senses, | 81 | 13 | 47 | 90 | 13 |
| Senses, and man a spirit in love | 173 | 2 | 88 | 193 | 2 |
| When all my five and country senses see | 81 | | 47 | 90 | |
| SENSUAL | | | | | |
| Born of the sensual root and sap; | 39 | 14 | 21 | 45 | 14 |
| The heart is sensual, though five eyes break. | 81 | 14 | 47 | 90 | 14 |
| Dressed to die, the sensual strut begun, | 99 | 6 | 60 | 110 | 6 |
| Saint carved and sensual among the scudding | 109 | 5 | 67 | 120 | 5 |
| And the sensual ruins make | 153 | 22 | 83 | 171 | 18 |
| SENT | | | | | |
| I sent my creature scouting on the globe, | 4 | 9 | 3 | 4 | 9 |
| I sent my own ambassador to light; | 5 | 9 | 3 | 5 | 9 |
| SENTENCE | | | | | |
| The dear, daft time I take to nudge the sentence, | 41 | 4 | 23 | 47 | 4 |
| SENTINEL | | | | | |
| The sexton sentinel, garrisoned under thistles, | 37 | 6 | 20 | 42 | 12 |
| SEPARATE | | | | | |
| A separate river breathes and runs; | 156 | 12 | 83 | 174 | 20 |
| SEPULCHRE | | | | | |
| Time's coral saint and the salt grief drown a foul sepulchre | 83 | 8 | 49 | 92 | 8 |
| SERAPHIM | | | | | |
| To seraphim | 165 | 8 | 86 | 184 | 16 |
| SERIAL | | | | | |
| Suit for a serial sum | 132 | 4 | 78 | 147 | 4 |
| SERMON | | | | | |
| Yard of the buttermilk rain on the pail! The sermon | 165 | 6 | 86 | 184 | 14 |

413

# SERPENT

| | U.K. | | | U.S. | |
|---|---|---|---|---|---|
| | Page | Line | Poem | Page | Line |
| **SERPENT** | | | | | |
| A serpent fiddled in the shaping-time. | 40 | 18 | 22 | 46 | 18 |
| This story's monster has a serpent caul, | 41 | 10 | 23 | 47 | 10 |
| Under a serpent cloud, | 171 | 5 | 88 | 191 | 5 |
| **SERPENT'S** | | | | | |
| Who was the serpent's | 131 | 3 | 77 | 145 | 9 |
| **SERPENTS** | | | | | |
| There shall be serpents in your tides, | 11 | 23 | 8 | 12 | 23 |
| Pour like a halo on the caps and serpents. | 75 | 24 | 44 | 84 | 24 |
| **SERVANT** | | | | | |
| How soon the servant sun, | 56 | 1 | 34 | 65 | 1 |
| How soon the servant sun | 56 | | 34 | 65 | |
| **SERVANTS** | | | | | |
| Child who was priest and servants, | 130 | 28 | 77 | 145 | 6 |
| **SERVE** | | | | | |
| All nerves to serve the sun, | 56 | 15 | 34 | 65 | 15 |
| Master the night nor serve the snowman's brain | 60 | 4 | 36 | 69 | 4 |
| Nutmeg, civet, and sea-parsley serve the plagued groom and bride | 84 | 5 | 49 | 93 | 11 |
| And serve me right as the preachers warn, | 175 | 9 | 89 | 195 | 14 |
| **SERVICE** | | | | | |
| The seas to service that her wood-tongued virtue | 87 | 22 | 52 | 96 | 22 |
| Silent in my service | 130 | 25 | 77 | 145 | 3 |
| **SET** | | | | | |
| Still set to scratch a laughter from my lung, | 12 | 5 | 9 | 13 | 5 |
| That set alight the weathers from a spark, | 22 | 14 | 14 | 27 | 14 |
| But time has set its maggot on their track. | 50 | 4 | 30 | 59 | 4 |
| Sailed and set dazzling by the handshaped ocean, | 78 | 5 | 46 | 87 | 5 |
| Myself to set foot | 102 | 8 | 63 | 113 | 8 |
| In the still sleeping town and set forth. | 102 | 10 | 63 | 113 | 10 |
| Suffer the first vision that set fire to the stars. | 108 | 18 | 66 | 119 | 18 |
| I set back the clock faced tailors, | 132 | 18 | 78 | 147 | 18 |
| **SETS** | | | | | |
| Poor peace as the sun sets | x | 6 | 1 | xviii | 12 |
| Over the sea-gut loudening, sets a rock alive; | 49 | 15 | 29 | 58 | 15 |
| Soon sets alight a long stick from the cradle; | 71 | 20 | 44 | 80 | 20 |
| **SETTING** | | | | | |
| Setting no store by harvest, freeze the soils; | 1 | 3 | 2 | 1 | 3 |
| **SETTLED** | | | | | |
| Settled on a virgin stronghold | 42 | 19 | 24 | 49 | 19 |
| **SETTLES** | | | | | |
| As they dive, the dust settles, | 36 | 19 | 20 | 41 | 19 |
| **SETTLING** | | | | | |
| Settling on a riddled stronghold | 42 | 26 | 24 | 50 | 5 |
| **SEVEN** | | | | | |
| That speak seven seas, | vii | 17 | 1 | xv | 17 |

| | U.K. | | | U.S. | |
|---|---|---|---|---|---|
| | *Page* | *Line* | *Poem* | *Page* | *Line* |
| Spelt out the seven seas, an evil index, | 74 | 12 | 44 | 83 | 12 |
| And into its talkative seven tombs | 157 | 19 | 83 | 176 | 11 |
| SEVENTY | | | | | |
| And sculptured Ann is seventy years of stone. | 88 | 7 | 52 | 97 | 7 |
| SEVERAL | | | | | |
| Of several near deaths, | 117 | 2 | 71 | 129 | 2 |
| SEVERERS | | | | | |
| And the second comers, the severers, the enemies from the deep | 115 | 22 | 69 | 127 | 22 |
| SEW | | | | | |
| When you sew the deep door. The bed is a cross place. | 97 | 13 | 59 | 108 | 13 |
| SEWING | | | | | |
| Soaks up the sewing tides), | 56 | 12 | 34 | 65 | 12 |
| Sewing a shroud for a journey | 99 | 4 | 60 | 110 | 4 |
| SEWN | | | | | |
| That, sewn to me by nerve and brain, | 4 | 11 | 3 | 4 | 11 |
| SEX | | | | | |
| The knobbly ape that swings along his sex | 13 | 9 | 9 | 14 | 16 |
| No third eye probe into a rainbow's sex | 67 | 25 | 41 | 76 | 25 |
| The climber of the water sex | 69 | 11 | 43 | 78 | 11 |
| SEXTON | | | | | |
| The sexton sentinel, garrisoned under thistles, | 37 | 6 | 20 | 42 | 12 |
| SHABBY | | | | | |
| Pulls down the shabby curtains of the skin; | 6 | 23 | 4 | 7 | 5 |
| The criers of Shabby and Shorten, | 132 | 27 | 78 | 148 | 2 |
| SHADE | | | | | |
| Sits in their double shade. | 6 | 21 | 4 | 7 | 3 |
| To shade and knit anew the patch of words | 21 | 10 | 13 | 25 | 10 |
| On that cloud coast to each grave-gabbing shade; | 26 | 18 | 16 | 31 | 18 |
| And this, nor this, is shade, the landed crow, | 51 | 19 | 31 | 60 | 19 |
| From your to-morrow-treading shade | 70 | 13 | 43 | 79 | 17 |
| Shade without shape? the shape of Pharaoh's echo? | 72 | 21 | 44 | 81 | 21 |
| Down the stacked sea and water-pillared shade, | 79 | 14 | 46 | 88 | 17 |
| Alcove of words out of cicada shade, | 82 | 4 | 48 | 91 | 4 |
| The shade of their trees was a word of many shades | 89 | 10 | 53 | 98 | 10 |
| And the cup and the cut bread in the dancing shade, | 120 | 3 | 72 | 132 | 8 |
| Bell believe or fear that the rustic shade or spell | 162 | 22 | 86 | 181 | 22 |
| Winds, from the dousing shade and the roarer at the latch, | 163 | 23 | 86 | 183 | 4 |
| SHADES | | | | | |
| There in the deep with quartered shades | 1 | 16 | 2 | 1 | 16 |
| Where fishes' food is fed the shades | 5 | 5 | 3 | 5 | 5 |

SHADES (continued)

|  | U.K. | | | U.S. | |
|---|---|---|---|---|---|
|  | *Page* | *Line* | *Poem* | *Page* | *Line* |
| There round about your stones the shades | 11 | 16 | 8 | 12 | 16 |
| The shades of girls, all flavoured from their shrouds, | 14 | 7 | 10 | 16 | 7 |
| The shade of their trees was a word of many shades | 89 | 10 | 53 | 98 | 10 |
| And for the woman in shades | 109 | 4 | 67 | 120 | 4 |
| About the saint in shades while the endless breviary | 109 | 26 | 67 | 120 | 26 |
| Of shades, symbol of desire beyond my hours | 110 | 7 | 67 | 121 | 9 |
| Once seen strangers or shades on a stair; | 113 | 15 | 69 | 125 | 15 |

SHADOW

|  |  |  |  |  |  |
|---|---|---|---|---|---|
| And cast a shadow crab upon the land, | 16 | 4 | 11 | 19 | 4 |
| The fellow seed and shadow as it babbled | 30 | 9 | 18 | 35 | 9 |
| Shall I let pray the shadow of a sound | 101 | 10 | 62 | 112 | 10 |
| Open as to the air to the naked shadow | 115 | 17 | 69 | 127 | 17 |
| A wind throws a shadow and it freezes fast. | 154 | 10 | 83 | 172 | 10 |
| Up to the swallow thronged loft by the shadow of my hand, | 160 | 25 | 85 | 180 | 2 |

SHADOWED

|  |  |  |  |  |  |
|---|---|---|---|---|---|
| And the shadowed head of pain | 138 | 7 | 82 | 155 | 7 |

SHADOWLESS

|  |  |  |  |  |  |
|---|---|---|---|---|---|
| Thus the shadowless man or ox, and the pictured devil, | 35 | 22 | 20 | 40 | 22 |

SHADOWS

|  |  |  |  |  |  |
|---|---|---|---|---|---|
| We watch the show of shadows kiss or kill, | 14 | 19 | 10 | 16 | 19 |
| Bisected shadows on the thunder's bone | 30 | 5 | 18 | 35 | 5 |
| Of psalms and shadows among the pincered sandcrabs prancing | 167 | 24 | 87 | 188 | 5 |

SHAFT

|  |  |  |  |  |  |
|---|---|---|---|---|---|
| The lovely gift of the gab bangs back on a blind shaft. | 94 | 6 | 57 | 104 | 6 |

SHAFTED

|  |  |  |  |  |  |
|---|---|---|---|---|---|
| Flies on the shafted disk, declaims the morning | 16 | 19 | 11 | 19 | 19 |

SHAKEN

|  |  |  |  |  |  |
|---|---|---|---|---|---|
| Through the shaken greensward lake, silent, on moonshod hooves, | 165 | 13 | 86 | 185 | 3 |

SHAKES

|  |  |  |  |  |  |
|---|---|---|---|---|---|
| Shakes, in crabbed burial shawl, by sorcerer's insect woken, | 83 | 23 | 49 | 93 | 5 |
| Shakes a desolate boy who slits his throat | 87 | 7 | 52 | 96 | 7 |

SHAKING

|  |  |  |  |  |  |
|---|---|---|---|---|---|
| Before the veins were shaking in their sieve, | 23 | 4 | 14 | 28 | 4 |
| Shaking the sea-hatched skull, | 38 | 22 | 20 | 44 | 12 |

SHALL

|  |  |  |  |  |  |
|---|---|---|---|---|---|
| I see that from these boys shall men of nothing | 1 | 19 | 2 | 1 | 19 |
| Shall calm her sores. | 9 | 18 | 6 | 10 | 18 |
| Shall not be latched while magic glides | 11 | 20 | 8 | 12 | 20 |

|  | U.K. | | | U.S. | |
| --- | --- | --- | --- | --- | --- |
|  | Page | Line | Poem | Page | Line |
| There shall be corals in your beds, | 11 | 22 | 8 | 12 | 22 |
| There shall be serpents in your tides, | 11 | 23 | 8 | 12 | 23 |
| Shall it be male or female? say the cells, | 12 | 8 | 9 | 13 | 8 |
| Shall it be male or female? say the fingers | 12 | 15 | 9 | 13 | 15 |
| Shall fall awake when cures and their itch | 15 | 2 | 10 | 17 | 2 |
| For we shall be a shouter like the cock, | 15 | 17 | 10 | 17 | 17 |
| Blowing the old dead back; our shots shall smack | 15 | 18 | 10 | 17 | 18 |
| And we shall be fit fellows for a life, | 15 | 20 | 10 | 17 | 20 |
| And who remain shall flower as they love, | 15 | 21 | 10 | 18 | 1 |
| The seed-at-zero shall not storm | 42 | 1 | 24 | 49 | 1 |
| The seed-at-zero shall not storm | 42 | 8 | 24 | 49 | 8 |
| Shall the star-flanked seed be riddled, | 42 | 16 | 24 | 49 | 16 |
| He shall grapple with the guard | 42 | 20 | 24 | 49 | 20 |
| Shall the star-flanked seed be riddled, | 42 | 23 | 24 | 50 | 2 |
| He shall grapple with the guard | 42 | 27 | 24 | 50 | 6 |
| Shall not thunder on the town | 43 | 17 | 24 | 51 | 3 |
| Shall the hero-in-tomorrow | 43 | 20 | 24 | 51 | 6 |
| Shall the hero-in-to-morrow | 43 | 27 | 24 | 51 | 13 |
| Shall gods be said to thump the clouds | 44 | 1 | 25 | 52 | 1 |
| Shall rainbows be their tunics' colour? | 44 | 4 | 25 | 52 | 4 |
| Shall it be said they sprinkle water | 44 | 6 | 25 | 52 | 6 |
| Shall it be said that, venuswise, | 44 | 8 | 25 | 52 | 8 |
| It shall be said that gods are stone. | 44 | 11 | 25 | 52 | 11 |
| Shall a dropped stone drum on the ground, | 44 | 12 | 25 | 52 | 12 |
| What shall it tell me if a timeless insect | 45 | 16 | 26 | 53 | 16 |
| Shall I still be love's house on the widdershin earth, | 47 | 5 | 27 | 55 | 5 |
| Shall not be known till windwell dries | 53 | 2 | 32 | 62 | 2 |
| The child shall question all his days, | 53 | 7 | 32 | 62 | 7 |
| Shall they clasp a comet in their fists? | 53 | 11 | 32 | 62 | 11 |
| Shall a white answer echo from the rooftops. | 53 | 15 | 32 | 62 | 15 |
| Shall raise a lamp | 56 | 25 | 34 | 66 | 4 |
| Shall I unbolt or stay | 58 | 5 | 35 | 67 | 5 |
| Shall I run to the ships | 58 | 21 | 35 | 67 | 21 |
| Shall I let in the stranger, | 59 | 4 | 35 | 68 | 4 |
| Shall I welcome the sailor, | 59 | 5 | 35 | 68 | 5 |
| Shall you turn cockwise on a tufted axle. | 60 | 24 | 36 | 69 | 24 |
| Shall I fall to death's feather. | 64 | 18 | 39 | 73 | 18 |
| All shall remain and on the graveward gulf | 67 | 27 | 41 | 76 | 27 |
| And death shall have no dominion. | 68 | 1 | 42 | 77 | 1 |
| Dead men naked they shall be one | 68 | 2 | 42 | 77 | 2 |
| They shall have stars at elbow and foot; | 68 | 5 | 42 | 77 | 5 |
| Though they go mad they shall be sane, | 68 | 6 | 42 | 77 | 6 |
| Though they sink through the sea they shall rise again; | 68 | 7 | 42 | 77 | 7 |
| Though lovers be lost love shall not; | 68 | 8 | 42 | 77 | 8 |
| And death shall have no dominion. | 68 | 9 | 42 | 77 | 9 |

| | U.K. | | | U.S. | |
|---|---|---|---|---|---|
| | Page | Line | Poem | Page | Line |
| And death shall have no dominion. | 68 | 10 | 42 | 77 | 10 |
| They lying long shall not die windily; | 68 | 12 | 42 | 77 | 12 |
| Strapped to a wheel, yet they shall not break; | 68 | 14 | 42 | 77 | 14 |
| Faith in their hands shall snap in two, | 68 | 15 | 42 | 77 | 15 |
| And death shall have no dominion. | 68 | 18 | 42 | 77 | 18 |
| And death shall have no dominion. | 68 | 19 | 42 | 77 | 19 |
| And death shall have no dominion. | 68 | 27 | 42 | 77 | 27 |
| 'Time shall not murder you,' He said, | 70 | 16 | 43 | 79 | 20 |
| So shall winged harbours through the rockbirds' eyes | 76 | 12 | 44 | 85 | 12 |
| Shall the blind horse sing sweeter? | 77 | 2 | 45 | 86 | 2 |
| Shall I, struck on the hot and rocking street, | 77 | 16 | 45 | 86 | 16 |
| Now my saying shall be my undoing, | 89 | 12 | 53 | 98 | 12 |
| Shall she receive a bellyful of weeds | 90 | 5 | 54 | 99 | 5 |
| Shall her smile breed that mouth, behind the mirror, | 90 | 13 | 54 | 99 | 13 |
| How shall my animal | 91 | 1 | 55 | 100 | 1 |
| How shall it magnetize, | 91 | 12 | 55 | 100 | 12 |
| Never shall beast be born to atlas the few seas | 92 | 4 | 55 | 101 | 10 |
| Will be the same grief flying. Whom shall they calm? | 100 | 11 | 61 | 111 | 11 |
| Shall the child sleep unharmed or the man be crying? | 100 | 12 | 61 | 111 | 12 |
| To-night shall find no dying but alive and warm | 100 | 15 | 61 | 111 | 15 |
| Shall drown in a grief as deep as his true grave, | 100 | 18 | 61 | 111 | 18 |
| Shall I let pray the shadow of a sound | 101 | 10 | 62 | 112 | 10 |
| I shall not murder | 101 | 14 | 62 | 112 | 14 |
| Never shall my self chant | 109 | 25 | 67 | 120 | 25 |
| Turns of your prayed flesh, nor shall I shoo the bird below me: | 109 | 27 | 67 | 121 | 1 |
| Both shall fail if I bow not to your blessing | 110 | 19 | 67 | 121 | 21 |
| One who called deepest down shall hold his peace | 117 | 9 | 71 | 129 | 9 |
| Till the blood shall spurt, | 129 | 21 | 77 | 143 | 21 |
| And the dust shall sing like a bird | 129 | 22 | 77 | 143 | 22 |
| Or we shall obey, and ride with you through the drowned. | 136 | 14 | 81 | 153 | 14 |
| I shall run lost in sudden | 139 | 11 | 82 | 156 | 11 |
| Breast I shall waken | 141 | 5 | 82 | 158 | 5 |
| Loping and bleating roughly and blithely shall leap, | 162 | 4 | 86 | 181 | 4 |
| Shall harrow and snow the blood while you ride wide and near, | 162 | 23 | 86 | 181 | 23 |
| And you shall wake, from country sleep, this dawn and each first dawn, | 166 | 11 | 86 | 186 | 11 |
| Wing, and blest shall | 168 | 5 | 87 | 188 | 9 |
| Shall gods be said to thump the clouds | 44 | | 25 | 52 | |

|  | U.K. | | | U.S. | |
|---|---|---|---|---|---|
|  | Page | Line | Poem | Page | Line |
| And death shall have no dominion | 68 | | 42 | 77 | |
| How shall my animal | 91 | | 55 | 100 | |
| SHALLOW | | | | | |
| Shallow and sedge, and 'dilly dilly,' calls the loft hawk, | 67 | 21 | 87 | 188 | 2 |
| SHAME | | | | | |
| Walking in wishes and lovely for shame | 153 | 9 | 83 | 171 | 5 |
| SHAMEFUL | | | | | |
| Is maiden in the shameful oak, omens | 78 | 21 | 46 | 87 | 21 |
| SHAMES | | | | | |
| Shames and the damp dishonours, the relic scraping. | 37 | 20 | 20 | 43 | 3 |
| SHANK | | | | | |
| An old man's shank one-marrowed with my bone, | 13 | 4 | 9 | 14 | 11 |
| SHAN'T | | | | | |
| Split all ends up they shan't crack; | 68 | 17 | 42 | 77 | 17 |
| SHAPE | | | | | |
| But when the stars, assuming shape, | 4 | 16 | 3 | 4 | 16 |
| And conjured up a carcass shape | 5 | 11 | 3 | 5 | 11 |
| And now the horns of England, in the sound of shape, | 49 | 13 | 29 | 58 | 13 |
| The dens of shape | 55 | 1 | 33 | 64 | 4 |
| Shape all her whelps with the long voice of water, | 55 | 2 | 33 | 64 | 5 |
| A nitric shape that leaps her, time and acid; | 55 | 7 | 33 | 64 | 10 |
| Who gave these seas their colour in a shape, | 61 | 1 | 36 | 70 | 1 |
| Shape with my fathers' thieves. | 67 | 28 | 41 | 76 | 28 |
| Death is all metaphors, shape in one history; | 71 | 15 | 44 | 80 | 15 |
| Shade without shape? the shape of Pharaoh's echo? | 72 | 21 | 44 | 81 | 21 |
| (My shape of age nagging the wounded whisper). | 72 | 22 | 44 | 81 | 22 |
| Time tracks the sound of shape on man and cloud, | 75 | 3 | 44 | 84 | 3 |
| Whose wizard shape I trace in the cavernous skull, | 91 | 2 | 55 | 100 | 2 |
| A limp and riderless shape to leap nine thinning months.' | 97 | 15 | 59 | 108 | 15 |
| And the star of the lost the shape of the eyes. | 147 | 1 | 82 | 164 | 1 |
| Sin who had a woman's shape | 153 | 14 | 83 | 171 | 10 |
| And surely he sails like the ship shape clouds. Oh he | 165 | 28 | 86 | 185 | 18 |
| SHAPED | | | | | |
| That shaped the Jordan near my home | 7 | 4 | 5 | 8 | 4 |
| Shaped my clayfellow, and the heaven's ark | 61 | 2 | 36 | 70 | 2 |
| Shaped in old armour and oak the countenance of a dunce | 85 | 7 | 50 | 94 | 7 |

|  | U.K. | | | U.S. | |
|---|---|---|---|---|---|
|  | Page | Line | Poem | Page | Line |
| And the harp shaped voice of the water's dust plucks in a fold | 121 | 24 | 72 | 134 | 19 |
| And air shaped Heaven where souls grow wild | 172 | 20 | 88 | 192 | 20 |
| SHAPELESS | | | | | |
| I who was shapeless as the water | 7 | 3 | 5 | 8 | 3 |
| With the womb of his shapeless people. | 34 | 3 | 19 | 39 | 9 |
| O who is glory in the shapeless maps, | 61 | 4 | 36 | 70 | 4 |
| 'Who could snap off the shapeless print | 70 | 12 | 43 | 79 | 16 |
| Child of the short spark in a shapeless country | 71 | 19 | 44 | 80 | 19 |
| SHAPES | | | | | |
| This rumpus of shapes | viii | 11 | I | xvi | 11 |
| Pack off the shapes of daylight and their starch, | 15 | 4 | 10 | 17 | 4 |
| The wordy shapes of women, and the rows | 16 | 11 | 11 | 19 | 11 |
| Shapes in a cinder death; love for his trick, | 19 | 23 | 12 | 23 | 8 |
| I learnt man's tongue, to twist the shapes of thoughts | 21 | 8 | 13 | 25 | 8 |
| All that shapes from the caul and suckle, | 34 | 4 | 19 | 39 | 10 |
| In shapes of sin forked out the bearded apple, | 40 | 4 | 22 | 46 | 4 |
| That shapes each bushy item of the air | 60 | 5 | 36 | 69 | 5 |
| And over the glazed lakes skated the shapes of fishes | 123 | 5 | 72 | 136 | 15 |
| Under the lighted shapes of faith and their moonshade | 176 | 17 | 90 | 197 | 17 |
| SHAPING-TIME | | | | | |
| In shaping-time the circle stung awake, | 40 | 3 | 22 | 46 | 3 |
| A serpent fiddled in the shaping-time. | 40 | 18 | 22 | 46 | 18 |
| SHARE | | | | | |
| And share my bed with Capricorn and Cancer. | 71 | 14 | 44 | 80 | 14 |
| To share my room in the house not right in the head, | 108 | 2 | 66 | 119 | 2 |
| Nor could share, for his pride, to the least | 114 | 21 | 69 | 126 | 21 |
| SHARK | | | | | |
| Glared through shark mask and navigating head, | 133 | 11 | 78 | 48 | 14 |
| SHARP | | | | | |
| Sharp in my second death I marked the hills, harvest | 28 | 17 | 17 | 33 | 17 |
| Where, wound in emerald linen and sharp wind, | 79 | 16 | 46 | 88 | 19 |
| Of the sharp, enamelled eyes and the spectacled claws | 85 | 2 | 50 | 94 | 2 |
| SHATTERED | | | | | |
| Rage shattered waters kick | 172 | 16 | 88 | 192 | 16 |
| SHAWL | | | | | |
| And, winding-footed in their shawl and sheet, | 14 | 4 | 10 | 16 | 4 |
| Shakes, in crabbed burial shawl, by sorcerer's insect woken, | 83 | 23 | 49 | 93 | 5 |
| To the kissed kite hems of his shawl, | 95 | 3 | 58 | 105 | 3 |

SHE

|  | U.K. | | | U.S. | |
|---|---|---|---|---|---|
|  | Page | Line | Poem | Page | Line |
| One by one in dust and shawl, | 155 | 1 | 83 | 173 | 5 |
| Nor blows back moon and midnight as she blows. | 2 | 6 | 2 | 2 | 6 |
| My busy heart who shudders as she talks | 16 | 7 | 11 | 19 | 7 |
| The boy she dropped from darkness at her side | 21 | 2 | 13 | 25 | 2 |
| Half of the fellow mother as she dabbles | 30 | 3 | 18 | 35 | 3 |
| She threads off the sap and needles, blood and bubble | 35 | 10 | 20 | 40 | 10 |
| You are all these, said she who gave me the long suck, | 46 | 17 | 27 | 54 | 17 |
| She who was who I hold, the fats and flower, | 54 | 2 | 33 | 63 | 2 |
| And she who lies, | 54 | 17 | 33 | 63 | 17 |
| Who then is she, | 54 | 25 | 33 | 64 | 1 |
| She holding me? The people's sea drives on her, | 54 | 26 | 33 | 64 | 2 |
| That she I have, | 55 | 3 | 33 | 64 | 6 |
| And salt-eyed stumble bedward where she lies | 67 | 12 | 41 | 76 | 12 |
| She makes for me a nettle's innocence | 78 | 16 | 46 | 87 | 16 |
| She would not have me sinking in the holy | 87 | 18 | 52 | 96 | 18 |
| Flood of her heart's fame; she would lie dumb and deep | 87 | 19 | 52 | 96 | 19 |
| Shall she receive a bellyful of weeds | 90 | 5 | 54 | 99 | 5 |
| The tombstone told when she died. | 93 | 1 | 56 | 102 | 1 |
| She married in this pouring place, | 93 | 4 | 56 | 102 | 4 |
| Before she lay on a stranger's bed | 93 | 11 | 56 | 102 | 11 |
| She cried her white-dressed limbs were bare | 93 | 17 | 56 | 102 | 17 |
| She wept in her pain and made mouths, | 93 | 19 | 56 | 102 | 19 |
| And the other full of tears that she will be dead, | 100 | 5 | 61 | 111 | 5 |
| She deludes the heaven-proof house with entering clouds | 108 | 6 | 66 | 119 | 6 |
| Yet she deludes with walking the nightmarish room, | 108 | 7 | 66 | 119 | 7 |
| She has come possessed | 108 | 10 | 66 | 119 | 10 |
| She sleeps in the narrow trough yet she walks the dust | 108 | 13 | 66 | 119 | 13 |
| The she mules bear their minotaurs, | 110 | 4 | 67 | 121 | 6 |
| Lucklessly she must lie patient | 110 | 25 | 67 | 122 | 3 |
| That she might stand in the night | 112 | 11 | 68 | 124 | 11 |
| Man was the burning England she was sleep-walking, and the enamouring island | 113 | 20 | 69 | 125 | 20 |
| Close and far she announced the theft of the heart | 114 | 16 | 69 | 126 | 16 |
| A she bird sleeping brittle by | 115 | 10 | 69 | 127 | 10 |
| O she lies alone and still, | 115 | 18 | 69 | 127 | 18 |
| A she bird rose and rayed like a burning bride. | 121 | 14 | 72 | 134 | 9 |
| A she bird dawned, and her breast with snow and scarlet downed. | 121 | 15 | 72 | 134 | 10 |

| | U.K. | | | U.S. | |
|---|---|---|---|---|---|
| | *Page* | *Line* | *Poem* | *Page* | *Line* |
| Of fields. For love, the long ago she bird rises. Look. | 121 | 25 | 72 | 134 | 20 |
| Was flying through the house as though the she bird praised | 122 | 3 | 72 | 135 | 3 |
| Listen and look where she sails the goose plucked sea, | 122 | 20 | 72 | 135 | 20 |
| In a choir of wings, as though she slept or died, | 123 | 12 | 72 | 137 | 2 |
| And she rose with him flowering in her melting snow. | 123 | 20 | 72 | 137 | 10 |
| Her deepsea pillow where once she married alone, | 127 | 9 | 75 | 141 | 9 |
| For a man sleeps where fire leapt down and she learns through his arm | 127 | 13 | 75 | 141 | 13 |
| She longs among horses and angels, | 150 | 9 | 83 | 167 | 13 |
| She nipped and dived in the nick of love, | 151 | 7 | 83 | 168 | 15 |
| Kill Time! She turns in her pain! | 155 | 10 | 83 | 173 | 14 |
| She is breaking with seasons and clouds; | 156 | 8 | 83 | 174 | 16 |
| In the coal black sky and she bore angels! | 175 | 26 | 89 | 196 | 7 |
| The tombstone told when she died | 93 | | 56 | 102 | |
| SHE-[BIRD] | | | | | |
| All night lost and long wading in the wake of the she- | 122 | 18 | 72 | 135 | 18 |
| SHEARWATER | | | | | |
| Oh the shearwater birds and their boatsized brood | 151 | 19 | 83 | 169 | 7 |
| SHEATH-DECKED | | | | | |
| The sheath-decked jacks, queen with a shuffled heart; | 73 | 13 | 44 | 82 | 13 |
| SHEBA'S | | | | | |
| And no-one stirs at Sheba's side | 153 | 12 | 83 | 171 | 8 |
| SHED | | | | | |
| The sun and moon shed one white light. | 20 | 9 | 13 | 24 | 9 |
| SHEDS | | | | | |
| Sheds the syllabic blood and drains her words. | 16 | 8 | 11 | 19 | 8 |
| In the dark of the coffin and sheds dry leaves, | 87 | 8 | 52 | 96 | 8 |
| SHEEP | | | | | |
| Sheep white hollow farms | viii | 25 | 1 | xvi | 25 |
| Of sheep and churches noise | x | 5 | 1 | xviii | 11 |
| Flocked with the sheep white smoke of the farm house cowl | 119 | 9 | 72 | 131 | 9 |
| But a black sheep with a crumpled horn, | 175 | 13 | 89 | 195 | 18 |
| SHEEPWHITE | | | | | |
| Fear or believe that the wolf in a sheepwhite hood | 162 | 3 | 86 | 181 | 3 |
| SHEET | | | | | |
| How at my sheet goes the same crooked worm. | 9 | 22 | 6 | 10 | 22 |
| And, winding-footed in their shawl and sheet, | 14 | 4 | 10 | 16 | 4 |

|  | U.K. | | | U.S. | |
|---|---|---|---|---|---|
|  | Page | Line | Poem | Page | Line |
| My Egypt's armour buckling in its sheet, | 31 | 10 | 18 | 36 | 10 |
| Trap I with coil and sheet, | 56 | 19 | 34 | 65 | 19 |
| I drew the white sheet over the islands | 134 | 29 | 79 | 151 | 7 |
| That came from the wound wrapped in the salt sheet. | 136 | 4 | 81 | 153 | 4 |
| And when the salt sheet broke in a storm of singing | 136 | 7 | 81 | 153 | 7 |
| We heard the sea sound sing, we saw the salt sheet tell. | 136 | 12 | 81 | 153 | 12 |
| SHELL | | | | | |
| Through the rotating shell, strong | 28 | 2 | 17 | 33 | 2 |
| And breaks his shell in the last shocked beginning; | 41 | 13 | 23 | 47 | 13 |
| Where bird and shell are babbling in my tower? | 46 | 14 | 27 | 54 | 14 |
| Twine in a moon-blown shell, | 69 | 15 | 43 | 78 | 15 |
| In the molested rocks the shell of virgins, | 78 | 18 | 46 | 87 | 18 |
| Its wringing shell, and let her eyelids fasten. | 79 | 9 | 46 | 88 | 12 |
| Down breeze and shell to a discordant beach, | 81 | 7 | 47 | 90 | 7 |
| Vessel of abscesses and exultation's shell, | 91 | 3 | 55 | 100 | 3 |
| Or saw in the looking-glass shell | 93 | 7 | 56 | 102 | 7 |
| And out of every domed and soil-based shell | 115 | 5 | 69 | 127 | 5 |
| And laid your cheek against a cloud-formed shell: | 125 | 23 | 74 | 139 | 23 |
| Till every turtle crushed from his shell | 151 | 10 | 83 | 168 | 18 |
| Valley and sahara in a shell, | 152 | 18 | 83 | 170 | 10 |
| Thrown to the sea in the shell of a girl | 152 | 20 | 83 | 170 | 12 |
| Always good-bye, cried the voices through the shell, | 154 | 1 | 83 | 172 | 1 |
| And read, in a shell, | 168 | 1 | 87 | 188 | 5 |
| SHELL-HUNG | | | | | |
| Of eels, saint heron hymning in the shell-hung distant | 168 | 12 | 87 | 188 | 16 |
| SHELLING | | | | | |
| As sunlight paints the shelling of their heads. | 1 | 18 | 2 | 1 | 18 |
| SHELLS | | | | | |
| Stabbing, and herons, and shells | vii | 16 | 1 | xv | 16 |
| On casting tides, are tangled in the shells, | 32 | 2 | 18 | 37 | 8 |
| The mazes of his praise and envious tongue were worked in flames and shells. | 95 | 17 | 58 | 105 | 17 |
| And load the throats of shells | 117 | 22 | 71 | 129 | 22 |
| And the coins on my eyelids sang like shells. | 134 | 30 | 79 | 151 | 8 |
| Through wynds and shells of drowned | 170 | 23 | 88 | 190 | 23 |
| SHELTER | | | | | |
| Woe to the windy masons at my shelter? | 47 | 6 | 27 | 55 | 6 |
| That night of time under the Christward shelter: | 71 | 12 | 44 | 80 | 12 |
| SHIELD | | | | | |
| To shield the glistening brain and blunt the examiners, | 85 | 8 | 50 | 94 | 8 |

| | | | U.K. | | | U.S. | |
| --- | --- | --- | --- | --- | --- | --- | --- |
| | | | *Page* | *Line* | *Poem* | *Page* | *Line* |
| **SHIELDED** | | | | | | | |
| | From the broomed witch's spume you are shielded by fern | | 162 | 17 | 86 | 181 | 17 |
| | Be shielded by chant and flower and gay may you | | 163 | 19 | 86 | 182 | 19 |
| **SHIFT** | | | | | | | |
| | Of bud of Adam through his boxy shift, | | 19 | 13 | 12 | 22 | 18 |
| | The secret child, I shift about the sea | | 32 | 11 | 18 | 37 | 17 |
| | O ring of seas, nor sorrow as I shift | | 60 | 20 | 36 | 69 | 20 |
| | Bent like three trees and bird-papped through her shift, | | 75 | 9 | 44 | 84 | 9 |
| **SHIFTING** | | | | | | | |
| | Stature by seedy shifting, | | 1 | 20 | 2 | 1 | 20 |
| | Shifting to light, turned on me like a moon. | | 26 | 3 | 16 | 31 | 3 |
| **SHINE** | | | | | | | |
| | Should lanterns shine, the holy face, | | 63 | 1 | 38 | 72 | 1 |
| | Should lanterns shine | | 63 | | 38 | 72 | |
| **SHINES** | | | | | | | |
| | Light breaks where no sun shines; | | 24 | 1 | 15 | 29 | 1 |
| | Light breaks where no sun shines | | 24 | | 15 | 29 | |
| **SHINGLE** | | | | | | | |
| | We grieve as the blithe birds, never again, leave shingle and elm, | | 168 | 9 | 87 | 188 | 13 |
| **SHINING** | | | | | | | |
| | Terror and shining from | | 139 | 12 | 82 | 156 | 12 |
| | Shining, it was Adam and maiden, | | 160 | 8 | 85 | 179 | 8 |
| | And my shining men no more alone | | 173 | 26 | 88 | 193 | 26 |
| **SHIP** | | | | | | | |
| | Snail of man in His ship of fires | | 69 | 8 | 43 | 78 | 8 |
| | In the fountain basin where I sailed my ship | | 111 | 10 | 68 | 123 | 10 |
| | And surely he sails like the ship shape clouds. Oh he | | 165 | 28 | 86 | 185 | 18 |
| | Ship towns to pastures of otters. He | | 170 | 24 | 88 | 190 | 24 |
| **SHIP'S** | | | | | | | |
| | Hears, there, this fox light, my flood ship's | | ix | 18 | 1 | xvii | 18 |
| **SHIP-RACKED** | | | | | | | |
| | Time's ship-racked gospel on the globe I balance: | | 76 | 11 | 44 | 85 | 11 |
| **SHIP-WORK** | | | | | | | |
| | The vanishing of the musical ship-work and the chucked bells, | | 95 | 8 | 58 | 105 | 8 |
| **SHIPPEN** | | | | | | | |
| | Trounced by his wings in the hissing shippen, long dead | | 177 | 19 | 90 | 198 | 18 |
| **SHIPS** | | | | | | | |
| | Ships anchor off the bay. | | 58 | 20 | 35 | 67 | 20 |
| | Shall I run to the ships | | 58 | 21 | 35 | 67 | 21 |

| | U.K. | | | U.S. | |
|---|---|---|---|---|---|
| | *Page* | *Line* | *Poem* | *Page* | *Line* |
| Ships, hold you poison or grapes? | 58 | 25 | 35 | 67 | 25 |
| Ships anchor off the bay, | 59 | 2 | 35 | 68 | 2 |
| Hands of the stranger and holds of the ships, | 59 | 7 | 35 | 68 | 7 |
| Said the dwindling ships. | 149 | 24 | 83 | 167 | 4 |
| Trees cool and dry in the whirlpool of ships | 156 | 2 | 83 | 174 | 10 |
| Dawn ships clouted aground, | 172 | 25 | 88 | 192 | 25 |
| SHIPS' | | | | | |
| Be by the ships' sea broken at the manstring anchored | 38 | 8 | 20 | 43 | 18 |
| SHIPWRECK | | | | | |
| In the shipwreck of muscle; | 38 | 10 | 20 | 43 | 20 |
| SHIPWRECKED | | | | | |
| The sun shipwrecked west on a pearl | 149 | 15 | 83 | 166 | 15 |
| SHIPYARDS | | | | | |
| And the shipyards of Galilee's footprints hide a navy of doves. | 127 | 7 | 75 | 141 | 7 |
| SHIRE | | | | | |
| Of many a thorny shire tell you notes, | 16 | 15 | 11 | 19 | 15 |
| My girl ranging the night in the rose and shire | 162 | 9 | 86 | 181 | 9 |
| SHOAL | | | | | |
| And tussle in a shoal of loves. | 150 | 6 | 83 | 167 | 10 |
| Whenever I dove in a breast high shoal, | 174 | 21 | 89 | 194 | 21 |
| SHOALS | | | | | |
| And dark shoals every holy field. | x | 7 | 1 | xviii | 13 |
| SHOCKED | | | | | |
| And breaks his shell in the last shocked beginning; | 41 | 13 | 23 | 47 | 13 |
| SHOED | | | | | |
| The singing breaks in the snow shoed villages of wishes | 123 | 3 | 72 | 136 | 13 |
| SHONE | | | | | |
| Shone in my ears the light of sound, | 20 | 20 | 13 | 24 | 20 |
| And nothing shone on the water's face | 150 | 20 | 83 | 168 | 4 |
| SHOO | | | | | |
| Turns of your prayed flesh, nor shall I shoo the bird below me: | 109 | 27 | 67 | 121 | 1 |
| SHOOK | | | | | |
| Laughing when he shook his paper | 111 | 20 | 68 | 123 | 20 |
| SHOOT | | | | | |
| Joy is the knock of dust, Cadaver's shoot | 19 | 12 | 12 | 22 | 17 |
| To shoot and sing your praise, | 117 | 8 | 71 | 129 | 8 |
| SHOOTING | | | | | |
| The child that sucketh long is shooting up, | 71 | 16 | 44 | 80 | 16 |
| Over the barbed and shooting sea assumed an army | 158 | 6 | 84 | 177 | 6 |
| SHOP | | | | | |
| Tasselled in cellar and snipping shop | 132 | 11 | 78 | 147 | 11 |

| | U.K. | | | U.S. | |
|---|---|---|---|---|---|
| | *Page* | *Line* | *Poem* | *Page* | *Line* |
| SHORE | | | | | |
| Seaports by a drunken shore | 43 | 6 | 24 | 50 | 13 |
| Seaports by a thirsty shore | 43 | 13 | 24 | 50 | 20 |
| Am I not you who front the tidy shore, | 46 | 15 | 27 | 54 | 15 |
| The strata of the shore and drown red rock; | 82 | 20 | 48 | 91 | 20 |
| Priested shore | 102 | 4 | 63 | 113 | 4 |
| Singly lie with the whole wide shore, | 115 | 3 | 69 | 127 | 3 |
| SHORES | | | | | |
| Of tides that never touch the shores. | 8 | 10 | 5 | 9 | 10 |
| Of the crotch of the squawking shores, | 96 | 2 | 58 | 106 | 2 |
| SHORN | | | | | |
| Sigh long, clay cold, lie shorn, | 92 | 6 | 55 | 101 | 12 |
| Flying. The rite is shorn | 123 | 6 | 72 | 136 | 16 |
| The waters shorn. | 164 | 5 | 86 | 183 | 12 |
| SHORT | | | | | |
| Child of the short spark in a shapeless country | 71 | 19 | 44 | 80 | 19 |
| The size of genesis? the short spark's gender? | 72 | 20 | 44 | 81 | 20 |
| Clips short the gesture of breath. | 92 | 11 | 55 | 101 | 17 |
| SHORTEN | | | | | |
| The criers of Shabby and Shorten, | 132 | 27 | 78 | 148 | 2 |
| SHOT | | | | | |
| Turns damp to dry; the golden shot | 6 | 2 | 4 | 6 | 2 |
| Blood shot and scattered to the winds of light | 23 | 5 | 14 | 28 | 5 |
| Shot through the leaf, | 54 | 12 | 33 | 63 | 12 |
| Shot in the wind, by tilted arcs, | 69 | 26 | 43 | 79 | 2 |
| When all the keys shot from the locks, and rang. | 135 | 8 | 80 | 152 | 8 |
| SHOTS | | | | | |
| Impose their shots, throwing the nights away; | 14 | 18 | 10 | 16 | 18 |
| Blowing the old dead back; our shots shall smack | 15 | 18 | 10 | 17 | 18 |
| SHOULD | | | | | |
| I should tell summer from the trees, the worms | 45 | 9 | 26 | 53 | 9 |
| I should learn spring by the cuckooing, | 45 | 12 | 26 | 53 | 12 |
| And the slug should teach me destruction. | 45 | 13 | 26 | 53 | 13 |
| Man should be cured of distemper. | 48 | 27 | 28 | 57 | 4 |
| Should he, for centre sake, hop in the dust, | 51 | 6 | 31 | 60 | 6 |
| Should he who split his children with a cure | 51 | 13 | 31 | 60 | 13 |
| Should lanterns shine, the holy face, | 63 | 1 | 38 | 72 | 1 |
| And many years should see some change. | 63 | 17 | 38 | 72 | 17 |
| Should cure our ills of the water | 82 | 12 | 48 | 91 | 12 |
| Who should be furious, | 91 | 6 | 55 | 100 | 6 |
| Old age should burn and rave at close of day; | 116 | 2 | 70 | 128 | 2 |
| And fires where he should prowl down the cloud | 120 | 12 | 72 | 132 | 17 |
| When cold as snow he should run the wended vales among | 120 | 20 | 72 | 133 | 5 |
| I should hear him fly with the high fields | 161 | 2 | 85 | 180 | 5 |
| O deepest wound of all that he should die | | | 91 | 201 | 16 |

| | U.K. | | | U.S. | |
|---|---|---|---|---|---|
| | Page | Line | Poem | Page | Line |
| Should lanterns shine | 63 | | 38 | 72 | |
| **SHOULDER** | | | | | |
| That rules from wrist to shoulder, | 10 | 2 | 7 | 11 | 2 |
| The mighty hand leads to a sloping shoulder, | 62 | 5 | 37 | 71 | 5 |
| On the hill's shoulder, | 102 | 25 | 63 | 113 | 25 |
| And steeples pierce the cloud on her shoulder | 157 | 1 | 83 | 175 | 13 |
| With the dew, come back, the cock on his shoulder: it was all | 160 | 7 | 85 | 179 | 7 |
| **SHOUT** | | | | | |
| In lairs and asylums of the tremendous shout. | 125 | 16 | 74 | 139 | 16 |
| Shout | 169 | 6 | 87 | 189 | 15 |
| **SHOUTER** | | | | | |
| For we shall be a shouter like the cock, | 15 | 17 | 10 | 17 | 17 |
| **SHOVED** | | | | | |
| And I shoved it into the coal black sky | 175 | 18 | 89 | 195 | 23 |
| **SHOW** | | | | | |
| We watch the show of shadows kiss or kill, | 14 | 19 | 10 | 16 | 19 |
| **SHOWER** | | | | | |
| Camped in the drug-white shower of nerves and food, | 77 | 8 | 45 | 86 | 8 |
| And walked abroad in a shower of all my days. | 102 | 16 | 63 | 113 | 16 |
| **SHOWN** | | | | | |
| Now shown and mostly bare I would lie down, | 133 | 21 | 78 | 149 | 4 |
| **SHOWS** | | | | | |
| Where no wax is, the candle shows its hairs. | 24 | 12 | 15 | 29 | 12 |
| Who shows to the selves asleep | 153 | 7 | 83 | 171 | 3 |
| **SHRAPNEL** | | | | | |
| I dreamed my genesis and died again, shrapnel | 28 | 13 | 17 | 33 | 13 |
| **SHRILL** | | | | | |
| And the shrill child's play | 167 | 5 | 87 | 187 | 5 |
| **SHRINE** | | | | | |
| In the shrine | 141 | 3 | 82 | 158 | 3 |
| To the shrine of his world's wound | 145 | 3 | 82 | 162 | 3 |
| **SHRINED** | | | | | |
| Oh, let me midlife mourn by the shrined | 172 | 22 | 88 | 192 | 22 |
| **SHRIVELLING** | | | | | |
| Hymned his shrivelling flock, | 95 | 13 | 58 | 105 | 13 |
| **SHROUD** | | | | | |
| Hauls my shroud sail. | 9 | 13 | 6 | 10 | 13 |
| Erect a walking centre in the shroud, | 56 | 27 | 34 | 66 | 6 |
| My camel's eyes will needle through the shroud. | 73 | 6 | 44 | 82 | 6 |
| Weighed in rock shroud, is my proud pyramid; | 79 | 15 | 46 | 88 | 18 |
| Sewing a shroud for a journey | 99 | 4 | 60 | 110 | 4 |
| Herons walk in their shroud, | 170 | 27 | 88 | 190 | 27 |
| **SHROUDED** | | | | | |
| That shrouded men might marrow as they fly. | 15 | 10 | 10 | 17 | 10 |

|  | U.K. | | | U.S. | |
| --- | Page | Line | Poem | Page | Line |
| **SHROUDING** | | | | | |
| The invoked, shrouding veil at the cap of the face, | 91 | 5 | 55 | 100 | 5 |
| **SHROUDS** | | | | | |
| The shades of girls, all flavoured from their shrouds, | 14 | 7 | 10 | 16 | 7 |
| **SHRUBBERIES** | | | | | |
| After the railings and shrubberies | 112 | 14 | 68 | 124 | 14 |
| **SHRUBBERY** | | | | | |
| Gabriel and radiant shrubbery as the morning grows joyful | 158 | 15 | 84 | 177 | 15 |
| **SHUT** | | | | | |
| When cameras shut they hurry to their hole | 14 | 15 | 10 | 16 | 15 |
| Shut, too, in a tower of words, I mark | 16 | 9 | 11 | 19 | 9 |
| O make me a mask and a wall to shut from your spies | 85 | 1 | 50 | 94 | 1 |
| The grave and my calm body are shut to your coming as stone, | 98 | 6 | 59 | 109 | 9 |
| To shut the sun, plunge, mount your darkened keys | 118 | 5 | 71 | 130 | 9 |
| **SHUDDERS** | | | | | |
| My busy heart who shudders as she talks | 16 | 7 | 11 | 19 | 7 |
| **SHUFFLED** | | | | | |
| From limbs that had the measure of the worm, shuffled | 28 | 5 | 17 | 33 | 5 |
| The sheath-decked jacks, queen with a shuffled heart; | 73 | 13 | 44 | 82 | 13 |
| **SHUFFLING** | | | | | |
| The black ram, shuffling of the year, old winter, | 72 | 15 | 44 | 81 | 15 |
| **SHY** | | | | | |
| The cattle stirring, the mousing cat stepping shy, | 119 | 22 | 72 | 132 | 2 |
| I tiptoed shy in the gooseberry wood, | 174 | 4 | 89 | 194 | 4 |
| Petticoats galed high, or shy with the rough riding boys, | 176 | 18 | 90 | 197 | 18 |
| **SHYEST** | | | | | |
| Brassily at my shyest secret, | 107 | 5 | 65 | 118 | 5 |
| **SICK** | | | | | |
| Of sick old manhood on the fallen jaws, | 12 | 24 | 9 | 14 | 3 |
| Quaked the sick sea and snouted deep, | 151 | 2 | 83 | 168 | 10 |
| **SIDE** | | | | | |
| My hero bares my side and sees his heart | 10 | 11 | 7 | 11 | 11 |
| A rooking girl who stole me for her side, | 12 | 2 | 9 | 13 | 2 |
| By the sea's side, hearing the noise of birds, | 16 | 5 | 11 | 19 | 5 |
| By the sea's side hear the dark-vowelled birds. | 17 | 8 | 11 | 20 | 8 |
| The boy she dropped from darkness at her side | 21 | 2 | 13 | 25 | 2 |
| Housed in the side. | 54 | 16 | 33 | 63 | 16 |
| At nightbreak born in the fat side, from an animal bed | 84 | 2 | 49 | 93 | 8 |

| | U.K. | | | U.S. | |
|---|---|---|---|---|---|
| | Page | Line | Poem | Page | Line |
| Soaked my table the uglier side of a hill | 89 | 2 | 53 | 98 | 2 |
| Before I heard in my mother's side | 93 | 6 | 56 | 102 | 6 |
| This side of the truth, | 105 | 1 | 64 | 116 | 1 |
| With immortality at my side like Christ the sky. | 110 | 21 | 67 | 121 | 23 |
| Celebrating at her side | 114 | 19 | 69 | 126 | 19 |
| Winter-locked side by side, | 126 | 2 | 74 | 140 | 2 |
| And no-one stirs at Sheba's side | 153 | 12 | 83 | 171 | 8 |
| To court the honeyed heart from your side before sunrise | 162 | 13 | 86 | 181 | 13 |
| Heart! Slyly, slowly, hearing the wound in her side go | 165 | 24 | 86 | 185 | 14 |
| Until I die he will not leave my side.) | | | 91 | 201 | 19 |
| This side of the truth (for Llewelyn) | 105 | | 64 | 116 | |

SIDED
| Into the sided lap of light grew strong, | 21 | 3 | 13 | 25 | 3 |
|---|---|---|---|---|---|

SIDES
| Out of the sides of the north | 153 | 18 | 83 | 171 | 14 |
|---|---|---|---|---|---|
| And falls, and flowers in the yawning wound at our sides, | 163 | 13 | 86 | 183 | 20 |

SIDLE
| To my man-iron sidle. | 35 | 6 | 20 | 40 | 6 |
|---|---|---|---|---|---|

SIEVE
| Before the veins were shaking in their sieve, | 23 | 4 | 14 | 28 | 4 |
|---|---|---|---|---|---|

SIGH
| Sigh long, clay cold, lie shorn, | 92 | 6 | 55 | 101 | 12 |
|---|---|---|---|---|---|
| One lean sigh when we heard | 126 | 5 | 74 | 140 | 5 |

SIGHED
| Under his downy arm you sighed as he struck, | 125 | 19 | 74 | 139 | 19 |
|---|---|---|---|---|---|
| (Sighed the old ram rod, dying of women), | 174 | 3 | 89 | 194 | 3 |
| (Sighed the old ram rod, dying of bitches), | 174 | 15 | 89 | 194 | 15 |
| (Sighed the old ram rod, dying of welcome), | 174 | 27 | 89 | 195 | 3 |
| (Sighed the old ram rod, dying of downfall), | 175 | 10 | 89 | 195 | 15 |
| (Sighed the old ram rod, dying of strangers), | 175 | 22 | 89 | 196 | 3 |

SIGHING
| There the dark blade and wanton sighing her down | 113 | 16 | 69 | 125 | 16 |
|---|---|---|---|---|---|

SIGHS
| Out of the sighs a little comes, | 48 | 1 | 28 | 56 | 1 |
|---|---|---|---|---|---|
| Beneath my life, that sighs for the seducer's coming | 109 | 13 | 67 | 120 | 13 |
| Out of the sighs | 48 | | 28 | 56 | |

SIGHT
| Grave men, near death, who see with blinding sight | 116 | 13 | 70 | 128 | 13 |
|---|---|---|---|---|---|

SIGN
| Touched the first cloud and left a sign. | 22 | 12 | 14 | 27 | 12 |
|---|---|---|---|---|---|

|  | U.K. | | | U.S. | |
| --- | --- | --- | --- | --- | --- |
|  | *Page* | *Line* | *Poem* | *Page* | *Line* |
| SIGNAL |  |  |  |  |  |
| The signal moon is zero in their voids. | 1 | 12 | 2 | 1 | 12 |
| The signal grass that tells me all I know | 16 | 22 | 11 | 19 | 22 |
| SIGNATURE |  |  |  |  |  |
| In the beginning was the pale signature, | 22 | 7 | 14 | 27 | 7 |
| SIGNED |  |  |  |  |  |
| The hand that signed the paper felled a city; | 62 | 1 | 37 | 71 | 1 |
| The hand that signed the treaty bred a fever, | 62 | 9 | 37 | 71 | 9 |
| The hand that signed the paper | 62 |  | 37 | 71 |  |
| SIGNS |  |  |  |  |  |
| Some let me make you of the meadow's signs; | 16 | 21 | 11 | 19 | 21 |
| SILENCE |  |  |  |  |  |
| In seizure of silence commit the dead nuisance: | 35 | 23 | 20 | 40 | 23 |
| And burned sea silence on a wick of words. | 74 | 4 | 44 | 83 | 4 |
| Lost in a limp-treed and uneating silence, | 79 | 2 | 46 | 88 | 5 |
| Tells with silence the last light breaking | 101 | 4 | 62 | 112 | 4 |
| Silence, silence to do, when earth grew loud, | 125 | 15 | 74 | 139 | 15 |
| Back to black silence melt and mourn | 140 | 10 | 82 | 157 | 10 |
| Sleeps till Silence blows on a cloud | 153 | 15 | 83 | 171 | 11 |
| As the world falls, silent as the cyclone of silence. | 164 | 14 | 86 | 183 | 21 |
| God in his whirlwind silence save, who marks the sparrows hail, | 168 | 21 | 87 | 189 | 6 |
| Wave's silence, wept white angelus knells. | 171 | 11 | 88 | 191 | 11 |
| SILENCES |  |  |  |  |  |
| The lunar silences, the silent tide | 82 | 9 | 48 | 91 | 9 |
| SILENT |  |  |  |  |  |
| The lunar silences, the silent tide | 82 | 9 | 48 | 91 | 9 |
| A thundering bullring of your silent and girl-circled island. | 96 | 26 | 58 | 107 | 9 |
| The colossal intimacies of silent | 113 | 14 | 69 | 125 | 14 |
| Silent in my service | 130 | 25 | 77 | 145 | 3 |
| From the chill, silent centre | 132 | 22 | 78 | 147 | 22 |
| On the silent sea we have heard the sound | 136 | 3 | 81 | 153 | 3 |
| As the world falls, silent as the cyclone of silence. | 164 | 14 | 86 | 183 | 21 |
| Through the shaken greensward lake, silent, on moonshod hooves, | 165 | 13 | 86 | 185 | 3 |
| SILK |  |  |  |  |  |
| Why silk is soft and the stone wounds | 53 | 6 | 32 | 62 | 6 |
| And a silk pigeon's guilt in her proud absence, | 78 | 17 | 46 | 87 | 17 |
| Unclenched, armless, silk and rough love that breaks all rocks. | 126 | 16 | 74 | 140 | 16 |
| Or rippling soft in the spinney moon as the silk | 177 | 7 | 90 | 198 | 6 |
| SILL |  |  |  |  |  |
| And the strutting fern lay seeds on the black sill. | 88 | 12 | 52 | 97 | 12 |
| SILLY |  |  |  |  |  |
| My silly suit, hardly yet suffered for, | 133 | 1 | 78 | 148 | 4 |

|  | U.K. | | | U.S. | |
|---|---|---|---|---|---|
|  | *Page* | *Line* | *Poem* | *Page* | *Line* |
| **SILVER** | | | | | |
| No silver whistles chase him down the weeks' | 67 | 21 | 41 | 76 | 21 |
| Time for the swimmers' hands, music for silver lock | 86 | 7 | 51 | 95 | 7 |
| **SIMMERING** | | | | | |
| With every simmering woman his mouse | 175 | 1 | 89 | 195 | 6 |
| **SIMPLE** | | | | | |
| And nightly under the simple stars | 160 | 1 | 85 | 179 | 1 |
| So it must have been after the birth of the simple light | 160 | 11 | 85 | 179 | 11 |
| They with the simple Jacks were a boulder of wives)— | 178 | 3 | 90 | 199 | 4 |
| **SIN** | | | | | |
| Skinny as sin, the foaming marrow, | 33 | 11 | 19 | 38 | 11 |
| In shapes of sin forked out the bearded apple, | 40 | 4 | 22 | 46 | 4 |
| For my tall turrets cárry as your sin? | 46 | 6 | 27 | 54 | 6 |
| I laid her down and told her sin, | 65 | 23 | 40 | 74 | 23 |
| Sin who had a woman's shape | 153 | 14 | 83 | 171 | 10 |
| **SIN-EATER** | | | | | |
| Lie all unknowing of the grave sin-eater. | 47 | 8 | 27 | 55 | 8 |
| **SINCE** | | | | | |
| With every cry since light | 117 | 23 | 71 | 129 | 23 |
| This night and each night since the falling star you were born, | 164 | 6 | 86 | 183 | 13 |
| Since you were born: | 166 | 10 | 86 | 186 | 10 |
| Than ever was since the world was said, | 173 | 17 | 88 | 193 | 17 |
| Who once, green countries since, were a hedge-row of joys. | 176 | 20 | 90 | 197 | 20 |
| **SINEW** | | | | | |
| Were that enough, bone, blood, and sinew, | 48 | 24 | 28 | 57 | 1 |
| **SINEWS** | | | | | |
| Twisting on racks when sinews give way, | 68 | 13 | 42 | 77 | 13 |
| **SING** | | | | | |
| At poor peace I sing | vii | 23 | 1 | xv | 23 |
| Shall the blind horse sing sweeter? | 77 | 2 | 45 | 86 | 2 |
| That her love sing and swing through a brown chapel, | 87 | 25 | 52 | 96 | 25 |
| To shoot and sing your praise, | 117 | 8 | 71 | 129 | 8 |
| Listen. The minstrels sing | 121 | 1 | 72 | 133 | 16 |
| Sing | 129 | 11 | 77 | 143 | 11 |
| And the dust shall sing like a bird | 129 | 22 | 77 | 143 | 22 |
| We heard the sea sound sing, we saw the salt sheet tell. | 136 | 12 | 81 | 153 | 12 |
| And the midwives of miracle sing | 138 | 9 | 82 | 155 | 9 |
| Sing through the water-spoken prow | 152 | 6 | 83 | 169 | 18 |
| Sing how the seal has kissed her dead! | 152 | 10 | 83 | 170 | 2 |
| Sing and howl through sand and anemone | 152 | 17 | 83 | 170 | 9 |

SING (continued)

| | U.K. | | | U.S. | |
|---|---|---|---|---|---|
| | *Page* | *Line* | *Poem* | *Page* | *Line* |
| Sing and strike his heavy haul | 154 | 17 | 83 | 172 | 17 |
| And the old men sing from newborn lips: | 155 | 8 | 83 | 173 | 12 |
| And he who taught their lips to sing | 155 | 18 | 83 | 174 | 2 |
| Strike and sing his catch of fields | 156 | 13 | 83 | 175 | 1 |
| That uncalm still it is sure alone to stand and sing | 158 | 21 | 84 | 177 | 21 |
| Thirty-five bells sing struck | 171 | 12 | 88 | 191 | 12 |
| Fall and the dew larks sing | 173 | 21 | 88 | 193 | 21 |
| SINGEING | | | | | |
| Drivelled down to one singeing tree | 95 | 20 | 58 | 105 | 20 |
| SINGERS | | | | | |
| Here were fond climates and sweet singers suddenly | 103 | 1 | 63 | 114 | 1 |
| Word, singers, and tongue | 131 | 1 | 77 | 145 | 7 |
| SINGING | | | | | |
| Green was the singing house. | 20 | 24 | 13 | 24 | 24 |
| High lord esquire, speak up the singing cloud, | 60 | 17 | 36 | 69 | 17 |
| And sirens singing from our lady's sea-straw. | 73 | 24 | 44 | 82 | 24 |
| The fats of midnight when the salt was singing; | 74 | 10 | 44 | 83 | 10 |
| The singing breaks in the snow shoed villages of wishes | 123 | 3 | 72 | 136 | 13 |
| I labour by singing light | 128 | 6 | 76 | 142 | 6 |
| With singing | 129 | 10 | 77 | 143 | 10 |
| And when the salt sheet broke in a storm of singing | 136 | 7 | 81 | 153 | 7 |
| About the happy yard and singing as the farm was home, | 159 | 11 | 85 | 178 | 11 |
| Of the dingle torn to singing and the surpliced | 165 | 4 | 86 | 184 | 12 |
| Earth, air, water, fire, singing into the white act, | 165 | 16 | 86 | 185 | 6 |
| SINGINGBIRDS | | | | | |
| Still in the water and singingbirds. | 104 | 8 | 63 | 115 | 10 |
| SINGLE | | | | | |
| My great blood's iron single | 38 | 15 | 20 | 44 | 5 |
| Have sought your single grave, | 117 | 28 | 71 | 130 | 4 |
| SINGLY | | | | | |
| Singly lie with the whole wide shore, | 115 | 3 | 69 | 127 | 3 |
| SINGS | | | | | |
| My ark sings in the sun | x | 17 | 1 | xviii | 23 |
| 'My fathers' globe knocks on its nave and sings.' | 26 | 11 | 16 | 31 | 11 |
| Sings to the treading hawk | 115 | 13 | 69 | 127 | 13 |
| Time sings through the intricately dead snow drop. Listen. | 121 | 10 | 72 | 134 | 5 |
| To the gold gut that sings on his reel | 149 | 19 | 83 | 166 | 19 |
| His fiery reel sings off its flames, | 151 | 16 | 83 | 169 | 4 |
| He sings towards anguish; finches fly | 170 | 20 | 88 | 190 | 20 |
| Chastity prays for me, piety sings, | 175 | 28 | 89 | 196 | 9 |
| SINGSONG | | | | | |
| You king singsong owls, who moonbeam. | ix | 3 | 1 | xvii | 3 |

|  | U.K. Page | U.K. Line | Poem | U.S. Page | U.S. Line |
|---|---|---|---|---|---|
| **SINGULAR** | | | | | |
| Bent like a beast to lap the singular floods | 90 | 3 | 54 | 99 | 3 |
| **SINK** | | | | | |
| Though they sink through the sea they shall rise again; | 68 | 7 | 42 | 77 | 7 |
| That cannot sink or cease | 117 | 10 | 71 | 129 | 10 |
| **SINKING** | | | | | |
| She would not have me sinking in the holy | 87 | 18 | 52 | 96 | 18 |
| Creep and harp on the tide, sinking their charmed, bent pin | 91 | 24 | 55 | 101 | 2 |
| **SINNERS** | | | | | |
| And all love's sinners in sweet cloth kneel to a hyleg image, | 84 | 4 | 49 | 93 | 10 |
| **SINNERS'** | | | | | |
| It is the sinners' dust-tongued bell claps me to churches | 83 | 1 | 49 | 92 | 1 |
| It is the sinners' dust-tongued bell | 83 | | 49 | 92 | |
| **SINS** | | | | | |
| Some let me tell you of the raven's sins. | 16 | 24 | 11 | 19 | 24 |
| The pyre yet to be lighted of my sins and days, | 109 | 3 | 67 | 120 | 3 |
| **SIPPING** | | | | | |
| By sipping at the vine of days. | 8 | 12 | 5 | 9 | 12 |
| **SIR** | | | | | |
| Joy is no knocking nation, sir and madam, | 19 | 6 | 12 | 22 | 11 |
| Sir, is your doom. | 19 | 15 | 12 | 22 | 20 |
| Sir no say, | 51 | 10 | 31 | 60 | 10 |
| No say sir | 51 | 17 | 31 | 60 | 17 |
| (Sir morrow mark), | 56 | 2 | 34 | 65 | 2 |
| Sir morrow at his sponge, | 56 | 8 | 34 | 65 | 8 |
| (Sir morrow stamps | 56 | 23 | 34 | 66 | 2 |
| This inward sir, | 57 | 2 | 34 | 66 | 9 |
| Over Sir John's hill, | 167 | 1 | 87 | 187 | 1 |
| Daws Sir John's just hill dons, and again the gulled birds hare | 167 | 15 | 87 | 187 | 15 |
| It is the heron and I, under judging Sir John's elmed | 168 | 16 | 87 | 189 | 1 |
| Now on Sir John's hill. The heron, ankling the scaly | 169 | 7 | 87 | 189 | 16 |
| Over Sir John's hill | 167 | | 87 | 187 | |
| **SIRE** | | | | | |
| You are your sisters' sire, said seaweedy, | 47 | 2 | 27 | 55 | 2 |
| **SIREN'S** | | | | | |
| And love plucked out the stinging siren's eye, | 74 | 7 | 44 | 83 | 7 |
| **SIREN-PRINTED** | | | | | |
| Glint in the staved and siren-printed caverns, | 78 | 20 | 46 | 87 | 20 |

| | | U.K. | | | U.S. | |
| --- | --- | --- | --- | --- | --- | --- |
| | | *Page* | *Line* | *Poem* | *Page* | *Line* |
| SIRENS | | | | | | |
| | And sirens singing from our lady's sea-straw. | 73 | 24 | 44 | 82 | 24 |
| SISTER | | | | | | |
| | And sister to the fathering worm. | 7 | 6 | 5 | 8 | 6 |
| | And the wind was my sister suitor; | 7 | 15 | 5 | 8 | 15 |
| | Do you not sister me, nor the erected crime | 46 | 5 | 27 | 54 | 5 |
| | Am I not sister, too, who is my saviour? | 46 | 12 | 27 | 54 | 12 |
| | Have brotherless his sister on the handsaw. | 51 | 14 | 31 | 60 | 14 |
| SISTERS' | | | | | | |
| | You are your sisters' sire, said seaweedy, | 47 | 2 | 27 | 55 | 2 |
| SIT | | | | | | |
| | I sit and watch the worm beneath my nail | 13 | 6 | 9 | 14 | 13 |
| SITS | | | | | | |
| | Sits in their double shade. | 6 | 21 | 4 | 7 | 3 |
| SITTING | | | | | | |
| | I astounded the sitting tailors, | 132 | 17 | 78 | 147 | 17 |
| SIX | | | | | | |
| | Of lover, mother, lovers, or his six | 13 | 13 | 9 | 14 | 20 |
| | Of the sky, king of your six years. | 106 | 4 | 64 | 117 | 4 |
| SIX-YEAR | | | | | | |
| | The boat swims into the six-year weather, | 154 | 9 | 83 | 172 | 9 |
| SIXTH | | | | | | |
| | Which sixth of wind blew out the burning gentry? | 73 | 1 | 44 | 82 | 1 |
| SIZE | | | | | | |
| | The size of genesis? the short spark's gender? | 72 | 20 | 44 | 81 | 20 |
| | And over the sea wet church the size of a snail | 103 | 7 | 63 | 114 | 7 |
| | For the country of death is the heart's size | 146 | 17 | 82 | 163 | 17 |
| | Out of the urn the size of a man | 154 | 21 | 83 | 173 | 1 |
| SIZZLING | | | | | | |
| | And the sizzling beds of the town cried, Quick!— | 174 | 20 | 89 | 194 | 20 |
| SKATED | | | | | | |
| | And over the glazed lakes skated the shapes of fishes | 123 | 5 | 72 | 136 | 15 |
| SKEIN | | | | | | |
| | With bridebait of gold bread, ɪ with a living skein, | 91 | 25 | 55 | 101 | 3 |
| SKELETON | | | | | | |
| | Rise of the skeleton and | 28 | 22 | 17 | 34 | 2 |
| | Unsex the skeleton this mountain minute, | 75 | 16 | 44 | 84 | 16 |
| | I make a weapon of an ass's skeleton | 79 | 5 | 46 | 88 | 8 |
| | White as the skeleton | 130 | 21 | 77 | 144 | 21 |
| SKELETON'S | | | | | | |
| | Through the waves of the fat streets nor the skeleton's thin ways. | 98 | 5 | 59 | 109 | 8 |
| SKIES | | | | | | |
| | Time upon time the towers of the skies | 53 | 19 | 32 | 62 | 19 |

| | U.K. | | | U.S. | |
|---|---|---|---|---|---|
| | Page | Line | Poem | Page | Line |
| And the golden ball spins out of the skies; | 90 | 10 | 54 | 99 | 10 |
| The natural circle of the discovered skies | 91 | 10 | 55 | 100 | 10 |
| Into the answering skies from the green ground, | 100 | 7 | 61 | 111 | 7 |
| Under the unminding skies, | 105 | 6 | 64 | 116 | 6 |
| Possessed by the skies | 108 | 12 | 66 | 119 | 12 |

SKIMMED

| | | | | | |
|---|---|---|---|---|---|
| Hill of cypresses! The din and tale in the skimmed | 165 | 5 | 86 | 184 | 13 |

SKIMS

| | | | | | |
|---|---|---|---|---|---|
| As the boat skims on with drinking wings! | 154 | 14 | 83 | 172 | 14 |

SKIN

| | | | | | |
|---|---|---|---|---|---|
| Pulls down the shabby curtains of the skin; | 6 | 23 | 4 | 7 | 5 |
| Of skin and vein around the well | 8 | 2 | 5 | 9 | 2 |
| (Give, summer, over), the cemented skin, | 19 | 19 | 12 | 23 | 4 |
| The word of the blood, the wily skin, | 65 | 15 | 40 | 74 | 15 |
| The terrible world my brother bares his skin. | 80 | 7 | 46 | 89 | 15 |

SKINNING

| | | | | | |
|---|---|---|---|---|---|
| Where no cold is, the skinning gales unpin | 24 | 22 | 15 | 29 | 22 |

SKINNY

| | | | | | |
|---|---|---|---|---|---|
| Skinny as sin, the foaming marrow, | 33 | 11 | 19 | 38 | 11 |

SKINS

| | | | | | |
|---|---|---|---|---|---|
| Grafts on its bride one-sided skins of truth; | 15 | 8 | 10 | 17 | 8 |

SKIPPED

| | | | | | |
|---|---|---|---|---|---|
| I skipped in a blush as the big girls rolled | 174 | 6 | 89 | 194 | 6 |

SKIRTS

| | | | | | |
|---|---|---|---|---|---|
| As a he-god's paddling water skirts, | 132 | 16 | 78 | 147 | 16 |

SKULKING

| | | | | | |
|---|---|---|---|---|---|
| For my sulking, skulking, coal black soul! | 175 | 7 | 89 | 195 | 12 |

SKULKS

| | | | | | |
|---|---|---|---|---|---|
| Or skulks in the dell moon but moonshine echoing clear | 163 | 2 | 86 | 182 | 2 |

SKULL

| | | | | | |
|---|---|---|---|---|---|
| And these poor nerves so wired to the skull | 10 | 6 | 7 | 11 | 6 |
| They dance between their arclamps and our skull, | 14 | 17 | 10 | 16 | 17 |
| No, no, you lover skull, descending hammer | 19 | 2 | 12 | 22 | 7 |
| You hero skull, Cadaver in the hanger | 19 | 4 | 12 | 22 | 9 |
| Love's twilit nation and the skull of state, | 19 | 14 | 12 | 22 | 19 |
| From poles of skull and toe the windy blood | 24 | 14 | 15 | 29 | 14 |
| The flight of the carnal skull | 37 | 24 | 20 | 43 | 7 |
| Shaking the sea-hatched skull, | 38 | 22 | 20 | 44 | 12 |
| Horned down with skullfoot and the skull of toes | 72 | 9 | 44 | 81 | 9 |
| With the wild breast and blessed and giant skull | 87 | 28 | 52 | 96 | 28 |
| Whose wizard shape I trace in the cavernous skull, | 91 | 2 | 55 | 100 | 2 |
| The skull of the earth is barbed with a war of burning brains and hair. | 96 | 9 | 58 | 106 | 9 |

SKULL (continued)

| | U.K. | | | U.S. | |
|---|---|---|---|---|---|
| | *Page* | *Line* | *Poem* | *Page* | *Line* |
| In the cinder of the little skull, | 130 | 16 | 77 | 144 | 16 |
| In the cinder of the little skull, | 131 | 2 | 77 | 145 | 8 |
| See what clings to hair and skull | 154 | 13 | 83 | 172 | 13 |
| On skull and scar where his loves lie wrecked, | 171 | 13 | 88 | 191 | 13 |

SKULLFOOT

| | U.K. | | | U.S. | |
|---|---|---|---|---|---|
| Horned down with skullfoot and the skull of toes | 72 | 9 | 44 | 81 | 9 |

SKY

| | U.K. | | | U.S. | |
|---|---|---|---|---|---|
| Who periscope through flowers to the sky. | 5 | 6 | 3 | 5 | 6 |
| Sage on the earth and sky; | 11 | 21 | 8 | 12 | 21 |
| And earth and sky were as one airy hill, | 20 | 8 | 13 | 24 | 8 |
| The earth and sky were as two mountains meeting. | 20 | 15 | 13 | 24 | 15 |
| From the divorcing sky I learnt the double, | 21 | 20 | 13 | 26 | 3 |
| Nor fenced, nor staked, the gushers of the sky | 24 | 16 | 15 | 29 | 16 |
| And dropped on dreaming and the upward sky. | 26 | 5 | 16 | 31 | 5 |
| Through the rampart of the sky | 42 | 15 | 24 | 49 | 15 |
| Through the rampart of the sky | 42 | 22 | 24 | 50 | 1 |
| Under the arc of the sky they are unsafe. | 50 | 5 | 30 | 59 | 5 |
| And the parliament of sky, | 65 | 10 | 40 | 74 | 10 |
| And the sky lays down her laws, | 66 | 10 | 40 | 75 | 10 |
| This was the sky, Jack Christ, each minstrel angle | 75 | 11 | 44 | 84 | 11 |
| Pierce the spilt sky with diving wing in weed and heel | 86 | 4 | 51 | 95 | 4 |
| Behind my head a square of sky sags over | 90 | 8 | 54 | 99 | 8 |
| The scudding base of the familiar sky, | 96 | 4 | 58 | 106 | 4 |
| And down the other air and the blue altered sky | 103 | 17 | 63 | 114 | 17 |
| Of the sky, king of your six years. | 106 | 4 | 64 | 117 | 4 |
| Water and light, the earth and sky, | 106 | 8 | 64 | 117 | 8 |
| With immortality at my side like Christ the sky. | 110 | 21 | 67 | 121 | 23 |
| Gentle in their clogs over the fallen sky, | 119 | 24 | 72 | 132 | 4 |
| He wept from the crest of grief, he prayed to the veiled sky | 120 | 7 | 72 | 132 | 12 |
| Past the statues of the stables and the sky roofed sties | 120 | 9 | 72 | 132 | 14 |
| And the sky of birds in the plumed voice charmed | 122 | 8 | 72 | 135 | 8 |
| The sky, the bird, the bride, | 122 | 21 | 72 | 136 | 1 |
| The sky is torn across | 124 | 1 | 73 | 138 | 1 |
| And this day's sun leapt up the sky out of her thighs | 127 | 4 | 75 | 141 | 4 |
| The sky stride of the always slain | 142 | 10 | 82 | 159 | 10 |
| The sky. | 148 | 8 | 82 | 165 | 8 |
| The sky gathered again | 160 | 9 | 85 | 179 | 9 |
| And nothing I cared, at my sky blue trades, that time allows | 160 | 20 | 85 | 179 | 20 |
| Lying the sky | 165 | 20 | 86 | 185 | 10 |

| | U.K. | | | U.S. | |
|---|---|---|---|---|---|
| | Page | Line | Poem | Page | Line |
| On a seizing sky; small fishes glide | 170 | 22 | 88 | 190 | 22 |
| And I shoved it into the coal black sky | 175 | 18 | 89 | 195 | 23 |
| In the coal black sky and she bore angels! | 175 | 26 | 89 | 196 | 7 |
| Light of his thighs, spreadeagle to the dunghill sky, | 177 | 3 | 90 | 198 | 2 |
| Here among the light of the lording sky | | | 91 | 201 | 8 |
| SKY-BLUE | | | | | |
| But wailed and nested in the sky-blue wall | 126 | 7 | 74 | 140 | 7 |
| SKY-SCRAPING | | | | | |
| Range on the sky-scraping place. | 43 | 21 | 24 | 51 | 7 |
| SKYSIGNS | | | | | |
| Under the skysigns they who have no arms | 50 | 7 | 30 | 59 | 7 |
| SKYWARD | | | | | |
| Her flesh was meek as milk, but this skyward statue | 87 | 27 | 52 | 96 | 27 |
| SLAIN | | | | | |
| The sky stride of the always slain | 142 | 10 | 82 | 159 | 10 |
| Stone for the sake of the souls of the slain birds sailing. | 169 | 12 | 87 | 189 | 21 |
| SLANT | | | | | |
| My images stalk the trees and the slant sap's tunnel, | 36 | 1 | 20 | 41 | 1 |
| In his slant, racking house | 170 | 25 | 88 | 190 | 25 |
| SLAPPED | | | | | |
| Slapped down the guillotine, the blood-red double | 41 | 6 | 23 | 47 | 6 |
| SLASH | | | | | |
| Suffer the slash of vision by the fin-green stubble, | 38 | 7 | 20 | 43 | 17 |
| SLASHED | | | | | |
| Slashed down the last snake as though | 134 | 13 | 79 | 150 | 13 |
| And I gave my soul a blind, slashed eye, | 175 | 16 | 89 | 195 | 21 |
| SLASHES | | | | | |
| Cartoon of slashes on the tide-traced crater, | 74 | 1 | 44 | 83 | 1 |
| SLATES | | | | | |
| Rain beats the sand and slates. | 59 | 3 | 35 | 68 | 3 |
| SLAUGHTERED | | | | | |
| And the funeral grains of the slaughtered floor. | 135 | 5 | 80 | 152 | 5 |
| SLAVED-FOR | | | | | |
| My paid-for slaved-for own too late | 132 | 6 | 78 | 147 | 6 |
| SLAVES | | | | | |
| Who slaves to his crouched, eternal end | 171 | 4 | 88 | 191 | 4 |
| SLAY | | | | | |
| And the maggot no man can slay.' | 65 | 16 | 40 | 74 | 16 |
| SLEEK | | | | | |
| Slides good in the sleek mouth | 171 | 9 | 88 | 191 | 9 |
| SLEEP | | | | | |
| Beasts who sleep good and thin, | ix | 26 | 1 | xvii | 26 |

|  | U.K. | | | U.S. | |
| --- | --- | --- | --- | --- | --- |
|  | Page | Line | Poem | Page | Line |
| Drew in his eyes the straws of sleep, | 4 | 17 | 3 | 4 | 17 |
| Sleep navigates the tides of time; | 5 | 1 | 3 | 5 | 1 |
| And sleep rolls mute above the beds | 5 | 4 | 3 | 5 | 4 |
| I fellowed sleep who kissed me in the brain, | 26 | 1 | 16 | 31 | 1 |
| Where still they sleep unknowing of their ghost. | 26 | 20 | 16 | 31 | 20 |
| I dreamed my genesis in sweat of sleep, breaking | 28 | 1 | 17 | 33 | 1 |
| The crutch that marrow taps upon their sleep, | 30 | 14 | 18 | 35 | 14 |
| Sprinkles in children's eyes a long-last sleep | 53 | 13 | 32 | 62 | 13 |
| And when blind sleep drops on the spying senses, | 81 | 13 | 47 | 90 | 13 |
| Morning smack of the spade that wakes up sleep, | 87 | 6 | 52 | 96 | 6 |
| Or a nacreous sleep among soft particles and charms | 97 | 17 | 59 | 108 | 17 |
| The one not caring to whom in his sleep he will move | 100 | 4 | 61 | 111 | 4 |
| For the sleep in a safe land and the love who dies | 100 | 10 | 61 | 111 | 10 |
| Shall the child sleep unharmed or the man be crying? | 100 | 12 | 61 | 111 | 12 |
| And mark the dark eyed wave, through the eyes of sleep, | 100 | 19 | 61 | 111 | 19 |
| Sleep to a newborn sleep in a swaddling loin-leaf stroked and sang | 113 | 22 | 69 | 125 | 22 |
| Forgotten dark, rest their pulse and bury their dead in her faithless sleep. | 115 | 23 | 69 | 127 | 23 |
| Back. Lines of age sleep on the stones till trumpeting dawn. | 123 | 8 | 72 | 136 | 18 |
| Spoilers and pokers of sleep, | 134 | 5 | 79 | 150 | 5 |
| Lie still, sleep becalmed, sufferer with the wound | 136 | 1 | 81 | 153 | 1 |
| Lie still, sleep becalmed, hide the mouth in the throat, | 136 | 13 | 81 | 153 | 13 |
| Blind host to sleep | 145 | 6 | 82 | 162 | 6 |
| As I rode to sleep the owls were bearing the farm away, | 160 | 2 | 85 | 179 | 2 |
| Nor that riding to sleep | 161 | 1 | 85 | 180 | 4 |
| Sleep, good, for ever, slow and deep, spelled rare and wise, | 162 | 8 | 86 | 181 | 8 |
| And flower of country sleep and the greenwood keep. | 162 | 18 | 86 | 181 | 18 |
| Never, my girl, until tolled to sleep by the stern | 162 | 21 | 86 | 181 | 21 |
| Lie in grace. Sleep spelled at rest in the lowly house | 163 | 20 | 86 | 183 | 1 |
| In the tower and tolls to sleep over the stalls | 164 | 3 | 86 | 183 | 10 |

|  | U.K. | | | U.S. | |
|---|---|---|---|---|---|
|  | Page | Line | Poem | Page | Line |
| And you shall wake, from country sleep, this dawn and each first dawn, | 166 | 11 | 86 | 186 | 11 |
| And I lie down but to sleep in bed, | 175 | 6 | 89 | 195 | 11 |
| I fellowed sleep | 26 |  | 16 | 31 |  |
| Lie Still, Sleep Becalmed | 136 |  | 81 | 153 |  |
| In country sleep | 162 |  | 86 | 181 |  |
| SLEEPER |  |  |  |  |  |
| Awake, my sleeper, to the sun, | 5 | 13 | 3 | 5 | 13 |
| The dream has sucked the sleeper of his faith | 15 | 9 | 10 | 17 | 9 |
| And the old dog sleeper | 112 | 1 | 68 | 124 | 1 |
| SLEEPER'S |  |  |  |  |  |
| Let fall the tear of time; the sleeper's eye, | 26 | 2 | 16 | 31 | 2 |
| SLEEPERS |  |  |  |  |  |
| And stake the sleepers in the savage grave | 30 | 17 | 18 | 35 | 17 |
| Of sleepers whose tongue I toll | 146 | 3 | 82 | 163 | 3 |
| Of the charting sleepers prays | 146 | 15 | 82 | 163 | 15 |
| SLEEPING |  |  |  |  |  |
| Slow in a sleeping wind. | 6 | 15 | 4 | 6 | 15 |
| How light the sleeping on this soily star, | 26 | 24 | 16 | 32 | 4 |
| Sleeping on either hand. | 82 | 8 | 48 | 91 | 8 |
| In the still sleeping town and set forth. | 102 | 10 | 63 | 113 | 10 |
| A she bird sleeping brittle by | 115 | 10 | 69 | 127 | 10 |
| Roosts sleeping chill till the flame of the cock crow | 119 | 19 | 72 | 131 | 19 |
| SLEEPINGS |  |  |  |  |  |
| Which is the world? Of our two sleepings, which | 15 | 1 | 10 | 17 | 1 |
| SLEEP-WALKING |  |  |  |  |  |
| Man was the burning England she was sleep-walking, and the enamouring island | 113 | 20 | 69 | 125 | 20 |
| SLEEPS |  |  |  |  |  |
| She sleeps in the narrow trough yet she walks the dust | 108 | 13 | 66 | 119 | 13 |
| For a man sleeps where fire leapt down and she learns through his arm | 127 | 13 | 75 | 141 | 13 |
| Sleeps till Silence blows on a cloud | 153 | 15 | 83 | 171 | 11 |
| SLEEPY |  |  |  |  |  |
| The sleepy man of winter pulls, | 2 | 5 | 2 | 2 | 5 |
| Unpacks the head that, like a sleepy ghost, | 10 | 3 | 7 | 11 | 3 |
| SLEET |  |  |  |  |  |
| The blind, clawed stare is cold as sleet. | 153 | 5 | 83 | 171 | 1 |
| SLEEVE |  |  |  |  |  |
| Death flashing from his sleeve, | 67 | 16 | 41 | 76 | 16 |
| From Jesu's sleeve trumped up the king of spots, | 73 | 12 | 44 | 82 | 12 |
| By the curve of the nude mouth or the laugh up the sleeve. | 85 | 12 | 50 | 94 | 12 |

| | U.K. | | | U.S. | |
|---|---|---|---|---|---|
| | *Page* | *Line* | *Poem* | *Page* | *Line* |
| SLEEVES | | | | | |
| The spittled eyes, the salt ponds in the sleeves, | 87 | 5 | 52 | 96 | 5 |
| The stream from the priest black wristed spinney and sleeves | 165 | 1 | 86 | 184 | 9 |
| SLEPT | | | | | |
| Slept at night in a dog kennel | 111 | 11 | 68 | 123 | 11 |
| In a choir of wings, as though she slept or died, | 123 | 12 | 72 | 137 | 2 |
| SLEW | | | | | |
| Under the milky mushrooms slew my hunger, | 73 | 18 | 44 | 82 | 18 |
| SLIDES | | | | | |
| Slides like a sea; | 24 | 15 | 15 | 29 | 15 |
| Slides good in the sleek mouth | 171 | 9 | 88 | 191 | 9 |
| SLIME | | | | | |
| Despair of blood, faith in the maiden's slime, | 18 | 23 | 12 | 22 | 3 |
| The wild pigs' wood, and slime upon the trees, | 30 | 20 | 18 | 35 | 20 |
| And the beak of slime | 143 | 13 | 82 | 160 | 13 |
| Tangling through this spun slime | 173 | 3 | 88 | 193 | 3 |
| SLIPPED | | | | | |
| Slipped the fins of those humpbacked tons | 151 | 4 | 83 | 168 | 12 |
| SLIPS | | | | | |
| Seaward the salmon, sucked sun slips, | viii | 8 | 1 | xvi | 8 |
| Harbours my anchored tongue, slips the quay-stone, | 78 | 3 | 46 | 87 | 3 |
| SLITS | | | | | |
| Shakes a desolate boy who slits his throat | 87 | 7 | 52 | 96 | 7 |
| SLOE | | | | | |
| Burning! Night and the vein of birds in the winged, sloe wrist | 164 | 21 | 86 | 184 | 7 |
| SLOPING | | | | | |
| The mighty hand leads to a sloping shoulder, | 62 | 5 | 37 | 71 | 5 |
| SLOW | | | | | |
| Slow in a sleeping wind. | 6 | 15 | 4 | 6 | 15 |
| Slow rounding of four seasons' coasts, | 45 | 6 | 26 | 53 | 6 |
| And all the elements of the slow fall rejoiced | 122 | 4 | 72 | 135 | 4 |
| Bird through the times and lands and tribes of the slow flakes. | 122 | 19 | 72 | 135 | 19 |
| Open a pathway through the slow sad sail, | 136 | 9 | 81 | 153 | 9 |
| Sleep, good, for ever, slow and deep, spelled rare and wise, | 162 | 8 | 86 | 181 | 8 |
| Makes all the music; and I who hear the tune of the slow, | 169 | 9 | 87 | 189 | 18 |
| SLOWLY | | | | | |
| Love in her gear is slowly through the house, | 18 | 3 | 12 | 21 | 3 |
| The plum my mother picked matured slowly, | 21 | 1 | 13 | 25 | 1 |
| That bury the sweet street slowly, see | 96 | 8 | 58 | 106 | 8 |

| | U.K. | | | U.S. | |
| --- | --- | --- | --- | --- | --- |
| | *Page* | *Line* | *Poem* | *Page* | *Line* |
| And the sabbath rang slowly | 159 | 17 | 85 | 178 | 17 |
| Heart! Slyly, slowly, hearing the wound in her side go | 165 | 24 | 86 | 185 | 14 |
| Crashes, and slowly the fishing holy stalking heron | 167 | 11 | 87 | 187 | 11 |
| SLUG | | | | | |
| And the slug should teach me destruction. | 45 | 13 | 26 | 53 | 13 |
| SLUG'S | | | | | |
| The slug's a living calendar of days; | 45 | 15 | 26 | 53 | 15 |
| SLUM | | | | | |
| Over the sun's hovel and the slum of fire | 131 | 16 | 77 | 145 | 22 |
| SLUNK | | | | | |
| Slunk pouting out when the limp time came; | 175 | 15 | 89 | 195 | 20 |
| SLY | | | | | |
| Cast high, stunned on gilled stone; sly scissors ground in frost | 92 | 7 | 55 | 101 | 13 |
| Be you sure the Thief will seek a way sly and sure | 163 | 26 | 86 | 183 | 7 |
| And sly as snow and meek as dew blown to the thorn, | 164 | 1 | 86 | 183 | 8 |
| Who comes as red as the fox and sly as the heeled wind. | 165 | 10 | 86 | 184 | 18 |
| Time by, their dust was flesh the swineherd rooted sly, | 177 | 1 | 90 | 197 | 21 |
| SLYLY | | | | | |
| Heart! Slyly, slowly, hearing the wound in her side go | 165 | 24 | 86 | 185 | 14 |
| SMACK | | | | | |
| Blowing the old dead back; our shots shall smack | 15 | 18 | 10 | 17 | 18 |
| Morning smack of the spade that wakes up sleep, | 87 | 6 | 52 | 96 | 6 |
| SMALL | | | | | |
| And gallows, up the rays of his eyes the small birds of the bay | 167 | 4 | 87 | 187 | 4 |
| On a seizing sky; small fishes glide | 170 | 22 | 88 | 190 | 22 |
| The scurrying, furred small friars squeal, in the dowse | 177 | 11 | 90 | 198 | 10 |
| SMELL | | | | | |
| On tips of thought where thoughts smell in the rain; | 25 | 2 | 15 | 30 | 2 |
| Bleed from my burning fork and smell my heels. | 32 | 4 | 18 | 37 | 10 |
| And the smell of hay in the snow, and the far owl | 119 | 7 | 72 | 131 | 7 |
| SMELLING | | | | | |
| And all the herrings smelling in the sea, | 13 | 5 | 9 | 14 | 12 |

|  | U.K. |  |  | U.S. |  |
|  | Page | Line | Poem | Page | Line |
| **SMELT** |  |  |  |  |  |
| I smelt the maggot in my stool. | 8 | 6 | 5 | 9 | 6 |
| **SMILE** |  |  |  |  |  |
| One smile of light across the empty face; | 22 | 2 | 14 | 27 | 2 |
| Three-syllabled and starry as the smile; | 22 | 8 | 14 | 27 | 8 |
| Divining in a smile the oil of tears. | 24 | 18 | 15 | 29 | 18 |
| From all my mortal lovers with a starboard smile; | 60 | 21 | 36 | 69 | 21 |
| The circular smile tossed from lover to lover | 90 | 9 | 54 | 99 | 9 |
| Shall her smile breed that mouth, behind the mirror, | 90 | 13 | 54 | 99 | 13 |
| **SMILED** |  |  |  |  |  |
| Talked and tore though her eyes smiled. | 93 | 20 | 56 | 102 | 20 |
| **SMILES** |  |  |  |  |  |
| In the jails and studies of his keyless smiles. | 125 | 8 | 74 | 139 | 8 |
| **SMILING** |  |  |  |  |  |
| Once close-up smiling in the wall of pictures, | 73 | 9 | 44 | 82 | 9 |
| With unforgettably smiling act, | 107 | 11 | 65 | 118 | 11 |
| **SMITE** |  |  |  |  |  |
| Clangour as I hew and smite | ix | 19 | 1 | xvii | 19 |
| **SMOKE** |  |  |  |  |  |
| Smoke hill and hophead's valley, | 38 | 4 | 20 | 43 | 14 |
| Flocked with the sheep white smoke of the farm house cowl | 119 | 9 | 72 | 131 | 9 |
| Old wives that spin in the smoke, | 150 | 2 | 83 | 167 | 6 |
| He saw the storm smoke out to kill | 150 | 17 | 83 | 168 | 1 |
| **SMOKING** |  |  |  |  |  |
| Daft with the drug that's smoking in a girl | 13 | 2 | 9 | 14 | 9 |
| **SMOOTH** |  |  |  |  |  |
| Safe be and smooth from the bellows of the rushy brood. | 162 | 20 | 86 | 181 | 20 |
| **SMOOTHE** |  |  |  |  |  |
| Strike and smoothe, for my decks are drums, | 152 | 5 | 83 | 169 | 17 |
| **SMOTHER** |  |  |  |  |  |
| Nor can I smother the sweet waking.' | 66 | 8 | 40 | 75 | 8 |
| **SNAIL** |  |  |  |  |  |
| In the glass bed of grapes with snail and flower, | 36 | 5 | 20 | 41 | 5 |
| The haring snail go giddily round the flower, | 36 | 17 | 20 | 41 | 17 |
| Snail of man in His ship of fires | 69 | 8 | 43 | 78 | 8 |
| Drunk as a vineyard snail, flailed like an octopus, | 91 | 7 | 55 | 100 | 7 |
| And over the sea wet church the size of a snail | 103 | 7 | 63 | 114 | 7 |
| **SNAIL-WAKED** |  |  |  |  |  |
| From pole to pole leapt round the snail-waked world. | 75 | 14 | 44 | 84 | 14 |
| **SNAKE** |  |  |  |  |  |
| Incarnate devil in a talking snake, | 40 | 1 | 22 | 46 | 1 |

|  | U.K. | | | U.S. | |
| --- | --- | --- | --- | --- | --- |
|  | Page | Line | Poem | Page | Line |
| Slashed down the last snake as though | 134 | 13 | 79 | 150 | 13 |
| SNAKES | | | | | |
| These stolen bubbles have the bites of snakes | 67 | 23 | 41 | 76 | 23 |
| And darkness hung the walls with baskets of snakes, | 114 | 4 | 69 | 126 | 4 |
| SNAP | | | | | |
| My wine you drink, my bread you snap. | 39 | 15 | 21 | 45 | 15 |
| Faith in their hands shall snap in two, | 68 | 15 | 42 | 77 | 15 |
| 'Who could snap off the shapeless print | 70 | 12 | 43 | 79 | 16 |
| SNAPPED | | | | | |
| Stills snapped by night in the bread-sided field, | 73 | 8 | 44 | 82 | 8 |
| SNAPPING | | | | | |
| On the snapping rims of the ashpit, | 132 | 8 | 78 | 147 | 8 |
| SNAPT | | | | | |
| As the snapt feathers snow, | 169 | 2 | 87 | 189 | 11 |
| SNARED | | | | | |
| I'll comb the snared woods with a glove on a lamp, | 97 | 7 | 59 | 108 | 7 |
| SNATCHED | | | | | |
| And Jonah's Moby snatched me by the hair, | 73 | 20 | 44 | 82 | 20 |
| SNEAK | | | | | |
| Sneak down the stallion grave, | 67 | 18 | 41 | 76 | 18 |
| SNIFFED | | | | | |
| In the sniffed and poured snow on the tip of the tongue of the year | 77 | 5 | 45 | 86 | 5 |
| SNIPPED | | | | | |
| And flesh was snipped to cross the lines | 7 | 22 | 5 | 8 | 22 |
| SNIPPING | | | | | |
| Tasselled in cellar and snipping shop | 132 | 11 | 78 | 147 | 11 |
| SNIVELLING | | | | | |
| In the snivelling hours with dead, humped Ann | 87 | 13 | 52 | 96 | 13 |
| SNOUT | | | | | |
| Tail, Nile, and snout, a saddler of the rushes, | 38 | 20 | 20 | 44 | 10 |
| And the mole snout blunt under his pilgrimage of domes, | 177 | 16 | 90 | 198 | 15 |
| SNOUTED | | | | | |
| Quaked the sick sea and snouted deep, | 151 | 2 | 83 | 168 | 10 |
| SNOW | | | | | |
| The darted hail, the childish snow, | 7 | 14 | 5 | 8 | 14 |
| By red-eyed orchards sow the seeds of snow, | 60 | 11 | 36 | 69 | 11 |
| In the sniffed and poured snow on the tip of the tongue of the year | 77 | 5 | 45 | 86 | 5 |
| Storm, snow, and fountain in the weather of fireworks, | 83 | 14 | 49 | 92 | 14 |
| That the snow blind twilight ferries over the lakes | 119 | 2 | 72 | 131 | 2 |

SNOW (continued)

| | U.K. | | | U.S. | |
|---|---|---|---|---|---|
| | *Page* | *Line* | *Poem* | *Page* | *Line* |
| And the smell of hay in the snow, and the far owl | 119 | 7 | 72 | 131 | 7 |
| As the food and flames of the snow, a man unrolled | 119 | 13 | 72 | 131 | 13 |
| In his firelit island ringed by the winged snow | 119 | 17 | 72 | 131 | 17 |
| Of his snow blind love and rush in the white lairs. | 120 | 13 | 72 | 132 | 18 |
| When cold as snow he should run the wended vales among | 120 | 20 | 72 | 133 | 5 |
| Parish of snow. The carved mouths in the rock are wind swept strings. | 121 | 9 | 72 | 134 | 4 |
| Time sings through the intricately dead snow drop. Listen. | 121 | 10 | 72 | 134 | 5 |
| A she bird dawned, and her breast with snow and scarlet downed. | 121 | 15 | 72 | 134 | 10 |
| On the departed, snow bushed green, wanton in moon light | 121 | 17 | 72 | 134 | 12 |
| Under the one leaved trees ran a scarecrow of snow | 122 | 14 | 72 | 135 | 14 |
| The singing breaks in the snow shoed villages of wishes | 123 | 3 | 72 | 136 | 13 |
| And she rose with him flowering in her melting snow. | 123 | 20 | 72 | 137 | 10 |
| Laid in her snow | 130 | 13 | 77 | 144 | 13 |
| The polar eagle with his tread of snow. | 152 | 8 | 83 | 169 | 20 |
| Toppling up the boatside in a snow of light! | 154 | 18 | 83 | 172 | 18 |
| Shall harrow and snow the blood while you ride wide and near, | 162 | 23 | 86 | 181 | 23 |
| And sly as snow and meek as dew blown to the thorn, | 164 | 1 | 86 | 183 | 8 |
| Ever and ever he finds a way, as the snow falls, | 164 | 7 | 86 | 183 | 14 |
| Round the sun, he comes to my love like the designed snow, | 165 | 25 | 86 | 185 | 15 |
| As the snapt feathers snow, | 169 | 2 | 87 | 189 | 11 |
| On whom a world of ills came down like snow. | | | 91 | 201 | 11 |
| SNOW'S | | | | | |
| Once where the soft snow's blood was turned to ice. | 80 | 12 | 46 | 89 | 20 |
| SNOWMAN'S | | | | | |
| Master the night nor serve the snowman's brain | 60 | 4 | 36 | 69 | 4 |
| SNOWY | | | | | |
| Summon your snowy horsemen, and the four-stringed hill, | 49 | 14 | 29 | 58 | 14 |
| SO | | | | | |
| And these poor nerves so wired to the skull | 10 | 6 | 7 | 11 | 6 |
| So, planing-heeled, I flew along my man | 26 | 4 | 16 | 31 | 4 |
| Alone's unhurt, so the blind man sees best. | 50 | 9 | 30 | 59 | 9 |

| | U.K. | | | U.S. | |
|---|---|---|---|---|---|
| | *Page* | *Line* | *Poem* | *Page* | *Line* |
| So star fall, | 51 | 24 | 31 | 61 | 3 |
| So the ball fail, | 51 | 25 | 31 | 61 | 4 |
| So solve the mystic sun, the wife of light, | 51 | 26 | 31 | 61 | 5 |
| So cross her hand with their grave gipsy eyes, | 55 | 12 | 33 | 64 | 15 |
| So fast I move defying time, the quiet gentleman | 63 | 14 | 38 | 72 | 14 |
| So shall winged harbours through the rockbirds' eyes | 76 | 12 | 44 | 85 | 12 |
| Bullies into rough seas you so gentle | 96 | 24 | 58 | 107 | 7 |
| And I saw in the turning so clearly a child's | 103 | 21 | 63 | 114 | 21 |
| Were once such a creature, so gay and frank | 107 | 14 | 65 | 118 | 14 |
| So loud to my own | 137 | 5 | 82 | 154 | 5 |
| So it must have been after the birth of the simple light | 160 | 11 | 85 | 179 | 11 |
| In all his tuneful turning so few and such morning songs | 160 | 21 | 85 | 179 | 21 |
| High riding, held and blessed and true, and so stilly | 165 | 19 | 86 | 185 | 9 |
| In the wains tonned so high that the wisps of the hay | 176 | 14 | 90 | 197 | 14 |

SOAKED
| Soaked my table the uglier side of a hill | 89 | 2 | 53 | 98 | 2 |

SOAKING
| With wild sea fillies and soaking bridles | 156 | 17 | 83 | 175 | 5 |

SOAKS
| Soaks up the sewing tides), | 56 | 12 | 34 | 65 | 12 |

SOAR
| Soar, with its two bark towers, to that Day | 76 | 20 | 44 | 85 | 20 |

SOARING
| Cawing from their black bethels soaring, the holy books | 164 | 19 | 86 | 184 | 5 |

SOCKET
| Socket and grave, the brassy blood, | 34 | 11 | 19 | 39 | 17 |
| You with a bad coin in your socket, | 107 | 2 | 65 | 118 | 2 |

SOCKETS
| Night in the sockets rounds, | 24 | 19 | 15 | 29 | 19 |

SODOM
| O Rome and Sodom To-morrow and London | 156 | 23 | 83 | 175 | 11 |

SOFT
| From love's first fever to her plague, from the soft second | 20 | 1 | 13 | 24 | 1 |
| Why silk is soft and the stone wounds | 53 | 6 | 32 | 62 | 6 |
| Once where the soft snow's blood was turned to ice. | 80 | 12 | 46 | 89 | 20 |
| Or a nacreous sleep among soft particles and charms | 97 | 17 | 59 | 108 | 17 |
| Above her folded head, and the soft feathered voice | 122 | 2 | 72 | 135 | 2 |

SOFT (continued)

|  | U.K. | | | U.S. | |
|---|---|---|---|---|---|
|  | *Page* | *Line* | *Poem* | *Page* | *Line* |
| Exiled in us we arouse the soft, | 126 | 15 | 74 | 140 | 15 |
| Or rippling soft in the spinney moon as the silk | 177 | 7 | 90 | 198 | 6 |
| SOFTEN |  |  |  |  |  |
| The five kings count the dead but do not soften | 62 | 13 | 37 | 71 | 13 |
| SOIL |  |  |  |  |  |
| The secret of the soil grows through the eye, | 25 | 4 | 15 | 30 | 4 |
| Dust be your saviour under the conjured soil.) | 37 | 9 | 20 | 42 | 15 |
| Let the soil squeal I am the biting man | 56 | 20 | 34 | 65 | 20 |
| Light through sea and soil | 146 | 5 | 82 | 163 | 5 |
| SOIL-BASED |  |  |  |  |  |
| And out of every domed and soil-based shell | 115 | 5 | 69 | 127 | 5 |
| SOILS |  |  |  |  |  |
| Setting no store by harvest, freeze the soils; | 1 | 3 | 2 | 1 | 3 |
| SOILY |  |  |  |  |  |
| How light the sleeping on this soily star, | 26 | 24 | 16 | 32 | 4 |
| SOLDERED |  |  |  |  |  |
| The brain was celled and soldered in the thought | 23 | 2 | 14 | 28 | 2 |
| SOLDIER |  |  |  |  |  |
| For her soldier stained with spilt words | 48 | 15 | 28 | 56 | 15 |
| SOLE |  |  |  |  |  |
| A man torn up mourns in the sole night. | 115 | 21 | 69 | 127 | 21 |
| SOLEMNIZING |  |  |  |  |  |
| Mutter and foul wingbeat of the solemnizing nightpriest | 114 | 22 | 69 | 126 | 22 |
| SOLID |  |  |  |  |  |
| Strange to our solid eye, | 14 | 13 | 10 | 16 | 13 |
| That from the solid bases of the light | 22 | 20 | 14 | 27 | 20 |
| Stage of the ice, the solid ocean, | 33 | 2 | 19 | 38 | 2 |
| Let her inhale her dead, through seed and solid | 55 | 10 | 33 | 64 | 13 |
| SOLITARY |  |  |  |  |  |
| A solitary mister | 111 | 2 | 68 | 123 | 2 |
| SOLVE |  |  |  |  |  |
| So solve the mystic sun, the wife of light, | 51 | 26 | 31 | 61 | 5 |
| SOMBRE |  |  |  |  |  |
| Until the Sunday sombre bell at dark | 111 | 6 | 68 | 123 | 6 |
| SOME |  |  |  |  |  |
| Some dead undid their bushy jaws, | 4 | 22 | 3 | 4 | 22 |
| Some let me make you of the vowelled beeches, | 16 | 13 | 11 | 19 | 13 |
| Some of the oaken voices, from the roots | 16 | 14 | 11 | 19 | 14 |
| Some let me make you of the water's speeches. | 16 | 16 | 11 | 19 | 16 |
| Some let me make you of the meadow's signs; | 16 | 21 | 11 | 19 | 21 |
| Some let me tell you of the raven's sins. | 16 | 24 | 11 | 19 | 24 |
| (Some let me make you of autumnal spells, | 17 | 2 | 11 | 20 | 2 |
| Some let me make you of the heartless words. | 17 | 5 | 11 | 20 | 5 |
| Like some pitch moon, the limit of the globes; | 24 | 20 | 15 | 29 | 20 |
| There must, be praised, some certainty, | 48 | 7 | 28 | 56 | 7 |
| Calls some content to travel with the winds, | 53 | 17 | 32 | 62 | 17 |

| | U.K. | | | U.S. | |
|---|---|---|---|---|---|
| | *Page* | *Line* | *Poem* | *Page* | *Line* |
| And many years should see some change. | 63 | 17 | 38 | 72 | 17 |
| Some life, yet unspent, might explode | 64 | 12 | 39 | 73 | 12 |
| Around some coffin carrying | 133 | 2 | 78 | 148 | 5 |
| SON | | | | | |
| Disturb no winding-sheets, my son, | 65 | 6 | 40 | 74 | 6 |
| Thrust, my daughter or son, to escape, there is none, none, none, | 97 | 19 | 59 | 108 | 19 |
| You may not see, my son, | 105 | 2 | 64 | 116 | 2 |
| Over the ghost and the dropped son | 137 | 8 | 82 | 154 | 8 |
| Time is bearing another son. | 155 | 9 | 83 | 173 | 13 |
| SON'S | | | | | |
| Walking in the meadows of his son's eye | | | 91 | 201 | 10 |
| SONG | | | | | |
| To you strangers (though song) | vii | 24 | 1 | xv | 24 |
| The unwinding, song by rock, | 95 | 5 | 58 | 105 | 5 |
| Under the burial song | 143 | 3 | 82 | 160 | 3 |
| For their souls' song. | 168 | 22 | 87 | 189 | 7 |
| SONGS | | | | | |
| Those craning birds are choice for you, songs that jump back | 86 | 9 | 51 | 95 | 9 |
| In all his tuneful turning so few and such morning songs | 160 | 21 | 85 | 179 | 21 |
| SONS | | | | | |
| We are the sons of flint and pitch. | 3 | 5 | 2 | 3 | 11 |
| And the living earth your sons. | 110 | 28 | 67 | 122 | 6 |
| Seed of sons in the loin of the black husk left. | 130 | 8 | 77 | 144 | 8 |
| And immemorial sons of the cudgelling, hacked | 176 | 11 | 90 | 197 | 11 |
| SOON | | | | | |
| Like leaves of trees and as soon | viii | 5 | 1 | xvi | 5 |
| How soon the servant sun, | 56 | 1 | 34 | 65 | 1 |
| How soon my level, lord, | 56 | 22 | 34 | 66 | 1 |
| 'Find meat on bones that soon have none, | 65 | 1 | 40 | 74 | 1 |
| Soon sets alight a long stick from the cradle; | 71 | 20 | 44 | 80 | 20 |
| How soon the servant sun | 56 | | 34 | 65 | |
| SOONER | | | | | |
| Sooner drop with the worm of the ropes round my throat | 97 | 4 | 59 | 108 | 4 |
| SOOTHE | | | | | |
| When that immortal hospital made one more move to soothe | 158 | 3 | 84 | 177 | 3 |
| SOOTHED | | | | | |
| Lie fast and soothed, | 162 | 19 | 86 | 181 | 19 |
| SORCERER'S | | | | | |
| Shakes, in crabbed burial shawl, by sorcerer's insect woken, | 83 | 23 | 49 | 93 | 5 |
| SORES | | | | | |
| Shall calm her sores. | 9 | 18 | 6 | 10 | 18 |

SORES (continued)

| | U.K. | | | U.S. | |
|---|---|---|---|---|---|
| | *Page* | *Line* | *Poem* | *Page* | *Line* |
| Flicked from the carbolic city puzzle in a bed of sores | 96 | 3 | 58 | 106 | 3 |
| SORROW | | | | | |
| O ring of seas, nor sorrow as I shift | 60 | 20 | 36 | 69 | 20 |
| SOUGHT | | | | | |
| Have sought your single grave, | 117 | 28 | 71 | 130 | 4 |
| Inhuman cradle and the bride bed forever sought | 120 | 24 | 72 | 133 | 9 |
| SOUL | | | | | |
| Of the hearthstone tales my own, lost love; and the soul walks | 164 | 4 | 86 | 183 | 11 |
| And every soul His priest, | 172 | 7 | 88 | 192 | 7 |
| From my sulking, skulking, coal black soul! | 175 | 7 | 89 | 195 | 12 |
| At last the soul from its foul mousehole | 175 | 14 | 89 | 195 | 19 |
| And I gave my soul a blind, slashed eye, | 175 | 16 | 89 | 195 | 21 |
| To find a woman's soul for a wife. | 175 | 19 | 89 | 195 | 24 |
| For, oh, my soul found a sunday wife | 175 | 25 | 89 | 196 | 6 |
| SOULS | | | | | |
| And the souls of all men | 105 | 19 | 64 | 116 | 19 |
| Is certain god, and the ceremony of souls | 109 | 23 | 67 | 120 | 23 |
| Stone for the sake of the souls of the slain birds sailing. | 169 | 12 | 87 | 189 | 21 |
| And air shaped Heaven where souls grow wild | 172 | 20 | 88 | 192 | 20 |
| SOULS' | | | | | |
| For their souls' song. | 168 | 22 | 87 | 189 | 7 |
| SOUND | | | | | |
| Shone in my ears the light of sound, | 20 | 20 | 13 | 24 | 20 |
| Called in my eyes the sound of light. | 20 | 21 | 13 | 24 | 21 |
| And now the horns of England, in the sound of shape, | 49 | 13 | 29 | 58 | 13 |
| The land lies out of sound | 58 | 13 | 35 | 67 | 13 |
| Time tracks the sound of shape on man and cloud, | 75 | 3 | 44 | 84 | 3 |
| Turns in the dark on the sound they know will arise | 100 | 6 | 61 | 111 | 6 |
| The sound about to be said in the two prayers | 100 | 9 | 61 | 111 | 9 |
| Shall I let pray the shadow of a sound | 101 | 10 | 62 | 112 | 10 |
| On out of sound | 111 | 18 | 68 | 123 | 18 |
| Though no sound flowed down the hand folded air | 120 | 15 | 72 | 132 | 20 |
| It was a hand or sound | 121 | 11 | 72 | 134 | 6 |
| On the silent sea we have heard the sound | 136 | 3 | 81 | 153 | 3 |
| To the sea sound flowing like blood from the loud wound | 136 | 6 | 81 | 153 | 6 |
| We heard the sea sound sing, we saw the salt sheet tell. | 136 | 12 | 81 | 153 | 12 |
| There is nothing left of the sea but its sound, | 157 | 13 | 83 | 176 | 5 |

|  | U.K. Page | Line | Poem | U.S. Page | Line |
|---|---|---|---|---|---|
| Last sound, the world going out without a breath: |  |  | 91 | 201 | 13 |
| **SOUNDING** |  |  |  |  |  |
| What had been one was many sounding minded. | 21 | 17 | 13 | 25 | 17 |
| **SOUNDS** |  |  |  |  |  |
| For my sawn, splay sounds), | viii | 2 | 1 | xvi | 2 |
| Sounds with the grains as they hurry | 82 | 15 | 48 | 91 | 15 |
| **SOUR** |  |  |  |  |  |
| Sour the boiling honey; | 1 | 8 | 2 | 1 | 8 |
| I know her scrubbed and sour humble hands | 88 | 3 | 52 | 97 | 3 |
| Milk in your mouth, at the sour floods | 96 | 7 | 58 | 106 | 7 |
| **SOURCE** |  |  |  |  |  |
| To cut the channels at their source | 11 | 11 | 8 | 12 | 11 |
| **SOUTH** |  |  |  |  |  |
| The Arctic scut, and basin of the South, | 31 | 20 | 18 | 37 | 2 |
| Drives forth my men, my children, from the hanging south. | 49 | 6 | 29 | 58 | 6 |
| Why east wind chills and south wind cools | 53 | 1 | 32 | 62 | 1 |
| **SOVEREIGN** |  |  |  |  |  |
| Five sovereign fingers taxed the breath, | 62 | 2 | 37 | 71 | 2 |
| Bound by a sovereign strip, we lie, | 82 | 18 | 48 | 91 | 18 |
| **SOW** |  |  |  |  |  |
| By red-eyed orchards sow the seeds of snow, | 60 | 11 | 36 | 69 | 11 |
| Or sow my salt seed | 101 | 11 | 62 | 112 | 11 |
| **SOWN** |  |  |  |  |  |
| Has sown a flying garden round that sea-ghost? | 76 | 18 | 44 | 85 | 18 |
| For the surge is sown with barley, | 156 | 14 | 83 | 175 | 2 |
| **SPACE** |  |  |  |  |  |
| And, burning ciphers on the round of space, | 22 | 5 | 14 | 27 | 5 |
| Now that my symbols have outelbowed space, | 41 | 2 | 23 | 47 | 2 |
| From the foreign fields of space, | 43 | 16 | 24 | 51 | 2 |
| From the star-flanked fields of space, | 43 | 23 | 24 | 51 | 9 |
| **SPADE** |  |  |  |  |  |
| Morning smack of the spade that wakes up sleep, | 87 | 6 | 52 | 96 | 6 |
| **SPADE'S** |  |  |  |  |  |
| Assembling waits for the spade's ring on the cage. | 135 | 11 | 80 | 152 | 11 |
| **SPADE-HANDED** |  |  |  |  |  |
| When blood, spade-handed, and the logic time | 18 | 13 | 12 | 21 | 13 |
| **SPADES** |  |  |  |  |  |
| Said the fake gentleman in suit of spades, | 73 | 14 | 44 | 82 | 14 |
| Stumble out with their spades, | 119 | 21 | 72 | 132 | 1 |
| **SPANNED** |  |  |  |  |  |
| More spanned with angels ride | 173 | 23 | 88 | 193 | 23 |
| **SPARK** |  |  |  |  |  |
| That set alight the weathers from a spark, | 22 | 14 | 14 | 27 | 14 |
| A three-eyed, red-eyed spark, blunt as a flower; | 22 | 15 | 14 | 27 | 15 |
| Child of the short spark in a shapeless country | 71 | 19 | 44 | 80 | 19 |

|  | U.K. | | | U.S. | |
|---|---|---|---|---|---|
|  | Page | Line | Poem | Page | Line |
| SPARK'S | | | | | |
| The size of genesis? the short spark's gender? | 72 | 20 | 44 | 81 | 20 |
| SPARROWFALL | | | | | |
| Mammoth and sparrowfall | 134 | 20 | 79 | 150 | 20 |
| SPARROWS | | | | | |
| Of the sparrows and such who swansing, dusk, in wrangling hedges. | 167 | 7 | 87 | 187 | 7 |
| God in his whirlwind silence save, who marks the sparrows hail, | 168 | 21 | 87 | 189 | 6 |
| SPAT | | | | | |
| Each golden grain spat life into its fellow, | 20 | 23 | 13 | 24 | 23 |
| Spat up from the resuffered pain. | 28 | 24 | 17 | 34 | 4 |
| SPEAK | | | | | |
| That speak seven seas, | vii | 17 | 1 | xv | 17 |
| And speak their midnight nothings as they swell; | 14 | 14 | 10 | 16 | 14 |
| Flung gravel chime? Let the stones speak | 44 | 13 | 25 | 52 | 13 |
| High lord esquire, speak up the singing cloud, | 60 | 17 | 36 | 69 | 17 |
| Who speak on a finger and thumb, | 70 | 1 | 43 | 79 | 5 |
| The rain through her cold heart speak | 93 | 8 | 56 | 102 | 8 |
| Heard her speak through the chipped beak | 93 | 24 | 56 | 103 | 4 |
| SPEAKS | | | | | |
| The sea speaks in a kingly voice, | 66 | 11 | 40 | 75 | 11 |
| SPEAR | | | | | |
| Herons spire and spear. | 170 | 9 | 88 | 190 | 9 |
| SPECTACLED | | | | | |
| Of the sharp, enamelled eyes and the spectacled claws | 85 | 2 | 50 | 94 | 2 |
| SPECTACLES | | | | | |
| Time at the city spectacles, and half | 41 | 3 | 23 | 47 | 3 |
| SPED | | | | | |
| Nor damned the sea that sped about my fist, | 4 | 3 | 3 | 4 | 3 |
| Storm her sped heart, hand with beheaded veins | 79 | 8 | 46 | 88 | 11 |
| He sped into the drinking dark; | 149 | 14 | 83 | 166 | 14 |
| SPEECH | | | | | |
| Of the pacing, famous sea but its speech, | 157 | 18 | 83 | 176 | 10 |
| SPEECHES | | | | | |
| Some let me make you of the water's speeches. | 16 | 16 | 11 | 19 | 16 |
| SPEEDED | | | | | |
| At God speeded summer's end | vii | 2 | 1 | xv | 2 |
| At God speeded summer's end | x | 18 | 1 | xviii | 24 |
| SPELL | | | | | |
| Bell believe or fear that the rustic shade or spell | 162 | 22 | 86 | 181 | 22 |
| SPELLBOUND | | | | | |
| In the first, spinning place, the spellbound horses walking warm | 160 | 12 | 85 | 179 | 12 |

| | U.K. | | | U.S. | |
|---|---|---|---|---|---|
| | *Page* | *Line* | *Poem* | *Page* | *Line* |
| SPELLED | | | | | |
| In the land of the hearthstone tales, and spelled asleep, | 162 | 2 | 86 | 181 | 2 |
| Sleep, good, for ever, slow and deep, spelled rare and wise, | 162 | 8 | 86 | 181 | 8 |
| Lie in grace. Sleep spelled at rest in the lowly house | 163 | 20 | 86 | 183 | 1 |
| SPELLING | | | | | |
| The heart is drained that, spelling in the scurry | 17 | 6 | 11 | 20 | 6 |
| Endure burial under the spelling wall, | 91 | 4 | 55 | 100 | 4 |
| SPELLS | | | | | |
| (Some let me make you of autumnal spells, | 17 | 2 | 11 | 20 | 2 |
| Curl-locked and animal cavepools of spells and bone, | 91 | 27 | 55 | 101 | 5 |
| And spells on the winds of the dead his winter's tale. | 121 | 4 | 72 | 133 | 19 |
| SPELT | | | | | |
| I spelt my vision with a hand and hair, | 26 | 23 | 16 | 32 | 3 |
| Spelt out the seven seas, an evil index, | 74 | 12 | 44 | 83 | 12 |
| SPENT | | | | | |
| From the hissing of the spent lie | 64 | 2 | 39 | 73 | 2 |
| SPENTOUT | | | | | |
| The root of tongues ends in a spentout cancer, | 21 | 13 | 13 | 25 | 13 |
| SPEWED | | | | | |
| One womb, one mind, spewed out the matter, | 21 | 18 | 13 | 26 | 1 |
| SPHERE | | | | | |
| And a high sphere be his bearer; | 43 | 11 | 24 | 50 | 18 |
| SPHERES | | | | | |
| Lulling of spheres in the seashell flesh, | 173 | 8 | 88 | 193 | 8 |
| SPHERES' | | | | | |
| He cried as he died, fearing at last the spheres' | | | 91 | 201 | 12 |
| SPIDER | | | | | |
| 'War on the spider and the wren! | 66 | 14 | 40 | 75 | 14 |
| SPIDER-TONGUED | | | | | |
| The spider-tongued, and the loud hill of Wales) | 17 | 3 | 11 | 20 | 3 |
| SPIES | | | | | |
| O make me a mask and a wall to shut from your spies | 85 | 1 | 50 | 94 | 1 |
| SPIKE | | | | | |
| In a spinney of ringed boys and ganders, spike and burn, | 162 | 14 | 86 | 181 | 14 |
| SPIKED | | | | | |
| Spiked with a mastiff collar, | 132 | 10 | 78 | 147 | 10 |
| SPILL | | | | | |
| That spill such acrid blood. | 48 | 16 | 28 | 56 | 16 |
| Spill the lank folly's hunter and the hard-held hope. | 49 | 18 | 29 | 58 | 18 |

|  | U.K. | | | U.S. | |
| --- | --- | --- | --- | --- | --- |
|  | Page | Line | Poem | Page | Line |
| **SPILLED** | | | | | |
| On the last rick's tip by spilled wine-wells | 95 | 14 | 58 | 105 | 14 |
| **SPILT** | | | | | |
| For her soldier stained with spilt words | 48 | 15 | 28 | 56 | 15 |
| Pierce the spilt sky with diving wing in weed and heel | 86 | 4 | 51 | 95 | 4 |
| Is gathered and spilt | 105 | 10 | 64 | 116 | 10 |
| **SPIN** | | | | | |
| Not spin to stare at an old year | 77 | 17 | 45 | 86 | 17 |
| The spin | 140 | 2 | 82 | 157 | 2 |
| Sun spin a grave grey | 147 | 14 | 82 | 164 | 14 |
| Old wives that spin in the smoke, | 150 | 2 | 83 | 167 | 6 |
| **SPINDRIFT** | | | | | |
| Sweetly the diver's bell in the steeple of spindrift | 37 | 11 | 20 | 42 | 17 |
| On these spindrift pages | 128 | 14 | 76 | 142 | 14 |
| **SPINE** | | | | | |
| The proud spine spurning turn and twist. | 10 | 5 | 7 | 11 | 5 |
| **SPINNEY** | | | | | |
| In a spinney of ringed boys and ganders, spike and burn, | 162 | 14 | 86 | 181 | 14 |
| The stream from the priest black wristed spinney and sleeves | 165 | 1 | 86 | 184 | 9 |
| Or rippling soft in the spinney moon as the silk | 177 | 7 | 90 | 198 | 6 |
| **SPINNING** | | | | | |
| How I, a spinning man, | viii | 13 | 1 | xvi | 13 |
| We summer boys in this four-winded spinning, | 2 | 13 | 2 | 2 | 13 |
| In the first, spinning place, the spellbound horses walking warm | 160 | 12 | 85 | 179 | 12 |
| **SPINNING-WHEELS** | | | | | |
| Bright as her spinning-wheels, the colic season | 35 | 8 | 20 | 40 | 8 |
| **SPINS** | | | | | |
| And the golden ball spins out of the skies; | 90 | 10 | 54 | 99 | 10 |
| Spins its morning of praise, | 173 | 18 | 88 | 193 | 18 |
| **SPIRAL** | | | | | |
| A quarrel of weathers and trees in the windy spiral. | 36 | 18 | 20 | 41 | 18 |
| Splitting the long eye open, and the spiral turnkey, | 36 | 26 | 20 | 42 | 5 |
| O spiral of ascension | 141 | 11 | 82 | 158 | 11 |
| **SPIRE** | | | | | |
| No tread more perilous, the green steps and spire | 36 | 2 | 20 | 41 | 2 |
| Hear by death's accident the clocked and dashed-down spire | 83 | 11 | 49 | 92 | 11 |
| The spire cranes. Its statue is an aviary. | 86 | 1 | 51 | 95 | 1 |
| An inch in froth. Chimes cheat the prison spire, pelter | 86 | 5 | 51 | 95 | 5 |
| Herons spire and spear. | 170 | 9 | 88 | 190 | 9 |

| | U.K. | | | U.S. | |
|---|---|---|---|---|---|
| | Page | Line | Poem | Page | Line |
| The spire cranes | 86 | | 51 | 95 | |
| SPIRE'S | | | | | |
| And mouth. Both note and plume plunge from the spire's hook. | 86 | 8 | 51 | 95 | 8 |
| SPIRIT | | | | | |
| Before the agony; the spirit grows, | 48 | 3 | 28 | 56 | 3 |
| Or spirit up a cloud, | 56 | 26 | 34 | 66 | 5 |
| Gold on such features, and the linen spirit | 76 | 3 | 44 | 85 | 3 |
| Bless her bent spirit with four, crossing birds. | 87 | 26 | 52 | 96 | 26 |
| Senses, and man a spirit in love | 173 | 2 | 88 | 193 | 2 |
| SPIRITS | | | | | |
| Scales the blue wall of spirits; | 83 | 21 | 49 | 93 | 3 |
| With the spirits of the horseshoe bay | 172 | 2 | 88 | 192 | 2 |
| SPIT | | | | | |
| By the spit and the black pot in the log bright light | 120 | 2 | 72 | 132 | 7 |
| By the spit and the black pot in the log bright light. | 122 | 7 | 72 | 135 | 7 |
| And the black spit of the chapel fold, | 174 | 2 | 89 | 194 | 2 |
| SPITTING | | | | | |
| Cut Christbread spitting vinegar and all | 95 | 16 | 58 | 105 | 16 |
| SPITTLE | | | | | |
| That clouts the spittle like bubbles with broken rooms, | 77 | 6 | 45 | 86 | 6 |
| SPITTLED | | | | | |
| The spittled eyes, the salt ponds in the sleeves, | 87 | 5 | 52 | 96 | 5 |
| SPLASHED | | | | | |
| And the splashed mothering maiden | 139 | 8 | 82 | 156 | 8 |
| SPLAY | | | | | |
| For my sawn, splay sounds), | viii | 2 | 1 | xvi | 2 |
| SPLICE | | | | | |
| Where once your green knots sank their splice | 11 | 7 | 8 | 12 | 7 |
| SPLINTERS | | | | | |
| Button your bodice on a hump of splinters, | 73 | 5 | 44 | 82 | 5 |
| SPLINTS | | | | | |
| The lamped calligrapher, the queen in splints, | 75 | 21 | 44 | 84 | 21 |
| SPLIT | | | | | |
| Split up the brawned womb's weathers, | 1 | 14 | 2 | 1 | 14 |
| Should he who split his children with a cure | 51 | 13 | 31 | 60 | 13 |
| Split all ends up they shan't crack; | 68 | 17 | 42 | 77 | 17 |
| By lava's light split through the oyster vowels | 74 | 3 | 44 | 83 | 3 |
| From an odd room in a split house stare, | 96 | 6 | 58 | 106 | 6 |
| SPLITTING | | | | | |
| Splitting the long eye open, and the spiral turnkey, | 36 | 26 | 20 | 42 | 5 |
| SPOILERS | | | | | |
| Spoilers and pokers of sleep, | 134 | 5 | 79 | 150 | 5 |

|  | U.K. | | | U.S. | |
| --- | --- | --- | --- | --- | --- |
|  | *Page* | *Line* | *Poem* | *Page* | *Line* |
| SPOKE | | | | | |
| When I woke, the town spoke. | 134 | 1 | 79 | 150 | 1 |
| No Time, spoke the clocks, no God, rang the bells, | 134 | 28 | 79 | 151 | 6 |
| SPOKEN | | | | | |
| Love is the last light spoken. Oh | 130 | 7 | 77 | 144 | 7 |
| SPONGE | | | | | |
| The mouth of time sucked, like a sponge, | 4 | 4 | 3 | 4 | 4 |
| Sir morrow at his sponge, | 56 | 8 | 34 | 65 | 8 |
| The scaled sea-sawers, fix in a naked sponge | 74 | 22 | 44 | 83 | 22 |
| Woe drip from the dishrag hands and the pressed sponge of the forehead, | 96 | 20 | 58 | 107 | 3 |
| SPORT | | | | | |
| Country, your sport is summer, and December's pools | 49 | 7 | 29 | 58 | 7 |
| Your sport is summer as the spring runs angrily. | 49 | 24 | 29 | 58 | 24 |
| SPOT | | | | | |
| Spot the blown word, and on the seas I image | 76 | 13 | 44 | 85 | 13 |
| SPOTS | | | | | |
| From Jesu's sleeve trumped up the king of spots, | 73 | 12 | 44 | 82 | 12 |
| SPOUT | | | | | |
| Spout to the rod | 24 | 17 | 15 | 29 | 17 |
| Bump on a spout let the bubbles jump out. | 97 | 3 | 59 | 108 | 3 |
| Spun on a spout like a long-legged ball | 151 | 8 | 83 | 168 | 16 |
| SPOUTED | | | | | |
| Life rose and spouted from the rolling seas, | 22 | 16 | 14 | 27 | 16 |
| SPRAWL | | | | | |
| Like an approaching wave I sprawl to ruin. | 79 | 12 | 46 | 88 | 15 |
| SPRAY | | | | | |
| Over the wakeward-flashing spray | 152 | 1 | 83 | 169 | 13 |
| SPRAY-BASED | | | | | |
| Or spray-based and rock-chested sea: | 77 | 24 | 45 | 86 | 24 |
| SPREADEAGLE | | | | | |
| Light of his thighs, spreadeagle to the dunghill sky, | 177 | 3 | 90 | 198 | 2 |
| SPRING | | | | | |
| In spring we cross our foreheads with the holly, | 2 | 19 | 2 | 3 | 1 |
| I who was deaf to spring and summer, | 7 | 7 | 5 | 8 | 7 |
| How at the mountain spring the same mouth sucks. | 9 | 10 | 6 | 10 | 10 |
| Nor the bad blood of spring. | 12 | 7 | 9 | 13 | 7 |
| Youth did condense; the tears of spring | 21 | 24 | 13 | 26 | 7 |
| The film of spring is hanging from the lids. | 24 | 24 | 15 | 29 | 24 |
| Corrosive spring out of the iceberg's crop, | 30 | 8 | 18 | 35 | 8 |
| City of spring, the governed flower, | 33 | 4 | 19 | 38 | 4 |
| Beginning with doom in the bulb, the spring unravels, | 35 | 7 | 20 | 40 | 7 |

|  | U.K. | | | U.S. | |
|---|---|---|---|---|---|
|  | *Page* | *Line* | *Poem* | *Page* | *Line* |
| Here in this spring, stars float along the void; | 45 | 1 | 26 | 53 | 1 |
| This summer buries a spring bird. | 45 | 4 | 26 | 53 | 4 |
| I should learn spring by the cuckooing, | 45 | 12 | 26 | 53 | 12 |
| Crack like a spring in a vice, bone breaking April, | 49 | 17 | 29 | 58 | 17 |
| Your sport is summer as the spring runs angrily. | 49 | 24 | 29 | 58 | 24 |
| (Fog by his spring | 56 | 11 | 34 | 65 | 11 |
| Murmur of spring nor crush the cockerel's eggs, | 60 | 7 | 36 | 69 | 7 |
| Said the antipodes, and twice spring chimed. | 72 | 18 | 44 | 81 | 18 |
| Of spring and summer were blooming in the tall tales | 103 | 11 | 63 | 114 | 11 |
| The voice of the dust of water from the withered spring | 121 | 5 | 72 | 133 | 20 |
| Exultation lies down. Time buries the spring weather | 123 | 9 | 72 | 136 | 19 |
| Praise that the spring time is all | 158 | 14 | 84 | 177 | 14 |
| And the mother and toppling house of the holy spring, | 158 | 23 | 84 | 177 | 23 |
| Taller this thunderclap spring, and how | 173 | 22 | 88 | 193 | 22 |
| And gone that barley dark where their clogs danced in the spring, | 177 | 20 | 90 | 198 | 19 |
| Here in this spring | 45 |  | 26 | 53 |  |
| Holy Spring | 158 |  | 84 | 177 |  |
| SPRINGFUL |  |  |  |  |  |
| A springful of larks in a rolling | 102 | 21 | 63 | 113 | 21 |
| SPRINGING |  |  |  |  |  |
| Beginning with doom in the ghost, and the springing marvels, | 35 | 13 | 20 | 40 | 13 |
| SPRINGS |  |  |  |  |  |
| Of nightingale and centaur dead horse. The springs wither | 123 | 7 | 72 | 136 | 17 |
| White springs in the dark. | 153 | 24 | 83 | 171 | 20 |
| SPRINGSHOOTS |  |  |  |  |  |
| And the craters of his eyes grew springshoots and fire | 135 | 7 | 80 | 152 | 7 |
| SPRINGTAILED |  |  |  |  |  |
| No springtailed tom in the red hot town | 174 | 29 | 89 | 195 | 5 |
| SPRINKLE |  |  |  |  |  |
| Shall it be said they sprinkle water | 44 | 6 | 25 | 52 | 6 |
| SPRINKLES |  |  |  |  |  |
| Sprinkles in children's eyes a long-last sleep | 53 | 13 | 32 | 62 | 13 |
| SPRINT |  |  |  |  |  |
| Peck, sprint, dance on fountains and duck time | 97 | 8 | 59 | 108 | 8 |
| SPROUT |  |  |  |  |  |
| Sprout from the stony lockers like a tree on Aran. | 37 | 27 | 20 | 43 | 10 |
| Nor sprout on owl-seed like a goblin-sucker, | 60 | 14 | 36 | 69 | 14 |

SPROUT (continued)

| | U.K. | | | U.S. | |
|---|---|---|---|---|---|
| | *Page* | *Line* | *Poem* | *Page* | *Line* |
| In quick, sweet, cruel light till the locked ground sprout out, | 91 | 18 | 55 | 100 | 18 |
| SPROUTED | | | | | |
| The winging bone that sprouted in the heels, | 12 | 11 | 9 | 13 | 11 |
| SPUME | | | | | |
| From the broomed witch's spume you are shielded by fern | 162 | 17 | 86 | 181 | 17 |
| SPUMING | | | | | |
| In the spuming | 140 | 4 | 82 | 157 | 4 |
| SPUN | | | | | |
| Spun to my screws, your dry ghost blows, | 11 | 2 | 8 | 12 | 2 |
| The two-framed globe that spun into a score; | 21 | 21 | 13 | 26 | 4 |
| Heaven and hell mixed as they spun. | 22 | 6 | 14 | 27 | 6 |
| In your every inch and glance is the globe of genesis spun, | 110 | 27 | 67 | 122 | 5 |
| Spun on a spout like a long-legged ball | 151 | 8 | 83 | 168 | 16 |
| Of paradise, in the spun bud of the world. | 123 | 19 | 72 | 137 | 9 |
| Tangling through this spun slime | 173 | 3 | 88 | 193 | 3 |
| SPURNING | | | | | |
| The proud spine spurning turn and twist. | 10 | 5 | 7 | 11 | 5 |
| SPURNS | | | | | |
| He celebrates and spurns | 170 | 7 | 88 | 190 | 7 |
| SPURT | | | | | |
| Till the blood shall spurt, | 129 | 21 | 77 | 143 | 21 |
| SPYING | | | | | |
| And when blind sleep drops on the spying senses, | 81 | 13 | 47 | 90 | 13 |
| SQUALL | | | | | |
| A squall of birds bellowed and fell, | 150 | 15 | 83 | 167 | 19 |
| SQUARE | | | | | |
| Square in these worlds the mortal circle. | 34 | 6 | 19 | 39 | 12 |
| Behind my head a square of sky sags over | 90 | 8 | 54 | 99 | 8 |
| SQUATTERS | | | | | |
| The flashing needle rock of squatters, | 132 | 26 | 78 | 148 | 1 |
| SQUAWK | | | | | |
| And blithely they squawk | 167 | 8 | 87 | 187 | 8 |
| SQUAWKING | | | | | |
| Of the crotch of the squawking shores, | 96 | 2 | 58 | 106 | 2 |
| SQUEAL | | | | | |
| Let the soil squeal I am the biting man | 56 | 20 | 34 | 65 | 20 |
| The scurrying, furred small friars squeal, in the dowse | 177 | 11 | 90 | 198 | 10 |
| SQUEEZE | | | | | |
| Claw of the crabbed veins squeeze from each red particle | 91 | 21 | 55 | 100 | 21 |
| SQUIRES | | | | | |
| And nail the merry squires to the trees; | 2 | 21 | 2 | 3 | 3 |

|  | U.K. | | | U.S. | |
| --- | Page | Line | Poem | Page | Line |
| SQUIRREL | | | | | |
| They see the squirrel stumble, | 36 | 16 | 20 | 41 | 16 |
| In the squirrel nimble grove, under linen and thatch | 163 | 21 | 86 | 183 | 2 |
| STABBING | | | | | |
| Stabbing, and herons, and shells | vii | 16 | 1 | xv | 16 |
| STABLE | | | | | |
| Out of the whinnying green stable | 160 | 13 | 85 | 179 | 13 |
| STABLES | | | | | |
| Past the statues of the stables and the sky roofed sties | 120 | 9 | 72 | 132 | 14 |
| All the moon long I heard, blessed among stables, the night-jars | 160 | 3 | 85 | 179 | 3 |
| STABS | | | | | |
| Where the elegiac fisherbird stabs and paddles | 167 | 19 | 87 | 187 | 19 |
| STACKED | | | | | |
| Down the stacked sea and water-pillared shade, | 79 | 14 | 46 | 88 | 17 |
| STAGE | | | | | |
| Stage of the ice, the solid ocean, | 33 | 2 | 19 | 38 | 2 |
| STAGES | | | | | |
| Crying, white gowned, from the middle moonlit stages | 114 | 14 | 69 | 126 | 14 |
| On the ivory stages | 128 | 9 | 76 | 142 | 9 |
| STAIN | | | | | |
| Halt among eunuchs, and the nitric stain | 18 | 24 | 12 | 22 | 4 |
| The lovers' house, lie suffering my stain? | 46 | 4 | 27 | 54 | 4 |
| STAINED | | | | | |
| For her soldier stained with spilt words | 48 | 15 | 28 | 56 | 15 |
| The stained flats of heaven hit and razed | 95 | 2 | 58 | 105 | 2 |
| STAIR | | | | | |
| Once seen strangers or shades on a stair; | 113 | 15 | 69 | 125 | 15 |
| STAIRS | | | | | |
| Up naked stairs, a turtle in a hearse, | 18 | 4 | 12 | 21 | 4 |
| You by the cavern over the black stairs, | 71 | 22 | 44 | 80 | 22 |
| By the child going to bed and the man on the stairs | 100 | 2 | 61 | 111 | 2 |
| From the man on the stairs and the child by his bed. | 100 | 8 | 61 | 111 | 8 |
| Turns on the quick and the dead, and the man on the stairs | 100 | 14 | 61 | 111 | 14 |
| Dragging him up the stairs to one who lies dead. | 100 | 20 | 61 | 111 | 20 |
| STAKE | | | | | |
| And stake the sleepers in the savage grave | 30 | 17 | 18 | 35 | 17 |
| STAKED | | | | | |
| Nor fenced, nor staked, the gushers of the sky | 24 | 16 | 15 | 29 | 16 |
| Worm in the scalp, the staked and fallow. | 33 | 9 | 19 | 38 | 9 |

|  | U.K. | | | U.S. | |
|---|---|---|---|---|---|
|  | Page | Line | Poem | Page | Line |
| **STALE** |  |  |  |  |  |
| Stale of Adam's brine until, vision | 29 | 3 | 17 | 34 | 7 |
| In a room with a stuffed fox and a stale fern, | 87 | 11 | 52 | 96 | 11 |
| **STALK** |  |  |  |  |  |
| My images stalk the trees and the slant sap's tunnel, | 36 | 1 | 20 | 41 | 1 |
| And opium head, crow stalk, puffed, cut, and blown, | 78 | 10 | 46 | 87 | 10 |
| **STALKED** |  |  |  |  |  |
| To the bait that stalked out of the sack, | 149 | 20 | 83 | 166 | 20 |
| **STALKING** |  |  |  |  |  |
| Comes, like a scissors stalking, tailor age, | 18 | 6 | 12 | 21 | 6 |
| Stalking my children's faces with a tail of blood, | 49 | 20 | 29 | 58 | 20 |
| Crashes, and slowly the fishing holy stalking heron | 167 | 11 | 87 | 187 | 11 |
| **STALKS** |  |  |  |  |  |
| Like stalks of tall, dry straw, | vii | 22 | 1 | xv | 22 |
| **STALLION** |  |  |  |  |  |
| Sneak down the stallion grave, | 67 | 18 | 41 | 76 | 18 |
| **STALLS** |  |  |  |  |  |
| In the tower and tolls to sleep over the stalls | 164 | 3 | 86 | 183 | 10 |
| Through the haygold stalls, as the dew falls on the wind- | 164 | 9 | 86 | 183 | 16 |
| **STAMMEL** |  |  |  |  |  |
| I blow the stammel feather in the vein. | 32 | 8 | 18 | 37 | 14 |
| **STAMMERED** |  |  |  |  |  |
| The ghost is dumb that stammered in the straw, | 31 | 4 | 18 | 36 | 4 |
| **STAMP** |  |  |  |  |  |
| Stamp of the minted face upon the moon; | 22 | 10 | 14 | 27 | 10 |
| Now stamp the Lord's Prayer on a grain of rice, | 74 | 15 | 44 | 83 | 15 |
| **STAMPS** |  |  |  |  |  |
| (Sir morrow stamps | 56 | 23 | 34 | 66 | 2 |
| **STAND** |  |  |  |  |  |
| And the naked egg stand straight, | 56 | 7 | 34 | 65 | 7 |
| I stand, for this memorial's sake, alone | 87 | 12 | 52 | 96 | 12 |
| Whom now I conjure to stand as thief | 107 | 9 | 65 | 118 | 9 |
| That she might stand in the night | 112 | 11 | 68 | 124 | 11 |
| The statues of great rain stand still, | 154 | 15 | 83 | 172 | 15 |
| That uncalm still it is sure alone to stand and sing | 158 | 21 | 84 | 177 | 21 |
| **STANDS** |  |  |  |  |  |
| These are your years' recorders. The circular world stands still.) | 37 | 21 | 20 | 143 | 4 |
| Who razed my wooden folly stands aghast, | 46 | 22 | 27 | 54 | 22 |
| Because there stands, one story out of the bum city, | 77 | 13 | 45 | 86 | 13 |
| He stands alone at the door of his home, | 157 | 23 | 83 | 176 | 15 |

|  |  | U.K. |  | Poem | U.S. |  |
|  | Page | Line |  |  | Page | Line |
| STAR |  |  |  |  |  |  |
| Glory also this star, bird | viii | 14 | I | xvi | 14 |
| In the beginning was the three-pointed star, | 22 | 1 | 14 | 27 | 1 |
| How light the sleeping on this soily star, | 26 | 24 | 16 | 32 | 4 |
| So star fall, | 51 | 24 | 31 | 61 | 3 |
| Cut to the still star in the order of the quick | 109 | 20 | 67 | 120 | 20 |
| On a star of faith pure as the drifting bread, | 119 | 12 | 72 | 131 | 12 |
| A star was broken | 129 | 14 | 77 | 143 | 14 |
| Star and country to the legion | 146 | 2 | 82 | 163 | 2 |
| And the star of the lost the shape of the eyes. | 147 | 1 | 82 | 164 | 1 |
| The star rise at pasture and nightlong the fables graze | 163 | 11 | 86 | 182 | 11 |
| And star: held and blessed, though you scour the high four | 163 | 22 | 86 | 183 | 3 |
| This night and each night since the falling star you were born, | 164 | 6 | 86 | 183 | 13 |
| Of the morning leaves, as the star falls, as the winged | 164 | 11 | 86 | 183 | 18 |
| STARBOARD |  |  |  |  |  |
| From all my mortal lovers with a starboard smile; | 60 | 21 | 36 | 69 | 21 |
| STARCH |  |  |  |  |  |
| Pack off the shapes of daylight and their starch, | 15 | 4 | 10 | 17 | 4 |
| STARE |  |  |  |  |  |
| Not spin to stare at an old year | 77 | 17 | 45 | 86 | 17 |
| From an odd room in a split house stare, | 96 | 6 | 58 | 106 | 6 |
| The blind, clawed stare is cold as sleet. | 153 | 5 | 83 | 171 | 1 |
| STARER |  |  |  |  |  |
| The boy of woman and the wanton starer | 46 | 10 | 27 | 54 | 10 |
| STARFISH |  |  |  |  |  |
| By scummed, starfish sands | vii | 9 | I | xv | 9 |
| STAR-FLANKED |  |  |  |  |  |
| Shall the star-flanked seed be riddled, | 42 | 16 | 24 | 49 | 16 |
| Shall the star-flanked seed be riddled, | 42 | 23 | 24 | 50 | 2 |
| With a star-flanked garrison, | 43 | 18 | 24 | 51 | 4 |
| From the star-flanked fields of space, | 43 | 23 | 24 | 51 | 9 |
| STAR-GESTURED |  |  |  |  |  |
| Of the star-gestured children in the park. | 16 | 12 | 11 | 19 | 12 |
| STARLIGHT |  |  |  |  |  |
| Fire on starlight, rake Jesu's stream; | 150 | 19 | 83 | 168 | 3 |
| STARRED |  |  |  |  |  |
| From the starred well? | 163 | 3 | 86 | 182 | 3 |
| STARRY |  |  |  |  |  |
| Three-syllabled and starry as the smile; | 22 | 8 | 14 | 27 | 8 |
| I scrape through resin to a starry bone | 31 | 11 | 18 | 36 | 11 |
| The night above the dingle starry, | 159 | 3 | 85 | 178 | 3 |

# STARS

| | U.K. | | Poem | U.S. | |
|---|---|---|---|---|---|
| | Page | Line | | Page | Line |
| **STARS** | | | | | |
| Under the stars of Wales, | x | 9 | 1 | xviii | 15 |
| Where, punctual as death, we ring the stars; | 2 | 3 | 2 | 2 | 3 |
| But when the stars, assuming shape, | 4 | 16 | 3 | 4 | 16 |
| The leaden stars, the rainy hammer | 7 | 11 | 5 | 8 | 11 |
| How time has ticked a heaven round the stars. | 9 | 20 | 6 | 10 | 20 |
| The fruit of man unwrinkles in the stars, | 24 | 10 | 15 | 29 | 10 |
| Reaching a second ground far from the stars; | 26 | 7 | 16 | 31 | 7 |
| Here in this spring, stars float along the void; | 45 | 1 | 26 | 53 | 1 |
| Though what the stars ask as they round | 53 | 18 | 32 | 62 | 18 |
| Is heard but little till the stars go out. | 53 | 20 | 32 | 62 | 20 |
| They shall have stars at elbow and foot; | 68 | 5 | 42 | 77 | 5 |
| And, manned by midnight, Jacob to the stars. | 71 | 24 | 44 | 80 | 24 |
| Husk of young stars and handfull zodiac, | 81 | 4 | 47 | 90 | 4 |
| Suffer the first vision that set fire to the stars. | 108 | 18 | 66 | 119 | 18 |
| Tongue of your translating eyes. The young stars told me, | 110 | 23 | 67 | 122 | 1 |
| With the incestuous secret brother in the seconds to perpetuate the stars, | 115 | 20 | 69 | 127 | 20 |
| And the stars falling cold, | 119 | 6 | 72 | 131 | 6 |
| The cloud, the need, the planted stars, the joy beyond | 122 | 22 | 72 | 136 | 2 |
| And nightly under the simple stars | 160 | 1 | 85 | 179 | 1 |
| Steered by the falling stars. | 171 | 14 | 88 | 191 | 14 |
| Masts and fishes to the still quick stars, | 172 | 17 | 88 | 192 | 17 |
| **STARS'** | | | | | |
| All things are known: the stars' advice | 53 | 16 | 32 | 62 | 16 |
| Fly like the stars' blood, | 105 | 24 | 64 | 116 | 24 |
| Or the stars' seashore dead, | 172 | 3 | 88 | 192 | 3 |
| **STAR-SET** | | | | | |
| Star-set at Jacob's angle, | 38 | 3 | 20 | 43 | 13 |
| **STAR-STRUCK** | | | | | |
| Venus lies star-struck in her wound | 153 | 21 | 83 | 171 | 17 |
| **STARVE** | | | | | |
| If the dead starve, their stomachs turn to tumble | 77 | 22 | 45 | 86 | 22 |
| **STARVED** | | | | | |
| Calls the starved fire herd, is cast in ice, | 79 | 1 | 46 | 88 | 4 |
| **STATE** | | | | | |
| Love's twilit nation and the skull of state, | 19 | 14 | 12 | 22 | 19 |
| **STATEMENT** | | | | | |
| Doom on deniers at the wind-turned statement. | 74 | 20 | 44 | 83 | 20 |
| **STATIONS** | | | | | |
| Nor blaspheme down the stations of the breath | 101 | 16 | 62 | 112 | 16 |
| **STATUARY** | | | | | |
| Secretly in statuary, | 77 | 15 | 45 | 86 | 15 |
| **STATUE** | | | | | |
| The spire cranes. Its statue is an aviary. | 86 | 1 | 51 | 95 | 1 |

| | U.K. | | | U.S. | |
|---|---|---|---|---|---|
| | *Page* | *Line* | *Poem* | *Page* | *Line* |
| Her flesh was meek as milk, but this skyward statue | 87 | 27 | 52 | 96 | 27 |
| STATUES | | | | | |
| Past the statues of the stables and the sky roofed sties | 120 | 9 | 72 | 132 | 14 |
| The statues of great rain stand still, | 154 | 15 | 83 | 172 | 15 |
| STATURE | | | | | |
| Stature by seedy shifting, | 1 | 20 | 2 | 1 | 20 |
| STAVED | | | | | |
| Glint in the staved and siren-printed caverns, | 78 | 20 | 46 | 87 | 20 |
| And staved, and riven among plumes my rider weep. | 162 | 16 | 86 | 181 | 16 |
| STAY | | | | | |
| In children's circuses could stay their troubles? | 50 | 2 | 30 | 59 | 2 |
| Shall I unbolt or stay | 58 | 5 | 35 | 67 | 5 |
| Or stay till the day I die | 58 | 23 | 35 | 67 | 23 |
| Or stay till the day I die? | 59 | 6 | 35 | 68 | 6 |
| STEADILY | | | | | |
| The cadaverous gravels, falls thick and steadily, | 36 | 20 | 20 | 41 | 20 |
| STEAL | | | | | |
| Comes designed to my love to steal not her tide raking | 166 | 1 | 86 | 186 | 1 |
| STEALS | | | | | |
| The knave of pain steals off | 67 | 3 | 41 | 76 | 3 |
| STEALTHY | | | | | |
| The pale breath of cattle at the stealthy sail, | 119 | 5 | 72 | 131 | 5 |
| STEEPLE | | | | | |
| Sweetly the diver's bell in the steeple of spindrift | 37 | 11 | 20 | 42 | 17 |
| Herons, steeple stemmed, bless. | 170 | 18 | 88 | 190 | 18 |
| STEEPLED | | | | | |
| This first and steepled season, to the summer's game. | 49 | 12 | 29 | 58 | 12 |
| STEEPLEJACK | | | | | |
| A steeplejack tower, bonerailed and masterless, | 35 | 20 | 20 | 40 | 20 |
| STEEPLES | | | | | |
| Into the organpipes and steeples | 131 | 9 | 77 | 145 | 15 |
| And steeples pierce the cloud on her shoulder | 157 | 1 | 83 | 175 | 13 |
| STEERED | | | | | |
| Steered by the falling stars. | 171 | 14 | 88 | 191 | 14 |
| STEERS | | | | | |
| Pushed up their hair, the dry wind steers | 11 | 5 | 8 | 12 | 5 |
| STEM | | | | | |
| A stem cementing, wrestled up the tower, | 54 | 5 | 33 | 63 | 5 |
| STEMMED | | | | | |
| Herons, steeple stemmed, bless. | 170 | 18 | 88 | 190 | 18 |
| STEPPED | | | | | |
| He put on his clothes and stepped out and he died, | 135 | 2 | 80 | 152 | 2 |

461

| | U.K. | | | U.S. | |
|---|---|---|---|---|---|
| | *Page* | *Line* | *Poem* | *Page* | *Line* |
| STEPPING | | | | | |
| The cattle stirring, the mousing cat stepping shy, | 119 | 22 | 72 | 132 | 2 |
| STEPS | | | | | |
| No tread more perilous, the green steps and spire | 36 | 2 | 20 | 41 | 2 |
| STERN | | | | | |
| From **salt-lipped** beak to the kick of the stern | 152 | 9 | 83 | 170 | 1 |
| Never, my girl, until tolled to sleep by the stern | 162 | 21 | 86 | 181 | 21 |
| This night and each vast night until the stern bell talks | 164 | 2 | 86 | 183 | 9 |
| STICK | | | | | |
| Tells the stick, 'fail.' | 19 | 5 | 12 | 22 | 10 |
| Brass and the bodiless image, on a stick of folly | 38 | 2 | 20 | 43 | 12 |
| Soon sets alight a long stick from the cradle; | 71 | 20 | 44 | 80 | 20 |
| With his stick that picked up leaves. | 111 | 24 | 68 | 123 | 24 |
| STICKS | | | | | |
| Nor the crossed sticks of war. | 12 | 14 | 9 | 13 | 14 |
| Hearing the raven cough in winter sticks, | 16 | 6 | 11 | 19 | 6 |
| The sticks of the house were his; his books he owned. | | | 91 | 201 | 4 |
| STIES | | | | | |
| Past the statues of the stables and the sky roofed sties | 120 | 9 | 72 | 132 | 14 |
| STIFF | | | | | |
| And mother milk was stiff as sand, | 5 | 8 | 3 | 5 | 8 |
| The words of death are dryer than his stiff, | 13 | 18 | 9 | 15 | 4 |
| STILL | | | | | |
| The redhaired cancer still alive, | 4 | 20 | 3 | 4 | 20 |
| Still set to scratch a laughter from my lung, | 12 | 5 | 9 | 13 | 5 |
| Where still they sleep unknowing of their ghost. | 26 | 20 | 16 | 31 | 20 |
| An old, mad man still climbing in his ghost, | 27 | 4 | 16 | 32 | 9 |
| These are your years' recorders. The circular world stands still.) | 37 | 21 | 20 | 143 | 4 |
| Shall I still be love's house on the widdershin earth, | 47 | 5 | 27 | 55 | 5 |
| Black night still ministers the moon, | 66 | 9 | 40 | 75 | 9 |
| Lapping the still canals, the dry tide-master | 82 | 10 | 48 | 91 | 10 |
| From the emerald, still bell; and from the pacing weather-cock | 83 | 17 | 49 | 92 | 17 |
| Magnified out of praise; her death was a still drop; | 87 | 17 | 52 | 96 | 17 |
| With a capsized field where a school sat still | 89 | 3 | 53 | 98 | 3 |
| Her two surnames stopped me still. | 93 | 2 | 56 | 102 | 2 |
| And the still hour | 101 | 5 | 62 | 112 | 5 |
| In the still sleeping town and set forth. | 102 | 10 | 63 | 113 | 10 |
| Still in the water and singingbirds. | 104 | 8 | 63 | 115 | 10 |
| Still be sung | 104 | 17 | 63 | 115 | 19 |
| Cut to the still star in the order of the quick | 109 | 20 | 67 | 120 | 20 |

|  | U.K. | | | U.S. | |
|---|---|---|---|---|---|
|  | Page | Line | Poem | Page | Line |
| And the vaulting bird be still. O my true love, hold me. | 110 | 26 | 67 | 122 | 4 |
| O she lies alone and still, | 115 | 18 | 69 | 127 | 18 |
| Exercised in the still night | 128 | 2 | 76 | 142 | 2 |
| Lie still, sleep becalmed, sufferer with the wound | 136 | 1 | 81 | 153 | 1 |
| Lie still, sleep becalmed, hide the mouth in the throat, | 136 | 13 | 81 | 153 | 13 |
| Still as stone | 138 | 3 | 82 | 155 | 3 |
| The statues of great rain stand still, | 154 | 15 | 83 | 172 | 15 |
| And stunned and still on the green, laid veil | 156 | 3 | 83 | 174 | 11 |
| That uncalm still it is sure alone to stand and sing | 158 | 21 | 84 | 177 | 21 |
| The hawk on fire hangs still; | 167 | 2 | 87 | 187 | 2 |
| Masts and fishes to the still quick stars, | 172 | 17 | 88 | 192 | 17 |
| Where barren as boulders women lie longing still | 176 | 4 | 90 | 197 | 4 |
| And the daughters of darkness flame like Fawkes fires still. | 178 | 19 | 90 | 199 | 20 |
| Or still all the numberless days of his death, though |  |  | 91 | 200 | 8 |
| Lie Still, Sleep Becalmed | 136 |  | 81 | 153 |  |
| STILLS |  |  |  |  |  |
| Stills snapped by night in the bread-sided field, | 73 | 8 | 44 | 82 | 8 |
| STILLY |  |  |  |  |  |
| High riding, held and blessed and true, and so stilly | 165 | 19 | 86 | 185 | 9 |
| STILT |  |  |  |  |  |
| And wharves of water where the walls dance and the white cranes stilt. | 168 | 15 | 87 | 188 | 19 |
| STILTS |  |  |  |  |  |
| My friends were enemies on stilts | 107 | 20 | 65 | 118 | 20 |
| In his house on stilts high among beaks | 170 | 4 | 88 | 190 | 4 |
| STINGING |  |  |  |  |  |
| And love plucked out the stinging siren's eye, | 74 | 7 | 44 | 83 | 7 |
| STIR |  |  |  |  |  |
| Yea the dead stir, | 51 | 18 | 31 | 60 | 18 |
| O we who could not stir | 126 | 4 | 74 | 140 | 4 |
| STIRRED |  |  |  |  |  |
| When no mouth stirred about the hanging famine, | 20 | 5 | 13 | 24 | 5 |
| STIRRING |  |  |  |  |  |
| The cattle stirring, the mousing cat stepping shy, | 119 | 22 | 72 | 132 | 2 |
| STIRS |  |  |  |  |  |
| Stirs the quicksand; that ropes the blowing wind | 9 | 12 | 6 | 10 | 12 |
| Where no seed stirs, | 24 | 9 | 15 | 29 | 9 |
| And no-one stirs at Sheba's side | 153 | 12 | 83 | 171 | 8 |
| STITCH |  |  |  |  |  |
| The famous stitch droppers. | 132 | 28 | 78 | 148 | 3 |

|  | U.K. |  |  | U.S. |  |
|---|---|---|---|---|---|
|  | Page | Line | Poem | Page | Line |
| **STITCHED** |  |  |  |  |  |
| In the stitched wound and clotted wind, muzzled | 28 | 15 | 17 | 33 | 15 |
| **STOCKED** |  |  |  |  |  |
| The stocked heart is forced, and agony has another mouth to feed. | 96 | 17 | 58 | 106 | 17 |
| **STOLE** |  |  |  |  |  |
| A rooking girl who stole me for her side, | 12 | 2 | 9 | 13 | 2 |
| **STOLEN** |  |  |  |  |  |
| These stolen bubbles have the bites of snakes | 67 | 23 | 41 | 76 | 23 |
| **STOMACHS** |  |  |  |  |  |
| If the dead starve, their stomachs turn to tumble | 77 | 22 | 45 | 86 | 22 |
| **STONE** |  |  |  |  |  |
| My pickbrain masters morsing on the stone | 18 | 22 | 12 | 22 | 2 |
| It shall be said that gods are stone. | 44 | 11 | 25 | 52 | 11 |
| Shall a dropped stone drum on the ground, | 44 | 12 | 25 | 52 | 12 |
| For my tall tower's sake cast in her stone? | 46 | 2 | 27 | 54 | 2 |
| Why silk is soft and the stone wounds | 53 | 6 | 32 | 62 | 6 |
| Can time unriddle, and the cupboard stone, | 56 | 3 | 34 | 65 | 3 |
| The long-tailed stone | 56 | 18 | 34 | 65 | 18 |
| But when the ladies are cold as stone | 65 | 7 | 40 | 74 | 7 |
| Proud as a sucked stone and huge as sandgrains. | 78 | 23 | 46 | 87 | 23 |
| Out of the font of bone and plants at that stone tocsin | 83 | 20 | 49 | 93 | 2 |
| From the stone nest it does not let the feathery | 86 | 2 | 51 | 95 | 2 |
| And sculptured Ann is seventy years of stone. | 88 | 7 | 52 | 97 | 7 |
| And every stone I wind off like a reel. | 89 | 13 | 53 | 98 | 13 |
| Cast high, stunned on gilled stone; sly scissors ground in frost | 92 | 7 | 55 | 101 | 13 |
| More the thick stone cannot tell. | 93 | 10 | 56 | 102 | 10 |
| Of the stone bird guarding her: | 93 | 25 | 56 | 103 | 5 |
| Throw your fear a parcel of stone | 96 | 12 | 58 | 106 | 12 |
| The grave and my calm body are shut to your coming as stone, | 98 | 6 | 59 | 109 | 9 |
| A stone lies lost and locked in the lark-high hill. | 115 | 16 | 69 | 127 | 16 |
| Under the sad breast of the head stone | 130 | 20 | 77 | 144 | 20 |
| Summoning a child's voice from a webfoot stone, | 133 | 18 | 78 | 149 | 1 |
| He dropped where he loved on the burst pavement stone | 135 | 4 | 80 | 152 | 4 |
| Still as stone | 138 | 3 | 82 | 155 | 3 |
| Endure the stone | 145 | 5 | 82 | 162 | 5 |
| Stone for the sake of the souls of the slain birds sailing. | 169 | 12 | 87 | 189 | 21 |
| And ducked and draked white lake that harps to a hail stone. | 177 | 8 | 90 | 198 | 7 |
| **STONED** |  |  |  |  |  |
| Where at night we stoned the cold and cuckoo | 89 | 8 | 53 | 98 | 8 |

| | U.K. | | | U.S. | |
|---|---|---|---|---|---|
| | Page | Line | Poem | Page | Line |

**STONE-NECKED**

Each ancient, stone-necked minute of love's season — 78, 2, 46, 87, 2

**STONES**

There round about your stones the shades — 11, 16, 8, 12, 16
Flung gravel chime? Let the stones speak — 44, 13, 25, 52, 13
With stones of odyssey for ash and garland — 76·, 7, 44, 85, 7
To the trees and the stones and the fish in the tide. — 104, 5, 63, 115, 7
To roar on the rockery stones — 112, 5, 68, 124, 5
He knelt on the cold stones, — 120, 6, 72, 132, 11
Leaves is dancing. Lines of age on the stones weave in a flock. — 121, 23, 72, 134, 18
Back. Lines of age sleep on the stones till trumpeting dawn. — 123, 8, 72, 136, 18
With moving fish and rounded stones — 156, 10, 83, 174, 18
Though the names on their weed grown stones are rained away, — 176, 8, 90, 197, 8

**STONING**

To glow after the god stoning night — 158, 11, 84, 177, 11

**STONY**

Into the stony idiom of the brain, — 21, 9, 13, 25, 9
Sprout from the stony lockers like a tree on Aran. — 37, 27, 20, 43, 10

**STOOD**

Lean time on tide and times the wind stood rough, — 67, 6, 41, 76, 6
Year to heaven stood there then in the summer noon — 104, 14, 63, 115, 16

**STOOL**

I smelt the maggot in my stool. — 8, 6, 5, 9, 6

**STOPPED**

Her two surnames stopped me still. — 93, 2, 56, 102, 2
Tell his street on its back he stopped a sun — 135, 6, 80, 152, 6

**STORE**

Setting no store by harvest, freeze the soils; — 1, 3, 2, 1, 3

**STORED**

At the breast stored with seas. No return — 98, 4, 59, 109, 7

**STORIES**

All legends' sweethearts on a tree of stories, — 41, 25, 23, 48, 7
Who tossed the high tide in a time of stories — 67, 13, 41, 76, 13
On the old seas from stories, thrashing my wings, — 133, 8, 78, 148, 11

**STORKS**

And a hundred storks perch on the sun's right hand. — 135, 14, 80, 152, 14

**STORM**

The seed-at-zero shall not storm — 42, 1, 24, 49, 1
The seed-at-zero shall not storm — 42, 8, 24, 49, 8

465

STORM (continued)

|  | U.K. | | | U.S. | |
|---|---|---|---|---|---|
|  | *Page* | *Line* | *Poem* | *Page* | *Line* |
| Storm her sped heart, hand with beheaded veins | 79 | 8 | 46 | 88 | 11 |
| Ribbed between desert and water storm, | 82 | 11 | 48 | 91 | 11 |
| Storm, snow, and fountain in the weather of fireworks, | 83 | 14 | 49 | 92 | 14 |
| Storm me forever over her grave until | 88 | 10 | 52 | 97 | 10 |
| And when the salt sheet broke in a storm of singing | 136 | 7 | 81 | 153 | 7 |
| His mouth and rocked him like a storm | 139 | 10 | 82 | 156 | 10 |
| He saw the storm smoke out to kill | 150 | 17 | 83 | 168 | 1 |
| STORMS | | | | | |
| Storms in the freezing tomb. | 6 | 3 | 4 | 6 | 3 |
| Tell, if at all, the winter's storms | 45 | 10 | 26 | 53 | 10 |
| STORY | | | | | |
| Because there stands, one story out of the bum city, | 77 | 13 | 45 | 86 | 13 |
| STORY'S | | | | | |
| This story's monster has a serpent caul, | 41 | 10 | 23 | 47 | 10 |
| STOVED | | | | | |
| The stoved bones' voyage downward | 38 | 9 | 20 | 43 | 19 |
| STRAIGHT | | | | | |
| In the straight grave, | 18 | 20 | 12 | 21 | 20 |
| And the naked egg stand straight, | 56 | 7 | 34 | 65 | 7 |
| Straight as a young elm | 112 | 9 | 68 | 124 | 9 |
| Straight and tall from his crooked bones | 112 | 10 | 68 | 124 | 10 |
| STRAIGHTENS | | | | | |
| Golden Glamorgan straightens, to the falling birds. | 49 | 23 | 29 | 58 | 23 |
| STRAIT | | | | | |
| Strait in the mazed bed | 108 | 5 | 66 | 119 | 5 |
| STRAND | | | | | |
| Flows to the strand of flowers like the dew's ruly sea, | 165 | 27 | 86 | 185 | 17 |
| STRANGE | | | | | |
| Strange to our solid eye, | 14 | 13 | 10 | 16 | 13 |
| Tells you and you, my masters, as his strange | 56 | 13 | 34 | 65 | 13 |
| When near and strange wounded on London's waves | 117 | 27 | 71 | 130 | 3 |
| STRANGER | | | | | |
| Shall I let in the stranger, | 59 | 4 | 35 | 68 | 4 |
| Hands of the stranger and holds of the ships, | 59 | 7 | 35 | 68 | 7 |
| And a stranger enter like iron. | 96 | 22 | 58 | 107 | 5 |
| A stranger has come | 108 | 1 | 66 | 119 | 1 |
| STRANGER-EYES | | | | | |
| Unseen by stranger-eyes | 58 | 7 | 35 | 67 | 7 |
| STRANGER'S | | | | | |
| Before she lay on a stranger's bed | 93 | 11 | 56 | 102 | 11 |
| STRANGERS | | | | | |
| To you strangers (though song | vii | 24 | 1 | xv | 24 |

| | U.K. | | | U.S. | |
|---|---|---|---|---|---|
| | *Page* | *Line* | *Poem* | *Page* | *Line* |
| When we were strangers to the guided seas, | 40 | 7 | 22 | 46 | 7 |
| Once seen strangers or shades on a stair; | 113 | 15 | 69 | 125 | 15 |
| Locking, unlocking, the murdered strangers weave, | 117 | 15 | 71 | 129 | 15 |
| (Sighed the old ram rod, dying of strangers), | 175 | 22 | 89 | 196 | 3 |
| STRANGERS' | | | | | |
| Our own true strangers' dust | 126 | 13 | 74 | 140 | 13 |
| STRAPPED | | | | | |
| Strapped to a wheel, yet they shall not break; | 68 | 14 | 42 | 77 | 14 |
| In a land strapped by hunger | 90 | 4 | 54 | 99 | 4 |
| STRATA | | | | | |
| The strata of the shore and drown red rock; | 82 | 20 | 48 | 91 | 20 |
| STRAW | | | | | |
| Like stalks of tall, dry straw, | vii | 22 | 1 | vx | 22 |
| And from the planted womb the man of straw. | 2 | 12 | 2 | 2 | 12 |
| The ghost is dumb that stammered in the straw, | 31 | 4 | 18 | 36 | 4 |
| STRAWBERRIES | | | | | |
| And the wild boys innocent as strawberries | 112 | 16 | 68 | 124 | 16 |
| STRAWS | | | | | |
| Drew in his eyes the straws of sleep, | 4 | 17 | 3 | 4 | 17 |
| Broke through her straws, breaking my bandaged string, | 12 | 3 | 9 | 13 | 3 |
| The straws of Asia, lose me as I turn | 31 | 23 | 18 | 37 | 5 |
| When the worm builds with the gold straws of venom | 76 | 21 | 44 | 85 | 21 |
| With a hold of leeches and straws, | 95 | 24 | 58 | 105 | 24 |
| STREAK | | | | | |
| The rippled seals streak down | 171 | 7 | 88 | 191 | 7 |
| STREAM | | | | | |
| Molten and mountainous to stream | viii | 23 | 1 | xvi | 23 |
| My world was christened in a stream of milk. | 20 | 7 | 13 | 24 | 7 |
| Stream with bells and baying water bounds. The dew rings | 121 | 7 | 72 | 134 | 2 |
| Furied by his stream | 139 | 5 | 82 | 156 | 5 |
| In the first fury of his stream | 140 | 8 | 82 | 157 | 8 |
| Stream upon his martyrdom | 147 | 16 | 82 | 164 | 16 |
| Fire on starlight, rake Jesu's stream; | 150 | 19 | 83 | 168 | 3 |
| Sussanah's drowned in the bearded stream | 153 | 11 | 83 | 171 | 7 |
| The stream from the priest black wristed spinney and sleeves | 165 | 1 | 86 | 184 | 9 |
| STREAMED | | | | | |
| Streamed again a wonder of summer | 103 | 18 | 63 | 114 | 18 |
| STREAMS | | | | | |
| Drives my red blood; that dries the mouthing streams | 9 | 7 | 6 | 10 | 7 |
| Of the golden ghost who ringed with his streams her mercury bone, | 127 | 11 | 75 | 141 | 11 |

|  | U.K. | | | U.S. | |
|---|---|---|---|---|---|
|  | Page | Line | Poem | Page | Line |
| In the pebbles of the holy streams. | 159 | 18 | 85 | 178 | 18 |
| **STREET** | | | | | |
| Limp in the street of sea, among the rabble | 30 | 15 | 18 | 35 | 15 |
| Shall I, struck on the hot and rocking street, | 77 | 16 | 45 | 86 | 16 |
| On the last street wave praised | 95 | 4 | 58 | 105 | 4 |
| That bury the sweet street slowly, see | 96 | 8 | 58 | 106 | 8 |
| Your polestar neighbor, sun of another street, | 117 | 17 | 71 | 129 | 17 |
| Among the street burned to tireless death | 129 | 4 | 77 | 143 | 4 |
| Street we chant the flying sea | 130 | 5 | 77 | 144 | 5 |
| Tell his street on its back he stopped a sun | 135 | 6 | 80 | 152 | 6 |
| **STREETS** | | | | | |
| Through the waves of the fat streets nor the skeleton's thin ways. | 98 | 5 | 59 | 109 | 8 |
| And the streets that the fisherman combed | 157 | 2 | 83 | 175 | 14 |
| Streets or hungering in the crumbled wood: to these | 178 | 16 | 90 | 199 | 17 |
| **STRENGTH** | | | | | |
| Of new man strength, I seek the sun. | 29 | 4 | 17 | 34 | 8 |
| Clack through the thicket of strength, love hewn in pillars drops | 92 | 8 | 55 | 101 | 14 |
| **STRETCH** | | | | | |
| Stretch the salt photographs, | 69 | 19 | 43 | 78 | 19 |
| **STREWING** | | | | | |
| Strewing their bowels from a hill of bones, | 31 | 17 | 18 | 36 | 17 |
| **STRIDE** | | | | | |
| Stride through Cadaver's country in my force, | 18 | 21 | 12 | 22 | 1 |
| I, in my intricate image, stride on two levels, | 35 | 1 | 20 | 40 | 1 |
| The sky stride of the always slain | 142 | 10 | 82 | 159 | 10 |
| **STRIDING** | | | | | |
| His striped and noon maned tribe striding to holocaust, | 110 | 3 | 67 | 121 | 5 |
| **STRIKE** | | | | | |
| Strike the sea hour through bellmetal. | 83 | 12 | 49 | 92 | 12 |
| Strike in the time-bomb town, | 96 | 10 | 58 | 106 | 10 |
| Strike light, and bloody a loud room. | 97 | 10 | 59 | 108 | 10 |
| Strike and smoothe, for my decks are drums, | 152 | 5 | 83 | 169 | 17 |
| Sing and strike his heavy haul | 154 | 17 | 83 | 172 | 17 |
| Strike and sing his catch of fields | 156 | 13 | 83 | 175 | 1 |
| **STRIKES** | | | | | |
| Carrying cloud, Death strikes their house. | 124 | 8 | 73 | 138 | 8 |
| **STRIKING** | | | | | |
| Carved birds blunt their striking throats on the salt gravel, | 86 | 3 | 51 | 95 | 3 |
| **STRING** | | | | | |
| Broke through her straws, breaking my bandaged string, | 12 | 3 | 9 | 13 | 3 |

| | U.K. | | | U.S. | |
|---|---|---|---|---|---|
| | *Page* | *Line* | *Poem* | *Page* | *Line* |
| STRINGED | | | | | |
| Had stringed my flask of matter to his rib. | 4 | 12 | 3 | 4 | 12 |
| STRINGS | | | | | |
| Parish of snow. The carved mouths in the rock are wind swept strings. | 121 | 9 | 72 | 134 | 4 |
| STRIP | | | | | |
| But strip the twelve-winded marrow from his circle; | 60 | 3 | 36 | 69 | 3 |
| Weans on an artery the gender's strip; | 71 | 18 | 44 | 80 | 18 |
| Strip to this tree: a rocking alphabet, | 74 | 17 | 44 | 83 | 17 |
| Bound by a sovereign strip, we lie, | 82 | 18 | 48 | 91 | 18 |
| STRIPED | | | | | |
| His striped and noon maned tribe striding to holocaust, | 110 | 3 | 67 | 121 | 5 |
| STRIPPING | | | | | |
| Stripping my loin of promise, | 10 | 14 | 7 | 11 | 14 |
| STRIPS | | | | | |
| Our strips of stuff that tatter as we move | 15 | 12 | 10 | 17 | 12 |
| STRODE | | | | | |
| Who strode for your own dead | 117 | 20 | 71 | 129 | 20 |
| STROKE | | | | | |
| Stroke of mechanical flesh on mine, | 34 | 5 | 19 | 39 | 11 |
| I am, the tower told, felled by a timeless stroke, | 46 | 21 | 27 | 54 | 21 |
| The crusted wound nor stroke the brow; | 62 | 14 | 37 | 71 | 14 |
| STROKED | | | | | |
| Sleep to a newborn sleep in a swaddling loin-leaf stroked and sang | 113 | 22 | 69 | 125 | 22 |
| STROKES | | | | | |
| In the sun strokes of summer, | 109 | 14 | 67 | 120 | 14 |
| STRONG | | | | | |
| Into the sided lap of light grew strong, | 21 | 3 | 13 | 25 | 3 |
| Through the rotating shell, strong | 28 | 2 | 17 | 33 | 2 |
| STRONGHOLD | | | | | |
| Settled on a virgin stronghold | 42 | 19 | 24 | 49 | 19 |
| Settling on a riddled stronghold | 42 | 26 | 24 | 50 | 5 |
| STRUCK | | | | | |
| And I was struck down by death's feather. | 8 | 15 | 5 | 9 | 15 |
| Shall I, struck on the hot and rocking street, | 77 | 16 | 45 | 86 | 16 |
| Refusal struck her loin and the lame flower | 90 | 2 | 54 | 99 | 2 |
| Refusal struck like a bell under water | 90 | 12 | 54 | 99 | 12 |
| That I struck one day by luck, | 93 | 5 | 56 | 102 | 5 |
| His naked need struck him howling and bowed | 120 | 14 | 72 | 132 | 19 |
| Under his downy arm you sighed as he struck, | 125 | 19 | 74 | 139 | 19 |
| Good-bye, good luck, struck the sun and the moon, | 157 | 21 | 83 | 176 | 13 |
| And I am struck as lonely as a holy maker by the sun. | 158 | 12 | 84 | 177 | 12 |

STRUCK (continued)

| | U.K. | | | U.S. | |
|---|---|---|---|---|---|
| | *Page* | *Line* | *Poem* | *Page* | *Line* |
| Thirty-five bells sing struck | 171 | 12 | 88 | 191 | 12 |
| STRUCTURE | | | | | |
| My throat knew thirst before the structure | 8 | 1 | 5 | 9 | 1 |
| STRUGGLE | | | | | |
| Give over, lovers, locking, and the seawax struggle, | 38 | 11 | 20 | 44 | 1 |
| STRUGGLING | | | | | |
| My second struggling from the grass. | 28 | 20 | 17 | 33 | 20 |
| STRUNG | | | | | |
| Strung by the flaxen whale-weed, from the hang- man's raft, | 37 | 14 | 20 | 42 | 20 |
| But only the wind strung | 120 | 16 | 72 | 133 | 1 |
| STRUT | | | | | |
| Dressed to die, the sensual strut begun, | 99 | 6 | 60 | 110 | 6 |
| Or the strut and trade of charms | 128 | 8 | 76 | 142 | 8 |
| STRUTTING | | | | | |
| And the strutting fern lay seeds on the black sill. | 88 | 12 | 52 | 97 | 12 |
| STUB | | | | | |
| With a stub of black buds, | 95 | 21 | 58 | 105 | 21 |
| STUBBLE | | | | | |
| Suffer the slash of vision by the fin-green stubble, | 38 | 7 | 20 | 43 | 17 |
| STUDDED | | | | | |
| Towards the studded male in a bent, midnight blaze | 91 | 13 | 55 | 100 | 13 |
| STUDIES | | | | | |
| In the jails and studies of his keyless smiles. | 125 | 8 | 74 | 139 | 8 |
| STUFF | | | | | |
| Our strips of stuff that tatter as we move | 15 | 12 | 10 | 17 | 12 |
| Lose the great pains or stuff the wound, | 48 | 12 | 28 | 56 | 12 |
| STUFFED | | | | | |
| In a room with a stuffed fox and a stale fern, | 87 | 11 | 52 | 96 | 11 |
| The stuffed lung of the fox twitch and cry Love | 88 | 11 | 52 | 97 | 11 |
| STUMBLE | | | | | |
| They see the squirrel stumble, | 36 | 16 | 20 | 41 | 16 |
| And salt-eyed stumble bedward where she lies | 67 | 12 | 41 | 76 | 12 |
| Stumble out with their spades, | 119 | 21 | 72 | 132 | 1 |
| STUMBLED | | | | | |
| Rasped at last, and I stumbled and sucked, | 107 | 8 | 65 | 118 | 8 |
| STUMBLING | | | | | |
| Dumbly and divinely stumbling | 42 | 6 | 24 | 49 | 6 |
| STUMP | | | | | |
| Invisible on the stump | 56 | 28 | 34 | 66 | 7 |
| STUNG | | | | | |
| In shaping-time the circle stung awake, | 40 | 3 | 22 | 46 | 3 |
| STUNNED | | | | | |
| Cast high, stunned on gilled stone; sly scissors ground in frost | 92 | 7 | 55 | 101 | 13 |

| | U.K. | | | U.S. | |
|---|---|---|---|---|---|
| | Page | Line | Poem | Page | Line |
| And stunned and still on the green, laid veil | 156 | 3 | 83 | 174 | 11 |

STY

| | Page | Line | Poem | Page | Line |
|---|---|---|---|---|---|
| Flared in the reek of the wiving sty with the rush | 177 | 2 | 90 | 198 | 1 |

STYLUS

| | Page | Line | Poem | Page | Line |
|---|---|---|---|---|---|
| The grooved land rotating, that the stylus of lightning | 37 | 17 | 20 | 42 | 23 |

SUBSTANCE

| | Page | Line | Poem | Page | Line |
|---|---|---|---|---|---|
| The substance forked that marrowed the first sun; | 22 | 4 | 14 | 27 | 4 |

SUBTLE

| | Page | Line | Poem | Page | Line |
|---|---|---|---|---|---|
| It were a wand or subtle bough; | 134 | 14 | 79 | 150 | 14 |

SUBWAY

| | Page | Line | Poem | Page | Line |
|---|---|---|---|---|---|
| Nor city tar and subway bored to foster | 19 | 9 | 12 | 22 | 14 |

SUCH

| | Page | Line | Poem | Page | Line |
|---|---|---|---|---|---|
| Gives up its dead to such a working sea; | 5 | 3 | 3 | 5 | 3 |
| A million minds gave suck to such a bud | 21 | 22 | 13 | 26 | 5 |
| After such fighting as the weakest know, | 48 | 10 | 28 | 56 | 10 |
| That spill such acrid blood. | 48 | 16 | 28 | 56 | 16 |
| Gold on such features, and the linen spirit | 76 | 3 | 44 | 85 | 3 |
| Were once such a creature, so gay and frank | 107 | 14 | 65 | 118 | 14 |
| But blessed by such heroic hosts in your every | 109 | 21 | 67 | 120 | 21 |
| In all his tuneful turning so few and such morning songs | 160 | 21 | 85 | 179 | 21 |
| Of the sparrows and such who swansing, dusk, in wrangling hedges. | 167 | 7 | 87 | 187 | 7 |

SUCK

| | Page | Line | Poem | Page | Line |
|---|---|---|---|---|---|
| One breast gave suck the fever's issue; | 21 | 19 | 13 | 26 | 2 |
| A million minds gave suck to such a bud | 21 | 22 | 13 | 26 | 5 |
| You are all these, said she who gave me the long suck, | 46 | 17 | 27 | 54 | 17 |

SUCKED

| | Page | Line | Poem | Page | Line |
|---|---|---|---|---|---|
| Seaward the salmon, sucked sun slips, | viii | 8 | 1 | xvi | 8 |
| The mouth of time sucked, like a sponge, | 4 | 4 | 3 | 4 | 4 |
| When the galactic sea was sucked | 4 | 7 | 3 | 4 | 7 |
| The dream has sucked the sleeper of his faith | 15 | 9 | 10 | 17 | 9 |
| The salt sucked dam and darlings of the land | 47 | 3 | 27 | 55 | 3 |
| Proud as a sucked stone and huge as sandgrains. | 78 | 23 | 46 | 87 | 23 |
| Rasped at last, and I stumbled and sucked, | 107 | 8 | 65 | 118 | 8 |

SUCKETH

| | Page | Line | Poem | Page | Line |
|---|---|---|---|---|---|
| The child that sucketh long is shooting up, | 71 | 16 | 44 | 80 | 16 |

SUCKING

| | Page | Line | Poem | Page | Line |
|---|---|---|---|---|---|
| Sucking the dark, kissed on the cyanide, | 30 | 21 | 18 | 35 | 21 |

SUCKLE

| | Page | Line | Poem | Page | Line |
|---|---|---|---|---|---|
| All that shapes from the caul and suckle, | 34 | 4 | 19 | 39 | 10 |

SUCKLING

| | Page | Line | Poem | Page | Line |
|---|---|---|---|---|---|
| Prides of to-morrow suckling in her eyes, | 80 | 14 | 46 | 89 | 22 |

|  |  | U.K. |  |  | U.S. |  |
|---|---|---|---|---|---|---|
|  |  | Page | Line | Poem | Page | Line |
| **SUCKS** |  |  |  |  |  |  |
|  | How at the mountain spring the same mouth sucks. | 9 | 10 | 6 | 10 | 10 |
|  | Who sucks the bell-voiced Adam out of magic, | 74 | 23 | 44 | 83 | 23 |
| **SUDDEN** |  |  |  |  |  |  |
|  | I shall run lost in sudden | 139 | 11 | 82 | 156 | 11 |
|  | In a blessing of the sudden | 148 | 2 | 82 | 165 | 2 |
| **SUDDENLY** |  |  |  |  |  |  |
|  | Here were fond climates and sweet singers suddenly | 103 | 1 | 63 | 114 | 1 |
| **SUFFER** |  |  |  |  |  |  |
|  | As yet ungotten, I did suffer; | 7 | 19 | 5 | 8 | 19 |
|  | They suffer the undead water where the turtle nibbles, | 37 | 22 | 20 | 43 | 5 |
|  | Suffer, my topsy-turvies, that a double angel | 37 | 26 | 20 | 43 | 9 |
|  | Suffer the slash of vision by the fin-green stubble, | 38 | 7 | 20 | 43 | 17 |
|  | Suffer the heaven's children through my heart-beat. | 75 | 18 | 44 | 84 | 18 |
|  | Convenient bird and beast lie lodged to suffer | 77 | 3 | 45 | 86 | 3 |
|  | Suffer the first vision that set fire to the stars. | 108 | 18 | 66 | 119 | 18 |
| **SUFFERED** |  |  |  |  |  |  |
|  | My silly suit, hardly yet suffered for, | 133 | 1 | 78 | 148 | 4 |
| **SUFFERER** |  |  |  |  |  |  |
|  | Lie still, sleep becalmed, sufferer with the wound | 136 | 1 | 81 | 153 | 1 |
| **SUFFERING** |  |  |  |  |  |  |
|  | The lovers' house, lie suffering my stain? | 46 | 4 | 27 | 54 | 4 |
|  | The hollow words could bear all suffering | 48 | 22 | 28 | 56 | 22 |
| **SUFFERS** |  |  |  |  |  |  |
|  | And the endless beginning of prodigies suffers open.' | 98 | 7 | 59 | 109 | 10 |
| **SUIT** |  |  |  |  |  |  |
|  | Said the fake gentleman in suit of spades, | 73 | 14 | 44 | 82 | 14 |
|  | Suit for a serial sum | 132 | 4 | 78 | 147 | 4 |
|  | My silly suit, hardly yet suffered for, | 133 | 1 | 78 | 148 | 4 |
| **SUITOR** |  |  |  |  |  |  |
|  | And the wind was my sister suitor; | 7 | 15 | 5 | 8 | 15 |
| **SULKING** |  |  |  |  |  |  |
|  | For my sulking, skulking, coal black soul! | 175 | 7 | 89 | 195 | 12 |
| **SULLEN** |  |  |  |  |  |  |
|  | In my craft or sullen art | 128 | 1 | 76 | 142 | 1 |
|  | In my Craft or Sullen Art | 128 |  | 76 | 142 |  |
| **SULPHUR** |  |  |  |  |  |  |
|  | Hell in a horn of sulphur and the cloven myth, | 40 | 16 | 22 | 46 | 16 |
|  | When, with his torch and hourglass, like a sulphur priest, | 83 | 2 | 49 | 92 | 2 |

| | U.K. | | | U.S. | |
|---|---|---|---|---|---|
| | *Page* | *Line* | *Poem* | *Page* | *Line* |
| **SULTRY** | | | | | |
| And the multitude's sultry tear turns cool on the weeping wall, | 158 | 17 | 84 | 177 | 17 |
| To the sultry, biding herds, I said, | 175 | 4 | 89 | 195 | 9 |
| **SUM** | | | | | |
| Suit for a serial sum | 132 | 4 | 78 | 147 | 4 |
| **SUMMER** | | | | | |
| I see the boys of summer in their ruin | 1 | 1 | 2 | 1 | 1 |
| I see the summer children in their mothers | 1 | 13 | 2 | 1 | 13 |
| O see the pulse of summer in the ice. | 1 | 24 | 2 | 1 | 24 |
| Death from a summer woman, | 2 | 8 | 2 | 2 | 8 |
| We summer boys in this four-winded spinning, | 2 | 13 | 2 | 2 | 13 |
| I see you boys of summer in your ruin. | 3 | 1 | 2 | 3 | 7 |
| I who was deaf to spring and summer, | 7 | 7 | 5 | 8 | 7 |
| The cancer's fusion, or the summer feather | 19 | 7 | 12 | 22 | 12 |
| (Give, summer, over), the cemented skin, | 19 | 19 | 12 | 23 | 4 |
| Dissolved in summer and the hundred seasons; | 21 | 25 | 13 | 26 | 8 |
| Incising summer. | 31 | 9 | 18 | 36 | 9 |
| Once in this wind the summer blood | 39 | 6 | 21 | 45 | 6 |
| This summer buries a spring bird. | 45 | 4 | 26 | 53 | 4 |
| I should tell summer from the trees, the worms | 45 | 9 | 26 | 53 | 9 |
| A worm tells summer better than the clock, | 45 | 14 | 26 | 53 | 14 |
| Adore my windows for their summer scene? | 46 | 8 | 27 | 54 | 8 |
| Marking the flesh and summer in the bay? | 46 | 11 | 27 | 54 | 11 |
| Country, your sport is summer, and December's pools | 49 | 7 | 29 | 58 | 7 |
| Your sport is summer as the spring runs angrily. | 49 | 24 | 29 | 58 | 24 |
| Forever it is a white child in the dark-skinned summer | 83 | 19 | 49 | 93 | 1 |
| Of spring and summer were blooming in the tall tales | 103 | 11 | 63 | 114 | 11 |
| Streamed again a wonder of summer | 103 | 18 | 63 | 114 | 18 |
| Year to heaven stood there then in the summer noon | 104 | 14 | 63 | 115 | 16 |
| In the sun strokes of summer, | 109 | 14 | 67 | 120 | 14 |
| Of summer come in his great good time | 175 | 3 | 89 | 195 | 8 |
| Manes, under his quenchless summer barbed gold to the bone, | 177 | 6 | 90 | 198 | 5 |
| I see the boys of summer | 1 | | 2 | 1 | |
| **SUMMER'S** | | | | | |
| At God speeded summer's end | vii | 2 | 1 | xv | 2 |
| At God speeded summer's end | x | 18 | 1 | xviii | 24 |
| This first and steepled season, to the summer's game. | 49 | 12 | 29 | 58 | 12 |
| **SUMMERS** | | | | | |
| Falls on a ring of summers and locked noons. | 79 | 4 | 46 | 88 | 7 |

|  | U.K. | | | U.S. | |
|---|---|---|---|---|---|
|  | *Page* | *Line* | *Poem* | *Page* | *Line* |
| SUMMERTIME | | | | | |
| Summertime of the dead whispered the truth of his joy | 104 | 4 | 63 | 115 | 6 |
| SUMMERY | | | | | |
| Summery | 102 | 24 | 63 | 113 | 24 |
| SUMMON | | | | | |
| We are the dark deniers, let us summon | 2 | 7 | 2 | 2 | 7 |
| Summon your snowy horsemen, and the four-stringed hill, | 49 | 14 | 29 | 58 | 14 |
| SUMMONING | | | | | |
| Summoning a child's voice from a webfoot stone, | 133 | 18 | 78 | 149 | 1 |
| SUN | | | | | |
| In the torrent salmon sun, | vii | 3 | 1 | xv | 3 |
| Seaward the salmon, sucked sun slips, | viii | 8 | 1 | xvi | 8 |
| Poor peace as the sun sets | x | 6 | 1 | xviii | 12 |
| My ark sings in the sun | x | 17 | 1 | xviii | 23 |
| There in the sun the frigid threads | 1 | 10 | 2 | 1 | 10 |
| Of sun and moon they paint their dams | 1 | 17 | 2 | 1 | 17 |
| And held a little sabbath with the sun, | 4 | 15 | 3 | 4 | 15 |
| Awake, my sleeper, to the sun, | 5 | 13 | 3 | 5 | 13 |
| A process blows the moon into the sun, | 6 | 22 | 4 | 7 | 4 |
| Who knew not sun and moon by name, | 7 | 8 | 5 | 8 | 8 |
| Caught by the crabbing sun I walk on fire | 16 | 3 | 11 | 19 | 3 |
| Ball of the foot depending from the sun, | 19 | 18 | 12 | 23 | 3 |
| The sun and moon shed one white light. | 20 | 9 | 13 | 24 | 9 |
| The sun was red, the moon was grey, | 20 | 14 | 13 | 24 | 14 |
| Itched in the noise of wind and sun. | 21 | 6 | 13 | 25 | 6 |
| One sun, one manna, warmed and fed. | 21 | 26 | 13 | 26 | 9 |
| The substance forked that marrowed the first sun; | 22 | 4 | 14 | 27 | 4 |
| Before the pitch was forking to a sun; | 23 | 3 | 14 | 28 | 3 |
| Light breaks where no sun shines; | 24 | 1 | 15 | 29 | 1 |
| And blood jumps in the sun; | 25 | 5 | 15 | 30 | 5 |
| There grows the hours' ladder to the sun, | 27 | 1 | 16 | 32 | 6 |
| Of new man strength, I seek the sun. | 29 | 4 | 17 | 34 | 8 |
| Man broke the sun, pulled the wind down. | 39 | 10 | 21 | 45 | 10 |
| All heaven in a midnight of the sun, | 40 | 17 | 22 | 46 | 17 |
| Or the funeral of the sun; | 45 | 11 | 26 | 53 | 11 |
| That made me happy in the sun, | 48 | 19 | 28 | 56 | 19 |
| So solve the mystic sun, the wife of light, | 51 | 26 | 31 | 61 | 5 |
| The sun that leaps on petals through a nought, | 51 | 27 | 31 | 61 | 6 |
| Sailed up the sun; | 54 | 8 | 33 | 63 | 8 |
| How soon the servant sun, | 56 | 1 | 34 | 65 | 1 |
| All nerves to serve the sun, | 56 | 15 | 34 | 65 | 15 |
| Dictatorship of sun. | 65 | 13 | 40 | 74 | 13 |
| Doom on the sun!' | 66 | 16 | 40 | 75 | 16 |
| Break in the sun till the sun breaks down, | 68 | 26 | 42 | 70 | 26 |

| | U.K. | | | U.S. | |
|---|---|---|---|---|---|
| | Page | Line | Poem | Page | Line |
| And by this blowclock witness of the sun | 75 | 17 | 44 | 84 | 17 |
| Round the parched worlds of Wales and drowned each sun | 87 | 15 | 52 | 96 | 15 |
| With carved bird, saint, and sun, the wrack-spiked maiden mouth | 92 | 9 | 55 | 101 | 15 |
| And the sun killed in her face. | 93 | 9 | 56 | 102 | 9 |
| And makes with a flick of the thumb and sun | 96 | 25 | 58 | 107 | 8 |
| By the light of the meat-eating sun. | 99 | 5 | 60 | 110 | 5 |
| Blackbirds and the sun of October | 102 | 23 | 63 | 113 | 23 |
| Of sun light | 103 | 24 | 63 | 114 | 24 |
| In the sun. | 104 | 12 | 63 | 115 | 14 |
| In the sun strokes of summer, | 109 | 14 | 67 | 120 | 14 |
| Wild men who caught and sang the sun in flight, | 116 | 10 | 70 | 128 | 10 |
| Your polestar neighbor, sun of another street, | 117 | 17 | 71 | 129 | 17 |
| To shut the sun, plunge, mount your darkened keys | 118 | 5 | 71 | 130 | 9 |
| Children kept from the sun | 125 | 4 | 74 | 139 | 4 |
| And this day's sun leapt up the sky out of her thighs | 127 | 4 | 75 | 141 | 4 |
| No longer will the vibrations of the sun desire on | 127 | 8 | 75 | 141 | 8 |
| That other sun, the jealous coursing of the unrivalled blood. | 127 | 14 | 75 | 141 | 14 |
| Night fall and the fruit like a sun, | 131 | 4 | 77 | 145 | 10 |
| Tell his street on its back he stopped a sun | 135 | 6 | 80 | 152 | 6 |
| Of the sun | 140 | 3 | 82 | 157 | 3 |
| Praised the sun | 142 | 3 | 82 | 159 | 3 |
| That he who learns now the sun and moon | 144 | 1 | 82 | 161 | 1 |
| Unbidden by the sun | 145 | 14 | 82 | 162 | 14 |
| Sun spin a grave grey | 147 | 14 | 82 | 164 | 14 |
| Sun. In the name of the damned | 148 | 3 | 82 | 165 | 3 |
| But the loud sun | 148 | 6 | 82 | 165 | 6 |
| One. The sun roars at the prayer's end | 148 | 17 | 82 | 165 | 17 |
| The sun shipwrecked west on a pearl | 149 | 15 | 83 | 166 | 15 |
| Weeps like the risen sun among | 155 | 19 | 83 | 174 | 3 |
| Good-bye, good luck, struck the sun and the moon, | 157 | 21 | 83 | 176 | 13 |
| And I am struck as lonely as a holy maker by the sun. | 158 | 12 | 84 | 177 | 12 |
| Sun the father his quiver full of the infants of pure fire, | 158 | 19 | 84 | 177 | 19 |
| In the sun that is young once only, | 159 | 12 | 85 | 178 | 12 |
| All the sun long it was running, it was lovely, the hay | 159 | 19 | 85 | 178 | 19 |
| And the sun grew round that very day. | 160 | 10 | 85 | 179 | 10 |
| In the sun born over and over, | 160 | 17 | 85 | 179 | 17 |
| Round the sun, he comes to my love like the designed snow, | 165 | 25 | 86 | 185 | 15 |

## SUN (continued)

| | U.K. | | | U.S. | |
|---|---|---|---|---|---|
| | Page | Line | Poem | Page | Line |
| He comes to leave her in the lawless sun awaking | 166 | 6 | 86 | 186 | 6 |
| Your faith as deathless as the outcry of the ruled sun. | 166 | 12 | 86 | 186 | 12 |
| In the mustardseed sun, | 170 | 1 | 88 | 190 | 1 |
| The louder the sun blooms | 173 | 12 | 88 | 193 | 12 |
| In the courters' lanes, or twined in the ox roasting sun | 176 | 13 | 90 | 197 | 13 |
| Off by the sun and Daughters no longer grieved | 178 | 14 | 90 | 199 | 15 |
| Light breaks where no sun shines | 24 | | 15 | 29 | |
| How soon the servant sun | 56 | | 34 | 65 | |

SUN'S

| | | | | | |
|---|---|---|---|---|---|
| Like the sun's tears, | 106 | 1 | 64 | 117 | 1 |
| Over the sun's hovel and the slum of fire | 131 | 16 | 77 | 145 | 22 |
| And a hundred storks perch on the sun's right hand. | 135 | 14 | 80 | 152 | 14 |
| Or with their orchard man in the core of the sun's bush | 177 | 4 | 90 | 198 | 3 |

SUNCOCK

| | | | | | |
|---|---|---|---|---|---|
| I tell her this: before the suncock cast | 55 | 8 | 33 | 64 | 11 |

SUNDAY

| | | | | | |
|---|---|---|---|---|---|
| For, Sunday faced, with dusters in my glove, | 18 | 16 | 12 | 21 | 16 |
| Until the Sunday sombre bell at dark | 111 | 6 | 68 | 123 | 6 |
| And on seesaw sunday nights I wooed | 174 | 8 | 89 | 194 | 8 |
| For, oh, my soul found a sunday wife | 175 | 25 | 89 | 196 | 6 |

SUNDAYS

| | | | | | |
|---|---|---|---|---|---|
| Who heard the tall bell sail down the Sundays of the dead | 178 | 10 | 90 | 199 | 11 |

SUNDERED

| | | | | | |
|---|---|---|---|---|---|
| When sunlight goes are sundered from the worm, | 14 | 8 | 10 | 16 | 8 |
| And through the sundered water crawls | 155 | 22 | 83 | 174 | 6 |
| To death, one man through his sundered hulks, | 173 | 11 | 88 | 193 | 11 |

SUNDERING

| | | | | | |
|---|---|---|---|---|---|
| The sundering ultimate kingdom of genesis' thunder. | 131 | 25 | 77 | 146 | 7 |

SUNDOWN

| | | | | | |
|---|---|---|---|---|---|
| Cudgel great air, wreck east, and topple sun-down, | 79 | 7 | 46 | 88 | 10 |

SUNG

| | | | | | |
|---|---|---|---|---|---|
| Still be sung | 104 | 17 | 63 | 115 | 19 |
| All praise of the hawk on fire in hawk-eyed dusk be sung, | 168 | 3 | 87 | 188 | 7 |

SUN-GLOVED

| | | | | | |
|---|---|---|---|---|---|
| Comes love's anatomist with sun-gloved hand | 79 | 18 | 46 | 88 | 21 |

SUN-LEAVED

| | | | | | |
|---|---|---|---|---|---|
| The sun-leaved holy candlewoods | 95 | 19 | 58 | 105 | 19 |

|  | U.K. Page | Line | Poem | U.S. Page | Line |
|---|---|---|---|---|---|
| **SUNKEN** |  |  |  |  |  |
| Riding the sea light on a sunken path, | 67 | 8 | 41 | 76 | 8 |
| **SUNLIGHT** |  |  |  |  |  |
| As sunlight paints the shelling of their heads. | 1 | 18 | 2 | 1 | 18 |
| When sunlight goes are sundered from the worm, | 14 | 8 | 10 | 16 | 8 |
| **SUNNY** |  |  |  |  |  |
| The sunny gentlemen, the Welshing rich, | 15 | 5 | 10 | 17 | 5 |
| **SUNRISE** |  |  |  |  |  |
| To court the honeyed heart from your side before sunrise | 162 | 13 | 86 | 181 | 13 |
| **SUNS** |  |  |  |  |  |
| Turns night to day; blood in their suns | 6 | 5 | 4 | 6 | 5 |
| Of suns in the man-melting night. | 28 | 8 | 17 | 33 | 8 |
| Is celebrated there, and communion between suns. | 109 | 24 | 67 | 120 | 24 |
| **SUNSET** |  |  |  |  |  |
| To the sunset nets, | vii | 14 | 1 | xv | 14 |
| **SUNSHINE** |  |  |  |  |  |
| Season and sunshine, grace and girl, | 66 | 7 | 40 | 75 | 7 |
| **SUPER-OR-NEAR** |  |  |  |  |  |
| Super-or-near man | 114 | 6 | 69 | 126 | 6 |
| **SUPPER** |  |  |  |  |  |
| The supper and knives of a mood. | 77 | 4 | 45 | 86 | 4 |
| **SURE** |  |  |  |  |  |
| That uncalm still it is sure alone to stand and sing | 158 | 21 | 84 | 177 | 21 |
| Be you sure the Thief will seek a way sly and sure | 163 | 26 | 86 | 183 | 7 |
| **SURELY** |  |  |  |  |  |
| And surely he sails like the ship shape clouds. Oh he | 165 | 28 | 86 | 185 | 18 |
| **SURGE** |  |  |  |  |  |
| For the surge is sown with barley, | 156 | 14 | 83 | 175 | 2 |
| **SURNAMES** |  |  |  |  |  |
| Her two surnames stopped me still. | 93 | 2 | 56 | 102 | 2 |
| **SURPLICED** |  |  |  |  |  |
| Of the dingle torn to singing and the surpliced | 165 | 4 | 86 | 184 | 12 |
| **SURPRISED** |  |  |  |  |  |
| Surprised in the opening of her nightlong eyes | 127 | 2 | 75 | 141 | 2 |
| **SURRENDER** |  |  |  |  |  |
| To surrender now is to pay the expensive ogre twice. | 94 | 10 | 57 | 104 | 10 |
| **SUSSANAH'S** |  |  |  |  |  |
| Sussanah's drowned in the bearded stream | 153 | 11 | 83 | 171 | 7 |
| **SWADDLING** |  |  |  |  |  |
| Sleep to a newborn sleep in a swaddling loin-leaf stroked and sang | 113 | 22 | 69 | 125 | 22 |

| | | U.K. | | | U.S. | |
|---|---|---|---|---|---|---|
| | | Page | Line | Poem | Page | Line |
| **SWAG** | | | | | | |
| | With swag of bubbles in a seedy sack | 67 | 17 | 41 | 76 | 17 |
| **SWALLOW** | | | | | | |
| | Up to the swallow thronged loft by the shadow of my hand, | 160 | 25 | 85 | 180 | 2 |
| **SWALLOWED** | | | | | | |
| | And swallowed dry the waters of the breast. | 4 | 6 | 3 | 4 | 6 |
| **SWALLOWER** | | | | | | |
| | Or decked on a cloud swallower, | 132 | 12 | 78 | 147 | 12 |
| **SWAM** | | | | | | |
| | The voices of all the drowned swam on the wind. | 136 | 8 | 81 | 153 | 8 |
| | And the moon swam out of its hulk. | 149 | 16 | 83 | 166 | 16 |
| **SWANKED** | | | | | | |
| | Then, bushily swanked in bear wig and tails, | 132 | 19 | 78 | 147 | 19 |
| **SWANS** | | | | | | |
| | And the dumb swans drub blue | viii | 9 | 1 | xvi | 9 |
| | Alone between nurses and swans | 112 | 2 | 68 | 124 | 2 |
| **SWANSING** | | | | | | |
| | Of the sparrows and such who swansing, dusk, in wrangling hedges. | 167 | 7 | 87 | 187 | 7 |
| **SWARMS** | | | | | | |
| | Swarms on the kingdom come | 139 | 6 | 82 | 156 | 6 |
| **SWEAT** | | | | | | |
| | I dreamed my genesis in sweat of sleep, breaking | 28 | 1 | 17 | 33 | 1 |
| | I dreamed my genesis in sweat of death, fallen | 29 | 1 | 17 | 34 | 5 |
| **SWEET** | | | | | | |
| | Sweet are their fathered faces in their wings.' | 26 | 14 | 16 | 31 | 14 |
| | Were vaguenesses enough and the sweet lies plenty, | 48 | 21 | 28 | 56 | 21 |
| | And all sweet hell, deaf as an hour's ear, | 57 | 5 | 34 | 66 | 12 |
| | Nor can I smother the sweet waking.' | 66 | 8 | 40 | 75 | 8 |
| | And all love's sinners in sweet cloth kneel to a hyleg image, | 84 | 4 | 49 | 93 | 10 |
| | In quick, sweet, cruel light till the locked ground sprout out, | 91 | 18 | 55 | 100 | 18 |
| | The sweet, fish-gilled boats bringing blood | 95 | 22 | 58 | 105 | 22 |
| | That bury the sweet street slowly, see | 96 | 8 | 58 | 106 | 8 |
| | Here were fond climates and sweet singers suddenly | 103 | 1 | 63 | 114 | 1 |
| | Till the sweet tooth of my love bit dry, | 107 | 7 | 65 | 118 | 7 |
| | It was sweet to drown in the readymade handy water | 133 | 16 | 78 | 148 | 19 |
| **SWEETENS** | | | | | | |
| | Innocence sweetens my last black breath, | 175 | 29 | 89 | 196 | 10 |
| **SWEETER** | | | | | | |
| | Shall the blind horse sing sweeter? | 77 | 2 | 45 | 86 | 2 |

|  | U.K. | | Poem | U.S. | |
|---|---|---|---|---|---|
|  | Page | Line |  | Page | Line |
| SWEETHEARTING |  |  |  |  |  |
| Time and the crabs and the sweethearting crib | 12 | 25 | 9 | 14 | 4 |
| SWEETHEARTS |  |  |  |  |  |
| All legends' sweethearts on a tree of stories, | 41 | 25 | 23 | 48 | 7 |
| SWEETHEARTS' |  |  |  |  |  |
| Dead on the sweethearts' toes. | 12 | 28 | 9 | 14 | 7 |
| SWEETLY |  |  |  |  |  |
| Sweetly the diver's bell in the steeple of spindrift | 37 | 11 | 20 | 42 | 17 |
| The present mouth, and the sweetly blown trumpet of lies, | 85 | 6 | 50 | 94 | 6 |
| SWELL |  |  |  |  |  |
| And speak their midnight nothings as they swell; | 14 | 14 | 10 | 16 | 14 |
| SWELTER |  |  |  |  |  |
| But a hillocky bull in the swelter | 175 | 2 | 89 | 195 | 7 |
| SWEPT |  |  |  |  |  |
| Ask the tall fish swept from the bible east, | 76 | 16 | 44 | 85 | 16 |
| Parish of snow. The carved mouths in the rock are wind swept strings. | 121 | 9 | 72 | 134 | 4 |
| And swept into our wounds and houses, | 158 | 7 | 84 | 177 | 7 |
| SWERVE |  |  |  |  |  |
| Till every beast blared down in a swerve | 151 | 9 | 83 | 168 | 17 |
| SWIFT |  |  |  |  |  |
| Then swift from a bursting sea with bottlecork boats | 132 | 13 | 78 | 147 | 13 |
| For we saw him throw to the swift flood | 149 | 21 | 83 | 167 | 1 |
| SWIMMERS' |  |  |  |  |  |
| Time for the swimmers' hands, music for silver lock | 86 | 7 | 51 | 95 | 7 |
| SWIMS |  |  |  |  |  |
| The boat swims into the six-year weather, | 154 | 9 | 83 | 172 | 9 |
| SWINE |  |  |  |  |  |
| That out of a bower of red swine | 66 | 4 | 40 | 75 | 4 |
| Of the hobnail tales: no gooseherd or swine will turn | 162 | 10 | 86 | 181 | 10 |
| SWINEHERD |  |  |  |  |  |
| Time by, their dust was flesh the swineherd rooted sly, | 177 | 1 | 90 | 197 | 21 |
| SWING |  |  |  |  |  |
| The swing of milk was tufted in the pap, | 30 | 10 | 18 | 35 | 10 |
| That her love sing and swing through a brown chapel, | 87 | 25 | 52 | 96 | 25 |
| SWINGS |  |  |  |  |  |
| The knobbly ape that swings along his sex | 13 | 9 | 9 | 14 | 16 |
| The dust of their kettles and clocks swings to and fro | 178 | 5 | 90 | 199 | 6 |
| SWINISH |  |  |  |  |  |
| The swinish plains of carrion | 143 | 2 | 82 | 160 | 2 |

|  | U.K. | | | U.S. | |
|  | Page | Line | Poem | Page | Line |
| SWITCHBACK | | | | | |
| By full tilt river and switchback sea | 170 | 2 | 88 | 190 | 2 |
| SWIVEL | | | | | |
| The fellow halves that, cloven as they swivel | 32 | 1 | 18 | 37 | 7 |
| SWUNG | | | | | |
| Swung by my father from his dome. | 7 | 12 | 5 | 8 | 12 |
| In a cavernous, swung | 171 | 10 | 88 | 191 | 10 |
| SYLLABIC | | | | | |
| Sheds the syllabic blood and drains her words. | 16 | 8 | 11 | 19 | 8 |
| SYLLABLES | | | | | |
| And, lashed to syllables, the lynx tongue cry | 81 | 8 | 47 | 90 | 8 |
| SYMBOL | | | | | |
| Of shades, symbol of desire beyond my hours | 110 | 7 | 67 | 121 | 9 |
| SYMBOLED | | | | | |
| Voyaging clockwise off the symboled harbour, | 36 | 8 | 20 | 41 | 8 |
| SYMBOLS | | | | | |
| Now that my symbols have outelbowed space, | 41 | 2 | 23 | 47 | 2 |
| Symbols are selected from the years' | 45 | 5 | 26 | 53 | 5 |
| SYNAGOGUE | | | | | |
| And the synagogue of the ear of corn | 101 | 9 | 62 | 112 | 9 |
| SYNTHETIC | | | | | |
| Fear not the flat, synthetic blood, | 33 | 14 | 19 | 38 | 14 |

# ENTRIES UNDER T

| TABLE | | | | | |
| Dazzle this face of voices on the moon-turned table, | 37 | 18 | 20 | 43 | 1 |
| Over the past table I repeat this present grace. | 77 | 25 | 45 | 86 | 25 |
| Soaked my table the uglier side of a hill | 89 | 2 | 53 | 98 | 2 |
| TACKLE | | | | | |
| And gale I tackle, the whole world of then, | 173 | 15 | 88 | 193 | 15 |
| TACKLED | | | | | |
| Tackled with clouds, who kneel | vii | 13 | 1 | xv | 13 |
| TAIL | | | | | |
| Tail, Nile, and snout, a saddler of the rushes, | 38 | 20 | 20 | 44 | 10 |
| Of head and tail made witnesses to this | 41 | 7 | 23 | 47 | 7 |
| Stalking my children's faces with a tail of blood, | 49 | 20 | 29 | 58 | 20 |
| With loud, torn tooth and tail and cobweb drum | 80 | 4 | 46 | 89 | 12 |
| TAILOR | | | | | |
| Comes, like a scissors stalking, tailor age, | 18 | 6 | 12 | 21 | 6 |

| | U.K. | | | U.S. | |
|---|---|---|---|---|---|
| | Page | Line | Poem | Page | Line |
| In the groin of the natural doorway I crouched like a tailor | 99 | 3 | 60 | 110 | 3 |
| TAILOR'S | | | | | |
| I was pierced by the idol tailor's eyes, | 133 | 10 | 78 | 148 | 13 |
| TAILORS | | | | | |
| I astounded the sitting tailors, | 132 | 17 | 78 | 147 | 17 |
| I set back the clock faced tailors, | 132 | 18 | 78 | 147 | 18 |
| TAILORS' | | | | | |
| The cloud perched tailors' master with nerves for cotton. | 133 | 7 | 78 | 148 | 10 |
| TAILS | | | | | |
| Then, bushily swanked in bear wig and tails, | 132 | 19 | 78 | 147 | 19 |
| TAKE | | | | | |
| Happy Cadaver's hunger as you take | 19 | 24 | 12 | 23 | 9 |
| The dear, daft time I take to nudge the sentence, | 41 | 4 | 23 | 47 | 4 |
| Before death takes you, O take back this. | 66 | 17 | 40 | 75 | 17 |
| I bitterly take to task my poverty and craft: | 94 | 3 | 57 | 104 | 3 |
| To take to give is all, return what is hungrily given | 94 | 4 | 57 | 104 | 4 |
| If I take to burn or return this world which is each man's work. | 94 | 12 | 57 | 104 | 12 |
| Nothing I cared, in the lamb white days, that time would take me | 160 | 24 | 85 | 180 | 1 |
| He comes to take | 166 | 4 | 86 | 186 | 4 |
| TAKEN | | | | | |
| And count the taken, forsaken mysteries in a bad dark. | 94 | 9 | 57 | 104 | 9 |
| And taken by light in her arms at long and dear last | 108 | 16 | 66 | 119 | 16 |
| In the taken body at many ages, | 114 | 17 | 69 | 126 | 17 |
| TAKES | | | | | |
| Before death takes you, O take back this. | 66 | 17 | 40 | 75 | 17 |
| TAKING | | | | | |
| On the consumptives' terrace taking their two farewells, | 36 | 10 | 20 | 41 | 10 |
| TALE | | | | | |
| In trust and tale have I divided sense, | 41 | 5 | 23 | 47 | 5 |
| It is a winter's tale | 119 | 1 | 72 | 131 | 1 |
| In the river wended vales where the tale was told. | 119 | 10 | 72 | 131 | 10 |
| And spells on the winds of the dead his winter's tale. | 121 | 4 | 72 | 133 | 19 |
| And the home of prayers and fires, the tale ended. | 122 | 30 | 72 | 136 | 10 |
| Of the nightingale's din and tale! The upgiven ghost | 165 | 3 | 86 | 184 | 11 |
| Hill of cypresses! The din and tale in the skimmed | 165 | 5 | 86 | 184 | 13 |

# TALE (continued)

|  | U.K. | | | U.S. | |
|---|---|---|---|---|---|
|  | *Page* | *Line* | *Poem* | *Page* | *Line* |
| A Winter's Tale | 119 | | 72 | 131 | |
| TALE'S | | | | | |
| Let the tale's sailor from a Christian voyage | 76 | 9 | 44 | 85 | 9 |
| TALES | | | | | |
| My cross of tales behind the fabulous curtain.' | 41 | 26 | 23 | 48 | 8 |
| Hold hard, my country children in the world of tales, | 49 | 10 | 29 | 58 | 10 |
| Of spring and summer were blooming in the tall tales | 103 | 11 | 63 | 114 | 11 |
| In the land of the hearthstone tales, and spelled asleep, | 162 | 2 | 86 | 181 | 2 |
| Of the hobnail tales: no gooseherd or swine will turn | 162 | 10 | 86 | 181 | 10 |
| Now the tales praise | 163 | 10 | 86 | 182 | 10 |
| Of the hearthstone tales my own, lost love; and the soul walks | 164 | 4 | 86 | 183 | 11 |
| TALK | | | | | |
| With tongues that talk all tongues. | 44 | 14 | 25 | 52 | 14 |
| That put an end to talk. | 62 | 8 | 37 | 71 | 8 |
| TALKATIVE | | | | | |
| And into its talkative seven tombs | 157 | 19 | 83 | 176 | 11 |
| TALKED | | | | | |
| Talked and tore though her eyes smiled. | 93 | 20 | 56 | 102 | 20 |
| TALKING | | | | | |
| Incarnate devil in a talking snake, | 40 | 1 | 22 | 46 | 1 |
| TALKS | | | | | |
| My busy heart who shudders as she talks | 16 | 7 | 11 | 19 | 7 |
| This night and each vast night until the stern bell talks | 164 | 2 | 86 | 183 | 9 |
| TALL | | | | | |
| Like stalks of tall, dry straw, | vii | 22 | 1 | xv | 22 |
| For my tall tower's sake cast in her stone? | 46 | 2 | 27 | 54 | 2 |
| For my tall turrets carry as your sin? | 46 | 6 | 27 | 54 | 6 |
| Ask the tall fish swept from the bible east, | 76 | 16 | 44 | 85 | 16 |
| Of spring and summer were blooming in the tall tales | 103 | 11 | 63 | 114 | 11 |
| Straight and tall from his crooked bones | 112 | 10 | 68 | 124 | 10 |
| And the tall grains foamed in their bills; | 153 | 1 | 83 | 170 | 16 |
| Who heard the tall bell sail down the Sundays of the dead | 178 | 10 | 90 | 199 | 11 |
| TALLER | | | | | |
| Taller this thunderclap spring, and how | 173 | 22 | 88 | 193 | 22 |
| TALLOW | | | | | |
| Till tallow I blew from the wax's tower | 74 | 9 | 44 | 83 | 9 |
| TALLOW-EYED | | | | | |
| He in a book of water tallow-eyed | 74 | 2 | 44 | 83 | 2 |

| | U.K. | | | U.S. | |
|---|---|---|---|---|---|
| | *Page* | *Line* | *Poem* | *Page* | *Line* |
| **TANGLED** | | | | | |
| Tangled with chirrup and fruit, | vii | 6 | 1 | xv | 6 |
| On casting tides, are tangled in the shells, | 32 | 2 | 18 | 37 | 8 |
| In the groin's endless coil a man is tangled.' | 79 | 27 | 46 | 89 | 8 |
| **TANGLING** | | | | | |
| Tangling through this spun slime | 173 | 3 | 88 | 193 | 3 |
| **TAP** | | | | | |
| Windshake of sailshaped ears, muffle-toed tap | 87 | 2 | 52 | 96 | 2 |
| Tap happily of one peg in the thick | 87 | 3 | 52 | 96 | 3 |
| **TAPE** | | | | | |
| Robbed of the foxy tongue, his footed tape | 18 | 9 | 12 | 21 | 9 |
| **TAPPED** | | | | | |
| With liquid hands tapped on the womb, | 7 | 2 | 5 | 8 | 2 |
| The code of night tapped on my tongue; | 21 | 16 | 13 | 25 | 16 |
| Death hairy-heeled,, and the tapped ghost in wood, | 52 | 5 | 31 | 61 | 12 |
| **TAPPING** | | | | | |
| With her rampart to his tapping, | 42 | 3 | 24 | 49 | 3 |
| With her rampart to his tapping, | 42 | 10 | 24 | 49 | 10 |
| **TAPS** | | | | | |
| The crutch that marrow taps upon their sleep, | 30 | 14 | 18 | 35 | 14 |
| **TAR** | | | | | |
| Nor city tar and subway bored to foster | 19 | 9 | 12 | 22 | 14 |
| **TARRED** | | | | | |
| As tarred with blood as the bright thorns I wept; | 75 | 7 | 44 | 84 | 7 |
| **TASK** | | | | | |
| I bitterly take to task my poverty and craft: | 94 | 3 | 57 | 104 | 3 |
| **TASSELLED** | | | | | |
| Tasselled in cellar and snipping shop | 132 | 11 | 78 | 147 | 11 |
| **TASTED** | | | | | |
| A little comes, is tasted and found good; | 48 | 5 | 28 | 56 | 5 |
| **TATTER** | | | | | |
| Our strips of stuff that tatter as we move | 15 | 12 | 10 | 17 | 12 |
| **TAUGHT** | | | | | |
| And he who taught their lips to sing | 155 | 18 | 83 | 174 | 2 |
| **TAUT** | | | | | |
| 'See,' drummed the taut masks, 'how the dead ascend: | 79 | 26 | 46 | 89 | 7 |
| **TAXED** | | | | | |
| Five sovereign fingers taxed the breath, | 62 | 2 | 37 | 71 | 2 |
| **TEACH** | | | | | |
| In autumn teach three seasons' fires | 45 | 7 | 26 | 53 | 7 |
| And the slug should teach me destruction. | 45 | 13 | 26 | 53 | 13 |
| Teach me the love that is evergreen after the fall leaved | 178 | 12 | 90 | 199 | 13 |
| **TEACHES** | | | | | |
| Teaches with no telling | 110 | 16 | 67 | 121 | 18 |

|  | U.K. | | Poem | U.S. | |
|---|---|---|---|---|---|
|  | Page | Line |  | Page | Line |
| **TEAR** | | | | | |
| Let fall the tear of time; the sleeper's eye, | 26 | 2 | 16 | 31 | 2 |
| Grief with dishevelled hands tear out the altar ghost | 83 | 5 | 49 | 92 | 5 |
| A blazing red harsh head tear up | 93 | 29 | 56 | 103 | 9 |
| Put a tear for joy in the unearthly flood | 125 | 22 | 74 | 139 | 22 |
| Now break a giant tear for the little known fall, | 126 | 8 | 74 | 140 | 8 |
| And the multitude's sultry tear turns cool on the weeping wall, | 158 | 17 | 84 | 177 | 17 |
| Fishing in the tear of the Towy. Only a hoot owl | 169 | 3 | 87 | 189 | 12 |
| **TEARDROPS** | | | | | |
| With pins for teardrops is the long wound's woman. | 75 | 10 | 44 | 84 | 10 |
| **TEAR-STAINED** | | | | | |
| And a tear-stained widower grief drooped from the lashes | 85 | 9 | 50 | 94 | 9 |
| **TEAR-STUFFED** | | | | | |
| After the feast of tear-stuffed time and thistles | 87 | 10 | 52 | 96 | 10 |
| **TEARS** | | | | | |
| Youth did condense; the tears of spring | 21 | 24 | 13 | 26 | 7 |
| Divining in a smile the oil of tears. | 24 | 18 | 15 | 29 | 18 |
| Hands have no tears to flow. | 62 | 16 | 37 | 71 | 16 |
| My dear would I change my tears on your iron head. | 97 | 18 | 59 | 108 | 18 |
| Twenty-four years remind the tears of my eyes. | 99 | 1 | 60 | 110 | 1 |
| And the other full of tears that she will be dead, | 100 | 5 | 61 | 111 | 5 |
| That his tears burned my cheeks and his heart moved in mine. | 103 | 28 | 63 | 115 | 2 |
| Like the sun's tears, | 106 | 1 | 64 | 117 | 1 |
| On the madhouse boards worn thin by my walking tears. | 108 | 15 | 66 | 119 | 15 |
| I see the tigron in tears | 110 | 1 | 67 | 121 | 3 |
| Curse, bless, me now with your fierce tears, I pray. | 116 | 17 | 70 | 128 | 17 |
| Will dive up to his tears. | 117 | 18 | 71 | 129 | 18 |
| In the churches of his tears, | 125 | 18 | 74 | 139 | 18 |
| Too proud to cry, too frail to check the tears, | | | 91 | 201 | 14 |
| The tears out of his eyes, too proud to cry. | | | 91 | 201 | 18 |
| **TEATS** | | | | | |
| Time's tune my ladies with the teats of music, | 74 | 21 | 44 | 83 | 21 |
| **TEETH** | | | | | |
| The body prospered, teeth in the marrowed gums, | 20 | 16 | 13 | 24 | 16 |
| Grave's foot, blinds down the lids, the teeth in black, | 87 | 4 | 52 | 96 | 4 |
| **TELL** | | | | | |
| And I am dumb to tell the crooked rose | 9 | 4 | 6 | 10 | 4 |

| | U.K. | | | U.S. | |
|---|---|---|---|---|---|
| | *Page* | *Line* | *Poem* | *Page* | *Line* |
| And I am dumb to tell the hanging man | 9 | 14 | 6 | 10 | 14 |
| And I am dumb to tell a weather's wind | 9 | 19 | 6 | 10 | 19 |
| And I am dumb to tell the lover's tomb | 9 | 21 | 6 | 10 | 21 |
| Of many a thorny shire tell you notes, | 16 | 15 | 11 | 19 | 15 |
| Some let me tell you of the raven's sins. | 16 | 24 | 11 | 19 | 24 |
| The wisemen tell me that the garden gods | 40 | 9 | 22 | 46 | 9 |
| I should tell summer from the trees, the worms | 45 | 9 | 26 | 53 | 9 |
| Tell, if at all, the winter's storms | 45 | 10 | 26 | 53 | 10 |
| What shall it tell me if a timeless insect | 45 | 16 | 26 | 53 | 16 |
| I tell her this: before the suncock cast | 55 | 8 | 33 | 64 | 11 |
| More the thick stone cannot tell. | 93 | 10 | 56 | 102 | 10 |
| Tell his street on its back he stopped a sun | 135 | 6 | 80 | 152 | 6 |
| We heard the sea sound sing, we saw the salt sheet tell. | 136 | 12 | 81 | 153 | 12 |
| Leaping! The gospel rooks! All tell, this night, of him | 165 | 9 | 86 | 184 | 17 |

**TELLING**

| | | | | | |
|---|---|---|---|---|---|
| I have heard many years of telling, | 63 | 16 | 38 | 72 | 16 |
| Teaches with no telling | 110 | 16 | 67 | 121 | 18 |
| Is telling. The wizened | 121 | 6 | 72 | 134 | 1 |
| In the rain telling its beads, and the gravest ghost | 163 | 8 | 86 | 182 | 8 |

**TELLS**

| | | | | | |
|---|---|---|---|---|---|
| And tells the page the empty ill. | 10 | 10 | 7 | 11 | 10 |
| Tells me the hour's word, the neural meaning | 16 | 18 | 11 | 19 | 18 |
| And tells the windy weather in the cock. | 16 | 20 | 11 | 19 | 20 |
| The signal grass that tells me all I know | 16 | 22 | 11 | 19 | 22 |
| Tells the stick, 'fail'. | 19 | 5 | 12 | 22 | 10 |
| A worm tells summer better than the clock, | 45 | 14 | 26 | 53 | 14 |
| Tells you and you, my masters, as his strange | 56 | 13 | 34 | 65 | 13 |
| Tells with silence the last light breaking | 101 | 4 | 62 | 112 | 4 |

**TELL-TALE**

| | | | | | |
|---|---|---|---|---|---|
| No tell-tale lover has an end more certain, | 41 | 24 | 23 | 48 | 6 |
| Hill, tell-tale the knelled | 168 | 17 | 87 | 189 | 2 |

**TELLTALE**

| | | | | | |
|---|---|---|---|---|---|
| The rude owl cried like a telltale tit, | 174 | 5 | 89 | 194 | 5 |

**TEMPERED**

| | | | | | |
|---|---|---|---|---|---|
| My blood upon the tempered dead, forcing | 28 | 19 | 17 | 33 | 19 |

**TEMPERS**

| | | | | | |
|---|---|---|---|---|---|
| Of light and love, the tempers of the heart, | 14 | 2 | 10 | 16 | 2 |

**TEMPLE-BOUND**

| | | | | | |
|---|---|---|---|---|---|
| Tongue and ear in the thread, angle the temple-bound | 91 | 26 | 55 | 101 | 4 |

**TEMPTER**

| | | | | | |
|---|---|---|---|---|---|
| The tempter under the eyelid | 153 | 6 | 83 | 171 | 2 |

**TENDRIL**

| | | | | | |
|---|---|---|---|---|---|
| And bear those tendril hands I touch across | 90 | 6 | 54 | 99 | 6 |

# TENTACLE

|  | U.K. | | Poem | U.S. | |
|---|---|---|---|---|---|
|  | Page | Line | | Page | Line |
| **TENTACLE** | | | | | |
| Trace out a tentacle, | 91 | 28 | 55 | 101 | 6 |
| **TERRACE** | | | | | |
| On the consumptives' terrace taking their two farewells, | 36 | 10 | 20 | 41 | 10 |
| **TERRIBLE** | | | | | |
| Growing more terrible as the day | 64 | 4 | 39 | 73 | 4 |
| The terrible world my brother bares his skin. | 80 | 7 | 46 | 89 | 15 |
| **TERRIBLY** | | | | | |
| Time kills me terribly. | 70 | 15 | 43 | 79 | 19 |
| And terribly lead him home alive | 157 | 6 | 83 | 175 | 18 |
| **TERROR** | | | | | |
| Terror and shining from | 139 | 12 | 82 | 156 | 12 |
| Lead her prodigal home to his terror, | 157 | 7 | 83 | 175 | 19 |
| Terror will rage apart | 171 | 16 | 88 | 191 | 16 |
| **TERRORS'** | | | | | |
| And the old terrors' continual cry | 64 | 3 | 39 | 73 | 3 |
| **THAMES** | | | | | |
| Of the riding Thames. | 101 | 23 | 62 | 112 | 23 |
| **THAN** | | | | | |
| The words of death are dryer than his stiff, | 13 | 18 | 9 | 15 | 4 |
| Of love am barer than Cadaver's trap | 18 | 8 | 12 | 21 | 8 |
| Black as the beast and paler than the cross. | 40 | 12 | 22 | 46 | 12 |
| A worm tells summer better than the clock, | 45 | 14 | 26 | 53 | 14 |
| There's more than dying; | 48 | 11 | 28 | 56 | 11 |
| Than bully ill love in the clouted scene. | 97 | 5 | 59 | 108 | 5 |
| Rarer than radium, | 125 | 2 | 74 | 139 | 2 |
| Commoner than water, crueller than truth; | 125 | 3 | 74 | 139 | 3 |
| With no more desire than a ghost. | 154 | 4 | 83 | 172 | 4 |
| Than ever was since the world was said, | 173 | 17 | 88 | 193 | 17 |
| To Others than You | 107 | | 65 | 118 | |
| **THATCH** | | | | | |
| in the squirrel nimble grove, under linen and thatch | 163 | 21 | 86 | 183 | 2 |
| **THEFT** | | | | | |
| Close and far she announced the theft of the heart | 114 | 16 | 69 | 126 | 16 |
| **THEM** | | | | | |
| And the unicorn evils run them through; | 68 | 16 | 42 | 77 | 16 |
| That though I loved them for their faults | 107 | 18 | 65 | 118 | 18 |
| Running when he had heard them clearly | 111 | 17 | 68 | 123 | 17 |
| The locks yawned loose and a blast blew them wide, | 135 | 3 | 80 | 152 | 3 |
| For his briared hands to hoist them | 145 | 2 | 82 | 162 | 2 |
| Leads them as children and as air | 155 | 5 | 83 | 173 | 9 |
| Trot and gallop with gulls upon them | 156 | 21 | 83 | 175 | 9 |
| In the coal black bush and let them grieve. | 174 | 12 | 89 | 194 | 12 |

|  | U.K. Page | Line | Poem | U.S. Page | Line |
|---|---|---|---|---|---|
| **THEN** |  |  |  |  |  |
| We will ride out alone, and then, | x | 8 | 1 | xviii | 14 |
| Then all the matter of the living air | 26 | 21 | 16 | 32 | 1 |
| If not of loving well, then not, | 48 | 8 | 28 | 56 | 8 |
| Who then is she, | 54 | 25 | 33 | 64 | 1 |
| Then hang a ram rose over the rags. | 65 | 8 | 40 | 74 | 8 |
| Then was my neophyte, | 69 | 1 | 43 | 78 | 1 |
| Then threw on that tide-hoisted screen | 70 | 6 | 43 | 79 | 10 |
| Then, penny-eyed, that gentleman of wounds, | 71 | 7 | 44 | 80 | 7 |
| Hairs of your head, then said the hollow agent, | 72 | 1 | 44 | 81 | 1 |
| Year to heaven stood there then in the summer noon | 104 | 14 | 63 | 115 | 16 |
| Death, and bad death, and then | 105 | 22 | 64 | 116 | 22 |
| Of fields. And burning then | 119 | 16 | 72 | 131 | 16 |
| Then swift from a bursting sea with bottlecork boats | 132 | 13 | 78 | 147 | 13 |
| Then, bushily swanked in bear wig and tails, | 132 | 19 | 78 | 147 | 19 |
| Then good-bye to the fishermanned | 149 | 5 | 83 | 166 | 5 |
| And then to awake, and the farm, like a wanderer white | 160 | 6 | 85 | 179 | 6 |
| And gale I tackle, the whole world of then, | 173 | 15 | 88 | 193 | 15 |
| Holier then their eyes, | 173 | 25 | 88 | 193 | 25 |
| Then was my neophyte | 69 |  | 43 | 78 |  |
| **THERE** |  |  |  |  |  |
| Out there, crow black, men | vii | 12 | 1 | xv | 12 |
| Hoo, there, in castle keep, | ix | 1 | 1 | xvii | 2 |
| Hears, there, this fox light, my flood ship's | ix | 18 | 1 | xvii | 18 |
| There in their heat the winter floods | 1 | 4 | 2 | 1 | 4 |
| There in the sun the frigid threads | 1 | 10 | 2 | 1 | 10 |
| There in the deep with quartered shades | 1 | 16 | 2 | 1 | 16 |
| There from their hearts the dogdayed pulse | 1 | 22 | 2 | 1 | 22 |
| There, in his night, the black-tongued bells | 2 | 4 | 2 | 2 | 4 |
| Into the tided cord, there goes | 11 | 8 | 8 | 12 | 8 |
| There round about your stones the shades | 11 | 16 | 8 | 12 | 16 |
| There shall be corals in your beds, | 11 | 22 | 8 | 12 | 22 |
| There shall be serpents in your tides, | 11 | 23 | 8 | 12 | 23 |
| And there we wept, I and a ghostly other, | 26 | 8 | 16 | 31 | 8 |
| There grows the hours' ladder to the sun, | 27 | 1 | 16 | 32 | 6 |
| And God walked there who was a fiddling warden | 40 | 5 | 22 | 46 | 5 |
| There must, be praised, some certainty, | 48 | 7 | 28 | 56 | 7 |
| For all there is to give I offer: | 48 | 28 | 28 | 57 | 5 |
| Was there a time when dancers with their fiddles | 50 | 1 | 30 | 59 | 1 |
| There was a time they could cry over books, | 50 | 3 | 30 | 59 | 3 |
| For there are ghosts in the air | 64 | 8 | 39 | 73 | 8 |
| First there was the lamb on knocking knees | 72 | 5 | 44 | 81 | 5 |
| Because there stands, one story out of the bum city, | 77 | 13 | 45 | 86 | 13 |

|  | U.K. | | | U.S. | |
|---|---|---|---|---|---|
|  | *Page* | *Line* | *Poem* | *Page* | *Line* |
| There is loud and dark directly under the dumb flame, | 83 | 13 | 49 | 92 | 13 |
| Thrust, my daughter or son, to escape, there is none, none, none, | 97 | 19 | 59 | 108 | 19 |
| Has a voice and a house, and there and here you must couch and cry. | 98 | 2 | 59 | 109 | 5 |
| After the first death, there is no other. | 101 | 24 | 62 | 112 | 24 |
| There could I marvel | 103 | 13 | 63 | 114 | 13 |
| And there could I marvel my birthday | 104 | 9 | 63 | 115 | 11 |
| Year to heaven stood there then in the summer noon | 104 | 14 | 63 | 115 | 16 |
| You my friend there with a winning air | 107 | 3 | 65 | 118 | 3 |
| Is celebrated there, and communion between suns. | 109 | 24 | 67 | 120 | 24 |
| Flew man-bearing there. | 113 | 6 | 69 | 125 | 6 |
| There the dark blade and wanton sighing her down | 113 | 16 | 69 | 125 | 16 |
| There where a numberless tongue | 114 | 1 | 69 | 126 | 1 |
| And you, my father, there on the sad height, | 116 | 16 | 70 | 128 | 16 |
| And there outside on the bread of the ground | 121 | 13 | 72 | 134 | 8 |
| There was a saviour | 125 | 1 | 74 | 139 | 1 |
| There was calm to be done in his safe unrest, | 125 | 11 | 74 | 139 | 11 |
| There was glory to hear | 125 | 17 | 74 | 139 | 17 |
| Now in the dark there is only yourself and myself. | 125 | 24 | 74 | 139 | 24 |
| There | 141 | 1 | 82 | 158 | 1 |
| There is thunder under its thumbs; | 151 | 14 | 83 | 169 | 2 |
| There is nothing left of the sea but its sound, | 157 | 13 | 83 | 176 | 5 |
| Call for confessor and wiser mirror but there is none | 158 | 10 | 84 | 177 | 10 |
| The leaping saga of prayer! And high, there, on the hare- | 164 | 17 | 86 | 184 | 3 |
| There | 167 | 18 | 87 | 187 | 18 |
| There he might wander bare | 172 | 1 | 88 | 192 | 1 |
| And there this night I walk in the white giant's thigh | 176 | 3 | 90 | 197 | 3 |
| Hill, under the grass, in love, and there grow |  |  | 91 | 200 | 6 |
| Was there a time | 50 |  | 30 | 59 |  |
| There was a Saviour | 125 |  | 74 | 139 |  |
| THERE'S |  |  |  |  |  |
| There's more than dying; | 48 | 11 | 28 | 56 | 11 |
| THESE |  |  |  |  |  |
| Out of these seathumbed leaves | viii | 3 | 1 | xvi | 3 |
| These boys of light are curdlers in their folly, | 1 | 7 | 2 | 1 | 7 |
| I see that from these boys shall men of nothing | 1 | 19 | 2 | 1 | 19 |
| And these poor nerves so wired to the skull | 10 | 6 | 7 | 11 | 6 |
| 'These are but dreaming men. Breathe, and they fade.' | 26 | 15 | 16 | 31 | 15 |

| | U.K. | | | U.S. | |
|---|---|---|---|---|---|
| | Page | Line | Poem | Page | Line |
| Square in these worlds the mortal circle. | 34 | 6 | 19 | 39 | 12 |
| These are your years' recorders. The circular world stands still.) | 37 | 21 | 20 | 143 | 4 |
| You are all these, said she who gave me the long suck, | 46 | 17 | 27 | 54 | 17 |
| All these, he said who sacked the children's town, | 46 | 18 | 27 | 54 | 18 |
| Hold hard, these ancient minutes in the cuckoo's month, | 49 | 1 | 29 | 58 | 1 |
| But graft these four-fruited ridings on your country; | 60 | 9 | 36 | 69 | 9 |
| Who gave these seas their colour in a shape, | 61 | 1 | 36 | 70 | 1 |
| These five kings did a king to death. | 62 | 4 | 37 | 71 | 4 |
| By these I would not care to die, | 64 | 19 | 39 | 73 | 19 |
| These stolen bubbles have the bites of snakes | 67 | 23 | 41 | 76 | 23 |
| Who in these labyrinths, | 69 | 13 | 43 | 78 | 13 |
| Over these groundworks thrusting through a pavement | 72 | 3 | 44 | 81 | 3 |
| These are her contraries: the beast who follows | 78 | 24 | 46 | 88 | 1 |
| These once-blind eyes have breathed a wind of visions, | 80 | 1 | 46 | 89 | 9 |
| These cloud-sopped, marble hands, this monumental | 88 | 8 | 52 | 97 | 8 |
| These were the woods the river and sea | 104 | 1 | 63 | 115 | 3 |
| On these spindrift pages | 128 | 14 | 76 | 142 | 14 |
| Streets or hungering in the crumbled wood: to these | 178 | 16 | 90 | 199 | 17 |
| Hold hard, these ancient minutes in the cuckoo's month | 49 | | 29 | 58 | |

THEY

| | | | | | |
|---|---|---|---|---|---|
| Of frozen loves they fetch their girls, | 1 | 5 | 2 | 1 | 5 |
| The jacks of frost they finger in the hives; | 1 | 9 | 2 | 1 | 9 |
| Of doubt and dark they feed their nerves; | 1 | 11 | 2 | 1 | 11 |
| Of sun and moon they paint their dams | 1 | 17 | 2 | 1 | 17 |
| But seasons must be challenged or they totter | 2 | 1 | 2 | 2 | 1 |
| O see the poles are kissing as they cross. | 3 | 6 | 2 | 3 | 12 |
| And speak their midnight nothings as they swell; | 14 | 14 | 10 | 16 | 14 |
| When cameras shut they hurry to their hole | 14 | 15 | 10 | 16 | 15 |
| They dance between their arclamps and our skull, | 14 | 17 | 10 | 16 | 17 |
| That shrouded men might marrow as they fly. | 15 | 10 | 10 | 17 | 10 |
| And who remain shall flower as they love, | 15 | 21 | 10 | 18 | 1 |
| Heaven and hell mixed as they spun. | 22 | 6 | 14 | 27 | 6 |
| 'These are but dreaming men. Breathe, and they fade.' | 26 | 15 | 16 | 31 | 15 |
| Where still they sleep unknowing of their ghost. | 26 | 20 | 16 | 31 | 20 |

489

|  | U.K. | | | U.S. | |
|  | Page | Line | Poem | Page | Line |
| The patchwork halves were cloven as they scudded | 30 | 19 | 18 | 35 | 19 |
| Rotating halves are horning as they drill | 30 | 23 | 18 | 35 | 23 |
| The fellow halves that, cloven as they swivel | 32 | 1 | 18 | 37 | 7 |
| They climb the country pinnacle, | 36 | 13 | 20 | 41 | 13 |
| They see the squirrel stumble, | 36 | 16 | 20 | 41 | 16 |
| As they dive, the dust settles, | 36 | 19 | 20 | 41 | 19 |
| Under the mask and the ether, they making bloody | 37 | 2 | 20 | 42 | 8 |
| As they drown, the chime travels, | 37 | 10 | 20 | 42 | 16 |
| Hear they the salt glass breakers and the tongues of burial. | 37 | 15 | 20 | 42 | 21 |
| They suffer the undead water where the turtle nibbles, | 37 | 22 | 20 | 43 | 5 |
| Shall it be said they sprinkle water | 44 | 6 | 25 | 52 | 6 |
| They said, who hacked and humoured, they were mine. | 46 | 20 | 27 | 54 | 20 |
| Love's house, they answer, and the tower death | 47 | 7 | 27 | 55 | 7 |
| There was a time they could cry over books, | 50 | 3 | 30 | 59 | 3 |
| Under the arc of the sky they are unsafe. | 50 | 5 | 30 | 59 | 5 |
| Under the skysigns they who have no arms | 50 | 7 | 30 | 59 | 7 |
| Shall they clasp a comet in their fists? | 53 | 11 | 32 | 62 | 11 |
| Though what the stars ask as they round | 53 | 18 | 32 | 62 | 18 |
| Dead men naked they shall be one | 68 | 2 | 42 | 77 | 2 |
| That he let the dead lie though they moan | 145 | 1 | 82 | 162 | 1 |
| They shall have stars at elbow and foot; | 68 | 5 | 42 | 77 | 5 |
| Though they go mad they shall be sane, | 68 | 6 | 42 | 77 | 6 |
| Though they sink through the sea they shall rise again; | 68 | 7 | 42 | 77 | 7 |
| They lying long shall not die windily; | 68 | 12 | 42 | 77 | 12 |
| Strapped to a wheel, yet they shall not break; | 68 | 14 | 42 | 77 | 14 |
| Split all ends up they shan't crack; | 68 | 17 | 42 | 77 | 17 |
| Though they be mad and dead as nails, | 68 | 24 | 42 | 77 | 24 |
| Sounds with the grains as they hurry | 82 | 15 | 48 | 91 | 15 |
| (Bury the dead for fear that they walk to the grave in labour.) | 99 | 2 | 60 | 110 | 2 |
| Turns in the dark on the sound they know will arise | 100 | 6 | 61 | 111 | 6 |
| Will be the same grief flying. Whom shall they calm? | 100 | 11 | 61 | 111 | 11 |
| And Mister they called Hey mister | 111 | 15 | 68 | 123 | 15 |
| Because their words have forked no lightning they | 116 | 5 | 70 | 128 | 5 |
| And learn, too late, they grieved it on its way, | 116 | 11 | 70 | 128 | 11 |
| They come together whom their love parted: | 124 | 10 | 73 | 138 | 10 |
| And blithely they squawk | 167 | 8 | 87 | 187 | 8 |
| Doing what they are told, | 170 | 12 | 88 | 190 | 12 |

| | U.K. | | | U.S. | |
|---|---|---|---|---|---|
| | Page | Line | Poem | Page | Line |
| To labour and love though they lay down long ago. | 176 | 5 | 90 | 197 | 5 |
| They yearn with tongues of curlews for the unconceived | 176 | 10 | 90 | 197 | 10 |
| Young as they in the after milking moonlight lay | 176 | 16 | 90 | 197 | 16 |
| They with the simple Jacks were a boulder of wives)— | 178 | 3 | 90 | 199 | 4 |
| They from houses where the harvest kneels, hold me hard, | 178 | 9 | 90 | 199 | 10 |
| THEY'LL | | | | | |
| Manned with their loves they'll move, | x | 12 | 1 | xviii | 18 |
| THICK | | | | | |
| But animals thick as thieves | ix | 23 | 1 | xvii | 23 |
| The cadaverous gravels, falls thick and steadily, | 36 | 20 | 20 | 41 | 20 |
| Tap happily of one peg in the thick | 87 | 3 | 52 | 96 | 3 |
| More the thick stone cannot tell. | 93 | 10 | 56 | 102 | 10 |
| THICKET | | | | | |
| Clack through the thicket of strength, love hewn in pillars drops | 92 | 8 | 55 | 101 | 14 |
| THICKETS | | | | | |
| And fast through the drifts of the thickets antlered like deer, | 122 | 15 | 72 | 135 | 15 |
| THIEF | | | | | |
| Grief thief of time crawls off, | 67 | 1 | 41 | 76 | 1 |
| And timelessly lies loving with the thief. | 67 | 14 | 41 | 76 | 14 |
| Whom now I conjure to stand as thief | 107 | 9 | 65 | 118 | 9 |
| The thief of adolescence, | 114 | 8 | 69 | 126 | 8 |
| And mire of love, but the Thief as meek as the dew. | 163 | 15 | 86 | 182 | 15 |
| Be you sure the Thief will seek a way sly and sure | 163 | 26 | 86 | 183 | 7 |
| The Thief fall on the dead like the willy nilly dew, | 165 | 22 | 86 | 185 | 12 |
| Grief thief of time | 67 | | 41 | 76 | |
| THIEVES | | | | | |
| But animals thick as thieves | ix | 23 | 1 | xvii | 23 |
| Of birth and death, the two sad knives of thieves, | 10 | 18 | 7 | 11 | 18 |
| Shape with my fathers' thieves. | 67 | 28 | 41 | 76 | 28 |
| I by the tree of thieves, all glory's sawbones, | 75 | 15 | 44 | 84 | 15 |
| THIGH | | | | | |
| The itch of man upon the baby's thigh, | 12 | 12 | 9 | 13 | 12 |
| Was muscled, matted, wise to the crying thigh | 21 | 4 | 13 | 25 | 4 |
| Dry in the half-tracked thigh. | 32 | 12 | 18 | 37 | 18 |
| And there this night I walk in the white giant's thigh | 176 | 3 | 90 | 197 | 3 |
| In the white giant's thigh | 176 | | 90 | 197 | |

|  | U.K. | | | U.S. | |
|---|---|---|---|---|---|
|  | *Page* | *Line* | *Poem* | *Page* | *Line* |
| **THIGHS** | | | | | |
| A candle in the thighs | 24 | 7 | 15 | 29 | 7 |
| And through the thighs of the engulfing bride, | 123 | 14 | 72 | 137 | 4 |
| And this day's sun leapt up the sky out of her thighs | 127 | 4 | 75 | 141 | 4 |
| Insects and valleys hold her thighs hard, | 156 | 6 | 83 | 174 | 14 |
| Modesty hides my thighs in her wings, | 175 | 30 | 89 | 196 | 11 |
| Light of his thighs, spreadeagle to the dunghill sky, | 177 | 3 | 90 | 198 | 2 |
| **THIMBLE** | | | | | |
| And prick the thumb-stained heaven through the thimble. | 31 | 3 | 18 | 36 | 3 |
| And the cell-stepped thimble; | 37 | 25 | 20 | 43 | 8 |
| **THIN** | | | | | |
| Beasts who sleep good and thin, | ix | 26 | 1 | xvii | 26 |
| Heart of Cadaver's candle waxes thin, | 18 | 12 | 12 | 21 | 12 |
| By a thin sea of flesh | 58 | 11 | 35 | 67 | 11 |
| My breasts are thin. | 65 | 21 | 40 | 74 | 21 |
| Through the waves of the fat streets nor the skeleton's thin ways. | 98 | 5 | 59 | 109 | 8 |
| On the madhouse boards worn thin by my walking tears. | 108 | 15 | 66 | 119 | 15 |
| Behind the wall thin as a wren's bone? | 137 | 9 | 82 | 154 | 9 |
| I lie down thin and hear the good bells jaw— | 175 | 24 | 89 | 196 | 5 |
| **THINGS** | | | | | |
| The things of light | 24 | 5 | 15 | 29 | 5 |
| All things are known: the stars' advice | 53 | 16 | 32 | 62 | 16 |
| **THINK** | | | | | |
| I never thought to utter or think | 107 | 16 | 65 | 118 | 16 |
| **THINNING** | | | | | |
| A limp and riderless shape to leap nine thinning months.' | 97 | 15 | 59 | 108 | 15 |
| **THIRD** | | | | | |
| No third eye probe into a rainbow's sex | 67 | 25 | 41 | 76 | 25 |
| **THIRST** | | | | | |
| My throat knew thirst before the structure | 8 | 1 | 5 | 9 | 1 |
| Both quench his thirst he'll have a black reply. | 53 | 9 | 32 | 62 | 9 |
| 'The thirst is quenched, the hunger gone, | 65 | 17 | 40 | 74 | 17 |
| **THIRSTY** | | | | | |
| Have their thirsty sailors hide him. | 43 | 7 | 24 | 50 | 14 |
| Seaports by a thirsty shore | 43 | 13 | 24 | 50 | 20 |
| **THIRTIETH** | | | | | |
| It was my thirtieth year to heaven | 102 | 1 | 63 | 113 | 1 |
| It was my thirtieth | 104 | 13 | 63 | 115 | 15 |
| **THIRTY-FIFTH** | | | | | |
| His driftwood thirty-fifth wind turned age; | 170 | 8 | 88 | 190 | 8 |
| **THIRTY-FIVE** | | | | | |
| Thirty-five bells sing struck | 171 | 12 | 88 | 191 | 12 |

|  | U.K. | | | U.S. | |
|  | Page | Line | Poem | Page | Line |
| **THISTLE** | | | | | |
| Your mouth, my love, the thistle in the kiss? | 13 | 16 | 9 | 15 | 2 |
| Of day, in the thistle aisles, till the white owl crossed | 177 | 12 | 90 | 198 | 11 |
| **THISTLEDOWN** | | | | | |
| In the thistledown fall, | 170 | 19 | 88 | 190 | 19 |
| **THISTLES** | | | | | |
| The sexton sentinel, garrisoned under thistles, | 37 | 6 | 20 | 42 | 12 |
| After the feast of tear-stuffed time and thistles | 87 | 10 | 52 | 96 | 10 |
| **THISTLING** | | | | | |
| Of thistling frost | 165 | 2 | 86 | 184 | 10 |
| **THORN** | | | | | |
| Or, water-lammed, from the scythe-sided thorn, | 54 | 3 | 33 | 63 | 3 |
| December's thorn screwed in a brow of holly. | 76 | 14 | 44 | 85 | 14 |
| Casting to-morrow like a thorn | 138 | 8 | 82 | 155 | 8 |
| And sly as snow and meek as dew blown to the thorn, | 164 | 1 | 86 | 183 | 8 |
| **THORNS** | | | | | |
| As tarred with blood as the bright thorns I wept; | 75 | 7 | 44 | 84 | 7 |
| **THORNY** | | | | | |
| My Jack of Christ born thorny on the tree? | 13 | 17 | 9 | 15 | 3 |
| Of many a thorny shire tell you notes, | 16 | 15 | 11 | 19 | 15 |
| **THOROUGHFARES** | | | | | |
| Coil from the thoroughfares of her hair | 157 | 5 | 83 | 175 | 17 |
| **THOSE** | | | | | |
| Those craning birds are choice for you, songs that jump back | 86 | 9 | 51 | 95 | 9 |
| And bear those tendril hands I touch across | 90 | 6 | 54 | 99 | 6 |
| Slipped the fins of those humpbacked tons | 151 | 4 | 83 | 168 | 12 |
| Among those Killed in the Dawn Raid was a Man Aged a Hundred | 135 | | 80 | 152 | |
| **THOUGH** | | | | | |
| To you strangers (though song | vii | 24 | 1 | xv | 24 |
| Though what the stars ask as they round | 53 | 18 | 32 | 62 | 18 |
| Though they go mad they shall be sane, | 68 | 6 | 42 | 77 | 6 |
| Though they sink through the sea they shall rise again; | 68 | 7 | 42 | 77 | 7 |
| Though lovers be lost love shall not; | 68 | 8 | 42 | 77 | 8 |
| Though they be mad and dead as nails, | 68 | 24 | 42 | 77 | 24 |
| And though my love pulls the pale, nippled air, | 80 | 13 | 46 | 89 | 21 |
| The heart is sensual, though five eyes break. | 81 | 14 | 47 | 90 | 14 |
| (Though this for her is a monstrous image blindly | 87 | 16 | 52 | 96 | 16 |
| Talked and tore though her eyes smiled. | 93 | 20 | 56 | 102 | 20 |
| Though the town below lay leaved with October blood. | 104 | 15 | 63 | 115 | 17 |
| That though I loved them for their faults | 107 | 18 | 65 | 118 | 18 |

| | U.K. | | | U.S. | |
|---|---|---|---|---|---|
| | Page | Line | Poem | Page | Line |
| Though the brawl of the kiss has not occurred | 109 | 7 | 67 | 120 | 7 |
| Though wise men at their end know dark is right, | 116 | 4 | 70 | 128 | 4 |
| Though no sound flowed down the hand folded air | 120 | 15 | 72 | 132 | 20 |
| Was flying through the house as though the she bird praised | 122 | 3 | 72 | 135 | 3 |
| In a choir of wings, as though she slept or died, | 123 | 12 | 72 | 137 | 2 |
| Though the moment of a miracle is unending lightning | 127 | 6 | 75 | 141 | 6 |
| Slashed down the last snake as though | 134 | 13 | 79 | 150 | 13 |
| I pray though I belong | 143 | 14 | 82 | 160 | 14 |
| That he let the dead lie though they moan | 145 | 1 | 82 | 162 | 1 |
| Though I sang in my chains like the sea. | 161 | 6 | 85 | 180 | 9 |
| And star: held and blessed, though you scour the high four | 163 | 22 | 86 | 183 | 3 |
| Yet, though I cry with tumbledown tongue, | 172 | 26 | 88 | 192 | 26 |
| To labour and love though they lay down long ago. | 176 | 5 | 90 | 197 | 5 |
| Though the names on their weed grown stones are rained away, | 176 | 8 | 90 | 197 | 8 |
| Or still all the numberless days of his death, though | | | 91 | 200 | 8 |
| **THOUGHT** | | | | | |
| The brain was celled and soldered in the thought | 23 | 2 | 14 | 28 | 2 |
| On tips of thought where thoughts smell in the rain; | 25 | 2 | 15 | 30 | 2 |
| I never thought to utter or think | 107 | 16 | 65 | 118 | 16 |
| **THOUGHTS** | | | | | |
| I learnt man's tongue, to twist the shapes of thoughts | 21 | 8 | 13 | 25 | 8 |
| On tips of thought where thoughts smell in the rain; | 25 | 2 | 15 | 30 | 2 |
| **THRASHED** | | | | | |
| Rough as cows' tongues and thrashed with brambles their buttermilk | 177 | 5 | 90 | 198 | 4 |
| **THRASHING** | | | | | |
| On the old seas from stories, thrashing my wings, | 133 | 8 | 78 | 148 | 11 |
| At his thrashing hair and whale-blue eye; | 149 | 3 | 83 | 166 | 3 |
| **THREAD** | | | | | |
| 'A lizard darting with black venom's thread | 79 | 23 | 46 | 89 | 4 |
| Tongue and ear in the thread, angle the temple-bound | 91 | 26 | 55 | 101 | 4 |
| And wind his globe out of your water thread | 117 | 21 | 71 | 129 | 21 |
| To the boy of common thread, | 133 | 13 | 78 | 148 | 16 |
| Gold gut is a lightning thread, | 151 | 15 | 83 | 169 | 3 |

| | U.K. | | | U.S. | |
| | Page | Line | Poem | Page | Line |
|---|---|---|---|---|---|
| **THREADBARE** | | | | | |
| Lie with religion in their cramp, her threadbare | 88 | 4 | 52 | 97 | 4 |
| **THREADS** | | | | | |
| There in the sun the frigid threads | I | 10 | 2 | I | 10 |
| She threads off the sap and needles, blood and bubble | 35 | 10 | 20 | 40 | 10 |
| **THREE** | | | | | |
| In autumn teach three seasons' fires | 45 | 7 | 26 | 53 | 7 |
| And three dead seasons on a climbing grave | 72 | 6 | 44 | 81 | 6 |
| Bent like three trees and bird-papped through her shift, | 75 | 9 | 44 | 84 | 9 |
| On no work of words now for three lean months in the bloody | 94 | I | 57 | 104 | I |
| Who moved for three years in tune | 124 | 3 | 73 | 138 | 3 |
| Her robin breasted tree, three Marys in the rays. | 163 | 6 | 86 | 182 | 6 |
| **THREE-COLOURED** | | | | | |
| Till the three-coloured rainbow from my nipples | 75 | 13 | 44 | 84 | 13 |
| **THREE-EYED** | | | | | |
| A three-eyed, red-eyed spark, blunt as a flower; | 22 | 15 | 14 | 27 | 15 |
| **THREE-POINTED** | | | | | |
| In the beginning was the three-pointed star, | 22 | I | 14 | 27 | I |
| **THREE-QUARTERS** | | | | | |
| (An old tormented man three-quarters blind, | | | 91 | 200 | 18 |
| **THREE-SYLLABLED** | | | | | |
| Three-syllabled and starry as the smile; | 22 | 8 | 14 | 27 | 8 |
| **THREW** | | | | | |
| The ball I threw while playing in the park | 63 | 18 | 38 | 72 | 18 |
| Then threw on that tide-hoisted screen | 70 | 6 | 43 | 79 | 10 |
| **THROAT** | | | | | |
| My throat knew thirst before the structure | 8 | I | 5 | 9 | I |
| Shakes a desolate boy who slits his throat | 87 | 7 | 52 | 96 | 7 |
| Sooner drop with the worm of the ropes round my throat | 97 | 4 | 59 | 108 | 4 |
| In the throat, burning and turning. All night afloat | 136 | 2 | 81 | 153 | 2 |
| Lie still, sleep becalmed, hide the mouth in the throat, | 136 | 13 | 81 | 153 | 13 |
| A cloud blew the rain from its throat; | 150 | 16 | 83 | 167 | 20 |
| **THROATS** | | | | | |
| Of love and light bursts in their throats. | I | 23 | 2 | I | 23 |
| Carved birds blunt their striking throats on the salt gravel, | 86 | 3 | 51 | 95 | 3 |
| And load the throats of shells | 117 | 22 | 71 | 129 | 22 |
| Through throats where many rivers meet, the curlews cry, | 176 | I | 90 | 197 | I |
| Through throats where many rivers meet, the women pray, | 176 | 6 | 90 | 197 | 6 |

|  | U.K. Page | Line | Poem | U.S. Page | Line |
|---|---|---|---|---|---|
| **THRONE** | | | | | |
| Crying at the man drenched throne | 140 | 7 | 82 | 157 | 7 |
| **THRONG** | | | | | |
| Hollow farms in a throng | ix | 28 | 1 | xviii | 2 |
| **THRONGED** | | | | | |
| Up to the swallow thronged loft by the shadow of my hand, | 160 | 25 | 85 | 180 | 2 |
| **THROW** | | | | | |
| Throw your fear a parcel of stone | 96 | 12 | 58 | 106 | 12 |
| Throw wide to the wind the gates of the wandering boat | 136 | 10 | 81 | 153 | 10 |
| For we saw him throw to the swift flood | 149 | 21 | 83 | 167 | 1 |
| The centuries throw back their hair | 155 | 7 | 83 | 173 | 11 |
| **THROWING** | | | | | |
| Impose their shots, throwing the nights away; | 14 | 18 | 10 | 16 | 18 |
| **THROWN** | | | | | |
| All but the briskest riders thrown, | 5 | 17 | 3 | 5 | 17 |
| Arc-lamped thrown back upon the cutting flood. | 73 | 10 | 44 | 82 | 10 |
| And the dark thrown | 138 | 14 | 82 | 155 | 14 |
| Thrown to the sea in the shell of a girl | 152 | 20 | 83 | 170 | 12 |
| **THROWS** | | | | | |
| A wind throws a shadow and it freezes fast. | 154 | 10 | 83 | 172 | 10 |
| **THRUST** | | | | | |
| Thrust, my daughter or son, to escape, there is none, none, none, | 97 | 19 | 59 | 108 | 19 |
| **THRUSTING** | | | | | |
| Thrusting the tom-thumb vision up the iron mile. | 38 | 6 | 20 | 43 | 16 |
| Over these groundworks thrusting through a pavement | 72 | 3 | 44 | 81 | 3 |
| **THUMB** | | | | | |
| Drive children up like bruises to the thumb, | 18 | 14 | 12 | 21 | 14 |
| Who speak on a finger and thumb, | 70 | 1 | 43 | 79 | 5 |
| And makes with a flick of the thumb and sun | 96 | 25 | 58 | 107 | 8 |
| **THUMB-STAINED** | | | | | |
| And prick the thumb-stained heaven through the thimble. | 31 | 3 | 18 | 36 | 3 |
| **THUMBS** | | | | | |
| Divide the night and day with fairy thumbs; | 1 | 15 | 2 | 1 | 15 |
| The fingers will forget green thumbs and mark | 81 | 2 | 47 | 90 | 2 |
| There is thunder under its thumbs; | 151 | 14 | 83 | 169 | 2 |
| **THUMP** | | | | | |
| Shall gods be said to thump the clouds | 44 | 1 | 25 | 52 | 1 |
| Shall gods be said to thump the clouds | 44 | | 25 | 52 | |
| **THUNDER** | | | | | |
| Shall not thunder on the town | 43 | 17 | 24 | 51 | 3 |

| | U.K. Page | U.K. Line | Poem | U.S. Page | U.S. Line |
|---|---|---|---|---|---|
| When clouds are cursed by thunder, | 44 | 2 | 25 | 52 | 2 |
| And the thunder of calls and notes. | 64 | 10 | 39 | 73 | 10 |
| The sundering ultimate kingdom of genesis' thunder. | 131 | 25 | 77 | 146 | 7 |
| There is thunder under its thumbs; | 151 | 14 | 83 | 169 | 2 |
| As the sails drank up the hail of thunder | 154 | 7 | 83 | 172 | 7 |
| THUNDER'S | | | | | |
| Bisected shadows on the thunder's bone | 30 | 5 | 18 | 35 | 5 |
| THUNDERBOLTS | | | | | |
| Will pull the thunderbolts | 118 | 4 | 71 | 130 | 8 |
| And thunderbolts in their manes. | 156 | 22 | 83 | 175 | 10 |
| THUNDERCLAP | | | | | |
| Taller this thunderclap spring, and how | 173 | 22 | 88 | 193 | 22 |
| THUNDERCLAPPING | | | | | |
| Flashed first across his thunderclapping eyes. | 117 | 24 | 71 | 129 | 24 |
| THUNDERING | | | | | |
| A thundering bullring of your silent and girl-circled island. | 96 | 26 | 58 | 107 | 9 |
| THUNDEROUS | | | | | |
| On thunderous pavements in the garden time; | 72 | 10 | 44 | 81 | 10 |
| THUNDERS | | | | | |
| Thunders on the foreign town | 43 | 24 | 24 | 51 | 10 |
| THUS | | | | | |
| Thus the shadowless man or ox, and the pictured devil, | 35 | 22 | 20 | 40 | 22 |
| THUD | | | | | |
| Felt thud beneath my flesh's armour, | 7 | 9 | 5 | 8 | 9 |
| TICKED | | | | | |
| How time has ticked a heaven round the stars. | 9 | 20 | 6 | 10 | 20 |
| TICKLE | | | | | |
| If the red tickle as the cattle calve | 12 | 4 | 9 | 13 | 4 |
| TICKLED | | | | | |
| If I were tickled by the rub of love, | 12 | 1 | 9 | 13 | 1 |
| If I were tickled by the hatching hair, | 12 | 10 | 9 | 13 | 10 |
| If I were tickled by the urchin hungers | 12 | 18 | 9 | 13 | 18 |
| If I were tickled by the lover's rub | 12 | 22 | 9 | 14 | 1 |
| I would be tickled by the rub that is: | 13 | 20 | 9 | 15 | 6 |
| If I were tickled by the rub of love | 12 | | 9 | 13 | |
| TICKLES | | | | | |
| And that's the rub, the only rub that tickles. | 13 | 8 | 9 | 14 | 15 |
| TIDE | | | | | |
| The cockerel's tide upcasting from the fire. | 51 | 21 | 31 | 60 | 21 |
| Lean time on tide and times the wind stood rough, | 67 | 6 | 41 | 76 | 6 |
| Who tossed the high tide in a time of stories | 67 | 13 | 41 | 76 | 13 |
| The lunar silences, the silent tide | 82 | 9 | 48 | 91 | 9 |
| Creep and harp on the tide, sinking their charmed, bent pin | 91 | 24 | 55 | 101 | 2 |

|  | U.K. | | | U.S. | |
|  | Page | Line | Poem | Page | Line |
| High tide and the heron dived when I took the road | 102 | 17 | 63 | 113 | 17 |
| To the trees and the stones and the fish in the tide. | 104 | 5 | 63 | 115 | 7 |
| Out to the tiered and hearing tide, | 114 | 15 | 69 | 126 | 15 |
| The country tide is cobbled with towns, | 156 | 24 | 83 | 175 | 12 |
| Comes designed to my love to steal not her tide raking | 166 | 1 | 86 | 186 | 1 |
| To kill and their own tide daubing blood | 171 | 8 | 88 | 191 | 8 |
| **TIDED** | | | | | |
| Into the tided cord, there goes | 11 | 8 | 8 | 12 | 8 |
| **TIDE-HOISTED** | | | | | |
| Then threw on that tide-hoisted screen | 70 | 6 | 43 | 79 | 10 |
| **TIDE-LOOPED** | | | | | |
| Or like the tide-looped breastknot reefed again | 78 | 11 | 46 | 87 | 11 |
| **TIDE-MASTER** | | | | | |
| Lapping the still canals, the dry tide-master | 82 | 10 | 48 | 91 | 10 |
| **TIDE-PRINT** | | | | | |
| Moonfall and sailing emperor, pale as their tide-print, | 83 | 10 | 49 | 92 | 10 |
| **TIDE-TONGUED** | | | | | |
| Of tide-tongued heads and bladders in the deep, | 30 | 16 | 18 | 35 | 16 |
| **TIDE-TRACED** | | | | | |
| Cartoon of slashes on the tide-traced crater, | 74 | 1 | 44 | 83 | 1 |
| **TIDES** | | | | | |
| And drown the cargoed apples in their tides. | 1 | 6 | 2 | 1 | 6 |
| To choke the deserts with her tides, | 2 | 17 | 2 | 2 | 17 |
| Sleep navigates the tides of time; | 5 | 1 | 3 | 5 | 1 |
| Of tides that never touch the shores. | 8 | 10 | 5 | 9 | 10 |
| Invisible, your clocking tides | 11 | 13 | 8 | 12 | 13 |
| There shall be serpents in your tides, | 11 | 23 | 8 | 12 | 23 |
| Push in their tides; | 24 | 3 | 15 | 29 | 3 |
| On casting tides, are tangled in the shells, | 32 | 2 | 18 | 37 | 8 |
| Soaks up the sewing tides), | 56 | 12 | 34 | 65 | 12 |
| But the hungry kings of the tides; | 153 | 13 | 83 | 171 | 9 |
| **TIDETHREAD** | | | | | |
| This tidethread and the lane of scales, | 69 | 14 | 43 | 78 | 14 |
| **TIDY** | | | | | |
| Am I not you who front the tidy shore, | 46 | 15 | 27 | 54 | 15 |
| Tidy and cursed in my dove cooed room | 175 | 23 | 89 | 196 | 4 |
| **TIERED** | | | | | |
| Out to the tiered and hearing tide, | 114 | 15 | 69 | 126 | 15 |
| **TIGERS** | | | | | |
| Made the tigers jump out of their eyes | 112 | 4 | 68 | 124 | 4 |
| **TIGRON** | | | | | |
| I see the tigron in tears | 110 | 1 | 67 | 121 | 3 |
| **TILER** | | | | | |
| Nor roof of sand, nor yet the towering tiler? | 46 | 16 | 27 | 54 | 16 |

| | U.K. | | | U.S. | |
|---|---|---|---|---|---|
| | *Page* | *Line* | *Poem* | *Page* | *Line* |
| **TILL** | | | | | |
| Unfailing till the blood runs foul; | 8 | 4 | 5 | 9 | 4 |
| Till all our sea-faiths die. | 11 | 24 | 8 | 12 | 24 |
| And, clapped in water till the triton dangles, | 37 | 13 | 20 | 42 | 19 |
| Shall not be known till windwell dries | 53 | 2 | 32 | 62 | 2 |
| Not till, from high and low, their dust | 53 | 12 | 32 | 62 | 12 |
| Is heard but little till the stars go out. | 53 | 20 | 32 | 62 | 20 |
| Alone till the day I die | 58 | 6 | 35 | 67 | 6 |
| Or stay till the day I die | 58 | 23 | 35 | 67 | 23 |
| Or stay till the day I die? | 59 | 6 | 35 | 68 | 6 |
| Till field and roof lie level and the same | 63 | 13 | 38 | 72 | 13 |
| Break in the sun till the sun breaks down, | 68 | 26 | 42 | 70 | 26 |
| Love's image till my heartbone breaks | 70 | 7 | 43 | 79 | 11 |
| Till tallow I blew from the wax's tower | 74 | 9 | 44 | 83 | 9 |
| Till the three-coloured rainbow from my nipples | 75 | 13 | 44 | 84 | 13 |
| In quick, sweet, cruel light till the locked ground sprout out, | 91 | 18 | 55 | 100 | 18 |
| Till the sweet tooth of my love bit dry, | 107 | 7 | 65 | 118 | 7 |
| Roosts sleeping chill till the flame of the cock crow | 119 | 19 | 72 | 131 | 19 |
| Back. Lines of age sleep on the stones till trumpeting dawn. | 123 | 8 | 72 | 136 | 18 |
| Till the blood shall spurt, | 129 | 21 | 77 | 143 | 21 |
| Till every beast blared down in a swerve | 151 | 9 | 83 | 168 | 17 |
| Till every turtle crushed from his shell | 151 | 10 | 83 | 168 | 18 |
| Till every bone in the rushing grave | 151 | 11 | 83 | 168 | 19 |
| Sleeps till Silence blows on a cloud | 153 | 15 | 83 | 171 | 11 |
| Of day, in the thistle aisles, till the white owl crossed | 177 | 12 | 90 | 198 | 11 |
| **TILT** | | | | | |
| By full tilt river and switchback sea | 170 | 2 | 88 | 190 | 2 |
| **TILTED** | | | | | |
| Shot in the wind, by tilted arcs, | 69 | 26 | 43 | 79 | 2 |
| In the river Towy below bows his tilted headstone. | 167 | 12 | 87 | 187 | 12 |
| **TILTING** | | | | | |
| Of dusk and water I see the tilting whispering | 168 | 24 | 87 | 189 | 9 |
| **TIME** | | | | | |
| The mouth of time sucked, like a sponge, | 4 | 4 | 3 | 4 | 4 |
| Sleep navigates the tides of time; | 5 | 1 | 3 | 5 | 1 |
| And time cast forth my mortal creature | 8 | 7 | 5 | 9 | 7 |
| The lips of time leech to the fountain head; | 9 | 16 | 6 | 10 | 16 |
| How time has ticked a heaven round the stars. | 9 | 20 | 6 | 10 | 20 |
| Time and the crabs and the sweethearting crib | 12 | 25 | 9 | 14 | 4 |
| When, like a running grave, time tracks you down, | 18 | 1 | 12 | 21 | 1 |
| When blood, spade-handed, and the logic time | 18 | 13 | 12 | 21 | 13 |

|  | U.K. | | Poem | U.S. | |
| --- | --- | --- | --- | --- | --- |
|  | Page | Line | Poem | Page | Line |
| Time is a foolish fancy, time and fool. | 19 | 1 | 12 | 22 | 6 |
| With whistler's cough contages, time on track | 19 | 22 | 12 | 23 | 7 |
| The time for breast and the green apron age | 20 | 4 | 13 | 24 | 4 |
| Let fall the tear of time; the sleeper's eye, | 26 | 2 | 16 | 31 | 2 |
| The sea and instrument, nicked in the locks of time, | 38 | 14 | 20 | 44 | 4 |
| Time in the hourless houses | 38 | 21 | 20 | 44 | 11 |
| Time at the city spectacles, and half | 41 | 3 | 23 | 47 | 3 |
| The dear, daft time I take to nudge the sentence, | 41 | 4 | 23 | 47 | 4 |
| As the green blooms ride upward, to the drive of time; | 49 | 3 | 29 | 58 | 3 |
| Time, in a folly's rider, like a county man | 49 | 4 | 29 | 58 | 4 |
| Time, in a rider rising, from the harnessed valley; | 49 | 21 | 29 | 58 | 21 |
| Was there a time when dancers with their fiddles | 50 | 1 | 30 | 59 | 1 |
| There was a time they could cry over books, | 50 | 3 | 30 | 59 | 3 |
| But time has set its maggot on their track. | 50 | 4 | 30 | 59 | 4 |
| Time upon time the towers of the skies | 53 | 19 | 32 | 62 | 19 |
| A nitric shape that leaps her, time and acid; | 55 | 7 | 33 | 64 | 10 |
| Can time unriddle, and the cupboard stone, | 56 | 3 | 34 | 65 | 3 |
| Farmer in time of frost the burning leagues, | 60 | 10 | 36 | 69 | 10 |
| In time at flood filled with his coloured doubles; | 61 | 3 | 36 | 70 | 3 |
| So fast I move defying time, the quiet gentleman | 63 | 14 | 38 | 72 | 14 |
| Grief thief of time crawls off, | 67 | 1 | 41 | 76 | 1 |
| The sea-halved faith that blew time to his knees, | 67 | 4 | 41 | 76 | 4 |
| Lean time on tide and times the wind stood rough, | 67 | 6 | 41 | 76 | 6 |
| Who tossed the high tide in a time of stories | 67 | 13 | 41 | 76 | 13 |
| Time on the canvas paths. | 69 | 24 | 43 | 78 | 24 |
| Time kills me terribly. | 70 | 15 | 43 | 79 | 19 |
| 'Time shall not murder you,' He said, | 70 | 16 | 43 | 79 | 20 |
| I saw time murder me. | 70 | 20 | 43 | 79 | 24 |
| That night of time under the Christward shelter: | 71 | 12 | 44 | 80 | 12 |
| On thunderous pavements in the garden time; | 72 | 10 | 44 | 81 | 10 |
| Time, milk, and magic, from the world beginning. | 74 | 24 | 44 | 83 | 24 |
| Time is the tune my ladies lend their heartbreak, | 75 | 1 | 44 | 84 | 1 |
| Time tracks the sound of shape on man and cloud, | 75 | 3 | 44 | 84 | 3 |
| Time marks a black aisle kindle from the brand of ashes, | 83 | 4 | 49 | 92 | 4 |
| Grief with drenched book and candle christens the cherub time | 83 | 16 | 49 | 92 | 16 |
| I mean by time the cast and curfew rascal of our marriage, | 84 | 1 | 49 | 93 | 7 |
| In time like outlaw rains on that priest, water, | 86 | 6 | 51 | 95 | 6 |

|  | U.K. |  |  | U.S. |  |
|  | Page | Line | Poem | Page | Line |
| Time for the swimmers' hands, music for silver lock | 86 | 7 | 51 | 95 | 7 |
| After the feast of tear-stuffed time and thistles | 87 | 10 | 52 | 96 | 10 |
| Peck, sprint, dance on fountains and duck time | 97 | 8 | 59 | 108 | 8 |
| Made all day until bell time | 112 | 7 | 68 | 124 | 7 |
| Or flower under the time dying flesh astride. | 120 | 30 | 72 | 133 | 15 |
| Time sings through the intricately dead snow drop. Listen. | 121 | 10 | 72 | 134 | 5 |
| The fields of seed and the time dying flesh astride, | 122 | 23 | 72 | 136 | 3 |
| Exultation lies down. Time buries the spring weather | 123 | 9 | 72 | 136 | 19 |
| Once below a time, | 132 | 1 | 78 | 147 | 1 |
| The warm-veined double of Time | 134 | 11 | 79 | 150 | 11 |
| No Time, spoke the clocks, no God, rang the bells, | 134 | 28 | 79 | 151 | 6 |
| To the burn and turn of time | 137 | 11 | 82 | 154 | 11 |
| Time is bearing another son. | 155 | 9 | 83 | 173 | 13 |
| Kill Time! She turns in her pain! | 155 | 10 | 83 | 173 | 14 |
| Time and places grip her breast bone, | 156 | 7 | 83 | 174 | 15 |
| Praise that the spring time is all | 158 | 14 | 84 | 177 | 14 |
| If only for a last time. | 158 | 24 | 84 | 177 | 24 |
| Time let me hail and climb | 159 | 4 | 85 | 178 | 4 |
| And once below a time I lordly had the trees and leaves | 159 | 7 | 85 | 178 | 7 |
| Time let me play and be | 159 | 13 | 85 | 178 | 13 |
| And nothing I cared, at my sky blue trades, that time allows | 160 | 20 | 85 | 179 | 20 |
| Nothing I cared, in the lamb white days, that time would take me | 160 | 24 | 85 | 180 | 1 |
| Time held me green and dying | 161 | 5 | 85 | 180 | 8 |
| Of summer come in his great good time | 175 | 3 | 89 | 195 | 8 |
| Of, time enough when the blood creeps cold, | 175 | 5 | 89 | 195 | 10 |
| Slunk pouting out when the limp time came; | 175 | 15 | 89 | 195 | 20 |
| Time by, their dust was flesh the swineherd rooted sly, | 177 | 1 | 90 | 197 | 21 |
| Was there a time | 50 |  | 30 | 59 |  |
| Grief thief of time | 67 |  | 41 | 76 |  |
| Once below a time | 132 |  | 78 | 147 |  |

TIME'S

| I, that time's jacket or the coat of ice | 18 | 18 | 12 | 21 | 18 |
| Adam, time's joker, on a witch of cardboard | 74 | 11 | 44 | 83 | 11 |
| Time's tune my ladies with the teats of music, | 74 | 21 | 44 | 83 | 21 |
| Time's nerve in vinegar, the gallow grave | 75 | 6 | 44 | 84 | 6 |
| Time's ship-racked gospel on the globe I balance: | 76 | 11 | 44 | 85 | 11 |
| Time's coral saint and the salt grief drown a foul sepulchre | 83 | 8 | 49 | 92 | 8 |

## TIME-BOMB

|  | U.K. | | | U.S. | |
|---|---|---|---|---|---|
|  | Page | Line | Poem | Page | Line |
| **TIME-BOMB** | | | | | |
| Strike in the time-bomb town, | 96 | 10 | 58 | 106 | 10 |
| **TIME-FACED** | | | | | |
| Now Jack my fathers let the time-faced crook, | 67 | 15 | 41 | 76 | 15 |
| **TIME-SHAKEN** | | | | | |
| Before the lunge of the night, the notes on this time-shaken | 169 | 11 | 87 | 189 | 20 |
| **TIMED** | | | | | |
| My fuses timed to charge his heart, | 4 | 13 | 3 | 4 | 13 |
| **TIMELESS** | | | | | |
| What shall it tell me if a timeless insect | 45 | 16 | 26 | 53 | 16 |
| I am, the tower told, felled by a timeless stroke, | 46 | 21 | 27 | 54 | 21 |
| And, Rip Van Winkle from a timeless cradle, | 72 | 13 | 44 | 81 | 13 |
| **TIMELESSLY** | | | | | |
| And timelessly lies loving with the thief. | 67 | 14 | 41 | 76 | 14 |
| **TIMES** | | | | | |
| Lean time on tide and times the wind stood rough, | 67 | 6 | 41 | 76 | 6 |
| Savours the lick of the times through a deadly wood of hair | 77 | 9 | 45 | 86 | 9 |
| Rode and whistled a hundred times | 113 | 18 | 69 | 125 | 18 |
| Bird through the times and lands and tribes of the slow flakes. | 122 | 19 | 72 | 135 | 19 |
| **TIMID** | | | | | |
| Deliver me who, timid in my tribe, | 18 | 7 | 12 | 21 | 7 |
| **TIP** | | | | | |
| In the sniffed and poured snow on the tip of the tongue of the year | 77 | 5 | 45 | 86 | 5 |
| On the last rick's tip by spilled wine-wells | 95 | 14 | 58 | 105 | 14 |
| **TIPS** | | | | | |
| On tips of thought where thoughts smell in the rain; | 25 | 2 | 15 | 30 | 2 |
| **TIPSY** | | | | | |
| Black-tongued and tipsy from salvation's bottle. | 73 | 15 | 44 | 82 | 15 |
| **TIPTOED** | | | | | |
| I tiptoed shy in the gooseberry wood, | 174 | 4 | 89 | 194 | 4 |
| **TIRELESS** | | | | | |
| Among the street burned to tireless death | 129 | 4 | 77 | 143 | 4 |
| **TIT** | | | | | |
| Tom tit and Dai mouse! | x | 16 | 1 | xviii | 22 |
| The rude owl cried like a telltale tit, | 174 | 5 | 89 | 194 | 5 |
| **TITHINGS** | | | | | |
| Lay the gold tithings barren, | 1 | 2 | 2 | 1 | 2 |
| **TOCSIN** | | | | | |
| Out of the font of bone and plants at that stone tocsin | 83 | 20 | 49 | 93 | 2 |
| **TO-DAY** | | | | | |
| To-day, this insect, and the world I breathe, | 41 | 1 | 23 | 47 | 1 |

| | U.K. | | | U.S. | |
|---|---|---|---|---|---|
| | *Page* | *Line* | *Poem* | *Page* | *Line* |
| To-day, this insect | 41 | | 23 | 47 | |
| **TOE** | | | | | |
| From poles of skull and toe the windy blood | 24 | 14 | 15 | 29 | 14 |
| **TOES** | | | | | |
| Dead on the sweethearts' toes. | 12 | 28 | 9 | 14 | 7 |
| Horned down with skullfoot and the skull of toes | 72 | 9 | 44 | 81 | 9 |
| **TOGETHER** | | | | | |
| Two sand grains together in bed, | 115 | 1 | 69 | 127 | 1 |
| They come together whom their love parted: | 124 | 10 | 73 | 138 | 10 |
| O Adam and Eve together | 130 | 18 | 77 | 144 | 18 |
| **TOILS** | | | | | |
| Toils towards the ambush of his wounds; | 170 | 17 | 88 | 190 | 17 |
| **TOLD** | | | | | |
| I am, the tower told, felled by a timeless stroke, | 46 | 21 | 27 | 54 | 21 |
| I have been told to reason by the heart, | 63 | 9 | 38 | 72 | 9 |
| I have been told to reason by the pulse, | 63 | 11 | 38 | 72 | 11 |
| I laid her down and told her sin, | 65 | 23 | 40 | 74 | 23 |
| The tombstone told when she died. | 93 | 1 | 56 | 102 | 1 |
| And the twice told fields of infancy | 103 | 26 | 63 | 115 | 1 |
| Tongue of your translating eyes. The young stars told me, | 110 | 23 | 67 | 122 | 1 |
| In the river wended vales where the tale was told. | 119 | 10 | 72 | 131 | 10 |
| Birdman or told ghost I hung. | 133 | 3 | 78 | 148 | 6 |
| Doing what they are told, | 170 | 12 | 88 | 190 | 12 |
| The tombstone told when she died | 93 | | 56 | 102 | |
| **TOLL** | | | | | |
| Of sleepers whose tongue I toll | 146 | 3 | 82 | 163 | 3 |
| **TOLLED** | | | | | |
| Never, my girl, until tolled to sleep by the stern | 162 | 21 | 86 | 181 | 21 |
| **TOLLS** | | | | | |
| In the tower and tolls to sleep over the stalls | 164 | 3 | 86 | 183 | 10 |
| Who tolls his birthday bell, | 170 | 16 | 88 | 190 | 16 |
| **TOM** | | | | | |
| Tom tit and Dai mouse! | x | 16 | 1 | xviii | 22 |
| No springtailed tom in the red hot town | 174 | 29 | 89 | 195 | 5 |
| **TOM-THUMB** | | | | | |
| Thrusting the tom-thumb vision up the iron mile. | 38 | 6 | 20 | 43 | 16 |
| **TOMB** | | | | | |
| The dry Sargasso of the tomb | 5 | 2 | 3 | 5 | 2 |
| Storms in the freezing tomb. | 6 | 3 | 4 | 6 | 3 |
| And I am dumb to tell the lover's tomb | 9 | 21 | 6 | 10 | 21 |
| Dry as a tomb, your coloured lids | 11 | 19 | 8 | 12 | 19 |
| By midnight pulleys that unhouse the tomb. | 14 | 10 | 10 | 16 | 10 |
| The cloud climb of the exhaling tomb | 141 | 8 | 82 | 158 | 8 |
| **TOMBS** | | | | | |
| Nor ever, as the wild tongue breaks its tombs, | 77 | 11 | 45 | 86 | 11 |

|  | U.K. | | | U.S. | |
|---|---|---|---|---|---|
|  | Page | Line | Poem | Page | Line |
| And into its talkative seven tombs | 157 | 19 | 83 | 176 | 11 |
| TOMBSTONE |  |  |  |  |  |
| The tombstone told when she died. | 93 | 1 | 56 | 102 | 1 |
| The tombstone told when she died | 93 |  | 56 | 102 |  |
| TO-MORROW |  |  |  |  |  |
| Prides of to-morrow suckling in her eyes, | 80 | 14 | 46 | 89 | 22 |
| Casting to-morrow like a thorn | 138 | 8 | 82 | 155 | 8 |
| O Rome and Sodom To-morrow and London | 156 | 23 | 83 | 175 | 11 |
| And to-morrow weeps in a blind cage | 171 | 15 | 88 | 191 | 15 |
| TO-MORROW'S |  |  |  |  |  |
| To-morrow's diver in her horny milk, | 30 | 4 | 18 | 35 | 4 |
| Bit out the mandrake with to-morrow's scream. | 71 | 6 | 44 | 80 | 6 |
| Her lover's wings that fold to-morrow's flight, | 115 | 11 | 69 | 127 | 11 |
| TO-MORROW-TREADING |  |  |  |  |  |
| From your to-morrow-treading shade | 70 | 13 | 43 | 79 | 17 |
| TONGUE |  |  |  |  |  |
| Robbed of the foxy tongue, his footed tape | 18 | 9 | 12 | 21 | 9 |
| I learnt man's tongue, to twist the shapes of thoughts | 21 | 8 | 13 | 25 | 8 |
| The code of night tapped on my tongue; | 21 | 16 | 13 | 25 | 16 |
| Lop, love, my fork tongue, said the pin-hilled nettle; | 74 | 6 | 44 | 83 | 6 |
| Old cock from nowheres lopped the minstrel tongue | 74 | 8 | 44 | 83 | 8 |
| In the sniffed and poured snow on the tip of the tongue of the year | 77 | 5 | 45 | 86 | 5 |
| Nor ever, as the wild tongue breaks its tombs, | 77 | 11 | 45 | 86 | 11 |
| Harbours my anchored tongue, slips the quay-stone, | 78 | 3 | 46 | 87 | 3 |
| 'His mother's womb had a tongue that lapped up mud,' | 79 | 20 | 46 | 89 | 1 |
| And, lashed to syllables, the lynx tongue cry | 81 | 8 | 47 | 90 | 8 |
| The bayonet tongue in this undefended prayer-piece, | 85 | 5 | 50 | 94 | 5 |
| Tongue and ear in the thread, angle the temple-bound | 91 | 26 | 55 | 101 | 4 |
| Or that rainy tongue beat back | 93 | 13 | 56 | 102 | 13 |
| The mazes of his praise and envious tongue were worked in flames and shells. | 95 | 17 | 58 | 105 | 17 |
| Tongue of your translating eyes. The young stars told me, | 110 | 23 | 67 | 122 | 1 |
| There where a numberless tongue | 114 | 1 | 69 | 126 | 1 |
| Assembled at his tongue | 125 | 5 | 74 | 139 | 5 |
| When the caught tongue nodded blind, | 129 | 13 | 77 | 143 | 13 |
| Word, singers, and tongue | 131 | 1 | 77 | 145 | 7 |
| Its tongue peeled in the wrap of a leaf. | 134 | 15 | 79 | 150 | 15 |
| Yet, though I cry with tumbledown tongue, | 172 | 26 | 88 | 192 | 26 |

|  | U.K. | | | U.S. | |
|---|---|---|---|---|---|
|  | *Page* | *Line* | *Poem* | *Page* | *Line* |
| Of sleepers whose tongue I toll | 146 | 3 | 82 | 163 | 3 |
| TONGUED |  |  |  |  |  |
| On a tongued puffball) | ix | 22 | 1 | xvii | 22 |
| And the rhymer in the long tongued room, | 170 | 15 | 88 | 190 | 15 |
| TONGUES |  |  |  |  |  |
| The root of tongues ends in a spentout cancer, | 21 | 13 | 13 | 25 | 13 |
| The tongues of heaven gossip as I glide | 32 | 5 | 18 | 37 | 11 |
| Hear they the salt glass breakers and the tongues of burial. | 37 | 15 | 20 | 42 | 21 |
| With tongues that talk all tongues. | 44 | 14 | 25 | 52 | 14 |
| In high corn and the harvest melting on their tongues. | 120 | 18 | 72 | 133 | 3 |
| They yearn with tongues of curlews for the unconceived | 176 | 10 | 90 | 197 | 10 |
| Rough as cows' tongues and thrashed with brambles their buttermilk | 177 | 5 | 90 | 198 | 4 |
| And the rain wring out its tongues on the faded yard, | 178 | 11 | 90 | 199 | 12 |
| TO-NIGHT |  |  |  |  |  |
| To-night shall find no dying but **alive** and warm | 100 | 15 | 61 | 111 | 15 |
| TONNED |  |  |  |  |  |
| In the wains tonned so high that the wisps of the hay | 176 | 14 | 90 | 197 | 14 |
| TONS |  |  |  |  |  |
| Slipped the fins of those humpbacked tons | 151 | 4 | 83 | 168 | 12 |
| TOO |  |  |  |  |  |
| Shut, too, in a tower of words, I mark | 16 | 9 | 11 | 19 | 9 |
| 'This that we tread was, too, your fathers' land.' | 26 | 12 | 16 | 31 | 12 |
| Am I not father, too, and the ascending boy, | 46 | 9 | 27 | 54 | 9 |
| Am I not sister, too, who is my saviour? | 46 | 12 | 27 | 54 | 12 |
| He'll ache too long | 48 | 13 | 28 | 56 | 13 |
| And learn, too late, they grieved it on its way, | 116 | 11 | 70 | 128 | 11 |
| Too late in the wrong rain | 124 | 9 | 73 | 138 | 9 |
| My paid-for slaved-for own too late | 132 | 6 | 78 | 147 | 6 |
| Too proud to die; broken and blind he died |  |  | 91 | 200 | 1 |
| I am not too proud to cry that He and he |  |  | 91 | 200 | 19 |
| Too proud to cry, too frail to check the tears, |  |  | 91 | 201 | 14 |
| The tears out of his eyes, too proud to cry. |  |  | 91 | 201 | 18 |
| TOOK |  |  |  |  |  |
| Who took my flesh and bone for armour | 8 | 21 | 5 | 9 | 21 |
| A merry girl took me for man, | 65 | 22 | 40 | 74 | 22 |
| Rip of the vaults, I took my marrow-ladle | 72 | 11 | 44 | 81 | 11 |
| High tide and the heron dived when I took the road | 102 | 17 | 63 | 113 | 17 |
| Blackened with birds took a last look | 149 | 2 | 83 | 166 | 2 |
| TOOTH |  |  |  |  |  |
| With loud, torn tooth and tail and cobweb drum | 80 | 4 | 46 | 89 | 12 |

505

TOOTH (continued)

| | U.K. | | | U.S. | |
|---|---|---|---|---|---|
| | Page | Line | Poem | Page | Line |
| Till the sweet tooth of my love bit dry, | 107 | 7 | 65 | 118 | 7 |
| TOOTHLESS | | | | | |
| Bread and milk mansion in a toothless town. | 78 | 15 | 46 | 87 | 15 |
| TOP | | | | | |
| A brute land in the cool top of the country days | 91 | 15 | 55 | 100 | 15 |
| High and dry by the top of the mast, | 149 | 8 | 83 | 166 | 8 |
| TOPLESS | | | | | |
| Cried the topless, inchtaped lips from hank and hood | 79 | 21 | 46 | 89 | 2 |
| TOPPLE | | | | | |
| Cudgel great air, wreck east, and topple sun-down, | 79 | 7 | 46 | 88 | 10 |
| TOPPLING | | | | | |
| Toppling and burning in the muddle of towers and galleries | 77 | 18 | 45 | 86 | 18 |
| Toppling up the boatside in a snow of light! | 154 | 18 | 83 | 172 | 18 |
| And the mother and toppling house of the holy spring, | 158 | 23 | 84 | 177 | 23 |
| TOPS | | | | | |
| My mothers-eyed, upon the tops of trees; | 26 | 9 | 16 | 31 | 9 |
| On to the blindly tossing tops; | 155 | 6 | 83 | 173 | 10 |
| TOPSY-TURVIES | | | | | |
| Suffer, my topsy-turvies, that a double angel | 37 | 26 | 20 | 43 | 9 |
| TORCH | | | | | |
| When, with his torch and hourglass, like a sulphur priest, | 83 | 2 | 49 | 92 | 2 |
| Quick in the wood at love, where a torch of foxes foams, | 177 | 14 | 90 | 198 | 13 |
| TORE | | | | | |
| Talked and tore though her eyes smiled. | 93 | 20 | 56 | 102 | 20 |
| TORMENTED | | | | | |
| (An old tormented man three-quarters blind, | | | 91 | 200 | 18 |
| TORN | | | | | |
| Roared, sea born, man torn, blood blest. | viii | 15 | 1 | xvi | 15 |
| And the limbs are torn. | 65 | 5 | 40 | 74 | 5 |
| With loud, torn tooth and tail and cobweb drum | 80 | 4 | 46 | 89 | 12 |
| A man torn up mourns in the sole night. | 115 | 21 | 69 | 127 | 21 |
| Torn and alone in a farm house in a fold | 119 | 15 | 72 | 131 | 15 |
| The sky is torn across | 124 | 1 | 73 | 138 | 1 |
| In love torn breeches and blistered jacket | 132 | 7 | 78 | 147 | 7 |
| And the winged wall is torn | 138 | 12 | 82 | 155 | 12 |
| Of the dingle torn to singing and the surpliced | 165 | 4 | 86 | 184 | 12 |
| TORRENT | | | | | |
| In the torrent salmon sun, | vii | 3 | 1 | xv | 3 |
| TORRID | | | | | |
| By his torrid crown | 138 | 13 | 82 | 155 | 13 |

| | U.K. Page | U.K. Line | Poem | U.S. Page | U.S. Line |
|---|---|---|---|---|---|
| **TOSSED** | | | | | |
| Who tossed the high tide in a time of stories | 67 | 13 | 41 | 76 | 13 |
| Fumed like a tree, and tossed a burning bird; | 80 | 3 | 46 | 89 | 11 |
| The circular smile tossed from lover to lover | 90 | 9 | 54 | 99 | 9 |
| **TOSSING** | | | | | |
| On to the blindly tossing tops; | 155 | 6 | 83 | 173 | 10 |
| **TOTTER** | | | | | |
| But seasons must be challenged or they totter | 2 | 1 | 2 | 2 | 1 |
| **TOUCH** | | | | | |
| Of tides that never touch the shores. | 8 | 10 | 5 | 9 | 10 |
| And bear those tendril hands I touch across | 90 | 6 | 54 | 99 | 6 |
| **TOUCHED** | | | | | |
| The blood that touched the crosstree and the grail | 22 | 11 | 14 | 27 | 11 |
| Touched the first cloud and left a sign. | 22 | 12 | 14 | 27 | 12 |
| **TOUCHES** | | | | | |
| A hill touches an angel. Out of a saint's cell | 163 | 4 | 86 | 182 | 4 |
| **TOWARDS** | | | | | |
| Towards the studded male in a bent, midnight blaze | 91 | 13 | 55 | 100 | 13 |
| Toils towards the ambush of his wounds; | 170 | 17 | 88 | 190 | 17 |
| He sings towards anguish; finches fly | 170 | 20 | 88 | 190 | 20 |
| **TOWER** | | | | | |
| Shut, too, in a tower of words, I mark | 16 | 9 | 11 | 19 | 9 |
| I damp the waxlights in your tower dome. | 19 | 11 | 12 | 22 | 16 |
| Everything ends, the tower ending and, | 19 | 16 | 12 | 23 | 1 |
| A steeplejack tower, bonerailed and masterless, | 35 | 20 | 20 | 40 | 20 |
| Like a tower on the town | 42 | 5 | 24 | 49 | 5 |
| Like a tower on the town | 42 | 12 | 24 | 49 | 12 |
| Where bird and shell are babbling in my tower? | 46 | 14 | 27 | 54 | 14 |
| I am, the tower told, felled by a timeless stroke, | 46 | 21 | 27 | 54 | 21 |
| Love's house, they answer, and the tower death | 47 | 7 | 27 | 55 | 7 |
| A stem cementing, wrestled up the tower, | 54 | 5 | 33 | 63 | 5 |
| Till tallow I blew from the wax's tower | 74 | 9 | 44 | 83 | 9 |
| In the tower and tolls to sleep over the stalls | 164 | 3 | 86 | 183 | 10 |
| **TOWER'S** | | | | | |
| For my tall tower's sake cast in her stone? | 46 | 2 | 27 | 54 | 2 |
| **TOWERING** | | | | | |
| Nor roof of sand, nor yet the towering tiler? | 46 | 16 | 27 | 54 | 16 |
| Nor for the towering dead | 128 | 15 | 76 | 142 | 15 |
| **TOWERS** | | | | | |
| Day's night whose towers will catch | vii | 20 | 1 | xv | 20 |
| Come unto sea-stuck towers, at the fibre scaling, | 37 | 23 | 20 | 43 | 6 |
| Time upon time the towers of the skies | 53 | 19 | 32 | 62 | 19 |
| Soar, with its two bark towers, to that Day | 76 | 20 | 44 | 85 | 20 |
| Toppling and burning in the muddle of towers and galleries | 77 | 18 | 45 | 86 | 18 |

TOWN

|  | U.K. | | Poem | U.S. | |
| --- | --- | --- | --- | --- | --- |
|  | Page | Line |  | Page | Line |
| **TOWN** | | | | | |
| A worker in the morning town, | 5 | 14 | 3 | 4 | 14 |
| In the pouring town, | 38 | 16 | 20 | 44 | 6 |
| That town of ghosts, the trodden womb | 42 | 2 | 24 | 49 | 2 |
| Like a tower on the town | 42 | 5 | 24 | 49 | 5 |
| That town of ghosts, the manwaged womb | 42 | 9 | 24 | 49 | 9 |
| Like a tower on the town | 42 | 12 | 24 | 49 | 12 |
| Shall not thunder on the town | 43 | 17 | 24 | 51 | 3 |
| Thunders on the foreign town | 43 | 24 | 24 | 51 | 10 |
| All these, he said who sacked the children's town, | 46 | 18 | 27 | 54 | 18 |
| Bread and milk mansion in a toothless town. | 78 | 15 | 46 | 87 | 15 |
| And walk the warring sands by the dead town, | 79 | 6 | 46 | 88 | 9 |
| Strike in the time-bomb town, | 96 | 10 | 58 | 106 | 10 |
| In the final direction of the elementary town | 99 | 8 | 60 | 110 | 8 |
| In the still sleeping town and set forth. | 102 | 10 | 63 | 113 | 10 |
| Of the town closed as the town awoke. | 102 | 20 | 63 | 113 | 20 |
| Though the town below lay leaved with October blood. | 104 | 15 | 63 | 115 | 17 |
| The truant boys from the town | 111 | 16 | 68 | 123 | 16 |
| When I woke, the town spoke. | 134 | 1 | 79 | 150 | 1 |
| Crossly out of the town noises | 134 | 24 | 79 | 151 | 2 |
| Cry my sea town was breaking. | 134 | 27 | 79 | 151 | 5 |
| The trodden town rang its cobbles for luck. | 149 | 4 | 83 | 166 | 4 |
| Out of the house that holds a town | 154 | 23 | 83 | 173 | 3 |
| And the sizzling beds of the town cried, Quick!— | 174 | 20 | 89 | 194 | 20 |
| No springtailed tom in the red hot town | 174 | 29 | 89 | 195 | 5 |
| **TOWNS** | | | | | |
| Towns around on a wheel of fire. | 33 | 6 | 19 | 38 | 6 |
| The country tide is cobbled with towns, | 156 | 24 | 83 | 175 | 12 |
| And honoured among wagons I was prince of the apple towns | 159 | 6 | 85 | 178 | 6 |
| Ship towns to pastures of otters. He | 170 | 24 | 88 | 190 | 24 |
| **TOWY** | | | | | |
| In the river Towy below bows his tilted headstone. | 167 | 12 | 87 | 187 | 12 |
| Fishing in the tear of the Towy. Only a hoot owl | 169 | 3 | 87 | 189 | 12 |
| **TOWY's** | | | | | |
| To the hawk on fire, the halter height, over Towy's fins, | 167 | 16 | 87 | 187 | 16 |
| **TRACE** | | | | | |
| Whose wizard shape I trace in the cavernous skull, | 91 | 2 | 55 | 100 | 2 |
| Trace out a tentacle, | 91 | 28 | 55 | 101 | 6 |
| **TRACK** | | | | | |
| With whistler's cough contages, time on track | 19 | 22 | 12 | 23 | 7 |
| But time has set its maggot on their track. | 50 | 4 | 30 | 59 | 4 |

| | U.K. | | | U.S. | |
|---|---|---|---|---|---|
| | Page | Line | Poem | Page | Line |
| **TRACKS** | | | | | |
| When, like a running grave, time tracks you down, | 18 | 1 | 12 | 21 | 1 |
| The greenwood dying as the deer fall in their tracks, | 49 | 11 | 29 | 58 | 11 |
| Time tracks the sound of shape on man and cloud, | 75 | 3 | 44 | 84 | 3 |
| In the claw tracks of hawks | 170 | 21 | 88 | 190 | 21 |
| **TRADE** | | | | | |
| Or the strut and trade of charms | 128 | 8 | 76 | 142 | 8 |
| And the hewn coils of his trade perceives | 170 | 26 | 88 | 190 | 26 |
| **TRADES** | | | | | |
| And all the woken farm at its white trades, | 119 | 25 | 72 | 132 | 5 |
| And nothing I cared, at my sky blue trades, that time allows | 160 | 20 | 85 | 179 | 20 |
| **TRAIL** | | | | | |
| Trail with daisies and barley | 159 | 8 | 85 | 178 | 8 |
| **TRAILED** | | | | | |
| Round her trailed wrist fresh water weaves, | 156 | 9 | 83 | 174 | 17 |
| **TRAILING** | | | | | |
| Trailing the frost bitten cloth, | 132 | 23 | 78 | 147 | 23 |
| **TRAILS** | | | | | |
| Flounders, gulls, on their cold, dying trails, | 170 | 11 | 88 | 190 | 11 |
| **TRANSLATING** | | | | | |
| The word flowed up, translating to the heart | 22 | 23 | 14 | 27 | 23 |
| Tongue of your translating eyes. The young stars told me, | 110 | 23 | 67 | 122 | 1 |
| **TRAP** | | | | | |
| Of love am barer than Cadaver's trap | 18 | 8 | 12 | 21 | 8 |
| Trap I with coil and sheet, | 56 | 19 | 34 | 65 | 19 |
| **TRASH** | | | | | |
| And lets their trash be honoured as the quick. | 15 | 15 | 10 | 17 | 15 |
| **TRAVEL** | | | | | |
| Calls some content to travel with the winds, | 53 | 17 | 32 | 62 | 17 |
| But do not travel down dumb wind like prodigals. | 86 | 11 | 51 | 95 | 11 |
| **TRAVELS** | | | | | |
| As they drown, the chime travels, | 37 | 10 | 20 | 42 | 16 |
| **TRAY** | | | | | |
| The tray of knives, the antiseptic funeral; | 37 | 3 | 20 | 42 | 9 |
| **TREAD** | | | | | |
| Tread, like a naked Venus, | 10 | 12 | 7 | 11 | 12 |
| 'This that we tread was, too, your fathers' land.' | 26 | 12 | 16 | 31 | 12 |
| 'But this we tread bears the angelic gangs, | 26 | 13 | 16 | 31 | 13 |
| Fear not the tread, the seeded milling, | 33 | 16 | 19 | 38 | 16 |
| The scales of this twin world tread on the double, | 35 | 4 | 20 | 40 | 4 |
| No tread more perilous, the green steps and spire | 36 | 2 | 20 | 41 | 2 |

TREAD (continued)

| | U.K. | | | U.S. | |
|---|---|---|---|---|---|
| | *Page* | *Line* | *Poem* | *Page* | *Line* |
| Horses, centaur dead, turn and tread the drenched white | 121 | 19 | 72 | 134 | 14 |
| The polar eagle with his tread of snow. | 152 | 8 | 83 | 169 | 20 |
| TREADING | | | | | |
| Sings to the treading hawk | 115 | 13 | 69 | 127 | 13 |
| TREASURES | | | | | |
| To lift to leave from the treasures of man is pleasing death | 94 | 7 | 57 | 104 | 7 |
| TREATY | | | | | |
| The hand that signed the treaty bred a fever, | 62 | 9 | 37 | 71 | 9 |
| TREE | | | | | |
| My Jack of Christ born thorny on the tree? | 13 | 17 | 9 | 15 | 3 |
| Lit on the cuddled tree, the cross of fever, | 19 | 8 | 12 | 22 | 13 |
| I with the wooden insect in the tree of nettles, | 36 | 4 | 20 | 41 | 4 |
| Sprout from the stony lockers like a tree on Aran. | 37 | 27 | 20 | 43 | 10 |
| This wine upon a foreign tree | 39 | 2 | 21 | 45 | 2 |
| Twined good and evil on an eastern tree; | 40 | 10 | 22 | 46 | 10 |
| All legends' sweethearts on a tree of stories, | 41 | 25 | 23 | 48 | 7 |
| Strip to this tree: a rocking alphabet, | 74 | 17 | 44 | 83 | 17 |
| I by the tree of thieves, all glory's sawbones, | 75 | 15 | 44 | 84 | 15 |
| My nest of mercies in the rude, red tree. | 76 | 22 | 44 | 85 | 22 |
| In that proud sailing tree with branches driven | 78 | 6 | 46 | 87 | 6 |
| Fumed like a tree, and tossed a burning bird; | 80 | 3 | 46 | 89 | 11 |
| Gag of a dumbstruck tree to block from bare enemies | 85 | 4 | 50 | 94 | 4 |
| Drivelled down to one singeing tree | 95 | 20 | 58 | 105 | 20 |
| Her robin breasted tree, three Marys in the rays. | 163 | 6 | 86 | 182 | 6 |
| Milled dust of the apple tree and the pounded islands | 164 | 10 | 86 | 183 | 17 |
| TREEFORK | | | | | |
| Within the nested treefork | 115 | 12 | 69 | 127 | 12 |
| TREE-TAILED | | | | | |
| Butt of the tree-tailed worm that mounted Eve, | 72 | 8 | 44 | 81 | 8 |
| TREES | | | | | |
| Like leaves of trees and as soon | viii | 5 | 1 | xvi | 5 |
| And nail the merry squires to the trees; | 2 | 21 | 2 | 3 | 3 |
| And worlds hang on the trees. | 5 | 18 | 3 | 5 | 18 |
| Drives my green age; that blasts the roots of trees | 9 | 2 | 6 | 10 | 2 |
| On the horizon walking like the trees | 16 | 10 | 11 | 19 | 10 |
| My mothers-eyed, upon the tops of trees; | 26 | 9 | 16 | 31 | 9 |
| The wild pigs' wood, and slime upon the trees, | 30 | 20 | 18 | 35 | 20 |
| My images stalk the trees and the slant sap's tunnel, | 36 | 1 | 20 | 41 | 1 |
| A quarrel of weathers and trees in the windy spiral. | 36 | 18 | 20 | 41 | 18 |
| I should tell summer from the trees, the worms | 45 | 9 | 26 | 53 | 9 |

| | U.K. | | | U.S. | |
|---|---|---|---|---|---|
| | *Page* | *Line* | *Poem* | *Page* | *Line* |
| By crane and water-tower by the seedy trees | 49 | 8 | 29 | 58 | 8 |
| A leg as long as trees, | 57 | 1 | 34 | 66 | 8 |
| And one light's language in the book of trees. | 74 | 19 | 44 | 83 | 19 |
| Bent like three trees and bird-papped through her shift, | 75 | 9 | 44 | 84 | 9 |
| A calm wind blows that raised the trees like hair | 80 | 11 | 46 | 89 | 19 |
| The shade of their trees was a word of many shades | 89 | 10 | 53 | 98 | 10 |
| Birds and the birds of the winged trees flying my name | 102 | 12 | 63 | 113 | 12 |
| To the trees and the stones and the fish in the tide. | 104 | 5 | 63 | 115 | 7 |
| Propped between trees and water | 111 | 3 | 68 | 123 | 3 |
| That lets the trees and water enter | 111 | 5 | 68 | 123 | 5 |
| The birds the grass the trees the lake | 112 | 15 | 68 | 124 | 15 |
| Under the one leaved trees ran a scarecrow of snow | 122 | 14 | 72 | 135 | 14 |
| Trees cool and dry in the whirlpool of ships | 156 | 2 | 83 | 174 | 10 |
| And once below a time I lordly had the trees and leaves | 159 | 7 | 85 | 178 | 7 |
| Love for ever meridian through the courters' trees | 178 | 18 | 90 | 199 | 19 |
| TREMBLE | | | | | |
| What colour is glory? death's feather? tremble | 31 | 1 | 18 | 36 | 1 |
| TREMBLED | | | | | |
| Under the mile off moon we trembled listening | 136 | 5 | 81 | 153 | 5 |
| TREMENDOUS | | | | | |
| In lairs and asylums of the tremendous shout. | 125 | 16 | 74 | 139 | 16 |
| TRESPASSER | | | | | |
| Trespasser and broken bride | 114 | 18 | 69 | 126 | 18 |
| TRIANGLE | | | | | |
| World in the sand, on the triangle landscape, | 76 | 6 | 44 | 85 | 6 |
| TRIANGLES | | | | | |
| The twelve triangles of the cherub wind | 54 | 23 | 33 | 63 | 23 |
| TRIBE | | | | | |
| Deliver me who, timid in my tribe, | 18 | 7 | 12 | 21 | 7 |
| His striped and noon maned tribe striding to holocaust, | 110 | 3 | 67 | 121 | 5 |
| TRIBES | | | | | |
| Bird through the times and lands and tribes of the slow flakes. | 122 | 19 | 72 | 135 | 19 |
| The liquid choirs of his tribes. | 155 | 20 | 83 | 174 | 4 |
| TRICK | | | | | |
| By trick or chance he fell asleep | 5 | 10 | 3 | 5 | 10 |
| Shapes in a cinder death; love for his trick, | 19 | 23 | 12 | 23 | 8 |
| TRIGGER | | | | | |
| The trigger and scythe, the bridal blade, | 33 | 17 | 19 | 38 | 17 |

TRITON

| | | U.K. | | | U.S. | |
|---|---|---|---|---|---|---|
| | | Page | Line | Poem | Page | Line |
| **TRITON** | | | | | | |
| | And, clapped in water till the triton dangles, | 37 | 13 | 20 | 42 | 19 |
| **TRIUMPHANT** | | | | | | |
| | With more triumphant faith | 173 | 16 | 88 | 193 | 16 |
| **TRODDEN** | | | | | | |
| | That town of ghosts, the trodden womb | 42 | 2 | 24 | 49 | 2 |
| | The trodden town rang its cobbles for luck. | 149 | 4 | 83 | 166 | 4 |
| **TROT** | | | | | | |
| | To trot with a loud mate the haybeds of a mile, | 91 | 16 | 55 | 100 | 16 |
| | Trot and gallop with gulls upon them | 156 | 21 | 83 | 175 | 9 |
| **TROUBLE** | | | | | | |
| | Out of the room the weight of his trouble | 154 | 22 | 83 | 173 | 2 |
| **TROUBLES** | | | | | | |
| | In children's circuses could stay their troubles? | 50 | 2 | 30 | 59 | 2 |
| **TROUGH** | | | | | | |
| | She sleeps in the narrow trough yet she walks the dust | 108 | 13 | 66 | 119 | 13 |
| **TROUNCED** | | | | | | |
| | Trounced by his wings in the hissing shippen, long dead | 177 | 19 | 90 | 198 | 18 |
| **TRUANT** | | | | | | |
| | The truant boys from the town | 111 | 16 | 68 | 123 | 16 |
| **TRUE** | | | | | | |
| | And that is true after perpetual defeat. | 48 | 9 | 28 | 56 | 9 |
| | Shall drown in a grief as deep as his true grave, | 100 | 18 | 61 | 111 | 18 |
| | Away but the weather turned around. And the true | 104 | 10 | 63 | 115 | 12 |
| | And the vaulting bird be still. O my true love, hold me. | 110 | 26 | 67 | 122 | 4 |
| | From every true or crater | 124 | 7 | 73 | 138 | 7 |
| | Our own true strangers' dust | 126 | 13 | 74 | 140 | 13 |
| | High riding, held and blessed and true, and so stilly | 165 | 19 | 86 | 185 | 9 |
| | Now will be ever is always true, | 171 | 24 | 88 | 191 | 24 |
| **TRULY** | | | | | | |
| | And truly he | 165 | 26 | 86 | 185 | 16 |
| **TRUMPED** | | | | | | |
| | From Jesu's sleeve trumped up the king of spots, | 73 | 12 | 44 | 82 | 12 |
| **TRUMPET** | | | | | | |
| | Hark: I trumpet the place, | viii | 16 | 1 | xvi | 16 |
| | He'll trumpet into meat), | 56 | 5 | 34 | 65 | 5 |
| | Blasts back the trumpet voice. | 57 | 6 | 34 | 66 | 13 |
| | The present mouth, and the sweetly blown trumpet of lies, | 85 | 6 | 50 | 94 | 6 |
| **TRUMPETING** | | | | | | |
| | Back. Lines of age sleep on the stones till trumpeting dawn. | 123 | 8 | 72 | 136 | 18 |

|  | U.K. Page | Line | Poem | U.S. Page | Line |
|---|---|---|---|---|---|
| **TRUMPETS** | | | | | |
| Leap, as to trumpets. Calligraphy of the old | 121 | 22 | 72 | 134 | 17 |
| **TRUST** | | | | | |
| In trust and tale have I divided sense, | 41 | 5 | 23 | 47 | 5 |
| **TRUTH** | | | | | |
| Grafts on its bride one-sided skins of truth; | 15 | 8 | 10 | 17 | 8 |
| The mankind of her going with a grave truth | 101 | 15 | 62 | 112 | 15 |
| Summertime of the dead whispered the truth of his joy | 104 | 4 | 63 | 115 | 6 |
| O may my heart's truth | 104 | 16 | 63 | 115 | 18 |
| This side of the truth, | 105 | 1 | 64 | 116 | 1 |
| Each truth, each lie, | 106 | 11 | 64 | 117 | 11 |
| While you displaced a truth in the air, | 107 | 17 | 65 | 118 | 17 |
| Commoner than water, crueller than truth; | 125 | 3 | 74 | 139 | 3 |
| This Side of the Truth (for Llewelyn) | 105 | | 64 | 116 | |
| **TUFT** | | | | | |
| Roll unmanly over this turning tuft, | 60 | 19 | 36 | 69 | 19 |
| **TUFTED** | | | | | |
| The swing of milk was tufted in the pap, | 30 | 10 | 18 | 35 | 10 |
| Shall you turn cockwise on a tufted axle. | 60 | 24 | 36 | 69 | 24 |
| **TUGGED** | | | | | |
| Tugged through the days | 54 | 20 | 33 | 63 | 20 |
| **TUMBLE** | | | | | |
| No god-in-hero tumble down | 42 | 4 | 24 | 49 | 4 |
| No god-in-hero tumble down | 42 | 11 | 24 | 49 | 11 |
| If the dead starve, their stomachs turn to tumble | 77 | 22 | 45 | 86 | 22 |
| **TUMBLEDOWN** | | | | | |
| Yet, though I cry with tumbledown tongue, | 172 | 26 | 88 | 192 | 26 |
| **TUMBLING** | | | | | |
| On God's rough tumbling grounds | ix | 24 | 1 | xvii | 24 |
| Is come of the sea tumbling in harness | 101 | 6 | 62 | 112 | 6 |
| **TUNE** | | | | | |
| Hubbub and fiddle, this tune | ix | 21 | 1 | xvii | 21 |
| Time's tune my ladies with the teats of music, | 74 | 21 | 44 | 83 | 21 |
| Time is the tune my ladies lend their heartbreak, | 75 | 1 | 44 | 84 | 1 |
| Who moved for three years in tune | 124 | 3 | 73 | 138 | 3 |
| Makes all the music; and I who hear the tune of the slow, | 169 | 9 | 87 | 189 | 18 |
| **TUNEFUL** | | | | | |
| In all his tuneful turning so few and such morning songs | 160 | 21 | 85 | 179 | 21 |
| **TUNES** | | | | | |
| Fields high as the house, the tunes from the chimneys, it was air | 159 | 20 | 85 | 178 | 20 |
| **TUNICS'** | | | | | |
| Shall rainbows be their tunics' colour? | 44 | 4 | 25 | 52 | 4 |

TUNNEL

|  | U.K. Page | Line | Poem | U.S. Page | Line |
|---|---|---|---|---|---|
| **TUNNEL** | | | | | |
| My images stalk the trees and the slant sap's tunnel, | 36 | 1 | 20 | 41 | 1 |
| **TURBULENT** | | | | | |
| Until the turbulent new born | 138 | 10 | 82 | 155 | 10 |
| **TURN** | | | | | |
| The proud spine spurning turn and twist. | 10 | 5 | 7 | 11 | 5 |
| The straws of Asia, lose me as I turn | 31 | 23 | 18 | 37 | 5 |
| Fear not the screws that turn the voice, | 33 | 23 | 19 | 39 | 5 |
| Turn the long sea arterial | 36 | 22 | 20 | 42 | 1 |
| (Turn the sea-spindle lateral, | 37 | 16 | 20 | 42 | 22 |
| Shall you turn cockwise on a tufted axle. | 60 | 24 | 36 | 69 | 24 |
| If the dead starve, their stomachs turn to tumble | 77 | 22 | 45 | 86 | 22 |
| The bowels turn turtle, | 91 | 20 | 55 | 100 | 20 |
| Horses, centaur dead, turn and tread the drenched white | 121 | 19 | 72 | 134 | 14 |
| To hear the golden note turn in a groove, | 125 | 6 | 74 | 139 | 6 |
| To the burn and turn of time | 137 | 11 | 82 | 154 | 11 |
| I turn the corner of prayer and burn | 148 | 1 | 82 | 165 | 1 |
| I would turn back and run | 148 | 4 | 82 | 165 | 4 |
| Of the hobnail tales: no gooseherd or swine will turn | 162 | 10 | 86 | 181 | 10 |
| The darkest way, and did not turn away, | | | 91 | 200 | 2 |
| **TURNED** | | | | | |
| When once the twilight screws were turned, | 5 | 7 | 3 | 5 | 7 |
| Shifting to light, turned on me like a moon. | 26 | 3 | 16 | 31 | 3 |
| Once where the soft snow's blood was turned to ice. | 80 | 12 | 46 | 89 | 20 |
| Away but the weather turned around. | 103 | 15 | 63 | 114 | 15 |
| It turned away from the blithe country | 103 | 16 | 63 | 114 | 16 |
| Away but the weather turned around. And the true | 104 | 10 | 63 | 115 | 12 |
| Once when the world turned old | 119 | 11 | 72 | 131 | 11 |
| His driftwood thirty-fifth wind turned age; | 170 | 8 | 88 | 190 | 8 |
| **TURNING** | | | | | |
| The world's turning wood, | viii | 1 | 1 | xvi | 1 |
| Turning a petrol face blind to the enemy | 36 | 23 | 20 | 42 | 2 |
| Turning the riderless dead by the channel wall. | 36 | 24 | 20 | 42 | 3 |
| Roll unmanly over this turning tuft, | 60 | 19 | 36 | 69 | 19 |
| And I saw in the turning so clearly a child's | 103 | 21 | 63 | 114 | 21 |
| On this high hill in a year's turning. | 104 | 18 | 63 | 115 | 20 |
| In the throat, burning and turning. All night afloat | 136 | 2 | 81 | 153 | 2 |
| In all his tuneful turning so few and such morning songs | 160 | 21 | 85 | 179 | 21 |
| Only for the turning of the earth in her holy | 165 | 23 | 86 | 185 | 13 |

|  | U.K. | | | U.S. | |
|---|---|---|---|---|---|
|  | Page | Line | Poem | Page | Line |
| **TURNIPS** | | | | | |
| With fists of turnips punishes the land, | 17 | 4 | 11 | 20 | 4 |
| **TURNKEY** | | | | | |
| Splitting the long eye open, and the spiral turnkey, | 36 | 26 | 20 | 42 | 5 |
| **TURNS** | | | | | |
| Turns damp to dry; the golden shot | 6 | 2 | 4 | 6 | 2 |
| Turns night to day; blood in their suns | 6 | 5 | 4 | 6 | 5 |
| Turns ghost to ghost; each mothered child | 6 | 20 | 4 | 7 | 2 |
| Turns mine to wax. | 9 | 8 | 6 | 10 | 8 |
| The dead turns up its eye; | 11 | 3 | 8 | 12 | 3 |
| Turns in the earth that turns the ashen | 33 | 5 | 19 | 38 | 5 |
| Turns in the dark on the sound they know will arise | 100 | 6 | 61 | 111 | 6 |
| Turns on the quick and the dead, and the man on the stairs | 100 | 14 | 61 | 111 | 14 |
| Turns of your prayed flesh, nor shall I shoo the bird below me: | 109 | 27 | 67 | 121 | 1 |
| Kill Time! She turns in her pain! | 155 | 10 | 83 | 173 | 14 |
| Turns the moon-chained and water-wound | 157 | 11 | 83 | 176 | 3 |
| And the multitude's sultry tear turns cool on the weeping wall, | 158 | 17 | 84 | 177 | 17 |
| **TURNTURTLE** | | | | | |
| Dolphins dive in their turnturtle dust, | 171 | 6 | 88 | 191 | 6 |
| **TURRETS** | | | | | |
| For my tall turrets carry as your sin? | 46 | 6 | 27 | 54 | 6 |
| Ears in the turrets hear | 58 | 1 | 35 | 67 | 1 |
| Ding dong from the mute turrets. | 83 | 24 | 49 | 93 | 6 |
| Ears in the turrets hear | 58 | | 35 | 67 | |
| **TURTLE** | | | | | |
| Up naked stairs, a turtle in a hearse, | 18 | 4 | 12 | 21 | 4 |
| They suffer the undead water where the turtle nibbles, | 37 | 22 | 20 | 43 | 5 |
| The bowels turn turtle, | 91 | 20 | 55 | 100 | 20 |
| Till every turtle crushed from his shell | 151 | 10 | 83 | 168 | 18 |
| **TUSKED** | | | | | |
| Nor the tusked prince, in the ruttish farm, at the rind | 163 | 14 | 86 | 182 | 14 |
| And the tusked, ramshackling sea exults; | 173 | 13 | 88 | 193 | 13 |
| **TUSSLE** | | | | | |
| And tussle in a shoal of loves. | 150 | 6 | 83 | 167 | 10 |
| **TWELVE** | | | | | |
| Twelve winds encounter by the white host at pasture, | 36 | 14 | 20 | 41 | 14 |
| The twelve triangles of the cherub wind | 54 | 23 | 33 | 63 | 23 |
| Ducked in the twelve, disciple seas | 69 | 4 | 43 | 78 | 4 |
| **TWELVE-WINDED** | | | | | |
| But strip the twelve-winded marrow from his circle; | 60 | 3 | 36 | 69 | 3 |

TWELVE-WINDED (continued)

| | U.K. | | | U.S. | |
|---|---|---|---|---|---|
| | *Page* | *Line* | *Poem* | *Page* | *Line* |
| Rippling in twelve-winded circles, | 131 | 12 | 77 | 145 | 18 |
| **TWENTY-FOUR** | | | | | |
| Twenty-four years remind the tears of my eyes. | 99 | 1 | 60 | 110 | 1 |
| Twenty-four years | 99 | | 60 | 110 | |
| **TWICE** | | | | | |
| Twice in the feeding sea, grown | 29 | 2 | 17 | 34 | 6 |
| Look twice before he fell from grace. | 63 | 4 | 38 | 72 | 4 |
| Said the antipodes, and twice spring chimed. | 72 | 18 | 44 | 81 | 18 |
| To surrender now is to pay the expensive ogre twice. | 94 | 10 | 57 | 104 | 10 |
| And the twice told fields of infancy | 103 | 26 | 63 | 115 | 1 |
| **TWIGS** | | | | | |
| An enamoured man alone by the twigs of his eyes, two fires, | 77 | 7 | 45 | 86 | 7 |
| **TWILIGHT** | | | | | |
| When once the twilight locks no longer | 4 | 1 | 3 | 4 | 1 |
| When once the twilight screws were turned, | 5 | 7 | 3 | 5 | 7 |
| That the snow blind twilight ferries over the lakes | 119 | 2 | 72 | 131 | 2 |
| When once the twilight locks no longer | 4 | | 3 | 4 | |
| **TWILIT** | | | | | |
| Love's twilit nation and the skull of state, | 19 | 14 | 12 | 22 | 19 |
| **TWIN** | | | | | |
| The scales of this twin world tread on the double, | 35 | 4 | 20 | 40 | 4 |
| Create this twin miracle. | 35 | 18 | 20 | 40 | 18 |
| **TWIN-BOXED** | | | | | |
| And free the twin-boxed grief, | 67 | 20 | 41 | 76 | 20 |
| **TWINE** | | | | | |
| Twine in a moon-blown shell, | 69 | 15 | 43 | 78 | 15 |
| **TWINED** | | | | | |
| Twined good and evil on an eastern tree; | 40 | 10 | 22 | 46 | 10 |
| In the courters' lanes, or twined in the ox roasting sun | 176 | 13 | 90 | 197 | 13 |
| **TWINKLING** | | | | | |
| Enticed with twinkling bits of the eye | 107 | 6 | 65 | 118 | 6 |
| **TWIST** | | | | | |
| Did twist into a living cipher, | 7 | 21 | 5 | 8 | 21 |
| The proud spine spurning turn and twist. | 10 | 5 | 7 | 11 | 5 |
| From damp love-darkness and the nurse's twist | 13 | 10 | 9 | 14 | 17 |
| I learnt man's tongue, to twist the shapes of thoughts | 21 | 8 | 13 | 25 | 8 |
| **TWISTED** | | | | | |
| The twisted brain, the fair-formed loin, | 48 | 25 | 28 | 57 | 2 |
| I whistled all night in the twisted flues, | 174 | 18 | 89 | 194 | 18 |
| **TWISTING** | | | | | |
| Twisting on racks when sinews give way, | 68 | 13 | 42 | 77 | 13 |

| | U.K. Page | U.K. Line | Poem | U.S. Page | U.S. Line |
|---|---|---|---|---|---|
| **TWITCH** | | | | | |
| The stuffed lung of the fox twitch and cry Love | 88 | 11 | 52 | 97 | 11 |
| **TWO** | | | | | |
| Move like two ghosts before the eye. | 6 | 18 | 4 | 6 | 18 |
| Of birth and death, the two sad knives of thieves, | 10 | 18 | 7 | 11 | 18 |
| Two one-dimensioned ghosts, love on a reel, | 14 | 12 | 10 | 16 | 12 |
| Which is the world? Of our two sleepings, which | 15 | 1 | 10 | 17 | 1 |
| The earth and sky were as two mountains meeting. | 20 | 15 | 13 | 24 | 15 |
| I, in my intricate image, stride on two levels, | 35 | 1 | 20 | 40 | 1 |
| On the consumptives' terrace taking their two farewells, | 36 | 10 | 20 | 41 | 10 |
| Two heels of water on the floor of seed), | 56 | 24 | 34 | 66 | 3 |
| And drink in the two milked crags, | 65 | 2 | 40 | 74 | 2 |
| Faith in their hands shall snap in two, | 68 | 15 | 42 | 77 | 15 |
| Soar, with its two bark towers, to that Day | 76 | 20 | 44 | 85 | 20 |
| An enamoured man alone by the twigs of his eyes, two fires, | 77 | 7 | 45 | 86 | 7 |
| The agonized, two seas. | 90 | 7 | 54 | 99 | 7 |
| Her two surnames stopped me still. | 93 | 2 | 56 | 102 | 2 |
| The sound about to be said in the two prayers | 100 | 9 | 61 | 111 | 9 |
| Good and bad, two ways | 105 | 13 | 64 | 116 | 13 |
| The death biding two lie lonely. | 109 | 28 | 67 | 121 | 2 |
| Two sand grains together in bed, | 115 | 1 | 69 | 127 | 1 |
| Innocent between two wars, | 115 | 19 | 69 | 127 | 19 |
| This ragged anniversary of two | 124 | 2 | 73 | 138 | 2 |
| Two proud, blacked brothers cry, | 126 | 1 | 74 | 140 | 1 |
| And caught between two nights, blindness and death. | | | 91 | 201 | 15 |
| **TWO-A-VEIN** | | | | | |
| The two-a-vein, the foreskin, and the cloud. | 52 | 7 | 31 | 61 | 14 |
| **TWO-FRAMED** | | | | | |
| The two-framed globe that spun into a score; | 21 | 21 | 13 | 26 | 4 |
| **TWO-GUNNED** | | | | | |
| And from the windy West came two-gunned Gabriel, | 73 | 11 | 44 | 82 | 11 |
| **TYBURN** | | | | | |
| To fiery tyburn over the wrestle of elms until | 167 | 9 | 87 | 187 | 9 |

# ENTRIES UNDER U

UGLIER
    Soaked my table the uglier side of a hill    89  2  53  98  2

ULTIMATE
    The sundering ultimate kingdom of genesis'
      thunder.    131  25  77  146  7

UNACCUSTOMED
    Caught in an octagon of unaccustomed light,    63  2  38  72  2

UNANGLED
    Breaks on unangled land.    6  12  4  6  12

UNBIDDEN
    Unbidden by the sun    145  14  82  162  14

UNBLESSED
    The darkest justice of death, blind and un-
      blessed.    91  200  11

UNBOLT
    Shall I unbolt or stay    58  5  35  67  5

UNBOLTS
    And love unbolts the dark    171  18  88  191  18

UNBORN
    Bolt for the salt unborn.    30  6  18  35  6
    Bearding the unborn devil,    32  3  18  37  9
    My clay unsuckled and my salt unborn,    32  10  18  37  16
    O green and unborn and undead?'    70  19  43  79  23
    In the name of the unborn    147  3  82  164  3
    With blessed, unborn God and His Ghost,    172  6  88  192  6

UNBUTTONED
    With bones unbuttoned to the half-way winds,    71  9  44  80  9

UNCAGED
    Of the uncaged sea bottom    141  7  82  158  7

UNCALM
    That uncalm still it is sure alone to stand and
      sing    158  21  84  177  21

UNCHRISTENED
    Lost on the unchristened mountain    144  16  82  161  16

UNCLENCHED
    Unclenched, armless, silk and rough love that
      breaks all rocks.    126  16  74  140  16

UNCONCEIVED
    They yearn with tongues of curlews for the un-
      conceived    176  10  90  197  10

|  | U.K. Page | Line | Poem | U.S. Page | Line |
|---|---|---|---|---|---|
| **UNCREDITED** |  |  |  |  |  |
| Uncredited blows Jericho on Eden. | 41 | 17 | 23 | 47 | 17 |
| **UNDEAD** |  |  |  |  |  |
| They suffer the undead water where the turtle nibbles, | 37 | 22 | 20 | 43 | 5 |
| And the undead eye-teeth, | 67 | 24 | 41 | 76 | 24 |
| O green and unborn and undead?' | 70 | 19 | 43 | 79 | 23 |
| **UNDEFENDED** |  |  |  |  |  |
| The bayonet tongue in this undefended prayer-piece, | 85 | 5 | 50 | 94 | 5 |
| **UNDER** |  |  |  |  |  |
| Under the stars of Wales, | x | 9 | 1 | xviii | 15 |
| Under the mask and the ether, they making bloody | 37 | 2 | 20 | 42 | 8 |
| The sexton sentinel, garrisoned under thistles, | 37 | 6 | 20 | 42 | 12 |
| Dust be your saviour under the conjured soil.) | 37 | 9 | 20 | 42 | 15 |
| Groping for matter under the dog's plate, | 48 | 26 | 28 | 57 | 3 |
| Under the lank, fourth folly on Glamorgan's hill, | 49 | 2 | 29 | 58 | 2 |
| Under the arc of the sky they are unsafe. | 50 | 5 | 30 | 59 | 5 |
| Under the skysigns they who have no arms | 50 | 7 | 30 | 59 | 7 |
| Under the windings of the sea | 68 | 11 | 42 | 77 | 11 |
| Under the bell of rocks, | 69 | 3 | 43 | 78 | 3 |
| That night of time under the Christward shelter: | 71 | 12 | 44 | 80 | 12 |
| Under the milky mushrooms slew my hunger, | 73 | 18 | 44 | 82 | 18 |
| There is loud and dark directly under the dumb flame, | 83 | 13 | 49 | 92 | 13 |
| Refusal struck like a bell under water | 90 | 12 | 54 | 99 | 12 |
| Endure burial under the spelling wall, | 91 | 4 | 55 | 100 | 4 |
| In the wood faraway under me. | 103 | 5 | 63 | 114 | 5 |
| Beyond the border and under the lark full cloud. | 103 | 12 | 63 | 114 | 12 |
| Under the unminding skies, | 105 | 6 | 64 | 116 | 6 |
| And my whole heart under your hammer, | 107 | 13 | 65 | 118 | 13 |
| Waiting with phoenix under | 109 | 2 | 67 | 120 | 2 |
| Under the cloud against love is caught and held and kissed | 109 | 17 | 67 | 120 | 17 |
| Under the encumbered eyelid, | 113 | 3 | 69 | 125 | 3 |
| Golden dissolving under the water veil. | 115 | 9 | 69 | 127 | 9 |
| Or flower under the time dying flesh astride. | 120 | 30 | 72 | 133 | 15 |
| Under the one leaved trees ran a scarecrow of snow | 122 | 14 | 72 | 135 | 14 |
| Under his downy arm you sighed as he struck, | 125 | 19 | 74 | 139 | 19 |
| Who under the lids of her windows hoisted his golden luggage, | 127 | 12 | 75 | 141 | 12 |
| Under the sad breast of the head stone | 130 | 20 | 77 | 144 | 20 |
| The masses of the sea under | 131 | 21 | 77 | 146 | 3 |
| Under the mile off moon we trembled listening | 136 | 5 | 81 | 153 | 5 |

UNDER (continued)

|  | U.K. Page | Line | Poem | U.S. Page | Line |
|---|---|---|---|---|---|
| Under the burial song | 143 | 3 | 82 | 160 | 3 |
| Under the night forever falling. | 145 | 17 | 82 | 162 | 17 |
| The lured fish under the foam | 150 | 23 | 83 | 168 | 7 |
| There is thunder under its thumbs; | 151 | 14 | 83 | 169 | 2 |
| Are making under the green, laid veil | 151 | 21 | 83 | 169 | 9 |
| The tempter under the eyelid | 153 | 6 | 83 | 171 | 2 |
| See what the gold gut drags from under | 154 | 11 | 83 | 172 | 11 |
| Down, down, down, under the ground, | 157 | 9 | 83 | 176 | 1 |
| Under the floating villages, | 157 | 10 | 83 | 176 | 2 |
| Under the earth the loud sea walks, | 157 | 14 | 83 | 176 | 6 |
| Now as I was young and easy under the apple boughs | 159 | 1 | 85 | 178 | 1 |
| And nightly under the simple stars | 160 | 1 | 85 | 179 | 1 |
| Under the new made clouds and happy as the heart was long, | 160 | 16 | 85 | 179 | 16 |
| Under the prayer wheeling moon in the rosy wood | 163 | 18 | 86 | 182 | 18 |
| In the squirrel nimble grove, under linen and thatch | 163 | 21 | 86 | 183 | 2 |
| When his viperish fuse hangs looped with flames under the brand | 168 | 4 | 87 | 188 | 8 |
| It is the heron and I, under judging Sir John's elmed | 168 | 16 | 87 | 189 | 1 |
| Under and round him go | 170 | 10 | 88 | 190 | 10 |
| Under a serpent cloud, | 171 | 5 | 88 | 191 | 5 |
| Under the conceiving moon, on the high chalk hill, | 176 | 2 | 90 | 197 | 2 |
| Under the lighted shapes of faith and their moon-shade | 176 | 17 | 90 | 197 | 17 |
| Manes, under his quenchless summer barbed gold to the bone, | 177 | 6 | 90 | 198 | 5 |
| And the mole snout blunt under his pilgrimage of domes, | 177 | 16 | 90 | 198 | 15 |
| Their breasts full of honey, under their gander king | 177 | 18 | 90 | 198 | 17 |
| Hill, under the grass, in love, and there grow |  |  | 91 | 200 | 6 |
| UNDERTAKER'S |  |  |  |  |  |
| Out of the wrinkled undertaker's van, | 72 | 12 | 44 | 81 | 12 |
| UNDESIRERS |  |  |  |  |  |
| And the undesirers | 147 | 4 | 82 | 164 | 4 |
| UNDID |  |  |  |  |  |
| Some dead undid their bushy jaws, | 4 | 22 | 3 | 4 | 22 |
| UNDIE |  |  |  |  |  |
| Crumble and undie | viii | 6 | 1 | xvi | 6 |
| UNDO |  |  |  |  |  |
| The gentle seaslides of saying I must undo | 89 | 5 | 53 | 98 | 5 |
| UNDOING |  |  |  |  |  |
| Now my saying shall be my undoing, | 89 | 12 | 53 | 98 | 12 |

| | | U.K. | | Poem | U.S. | |
|---|---|---|---|---|---|---|
| | | Page | Line | | Page | Line |
| **UNDONE** | | | | | | |
| | That all is undone, | 105 | 5 | 64 | 116 | 5 |
| | His faith around her flew undone | 114 | 3 | 69 | 126 | 3 |
| | Man and woman undone, | 131 | 5 | 77 | 145 | 11 |
| **UNEARTHLY** | | | | | | |
| | Put a tear for joy in the unearthly flood | 125 | 22 | 74 | 139 | 22 |
| **UNEATING** | | | | | | |
| | Lost in a limp-treed and uneating silence, | 79 | 2 | 46 | 88 | 5 |
| **UNENDING** | | | | | | |
| | Though the moment of a miracle is unending lightning | 127 | 6 | 75 | 141 | 6 |
| **UNENTERED** | | | | | | |
| | Ride through the doors of our unentered house. | 126 | 14 | 74 | 140 | 14 |
| **UNFAILING** | | | | | | |
| | Unfailing till the blood runs foul; | 8 | 4 | 5 | 9 | 4 |
| **UNFIRED** | | | | | | |
| | Continence. I see the unfired phoenix, herald | 110 | 9 | 67 | 121 | 11 |
| **UNFOLDING** | | | | | | |
| | From the unfolding to the scissored caul, | 20 | 3 | 13 | 24 | 3 |
| **UNFORGETTABLY** | | | | | | |
| | With unforgettably smiling act, | 107 | 11 | 65 | 118 | 11 |
| **UNFREE** | | | | | | |
| | To the anguish and carrion, to the infant forever unfree, | 97 | 22 | 59 | 109 | 2 |
| **UNGOTTEN** | | | | | | |
| | Ungotten I knew night and day. | 7 | 18 | 5 | 8 | 18 |
| | As yet ungotten, I did suffer; | 7 | 19 | 5 | 8 | 19 |
| **UNHARMED** | | | | | | |
| | Shall the child sleep unharmed or the man be crying? | 100 | 12 | 61 | 111 | 12 |
| **UNHOLY** | | | | | | |
| | Her holy unholy hours with the always anonymous beast. | 114 | 23 | 69 | 126 | 23 |
| **UNHOUSE** | | | | | | |
| | By midnight pulleys that unhouse the tomb. | 14 | 10 | 10 | 16 | 10 |
| **UNHURT** | | | | | | |
| | Alone's unhurt, so the blind man sees best. | 50 | 9 | 30 | 59 | 9 |
| **UNICORN** | | | | | | |
| | And the unicorn evils run them through; | 68 | 16 | 42 | 77 | 16 |
| **UNJUDGING** | | | | | | |
| | Die in unjudging love. | 106 | 12 | 64 | 117 | 12 |
| **UNKIND** | | | | | | |
| | And Noah's rekindled now unkind dove | 113 | 5 | 69 | 125 | 5 |
| **UNKNOWING** | | | | | | |
| | Where still they sleep unknowing of their ghost. | 26 | 20 | 16 | 31 | 20 |
| | Lie all unknowing of the grave sin-eater. | 47 | 8 | 27 | 55 | 8 |

|  | U.K. | | | U.S. | |
|---|---|---|---|---|---|
|  | Page | Line | Poem | Page | Line |
| UNKNOWN | | | | | |
| One who is most unknown, | 117 | 16 | 71 | 129 | 16 |
| In the birth bloody room unknown | 137 | 10 | 82 | 154 | 10 |
| In the unknown, famous light of great | 171 | 20 | 88 | 191 | 20 |
| UNLOCKED | | | | | |
| And all the dry seabed unlocked, | 4 | 8 | 3 | 4 | 8 |
| UNLOCKING | | | | | |
| Locking, unlocking, the murdered strangers weave, | 117 | 15 | 71 | 129 | 15 |
| UNLUCKILY | | | | | |
| Unluckily for a death | 109 | 1 | 67 | 120 | 1 |
| Unluckily for a Death | 109 | | 67 | 120 | |
| UNMADE | | | | | |
| All night in the unmade park | 112 | 13 | 68 | 124 | 13 |
| UNMANLY | | | | | |
| Roll unmanly over this turning tuft, | 60 | 19 | 36 | 69 | 19 |
| UNMANNINGLY | | | | | |
| For who unmanningly haunts the mountain ravened eaves | 163 | 1 | 86 | 182 | 1 |
| UNMINDING | | | | | |
| Under the unminding skies, | 105 | 6 | 64 | 116 | 6 |
| UNMORTAL | | | | | |
| My man of leaves and the bronze root, mortal, unmortal, | 35 | 16 | 20 | 40 | 16 |
| UNMOURNING | | | | | |
| Secret by the unmourning water | 101 | 22 | 62 | 112 | 22 |
| UNPACKS | | | | | |
| Unpacks the head that, like a sleepy ghost, | 10 | 3 | 7 | 11 | 3 |
| UNPIN | | | | | |
| Where no cold is, the skinning gales unpin | 24 | 22 | 15 | 29 | 22 |
| UNPLANTED | | | | | |
| And the unplanted ghost. | 30 | 12 | 18 | 35 | 12 |
| UNPRICKED | | | | | |
| Pack back the downed bone. If the unpricked ball of my breath | 97 | 2 | 59 | 108 | 2 |
| UNRAVEL | | | | | |
| Rage me back to the making house. My hand unravel | 97 | 12 | 59 | 108 | 12 |
| UNRAVELLER | | | | | |
| The green unraveller | 11 | 9 | 8 | 12 | 9 |
| UNRAVELS | | | | | |
| Beginning with doom in the bulb, the spring unravels, | 35 | 7 | 20 | 40 | 7 |
| UNREINED | | | | | |
| Whales unreined from the green grave | 113 | 8 | 69 | 125 | 8 |
| UNREST | | | | | |
| There was calm to be done in his safe unrest, | 125 | 11 | 74 | 139 | 11 |

| | U.K. | | | U.S. | |
|---|---|---|---|---|---|
| | *Page* | *Line* | *Poem* | *Page* | *Line* |

UNRIDDLE

| | | | | | |
|---|---|---|---|---|---|
| Can time unriddle, and the cupboard stone, | 56 | 3 | 34 | 65 | 3 |

UNRIVALLED

| | | | | | |
|---|---|---|---|---|---|
| That other sun, the jealous coursing of the un-rivalled blood. | 127 | 14 | 75 | 141 | 14 |

UNROLLED

| | | | | | |
|---|---|---|---|---|---|
| As the food and flames of the snow, a man un-rolled | 119 | 13 | 72 | 131 | 13 |

UNRULY

| | | | | | |
|---|---|---|---|---|---|
| I hug to love with my unruly scrawl | 10 | 8 | 7 | 11 | 8 |

UNSACRED

| | | | | | |
|---|---|---|---|---|---|
| Her faith that this last night for his unsacred sake | 166 | 5 | 86 | 186 | 5 |

UNSAFE

| | | | | | |
|---|---|---|---|---|---|
| Under the arc of the sky they are unsafe. | 50 | 5 | 30 | 59 | 5 |

UNSEEING

| | | | | | |
|---|---|---|---|---|---|
| Through his unseeing eyes to the roots of the sea. | | | 91 | 200 | 17 |

UNSEEN

| | | | | | |
|---|---|---|---|---|---|
| Unseen by stranger-eyes | 58 | 7 | 35 | 67 | 7 |

UNSEX

| | | | | | |
|---|---|---|---|---|---|
| Unsex the skeleton this mountain minute, | 75 | 16 | 44 | 84 | 16 |

UNSHELVE

| | | | | | |
|---|---|---|---|---|---|
| Unshelve that all my gristles have a gown | 56 | 6 | 34 | 65 | 6 |

UNSHODDEN

| | | | | | |
|---|---|---|---|---|---|
| From the first print of the unshodden foot, the lifting | 20 | 10 | 13 | 24 | 10 |

UNSKATED

| | | | | | |
|---|---|---|---|---|---|
| Lie this fifth month unskated, and the birds have flown; | 49 | 9 | 29 | 58 | 9 |

UNSPENT

| | | | | | |
|---|---|---|---|---|---|
| Some life, yet unspent, might explode | 64 | 12 | 39 | 73 | 12 |

UNSUCKED

| | | | | | |
|---|---|---|---|---|---|
| Who could hack out your unsucked heart, | 70 | 18 | 43 | 79 | 22 |

UNSUCKLED

| | | | | | |
|---|---|---|---|---|---|
| My clay unsuckled and my salt unborn, | 32 | 10 | 18 | 37 | 16 |

UNTIL

| | | | | | |
|---|---|---|---|---|---|
| Stale of Adam's brine until, vision | 29 | 3 | 17 | 34 | 7 |
| Lie watching yellow until the golden weather | 82 | 23 | 48 | 91 | 23 |
| Storm me forever over her grave until | 88 | 10 | 52 | 97 | 10 |
| Never until the mankind making | 101 | 1 | 62 | 112 | 1 |
| Until the Sunday sombre bell at dark | 111 | 6 | 68 | 123 | 6 |
| Made all day until bell time | 112 | 7 | 68 | 124 | 7 |
| Until that one loved least | 118 | 7 | 71 | 130 | 11 |
| Until the turbulent new born | 138 | 10 | 82 | 155 | 10 |
| Never, my girl, until tolled to sleep by the stern | 162 | 21 | 86 | 181 | 21 |
| This night and each vast night until the stern bell talks | 164 | 2 | 86 | 183 | 9 |
| To fiery tyburn over the wrestle of elms until | 167 | 9 | 87 | 187 | 9 |

UNTIL (continued)

| | U.K. | | | U.S. | |
|---|---|---|---|---|---|
| | Page | Line | Poem | Page | Line |
| Until I die he will not leave my side.) | | | 91 | 201 | 19 |
| UNTO | | | | | |
| And I am dumb to mouth unto my veins | 9 | 9 | 6 | 10 | 9 |
| Come unto sea-stuck towers, at the fibre scaling, | 37 | 23 | 20 | 43 | 6 |
| Faithlessly unto Him | 172 | 18 | 88 | 192 | 18 |
| UNWHOLESOME | | | | | |
| All, men my madmen, the unwholesome wind | 19 | 21 | 12 | 23 | 6 |
| UNWINDING | | | | | |
| The unwinding, song by rock, | 95 | 5 | 58 | 105 | 5 |
| UNWRINKLES | | | | | |
| The fruit of man unwrinkles in the stars, | 24 | 10 | 15 | 29 | 10 |
| UNWRINKLING | | | | | |
| A chrysalis unwrinkling on the iron, | 54 | 10 | 33 | 63 | 10 |
| UP | | | | | |
| Split up the brawned womb's weathers, | 1 | 14 | 2 | 1 | 14 |
| Hold up the noisy sea and drop her birds, | 2 | 15 | 2 | 2 | 15 |
| Gives up its dead to such a working sea; | 5 | 3 | 3 | 5 | 3 |
| And conjured up a carcass shape | 5 | 11 | 3 | 5 | 11 |
| Lights up the living worm. | 6 | 6 | 4 | 6 | 6 |
| And the heart gives up its dead. | 6 | 24 | 4 | 7 | 6 |
| The dead turns up its eye; | 11 | 3 | 8 | 12 | 3 |
| Pushed up their hair, the dry wind steers | 11 | 5 | 8 | 12 | 5 |
| Raise up this red-eyed earth? | 15 | 3 | 10 | 17 | 3 |
| Up naked stairs, a turtle in a hearse, | 18 | 4 | 12 | 21 | 4 |
| Drive children up like bruises to the thumb, | 18 | 14 | 12 | 21 | 14 |
| The word flowed up, translating to the heart | 22 | 23 | 14 | 27 | 23 |
| Raised up a voice, and, climbing on the words, | 26 | 22 | 16 | 32 | 2 |
| Spat up from the resuffered pain. | 28 | 24 | 17 | 34 | 4 |
| Thrusting the tom-thumb vision up the iron mile. | 38 | 6 | 20 | 43 | 16 |
| Up rose the Abraham-man, mad for my sake, | 46 | 19 | 27 | 54 | 19 |
| A stem cementing, wrestled up the tower, | 54 | 5 | 33 | 63 | 5 |
| Sailed up the sun; | 54 | 8 | 33 | 63 | 8 |
| Soaks up the sewing tides), | 56 | 12 | 34 | 65 | 12 |
| Or spirit up a cloud, | 56 | 26 | 34 | 66 | 5 |
| High lord esquire, speak up the singing cloud, | 60 | 17 | 36 | 69 | 17 |
| Would wither up, and any boy of love | 63 | 3 | 38 | 72 | 3 |
| Split all ends up they shan't crack; | 68 | 17 | 42 | 77 | 17 |
| The child that sucketh long is shooting up, | 71 | 16 | 44 | 80 | 16 |
| From Jesu's sleeve trumped up the king of spots, | 73 | 12 | 44 | 82 | 12 |
| Her molten flight up cinder-nesting columns, | 78 | 26 | 46 | 88 | 3 |
| 'His mother's womb had a tongue that lapped up mud,' | 79 | 20 | 46 | 89 | 1 |
| By the curve of the nude mouth or the laugh up the sleeve. | 85 | 12 | 50 | 94 | 12 |
| Morning smack of the spade that wakes up sleep, | 87 | 6 | 52 | 96 | 6 |
| You have kicked from a dark den, leaped up the whinnying light, | 92 | 15 | 55 | 101 | 21 |

524

| | U.K. | | | U.S. | |
|---|---|---|---|---|---|
| | *Page* | *Line* | *Poem* | *Page* | *Line* |
| A blazing red harsh head tear up | 93 | 29 | 56 | 103 | 9 |
| Puffing the pounds of manna up through the dew to heaven, | 94 | 5 | 57 | 104 | 5 |
| Dragging him up the stairs to one who lies dead. | 100 | 20 | 61 | 111 | 20 |
| But nobody chained him up. | 111 | 12 | 68 | 123 | 12 |
| With his stick that picked up leaves. | 111 | 24 | 68 | 123 | 24 |
| In fountains of origin gave up their love, | 113 | 9 | 69 | 125 | 9 |
| A man torn up mourns in the sole night. | 115 | 21 | 69 | 127 | 21 |
| Will dive up to his tears. | 117 | 18 | 71 | 129 | 18 |
| Him up and he ran like a wind after the kindling flight | 122 | 9 | 72 | 135 | 9 |
| And this day's sun leapt up the sky out of her thighs | 127 | 4 | 75 | 141 | 4 |
| Up through the lubber crust of Wales | 132 | 24 | 78 | 147 | 24 |
| Up to his head in his blood, | 134 | 9 | 79 | 150 | 9 |
| As the sails drank up the hail of thunder | 154 | 7 | 83 | 172 | 7 |
| Toppling up the boatside in a snow of light! | 154 | 18 | 83 | 172 | 18 |
| Up and down the greater waves | 156 | 11 | 83 | 174 | 19 |
| Up to the swallow thronged loft by the shadow of my hand, | 160 | 25 | 85 | 180 | 2 |
| And gallows, up the rays of his eyes the small birds of the bay | 167 | 4 | 87 | 187 | 4 |
| UPCASTING | | | | | |
| The cockerel's tide upcasting from the fire. | 51 | 21 | 31 | 60 | 21 |
| UPCOMING | | | | | |
| Yawn to his upcoming. | 144 | 14 | 82 | 161 | 14 |
| UPGIVEN | | | | | |
| Of the nightingale's din and tale! The upgiven ghost | 165 | 3 | 86 | 184 | 11 |
| UPHEAVAL | | | | | |
| But blessed be hail and upheaval | 158 | 20 | 84 | 177 | 20 |
| UPON | | | | | |
| To drift or drown upon the seas | 8 | 8 | 5 | 9 | 8 |
| The itch of man upon the baby's thigh, | 12 | 12 | 9 | 13 | 12 |
| Rehearsing heat upon a raw-edged nerve. | 12 | 19 | 9 | 13 | 19 |
| And cast a shadow crab upon the land, | 16 | 4 | 11 | 19 | 4 |
| Stamp of the minted face upon the moon; | 22 | 10 | 14 | 27 | 10 |
| My mothers-eyed, upon the tops of trees; | 26 | 9 | 16 | 31 | 9 |
| My blood upon the tempered dead, forcing | 28 | 19 | 17 | 33 | 19 |
| The crutch that marrow taps upon their sleep, | 30 | 14 | 18 | 35 | 14 |
| The wild pigs' wood, and slime upon the trees, | 30 | 20 | 18 | 35 | 20 |
| This wine upon a foreign tree | 39 | 2 | 21 | 45 | 2 |
| Time upon time and towers of the skies | 53 | 19 | 32 | 62 | 19 |
| Arc-lamped thrown back upon the cutting flood. | 73 | 10 | 44 | 82 | 10 |
| His golden yesterday asleep upon the iris | 127 | 3 | 75 | 141 | 3 |
| Sang upon origin! | 142 | 6 | 82 | 159 | 6 |
| Stream upon his martyrdom | 147 | 16 | 82 | 164 | 16 |

UPON (continued)

|  | U.K. | | | U.S. | |
|---|---|---|---|---|---|
|  | *Page* | *Line* | *Poem* | *Page* | *Line* |
| Trot and gallop with gulls upon them | 156 | 21 | 83 | 175 | 9 |
| UPRIGHT | | | | | |
| An upright man in the antipodes | 77 | 23 | 45 | 86 | 23 |
| And upright Adam | 142 | 5 | 82 | 159 | 5 |
| UPROAR | | | | | |
| All birds and beasts of the linked night uproar and chime | 177 | 15 | 90 | 198 | 14 |
| UPSAILING | | | | | |
| And the bidden dust upsailing | 141 | 9 | 82 | 158 | 9 |
| UPWARD | | | | | |
| And dropped on dreaming and the upward sky. | 26 | 5 | 16 | 31 | 5 |
| As the green blooms ride upward, to the drive of time; | 49 | 3 | 29 | 58 | 3 |
| URCHIN | | | | | |
| If I were tickled by the urchin hungers | 12 | 18 | 9 | 13 | 18 |
| Who have brought forth the urchin grief. | 84 | 6 | 49 | 93 | 12 |
| URN | | | | | |
| Over the urn of sabbaths | 131 | 14 | 77 | 145 | 20 |
| From the vultured urn | 141 | 12 | 82 | 158 | 12 |
| Out of the urn the size of a man | 154 | 21 | 83 | 173 | 1 |
| US | | | | | |
| We are the dark deniers, let us summon | 2 | 7 | 2 | 2 | 7 |
| Now see, alone in us, | 126 | 12 | 74 | 140 | 12 |
| Exiled in us we arouse the soft, | 126 | 15 | 74 | 140 | 15 |
| Us forgive | 129 | 18 | 77 | 143 | 18 |
| Us your death that myselves the believers | 129 | 19 | 77 | 143 | 19 |
| Come let us die.' | 168 | 8 | 87 | 188 | 12 |
| UTTER | | | | | |
| I never thought to utter or think | 107 | 16 | 65 | 118 | 16 |
| Erupt, fountain, and enter to utter for ever | 131 | 23 | 77 | 146 | 5 |
| UTTERS | | | | | |
| That utters all love hunger | 10 | 9 | 7 | 11 | 9 |

# ENTRIES UNDER V

| | | | | | |
|---|---|---|---|---|---|
| VAGUENESSES | | | | | |
| Were vaguenesses enough and the sweet lies plenty, | 48 | 21 | 28 | 56 | 21 |
| VAIN | | | | | |
| Is corner-cast, breath's rag, scrawled weed, a vain | 78 | 9 | 46 | 87 | 9 |
| Crying in vain | 139 | 14 | 82 | 156 | 14 |

|  | U.K. | | | U.S. | |
|---|---|---|---|---|---|
|  | Page | Line | Poem | Page | Line |
| **VALE** | | | | | |
| As the rain falls, hail on the fleece, as the vale mist rides | 164 | 8 | 86 | 183 | 15 |
| Crystal harbour vale | 168 | 13 | 87 | 188 | 17 |
| **VALES** | | | | | |
| And floating fields from the farm in the cup of the vales, | 119 | 3 | 72 | 131 | 3 |
| In the river wended vales where the tale was told. | 119 | 10 | 72 | 131 | 10 |
| When cold as snow he should run the wended vales among | 120 | 20 | 72 | 133 | 5 |
| That a man knelt alone in the cup of the vales, | 122 | 5 | 72 | 135 | 5 |
| Vales where he prayed to come to the last harm | 122 | 29 | 72 | 136 | 9 |
| **VALLEY** | | | | | |
| My world is cypress, and an English valley. | 31 | 13 | 18 | 36 | 13 |
| Smoke hill and hophead's valley, | 38 | 4 | 20 | 43 | 14 |
| Time, in a rider rising, from the harnessed valley; | 49 | 21 | 29 | 58 | 21 |
| In the least valley of sackcloth to mourn | 101 | 12 | 62 | 112 | 12 |
| Valley and sahara in a shell, | 152 | 18 | 83 | 170 | 10 |
| **VALLEYS** | | | | | |
| Insects and valleys hold her thighs hard, | 156 | 6 | 83 | 174 | 14 |
| **VAMPIRE** | | | | | |
| That the vampire laugh. | 30 | 18 | 18 | 35 | 18 |
| **VAN** | | | | | |
| Out of the wrinkled undertaker's van, | 72 | 12 | 44 | 81 | 12 |
| And, Rip Van Winkle from a timeless cradle, | 72 | 13 | 44 | 81 | 13 |
| **VANISHED** | | | | | |
| All blood-signed assailings and vanished marriages in which he had no lovely part | 114 | 20 | 69 | 126 | 20 |
| **VANISHING** | | | | | |
| The vanishing of the musical ship-work and the chucked bells, | 95 | 8 | 58 | 105 | 8 |
| **VANITY** | | | | | |
| Crowing to Lazarus the morning is vanity, | 37 | 8 | 20 | 42 | 14 |
| He films my vanity. | 69 | 25 | 43 | 79 | 1 |
| **VAST** | | | | | |
| This night and each vast night until the stern bell talks | 164 | 2 | 86 | 183 | 9 |
| But her faith that each vast night and the saga of prayer | 166 | 3 | 86 | 186 | 3 |
| **VAULT** | | | | | |
| Over the vault of ridings with his hound at heel, | 49 | 5 | 29 | 58 | 5 |
| Through the last vault and vegetable groyne, | 78 | 7 | 46 | 87 | 7 |
| **VAULTED** | | | | | |
| Is always lost in her vaulted breath, | 153 | 20 | 83 | 171 | 16 |
| **VAULTING** | | | | | |
| And the vaulting bird be still. O my true love, hold me. | 110 | 26 | 67 | 122 | 4 |

|  | U.K. | | | U.S. | |
|  | Page | Line | Poem | Page | Line |
| Their breast, the vaulting does roister, the horned bucks climb | 177 | 13 | 90 | 198 | 12 |
| VAULTS | | | | | |
| Rip of the vaults, I took my marrow-ladle | 72 | 11 | 44 | 81 | 11 |
| VEGETABLE | | | | | |
| In your young years the vegetable century. | 60 | 12 | 36 | 69 | 12 |
| Through the last vault and vegetable groyne, | 78 | 7 | 46 | 87 | 7 |
| How, through the halfmoon's vegetable eye, | 81 | 3 | 47 | 90 | 3 |
| VEIL | | | | | |
| Foster the light nor veil the manshaped moon, | 60 | 1 | 36 | 69 | 1 |
| Through veil and fin and fire and coil | 69 | 23 | 43 | 78 | 23 |
| To veil belladonna and let the dry eyes perceive | 85 | 10 | 50 | 94 | 10 |
| The invoked, shrouding veil at the cap of the face, | 91 | 5 | 55 | 100 | 5 |
| Golden dissolving under the water veil. | 115 | 9 | 69 | 127 | 9 |
| Are making under the green, laid veil | 151 | 21 | 83 | 169 | 9 |
| And stunned and still on the green, laid veil | 156 | 3 | 83 | 174 | 11 |
| VEILED | | | | | |
| He wept from the crest of grief, he prayed to the veiled sky | 120 | 7 | 72 | 132 | 12 |
| VEIN | | | | | |
| Of skin and vein around the well | 8 | 2 | 5 | 9 | 2 |
| I blow the stammel feather in the vein. | 32 | 8 | 18 | 37 | 14 |
| Make desolation in the vein, | 39 | 12 | 21 | 45 | 12 |
| Burning! Night and the vein of birds in the winged, sloe wrist | 164 | 21 | 86 | 184 | 7 |
| Of blood! The bird loud vein! The saga from mermen | 165 | 7 | 86 | 184 | 15 |
| VEINED | | | | | |
| (But nothing bore, no mouthing babe to the veined hives | 178 | 1 | 90 | 199 | 2 |
| Veined his poor hand I held, and I saw | | | 91 | 200 | 16 |
| VEINS | | | | | |
| A weather in the quarter of the veins | 6 | 4 | 4 | 6 | 4 |
| My veins flowed with the Eastern weather; | 7 | 17 | 5 | 8 | 17 |
| And I am dumb to mouth unto my veins | 9 | 9 | 6 | 10 | 9 |
| Before the veins were shaking in their sieve, | 23 | 4 | 14 | 28 | 4 |
| Heir to the scalding veins that hold love's drop, costly | 28 | 9 | 17 | 33 | 9 |
| Storm her sped heart, hand with beheaded veins | 79 | 8 | 46 | 88 | 11 |
| Claw of the crabbed veins squeeze from each red particle | 91 | 21 | 55 | 100 | 21 |
| With my red veins full of money, | 99 | 7 | 60 | 110 | 7 |
| The grains beyond age, the dark veins of her mother, | 101 | 21 | 62 | 112 | 21 |
| VELVET | | | | | |
| And the velvet dead inch out. | 56 | 21 | 34 | 65 | 21 |

|  | U.K. | | | U.S. | |
|---|---|---|---|---|---|
|  | Page | Line | Poem | Page | Line |
| Quickness of hand in the velvet glove | 107 | 12 | 65 | 118 | 12 |
| VENOM | | | | | |
| When the worm builds with the gold straws of venom | 76 | 21 | 44 | 85 | 21 |
| VENOM'S | | | | | |
| 'A lizard darting with black venom's thread | 79 | 23 | 46 | 89 | 4 |
| VENUS | | | | | |
| Tread, like a naked Venus, | 10 | 12 | 7 | 11 | 12 |
| Or, masted venus, through the paddler's bowl | 54 | 7 | 33 | 63 | 7 |
| Venus lies star-struck in her wound | 153 | 21 | 83 | 171 | 17 |
| VENUSWISE | | | | | |
| Shall it be said that, venuswise, | 44 | 8 | 25 | 52 | 8 |
| VERBS | | | | | |
| I learnt the verbs of will, and had my secret; | 21 | 15 | 13 | 25 | 15 |
| VERGE | | | | | |
| Now the heron grieves in the weeded verge. Through windows | 168 | 23 | 87 | 189 | 8 |
| VERTICALS | | | | | |
| Rung bone and blade, the verticals of Adam, | 71 | 23 | 44 | 80 | 23 |
| VERY | | | | | |
| And the sun grew round that very day. | 160 | 10 | 85 | 179 | 10 |
| VESSEL | | | | | |
| Vessel of abscesses and exultation's shell, | 91 | 3 | 55 | 100 | 3 |
| VIBRATIONS | | | | | |
| No longer will the vibrations of the sun desire on | 127 | 8 | 75 | 141 | 8 |
| VICE | | | | | |
| Know now the flesh's lock and vice, | 33 | 20 | 19 | 39 | 2 |
| Crack like a spring in a vice, bone breaking April, | 49 | 17 | 29 | 58 | 17 |
| VILLAGE | | | | | |
| May a humble village labour | 43 | 1 | 24 | 50 | 8 |
| A village green may scold him | 43 | 10 | 24 | 50 | 17 |
| VILLAGES | | | | | |
| In the departed villages. The nightingale, | 121 | 2 | 72 | 133 | 17 |
| The singing breaks in the snow shoed villages of wishes | 123 | 3 | 72 | 136 | 13 |
| Under the floating villages, | 157 | 10 | 83 | 176 | 2 |
| VINE | | | | | |
| By sipping at the vine of days. | 8 | 12 | 5 | 9 | 12 |
| Knocked in the flesh that decked the vine, | 39 | 7 | 21 | 45 | 7 |
| VINEGAR | | | | | |
| Time's nerve in vinegar, the gallow grave | 75 | 6 | 44 | 84 | 6 |
| Cut Christbread spitting vinegar and all | 95 | 16 | 58 | 105 | 16 |
| VINEYARD | | | | | |
| Drunk as a vineyard snail, flailed like an octopus, | 91 | 7 | 55 | 100 | 7 |
| VIPERISH | | | | | |
| When his viperish fuse hangs looped with flames under the brand | 168 | 4 | 87 | 188 | 8 |

VIRGIL

| | U.K. | | | U.S. | |
| | *Page* | *Line* | *Poem* | *Page* | *Line* |
|---|---|---|---|---|---|
| VIRGIL | | | | | |
| By waste seas where the white bear quoted Virgil | 73 | 23 | 44 | 82 | 23 |
| VIRGIN | | | | | |
| May fail to fasten with a virgin o | 18 | 19 | 12 | 21 | 19 |
| Settled on a virgin stronghold | 42 | 19 | 24 | 49 | 19 |
| Quickening for the virgin sea; | 42 | 25 | 24 | 50 | 4 |
| A virgin married at rest. | 93 | 3 | 56 | 102 | 3 |
| Or the chosen virgin | 130 | 12 | 77 | 144 | 12 |
| Sand with legends in its virgin laps | 156 | 4 | 83 | 174 | 12 |
| On the Marriage of a Virgin | 127 | | 75 | 141 | |
| VIRGINITY | | | | | |
| Was miraculous virginity old as loaves and fishes, | 127 | 5 | 75 | 141 | 5 |
| VIRGINS | | | | | |
| In the molested rocks the shell of virgins, | 78 | 18 | 46 | 87 | 18 |
| VIRTUE | | | | | |
| The seas to service that her wood-tongued virtue | 87 | 22 | 52 | 96 | 22 |
| VIRTUES | | | | | |
| And all the deadly virtues plague my death! | 175 | 31 | 89 | 196 | 12 |
| VISION | | | | | |
| I spelt my vision with a hand and hair, | 26 | 23 | 16 | 32 | 3 |
| Through vision and the girdered nerve. | 28 | 4 | 17 | 33 | 4 |
| Stale of Adam's brine until, vision | 29 | 3 | 17 | 34 | 7 |
| And the flame in the flesh's vision. | 34 | 9 | 19 | 39 | 15 |
| Thrusting the tom-thumb vision up the iron mile. | 38 | 6 | 20 | 43 | 16 |
| Suffer the slash of vision by the fin-green stubble, | 38 | 7 | 20 | 43 | 17 |
| John's beast, Job's patience, and the fibs of vision, | 41 | 21 | 23 | 48 | 3 |
| Suffer the first vision that set fire to the stars. | 108 | 18 | 66 | 119 | 18 |
| Of saints to their vision! | 142 | 12 | 82 | 159 | 12 |
| Vision and Prayer | 137 | | 82 | 154 | |
| VISIONS | | | | | |
| These once-blind eyes have breathed a wind of visions, | 80 | 1 | 46 | 89 | 9 |
| VOICE | | | | | |
| And to the voice that, like a voice of hunger, | 21 | 5 | 13 | 25 | 5 |
| Raised up a voice, and, climbing on the words, | 26 | 22 | 16 | 32 | 2 |
| Fear not the screws that turn the voice, | 33 | 23 | 19 | 39 | 5 |
| Greek in the Irish sea the ageless voice: | 41 | 22 | 23 | 48 | 4 |
| Shape all her whelps with the long voice of water, | 55 | 2 | 33 | 64 | 5 |
| Blasts back the trumpet voice. | 57 | 6 | 34 | 66 | 13 |
| The sea speaks in a kingly voice, | 66 | 11 | 40 | 75 | 11 |
| The voice of bird on coral prays. | 83 | 18 | 49 | 92 | 18 |

|  | U.K. | | | U.S. | |
|  | Page | Line | Poem | Page | Line |
| To the built voice, or fly with winter to the bells, | 86 | 10 | 51 | 95 | 10 |
| Argument of the hewn voice, gesture and psalm, | 88 | 9 | 52 | 97 | 9 |
| The parched and raging voice? | 91 | 22 | 55 | 100 | 22 |
| Has a voice and a house, and there and here you must couch and cry. | 98 | 2 | 59 | 109 | 5 |
| One voice in chains declaims | 115 | 6 | 69 | 127 | 6 |
| The voice of the dust of water from the withered spring | 121 | 5 | 72 | 133 | 20 |
| And the harp shaped voice of the water's dust plucks in a fold | 121 | 24 | 72 | 134 | 19 |
| Above her folded head, and the soft feathered voice | 122 | 2 | 72 | 135 | 2 |
| And the sky of birds in the plumed voice charmed | 122 | 8 | 72 | 135 | 8 |
| The voice of children says | 125 | 9 | 74 | 139 | 9 |
| Summoning a child's voice from a webfoot stone, | 133 | 18 | 78 | 149 | 1 |
| A voice in the erected air, | 134 | 25 | 79 | 151 | 3 |
| Cry. My voice burns in his hand. | 148 | 15 | 82 | 165 | 15 |
| VOICES | | | | | |
| Some of the oaken voices, from the roots | 16 | 14 | 11 | 19 | 14 |
| Dazzle this face of voices on the moon-turned table, | 37 | 18 | 20 | 43 | 1 |
| Of mortal voices to the ninnies' choir, | 60 | 16 | 36 | 69 | 16 |
| The voices of all the drowned swam on the wind. | 136 | 8 | 81 | 153 | 8 |
| Always good-bye, cried the voices through the shell, | 154 | 1 | 83 | 172 | 1 |
| VOID | | | | | |
| Abstracted all the letters of the void; | 22 | 21 | 14 | 27 | 21 |
| Here in this spring, stars float along the void; | 45 | 1 | 26 | 53 | 1 |
| And, in that brambled void, | 171 | 25 | 88 | 191 | 25 |
| VOIDS | | | | | |
| The signal moon is zero in their voids. | 1 | 12 | 2 | 1 | 12 |
| Of children go who, from their voids, | 11 | 17 | 8 | 12 | 17 |
| VOLLEY | | | | | |
| Red in an Austrian volley. | 31 | 15 | 18 | 36 | 15 |
| VOWS | | | | | |
| Down the long walks of their vows. | 124 | 4 | 73 | 138 | 4 |
| Cool in your vows. | 163 | 24 | 86 | 183 | 5 |
| Ever and ever by all your vows believe and fear | 166 | 8 | 86 | 186 | 8 |
| And druid herons' vows | 172 | 23 | 88 | 192 | 23 |
| VOWELLED | | | | | |
| Some let me make you of the vowelled beeches, | 16 | 13 | 11 | 19 | 13 |
| VOWELS | | | | | |
| By Lava's light split through the oyster vowels | 74 | 3 | 44 | 83 | 3 |
| VOYAGE | | | | | |
| The stoved bones' voyage downward | 38 | 9 | 20 | 43 | 19 |

VOYAGE (continued)

|  | U.K. |  |  | U.S. |  |
|  | Page | Line | Poem | Page | Line |
| Let the tale's sailor from a Christian voyage | 76 | 9 | 44 | 85 | 9 |
| For my voyage to begin to the end of my wound, | 136 | 11 | 81 | 153 | 11 |
| The voyage to ruin I must run, | 172 | 24 | 88 | 192 | 24 |
| VOYAGING |  |  |  |  |  |
| Voyaging clockwise off the symboled harbour, | 36 | 8 | 20 | 41 | 8 |
| VULTURED |  |  |  |  |  |
| From the vultured urn | 141 | 12 | 82 | 158 | 12 |

# ENTRIES UNDER W

| WADED |  |  |  |  |  |
| Pleading in the waded bay for the seed to flow | 176 | 7 | 90 | 197 | 7 |
| WADING |  |  |  |  |  |
| All night lost and long wading in the wake of the she- | 122 | 18 | 72 | 135 | 18 |
| WAGES |  |  |  |  |  |
| But for the common wages | 128 | 10 | 76 | 142 | 10 |
| Who pay no praise or wages | 128 | 19 | 76 | 142 | 19 |
| WAGGED |  |  |  |  |  |
| Rounds to look at the red, wagged root. | 77 | 12 | 45 | 86 | 12 |
| WAGGING |  |  |  |  |  |
| Behind a pot of ferns the wagging clock | 16 | 17 | 11 | 19 | 17 |
| WAGONS |  |  |  |  |  |
| And honoured among wagons I was prince of the apple towns | 159 | 6 | 85 | 178 | 6 |
| WAGS |  |  |  |  |  |
| Whose beard wags in Egyptian wind. | 63 | 15 | 38 | 72 | 15 |
| WAIL |  |  |  |  |  |
| Lapped among herods wail | 96 | 14 | 58 | 106 | 14 |
| WAILED |  |  |  |  |  |
| But wailed and nested in the sky-blue wall | 126 | 7 | 74 | 140 | 7 |
| WAINS |  |  |  |  |  |
| In the wains tonned so high that the wisps of the hay | 176 | 14 | 90 | 197 | 14 |
| WAITING |  |  |  |  |  |
| Through no regret of leaving woman waiting | 48 | 14 | 28 | 56 | 14 |
| Waiting with phoenix under | 109 | 2 | 67 | 120 | 2 |
| WAITS |  |  |  |  |  |
| Assembling waits for the spade's ring on the cage. | 135 | 11 | 80 | 152 | 11 |
| WAKE |  |  |  |  |  |
| O wake in me in my house in the mud | 96 | 1 | 58 | 106 | 1 |
| O wake to see, after a noble fall, | 96 | 18 | 58 | 107 | 1 |

|  | U.K. | | | U.S. | |
|---|---|---|---|---|---|
|  | Page | Line | Poem | Page | Line |
| All night lost and long wading in the wake of the she- | 122 | 18 | 72 | 135 | 18 |
| But heard his bait buck in the wake | 150 | 5 | 83 | 167 | 9 |
| Whales in the wake like capes and Alps | 151 | 1 | 83 | 168 | 9 |
| And wake to the farm forever fled from the childless land. | 161 | 3 | 85 | 180 | 6 |
| And you shall wake, from country sleep, this dawn and each first dawn, | 166 | 11 | 86 | 186 | 11 |
| **WAKEN** |  |  |  |  |  |
| Breast I shall waken | 141 | 5 | 82 | 158 | 5 |
| **WAKES** |  |  |  |  |  |
| Morning smack of the spade that wakes up sleep, | 87 | 6 | 52 | 96 | 6 |
| In the winds' wakes. | 164 | 14 | 86 | 185 | 4 |
| **WAKEWARD-FLASHING** |  |  |  |  |  |
| Over the wakeward-flashing spray | 152 | 1 | 83 | 169 | 13 |
| **WAKING** |  |  |  |  |  |
| How deep the waking in the worlded clouds. | 26 | 25 | 16 | 32 | 5 |
| Nor can I smother the sweet waking.' | 66 | 8 | 40 | 75 | 8 |
| Waking alone in a multitude of loves when morning's light | 127 | 1 | 75 | 141 | 1 |
| I heard, this morning, waking, | 134 | 23 | 79 | 151 | 1 |
| When the morning was waking over the war | 135 | 1 | 80 | 152 | 1 |
| **WALES** |  |  |  |  |  |
| To Wales in my arms. | ix | 1 | 1 | xvii | 1 |
| Under the stars of Wales, | x | 9 | 1 | xviii | 15 |
| The spider-tongued, and the loud hill of Wales) | 17 | 3 | 11 | 20 | 3 |
| Round the parched worlds of Wales and drowned each sun | 87 | 15 | 52 | 96 | 15 |
| Up through the lubber crust of Wales | 132 | 24 | 78 | 147 | 24 |
| **WALK** |  |  |  |  |  |
| Caught by the crabbing sun I walk on fire | 16 | 3 | 11 | 19 | 3 |
| And walk the warring sands by the dead town, | 79 | 6 | 46 | 88 | 9 |
| (Bury the dead for fear that they walk to the grave in labour.) | 99 | 2 | 60 | 110 | 2 |
| Nor walk in the cool of your mortal garden | 110 | 20 | 67 | 121 | 22 |
| After a water-face walk, | 134 | 18 | 79 | 150 | 18 |
| And all the lifted waters walk and leap. | 153 | 16 | 83 | 171 | 12 |
| Herons walk in their shroud, | 170 | 27 | 88 | 190 | 27 |
| And there this night I walk in the white giant's thigh | 176 | 3 | 90 | 197 | 3 |
| **WALKED** |  |  |  |  |  |
| And God walked there who was a fiddling warden | 40 | 5 | 22 | 46 | 5 |
| And walked abroad in a shower of all my days. | 102 | 16 | 63 | 113 | 16 |
| Forgotten mornings when he walked with his mother | 103 | 22 | 63 | 114 | 22 |

WALKED (continued)

| | U.K. | | | U.S. | |
|---|---|---|---|---|---|
| | Page | Line | Poem | Page | Line |
| Or walked on the earth in the evening | 155 | 15 | 83 | 173 | 19 |

WALKING

| | | | | | |
|---|---|---|---|---|---|
| On the horizon walking like the trees | 16 | 10 | 11 | 19 | 10 |
| Erect a walking centre in the shroud, | 56 | 27 | 34 | 66 | 6 |
| A merry manshape of your walking circle. | 61 | 6 | 36 | 70 | 6 |
| Scraped at my cradle in a walking word | 71 | 11 | 44 | 80 | 11 |
| Yet she deludes with walking the nightmarish room, | 108 | 7 | 66 | 119 | 7 |
| On the madhouse boards worn thin by my walking tears. | 108 | 15 | 66 | 119 | 15 |
| The octopus walking into her limbs | 152 | 7 | 83 | 169 | 19 |
| Walking in wishes and lovely for shame | 153 | 9 | 83 | 171 | 5 |
| In the first, spinning place, the spellbound horses walking warm | 160 | 12 | 85 | 179 | 12 |
| Walking in the meadows of his son's eye | | | 91 | 201 | 10 |

WALKS

| | | | | | |
|---|---|---|---|---|---|
| Walks with no wound, nor lightning in her face, | 80 | 10 | 46 | 89 | 18 |
| She sleeps in the narrow trough yet she walks the dust | 108 | 13 | 66 | 119 | 13 |
| Paddocks in the farms of birds. The dead oak walks for love. | 121 | 20 | 72 | 134 | 15 |
| Down the long walks of their vows. | 124 | 4 | 73 | 138 | 4 |
| Under the earth the loud sea walks, | 157 | 14 | 83 | 176 | 6 |
| Of the hearthstone tales my own, lost love; and the soul walks | 164 | 4 | 86 | 183 | 11 |

WALL

| | | | | | |
|---|---|---|---|---|---|
| Turning the riderless dead by the channel wall. | 36 | 24 | 20 | 42 | 3 |
| Measures his own length on the garden wall | 41 | 12 | 23 | 47 | 12 |
| Once close-up smiling in the wall of pictures, | 73 | 9 | 44 | 82 | 9 |
| Scales the blue wall of spirits; | 83 | 21 | 49 | 93 | 3 |
| O make me a mask and a wall to shut from your spies | 85 | 1 | 50 | 94 | 1 |
| Endure burial under the spelling wall, | 91 | 4 | 55 | 100 | 4 |
| Meet once on a mortal wall | 93 | 23 | 56 | 103 | 3 |
| Of the woven wall | 95 | 6 | 58 | 105 | 6 |
| And the knock of sailing boats on the net webbed wall | 102 | 7 | 63 | 113 | 7 |
| Who admits the delusive light through the bouncing wall, | 108 | 11 | 66 | 119 | 11 |
| But wailed and nested in the sky-blue wall | 126 | 7 | 74 | 140 | 7 |
| Behind the wall thin as a wren's bone? | 137 | 9 | 82 | 154 | 9 |
| Wall hearing the moan | 138 | 5 | 82 | 155 | 5 |
| And the winged wall is torn | 138 | 12 | 82 | 155 | 12 |
| And the multitude's sultry tear turns cool on the weeping wall, | 158 | 17 | 84 | 177 | 17 |

WALL'S

| | | | | | |
|---|---|---|---|---|---|
| Behind the wall's wren | 144 | 5 | 82 | 161 | 5 |

| | U.K. | | | U.S. | |
|---|---|---|---|---|---|
| | *Page* | *Line* | *Poem* | *Page* | *Line* |
| **WALLS** | | | | | |
| That chalk the walls with green girls and their men. | 12 | 16 | 9 | 13 | 16 |
| Bow down the walls of the ferned and foxy woods | 87 | 24 | 52 | 96 | 24 |
| And darkness hung the walls with baskets of snakes, | 114 | 4 | 69 | 126 | 4 |
| And wharves of water where the walls dance and the white cranes stilt. | 168 | 15 | 87 | 188 | 19 |
| **WAND** | | | | | |
| It were a wand or subtle bough, | 134 | 14 | 79 | 150 | 14 |
| **WANDER** | | | | | |
| There he might wander bare | 172 | 1 | 88 | 192 | 1 |
| **WANDERED** | | | | | |
| Come in the morning where I wandered and listened | 103 | 2 | 63 | 114 | 2 |
| **WANDERER** | | | | | |
| And then to awake, and the farm, like a wanderer white | 160 | 6 | 85 | 179 | 6 |
| **WANDERING** | | | | | |
| Throw wide to the wind the gates of the wandering boat | 136 | 10 | 81 | 153 | 10 |
| **WANTING** | | | | | |
| I see the wanting nun saint carved in a garb | 110 | 6 | 67 | 121 | 8 |
| Pool at the wanting centre, in the folds | 123 | 18 | 72 | 137 | 8 |
| Oh all the wanting flesh his enemy | 152 | 19 | 83 | 170 | 11 |
| **WANTON** | | | | | |
| The boy of woman and the wanton starer | 46 | 10 | 27 | 54 | 10 |
| There the dark blade and wanton sighing her down | 113 | 16 | 69 | 125 | 16 |
| On the departed, snow bushed green, wanton in moon light | 121 | 17 | 72 | 134 | 12 |
| In the name of the wanton | 144 | 15 | 82 | 161 | 15 |
| **WAR** | | | | | |
| And barnroofs cockcrow war! | ix | 30 | 1 | xviii | 4 |
| Nor the crossed sticks of war. | 12 | 14 | 9 | 13 | 14 |
| 'War on the spider and the wren! | 66 | 14 | 40 | 75 | 14 |
| War on the destiny of man! | 66 | 15 | 40 | 75 | 15 |
| The skull of the earth is barbed with a war of burning brains and hair. | 96 | 9 | 58 | 106 | 9 |
| When the morning was waking over the war | 135 | 1 | 80 | 152 | 1 |
| I climb to greet the war in which I have no heart but only | 158 | 8 | 84 | 177 | 8 |
| **WARBEARING** | | | | | |
| Over the warbearing line | 42 | 14 | 24 | 49 | 14 |
| **WARDEN** | | | | | |
| And God walked there who was a fiddling warden | 40 | 5 | 22 | 46 | 5 |

WARDS

| | U.K. | | | U.S. | |
|---|---|---|---|---|---|
| | Page | Line | Poem | Page | Line |
| **WARDS** | | | | | |
| Or rides the imagined oceans of the male wards. | 108 | 9 | 66 | 119 | 9 |
| **WARM** | | | | | |
| To-night shall find no dying but alive and warm | 100 | 15 | 61 | 111 | 15 |
| In the first, spinning place, the spellbound horses walking warm | 160 | 12 | 85 | 179 | 12 |
| **WARMED** | | | | | |
| One sun, one manna, warmed and fed. | 21 | 26 | 13 | 26 | 9 |
| **WARM-VEINED** | | | | | |
| The warm-veined double of Time | 134 | 11 | 79 | 150 | 11 |
| **WARMS** | | | | | |
| Warms youth and seed and burns the seeds of age; | 24 | 8 | 15 | 29 | 8 |
| **WARMTH** | | | | | |
| Need no word's warmth. | 21 | 12 | 13 | 25 | 12 |
| **WARN** | | | | | |
| And serve me right as the preachers warn, | 175 | 9 | 89 | 195 | 14 |
| **WARNED** | | | | | |
| Of chemic blood, warned of the coming fury. | 17 | 7 | 11 | 20 | 7 |
| **WARNING** | | | | | |
| From the first secret of the heart, the warning ghost, | 20 | 12 | 13 | 24 | 12 |
| Warning among the folds, and the frozen hold | 119 | 8 | 72 | 131 | 8 |
| **WARRING** | | | | | |
| I make this in a warring absence when | 78 | 1 | 46 | 87 | 1 |
| And walk the warring sands by the dead town, | 79 | 6 | 46 | 88 | 9 |
| I make this in a warring absence | 78 | | 46 | 87 | |
| **WARS** | | | | | |
| Her ropes of heritage, the wars of pardon, | 54 | 21 | 33 | 63 | 21 |
| Innocent between two wars, | 115 | 19 | 69 | 127 | 19 |
| Wars | 167 | 6 | 87 | 187 | 6 |
| **WASTE** | | | | | |
| Above the waste allotments the dawn halts. | 25 | 6 | 15 | 30 | 6 |
| By waste seas where the white bear quoted Virgil | 73 | 23 | 44 | 82 | 23 |
| **WASTED** | | | | | |
| Feeling regret when this is wasted | 48 | 18 | 28 | 56 | 18 |
| **WATCH** | | | | | |
| I sit and watch the worm beneath my nail | 13 | 6 | 9 | 14 | 13 |
| We watch the show of shadows kiss or kill, | 14 | 19 | 10 | 16 | 19 |
| The whispering ears will watch love drummed away | 81 | 6 | 47 | 90 | 6 |
| Watch yellow, wish for wind to blow away | 82 | 19 | 48 | 91 | 19 |
| **WATCHED** | | | | | |
| In the watched dark, quivering through locks and caves, | 118 | 3 | 71 | 130 | 7 |
| **WATCHING** | | | | | |
| We lying by seasand, watching yellow | 82 | 1 | 48 | 91 | 1 |

WATER

| | U.K. | | | U.S. | |
|---|---|---|---|---|---|
| | Page | Line | Poem | Page | Line |
| Lie watching yellow until the golden weather | 82 | 23 | 48 | 91 | 23 |

WATER

| | Page | Line | Poem | Page | Line |
|---|---|---|---|---|---|
| The water lidded lands, | x | 11 | 1 | xviii | 17 |
| I who was shapeless as the water | 7 | 3 | 5 | 8 | 3 |
| Where words and water make a mixture | 8 | 3 | 5 | 9 | 3 |
| The force that drives the water through the rocks | 9 | 6 | 6 | 10 | 6 |
| The hand that whirls the water in the pool | 9 | 11 | 6 | 10 | 11 |
| And after came the imprints on the water, | 22 | 9 | 14 | 27 | 9 |
| Finding the water final, | 36 | 9 | 20 | 41 | 9 |
| The highroad of water where the seabear and Mackerel | 36 | 21 | 20 | 41 | 21 |
| And, clapped in water till the triton dangles, | 37 | 13 | 20 | 42 | 19 |
| They suffer the undead water where the turtle nibbles, | 37 | 22 | 20 | 43 | 5 |
| Shall it be said they sprinkle water | 44 | 6 | 25 | 52 | 6 |
| The horn and ball of water on the frog | 54 | 15 | 33 | 63 | 15 |
| Shape all her whelps with the long voice of water, | 55 | 2 | 33 | 64 | 5 |
| Two heels of water on the floor of seed), | 56 | 24 | 34 | 66 | 3 |
| The climber of the water sex | 69 | 11 | 43 | 78 | 11 |
| Over the water come | 69 | 27 | 43 | 79 | 3 |
| Blunt scythe and water blade. | 70 | 11 | 43 | 79 | 15 |
| He in a book of water tallow-eyed | 74 | 2 | 44 | 83 | 2 |
| Ribbed between desert and water storm, | 82 | 11 | 48 | 91 | 11 |
| Should cure our ills of the water | 82 | 12 | 48 | 91 | 12 |
| In time like outlaw rains on that priest, water, | 86 | 6 | 51 | 95 | 6 |
| Refusal struck like a bell under water | 90 | 12 | 54 | 99 | 12 |
| Zion of the water bead | 101 | 8 | 62 | 112 | 8 |
| Secret by the unmourning water | 101 | 22 | 62 | 112 | 22 |
| With water praying and call of seagull and rook | 102 | 6 | 63 | 113 | 6 |
| Still in the water and singingbirds. | 104 | 8 | 63 | 115 | 10 |
| Water and light, the earth and sky, | 106 | 8 | 64 | 117 | 8 |
| Propped between trees and water | 111 | 3 | 68 | 123 | 3 |
| That lets the trees and water enter | 111 | 5 | 68 | 123 | 5 |
| Drinking water from the chained cup | 111 | 8 | 68 | 123 | 8 |
| Like the water he sat down | 111 | 14 | 68 | 123 | 14 |
| Golden dissolving under the water veil. | 115 | 9 | 69 | 127 | 9 |
| And wind his globe out of your water thread | 117 | 21 | 71 | 129 | 21 |
| Hunger of birds in the fields of the bread of water, | 120 | 17 | 72 | 133 | 2 |
| The voice of the dust of water from the withered spring | 121 | 5 | 72 | 133 | 20 |
| Stream with bells and baying water bounds. The dew rings | 121 | 7 | 72 | 134 | 2 |
| Commoner than water, crueller than truth; | 125 | 3 | 74 | 139 | 3 |
| As a he-god's paddling water skirts, | 132 | 16 | 78 | 147 | 16 |

## WATER (continued)

| | U.K. | | | U.S. | |
|---|---|---|---|---|---|
| | Page | Line | Poem | Page | Line |
| It was sweet to drown in the readymade handy water | 133 | 16 | 78 | 148 | 19 |
| Over the graveyard in the water | 152 | 13 | 83 | 170 | 5 |
| Is old as water and plain as an eel; | 152 | 21 | 83 | 170 | 13 |
| And through the sundered water crawls | 155 | 22 | 83 | 174 | 6 |
| Round her trailed wrist fresh water weaves, | 156 | 9 | 83 | 174 | 17 |
| Earth, air, water, fire, singing into the white act, | 165 | 16 | 86 | 185 | 6 |
| I open the leaves of the water at a passage | 167 | 23 | 87 | 188 | 4 |
| And wharves of water where the walls dance and the white cranes stilt. | 168 | 15 | 87 | 188 | 19 |
| Of dusk and water I see the tilting whispering | 168 | 24 | 87 | 189 | 9 |
| **WATER'S** | | | | | |
| Some let me make you of the water's speeches. | 16 | 16 | 11 | 19 | 16 |
| And the harp shaped voice of the water's dust plucks in a fold | 121 | 24 | 72 | 134 | 19 |
| And nothing shone on the water's face | 150 | 20 | 83 | 168 | 4 |
| **WATER-[BIRDS]** | | | | | |
| My birthday began with the water- | 102 | 11 | 63 | 113 | 11 |
| **WATER-CLOCKS** | | | | | |
| The winder of the water-clocks | 69 | 5 | 43 | 78 | 5 |
| **WATER-FACE** | | | | | |
| After a water-face walk, | 134 | 18 | 79 | 150 | 18 |
| **WATER-LAMMED** | | | | | |
| Or, water-lammed, from the scythe-sided thorn, | 54 | 3 | 33 | 63 | 3 |
| **WATER-PILLARED** | | | | | |
| Down the stacked sea and water-pillared shade, | 79 | 14 | 46 | 88 | 17 |
| **WATER-SPOKEN** | | | | | |
| Sing through the water-spoken prow | 152 | 6 | 83 | 169 | 18 |
| **WATER-TOWER** | | | | | |
| By crane and water-tower by the seedy trees | 49 | 8 | 29 | 58 | 8 |
| **WATER-WOUND** | | | | | |
| Turns the moon-chained and water-wound | 157 | 11 | 83 | 176 | 3 |
| **WATERED** | | | | | |
| My grave is watered by the crossing Jordan. | 31 | 19 | 18 | 37 | 1 |
| **WATERFALLS** | | | | | |
| With men and women and waterfalls | 156 | 1 | 83 | 174 | 9 |
| **WATERS** | | | | | |
| Eternal waters away | vii | 18 | 1 | xv | 18 |
| Of waters cluck and cling, | ix | 29 | 1 | xviii | 3 |
| And swallowed dry the waters of the breast. | 4 | 6 | 3 | 4 | 6 |
| Where once the waters of your face | 11 | 1 | 8 | 12 | 1 |
| Where no sea runs, the waters of the heart | 24 | 2 | 15 | 29 | 2 |
| In sacred waters that no frost could harden, | 40 | 14 | 22 | 46 | 14 |
| Nor when all ponderous heaven's host of waters breaks. | 97 | 20 | 59 | 108 | 20 |
| And all the lifted waters walk and leap. | 153 | 16 | 83 | 171 | 12 |
| The waters shorn. | 164 | 5 | 86 | 183 | 12 |

|  | U.K. | | | U.S. | |
|---|---|---|---|---|---|
|  | *Page* | *Line* | *Poem* | *Page* | *Line* |
| Rage shattered waters kick | 172 | 16 | 88 | 192 | 16 |
| Where once the waters of your face | 11 |  | 8 | 12 |  |
| WATERY |  |  |  |  |  |
| And playing, lovely and watery | 159 | 21 | 85 | 178 | 21 |
| WAVE |  |  |  |  |  |
| Pick the world's ball of wave and froth | 2 | 16 | 2 | 2 | 16 |
| Like an approaching wave I sprawl to ruin. | 79 | 12 | 46 | 88 | 15 |
| In a holy room in a wave; | 84 | 3 | 49 | 93 | 9 |
| On the last street wave praised | 95 | 4 | 58 | 105 | 4 |
| And mark the dark eyed wave, through the eyes of sleep, | 100 | 19 | 61 | 111 | 19 |
| Last night in a raping wave | 113 | 7 | 69 | 125 | 7 |
| Good men, the last wave by, crying how bright | 116 | 7 | 70 | 128 | 7 |
| On my cleaving arm as I blasted in a wave. | 133 | 20 | 78 | 149 | 3 |
| Gull, on the wave with sand in its eyes! And the foal moves | 165 | 12 | 86 | 185 | 2 |
| And every wave of the way | 173 | 14 | 88 | 193 | 14 |
| WAVE'S |  |  |  |  |  |
| Wave's silence, wept white angelus knells. | 171 | 11 | 88 | 191 | 11 |
| WAVES |  |  |  |  |  |
| Or waves break loud on the seashores; | 68 | 21 | 42 | 77 | 21 |
| Through the waves of the fat streets nor the skeleton's thin ways. | 98 | 5 | 59 | 109 | 8 |
| When near and strange wounded on London's waves | 117 | 27 | 71 | 130 | 3 |
| In the praying windows of waves | 150 | 4 | 83 | 167 | 8 |
| Huge weddings in the waves, | 151 | 24 | 83 | 169 | 12 |
| Up and down the greater waves | 156 | 11 | 83 | 174 | 19 |
| The hills have footed the waves away, | 156 | 16 | 83 | 175 | 4 |
| Lowlands of the waves, | 169 | 8 | 87 | 189 | 17 |
| Curlews aloud in the congered waves | 170 | 13 | 88 | 190 | 13 |
| WAXLIGHTS |  |  |  |  |  |
| I damp the waxlights in your tower dome. | 19 | 11 | 12 | 22 | 16 |
| WAX |  |  |  |  |  |
| Turns mine to wax. | 9 | 8 | 6 | 10 | 8 |
| Where no wax is, the candle shows its hairs. | 24 | 12 | 15 | 29 | 12 |
| Let the wax disk babble | 37 | 19 | 20 | 43 | 2 |
| WAX'S |  |  |  |  |  |
| Till tallow I blew from the wax's tower | 74 | 9 | 44 | 83 | 9 |
| WAXES |  |  |  |  |  |
| Heart of Cadaver's candle waxes thin, | 18 | 12 | 12 | 21 | 12 |
| WAY |  |  |  |  |  |
| Twisting on racks when sinews give way, | 68 | 13 | 42 | 77 | 13 |
| The grain that hurries this way from the rim of the grave | 98 | 1 | 59 | 109 | 4 |
| And learn, too late, they grieved it on its way, | 116 | 11 | 70 | 128 | 11 |
| Be you sure the Thief will seek a way sly and sure | 163 | 26 | 86 | 183 | 7 |

## WAY (continued)

|  | U.K. Page | U.K. Line | Poem | U.S. Page | U.S. Line |
|---|---|---|---|---|---|
| Ever and ever he finds a way, as the snow falls, | 164 | 7 | 86 | 183 | 14 |
| Dark is a way and light is a place, | 171 | 22 | 88 | 191 | 22 |
| But dark is a long way. | 172 | 10 | 88 | 192 | 10 |
| And every wave of the way | 173 | 14 | 88 | 193 | 14 |
| The darkest way, and did not turn away, |  |  | 91 | 200 | 2 |

WAYS

|  | U.K. Page | U.K. Line | Poem | U.S. Page | U.S. Line |
|---|---|---|---|---|---|
| Through the waves of the fat streets nor the skeleton's thin ways. | 98 | 5 | 59 | 109 | 8 |
| Good and bad, two ways | 105 | 13 | 64 | 116 | 13 |
| Ways | 146 | 9 | 82 | 163 | 9 |
| I ran my heedless ways, | 160 | 18 | 85 | 179 | 18 |
| Work at their ways to death, | 170 | 14 | 88 | 190 | 14 |

WAYSIDE

|  | U.K. Page | U.K. Line | Poem | U.S. Page | U.S. Line |
|---|---|---|---|---|---|
| Who once were a bloom of wayside brides in the hawed house | 177 | 9 | 90 | 198 | 8 |

WE

|  | U.K. Page | U.K. Line | Poem | U.S. Page | U.S. Line |
|---|---|---|---|---|---|
| We will ride out alone, and then, | x | 8 | 1 | xviii | 14 |
| Where, punctual as death, we ring the stars; | 2 | 3 | 2 | 2 | 3 |
| We are the dark deniers, let us summon | 2 | 7 | 2 | 2 | 7 |
| We summer boys in this four-winded spinning, | 2 | 13 | 2 | 2 | 13 |
| In spring we cross our foreheads with the holly, | 2 | 19 | 2 | 3 | 1 |
| We are the sons of flint and pitch. | 3 | 5 | 2 | 3 | 11 |
| We watch the show of shadows kiss or kill, | 14 | 19 | 10 | 16 | 19 |
| Our strips of stuff that tatter as we move | 15 | 12 | 10 | 17 | 12 |
| For we shall be a shouter like the cock, | 15 | 17 | 10 | 17 | 17 |
| And we shall be fit fellows for a life, | 15 | 20 | 10 | 17 | 20 |
| And there we wept, I and a ghostly other, | 26 | 8 | 16 | 31 | 8 |
| 'This that we tread was, too, your fathers' land.' | 26 | 12 | 16 | 31 | 12 |
| 'But this we tread bears the angelic gangs, | 26 | 13 | 16 | 31 | 13 |
| When we were strangers to the guided seas, | 40 | 7 | 22 | 46 | 7 |
| We in our Eden knew the secret guardian | 40 | 13 | 22 | 46 | 13 |
| We make me mystic as the arm of air, | 52 | 6 | 31 | 61 | 13 |
| We rung our weathering changes on the ladder, | 72 | 17 | 44 | 81 | 17 |
| We lying by seasand, watching yellow | 82 | 1 | 48 | 91 | 1 |
| Bound by a sovereign strip, we lie, | 82 | 18 | 48 | 91 | 18 |
| Can we fend off rock arrival, | 82 | 22 | 48 | 91 | 22 |
| Where at night we stoned the cold and cuckoo | 89 | 8 | 53 | 98 | 8 |
| We hid our fears in that murdering breath, | 125 | 14 | 74 | 139 | 14 |
| O we who could not stir | 126 | 4 | 74 | 140 | 4 |
| One lean sigh when we heard | 126 | 5 | 74 | 140 | 5 |
| Exiled in us we arouse the soft, | 126 | 15 | 74 | 140 | 15 |
| Street we chant the flying sea | 130 | 5 | 77 | 144 | 5 |
| On the silent sea we have heard the sound | 136 | 3 | 81 | 153 | 3 |
| Under the mile off moon we trembled listening | 136 | 5 | 81 | 153 | 5 |
| We heard the sea sound sing, we saw the salt sheet tell. | 136 | 12 | 81 | 153 | 12 |

|  | U.K. | | | U.S. | |
|---|---|---|---|---|---|
|  | Page | Line | Poem | Page | Line |
| Or we shall obey, and ride with you through the drowned. | 136 | 14 | 81 | 153 | 14 |
| And we have come | 146 | 6 | 82 | 163 | 6 |
| For we saw him throw to the swift flood | 149 | 21 | 83 | 167 | 1 |
| We grieve as the blithe birds, never again, leave shingle and elm, | 168 | 9 | 87 | 188 | 13 |
| We lying by seasand | 82 |  | 48 | 91 |  |
| **WEAK** |  |  |  |  |  |
| And this weak house to marrow-columned heaven, | 78 | 8 | 46 | 87 | 8 |
| **WEAKEST** |  |  |  |  |  |
| After such fighting as the weakest know, | 48 | 10 | 28 | 56 | 10 |
| **WEANS** |  |  |  |  |  |
| Weans on an artery the gender's strip; | 71 | 18 | 44 | 80 | 18 |
| **WEAPON** |  |  |  |  |  |
| I make a weapon of an ass's skeleton | 79 | 5 | 46 | 88 | 8 |
| **WEARING** |  |  |  |  |  |
| Wearing the quick away. | 13 | 7 | 9 | 14 | 14 |
| **WEARS** |  |  |  |  |  |
| Says the world wears away? | 45 | 17 | 26 | 53 | 17 |
| **WEAR-WILLOW** |  |  |  |  |  |
| Wear-willow river, grave, | 169 | 10 | 87 | 189 | 19 |
| **WEATHER** |  |  |  |  |  |
| A process in the weather of the heart | 6 | 1 | 4 | 6 | 1 |
| A weather in the quarter of the veins | 6 | 4 | 4 | 6 | 4 |
| A darkness in the weather of the eye | 6 | 10 | 4 | 6 | 10 |
| A weather in the flesh and bone | 6 | 16 | 4 | 6 | 16 |
| A process in the weather of the world | 6 | 19 | 4 | 7 | 1 |
| My veins flowed with the Eastern weather; | 7 | 17 | 5 | 8 | 17 |
| And tells the windy weather in the cock. | 16 | 20 | 11 | 19 | 20 |
| I fled the earth and, naked, climbed the weather, | 26 | 6 | 16 | 31 | 6 |
| Hearing the weather fall. | 36 | 6 | 20 | 41 | 6 |
| Be said to weep when weather howls? | 44 | 3 | 25 | 52 | 3 |
| Down pelts the naked weather; | 45 | 3 | 26 | 53 | 3 |
| Nor weather winds that blow not down the bone, | 60 | 2 | 36 | 69 | 2 |
| Lie watching yellow until the golden weather | 82 | 23 | 48 | 91 | 23 |
| Storm, snow, and fountain in the weather of fireworks, | 83 | 14 | 49 | 92 | 14 |
| Away but the weather turned around. | 103 | 15 | 63 | 114 | 15 |
| Away but the weather turned around. And the true | 104 | 10 | 63 | 115 | 12 |
| Exultation lies down. Time buries the spring weather | 123 | 9 | 72 | 136 | 19 |
| The boat swims into the six-year weather, | 154 | 9 | 83 | 172 | 9 |
| A process in the weather of the heart | 6 |  | 4 | 6 |  |
| **WEATHER'S** |  |  |  |  |  |
| And I am dumb to tell a weather's wind | 9 | 19 | 6 | 10 | 19 |

|  |  | U.K. |  |  | U.S. |  |
|---|---|---|---|---|---|---|
|  |  | Page | Line | Poem | Page | Line |
| WEATHERCOCKS' | | | | | | |
| | Into the weathercocks' molten mouths | 131 | 11 | 77 | 145 | 17 |
| WEATHERING | | | | | | |
| | We rung our weathering changes on the ladder, | 72 | 17 | 44 | 81 | 17 |
| WEATHER-COCK | | | | | | |
| | From the emerald, still bell; and from the pacing weather-cock | 83 | 17 | 49 | 92 | 17 |
| WEATHERS | | | | | | |
| | Split up the brawned womb's weathers, | 1 | 14 | 2 | 1 | 14 |
| | That set alight the weathers from a spark, | 22 | 14 | 14 | 27 | 14 |
| | A quarrel of weathers and trees in the windy spiral. | 36 | 18 | 20 | 41 | 18 |
| | Down fall four padding weathers on the scarlet lands, | 49 | 19 | 29 | 58 | 19 |
| | And hemlock-headed in the wood of weathers. | 72 | 4 | 44 | 81 | 4 |
| | With the outside weathers, | 91 | 9 | 55 | 100 | 9 |
| WEAVE | | | | | | |
| | Locking, unlocking, the murdered strangers weave, | 117 | 15 | 71 | 129 | 15 |
| | Leaves is dancing. Lines of age on the stones weave in a flock. | 121 | 23 | 72 | 134 | 18 |
| WEAVES | | | | | | |
| | Round her trailed wrist fresh water weaves, | 156 | 9 | 83 | 174 | 17 |
| WEAVING | | | | | | |
| | And fled their love in a weaving dip. | 151 | 5 | 83 | 168 | 13 |
| WEB | | | | | | |
| | Yet out of the beaked, web dark and the pouncing boughs | 163 | 25 | 86 | 183 | 6 |
| WEBBED | | | | | | |
| | And the knock of sailing boats on the net webbed wall | 102 | 7 | 63 | 113 | 7 |
| WEBFOOT | | | | | | |
| | Summoning a child's voice from a webfoot stone, | 133 | 18 | 78 | 149 | 1 |
| WEDDED | | | | | | |
| | And the wings glided wide and he was hymned and wedded, | 123 | 13 | 72 | 137 | 3 |
| WEDDING | | | | | | |
| | On a Wedding Anniversary | 124 | | 73 | 138 | |
| WEDDINGS | | | | | | |
| | Huge weddings in the waves, | 151 | 24 | 83 | 169 | 12 |
| WEDDINGS' | | | | | | |
| | All the green leaved little weddings' wives | 174 | 11 | 89 | 194 | 11 |
| WEDS | | | | | | |
| | Weds my long gentlemen to dusts and furies; | 76 | 4 | 44 | 85 | 4 |
| WEED | | | | | | |
| | The weed of love's left dry; | 11 | 15 | 8 | 12 | 15 |

| | U.K. | | | U.S. | |
|---|---|---|---|---|---|
| | Page | Line | Poem | Page | Line |
| Is corner-cast, breath's rag, scrawled weed, a vain | 78 | 9 | 46 | 87 | 9 |
| Pierce the spilt sky with diving wing in weed and heel | 86 | 4 | 51 | 95 | 4 |
| Nailed with an open eye, in the bowl of wounds and weed | 92 | 1 | 55 | 101 | 7 |
| Though the names on their weed grown stones are rained away, | 176 | 8 | 90 | 197 | 8 |
| **WEEDED** | | | | | |
| Now the heron grieves in the weeded verge. Through windows | 168 | 23 | 87 | 189 | 8 |
| **WEEDS** | | | | | |
| Break on the lovebeds of the weeds; | 11 | 14 | 8 | 12 | 14 |
| Shall she receive a bellyful of weeds | 90 | 5 | 54 | 99 | 5 |
| **WEEKS'** | | | | | |
| No silver whistles chase him down the weeks' | 67 | 21 | 41 | 76 | 21 |
| **WEEP** | | | | | |
| Be said to weep when weather howls? | 44 | 3 | 25 | 52 | 3 |
| And staved, and riven among plumes my rider weep. | 162 | 16 | 86 | 181 | 16 |
| Might cross its planets, the bell weep, night gather her eyes, | 165 | 21 | 86 | 185 | 11 |
| **WEEPING** | | | | | |
| And the multitude's sultry tear turns cool on the weeping wall, | 158 | 17 | 84 | 177 | 17 |
| **WEEPS** | | | | | |
| Weeps on the desert ochre and the salt | 31 | 8 | 18 | 36 | 8 |
| Weeps like the risen sun among | 155 | 19 | 83 | 174 | 3 |
| And to-morrow weeps in a blind cage | 171 | 15 | 88 | 191 | 15 |
| **WEIGHED** | | | | | |
| Weighed in rock shroud, is my proud pyramid; | 79 | 15 | 46 | 88 | 18 |
| **WEIGHT** | | | | | |
| Out of the room the weight of his trouble | 154 | 22 | 83 | 173 | 2 |
| **WEIRD** | | | | | |
| Draw down to its weird eyes? | 91 | 11 | 55 | 100 | 11 |
| **WELCOME** | | | | | |
| And welcome no sailor? | 58 | 24 | 35 | 67 | 24 |
| Shall I welcome the sailor, | 59 | 5 | 35 | 68 | 5 |
| (Sighed the old ram rod, dying of welcome), | 174 | 27 | 89 | 195 | 3 |
| **WELL** | | | | | |
| Of skin and vein around the well | 8 | 2 | 5 | 9 | 2 |
| If not of loving well, then not, | 48 | 8 | 28 | 56 | 8 |
| One enemy, of many, who knows well | 118 | 1 | 71 | 130 | 5 |
| From the starred well? | 163 | 3 | 86 | 182 | 3 |
| **WELSH** | | | | | |
| With Welsh and reverent rook, | ix | 9 | 1 | xvii | 9 |
| **WELSHING** | | | | | |
| The sunny gentlemen, the Welshing rich, | 15 | 5 | 10 | 17 | 5 |

|  | U.K. | | | U.S. | |
| --- | --- | --- | --- | --- | --- |
|  | Page | Line | Poem | Page | Line |
| WENDED | | | | | |
| In the river wended vales where the tale was told. | 119 | 10 | 72 | 131 | 10 |
| When cold as snow he should run the wended vales among | 120 | 20 | 72 | 133 | 5 |
| And the lakes and floating fields and the river wended | 122 | 28 | 72 | 136 | 8 |
| WENT | | | | | |
| Funnels and masts went by in a whirl. | 149 | 17 | 83 | 166 | 17 |
| WEPT | | | | | |
| And there we wept, I and a ghostly other, | 26 | 8 | 16 | 31 | 8 |
| All-hollowed man wept for his white apparel | 38 | 24 | 20 | 44 | 14 |
| As tarred with blood as the bright thorns I wept; | 75 | 7 | 44 | 84 | 7 |
| She wept in her pain and made mouths, | 93 | 19 | 56 | 102 | 19 |
| He knelt, he wept, he prayed, | 120 | 1 | 72 | 132 | 6 |
| He wept from the crest of grief, he prayed to the veiled sky | 120 | 7 | 72 | 132 | 12 |
| Wave's silence, wept white angelus knells. | 171 | 11 | 88 | 191 | 11 |
| WERE | | | | | |
| When once the twilight screws were turned, | 5 | 7 | 3 | 5 | 7 |
| If I were tickled by the rub of love, | 12 | 1 | 9 | 13 | 1 |
| If I were tickled by the hatching hair, | 12 | 10 | 9 | 13 | 10 |
| If I were tickled by the urchin hungers | 12 | 18 | 9 | 13 | 18 |
| If I were tickled by the lovers' rub | 12 | 22 | 9 | 14 | 1 |
| And earth and sky were as one airy hill, | 20 | 8 | 13 | 24 | 8 |
| The earth and sky were as two mountains meeting. | 20 | 15 | 13 | 24 | 15 |
| Before the veins were shaking in their sieve, | 23 | 4 | 14 | 28 | 4 |
| The patchwork halves were cloven as they scudded | 30 | 19 | 18 | 35 | 19 |
| Were oat and grape | 39 | 13 | 21 | 45 | 13 |
| When we were strangers to the guided seas, | 40 | 7 | 22 | 46 | 7 |
| They said, who hacked and humoured, they were mine. | 46 | 20 | 27 | 54 | 20 |
| Were that enough, enough to ease the pain, | 48 | 17 | 28 | 56 | 17 |
| Were vaguenesses enough and the sweet lies plenty, | 48 | 21 | 28 | 56 | 21 |
| Were that enough, bone, blood, and sinew, | 48 | 24 | 28 | 57 | 1 |
| She cried her white-dressed limbs were bare | 93 | 17 | 56 | 102 | 17 |
| And her red lips were kissed black, | 93 | 18 | 56 | 102 | 18 |
| The mazes of his praise and envious tongue were worked in flames and shells. | 95 | 17 | 58 | 105 | 17 |
| Here were fond climates and sweet singers suddenly | 103 | 1 | 63 | 114 | 1 |
| Of spring and summer were blooming in the tall tales | 103 | 11 | 63 | 114 | 11 |
| These were the woods the river and sea | 104 | 1 | 63 | 115 | 3 |

|  | U.K. | | | U.S. | |
| --- | --- | --- | --- | --- | --- |
|  | Page | Line | Poem | Page | Line |
| Were once such a creature, so gay and frank | 107 | 14 | 65 | 118 | 14 |
| My friends were enemies on stilts | 107 | 20 | 65 | 118 | 20 |
| And the groves were blue with sailors | 112 | 6 | 68 | 124 | 6 |
| And the wild wings were raised | 122 | 1 | 72 | 135 | 1 |
| It were a wand or subtle bough, | 134 | 14 | 79 | 150 | 14 |
| All the fishes were rayed in blood, | 149 | 23 | 83 | 167 | 3 |
| As I rode to sleep the owls were bearing the farm away, | 160 | 2 | 85 | 179 | 2 |
| This night and each night since the falling star you were born, | 164 | 6 | 86 | 183 | 13 |
| Since you were born: | 166 | 10 | 86 | 186 | 10 |
| Who once, green countries since, were a hedgerow of joys. | 176 | 20 | 90 | 197 | 20 |
| Who once were a bloom of wayside brides in the hawed house | 177 | 9 | 90 | 198 | 8 |
| They with the simple Jacks were a boulder of wives)— | 178 | 3 | 90 | 199 | 4 |
| The sticks of the house were his; his books he owned. |  |  | 91 | 201 | 4 |
| If I were tickled by the rub of love | 12 |  | 9 | 13 |  |
| WEST |  |  |  |  |  |
| With the man in the wind and the west moon; | 68 | 3 | 42 | 77 | 3 |
| And from the windy West came two-gunned Gabriel, | 73 | 11 | 44 | 82 | 11 |
| The sun shipwrecked west on a pearl | 149 | 15 | 83 | 166 | 15 |
| WEST'S |  |  |  |  |  |
| And west's no longer drowned | 53 | 3 | 32 | 62 | 3 |
| WETHER |  |  |  |  |  |
| That Adam's wether in the flock of horns, | 72 | 7 | 44 | 81 | 7 |
| WET |  |  |  |  |  |
| And lay the wet fruits low. | 11 | 12 | 8 | 12 | 12 |
| The wet night scolds me like a nurse? | 44 | 10 | 25 | 52 | 10 |
| Is carved from her in a room with a wet window | 88 | 1 | 52 | 97 | 1 |
| And over the sea wet church the size of a snail | 103 | 7 | 63 | 114 | 7 |
| WHACK |  |  |  |  |  |
| Whack their boys' limbs, | 14 | 3 | 10 | 16 | 3 |
| In a whack of wind. | 167 | 17 | 87 | 187 | 17 |
| WHALE |  |  |  |  |  |
| Mirror from man to whale | 69 | 21 | 43 | 78 | 21 |
| WHALEBED |  |  |  |  |  |
| Whalebed and bulldance, the gold bush of lions, | 78 | 22 | 46 | 87 | 22 |
| WHALE-BLUE |  |  |  |  |  |
| At his thrashing hair and whale-blue eye; | 149 | 3 | 83 | 166 | 3 |
| WHALE-WEED |  |  |  |  |  |
| Strung by the flaxen whale-weed, from the hangman's raft, | 37 | 14 | 20 | 42 | 20 |

|  | U.K. | | | U.S. | |
|---|---|---|---|---|---|
|  | *Page* | *Line* | *Poem* | *Page* | *Line* |
| WHALES | | | | | |
| Whales unreined from the green grave | 113 | 8 | 69 | 125 | 8 |
| Of the sea is hilly with whales, | 150 | 8 | 83 | 167 | 12 |
| Whales in the wake like capes and Alps | 151 | 1 | 83 | 168 | 9 |
| Marrow of eagles, the roots of whales | 172 | 4 | 88 | 192 | 4 |
| WHARVES | | | | | |
| And wharves of water where the walls dance and the white cranes stilt. | 168 | 15 | 87 | 188 | 19 |
| WHAT | | | | | |
| What had been one was many sounding minded. | 21 | 17 | 13 | 25 | 17 |
| What colour is glory? death's feather? tremble | 31 | 1 | 18 | 36 | 1 |
| Who blows death's feather? What glory is colour? | 32 | 7 | 18 | 37 | 13 |
| What shall it tell me if a timeless insect | 45 | 16 | 26 | 53 | 16 |
| Though what the stars ask as they round | 53 | 18 | 32 | 62 | 18 |
| What is the metre of the dictionary? | 72 | 19 | 44 | 81 | 19 |
| What of a bamboo man among your acres? | 73 | 3 | 44 | 82 | 3 |
| What rhubarb man peeled in her foam-blue channel | 76 | 17 | 44 | 85 | 17 |
| To take to give is all, return what is hungrily given | 94 | 4 | 57 | 104 | 4 |
| See what the gold gut drags from under | 154 | 11 | 83 | 172 | 11 |
| See what clings to hair and skull | 154 | 13 | 83 | 172 | 13 |
| Doing what they are told, | 170 | 12 | 88 | 190 | 12 |
| Hating his God, but what he was was plain: | | | 91 | 201 | 2 |
| WHAT'S | | | | | |
| And what's the rub? Death's feather on the nerve? | 13 | 15 | 9 | 15 | 1 |
| What's never known is safest in this life. | 50 | 6 | 30 | 59 | 6 |
| WHATSOEVER | | | | | |
| Whatsoever I did in the coal- | 174 | 23 | 89 | 194 | 23 |
| WHEATFIELD | | | | | |
| Into the bread in a wheatfield of flames, | 131 | 18 | 77 | 145 | 24 |
| WHEEL | | | | | |
| Towns around on a wheel of fire. | 33 | 6 | 19 | 38 | 6 |
| Strapped to a wheel, yet they shall not break; | 68 | 14 | 42 | 77 | 14 |
| WHEELING | | | | | |
| Under the prayer wheeling moon in the rosy wood | 163 | 18 | 86 | 182 | 18 |
| WHELPS | | | | | |
| Shape all her whelps with the long voice of water, | 55 | 2 | 33 | 64 | 5 |
| WHEN | | | | | |
| When once the twilight locks no longer | 4 | 1 | 3 | 4 | 1 |
| When the galactic sea was sucked | 4 | 7 | 3 | 4 | 7 |
| But when the stars, assuming shape, | 4 | 16 | 3 | 4 | 16 |
| When once the twilight screws were turned, | 5 | 7 | 3 | 5 | 7 |

| | U.K. | | | U.S. | |
|---|---|---|---|---|---|
| | Page | Line | Poem | Page | Line |
| Nor when he finds a beauty in the breast | 13 | 12 | 9 | 14 | 19 |
| When sunlight goes are sundered from the worm, | 14 | 8 | 10 | 16 | 8 |
| When cameras shut they hurry to their hole | 14 | 15 | 10 | 16 | 15 |
| Shall fall awake when cures and their itch | 15 | 2 | 10 | 17 | 2 |
| Especially when the October wind | 16 | 1 | 11 | 19 | 1 |
| Especially when the October wind | 17 | 1 | 11 | 20 | 1 |
| When, like a running grave, time tracks you down, | 18 | 1 | 12 | 21 | 1 |
| When blood, spade-handed, and the logic time | 18 | 13 | 12 | 21 | 13 |
| When no mouth stirred about the hanging famine, | 20 | 5 | 13 | 24 | 5 |
| When logics die, | 25 | 3 | 15 | 30 | 3 |
| When we were strangers to the guided seas, | 40 | 7 | 22 | 46 | 7 |
| And when the moon rose windily it was | 40 | 11 | 22 | 46 | 11 |
| When clouds are cursed by thunder, | 44 | 2 | 25 | 52 | 2 |
| Be said to weep when weather howls? | 44 | 3 | 25 | 52 | 3 |
| When it is rain where are the gods? | 44 | 5 | 25 | 52 | 5 |
| Feeling regret when this is wasted | 48 | 18 | 28 | 56 | 18 |
| Was there a time when dancers with their fiddles | 50 | 1 | 30 | 59 | 1 |
| When cometh Jack Frost? the children ask. | 53 | 10 | 32 | 62 | 10 |
| Nor when my love lies in the cross-boned drift | 60 | 22 | 36 | 69 | 22 |
| And, when it quickens, alter the actions' pace | 63 | 12 | 38 | 72 | 12 |
| But when the ladies are cold as stone | 65 | 7 | 40 | 74 | 7 |
| When their bones are picked clean and the clean bones gone, | 68 | 4 | 42 | 77 | 4 |
| Twisting on racks when sinews give way, | 68 | 13 | 42 | 77 | 13 |
| The fats of midnight when the salt was singing; | 74 | 10 | 44 | 83 | 10 |
| When the worm builds with the gold straws of venom | 76 | 21 | 44 | 85 | 21 |
| I make this in a warring absence when | 78 | 1 | 46 | 87 | 1 |
| When, praise is blessed, her pride in mast and fountain | 78 | 4 | 46 | 87 | 4 |
| When all my five and country senses see, | 81 | 1 | 47 | 90 | 1 |
| And when blind sleep drops on the spying senses, | 81 | 13 | 47 | 90 | 13 |
| When, with his torch and hourglass, like a sulphur priest, | 83 | 2 | 49 | 92 | 2 |
| When I whistled with mitching boys through a reservoir park | 89 | 7 | 53 | 98 | 7 |
| Die in red feathers when the flying heaven's cut, | 92 | 12 | 55 | 101 | 18 |
| The tombstone told when she died. | 93 | 1 | 56 | 102 | 1 |
| When you sew the deep door. The bed is a cross place. | 97 | 13 | 59 | 108 | 13 |
| Nor when all ponderous heaven's host of waters breaks. | 97 | 20 | 59 | 108 | 20 |
| High tide and the heron dived when I took the road | 102 | 17 | 63 | 113 | 17 |

547

| | U.K. | | | U.S. | |
|---|---|---|---|---|---|
| | *Page* | *Line* | *Poem* | *Page* | *Line* |
| Forgotten mornings when he walked with his mother | 103 | 22 | 63 | 114 | 22 |
| Who palmed the lie on me when you looked | 107 | 4 | 65 | 118 | 4 |
| Running when he had heard them clearly | 111 | 17 | 68 | 123 | 17 |
| Laughing when he shook his paper | 111 | 20 | 68 | 123 | 20 |
| When one at the great least of your best loved | 117 | 3 | 71 | 129 | 3 |
| When at your lips and keys, | 117 | 14 | 71 | 129 | 14 |
| When near and strange wounded on London's waves | 117 | 27 | 71 | 130 | 3 |
| Once when the world turned old | 119 | 11 | 72 | 131 | 11 |
| When cold as snow he should run the wended vales among | 120 | 20 | 72 | 133 | 5 |
| When black birds died like priests in the cloaked hedge row | 122 | 12 | 72 | 135 | 12 |
| When hindering man hurt | 125 | 12 | 74 | 139 | 12 |
| Silence, silence to do, when earth grew loud, | 125 | 15 | 74 | 139 | 15 |
| On to the ground when a man died | 125 | 21 | 74 | 139 | 21 |
| One lean sigh when we heard | 126 | 5 | 74 | 140 | 5 |
| Waking alone in a multitude of loves when morning's light | 127 | 1 | 75 | 141 | 1 |
| When only the moon rages | 128 | 3 | 76 | 142 | 3 |
| When the caught tongue nodded blind, | 129 | 13 | 77 | 143 | 13 |
| When my pinned-around-the-spirit | 132 | 2 | 78 | 147 | 2 |
| When I woke, the town spoke. | 134 | 1 | 79 | 150 | 1 |
| When the morning was waking over the war | 135 | 1 | 80 | 152 | 1 |
| When all the keys shot from the locks, and rang. | 135 | 8 | 80 | 152 | 8 |
| And when the salt sheet broke in a storm of singing | 136 | 7 | 81 | 153 | 7 |
| When | 139 | 1 | 82 | 156 | 1 |
| Of man when | 141 | 14 | 82 | 158 | 14 |
| When his long-legged flesh was a wind on fire | 157 | 3 | 83 | 175 | 15 |
| When that immortal hospital made one more move to soothe | 158 | 3 | 84 | 177 | 3 |
| When his viperish fuse hangs looped with flames under the brand | 168 | 4 | 87 | 188 | 8 |
| When I was a windy boy and a bit | 174 | 1 | 89 | 194 | 1 |
| When I was a gusty man and a half | 174 | 13 | 89 | 194 | 13 |
| When I was a man you could call a man | 174 | 25 | 89 | 195 | 1 |
| Of, time enough when the blood creeps cold, | 175 | 5 | 89 | 195 | 10 |
| When I was a half the man I was | 175 | 8 | 89 | 195 | 13 |
| Slunk pouting out when the limp time came; | 175 | 15 | 89 | 195 | 20 |
| When once the twilight locks no longer | 4 | | 3 | 4 | |
| Especially when the October wind | 16 | | 11 | 19 | |
| When, like a running grave | 18 | | 12 | 21 | |
| When all my five and country senses see | 81 | | 47 | 90 | |
| The tombstone told when she died | 93 | | 56 | 102 | |
| When I Woke | 134 | | 79 | 150 | |

|  | U.K. | | | U.S. | |
|  | *Page* | *Line* | *Poem* | *Page* | *Line* |
| **WHENEVER** | | | | | |
| Whenever I dove in a breast high shoal, | 174 | 21 | 89 | 194 | 21 |
| **WHERE** | | | | | |
| Where, punctual as death, we ring the stars; | 2 | 3 | 2 | 2 | 3 |
| Where fishes' food is fed the shades | 5 | 5 | 3 | 5 | 5 |
| And leave the poppied pickthank where he lies; | 5 | 15 | 3 | 5 | 15 |
| Where words and water make a mixture | 8 | 3 | 5 | 9 | 3 |
| Where once the waters of your face | 11 | 1 | 8 | 12 | 1 |
| Where once the mermen through your ice | 11 | 4 | 8 | 12 | 4 |
| Where once your green knots sank their splice | 11 | 7 | 8 | 12 | 7 |
| That but a name, where maggots have their X. | 21 | 14 | 13 | 25 | 14 |
| Light breaks where no sun shines; | 24 | 1 | 15 | 29 | 1 |
| Where no sea runs, the waters of the heart | 24 | 2 | 15 | 29 | 2 |
| File through the flesh where no flesh decks the bones. | 24 | 6 | 15 | 29 | 6 |
| Where no seed stirs, | 24 | 9 | 15 | 29 | 9 |
| Where no wax is, the candle shows its hairs. | 24 | 12 | 15 | 29 | 12 |
| Where no cold is, the skinning gales unpin | 24 | 22 | 15 | 29 | 22 |
| On tips of thought where thoughts smell in the rain; | 25 | 2 | 15 | 30 | 2 |
| Where still they sleep unknowing of their ghost. | 26 | 20 | 16 | 31 | 20 |
| The highroad of water where the seabear and mackerel | 36 | 21 | 20 | 41 | 21 |
| They suffer the undead water where the turtle nibbles, | 37 | 22 | 20 | 43 | 5 |
| When it is rain where are the gods? | 44 | 5 | 25 | 52 | 5 |
| Where bird and shell are babbling in my tower? | 46 | 14 | 27 | 54 | 14 |
| And salt-eyed stumble bedward where she lies | 67 | 12 | 41 | 76 | 12 |
| Where blew a flower may a flower no more | 68 | 22 | 42 | 77 | 22 |
| By waste seas where the white bear quoted Virgil | 73 | 23 | 44 | 82 | 23 |
| Where, wound in emerald linen and sharp wind, | 79 | 16 | 46 | 88 | 19 |
| In that bright anchorground where I lay linened, | 79 | 22 | 46 | 89 | 3 |
| Once where the soft snow's blood was turned to ice. | 80 | 12 | 46 | 89 | 20 |
| With a capsized field where a school sat still | 89 | 3 | 53 | 98 | 3 |
| Where at night we stoned the cold and cuckoo | 89 | 8 | 53 | 98 | 8 |
| Come in the morning where I wandered and listened | 103 | 2 | 63 | 114 | 2 |
| Where a boy | 104 | 2 | 63 | 115 | 4 |
| In the fountain basin where I sailed my ship | 111 | 10 | 68 | 123 | 10 |
| There where a numberless tongue | 114 | 1 | 69 | 126 | 1 |
| In the river wended vales where the tale was told. | 119 | 10 | 72 | 131 | 10 |
| And fires where he should prowl down the cloud | 120 | 12 | 72 | 132 | 17 |
| Listen and look where she sails the goose plucked sea, | 122 | 20 | 72 | 135 | 20 |

|  | U.K. Page | Line | Poem | U.S. Page | Line |
|---|---|---|---|---|---|
| Vales where he prayed to come to the last harm | 122 | 29 | 72 | 136 | 9 |
| Her deepsea pillow where once she married alone, | 127 | 9 | 75 | 141 | 9 |
| For a man sleeps where fire leapt down and she learns through his arm | 127 | 13 | 75 | 141 | 13 |
| Where birds ride like leaves and boats like ducks | 134 | 22 | 79 | 150 | 22 |
| He dropped where he loved on the burst pavement stone | 135 | 4 | 80 | 152 | 4 |
| Where the anchor rode like a gull | 150 | 13 | 83 | 167 | 17 |
| Where the elegiac fisherbirds stabs and paddles | 167 | 19 | 87 | 187 | 19 |
| Where the sea cobbles sail, | 168 | 14 | 87 | 188 | 18 |
| And wharves of water where the walls dance and the white cranes stilt. | 168 | 15 | 87 | 188 | 19 |
| Where the cormorants scud, | 170 | 3 | 88 | 190 | 3 |
| On skull and scar where his loves lie wrecked, | 171 | 13 | 88 | 191 | 13 |
| And air shaped Heaven where souls grow wild | 172 | 20 | 88 | 192 | 20 |
| Through throats where many rivers meet, the curlews cry, | 176 | 1 | 90 | 197 | 1 |
| Where barren as boulders women lie longing still | 176 | 4 | 90 | 197 | 4 |
| Through throats where many rivers meet, the women pray, | 176 | 6 | 90 | 197 | 6 |
| Quick in the wood at love, where a torch of foxes foams, | 177 | 14 | 90 | 198 | 13 |
| And gone that barley dark where their clogs danced in the spring, | 177 | 20 | 90 | 198 | 19 |
| Where the hay rides now or the bracken kitchens rust | 178 | 6 | 90 | 199 | 7 |
| They from houses where the harvest kneels, hold me hard, | 178 | 9 | 90 | 199 | 10 |
| An old blind man is with me where I go | | | 91 | 201 | 9 |
| Where once the waters of your face | 11 | | 8 | 12 | |
| Light breaks where no sun shines | 24 | | 15 | 29 | |
| **WHEREVER** | | | | | |
| Wherever I ramped in the clover quilts, | 174 | 22 | 89 | 194 | 22 |
| **WHETHER** | | | | | |
| I know not whether | 130 | 9 | 77 | 144 | 9 |
| **WHICH** | | | | | |
| Which is the world? Of our two sleepings, which | 15 | 1 | 10 | 17 | 1 |
| Which sixth of wind blew out the burning gentry? | 73 | 1 | 44 | 82 | 1 |
| If I take to burn or return this world which is each man's work. | 94 | 12 | 57 | 104 | 12 |
| All blood-signed assailings and vanished marriages in which he had no lovely part | 114 | 20 | 69 | 126 | 20 |
| I climb to greet the war in which I have no heart but only | 158 | 8 | 84 | 177 | 8 |

| | U.K. | | | U.S. | |
|---|---|---|---|---|---|
| | *Page* | *Line* | *Poem* | *Page* | *Line* |
| Which was rest and dust, and in the kind ground | | | 91 | 200 | 10 |
| WHILE | | | | | |
| Shall not be latched while magic glides | 11 | 20 | 8 | 12 | 20 |
| How much was happy while it lasted, | 48 | 20 | 28 | 56 | 20 |
| The ball I threw while playing in the park | 63 | 18 | 38 | 72 | 18 |
| While you displaced a truth in the air, | 107 | 17 | 65 | 118 | 17 |
| About the saint in shades while the endless breviary | 109 | 26 | 67 | 120 | 26 |
| While the boys among willows | 112 | 3 | 68 | 124 | 3 |
| While a man outside with a billhook, | 134 | 8 | 79 | 150 | 8 |
| Shall harrow and snow the blood while you ride wide and near, | 162 | 23 | 86 | 181 | 23 |
| WHINNYING | | | | | |
| You have kicked from a dark den, leaped up the whinnying light, | 92 | 15 | 55 | 101 | 21 |
| Out of the whinnying green stable | 160 | 13 | 85 | 179 | 13 |
| WHIRL | | | | | |
| Funnels and masts went by in a whirl. | 149 | 17 | 83 | 166 | 17 |
| WHIRLED | | | | | |
| The whirled boat in the burn of his blood | 151 | 17 | 83 | 169 | 5 |
| WHIRLING | | | | | |
| Over the whirling ditch of daybreak | 131 | 15 | 77 | 145 | 21 |
| WHIRL-[POOL] | | | | | |
| Burning in the bride bed of love, in the whirl- | 123 | 17 | 72 | 137 | 7 |
| WHIRLPOOL | | | | | |
| And a whirlpool drives the prayerwheel; | 83 | 9 | 49 | 92 | 9 |
| Trees cool and dry in the whirlpool of ships | 156 | 2 | 83 | 174 | 10 |
| WHIRLS | | | | | |
| The hand that whirls the water in the pool | 9 | 11 | 6 | 10 | 11 |
| WHIRLWIND | | | | | |
| God in his whirlwind silence save, who marks the sparrows hail, | 168 | 21 | 87 | 189 | 6 |
| WHIRRING | | | | | |
| On the angelic etna of the last whirring feather-lands, | 95 | 11 | 58 | 105 | 11 |
| WHISKING | | | | | |
| Whisking hare! who | ix | 17 | 1 | xvii | 17 |
| WHISPER | | | | | |
| (My shape of age nagging the wounded whisper). | 72 | 22 | 44 | 81 | 22 |
| Whisper in a damp word, her wits drilled hollow, | 88 | 5 | 52 | 97 | 5 |
| WHISPERED | | | | | |
| Summertime of the dead whispered the truth of his joy | 104 | 4 | 63 | 115 | 6 |
| Whispered the affectionate sand | 149 | 9 | 83 | 166 | 9 |

| | U.K. | | | U.S. | |
|---|---|---|---|---|---|
| | Page | Line | Poem | Page | Line |
| **WHISPERING** | | | | | |
| The whispering ears will watch love drummed away | 81 | 6 | 47 | 90 | 6 |
| Of dusk and water I see the tilting whispering | 168 | 24 | 87 | 189 | 9 |
| **WHISTLED** | | | | | |
| When I whistled with mitching boys through a reservoir park | 89 | 7 | 53 | 98 | 7 |
| Rode and whistled a hundred times | 113 | 18 | 69 | 125 | 18 |
| I whistled all night in the twisted flues, | 174 | 18 | 89 | 194 | 18 |
| **WHISTLER'S** | | | | | |
| With whistler's cough contages, time on track | 19 | 22 | 12 | 23 | 7 |
| **WHISTLES** | | | | | |
| No silver whistles chase him down the weeks' | 67 | 21 | 41 | 76 | 21 |
| Because the pleasure-bird whistles after the hot wires, | 77 | 1 | 45 | 86 | 1 |
| Of the led-astray birds whom God, for their breast of whistles, | 168 | 19 | 87 | 189 | 4 |
| Because the pleasure-bird whistles | 77 | | 45 | 86 | |
| **WHISTLING** | | | | | |
| Cloud and the roadside bushes brimming with whistling | 102 | 22 | 63 | 113 | 22 |
| **WHITE** | | | | | |
| Sheep white hollow farms | viii | 25 | 1 | xvi | 25 |
| The sun and moon shed one white light. | 20 | 9 | 13 | 24 | 9 |
| Twelve winds encounter by the white host at pasture, | 36 | 14 | 20 | 41 | 14 |
| All-hollowed man wept for his white apparel | 38 | 24 | 20 | 44 | 14 |
| Shall a white answer echo from the rooftops. | 53 | 15 | 32 | 62 | 15 |
| In this white house? | 58 | 8 | 35 | 67 | 8 |
| Child in white blood bent on its knees | 69 | 2 | 43 | 78 | 2 |
| By waste seas where the white bear quoted Virgil | 73 | 23 | 44 | 82 | 23 |
| Forever it is a white child in the dark-skinned summer | 83 | 19 | 49 | 93 | 1 |
| And a black and white patch of girls grew playing; | 89 | 4 | 53 | 98 | 4 |
| The breath draw back like a bolt through white oil | 96 | 21 | 58 | 107 | 4 |
| Above the farms and the white horses | 102 | 13 | 63 | 113 | 13 |
| Crying, white gowned, from the middle moonlit stages | 114 | 14 | 69 | 126 | 14 |
| Flocked with the sheep white smoke of the farm house cowl | 119 | 9 | 72 | 131 | 9 |
| And the dung hills white as wool and the hen | 119 | 18 | 72 | 131 | 18 |
| And all the woken farm at its white trades, | 119 | 25 | 72 | 132 | 5 |
| May his hunger go howling on bare white bones | 120 | 8 | 72 | 132 | 13 |
| Of his snow blind love and rush in the white lairs. | 120 | 13 | 72 | 132 | 18 |

|  | U.K. | | | U.S. | |
| --- | --- | --- | --- | --- | --- |
|  | *Page* | *Line* | *Poem* | *Page* | *Line* |
| In the always desiring centre of the white | 120 | 23 | 72 | 133 | 8 |
| Never to flourish in the fields of the white seed | 120 | 29 | 72 | 133 | 14 |
| Horses, centaur dead, turn and tread the drenched white | 121 | 19 | 72 | 134 | 14 |
| On a bread white hill over the cupped farm | 122 | 27 | 72 | 136 | 7 |
| On the white, no longer growing green, and, minstrel dead, | 123 | 2 | 72 | 136 | 12 |
| Or the white ewe lamb | 130 | 11 | 77 | 144 | 11 |
| White as the skeleton | 130 | 21 | 77 | 144 | 21 |
| I drew the white sheet over the islands | 134 | 29 | 79 | 151 | 7 |
| Sails drank the wind, and white as milk | 149 | 13 | 83 | 166 | 13 |
| White springs in the dark. | 153 | 24 | 83 | 171 | 20 |
| And then to awake, and the farm, like a wanderer white | 160 | 6 | 85 | 179 | 6 |
| Nothing I cared, in the lamb white days, that time would take me | 160 | 24 | 85 | 180 | 1 |
| Earth, air, water, fire, singing into the white act, | 165 | 16 | 86 | 185 | 6 |
| And wharves of water where the walls dance and the white cranes stilt. | 168 | 15 | 87 | 188 | 19 |
| Wave's silence, wept white angelus knells. | 171 | 11 | 88 | 191 | 11 |
| And there this night I walk in the white giant's thigh | 176 | 3 | 90 | 197 | 3 |
| And ducked and draked white lake that harps to a hail stone. | 177 | 8 | 90 | 198 | 7 |
| Of day, in  he thistle aisles, till the white owl crossed | 177 | 12 | 90 | 198 | 11 |
| In the white giant's thigh | 176 |  | 90 | 197 |  |
| WHITE-DRESSED |  |  |  |  |  |
| She cried her white-dressed limbs were bare | 93 | 17 | 56 | 102 | 17 |
| WHO |  |  |  |  |  |
| Tackled with clouds, who kneel | vii | 13 | 1 | xv | 13 |
| You king singsong owls, who moonbeam. | ix | 3 | 1 | xvii | 3 |
| Who moons her blue notes from her nest | ix | 11 | 1 | xvii | 11 |
| Whisking hare! who | ix | 17 | 1 | xvii | 17 |
| Beasts who sleep good and thin, | ix | 26 | 1 | xvii | 26 |
| From the fair dead who flush the sea | 2 | 10 | 2 | 2 | 10 |
| Who periscope through flowers to the sky. | 5 | 6 | 3 | 5 | 6 |
| I who was shapeless as the water | 7 | 3 | 5 | 8 | 3 |
| I who was deaf to spring and summer, | 7 | 7 | 5 | 8 | 7 |
| Who knew not sun and moon by name, | 7 | 8 | 5 | 8 | 8 |
| I who was rich was made the richer | 8 | 11 | 5 | 9 | 11 |
| You who bow down at cross and altar, | 8 | 19 | 5 | 9 | 19 |
| Who took my flesh and bone for armour | 8 | 21 | 5 | 9 | 21 |
| Of children go who, from their voids, | 11 | 17 | 8 | 12 | 17 |
| A rooking girl who stole me for her side, | 12 | 2 | 9 | 13 | 2 |
| And who remain shall flower as they love, | 15 | 21 | 10 | 18 | 1 |
| My busy heart who shudders as she talks | 16 | 7 | 11 | 19 | 7 |

|  | U.K. | | | U.S. | |
| --- | --- | --- | --- | --- | --- |
|  | Page | Line | Poem | Page | Line |
| Deliver me who, timid in my tribe, | 18 | 7 | 12 | 21 | 7 |
| Left by the dead who, in their moonless acre, | 21 | 11 | 13 | 25 | 11 |
| I fellowed sleep who kissed me in the brain, | 26 | 1 | 16 | 31 | 1 |
| Who seek me landward, marking in my mouth | 31 | 22 | 18 | 37 | 4 |
| Who blows death's feather? What glory is colour? | 32 | 7 | 18 | 37 | 13 |
| And God walked there who was a fiddling warden | 40 | 5 | 22 | 46 | 5 |
| Am I not sister, too, who is my saviour? | 46 | 12 | 27 | 54 | 12 |
| Am I not you who front the tidy shore, | 46 | 15 | 27 | 54 | 15 |
| You are all these, said she who gave me the long suck, | 46 | 17 | 27 | 54 | 17 |
| All these, he said who sacked the children's town, | 46 | 18 | 27 | 54 | 18 |
| They said, who hacked and humoured, they were mine. | 46 | 20 | 27 | 54 | 20 |
| Who razed my wooden folly stands aghast, | 46 | 22 | 27 | 54 | 22 |
| Who play the proper gentleman and lady. | 47 | 4 | 27 | 55 | 4 |
| Under the skysigns they who have no arms | 50 | 7 | 30 | 59 | 7 |
| Should he who split his children with a cure | 51 | 13 | 31 | 60 | 13 |
| She who was who I hold, the fats and flower, | 54 | 2 | 33 | 63 | 2 |
| Who is my grief, | 54 | 9 | 33 | 63 | 9 |
| Was who was folded on the rod the aaron | 54 | 13 | 33 | 63 | 13 |
| And she who lies, | 54 | 17 | 33 | 63 | 17 |
| Who then is she, | 54 | 25 | 33 | 64 | 1 |
| Who gave these seas their colour in a shape, | 61 | 1 | 36 | 70 | 1 |
| O who is glory in the shapeless maps, | 61 | 4 | 36 | 70 | 4 |
| Who tossed the high tide in a time of stories | 67 | 13 | 41 | 76 | 13 |
| Who in these labyrinths, | 69 | 13 | 43 | 78 | 13 |
| Who speak on a finger and thumb, | 70 | 1 | 43 | 79 | 5 |
| Who kills my history? | 70 | 9 | 43 | 79 | 13 |
| 'Who could snap off the shapeless print | 70 | 12 | 43 | 79 | 16 |
| Who could hack out your unsucked heart, | 70 | 18 | 43 | 79 | 22 |
| Who sucks the bell-voiced Adam out of magic, | 74 | 23 | 44 | 83 | 23 |
| These are her contraries: the beast who follows | 78 | 24 | 46 | 88 | 1 |
| Who scales a hailing hill in her cold flintsteps | 79 | 3 | 46 | 88 | 6 |
| Who picks the live heart on a diamond. | 79 | 19 | 46 | 88 | 22 |
| And the grave sea, mock who deride | 82 | 2 | 48 | 91 | 2 |
| Who follow the red rivers, hollow | 82 | 3 | 48 | 91 | 3 |
| Who have brought forth the urchin grief. | 84 | 6 | 49 | 93 | 12 |
| Shakes a desolate boy who slits his throat | 87 | 7 | 52 | 96 | 7 |
| Who should be furious, | 91 | 6 | 55 | 100 | 6 |
| I who saw in a hurried film | 93 | 21 | 56 | 103 | 1 |
| Who climbs to his dying love in her high room, | 100 | 3 | 61 | 111 | 3 |
| For the sleep in a safe land and the love who dies | 100 | 10 | 61 | 111 | 10 |
| Dragging him up the stairs to one who lies dead. | 100 | 20 | 61 | 111 | 20 |
| Who palmed the lie on me when you looked | 107 | 4 | 65 | 118 | 4 |

| | U.K. | | | U.S. | |
| | *Page* | *Line* | *Poem* | *Page* | *Line* |
|---|---|---|---|---|---|
| Who admits the delusive light through the bouncing wall, | 108 | 11 | 66 | 119 | 11 |
| Wild men who caught and sang the sun in flight, | 116 | 10 | 70 | 128 | 10 |
| Grave men, near death, who see with blinding sight | 116 | 13 | 70 | 128 | 13 |
| One who called deepest down shall hold his peace | 117 | 9 | 71 | 129 | 9 |
| One who is most unknown, | 117 | 16 | 71 | 129 | 16 |
| Who strode for your own dead | 117 | 20 | 71 | 129 | 20 |
| One enemy, of many, who knows well | 118 | 1 | 71 | 130 | 5 |
| Who moved for three years in tune | 124 | 3 | 73 | 138 | 3 |
| O you who could not cry | 125 | 20 | 74 | 139 | 20 |
| O we who could not stir | 126 | 4 | 74 | 140 | 4 |
| Of the golden ghost who ringed with his streams her mercury bone, | 127 | 11 | 75 | 141 | 11 |
| Who under the lids of her windows hoisted his golden luggage, | 127 | 12 | 75 | 141 | 12 |
| Who pay no praise or wages | 128 | 19 | 76 | 142 | 19 |
| Child who was priest and servants, | 130 | 28 | 77 | 145 | 6 |
| Who was the serpent's | 131 | 3 | 77 | 145 | 9 |
| Who | 137 | 1 | 82 | 154 | 1 |
| Who is born | 137 | 3 | 82 | 154 | 3 |
| Who bore him with a bonfire in | 139 | 9 | 82 | 156 | 9 |
| For I was lost who am | 140 | 6 | 82 | 157 | 6 |
| For I was lost who have come | 140 | 11 | 82 | 157 | 11 |
| In the name of the lost who glory in | 143 | 1 | 82 | 160 | 1 |
| That he who learns now the sun and moon | 144 | 1 | 82 | 161 | 1 |
| Who shows to the selves asleep | 153 | 7 | 83 | 171 | 3 |
| Sin who had a woman's shape | 153 | 14 | 83 | 171 | 10 |
| He who blew the great fire in | 155 | 13 | 83 | 173 | 17 |
| And he who taught their lips to sing | 155 | 18 | 83 | 174 | 2 |
| For who unmanningly haunts the mountain ravened eaves | 163 | 1 | 86 | 182 | 1 |
| Who comes as red as the fox and sly as the heeled wind. | 165 | 10 | 86 | 184 | 18 |
| Of the sparrows and such who swansing, dusk, in wrangling hedges. | 167 | 7 | 87 | 187 | 7 |
| God in his whirlwind silence save, who marks the sparrows hail, | 168 | 21 | 87 | 189 | 6 |
| Makes all the music; and I who hear the tune of the slow, | 169 | 9 | 87 | 189 | 18 |
| Who tolls his birthday bell, | 170 | 16 | 88 | 190 | 16 |
| Who slaves to his crouched, eternal end | 171 | 4 | 88 | 191 | 4 |
| Who knows the rocketing wind will blow | 172 | 13 | 88 | 192 | 13 |
| Who is the light of old | 172 | 19 | 88 | 192 | 19 |
| Hill. Who once in gooseskin winter loved all ice leaved | 176 | 12 | 90 | 197 | 12 |

WHO (continued)

<table>
<tr><td></td><td colspan="2">U.K.</td><td></td><td colspan="2">U.S.</td></tr>
<tr><td></td><td>*Page*</td><td>*Line*</td><td>*Poem*</td><td>*Page*</td><td>*Line*</td></tr>
<tr><td>Who once, green countries since, were a hedge-<br>row of joys.</td><td>176</td><td>20</td><td>90</td><td>197</td><td>20</td></tr>
<tr><td>Who once were a bloom of wayside brides in the<br>hawed house</td><td>177</td><td>9</td><td>90</td><td>198</td><td>8</td></tr>
<tr><td>Who heard the tall bell sail down the Sundays<br>of the dead</td><td>178</td><td>10</td><td>90</td><td>199</td><td>11</td></tr>
<tr><td>WHO'D</td><td></td><td></td><td></td><td></td><td></td></tr>
<tr><td>Who'd raise the organs of the counted dust</td><td>117</td><td>7</td><td>71</td><td>129</td><td>7</td></tr>
<tr><td>WHOEVER</td><td></td><td></td><td></td><td></td><td></td></tr>
<tr><td>Whoever I would with my wicked eyes,</td><td>174</td><td>9</td><td>89</td><td>194</td><td>9</td></tr>
<tr><td>WHOLE</td><td></td><td></td><td></td><td></td><td></td></tr>
<tr><td>And my whole heart under your hammer,</td><td>107</td><td>13</td><td>65</td><td>118</td><td>13</td></tr>
<tr><td>Singly lie with the whole wide shore,</td><td>115</td><td>3</td><td>69</td><td>127</td><td>3</td></tr>
<tr><td>And the whole pain</td><td>142</td><td>14</td><td>82</td><td>159</td><td>14</td></tr>
<tr><td>Now cast down your rod, for the whole</td><td>150</td><td>7</td><td>83</td><td>167</td><td>11</td></tr>
<tr><td>And gale I tackle, the whole world of then,</td><td>173</td><td>15</td><td>88</td><td>193</td><td>15</td></tr>
<tr><td>The whole of the moon I could love and<br>leave</td><td>174</td><td>10</td><td>89</td><td>194</td><td>10</td></tr>
<tr><td>WHOLLY</td><td></td><td></td><td></td><td></td><td></td></tr>
<tr><td>Not wholly to that lamenting</td><td>143</td><td>15</td><td>82</td><td>160</td><td>15</td></tr>
<tr><td>WHOM</td><td></td><td></td><td></td><td></td><td></td></tr>
<tr><td>The one not caring to whom in his sleep he will<br>move</td><td>100</td><td>4</td><td>61</td><td>111</td><td>4</td></tr>
<tr><td>Will be the same grief flying. Whom shall they<br>calm?</td><td>100</td><td>11</td><td>61</td><td>111</td><td>11</td></tr>
<tr><td>And the child not caring to whom he climbs his<br>prayer</td><td>100</td><td>17</td><td>61</td><td>111</td><td>17</td></tr>
<tr><td>Whom now I conjure to stand as thief</td><td>107</td><td>9</td><td>65</td><td>118</td><td>9</td></tr>
<tr><td>They come together whom their love parted:</td><td>124</td><td>10</td><td>73</td><td>138</td><td>10</td></tr>
<tr><td>Of the led-astray birds whom God, for their<br>breast of whistles,</td><td>168</td><td>19</td><td>87</td><td>189</td><td>4</td></tr>
<tr><td>On whom a world of ills came down like snow.</td><td></td><td></td><td>91</td><td>201</td><td>11</td></tr>
<tr><td>WHOSE</td><td></td><td></td><td></td><td></td><td></td></tr>
<tr><td>Day's night whose towers will catch</td><td>vii</td><td>20</td><td>1</td><td>xv</td><td>20</td></tr>
<tr><td>Whose beard wags in Egyptian wind.</td><td>63</td><td>15</td><td>38</td><td>72</td><td>15</td></tr>
<tr><td>That frozen wife whose juices drift like a fixed<br>sea</td><td>77</td><td>14</td><td>45</td><td>86</td><td>14</td></tr>
<tr><td>Whose hooded, fountain heart once fell in<br>puddles</td><td>87</td><td>14</td><td>52</td><td>96</td><td>14</td></tr>
<tr><td>Whose wizard shape I trace in the cavernous<br>skull,</td><td>91</td><td>2</td><td>55</td><td>100</td><td>2</td></tr>
<tr><td>Of sleepers whose tongue I toll</td><td>146</td><td>3</td><td>82</td><td>163</td><td>3</td></tr>
<tr><td>WHY</td><td></td><td></td><td></td><td></td><td></td></tr>
<tr><td>Why east wind chills and south wind cools</td><td>53</td><td>1</td><td>32</td><td>62</td><td>1</td></tr>
<tr><td>Why silk is soft and the stone wounds</td><td>53</td><td>6</td><td>32</td><td>62</td><td>6</td></tr>
<tr><td>Why night-time rain and the breast's blood</td><td>53</td><td>8</td><td>32</td><td>62</td><td>8</td></tr>
<tr><td>Why east wind chills</td><td>53</td><td></td><td>32</td><td>62</td><td></td></tr>
</table>

|  | U.K. | | | U.S. | |
|  | Page | Line | Poem | Page | Line |
| **WICK** | | | | | |
| And burned sea silence on a wick of words. | 74 | 4 | 44 | 83 | 4 |
| **WICK-[DIPPING]** | | | | | |
| Not a boy and a bit in the wick- | 174 | 16 | 89 | 194 | 16 |
| **WICKED** | | | | | |
| The kingcrafts of the wicked sea, | 65 | 11 | 40 | 74 | 11 |
| And the wicked wish, | 106 | 5 | 64 | 117 | 5 |
| Whoever I would with my wicked eyes, | 174 | 9 | 89 | 194 | 9 |
| **WIDDERSHIN** | | | | | |
| Shall I still be love's house on the widdershin earth, | 47 | 5 | 27 | 55 | 5 |
| **WIDE** | | | | | |
| Her constant, nor the winds of love broken wide | 109 | 10 | 67 | 120 | 10 |
| Singly lie with the whole wide shore, | 115 | 3 | 69 | 127 | 3 |
| In the long ago land that glided the dark door wide | 121 | 12 | 72 | 134 | 7 |
| In the far ago land the door of his death glided wide, | 122 | 25 | 72 | 136 | 5 |
| And the wings glided wide and he was hymned and wedded, | 123 | 13 | 72 | 137 | 3 |
| The locks yawned loose and a blast blew them wide, | 135 | 3 | 80 | 152 | 3 |
| Throw wide to the wind the gates of the wandering boat | 136 | 10 | 81 | 153 | 10 |
| Shall harrow and snow the blood while you ride wide and near, | 162 | 23 | 86 | 181 | 23 |
| **WIDOWER** | | | | | |
| And a tear-stained widower grief drooped from the lashes | 85 | 9 | 50 | 94 | 9 |
| **WIDOWS** | | | | | |
| Groom the dark brides, the widows of the night | 14 | 5 | 10 | 16 | 5 |
| **WIFE** | | | | | |
| So solve the mystic sun, the wife of light, | 51 | 26 | 31 | 61 | 5 |
| That frozen wife whose juices drift like a fixed sea | 77 | 14 | 45 | 86 | 14 |
| To find a woman's soul for a wife. | 175 | 19 | 89 | 195 | 24 |
| For, oh, my soul found a sunday wife | 175 | 25 | 89 | 196 | 6 |
| **WIG** | | | | | |
| Then, bushily swanked in bear wig and tails, | 132 | 19 | 78 | 147 | 19 |
| **WILD** | | | | | |
| The wild pigs' wood, and slime upon the trees, | 30 | 20 | 18 | 35 | 20 |
| Nor ever, as the wild tongue breaks its tombs, | 77 | 11 | 45 | 86 | 11 |
| With the wild breast and blessed and giant skull | 87 | 28 | 52 | 96 | 28 |
| And the wild boys innocent as strawberries | 112 | 16 | 68 | 124 | 16 |
| Wild men who caught and sang the sun in flight, | 116 | 10 | 70 | 128 | 10 |
| And the wild wings were raised | 122 | 1 | 72 | 135 | 1 |
| The wild | 137 | 16 | 82 | 154 | 16 |

# WILD (continued)

|  | U.K. |  |  | U.S. |  |
|---|---|---|---|---|---|
|  | Page | Line | Poem | Page | Line |
| With wild sea fillies and soaking bridles | 156 | 17 | 83 | 175 | 5 |
| And wishbones of wild geese, | 172 | 5 | 88 | 192 | 5 |
| And air shaped Heaven where souls grow wild | 172 | 20 | 88 | 192 | 20 |
| **WILDERNESS** |  |  |  |  |  |
| From a lost wilderness | 125 | 10 | 74 | 139 | 10 |
| Of the garden of wilderness. | 131 | 8 | 77 | 145 | 14 |
| **WILL** |  |  |  |  |  |
| Day's night whose towers will catch | vii | 20 | I | xv | 20 |
| That will fly and fall | viii | 4 | I | xvi | 4 |
| We will ride out alone, and then, | x | 8 | I | xviii | 14 |
| I learnt the verbs of will, and had my secret; | 21 | 15 | 13 | 25 | 15 |
| My camel's eyes will needle through the shroud. | 73 | 6 | 44 | 82 | 6 |
| The fingers will forget green thumbs and mark | 81 | 2 | 47 | 90 | 2 |
| The whispering ears will watch love drummed away | 81 | 6 | 47 | 90 | 6 |
| In all love's countries, that will grope awake; | 81 | 12 | 47 | 90 | 12 |
| That will rake at last all currencies of the marked breath | 94 | 8 | 57 | 104 | 8 |
| The one not caring to whom in his sleep he will move | 100 | 4 | 61 | 111 | 4 |
| And the other full of tears that she will be dead, | 100 | 5 | 61 | 111 | 5 |
| Turns in the dark on the sound they know will arise | 100 | 6 | 61 | 111 | 6 |
| Will be the same grief flying. Whom shall they calm? | 100 | 11 | 61 | 111 | 11 |
| Yet raves at her will | 108 | 14 | 66 | 119 | 14 |
| Will dive up to his tears. | 117 | 18 | 71 | 129 | 18 |
| Will pull the thunderbolts | 118 | 4 | 71 | 130 | 8 |
| No longer will the vibrations of the sun desire on | 127 | 8 | 75 | 141 | 8 |
| Of the hobnail tales: no gooseherd or swine will turn | 162 | 10 | 86 | 181 | 10 |
| Be you sure the Thief will seek a way sly and sure | 163 | 26 | 86 | 183 | 7 |
| Naked and forsaken to grieve he will not come. | 166 | 7 | 86 | 186 | 7 |
| Terror will rage apart | 171 | 16 | 88 | 191 | 16 |
| Now will be ever is always true, | 171 | 24 | 88 | 191 | 24 |
| Who knows the rocketing wind will blow | 172 | 13 | 88 | 192 | 13 |
| Will never go out of my mind: |  |  | 91 | 200 | 20 |
| Until I die he will not leave my side.) |  |  | 91 | 201 | 19 |
| **WILLOW** |  |  |  |  |  |
| Through the loud zoo of the willow groves | 111 | 22 | 68 | 123 | 22 |
| **WILLOWS** |  |  |  |  |  |
| While the boys among willows | 112 | 3 | 68 | 124 | 3 |
| **WILLY** |  |  |  |  |  |
| The thief fall on the dead like the willy nilly dew, | 165 | 22 | 86 | 185 | 12 |
| **WILY** |  |  |  |  |  |
| The word of the blood, the wily skin, | 65 | 15 | 40 | 74 | 15 |

|  | U.K. | | | U.S. | |
|  | Page | Line | Poem | Page | Line |
|---|---|---|---|---|---|
| WIND | | | | | |
| In the religious wind | vii | 21 | 1 | xv | 21 |
| Slow in a sleeping wind. | 6 | 15 | 4 | 6 | 15 |
| And the wind was my sister suitor; | 7 | 15 | 5 | 8 | 15 |
| Wind in me leaped, the hellborn dew; | 7 | 16 | 5 | 8 | 16 |
| Stirs the quicksand; that ropes the blowing wind | 9 | 12 | 6 | 10 | 12 |
| And I am dumb to tell a weather's wind | 9 | 19 | 6 | 10 | 19 |
| The beach of flesh, and wind her bloodred plait; | 10 | 13 | 7 | 11 | 13 |
| Pushed up their hair, the dry wind steers | 11 | 5 | 8 | 12 | 5 |
| Especially when the October wind | 16 | 1 | 11 | 19 | 1 |
| Especially when the October wind | 17 | 1 | 11 | 20 | 1 |
| (Have with the house of wind), the leaning scene, | 19 | 17 | 12 | 23 | 2 |
| All, men my madmen, the unwholesome wind | 19 | 21 | 12 | 23 | 6 |
| Itched in the noise of wind and sun. | 21 | 6 | 13 | 25 | 6 |
| In the stitched wound and clotted wind, muzzled | 28 | 15 | 17 | 33 | 15 |
| I, in a wind on fire, from green Adam's cradle, | 38 | 17 | 20 | 44 | 7 |
| Man in the day or wind at night | 39 | 4 | 21 | 45 | 4 |
| Once in this wind the summer blood | 39 | 6 | 21 | 45 | 6 |
| The oat was merry in the wind; | 39 | 9 | 21 | 45 | 9 |
| Man broke the sun, pulled the wind down. | 39 | 10 | 21 | 45 | 10 |
| Why east wind chills and south wind cools | 53 | 1 | 32 | 62 | 1 |
| Hell wind and sea, | 54 | 4 | 33 | 63 | 4 |
| The twelve triangles of the cherub wind | 54 | 23 | 33 | 63 | 23 |
| The wind pass like a fire, | 58 | 18 | 35 | 67 | 18 |
| With the wind in my hair, | 58 | 22 | 35 | 67 | 22 |
| Whose beard wags in Egyptian wind. | 63 | 15 | 38 | 72 | 15 |
| Lean time on tide and times the wind stood rough, | 67 | 6 | 41 | 76 | 6 |
| With the man in the wind and the west moon; | 68 | 3 | 42 | 77 | 3 |
| Shot in the wind, by tilted arcs, | 69 | 26 | 43 | 79 | 2 |
| Which sixth of wind blew out the burning gentry? | 73 | 1 | 44 | 82 | 1 |
| In a wind that plucked a goose, | 77 | 10 | 45 | 86 | 10 |
| Where, wound in emerald linen and sharp wind, | 79 | 16 | 46 | 88 | 19 |
| These once-blind eyes have breathed a wind of visions, | 80 | 1 | 46 | 89 | 9 |
| A calm wind blows that raised the trees like hair | 80 | 11 | 46 | 89 | 19 |
| A calling for colour calls with the wind | 82 | 6 | 48 | 91 | 6 |
| Watch yellow, wish for wind to blow away | 82 | 19 | 48 | 91 | 19 |
| But do not travel down dumb wind like prodigals. | 86 | 11 | 51 | 95 | 11 |
| And every stone I wind off like a reel. | 89 | 13 | 53 | 98 | 13 |
| Wind blow cold | 103 | 4 | 63 | 114 | 4 |

WIND (continued)

|  | U.K. | | | U.S. | |
|---|---|---|---|---|---|
|  | Page | Line | Poem | Page | Line |
| To the wind the choir and cloister | 109 | 11 | 67 | 120 | 11 |
| And wind his globe out of your water thread | 117 | 21 | 71 | 129 | 21 |
| But only the wind strung | 120 | 16 | 72 | 133 | 1 |
| Parish of snow. The carved mouths in the rock are wind swept strings. | 121 | 9 | 72 | 134 | 4 |
| Him up and he ran like a wind after the kindling flight | 122 | 9 | 72 | 135 | 9 |
| The voices of all the drowned swam on the wind. | 136 | 8 | 81 | 153 | 8 |
| Throw wide to the wind the gates of the wandering boat | 136 | 10 | 81 | 153 | 10 |
| Sails drank the wind, and white as milk | 149 | 13 | 83 | 166 | 13 |
| A wind throws a shadow and it freezes fast. | 154 | 10 | 83 | 172 | 10 |
| When his long-legged flesh was a wind on fire | 157 | 3 | 83 | 175 | 15 |
| Who comes as red as the fox and sly as the heeled wind. | 165 | 10 | 86 | 184 | 18 |
| In a whack of wind. | 167 | 17 | 87 | 187 | 17 |
| His driftwood thirty-fifth wind turned age; | 170 | 8 | 88 | 190 | 8 |
| Who knows the rocketing wind will blow | 172 | 13 | 88 | 192 | 13 |
| Especially when the October wind | 16 |  | 11 | 19 |  |
| Why east wind chills | 53 |  | 32 | 62 |  |
| WIND-HEELED |  |  |  |  |  |
| Wind-heeled foot in the hole of a fireball, | 95 | 12 | 58 | 105 | 12 |
| WIND-[MILLED] |  |  |  |  |  |
| Through the haygold stalls, as the dew falls on the wind- | 164 | 9 | 86 | 183 | 16 |
| WIND-TURNED |  |  |  |  |  |
| Doom on deniers at the wind-turned statement. | 74 | 20 | 44 | 83 | 20 |
| WINDER |  |  |  |  |  |
| The winder of the water-clocks | 69 | 5 | 43 | 78 | 5 |
| The winder of the clockwise scene | 70 | 4 | 43 | 79 | 8 |
| WINDFALL |  |  |  |  |  |
| Down the rivers of the windfall light. | 159 | 9 | 85 | 178 | 9 |
| WINDILY |  |  |  |  |  |
| Windily master of man was the rotten fathom, | 38 | 26 | 20 | 44 | 16 |
| And when the moon rose windily it was | 40 | 11 | 22 | 46 | 11 |
| They lying long shall not die windily; | 68 | 12 | 42 | 77 | 12 |
| WINDING |  |  |  |  |  |
| This day winding down now | vii | 1 | 1 | xv | 1 |
| Into the winding dark | 105 | 11 | 64 | 116 | 11 |
| The world winding home! | 142 | 13 | 82 | 159 | 13 |
| WINDING-FOOTED |  |  |  |  |  |
| And, winding-footed in their shawl and sheet, | 14 | 4 | 10 | 16 | 4 |
| WINDING-SHEETS |  |  |  |  |  |
| Disturb no winding-sheets, my son, | 65 | 6 | 40 | 74 | 6 |
| WINDINGS |  |  |  |  |  |
| Under the windings of the sea | 68 | 11 | 42 | 77 | 11 |

| | U.K. | | | U.S. | |
|---|---|---|---|---|---|
| | *Page* | *Line* | *Poem* | *Page* | *Line* |
| WINDLESS | | | | | |
| Gliding windless through the hand folded flakes, | 119 | 4 | 72 | 131 | 4 |
| Past the blind barns and byres of the windless farm. | 122 | 10 | 72 | 135 | 10 |
| WINDMILL | | | | | |
| An air-drawn windmill on a wooden horse, | 41 | 20 | 23 | 48 | 2 |
| WINDOW | | | | | |
| Is carved from her in a room with a wet window | 88 | 1 | 52 | 97 | 1 |
| WINDOWS | | | | | |
| Adore my windows for their summer scene? | 46 | 8 | 27 | 54 | 8 |
| The windows pour into their heart | 124 | 11 | 73 | 138 | 11 |
| Who under the lids of her windows hoisted his golden luggage, | 127 | 12 | 75 | 141 | 12 |
| In the praying windows of waves | 150 | 4 | 83 | 167 | 8 |
| Now the heron grieves in the weeded verge. Through windows | 168 | 23 | 87 | 189 | 8 |
| WINDS | | | | | |
| And the four winds, that had long blown as one, | 20 | 19 | 13 | 24 | 19 |
| Blood shot and scattered to the winds of light | 23 | 5 | 14 | 28 | 5 |
| Twelve winds encounter by the white host at pasture, | 36 | 14 | 20 | 41 | 14 |
| In winds that bring the fruit and rind | 53 | 4 | 32 | 62 | 4 |
| Calls some content to travel with the winds, | 53 | 17 | 32 | 62 | 17 |
| Nor weather winds that blow not down the bone, | 60 | 2 | 36 | 69 | 2 |
| With bones unbuttoned to the half-way winds, | 71 | 9 | 44 | 80 | 9 |
| By magnet winds to her blind mother drawn, | 78 | 14 | 46 | 87 | 14 |
| Her constant, nor the winds of love broken wide | 109 | 10 | 67 | 120 | 10 |
| And spells on the winds of the dead his winter's tale. | 121 | 4 | 72 | 133 | 19 |
| And the fisherman winds his reel | 154 | 3 | 83 | 172 | 3 |
| Winds, from the dousing shade and the roarer at the latch, | 163 | 23 | 86 | 183 | 4 |
| Heeled winds the rooks | 164 | 18 | 86 | 184 | 4 |
| WINDS' | | | | | |
| In the winds' wakes. | 164 | 14 | 86 | 185 | 4 |
| WINDSHAKE | | | | | |
| Windshake of sailshaped ears, muffle-toed tap | 87 | 2 | 52 | 96 | 2 |
| WINDWELL | | | | | |
| Shall not be known till windwell dries | 53 | 2 | 32 | 62 | 2 |
| WINDY | | | | | |
| And tells the windy weather in the cock. | 16 | 20 | 11 | 19 | 20 |
| All world was one, one windy nothing, | 20 | 6 | 13 | 24 | 6 |
| From poles of skull and toe the windy blood | 24 | 14 | 15 | 29 | 14 |
| A quarrel of weathers and trees in the windy spiral. | 36 | 18 | 20 | 41 | 18 |
| Woe to the windy masons at my shelter? | 47 | 6 | 27 | 55 | 6 |
| Hatched from the windy salvage on one leg, | 71 | 10 | 44 | 80 | 10 |

WINDY (continued)

| | U.K. | | | U.S. | |
|---|---|---|---|---|---|
| | *Page* | *Line* | *Poem* | *Page* | *Line* |
| And from the windy West came two-gunned Gabriel, | 73 | 11 | 44 | 82 | 11 |
| When I was a windy boy and a bit | 174 | 1 | 89 | 194 | 1 |
| WINE | | | | | |
| This wine upon a foreign tree | 39 | 2 | 21 | 45 | 2 |
| My wine you drink, my bread you snap. | 39 | 15 | 21 | 45 | 15 |
| Into the wine burning like brandy, | 131 | 19 | 77 | 146 | 1 |
| WINE-WELLS | | | | | |
| On the last rick's tip by spilled wine-wells | 95 | 14 | 58 | 105 | 14 |
| WING | | | | | |
| Pierce the spilt sky with diving wing in weed and heel | 86 | 4 | 51 | 95 | 4 |
| Cyclone of his wing | 140 | 5 | 82 | 157 | 5 |
| Wing, and blest shall | 168 | 5 | 87 | 188 | 9 |
| WINGBEAT | | | | | |
| Mutter and foul wingbeat of the solemnizing nightpriest | 114 | 22 | 69 | 126 | 22 |
| WINGED | | | | | |
| Winged like a sabbath ass this children's piece | 41 | 16 | 23 | 47 | 16 |
| So shall winged harbours through the rockbirds' eyes | 76 | 12 | 44 | 85 | 12 |
| Birds and the birds of the winged trees flying my name | 102 | 12 | 63 | 113 | 12 |
| In his firelit island ringed by the winged snow | 119 | 17 | 72 | 131 | 17 |
| And the winged wall is torn | 138 | 12 | 82 | 155 | 12 |
| Of the morning leaves, as the stars falls, as the winged | 164 | 11 | 86 | 183 | 18 |
| Burning! Night and the vein of birds in the winged, sloe wrist | 164 | 21 | 86 | 184 | 7 |
| WINGING | | | | | |
| The winging bone that sprouted in the heels, | 12 | 11 | 9 | 13 | 11 |
| WINGS | | | | | |
| Sweet are their fathered faces in their wings.' | 26 | 14 | 16 | 31 | 14 |
| Her lover's wings that fold to-morrow's flight, | 115 | 11 | 69 | 127 | 11 |
| Dust in the buried wood, flies on the grains of her wings | 121 | 3 | 72 | 133 | 18 |
| And the wild wings were raised | 122 | 1 | 72 | 135 | 1 |
| In a choir of wings, as though she slept or died, | 123 | 12 | 72 | 137 | 2 |
| And the wings glided wide and he was hymned and wedded, | 123 | 13 | 72 | 137 | 3 |
| On the old seas from stories, thrashing my wings, | 133 | 8 | 78 | 148 | 11 |
| The morning is flying on the wings of his age | 135 | 13 | 80 | 152 | 13 |
| O the wings of the children! | 142 | 7 | 82 | 159 | 7 |
| As the boat skims on with drinking wings! | 154 | 14 | 83 | 172 | 14 |
| And the wings of the great roc ribboned for the fair! | 164 | 16 | 86 | 184 | 2 |

|  | U.K. | | | U.S. | |
|---|---|---|---|---|---|
|  | *Page* | *Line* | *Poem* | *Page* | *Line* |
| Modesty hides my thighs in her wings, | 175 | 30 | 89 | 196 | 11 |
| Trounced by his wings in the hissing shippen, long dead | 177 | 19 | 90 | 198 | 18 |
| **WINKLE** | | | | | |
| And, Rip Van Winkle from a timeless cradle, | 72 | 13 | 44 | 81 | 13 |
| **WINNING** | | | | | |
| You my friend there with a winning air | 107 | 3 | 65 | 118 | 3 |
| **WINTER** | | | | | |
| There in their heat the winter floods | 1 | 4 | 2 | 1 | 4 |
| The sleepy man of winter pulls, | 2 | 5 | 2 | 2 | 5 |
| I knew the message of the winter, | 7 | 13 | 5 | 8 | 13 |
| Hearing the raven cough in winter sticks, | 16 | 6 | 11 | 19 | 6 |
| Breaks with the wormy winter through the eye. | 16 | 23 | 11 | 19 | 23 |
| Here in this ornamental winter | 45 | 2 | 26 | 53 | 2 |
| The black ram, shuffling of the year, old winter, | 72 | 15 | 44 | 81 | 15 |
| From blank and leaking winter sails the child in colour, | 83 | 22 | 49 | 93 | 4 |
| To the built voice, or fly with winter to the bells, | 86 | 10 | 51 | 95 | 10 |
| Hill. Who once in gooseskin winter loved all ice leaved | 176 | 12 | 90 | 197 | 12 |
| **·WINTER-LOCKED** | | | | | |
| Winter-locked side by side, | 126 | 2 | 74 | 140 | 2 |
| **WINTER'S** | | | | | |
| The winter's robes; | 24 | 23 | 15 | 29 | 23 |
| Tell, if at all, the winter's storms | 45 | 10 | 26 | 53 | 10 |
| It is a winter's tale | 119 | 1 | 72 | 131 | 1 |
| And spells on the winds of the dead his winter's tale. | 121 | 4 | 72 | 133 | 19 |
| A Winter's Tale | 119 | | 72 | 131 | |
| **WINTERED** | | | | | |
| Love in the frost is pared and wintered by, | 81 | 5 | 47 | 90 | 5 |
| **WINTRY** | | | | | |
| My youth is bent by the same wintry fever. | 9 | 5 | 6 | 10 | 5 |
| Of the wintry nunnery of the order of lust | 109 | 12 | 67 | 120 | 12 |
| **WIPES** | | | | | |
| That wipes away not crow's-foot nor the lock | 12 | 23 | 9 | 14 | 2 |
| **WIRE** | | | | | |
| He holds the wire from this box of nerves | 10 | 16 | 7 | 11 | 16 |
| **WIRED** | | | | | |
| And these poor nerves so wired to the skull | 10 | 6 | 7 | 11 | 6 |
| **WIRES** | | | | | |
| Because the pleasure-bird whistles after the hot wires, | 77 | 1 | 45 | 86 | 1 |
| **WISE** | | | | | |
| Was muscled, matted, wise to the crying thigh | 21 | 4 | 13 | 25 | 4 |
| Though wise men at their end know dark is right, | 116 | 4 | 70 | 128 | 4 |

# WISE (continued)

| | | U.K. | | | U.S. | |
|---|---|---|---|---|---|---|
| | | *Page* | *Line* | *Poem* | *Page* | *Line* |
| Sleep, good, for ever, slow and deep, spelled rare and wise, | | 162 | 8 | 86 | 181 | 8 |
| **WISEMEN** | | | | | | |
| The wisemen tell me that the garden gods | | 40 | 9 | 22 | 46 | 9 |
| **WISER** | | | | | | |
| Call for confessor and wiser mirror but there is none | | 158 | 10 | 84 | 177 | 10 |
| **WISH** | | | | | | |
| Watch yellow, wish for wind to blow away | | 82 | 19 | 48 | 91 | 19 |
| And the wicked wish, | | 106 | 5 | 64 | 117 | 5 |
| **WISHBONES** | | | | | | |
| And wishbones of wild geese, | | 172 | 5 | 88 | 192 | 5 |
| **WISHES** | | | | | | |
| But wishes breed not, neither | | 82 | 21 | 48 | 91 | 21 |
| The singing breaks in the snow shoed villages of wishes | | 123 | 3 | 72 | 136 | 13 |
| Prisoners of wishes locked their eyes | | 125 | 7 | 74 | 139 | 7 |
| Walking in wishes and lovely for shame | | 153 | 9 | 83 | 171 | 5 |
| My wishes raced through the house high hay | | 160 | 19 | 85 | 179 | 19 |
| **WISPS** | | | | | | |
| In the wains tonned so high that the wisps of the hay | | 176 | 14 | 90 | 197 | 14 |
| **WITCH** | | | | | | |
| Adam, time's joker, on a witch of cardboard | | 74 | 11 | 44 | 83 | 11 |
| **WITCH'S** | | | | | | |
| From the broomed witch's spume you are shielded by fern | | 162 | 17 | 86 | 181 | 17 |
| **WITCHLIKE** | | | | | | |
| Cry joy that this witchlike midwife second | | 96 | 23 | 58 | 107 | 6 |
| **WITHER** | | | | | | |
| Would wither up, and any boy of love | | 63 | 3 | 38 | 72 | 3 |
| Of nightingale and centaur dead horse. The springs wither | | 123 | 7 | 72 | 136 | 17 |
| **WITHERED** | | | | | | |
| My lips are withered with a kiss, | | 65 | 20 | 40 | 74 | 20 |
| The voice of the dust of water from the withered spring | | 121 | 5 | 72 | 133 | 20 |
| **WITHIN** | | | | | | |
| Within the hallowed gland, blood blessed the heart, | | 20 | 18 | 13 | 24 | 18 |
| Within the nested treefork | | 115 | 12 | 69 | 127 | 12 |
| Brethren for joy has moved within | | 143 | 16 | 82 | 160 | 16 |
| **WITHOUT** | | | | | | |
| Shade without shape? the shape of Pharaoh's echo? | | 72 | 21 | 44 | 81 | 21 |
| I may without fail | | 108 | 17 | 66 | 119 | 17 |
| A woman figure without fault | | 112 | 8 | 68 | 124 | 8 |

|  | U.K. | | | U.S. | |
| --- | --- | --- | --- | --- | --- |
|  | Page | Line | Poem | Page | Line |
| My dear this night he comes and night without end my dear | 166 | 9 | 86 | 186 | 9 |
| Last sound, the world going out without a breath: |  |  | 91 | 201 | 13 |
| WITNESS |  |  |  |  |  |
| And by this blowclock witness of the sun | 75 | 17 | 44 | 84 | 17 |
| WITNESSED |  |  |  |  |  |
| Witnessed with a kiss. | 150 | 24 | 83 | 168 | 8 |
| WITNESSES |  |  |  |  |  |
| Of head and tail made witnesses to this | 41 | 7 | 23 | 47 | 7 |
| My one and noble heart has witnesses | 81 | 11 | 47 | 90 | 11 |
| WITS |  |  |  |  |  |
| Whisper in a damp word, her wits drilled hollow, | 88 | 5 | 52 | 97 | 5 |
| WIVING |  |  |  |  |  |
| Flared in the reek of the wiving sty with the rush | 177 | 2 | 90 | 198 | 1 |
| WIVES |  |  |  |  |  |
| Old wives that spin in the smoke, | 150 | 2 | 83 | 167 | 6 |
| The long-legged beautiful bait their wives. | 151 | 22 | 83 | 169 | 10 |
| All the green leaved little weddings' wives | 174 | 11 | 89 | 194 | 11 |
| They with the simple Jacks were a boulder of wives)— | 178 | 3 | 90 | 199 | 4 |
| WIZARD |  |  |  |  |  |
| Whose wizard shape I trace in the cavernous skull, | 91 | 2 | 55 | 100 | 2 |
| WIZARD'S |  |  |  |  |  |
| But rail with your wizard's ribs the heart-shaped planet; | 60 | 15 | 36 | 69 | 15 |
| WIZENED |  |  |  |  |  |
| Is telling. The wizened | 121 | 6 | 72 | 134 | 1 |
| WOE |  |  |  |  |  |
| Agape, with woe | ix | 14 | 1 | xvii | 14 |
| Woe to the windy masons at my shelter? | 47 | 6 | 27 | 55 | 6 |
| Woe drip from the dishrag hands and the pressed sponge of the forehead, | 96 | 20 | 58 | 107 | 3 |
| WOEBEGONE |  |  |  |  |  |
| Out of the woebegone pyre | 158 | 16 | 84 | 177 | 16 |
| WOKE |  |  |  |  |  |
| Woke to my hearing from harbour and neighbour wood | 102 | 2 | 63 | 113 | 2 |
| When I woke, the town spoke. | 134 | 1 | 79 | 150 | 1 |
| When I Woke | 134 |  | 79 | 150 |  |
| WOKEN |  |  |  |  |  |
| Shakes, in crabbed burial shawl, by sorcerer's insect woken, | 83 | 23 | 49 | 93 | 5 |
| And all the woken farm at its white trades, | 119 | 25 | 72 | 132 | 5 |
| WOLF |  |  |  |  |  |
| Fear or believe that the wolf in a sheepwhite hood | 162 | 3 | 86 | 181 | 3 |

| | U.K. | | | U.S. | |
|---|---|---|---|---|---|
| | *Page* | *Line* | *Poem* | *Page* | *Line* |
| For ever of all not the wolf in his baaing hood | 163 | 13 | 86 | 182 | 13 |
| WOMAN | | | | | |
| Death from a summer woman, | 2 | 8 | 2 | 2 | 8 |
| The boy of woman and the wanton starer | 46 | 10 | 27 | 54 | 10 |
| Through no regret of leaving woman waiting | 48 | 14 | 28 | 56 | 14 |
| With pins for teardrops is the long wound's woman. | 75 | 10 | 44 | 84 | 10 |
| And for the woman in shades | 109 | 4 | 67 | 120 | 4 |
| A woman figure without fault | 112 | 8 | 68 | 124 | 8 |
| The woman breasted and the heaven headed | 123 | 15 | 72 | 137 | 5 |
| Man and woman undone, | 131 | 5 | 77 | 145 | 11 |
| With every simmering woman his mouse | 175 | 1 | 89 | 195 | 6 |
| WOMAN'S | | | | | |
| Sin who had a woman's shape | 153 | 14 | 83 | 171 | 10 |
| To find a woman's soul for a wife. | 175 | 19 | 89 | 195 | 24 |
| WOMAN-LUCK | | | | | |
| Frogs and satans and woman-luck, | 134 | 7 | 79 | 150 | 7 |
| WOMB | | | | | |
| And from the planted womb the man of straw. | 2 | 12 | 2 | 2 | 12 |
| The bones of blindness; and the womb | 6 | 8 | 4 | 6 | 8 |
| With liquid hands tapped on the womb, | 7 | 2 | 5 | 8 | 2 |
| And double-crossed my mother's womb. | 8 | 22 | 5 | 9 | 22 |
| And to the hollow minute of the womb, | 20 | 2 | 13 | 24 | 2 |
| One womb, one mind, spewed out the matter, | 21 | 18 | 13 | 26 | 1 |
| With the womb of his shapeless people. | 34 | 3 | 19 | 39 | 9 |
| That town of ghosts, the trodden womb | 42 | 2 | 24 | 49 | 2 |
| That town of ghosts, the manwaged womb | 42 | 9 | 24 | 49 | 9 |
| 'His mother's womb had a tongue that lapped up mud,' | 79 | 20 | 46 | 89 | 1 |
| But my womb was bellowing | 93 | 27 | 56 | 103 | 7 |
| That I can hear the womb | 137 | 6 | 82 | 154 | 6 |
| And the womb | 144 | 7 | 82 | 161 | 7 |
| Harpies around me out of her womb! | 175 | 27 | 89 | 196 | 8 |
| WOMB-EYED | | | | | |
| The womb-eyed, cries, | 57 | 4 | 34 | 66 | 11 |
| WOMB'S | | | | | |
| Split up the brawned womb's weathers, | 1 | 14 | 2 | 1 | 14 |
| WOMEN | | | | | |
| The wordy shapes of women, and the rows | 16 | 11 | 11 | 19 | 11 |
| Mast-high moon-white women naked | 153 | 8 | 83 | 171 | 4 |
| With men and women and waterfalls | 156 | 1 | 83 | 174 | 9 |
| (Sighed the old ram rod, dying of women), | 174 | 3 | 89 | 194 | 3 |
| Where barren as boulders women lie longing still | 176 | 4 | 90 | 197 | 4 |
| Through throats where many rivers meet, the women pray, | 176 | 6 | 90 | 197 | 6 |
| Hale dead and deathless do the women of the hill | 178 | 17 | 90 | 199 | 18 |

|  | U.K. Page | Line | Poem | U.S. Page | Line |
|---|---|---|---|---|---|
| **WONDER** | | | | | |
| And to the first dumb wonder at the flesh, | 20 | 13 | 13 | 24 | 13 |
| Streamed again a wonder of summer | 103 | 18 | 63 | 114 | 18 |
| **WOOD** | | | | | |
| The world's turning wood, | viii | 1 | 1 | xvi | 1 |
| The wild pigs' wood, and slime upon the trees, | 30 | 20 | 18 | 35 | 20 |
| Death hairy-heeled, and the tapped ghost in wood, | 52 | 5 | 31 | 61 | 12 |
| And hemlock-headed in the wood of weathers. | 72 | 4 | 44 | 81 | 4 |
| Savours the lick of the times through a deadly wood of hair | 77 | 9 | 45 | 86 | 9 |
| Woke to my hearing from harbour and neighbour wood | 102 | 2 | 63 | 113 | 2 |
| In the wood faraway under me. | 103 | 5 | 63 | 114 | 5 |
| Dust in the buried wood, flies on the grains of her wings | 121 | 3 | 72 | 133 | 18 |
| To eat your heart in the house in the rosy wood. | 162 | 7 | 86 | 181 | 7 |
| Sanctum sanctorum the animal eye of the wood | 163 | 7 | 86 | 182 | 7 |
| Under the prayer wheeling moon in the rosy wood | 163 | 18 | 86 | 182 | 18 |
| Of the wood! Pastoral beat of blood through the laced leaves! | 164 | 22 | 86 | 184 | 8 |
| I tiptoed shy in the gooseberry wood, | 174 | 4 | 89 | 194 | 4 |
| Quick in the wood at love, where a torch of foxes foams, | 177 | 14 | 90 | 198 | 13 |
| Streets or hungering in the crumbled wood: to these | 178 | 16 | 90 | 199 | 17 |
| **WOOD'S** | | | | | |
| At a wood's dancing hoof, | vii | 8 | 1 | xv | 8 |
| **WOOD-TONGUED** | | | | | |
| The seas to service that her wood-tongued virtue | 87 | 22 | 52 | 96 | 22 |
| **WOODEN** | | | | | |
| Like wooden islands, hill to hill. | x | 13 | 1 | xviii | 19 |
| I with the wooden insect in the tree of nettles, | 36 | 4 | 20 | 41 | 4 |
| An air-drawn windmill on a wooden horse, | 41 | 20 | 23 | 48 | 2 |
| Who razed my wooden folly stands aghast, | 46 | 22 | 27 | 54 | 22 |
| **WOODS** | | | | | |
| Hist, in hogsback woods! The haystacked | ix | 27 | 1 | xviii | 1 |
| A Bible-leaved of all the written woods | 74 | 16 | 44 | 83 | 16 |
| Bow down the walls of the ferned and foxy woods | 87 | 24 | 52 | 96 | 24 |
| Ancient woods of my blood, dash down to the nut of the seas | 94 | 11 | 57 | 104 | 11 |
| I'll comb the snared woods with a glove on a lamp, | 97 | 7 | 59 | 108 | 7 |

# WOODS (continued)

|  | U.K. | | Poem | U.S. | |
|---|---|---|---|---|---|
|  | Page | Line | Poem | Page | Line |
| These were the woods the river and sea | 104 | 1 | 63 | 115 | 3 |
| Plenty as blackberries in the woods | 171 | 26 | 88 | 191 | 26 |
| WOODS' | | | | | |
| Coo rooing the woods' praise, | ix | 10 | 1 | xvii | 10 |
| WOOED | | | | | |
| Nor the innocent lie in the rooting dingle wooed | 162 | 15 | 86 | 181 | 15 |
| And on seesaw sunday nights I wooed | 174 | 8 | 89 | 194 | 8 |
| And heard the lewd, wooed field flow to the coming frost, | 177 | 10 | 90 | 198 | 9 |
| WOOL | | | | | |
| And the dung hills white as wool and the hen | 119 | 18 | 72 | 131 | 18 |
| WORD | | | | | |
| Tells me the hour's word, the neural meaning | 16 | 18 | 11 | 19 | 18 |
| In the beginning was the word, the word | 22 | 19 | 14 | 27 | 19 |
| The word flowed up, translating to the heart | 22 | 23 | 14 | 27 | 23 |
| The word of the blood, the wily skin, | 65 | 15 | 40 | 74 | 15 |
| Scraped at my cradle in a walking word | 71 | 11 | 44 | 80 | 11 |
| Genesis in the root, the scarecrow word, | 74 | 18 | 44 | 83 | 18 |
| Spot the blown word, and on the seas I image | 76 | 13 | 44 | 85 | 13 |
| Whisper in a damp word, her wits drilled hollow, | 88 | 5 | 52 | 97 | 5 |
| The shade of their trees was a word of many shades | 89 | 10 | 53 | 98 | 10 |
| Word, singers, and tongue | 131 | 1 | 77 | 145 | 7 |
| WORD'S | | | | | |
| Need no word's warmth. | 21 | 12 | 13 | 25 | 12 |
| WORDS | | | | | |
| Where words and water make a mixture | 8 | 3 | 5 | 9 | 3 |
| The words of death are dryer than his stiff, | 13 | 18 | 9 | 15 | 4 |
| Sheds the syllabic blood and drains her words. | 16 | 8 | 11 | 19 | 8 |
| Shut, too, in a tower of words, I mark | 16 | 9 | 11 | 19 | 9 |
| Some let me make you of the heartless words. | 17 | 5 | 11 | 20 | 5 |
| To shade and knit anew the patch of words | 21 | 10 | 13 | 25 | 10 |
| Raised up a voice, and, climbing on the words, | 26 | 22 | 16 | 32 | 2 |
| For her soldier stained with spilt words | 48 | 15 | 28 | 56 | 15 |
| The hollow words could bear all suffering | 48 | 22 | 28 | 56 | 22 |
| And burned sea silence on a wick of words. | 74 | 4 | 44 | 83 | 4 |
| Alcove of words out of cicada shade, | 82 | 4 | 48 | 91 | 4 |
| On no work of words now for three lean months in the bloody | 94 | 1 | 57 | 104 | 1 |
| And all your deeds and words, | 106 | 10 | 64 | 117 | 10 |
| Because their words have forked no lightning they | 116 | 5 | 70 | 128 | 5 |
| On no work of words | 94 | | 57 | 104 | |
| WORDY | | | | | |
| My wordy wounds are printed with your hair | 13 | 19 | 9 | 15 | 5 |

568

|  | U.K. | | | U.S. | |
|---|---|---|---|---|---|
|  | Page | Line | Poem | Page | Line |
| The wordy shapes of women, and the rows | 16 | 11 | 11 | 19 | 11 |
| WORE |  |  |  |  |  |
| Never never oh never to regret the bugle I wore | 133 | 19 | 78 | 149 | 2 |
| WORK |  |  |  |  |  |
| Work ark and the moonshine | x | 1 | 1 | xviii | 7 |
| On no work of words now for three lean months in the bloody | 94 | 1 | 57 | 104 | 1 |
| If I take to burn or return this world which is each man's work. | 94 | 12 | 57 | 104 | 12 |
| Work at their ways to death, | 170 | 14 | 88 | 190 | 14 |
| On no work of words | 94 |  | 57 | 104 |  |
| WORKED |  |  |  |  |  |
| Worked on a world of petals; | 35 | 9 | 20 | 40 | 9 |
| The mazes of his praise and envious tongue were worked in flames and shells. | 95 | 17 | 58 | 105 | 17 |
| In the memory worked by mirrors, | 107 | 10 | 65 | 118 | 10 |
| In grottoes I worked with birds, | 132 | 9 | 78 | 147 | 9 |
| WORKER |  |  |  |  |  |
| A worker in the morning town, | 5 | 14 | 3 | 5 | 14 |
| WORKING |  |  |  |  |  |
| Gives up its dead to such a working sea; | 5 | 3 | 3 | 5 | 3 |
| The loin is glory in a working pallor. | 32 | 9 | 18 | 37 | 15 |
| Fear not the working world, my mortal, | 33 | 13 | 19 | 38 | 13 |
| WORLD |  |  |  |  |  |
| A process in the weather of the world | 6 | 19 | 4 | 7 | 1 |
| Which is the world? Of our two sleepings, which | 15 | 1 | 10 | 17 | 1 |
| This is the world: the lying likeness of | 15 | 11 | 10 | 17 | 11 |
| This is the world. Have faith. | 15 | 16 | 10 | 17 | 16 |
| This world is half the devil's and my own, | 13 | 1 | 9 | 14 | 8 |
| This kissproof world. | 19 | 25 | 12 | 23 | 10 |
| All world was one, one windy nothing, | 20 | 6 | 13 | 24 | 6 |
| My world was christened in a stream of milk. | 20 | 7 | 13 | 24 | 7 |
| My world is pyramid. The padded mummer | 31 | 7 | 18 | 36 | 7 |
| My world is cypress, and an English valley. | 31 | 13 | 18 | 36 | 13 |
| Fear not the working world, my mortal, | 33 | 13 | 19 | 38 | 13 |
| The scales of this twin world tread on the double, | 35 | 4 | 20 | 40 | 4 |
| Worked on a world of petals; | 35 | 9 | 20 | 40 | 9 |
| These are your years' recorders. The circular world stands still.) | 37 | 21 | 20 | 143 | 4 |
| To-day, this insect, and the world I breathe, | 41 | 1 | 23 | 47 | 1 |
| Says the world wears away? | 45 | 17 | 26 | 53 | 17 |
| Hold hard, my country children in the world of tales, | 49 | 10 | 29 | 58 | 10 |
| Now make the world of me as I have made | 61 | 5 | 36 | 70 | 5 |
| Time, milk, and magic, from the world beginning. | 74 | 24 | 44 | 83 | 24 |

| | U.K. | | | U.S. | |
|---|---|---|---|---|---|
| | Page | Line | Poem | Page | Line |
| From pole to pole leapt round the snail-waked world. | 75 | 14 | 44 | 84 | 14 |
| World in the sand, on the triangle landscape, | 76 | 6 | 44 | 85 | 6 |
| The terrible world my brother bares his skin. | 80 | 7 | 46 | 89 | 15 |
| If I take to burn or return this world which is each man's work. | 94 | 12 | 57 | 104 | 12 |
| Once when the world turned old | 119 | 11 | 72 | 131 | 11 |
| Of paradise, in the spun bud of the world. | 123 | 19 | 72 | 137 | 9 |
| The world winding home! | 142 | 13 | 82 | 159 | 13 |
| Seasons over the liquid world, | 153 | 23 | 83 | 171 | 19 |
| As the world falls, silent as the cyclone of silence. | 164 | 14 | 86 | 183 | 21 |
| And gale I tackle, the whole world of then, | 173 | 15 | 88 | 193 | 15 |
| Than ever was since the world was said, | 173 | 17 | 88 | 193 | 17 |
| On whom a world of ills came down like snow. | | | 91 | 201 | 11 |
| Last sound, the world going out without a breath: | | | 91 | 201 | 13 |
| My world is pyramid | 30 | | 18 | 35 | |

WORLD'S

| | Page | Line | Poem | Page | Line |
|---|---|---|---|---|---|
| The world's turning wood, | viii | 1 | 1 | xvi | 1 |
| Pick the world's ball of wave and froth | 2 | 16 | 2 | 2 | 16 |
| I am the long world's gentleman, he said, | 71 | 13 | 44 | 80 | 13 |
| The world's my wound, God's Mary in her grief, | 75 | 8 | 44 | 84 | 8 |
| To the shrine of his world's wound | 145 | 3 | 82 | 162 | 3 |
| Me in his world's wound. | 148 | 13 | 82 | 165 | 13 |

WORLDED

| | Page | Line | Poem | Page | Line |
|---|---|---|---|---|---|
| How deep the waking in the worlded clouds. | 26 | 25 | 16 | 32 | 5 |

WORLDS

| | Page | Line | Poem | Page | Line |
|---|---|---|---|---|---|
| And worlds hang on the trees. | 5 | 18 | 3 | 5 | 18 |
| All all and all the dry worlds lever, | 33 | 1 | 19 | 38 | 1 |
| All of the flesh, the dry worlds lever. | 33 | 12 | 19 | 38 | 12 |
| All all and all the dry worlds couple, | 34 | 1 | 19 | 39 | 7 |
| Square in these worlds the mortal circle. | 34 | 6 | 19 | 39 | 12 |
| Round the parched worlds of Wales and drowned each sun | 87 | 15 | 52 | 96 | 15 |
| All all and all the dry worlds lever | 33 | | 19 | 38 | |

WORM

| | Page | Line | Poem | Page | Line |
|---|---|---|---|---|---|
| The bright-eyed worm on Davy's lamp, | 2 | 11 | 2 | 2 | 11 |
| Locked in the long worm of my finger | 4 | 2 | 3 | 4 | 2 |
| Lights up the living worm. | 6 | 6 | 4 | 6 | 6 |
| And sister to the fathering worm. | 7 | 6 | 5 | 8 | 6 |
| How at my sheet goes the same crooked worm. | 9 | 22 | 6 | 10 | 22 |
| I sit and watch the worm beneath my nail | 13 | 6 | 9 | 14 | 13 |
| When sunlight goes are sundered from the worm, | 14 | 8 | 10 | 16 | 8 |
| From limbs that had the measure of the worm, shuffled | 28 | 5 | 17 | 33 | 5 |
| Worm in the scalp, the staked and fallow. | 33 | 9 | 19 | 38 | 9 |

|  | U.K. |  |  | U.S. |  |
|---|---|---|---|---|---|
|  | Page | Line | Poem | Page | Line |
| A worm tells summer better than the clock, | 45 | 14 | 26 | 53 | 14 |
| Butt of the tree-tailed worm that mounted Eve, | 72 | 8 | 44 | 81 | 8 |
| When the worm builds with the gold straws of venom | 76 | 21 | 44 | 85 | 21 |
| Sooner drop with the worm of the ropes round my throat | 97 | 4 | 59 | 108 | 4 |
| WORMS |  |  |  |  |  |
| I should tell summer from the trees, the worms | 45 | 9 | 26 | 53 | 9 |
| WORMY |  |  |  |  |  |
| Breaks with the wormy winter through the eye. | 16 | 23 | 11 | 19 | 23 |
| WORN |  |  |  |  |  |
| On the madhouse boards worn thin by my walking tears. | 108 | 15 | 66 | 119 | 15 |
| WOULD |  |  |  |  |  |
| I would not fear the apple nor the flood | 12 | 6 | 9 | 13 | 6 |
| I would not fear the gallows nor the axe | 12 | 13 | 9 | 13 | 13 |
| I would not fear the muscling-in of love | 12 | 17 | 9 | 13 | 17 |
| I would not fear the devil in the loin | 12 | 20 | 9 | 13 | 20 |
| Would leave me cold as butter for the flies, | 12 | 26 | 9 | 14 | 5 |
| I would be tickled by the rub that is: | 13 | 20 | 9 | 15 | 6 |
| Would wither up, and any boy of love | 63 | 3 | 38 | 72 | 3 |
| By these I would not care to die, | 64 | 19 | 39 | 73 | 19 |
| She would not have me sinking in the holy | 87 | 18 | 52 | 96 | 18 |
| Flood of her heart's fame; she would lie dumb and deep | 87 | 19 | 52 | 96 | 19 |
| My dear would I change my tears on your iron head. | 97 | 18 | 59 | 108 | 18 |
| Night, and enjoyed as he would. | 114 | 13 | 69 | 126 | 13 |
| Now shown and mostly bare I would lie down, | 133 | 21 | 78 | 149 | 4 |
| I would turn back and run | 148 | 4 | 82 | 165 | 4 |
| Nothing I cared, in the lamb white days, that time would take me | 160 | 24 | 85 | 180 | 1 |
| Whoever I would with my wicked eyes, | 174 | 9 | 89 | 194 | 9 |
| WOUND |  |  |  |  |  |
| Over the wound asleep | viii | 24 |  | xvi | 24 |
| In the stitched wound and clotted wind, muzzled | 28 | 15 | 17 | 33 | 15 |
| Lose the great pains or stuff the wound, | 48 | 12 | 28 | 56 | 12 |
| (The wound records), | 56 | 9 | 34 | 65 | 9 |
| The crusted wound nor stroke the brow; | 62 | 14 | 37 | 71 | 14 |
| Wound like a ball of lakes | 70 | 5 | 43 | 79 | 9 |
| Blew out the blood gauze through the wound of man wax. | 74 | 14 | 44 | 83 | 14 |
| The world's my wound, God's Mary in her grief, | 75 | 8 | 44 | 84 | 8 |
| With priest and pharaoh bed my gentle wound, | 76 | 5 | 44 | 85 | 5 |
| Where, wound in emerald linen and sharp wind, | 79 | 16 | 46 | 88 | 19 |
| Walks with no wound, nor lightning in her face, | 80 | 10 | 46 | 89 | 18 |

## WOUND (continued)

| | U.K. Page | Line | Poem | U.S. Page | Line |
|---|---|---|---|---|---|
| Inch and glance that the wound | 109 | 22 | 67 | 120 | 22 |
| Wound their room with a male moan, | 114 | 2 | 69 | 126 | 2 |
| Endlessly to his wound | 117 | 11 | 71 | 129 | 11 |
| The heavenly ambulance drawn by a wound | 135 | 10 | 80 | 152 | 10 |
| Lie still, sleep becalmed, sufferer with the wound | 136 | 1 | 81 | 153 | 1 |
| That came from the wound wrapped in the salt sheet. | 136 | 4 | 81 | 153 | 4 |
| To the sea sound flowing like blood from the loud wound | 136 | 6 | 81 | 153 | 6 |
| For my voyage to begin to the end of my wound, | 136 | 11 | 81 | 153 | 11 |
| Of his wound | 140 | 15 | 82 | 157 | 15 |
| To the shrine of his world's wound | 145 | 3 | 82 | 162 | 3 |
| Me in his world's wound. | 148 | 13 | 82 | 165 | 13 |
| Venus lies star-struck in her wound | 153 | 21 | 83 | 171 | 17 |
| And falls, and flowers in the yawning wound at our sides, | 163 | 13 | 86 | 183 | 20 |
| Heart! Slyly, slowly, hearing the wound in her side go | 165 | 24 | 86 | 185 | 14 |
| Wound, nor her riding high, nor her eyes, nor kindled hair, | 166 | 2 | 86 | 186 | 2 |
| Nor did he now, save to his secret wound. | | | 91 | 201 | 6 |
| O deepest wound of all that he should die | | | 91 | 201 | 16 |

### WOUND'S
| | | | | | |
|---|---|---|---|---|---|
| With pins for teardrops is the long wound's woman. | 75 | 10 | 44 | 84 | 10 |

### WOUND-DOWN
| | | | | | |
|---|---|---|---|---|---|
| The wound-down cough of the blood-counting clock | 95 | 9 | 58 | 105 | 9 |

### WOUNDED
| | | | | | |
|---|---|---|---|---|---|
| (My shape of age nagging the wounded whisper). | 72 | 22 | 44 | 81 | 22 |
| When near and strange wounded on London's waves | 117 | 27 | 71 | 130 | 3 |

### WOUNDS
| | | | | | |
|---|---|---|---|---|---|
| My wordy wounds are printed with your hair | 13 | 19 | 9 | 15 | 5 |
| Why silk is soft and the stone wounds | 53 | 6 | 32 | 62 | 6 |
| Then, penny-eyed, that gentleman of wounds, | 71 | 7 | 44 | 80 | 7 |
| That her fond wounds are mended bitterly. | 81 | 9 | 47 | 90 | 9 |
| Nailed with an open eye, in the bowl of wounds and weed | 92 | 1 | 55 | 101 | 7 |
| And swept into our wounds and houses, | 158 | 7 | 84 | 177 | 7 |
| Toils towards the ambush of his wounds; | 170 | 17 | 88 | 190 | 17 |

### WOUNDWARD
| | | | | | |
|---|---|---|---|---|---|
| The woundward flight of the ancient | 142 | 8 | 82 | 159 | 8 |

### WOVEN
| | | | | | |
|---|---|---|---|---|---|
| Of the woven wall | 95 | 6 | 58 | 105 | 6 |

|  | U.K. | | | U.S. | |
|---|---|---|---|---|---|
|  | *Page* | *Line* | *Poem* | *Page* | *Line* |
| **WRACK** | | | | | |
| The ringed-sea ghost, rise grimly from the wrack. | 46 | 24 | 27 | 54 | 24 |
| **WRACKSPIKED** | | | | | |
| With carved bird, saint, and sun, the wrack-spiked maiden mouth | 92 | 9 | 55 | 101 | 15 |
| **WRANGLING** | | | | | |
| Of the sparrows and such who swansing, dusk, in wrangling hedges. | 167 | 7 | 87 | 187 | 7 |
| **WRAP** | | | | | |
| Its tongue peeled in the wrap of a leaf. | 134 | 15 | 79 | 150 | 15 |
| **WRAPPED** | | | | | |
| That came from the wound wrapped in the salt sheet. | 136 | 4 | 81 | 153 | 4 |
| **WREATH** | | | | | |
| And comb the county gardens for a wreath. | 2 | 18 | 2 | 2 | 18 |
| **WREATHING** | | | | | |
| Of minnows wreathing around their prayer; | 171 | 2 | 88 | 191 | 2 |
| **WRECK** | | | | | |
| Cudgel great air, wreck east, and topple sun-down, | 79 | 7 | 46 | 88 | 10 |
| **WRECKED** | | | | | |
| On skull and scar where his loves lie wrecked, | 171 | 13 | 88 | 191 | 13 |
| **WREN** | | | | | |
| 'War on the spider and the wren! | 66 | 14 | 40 | 75 | 14 |
| By the wren bone | 138 | 4 | 82 | 155 | 4 |
| The wren | 139 | 2 | 82 | 156 | 2 |
| Behind the wall's wren | 144 | 5 | 82 | 161 | 5 |
| And the hawk in the egg kills the wren. | 155 | 12 | 83 | 173 | 16 |
| **WREN'S** | | | | | |
| Behind the wall thin as a wren's bone? | 137 | 9 | 82 | 154 | 9 |
| **WRENCHED** | | | | | |
| Wrenched by my fingerman, the leaden bud | 54 | 11 | 33 | 63 | 11 |
| **WRESTLE** | | | | | |
| To fiery tyburn over the wrestle of elms until | 167 | 9 | 87 | 187 | 9 |
| **WRESTLED** | | | | | |
| A stem cementing, wrestled up the tower, | 54 | 5 | 33 | 63 | 5 |
| **WRING** | | | | | |
| And the rain wring out its tongues on the faded yard, | 178 | 11 | 90 | 199 | 12 |
| **WRINGING** | | | | | |
| And brambles in the wringing brains | 7 | 24 | 5 | 8 | 24 |
| Its wringing shell, and let her eyelids fasten. | 79 | 9 | 46 | 88 | 12 |
| To the rain wringing | 103 | 3 | 63 | 114 | 3 |
| **WRINKLED** | | | | | |
| Out of the wrinkled undertaker's van, | 72 | 12 | 44 | 81 | 12 |
| **WRIST** | | | | | |
| My hero bares his nerves along my wrist | 10 | 1 | 7 | 11 | 1 |

WRIST (continued)

| | U.K. | | | U.S. | |
|---|---|---|---|---|---|
| | Page | Line | Poem | Page | Line |
| That rules from wrist to shoulder, | 10 | 2 | 7 | 11 | 2 |
| Round her trailed wrist fresh water weaves, | 156 | 9 | 83 | 174 | 17 |
| Burning! Night and the vein of birds in the winged, sloe wrist | 164 | 21 | 86 | 184 | 7 |
| WRISTED | | | | | |
| The stream from the priest black wristed spinney and sleeves | 165 | 1 | 86 | 184 | 9 |
| WRITE | | | | | |
| From the raging moon I write | 128 | 13 | 76 | 142 | 13 |
| WRITHES | | | | | |
| Bone writhes down | 139 | 3 | 82 | 156 | 3 |
| WRITTEN | | | | | |
| A Bible-leaved of all the written woods | 74 | 16 | 44 | 83 | 16 |
| WRONG | | | | | |
| Too late in the wrong rain | 124 | 9 | 73 | 138 | 9 |
| WYNDS | | | | | |
| Through wynds and shells of drowned | 170 | 23 | 88 | 190 | 23 |

# ENTRY UNDER X

X

| | | | | | |
|---|---|---|---|---|---|
| That but a name, where maggots have their X. | 21 | 14 | 13 | 25 | 14 |

# ENTRIES UNDER Y

YARD

| | | | | | |
|---|---|---|---|---|---|
| Down in the yard of day. | 14 | 16 | 10 | 16 | 16 |
| About the happy yard and singing as the farm was home, | 159 | 11 | 85 | 178 | 11 |
| Yard of the buttermilk rain on the pail! The sermon | 165 | 6 | 86 | 184 | 14 |
| And the rain wring out its tongues on the faded yard, | 178 | 11 | 90 | 199 | 12 |

| | U.K. | | | U.S. | |
|---|---|---|---|---|---|
| | Page | Line | Poem | Page | Line |
| **YARDS** | | | | | |
| I piece my flesh that rattled on the yards | 31 | 14 | 18 | 36 | 14 |
| Combs through the mantled yards and the morning men | 119 | 20 | 72 | 131 | 20 |
| **YAWN** | | | | | |
| Yawn to his upcoming. | 144 | 14 | 82 | 161 | 14 |
| **YAWNED** | | | | | |
| The locks yawned loose and a blast blew them wide, | 135 | 3 | 80 | 152 | 3 |
| **YAWNING** | | | | | |
| And falls, and flowers in the yawning wound at our sides, | 163 | 13 | 86 | 183 | 20 |
| **YEA** | | | | | |
| Yea the dead stir, | 51 | 18 | 31 | 60 | 18 |
| **YEAR** | | | | | |
| The black ram, shuffling of the year, old winter, | 72 | 15 | 44 | 81 | 15 |
| In the sniffed and poured snow on the tip of the tongue of the year | 77 | 5 | 45 | 86 | 5 |
| Not spin to stare at an old year | 77 | 17 | 45 | 86 | 17 |
| In a fiercely mourning house in a crooked year. | 88 | 2 | 52 | 97 | 2 |
| Belly of the rich year and the big purse of my body | 94 | 2 | 57 | 104 | 2 |
| It was my thirtieth year to heaven | 102 | 1 | 63 | 113 | 1 |
| Year to heaven stood there then in the summer noon | 104 | 14 | 63 | 115 | 16 |
| In the poles of the year | 122 | 11 | 72 | 135 | 11 |
| To this inhospitable hollow year, | 126 | 3 | 74 | 140 | 3 |
| Out of a lair in the flocked leaves in the dew dipped year | 162 | 6 | 86 | 181 | 6 |
| **YEAR'S** | | | | | |
| On this high hill in a year's turning. | 104 | 18 | 63 | 115 | 20 |
| **YEAR-HEDGED** | | | | | |
| The year-hedged row is lame with flint, | 70 | 10 | 43 | 79 | 14 |
| **YEARN** | | | | | |
| They yearn with tongues of curlews for the unconceived | 176 | 10 | 90 | 197 | 10 |
| **YEARS** | | | | | |
| In your young years the vegetable century. | 60 | 12 | 36 | 69 | 12 |
| I have heard many years of telling, | 63 | 16 | 38 | 72 | 16 |
| And many years should see some change. | 63 | 17 | 38 | 72 | 17 |
| The moon-drawn grave, with the seafaring years, | 67 | 2 | 41 | 76 | 2 |
| And sculptured Ann is seventy years of stone. | 88 | 7 | 52 | 97 | 7 |
| Through the devilish years and innocent deaths | 93 | 14 | 56 | 102 | 14 |
| Twenty-four years remind the tears of my eyes. | 99 | 1 | 60 | 110 | 1 |
| Of the sky, king of your six years. | 106 | 4 | 64 | 117 | 4 |
| Who moved for three years in tune | 124 | 3 | 73 | 138 | 3 |

YEARS (continued)

| | | U.K. | | | U.S. | |
| --- | --- | --- | --- | --- | --- | --- |
| | | Page | Line | Poem | Page | Line |
| Twenty-four years | | 99 | | 60 | 110 | |
| YEARS' | | | | | | |
| These are your years' recorders. The circular world stands still.) | | 37 | 21 | 20 | 143 | 4 |
| Symbols are selected from the years' | | 45 | 5 | 26 | 53 | 5 |
| YELLOW | | | | | | |
| And yellow was the multiplying sand, | | 20 | 22 | 13 | 24 | 22 |
| We lying by seasand, watching yellow | | 82 | 1 | 48 | 91 | 1 |
| For in this yellow grave of sand and sea | | 82 | 5 | 48 | 91 | 5 |
| Watch yellow, wish for wind to blow away | | 82 | 19 | 48 | 91 | 19 |
| Lie watching yellow until the golden weather | | 82 | 23 | 48 | 91 | 23 |
| YES | | | | | | |
| Death to the yes, | | 51 | 11 | 31 | 60 | 11 |
| The yes to death, the yesman and the answer, | | 51 | 12 | 31 | 60 | 12 |
| YESMAN | | | | | | |
| The yes to death, the yesman and the answer, | | 51 | 12 | 31 | 60 | 12 |
| YESTERDAY | | | | | | |
| His golden yesterday asleep upon the iris | | 127 | 3 | 75 | 141 | 3 |
| YET | | | | | | |
| As yet was in a molten form, | | 7 | 10 | 5 | 8 | 10 |
| As yet ungotten, I did suffer; | | 7 | 19 | 5 | 8 | 19 |
| Nor roof of sand, nor yet the towering tiler? | | 46 | 16 | 27 | 54 | 16 |
| Has not yet reached the ground. | | 63 | 19 | 38 | 72 | 19 |
| Some life, yet unspent, might explode | | 64 | 12 | 39 | 73 | 12 |
| Strapped to a wheel, yet they shall not break; | | 68 | 14 | 42 | 77 | 14 |
| Yet this I make in a forgiving presence. | | 80 | 15 | 46 | 89 | 23 |
| Yet she deludes with walking the nightmarish room; | | 108 | 7 | 66 | 119 | 7 |
| She sleeps in the narrow trough yet she walks the dust | | 108 | 13 | 66 | 119 | 13 |
| Yet raves at her will | | 108 | 14 | 66 | 119 | 14 |
| The pyre yet to be lighted of my sins and days, | | 109 | 3 | 67 | 120 | 3 |
| My silly suit, hardly yet suffered for, | | 133 | 1 | 78 | 148 | 4 |
| Yet out of the beaked, web dark and the pouncing boughs | | 163 | 25 | 86 | 183 | 6 |
| Yet, though I cry with tumbledown tongue, | | 172 | 26 | 88 | 192 | 26 |
| YOLK | | | | | | |
| Carrion, paradise, chirrup my bright yolk. | | 115 | 14 | 69 | 127 | 14 |
| YOU | | | | | | |
| To you strangers (though song | | vii | 24 | 1 | xv | 24 |
| For you to know | | viii | 12 | 1 | xvi | 12 |
| You king singsong owls, who moonbeam. | | ix | 3 | 1 | xvii | 3 |
| I see you boys of summer in your ruin. | | 3 | 1 | 2 | 3 | 7 |
| You who bow down at cross and altar, | | 8 | 19 | 5 | 9 | 19 |
| Some let me make you of the vowelled beeches, | | 16 | 13 | 11 | 19 | 13 |
| Of many a thorny shire tell you notes, | | 16 | 15 | 11 | 19 | 15 |
| Some let me make you of the water's speeches. | | 16 | 16 | 11 | 19 | 16 |

|  | U.K. | | | U.S. | |
|---|---|---|---|---|---|
|  | Page | Line | Poem | Page | Line |
| Some let me make you of the meadow's signs; | 16 | 21 | 11 | 19 | 21 |
| Some let me tell you of the raven's sins. | 16 | 24 | 11 | 19 | 24 |
| (Some let me make you of autumnal spells, | 17 | 2 | 11 | 20 | 2 |
| Some let me make you of the heartless words. | 17 | 5 | 11 | 20 | 5 |
| When, like a running grave, time tracks you down, | 18 | 1 | 12 | 21 | 1 |
| No, no, you lover skull, descending hammer | 19 | 2 | 12 | 22 | 7 |
| You hero skull, Cadaver in the hanger | 19 | 4 | 12 | 22 | 9 |
| Happy Cadaver's hunger as you take | 19 | 24 | 12 | 23 | 9 |
| This flesh you break, this blood you let | 39 | 11 | 21 | 45 | 11 |
| My wine you drink, my bread you snap. | 39 | 15 | 21 | 45 | 15 |
| Do you not father me, nor the erected arm | 46 | 1 | 27 | 54 | 1 |
| Do you not mother me, nor, as I am, | 46 | 3 | 27 | 54 | 3 |
| Do you not sister me, nor the erected crime | 46 | 5 | 27 | 54 | 5 |
| Do you not brother me, nor, as you climb, | 46 | 7 | 27 | 54 | 7 |
| Am I not all of you by the directed sea | 46 | 13 | 27 | 54 | 13 |
| Am I not you who front the tidy shore, | 46 | 15 | 27 | 54 | 15 |
| You are all these, said she who gave me the long suck, | 46 | 17 | 27 | 54 | 17 |
| Do you not father me on the destroying sand? | 47 | 1 | 27 | 55 | 1 |
| You are your sisters' sire, said seaweedy, | 47 | 2 | 27 | 55 | 2 |
| Tells you and you, my masters, as his strange | 56 | 13 | 34 | 65 | 13 |
| Hands, hold you poison or grapes? | 58 | 9 | 35 | 67 | 9 |
| Ships, hold you poison or grapes? | 58 | 25 | 35 | 67 | 25 |
| Hold you poison or grapes: | 59 | 8 | 35 | 68 | 8 |
| Shall you turn cockwise on a tufted axle. | 60 | 24 | 36 | 69 | 24 |
| Before death takes you, O take back this. | 66 | 17 | 40 | 75 | 17 |
| 'Time shall not murder you,' He said, | 70 | 16 | 43 | 79 | 20 |
| You by the cavern over the black stairs, | 71 | 22 | 44 | 80 | 22 |
| Those craning birds are choice for you, songs that jump back | 86 | 9 | 51 | 95 | 9 |
| You have kicked from a dark den, leaped up the whinnying light, | 92 | 15 | 55 | 101 | 21 |
| Bullies into rough seas you so gentle | 96 | 24 | 58 | 107 | 7 |
| When you sew the deep door. The bed is a cross place. | 97 | 13 | 59 | 108 | 13 |
| Has a voice and a house, and there and here you must couch and cry. | 98 | 2 | 59 | 109 | 5 |
| You may not see, my son, | 105 | 2 | 64 | 116 | 2 |
| Before you move to make | 105 | 8 | 64 | 116 | 8 |
| Go crying through you and me | 105 | 18 | 64 | 116 | 18 |
| Is cast before you move, | 106 | 9 | 64 | 117 | 9 |
| Friend by enemy I call you out. | 107 | 1 | 65 | 118 | 1 |
| You with a bad coin in your socket, | 107 | 2 | 65 | 118 | 2 |
| You my friend there with a winning air | 107 | 3 | 65 | 118 | 3 |
| Who palmed the lie on me when you looked | 107 | 4 | 65 | 118 | 4 |
| While you displaced a truth in the air, | 107 | 17 | 65 | 118 | 17 |

YOU (continued)

|  | U.K. | | | U.S. | |
|  | Page | Line | Poem | Page | Line |
| And you, my father, there on the sad height, | 116 | 16 | 70 | 128 | 16 |
| Under his downy arm you sighed as he struck, | 125 | 19 | 74 | 139 | 19 |
| O you who could not cry | 125 | 20 | 74 | 139 | 20 |
| Or we shall obey, and ride with you through the drowned. | 136 | 14 | 81 | 153 | 14 |
| Are you | 137 | 2 | 82 | 154 | 2 |
| From the broomed witch's spume you are shielded by fern, | 162 | 17 | 86 | 181 | 17 |
| Shall harrow and snow the blood while you ride wide and near, | 162 | 23 | 86 | 181 | 23 |
| Be shielded by chant and flower and gay may you | 163 | 19 | 86 | 182 | 19 |
| And star: held and blessed, though you scour the high four | 163 | 22 | 86 | 183 | 3 |
| Be you sure the Thief will seek a way sly and sure | 163 | 26 | 86 | 183 | 7 |
| This night and each night since the falling star you were born, | 164 | 6 | 86 | 183 | 13 |
| Since you were born: | 166 | 10 | 86 | 186 | 10 |
| And you shall wake, from country sleep, this dawn and each first dawn, | 166 | 11 | 86 | 186 | 11 |
| When I was a man you could call a man | 174 | 25 | 89 | 195 | 1 |
| Do you not father me | 46 | | 27 | 54 | |
| To Others than You | 107 | | 65 | 118 | |
| YOUNG | | | | | |
| In your young years the vegetable century. | 60 | 12 | 36 | 69 | 12 |
| Husk of young stars and handfull zodiac, | 81 | 4 | 47 | 90 | 4 |
| Tongue of your translating eyes. The young stars told me, | 110 | 23 | 67 | 122 | 1 |
| Straight as a young elm | 112 | 9 | 68 | 124 | 9 |
| Juan aflame and savagely young King Lear, | 113 | 11 | 69 | 125 | 11 |
| Young from the canyons of oblivion! | 142 | 9 | 82 | 159 | 9 |
| Now as I was young and easy under the apple boughs | 159 | 1 | 85 | 178 | 1 |
| In the sun that is young once only, | 159 | 12 | 85 | 178 | 12 |
| Oh as I was young and easy in the mercy of his means, | 161 | 4 | 85 | 180 | 7 |
| Young | 168 | 6 | 87 | 188 | 10 |
| I young Aesop fabling to the near night by the dingle | 168 | 11 | 87 | 188 | 15 |
| Gulled and chanter in young Heaven's fold | 172 | 8 | 88 | 192 | 8 |
| Young as they in the after milking moonlight lay | 176 | 16 | 90 | 197 | 16 |
| Young among the long flocks, and never lie lost | | | 91 | 200 | 7 |
| YOURSELF | | | | | |
| Now in the dark there is only yourself and myself. | 125 | 24 | 74 | 139 | 24 |
| YOUTH | | | | | |
| My youth is bent by the same wintry fever. | 9 | 5 | 6 | 10 | 5 |

| | U.K. | | | U.S. | |
|---|---|---|---|---|---|
| | Page | Line | Poem | Page | Line |
| Youth did condense; the tears of spring | 21 | 24 | 13 | 26 | 7 |
| Warms youth and seed and burns the seeds of age; | 24 | 8 | 15 | 29 | 8 |
| Cast back the bone of youth | 67 | 11 | 41 | 76 | 11 |
| Elegy of innocence and youth. | 101 | 18 | 62 | 112 | 18 |
| In the blinding country of youth, | 105 | 4 | 64 | 116 | 4 |

# ENTRIES UNDER Z

ZENITH
| | | | | | |
|---|---|---|---|---|---|
| O light in zenith, the coupled bud, | 34 | 8 | 19 | 39 | 14 |

ZERO
| | | | | | |
|---|---|---|---|---|---|
| The signal moon is zero in their voids. | 1 | 12 | 2 | 1 | 12 |

ZION
| | | | | | |
|---|---|---|---|---|---|
| Zion of the water bead | 101 | 8 | 62 | 112 | 8 |

ZODIAC
| | | | | | |
|---|---|---|---|---|---|
| Husk of young stars and handfull zodiac, | 81 | 4 | 47 | 90 | 4 |
| Looms the last Samson of your zodiac. | 118 | 8 | 71 | 130 | 12 |

ZOO
| | | | | | |
|---|---|---|---|---|---|
| Through the loud zoo of the willow groves | 111 | 22 | 68 | 123 | 22 |